COOKERY YEAR

Cookery Year
was revised, edited and designed by
Tucker Slingsby Ltd, London

First edition copyright © 1973
Revised edition copyright © 1996 The Reader's Digest Association Limited,
11 Westferry Circus, Canary Wharf,
London E14 4HE

First paperback edition copyright © 2004

Reprinted 2009

We are committed both to the quality of our products and the service we provide to our customers.
We value your comments, so please do contact us on 08705 113366 or via our website at www.readersdigest.co.uk

If you have any comments or suggestions about the content of our books, email us at gbeditorial@readersdigest.co.uk

Printed and bound in China

ISBN 978 0 276 42893 7
Book code 400-475 UP0000-1
Oracle code 250014508S.00.24

COOKERY YEAR

A month-by-month collection of delicious seasonal recipes

Published by The Reader's Digest Association Limited

London • New York • Sydney • Montreal

COOKERY YEAR

The Publishers wish to thank the following people
for their contribution in preparing this book:

Editorial consultant: Bridget Jones

Home economist: Moya Clarke

Writers: Bridget Jones
Judy Ridgway

Artists: Dale Evans, Wildlife Art Agency;
Sally Goodden, Wildlife Art
Agency; Andy Peck, Wildlife Art
Agency; King & King Associates

New photography: James Duncan
Home economist: Carole Handslip
Stylist: Susie Gittins

Jacket photography: Vernon Morgan

Editorial directors: Janet Slingsby
Del Tucker
Project editor: Katie Preston
Editorial team: Deirdre Clark
Michèle Clarke
Jenni Fleetwood
Alison Leach
Yungjoo Rhee

Design director: Jo Tapper
Design team: Alan Hamp
Stewart Perry
Steve Rowling

Index: Robert Hood

Thanks also to the following organisations for their
help: Fresh Fruit and Vegetable Information Bureau,
British Meat, Sea Fish Industry Authority.

Credits and acknowledgements for the original edition
appear on page 440.

ABOUT THIS BOOK

Three major sections provide a wealth of delicious seasonal recipes and culinary advice:

• *Buying for Quality* is a guide to selecting the best and freshest ingredients.

• *Twelve Months of Recipes* features hundreds of ideas for dishes featuring seasonal ingredients.

• *Methods and Techniques* is an illustrated guide to basic cooking techniques. When a recipe requires a particular technique or method a page number is given referring you to this section.

In addition, the *A to Z of Cookery Terms* explains specialist terms: throughout the recipes, words marked with an asterisk* are listed in this glossary. A comprehensive index allows you to find recipes by name or by major ingredients.

The recipes

• Metric and Imperial measures are given throughout: use only one set of measures when following a recipe as the conversions are not always interchangeable.

• Can sizes are given as listed on labels. Sizes and conversion vary slightly according to the brand – if a can of an identical weight is not available, use one which is approximately the same size.

• Teaspoons and tablespoons refer to measuring spoons, and quantities are level unless otherwise stated. Table cutlery does not hold a standard volume and should not be used for measuring.

• Oven temperatures are given in metric (°C), Imperial (°F) and for gas; they refer to standard ovens. Reduce time or temperature according to manufacturer's guidelines for a fan assisted oven.

• Each recipe includes a guide to times for preparation, cooking, chilling, marinating and other processes as appropriate. Timings are not included for preparing and cooking recipes, such as a basic sauce, which are listed in the ingredients. The cooking time given is a guide to the approximate total time required for cooking the recipe.

• The following abbreviations are used throughout the book:

ml = millilitres	g = grams
kg = kilograms	mm = millimetres
cm = centimetres	pt = pint
oz = ounce	lb = pound
in = inch	

CONTENTS

Fish, Shellfish & Seafood 10

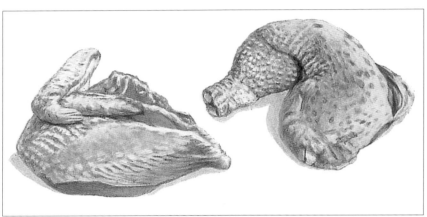

Poultry 17

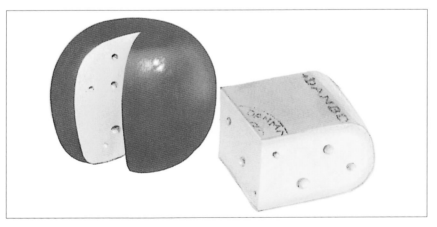

Cheese 31

Vegetables 38

QUALITY

Game 19

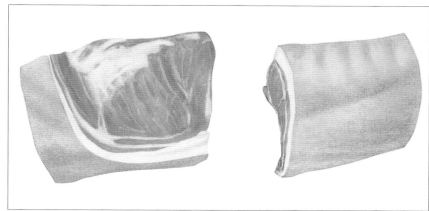

Meat 21

Fruit 45

FISH, SHELLFISH & SEAFOOD

Fish can be divided into freshwater and sea fish, the latter being grouped according to whether they are white or oily. There are also flat or round species of white fish. Shellfish can be grouped according to whether they are crustaceans or molluscs.

There are a few useful guidelines to bear in mind when buying and using seafood. Firstly, buy from a reputable supplier. A fishmonger or fish counter should smell fresh and look clean – a stale and strong fishy smell is an indication of poor standards.

Fresh fish should look it: whole fish should look shiny, moist and bright, with clear markings where applicable. The eyes should be bright and moist. Fillets and steaks should have a good shape – they should not be damaged or broken. The fish should have a good texture – firm rather than soft or flabby – and it should look moist and succulent. White fish should look translucent and white, not off-white. Types of fish that tend to be dry (such as tuna or swordfish) should not be dried out on the surface.

Shellfish should have undamaged tightly closed shells. Live crustaceans, such as lobster, crawfish and crab, should be lively and react quickly when touched. Cooked shellfish should be carefully displayed – remember that cooked prawns or crab should appear good enough to eat even before cooking.

Smoked fish, such as salmon and mackerel, should have a good colour and not look dried out, wrinkled or curled.

Frozen Fish and Seafood

Some years ago all frozen fish was considered to be second-rate, but technology and handling systems have improved immensely since those early days. Factory ships are now capable of processing fish expertly – with greater skill than a second-rate retailer – and freezing it at its prime. So good-quality frozen fish is well worth buying, but check to make sure that this is what you are getting. Look for thick, well sealed and undamaged packaging which is stored properly in a shop with a good turnover. Avoid any fish that shows signs of freezer burn – dehydrated and slightly discoloured patches, especially around the edge or at the thin end of fillets.

As a guide, white fish may be frozen for up to 3 months, oily fish for 2 months, smoked fish for 3 months and shellfish for 2 months. Thaw fish in a covered container overnight in the refrigerator. Do not refreeze raw thawed fish.

The Fishmonger

A good fishmonger should provide a professional service; you should be able to rely on him or her for reliable advice and to prepare fish for you the way you want it. Large supermarkets with 'manned' fish counters should offer the same level of service as a traditional fishmonger: if you find fault with the fish, or have doubts about the level of knowledge and skill, then you should talk to the store manager or write to the head office.

Given a few days' notice, a fishmonger will be able to advise of availability in advance and order unusual or expensive items. For example, a fishmonger (including supermarket counters) will obtain live lobsters, advising you and agreeing in advance about their size, or prepare a whole salmon for pickling or poaching. Cleaning, gutting and beheading whole fish are quickly carried out while you wait. If you want a large fish scaled, or several fish filleted or skinned, then it is helpful to give the fishmonger some time to do this, especially during busy periods, and to come back to collect the fish when you have finished the rest of your shopping.

Seasons

Like most produce, fish and seafood are no longer seasonal foods. Worldwide food transportation means that the majority of fish and seafood is available throughout the year. However, weather conditions do affect the availability and price of fish and seafood, so although a large specialist supplier may provide anything (at a price), the choice at an average fishmonger varies throughout the year. The spawning and shoaling habits of the fish also affect quality and availability. The seasons given here reflect the main source of supply and times when fish is likely to be at its best.

Cuts of Fish

Fillets are easily recognised as the flat pieces of fish which are cut off the bones of the fish. A fish steak is a solid round of fish, a slice down through the rear end of the body. A cutlet is a slice down through the middle of the body and has two flaps of flesh which curve around the (gutted) belly area.

BRILL

TURBOT

White Fish – Flat

Brill This delicate flat fish is smaller than, and inferior to, turbot. Sold whole or filleted. Bake, grill, fry or poach. Season: June to February.

Dab A flat fish that is smaller than plaice and has small, rough scales. Sold whole or filleted. Grill, fry or bake. Season: September to May.

Flounder (fluke) A European flat fish of the same family as brill and plaice. The light brown upper side has orange-red spots and the underside should be creamy white. Season: March to November.

Halibut This is the largest flat fish and it is sold in steaks or fillets. Chicken halibut is smaller, as is Greenland or mock halibut.

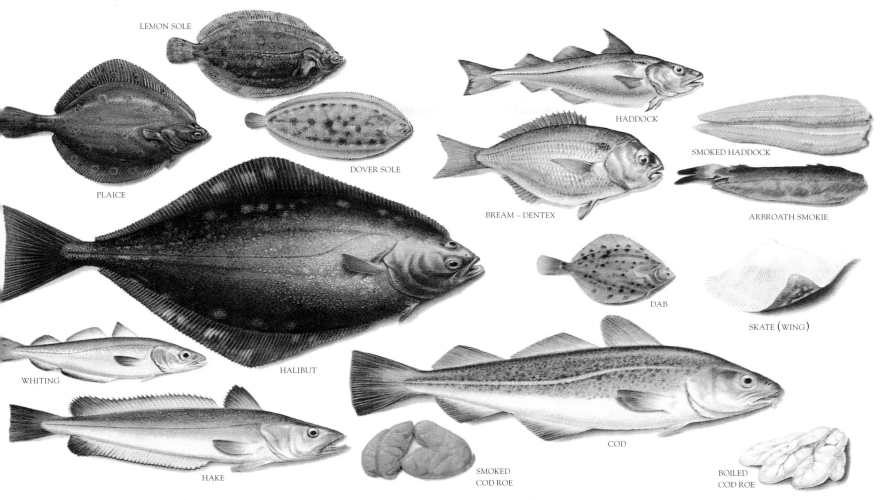

LEMON SOLE

HADDOCK

SMOKED HADDOCK

DOVER SOLE

PLAICE

BREAM – DENTEX

ARBROATH SMOKIE

DAB

SKATE (WING)

WHITING

HALIBUT

HAKE

SMOKED
COD ROE

COD

BOILED
COD ROE

The latter has dark skin on both sides unlike true halibut which has a creamy white underside. Greenland halibut is inferior and less expensive than true halibut. Season: June to March.

Lemon sole A well-flavoured European flat fish with a good texture. Lemon sole is not a true sole and should not be confused with Dover sole, the only true sole, which is of higher quality. Season: May to March.

Megrim This fish comes from the same family as brill and turbot. Megrim has a good flavour and texture. Quality-wise, compare this fish with plaice or lemon sole rather than sole. Season: May to February.

Plaice Grey-brown with orange spots on the upper side and creamy-white on the underside. Sold whole or as fillets. Grill, poach, bake or fry. Season: May to February.

Skate This flat, ray-shaped fish is a member of the shark family, Skate is never cooked freshly caught, it is kept for a day before the wings are skinned and sold for cooking. Like huss and shark, skate has a cartilaginous skeleton and the wings have prominent spines that are easily removed or avoided when the flesh is eaten. The wings have a distinct smell which is 'fresh' and mild when they are ready for eating. If skate

has a strong, unpleasant ammoniacal smell, it is stale and has been kept for too long. Poaching in water to which a little vinegar has been added counteracts a slightly strong aroma but if the smell is very pronounced the fish should be avoided or discarded. Braise, poach, grill or fry. Season: May to February.

Sole or Dover sole The tough dark skin on the top of sole is always removed, usually by the

fishmonger who strips it off the whole fish. The white underskin may be left on or it can be removed. The flesh is finely textured and delicate in flavour, making this the most superior of the flat fish. Sold whole or in fillets. Poach, bake, grill or fry. Season: May to February.

Turbot A large flat fish with raised nobbly growths on its back and a creamy white underside. The white, firm flesh has an

11

excellent flavour. Sold whole, as steaks or fillets. A special, turbot-shaped fish kettle is available for poaching whole fish. Poach, bake, grill or fry. Season: April to February.

Witch (Torbay sole) Similar to lemon sole, but slightly smaller. Season: May to February.

White Fish – Round

Bass, sea (sea wolf or *loup de mer*, white salmon or bass salmon) A round silvery fish with greyish-blue back and light underside. The firm white flesh has a delicate flavour. Scrape off scales and cook whole or in fillets. Bake, poach or grill. Season: August to March.

Bream There are many types of sea bream. Red bream has a red or red-tinged back and a black spot on the side behind the head. Black bream is a better-quality fish than red bream; it has a dark grey back and pale gold stripe or stripes along the side. Gilt-head bream (*daurade*) is one of the best. The latter has a gold mark on the front of the head and a gold spot on each cheek. Dentex is the other prized variety. Porgy is the American name for bream. Bake, grill or fry. Seasons: red bream – June to February; black bream – July to December.

Cod Large fish with an elongated body which may weigh up to 36 kg/80 lb. It has a brown back with yellow and brown spots, small soft grey scales and a white underside. The firm white flesh separates into large flakes. Sold whole, in fillets, steaks or cutlets. Suitable for all cooking methods. Season: June to February.

Cod roe The pinkish hard roe is the ovaries of the female fish and soft roe, or milt, is the testis of the male fish. The latter is also known as chitterling. Roe is sold uncooked or boiled. The hard roe is also smoked.

Coley (coalfish or saithe) This fish has near-black skin and pinkish-grey flesh which whitens when cooked. Coley has a strong flavour, larger flakes and coarser texture than cod, and is generally considered to be inferior. Bake, fry or grill; useful for fish cakes and pies or spiced dishes. Season: August to February.

Conger eel The most common sea eel, this fish has pale grey to jet-black skin. The white flesh is tough and is best cooked by stewing or braising, usually with flavoursome ingredients and seasonings. Sold in steaks or larger pieces for baking. Season: March to October.

Grey mullet There are many varieties of grey mullet, some of which swim up river estuaries. The flesh is firm and white. Bake, poach or grill. Season: September to February.

Haddock A grey-skinned fish of the cod family. A dark line runs along both flanks and there is a dark smudge behind the gills. The firm white flesh breaks into flakes that are finer than those in cod. Sold whole or as steaks and fillets. Poach, bake, grill or fry. Season: May to February.

Hake A round, long and slender fish with scaly silver-grey skin and tender, white flesh. Cuts from the tail end tend to be slightly bony but the main part of the fish has few bones other than

RED MULLET

GREY MULLET

SPRAT

SMOKED SPRAT

CARP

TROUT

PILCHARD

SARDINE

SMOKED TROUT

SEA TROUT

the backbone. Sold whole, as fillets, steaks and cutlets. Bake, poach, fry or grill. Season: June to March.

Huss (dogfish, rigg, flake or rock salmon) Related to the shark family, huss has a cartilaginous backbone which is removed by the fishmonger. The fish is always sold skinned and split through. The firm white flesh has a distinct, if not strong, flavour. It is a traditional fish in British fish and chip shops, sold

battered and fried, but it can also be braised or stewed. Season: throughout the year.

Red mullet Unrelated to, and smaller than, grey mullet, red mullet has firm white flesh with a good, though delicate, flavour. Bake, grill or fry. Season: May to November.

Rockfish (catfish or wolf fish) This is a blue-grey fish with firm flesh tinged with pink. It is a fearsome-looking fish with large pointed front teeth. Its diet of sea

urchins, clams and molluscs gives its flesh a good flavour. It is usually sold filleted. Fry, bake or poach. Season: September to February.

Whiting A member of the cod family, whiting is a small fish compared to cod and hake. When fresh, the soft flesh is flaky, but it deteriorates rapidly. Whiting has a very delicate flavour and is considered to be rather bland. Poach, bake or fry. Season: June to February.

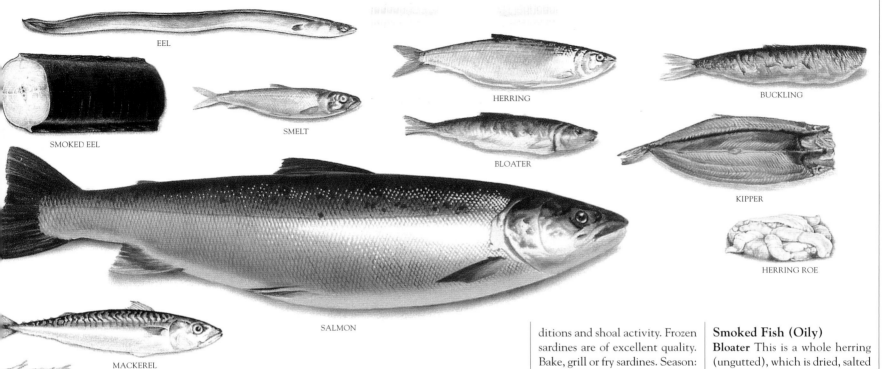

EEL

SMOKED EEL

SMELT

HERRING

BLOATER

BUCKLING

KIPPER

HERRING ROE

SALMON

MACKEREL

WHITEBAIT

SMOKED MACKEREL

Smoked White Fish

Arbroath smokie These smoked fish are small whole haddock hot-smoked to a brown colour. Poach or grill.

Smoked haddock These smoked fillets are pale yellow in colour. Finnan haddock is smoked on the bone. Very yellow haddock has probably been artificially coloured. Smoked haddock loses its flavour quickly. Poach, steam or use it in sauced dishes, such as pies, and fish cakes.

Oily Fish

Herring A small bony fish with a good flavour. Sold whole or ask the fishmonger to fillet the fish, then remove any stray fine bones before cooking. Bake, fry or grill. Season: May to December.

Herring roes Both hard and soft roes are in variable supply, depending on whether the fishmonger prepares the whole fish or not.

Mackerel Mackerel must be used on the day of purchase. Sold whole. Grill, fry, bake or souse.

Season: throughout the year.

Pilchard Adult sardines. They deteriorate quickly and are mainly sold canned.

Salted herring This is a whole or gutted herring preserved in heavy salt brine. It usually needs soaking for 24 hours before filleting and serving.

Sardine This is a small, immature pilchard. Fresh sardines are available throughout the year, but the local catch is spasmodic, and depends on weather con-

ditions and shoal activity. Frozen sardines are of excellent quality. Bake, grill or fry sardines. Season: throughout the year.

Sprat Small, silvery-skinned fish of the herring family. Prepare and cook sprats in the same way as smelts. Young sprats are often sold as whitebait. The young fish are also known as brislings, and are often sold canned in oil or a sauce, sometimes after being lightly smoked. Whole smoked sprats are also available in late autumn and winter. Season: October to March.

Whitebait The 'fry' or young of the herring or sprat. About 3.5 cm/1½ in long, and silvery in colour. Whitebait are cooked and eaten whole. They are coated in seasoned flour and then deep fried until crisp. Season: throughout the year.

Smoked Fish (Oily)

Bloater This is a whole herring (ungutted), which is dried, salted and then cold-smoked. Must be cleaned, grilled or fried on the day of purchase.

Buckling Hot-smoked herring. Gutted and head removed before smoking. Ready to eat.

Kipper This is the most common form of smoked herring. It is split and salted before being smoked. Some kippers look dark because artificial colouring is added. These should be eaten as soon as possible after buying. Some kippers are not dyed at all and will keep well. All kippers should have a sheen to them and the flesh should be soft to the touch. Kippers are sold whole, traditionally in pairs, or as fillets which are also available vacuum-packed and frozen.

Red herring Whole dried and smoked herring, dyed red. Strong and salty flavour, mainly used for mousses and pâtés.

Smoked eel This is sold whole (in lengths) or as fillets. The hot-smoked fish has a delicate flavour and is ready to eat.

Smoked mackerel Hot-smoked and ready for eating, either whole (gutted) or in fillets.

Smoked salmon This varies in quality and price. It may be sold as whole sides, sliced or as offcuts (useful for cooking), but as a general rule price is a guide to quality. Hot-smoked salmon, cut in small thick slices through the fillet, is cooked with a mild smoked flavour.

Smoked trout Rainbow trout smoked to a rich brown colour. Sold whole or in fillets. Requires no cooking.

Exotic Fish

The availability of fish from Africa, the Seychelles, the Pacific and Indian Oceans has increased greatly and is well worth trying if you are looking for something unusual and different. Some types are regularly available, but others are stocked only for a short period, then dropped by a particular fishmonger or only obtainable to order. These exotic fish are usually available all year.

Emperor (Emperor bream) These are related to sea bream and are scaly fish with pointed faces. They may be grey or colourful, with spots or stripes. The flesh is normally white, but the variety called Capitaine Rouge has pink flesh. Available whole or in fillets. Bake, grill or poach.

Grouper (including red grouper and a number of other fish of this type) These fish have white flesh with a good flavour. They are available whole or in steaks or cutlets. Bake, grill, fry or poach.

Hoki From New Zealand, hoki fillets are similar to cod or haddock. The fish is sold as prepared skinned fillets. Breaded fillets and other similar products are also popular.

Parrotfish This fish has a parrot-like mouth and face, and is brightly coloured in blues, golds and greens. Parrotfish are sold whole. Because the soft, delicate flesh deteriorates quickly, the fish should be cooked promptly. Bake, braise, grill or poach.

Snapper (including red snapper and several varieties of fish of this type) These colourful, scaly fish have firm white flesh which is ideal for cooking with spices or braising in full-flavoured sauces. Usually sold whole. Bake, braise, stew or grill.

Shark A firm, dry fish sold skinned and cut in steaks. It is best cooked with spices or with a well-flavoured sauce, and is ideal for stewing or braising. Marinating with oil and seasonings is recommended.

Swordfish A firm-textured fish which is sold as steaks. The fish should be marinated and basted with oil, lemon juice and seasonings during cooking to keep it moist and well-flavoured. Grill, fry, bake or braise.

Tuna A dark-fleshed fish, sold in steaks. The flesh can be dry, so it benefits from being marinated before being grilled or fried. It may also be braised or baked.

Freshwater Fish

Carp There are several varieties of carp, including mirror or king carp. The quality of wild carp depends on the habitat and fish from stagnant or poor-flowing lakes, ponds and sluggish rivers often have a muddy smell and taste. The flavour of the fish can be improved by soaking the fish for 3 hours in salted water before cooking but it will be inferior. Farmed carp usually weighs 1–2 kg/2¼–4 lb 6 oz, but they can be larger. It is usually necessary to order carp several days in advance, and it is sensible to check the availability with the fishmonger. Poach, braise or bake. Season: mid-June to March.

Eel, common A richly flavoured fish with shiny grey-black skin and firm white flesh. Freshwater eel should be cooked as soon as possible after killing, therefore it is killed and skinned by the fishmonger. Unlike conger eel, freshwater eel is tender, oily and better flavoured. Grill, bake, stew or braise. Season: throughout the year.

Pike A large, long fish with a large, flat jaw, a mouth that stretches to the eyes, and with numerous strong teeth. It has coarse, very bony flesh which needs soaking before being baked or boiled. It is usually puréed and sieved, then used to make quenelles or the fish mixture can be stuffed back into the skin and baked to make gefilte fish.

Salmon The 'king of fish', the wild salmon is caught in cool, fast-running rivers. It is a saltwater fish which travels up rivers to spawn. Salmon farming has increased availability and reduced the price of the fish, making it a comparatively everyday ingredient rather than a rare treat. A fresh salmon has bright silvery scales, red gills and pink-red, close-textured flesh. Sold whole (3.62–9 kg/8–20 lb) or as steaks. Avoid steaks with watery, grey-looking flesh. A small salmon (1.8–3.62 kg/4–8 lb) is known as a grilse. Season: farmed – all year; wild – spring to autumn subject to local authority permits.

Smelt or sparling Tiny saltwater fish which, like salmon, spawns and is caught in rivers. It has bright silvery scales and pure white flesh when quite fresh. It has a strong aroma which has been compared to that of violets and cucumbers, and a delicate flavour. Clean by pressing the entrails out through a cut just below the gills, and serve smelts shallow or deep-fried. Season: January to March.

Trout, rainbow This is the most common trout, reared on fish farms. It is green-gold in colour with whitish flesh. Bake, grill, poach or fry. Season: throughout the year.

Trout, river or brown This has darker skin than rainbow trout and is spotted. The flesh is superior to that of rainbow trout. Grill or fry. Season: March to September, but in scant supply.

Trout, sea or salmon Similar to salmon, with silvery scales when fresh. The firm flesh has a delicate salmon flavour and is pale pink. Always sold whole, at an average weight of 900 g–2.72 kg/2–6 lb. Bake or poach. Season: March to July.

SHELLFISH

Crustaceans

Crab The common crab or brown crab is grey-brown when alive, brownish-red when cooked. It is usually sold cooked or dressed, that is prepared ready for eating. The weight of a crab varies from 675 g/1½lb to 3.62 kg/8 lb. The claws provide white meat and the shell, brown meat. Male crabs (cocks) have larger claws, and the female crabs (hens) often contain edible roes or red coral. Crabs are best when medium-sized (1.4 kg/3 lb) and should have both claws attached. When buying crab, shake it lightly; it should feel heavy but with no sound of water inside. Season: April to December.

Crawfish (spiny lobster or rock lobster) Similar to lobster, but heavier, weighing 2.27–2.72 kg/5–6 lb. It lacks the large claws, and all the meat is contained in the tail. The flesh is coarser in texture than lobster meat, but should be prepared in the same way. Sold live or cooked, but in scant supply, and most crawfish tails are sold frozen. Season: April to October.

Crayfish These freshwater crustaceans naturally live in rivers and lakes, but they are farmed for the fish trade. Crayfish are brown when alive and bright red when cooked. These shellfish look like miniature lobsters as they have claws; however, the claws do not contain much meat and the tail is the part that is eaten. Farmed crayfish are usually purged, otherwise the black intestine running along the tail has to be removed.

Crayfish are sold live or cooked; live crayfish should be plunged into boiling water and cooked for 5 minutes. Remove the black intestine when peeling the crayfish (peel them in the same way as prawns). Not to be confused with sea water *crawfish*.

Dublin Bay prawns (scampi, Norway lobsters or *langoustines*) About 10 cm/4 in long, these look like miniature lobsters because of their long claws. They are pale pink when alive and pink when boiled. Dublin Bay prawns are sold mainly shelled, as scampi tails, and generally breaded, frozen and are available all year round. Season: April to November.

Lobster Sold live or cooked. This shellfish is dark blue when alive and scarlet when boiled. The male lobster is brighter in colour and smaller than the female, but with larger claws. The female has a broader tail and more tender flesh. The female also contains the red coral, spawn or eggs, used for lobster butter. Buy a medium-sized one which feels heavy for its size. Best at an average weight of 450–900 g/1–2 lb. The tail should spring back when it is straightened out. Avoid lobsters with white shells on their backs as this is a sign of old age. Season: April to November.

Prawns Popular, comparatively inexpensive and available in many forms. Uncooked prawns are a grey-beige colour, they turn pink when they are cooked. It is easiest to group the types of prawns into cold water and warm water varieties.

The cold water prawns include peeled cooked prawns and the cooked unpeeled prawns of average size. There are different qualities of peeled cooked prawns, from small and poorly shelled examples to medium-sized prawns which should be used for the majority of dishes.

Prawns that live in warm waters are usually larger than cold water types. They come from many countries and include the medium-sized cooked prawns in their shells, which are sometimes called Mediterranean prawns. Large Mediterranean prawns in the shell are not as curved as the medium-sized ones.

Tiger prawns are so named because of their striped markings. These vary slightly in size: they are larger than the average prawn but they are usually smaller than the large Mediterranean prawns. Tiger prawns are available cooked with or without their shells and raw in the shell, with or without their heads. Available all year.

Shrimps Brown shrimps are small crustaceans with almost translucent shells which turn brown when they are boiled. These shellfish are not readily available from fishmongers countrywide, but they are sold by better outlets and in areas where they are landed. Brown shrimps are difficult to peel, but they do have an excellent flavour. Season: February to October.

Pink shrimps have grey shells and turn rosy-pink when boiled. They are not as tasty as brown shrimps and are usually sold cooked but unpeeled. Shrimps are less widely available than prawns.

DUBLIN BAY PRAWN

SHRIMPS

WINKLES

COCKLES

CRAB

Molluscs

Clams There are many varieties of clam, ranging from small cockle-sized shellfish to large clams, each weighing several kilos or pounds. Small clams, such as the warty venus or *prairie*, are often eaten raw, like oysters.

Carpet shell is another small clam which may be served raw. Quahog is a larger clam. Razor shell is the long narrow clam with the familiar pale shell. Clams are sold live: for serving raw, they can be opened in the same way as oysters. Otherwise,

prepare and cook them in the same way as mussels. Large tough clams then have to be diced or chopped and stewed until tender. Season: throughout the year.

Cockles Small shellfish with white, fluted shells. They are usually sold cooked and shelled.

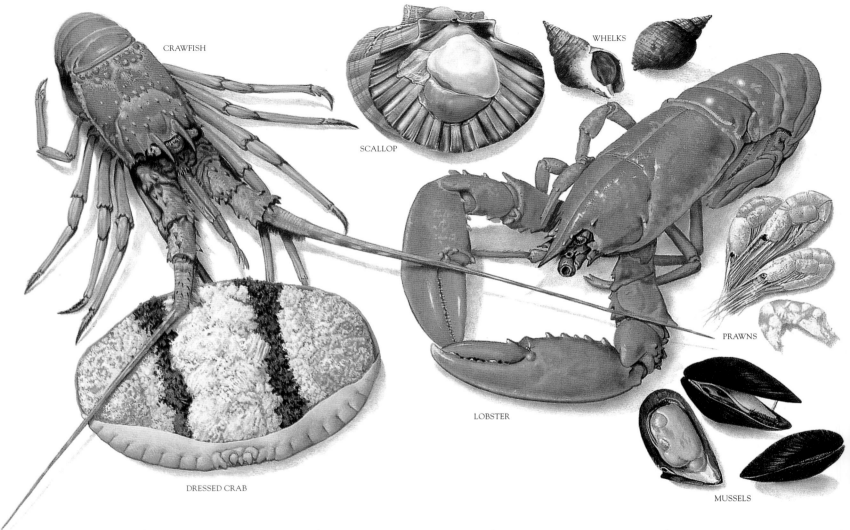

CRAWFISH

WHELKS

SCALLOP

PRAWNS

LOBSTER

DRESSED CRAB

MUSSELS

Fresh cockles should be prepared in the same way as mussels. Season: May to December.

Mussels These are sold live or cooked. Cooked mussels are also sold frozen on the half shell. Since mussels rapidly deteriorate once they are killed, they must be alive when cooked: discard any with broken shells and any which do not close when tapped. Mussels are traditionally sold by the pint (allow 900 ml/1½ pt per person), but are now more commonly available by weight and 450 g/1 lb will serve two as a starter or one as a main course. Large New Zealand green-shelled mussels are sold cooked on the half shell. They may be stuffed or topped with a savoury butter (page 307) and then grilled or baked in the oven. Season: September to March.

Oysters The European or native oyster is considered to be the finest variety and it is more expensive than the Portuguese or cupped oyster which is readily available all year. The native oyster is more rounded in shape and it has a shallow shell. Native oysters are available only during the season given opposite. These molluscs are traditionally eaten raw. They are sold live and have to be opened just before serving or cooking. Shells should be closed, or should shut when tapped. Some gourmets maintain that a raw oyster should be swallowed whole, while others believe that it should be chewed to release the full flavours. Oysters must be absolutely fresh and should be opened just before serving. Allow six for each person. Oysters are readily available at a reasonable price and are generally more popular cooked than raw. Grill or poach them in stock. Season: September to April.

Scallops Native molluscs with white flesh and orange roe. The smaller round nuggets of white meat without the roes are known as queen scallops or queens. They are enclosed in pinkish-brown shells, but are usually sold opened. Look for firm white flesh and bright orange roe. Suitable for poaching, baking and grilling. Season: September to March.

Whelks These molluscs are nearly always sold cooked and shelled. They are eaten with vinegar and brown bread. Season: February to August.

Winkles (periwinkle) Similar to whelks, but smaller. They are sold cooked and shelled. A large pin is needed to remove the cap or scale at the top of the shell and to unwind the winkle inside. Season: September to April.

Other Seafood

There are many types of food taken from the sea, and a host of different creatures that are occasionally sold by fishmongers. Sea plants, such as seaweed, are also popular foods. The following seafood is readily available, although availability may depend on the region where you live.

Laver This is a seaweed product. The seaweed is gathered around the south coast of Wales. The cooked seaweed is mixed with oatmeal and shaped into small cakes that are shallow fried and traditionally served with bacon.

Samphire Bright green rock samphire is found on rocks and cliffs around the east coast of England. Marsh samphire is another variety found in salt water marshland. Fishmongers occasionally pack samphire as a 'garnish' with shellfish purchases. The samphire should be washed and cooked in boiling water and served as a vegetable. Samphire may also be pickled in vinegar.

Squid These are sold whole or prepared. The cleaned squid is sold as a clean, white body sac which may be sliced into rings or stuffed. To clean whole squid, the head and tentacles should be pulled out of the body sac and the head part removed. A translucent quill or pen runs down the length of the body and this should be pulled out, then the mottled skin should be rubbed off the outside of the sac and from the wing-like fins. The tentacles can be rubbed with salt and washed, then reserved. The head parts are discarded.

POULTRY

Poultry is the term used to describe domestic birds, bred for food purposes; it covers chicken, guinea fowl, duck, turkey and goose. The last is only much in demand at Christmas time and therefore not stocked by the average butcher or supermarket for most of the year, but can usually be ordered. There is an excellent choice of fresh and frozen poultry, including joints, diced and minced meat as well as whole birds.

Handling Poultry

Chicken and turkey can carry salmonella bacteria, but this will not cause problems if the poultry is kept chilled, used by the recommended date and thoroughly cooked before being served. You should ensure that cooked food or ingredients to be served uncooked do not come into contact with uncooked poultry or any similar foods, such as raw eggs, meat and fish that require cooking.

Buy fresh poultry from a reputable butcher or supermarket, where it is well handled and kept chilled or frozen in a freezer that is not over-stacked with food. Chill fresh poultry or place frozen poultry in the freezer promptly after purchase. Keep raw foods and cooked foods (or ingredients that are eaten un-cooked, such as salad ingredients, cheese or butter) quite separate in the refrigerator. Place poultry in a dish which will contain any juices and cover it, then store it towards the bottom of the refrigerator which tends to be colder than the top (or right under the ice compartment in some appliances).

Always cook the poultry by the date recommended on the pack. If the poultry is not pre-packed, use it within 1–2 days. Thoroughly wash your hands, surfaces and all utensils after handling raw poultry.

Chicken Available fresh or frozen, and sold oven-ready. Today, the majority of chickens are sold without their giblets. Some butchers will include the giblets, if required. A fresh chicken should have a plump, white breast, smooth and pliable legs and a pliable beak and breast-bone. Young birds will have short, sharp claws.

Chickens are often sold under different names, according to their age and weight, and/or according to the rearing method. Free-range birds have a better flavour than, and are superior in quality to, battery chickens. Corn-fed birds have a distinctive yellow skin.

Various terms are used for rearing methods. 'Free-range' indicates that a maximum number of birds are housed per square metre and that they have access to open air for at least half their lifetime. 'Traditional free-range' is a term used for chickens reared with slightly more space in their houses and they must have access to open air from the age of 6 weeks onwards. Traditional free-range chickens are allocated more space per bird in the open air than free-range birds. 'Free-range total freedom' indicates that birds have access to the outside without being fenced into a minimum area. Regulations and information change; however, the important point is that it is worth reading labels on food and comparing items within the full range available. At first glance, a 'free-range' chicken may seem to be the best choice, but stop to read the other labels and you may find that there are better alternatives on offer.

Poussin A baby chicken, four to six weeks old and weighing up to 450 g/1 lb. Allow one poussin per person. Suitable for roasting, spit-roasting and grilling.

Spring chicken Small, young birds with an average weight of 1.15 kg/2½ lb, these yield only a small amount of meat – when roasted they will serve three people at the most. Suitable for grilling or frying.

Roasting chicken (or broiler) The most popular size, weighing 1.4–1.8 kg/3–4 lb, is enough for four people. The larger roasting chicken, weighing 1.8–2.72 kg/4–6 lb, serves about six people.

Boiling fowl An older bird, usually a hen after the laying season and about eight months old, with an average weight of 2.72 kg/6 lb. A boiling fowl has a good flavour and is suitable for soups or stews. However, boiling fowl are not available through most supermarkets, but they can be ordered from good butchers.

Duck The most famous breed is the Aylesbury duck. It is usually sold at a weight of 1.8–2.72 kg/ 4–6 lb, but a duck does not serve as many as a chicken of similar weight. A 2.72 kg/6 lb roast duck is only just enough for four people and is not an easy bird to carve for a dinner party as the breast meat will not provide generous portions, so the joints are usually served as well.

Duck is naturally more fatty than chicken or turkey; however, birds are now bred to have a reduced fat content. As well as whole birds, joints and portions are also readily available.

Duckling A young duck which weighs 1.6–1.8 kg/3½–4 lb, and is at its best from April to July. It is always roasted and will serve no more than two people.

Goose This is a fatty bird with flesh which cooks to a light brown and has a slightly gamey flavour. The average weight of a goose is 2.72–5.45 kg/6–12 lb, but the proportion of meat is small. Much of the weight is lost in fat rendered during roasting. A goose will serve six people; a larger bird may provide eight portions, but they will not be generous. Choose a young bird with soft yellow feet and legs which still have a little down on them. Older birds have stiff, dry webs. Goose is readily available over the Christmas season, but is not generally offered by supermarkets or average butchers at other times. However, they can usually be ordered in advance.

Guinea fowl Originally a game bird, guinea fowl is now farmed. The flesh is firm and creamy-white with a delicate flavour, not dissimilar to chicken, but slightly more 'gamey' and so reminiscent of turkey.

Guinea fowl is sometimes sold as squabs (weight 575 g/ 1¼ lb), chicks (up to 1 kg/2¼ lb) and fowls (up to 1.7 kg/3¾ lb). It is suitable for roasting, braising and casseroles.

Turkey This bird is now on sale all year round, fresh or frozen, whole or in joints, in small as well as large sizes. The weight of a turkey ranges from 2.72 kg/6 lb to 13.6–18.14 kg/30–40 lb, the average weight being 4.5–6.35 kg/ 10–14 lb. Allow 275–350 g/ 10–12 oz for each person. Drumsticks, large breast joints, breast fillets, diced and minced turkey are all readily available.

Cuts of Poultry

These are some of the popular joints and cuts.

Quarters These include either a wing or leg joint and part of the breast. The wing joint includes the larger part of the breast, the leg has the thigh and a small amount of breast meat.

Part-boned breast The breast bone is removed, leaving a neat fillet of meat but the wing joint is left in place. This is the traditional joint for making Chicken Kiev (page 248).

Boneless breasts or breast fillets Neat portions of meat, which are sometimes sold skinned. Whole breasts are removed from small birds, single-portion fillets are cut from large birds.

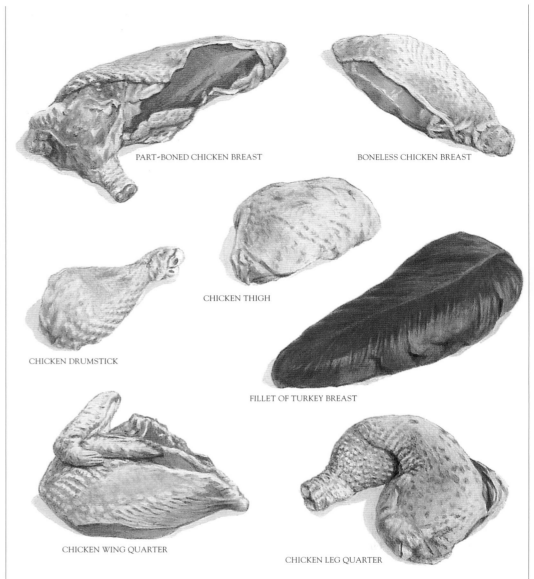

PART-BONED CHICKEN BREAST

BONELESS CHICKEN BREAST

CHICKEN THIGH

CHICKEN DRUMSTICK

FILLET OF TURKEY BREAST

CHICKEN WING QUARTER

CHICKEN LEG QUARTER

Drumsticks This cut is available from both chicken and turkey. Turkey drumsticks are quite tough and so they benefit from braising or slow roasting. After braising, all the meat can be removed, cut up and added to a sauce. Chicken drumsticks also take a comparatively long time to cook well.

Serve two chicken drumsticks per portion. A small turkey drumstick will serve two people and a large one three or four.

Thighs Small, neat chicken portions sold on the bone or boned with the skin on to hold the meat together. These provide a small portion of white meat. Serve one or two thighs per person, baked, braised or grilled.

GAME

The term game is applied to wild animals and birds which are hunted and eaten. In Britain, there is a close season for most game, when hunting is forbidden. Only rabbits and pigeons are not protected by law and are available fresh throughout the year. The seasons apply not only to the act of killing the game but also to selling it. Game must not be sold more than 10 days after the end of the season. Game 'farming', freezing and the importing of game provide a supply of farmed venison and frozen game all year.

Most game is bought from licensed supermarkets, butchers and, traditionally, fishmongers. It is sold prepared (dressed) ready for cooking. Customers rely on the retailer for quality products, and for their guidance as to whether birds are tender and suitable for roasting or older, tough birds for braising or stewing.

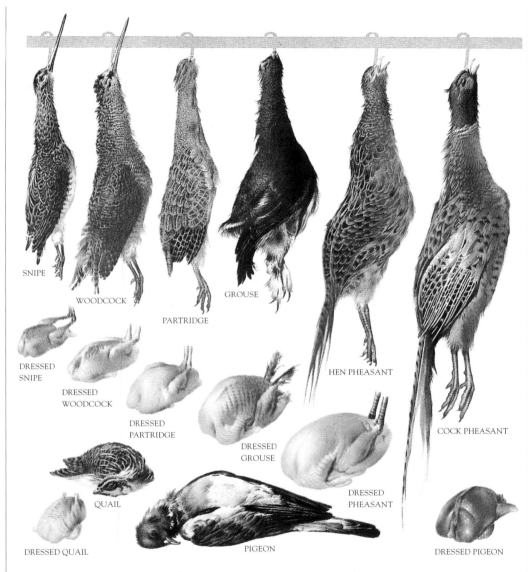

SNIPE

WOODCOCK

PARTRIDGE

GROUSE

HEN PHEASANT

COCK PHEASANT

DRESSED SNIPE

DRESSED WOODCOCK

DRESSED PARTRIDGE

DRESSED GROUSE

DRESSED PHEASANT

QUAIL

DRESSED QUAIL

PIGEON

DRESSED PIGEON

Game Birds

Grouse, red or **Scottish** This is the most common and popular grouse. Young birds, with soft downy breast feathers and pointed flight wings, are roasted and served, one per person. Older birds, with rounded tips to their wings, are better casseroled. Season: 12 August–10 December; best, August to October.

Mallard The largest wild duck, with lean, dry flesh. The flight feathers are pointed and the breast is downy in young birds. Hang mallard for one day only. Serve roasted, allowing one bird for two or three people. Season: 1 September–31 January, extended to 20 February in or over areas below high water mark of ordinary spring tides; best, November and December.

Partridge There are two varieties, the English or grey partridge, which has the better flavour, and the slightly larger, red-legged French variety. Young birds have pointed tips to the feathers, yellow-brown pliable feet and light-coloured plump flesh. Serve one bird per person. Season: 1 September–1 February; best, October and November.

Pheasant The cock and hen may be sold singly or as a brace. Young birds of both sexes have pliable beaks and feet, soft and pointed feathers; on cocks the short spurs are rounded. A hen pheasant, which is considered the tastiest and more tender, will serve three, and a cock pheasant three to four people. Young birds and hens may be roasted, older birds and cock pheasants are better braised or casseroled as they tend to be rather tough. Season: 1 October–1 February; best, November and December.

Pigeon Wood pigeons are inexpensive game birds, often tough and best casseroled. Very young birds, with pink legs, downy feathers and plump breast, may be roasted or grilled. Serve one bird per person. Season: all year round; best, August to October.

Quail Wild quail is protected by law and so must not be shot. Farmed quail is available throughout the year. Roast, braise or grill this game bird. Serve one per person. Season: all year round.

Snipe This small bird is not often seen in the shops. Some gourmets maintain that snipe should not be drawn before being cooked; the head is twisted round so that the long bill can be pushed like a skewer between the legs and into the body. Serve one roast snipe per person. Season: 12 August–31 January; best, November.

Teal The most common wild duck, with short pointed feathers and thin soft feet in young birds.

TEAL

DRESSED TEAL

MALLARD

RABBIT

VENISON

LEG

SADDLE

LOIN CHOPS

SHOULDER

HARE

DRESSED MALLARD

FORE AND
HIND LEGS
OF RABBIT

SADDLE OF
RABBIT

SADDLE OF HARE

QUAIL'S EGGS

Teal is excellent for roasting and for grilling. Serve one teal per person. Season: as mallard; best, December.

Wild goose These game birds are protected by law and so it is illegal to sell, or offer for sale, dead wild geese.

Woodcock This bird (average weight 350 g/12 oz) is slightly larger than snipe, which it resembles, with a plumper breast. It may be roasted undrawn, trussed with its long bill. Season: 1 October–31 January; best, November and December.

Furred Game

Hare There are two types, the English or brown hare and the Scottish or blue hare. A young hare (weighing 2.72–3.25 kg/ 6–7 lb), known as a leveret, can be recognised by its small, sharp, white teeth, smooth fur and

hidden claws; the soft ears tear easily. Young hares may be roasted whole, to serve 4–6 people; older animals are better casseroled although a saddle of hare can be roasted. Season: 1 August–28 February; best, October onwards.

Rabbit The flesh of the wild rabbit often has a gamey flavour. Smaller than the hare (serves three people), a young rabbit can be recognised by the same signs. Wild rabbit is prepared and cooked in the same way as hare. Rabbits in the shops are farmed and have a flavour similar to chicken. They are sold whole or jointed. Season: throughout the year.

Venison The best meat comes from the young male deer (buck), at an age of 1½–2 years when the hooves are small and smooth. The lean meat is dark red and close-grained, with firm white fat which is removed before cooking as it has an unpleasant taste. Venison is sold in joints, the leg and saddle being the choicest cuts. Loin chops, neck cutlets and shoulder may be braised. Cubed venison is available for stews, minced venison is ideal for pies and venison sausages are also made. The seasons vary according to the type of deer and also differ between Scotland and England and Wales. The seasons overlap, providing a supply of wild venison all year round; however, the majority is available from November to February.
England and Wales: Red deer: stag – 1 August–30 April; hind – 1 November–28 February. Fallow deer: buck – 1 August–30 April; doe – 1 November–28 February. Roe deer: buck – 1 April–31 October; doe – 1 November–30 April. Sika deer: stag – 1 August–30 April; hind – 1 November–30 April.
Scotland: Red deer: stag – 1 July–20 October; hind – 21 October–15 February. Fallow deer: buck – 1 August–30 April; doe – 21 October–15 February. Roe deer: buck – 1 April–20 October; doe – 21 October–31 March. Sika deer: stag – 1 July–20 October; hind – 21 October–15 February.

MEAT

Traditionally, meat was one area in which knowledge was important to make a prize purchase; 'the housewife' went to 'the butcher' and asked for a weekly joint of meat by name, weight and gave specific orders for its preparation – trimmed, chined, scored, boned and rolled, and so on. Today, you do not have to be an expert to buy good-quality meat: supermarkets sell prepacked meat, ready for cooking and with guidance on the best cooking methods on the label. Independent butchers provide the same service offered by supermarkets – and more. They often display a small selection of different cuts but they are always ready to give the best possible advice on the complete range of meat.

Few butchers now expect customers to have specialist knowledge, so they are ready to respond with suggestions for choosing meat for cheap or grand meals, for anything from a single portion to a dinner party for a dozen guests; for stews or braises, international dishes, roasts, grills and barbecues. A butcher will quickly explain and demonstrate the alternative ways in which he can prepare meat for you – even an economical breast of lamb can be adapted to give several completely different types of meals, from a traditional stuffed and rolled roast to spicy ribs.

Understanding Meat
Knowing all the cuts of meat, the regional variations and individual butchers' favourite terms is not practical, but understanding the different types of meat means that ideas for meals and recipes can be translated into a shopping list of specific cuts of meat simply by checking the details in this section. Recognising names of cuts, even if you would not remember them in order to ask for them, means that full advantage can be taken of the supermarket range or the butcher's suggestions and special offers. Many butchers prepare half or whole carcasses of pork for freezing or offer a discount on packs of different cuts; knowing how to prepare the different joints means that you can buy with confidence.

Tough or tender? Meat with a high percentage of connective tissue and/or gristle requires long, slow, moist cooking to break this down and make the meat tender. Meat with less connective tissue can be roasted or grilled to give tender results. It is a mistake always to think of tenderness as an indication of flavour and quality: braising a joint which may be slightly too tough for roasting (for example a joint of beef chuck or chuck steak) can make a dish with a great deal of flavour. As a buying guide, connective tissue can be recognised as a fine silvery sheath around lean muscle meat or sometimes it can be seen as slim strands of gristle. The more obvious the connective tissue, then the longer the meat should be cooked. These days, large areas of gristle are usually trimmed off the meat as part of the butchering process.

Beef is the meat with the most variation in texture and applying the wrong cooking method to the cut will give poor results, for example roasting a stewing cut will give inedibly tough meat. The tenderness of lamb (with the exception of scrag end of neck) and pork is less variable and the majority of cuts are suitable for roasting if not for grilling. In these cases, the main differences between the cuts are the fat content and, in some cuts of pork, sinews.

Fat and lean Meat is now both bred and butchered to provide leaner cuts. The fat content is important to give the traditional full flavour, especially in roasting where the fat bastes the meat and reaches a high temperature to give the dark caramelised colour and flavour. However, tastes change and requirements are now more variable than they once were. A rich and succulent traditional rib roast encrusted with a crisp and golden edge of fat may still be some people's choice, but many prefer a lighter-flavoured roast cooked at a lower temperature for a comparatively longer period – a lean joint of topside, for example. As a buying guide, a certain percentage of fat will enrich the flavour of the meat. Cuts without a visible area of fat will have a lighter taste.

Colour Beef is a dark red, lamb a lighter, fresher colour, and pork is pink. Particularly when buying beef, it is worth knowing that the colour of the meat darkens with hanging and meat that is bright red is both young and hung for the minimum time to render it tender. There is nothing wrong with this: the majority of supermarket and butchers' beef is younger (therefore more tender) and not hung for as long as it once was. However, some independent butchers do hang their meat or will at least provide well hung meat to order. The beef will look a deeper red-brown colour when well hung and, in general, the flavour will be richer and the texture more 'melt-in-the-mouth'.

Cuts for all occasions As well as the traditional cuts of meat, there is now a wide selection of meats specifically prepared for quick cooking and to provide different eating options. For quick stir frying, there is usually a choice of diced meat or strips of meat, particularly pork. Braising and stewing meat is available trimmed and cut into casserole-ready cubes. Minced meat comes in a range of types and qualities: pork, lamb and veal are offered as well as beef or steak, either finely ground or coarsely minced with a low fat content if required. Slices of meat or escalopes, minute steaks, ready-skewered meat for kebabs and trimmed nuggets of meat for grilling or frying are all typical products.

Cutting methods British joints are prepared by cutting across the grain of the meat, often giving the customary proportion of fat to lean and producing the tender, short-grained eating quality associated with cooked meat, particularly roasts. The method of cutting meat varies according to the country, with joints taken from different parts of the animal, and the meat may be cut in line with the grain rather than across it. Meat cut with the grain may be trimmed of *all* fat and connective tissue, then a separate barding of fat may be wrapped around it to keep it moist during roasting.

BEEF

The best beef comes from young animals, but even so it must, after slaughtering, be matured or 'hung', at low temperatures, to tenderise the meat with the minimum loss of weight and to improve its keeping qualities. At one time, a hanging period of 12–14 days was considered ideal, but with the trend towards slaughtering younger animals, the hanging period is now a good deal less. On properly hung beef, the lean meat should be plum-red in colour and slightly moist. Very bright red meat denotes that the beef has not been hung sufficiently and is therefore not as tender as it should be, also the flavour will not be as good. For well-hung beef it is essential to visit – and usually to know – a good independent butcher who will provide well-hung beef to order if not on a regular 'everyday' basis. Dark red, lean

and sinewy beef indicates cuts from an animal not of prime quality and likely to be tough. Such cuts are, however, suitable for slow cooking, provided they are well flecked with fat, which will give tenderness, heighten flavour and prevent the meat becoming too dry.

Cuts of beef – and the names by which they are known – vary considerably in different parts of the United Kingdom. In Scotland and the North of England, for example, leg and shin of beef is known as hough.

Many traditional cuts, which are favoured for stewing or boiling, are not as popular as they once were. Therefore such cuts, especially ones with a high gristle content, are minced. Independent butchers sometimes use these tough cuts to make excellent sausages or burgers.

The cuts and joints illustrated here may not always be available from your local supermarket, which will specialise in pre-packed meats, but a good butcher will supply any of them given a few days' notice.

Blade bone Sold as braising steak and often included with chuck which is similar (in Scotland, the blade and chuck together are known as a shoulder). Many butchers dice blade of beef and mix it with chopped kidney to be sold as steak and kidney. Blade is also excellent for slow-cooked casseroles and stews.

Brisket on the bone A whole brisket weighs 7.25–8.16 kg/ 16–18 lb; it is usually cut up into joints, ideally of 2.05–2.27 kg/ 4½–5 lb because of the amount of

bone and meat. Choose a joint with a good proportion of meat to fat and bone. Cook by boiling, pot-roasting or braising.

Brisket, rolled Boned and rolled joints are suitable for slow pot-roasting and braising. Brisket is an excellent economical buy, especially when catering for large numbers. Ask the butcher to trim the joint of excess fat. Traditionally, brisket was readily available salted, but this is now not as common. High-quality butchers still offer salted beef. The meat is then boiled with vegetables and it may be pressed to serve cold.

Chuck This is the more tender cut of stewing steak and is also suitable for braising, known in the North of England as a chine. Braise, stew or use for pie and pudding fillings.

Clod or **sticking** Also known as **neck.** This muscular cut is useful for stewing or casseroles. It is usually fairly inexpensive, but has a high proportion of gristle which must be trimmed off.

Fillet This lean and boneless piece of beef, which lies below the ribs of the sirloin, is the most expensive. It is usually sliced into steaks of about 175–225 g/6–8 oz each. Tiny flecks of fat running through the lean are good signs that the steaks will grill well. It can also be ordered whole or in large portions for such dishes as boeuf en croûte, larded with thin strips of bacon fat.

Flank Not to be confused with thick flank or top rump, this is an inexpensive, fatty joint. It is used mainly for minced beef, sausages and burgers.

Fore rib One of the larger roasting joints, fore rib can be cooked either on the bone or boned and rolled.

Leg This always refers to one of the hind legs, which contain a large proportion of tissue and gristle. The meat is lean and has a good flavour but it needs long and slow cooking. It makes excellent, full-flavoured stews and casseroles, and it is also used for consommé and beef tea.

Shin This comes from the foreleg and is usually fairly gristly. It is normally sold for stews, casseroles, puddings or pies and, because of its high gelatine content, for brawns. Shin is a relatively inexpensive cut of beef, but also wasteful.

Silverside This boned joint is traditionally used for spiced or salted beef for slow-boiling to serve hot or, after pressing, cold. Unsalted, the joint may be pot-roasted or barded and used for boeuf à la mode.

Sirloin This is the traditional roast beef of old England. It is the ideal roast for quick cooking and tenderness, but also the most expensive. Can be bought on the bone or boned and rolled. It is sold with the fillet attached; if bought on the bone, the fillet can be removed and cooked separately.

Skirt Taken from the flank area, this is a coarse-grained cut which is suitable for stewing or braising. Goose skirt is a thinner, flat cut from the same area and this tends to have a lower proportion of gristle and membranes.

Top and back rib Usually known as middle rib, this cut comes

from the ribs between the fore ribs and the shoulder. The joint is divided into two: top and back ribs which are partially boned and rolled for easier carving. These joints have less bone than fore ribs do and they are good slow-roasted.

Top rump A large joint from the hind leg, also known as thick flank. It is usually cut into two joints and tied with fat. May be slow-roasted at low temperature, but is better pot-roasted. Can also be sliced for braising or cubed for casseroles and stews.

Topside A very lean, boneless joint with a fine grain to the meat. It is best slow-roasted or pot-roasted, but it may also be braised. If topside of beef is used for roasting, ask the butcher to tie a piece of good larding fat round the joint to keep it moist during cooking.

Wing or prime rib This large joint, from between the fore ribs and sirloin, is one of the most expensive cuts. It is an excellent joint for roasting (a standing rib roast), weighing 1.8 kg – 5.45 kg/ 4 – 12 lb. It should have a good eye muscle of meat and a good outer layer of firm and creamy yellow fat.

Steak

Châteaubriand This tender, expensive steak is ideally about 3 cm/1¼ in thick and is cut from the centre of the fillet. Grill or fry. It is generally large enough to serve two people.

Entrecôte The lean, tender eye muscle from a boneless sirloin. Usually 2.5–3.5 cm/1–1½ in thick, and one of the most pop-

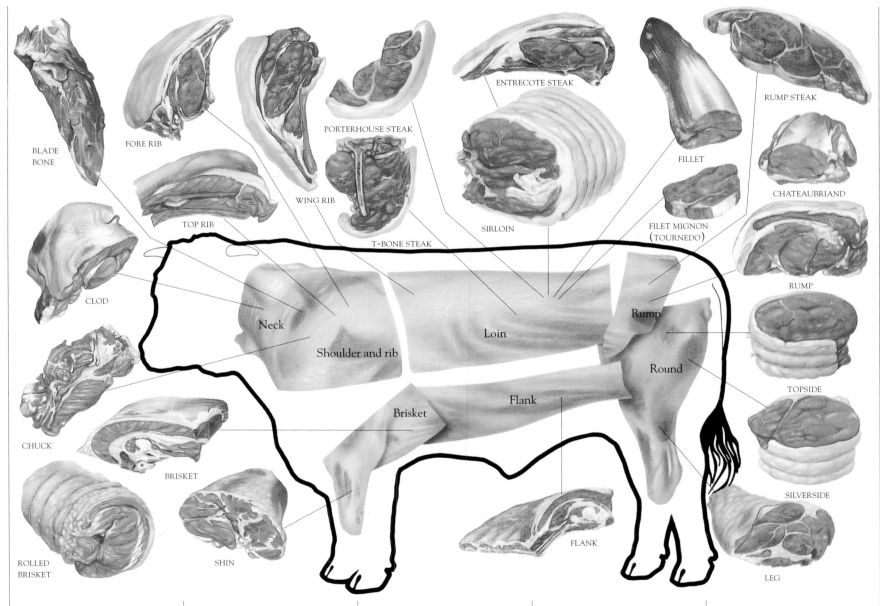

BLADE BONE

FORE RIB

TOP RIB

PORTERHOUSE STEAK

WING RIB

T-BONE STEAK

ENTRECOTE STEAK

SIRLOIN

FILLET

FILET MIGNON (TOURNEDO)

RUMP STEAK

CHATEAUBRIAND

RUMP

TOPSIDE

SILVERSIDE

LEG

CLOD

CHUCK

BRISKET

ROLLED BRISKET

SHIN

FLANK

Neck

Shoulder and rib

Brisket

Loin

Flank

Rump

Round

ular steaks as it can be cut to uniform weight and size.

Fillet See opposite page. Small steaks from the thin end of the fillet or the eye of meat from the thicker end of the fillet are

known as filet mignon or tournedos. Tournedos are usually barded, tied and skewered to keep their shape during cooking. **Porterhouse** A thick steak cut from the chump end of the

sirloin, containing part of the fillet. Usually 1.5–2.5 cm/¾–1 in thick, this steak is excellent for grilling, especially over charcoal. Make sure the butcher trims off all excess fat.

Rump This is considered the best-flavoured steak, excellent for grilling, or frying with onions. This steak should have about 5 mm/¼ in fat on the outside edge and no gristle.

T-bone This thick steak is cut on the bone, from between the chump end and wing rib. It is usually cut to serve two portions, but may also be cut out as individual steaks. Grill or fry.

23

VEAL

Historically, veal has never been a popular meat in the UK, and certainly is not to everyone's taste today. For this reason, British supermarkets and average butchers do not provide the variety of cuts you would find in other European countries, though there is a choice between home-produced and imported meat. There is also a move to provide meat from home-reared cattle, meeting British welfare standards, rather than relying largely on imported meat.

Veal is a pale meat with a light flavour. Escalopes, diced and minced veal are particularly popular in supermarkets, but joints and stewing meat on the bone are also on offer. Larger, high-class butchers sometimes offer a full range of cuts of veal.

Best end neck A medium-priced cut sold on the bone for roasting. It can also be boned, stuffed and rolled for roasting whole, but is more often sold as neck cutlets.

Best end neck cutlets These cutlets should have the tip of the chine bone removed before being cut about 2.5 cm/1 in thick. Each cutlet should have a good round eye of meat; grill or fry, allowing two cutlets per person.

Breast One of the most economical cuts of veal. It may be roasted on the bone or boned, stuffed and rolled first. Cut into 2.5 cm/1 in thick strips, it is excellent for braising or stewing.

Escalopes From the prime muscle of the leg, such as the topside. They are cut, with the grain, no more than 5 mm/¼ in thick and beaten into thin slices.

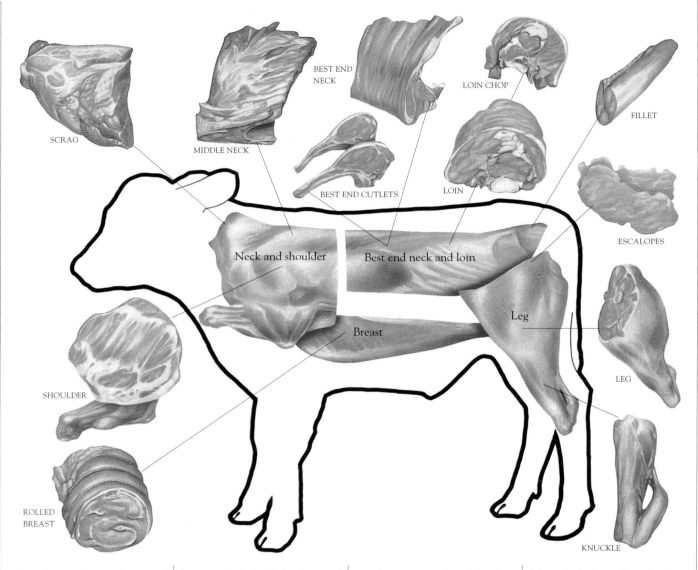

SCRAG

MIDDLE NECK

BEST END NECK

LOIN CHOP

FILLET

BEST END CUTLETS

LOIN

ESCALOPES

Neck and shoulder

Best end neck and loin

SHOULDER

Breast

Leg

LEG

ROLLED BREAST

KNUCKLE

Fillet This cut lies at the top of the hind leg and is the most expensive of veal cuts, usually weighing 225–350 g/8–12 oz. There is, however, no wastage with fillet, and it is both tender and delicately flavoured. It is normally cut into fillet steaks, but may also be barded and roasted whole.

Knuckle One of the cheaper cuts, this comes from the lower part of the hind or fore leg. The hind knuckle is the more tender; it can be slow-roasted on the bone or cut into 3.5–5 cm/ 1½–2 in pieces and used for Osso Buco (page 270). The fore leg knuckle (shin) is only suitable for boiling, or it may be boned and used for stews and casseroles.

Leg This is one of the largest and most expensive joints with a high proportion of meat to bone. The whole leg, after the hind knuckle has been removed, may be roasted on the bone. It is a very large joint and usually the topside, known as cushion of veal, is cut off for escalopes and the remainder boned and rolled for smaller roasting joints.

Loin A prime cut, taken from between the best end and the leg. It is sold as a whole joint on the bone, and is also sold boned. Loin is suitable for roasting. It may also be cut into single bone portions, as individual chops.

Loin chops Single bone portions, cut 2.5 cm/1 in thick for grilling and frying. They sometimes include the kidney.

Middle neck An economical cut, but with a high proportion of bone. It is usually sold in cutlets for braising or boned as pie veal.

Scrag Mainly sold in one piece for boiling or stewing. This cut is inexpensive, but there is a high percentage of bone to meat. Most butchers chop scrag and offer it for casseroles.

Shoulder This is also known as the oyster of veal after the fore knuckle has been removed. It is the cheapest veal roasting joint, sold on the bone, but better boned, stuffed and rolled.

LAMB

Lamb is a tender meat with a distinctive flavour and aroma. Mutton, the term for meat from older sheep, has a stronger flavour and is tougher than lamb. It is rarely available today as people generally prefer lamb for its tenderness and lighter taste. Welsh lamb is a particular speciality, valued for its sweet fresh flavour which comes out well when it is roasted.

Lamb is light red in colour. It should look fresh and moist with creamy-white, firm fat. Joints should have a plump layer of meat under a thin, pliable skin with a light sheen.

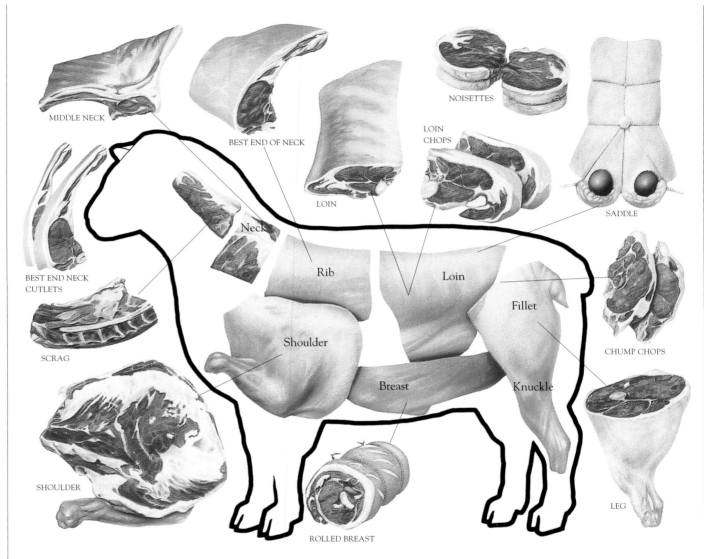

MIDDLE NECK

BEST END OF NECK

NOISETTES

LOIN CHOPS

LOIN

SADDLE

BEST END NECK CUTLETS

SCRAG

CHUMP CHOPS

SHOULDER

Neck

Rib

Loin

Fillet

Shoulder

Breast

Knuckle

LEG

ROLLED BREAST

Best end of neck A tasty and versatile cut from between the middle neck and the loin. It may be braised and is excellent as a small roast on the bone. For a whole roast, the butcher will saw through the vertebrae – the bone known as the chine bone –

without removing it from the joint. He will also strip off the outer thin skin.

Two best ends of neck are used to shape a crown, from which the skin and excess fat have been removed. The top of the rib bones are cleaned.

A guard of honour (pages 330 and 126) is another popular roast. It is shaped from two best ends and joined in such a way that the trimmed rib bones crisscross on top. Give the butcher a few days' notice to prepare either of these joints.

Breast An economical cut, which is usually sold boned, stuffed and rolled, for roasting or braising. It is fatty, so is not much in demand.

Chops These individual cuts come either from the loin or the leg. They are suitable for grilling, frying or braising.

Chump chops, which are 1.5–2.5 cm/¾–1 in thick, are cut from between the leg and the loin. They are oval with a small central bone, and are more expensive than loin chops because each leg of the animal gives only two chops.

Chops cut from the loin, about 2.5 cm/1 in thick, have a small T-shaped bone. They should be fairly lean with a thin layer of fat on the outside edge.

Cutlets These are taken from the best end neck, as individual cuts. They have a characteristic long bone, a thin layer of fat and a small round eye of sweet lean meat. Suitable for grilling and frying; allow two cutlets per person. Cutlet frills are placed on the bare rib ends after cooking.

Fillet off the leg This is the upper part of the leg and is frequently sold as a separate joint. It has lean meat, little bone and no gristle. It is suitable for roasting whole on the bone.

Knuckle The lower part of the hind leg, usually sold as a separate, fairly expensive joint for roasting on the bone. It may also be boned, stuffed and rolled.

Leg This is the most popular large roasting joint, weighing 1.8–2.5 kg/4–5½ lb. It is sold on the bone and can also be ordered boned and rolled. The leg, being large, is often divided into two joints: knuckle and fillet. Whole leg of lamb is suitable for roasting, braising and boiling. Lamb steaks are cut from the leg, either on the bone or boned.

In Scotland, the leg is known as gigot; it includes the chump end of the loin. It is usually divided into three portions: chump, centre and knuckle.

Loin This prime joint is usually sold on the bone for roasting whole. A complete loin weighs about 1.8 kg/4 lb, but it is also sold in smaller portions. It has a thin even layer of fat just below the skin. Ask the butcher to saw through the chine bone for easier carving. The loin can also be ordered boned, then stuffed with the chopped kidneys and rolled to make a good roast for a small number of people.

Middle neck This comes from between the best end of neck and the scrag; it is sometimes sold in one piece including the scrag. It has a large proportion of bone and fat to meat and is best used for stews; boned, it may also be sliced and fried.

Noisettes These are small round and thick slices cut from the boned and rolled loin or best end. Many supermarkets and butchers stock noisettes but it is wise to order them in advance if in doubt. They are suitable for grilling or frying.

Rib The complete rib section is seldom sold whole, but cut into three portions: best end of neck, middle neck and scrag.

Saddle A large prime joint made up of both loins and cut from the best end to the legs, with the tail left on. The butcher requires a few days' notice to dress a saddle. The meat is skinned and the cleaned kidneys are skewered and tied to the end of the loins, with the slit tail wrapped round them. A saddle weighs about 3.62 kg/8 lb and makes an ideal, if expensive, large roast.

Scrag end of neck This cut nearest the head contains much bone and gristle. It is sold already chopped and used for stews and soups and broths.

Shoulder A roasting joint from the fore-quarter which usually weighs 1.6–1.8 kg/3½–4 lb. It is the least expensive of the roasting joints, fattier than the leg, but with a sweeter flavour. It is more difficult to carve than the leg and is therefore often boned and rolled.

In Scotland, a shoulder is cut as a larger joint, to include part of the neck and the breast. It is then divided into two or three joints and often boned, stuffed and rolled for roasting.

PORK

The majority of pork is fine-grained and tender. Traditionally, pork was a seasonal meat which was not available during summer months (only being available when there was an 'r' in the month), as it did not keep as well as beef or lamb. Much was salted and preserved – hence the continuing popularity of bacon and gammon.

Pork is not as fatty as it used to be – even a joint of belly pork has only a small percentage of fat to meat. The meat should be pale pink, firm, smooth and moist. The fat on pork is softer and smoother than on beef or lamb; it should be an opaque, creamy white or 'milky' in appearance. The rind should be pliable and smooth, not too thick and slightly pink. It should not be hairy. On joints of pork, the rind should be evenly scored, or cut,

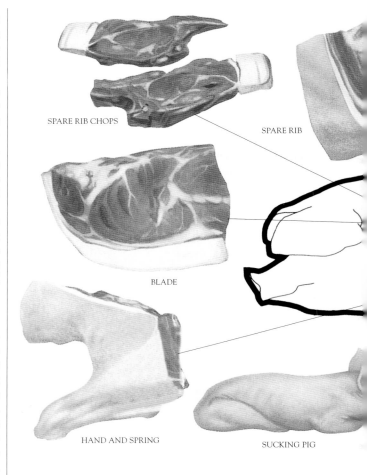

SPARE RIB CHOPS

SPARE RIB

BLADE

HAND AND SPRING

SUCKING PIG

into narrow strips, but the cuts should not extend right down into the fat.

Belly This is sometimes known as streaky, draft or flank pork. It is fairly fatty, and the best cut is the thicker part of the belly which has a good proportion of lean meat. It is a cheap cut which is sold fresh or, traditionally, salted. Belly pork is good for roasting and can be boned, stuffed and rolled. It can also be chopped up for stews or sliced for

grilling. Salted belly pork should be soaked before boiling.

Blade A small, reasonably priced joint cut from the shoulder. It weighs about 900 g/2 lb and may be roasted on the bone, or boned, stuffed and rolled for roasting.

Chops These large, fairly expensive slices, generally about 2.5 cm/1 in thick, come from the loin or the spare rib joints. They are all suitable for grilling, frying or baking. There are three cuts sold as chops. Chump chops are cut

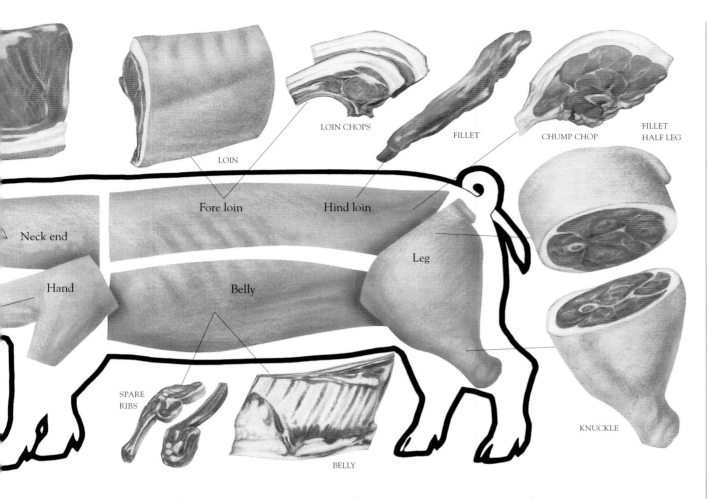

LOIN CHOPS

FILLET

CHUMP CHOP

FILLET
HALF LEG

LOIN

Fore loin

Hind loin

Leg

Neck end

Hand

Belly

SPARE
RIBS

KNUCKLE

BELLY

fleshed with fat. It is particularly economical when bought whole. The knuckle end can be cut off and salted for boiling; two or three steaks can be cut from the thin end and used for grilling or frying, while the centre portion can be roasted whole.

In Scotland, the hand and spring is known as a runner.

Knuckle In Scotland this large pork joint is known as hough. It is cut from the lower part of the leg. Knuckle is fairly expensive and can be roasted whole or boned and then stuffed. It is also an excellent choice for boiling and stewing. On a prime joint, the knuckle bone should have a tinge of blue.

Leg A prime, expensive roasting joint known as gigot in Scotland. A whole leg weighs 4.5–6.8 kg/ 10–15 lb and is usually sold cut into two joints: the fillet half leg and the knuckle half. Both are excellent roasted on the bone. Whole legs are sometimes partly boned and tied by the butcher so that smaller roasting joints from 1.5 kg/2½ lb upwards can be cut.

Loin Considered by many people to be the choicest cut of pork, the loin is also the most expensive. The whole loin weighs 4.08–4.5 kg/9–10 lb and may be roasted whole, but it is more often cut into smaller joints.

The hind loin is the choicest part of the pork loin, and it usually has the kidney and fillet attached. The fore loin or rib end is similar in appearance to best end of lamb, although much larger. It can be prepared by the butcher as a large crown roast to serve at least ten people.

from the chump end which lies between the loin and the leg. They have a round central bone. A boned chump chop is cut into 1.5 cm/¾ in thick pork steaks, or even thinner, and beaten flat into pork escalopes.

Loin chops are cuts from either the end of the fore loin or from the hind loin. They all have a T-bone, and chops from the hind loin usually come with the kidney left in. If the chops are bought with rind on, it is

advisable to snip through it with scissors to prevent the chop curling during cooking.

Spare rib chops are cuts from the spare rib joint which have a smaller eye of meat than chump and loin chops. They contain little bone, however, and have a sweeter taste. Grill or fry. Do not confuse them with spare ribs which come from the belly.

Fillet or tenderloin This is the lean and tender muscle which lies underneath the backbone in

the hind loin. This choice cut for roasting, braising, grilling and frying is covered in a near-transparent thin skin which must be peeled off. For roasting whole, the fillet is best cut through half its thickness, spread with a filling and rolled up.

Fillet half leg The top end of the hind leg. It is roasted whole on the bone or cut into steaks.

Hand The lower part of the shoulder, usually more expensive than the complete hand and

spring. It has a large area of rind for crisp crackling and is also ideal, boned, stuffed and rolled, for roasting.

Hand and spring In north-east England this is known as the shoulder. It is the lower shoulder (the hand), with the jowl, the knuckle and trotter as well as the first three or four bones of the belly. Sold fresh or salted and relatively inexpensive. When buying this joint, look for one which is compact and well

Neck end A fairly inexpensive joint which is the upper part of the shoulder and consists of the blade and spare rib. It is known in north-east England as a chine. In Scotland it is called shoulder and is cut larger, weighing up to 9 kg/20 lb. Look for a compact joint, with an even distribution of fat and a large amount of lean meat. It can be boned and rolled and cut into joints of varying sizes, or sold separately as blade and spare rib. Also used cubed for kebabs.

Spare rib The cut left on the upper part of the shoulder after the blade has been removed from the neck end. Suitable for roasting, braising or stewing.

Spare ribs In spite of its name, these do not come from the spare rib, but are cut from the rib part of the belly. Rind and all excess fat are removed and the ribs are cut into single bone strips. Used in Chinese cooking, for roasting and for barbecues.

Sucking (suckling) pig A young pig from three weeks to two months old when slaughtered. It is usually spit-roasted to obtain the golden crisp skin.

BACON, GAMMON AND HAM

Bacon, gammon and ham come from pigs especially reared to produce certain proportions of lean meat to fat. Bacon comes from the body of the pig, and the gammon comes from the hind legs. Ham is the term used for the hind legs, usually to refer to cooked joints. However, ham is often used instead of gammon to refer to steaks; so, in some instances 'ham and eggs' refers to gammon steak with eggs rather than cooked ham with eggs.

Bacon and gammon are cured in brine and then matured. At this stage bacon is known as green or unsmoked bacon, and rind is pale, the flesh pink and the flavour is delicate. Gammon is cut from the carcass after brining. Further processing by drying and smoking produces smoked gammon or bacon, which has dark pink flesh and a golden-brown rind. Whether green or smoked, bacon and gammon should have firm moist flesh and the fat should be white to cream with no yellow or green tinges. Bacon and gammon are sold in joints, boned and rolled, or in rashers and steaks.

Regional hams are produced by different curing methods, when seasonings, spices and sugar or other sweetening may be added. Contemporary curing is quicker than the traditional soaking in brine and maturing method, and it involves injecting a curing solution into the meat. The bacon is usually sold in vacuum packs as 'mild', 'tender' or 'sweet cure'.

Modern curing, even when using traditional methods, gives a far less salty result. For this reason, it is rarely necessary to soak joints of bacon or gammon in water before cooking. Soaking for many hours can result in a mild joint of gammon being rather tasteless when cooked. As a general guide, parboiling or soaking can give a good result when baking a joint which might otherwise taste salty.

Collar

One of the more inexpensive bacon joints, suitable for boiling or parboiling and roasting. The whole collar has an average weight of 3.62 kg/8 lb. It may also be sold in smaller joints.

End collar A small cut usually weighing up to 900 g/2 lb. A good boiling joint, also used as a base for soups.

Middle collar This is a slightly larger and thicker cut than the end collar, and may be cooked in the same way.

Prime collar An excellent small joint for boiling and roasting, equally good cold or hot, but carves easiest when cold. Also cut into rashers.

Back

A lean joint, up to 3.62 kg/8 lb in weight, sold in some parts of the country as a whole joint, usually with the rib bones cut out. It is rolled for boiling, braising or baking. More often, however, back is cut into rashers known by various names.

Top back rashers Taken from the widest part of the back, nearest to the shoulder, these rashers are always lean. They have a sweeter flavour and a more distinctive taste than other rashers. Best grilled.

Middle or **through cut** Usually cheaper than short back as it is a combination of back and streaky bacon. A joint is ideal for baking whole, or it may be cut into rashers and divided into meaty and streaky rashers. The meaty rashers can be grilled, and the streaky ones used for bacon rolls and for barding.

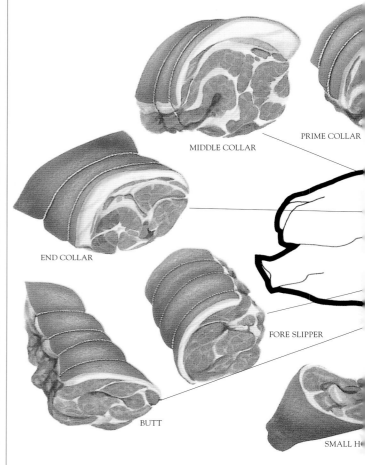

PRIME COLLAR

MIDDLE COLLAR

END COLLAR

FORE SLIPPER

BUTT

SMALL H

Short back Considered to be the prime cut of the back, this is nearly always sold as rashers which are fairly expensive. It may also be cut into 1–1.5 cm/ ½–¾ in thick chops for grilling.

Oyster cut This comes from the rear part of the back after the long back has been removed. It is sometimes sold as a small joint with the bone in, weighing about 675 g/1½ lb, and is suitable for boiling. Oyster cut is also sold as small rashers.

Long back This is another choice cut of bacon. It comes from just above the gammon joint and is equally expensive. Long back rashers are cut thinly for grilling and frying; they may also be cut into thick steaks.

Gammon

A whole gammon, 5.45–6.35 kg/ 12–14 lb, is the hind leg of a bacon pig and is cut square at the top, unlike ham. Gammon is more expensive than other bacon

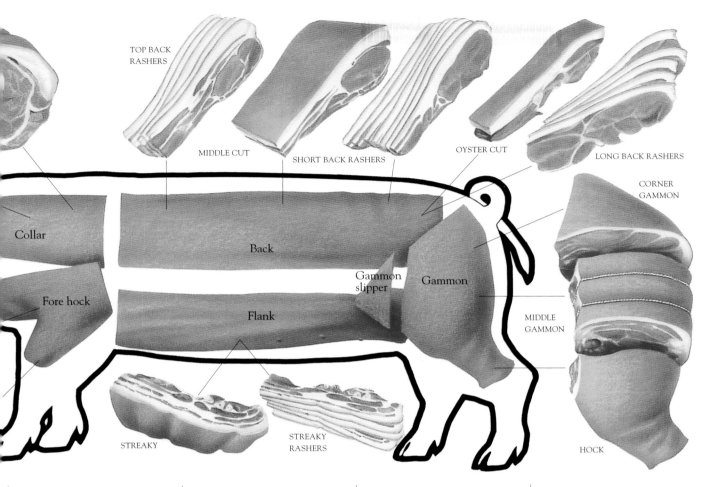

TOP BACK
RASHERS

MIDDLE CUT

SHORT BACK RASHERS

OYSTER CUT

LONG BACK RASHERS

CORNER
GAMMON

Collar

Back

Fore hock

Gammon
slipper

Gammon

Flank

MIDDLE
GAMMON

STREAKY

STREAKY
RASHERS

HOCK

Ham

A whole ham weighs 4.5–7.25 kg/ 10–16 lb and is sold whole or cut into slices. Some butchers will boil whole hams at no extra charge, but as cooking depends on the type of curing, most hams come with instructions. The following are examples of regional hams. They are not widely available, but they can be found in good delicatessens or larger supermarkets. These hams are more expensive than plain boiled or baked ham, but their flavours are individual.

Bradenham ham Smaller than most other hams, this is soaked in molasses rather than salt, which turns its skin black. The meat is more red than pink. Bradenham hams are hung for months to develop their distinctive, slightly sweet flavour.

Suffolk ham Like the Bradenham ham, this is also soaked in molasses. This ham has a full yet delicate flavour.

Wiltshire ham Mild cured, the Wiltshire ham has a delicate taste, but it does not keep as well as other hams.

York ham This ham is cured with dry salt, lightly smoked and matured for months. It is firm and tender, and has a delicate pink meat with a mild flavour. York hams weigh about 8.16 kg/ 18 lb, and are usually sold at Christmas, although smaller ones, weighing about 5.45 kg/ 12 lb, are available. The name 'York ham' is sometimes loosely used to indicate any type of ham suitable for cooking, and to distinguish it from smoked ham, which is eaten raw.

---

joints; it may be parboiled and baked whole, but is usually cut into four different joints.

Corner gammon This triangular joint is cut from the top of the leg and weighs about 1.8 kg/4 lb. It is a lean joint, suitable for boiling and baking.

Middle gammon A succulent and lean gammon joint from the middle of the leg, of even shape and excellent flavour. It weighs on average 2.27 kg/5 lb and is an ideal joint for boiling and

baking, studded with cloves. Rashers and steaks for grilling and frying are cut from the joint.

Hock or gammon knuckle The cheapest of the gammon joints, with a high proportion of bone. Usually sold on the bone for boiling and suitable for dishes with chopped ham.

Gammon slipper This small and lean triangular joint comes from the inside of the hind leg. It is an economical buy and the traditional joint for boiling.

Streaky

Streaky or **flank** The streaky belly joint has alternate layers of fat and lean meat and always contains some gristle which must be snipped out. It is most often sold as rashers. Flank, the end of the streaky joint where there are no rib bones, is invariably fatty and best used for barding only.

Fore hock

This is the whole fore-leg of a bacon pig. It is one of the cheap-

est joints, weighing about 3.62kg/ 8 lb. Usually cut up and sold in three smaller joints:

Butt The largest of the fore hock joints, weighing up to 1.8 kg/4 lb. Suitable for boiling or baking.

Fore slipper The fattier joint of the fore hock. Like butt, it is best boiled, but served cold.

Small hock The knuckle end, weighing 900g–1.4 kg/2–3 lb. It is a tough bony joint, and the flesh is best cut from the bone and used in casseroles.

OFFAL

The term 'offal' comes from 'off-all' and refers to those edible parts of the animal that remain when the meat has been cut off the carcass. This includes internal organs: tongue, kidneys, heart and liver, which all have their own distinctive flavour; brains and sweetbreads, which are quite different and more delicate; the stomach lining from ox which is prepared and sold as tripe; intestines, which are used as sausage skins; and blood, which is used in black pudding. Offal also covers pig's head (for brawn) and cheek (the latter cooked and coated with crumbs to make Bath chap, a small ham); ox tail; and feet, pig's or bacon trotters and calf's foot, the latter being valued for their gelatine content as well as flavour when making stocks and soups.

All offal is highly perishable – more so than any other food – so it should be used on the day of purchase or certainly within 24 hours. On pre-packed offal, take care to scrupulously observe the recommended dates by which the product should be sold and used. Chill offal promptly after shopping, placing loose-packed items in a covered container but leaving sealed supermarket packs as purchased.

The majority of offal is sold already prepared for cooking, with only minor trimming necessary, for example snipping out the small white fatty core in lamb's kidneys, peeling off thin membranes or snipping out tubes from hearts. Some offal, particularly hearts, requires long slow cooking for tender results, but the majority is tender and cooks quickly. Tripe is sold ready blanched and often has already been boiled until tender.

Brains

Currently, brains from British cattle are not sold, but imported brains and sweetbreads are available. This does, however, mean that this form of offal is in limited supply and expensive: larger, high-class butchers will provide a complete range of offal. Calf's brains are considered to have the most delicate, superior, flavour, but lamb's brains can be substituted for them.

Feet

Pig's trotters are the ones most frequently seen in butchers, either fresh or brined. Cow heel, once a favourite ingredient for jellied stock, is now rarely seen. Calf's foot, too, is rare and must be ordered well in advance.

Calf's foot This type of offal contains a high proportion of gelatine and is ideal for making stock to be used with jellied moulds of meat or poultry.

Pig's trotters This offal may be used instead of a calf's foot for making jellied stock and as a base for lentil soups. Pig's trotters are also suitable, after boiling, as an ingredient for setting brawns. Alternatively, trotters may be boned, stuffed and slow-roasted.

Heads

Pig's heads are the only offal of this type now sold; the others are no longer available in butchers. Pig's head is prepared by boiling

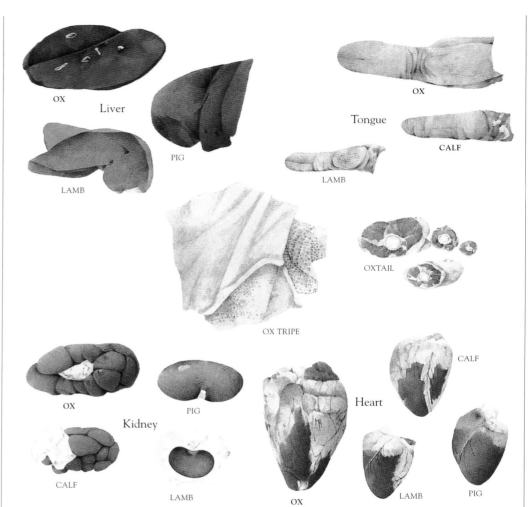

OX — Liver — PIG — LAMB

OX — Tongue — CALF — LAMB

OX TRIPE

OXTAIL

OX — Kidney — PIG — CALF — LAMB

CALF — Heart — OX — LAMB — PIG

with vegetables and spices, then all the meat is removed and set in the reduced jellied stock to make brawn. A pig's head from the butcher comes cleaned, trimmed and chopped into pieces ready for boiling.

Hearts

All hearts make good eating, but require long slow cooking.

Calf's heart Available only from specialist, high-class butchers. Ask the butcher to cut out the coarse fibres.

Lamb's heart This is the smallest and most tender heart. Choose bright red and firm hearts, avoiding any that are grey.

Ox heart A muscular and coarse piece of offal weighing up to 1.8 kg/4 lb. It is best used chopped in stews and casseroles.

Pig's heart This is larger and less tender than lamb's heart, usually inexpensive and may be stuffed and slowly braised.

Kidneys

Ox kidney is the largest and coarsest, followed by the similar but smaller and more tender calf's kidney. Lamb's kidney is far smaller, and is surrounded by a thick, white deposit of suet which is usually removed before the kidneys are sold. Pig's kidney is similar to lamb's in colour and texture, but is more elongated and flatter with no suet covering.

Calf's kidney Prepare and use as for ox kidney. Calf's kidney, being more tender, may also be braised or stewed. It is light brown with creamy-white suet.

Lamb's kidney This is the best kidney for grilling or frying. Choose light brown and firm kidneys, avoiding any that are dark or strong-smelling.

Pig's kidney May be grilled or fried or chopped up for stews and casseroles. Cut in half and snip out the gristly cores before grilling or serving.

Ox kidney This large kidney, about 675 g/1½ lb in weight, is usually tough and suitable only for slow-cooking stews, pies and meat puddings.

Liver

The best and most expensive is calf's liver, the cheapest ox. The latter has the strongest flavour, followed by pig's, lamb's and calf's liver in that order.

Calf's liver This is pale milky brown in colour and soft to the touch. Make sure the butcher removes the inedible main pipes. Grill or fry.

Lamb's liver Less expensive than calf's liver and excellent for frying and grilling. Choose liver light brown in colour and avoid any that is dark brown and therefore from an older animal.

Pig's liver Stronger in flavour and softer in texture than both calf's and lamb's, pig's liver may be grilled or fried. It is, however, better used for pâtés or included in stews and casseroles.

Ox liver A coarse and tough liver, not recommended for grilling or frying. It should be soaked in milk or lightly salted water for a few hours to mellow the strong flavour. It can then be stewed or braised, either on its own or with stewing steak.

Oxtail

This is sold ready skinned and jointed; the fat should be a creamy-white and the lean meat deep red. Excellent braised or in casseroles, and as a basis for rich, meaty soups.

Sausages

These are made by blending lean and fat meat with bread or cereal and seasonings. Preservatives may be added, but many butchers make sausages which have to be used promptly or frozen. There is a vast array of sausages on offer, from simple pork chipolatas to game sausages and others with herbs, seasonings or vegetables.

The meat content of sausages is controlled by law and has to relate to the title given to the sausages: pork sausages have to contain a minimum amount of pork, similarly beef sausages, and there is a limit to the percentage of fat to lean that can be used.

Chipolatas are slim, fine-textured pork sausages. Cocktail sausages are short chipolatas.

There are many regional variations, including black pudding, a sausage made with pig's blood, and haggis, made with sheep's offal, oatmeal and spices packed into a sheep's stomach.

Sweetbreads

Currently, sweetbreads taken from British cattle are not sold; however, imported sweetbreads are available. This is the term used for the thymus gland and the sweetbreads of calf and lamb are considered to be a delicacy as they have a light flavour and texture. Ox sweetbreads are tough and stronger in flavour.

Tongue

Ox and lamb's tongues are the most readily available.

Lamb's tongue A small tongue weighing only about 225 g/8 oz. Should be soaked in lightly salted water before boiling or braising. Skin before pressing the tongue between heavy weights and serving it cold cut into slices.

Ox tongue A single ox tongue weighs 1.8–2.72 kg/ 4–6 lb and can be bought fresh or salted. It must be slowly boiled for several hours, and the rough skin and bones removed before serving.

Tripe

This comes from the ox and is the lining of the stomach. Tripe from the first stomach is the smoothest and is known as blanket tripe. From the second stomach comes the honeycomb tripe. Both types of tripe should be thick, firm and white; avoid any that is slimy and grey or has a flabby appearance.

Tripe is sold blanched, rinsed and partly boiled – ask the butcher how much longer it should be cooked as it may require short braising. It can be stewed, boiled in milk, or sliced and deep fried.

CHEESE

Look on any large supermarket cold shelf and you will find a wide choice of cheeses from all over the world, including both the classics and many new varieties. The range varies according to trends in cooking and eating as well as fluctuations in the manufacture and availability of the raw ingredients, in this case milk from cows, ewes, goats or even buffalo (for traditional Italian mozzarella). Vegetarian cheeses, made without animal rennet, are also readily available. This listing highlights the best-known cheeses.

The majority of cheese is cut and pre-packed either by the manufacturer, distributor or the store staff. Generally, cheese that is vacuum-packed by the manufacturer or a central distributor will be of better quality than the chunks that are wrapped in plastic film actually at the delicatessen counter. If whole cheeses are available, it is also best to have a piece freshly cut. This allows you to select precisely the quantity you need, while the cheese is usually cut with more care; it is also freshly wrapped and not allowed to dry out or sweat. Avoid cheese which looks dried-out on the surface or with darkened corners or edges that have dried, shrunk and cracked.

Semi-soft cheeses, such as brie, that have a chalky layer running through the middle are not ripe, and will taste dry and tangy. A semi-soft cheese that looks very chalky and under-ripe will rarely ripen properly – the process of ripening should be carried out in controlled conditions by its maker and is something that can never be replicated satisfactorily at home.

When ripe, this kind of cheese should 'give' slightly when it is pressed, it should look smooth and the sides should bulge out slightly; when it is very ripe, the centre will run slightly, while extremely ripe cheese will have darkened patches (beige instead of creamy white) on the rind and the taste may be quite strong.

A ripe hard blue cheese, such as Stilton, should be creamy rather than crumbly and white and the rind should be slightly darkened. If there is a distinctly dark and slightly softened area running into the cheese from the rind, then the cheese will be very ripe, creamy and quite strong.

When storing cheese at home, wrap it in greaseproof paper and cling film or a sealed polythene bag, or place it in an airtight container, and store it in the refrigerator. Cheese for cooking can be used straight from the refrigerator. For eating, cheese is best served at room temperature: unwrap it about 1 hour before serving, place it on a cheeseboard or plate and cover loosely with cling film or greaseproof paper. If the cheese is left tightly

ENGLISH CHEDDAR

LEICESTER

CAERPHILLY

DERBY

SAGE DERBY

CHESHIRE

RED WINDSOR

CAITHNESS

STILTON

WENSLEYDALE

MORVEN

BLUE CHESHIRE

packed in a sealed container it will sweat. Chill any leftover cheese again promptly. Use the cheese by the recommended date printed on the packaging.

Grated hard cheese freezes well for cooking purposes and it can be used straight from frozen. Parmesan and Pecorino cheeses are excellent freezer candidates – buy and finely grate a large chunk of cheese, then thaw small amounts as required or use from frozen.

BRITISH CHEESES

An enormous variety of cheese is produced in Britain, from traditional favourites, like Cheddar and Stilton, to cheeses that were once available only as imports, for example brie, feta and paneer. Supermarkets offer an excellent range of home-produced cheese, but there are more to be found in independent delicatessen shops and markets. Cheeses such as Caithness may be found locally,

but others, such as Morven, are rarely made commercially. This list covers the traditional cheeses and some of the modern classics.

Applewood, smoked Smoked Cheddar with a rich flavour.

Blue Cheshire A golden-yellow cheese, deeply veined, with a strong flavour and slightly creamy texture. It has a stronger flavour than Stilton.

Blue Wensleydale An old cheese which is still made, but it is not

as common as ordinary (white) Wensleydale.

Caboc A soft, buttery, full-cream cheese, Caboc is seldom seen south of Scotland. The cheese is rolled in toasted oatmeal, and is best when eaten spread on biscuits without butter.

Caerphilly This crumbly white cheese from Wales has a mild, slightly tangy flavour.

Cheddar This is probably the most popular and best-known of

cheeses. English Cheddar has a strong yellow colour and a close, creamy texture. Its full, nutty flavour, which varies in strength, makes it a good all-purpose cheese. English Cheddar is at its best at six months old.

Scottish Cheddar has a firmer texture than English and often a stronger flavour. There are many imported Cheddars from areas as far apart as Ireland and Canada. All varieties are labelled with their country of origin and a guide to strength, from mild to extra mature.

In addition to the main Cheddar varieties, it is worth looking out for local Cheddars, produced on a smaller scale and usually rinded cheeses. They often have an excellent texture and flavour which tends to be firmer and less 'soapy' than some of the run-of-the-mill Cheddars.

Cheshire The oldest known British cheese, Cheshire has a mild, mellow and slightly salty taste. Cheshire is a crumbly cheese. Red Cheshire is also available.

Cornish Yarg A mild, pale hard cheese with a slightly tangy taste. The cheese is wrapped in nettles producing a dark grey-black rind.

Cottage cheese Low-fat soft cheese made from skimmed milk. The curd is cut up and heated in the whey, then drained and washed. Cottage cheese is very mild and slightly tangy.

Crowdie A Scottish soft cheese, with a finer texture than cottage cheese; made from skimmed milk and enriched with cream.

Curd cheese Tangy soft cheese with a smooth texture and, usually, a medium fat content.

Derby This is a honey-coloured and close-textured cheese. Derby cheese is allowed to mature for up to six months and during this time, its mild, distinctive flavour develops to the full.

Double Gloucester Vegetable colouring gives this firm, smooth, mature cheese a rich golden hue. Double Gloucester is made from the milk of Gloucester cattle and the cheese is matured for between three and six months.

Dunlop A moist Scottish cheese, rather like English Cheddar but with a softer texture and usually milder. It has the colour of pale butter. Good for grilling.

Huntsman A layered cheese, with Double Gloucester sandwiching a layer of Stilton.

Ilchester Flavoured Cheddar, originally with beer and chives.

Lancashire This crumbly, pale-coloured cheese has a mild, yet rich, and slightly salty flavour. Made and matured by traditional methods, Lancashire can be quite buttery, but the majority is not matured to this extent.

Leicester A mild cheese, a true Leicester is characterised by its fine grainy texture. Red Leicester has vegetable colouring added.

Low-fat soft cheese There is a wide variety of cheese in this category, including 'spreading' soft cheeses which can be useful in cooking. However, note the difference between a 'low-fat soft cheese' and a 'low-fat cheese spread' as the latter may have starch added and it will probably have a different taste. A spread with starch will also behave differently in cooking.

Pencarreg Brie A Welsh brie. It ripens to a soft creamy texture and has a rich flavour.

Red Windsor This Cheddar has red wine added to give it a slightly sweet 'cheese and wine' flavour and a pink-red colour.

Sage Derby This variation of Derby is now more widely available than the original cheese. Sage Derby is flavoured with the herb sage, giving it a full savoury flavour, and is coloured to give its distinctive green marbling.

Sheviok Cornish ewes' milk cheese with a firm texture.

Shropshire Blue A serious blue cheese, with a dark veining of blue in a rich, golden cheese. Mature and powerful.

Somerset Brie A creamy brie with a good flavour.

Stilton Between the distinctive patches of slate-blue mould, Stilton is a rich creamy colour when mature, not white which is a sign of immaturity. Traditionally at its best for Christmas, when cheeses made in September, from rich late-summer milk, were mature. Good Stilton is available throughout the year. It has a distinctive 'musty' blue flavour which is unmatched by any other blue cheese. Production is protected and carefully regulated by members of the Stilton Cheese-makers' Association. White Stilton is also available – it has a mild, slightly tangy flavour.

Swaledale A Yorkshire cheese with a smooth, soft texture and creamy flavour.

Teifi A Welsh cheese similar in texture to Gouda and enclosed in a pale wax rind. When mature, Teifi has a full, rich flavour and a smooth texture. There are varieties flavoured with herbs or with peppercorns. A variety flavoured with cumin seeds is made to an old medieval Dutch recipe, but it is not made in the same quantity as the plain cheese.

Wensleydale Crumbly in texture, Wensleydale is a pale cheese from Yorkshire. It is consistently mild in taste and is traditionally served with apple pie. Wensleydale was originally a blue cheese and a blue variety is available.

FAMOUS INTERNATIONAL CHEESES

Larger supermarkets offer a range of cheeses that differ widely in style, from creamy French and Italian cheeses to serve with biscuits, to tough ewes' cheese for grilling or creamy Indian cheese for frying. Not only are cheeses exported from their traditional countries of origin, but they are also made all over the world, so you may well buy a British 'Indian' paneer or 'Greek' feta. Sometimes it pays to check the origin of the product on the label as the cheese made in its native land can be far superior to the one made abroad: Italian mozzarella and Dutch mozzarella are good examples, the latter being inferior to the former in every respect.

French Cheeses

Banon A pungent-tasting cheese, originally made from goats' milk, but now made from a mixture of cows' and goats' milk, or solely cows' milk. Banon is dipped in brandy or wine and coated with rosemary and winter savory, then wrapped in chestnut leaves. Traditionally, Banon is left to mature for a couple of months in stone jars.

Bleu d'Auvergne This creamy textured blue cheese has green-blue veins and is produced by the same mould as Roquefort. Bleu d'Auvergne is salted outside and pricked before the mould is allowed to develop.

Bleu de Bresse Small, soft, creamy, dark-veined blue cheese with a rich, fairly mild taste.

Bleu des Causses This firm-textured blue cheese is made from cows' milk and matured in caves in the same way as Roquefort. Being made from cows' milk, this cheese has a less piquant taste than Roquefort which is made with ewes' milk.

Boulette d'Avesnes A sharp, matured buttermilk cheese which is flavoured with herbs.

Boursault This is a mild triple cream cheese with a slightly pink soft rind.

Boursin A triple cream cheese flavoured with garlic, herbs or peppercorns.

Brie A large, round semi-soft, pale yellow cheese, about 7.5 cm/ 3 in thick, with a slightly reddish edible crust and a delicate flavour. One of the world's great cheeses, brie is made from cows' milk. The majority of brie is factory-made, and there are many varieties. The quality varies enormously, and French brie is not necessarily better than British brie; in fact, there are many good British bries which are without doubt superior to some inferior French cheeses. French farmhouse brie is considered to be better than factory-made cheese. Brie de Meaux is thought of as the king of bries.

Camembert Small round, semi-soft and creamy cheese with a white mould on a pale yellow crust. Camembert has a stronger flavour than brie – it is said to be reminiscent of mushrooms – and it certainly becomes more pronounced as the cheese ripens. Sold whole in boxes or in individually wrapped portions. Press the cheese gently and it

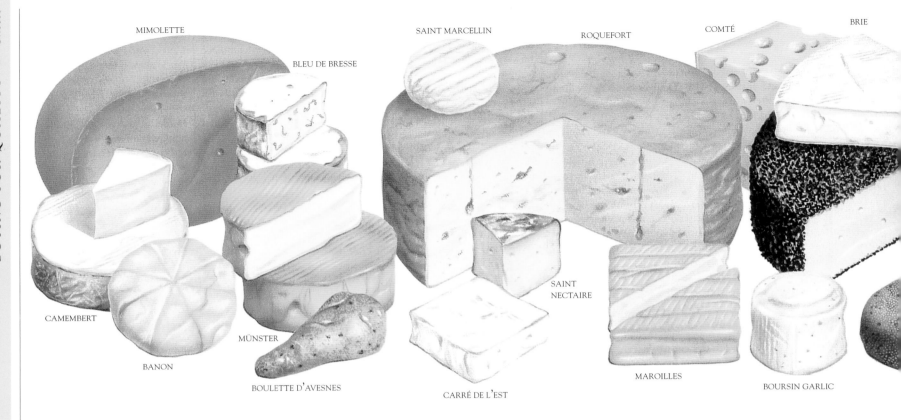

MIMOLETTE

BLEU DE BRESSE

SAINT MARCELLIN

ROQUEFORT

COMTÉ

BRIE

CAMEMBERT

BANON

MÜNSTER

BOULETTE D'AVESNES

CARRÉ DE L'EST

SAINT NECTAIRE

MAROILLES

BOURSIN GARLIC

will give when ripe. If the rind is visible, slightly yellow patches on at least one edge should break the white crust. Camembert that is over-ripe has dark patches, a very runny texture, is pungent and has a quite acrid taste.

Cantal, Fourme de Salers This is a hard, strong, pale yellow cheese which is made from cows' milk. It is one of the largest French cheeses, with a flavour similar to that of Cheddar.

Carré de l'Est A square, soft cheese, with a high fat content; it is similar to Camembert but milder in flavour.

Chaumes A semi-soft creamy cheese with an orange rind from the Dordogne region. Chaumes has a full, nutty flavour and strong aroma when ripe.

Comté A type of Swiss Gruyère: this firm, yellowish cheese has large holes.

Coulommiers A soft, yellowish cream cheese which has a white crust tinged with grey. This cheese has a stronger, less mellow flavour than brie, with a faint taste of almond.

Epoisses This soft, round cheese has an orange crust. It is made from curdled milk and is sometimes flavoured with clove, fennel or black pepper, then soaked in wine or *eau de vie*.

Fourme d'Ambert This veined sharp blue cheese, shaped like a drum, is crumbly in texture and slightly salty.

Gaperon or Gaperon d'Auvergne Small domed, basin-shaped cheese, with an edible white rind and semi-soft texture. Strongly flavoured with garlic and black peppercorns.

Langres A semi-hard or creamy cheese, usually sold in slices.

Livarot A soft, yellow cheese with a dark reddish-brown rind; made from skimmed milk. This cheese has a strong flavour, more pungent than Camembert.

Maroilles A square, semi-soft, slightly salted, yellow cheese with a reddish-brown rind, and a full flavour.

Mimolette A round cheese, orange in colour, with a grey rind; similar to a hard dry Cheddar.

Münster A semi-soft, creamy-textured and pungent cheese with reddish rind and strong flavour. Münster is sometimes flavoured with cumin or aniseed. Best eaten from November to April.

Petit Suisse A very creamy unsalted cheese, made from whole milk and extra cream, it has a faintly sour flavour and is often eaten with sugar.

Pipo Crem' A large, cylindrical blue cheese, sold in circular slices, this has a soft, edible white rind and a creamy texture. Pipo crem' has a mild flavour and a soft texture; it is similar to Italian dolcelatte.

Pont l'Evêque This square-shaped, semi-soft, pale yellow cheese has a crinkled yellow crust. Pont l'Evêque has a rich, flavour similar to that of Camembert.

Port-Salut A semi-hard, yellow cheese with a reddish rind and a bland taste.

Réblochon A soft cheese, pale cream in colour with an orange to chestnut rind. It has a bland

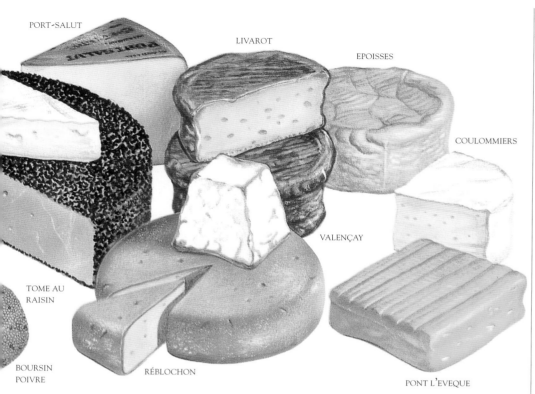

PORT-SALUT

LIVAROT

EPOISSES

COULOMMIERS

VALENÇAY

TOME AU RAISIN

BOURSIN POIVRE

RÉBLOCHON

PONT L'EVEQUE

taste which turns bitter when it is over ripe.

Roquefort A creamy-textured, tangy and powerful blue cheese which is made from ewes' milk. The cheese is ripened inside limestone caves.

Saint Marcellin A small, round, crumbly cream cheese made from goats' milk. Saint Marcellin has a mild taste with a touch of salt.

Saint Nectaire A semi-hard, pale yellow cheese with a rind coloured red, white and yellow and a bland but subtle flavour.

Saint Paulin A semi-hard, yellow cheese with a bland taste, similar to Port-Salut.

Tome, Tomme There are many cheeses of this type, including ewes' and cows' milk cheeses, and soft or semi-hard varieties.

Tome de Savoie A semi-hard yellow, strong-flavoured cheese with a reddish rind.

Tome au Raisin This white, processed cheese is covered with a mixture of dried black grape skins and pips.

Valençay or **Levroux** A creamy goat cheese, full-flavoured with a grey crust made by dusting the cheese with charcoal.

Italian Cheeses

Bel Paese Small whole buttery and mild cheese. Bel Paese has thin, dark yellow rind.

Caciocavallo This hard cheese is usually made in a pear shape. The cheese is white to straw-coloured, sometimes with a few holes, and the rind is smooth and thin with thread-like marks on the surface. It has a mild, semi-sweet flavour.

Dolcelatte Off-white in colour with blue-green veins running through it. It is a creamy, white soft cheese and far milder than Gorgonzola, its parent blue cheese. Dolcelatte was invented as a rich and creamy, milder alternative to Gorgonzola.

Fontina A semi-hard, pale cheese with a creamy texture and a nutty, slightly sweet flavour. The orange-coloured rind is often slightly thicker than on other cheeses. Imitations of this cheese are Fontal and Fontinella.

Gorgonzola The cheese is straw-coloured, mottled with blue-green and has a coarse brown rind. Gorgonzola has a pungent aroma and sharp flavour.

Mascarpone A rich cream cheese used in desserts.

Mozzarella Small round fresh cheese. Mozzarella was originally made from buffalo milk, but now both cows' and buffalo milk mozzarella are available.

The unsalted cheese has an elastic texture and a creamy flavour. It is packed in water and should be moist. Known for its use as a topping on pizza, when it melts to a creamy consistency, mozzarella is delicious marinated in oil and served with tomatoes or other salad ingredients.

Parmesan This is a well-matured cheese, which is kept for two years and is known as Parmigiano Reggiano. Fresh Parmesan is a hard cheese which breaks easily but it is not dried out and tough. It has a sweet, strong flavour.

Parmesan should always be purchased in pieces or freshly grated. The dried powdery cheese has a very strong (old socks) smell and the flavour is far inferior to good, freshly grated Parmesan.

Pecorino A hard cheese made from ewes' milk, this is pale in colour and crumbly in texture. Pecorino has a tangy flavour. There are many varieties of Pecorino; Pecorino Sardo is available as a young cheese or matured and almost as strong as Parmesan. Pecorino Romano is a strong, matured variety.

Provolone A hard curd cheese made in many different shapes – truncated cone, pear, melon or sausage – and tied with strings. The thin, smooth rind varies from yellow to brown, while the cheese itself is creamy-white.

Delicate and sweet after an average ripening of two or three months, it becomes spicy and almost sharp if kept longer, or if the curd has been prepared with kids' rennet. A lightly smoked variety is also obtainable.

Ricotta Ricotta is a fresh cheese made from whey left after the curds are strained. The whey may be from ewes' or cows' milk. Milk is added to the whey to give the characteristic creamy texture of the cheese.

There are two types of ricotta: a soft cheese with a smooth, light texture and a hard cheese which has a pale colour and is lightly salted. Both types of ricotta are sold in supermarkets; however, the soft white cheese is most common. Another matured variety is produced in Italy. Soft white ricotta is used in cooking as a filling for pasta, to make cheesecakes or in gnocchi. Unlike cream cheeses and curd cheeses, ricotta does not melt and run on heating.

Torta di Dolcelatte Although this is often sold *as* dolcelatte it is *not* dolcelatte. This cheese consists of layers of dolcelatte and mascarpone. It is very mild, lightly flavoured and creamy.

DOLCELATTE
FONTINA
PARMESAN
RICOTTA
CACIOCAVALLO
EDAM
GOUDA
DANISH BLUE
EMMENTHAL
GORGONZOLA
PROVOLONE
BEL PAESE
MOZZARELLA
GRUYERE
SAMSOE

Austrian Cheeses
Bergkäse Dull yellow with a dark brown rind, this hard cheese has a high fat content and a mild, nutty flavour.
Quargel This cheese is made in small rounds, which are yellow at the edges and white in the centre. Quargel has a piquant flavour.
Schlosskäse A mild-flavoured soft cheese, this cheese is pale yellow in colour with a heavily creased rind.

Danish Cheeses
Danbo Mild flavoured and firm textured, this cheese is easily recognised by its regular, even-sized holes. Sometimes it is given an added – and unusual – taste with caraway seeds.
Danish Blue This is a popular white cheese with close blue veins, with a salty flavour which diminishes as it matures. Danish blue has a soft, slightly crumbly texture.
Havarti This is a semi-hard

cheese with small holes, similar to Tilsit. The whole cheese may be cylindrical or loaf-shaped. it has a rich buttery taste with a slight tang.
Molbo A mild-flavoured cheese which has a slightly acid after-taste. Close-textured with a sprinkling of holes, Molbo is pale yellow with a red rind.
Samsoe A mild-flavoured cheese with a sweet, nutty flavour. Yellow colour with a firm texture and shiny round holes.

Dutch Cheeses
Edam This cheese has a mild flavour and a slightly rubbery consistency. It is always encased in a wax rind, which is red for the basic cheese. Matured Edam, with a stronger flavour, and varieties flavoured with herbs and/or spices are also available; these have black or green rinds. It is not recommended for cooking as Edam becomes stringy when it melts.
Gouda A creamy-tasting soft

cheese with a high butter-fat content. Produced in squat moulds, it is golden-yellow in colour. Gouda has far more flavour than Edam and there are several varieties, including a very well matured type with a strong flavour which cheese-sellers sometimes compare to Parmesan for strength. This cheese is not recommended for cooking.
Leerdamer Similar in appearance to Jarlsberg, this pale yellow cheese has a golden rind and a

ACHERIN
TRAPPISTENKÄSE
EDELPILZ
LIMBURGER
HALLOUMI
BERGKÄSE
FETA
TILSIT
SCHLOSSKÄSE
MOLBO
QUARGEL
DANBO

buttery, slightly waxy texture with even holes running through it. The flavour is only slightly sweet and very mild, without the rich, nutty taste of Jarlsberg.
Leiden A mellow cheese, with a slightly sharp taste when well ripened, flavoured with cumin.

Swiss Cheeses
Emmenthal Originally from Switzerland, Emmenthal is now also produced in Germany and Denmark, but there is little

difference in the flavour. The best kind of Emmenthal is made from milk of the highest quality. The cheese is dull yellow, with holes the size of cherries. It has a distinctly nutty taste.
Gruyère Widely used in cooking because of its full, nutty flavour, Gruyère is a hard cheese, pale yellow in colour, honeycombed with holes and having a brown, wrinkled rind. It is richer and more dense than Emmenthal and has smaller holes.

Vacherin This cheese is off-white in colour and has a rough, mottled rind. It is a semi-soft cheese with a mild flavour.

German Cheeses
Edelpilz A cows' milk cheese which is white around the edges, mottled blue at the centre, this cheese has a strong, sharp flavour and crumbly texture.
Limburger A soft cheese with a very strong smell and a spicy taste. It is made from whole

cows' milk. The rind is brown and shiny, and the cheese inside is bright yellow, with few holes.
Tilsit Originally made by Dutch settlers in East Prussia, this semi-hard cheese is also produced in Switzerland and Scandinavia.
Trappistenkäse A pale yellow cheese with a rich yellow rind, Trappistenkäse is a semi-soft cheese with a mild-flavour. It is made into loaves or bars and has a firm consistency with round or slitted holes.

Norwegian Cheeses
Gjetost This is a whey cheese, one in which the whey is cooked until its natural sugar content caramelises. Milk or cream may be added to the paste to make the cheese. Gjetost is made from goats' milk or cows' milk. It looks like dark brown fudge and it has a smooth, close, heavy texture. It tastes quite sweet and should be scraped into the thinnest of slices to serve because it is quite rich.
Jarlsberg A mild, smooth cheese with even holes through it. Jarlsberg has a rich nutty flavour with a slightly 'musty' aftertaste.
Ridder A yellow-rinded cheese with a semi-hard texture, this is similar to Saint Paulin. It has a mild, rich buttery flavour with a slight tang.

Greek Cheeses
Feta A semi-soft white curd cheese made from ewes' milk. White and firm but crumbly, feta can be quite creamy or dry and very salty. Packed in water to keep the cheese moist. Feta is full-flavoured and ideal for salads or it can be served as an appetiser

with black olives. Feta may be marinated in olive oil with herbs and garlic.
Halloumi This is a tough, white ewes' milk cheese which softens inside and forms a crisp golden crust when grilled. It has a slightly salty taste. Halloumi is also made in Turkey and the Middle East.

Cheeses from Other Countries
Manchego This is a Spanish cheese. It is a pale, creamy-white coloured hard cheese with a brown-gold textured, waxy rind. It has a good flavour with a hint of caramel-like sweetness, which is matched by a nutty, dry taste.
Monterey, Monterey Jack This cheese originates from California in the USA. It is similar in texture and flavour to Cheddar.
Paneer A fresh Indian cheese. The unsalted curds are pressed and cut into small cubes for frying in ghee. Neat blocks of the cheese are sold in vacuum packs which have a long shelf life. The fried cheese is golden and creamy, with a bland taste which goes well with spicy vegetables or rice dishes. Paneer is also used to make desserts.

VEGETABLES

To provide a year-round supply, vegetables today are imported from all over the world, including tropical countries as well as the Channel Islands and southern Europe. Despite the high standards of quality demanded by supermarkets, nothing can ever quite match the flavour of freshly picked vegetables in season. Take advantage of pick-your-own farms and farm shops. A good farm shop will probably have a fairly limited range of fresh vegetables either from one farm or from a number of local growers; some, however, are simply stores set up on farm land and the produce is not necessarily more local or any fresher than the vegetables you find in the supermarket. Country markets or farmers' markets are often good places to shop for fresh produce; this may not be washed, trimmed and as neat as that in a supermarket, but it can be extremely fresh and good value for money.

Supermarkets, though, must be given credit for stocking an enormous variety of exciting vegetables from across the world, and often for providing guidance on their preparation and cooking. Check the reverse of labels on vegetable wrappers, as these often contain useful information. This is a guide to popular vegetables with notes on the British commercial seasons.

Asparagus The English asparagus season is short, but imported asparagus is available throughout the year. Asparagus is a choice, but expensive, vegetable. It is sold loose or in bundles, and graded according to thickness of stem and plumpness of buds. Look for asparagus with tight, well-formed heads and avoid any with thin, woody, dry and dirty stems. Season: May and June.

Aubergines Oblong and almost round varieties of these distinctive, purple or white vegetables are available. Prime quality aubergines have a slight bloom to the shiny tough skin; the slightly fibrous flesh is pale creamy yellow. Season: May to September.

Avocados These fruits are shaped like pears. They are used as a vegetable rather than a dessert fruit. Avocados have green to purple skins. The oily, pale green, soft flesh surrounds a large stone. Avocados are not always ripe when bought: test them for ripeness by pressing the flesh gently at the rounded end – it should yield slightly. Avoid avocados with blotched, dry skins. Season: throughout the year.

Beans These may be eaten in the pod or shelled according to type, age and freshness.

Broad beans can be slender pods, up to 30 cm/12 in long with kidney-shaped, green-white or dark green seeds, or shorter

JERUSALEM ARTICHOKE

BEETROOT

SUMMER CABBAGE

SPRING CABBAGE

WINTER CABBAGE

BRUSSELS SPROUTS

WHITE CABBAGE

RED CABBAGE

SAVOY CABBAGE

CHICORY

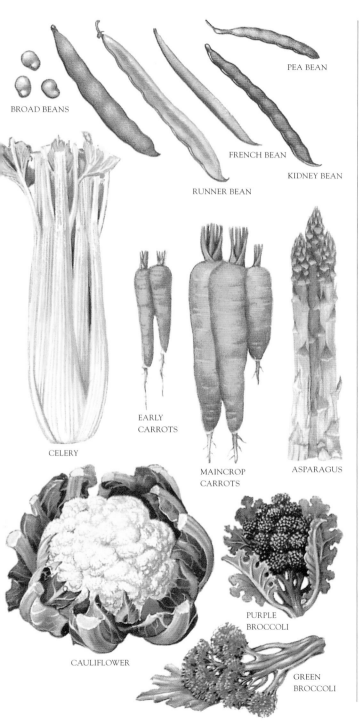

BROAD BEANS

PEA BEAN

FRENCH BEAN

KIDNEY BEAN

RUNNER BEAN

CELERY

EARLY
CARROTS

MAINCROP
CARROTS

ASPARAGUS

CAULIFLOWER

PURPLE
BROCCOLI

GREEN
BROCCOLI

pods, about 15 cm/6 in long, with round seeds. All pods should have a uniform bright green colour, which is free from black markings. Avoid shrivelled, dry-looking pods.

Blanch* broad beans before freezing them and use them within 2–3 months. Although young broad beans are a delicacy cooked complete with their pods, broad beans are usually shelled. Season: June and July.

French beans include a number of types, varying from almost flat pods, up to 13 cm/5 in long, to shorter and plumper beans; their colour varies from pale to mid-green. Most of them are stringless when young. Yellow French beans are also available in small quantities. Always buy young, crisp French beans. Season: June to September.

Kidney beans are heavy-podded, with the kidney-shaped beans showing through. The most popular variety is the purple kidney bean, which turns green when cooked. Choose kidney beans with a distinct bloom. Season: June to October.

Runner beans are larger, coarser and have more flavour than French beans. At their best they have bright green, succulent pods which need stringing before they are cooked. A runner bean should snap between the fingers. Avoid runner beans which are tough, limp, misshapen, dirty, or pitted with brown or black. Season: June to October.

Beetroot Two types of beetroot are available: long beetroot and globe-shaped. Small globe-shaped beetroot are sold in bunches from June onwards, but maincrop beetroot is sold by weight, either cooked or raw. Buy cooked beetroot with fresh skin which looks slightly moist, and avoid shrivelled beetroot which is usually tough and woody.

Uncooked beetroot bleeds easily, and care must be taken not to tear the skin when preparing beetroot for cooking. Plain, vacuum-packed cooked beetroot (without any vinegar or acid-based preservative) is an excellent vegetable to keep in the store cupboard as it has a long shelf life and a good flavour. Season: throughout the year.

Broccoli While cauliflower has one fused head of curds, broccoli develops into numerous shoots, each terminating in a small floret. There are white or green sprouted broccoli, as well as purple broccoli. Choose broccoli with small, fresh-looking heads and brittle stalks which snap easily in the fingers. Season: throughout the year.

Brussels sprouts This vegetable is popular in autumn and winter. The flavour is improved by frost. Look for firm, green sprouts and avoid those with loose leaves and any which show signs of yellowing and wilting. Season: August to April.

Cabbages There are green, white and red varieties, which may be conical or round, loose-leafed or tightly packed.

Use red cabbages for braising, marinating or for pickling. Fresh red cabbages have a good bloom. Season: October to June.

Savoy cabbages should have firm green heads with crisp and curling outer leaves. Pale green Savoys are almost certainly not fresh. Season: August to May.

Spring cabbages should have bright green and crisp leaves. Season: April and May.

Spring greens are young, mid-green cabbages sold before the hearts have developed. Use them on the day of purchase, as they wilt quickly. Season: November to April.

Summer and autumn cabbages follow spring cabbages, but have larger, more solid heads. Choose only firm, crisp-looking cabbages and check that the base of the stalk is clean. Avoid cabbages with slimy stalk ends and leaves pitted with holes. Season: June to October.

White cabbages are excellent both for cooking and for using in salads. Choose firm, compact heads, and avoid any with loose curling leaves or those with brown smudges. Season: throughout the year.

Winter cabbages are popular, particularly the round drumhead types. See that the heads are firm, and avoid any with wilting outer leaves. Season: November to March.

Calabrese This vegetable has a compact head of white, green or purple firm curds. Buy only well-coloured heads, avoiding any with limp leaves. Season: May to November.

Carrots Young and slender carrots are available in bunches with the foliage intact; they are tender and need only scrubbing before cooking. Maincrop carrots are larger and coarser; they are sold without the leaves and by weight. Maincrop carrots are available washed and unwashed, but require scraping or peeling. Avoid pitted and broken carrots. Season: July to May.

Cauliflowers Both summer and winter varieties are available; on winter cauliflowers (sometimes wrongly called broccoli) the dark green leaves are folded over the white curds, on summer cauliflowers the leaves are opened out. Choose cauliflowers with the creamy-white heads not fully developed and with clean white stalks. Avoid any cauliflowers with limp leaves and loose, brown, grey or damaged curds. Season: throughout the year.

Celeriac This is the edible root of a variety of celery. It has become more popular in Britain. Celeriac, which varies in size from an apple to a coconut, has a brown fibrous skin and creamy white flesh with a celery flavour. Look for firm roots showing no signs of mushy flesh. Season: August to January.

Celery The stalks of this vegetable are used raw in salads, or braised and used in soups and stews. The common varieties are white or pink, but pale green celery is also available, blanched, self-blanched or all green. Choose thick celery, plump at the base and with smooth sticks. The leaves indicate the freshness of celery: on prime celery the leaves are pale green and straight. Season: July to November (glasshouse May to July).

Chinese leaves These are a cross between a crunchy lettuce and a cabbage. The tall compact leaves have wide central stalks which

are tender and edible with pale green, frilly leaf surrounds. They keep well in a polythene bag in the refrigerator for about a week. Shred the leaves and use them raw or cook by stir frying or braising them for a short time. Season: April to December.

Chicory A salad vegetable with a conical white head of crisp leaves packed firmly together. Choose heads that are firmly packed and avoid any which show yellow, curling leaves. Season: April to November.

Courgettes Distinct type of vegetable marrow, specially grown and harvested at about 15 cm/ 6 in long. Prime courgettes are straight, firm and light green. Season: May to October.

Cucumbers Hothouse cucumbers are the ones usually seen in the shops and supermarkets, although small numbers of ridge or outdoor cucumbers also appear. Choose straight, firm cucumbers with a diameter no greater than 5 cm/2 in; the skin should have a bloom to it. Season: January to November.

Endive A salad vegetable with pale green, almost yellow and curly, bitter leaves. Choose dry, firm endive, avoiding any which look greasy at the base. Endive should not be confused with chicory (Belgian endive). Season: May to October.

Fennel, Florence fennel These are swollen stem bases with top leaves removed. They have a distinct aniseed flavour. Choose rounded ones, ranging in colour from pale green to white, avoiding deep green ones. Season: August to October.

Garlic A member of the onion family, which is only sold dried. The white or pink skin encloses small, curved segments known as cloves. These are surrounded by a thin layer of skin which must be peeled off. Store in a dry, dark place. Season: July to January.

Globe artichokes The artichoke is the leafy flower head of a thistle-like plant. The grey-green, stiff leaves overlap each other, and the edible parts of the leaves are the fleshy bases of each leaf. Below the leaves is the bottom, or fond of the artichoke, which has the finest flavour. Buy artichokes with stiff leaves which have a slight bloom. Season: June to June.

Horseradish This long, strongly flavoured root is seldom seen fresh in shops and markets. It is not used as a vegetable on its own, but as an ingredient of cold sauces. Horseradish at its best has straight roots, 2.5–5 cm/1–2 in thick at the top. Season: June to September.

Jerusalem artichokes These tubers are covered with a thin white or purple skin. The crisp sweet flesh is white. Prime tubers are fairly regular in shape, and measure up to 10 cm/4 in in length and about 5 cm/2 in across. Avoid Jerusalem artichokes that are very knobbly or misshapen, small and/or covered in dirt. Season: October to March.

Kale The broad leaves vary in colour from dark green to purple. They are heavily crimped and have prominent pale green or white mid-ribs. Avoid kale with yellow, drooping or damaged leaves. Season: October to April.

CHINESE LEAVES

LAMB'S LETTUCE

LOLLO ROSSO

ROCKET

OAK LEAF LETTUCE

RADICCHIO

Kohl-rabi This has a swollen stem, with a turnip-like flavour. The white or purple-skinned vegetables should be bought young, when they are the size of an orange. Avoid large coarse kohl-rabi and any with decayed leaves. Season: July to February.

Leeks These are composed of tightly packed skin layers which branch at the top into dark green leaves. The stems are white with an onion flavour. Look for well-shaped, straight leeks, trimmed at the top and avoid those with yellow, discoloured and slimy leaves. Season: July to May.

Lettuces and salad leaves An exciting array of salad leaves is sold throughout the year.

As well as the somewhat tasteless round or cabbage lettuce, there are cos, which has crisp, long, loose leaves; iceberg, with tightly packed, pale green and very crisp leaves which have a good, sweet flavour; and sweet-flavoured Little Gem lettuce hearts. Oak leaf lettuce has decorative soft leaves tinged dark red, which are more valued for appearance than flavour. Frisée or curly endive is a tight, frilly lettuce with pale green leaves

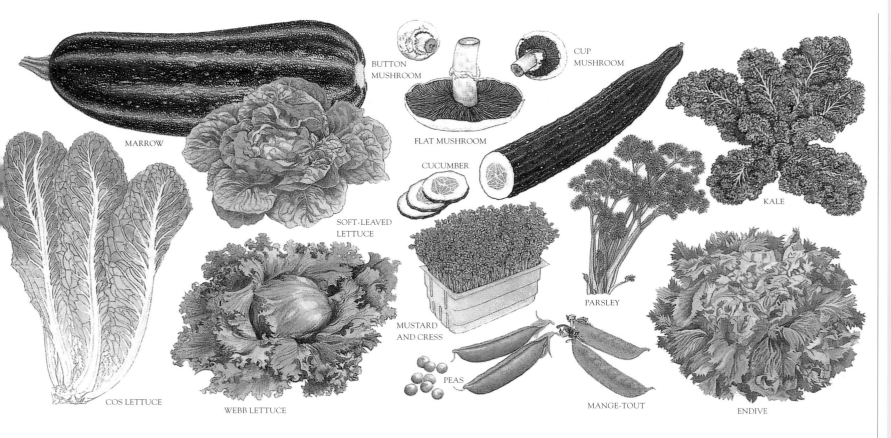

MARROW

BUTTON MUSHROOM

CUP MUSHROOM

FLAT MUSHROOM

CUCUMBER

KALE

SOFT-LEAVED LETTUCE

PARSLEY

MUSTARD AND CRESS

COS LETTUCE

WEBB LETTUCE

PEAS

MANGE-TOUT

ENDIVE

and a crunchy texture. Lollo biondo and lollo rosso are two attractive lettuces with a sweet flavour, the latter being tinged with red. The small oval leaves of lamb's lettuce or corn salad have a sweet flavour. Radicchio, though classed with the salad leaves, is actually a variety of chicory with red leaves and a bitter flavour. Rocket is a cross between a herb and a salad vegetable. It has a strong, rather peppery flavour, which is excellent in salads, but the plant should be used only in small amounts for that reason.

Mange-tout These are flat, bright green pods, about the length of pea pods, containing small round pea seeds. The ends are trimmed, then the pods are cooked and eaten whole. Season: July to September.

Marrows The skin of a marrow should be soft, with a dull bloom to it. Avoid awkwardly shaped and flabby marrows. Season: May to October.

Mooli Also known as daikon, this is a long white radish. It has the same peppery flavour as the familiar red radish, but it is not quite as hot. Use raw or shred

and cook in stir fries. Mooli can be cooked in the same way as turnips. Season: June to October.

Mushrooms These are sold either as buttons, open cup, open or flat according to age.

White and brown types are available, with brown, or chestnut, mushrooms having slightly more flavour than small white mushrooms. Large flat mushrooms have more flavour than the young button mushrooms. Choose mushrooms carefully as they turn limp quickly and soon lose their flavour. Avoid limp, broken mushrooms.

A good selection of specialist mushrooms are available from supermarkets. These may include oyster mushrooms, pale cream or yellow in colour with a delicate mushroom flavour; and shiitake, a dark, fairly small and close-textured mushroom with a strong flavour and used in oriental cooking. Wild mushrooms are also sold in some larger supermarkets, and the following are examples of those currently available. These must be cleaned carefully to remove all dirt and to ensure that the mushrooms are free from maggots (look for

tiny holes). *Trompettes des morts* are slim, black horn-shaped mushrooms with a rich flavour. They are also known as horn of plenty or black trumpet mushrooms. *Chanterelles* are a pale golden colour and have a slight hint of apricot in their flavour. *Pied de mouton* are also known as hedgehog fungus, and have pale creamy yellow caps that are pale underneath. The fins or spines do not grow from the stem out to the edge of the cap, but vertically, giving the underside of the mushrooms a spongy appearance. *Pied de mouton* have a

PEPPERS

SALSIFY

CELERIAC

AVOCADO

GLOBE ARTICHOKE

AUBERGINE

OKRA

COURGETTE

SWEET POTATO

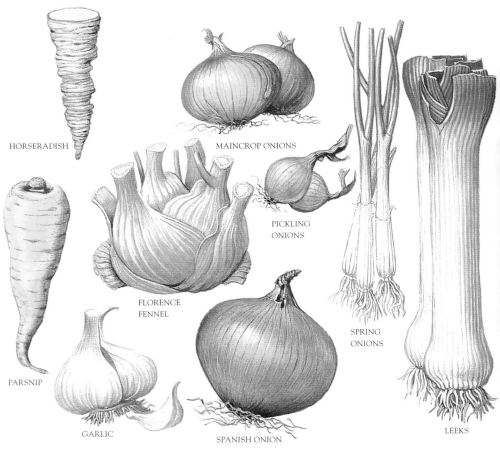

HORSERADISH

MAINCROP ONIONS

PICKLING ONIONS

FLORENCE FENNEL

SPRING ONIONS

PARSNIP

GARLIC

SPANISH ONION

LEEKS

delicious 'savoury' flavour which is not too strong. The raw mushrooms can taste bitter, but this bitterness disappears when the mushrooms are cooked, unless they are very large, in which case they may still taste bitter even after cooking. Season: throughout the year.

Mustard and cress (salad cress) This is another misnamed vegetable, because boxes of mustard and cress usually contain salad rape only. Buy mustard and cress in punnets; it should have a

bright green colour. Season: throughout the year.

Okra, ladies' fingers These vegetables are curved seed pods up to 23 cm/9 in long. They are usually eaten green, pod and seeds, when they are slightly under-ripe, and are served either whole or sliced, quickly sautéed or long braised. Season: throughout the year.

Onions Ordinary onions vary in shape and colour from flattish bulbs with brown skins to round bulbs with red-brown or pale

straw-coloured skins. As a very rough guide, the smaller the onion, the stronger the flavour. Large 'Spanish' onions have a mild, sweeter flavour than the traditional small British types. Choose onions which are firm and regular in shape and have feathery skins. Onions with shrivelled skins and softness around the neck are likely to be bad.

Red or white salad onions are also available. These have very fine skins and a lighter, slightly sweeter, flavour than the average

'cooking' onion. They can be cooked as well as eaten raw. Season: throughout the year.

Small pickling onions are available from early autumn into the beginning of winter.

Parsnips These vegetables are sold both washed and unwashed. The flavour is improved by a touch of frost, so they are best from October onwards, but before the central cores become woody. Buy parsnips with a crisp clean look; avoid any with a split or dried-up root, or with soft

brown patches on the crown. Season: July to April.

Peas Early peas (May) have round seeds, while maincrop and late varieties usually have wrinkled seeds. Buy peas with bright crisp pods and avoid any which are so large that they show through the pods. Test for freshness by eating the peas raw when they should be sweet and tender. Season: May to October.

Peppers These vegetable fruits have green, yellow, orange or red skins. They are sold with the

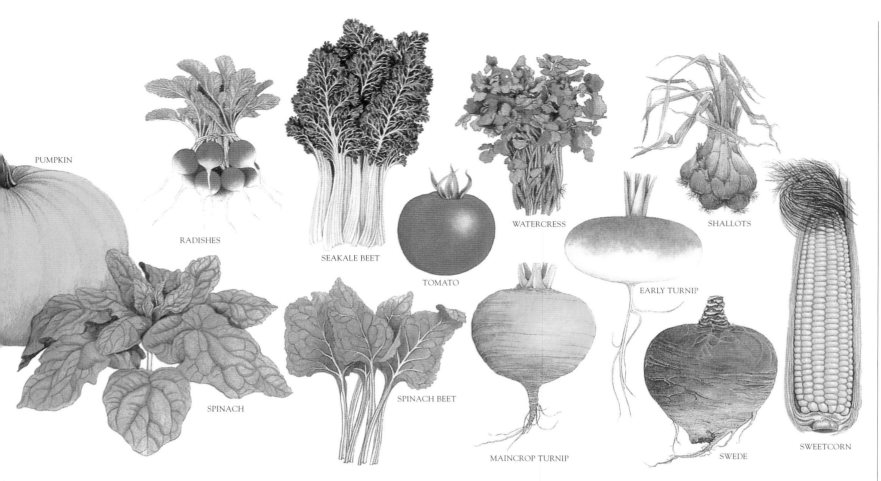

PUMPKIN

RADISHES

SEAKALE BEET

TOMATO

WATERCRESS

SHALLOTS

SPINACH

SPINACH BEET

EARLY TURNIP

MAINCROP TURNIP

SWEDE

SWEETCORN

stalk ends attached, and before use these must be cut off and the inner white mid-ribs and seeds removed. Choose firm, shiny peppers and avoid any which are misshapen and dull-looking. Season: May to October.

Potatoes Many varieties are grown commercially in Britain, and the name of the potato has to be displayed or included on the label when these vegetables are offered for sale. There is more emphasis on varieties which are good for baking these days,

especially as there is a year-round supply of 'new' potatoes or small, interesting, varieties which boil well and have a superior flavour.

As a general rule, King Edward potatoes are an excellent 'all-round' potato, giving good results when cooked by boiling, frying or baking. Both maincrop and early potatoes are now available throughout the year, and home-grown varieties come into season in May.

Early potatoes should be purchased in small quantities as they

quickly lose their earthy, crisp flavour. Early potato varieties include *Arran, Home Guard, Comet* and *Maris Bard*.

Maincrop potatoes are available from August to May. They may be bought in larger quantities than early potatoes. After they have been stored for a long time, the red-skinned varieties tend to lose their colour.

Maincrop varieties include *Cara, Desirée, King Edward, Maris Piper, Pentland Crown, Pentland Dell* and *Wilja*.

Pumpkins American pumpkins may weigh up to 45 kg/100 lb, but those seen in Britain weigh much less. Choose close-textured, non-stringy pumpkin. They are cooked like marrow or used for as pie fillings. Harvested in September and October, pumpkins can be stored to provide a supply for several months.

Radishes Small, pungent vegetables, used fresh in salads. Radishes may be round and red, tapering and white, bright red with white tips or black with

white flesh. Choose crisp, young, not too large radishes. Season: throughout the year.

Salsify This root vegetable has soft, white flesh. Look for young, regular-tapered roots with fresh grey-green leaves which can be added to salads. Season: October to April.

Scorzonera, black salsify Similar to salsify, this long, slender root vegetable has black skin and white flesh. Avoid small roots or those with shrivelled dry skins. Season: October to March.

43

Seakale beet, chard or Swiss chard This vegetable has spinach-like, dark green crisp and crinkled leaves with prominent white mid-ribs like celery stalks. Both the stalks and leaves are used. Season: August and September.

Shallots These small onions are chiefly used to flavour sauces. The smooth and firm bulbs have a slight garlic flavour. Choose hard, rounded bulbs, avoiding any with thick necks. Season: August to March.

Spinach There are two types of true spinach, the round-leafed summer variety and the prickly-leafed winter spinach. Both have tender dark green leaves which must be handled carefully as they easily bruise. Spinach wilts very quickly, and should be crisp to the touch. New Zealand spinach is similar to other leaf spinach, but it has smaller, drier and tougher leaves. Season: April to October.

Spinach beet Although seldom seen in the shops, this all-year-round spinach is a favourite vegetable in many gardens.

Spring onions The term spring onion is a misnomer, as this vegetable is in season throughout the year. Spring onions are essentially salad vegetables, but they are also popular for stir fries as well as for use in lightly cooked dishes or mixtures in which ordinary onions would taste very strong or 'raw'. The mild-flavoured bulbs have thin skin, which peels off easily. Choose spring onions with small bulbs and fresh green foliage, and avoid any with traces of worms or wilting or dark leaves.

Season: throughout the year.

Sprouting beans and seeds Beansprouts and alfalfa sprouts are dried seeds which are soaked and germinated. They are then used after a few days, before the young sprouts develop any signs of green growth. If the shoots are allowed to grow too long, the flavour can be bitter. The sprouts may be used in salads or stir fries, or quickly braised. Any cooking must be brief to retain the crunchy texture of the sprouts. Sprouting seeds have a high protein content.

Squashes These come from the same family as pumpkins, marrows and courgettes. The following are some of the types available throughout the year, according to type and imports. They can be cooked in the same way as marrow or pumpkin.

Pear-shaped and orange-beige in colour, butternut squash can be as small as a potato or as large as a melon. It has a small central hole and bright orange, sweet-tasting flesh.

Acorn squash is dark green, oval and ridged lengthways. Patty pan are small, green and yellow, and shaped like flying-saucers. They are cooked as for courgettes and have firm flesh and a good flavour. Custard squashes are pale-skinned and look like large patty pan squashes – they are sometimes called patty pan – but the flavour is not as good.

Spaghetti squash looks like a large melon; it is boiled whole, then cut to reveal the flesh which is in pale fine strands, hence the name. The flesh is delicious with butter and cheese,

KOHL-RABI

MOOLI

ACORN SQUASH

PATTY PAN SQUASH

SPAGHETTI SQUASH

BUTTERNUT SQUASH

GEM SQUASH

or it can be topped with a variety of sauces. Gem squash are small, round and dark green.

Sugar-snap peas These peas are similar to mange-tout, but the edible pods contain slightly larger peas. Delicious and sweet. Season: July to September.

Swedes These winter vegetables are similar to turnips, but the yellow flesh is milder in flavour. Avoid roots which are forked. Season: July to May.

Sweetcorn, corn on the cob The best cobs should be creamy and shiny within the bright green stiff outer leaves. The tassels at the top of the cob should be black and withered. Season: July to November.

Sweet potatoes These are not related to ordinary potatoes, the only resemblance being that they are both tubers. However, sweet potatoes are cooked by boiling, peeled or in their skins and they take about the same time to cook as large ordinary potatoes. Season: throughout the year.

Sweet potatoes are globular or elongated and may be white, pink, red or purple. The yellow or orange flesh is firm and slightly sweet. Sweet potatoes should not to be confused with the coarse-skinned, earthy-brown yam, which has white flesh.

Tomatoes Imported tomatoes are available throughout the year, but the best tomatoes are homegrown, in hothouses or in the open. There are a number of varieties that are commonly available, including small cherry tomatoes with a full flavour, also available as yellow fruit as well as red; plum tomatoes, with a good

flavour and a 'solid' fleshy texture; and very large beefsteak or Mediterranean tomatoes that tend to have a weak flavour and rather watery, seedy texture. Season: June to September.

Turnips There are two types of this root vegetable: early and maincrop. Early turnips have tender, mustard-flavoured flesh, which may be eaten both raw and cooked. They are usually sold washed, in bunches, and appear in the shops from April until July.

Maincrop turnips have a coarser flesh, but are excellent boiled and in soups and stews. Avoid turnips with brown spots and holes, and any with spongy patches. Season: August to May.

Watercress This small-leafed vegetable is mainly used in salads, soups and for garnishing dishes. Avoid watercress in flower or with a high proportion of yellow or wilting leaves. Use watercress within 24 hours of purchase. Season: throughout the year.

Yam These large, dark brown tubers have a thick, coarse skin. Yams should not be confused with thin-skinned sweet potatoes. Yams are usually sold whole in supermarkets (they are about the size of three or four potatoes) but in some markets, very large yams are cut up and sold by weight. They are related to cassava, a similar vegetable with white flesh which is cut into chunks and boiled. Yams taste very much like potatoes when they are cooked. Season: throughout the year. **Note** Never eat raw yam as it contains a natural toxin that is destroyed by cooking.

FRUIT

A wide variety of excellent-quality fruit is available throughout the year. Even soft fruit and currants are now on sale well out of their domestic seasons, their flavour usually standing up well to comparison with home-grown varieties. They can be expensive, however, so are not for everyday eating.

This section gives descriptions of different fruit and, where relevant, when home-grown produce is available, along with traditional favourite varieties. As with other produce, fruit should be eaten as soon as possible after purchase, and its keeping quality depends on type as well as how ripe it is when bought.

Soft fruit and stone fruit are particularly vulnerable to decay. Soft fruit should be chilled and eaten within a day of purchase; sometimes the fruit will keep for a couple of days in the refrigerator. Stone fruit should be kept in a cool room where it will keep for 2–3 days, according to its ripeness when purchased. The same watchpoint applies to many types of exotic fruit – use them promptly after purchase.

Apples keep well in a cool place but they dry out rapidly in the warm. In a cool kitchen, good-quality, unbruised, unblemished apples will keep for about a week, but prime-quality, freshly picked apples can be stored in a cool cellar, outhouse or garden shed. Fruit which is free from blemishes and wrapped in paper will keep for several months. Fruit with even the slightest sign of damage will rot from the point of the blemish. The fruit must be kept separate for this reason, or otherwise the damage will spread rapidly from one to another. To keep fruit in peak condition for a

long storage period involves keeping it very slightly damp and cool, away from frost and safe from wet and out of reach of vermin. Pears ripen quickly and should be eaten within 3–5 days, again depending on their condition when they were purchased.

Citrus fruit will keep for up to 2 weeks in a cool room. Lemons and limes should be kept in the refrigerator, where they will keep well until they are cut. Cut citrus fruit should be wrapped in cling film and stored in the refrigerator; it will keep for up to a week, but it will be far less juicy than when it has been freshly cut. If kept in a warm room, particularly stacked in a bowl, citrus fruit will dry out and squashed fruit underneath will become mouldy.

Soft fruit and apples will freeze well; stone fruit tends to become very soft once it has thawed. Stewed fruit and fruit purées freeze well.

All fruit should be washed or quickly rinsed and drained before it is eaten or used in cooking.

TOP FRUIT

Top fruit, which is the term used by fruit growers for all tree fruits, includes apples and pears, and also stone fruits such as cherries, nectarines, plums and peaches, as well as nuts.

Apples These are probably the most popular fruit. Apples are divided into dessert (or eating) and cooking apples. While cooking apples can only be used for culinary purposes, many dessert apples are also excellent for certain recipes. Look for apples with smooth skins and avoid any with brownish bruises.

Popular imported varieties of apple include *Granny Smith*, bright green skin with crisp juicy flesh and sharp flavour; *Golden Delicious*, smooth yellow-green skin with slightly woolly flesh and a fairly weak flavour; *Red Delicious*, which is similar to Golden Delicious, but sweeter; *Royal Gala*, which has red skin and a sweet crunchy flesh; and *Idared*, which has yellow-green skin streaked with red and sweet, crisp and juicy flesh. Traditional British varieties are still very popular, particularly *Worcester Pearmain*, which has a thick skin of pale green-yellow, heavily fused with crimson, and tough, white, sweet flesh (season: September to November); *Laxton's Superb*, with a yellow-green to pale lemon skin, marked with dull red, and firm juicy flesh (season: November to April); *Egremont Russet*, with a reddish-brown skin and crisp firm flesh (season: October to December); and *Cox's Orange Pippin*, with yellow-green to golden-yellow skin, flushed and streaked with orange or red, and firm, crisp, juicy and aromatic flesh (season: September to May).

Cooking apples are very much a British fruit as other countries use 'dessert' fruit for cooking. The main difference between the two types of apple is that cooking apples quickly reduce to a pulp whereas dessert apples require far longer stewing before they lose their shape. Cooking apples also have a sharp, intense flavour and usually need to be well sweetened during cooking.

The favourite variety of cooking apple is the *Bramley's Seedling* (season: end October to July). Other varieties include: *Grenadier* (season: August and September); *Lord Derby* (season: from October onwards); *Newton Wonder* (season: December until March); and *Early Victory* (season: July and August).

Apricots These small stone fruits have yellow, juicy and sweet flesh. Buy firm apricots, avoiding any fruit with bruised or squashy, brown skins. Season: throughout the year.

Cherries Buy firm, dry cherries and avoid containers with a high percentage of leaves to berries.

Dessert cherry varieties are either white (or pink) and black. The berries have juicy flesh, which varies from white-yellow to dark red.

Among the many home-grown varieties, the following are most often seen: *Napoleon Bigarreau* (season: mid to late June); *Frogmore Early* (season: late June); and *Merton Heart* (season: late June to end July).

The sour morello cherry is suitable for jam-making (season: July to August). Imported cherries are available all year round.

Crab apples These small, apple-like fruits are not usually available in the shops. The acid flesh has an excellent flavour when used for making preserves, such as crab apple jelly. Season: September and October.

Nectarines These stone fruits are a variety of peach. They have smooth skins and juicy, sweet flesh. Nectarines are served as a dessert fruit. Most nectarines are imported and are in season throughout the year.

Peaches There are two types. Free-stone peaches have juicy, soft flesh which comes easily away from the stone. Cling stone peaches have firmer flesh which adheres tightly to the stone. Free-stone peaches are considered to have a better flavour but are seen in the shops less frequently. Avoid any which have split or those with bruised skins and brown or soft spots. Imported peaches are available throughout the year and English hothouse peaches are in the shops from May until October.

Pears Many pears are home-grown and, with the addition of imported supplies, pears are now available throughout the year.

All pears can be served as dessert fruit or used for cooking. The term 'cooking pears' refers to slightly under-ripe fruit or firm varieties. Fruit with tough skin is often preferred for cooking. Pears bruise easily and should be handled with care. If pears are bought before they are fully ripe

EGREMONT RUSSET

GRANNY SMITH

CRAB APPLE

COX'S ORANGE PIPPIN

WORCESTER PEARMAIN

GOLDEN DELICIOUS

BRAMLEY'S SEEDLING

LAXTON'S SUPERB

they should be left in a warm room for 2–3 days when they will be ready for eating. Ripe pears will yield when gently pressed at the pointed stalk end.

The following are examples of popular home-grown varieties. Traditionally, Conference pears are the most widely grown for commercial purposes. Other varieties are available in smaller quantities, for shorter periods. *Conference*, a tapering dark green pear, heavily spotted with russet; creamy-pink, with juicy, sweet flesh (season: end September to

February). *Doyenne du Comice*, large, oval-shaped pear with pale yellow skin, occasionally flushed with red or russet; this variety has pale yellow, juicy, cinnamon-flavoured flesh (season: end October to December). *Williams' Bon Chrétien*, medium tapering pear with pale green skin turning yellow; juicy and sweet flesh (season: August).

Plums This group of top fruits includes both dessert and culinary varieties. Gages are a type of plum, round and green to yellow in colour. Damsons, too, are

plums with dark blue to black skin; damsons are oval in shape and smaller than gages, and should only be used cooked and for jam-making.

Plums should be firm to the touch, with a bloom on the skin; they are often sold slightly under-ripe and can be kept in a cool room for 1–3 days before serving. Imported plums are available throughout the year; they should be used at once.

Czar, large, dark blue plum with golden flesh and red juice (season: early August). *Pershore*,

SWEET CHERRY

KIRKE'S BLUE

MORELLO CHERRY

CZAR

PERSHORE

VICTORIA

DAMSON

CONFERENCE

DOYENNE DU COMICE

WILLIAM'S BON CHRÉTIEN

GAGE

NECTARINE

APRICOT

PEACH, IMPORTED

PEACH, ENGLISH

CHESTNUTS

HAZELNUTS

WALNUTS

FILBERT NUTS

tapering dessert plum, with yellow, faintly red-tinted skin and sometimes rather mealy flesh (season: August). *Victoria*, large oval plum, with a yellow skin flushed with scarlet; sweet and juicy flesh (season: late August). *Kirke's Blue*, a large, purple-black plup with a distinct bloom and juicy dark flesh.

Among the varieties of gages are: *Ouillin's Golden Gage* (season: August) and *Cambridge Gage* (season: August).

Quinces These fruits are sometimes available during October

and November. They have tough golden skin when ripe, and the firm, sour flesh is highly aromatic. Used for jams and jellies, or to flavour pies.

Sloes A member of the plum family. These are small fruit with blue-black skin. They have a dry, very sharp flavour and are usually used in preserves or for making sloe gin made by macerating the fruit in gin for several months.

For sloe gin the sloes are pricked all over before macerating, and sugar is added to make a rich, fruity liqueur.

NUTS

Chestnuts The shiny brown fruits of the sweet chestnut are enclosed in a fleshy outer covering which breaks open when the nuts are ripe. Avoid any chestnuts that look dried out and shrivelled. Season: October to December.

The large French chestnuts, called *marrons*, are sold boiled, peeled and vacuum packed or canned in brine or syrup. They are also sold puréed (unsweetened or with sugar) or candied (*marrons glacés*).

Hazelnuts or cob nuts These small, grey-brown nuts are partly covered with leafy husks. Ripe fresh hazelnuts should have firm, not shrivelled, husks. Available throughout the autumn.

Filbert nuts or filberts These are a variety of hazelnut, but the fruits are flask-shaped and should only be bought if they are completely covered by firm husks.

Walnuts Most of these nuts are imported for the Christmas trade. Avoid any which rattle, as they will be dry and shrivelled when you crack them open.

Walnut trees can be found in some parks or gardens of large houses (or where large properties once stood). The nuts drop off when ripe in late autumn and the outer green covering has to be removed (October to November). The nuts can be eaten fresh or dried for several days and stored. Unripe walnuts, on which the shell is not formed, can be pickled. The nuts have to be picked in early July and pricked all over, then soaked in brine for up to 2 weeks before they can be drained and bottled in vinegar.

SOFT FRUIT

Soft fruit, with the exception of gooseberries, leave stains on the bottom of the container; avoid any badly stained containers as the fruits are probably mushy or even mouldy. As soon as possible after buying, tip the berries carefully on to a plate, pick out any inferior fruit and set the remainder well apart on a tray until serving.

Bilberries A small quantity of these berries, also known as whortle berries, find their way into the shops. Bilberries are similar to blackcurrants, but they are firmer, smaller and dark blue. They are sour and suitable for pie fillings. Season: July and August.

Blackberries The berries are purple to black, juicy and sweet. Being extremely soft, they deteriorate quickly and must be used as fresh dessert berries as soon as possible after picking or purchase. Avoid using too many red and unripe blackberries. Season: July to October.

Blackcurrants These berries are usually sold stripped from their stalks. Look for containers with large berries and no more than 15 per cent dark red and 5 per cent green berries turning red. Blackcurrants are used for cooking and for making jams and preserves. The berries are dark, almost black, with fairly tough skin and juicy, slightly acid, flesh. Season: July and August.

Blueberries Slightly larger than currants, these dark blue berries have a white bloom. They are recognised by their clear juice which distinguishes them from other (different) types of tiny wild, blue-coloured berries. Blueberries can be served fresh, with cream, or used for desserts, either raw or lightly poached and sweetened. They can also be made into jelly. Season: July to September.

Gooseberries These are used as fillings for pies and tarts, and for jam and jelly-making. Avoid squashy berries or any with splits and blemishes to the skin. The majority of gooseberries are green or yellow-green and quite bitter, but larger, slightly more oval-shaped, berries with a blush of red are sweeter and they can be eaten raw, unsweetened if liked. The sweeter, dessert, berries tend to ripen later than the spring fruit. Season: end April to end August or early September.

Loganberries These tangy, juicy fruits are the same shape as blackberries, but the colour of raspberries. They are up to 5 cm/ 2 in long, tapering and seedless. Loganberries are usually sold in 450 g/1 lb punnets, with the hulls or centres in; avoid containers with heavy fruit stains. Season: early July to late August.

Mulberries These look like large, long blackberries, but they are slightly paler in colour. There is also a white variety. Mulberries may be used to make jams and jellies or as a filling for pies and similar cooked desserts. They may also be served raw, in fruit salads or sweetened to taste with icing sugar and served with cream. Season: August and September.

Raspberries Avoid berries which show cracks or pits near the top and any that are squashy. Raspberries are usually served fresh as a dessert, with cream; they may

LOGANBERRY

RASPBERRY

BLACKBERRY

COOKING GOOSEBERRY
– HOWARD'S LEVELLER

DESSERT GOOSEBERRY–
WHINHAM'S INDUSTRY

ROYAL SOVEREIGN

CAMBRIDGE VIGOUR

Strawberry
varieties

REDGAUNTLET

GRANDEE

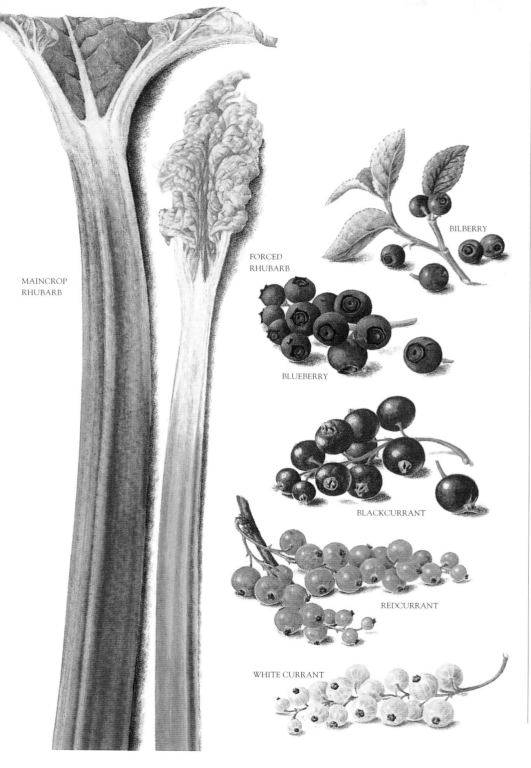

MAINCROP RHUBARB

FORCED RHUBARB

BILBERRY

BLUEBERRY

BLACKCURRANT

REDCURRANT

WHITE CURRANT

also be used to make pies, trifles, sauces and jams. Season: June to September.

Redcurrants These small, bright red, glossy berries may be served fresh with cream as a dessert or used in cooking. Avoid punnets with wet berries and with a high proportion of leaves. Redcurrants are also suitable for making compôtes and fruit salads, and are excellent for jelly-making. Season: July and August.

Rhubarb Although strictly a vegetable, rhubarb is used as a fruit. It is extremely acid and must be stewed or poached before being eaten. The leaves are highly poisonous. Early or forced rhubarb has tender, pink and delicately flavoured stalks which do not need to be peeled. Maincrop rhubarb has a stronger flavour and tough brittle stalks. Avoid limp and split rhubarb stalks. Season: (forced) mid-December to mid-April; (maincrop) mid-March to end of June.

Strawberries The most popular and eagerly awaited fruit of the berry season. Fresh strawberries are served with cream and sugar, used fresh to decorate and fill cakes and tarts, eaten with ice cream and water ices and used for jams. The sweet, juicy red berries should be used on the day they are bought. Choose berries with fresh-looking leaves and avoid over and under-ripe fruit and any with grey mould. Season: end May to July and again in autumn.

White currants These berries are usually served as a dessert fruit, stripped or left on their stalks and served with plenty of sugar. Season: July and August.

CITRUS FRUIT

All citrus fruit is imported from a wide variety of countries and the majority is available throughout the year. Most citrus fruit has a wide variety of uses, from serving fresh as a 'dessert' fruit to flavouring both sweet and savoury dishes and baking. The rind and juice are often valuable ingredients as well as the flesh. The rind may be pared in strips, then cut into fine shreds or it may be coarsely or finely grated. Both rind and juice can be frozen together or separately.

To prevent loss of moisture by evaporation through the skin, citrus fruit is often coated with a harmless wax covering. Always wash citrus fruit before grating the rind or using the peel – this applies to unwaxed as well as wax-coated fruit.

Clementines These fruits are a cross between an orange and a tangerine, with an orange-like skin. They are almost seedless and the pink-tinged flesh is slightly acidic. Clementines are popular for Christmas.

Grapefruit The largest of the citrus fruits, grapefruit are squat, round fruit with pale yellow skins which vary in thickness; the juicy flesh is pale yellow and sharp. A spongy soft skin is often an indication of thick peel and a lack of fruit juice and flesh.

Grapefruit are usually served fresh, cut in half, as a breakfast dish or a starter, with honey or sugar. They are also used in preparing marmalade. Pink grapefruit, which have sweet, pale pink flesh, are sweeter than ordinary yellow grapefruit.

Kumquats These are small, oval, orange-like fruits with yellow skin and juicy, slightly bitter flesh. Kumquats may be poached, when they are eaten with the skin, or used for marmalades, bottled and preserved in sugar syrup.

Lemons The fruits are large or small with smooth, thin or thick knobbly skin. Generally, plump lemons, which are heavy for their size and have smooth, oily skins, have less peel and will give more juice than large, knobbly-skinned lemons.

Limes A small fruit, similar to lemon but rounder, and with green-yellow thin skin and tart yellow flesh with a characteristic tangy flavour.

Limquats Small fruit, similar to kumquats, but bright green and lime-flavoured.

Mandarins These are another citrus fruit popular at Christmas for desserts. Mandarins are a type of orange, round but flattened in shape, with loose, oily, bright orange skin and pinkish white flesh, with lots of pips.

Naartjes Small, seedless orange-like fruit from South Africa, with loose, bright orange skin. They occasionally appear in the shops, but are more often available as crystallised whole fruit.

Oranges The shape and flavour of sweet oranges vary according to their country of origin. A choice is usually available throughout the year. Israel exports the world-famous Jaffa oranges. Shamouti oranges, which are a variety of Jaffa orange, are large, oval and thick-skinned. They are almost seedless, with very juicy and sweet flesh.

Navel oranges have thin, smooth skins and are distinguished by the raised embryo growth at one end; they have juicy flesh. Navels are seedless or they have only a few pips.

Blood oranges are small, with slightly rough skin flushed with red, and have sweet juicy flesh, flecked with red, usually with a number of pips.

Valencias are thin-skinned oranges with a rounded shape. They have sweet, very juicy and practically seedless flesh.

Bitter oranges are seasonal and only available for a short period during January and February. These oranges are smaller, more round and have rougher skins than sweet fruit. They generally appear to be second-quality oranges, but they have a strong flavour and bitter juice which can be valuable in cook-ing. Bitter oranges are used to make marmalade. They can be used in other cooking, the main example being Bigarade sauce. Seville oranges are the traditional variety.

Ortaniques These fruits are a cross between an orange and tangerine. They are similar in size to Navel oranges and have orange-yellow, thin skin and sweet, juicy, orange-coloured flesh. Use them fresh as a dessert fruit and also for making marmalade.

Pomelos These fruits look like large grapefruit and have thick skin surrounding the tangy flesh. The flesh is similar to grapefruit.

Satsumas Similar to a tangerine, these round and squat oranges have smooth, thick skin and pale orange-yellow flesh without pips.

CLEMENTINE

KUMQUAT

LIME

GRAPEFRUIT

LEMON

Tangerines A small type of sweet orange distinguished by its loose, bright-orange to red skin and small, juicy segments. Tangerines contain numerous pips, but they are a delicious dessert fruit. Also used for marmalades.

Uglis, tangelos A grapefruit-sized cross between a tangerine and a grapefruit. Uglis have thick, greenish-yellow skin; the juicy yellow flesh is sweeter than grapefruit and has only a few pips.

EXOTIC FRUIT AND NUTS

Many large supermarkets offer a variety of exciting fruit which are not seasonal, so they tend to be available throughout the year. The following is a selection of the widely available fruit, but there is often other interesting produce to sample – try unusual fruit when you see it, as it may not be in stock when you next visit the shop.

Almonds Small, oval, flat nuts in light brown pitted shells. They are available bitter and sweet, shelled and unshelled, and are best bought with the thin brown skin on. Available all year round.

Bananas These are normally picked and shipped green, then stored and sold in varying stages of ripeness. The starchy flesh becomes sweeter as it matures. The flavour is best when the skin is golden-yellow, flecked with

BLOOD ORANGE

VALENCIA ORANGE

NAVEL ORANGE

JAFFA ORANGE

ORTANIQUE

SEVILLE ORANGE

UGLI

MANDARIN

SATSUMA

brown. Avoid any with black spots or patches, and damaged and squashy fruit.

Brazil nuts Hard, dark brown, three-edged shells enclose firm, slightly oily nuts with a flavour similar to coconut and hazelnut. Brazil nuts are sold unshelled and shelled. Avoid any which feel light or rattle in the shells.

Coconuts These large nuts have a hard, dark brown outer shell closely covered with tough fibres.

At the top of each nut are three small indentations which must be punctured so that the colourless liquid (coconut water, not to be confused with coconut milk) can be shaken out. This is served chilled as a drink. Crack the tough shell by hitting it with a cleaver about one-third of the way down from the top. Prise the shells open, and cut out the tough flesh with a small sharp knife. To test a whole coconut

for freshness, shake it to make sure it contains liquid.

Cranberries Small, firm, bright red berries which have a sharp, slightly bitter flavour. Cranberries are stewed with sugar to make sauces and preserves. The berries can also be used in desserts. Cranberry sauce is a classic accompaniment for roast turkey and the fruit is primarily available from October to February. Cranberries freeze well.

Dates Fresh dates are plump, shiny and yellow-red to golden brown with smooth papery skins. The flesh is sweet and firm.

Dried dates should be plump, 2.5–5 cm/1–2 in long, and have shiny skins. Medjool dates are not as sweet as ordinary dried dates, they are moist and have an excellent flavour. They are available from September to March.

Figs Fresh purple or green figs are squat, pear-shaped fruits. They

are soft to the touch when ripe, and the skin, which is either white, red or purple, has a bloom to it. The juicy pulp is sweet, deep red and heavily seeded. Dried figs are very sweet and the seeds give the fruit a pleasant, slightly crunchy texture.

Grapes There is a wide range of black, red and white dessert grapes; most grapes are imported, but a few are grown in Britain under hothouse conditions. The

51

juicy, thin-skinned grapes should have a distinct bloom to them. Seedless varieties are sold for both black and green fruit. Avoid any with shrivelled, split or squashed berries, or those which show mould near the stems. Seedless grapes are available as blue, black, red, amber and green grapes.

Grenadillos These are smooth, orange-yellow skinned fruits with fragrant, pulpy flesh surrounding tiny black edible seeds. Grenadillos come from the same family as passion fruit.

Guavas Oval or pear-shaped fruit with creamy-white, lightly scented flesh. The skin is green or yellow and when ripe, the fruit should feel tender rather than hard. The guava has a core of edible seeds similar to a pear and these are usually removed when the fruit is prepared.

Kiwi fruit Also known as Chinese gooseberries, these brown, furry-skinned fruit have juicy, sweet, green flesh, pitted with black edible seeds.

Loquats These stone fruits, also known as Japanese medlars, are imported from Israel. They are similar in shape and size to plums, and they have smooth, golden-yellow, orange or red-brown skins. The juicy cream-coloured flesh is slightly tart. Choose firm fruit.

Lungans or longans Very similar to lychees, but slightly smaller and with smooth, light brown skin. The fruit has a central stone as lychees do.

Lychees These stone fruits are the size of large cherries, with hard, scaly skins, turning from pink through to brown. The white flesh is firm, juicy and slippery with an aromatic or scented flavour. Slit the skin and peel it off, then slit the flesh lengthways and carefully slip the stone out.

Mangoes These large stone fruits come in different shapes and sizes; some are round, others long and narrow, kidney or pear-shaped. The largest fruits may weigh up to 1.4 kg/3 lb, and the smallest are the size of an average peach. The skins range in colour from green to yellow, orange and red, flushed with pink. The orange-yellow, juicy flesh is fragrant and fully flavoured, with a pleasing tang when just ripe. Fruit that is very ripe has very soft flesh that becomes slightly fibrous and too sweet.

Mangosteens Dark purple, crisp skin surrounds opaque, creamy-white segments of fruit which are sweet and scented. Occasional large, dark and shiny pips should be removed.

Melons A ripe melon will yield to pressure applied gently at the stalk end. Melons are generally available throughout the year, with the exception of watermelons which are available only from May to September.

The Cantaloup melon has a slightly flattened shape, with green to yellow rough skin. The flesh is heavily scented, succulent and orange-yellow.

Charentais melon is perfectly round and small. The yellow-green skin, which is rather rough, is marked with downward indentations, and the deep orange flesh is faintly scented.

WATERMELON

HONEYDEW

OGEN

CHARENTAIS

LYCHEES

BANANA

POMEGRANATE

BRAZIL NUTS

BLACK GRAPES

RED GRAPES

GREEN GRAPES

ALMONDS

DRIED DATE

FRESH DATES

DRIED FIG

FRESH FIGS

PASSION FRUIT

PINEAPPLE

PAWPAW

PERSIMMON

COCONUT

MANGO

LOQUAT

PHYSALIS

CRANBERRIES

KIWI
FRUIT

Honeydew melon is the most widely available variety of melon. It is shaped like a rugby ball and has green, yellow or white wrinkled skin. The sweet flesh is pale green to pink.

Ogen melon is round and has yellow to orange skin which is marked with faint green stripes. The pale yellow flesh is very sweet and juicy.

Watermelon is the largest of all the melons. The glossy, dark skin surrounds the scarlet and juicy, almost watery, flesh and prominent black seeds.

Passion fruit These are small, aromatic fruit about the same size as large plums. There is a purple variety and a yellow type, the latter having the smoother skin. Both contain a sweet, juicy pulp laced with small black, crunchy seeds. The pulp may be sieved to make a dessert sauce and some of the seeds may be returned to it for a crunchy texture if liked.

Pawpaws These fruits are also known as papayas. Pawpaws are about the size of cooking apples, but they are pear-shaped. They have smooth skins which ripen and change colour from green through to yellow or orange. The sweet, orange-pink flesh has a delicate flavour which can sometimes be disappointing. Brown-black, inedible seeds lie in the centre and these may be scooped out with a teaspoon when the fruit is halved. Avoid fruits with dry or blemished skins.

Persimmons These tropical fruits look like large tomatoes with their leathery skins which turn from yellow to bright red. The orange-yellow juicy and soft flesh

has a sharp flavour. Fruits with pitted or cracked skins should not be bought.

Physalis These fruits are also known as Cape gooseberries. The yellow berries, which are about the size of cherries, are covered by papery husks in the shape of Chinese lanterns. The plump golden berries are served as a dessert fruit, stewed or made into preserves. They keep well for two or three weeks if bought unripe.

Pineapples Large oval fruits with hard, knobbly top skin, which varies from deep yellow to almost orange-brown. The firm, yellow to cream flesh is sweet and juicy. Look for fruits with stiff leaves. Miniature pineapples are ideal for halving, scooping out and serving as containers for desserts.

Pomegranates These fruits are the size of oranges with thin, but tough rinds. Prime pomegranates have bright, smooth skin which is golden to yellow or deep red in colour. The fruit consists of dark seeds surrounded by red, juicy and tangy flesh. The seeds and flesh have to be scooped out of the surrounding, cream-coloured membrane-like skin which has a bitter taste.

Prickly pears The fruit of a cactus, prickly pears are oval and yellow, blushed slightly pink in colour, with sharp spines. Once cut in half lengthways, the skin reveals flesh which is pale orange to red when ripe, with lots of edible seeds. The flavour is weak and slightly watery. Protect your hands with absorbent kitchen paper and an oven glove, then scrape or rub off the spines before cutting the fruit.

Rambutans These taste the same as lychees, but they have a bright rust-coloured covering of long hairs and are slightly larger than lychees. Prepare as for lychees.

Star fruits Also known as carambola, these yellow-skinned fruits are oval and ridged, giving star-shaped slices when cut. The skin is edible as are the occasional small seeds. Star fruit has a delicate, refreshing flavour. Slices dry out fairly quickly and discolour slightly when allowed to stand for long, so the fruit is best added to a salad or used as a decoration shortly before the dish is served. However, the time the fruit takes to discolour is not as fast as that for cooking apples and avocados.

Tamarillos These oval-shaped, red-skinned fruits are about the size of plum tomatoes. There is also a yellow or orange variety. The fruit also slightly resembles tomato, with thin, edible skin, dark seeds and tangy flesh.

TWELVE MONTHS

January
PAGES 56–77

February
PAGES 78–97

May
PAGES 138–157

June
PAGES 158–179

September
PAGES 220–239

October
PAGES 240–259

OF RECIPES

JANUARY

Winter Salad, Potage Paysanne, Stilton and Brussels Sprout Timbales.

January

Following the Christmas holiday and with the strong likelihood of bad weather, sea fishing is not at its peak. Consequently January is not one of the best months for fish and seafood. Oily fish are usually economical, with herring, mackerel and sprats as best buys. Mussels are also readily available at this time of year, and it is worth trying halibut as well as cod or haddock.

In spite of the year-round availability of turkey, demand still tends to fall in January, so prices are usually below those being charged in December. Venison is another former luxury food that is now farmed and is readily available throughout the year in most supermarkets. It is a good choice for special meals over the New Year, when a perfectly roasted joint will make a memorable meal. Because it is towards the end of the season, game birds are generally tougher and are best suited to use in casseroles and stews.

Take full advantage of traditional winter vegetables for hearty soups and hot pots – parsnips are in prime condition following a frost and other root vegetables, particularly home-grown Jerusalem artichokes, are in plentiful supply. British celeriac and kohl-rabi are still available, while this is also a good time to experiment with different ways with cabbage and Brussels sprouts.

Citrus fruits are at their best in the heart of winter, with juicy seedless oranges (navels), limes and lemons all available at good prices. The short season for bitter oranges begins, with the fruit coming into the shops from the end of January through February, so now is the time to stock up with them. If you do not have time to make marmalade during January or February, then freeze the fruit. Freeze marmalade oranges whole, cut up in preparation for making marmalade, or boiled ready for adding sugar and completing the cooking when time allows. It is also a good idea to freeze the pared rind and juice from bitter oranges for making Bigarade Sauce (page 84), for flavouring rich casseroles or for use in sweet dishes.

After the round of entertaining and feasting of Christmas and New Year, most people feel inclined to eat slightly lighter meals once they have settled down to January proper, so this is very much a month for simple home cooking. Baked potatoes, rice, pasta, beans and pulses combine well with seasonal vegetables in dishes that are satisfying and bulky without being too rich. Vegetable soups and casseroles are ideal for everyday meals, and the occasional vegetarian main course brings balance to a meat-based diet.

Menu suggestions *All the main recipes in the menus are found in this chapter. Any additional recipes from the back of the book or other chapters are accompanied by a page reference.*

Special Sunday Lunch

~

Stilton and Brussels Sprout Timbales

~

Stuffed Pork with Apricot Sauce
Baked Jerusalem Artichokes
Glazed Carrots (page 110)
Celeriac and Potato Purée (page 273)

~

Treacle Tart with Custard Sauce (page 338)
or
Grape Jelly (page 378)

This is a menu to serve family or friends after the festive season. The timbales can be made the day before and chilled overnight before cooking. The choice of desserts caters to cooks who want to plan ahead as well as to those who love traditional puddings.

Traditional Dinner Party

~

Cream of Brussels Sprout Soup

~

Marinated Venison
Parsnip Croquettes
Braised Red Cabbage (page 90)
Boiled Potatoes

~

Iced Tangerines
Cheese and Biscuits

Classic dishes have been carefully selected for this menu to ensure that the cook has plenty of time to relax with the guests. Both the first course and the dessert can be prepared ahead of time, while the croquettes can be fried in advance for reheating just before serving. The venison is the only dish that needs last-minute attention.

Vegetarian Dinner Party

~

Onion flan (page 130)

~

Celeriac and Bean Terrine with Pepper Relish
Brussels Sprouts topped with toasted almonds
Anna Potatoes (page 347)

~

Chilled Chocolate Soufflé (page 338)

By opening the meal with a classic onion flan, even people with traditional tastes will feel assured that they are going to enjoy the rest of this vegetarian dinner party menu. If you have individual quiche dishes, make miniature flans which look much more appealing than wedges.

Carbonnade à la Flamande (page 66).

SOUPS

Cream of Brussels Sprout Soup

A generous garnish of toasted almonds adds texture to this smooth soup. It can be served hot or chilled.

SERVES: 6
PREPARATION: 40 minutes
COOKING: 2¼ hours

For the stock
1.12 litres/2 pt water
100 g/4 oz belly pork
1 carrot
1 small turnip
1 clove garlic
1 onion studded with 2 cloves
6 sprigs parsley
1 bouquet garni*
6 peppercorns
1 bay leaf
1 teaspoon salt

For the soup
900 g/2 lb Brussels sprouts
225 g/8 oz potatoes
1 onion
50 g/2 oz butter
300 ml/½ pt milk
black pepper
2.5 ml/½ teaspoon grated nutmeg
150 ml/¼ pt single cream
100 g/4 oz flaked almonds to garnish

For the stock, put the water into a heavy-based saucepan and add the belly pork; cover with a lid and bring to the boil. Peel and slice the carrot and turnip, crush the garlic and add to the stock, along with the onion, parsley, bouquet garni, peppercorns, bay leaf and salt. Bring to the boil again and remove any scum. Cover and simmer for 1½ hours, then strain the liquid through muslin into a jug or basin. The stock should yield about 900 ml/1½ pt; if it yields less, top up with boiling water.

Trim and wash the Brussels sprouts, removing any damaged parts, and thinly slice the potatoes and onion. Melt the butter in a large saucepan and cook the onion and potatoes slowly for 10 minutes, until the onion is slightly softened but not coloured. Toss the Brussels sprouts with the potatoes and onion, then pour in the reserved stock and the milk. Bring this mixture to the boil; cover and simmer for 20 minutes. Add pepper and more salt to taste.

Allow the soup to cool for a few minutes before liquidising or rubbing it through a sieve. Stir the nutmeg and cream into the soup; reheat carefully without boiling or chill in the refrigerator for a few hours.

Put the flaked almonds on a baking sheet or a grill pan lined with a piece of cooking foil. Place under a heated grill, keeping the sheet well away from the heat so that the almonds toast slowly and evenly. Turn the almonds several times until they take on a deep amber colour.

Serve the soup in individual bowls and sprinkle generously with the cold toasted almonds.

Note Do not add the clove of garlic if the cream of Brussels sprout soup is to be frozen for later use. Freeze the puréed soup before adding the nutmeg and cream. Thaw the soup, reheat it, then stir in the nutmeg and cream, and heat gently.

Potage Paysanne

This farmhouse vegetable soup makes a filling and warming meal on its own. Select vegetables according to their availability and to your own taste – the quantities in the recipe are merely a guide. Peas, green beans and watercress may be added when the soup comes to the boil.

SERVES: 6
PREPARATION: 30 minutes
COOKING: 1 hour

3 carrots
1–2 turnips
2–3 parsnips
2 leeks
½ small head of celery
1 large onion
50 g/2 oz mushrooms
2 rashers streaky bacon
225 g/8 oz tomatoes
50 g/2 oz butter or 30 ml/
*   2 tablespoons oil*
30 ml/2 tablespoons plain flour
150 ml/¼ pt milk
900 ml/1½ pt White Stock
*   (page 310)*
salt and black pepper
lemon juice to taste
pinch mixed herbs

Garnish
10 ml/2 teaspoons chopped mint
*   or parsley*
Croûtons (page 313)

Wash and peel the carrots, turnips and parsnips; dice them finely. Remove the roots and outer coarse leaves from the leeks, wash them thoroughly under cold running water and chop roughly. Scrub the celery and slice the sticks finely; peel and roughly chop the onion. Trim and slice the mushrooms finely. Take the rind off the bacon and dice the rashers. Skin and roughly chop the tomatoes.

Melt the butter or heat the oil in a large heavy-based pan and fry the bacon, onion, celery and mushrooms over moderate heat until soft, but not browned. Add the prepared carrots, turnips, parsnips and leeks and fry them lightly. Remove the pan from the heat and mix in the plain flour. Gradually stir in the milk. Return the pan to the heat, add the hot stock and bring the soup to the

Potage Paysanne.

boil, stirring continuously. Add the chopped tomatoes, stir well and bring the soup to simmering point over low heat.

If necessary, thin the soup with water or more milk. Season to taste with salt, pepper, lemon juice and mixed herbs. Cover the pan and simmer the soup over very low heat, until the root vegetables are well cooked. This will take about 45 minutes.

Serve the soup hot, garnished with fresh mint or parsley and crisp croûtons.

■ Garlic bread (see Mexican Hot Pot Soup, page 243) or a separate bowl of grated cheese will make the soup even more substantial. Any leftover soup can be pressed through a sieve or liquidised and thinned to taste with milk or tomato juice.

Lentil Soup with Spiced Pecans

Lemon rind adds a refreshing flavour to this vegetarian lentil soup, and it is complemented by the flavour and texture of the spiced pecan nuts used as a garnish. You can choose between water or stock: water gives perfectly good results if the soup is well seasoned with salt and the same rule applies when you are using home-made unseasoned vegetable or chicken stock.

SERVES: 6
PREPARATION: 20 minutes
COOKING: 45 minutes

2 onions
2 carrots
2 sticks celery
pared rind of ½ lemon
15 ml/1 tablespoon oil
1 clove garlic (optional)
1 bay leaf
1 thyme sprig
15 ml/1 tablespoon tomato paste
225 g/8 oz red lentils
1.4 litres/2½ pt stock or water
salt and pepper
Spiced pecans
100 g/4 oz shelled pecan nuts
25 g/1 oz butter
2.5 ml/½ teaspoon ground mace
2.5 ml/½ teaspoon paprika
5 ml/1 teaspoon ground coriander
1.25 ml/¼ teaspoon chilli powder
150 ml/¼ pt Greek yogurt to serve

Roughly chop the onions, carrots and celery. Cut the lemon rind into thin strips. Heat the oil in a large saucepan. Add the garlic, bay leaf, thyme and all the prepared vegetables. Stir well,

cover the pan closely and cook gently for 20 minutes, shaking the pan occasionally.

Stir the tomato paste and lentils into the vegetables, then pour in the stock or water and bring to the boil, stirring. Reduce the heat, cover the pan and simmer the soup gently for 30 minutes. Add seasoning to taste, re-cover the pan and continue to cook for a further 15 minutes.

Prepare the nuts while the soup is cooking. Roughly chop the pecans. Melt the butter in a small saucepan, add the nuts, stir well to coat them in butter, then cook over gentle heat for 5 minutes. Add the mace, paprika, coriander and chilli powder, then continue to cook, stirring continuously, for 10 minutes. Set the pan aside.

Purée the soup in a liquidiser or food processor, or rub it through a sieve. Reheat and taste for seasoning before serving. Swirl a little Greek yogurt into each portion and sprinkle with some of the spiced pecans.

STARTERS, SAVOURIES & LIGHT DISHES

Terrine of Hare

SERVES: 6–8
MARINATING: 8–10 hours
PREPARATION: 45 minutes
OVEN: 190°C/375°F/gas 5
COOKING: 1½ hours

Marinade
4 bay leaves
8 juniper berries, crushed
5 ml/1 teaspoon salt
6 peppercorns
½ wine-glass brandy
Terrine
1 hare, skinned, cleaned and
    jointed, with liver, heart
    and kidneys
450 g/1 lb veal
450 g/1 lb belly pork
350 g/12 oz rashers streaky bacon
10 ml/2 teaspoons chopped thyme
10 ml/2 teaspoons chopped
    marjoram
5 ml/1 teaspoon dried basil

In a large bowl, mix together the marinade* ingredients. Cut 450–675 g/1–1½ lb of meat from the saddle and hind legs of the hare into thin slices and leave for 8–10 hours in the marinade.

Mince the veal with the liver, heart and kidneys. Remove the rind and bones from the pork and mince it separately.

Remove the rind from the bacon and use it to line one 1.12 litre/2 pt, or two 600 ml/1 pt, terrines or ovenproof dishes,

setting three or four rashers aside. Drain the marinade from the hare, strain and reserve it with the bay leaves. Lay half the minced pork on the bacon, followed by a layer of the veal mixture. Sprinkle each layer with thyme, marjoram, basil, salt and pepper. Lay the hare meat over the veal, pour the strained marinade over, and top with the other half of the pork; sprinkle with the remaining seasoning.

Top with the reserved bacon and bay leaves, and cover with buttered greaseproof paper before putting on the lid. Place in a bain marie* or a roasting pan containing boiling water that reaches just above half-way up the sides of the dish.

Set the bain marie in a pre-heated oven, cook for 1½ hours at 190°C/375°F/gas 5 or until a skewer pushed gently into the terrine comes away clean and the juices run clear. About 15 minutes before cooking is completed, remove the lid and greaseproof paper to allow the top of the terrine to brown.

Remove from the oven and leave to cool for about 30 minutes; cover the terrine with clean greaseproof paper and weight down with a 900 g/2 lb weight set on a plate.

■ Serve cold, with hot toast for a first course or a salad and crusty bread for lunch.

Stilton and Brussels Sprout Timbales

Leftover cooked Brussels sprouts may also be used in these timbales. They make a creamy first course or a light dish for lunch or supper.

SERVES: 6
PREPARATION: 40 minutes
OVEN: 180°C/350°F/gas 4
COOKING: about 1 hour

175 g/6 oz small Brussels sprouts
salt and black pepper
100 g/4 oz Stilton cheese
300 ml/½ pt thick coating White
    Sauce (page 352)
30 ml/2 tablespoons snipped chives
30 ml/2 tablespoons dry sherry
2 eggs
Lemon dressing
1 lemon
2.5 ml/½ teaspoon caster sugar
5 ml/1 teaspoon chopped winter
    savory or thyme
300 ml/½ pt fromage frais
Garnish
savory or thyme sprigs
fine strips of lemon rind

Cut a cross in the base of each sprout. Bring a small saucepan of salted water to the boil. Add the sprouts and bring back to the boil. then cook for 8 minutes. Drain the sprouts well and reduce them to a coarse purée in a food processor or liquidiser; if you do not have either of these appliances, chop up the sprouts very finely.

Crumble the Stilton cheese and stir it into the white sauce, keeping the pan over low heat until the cheese has melted and the sauce is smooth. Remove from the heat and stir in the sprout purée. Add the chives and sherry with seasoning to taste. Beat the eggs, then strain them into the mixture and stir until combined thoroughly.

Line the bottom of six individual ramekin dishes with circles of greaseproof paper. Grease the dishes and paper them well, then divide the Brussels sprout and cheese mixture between them. Place the ramekins in a roasting tin and pour in boiling water from a kettle to come about two-thirds of the way up the outside of the ramekins. Bake in a preheated oven at 180°C/350°F/gas 4 for about 30 minutes, until the mixture is just firm.

While the sprout timbales are cooking, pare a thin strip off the lemon, working from top to bottom on the fruit. Cut it into fine shreds and cook these in boiling water for 15 minutes, until tender. Drain and set aside. Mix the caster sugar, savory or thyme and 15 ml/1 tablespoon of juice squeezed from the lemon. Stir in the fromage frais and lemon rind.

To serve the timbales, slide a knife around the inside of the ramekin, between the mixture and the dish, then invert them on to warmed serving plates. Serve a little of the lemon dressing beside each timbale. Garnish with savory or thyme sprigs and fine strips of lemon rind. Offer the rest of the lemon dressing separately.

■ Crisp toast triangles or Melba Toast (page 313) complement the timbales.

Blini with Caviar

In Russia, where this hors d'oeuvre originates, blini – crisp, light, yeast-raised pancakes – are traditionally served with caviar, soured cream and onions.

SERVES: 8–12
PREPARATION: 40 minutes
RISING: about 1½ hours
COOKING: 20 minutes

350 g/12 oz plain flour
10 ml/2 teaspoons fast-action
*   easy-blend dried yeast*
pinch salt
15 ml/1 tablespoon caster sugar
2 large eggs
300 ml/½ pt milk
370 ml/13 fl oz hand-hot water
25 g/1 oz unsalted butter
2 large onions
300 ml/½ pt soured cream
200 g/7 oz lumpfish roe
1 large lemon
oil for frying

Sift the flour into a bowl. Mix in the yeast, salt and sugar. Make a well in the dry ingredients.

Separate the eggs and beat the yolks with the milk and water. Melt the butter, add it to the liquid and pour about half into the well in the flour mixture. Gradually beat in the flour to make a smooth batter and add the remaining liquid in stages as the batter thickens and becomes smooth with beating.

Cover the bowl with a clean cloth and leave the batter to rise in a warm place until it has doubled in volume.

Meanwhile, peel and roughly chop the onions, and put them in a serving bowl. Spoon the soured cream and lumpfish roe into serving bowls. Wash the lemon, cut it into wedges and arrange them in another bowl. Chill until serving.

Whisk the egg whites until they stand in soft peaks, and fold them into the risen batter.

Heat a little oil in a large heavy frying pan over high heat. Drop 2 spoonfuls of batter well apart in the pan at a time, to

Blini with Caviar.

make two pancakes, each about 10 cm/4 in wide. Cook the pancakes for about 1 minute on each side or until they are golden brown. Stir the batter occasionally between cooking the batches. Keep the blini hot on a wire rack in the oven until all the batter is used – it should make about 30 pancakes.

Serve the blini with the bowls of onions, cream, lumpfish roe and lemon separately.

Pytt i Panna

This classic Swedish dish makes good use of leftover cooked meat and potatoes.

SERVES: 4
PREPARATION: 10 minutes
COOKING: 20 minutes

5 boiled potatoes
40 g/1½ oz butter
15 ml/1 tablespoon olive oil
450 g/1 lb cooked beef or lamb
225 g/8 oz streaky bacon
1 large onion
salt and black pepper
15 ml/1 tablespoon chopped parsley
5 ml/1 teaspoon
*   Worcestershire sauce*
4 fried eggs to garnish

Chop the potatoes and fry in the butter and oil, over a high heat, until golden. Drain on absorbent kitchen paper and keep warm.

Dice the meat and bacon and fry with the chopped onion over medium heat until the onion softens, and the bacon is cooked. Return the potatoes to the pan, mix the ingredients carefully and season to taste. Cook for another

5 minutes, shaking the pan to prevent sticking. Stir in the chopped parsley and Worcestershire sauce, mixing well.

Spoon the mixture into a warm serving dish and top with fried eggs. Serve at once.

Pizza Baps

These savoury baked baps make a satisfying hot snack.

SERVES: 4
PREPARATION: 15 minutes
OVEN: 180°C/350°F/gas 4
COOKING: 20–25 minutes

4 large baps
60 ml/4 tablespoons olive oil
1 large onion
50 g/2 oz mushrooms
2 large tomatoes
salt and black pepper
pinch dried marjoram (optional)
175 g/6 oz quick-melting cheese,
*   thinly sliced*
8 anchovy fillets

Slice the baps in half and brush the surface with three-quarters of the olive oil. Slice the onion and cook in the remaining oil until soft; add the sliced mushrooms and cook for another 2 minutes.

Skin the tomatoes (page 302), slice and arrange them on top of the bap halves, season with salt, pepper and a little marjoram. Spoon the onion and mushroom mixture on top and cover with the cheese. Halve each anchovy fillet and arrange on the cheese.

Bake the pizza baps in a preheated oven at 180°C/350°F/gas 4 for 20–25 minutes or until the cheese is golden.

Baked Samosas

Filo pastry, which is convenient and easy to use, has been substituted for the traditional Indian pastry. Recipes are given for two alternative fillings: spicy chicken and vegetable.

MAKES: 30
PREPARATION: 1 hour
OVEN: 200°C/400°F/gas 6
COOKING: 40–45 minutes

1 onion
2 cloves garlic
2.5 cm/1 in piece of fresh
    root ginger
60 ml/4 tablespoons oil
15ml/1 tablespoon ground cumin
30 ml/2 tablespoons ground
    coriander
2.5 ml/½ teaspoon turmeric
450 g/1 lb lean minced beef
    or lamb
30 ml/2 tablespoons water
2.5 ml/½ teaspoon salt
15 ml/1 tablespoon lemon juice
30 ml/2 tablespoons chopped mint
2.5 ml/½ teaspoon Garam Masala
    (page 239)
75 g/3 oz butter
275 g/10 oz packet filo pastry,
    thawed if necessary

Finely chop the onion, crush the garlic and grate the ginger. Heat 30 ml/2 tablespoons of the oil in a saucepan, add the onion, garlic and ginger and cook gently for 5 minutes. Stir in the cumin, coriander and turmeric, cook for a few seconds, then stir in the minced beef or lamb. Cook, stirring, until the meat has changed colour, then add the water and salt. Cover and cook gently,

stirring occasionally, for 25 minutes, then remove the pan from the heat. Stir in the lemon juice, mint and garam masala. Allow the mixture to cool.

Melt the butter with the rest of the oil. Using a single sheet of filo at a time and keeping the rest covered to prevent it from drying out, brush with a little of the butter and oil. Cut the filo into three lengthways strips, each measuring about 7.5 × 30 cm/3 × 12 in. Place a teaspoonful of the filling at one end of a filo strip. Fold the strip over to make a triangle and continue to fold it over on itself to make a triangular pastry, completely enclosing the filling. Brush lightly with the melted butter and oil and place on a baking sheet. Repeat, using the remaining filo pastry and filling. Bake in a preheated oven at 200°C/400°F/gas 6 for about 8 minutes or until the samosas are golden.

Spicy Chicken Filling

375 g/12 oz skinned and boned
    chicken breasts
1 onion, about 100 g/4 oz
2.5 cm/1 in piece of fresh root
    ginger
1 small green chilli
60 ml/4 tablespoons oil
30 ml/2 tablespoons ground
    coriander
30 ml/2 tablespoons plain yogurt
2.5 ml/½ teaspoon salt
15 ml/1 tablespoon chopped
    fresh coriander
5 ml/1 teaspoon lemon juice
black pepper
2.5 ml/½ teaspoon Garam Masala
    (page 239)

Cut the chicken breasts into extremely small pieces or mince them coarsely. Chop the onion very finely, grate the ginger, then remove the seeds from the chilli and finely chop the flesh.

Heat the oil in a saucepan. Add the onion, ginger and chilli, cook gently for about 5 minutes, stirring. Add the chicken breast, stir until the meat becomes opaque, then stir in the coriander, yogurt and salt.

Cook the mixture gently, stirring every now and then, for 10 minutes. If the chicken starts to stick to the bottom of the pan, add 15 ml/1 tablespoon water. Remove from the heat, stir in the remaining ingredients and allow to cool. Use as an alternative filling for Baked Samosas (left).

Vegetable Filling

225 g/8 oz potatoes
salt and black pepper
100 g/4 oz frozen peas
50 g/2 oz onion
2.5 cm/1 in piece of fresh
    root ginger
1 small green chilli
30 ml/2 tablespoons oil
2.5 ml/½ teaspoon black
    mustard seeds
5 ml/1 teaspoon cumin seeds

Peel the potatoes, cut them in half and cook in a saucepan of boiling water for about 10 minutes or until cooked through but still holding their shape. Do not allow them to become floury. Boil the peas for 2–3 minutes. Drain both vegetables and cool.

Baked Samosas with cucumber and mint in plain yogurt.

Finely chop the onion and grate the fresh root ginger. Chop the green chilli finely. If a milder flavour is preferred, remove the chilli seeds. Heat the oil, add the mustard and cumin seeds and allow them to sizzle briefly. As soon as the mustard seeds pop and the cumin seeds start to brown, add the onion, ginger and chilli. Cook gently for 7 minutes, stirring occasionally. Remove the pan from the heat.

Cut the potatoes into very small dice. Add to the pan with the peas, stirring lightly. Cool, then add salt and pepper to taste. Use as an alternative filling for Baked Samosas (left).

FISH, SHELLFISH & SEAFOOD

Fish Pie with Prawns

SERVES: 4–5
PREPARATION: 45 minutes
COOKING: 30–45 minutes

675 g/1½ lb potatoes
salt and black pepper
450 g/1 lb cod fillet
50 g/2 oz butter or margarine
25 g/1 oz plain flour
300 ml/½ pt milk plus 30 ml/
    2 tablespoons
100 g/4 oz peeled cooked prawns,
    thawed if frozen
10 ml/2 teaspoons lemon juice
30 ml/2 tablespoons chopped
    parsley
60 ml/4 tablespoons grated
    Parmesan cheese
30 ml/2 tablespoons dried
    breadcrumbs

Peel and slice the potatoes. Bring a saucepan of salted water to the boil, add the potatoes and cook for about 10 minutes until just cooked. Drain well, keep warm.

Meanwhile skin the fish, removing any obvious bones. Cut the fish into 2.5 cm/1 in chunks. Melt 40 g/1½ oz of the butter or margarine in a saucepan, stir in the flour and cook the paste for 1 minute. Gradually stir in 300 ml/½ pt milk, beat until the sauce is smooth, then bring to the boil, stirring. Cook for 2 minutes, still stirring, to thicken the sauce. Gently stir in the cubed fish, add salt and pepper to taste, cover and cook gently for 10 minutes, stirring once or twice to prevent the fish from sticking.

Drain the prawns well if necessary. Remove the pan from the heat and add the prawns and lemon juice to the sauce. Gently stir in half the parsley, taste and adjust the seasoning. Pour into a 900 ml/1½ pt ovenproof dish. Mash the potatoes, stir in the remaining butter and parsley, then add the remaining milk and freshly ground pepper to taste. Stir in half the Parmesan. Using a fork, spread the mixture evenly over the top of the fish.

Mix the remaining Parmesan and breadcrumbs together and sprinkle over the top of the potato mixture. Place under a preheated moderately hot grill and cook for about 10 minutes to heat through and brown the top. Serve at once.

Note The pie may be made in advance, in which case it should be heated and browned in a preheated oven at 180°C/ 350°F/ gas 4 for about 25 minutes.

Curried Fish Bombay Style

SERVES: 4
PREPARATION: 20 minutes
COOKING: 35 minutes

900 g/2 lb thick white fish fillets
    (cod, halibut or coley)
1 onion
2 cloves garlic
1–2 dried chillies
50 g/2 oz ghee*
5 ml/1 teaspoon ground coriander
2.5 ml/½ teaspoon ground turmeric
2.5 ml/½ teaspoon ground
    mustard seeds
5 ml/1 teaspoon rice flour
300 ml/½ pt Coconut Milk
    (page 239)
juice of ½ lemon
salt

Cut the fish fillets into 5 cm/2 in pieces. Peel and chop the onion; chop the garlic and dried chillies. Heat the ghee over moderate heat and fry the onion until it is soft and transparent. Add the garlic, the dried chillies, and the ground coriander, turmeric and mustard seeds. Stir the mixture and reduce the heat.

Mix the rice flour to a thin paste with a little of the coconut milk, then stir in the remaining coconut milk and pour it over the contents in the pan, stirring continuously. Bring the mixture to the boil, add the lemon juice and season to taste with salt. Reduce the heat to simmer the sauce gently, add the pieces of white fish, and cover the pan. Simmer for 15 minutes or until the fish is cooked.

Cod in Cider

SERVES: 4
PREPARATION: 15 minutes
COOKING: 25 minutes

2 carrots
2 leeks
50 g/2 oz mushrooms
30 ml/2 tablespoons oil
300 ml/½ pt dry cider
4 cod steaks
salt and black pepper
15 g/½ oz butter
15 ml/1 tablespoon plain flour
15 ml/1 tablespoon chopped parsley

Peel the carrots and cut them into 5 mm/¼ inch slices. Trim the leeks, cut them into 1 cm/½ inch thick slices and wash thoroughly. Drain well. Slice the mushrooms.

Heat the oil in a saucepan or frying pan large enough to hold the cod steaks in a single layer. Add the carrots and cook for 2 minutes, then add the leeks, stir and cook for 1 minute. Stir in the cider. Arrange the cod on top, season with salt and freshly ground pepper and spread the mushrooms over the top. Cover the pan and cook gently for 15 minutes until the fish becomes opaque. Lift the fish out on to a warm serving dish and keep hot.

Mix the butter and flour to a smooth paste. Add a small piece of this beurre manié to the vegetables and cider, stirring until it has been absorbed. Repeat until all the beurre manié has been added, then bring to the boil, stirring, and cook for 3 minutes. Taste for seasoning. Spoon the sauce over the fish, sprinkle with parsley and serve.

Smelts with Almonds

These small salt-water fish are at their best when caught at spawning time in late winter. Their delicate flavour is most apparent when baked or fried.

SERVES: 6
PREPARATION: 10 minutes
COOKING: 10 minutes

18 smelts
90 ml/3 fl oz single cream
flour
salt and black pepper
40 g/1½ oz butter
15 ml/1 tablespoon olive oil
100 g/4 oz flaked almonds

Lightly wash the fish in cold water; cut off the heads and squeeze out the entrails. Dry the smelts on absorbent kitchen paper. Season a little flour with salt and pepper; dip the fish in the cream and roll in flour. Melt the butter in a heavy-based frying pan, add the olive oil and gently fry the smelts for 4 minutes on each side.

Remove the smelts from the pan and keep them warm. Turn up the heat slightly and fry the flaked almonds in the fat in which the fish has been cooked until they turn golden. Sprinkle the smelts with the almonds and pour over the butter.

■ Serve the smelts with thin slices of buttered brown bread.

Matelote of Eels

A matelote – not to be confused with matelot (a sailor) – is the French culinary term for a fish stew. In this recipe, eels are used.

SERVES: 4–6
PREPARATION: 20 minutes
COOKING: 45 minutes

675 g/1½ lb eels
2 small onions
50 g/2 oz butter
370 ml/13 fl oz dry white wine
1 carrot
1 clove garlic
1 bouquet garni*
2.5 ml/½ teaspoon ground rice
salt and black pepper
1 egg yolk
150 ml/¼ pt double cream
Garnish
12 button mushrooms
12 button onions
2–3 slices bread

Ask the fishmonger to skin and clean the eels. Peel and thinly slice the onions; fry half in half the butter until golden.

Wash and dry the eels and cut them into 5 cm/2 in pieces. Add to the onion and continue frying gently, for about 10 minutes, turning the eels until they are lightly browned. Pour in the wine and bring to a simmer.

Peel, slice and chop the carrot, peel and crush the garlic and add to the pan, with the remaining onion, bouquet garni, mace and seasoning. Cover and simmer for 25 minutes.

Trim the mushrooms and peel the button onions. Cut the crusts off the bread and cut the slices into small triangles. Fry the mushrooms and onions in the remaining butter, then remove them from the pan and keep hot. Fry the bread and keep hot. Remove the fish from the liquid and keep hot on a serving dish.

Beat the egg yolk and cream together and add a little of the fish liquid. Stir this into the mixture in the pan and continue gently stirring to heat the egg and cream without boiling. Pour the sauce over the eels and serve garnished with the mushrooms, onions and bread triangles.

Herrings in Oatmeal

SERVES: 6
PREPARATION: 15 minutes
COOKING: 20 minutes

4 small herrings
salt and black pepper
45–60 ml/3–4 tablespoons milk
60 ml/4 tablespoons coarse oatmeal
50 g/2 oz butter
lemon wedges to garnish

Scale, wash and clean the herrings (page 313); cut off the heads and carefully remove the backbones (page 314). Sprinkle a little salt and black pepper over the herrings, dip them in milk and coat evenly with the oatmeal, pressing it on firmly.

Melt the butter in a large heavy-based frying pan; fry the herrings over gentle heat for about 10 minutes on each side. Lift the fish from the pan and serve them immediately, garnished with lemon wedges.

POULTRY & GAME

Chicken Supreme St Sylvestre

SERVES: 4
PREPARATION: 20 minutes
COOKING: 35 minutes

4 boned chicken breasts
150 g/5 oz butter
1 shallot
150 ml/¼ pt red wine
150 ml/¼ pt chicken stock
salt and black pepper

Cook the chicken breasts in 50 g/ 2 oz of the butter over gentle heat for 25 minutes, or until they are tender.

Arrange the chicken on a serving dish. Finely chop the shallot and add to the pan, with the wine. Bring to the boil and continue boiling for 1 minute. Add the stock and boil briskly until reduced by half. Stir in the remaining butter, in small knobs, and season to taste.

Just before serving, pour the sauce over the chicken.

Partridge in Vine Leaves

Vine leaves impart an unusual flavour to these succulent game birds. Order the partridges ready for cooking and have the giblets included with the order.

SERVES: 4
PREPARATION: 25 minutes
COOKING: 1¼–1½ hours

2 young partridges
salt and black pepper
6 lemon slices
20 ml/4 teaspoons quince, crab
    apple or redcurrant jelly
8–10 vine leaves
350 g/12 oz fat bacon rashers
300 ml/½ pt white wine
900 ml/1½ pt chicken stock
Garnish
watercress
lemon spirals (page 412)

Wipe the partridges inside and out with absorbent kitchen paper and season with salt and pepper. Put 3 lemon slices and half the quince jelly inside each bird. Rinse and drain the vine leaves, then pat them dry on absorbent kitchen paper. Selecting large vine leaves to wrap around the birds, wrap each bird completely in leaves, then cover them with bacon rashers and tie firmly with fine string.

Place the white wine, stock and giblets from the partridges (if available) in a large saucepan and bring to the boil. Put the partridge parcels into the boiling liquid, bring back to the boil, reduce the heat and simmer, covered, for 1–1¼ hours, until they are tender.

Chill the partridges quickly by immersing them in a bowl of iced water until quite cold. Remove from the water, unwrap the bacon and vine leaves; dry the partridges thoroughly with absorbent kitchen paper.

Serve the partridges whole, on a bed of watercress, garnished with lemon spirals.
■ Offer some Cumberland Sauce (page 356) and a Lettuce and Celery Salad (page 213) with the partridges.

Chicken Supreme St Sylvestre.

Guinea Fowl in Red Wine

Guinea fowl are now classified as poultry and are raised like free-range chickens; they are also available frozen. The somewhat dry flesh is made tender by cooking the fowl in wine.

SERVES: 4–6
PREPARATION: 20 minutes
COOKING: 1 hour

75 g/3 oz belly pork
25 g/1 oz butter
1 or 2 guinea fowl (jointed)
salt and black pepper
16 button onions
2 cloves garlic
90 ml/3 fl oz brandy
1 bottle Beaujolais
150 ml/¼ pt chicken stock
1 bouquet garni*
15 ml/1 tablespoon soft
      brown sugar
100 g/4 oz mushrooms
Sauce
25 g/1 oz plain flour
25 g/1 oz butter
parsley sprigs to garnish

Cut the belly pork into small cubes and fry in the butter in a flameproof casserole. Wipe the poultry joints with absorbent kitchen paper and season with salt and pepper. Remove the pork from the pan and slowly brown the guinea fowl in the butter over gentle heat.

Peel the onions and crush the garlic, then add to the pan, turn them until they are glazed, then stir in the fried pork and heat for 1–2 minutes. Warm the brandy, pour over the guinea fowl and set

Guinea Fowl in Red Wine.

alight. As soon as the flames have died down, pour over the wine and chicken stock; add the bouquet garni. Stir in the brown sugar; increase the heat to bring the contents of the pan slowly to boiling point. Season to taste with salt and freshly ground pepper, then cover the pan and simmer for 30 minutes.

Meanwhile, trim and clean the mushrooms and add to the guinea fowl. Cover and cook for a further 15 minutes or until the guinea fowl is tender. Use a draining spoon to transfer the guinea fowl, button onions and mushrooms to a heated serving dish, cover and keep hot.

Turn up the heat and boil the cooking liquid rapidly until it is reduced by about half. Work the flour and butter together to form a paste. Reduce the heat so that the sauce simmers very gently. Whisking continuously, add the paste in small knobs. Whisk in each addition until it has melted and combined with the sauce before adding the next. Whisk lightly until the sauce boils, then simmer for 2–3 minutes. Pour the sauce over the guinea fowl and garnish with parsley.
■ Serve with boiled potatoes and Brussels sprouts or broccoli.

Pigeons with Pâté

SERVES: 6
MARINATING: 12 hours
PREPARATION: 40 minutes
OVEN: 140°C/275°F/gas 1
COOKING: 2 hours 40 minutes

6 young pigeons
½ bottle dry white wine
2 carrots
1 onion
2 bay leaves
4 sprigs parsley
2 sprigs thyme
pared rind of ½ orange
pared rind of ½ lemon
25 g/1 oz butter
Stuffing
15 ml/1 tablespoon port
1 egg yolk
225 g/8 oz smooth pâté
2.5 ml/½ teaspoon ground
      mixed spice
salt and black pepper
Long-cooked Cabbage
100 g/4 oz belly pork
1 large white cabbage
6 juniper berries
150 ml/¼ pt dry white wine or
      chicken stock
orange wedges to garnish

Wash the pigeons thoroughly inside and out, and remove the giblets, if necessary. Put the birds in a bowl and pour over the wine. Peel and thinly slice the carrots and onion and add to the pigeons, with the bay leaves, parsley, thyme, orange and lemon rind. Marinate* the pigeons for about 12 hours.

To make the stuffing, stir the port and egg yolk into the pâté. Add the spice and seasoning. Drain the pigeons and dry them with absorbent kitchen paper. Spoon the stuffing into the birds and sew them up; pepper them thoroughly.

Melt the butter in a large flameproof casserole and brown the birds quickly. Pour over the marinade, bring to simmering point and add salt and freshly ground black pepper to taste. Cover with a tight-fitting lid, and cook in a preheated oven at 140°C/275°F/gas 1 for 2½ hours.

For the cabbage, dice the belly pork and put in a heavy-based casserole in the oven. When the pork is crisp, swirl the fat around the sides of the casserole before removing and reserving the pork. Trim, wash and shred the white cabbage, then add it to the fat in the casserole.

Lightly crush the juniper berries in a mortar with a pestle. Add them to the cabbage with the pieces of belly pork, salt and pepper. Mix well, then pour over the white wine (or stock) and cover closely with foil. Cook in the oven at the same time as the pigeons, for 2¼–2½ hours.

About half-way through the cooking time, check the moisture content of the cabbage, stir well and add a little water if necessary. If the casserole is tightly covered to retain the cooking juices this should not be necessary. However, if the oven is slightly too fierce the cabbage may cook too quickly.

Spread the cooked cabbage and pork over the base of a warm serving dish, place the pigeons on top and pour over the liquid. Arrange a garnish of orange wedges on the cabbage.

Marinated Venison

SERVES: 6
PREPARATION: 25 minutes
MARINATING: 2–5 hours
OVEN: 190°C/375°F/gas 5
COOKING: about 1¾ hours

2 carrots
1 Spanish onion
2 sticks celery
1 clove garlic
30 ml/2 tablespoons olive oil
1 bay leaf
1 sprig thyme
12 juniper berries
450 ml/¾ pt port
300 ml/½ pt water
salt and black pepper
1.4 kg/3 lb boned and rolled joint
    of saddle or haunch of venison
30 ml/2 tablespoons plain flour
25 g/1 oz butter
15 ml/1 tablespoon redcurrant jelly

Venison in port is an excellent choice for that special dinner. A joint of boned and rolled saddle or haunch can serve any number from four to over a dozen people. A small whole saddle can be marinated and cooked on the bone; a 4.5 kg/10 lb joint, from a fallow deer, will serve ten to twelve, handsomely. Reduce the cooking time per 450 g/1 lb for joints over 1.4 kg/3 lb, allowing 15 minutes per 450 g/1 lb, plus an additional 15 minutes.

Peel and chop the carrots, onion and celery. Peel and crush the garlic. Heat the olive oil in a saucepan and add the prepared vegetables, garlic, bay leaf and thyme. Cook for 5 minutes without browning. Crush the juniper berries in a mortar and add them

to the vegetables. Pour in the port and bring to the boil. Reduce the heat and simmer for 5 minutes. Remove the pan from the heat, stir in the water and salt and pepper to taste.

Place the venison in a bowl and pour in the port mixture. Cover and leave for 2–5 hours, turning the meat occasionally.

Cut the rind off the bacon and stretch the rashers with a knife blade. Lift the venison out of the marinade and place it in a roasting tin. Cover the top of the joint with the bacon. Strain the marinade, add the vegetables to the tin and pour in about a third of the marinade. Cover with foil, making sure it is tightly sealed. Cook in a preheated oven at 190°C/375°F/gas 5 for 1 hour 20 minutes.

Meanwhile, cream the flour and butter to a smooth paste. Transfer the venison to a dish and keep it hot in the oven while making the sauce.

Strain the liquid from the roasting pan into a saucepan and pour in the remaining marinade. Bring to the boil, then reduce the heat so that the sauce simmers. Whisk in knobs of the butter and flour mixture to thicken the sauce, and bring the sauce to the boil. Simmer for 3–5 minutes. Finally, mix in the redcurrant jelly, and as soon as this has dissolved, season the sauce with salt and freshly ground black pepper if necessary.

Carve the joint and arrange the slices on a serving dish. Pour some of the sauce over the meat. Serve the remainder of the sauce in a separate dish.

MEAT

Braised Oxtail

Oxtail is an inexpensive, nourishing but fatty meat. This stew is best cooked the day before so that the fat can settle and be lifted from the top before the stew is reheated.

SERVES: 6
PREPARATION: 40 minutes
OVEN: 140°C/275°F/gas 1
COOKING: 4¾ hours

2 oxtails
flour
salt and black pepper
2 onions
40 g/1½ oz beef dripping or 30 ml/
    2 teaspoons oil
1 bottle red wine or 900 ml/1½ pt
    beef stock
1 bouquet garni*
2 bay leaves
15 ml/1 tablespoon redcurrant jelly
pared rind of ½ lemon and ½ orange
350 g/12 oz carrots
2 small turnips
15 ml/1 tablespoon lemon juice
15 ml/1 tablespoon tomato paste
175 g/6 oz mushrooms
Garnish
45 ml/3 tablespoons chopped
    fresh parsley
10 ml/2 teaspoons grated
    lemon rind

Cut the excess fat from the two oxtails. Chop them into 5 cm/ 2 in lengths if they have not already been cut up. Season a little flour with salt and freshly ground black pepper and use to

coat the oxtails. Peel and slice the onions.

Melt the dripping or oil in a large saucepan and brown the oxtail pieces in the hot fat. Then transfer to a large flameproof casserole. Fry the onions in the residue of the fat, and as soon as they begin to brown add them to the oxtail. Pour the wine or beef stock over the oxtail and onions, put the pot over the heat and bring the wine to the boil. Add the bouquet garni, salt, freshly ground black pepper, bay leaves, redcurrant jelly and rind. Cover the pot and simmer for 2 hours. Drain off the liquid into a wide bowl and leave to cool.

Peel and slice the carrots and turnips and add to the oxtail. Spoon as much fat as possible from the cooled liquid. (If it is thoroughly cold, the fat will have settled in a layer on top and can easily be lifted off.) Pour the liquid over the oxtail. Add the lemon juice and tomato paste; bring to the boil. Transfer to a preheated oven and cook at 140°C/275°F/gas 1 for 2½ hours, or until the oxtails are very tender. Add the trimmed and sliced mushrooms for the last 10 minutes of cooking time.

Serve sprinkled with parsley mixed with the grated lemon.
■ Fried Rice with Leeks (page 73) is a tasty accompaniment to this dish.

Carbonnade à la Flamande

This is an adaptation of a Belgian recipe for beef in beer. The ale gives the meat a distinctly nutty flavour, heightened by the garlic crust. This dish is best prepared in advance and reheated later.

SERVES: 6
PREPARATION: 55 minutes
OVEN: 160°C/325°F/gas 3
COOKING: 3¼ hours

1.4 kg/3 lb lean blade of beef or
    chuck steak, in one piece
3 large onions
4 cloves garlic (optional)
50 g/2 oz dripping or 45 ml/
    3 tablespoons oil
salt and black pepper
30 ml/2 tablespoons plain flour
15 ml/1 tablespoon soft
    brown sugar
300 ml/½ pt strong beef stock
450 ml/¾ pt brown ale
15 ml/1 tablespoon wine vinegar
1 bouquet garni*
2 bay leaves
Garlic Crust
100 g/4 oz butter
3 cloves garlic
1 French loaf

Cut the beef into 1 cm/½ in thick slices, about 7.5 cm/3 in long and 3.5 cm/1½ in wide. Peel and finely slice the onions; crush the cloves of garlic.

Melt the dripping or heat the oil in a large frying pan. Quickly brown the beef slices and put to one side. Lower the heat and cook the onions in the remaining fat until golden. Then add the garlic and cook for 2 minutes, stirring

Boiled Beef and Carrots with Suet Dumplings

This is one of the classic dishes from the English kitchen. Carrots and onions are always cooked with the beef.

SERVES: 6
PREPARATION: 30 minutes
COOKING: 3–3½ hours

1.8 kg/4 lb piece salt brisket
1 large onion
4 cloves
1 bouquet garni*
6 peppercorns
2 bay leaves
1 rasher streaky bacon
10 small carrots
12 small onions
2 small turnips
150 ml/¼ pt dry cider
2.5 ml/½ teaspoon dry mustard
2.5 ml/½ teaspoon ground cinnamon
1½ quantities Dumplings (page 369)

Buy lean brisket; ask the butcher how long the meat has been in brine and soak it in cold water overnight if the meat has been brined for more than three days; otherwise soak for 30 minutes.

Put the brisket in a large saucepan; peel the large onion, stud it with the cloves and add it to the beef, together with the bouquet garni, peppercorns, bay leaves and bacon. Cover with cold water, bring to the boil and after a few minutes remove the scum; keep the meat on the boil and continue skimming for about 10 minutes. Cover the pan and reduce the heat; simmer for 1¾ hours. Remove from the heat and lift out the meat; strain the liquid into a large bowl. Leave the liquid to settle until the fat rises to the surface. Skim the fat off the liquid, then mop the remaining fat off the liquid by skimming it gently with absorbent kitchen paper.

Peel the carrots and onions, and peel and coarsely slice the turnips. Arrange the vegetables in a deep pan, with the beef on top. Pour over enough strained liquid and the cider to cover. Sprinkle in the mustard and ground cinnamon, and cover the pan. Bring to the boil, then reduce the heat and simmer for 45 minutes.

Meanwhile, make the dumplings, adding parsley to the mixture instead of cheese. Add the dumplings to the simmering liquid, cover and cook gently for a further 15 minutes. If the pan is not large enough to hold both the meat and suet dumplings comfortably, complete the cooking time without adding the dumplings. Transfer the meat and vegetables to a serving dish, cover and keep hot. Then cook the dumplings.

Arrange the piece of beef in the centre of a serving dish and surround with the vegetables and dumplings; serve the liquid separately in a sauceboat.

■ Winter cabbage, cut into large chunks, may also be added to the simmering beef for the last 15 minutes of cooking. Plain boiled potatoes may be served instead of the dumplings.

continuously. Layer the onions and beef in a deep casserole, beginning with the onions and finishing with meat; season each layer lightly.

Stir the flour and sugar into the fat and the juices in the pan in which the beef and onions were cooked. Stir well, scraping all the sediment off the pan. Gradually pour in the stock, stirring continuously, until the sauce begins to thicken and is smooth; bring to the boil. Add the ale and the vinegar; bring back to the boil, then simmer for

a few minutes. Put the bouquet garni and bay leaves in the casserole and pour over the sauce. Cover the casserole and cook in a preheated oven for 2½ hours at 160°C/325°F/gas 3.

The flavour is improved if the casserole is cooled and chilled overnight at this stage, then reheated the next day, before making the garlic crust.

For the garlic crust, melt the butter in a frying pan over low heat. Crush the three cloves of garlic and stir into the butter. Cut the French bread into

Carbonnade à la Flamande.

1 cm/½ in thick slices and soak in the garlic butter, until this is completely absorbed. Put the bread on top of the carbonnade and cook in a preheated oven at 160°C/325°F/gas 3 for about 30 minutes. The meat should then be thoroughly heated and the garlic crust should be crisp with a golden tinge.

■ Serve the carbonnade direct from the casserole. Cauliflower with Almonds (page 71) works well as an accompaniment.

Roghan Josh (Kashmir)

SERVES: 4–6
PREPARATION: 25 minutes
COOKING: about 1½ hours

900 g/2 lb boned leg of lamb
2.5 cm/1 in piece of fresh
*   root ginger*
75 g/3 oz ghee*
10 ml/2 teaspoons ground
*   coriander*
7.5 ml/1½ teaspoons Garam
*   Masala (page 239)*
salt
chilli powder
600 ml/1 pt water
50 g/2 oz blanched almonds
60 ml/4 tablespoons double cream
*   or plain yogurt*
25 g/1 oz pistachio nuts

Cut the meat into 2.5 cm/1 in pieces. Peel and chop the ginger. Heat the ghee in a flameproof casserole and brown the lamb and ginger. Add the ground coriander and garam masala; season with salt and chilli powder and stir in the water. Bring to the boil, simmer gently, covered, for about 1½ hours.

Pound half the almonds in a mortar, adding 5 ml/1 teaspoon iced water occasionally to make a smooth paste. Mix in the cream or yogurt. Alternatively, the paste can be prepared in a liquidiser or food processor. Stir the paste mixture into the lamb. Cook for another 5 minutes over lowest possible heat. Chop the remaining almonds and the pistachio nuts, and sprinkle over the lamb and sauce to serve.

Durham Lamb Squab Pie

Originally, this recipe probably contained squabs – or young pigeons – but, in the course of time, meat was substituted. There are several variations of this English farmhouse dish; the following comes from Durham.

SERVES: 4–6
PREPARATION: 30 minutes
OVEN: 180°C/350°F/gas 4
COOKING: about 1½ hours

900 g/2 lb potatoes
8 lamb chops
1 large onion
3 cooking apples
40 g/1½ oz butter
5 ml/1 teaspoon brown sugar
salt and pepper
200 ml/7 fl oz chicken stock

Peel and thinly slice the potatoes and cover with cold water. Trim excess fat from the lamb chops. Peel and finely chop the onion, and peel, core and chop the apples. Melt 15 g/½ oz of the butter in a pan and fry the chops lightly on both sides. Remove them as soon as the blood starts to run. Fry the apples and onion in the fat for about 5 minutes.

Use half the remaining butter to grease the inside of a pie dish. Drain the sliced potatoes, dry on absorbent kitchen paper and line the base of the dish with half of them. Arrange the chops on the potato bed and spoon the apple and onion mixture over them. Sprinkle over the sugar, a little salt and a couple of twists of pepper from the mill. Cover with the rest of the potatoes and pour over the chicken stock. Melt the remaining butter and brush it over the potato layer. Cook the pie in a preheated oven at 180°C/350°F/gas 4 for about 1¼ hours or until the potatoes are tender and golden brown.
■ Brussels sprouts tossed in soft brown sugar and allspice could be served with the pie.

Durham Lamb Squab Pie.

Suffolk Stew

This is one of those hearty, satisfying stews that requires nothing before it, and very little afterwards. Order the best end of lamb chined*, and begin preparations a day in advance.

SERVES: 4–6
SOAKING: 8–10 hours
PREPARATION: 30 minutes
COOKING: 3 hours

50 g/2 oz green or brown lentils
50 g/2 oz haricot beans
25 g/1 oz pearl barley
1 large turnip
4 carrots
4 onions
1 best end of lamb
2 bay leaves
1 clove garlic
5 ml/1 teaspoon dried mixed herbs
salt and pepper
1.7 litres/3 pt water
4 large potatoes

Soak the lentils, haricot beans and pearl barley in cold water overnight. The following day, peel and roughly chop the turnip, carrots and onions; put them in a large saucepan. Trim any excess fat from the lamb and cut the meat into single chops. Add these, together with the bay leaves, crushed garlic, herbs and pepper to the vegetables.

Drain the lentils, beans and pearl barley and add them to the pan. Pour over the water, cover the pan and bring to the boil. Simmer gently for 2 hours. Peel the potatoes and cut them into large chunks, then add them to the stew with salt and pepper.

Bring back to simmering point, cover the pan and simmer gently for a further 1 hour.
■ Warmed bread or muffins may be served with the stew.

Spare Rib Chops in Marsala

Spare rib chops are meaty pork chops without bones and lightly marbled with fat. They are an economical, well-flavoured cut.

SERVES: 6
PREPARATION: 40 minutes
OVEN: 180°C/350°F/gas 4
COOKING: about 1 hour

15 ml/1 tablespoon olive oil
2 cloves garlic
6 spare rib chops of pork
30 ml/2 tablespoons
*   chopped parsley*
5 ml/1 teaspoon ground
*   fennel seeds*
salt and black pepper
150 ml/¼ pt fresh orange juice
150 ml/¼ pt chicken stock
45 ml/3 tablespoons Marsala wine

Heat the oil in a heavy-based flameproof casserole which may be placed in the oven. Peel and crush the cloves of garlic and rub over the chops. Mix the parsley with the fennel seeds; rub into the chops. Put the chops in the pan, pepper each well, and cook on both sides until browned. Do this in batches if the pan is not large enough to hold the chops in a single layer. Then return all the chops to the pan. Pour the orange juice, stock and Marsala over the chops. Add salt and pepper to taste.

Cook the chops in a pre-heated oven for 45 minutes at 180°C/350°F/gas 4, until the chops are tender. Serve from the casserole or transfer to a warmed serving dish.

■ Plain cooked pasta or creamy mashed potatoes are good accompaniments; diced buttered swede, broccoli or Brussels sprouts are suitable vegetables.

Cassoulet

Pork, beans and poultry are the ingredients of this classic farm-house dish from Languedoc in southern France. Preserved goose – confit d'oie – is the traditional poultry, but other poultry or game can be substituted. A deep ovenproof casserole with a capacity of at least 2.9 litres/5 pt is essential for this dish. Begin by soaking the beans overnight. The poultry portions may be skinned, if preferred.

SERVES: 6–8
PREPARATION: 30 minutes
SOAKING: 12 hours
OVEN: 180°C/350°F/gas 4
COOKING: 3¼–3½ hours

275 g/10 oz haricot beans
675 g/1½ lb piece bacon for boiling
3–4 cloves garlic
2 onions
4 sticks celery
1 large bouquet garni*
10 ml/2 teaspoons made mustard
6 small joints of chicken, duck
   or rabbit
225 g/8 oz Toulouse sausage or
   garlic sausage
salt and black pepper
100 g/4 oz fresh white breadcrumbs

Soak the haricot beans in cold water for 12 hours. Drain the beans, put them in a pan with some fresh water, bring to the boil and boil steadily for 20 minutes. Meanwhile, peel and chop the garlic and onions, and slice the celery. Drain the beans and place them, with the bacon, garlic, onions, celery, bouquet garni and mustard in a deep ovenproof casserole.

Do not add any salt at this stage as it will toughen the haricot beans and prevent them from becoming tender during further cooking. Pour in enough boiling water (from a kettle) to cover the ingredients. Cover and cook in a preheated oven at 180°C/350°F/gas 4 for 1½ hours.

Taste the cooking liquid and add seasoning if necessary. Add the poultry or game, pushing the joints well down into the beans. Add a little extra water, if necessary, so that the poultry or game portions are three-quarters submerged in liquid. Cut up the Toulouse or garlic sausage and add it to the casserole, pushing the pieces down between the other ingredients. Sprinkle the breadcrumbs over the top and cover the casserole. Continue to cook for a further 1 hour, then remove the lid and cook for a final 15–30 minutes to brown the breadcrumb crust.

■ Serve the cassoulet straight from the casserole dish. Crisp, hot French bread is all that is necessary to complement this substantial dish.

Stuffed Pork with Apricot Sauce

The fillet – or tenderloin – of pork is a lean cut weighing about 350–450 g/12–16 oz. A pair of tenderloins, each weighing about 450 g/1 lb, is used here.

SERVES: 6
PREPARATION: 30 minutes
OVEN: 160°C/325°F/gas 3
COOKING: about 1¾ hours

225 g/8 oz no-need-to-presoak
   dried apricots
15 ml/1 tablespoon sultanas
   or raisins
100 g/4 oz fine white breadcrumbs
15 ml/1 tablespoon finely
   chopped parsley
15 ml/1 tablespoon finely
   chopped onion
1–2 cloves garlic (optional)
7.5 ml/1½ teaspoons chopped
   tarragon
50 g/2 oz melted butter
1 orange
1 small egg
salt and black pepper
900 g/2 lb pork tenderloin
50 g/2 oz unsalted butter
600 ml/1 pt water
15 ml/1 tablespoon soft
   brown sugar
juice of 1 lemon
15 ml/1 tablespoon aniseed-
   flavoured liqueur or 30 ml/
   2 tablespoons dry sherry

Chop 40 g/1½ oz of the dried apricots and sultanas or raisins; mix with the breadcrumbs, parsley, onion, 1 crushed clove of garlic (if liked) and the tarragon. Stir in the melted butter. Grate the rind off the orange and add it

Stuffed Pork with Apricot Sauce.

to the stuffing. Cut all peel and pith from the fruit. Hold the orange over a basin and cut out the segments, slicing between each membrane. Squeeze any juice from the core and membranes before discarding them. Cut up the orange segments and add them to the stuffing with the collected juice. Beat the egg lightly and use it to bind the mixture. Season with salt and freshly ground pepper.

Trim any fat off each tenderloin and remove the transparent skin. Take the larger of the tenderloins and slit the meat lengthways through half its thickness, then open it out. Lay the meat between two sheets of greaseproof paper and beat it flat with a meat mallet or rolling pin until it is large and thin.

Spread the stuffing over the flattened tenderloin and lay the second tenderloin down the middle. Fold the flattened meat around the tenderloin, enclosing it completely. Tie with string, taking care not to squeeze out the stuffing.

Melt the butter in a large frying pan. Peel and slice the remaining garlic and fry until brown, then remove. Brown the pork in the butter, then transfer it to the roasting tin with the pan juices. Cover with foil and roast for about 1 hour 20 minutes (40 minutes for each 450 g/1 lb) in a preheated oven at 160°C/325°F/gas 3. Remove the cover for the last 10 minutes.

Place the remaining apricots in a saucepan. Add the water and bring to the boil. Simmer for about 20 minutes. Cool the apricots slightly, then purée them with the cooking liquid.

Transfer the pork to a serving plate, cover and keep hot. Mix the puréed apricots, sugar, lemon juice and liqueur or sherry in the tin. Bring to the boil, stirring, and simmer for 1–2 minutes.

Remove the string and slice the meat. Arrange on a serving dish and spoon over a little of the sauce. Offer the remaining sauce in a separate dish.

VEGETABLES & SALADS

Baked Jerusalem Artichokes

SERVES: 6
PREPARATION: 30 minutes
OVEN: 180°C/350°F/gas 4
COOKING: 45 minutes

juice of 1 lemon
675 g/1½ lb Jerusalem artichokes
salt and black pepper
50 g/2 oz butter
flour

Strain the lemon juice into a bowl of cold water. Wash and thinly peel the artichokes, cut them into 5 mm/¼ in slices and drop into the water and lemon juice to prevent them from going brown. Bring a large pan of salted water to the boil. Drain the artichokes and drop into the boiling water. Boil for 4 minutes, then drain in a colander.

Melt the butter in a fairly large, shallow ovenproof dish in an oven preheated to 180°C/350°F/gas 4. Season a little flour with salt and pepper and use it to coat the artichokes; turn in the butter. Return the dish to the oven and cook the vegetables for about 40 minutes.

Parsnip Croquettes

Parsnip is one of the traditional staple winter vegetables in Britain, and it is often served as a mash or purée. These crisp croquettes, which should be prepared in advance, go well with roast or braised meat.

SERVES: 4–6
PREPARATION: 30 minutes
CHILLING: 1½ hours
COOKING: about 30 minutes

900 g/2 lb parsnips
salt and black pepper
50 g/2 oz butter
5 ml/1 teaspoon grated nutmeg
fresh white breadcrumbs
2 eggs
oil for deep-frying

Peel and slice the parsnips. Place in a saucepan and pour in water to cover the vegetables. Add salt to taste and bring to the boil. Reduce the heat, part-cover the pan and simmer for 15–20 minutes, or until the parsnips are tender. Drain thoroughly, return the parsnips to the saucepan and mash them with a potato masher, then press them through a coarse sieve. Melt the butter, then beat it into the parsnips with pepper and the nutmeg. Allow to cool and chill for 1 hour.

To shape the croquettes, sprinkle a thick layer of the breadcrumbs on a plate. Beat the eggs in a wide, shallow dish. Place a spoonful of the parsnips on the breadcrumbs, then shape the mixture into a croquette measuring about 6 cm/2½ in long and about 2.5 cm/1 in wide. Use the crumbs to prevent the mixture sticking as you roll it into a neat cylinder shape.

Roll the crumbed croquette through the beaten egg, then coat it in a second layer of breadcrumbs. Shape the rest of the mixture in the same way to make 14 croquettes. Chill for at least 1½ hours before cooking the croquettes.

Heat the oil for deep frying to 190°C/375°F or until a cube of day-old bread browns in 1 minute. Deep fry the croquettes a few at a time until crisp and golden– the fresh crumb coating browns fairly quickly, so take care not to overcook it. If using a wire basket, dip it into the hot oil for 30 seconds before placing the croquettes in it. Drain the fried croquettes on absorbent kitchen paper and keep hot while frying the remaining croquettes.

Note The shaped and coated croquettes freeze well. Lay them on a baking sheet lined with cling film and freeze until firm. Then pack in sealed polythene bags and store for up to 3 months. Deep fry from frozen, reducing the heat once the coating has lightly browned and cooking until golden brown.

Savoury Parsnip Pie

Lightly smoked tofu complements the slightly sweet flavour of parsnips in this simple pie. Filo pastry is quick and easy to use and it gives impressive results; it is also less rich than puff or short crust pastry.

SERVES: 6
PREPARATION: 30 minutes
OVEN: 180°C/350°F/gas 4
COOKING: about 1¼ hours

450 g/1 lb parsnips
salt and black pepper
1 leek (about 175 g/6 oz)
2 sticks celery
1 onion
60 ml/4 tablespoons olive oil
1 bay leaf
30 ml/2 tablespoons plain flour
150 ml/¼ pt dry cider
150 ml/¼ pt milk
30 ml/2 tablespoons chopped parsley
60 ml/4 tablespoons grated Parmesan cheese
25 g/1 oz butter
6 sheets filo pastry (38 × 30 cm/ 15 × 12 in each; a 225 g/8 oz packet)
225 g/8 oz smoked tofu

Peel the parsnips and cut them into quarters lengthways. Hold the pieces together and slice them. Place the parsnips in a saucepan and pour in cold water to cover. Add salt to taste and bring to the boil. Reduce the heat slightly, cover the pan and boil the parsnips for 5 minutes. Drain and set aside. Slit the leek part through lengthways, wash it thoroughly to remove any dirt from between the layers and slice it thinly. Dice the celery and chop the onion. Heat half the olive oil in a large saucepan. Add the bay leaf, leek, celery and onion. Stir for 2 minutes, then cover the pan and cook for 20 minutes, shaking the pan occasionally. Stir in the flour and cook gently for 2 minutes. Pour in the cider and bring the mixture to the boil, stirring all the time. Gradually stir in the milk once the sauce has boiled, then bring it back to the boil again. Add the parsnips and seasoning to taste, then stir in the parsley and Parmesan. Remove the pan from the heat and leave to stand for 5 minutes.

Heat the remaining olive oil with the butter in a small pan. Brush a little of the butter mixture on to a 25 cm/10 in flan dish or tin. Use four sheets of filo to line the dish, overlapping them so that each sheet covers half the base, and leaving the edges of the pastry overhanging the edge of the dish. As each sheet is placed in the dish brush it very lightly with a little of the butter mixture. Cut the smoked tofu into 1–2.5 cm/½–1 in cubes and distribute them over the pastry base. Remove the bay leaf from the parsnip mixture, then spoon it into the pie, over and around the tofu.

Lay one of the remaining sheets of filo over the filling and brush it lightly with some of the butter mixture. Then fold the overhanging filo pastry over the top, brushing each piece with butter as you do so. Lay the last sheet of filo on top of the pie and pinch it into creases and folds with your fingers. Brush with the remaining butter mixture and bake the pie in a preheated oven at 180°C/350°F/gas 4 for 30 minutes. Cover the top loosely with a square of cooking foil to prevent the pastry from over-browning, then continue to cook for a further 20 minutes.

■ Spinach or cabbage and boiled or baked potatoes with soured cream are suitable vegetables for serving with the pie as a main meal.

Cauliflower with Almonds

Almonds browned in butter complement the delicate flavour of cauliflower.

SERVES: 4
PREPARATION: 10 minutes
COOKING: 12 minutes

1 large white cauliflower
salt
50 g/2 oz flaked almonds
25–50 g/1–2 oz butter

Cut away the coarse outer leaves from the cauliflower and break the individual florets from the central stem, leaving a short stalk on each.

Bring a large pan of salted water to the boil; cook the cauliflower for 5–7 minutes. Drain through a colander.

Meanwhile, fry the almonds in the butter over low heat until they are golden brown. Put the cauliflower in a dish and spoon over the almonds and butter.

Celeriac and Bean Terrine with Pepper Relish

This vegetarian terrine has a good creamy texture and delicate flavour; the relish of skinned peppers tossed in a piquant dressing perfectly complements both these qualities. The terrine can be served hot or cold.

SERVES: 6
PREPARATION: 30 minutes
OVEN: 180°C/350°F/gas 4
COOKING: about 1½ hours

350 g/12 oz celeriac root
salt and black pepper
225 g/8 oz curd cheese
1 onion
25 g/1 oz butter or 30 ml/
  2 tablespoons oil
400 g/14 oz can soya beans
2 eggs
100 g/4 oz fresh white breadcrumbs
50 g/2 oz mature Cheddar cheese
2.5 ml/½ teaspoon grated nutmeg
Pepper Relish
2 red peppers
2 green peppers
1 clove garlic
5 ml/1 teaspoon caster sugar
10 ml/2 teaspoons made
  English mustard
15 ml/1 tablespoon cider vinegar
60 ml/4 tablespoons olive oil
15 ml/1 tablespoon finely
  chopped capers
30 ml/2 tablespoons finely
  chopped onion
dash of Tabasco sauce (optional)
fresh herb sprigs to garnish

Peel the celeriac and cut it into thick slices. Cut the slices into chunks and place them in a saucepan. Pour in cold water to cover and add a little salt. Bring to the boil, reduce the heat and cover the pan. Boil the celeriac for 10–15 minutes, until it is tender. Drain well and mash until smooth. Beat the curd cheese into the hot celeriac.

Chop the onion. Heat the butter or oil in a saucepan. Add the onion and cook, stirring occasionally, for 10 minutes. Drain the soya beans in a sieve, add them to the onion and stir well. Purée the beans and onion in a liquidiser or food processor, then beat in the eggs. Stir the bean purée into the celeriac, then add the breadcrumbs and cheese with seasoning to taste and nutmeg.

Line the bottom of a 900 g/ 2 lb loaf tin or terrine with non-stick baking parchment. Grease the container well and turn the mixture into it. Press the mixture down evenly and level the top.

Bake in a preheated oven at 180°C/350°F/gas 4 for 1¼ hours, until browned on top, risen and firm to the touch. Slide a knife between the container and the terrine to loosen it around the sides, then leave to stand for 10 minutes before turning out.

Prepare the pepper relish as soon as the terrine is in the oven. Skewer each of the peppers in turn on a metal fork and hold them over a gas burner on the hob until the skin is charred and blistered. Alternatively, the peppers may be charred under a hot grill, in which case you should turn them regularly. Scrape and rub off the charred skin under cold water.

Halve the peppers and cut out their cores, seeds and pith, then chop or finely dice the flesh. Peel and crush the garlic clove, then place it in a basin and add the caster sugar, mustard and cider vinegar. Add salt and pepper to taste, then stir with a whisk until the sugar has dissolved. Gradually pour in the olive oil, whisking continuously, to make a thick dressing. Stir the peppers, capers and onion into the dressing, and add a dash of Tabasco sauce if liked. Cover and leave to stand for about 1 hour or longer before serving.

Cut the terrine into thick slices. Stir the pepper relish, spoon a little on the plates besides the terrine slices, transfer the remainder to a serving dish and offer it separately. Garnish with herb sprigs.

■ The terrine may be served as a starter or main course. A salad of grated carrots goes well with the cold terrine. Stir-fried seasonal vegetables are a crunchy accompaniment for the hot terrine – include carrots, cabbage and leeks for colour and flavour.

Vegetables with Borlotti Beans (overleaf) and Celeriac and Bean Terrine with Pepper Relish.

Vegetables with Borlotti Beans

If you find it difficult to get hold of dried ceps, use fresh brown cap mushrooms instead, but they must be cooked thoroughly in the butter before being added to the other vegetables. Continue cooking the mushrooms until the liquor they yield has completely evaporated.

SERVES: 4
PREPARATION: 20 minutes
COOKING: 45 minutes

2 leeks (about 350 g/12 oz)
2 carrots
1 green pepper
1 turnip (about 225 g/8 oz)
small swede or ½ large swede
1 celeriac root (about 350 g/12 oz)
8 sun-dried tomatoes
8 slices dried ceps or porcini
25 g/1 oz butter
1 clove garlic
1 bay leaf
2 sprigs winter savory or thyme
2.5 ml/½ teaspoon dried oregano
45 ml/3 tablespoons plain flour
300 ml/½ pt cider or white wine
salt and black pepper
400 g/14 oz can borlotti beans
fresh herb sprigs to garnish

Slit the leeks part through lengthways, wash them thoroughly under running water to remove dirt trapped between the layers, then slice them thinly. Cut the carrots into large dice. Halve the pepper, discard the core, seeds and pith, then dice the flesh.

Peel the turnip, swede and celeriac and cut them into cubes measuring about 1 cm/½ in, then place these vegetables in a saucepan and pour in cold water to cover. Add a little salt to taste and bring to the boil. Reduce the heat, cover the pan and simmer for 3 minutes. Meanwhile, place the sun-dried tomatoes and dried mushrooms in a basin. Drain the root vegetables; reserve 300 ml/ ½ pt of the cooking water, pouring it over the tomatoes and mushrooms. Set these aside to soak for 15 minutes.

Melt the butter in a large casserole. Crush the garlic clove and add it to the casserole with the bay leaf, savory or thyme, oregano, leeks, carrots and green pepper. Stir well, then cook for about 10 minutes, stirring often. Remove the tomatoes and mushrooms, chop them and set them aside. Strain the liquid through muslin to remove grit.

Stir the flour into the leek mixture. Then gradually pour in the strained soaking liquor and the wine or cider, stirring continuously and heating until the sauce thickens before adding more liquid. When all the liquid is added, bring the sauce to the boil. Add the tomatoes and mushrooms, the boiled root vegetables and seasoning. Stir gently until the mixture is just boiling again. Reduce the heat and cover the casserole, then simmer gently for 15 minutes. Drain the borlotti beans and stir them into the casserole. Cover and cook gently for a further 15 minutes, until the vegetables are tender. Taste for seasoning, garnish with fresh herbs.
■ Serve the braised vegetables with pasta, rice or boiled barley.

Soufflé Potatoes

SERVES: 6
PREPARATION: 15 minutes
OVEN: 200°C/400°F/gas 6
COOKING: 1¾ hours

6 large potatoes
50 g/2 oz melted butter
salt and black pepper
120 ml/4 fl oz milk or single cream
3 eggs, separated

Wash and dry the potatoes, prick them lightly with a fork and bake in a preheated oven at 200°C/ 400°F/gas 6 for 1½ hours or until tender. Cut a lid lengthways off the baked potatoes, scoop the flesh out into a bowl and mix in the melted butter, seasoning and milk or cream. Stir the egg yolks into the potato mixture. Whisk the egg whites with a little salt until stiff. Beat a quarter of the whites into the potatoes, then use a metal spoon to fold in the remainder.

Pile this soufflé mixture back into the hollow potato skins, return to the oven and bake at the same temperature for 15 minutes, or until the soufflés are well risen.

Serve immediately, before the soufflés have time to collapse.

Cabbage with Italian Dressing

This quickly made winter salad can be served with a selection of cold meats or as a side dish with a plain omelette.

SERVES: 4–6
PREPARATION: 10 minutes

1 white cabbage
1 small clove garlic
90 ml/6 tablespoons olive oil
30 ml/2 tablespoons white
    wine vinegar
1.25 ml/¼ teaspoon dried oregano
    or 2.5 ml/½ teaspoon chopped
    fresh oregano
1.25 ml/¼ teaspoon crushed
    fennel seeds
1.25 ml/¼ teaspoon celery salt
salt and black pepper

Cut away the coarse outer leaves, remove the core and finely shred the cabbage. Turn the vegetable into a serving bowl.

Crush the garlic and put it, with all the other ingredients, in a screw-top jar and shake vigorously. Pour this dressing over the cabbage, toss and serve.

Soufflé Potatoes.

Winter Salad

A crisp salad for lunch is welcome even on a winter's day. This salad has both contrasting colours and textures.

SERVES: 6
PREPARATION: 20 minutes
CHILLING: 30 minutes

275–350 g/10–12 oz cooked ham
    or poultry
½ small white cabbage
2 large carrots
4 sticks celery
1 crisp dessert apple
15 ml/1 tablespoon sultanas
juice of ½ lemon
30 ml/2 tablespoons single cream
    or plain yogurt
300 ml/½ pt mayonnaise
salt and black pepper
chopped parsley to garnish
    (optional)

Dice the ham or poultry. Shred the cabbage. Coarsely grate the carrot, thinly slice the celery and then dice the apple.

Mix the chopped meat, all the vegetables, the apple and the sultanas together in a large salad bowl. Whisk the lemon juice and cream or yogurt into the mayonnaise; season. Pour this dressing over the salad and mix it in thoroughly. Garnish the top with chopped parsley if liked.
■ Serve with baked potatoes or crusty bread for a complete meal.

RICE & PASTA

Rice with Garlic and Walnuts

This lightly flavoured rice dish goes well with grilled fish or meat, especially when a crisp salad completes the menu.

SERVES: 4–6
PREPARATION: 15 minutes
COOKING: 20 minutes

225 g/8 oz long-grain rice
600 ml/1 pt water or chicken stock
juice of ½ lemon
salt and black pepper
45 ml/3 tablespoons finely
    chopped parsley
2 cloves garlic
25 g/1 oz shelled walnuts
45 ml/3 tablespoons olive oil
50 g/2 oz Parmesan cheese

Place the rice in a pan, pour in the water or stock and lemon juice, and add a little salt. Bring the liquid to the boil, stir the rice and cover the pan with a close-fitting lid. Reduce the heat to a minimum setting and cook for 20 minutes. Turn the heat off and leave the rice to stand, covered, for a further 5 minutes.

Meanwhile, purée the chopped parsley, peeled garlic and walnuts with the olive oil. Grate the Parmesan cheese. Fork the paste and the Parmesan cheese into the rice, adding a generous grinding of black pepper. Do not overmix the rice as this will make the grains sticky. Serve immediately.

Fried Rice with Leeks

This simple rice dish is especially good with meat courses that contain a lot of sauce, such as casseroles and braised oxtail stews. If preferred, the rice and leeks can be spiced by cooking 2.5 ml/½ teaspoon good-quality curry powder with the leeks.

SERVES: 6
PREPARATION: 15 minutes
COOKING: 30 minutes

900 g/2 lb leeks
175 g/6 oz long-grain rice
450 ml/ ¾ pt water
25–50 g/1–2 oz butter
salt and black pepper

Remove the coarse outer leaves, roots and tops from the leeks and cut into 5 mm/¼ in thick slices. Wash well under cold running water, flushing away any dirt.

Place the rice in a pan, pour in the water and add a little salt. Bring the water to the boil, stir the rice and cover the pan with a close-fitting lid. Reduce the heat to a minimum setting and cook for 20 minutes. Turn the heat off and leave the rice to stand, covered, for a further 5 minutes.

Meanwhile, melt the butter in a large saucepan, and fry the leeks, stirring frequently, for 8 minutes or until just tender.

Fork up the rice and add the leeks. Season with freshly ground pepper and serve.

Macaroni Cheese with Ham and Tomatoes

Ham and fresh tomatoes add colour and flavour to a plain macaroni cheese.

SERVES: 4
PREPARATION: 20 minutes
OVEN: 200°C/400°F/gas 6
COOKING: 35 minutes

225 g/8 oz macaroni
salt and black pepper
175 g/6 oz grated Cheddar or
    Double Gloucester cheese
450 ml/¾ pt pouring White Sauce
    (page 352)
4 large tomatoes
100 g/4 oz cooked, diced ham
30 ml/2 tablespoons fresh white
    breadcrumbs
25 g/1 oz butter, melted

Cook the macaroni, uncovered, in plenty of boiling salted water for about 15 minutes. Stir two-thirds of the cheese into the white sauce; season to taste.

Skin the tomatoes (page 302) and chop them. Drain the macaroni and mix it into the sauce with the ham and tomatoes. Spoon the mixture into a buttered ovenproof dish. Mix the rest of the cheese with the breadcrumbs, sprinkle over the macaroni, and pour the melted butter over. Bake in a preheated oven at 200°C/400°F/gas 6 for 20 minutes or until the top is crisp and golden.

■ Serve hot, with a crisp winter salad or cooked vegetables, such as spinach or cauliflower.

Spaghetti with Aubergine

In Italy, pasta – and in particular spaghetti – frequently forms the main meal of the day.

SERVES: 4–6
PREPARATION: 10 minutes
COOKING: 15 minutes

1 large aubergine
salt and black pepper
flour
350 g/12 oz spaghetti
2 cloves garlic
90 ml/6 tablespoons olive oil
freshly ground Parmesan cheese
    to serve

Remove the stalk end of the aubergine. Cut the aubergine into thin slices and place these in layers in a colander. Sprinkle salt over each layer and leave for 30 minutes. Rinse the aubergine and wipe the slices dry on absorbent kitchen paper. Cut the slices into 5 mm/¼ in wide strips. Season a

Spaghetti with Aubergine.

little flour with plenty of salt and freshly ground pepper and use to coat the strips.

Bring a large saucepan of salted water to the boil. Lower the spaghetti into the boiling water, pushing it down as it softens. Bring back to the boil, stir once, then boil steadily for about 10 minutes, or until the spaghetti is tender but not soft.

While the spaghetti is cooking, peel and finely chop the garlic cloves, then heat the olive oil in a frying pan. Add the garlic and aubergine strips and cook, stirring often, until the aubergine is tender and browned.

Drain the spaghetti well and turn it into a warmed serving dish. Season with pepper and pour over the aubergine mixture with all the oil from the pan. Use a spoon and fork to mix the spaghetti and aubergine. Serve immediately, with freshly grated Parmesan cheese.

PUDDINGS & DESSERTS

Treacle Tart

The popularity of this traditional lattice tart has never diminished. It is, in spite of its name, always made with golden syrup.

SERVES: 6
PREPARATION: 20 minutes
OVEN: 200°C/400°F/gas 6
COOKING: 25–30 minutes

225 g/8 oz plain flour
pinch salt
150 g/5 oz butter
1 egg yolk
15–30 ml/1–2 tablespoons
    cold water
105 ml/7 tablespoons golden syrup
50 g/2 oz fresh white breadcrumbs
finely grated rind of 1 small lemon
15 ml/1 tablespoon lemon juice

Sift the flour and salt into a mixing bowl. Cut the butter into small knobs and rub into the flour until the mixture resembles breadcrumbs. Mix in the egg yolk with a fork, and add just enough cold water to the mixture to make a short dough. Lightly gather the dough into a ball.

Cut off a quarter of the pastry and set it aside for the lattice. Roll out the rest large enough to line a 20 cm/8 in shallow pie plate and prick the base.

Warm the syrup in a small saucepan until it is runny. Remove from the heat, stir in the other ingredients and spread over the pastry. Roll out any pastry trimmings with the reserved

Treacle Tart.

pastry and cut out 1 cm/½ in wide strips long enough to cover the tart. Dampen the pastry rim of the tart. Lay the pastry strips in a lattice pattern over the tart and trim the edges neatly. Bake the treacle tart in a preheated oven at 200°C/400°F/gas 6 for 25–30 minutes, until golden brown and cooked through.

■ Serve the tart hot or cold with Custard Sauce (page 338).

Bread Pudding

SERVES: 4–6
PREPARATION: 35 minutes
OVEN: 180°C/350°F/gas 4
COOKING: 2 hours

225 g/8 oz dry white bread
300 ml/½ pt milk
50 g/2 oz candied peel
grated rind of 1 small orange
grated rind of 1 lemon
100 g/4 oz currants
50 g/2 oz sultanas
75 g/3 oz shredded suet
50 g/2 oz demerara sugar
10 ml/2 teaspoons ground
    mixed spice
1 large egg
nutmeg
caster sugar

Cut off the crusts and break the bread into small pieces. Place in a large mixing bowl and pour over the milk; leave to soak for 20 minutes. Finely chop the candied peel and add to the bread with the grated orange and lemon rind; mix well. Add the dried fruit, suet, demerara sugar and mixed spice; stir well. Beat the egg and stir it into

the mixture to a dropping consistency. If necessary, add a little more milk.

Spoon the bread mixture into a well-greased 1.12 litre/2 pt pie dish and grate a little nutmeg over it. Bake in a preheated oven at 180°C/350°F/gas 4 for 1¾–2 hours or until browned.

Serve hot or cold, liberally sprinkled with caster sugar.

Peaches with Chestnut Cream

SERVES: 4
PREPARATION: 20 minutes
CHILLING: 30 minutes

8 canned white peach halves or
poached fresh peaches (see
Peaches with Soured Cream,
page 216)
30 ml/2 tablespoons icing sugar
225 g/8 oz unsweetened
    chestnut purée
30 ml/2 tablespoons brandy
150 ml/¼ pt double cream
cocoa powder (optional)

Drain the peach halves and place in four individual serving dishes, cut sides uppermost. Beat the icing sugar into the chestnut purée until smooth, then stir in the brandy.

Whip the cream until it stands in soft peaks, then fold it into the chestnut purée. Spoon or pipe the mixture into the peach halves and chill for 30 minutes. If liked, place a little cocoa powder in a tea strainer or small sieve and sift a little over the top of the chestnut cream before serving.

Chocolate Cream Pie

SERVES: 6
PREPARATION: 20 minutes
CHILLING: 1 hour

1 portion Biscuit Crust (page 380)
Filling
25 g/1 oz caster sugar
25 g/1 oz plain flour
2 egg yolks
300 ml/½ pt milk
25 g/1 oz unsalted butter
100 g/4 oz dark plain chocolate,
    grated
15 ml/1 tablespoon brandy or rum
icing sugar
Topping
150 ml/¼ pt double cream
15 ml/1 tablespoon milk
grated chocolate

Make up the biscuit crust according to the basic recipe and use it to line a 20 cm/8 in round flan tin or dish.

Mix the sugar, flour, and yolks with a little of the milk in a bowl until thoroughly combined and smooth. Heat the remaining milk until hot but not boiling, then pour it into the flour mixture, stirring continuously. Return this mixture to the pan and cook over low heat, stirring continuously, until the mixture thickens and just comes to the boil. Remove the pan from the heat and stir in the butter, cut into small pieces, the chocolate and brandy or rum. Stir until the chocolate has melted and the sauce is smooth. Spoon the filling into the biscuit crust, smoothing the top and dusting it with icing sugar to prevent a skin forming. Cool, then chill.

Just before serving, whip the cream with the milk until thick enough to hold its shape. Spoon this in an even layer over the chocolate filling. Sprinkle with coarsely grated chocolate.

Kulfi

A fragrant Indian ice-cream made with rose water, which gives, with the cooked milk, the traditional flavour. Adding cream, although not authentic, does give a better texture. Kulfi is traditionally made in small conical moulds but yogurt cartons may be used instead.

SERVES: 6
PREPARATION: 30 minutes
COOKING: 2–2½ hours
FREEZING: 12 hours

1.7 litres/3 pt milk
20 green cardamoms
60 ml/4 tablespoons caster sugar
25 g/1 oz pistachio nuts
15 g/½ oz blanched almonds
15 ml/1 tablespoon rose water
150 ml/¼ pt single cream
pistachio nuts to decorate
(optional)

Place the milk with the cardamoms in a large 2.9 litres/ 5 pt heavy-based saucepan. Bring to the boil, lower the heat but allow to simmer vigorously, without boiling over, until the milk has reduced by one third. This is a slow process which cannot be rushed. It can take as long as 2½ hours. Stir frequently, stirring in the skin as it forms.

When the milk has reduced remove the cardamoms with a perforated spoon. Stir in the sugar. Allow to cool while preparing the nuts. Place the pistachios in a heatproof bowl and pour in boiling water to cover. Soak for a few minutes, then drain the pistachios and remove the skins. Finely chop the pistachios with the almonds and add to the milk with the rose water. Stir in the cream. Pour into a suitable container for the freezer. When quite cold, freeze until the mixture becomes slushy and ice crystals start to form around the edges. Stir well, then return to the freezer. Repeat this process two or three times, by which time the kulfi will start to firm up. Quickly spoon it into suitable individual moulds or a freezerproof basin. Freeze until the kulfi is solid.

Transfer the kulfi to the refrigerator 30–60 minutes before serving, depending on the size of the container, to soften. Decorate with roughly chopped pistachio nuts, if liked.

Note The kulfi may be stored in the freezer for 2–3 months. Pack the moulds in a freezer bag. Alternatively, unmould the ice cream without softening it first, then wrap each ice cream in cling film before packing several together in a freezer bag.

Iced Tangerines

For a special dinner party, this refreshingly tangy and impressive looking ice cream is a fitting ending. Prepare the ice cream a day ahead.

SERVES: 6
PREPARATION: 30 minutes
COOKING: 25 minutes
FREEZING: overnight

8 medium-sized tangerines
175 g/6 oz caster sugar
300 ml/½ pt water
juice of ½ lemon
1 egg yolk
300 ml/½ pt double cream
Decoration
camellia leaves
crystallised violets
langues de chat

Wipe the tangerines, grate and reserve the rind from two fruit. Cut off the tops off all the tangerines and carefully scoop out and reserve the flesh from both tops and bottoms. Discard the tangerines which were grated and place the remaining six shells and lids in a polythene bag in the refrigerator. Squeeze about 300 ml/½ pt of juice from the tangerine flesh. Boil the sugar and water in a saucepan over a high heat for 10 minutes to make a syrup. Remove from the heat and allow to cool.

Stir the tangerine and lemon juices into the cooled syrup. Beat the egg yolk and stir into the syrup. Return to the heat and cook gently for 5 minutes, stirring continuously. Cool, pour into a freezing container, cover tightly with a lid and place in the freezer until the syrup is part frozen and slushy.

Whip the cream until thick but not stiff. Break the frozen syrup into a bowl and beat vigorously until it has an even texture. A food processor may be used to break up the ice quickly and smoothly. Stir in the cream and tangerine rind. Spoon this ice cream back into the freezing container, cover with a lid and freeze again until part frozen.

Turn out the mixture, break it down as before and beat until smooth. Return to the freezer and leave until firm, preferably overnight. At least 1 hour before

Iced Tangerines.

serving, scoop the ice cream into the empty tangerine shells and fix on the lids at an angle.

Brush the outsides of the tangerines with water and place in the freezer. Ten minutes before serving, remove the iced tangerines from the freezer in order to let the frost on the tangerine skins settle.

Serve on a tray decorated with well-washed camellia (or other glossy evergreen) leaves and crystallised violets. A dish of langues de chat or other dessert biscuits could be served with the ice cream.

A New-Year Dinner Party

*D*inner parties should be planned so that the cook is not trapped in the kitchen once the guests arrive. On some informal occasions, a completely cook-ahead menu is possible, leaving the cook free to relax and serve the meal as and when everyone is ready. It is also a good idea to include one or two dishes that are prepared in advance on a formal occasion when a traditional-style menu is served. This menu is a good example of one which balances the need for finishing touches with cook-ahead preparation without forfeiting quality or style. It is centred on roast duck, for which last-minute attention is essential, but the first course and dessert can both be prepared and completed earlier in the day.

Menu
~

Prawn Salad
with
Warm Bread Rolls

~

Duck with Orange
Parsnip Croquettes
Glazed Carrots (page 110)
Potatoes with Parsley

~

Floating Island

Preparation notes

● The parsnip croquettes can be made in advance and frozen. Deep fry them from frozen early on the day of the dinner party, until they are just crisp and golden. Drain them thoroughly on absorbent kitchen paper and leave them to cool on fresh kitchen paper. Then place them on a baking sheet, cover and set aside ready for reheating before serving. Place the croquettes in the oven with the duck when the first course is about to be served. The croquettes will heat through and their coating will be crisp.

● Prepare the dessert early on the day of the party, leaving the meringue in the tin ready to turn out at the last minute. Prepare the custard and leave it in a jug, covering the surface with dampened greaseproof paper to prevent a skin from forming. The dessert can be assembled quickly and easily just before serving.

Coordinate all the elements of your table decoration, from napkins to cutlery.

● Prepare the orange for the sauce to accompany the duck well ahead on the day of the dinner party. Leave the cooked rind and segments in a covered dish ready for garnishing.

● Prepare the potatoes for boiling, cutting them into neat, even-sized pieces, and cover them with cold water. Place a wedge of lemon in the potato water as well as salt to taste. Cook the potatoes just before serving the main course, drain them and transfer them to a heated serving dish. Dot with a little butter and cover closely. Keep the potatoes hot in a warm oven or place them over a saucepan of hot water. Alternatively, use a dish suitable for microwave cooking and heat them for about 3–5 minutes just before serving – they can be heating while the sauce for the duck is finished. Sprinkle chopped parsley over the potatoes before taking them to the table and top with a little fresh butter.

● Prepare the carrots in before hand, cutting them finely so that they cook very quickly. Place them in a saucepan with the glazing ingredients ready for cooking. Cook the carrots at the last minute, after clearing the first course and while the sauce for the duck is finished.

● Do not make the prawn salad too far in advance. This is best left until everything else is organised, about an hour before guests arrive. Make sure the ingredients are well tossed in the dressing and leave the salad in its serving bowl in the refrigerator.

Add the garnish just before taking the dish to the table. If you have sufficient space in the refrigerator, the salad can be spooned into individual dishes, each covered with cling film and chilled. Individual portions of salad always look neat and appetising when they are served as a first course. Remove the salad from the refrigerator about 15 minutes before the guests sit down to eat to take the chill off the salad ingredients, particularly the apples.

Prawn Salad

SERVES: 4
PREPARATION: 20 minutes

45 ml/3 tablespoons mayonnaise
60 ml/4 tablespoons double cream
juice of ½ lemon
salt and black pepper
2 large dessert apples
1 celery heart
450 g/1 lb peeled prawns
12 walnuts to garnish

Mix the mayonnaise in a bowl with the cream, add the lemon juice and season to taste with salt and pepper.

Peel and finely shred the apples; thinly slice the celery. Thoroughly drain thawed frozen prawns, if necessary, and mop them dry on absorbent kitchen paper. Fold the apples, celery and prawns into the seasoned mayonnaise mixture.

Spoon the salad into a serving bowl or into individual dishes and garnish with the walnuts. Place in the refrigerator until 15 minutes before serving.

Duck with Orange

SERVES: 4
PREPARATION: 45 minutes
OVEN: 200°C/400°F/gas 6
COOKING: about 2 hours

4 oranges
2 ducks (about 1.8–2.27 kg/
*   4–5 lb each)*
15 ml/1 tablespoon caster sugar
120 ml/4 fl oz red wine vinegar
300 ml/½ pt giblet stock
juice of ½ lemon
15 ml/1 tablespoon arrowroot
30 ml/2 tablespoons water
45 ml/3 tablespoons orange
*   liqueur, such as Curaçao*

Pare the rind thinly from the oranges and reserve it. Cut all peel and pith from the oranges. Hold each orange in turn over a basin and cut out the segments, slicing between each membrane. Squeeze any juice from the core and membranes before discarding them. Reserve the orange juice. Cut the rind into strips and boil them for 10 minutes in a little water. Drain the orange strips and set them aside, with the orange segments, for garnishing the duck.

Truss the ducks and place them on their sides in a greased roasting tin. Cook in a preheated

Duck with Orange.

oven at 200°C/400°F/gas 6 for 40 minutes, then turn each of the ducks on to the other side and cook for a further 30 minutes. Finally place the ducks on their backs and cook for a further 30 minutes. Baste the ducks frequently during cooking.

Boil the sugar and vinegar until reduced to a light caramel. Add the stock, reserved orange juice and lemon juice; boil for 5 minutes. Mix the arrowroot to a smooth paste with the water. Add a little of the hot sauce to the arrowroot, then pour the

mixture into the sauce and bring to the boil, stirring continuously. Remove the pan from the heat as soon as the sauce reaches boiling point. Stir in the orange liqueur and taste for seasoning.

Transfer the ducks to a heated dish, pour over the sauce and garnish with the orange segments and strips of rind.

Floating Island

SERVES: 4
PREPARATION: 1 hour
OVEN: 180°C/350°F/gas 4
COOKING: 40 minutes

75 g/3 oz coloured sugar almonds
4 egg whites
225 g/8 oz caster sugar
Custard
4 egg yolks
25 g/1 oz caster sugar
300 ml/½ pt milk
2.5 ml/½ teaspoon natural
*   vanilla essence*

Line the base of a 15 cm/6 in round, deep cake tin with non-stick baking parchment. With a rolling pin, coarsely crush the sugared almonds in a clean cloth. Whisk the egg whites until stiff, then gradually whisk in half the sugar; fold the remaining sugar gently into the stiff egg whites with a metal spoon. Spread a layer of this meringue mixture over the base of the prepared cake tin; follow with a layer of crushed almonds. Repeat until all the meringue and almonds are used up, finishing with a layer of the meringue.

Set the filled tin in a shallow baking or roasting tin with

boiling water to a depth of 2.5 cm/1 in. Bake in a preheated oven at 180°C/350°F/gas 4 for 30 minutes. Remove the tin from the oven and leave to cool. As the meringue cools it will shrink and should be gently eased away from the sides with the fingers.

To make the custard, beat the egg yolks with the sugar. Heat the milk in a saucepan until almost boiling, then stir it into the egg mixture until thoroughly mixed and strain into a bowl. Set this bowl over a saucepan half-filled with simmering water, and stir the custard gently until cooked and thickened slightly – about 10 minutes. Remove from the heat, add the vanilla essence and cover the surface of the custard with dampened grease-proof paper.

Just before serving the sweet, loosen the meringue with the tip of a knife and lift it on to a round deep serving plate. Pour the custard around the meringue, lifting this with a spatula or knife so that the custard runs beneath and around the meringue island.

FEBRUARY

Beetroot with Orange, Duck with Bigarade Sauce,
Three-fruit Marmalade.

February

February is thought of as the dullest month, when everyone has had enough of winter and even the crisp, clear weather subsides into cold, damp days. This is definitely the time of year to raid the store cupboard for the preserves of last year – fruity chutneys to match the tang of mature Cheddar cheese, crisp pickled cabbage to sharpen cold meats, or bright fruit jams to top freshly toasted muffins.

The culinary event of February is the availability of bitter oranges, heralding the annual marmalade-making session. Fruit that cannot be processed promptly can always be frozen whole, or grated rind and squeezed juice can be frozen for use in savoury and sweet dishes.

Depending on the calendar, Shrove Tuesday may fall at the end of February. This is the eve of Ash Wednesday, the first of the forty days of Lent leading up to Easter, and traditionally a day for using up rich ingredients in preparation for the Lenten fast by making pancakes. Stacks of piping hot pancakes served with fresh lemon juice, a sprinkling of caster sugar and a few currants are a terrific treat, and one for which it is well worth giving up a proper evening meal if you are not at home in time to make them for tea.

If Shrove Tuesday falls into the later month of March, the other excuse for indulging in a February cooking extravaganza is Saint Valentine's Day, when romantic cooks can take the opportunity of preparing a special meal. Those with limited kitchen skills can still impress their partner with a simple seafood offering, such as smoked salmon or a tiny pot of caviar with rye bread and soured cream served with chilled champagne. Oysters, the other classic food of love, may be lightly grilled with a little butter and seasoning; or mussels, once known as the poor-man's oysters, can be cooked plainly, *à la marinière*, as a treat for someone special who savours their flavour but loathes the somewhat time-consuming task of scrubbing and cleaning them. Shrimps are also a good buy, especially the tasty brown variety usually sold by smaller fishmongers and on market stalls. Small whole plaice, lemon sole and skate, also good value this month, tend to be more widely available than shrimps.

For everyday meals, there is still a plentiful supply of winter vegetables, with leeks and red cabbage as well as artichokes and the larger roots, such as swede. The first garden rhubarb is showing through, while forced rhubarb is at its best and ideal for poaching or combining with other fruits in compôtes. This is a better use for the rhubarb than using it as filling for hearty pies and crumbles.

Menu suggestions *All the main recipes are found in this chapter. Any additional recipes from the back of the book or other chapters are accompanied by a page reference.*

A Traditional Treat
~

Steak and Kidney Pudding
with Rich Gravy
Boiled Potatoes
Brussels Sprouts

~

Compôte of Rhubarb
and Bananas
Custard Sauce (page 354)

Old-fashioned favourites, such as suet puddings, take time to prepare, so they have become something of a treat for modern cooks, their families and their guests. This hearty menu will go down well instead of the usual Sunday roast; it does not include a starter, as the main course is extremely satisfying, but if you are entertaining, offer a dish of vegetable crudités with drinks before the meal.

Celebration Meal
~

Celeriac Salad with
Parma Ham

~

Duck with Bigarade Sauce
Duchesse Potatoes (page 347)
Brussels Sprouts
Glazed Carrots (page 110)

~

Chocolate Cake Mousse
(page 155)
or
Fresh Fruit

Wild duck is a good choice for a Sunday luncheon gathering or a very special dinner party. This menu takes advantage of the availability of bitter oranges to make a classic Bigarade Sauce.

Warm Mushroom Salad (page 90) and Cauliflower and Leek Lasagne (page 92).

Dinner Party
~

Moules Marinière
or
Leeks Vinaigrette

~

Pork Tenderloin with
Mushrooms
Mixed Grain Pilaf
Aubergine and Tomato
Ragoût (page 111)

~

Caramelised Oranges
Grand Marnier
Jumbles (page 391)

If you know all the guests invited to the dinner party well and are sure they will all appreciate mussels, then there is no need to offer an alternative first course; however, if there is a chance that someone may not like seafood on the shell, a simple dish of marinated leeks makes an excellent alternative first course.

SOUPS

Vegetable Soup with Ricotta Dumplings

The dumplings are spiced with a little coriander and spiked with lemon rind, so they contribute a delicious flavour to the soup as well as adding bulk.

SERVES: 4
PREPARATION: 25 minutes
COOKING: 40–45 minutes

450 g/1 lb potatoes
450 g/1 lb swede
1 large carrot
1 large leek
1 celery stick
1 onion
1 clove garlic (optional)
15 ml/1 tablespoon olive oil
1 bay leaf
4 sprigs parsley
100 g/4 oz Brussels sprouts
1.12 litres/2 pt stock (chicken or vegetable)
salt and black pepper
Ricotta Dumplings
175 g/6 oz fresh white breadcrumbs
40 g/1½ oz freshly grated Parmesan cheese
grated rind of 1 lemon
10 ml/2 teaspoons ground coriander
225 g/8 oz ricotta cheese
1 egg

Peel and dice the potatoes, swede and carrot. Trim and wash the leek, then cut it into thin slices. Thinly slice the celery, finely chop the onion and crush the garlic, if used.

Heat the olive oil in a large saucepan. Add the prepared ingredients, bay leaf and parsley, then stir well and cover the pan. Cook the vegetables over low to medium heat, shaking the pan occasionally, for 10 minutes. Meanwhile, trim and thinly slice the sprouts, then set them aside.

Add the stock to the vegetables with seasoning to taste. Bring to the boil, reduce the heat so that the soup simmers and give it a good stir. Cover the pan and cook the soup gently for 10 minutes. Add the sliced sprouts and continue to simmer gently for a further 10 minutes.

Prepare and cook the ricotta dumplings while the soup is simmering. Heat a large saucepan of salted water. Mix the breadcrumbs, Parmesan, lemon rind and coriander with a little seasoning, remembering that the Parmesan can be quite salty. Drain any surface liquid from the ricotta cheese before adding it to the mixture, then pound all the ingredients together until well combined. The mixture will come together but it will be very dry at this stage; taste a little to check the seasoning and add more salt if necessary. Mix in the egg until all the ingredients are thoroughly and evenly combined. Shape the mixture into 28 small dumplings.

Bring the saucepan of water to the boil, then reduce the heat so that is is just bubbling. Cook the dumplings in two or three batches, depending on the size of the pan. Add them to the water, then increase the heat slightly to bring it back to simmering point. Do not boil the water rapidly as vigorous bubbling will break up the dumplings. The dumplings cook in 3–5 minutes, rising to the surface of the water after about 2 minutes. Drain and transfer them to a warmed dish, cover and keep hot until all the dumplings are cooked.

Taste the soup for seasoning before ladling it into large bowls, discarding the herbs. Divide the dumplings between the bowls and serve at once.

Cock-a-Leekie Soup

Legend has it that this traditional Scottish soup originated in the days when cockfighting was a favourite sport. The loser was thrown into the stock pot together with leeks; prunes were a later addition for extra flavour. A boiling fowl does give the soup a superior flavour, if available, but the cooking time should be increased by 1 hour.

SERVES: 6
PREPARATION: 10–15 minutes
SOAKING: 6 hours (optional)
COOKING: 2 hours

6 prunes
1.4 kg/3 lb chicken (with giblets)
1 bouquet garni*
salt and black pepper
6 leeks
chopped fresh parsley to garnish

Soak the prunes for 6 hours in cold water or use the type that do not need soaking. Wipe the trussed chicken with absorbent kitchen paper, rinse the giblets and place both in a deep saucepan. Add the bouquet garni. Pour over enough cold water to cover the chicken (if necessary, split the bird in half so that it all remains submerged). Season the cooking water generously with salt and add a little freshly ground black pepper. Bring to the boil. Remove any scum from the surface, cover the pan with a tight-fitting lid and simmer for about 1½ hours, or until the chicken is tender.

Meanwhile, trim the coarse leaves off the leeks to within 5 cm/2 in of the top of the white

Cock-a-Leekie Soup.

stems and cut off the roots. Slit the leeks part way through lengthways, wash them well under running cold water, then cut them into 2.5 cm/1 in pieces. Skim the soup again, add the leeks and the prunes, which may be stoned or left whole. Simmer for another 30 minutes.

Lift the chicken and giblets from the soup; remove skin and bones from the chicken flesh. Reserve the best breast pieces for another recipe, and cut the remaining meat into small pieces. Add these to the soup and taste for seasoning.

Just before serving the hot soup, sprinkle finely chopped parsley over it.

STARTERS, SAVOURIES & LIGHT DISHES

Oeufs en Cocotte

In this classic French recipe, each egg is baked with a little cream in a small ovenproof dish.

SERVES: 4
PREPARATION: 5 minutes
OVEN: 180°C/350°F/gas 4
COOKING: 12 minutes

25 g/1 oz butter
8 eggs
salt and black pepper
120 ml/4 fl oz double cream

Warm eight ramekin dishes and butter them thoroughly. Crack an egg into each dish, season well with salt and freshly ground pepper and spoon a tablespoon of cream over each egg.

Place the ramekins in a large roasting tin, and fill with hot water to within 1 cm/½ in of the rims of the dishes. Cover the tin closely with kitchen foil and bake in a preheated oven at 180°C/350°F/gas 4, for about 12 minutes.

When cooked, the egg whites should be just set, and the yolks still runny. Serve at once.
■ Serve Melba Toast (page 313) or crisp triangles of toast with the eggs for a first course; thick slices of hot buttered toast are a more substantial accompaniment to the eggs for lunch or supper.

Eggs with Tuna Mayonnaise

SERVES: 4
PREPARATION: 20 minutes
COOKING: 8–10 minutes

4 eggs
99 g/3½ oz can tuna
juice of ½ lemon
6 anchovy fillets
150 ml/¼ pt mayonnaise
black pepper
4 crisp lettuce leaves
finely chopped fresh parsley
to garnish

Put the eggs in a saucepan, cover with cold water, bring to the boil, then simmer for 8–10 minutes to hard boil. Drain the eggs and cover them with cold water immediately to prevent further cooking. Shell the eggs.

Drain the oil from the tuna and mash the fish with a fork. Mix in the lemon juice, then chop and add two of the anchovy fillets. Rub the mixture through a coarse sieve into a basin and beat until it is a smooth purée. Alternatively, purée the tuna with the lemon juice and anchovy fillets in a food processor or liquidiser, adding about half the mayonnaise to give a smooth paste. Stir in the rest of the mayonnaise. Season to taste with black pepper.

Cut the eggs in half lengthways. Arrange the halves in pairs, rounded sides upwards, on the lettuce leaves, and coat them with the tuna fish mayonnaise. Cut the remaining anchovy fillets in half lengthways and arrange them over the egg halves; sprinkle with parsley.

Corn and Ham Fritters

MAKES: 12
PREPARATION: 25–30 minutes
COOKING: 25–30 minutes

150 g/5 oz plain flour
15 ml/1 tablespoon oil
150 ml/¼ pt tepid water
2 eggs
salt and black pepper
100 g/4 oz cooked ham
200 g/7 oz can sweetcorn
oil for shallow frying

Place the flour in a bowl. Make a well in the centre of the flour and add the oil, water, eggs and seasoning. Beat the eggs and liquid, gradually incorporating the surrounding flour to make a smooth batter.

Cut the ham into small dice, drain the sweetcorn, and add both to the batter, mixing well.

Heat a little oil in a large frying pan. Add spoonfuls of the mixture, keeping them well apart, and cook until set and golden underneath, about 3–4 minutes. Then turn and cook the second side for 2–3 minutes until golden. Continue cooking the batter, keeping each batch hot while cooking the next.

FISH, SHELLFISH & SEAFOOD

Hot Fish Curry

SERVES: 4
PREPARATION: 15 minutes
COOKING: about 30 minutes

2 onions
2.5 cm/1 in piece fresh root ginger
1 clove garlic
25 g/1 oz butter
15 ml/1 tablespoon good-quality curry powder
2.5 ml/½ teaspoon chilli powder
1 bay leaf
600 ml/1 pt chicken stock
30 ml/2 tablespoons tomato paste
juice of 1 lemon
1 piece star anise (optional)
675 g/1½ lb white fish fillet (cod or haddock) or 350 g/12 oz peeled cooked prawns
salt and black pepper

Peel and chop the onions, grate the ginger and peel and crush the garlic clove.

Melt the butter in a heavy-based pan and fry the curry and chilli powders over low heat for 1 minute. Add the onions, ginger, garlic and bay leaf, and cook, stirring often, for a further 15 minutes. Gradually stir in the stock and add the tomato paste and lemon juice. Add the star anise (if used) and simmer this sauce, covered, for about 1 hour.

If using white fish, skin the fillets and remove stray bones, then cut the flesh into chunks.

Remove the anise, stir in the fish or prawns and cook the fish for about 10 minutes. Cook the prawns for 5 minutes or until they are heated through – do not overcook. Season to taste.
■ Serve with Basmati rice and a bowl of cucumber with yogurt.

Raie au Beurre Noir

Skate should not be used when absolutely fresh as the flavour is more pronounced when the fish is slightly high. However, avoid stale skate which has a strong ammonia-like aroma.

SERVES: 4
PREPARATION: 10 minutes
COOKING: 30 minutes

900 g/2 lb wing of skate
300 ml/½ pt water
½ lemon
1 small onion
1 small bay leaf
2–3 peppercorns
3–4 sprigs parsley
2.5 ml/½ teaspoon salt
Beurre Noir
75 g/3 oz butter
15 ml/1 tablespoon white wine vinegar
15 ml/1 tablespoon finely chopped parsley

Rinse the skate, wipe it dry and cut into four portions. Place in a saucepan with the water. Slice the lemon; peel and slice the onion and add these to the pan, together with the bay leaf, peppercorns, sprigs of parsley and salt. Bring slowly to simmering point, reduce the heat so that the liquid does not boil and cook gently for 10–15 minutes, or until the skate is tender.

Make the sauce a few minutes before the skate is ready so that it can be used immediately after the fish has been drained. Heat the butter in a frying pan over low heat until nut brown in colour; do not allow it to scorch. Drain the fish with a perforated spoon and arrange on a hot serving dish. Remove the butter from the heat; stir in the vinegar and chopped parsley and pour the sauce over the skate.

■ Serve with boiled potatoes and green beans or peas.

Raie au Beurre Noir.

Herrings with Mustard Sauce

SERVES: 4
PREPARATION: 25 minutes
OVEN: 200°C/400°F/gas 6
COOKING: about 45 minutes

4 large herrings
100 g/4 oz fresh white breadcrumbs
60 ml/4 tablespoons finely
    chopped parsley
grated rind and juice of 1 lemon
salt and black pepper
25 g/1 oz butter
oil
Mustard Sauce
40 g/1½ oz butter
25 g/1 oz plain flour
450 ml/¾ pt milk
salt and black pepper
15 ml/1 tablespoon made
    English mustard
Garnish
lemon wedges
parsley sprigs

Remove the heads from the herrings, clean, gut and bone them (pages 313 and 314). Wash the herrings and pat them dry with absorbent kitchen paper.

Put the breadcrumbs, parsley, lemon rind and juice in a basin; season lightly with salt and freshly ground black pepper. Melt the butter and stir into the breadcrumbs to bind the mixture, which should now be moist, but crumbly. Stuff the herrings with the breadcrumb mixture and, if necessary, secure them with wooden cocktail sticks. Slash the skins crossways two or three times on each side; brush the herrings with oil and wrap each one in foil. Put the herrings in a well-buttered deep baking dish and bake in a preheated oven at 200°C/400°F/gas 6 for 35–40 minutes.

For the sauce, melt the butter in a pan; stir in the flour and cook for 1 minute. Gradually stir in the milk, beating well until the sauce is quite smooth. Bring to the boil and simmer for 2–3 minutes; season with salt and pepper. Stir in the mustard.

Transfer the baked herrings to a hot serving dish and garnish with wedges of lemon and sprigs of parsley. Serve the mustard sauce separately.

■ Boiled potatoes or Galette Lyonnaise (page 273) are good accompaniments.

Moules Marinière

The choice of flavouring ingredients may be varied in this classic dish of steamed mussels – a chopped garlic clove and a sprig of thyme may be added.

SERVES: 4
PREPARATION: 30 minutes
COOKING: 10 minutes

2.3 litres/4 pt mussels
50 g/2 oz butter
20 ml/4 teaspoons plain flour
1 small onion
1 bay leaf
2 sprigs parsley
250 ml/8 fl oz dry white wine
salt and black pepper
15 ml/1 teaspoon chopped parsley

Wash the mussels in cold water, scrub the shells thoroughly, scraping off any barnacles or tough dirt, and rinse several times to remove all grit. Pull away the beards, the black or brown hairy strands protruding from the shell. Discard any mussels with broken shells, and any which remain open when tapped sharply. Cream half the butter with the flour to make a smooth paste.

Melt the remaining butter in a large saucepan. Peel and finely chop the onion and cook it in the butter for 5 minutes, stirring occasionally. Add the bay leaf and parsley sprigs, then pour in the wine. Stir in salt and freshly ground black pepper to taste and heat until simmering. Place all the mussels in the pan at once, cover the pan and turn the heat to the highest setting. Cook the mussels for 5 minutes, shaking the pan occasionally, until all the mussels have opened. Take the pan from the heat and lift out the mussels, discarding any that have not opened. Remove the empty half shells from each mussel and place the other half with the mussel attached in individual soup plates. Cover and keep hot.

Strain the cooking liquor through a sieve lined with muslin or a coffee filter paper, then pour it back into the rinsed saucepan. Heat the liquid until simmering and then whisk in small lumps of the butter and flour paste. Whisk until each lump has melted before adding the next and keep the liquid just about simmering. Increase the heat slightly to boil and thicken the sauce, cook it for 2 minutes and add the chopped parsley. Pour the sauce over the mussels and serve at once.

■ Offer crisp, warmed French bread with the moules marinière, to mop up the delicious sauce. Remember to set out plates or dishes for the empty shells.
Note Shelled, cooked mussels may be frozen in their cooking liquor or a sauce. They keep well for 1–2 months and are very useful for adding to risotto, paella or pasta dishes.

POULTRY & GAME

Crisp Garlic Chicken

SERVES: 4
PREPARATION: 30 minutes
OVEN: 190°C/375°F/gas 5
COOKING: 30–40 minutes

2 cloves garlic
50 g/2 oz fresh white breadcrumbs
30 ml/2 tablespoons chopped
    parsley
grated rind of ½ lemon
salt and black pepper
4 chicken quarters or 8 drumsticks
    or thighs
30 ml/2 tablespoons clear honey

Crush the garlic and mix it with the breadcrumbs, parsley, grated lemon rind, salt and pepper.

Skin the pieces of chicken. Brush them with the honey and then dip into the crumb mixture, pressing the crumbs on firmly. Place on a baking sheet and cook in a preheated oven at 190°C/375°F/gas 5 for 30–40 minutes, or until the coating is crisp and the chicken is cooked.

Crisp Garlic Chicken can be served Maryland-style, with Corn and Ham Fritters (page 82), Bacon Rolls (page 331) and bananas fried in a little butter.

Coq au Vin

A classic stew of chicken in wine, traditionally this would have been made using an old boiling fowl and the cooking time would have been double that for a roasting bird.

SERVES: 4
MARINATING: 12–24 hours
PREPARATION: 40 minutes
OVEN: 150°C/300°F/gas 2
COOKING: 1¾–2¼ hours

1 chicken (about 1.6 kg/3½ lb)
600 ml/1 pt red wine, preferably
    Burgundy
bouquet garni*
salt and black pepper
100 g/4 oz pickled belly pork or
    100 g/4 oz streaky bacon
100 g/4 oz button onions
1 large clove garlic
100 g/4 oz mushrooms
15 ml/1 tablespoon olive oil
30 ml/2 tablespoons brandy
about 300 ml/½ pt stock
Beurre Manié made with 25 g/1 oz
    each of butter and plain flour
    (page 355)

Garnish
100 g/4 oz Glazed Onions
    (page 252)
50 g/2 oz fried or grilled button
    mushrooms
15 ml/1 tablespoon chopped
    parsley

Clean and truss the bird. Place it in a deep casserole or bowl and pour the wine over it. Cover and marinate* in the refrigerator for up to 24 hours. Dice the pickled pork or bacon, removing the rind first. Peel the onions and garlic. Trim and slice the mushrooms.

Heat the oil in a flameproof casserole or pan and fry the pork or bacon until the fat runs. Remove the meat from the casserole and put it to one side.

Drain the chicken, reserving the wine. Brown the bird all over in the hot fat, then spoon off any surplus fat. Warm the brandy in a metal ladle or small pan, set it alight and pour it flaming over the bird. As soon as the flames subside, pour in the wine and add the pork, onions, mushrooms and crushed garlic. Pour over enough stock to make the liquid come halfway up the bird. Bring just to boiling point, then reduce the heat so that the liquid barely simmers. Cover and cook over low heat on top of the stove, or in a preheated oven at 150°C/300°F/gas 2, for 1½–2 hours or until the bird is cooked through, turning it occasionally.

Remove the bird and divide it into joints; keep these warm on a serving dish. Lift out the onions, bacon and mushrooms with a perforated spoon and arrange them over the chicken. Reduce the cooking liquid by brisk boiling, then lower the heat and gradually whisk in pieces of beurre manié. Bring to the boil and simmer for 3 minutes until thickened. Add salt and freshly ground pepper to taste and pour the sauce over the chicken.

Serve the chicken garnished with the glazed onions, mushrooms and chopped parsley.

Note If available, use the chicken giblets with the bouquet garni, a little salt and freshly ground black pepper to make the stock for this stew.

Duck with Bigarade Sauce

The rich sauce is traditionally made with bitter oranges (such as Seville oranges), but when they are not in season sharpen sweet oranges with lemon juice.

SERVES: 4
PREPARATION: 25 minutes
OVEN: 200°C/400°F/gas 6
COOKING: about 1¾ hours

1 large or 2 small wild duck or 1
    farmed duck (with giblets)
1 or 2 oranges
poultry dripping or cooking fat
bouquet garni*
salt and black pepper
Bigarade Sauce
1 large onion
1 stick celery
50 g/2 oz mushrooms
2 rashers streaky bacon
100 g/4 oz carrots
2 small or 1 large orange
1 small or ½ large lemon if using
    sweet oranges
45 ml/3 tablespoons plain flour
120 ml/4 fl oz red wine
120 ml/4 fl oz tomato juice
150 ml/¼ pt giblet stock
15–30 ml/1–2 tablespoons
    redcurrant jelly
60 ml/2 fl oz port
Garnish
1 orange, sliced
fresh herb sprigs

Wipe the duck inside and out with absorbent kitchen paper. Peel and quarter the orange and put it inside the duck. Spread the duck breast with dripping or fat and place the bird in a greased roasting tin. Cover the tin with foil and roast in a preheated oven at 200°C/400°F/gas 6 for 45 minutes or longer, according to size. The duck is cooked if the juices run clear when a skewer is inserted in the thigh. Uncover after 30 minutes' roasting.

While the duck is cooking, roughly chop the duck liver and set it aside. Put the neck and giblets in a pan with enough water to cover them, the bouquet garni and seasoning. Bring the stock to the boil, reduce the heat, cover the pan and simmer for 20 minutes. Strain the stock.

For the sauce, peel and finely chop the onion, scrub and chop the celery stick and trim the mushrooms before slicing them. Remove the rind and chop the bacon finely.

Scrape or peel the carrots and chop them finely. Grate the rind from the orange(s) and lemon (if using), squeeze the juices and set both aside. Pour a thin layer of dripping from the duck into a heavy-based saucepan and fry the onion, celery, mushrooms and bacon until soft. Add the carrots to the pan and continue cooking until the onion begins to colour.

Stir in the flour and cook, stirring continuously, until the mixture is lightly browned. Gradually stir in the wine, tomato juice, duck livers and 150 ml/¼ pt giblet stock. Bring the sauce slowly to the boil, stirring all the time. Add the orange and lemon rind, and juices. Cover, reduce heat and simmer gently for 30 minutes.

When the duck is cooked, lift it carefully from the roasting tin, tail downwards so that the juices run back into the pan. Put the duck on a serving dish and keep hot. Carefully pour excess fat from the pan, and add the remaining giblet stock. Boil rapidly, scraping in all the brown residue from the bottom and sides of the pan, until the liquid is well-flavoured and reduced to a shallow layer in the base of the pan. Then stir it into the bigarade sauce. Stir in the red-currant jelly and port, and continue cooking over low heat until the jelly has dissolved. Taste and adjust the seasoning.

Garnish the duck with orange slices and fresh herb sprigs.

Wild Duck Salmi

SERVES: 4–6
PREPARATION: 1 hour
OVEN: 190°C/375°F/gas 5
       180°C/350°F/gas 4
COOKING: about 2 hours

2 wild duck (with giblets)
coarse salt
3 carrots
2 large onions
4 rashers streaky bacon
1 bay leaf
Sauce
50 g/2 oz butter
40 g/1½ oz plain flour
15 ml/ 1 tablespoon mushroom
    ketchup (optional)
45–60 ml/3–4 tablespoons medium
    dry sherry or port
squeeze lemon juice
salt and black pepper
6–8 stoned green olives

Wipe the ducks inside and out with absorbent kitchen paper and rub the skin with coarse salt. Peel and slice a carrot and onion and put them in a saucepan with the duck giblets. Pour over about 900 ml/1½ pt cold water, cover, bring to the boil and simmer for 30 minutes to make the stock.

Meanwhile, cut the rind off the bacon and cover the breasts of the ducks with the rashers. Peel and slice the remaining carrots and onion and use them to cover the base of a lightly greased roasting pan. Add the bay leaf, place the birds on the bed of vegetables and roast for 30 minutes only, in a preheated oven at 190°C/375°F/gas 5. Take out the birds, discarding the bacon; carve each duck into four portions and place in a casserole.

Strain the fat from the roasting pan, but keep back the vegetables. Pour 600 ml/1 pt of strained duck stock into the pan and stir over moderate heat until boiling. Simmer gently until it has reduced by about one third. Meanwhile, melt the butter in a saucepan over low heat. Stir in the flour and cook gently for 5–10 minutes, stirring the mixture occasionally until it is nutty brown. Gradually stir in the duck stock and continue to stir until boiling, then add the mushroom ketchup (if used), sherry or port, a squeeze of lemon and salt and pepper to taste. Strain the sauce over the ducks, cover and cook in a preheated oven at 180°C/350°F/gas 4 for about 50 minutes or until the ducks are tender. Add the olives and heat for a few moments.

■ Serve with creamed potatoes and broccoli.

Civet of Hare

This is a classic French farmhouse recipe, reminiscent of the traditional English jugged hare. The ingredients can be either a whole jointed hare or the legs and rib joints. Start preparation a day in advance.

SERVES: 6
MARINATING: 24 hours
PREPARATION: 45 minutes
COOKING: 3–3½ hours

1.15–1.4 kg/2½–3 lb hare pieces
2–3 carrots
2 onions
1 clove garlic
1 shallot
3 bay leaves
3 sprigs thyme
6 sprigs parsley
salt and black pepper
45 ml/3 tablespoons olive oil
1 bottle red wine
25 g/1 oz plain flour
25 g/1 oz butter
2 liqueur glasses brandy
200 ml/7 fl oz chicken stock
100 g/4 oz streaky bacon
450 g/1 lb small pickling onions
100 g/4 oz small mushrooms
chopped fresh parsley to garnish

Wipe the hare pieces with absorbent kitchen paper and put them in a large basin. Peel and finely slice the carrots and the onions. Skin and finely chop the garlic and the shallot. Add these vegetables, together with the bay leaves, thyme, parsley and freshly ground black pepper to the pieces of hare. Pour over the olive oil and wine and marinate* for 24 hours.

Remove the meat from the marinade and pat it dry on absorbent kitchen paper. Coat the meat with the flour, adding a generous sprinkling of salt. Melt the butter in a large saucepan and fry the meat gently for about 15 minutes, until browned on all sides. Pour the brandy over the meat and, when hot, set it alight. As soon as the flames have died down, sprinkle in any flour remaining from coating the meat and stir it into the juices around the hare joints.

Gradually add the marinade, stirring the wine into the flour paste in the pan as best you can, then pour in sufficient stock to just cover the meat. Bring to the boil, cover and simmer for 2½–3 hours or until the hare is tender.

Cut the bacon piece into strips, 2.5 cm/1 in long. Peel the pickling onions, leaving them whole. Put the bacon strips in a dry pan and fry gently until the fat runs. Add the onions and fry until lightly brown. Wipe and trim the mushrooms, cut each in half and add to the pan. Fry gently for a few minutes before seasoning, then remove from the pan and set aside.

Lift the hare pieces from the pan and keep them hot. Strain off the liquid and return it to the saucepan. Add more salt and pepper if necessary; if the sauce appears too thin, thicken with a little beurre manié. Put the hare into the pan, with the bacon, mushrooms and pickling onions. Reheat gently.

Arrange the meat on a hot serving dish, pour over the sauce and sprinkle with parsley.

MEAT

Daube de Boeuf

SERVES: 6
PREPARATION: 45 minutes
OVEN: 150°C/300°F/gas 2
COOKING: 3¼ hours

900 g/2 lb lean stewing steak
100 g/4 oz streaky bacon
½ bottle red wine
450 g/1 lb carrots
450 g/1 lb onions
45 g/1½ oz butter or 45 ml/
    3 tablespoons oil
1–2 cloves garlic
bouquet garni*
450 ml/¾ pt beef stock
2 tablespoons tomato paste
15 ml/1 tablespoon chopped
    fresh parsley
salt and black pepper

Trim the fat from the beef and cut the meat into 2.5 cm/1 in pieces. Cut off the rind and dice the bacon. Put the meat and bacon in a bowl, add the wine and marinate* for 3–4 hours.

Lift the meat out of the marinade and reserve the liquid. Peel or scrape the carrots and cut them into 5 mm/¼ in slices; peel and finely slice the onions. Using half the butter or oil, fry the beef and the bacon in a heavy-based frying pan until all the pieces of meat are evenly brown.

Lift out the beef and bacon, then fry the prepared carrots and onions in the remainder of the butter or oil. Peel and chop the garlic and add this to the vegetables during frying.

Cover the base of a large casserole with half the fried vegetables, then add the beef and bacon and top with the remaining vegetables. Pour the marinade into the casserole and add the bouquet garni.

Rinse out the frying pan with the stock. Stir to loosen all sediment, and bring the stock to the boil. Stir in the tomato paste and pour this liquid over the casserole. Add the parsley, cover and cook for 3 hours in a preheated oven at 150°C/300°F/gas 2. Check the seasoning and remove the bouquet garni.

Steak and Kidney Pudding

The traditional English beefsteak and kidney pudding is always served from the basin in which it was steamed. Have ready a white folded napkin or cloth to tie around the hot pudding basin.

SERVES: 4
PREPARATION: 30 minutes
COOKING: 3½–4 hours

450 g/1 lb lean stewing steak
100 g/4 oz ox kidney
1 onion
30 ml/2 tablespoons plain flour
salt and black pepper
225 g/8 oz Suet Crust Pastry
    (page 368)
25 g/1 oz butter

Trim away any fat or gristle from the beef, then cut it into 1 cm/½ in pieces. Remove the core from the kidney and cut it into 1 cm/½ in pieces. Peel and finely chop the onion. Coat the steak and kidney with the flour and mix with the onion.

Prepare the suet crust pastry and set aside a quarter for the pudding top. Roll out the remainder to a circle, 1 cm/½ in thick. Grease a 900 ml/1½ pt pudding basin well, and fit the pastry to the bottom and sides, allowing it to overhang the edge of the basin by about 1 cm/½ in. Spoon the meat and onion mixture, with a generous seasoning of salt and freshly ground pepper, into the basin; pour over enough cold water to come three-quarters up the sides of the basin.

Roll out the remaining pastry to a circle to fit the top of the basin. Damp the edges of the suet crust lining, cover with the pastry lid and pinch the edges of the lining and the lid tightly together to seal. Cover the top of the basin with a double thickness of buttered greaseproof paper, folding in a wide pleat across the centre, to allow the pudding to rise during cooking; secure the paper tightly with string.

Put the basin in a saucepan and pour boiling water around it until it reaches one-third up the sides. Steam briskly for 3½–4 hours, topping up with boiling water when necessary.
■ The meat pudding is usually accompanied by boiled potatoes and Brussels sprouts.

Savoury Mince

Use this tasty mixture as a filling for pancakes, the basis of a cottage pie or as a topping for baked jacket potatoes.

SERVES: 3–4
PREPARATION: 15 minutes
COOKING: about 50 minutes

1 onion
1 clove garlic (optional)
100 g/4 oz mushrooms
100 g/4 oz carrots
15 ml/1 tablespoon oil
1 bay leaf
450 g/1 lb lean minced beef
5 ml/1 teaspoon dried mixed herbs
15 ml/1 tablespoon plain flour
150 ml/¼ pt beef stock
10 ml/2 teaspoons
    Worcestershire sauce
10 ml/2 teaspoons tomato paste
salt and black pepper

Peel and finely chop the onion, crush the garlic and chop the mushrooms. Peel and dice the carrots. Heat the oil, add the onion, garlic, if liked, and bay leaf, and cook until lightly browned. Add the minced beef and cook, stirring, until the meat has changed colour. Stir in the mushrooms, carrots, herbs and flour. Gradually stir in the stock, Worcestershire sauce and tomato paste. Cover and cook gently, stirring every now and then, for 40 minutes. Taste and adjust seasoning if necessary. Remove the bay leaf before serving.

Shepherds Pie

As roast beef traditionally graces the Sunday lunch table, so this leftover dish follows for Monday night's supper. Remember you will need to make a generous quantity of gravy with the roast beef so that there is plenty left for the pie filling.

SERVES: 4
PREPARATION: 20 minutes
OVEN: 220°C/425°F/gas 7
COOKING: about 1 hour

2 onions
75 g/3 oz butter
350 g/12 oz cooked beef or
    lamb, minced
300 ml/½ pt beef gravy
15 ml/1 tablespoon tomato ketchup
1.25 ml/¼ teaspoon
    Worcestershire sauce
salt and black pepper
675 g/1½ lb potatoes
30–45 ml/2–3 tablespoons milk

Peel and finely chop the onions. Cook the onions in 25 g/1 oz of the butter until soft; add the meat and cook until lightly brown. Stir in the gravy, ketchup and Worcestershire sauce; season with salt and freshly ground black pepper. Put the meat in an ovenproof dish.

Peel the potatoes and cut them into chunks. Place in a saucepan, cover with water and add salt to taste. Bring to the boil, then cook for 10–15 minutes, or until tender. Drain and mash the potatoes, adding the remaining butter. Beat well until the butter has melted, then beat in the milk. Spoon the potatoes over the meat mixture to cover the top completely and press down gently with a fork to make a neat, ridged topping.

Bake in a preheated oven at 220°C/425°F/gas 7 for 30 minutes or until brown.

■ Serve the pie hot, on its own, or with a green vegetable.

Lancashire Hot Pot

In Northern England, the 'hot pot' was a tall earthenware pot. Mutton chops were stood upright round the inside and the centre was filled with vegetables. It was usual, too, in the days when they were cheap, to put a layer of oysters beneath the potato crust.

SERVES: 4–6
PREPARATION: 30 minutes
OVEN: 180°C/350°F/gas 4
          200°C/400°F/gas 6
COOKING: 2¼–2¾ hours

900 g/2 lb middle neck of lamb
flour
salt and black pepper
25 g/1 oz dripping or 30 ml/
    2 tablespoons oil
675 g/1½ lb potatoes
2 onions
6–8 carrots
2 sticks celery
1 leek
2.5 ml/¼ tablespoon dried
    mixed herbs
chopped fresh parsley to garnish

Bone the neck of lamb (follow the information on preparing noisettes as a guide, page 330) or ask the butcher to do this for you, saving the bones. Put the bones in a saucepan and cover with cold water. Bring the water to the boil, and after a few minutes remove the scum; cover with a lid and let the bones simmer while the vegetables and meat are being prepared.

Trim away any fat from the meat and cut the lamb into small pieces. Season a little flour with salt and pepper and use it to coat the meat. Fry in hot dripping or oil until browned and sealed on all sides. Peel the potatoes and cut into 5 mm/¼ in slices. Put aside half the slices for the top and place the remainder in the base of a deep buttered casserole.

Peel and coarsely chop the onions. Scrape or peel the carrots and slice them thinly. Scrub the celery sticks and chop them finely. Remove the outer coarse leaves and the root of the leek, wash it well and cut it across into thin slices. Mix all the vegetables together in a deep bowl, season with salt and pepper and sprinkle the herbs over them. Arrange layers of seasoned vegetables and meat in the casserole, beginning and ending with a layer of vegetables. Top with the remaining potato slices, arranging them neatly in overlapping circles. Strain the liquid from the bones and pour 450 ml/¾ pt into the casserole until it just reaches the upper potato layer. Cover with buttered greaseproof paper and a tight-fitting lid. Place in the centre of a preheated oven at 180°C/350°F/gas 4 and cook for 2–2½ hours.

About 30 minutes before serving, remove the lid and paper from the casserole. Brush the potatoes with a little melted dripping and sprinkle with coarse salt. Raise the oven heat to 200°C/400°F/gas 6 and return the uncovered casserole to the oven, so that the potatoes will crisp and brown slightly.

Sprinkle with finely chopped parsley just before serving.

■ The hot pot is a meal on its own, but is traditionally served with pickled red cabbage.

Pork Tenderloin with Mushrooms

The lean fillet or tenderloin of pork can be cooked whole, or cut into thick slices for a quick and delicious main course.

SERVES: 6
MARINATING: 30 minutes
PREPARATION: 30 minutes
COOKING: 20 minutes

675 g/1½ lb pork tenderloin
30 ml/2 tablespoons oil
15 ml/1 tablespoon lemon juice
black pepper
1 small clove garlic (optional)
Sauce
175 g/6 oz mushrooms
1 onion
50 g/2 oz butter
30 ml/2 tablespoons dry sherry
salt and black pepper
150 ml/¼ pt double cream

Trim away the thin skin, or sinew, and fat from the pork. Cut the meat crossways into 5 cm/ 2 in slices. Lay the slices between two sheets of damp greaseproof paper and beat them flat with a rolling pin. Arrange the slices in a shallow dish. Measure the oil and lemon juice into a basin and season with black pepper. Skin and crush the garlic, and mix it into the oil and lemon juice. Spoon this marinade* over the pork and leave for 30 minutes.

Meanwhile, trim and thinly slice the mushrooms. Peel the onion and chop it finely. Melt the butter in a frying pan and gently fry the onion for 5 minutes until it is soft, but not brown. Add the mushrooms and fry for a few minutes. Lift the vegetables from the pan and keep them hot. Drain the pork pieces from the marinade and fry gently in the hot butter for 3–4 minutes, turning once. Transfer the pork to a hot serving dish and keep it warm.

Measure the dry sherry into the frying pan and heat briskly, stirring continuously, until the liquid has been reduced to about 15 ml/1 tablespoon. Return the onion and mushrooms to the pan and season with salt and freshly ground black pepper. Stir in the cream. Heat gently, stirring until the sauce is heated through. Remove from the heat and pour the sauce over the pork.

■ Serve surrounded by boiled rice or pasta.

Pork Tenderloin with Mushrooms.

Kidneys Turbigo

SERVES: 4
PREPARATION: 25 minutes
COOKING: about 45 minutes

6 lamb kidneys
4 chipolata sausages
25 g/1 oz butter
8 button onions
15 ml/1 tablespoon plain flour
300 ml/½ pt chicken or beef stock
150 ml/¼ pt dry white wine
5 ml/1 teaspoon tomato paste
30 ml/2 tablespoons dry sherry
salt and black pepper
1 bay leaf
chopped fresh parsley
Croûtons to garnish (page 313)

Skin the kidneys, cut them in half and snip out the white core with a pair of scissors. Twist each sausage in half.

Kidneys Turbigo.

Melt the butter in a flame-proof casserole. Gently fry the sausages until brown all over, then remove from the pan and keep them hot.

Meanwhile, peel the onions, leaving them whole; add them to the fat in the casserole and cook, stirring frequently, until they are beginning to brown in parts. Remove the onions from the pan and set them aside with the sausages. Cook the kidneys in the fat until sealed, then remove them and set them aside with the sausages and onions.

Stir the flour into the fat remaining in the pan and cook gently for a few minutes. Gradually add the stock and wine, stirring well until the sauce is smooth. Bring to the boil, stir in the tomato paste and sherry; season to taste with salt and freshly ground black pepper.

Put the kidneys, sausages and onions back into the pan; add the bay leaf and heat to simmering point. Cover and simmer for 20–25 minutes.

Remove the bay leaf, check seasoning and sprinkle with parsley. Garnish with crisp croûtons.
■ Spiced Rice (see Sesame Chicken with Spiced Rice, page 188) or creamed potatoes and broccoli go well with this dish.

Liver in Tomato Sauce

SERVES: 3–4
PREPARATION: 25 minutes
COOKING: about 30 minutes

1 onion
45 ml/3 tablespoons oil
100 g/4 oz lean streaky bacon
450 g/1 lb lamb liver
10 ml/2 teaspoons chopped sage
25 g/1 oz plain flour
60 ml/2 fl oz red or white wine
150 ml/¼ pt lamb or beef stock
227 g/8 oz can chopped tomatoes
salt and black pepper
5 ml/1 teaspoon sugar
chopped parsley

Chop the onion. Heat the oil in a large frying pan, add the onion and cook gently until softened and lightly browned. Remove the rind from the bacon, chop it roughly and set aside. Lightly flour the liver.

When the onion has softened push it to one side of the pan, and add the liver in a single layer. Cook it fairly quickly to seal in the juices, turning once. Using a perforated spoon transfer the liver to a plate. Stir the bacon and sage into the pan. Cook for 2 minutes, stir in the flour and cook for 1 minute. Gradually add the wine, stock and tomatoes, with seasoning to taste and the sugar. Bring to the boil, stirring constantly, and cook for 2 minutes. Reduce the heat and return the liver to the pan, spooning the sauce over to cover. Cook gently for 5–8 minutes. The liver will toughen if cooked too rapidly or for too long. Sprinkle with parsley.

Chorizo Stir Fry

Chorizo is a spicy Spanish sausage flavoured with paprika or pimientos. It is quite red and is available in a variety of sizes either loose or prepacked.

SERVES: 4
PREPARATION: 20 minutes
COOKING: about 30 minutes

6 chorizo sausages (about 350 g/
    12 oz in weight)
1 cauliflower
1 onion
3 cloves garlic
1 leek
2 carrots
1 large bulb fennel
60 ml/4 tablespoons olive oil
45 ml/3 tablespoons plain flour
300 ml/½ pt dry cider
150 ml/¼ pt water
salt and black pepper

Fry or grill the sausages for 6–8 minutes or until cooked through.

Prepare the vegetables for stir frying. Trim the large stalks off the cauliflower and separate the florets, then cook them in boiling salted water for 2 minutes; drain well. Peel the onion and slice it thinly; peel and crush the garlic. Trim, slice and wash the leeks, peel and slice the carrots and trim and slice the bulb of fennel.

Heat the oil in a large frying pan or wok, add the onion and stir fry for 5 minutes. Stir in the garlic and leek, stir fry for 3 minutes. Add the carrots and fennel and stir fry for 5 minutes, then stir in the cauliflower.

Stir in the flour and cook for 1 minute, then gradually add the cider and water. Bring slowly to the boil, stirring all the time. Slice the chorizo sausages and add them to the stir fry mixture. Simmer gently for 3–5 minutes, depending on how crisp you like your vegetables. Make sure the slices of chorizo have heated right through.
■ Serve with brown rice, or Chinese egg noodles.

VEGETABLES & SALADS

Rich Mushroom Pancakes

SERVES: 4
PREPARATION: 45 minutes
COOKING: 30 minutes plus
time for preparing pancakes

8 Pancakes (page 339)
675 g/1½ lb chestnut mushrooms
50 g/2 oz black olives
1 onion
1 clove garlic
25 g/1 oz butter or 30 ml/
2 tablespoons olive oil
25 g/1 oz pine kernels
1 bay leaf
1 sprig thyme
4 tomatoes
salt and black pepper
60 ml/4 tablespoons chopped
parsley
600 ml/1 pt hot Béchamel Sauce
(page 353)
25 g/1 oz fresh white breadcrumbs
25 g/1 oz Cheddar cheese

Make the pancakes. To prevent them sticking together as you stack them up, lay a sheet of absorbent kitchen paper between each one.

Trim the stalk ends of the mushrooms, rinse them quickly under cold running water and drain well; then slice them thinly. Stone and thinly slice the black olives. Finely chop the onion and crush the garlic into a large saucepan. Add the butter or oil to the pan and heat gently. Fry the pine kernels with the garlic until lightly browned. Add the onion, bay leaf and thyme, and cook, stirring occasionally, for 5 minutes.

Add the mushrooms and turn the slices carefully to coat them with the butter or oil. Cook the mushrooms for about 20 minutes, until they have reduced in volume and their cooking juices have evaporated. Stir occasionally to prevent the mixture from sticking to the pan and regulate the heat so that it is high enough to evaporate the cooking liquid, but not fierce enough to brown the mixture.

Meanwhile, skin the four tomatoes (page 302) and cut each one in half. Scoop out the tomato seeds with the point of a knife and roughly chop the tomato shells.

Add the olives, tomatoes and a seasoning of salt and freshly ground black pepper to the mushroom mixture. Stir until the tomatoes are hot, but do not overcook the mixture at this stage. Stir in the parsley.

Fill the pancakes with the mushroom mixture, rolling each one up neatly, and place in a greased flameproof or gratin dish. Pour the hot Béchamel sauce over the pancakes to cover them evenly. Mix the breadcrumbs and cheese and sprinkle this over the top. Place under the grill, not too close to the heat source, and cook until the sauce is bubbling hot and the topping is crisp and golden. Serve immediately.

Stuffed Green Peppers

For this recipe, select squat round peppers that will stand upright neatly.

SERVES: 4
PREPARATION: 20 minutes
OVEN: 180°C/350°F/gas 4
COOKING: about 1 hour

4 even-sized green peppers
75 g/3 oz long-grain rice
1 small onion
50 g/2 oz mushrooms
2 rashers lean bacon
25 g/1 oz butter
225 g/8 oz chicken livers
salt and black pepper
5 ml/1 teaspoon chopped
fresh parsley
1 small egg
25–50 g/1–2 oz grated
Parmesan cheese

Cut the stalk ends off the peppers, removing as thin a slice as possible. Cut out the core of seeds and pith from inside the peppers, then rinse and drain them. Bring a saucepan of water to the boil, add the peppers and bring the water back to the boil. Cook for 5 minutes. Drain the peppers in a colander then place them upside-down on a double layer of absorbent kitchen paper.

For the stuffing, first cook the rice in a large pan of boiling salted water for 8–10 minutes, until tender; drain well. Peel the onion, wash and trim the mushrooms and chop up both finely. Cut the rind from the bacon and dice the flesh.

Melt the butter in a heavy-based pan and add the chicken livers whole; cook for a few minutes then remove and chop them into tiny pieces. Fry the bacon, onion and mushrooms for a few minutes. Return the chicken livers to the pan. Stir in the cooked rice, salt, pepper and parsley; remove the pan from the

Stuffed Green Peppers.

heat. Lightly beat the egg and stir it into the rice mixture.

Stand the green peppers in a buttered ovenproof dish. Spoon the rice into the peppers, and sprinkle with half the cheese.

Spoon 30 ml/2 tablespoons of cold water into the dish and place in a preheated oven at 180°C/350°F/gas 4; cook for 35–40 minutes. Sprinkle with the remaining cheese.

■ Serve a tomato sauce with the peppers – see Stuffed Peppers with Pork and Beef (page 229) or Compound Brown Sauce chart (page 354).

Colcannon

SERVES: 4
PREPARATION: 10 minutes
COOKING: 20 minutes

1 onion
4 rashers lean bacon
40 g/1½ oz fat or dripping or
30–45 ml/2–3 tablespoons oil
225 g/8 oz cooked cabbage
450 g/1 lb mashed potatoes
salt and black pepper
flour

Peel and chop the onion. Dice the bacon. Fry both in the fat until the onion is soft. Lift them out with a perforated spoon.

Chop the cooked cabbage and mix with the potato, bacon and onion; season with salt and black pepper. Shape the mixture into four flat cakes, about 1 cm/½ in thick. Coat with a little flour. Fry until golden brown.

■ Serve topped with a fried egg, or as a vegetable with cold meat.

Savoury Potato Cakes

MAKES: 8
PREPARATION: 35 minutes
OVEN: 200°C/400°F/gas 6
COOKING: 30–35 minutes

675 g/1½ lb potatoes
1 onion
salt
4 black olives
30 ml/2 tablespoons snipped chives
30 ml/2 tablespoons chopped
    parsley
1 egg
black pepper
plain flour
50 g/2 oz fresh breadcrumbs
30 ml/2 tablespoons olive oil

Peel and slice the potatoes and the onion. Cook in boiling salted water for 10–15 minutes until the potatoes are just cooked. Drain well. Mash the vegetables and allow to cool.

Stone and chop the olives and add them to the mashed potato with the chives, parsley and seasoning to taste. Beat the egg in a shallow bowl.

Divide the mixture into 8 equal piepes. Shape each piece into a cake using a little flour if required. Dip each potato cake in beaten egg and coat with the breadcrumbs. Reshape the cakes if necessary, pressing the crumbs on to make an even coating. Place on a baking sheet. Dab the cakes carefully with oil and bake in a preheated oven at 200°C/400°F/gas 6 for 20 minutes or until the coating is crisp and golden.

Braised Red Cabbage

A small amount of blackcurrant syrup (the type which can be diluted to make drinks), or cassis (blackcurrant liqueur), is delicious in braised red cabbage. As well as enriching the dish it adds a slightly fruity flavour to it.

SERVES: 4–6
PREPARATION: 20 minutes
COOKING: about 1 hour

575 g/1¼ lb red cabbage
1 large onion
45 ml/3 tablespoons olive oil
10 ml/2 teaspoons caraway seeds
    (optional)
1 large bay leaf
120 ml/4 fl oz water
30 ml/2 tablespoons blackcurrant
    syrup or cassis
15 ml/1 tablespoon soft
    brown sugar
2 Cox's or other sweet
    eating apples
15 ml/1 tablespoon red
    wine vinegar
salt and black pepper

Removing any faded outer leaves from the cabbage, cut it into quarters, remove the coarse stalk and finely shred the remainder. Peel and thinly slice the onion.

Heat the oil in a heavy-based flameproof casserole. Add the onion, caraway seeds, if liked, and bay leaf and cook gently, stirring, for 5 minutes to soften the onion without browning.

Add the shredded cabbage, water, blackcurrant syrup or cassis and sugar. Stir well, bring to a simmer, cover with a lid and cook gently for 30 minutes, stirring occasionally.

Cut the apples into quarters, remove the cores and slice them thinly. Add to the cabbage with the vinegar, salt and pepper to taste. Stir well, cover and cook for 10 minutes, then remove the lid, stir and cook for a further 10 minutes to allow some of the liquid to evaporate.

Leeks Vinaigrette

This cold, marinated leek dish may be served as a first course or as an accompaniment for grilled meats, such as chops.

SERVES: 4
PREPARATION: 15 minutes
COOKING: 30 minutes
MARINATING: 1–2 hours

8 small leeks
1 bay leaf
salt and black pepper
5 ml/1 teaspoon caster sugar
30 ml/2 tablespoons wine vinegar
1.25 ml/¼ teaspoon French
    mustard
45–60 ml/3–4 tablespoons olive oil
15 ml/1 tablespoon chopped
    parsley
2 hard-boiled eggs to garnish

Remove the coarse outer leaves from the leeks; trim off the roots and cut away the green tops, leaving about 10 cm/4 in of white stem on each leek. Slice the leeks in half lengthways, open them carefully and wash well under cold running water to remove all traces of grit.

Tie the halved leeks in four bundles using strong thread or cook's string; put them in a pan of boiling salted water and add the bay leaf. Bring back to the boil, then lower the heat to simmering point. Cover and cook the leeks for 30 minutes or until tender. Lift them carefully from the water and leave to drain.

Arrange the leeks in a serving dish and prepare the dressing; put salt and freshly ground pepper in a mixing bowl, add the sugar, vinegar and mustard. Blend thoroughly before adding the oil, mixing well. Stir in the chopped parsley, and spoon the dressing over the leeks. Leave to marinate* until cold, then cover and chill until ready to serve.

Garnish the leeks with slices of hard-boiled eggs.

Beetroot with Orange

In this recipe, cooked beetroot is combined with either fine-shred or sweet orange marmalade. The two flavours blend surprisingly well and suit any strong game, goose or duck.

SERVES: 4
PREPARATION: 5 minutes
COOKING: 10–15 minutes

450 g/1 lb cooked beetroot
25 g/1 oz butter
15 ml/1 tablespoon marmalade
juice of ½ orange
slice of orange to garnish

Peel and dice the cooked beetroot. Measure the butter, marmalade and orange juice into a saucepan, heat until the butter melts, then add the beetroot. Cook gently, stirring every now and then, for about 10 minutes, until the beetroot is evenly glazed.

Spoon the beetroot into a hot serving dish. Cut towards the centre of a thin orange slice, twist the two halves in opposite directions and place it on the beetroot as a garnish.

Warm Mushroom Salad

Other mushrooms can be used instead of button mushrooms. *Trompettes de mort*, the black, wild mushrooms, will give a rich flavour; the delicate-flavoured oyster variety are less expensive and can be mixed with button mushrooms for contrasting shape and texture.

SERVES: 4
PREPARATION: 20 minutes
COOKING: 5 minutes

grated rind and juice of 1 lime
5 ml/1 teaspoon caster sugar
salt and black pepper
100 g/4 oz leeks (1 medium)
2 carrots
1 red pepper
1 yellow pepper
1 green pepper
350 g/12 oz button mushrooms
2 garlic cloves
60 ml/4 tablespoons olive oil
flat-leafed parsley to garnish
    (optional)

Mix the lime rind and juice with the caster sugar and a little seasoning in a mixing bowl, whisking until the sugar and salt dissolves in the lime juice.

Trim and wash the leeks, then slice them thinly and separate the slices into rings. Bring a saucepan of salted water to the boil, add the leeks and bring the water back to the boil. Boil the leeks for 1 minute, then drain them well and toss them with the lime juice in the bowl. Peel or scrape and coarsely grate the carrots, then toss them with the leeks.

Skin the peppers by charring their skin over a gas burner on the hob or by cooking under a preheated grill until black and blistered. If using a hob, skewer the peppers one by one on a metal fork and rotate them over the flame. Rub or scrape off the skin under gently running cold water. Cut the stalk ends off the peppers, scoop out all pith and seeds from inside, then slice the flesh thinly into rings.

Turn the leek and carrot mixture into a large, shallow serving dish or divide it between four plates, and top with the pepper slices. Rinse the mushrooms very briefly under cold running water, then pat them dry on a clean tea-towel or absorbent kitchen paper. Crush the garlic into a large saucepan and add the oil. Heat the oil gently and cook the garlic for about 30 seconds. Increase the heat and add the mushrooms with seasoning to taste, then toss them over high heat for about 1 minute, until they are hot and very lightly cooked. Spoon the hot mushrooms over the salad, scraping out all the oil from the pan. Garnish with flat-leafed parsley if liked and serve at once.

Celeriac Salad with Parma Ham

The large celery-flavoured root may be boiled or stir fried and can also be served raw in a salad.

SERVES: 4
PREPARATION: 20 minutes
COOKING: 2–3 minutes

1 small celeriac root (about 350 g/12 oz)
30–45 ml/2–3 tablespoons mayonnaise
1.25 ml/¼ teaspoon French mustard
225 g/8 oz prosciutto (Parma) ham, thinly sliced

Peel the celeriac. Cut it into thin slices and then into matchstick-

Celeriac Salad with Parma Ham.

thin pieces. Add the celeriac to a pan of boiling salted water and blanch* for 2–3 minutes; drain in a colander and allow to cool. Blend together the mayonnaise and French mustard and toss the celeriac in this dressing.

Arrange the Parma ham on individual plates, allowing three thin slices per person. Divide the salad between the portions.

■ For a delicious, and satisfying, supper dish, substitute salami for the prosciutto. Cut the salami into thin strips and serve the salad in baked potatoes.

RICE & PASTA

Mixed Grain Pilaf

Cracked wheat and wild rice give this pilaf a nutty flavour and a bit of bite. Cracked wheat is the broken, uncooked grain, not to be confused with bulgur, the cooked variety.

SERVES: 4–6
PREPARATION: 30 minutes
COOKING: about 45 minutes

75 g/3 oz wild rice
salt and black pepper
1 onion
2 celery sticks
1 carrot
1 green pepper
100 g/4 oz white cabbage
1–2 cloves garlic
45 ml/3 tablespoons olive oil
1 bay leaf
2.5 ml/½ teaspoon dried oregano
75 g/3 oz no-need-to-presoak dried apricots
50 g/2 oz raisins
175 g/6 oz long-grain rice
75 g/3 oz cracked wheat
900 ml/1½ pt stock (chicken or vegetable)
50 g/2 oz shelled pecan nuts or blanched almonds
75 g/3 oz cashew nuts
60 ml/4 tablespoons chopped parsley

Cook the wild rice before making the pilaf. Add it to a saucepan of boiling salted water. Bring the water back to the boil, stir, then simmer for 10 minutes. Drain the rice through a sieve.

Meanwhile, chop the onion, thinly slice the celery and dice the carrot. Cut the pepper in half, cut out the stalk, pith and seeds, then dice the flesh. Shred the cabbage and chop the garlic. Heat the oil in a large saucepan. Add all the prepared ingredients, the bay leaf and oregano. Stir well, then cook for 5 minutes. Chop the apricots and add them with the raisins. Continue to cook, stirring occasionally for a further 5 minutes.

Mix the rice, wheat and wild rice into the vegetables. Pour in the stock, add seasoning to taste and bring to the boil. Stir the mixture once, then reduce the heat to the lowest setting and cover the pan tightly. Leave the pilaf to cook for 20 minutes, then turn the heat off or remove the pan from the heat and leave it to stand, covered, for 5 minutes.

Roughly chop the pecan nuts or split the almonds lengthways into four. Roast the pecans or almonds and cashews together in a heavy-based saucepan or frying pan while the rice is standing. Shake the pan frequently over low to medium heat until the nuts are lightly browned; the pecans will darken slightly. Take care not to burn the nuts.

Fork the nuts and chopped parsley into the pilaf; the grains should be tender and the mixture juicy, not completely dry.

■ Beetroot with Orange (page 90) is a tangy accompaniment to the pilaf.

Spanish Rice

This mixture of rice, onion and tomato is particularly good with grilled or fried chops, steak or hamburgers. It is also ideal for a quick supper dish.

SERVES: 4
PREPARATION: 10 minutes
COOKING: 20 minutes

175 g/6 oz long-grain rice
450 ml/¾ pt water
salt
1 onion
1 green pepper
25 g/1 oz butter
400 g/14 oz can chopped tomatoes
10 ml/2 teaspoons caster sugar
1 bay leaf
freshly grated Parmesan cheese
    to serve

Measure the rice into a large pan. Pour in the water and add a little salt. Bring the water to the boil, stir and cover the pan with a close-fitting lid. Reduce the heat to a minimum setting and cook for 15–20 minutes. At the end of cooking, remove the pan from the heat but do not remove the lid. Leave the rice to stand for a further 5 minutes.

Meanwhile, peel and finely slice the onion. Halve the green pepper, remove the stem, seeds and white midribs and finely shred the flesh.

Melt the butter in a saucepan and add the onion and green pepper. Cover and cook gently for about 15 minutes or until the onion is soft. Stir in the tomatoes, 2.5 ml/½ teaspoon salt, the sugar and bay leaf. Simmer, covered, for 15 minutes. Add the rice and mix it into the sauce using a fork and a cutting action rather than a stirring motion. Heat gently for 1–2 minutes without replacing the lid.

Remove the bay leaf and arrange the rice mixture on a hot serving dish. Offer freshly grated Parmesan cheese with the rice.
■ For a simple supper, serve with a crisp green salad and warmed ciabatta.

Cauliflower and Leek Lasagne

SERVES: 6
PREPARATION: 40 minutes
OVEN: 180°C/350°F/gas 4
COOKING: about 1 hour

8–12 sheets lasagne
    (see note below)
1 cauliflower
salt and black pepper
450 g/1 lb leeks
1 clove garlic
25 g/1 oz butter
5 ml/1 teaspoon dried or
    15 ml/1 tablespoon
    chopped fresh marjoram
1 bay leaf
30 ml/2 tablespoons tomato paste
2 × 400 g/14 oz cans
    chopped tomatoes
30 ml/2 tablespoons
    chopped parsley
75 g/3 oz Lancashire, Cheshire
    or Caerphilly cheese
600 ml/1 pt coating White Sauce
    (page 352)
60 ml/4 tablespoons freshly grated
    Parmesan cheese
marjoram sprigs to garnish
    (optional)

Cook the lasagne if necessary (see note). Trim the cauliflower, then cut it into quarters and cook these in a saucepan of boiling salted water for 5 minutes. Drain thoroughly in a colander while preparing the remaining ingredients.

Trim and thoroughly clean the leeks, then slice them thinly. Crush the garlic. Melt the butter in a large saucepan, add the leeks, garlic, marjoram and bay leaf, and cook, stirring often, for 10 minutes, until the leeks are softened and greatly reduced in volume. Stir in the tomato paste, canned tomatoes and seasoning. Heat until simmering, cover and cook gently for 10 minutes.

Meanwhile, cut the cauliflower into small florets, dicing or slicing the stalk according to size. Stir the cauliflower and parsley into the leek mixture, then remove the pan from the heat. Finely crumble the piece of cheese and stir it into the white sauce with the Parmesan.

Layer the leek mixture and pasta in a large baking dish. Ideally the dish should measure about 30 × 20 cm/12 × 8 in and it should be at least 5 cm/2 in deep. Many dishes sold for baking lasagne are too shallow to hold the layers and sauce topping. If necessary, use a roasting tin lined with foil. Begin with a thin layer of leek mixture on the bottom of the dish and finish with a layer of pasta on top. Pour the cheese sauce over the pasta and bake in a preheated oven at 180°C/350°F/gas 4 for about 40 minutes, or until the lasagne is golden brown. Fresh marjoram sprigs may be used as a garnish.

Warm Mushroom Salad (page 90) and Cauliflower and Leek Lasagne.

Note These days, you will find that most dried lasagne does not need to be boiled before it is layered in the baking dish. The quality, though, varies enormously depending on the brand. Beware of the types which look white and rather like perforated cardboard. They give very poor results! It is possible to find dried pasta which needs boiling first, but usually in Italian delicatessens; however, many supermarkets stock fresh lasagne, which is the best choice. Follow the packet instructions for preparing the pasta, boiling the dried type which needs cooking in a large volume of salted water, draining and rinsing it before setting it out on a clean tea-towel to keep the sheets separate. The bought fresh pasta may be placed in a large bowl, covered with plenty of freshly boiled water from a kettle and left to stand for about 5 minutes, then drained before use. Home-made pasta, which may be slightly thicker than bought fresh lasagne, should be boiled for about 2 minutes, drained and rinsed as for dried pasta.

Buttered Noodles

Plain noodles, dressed only with a little butter, are an excellent accompaniment for moist main dishes, like stews or meaty sauces. Add a little Parmesan cheese to the noodles and they also make a simple supper dish.

SERVES: 4
PREPARATION: 5 minutes
COOKING: 12 minutes

225 g/8 oz ribbon noodles
salt and black pepper
25 g/1 oz butter
25–50 g/1–2 oz Parmesan cheese, grated, to serve (optional)

Put the noodles in a large saucepan of boiling salted water, bring back to the boil and cook over moderate heat for about 12 minutes. If using fresh noodles, allow about 3 minutes' cooking once the water comes back to the boil. As soon as the noodles are tender, but while they retain a bit of 'bite' (al dente), drain them in a colander.

Melt the butter in a large saucepan; remove it from the heat and tip in the cooked noodles; season with freshly ground pepper.

Using two forks, lift and turn the noodles in the melted butter. transfer to a hot serving dish and sprinkle with the grated fresh Parmesan cheese, if liked.

■ Buttered noodles are an excellent accompaniment to Hungarian Goulash (page 250), Boeuf Stroganoff (page 250) and similar meat or poultry dishes which are cooked in or served with plenty of rich sauce.

Tagliatelle alla Bolognese

Egg noodles or tagliatelle are frequently served in Italy with a substantial sauce of minced beef.

SERVES: 4–6
PREPARATION: 25 minutes
COOKING: 45–60 minutes

1 onion
1 carrot
1 clove garlic
100 g/4 oz chicken livers
100 g/4 oz mushrooms
30 ml/2 tablespoons olive oil
450 g/1 lb lean minced beef
30 ml/2 tablespoons plain flour
400 g/14 oz can chopped tomatoes
black pepper
1 bay leaf
2.5 ml/½ teaspoon dried marjoram or oregano
30 ml/2 tablespoons tomato paste
150 ml/¼ pt red wine
300 ml/½ pt beef stock
30 ml/2 tablespoons chopped parsley
225–350 g/8–12 oz ribbon noodles
freshly grated Parmesan cheese to serve

Peel and finely chop the onion, carrot and the garlic. Trim and chop the chicken livers. Wipe and trim the mushrooms; slice them thinly.

Heat the oil in a heavy-based saucepan, and add the onion and carrot. Cover and cook gently for about 5 minutes or until the onion is tender. Add the garlic, chicken livers and minced beef, stirring until the meat is thoroughly browned, then add the mushrooms and fry for a few minutes. Mix in the flour, add the tomatoes, seasoning, the bay leaf, marjoram or oregano and tomato paste. Pour over the red wine and stock and bring to the boil. Lower the heat, cover the pan and simmer gently for 45–60 minutes. About 15 minutes before the sauce is ready, stir in the parsley. Put the tagliatelle in a large pan of boiling salted water. Bring back to the boil and cook for 12 minutes. Drain before piling on a hot serving dish. Pour the sauce over the noodles and serve with a bowl of grated cheese.

Note Bolognese sauce is a traditional accompaniment for long, slim pasta. It is also used in layered pasta dishes, such as traditional lasagne al forno. This delicious meat sauce may be made in large batches and frozen for up to 3 months.

PUDDINGS & DESSERTS

Crêpes Suzette

Cooked in a chafing dish over a burner at the table, Crêpes Suzette are a flamboyant dessert.

SERVES: 6
PREPARATION: 30 minutes
COOKING: 2–3 minutes plus time for preparing pancakes

12 Pancakes (page 339)
25 g/1 oz unsalted butter
50 g/2 oz caster sugar
juice of 2 oranges
juice of ½ lemon
30–45 ml/2–3 tablespoons orange liqueur

Cook the pancakes first and keep them hot between two plates over a pan of simmering water.

Melt the butter in a frying pan, stir in the sugar and cook gently until it is a golden-brown caramel. Add the strained orange and lemon juice and stir until the caramel has dissolved and makes a thick sauce. Drop a pancake into the pan, fold it in half and in half again. Push to the side of the pan and add the next pancake. When all the pancakes are in the pan, add the liqueur and set it alight after a few seconds. Shake the pan to incorporate the flamed liqueur in the sauce.

Transfer the pancakes to a hot serving dish, pour over the sauce from the pan and serve.

Crêpes Suzette.

Citron Fromage

Shiny, firm lemons are plentiful and good value this month. They can be used for a light mousse to follow a rich main course.

SERVES: 4
PREPARATION: 30 minutes
CHILLING: 2 hours

15 ml/1 tablespoon
    powdered gelatine
3 eggs
2 large lemons
100 g/4 oz caster sugar
150 ml/¼ pt double cream

Sprinkle the powdered gelatine over 30 ml/2 tablespoons of water in a small heatproof basin. Do not stir. Leave to stand for 15 minutes until the gelatine has absorbed the water. Separate the eggs, putting the yolks into a large bowl and the whites into another. Finely grate the rind from the lemons, and mix it into the egg yolks, together with the caster sugar. Squeeze the lemons and strain the juice. Place the basin of sponged gelatine over a pan of simmering water and stir until the gelatine has dissolved completely.

Beat the egg yolks and sugar until pale and creamy. Beat in the lemon juice. Slowly pour in the dissolved gelatine, beating continuously. Lightly whip the double cream and fold it into the mixture. Whisk the egg whites until stiff, then fold them in evenly and lightly.

Spoon the mousse into a serving dish or individual dishes and chill until set.

Apricot and Almond Puffs

Crushed ratafia biscuits give these light pastries a delicious almond flavour.

MAKES: 6
PREPARATION: 25 minutes
STANDING: 20 minutes
OVEN: 200°C/400°F/gas 6
COOKING: 15–20 minutes

100 g/4 oz no-need-to-presoak
    dried apricots
juice of 2 lemons
2 small Cox's apples
15 g/½ oz butter
50 g/2 oz ratafia biscuits
275 g/10 oz home-made Puff
    Pastry (page 374) or thawed
    frozen puff pastry
beaten egg white
caster sugar

Cut the apricots into small pieces and place in a bowl. Add the lemon juice, stir, then set aside to macerate for 20 minutes.

Peel, core and dice the apples. Melt the butter in a small saucepan, add the apples and apricots with the lemon juice. Cook, stirring continuously, for about 5 minutes. Remove from the heat. Crush the ratafia biscuits and stir them into the mixture. Set aside to cool.

On a lightly floured surface, roll out the pastry to a rectangle measuring 34 × 25 cm/13½ × 10 in. Cut out six 11 cm/4½ in rounds. Roll each round to an oval. Divide the filling between the pastry shapes, placing it on one half of the pastry only. Brush the edges with a little egg white, fold over the pastry to enclose the filling, then press and crimp the edges. Place on a damp baking sheet. Brush each pastry with egg white, then sprinkle with sugar. Bake in a preheated oven at 200°C/400°F/gas 6 for about 15 minutes or until well puffed and golden. Serve hot, or cool on a wire rack.

Caramelised Oranges Grand Marnier

This classic dinner party dessert can be prepared the day before the meal and chilled overnight; the result is better than when the fruit is merely chilled briefly.

SERVES: 6
PREPARATION: 15 minutes
COOKING: 45 minutes
CHILLING: 3 hours or more

6 oranges
175 g/6 oz caster sugar
150 ml/¼ pt water
juice of ½ lemon
30 ml/2 tablespoons Grand
    Marnier (or other
    orange liqueur)

Cut a slice from the top and bottom of each orange so that it will stand upright neatly. Slice downwards through the orange skin, cutting away the peel and all the white pith, leaving only the orange flesh. Cut the oranges crossways into slices and place them in a serving dish.

Select six of the larger pieces of peel and carefully cut away the pith. Shred the rind finely and put it in a saucepan. Cover with cold water, bring to the boil, then drain – this removes the bitter flavour of the rind. Cover the rind with fresh cold water; bring to the boil and simmer for about 30 minutes or until the orange rind is tender. Drain and set aside.

Put the sugar into a heavy-based saucepan, then stir with a wooden spoon over moderate heat until the sugar has melted and turned to caramel. Remove from the heat and carefully add the water – it will boil furiously. When the bubbling stops, return the pan to the heat and stir until the caramel has dissolved and a syrup has formed. Add the shredded orange rind and bring to the boil. Simmer for 2–3 minutes until the rind is glazed. Draw off the heat, cool for a few moments, then add the lemon juice and the Grand Marnier or other orange liqueur.

Spoon the syrup and candied rind over the prepared oranges. Set aside until cold, basting the oranges occasionally with the syrup. Chill for several hours before serving.
■ Serve with whipped cream or vanilla ice cream.

Compôte of Rhubarb and Bananas

Tender pink rhubarb is readily available early in the year. It should be cooked slowly to keep its shape for a compôte.

SERVES: 4
PREPARATION: 15 minutes
OVEN: 160°C/325°F/gas 3
COOKING: 35 minutes
CHILLING: 2 hours

450 g/1 lb rhubarb
175 g/6 oz caster sugar
juice of 1 orange
450 g/1 lb bananas

Trim the tops and bottoms off the rhubarb, wash the stalks and cut them into 2.5 cm/1 in lengths. Place in a casserole or ovenproof dish and add the sugar and strained orange juice. Stir the ingredients thoroughly, and cover with a lid. Bake for 35 minutes in a preheated oven at 160°C/325°F/gas 3. Remove the casserole from the oven and leave it to stand, covered, for 5–10 minutes.

Peel and thinly slice the bananas into a serving dish. Pour over the hot rhubarb and the juices. Cool and then chill.
■ A bowl of whipped cream or vanilla ice cream could be served with the compôte.

Tarte Tatin

This is an upside-down apple tart, made with dessert apples which remain in neat pieces. This quick version uses brown sugar for colour instead of caramelising the apples first.

SERVES: 4
PREPARATION: 30 minutes
OVEN: 180°C/350°F/gas 4
COOKING: 35–40 minutes

15 g/½ oz unsalted butter
50–75 g/2–3 oz soft brown sugar
450 g/1 lb dessert apples
Pastry
100 g/4 oz plain flour
50 g/2 oz unsalted butter
25 g/1 oz icing sugar
1 egg yolk

Melt the butter and brush a little over the inside of a 19–20 cm/7½–8 in shallow sponge tin. Line the base with greaseproof paper and brush with more melted butter. Sprinkle the brown sugar over the paper and press down.

Sift the flour into a basin. Rub the butter into the flour. Sift in the icing sugar and stir in the egg yolk and 15 ml/1 tablespoon of water. Mix to a rough dough before kneading it on a floured surface until smooth. Roll the pastry out to a circle the size of the tin and trim neatly.

Peel, core and thinly slice the apples. Arrange the slices in circles over the brown sugar. Carefully lift the pastry over the apple slices and press down. Bake in the centre of a preheated oven at 180°C/ 350°F/gas 4 for 35–40 minutes or until golden brown.

Cool the tart for about 5 minutes, then turn out, upside-down, on to a serving plate. Remove the paper.
■ Serve the tart hot, with a bowl of cream.

Rum and Butter Tarts

MAKES: 12–14
PREPARATION: 15 minutes
OVEN: 190°C/375°F/gas 5
COOKING: 15–20 minutes

75 g/3 oz currants
100 g/4 oz Shortcrust Pastry
(page 365)
25 g/1 oz butter
75 g/3 oz light soft brown sugar
15 ml/1 tablespoon single cream
or milk
45 ml/3 tablespoons rum
1 egg yolk

Cover the currants with boiling water and leave them to stand until they are plump – about 10 minutes; drain thoroughly.

Roll out the pastry and stamp out circles large enough to line 12–14 patty tins.

Melt the butter in a small pan, remove from the heat and stir in the sugar, cream and rum to taste. Add the currants and stir in the egg yolk until thoroughly combined.

Using a teaspoon, divide the currant mixture evenly between the tarts. Do not make the tarts more than three-quarters full. Bake in a preheated oven at 190°C/375°F/gas 5 for 15–20 minutes or until the pastry is crisp and the filling is set.

American Cheesecake

This transatlantic cheesecake is not baked like the continental version, but set with gelatine. A combination of cottage cheese and cream cheese is used but curd cheese may be substituted for both if preferred.

SERVES: 6
PREPARATION: 35 minutes
CHILLING: 3 hours

75 g/3 oz unsalted butter
75 g/3 oz crushed cornflakes
100 g/4 oz caster sugar
15 g/½ oz powdered gelatine
225 g/8 oz cottage cheese
100 g/4 oz fresh cream cheese
rind and juice of 1 small lemon
2 eggs
150 ml/¼ pt double cream
Decoration
halved black grapes
mandarin orange segments

Melt the butter in a small saucepan over low heat. Remove the pan from the heat and stir in the cornflake crumbs and 25 g/ 1 oz of sugar. Press this mixture over the base of a 20 cm/8 in round loose-bottomed flan dish or tin or cake tin. Put the cheesecake base in the refrigerator to chill while preparing the cheese mixture.

Sprinkle the gelatine over 45 ml/3 tablespoons water in a small heatproof basin. Do not stir. Leave to stand for 15 minutes until the gelatine has absorbed the water.

Meanwhile, rub the cottage cheese through a sieve into a bowl and add the cream cheese. Finely grate the lemon rind and mix in well.

Separate the eggs; add 40 g/ 1½ oz of sugar to the yolks and beat until creamy and light. Set the basin with the gelatine over a pan of simmering water and stir

American Cheesecake.

until the gelatine has dissolved completely.

Remove from the heat once the gelatine has dissolved, and add the strained lemon juice. Gradually whisk this liquid into the egg yolks, before blending it all into the cheese mixture. Lightly whip the cream until it stands in soft peaks, then fold it into the cheese mixture.

Using an electric beater, whisk the egg whites until stiff, then whisk in the remaining sugar until the mixture is glossy and stiff. Fold the egg whites into the cheese mixture. Pour over the chilled cheesecake base and level the top. Chill until firm.

When ready to serve, loosen the sides of the cheesecake with a knife blade. Remove the cake from the tin and decorate the top with halved black grapes and mandarin orange segments.

Home-made Marmalade

Marmalade making is time-consuming but economical, and the result, both in flavour and texture, is well worth the trouble. Marmalades from citrus fruits are basically made in the same way as jams and jellies, but the tough rind, which is an integral part of marmalade, needs long, slow cooking.

If the rind is not thoroughly softened during the first cooking stage, it becomes tough and unpleasant once it is cooked with the sugar.

Setting

Like jams and jellies, marmalade depends on pectin*, acid and sugar for setting. Since citrus fruits are rich sources of both pectin and acid, they always set well if the right proportions of ingredients are used and the preserve is properly tested for setting point. Pectin is found in the pith* (the yellow-white layer underneath the peel and surrounding the fruit pulp) and in the pips. Both should be tied in a muslin bag and boiled with the chopped peel.

Testing for Setting

Use a sugar thermometer to gauge setting point (104°C/220°F). This is the temperature reached when the marmalade has boiled sufficiently to give the correct concentration of sugar for setting. In addition to checking the temperature, use the saucer test: pour a little of the marmalade on to a cool saucer – if a skin which wrinkles when gently pushed with your fingertip forms in a few minutes, setting point has been reached.

A common problem when creating your own marmalade is overcooking, resulting in a dark, very thick preserve. If any preserve is boiled well beyond setting point, it loses its jelly-like quality and becomes sticky and syrupy. Remember that the marmsalade can be boiled after you have tested for setting, so it is a good idea to check sooner rather than later. Finally, it is worth investing in a sugar thermometer as it does give the most reliable information and, given that you use it early in the cooking and frequently, it will help to prevent overboiling.

Skimming and Potting

Remove the preserve from the heat immediately setting point is reached. Use a flat-bowled metal spoon to skim the surface, removing any scum, especially around the edge of the preserve. After skimming the marmalade, leave it to stand for about 30 minutes, then stir to distribute the peel evenly.

If marmalade is potted too soon, the rind floats; having a standing time allows the liquid preserve to set slightly – just enough to support the pieces of rind in suspension.

Pour into dry, warm jars and cover with waxed paper discs, wax side down. Leave the jars until completely cold before covering them with lids or with clear cellophane circles; secure the cellophane with rubber bands or fine string. Store the marmalade in a cool, dry place.

Always leave the marmalade covered with waxed discs, with sheets of absorbent kitchen paper laid loosely over the tops of the pots, until completely cold before putting on the lids. A warm preserve gives off moisture and this will later allow mould to grow on the marmalade.

Chunky Seville Orange

MAKES: about 45 kg/10 lb
PREPARATION: 1¼ hours
COOKING: about 2½ hours

*1.4 kg/3 lb Seville or bitter oranges
juice of 2 lemons
3.4 litres/6 pt water
2.72 kg/6 lb preserving sugar*

Remove any stalk ends from the oranges, scrub and dry them thoroughly. Using a potato peeler or sharp, narrow knife, peel off the rind in thin downward strips, being careful to leave all the white pith behind. Cut the rind into 5 mm/¼ in wide strips and set them aside.

Cut the oranges in half and squeeze out all the juice, saving the pips. Cut away the pith with a sharp knife, leaving the orange pulp. Chop the pith roughly and tie it in a large piece of muslin, together with the orange pips.

A selection of marmalades, showing the difference between a clear, fine cut, preserve and a dense, chunky marmalade.

Cut the orange pulp into small chunks and put them in a pan, with the chopped peel and the muslin bag. Strain the orange juice into the pan and add the strained lemon juice and water.

Bring the fruit mixture to the boil over low heat and simmer, uncovered, for about 2 hours or until the peel is quite soft and the contents of the pan have reduced by about half.

Remove the muslin bag, and add the sugar, stirring continuously until it has dissolved. Turn up the heat and boil the marmalade until it reaches a temperature of 104°C/220°F and setting point is reached, after about 15–20 minutes. Skim, stand, pot and cover when cold.

Dundee

MAKES: about 4.5 kg/10 lb
PREPARATION: 35 minutes
COOKING: about 2½ hours

1.4 kg/3 lb Seville or bitter oranges
3 lemons
3 sweet oranges
3.4 litres/6 pt water
2.72 kg/6 lb preserving sugar
10 ml/2 teaspoons black treacle

Wash all the fruit thoroughly. Place the whole fruits in a large pan with the water and cover. Bring to the boil and cook over low heat for about 1½ hours or until the fruit pierces easily.

Lift out the fruit and leave until cool enough to handle. Slice the fruit, scraping out all the pips and adding them to the pan with the cooking liquid. Chop the fruit roughly.

Boil the fruit juices rapidly for 15 minutes or until reduced by about half. Strain the liquid into a preserving pan, add the chopped fruit and bring to the boil. Stir in the sugar and black treacle and boil the marmalade until it reaches a temperature of 104°C/220°F and setting point is reached. Skim, stand, pot and then cover when cold.

Clear Seville Orange

MAKES: about 3.6 kg/8 lb
PREPARATION: 45 minutes
COOKING: about 2¼ hours

1.4 kg/3 lb Seville oranges
3.4 litres/6 pt water
juice of 2 lemons
2.72 kg/6 lb preserving sugar

Prepare the oranges as for Chunky Seville Orange. Put the finely shredded peel in a pan with half the water and the strained lemon juice. Bring to the boil and simmer, covered, over low heat for 2 hours, until the peel is tender.

Meanwhile, chop the peeled oranges roughly and put them in another pan with the remaining water. Bring to the boil, cover and simmer for 1½ hours.

Strain the liquid from the orange pulp through a fine sieve or muslin into the pan with the soft peel. Bring the marmalade mixture to the boil and reduce slightly before stirring in the sugar. Boil rapidly until the marmalade reaches a temperature of 104°C/220°F and setting point is reached. Skim, stand, pot and cover when cold.

Grapefruit

The thick layer of pith beneath grapefruit skin ensures a good set for this sweet marmalade.

MAKES: about 4.5 kg/10 lb
PREPARATION: 45 minutes
COOKING: about 2¼ hours

1.4 kg/3 lb grapefruit
225 g/8 oz lemons
3.4 litres/6 pt water
2.72 kg/6 lb preserving sugar

Proceed as for Clear Seville Orange Marmalade.

Three-fruit

MAKES: about 3.25 kg/7lb
PREPARATION: 1 hour
STANDING: 24 hours
COOKING: about 2 hours

2 lemons
2 oranges
2 grapefruit
1.7 litres/3 pt water
2.27 kg/5 lb preserving sugar

Wash and dry the fruit, cut off and reserve the ends of each fruit, then cut them into quarters. Slice the fruit quarters thinly, setting the pips aside. Place the fruit in a large bowl, with the water. Tie the reserved fruit ends and pips in muslin, add to the bowl, cover and leave to stand for 24 hours.

Put the contents of the bowl into a large saucepan and bring to the boil; reduce the heat, cover and simmer for 1½ hours. Remove the muslin bag and squeeze the juice from it back into the pan.

Add the sugar. Stir until it has dissolved, then boil rapidly until setting point is reached. Skim, stand, pot and then cover when cold.

Tangerine

MAKES: about 2.27 kg/5 lb
PREPARATION: 1¼ hours
COOKING: about 1¾ hours

1.4 kg/3 lb tangerines
6 lemons
2.9 litres/5 pt water
1.4 kg/3 lb preserving sugar

Clean the fruit and cut in half; squeeze out the juice, setting the pips aside. Remove the membranes from the tangerines, with a teaspoon, and put them in a bowl, together with the pips and 300 ml/½ pt of cold water.

Cut the tangerine peel into narrow strips (there is no pith on these fruits). Peel the lemons and add the pith to the pips.

Leave the peel, the fruit juices and the remaining water in a large bowl for about 8 hours.

Boil the contents of the large bowl, with the fruit membranes, pith and peel tied in muslin, for 1 hour or until reduced by half. Remove the muslin bag and add the sugar. Boil until setting point is reached. Skim, strain, pot and then cover when cold.

Lemon or Lime

Choose firm, unblemished fruits with smooth skins.

MAKES: about 4.5 kg/10 lb
PREPARATION: 1½ hours
COOKING: about 2 hours

1.4 kg/3 lb lemons or limes
3.4 litres/6 pt water
2.72 kg/6 lb preserving sugar

Proceed as for Chunky Seville Orange Marmalade. For a more jelly-like marmalade, follow the instructions for Clear Seville Orange Marmalade.

For Three Fruit Marmalade, slice the quartered grapefruit, oranges and lemons.

MARCH

Broccoli Spears au Gratin, Sprouting Broccoli with Fresh Pasta, Chicken Pie.

March

A month of change, March brings longer days and bright spells, while bitter winds and driving rain show that winter has not yet given way to spring. Despite the cold weather, exciting things are happening in the garden in March and there is always something to discover when the weather permits. Herb shoots begin to show through, especially mint which starts spreading into new ground if it is not contained, while the budding sage looks less woody and dead than it did during the first months of the year.

Purple sprouting broccoli is the real vegetable treat of the month, absolutely bursting with flavour even though it looks so insignificant. Spinach is also worthy of a place on the menu, either as a main ingredient in a pasta dish, such as lasagne or cannelloni, or as a vegetable accompaniment. British cucumbers are now available in the shops. Rhubarb will be in plentiful supply, just in time to provide inexpensive and warming puddings to round off simple meals.

On the fishmonger's slab, mussels are usually still a good seafood buy, along with cod and whiting as well as economical oily fish, such as herring, mackerel and sardines.

Annual festivities include Saint David's Day on March 1st, when the Welsh celebrate not only by sporting their national emblem, the leek, on their lapels but also by eating it in a hearty soup, or cawl, of mixed vegetables and lamb or other meat. Mothering Sunday usually gives young cooks the excuse they are looking for to be left alone in the kitchen to decorate a cake; while according to Lancashire tradition, the Lenten fast was broken on this day by making a fig pie.

Even though warmer weather is just around the corner, March is still a time for hot food and hearty cooking. The recipes in this chapter offer a change from traditional British favourites, with satisfying French Onion Soup, a colourful pot of Minestrone and Sauerbraten with piping hot noodles.

Menu suggestions *The theme for this month's menus is to provide piping hot meals and to introduce a few new flavours to lift the spirits out of the winter gloom. The majority of the recipes are featured in this chapter; page references are given if they are to be found elsewhere in the book.*

Dinner for Two
~

Avocados with Prawns

~

Steak au Poivre
Potato Croquettes (page 347)
Mixed Salad

~

Spiced Vanilla Soufflé
(page 134)

Arrange a stylish table, complete with candles and flowers, to set the scene for this classic culinary combination. The dessert can be replaced by a bowl of fresh fruit and a cheeseboard if you do not feel sufficiently confident to invite your guest into the kitchen to chat as you complete the final preparation of the soufflé mixture. All the recipes chosen can easily be made in half the original quantities and the potato croquettes can be prepared and cooked in advance.

Indian Supper
~

Prawns in Curry Sauce
with
Hot Nan Bread

~

Beef Kofta
Mixed Vegetable Curry
Aubergines with Yogurt
Boiled Basmati Rice
Lime Pickle
Mango Chutney

~

Kulfi (page 75)
or
Orange Caramel Custards
(page 277)

Make a half quantity of the curried prawn dish and serve it on small individual plates for the first course, offering the bread instead of rice as an accompaniment. Kulfi, which is the traditional Indian ice cream, may be prepared in advance.

Hearty Lunch
~

Minestrone
Poppy-seed Plait (page 397)

~

Glazed Lemon Tart

This is a good menu for busy weekends, especially on a relaxing Saturday after a morning walk. The soup can be made a day ahead, and the pasta added at the last minute when the soup is reheated, while the bread can be made several days in advance and frozen. The combination of dishes also translates well into an informal supper party by serving a platter of mixed salami, Parma ham and Italian cheeses to follow the soup, with a green salad for variety in texture.

Cous Cous with Vegetables (page 111) and Split Pea Biriani (page 113).

SOUPS

Malayan Beef and Prawn Soup

SERVES: 6
PREPARATION: 30 minutes
COOKING: about 2 hours

450 g/1 lb lean braising beef
1.4 litres/2½ pt water
3 onions
2 cloves garlic
2.5 cm/1 piece of fresh root ginger
3.75 ml/¾ teaspoon turmeric
5 ml/1 teaspoon ground coriander
225 g/8 oz peeled cooked prawns
45 ml/3 tablespoons butter
salt
15 ml/1 tablespoon fresh lime or
    lemon juice

Put the beef in a pan with the water. Peel and quarter 1 onion, and bruise 1 clove of garlic without peeling it; add both to the beef. Bring to the boil, cover pan and simmer for 1 hour.

Peel and grate 1 onion and pound it with the second garlic clove and the spices. Chop the prawns and fry them in 30 ml/ 2 tablespoons of butter for 2 minutes. Add the onion mixture and fry for a further 3–4 minutes.

Lift out the onion and garlic from the soup. Add the prawn mixture and simmer for 1 hour, or until the beef is tender. Take out the beef, slice it thinly and return it to the soup. Season with salt. Slice the last onion and fry in butter until crisp; add to the soup with the lime juice.

French Onion Soup

This traditional soup is always associated with the famous market, which no longer exists, at Les Halles in Paris. The porters kept out the cold of a raw winter's morning by drinking vast mugs of this onion soup.

SERVES: 4
PREPARATION: 20 minutes
COOKING: about 1 hour

675 g/1½ lb onions
50–75 g/2–3 oz butter
1.12 litres/2 pt beef stock
salt
4 slices French bread,
    1 cm/½ in thick
100 g/4 oz Gruyère cheese

Peel and thinly slice the onions. Melt the butter in a large saucepan and add the onions. Cover with a lid and cook over low heat for about 15 minutes, until the onions are soft and transparent. Remove the lid and continue frying the onions, stirring every now and then, for 15–20 minutes more, until they are golden brown. Stir in the beef stock and add salt to taste. Replace the lid and simmer the soup for 30 minutes.

Meanwhile, toast the French bread slices on one side only under the grill. Grate the cheese. Turn the bread slices over and top with half the cheese. Return to the grill until the cheese has melted. Arrange the bread in individual bowls and pour over the hot onion soup.

Serve the remaining grated cheese in a separate bowl.

Minestrone

This soup, of Italian origin and with numerous regional variations, is substantial enough to serve as a meal on its own.

SERVES: 4
PREPARATION: 15 minutes
COOKING: 30–35 minutes

1–2 carrots
1–2 sticks celery
1 onion
1 small turnip
1 potato
25 g/1 oz butter or 30 ml/
    2 tablespoons olive oil
1 clove garlic
900 ml/1½ pt ham or beef stock
2 large tomatoes
1 small leek
100 g/4 oz green cabbage or
    Brussels sprouts
25 g/1 oz spaghetti or quick-
    cooking macaroni
salt and black pepper
freshly grated Parmesan cheese
    to serve

Peel or scrape the carrot, wash the celery and chop both finely. Peel and finely chop the onion, turnip and potato.

Heat the butter or oil in a large, heavy-based pan and add the prepared vegetables, together with the peeled and crushed garlic. Fry the vegetables for a few minutes until they begin to soften, then add the hot stock. Bring to the boil, then cover the pan and simmer the soup over low heat for 15 minutes or until the vegetables are almost tender.

Skin the tomatoes (page 302); cut them in half, remove all seeds and chop up the tomato flesh. Trim the roots and coarse outer leaves from the leek, wash thoroughly under cold running water, then shred finely. Finely shred the cabbage or Brussels sprouts. Add the tomatoes, the

Minestrone.

leek and cabbage or sprouts to the pan; bring the soup back to the boil. Add the spaghetti, breaking it into small pieces, or the macaroni.

Simmer the soup, uncovered, over low heat for a further 10–15 minutes. Season to taste and serve with a bowl of grated Parmesan cheese.

STARTERS, SAVOURIES & LIGHT DISHES

Melon and Prawn Basket

SERVES: 8
PREPARATION: 20 minutes
CHILLING: about 1 hour

1 large melon
French Dressing (page 356)
675 g/1½ lb peeled cooked prawns
90 ml/6 tablespoons chopped celery
15 ml/1 tablespoon oil
5 ml/1 teaspoon curry powder
300 ml/½ pt soured cream
90 ml/6 tablespoons mayonnaise
grated coconut
Garnish
6 whole cooked prawns
Orange Butterflies (page 412)
1 bunch watercress

Cut a thin sliver off the base of the melon so that it stands steadily on a serving plate. To shape the basket, cut two wedges from the top, about a third of the way down into the fruit. Leave a 1–2.5 cm/½–1 in strip in place across the top of the fruit to form the handle. Cut the flesh from under the handle. Remove the pips and scoop the flesh out of the melon in balls. Toss the melon in the French dressing and set aside for 15 minutes. Drain the melon balls.

Mix the prawns with the celery and melon balls. Chill the mixture for about 30 minutes, or until ready to serve.

Melon and Prawn Basket.

Heat the oil in a small pan. Add the curry powder and cook gently, stirring, for 3 minutes. Remove from the heat and cool for a few minutes. Stir in the soured cream and mayonnaise. Chill until ready to serve. Gently stir the dressing into the prawn and melon mixture. Spoon the mixture into the basket, sprinkle with grated coconut and chill.

Garnish with prawns, orange butterflies and watercress. Serve within 1 hour of filling.

Duck Pâté

SERVES: 4
PREPARATION: 40 minutes
OVEN: 160°C/325°F/gas 3
COOKING: 1¼ hours

225 g/8 oz cooked meat from
    1 duck carcass or 1 boneless
    duck breast
100 g/4 oz minced pork
25 g/1 oz fresh white breadcrumbs
15 ml/1 tablespoon finely
    chopped onion
15 ml/1 tablespoon chopped chervil
30 ml/2 tablespoons
    chopped parsley
salt and black pepper
grated rind of ½ orange
15 ml/1 tablespoon brandy or
    dry sherry
1 egg
175–225 g/6–8 oz thin
    streaky bacon

Mince the duck coarsely. Mix with the minced pork, bread-crumbs, chopped onion, chervil and parsley. Season to taste with salt and freshly ground pepper. Stir in the grated orange rind and

brandy or dry sherry. Bind the pâté with the egg.

Cut the rind off the bacon and stretch the rashers with the back of a knife. Use to line a terrine or ovenproof dish. Spoon the pâté into the dish, pressing it down well. Fold the ends of the bacon rashers over the top. Put the dish in a roasting tin half filled with boiling water. Bake in a preheated oven at 160°C/325°F/gas 3 for 1¼ hours.

Potted Ham or Game

Potted meat is a 16th-century means of stretching leftovers.

SERVES: 4–6
PREPARATION: 10 minutes
COOKING: 5 minutes
CHILLING: 4–6 hours

275–350 g/10–12 oz cooked ham
    or game
pinch each of dried marjoram,
    thyme and mace
salt and black pepper
75 g/3 oz butter

Chop the meat and put it through the fine blade of a mincer twice. Season to taste with the herbs, mace, salt and pepper. Cook in 50 g/2 oz of the butter for about 5 minutes. Pack the meat into an earthenware jar or pot and set aside to cool.

Heat the remaining butter until foaming, strain through muslin and pour over the meat. Leave the pot in a refrigerator to set. The potted meat can be used for sandwich fillings, or served as a first course with hot toast.

Deep-fried Cheese Gnocchi

SERVES: 4
PREPARATION: 30 minutes
CHILLING: 2 hours
COOKING: 5 minutes

1 small onion
1 clove
1 bay leaf
6 parsley sprigs
600 ml/1 pt milk
175 g/6 oz Cheddar cheese
175 g/6 oz semolina
15 ml/1 tablespoon chopped parsley
salt and black pepper
cayenne pepper
1 egg
50 g/2 oz dry white or golden
    breadcrumbs
oil for deep frying

Peel the onion, leaving it whole, and stick the clove into it. Put the onion, bay leaf and parsley sprigs in the milk. Heat until almost boiling, then draw the pan off the heat, cover and leave to infuse for 15 minutes.

Grate the cheese. Strain and reheat the milk to boiling point. Sprinkle in the semolina, stirring continuously and cook for about 3 minutes until the mixture boils and becomes very thick. Draw the pan off the heat and stir in the grated cheese and chopped parsley; season to taste with salt, black pepper and cayenne pepper. Smooth this gnocchi mixture over a moistened dinner plate, shaping it into a neat circle. Chill for 1¼–2 hours.

Using a wet knife, cut the gnocchi into eight equal-sized

wedges, wiping and rinsing the knife after each cut. Beat the egg. Coat the wedges with the egg and then with the breadcrumbs. Shake off any loose crumbs.

Heat the oil for deep frying to 190°C/375°F or until a cube of day-old bread browns in 1 minute. Deep fry the gnocchi until crisp and golden, about 1–2 minutes. Drain them thoroughly on crumpled absorbent kitchen paper before arranging on a hot serving dish.

Gougère au Fromage

A gougère is a savoury choux pastry, flavoured with cheese. The paste is shaped in a ring or round, then cut into portions when served. Individual gougères are a traditional snack at wine tastings in the Burgundy region of France, where the round buns are served cold. The term is also used for savoury dishes consisting of a baked choux pastry border with a sauced filling.

SERVES: 4–6
PREPARATION: 15 minutes
OVEN: 220°C/425°F/gas 7
    190°C/375°F/gas 5
COOKING: about 45 minutes

150 ml/¼ pt water
100 g/4 oz butter
100 g/4 oz plain flour
5 ml/1 teaspoon salt
4 eggs
100 g/4 oz Gruyère cheese
egg and milk for glazing

Put the water in a heavy-based saucepan and add the butter, cut

into small knobs. Sift the flour and salt. Place the pan of water and butter over gentle heat; as soon as the butter has melted bring the contents to a brisk boil. Quickly tip in all the flour and, with a wooden spoon, beat for 1 minute over moderate heat until all the ingredients are thoroughly blended and the mixture leaves the sides of the pan clean. Allow to cool for about 15 minutes, so that the paste does not cook the eggs when they are added.

Beat the eggs, one at a time, into the paste. You must blend each one in thoroughly before adding the next. Continue to beat until the paste is smooth and glossy; it should be stiff enough to hold its shape when piped. Grate the Gruyère cheese and beat all but 25 g/1 oz into the choux paste.

Gougère au Fromage.

Grease and lightly flour a baking tray; trace a circle, about 20 cm/8 in across on it. Fit a large nylon piping bag with a 2.5 cm/1 in plain nozzle and fill the bag with the paste.

Pipe a circle of the choux paste on to the tray, following the guide line; if necessary, pipe a second layer on top or alongside the first to use up all the paste. Brush the surface with a lightly beaten egg mixed with a little milk; sprinkle with the rest of the cheese. Place in a preheated oven and bake for 15 minutes at 220°C/425°F/gas 7. Reduce the temperature to 190°C/375°F/gas 5 and cook for another 25–30 minutes. Lift from the baking tray on to a plate, and serve hot, warm or cold, cut in slices.

Smoked Haddock Mousse

SERVES: 6–8
PREPARATION: 45 minutes
CHILLING: 2–3 hours

900 g/2 lb smoked haddock fillet
1 small onion
450 ml/¾ pt milk
1 bay leaf
40 g/1½ oz butter
40 g/1½ oz plain flour
salt and black pepper
cayenne pepper
60 ml/4 tablespoons water
15 g/½ oz powdered gelatine
grated rind and juice of 1 lemon
300 ml/½ pt double cream
Aspic
30 ml/2 tablespoons water
2.5 ml/½ teaspoon powdered gelatine
15 ml/1 tablespoon lemon juice or vinegar
½ cucumber to garnish

Cut the haddock fillet into 8–10 pieces and put them in a saucepan; peel and slice the onion and add, with the milk and bay leaf, to the fish. Cover and simmer for about 10 minutes. Strain the fish through a colander and set the milk aside. Remove all skin and bones, and flake finely.

Melt the butter over low heat; stir in the flour and cook for a few minutes. Gradually stir in the milk, beating continuously to get a smooth sauce. Bring this to the boil and cook gently for 2–3 minutes. Season to taste with salt, pepper and cayenne. Pour the sauce into a large bowl, cover with buttered greaseproof paper and leave to cool. Pour the water into a small heatproof basin and sprinkle the gelatine over. Do not stir. Leave to stand for 15 minutes until the gelatine has absorbed the water. Set the basin over simmering water and stir until the gelatine has dissolved.

Remove the paper. Stir the sauce. Mix in the fish, gelatine and lemon rind and juice. Taste for seasoning. Whip the cream lightly and fold it into the mixture; pour into a 1.4–1.7 litre/2½–3 pt dish and chill until set.

For the aspic, pour the water into a small heatproof basin and sprinkle the gelatine over. Do not stir. Leave to stand for 15 minutes, until the gelatine has absorbed all the water. Set the basin over a pan of simmering water and stir until the gelatine has dissolved. Stir in the lemon juice or vinegar. Cool until the aspic is just beginning to set. Pour a little on top of the mousse. While this is setting, thinly slice the cucumber. Arrange the slices on the aspic. Spoon over the rest of the aspic and chill.

■ Serve with thin brown bread and butter or a green salad.

Goujons of Sole with Tartare Sauce

In France, small, smelt-like goujons or gudgeons are deep-fried and served like whitebait. The term 'goujons' is used for strips of thin fish fillets that are coated and deep fried in this way.

SERVES: 4
PREPARATION: 20 minutes
COOKING: 2–3 minutes

1 large Dover sole
flour
salt and black pepper
1 large egg
10 ml/2 teaspoons olive oil
golden breadcrumbs
oil for deep frying
Tartare Sauce
15 ml/1 tablespoon mayonnaise
15 ml/1 tablespoon double cream
5 ml/1 teaspoon chopped parsley
5 ml/1 teaspoon each chopped
   gherkins and capers
7.5 ml/1½ teaspoons chopped onion
lemon wedges to garnish

Goujons of Sole with Tartare Sauce.

Ask the fishmonger to skin and fillet the sole. Making a slanting cut, slice each fillet in half and then cut each half lengthways into three or four narrow strips.

Season a little flour with salt and freshly ground pepper to coat the fish thoroughly, shaking off any surplus. Beat the egg lightly and mix in the olive oil; dip the fish pieces in this mixture before rolling them in the breadcrumbs. Set the fish aside in a cool place.

For the tartare sauce, mix the mayonnaise, cream, parsley, gherkins, capers and onions. Spoon into a serving dish and chill.

Heat the oil for deep frying to 190°C/375°F or until a cube of day-old bread browns in 1 minute. Put the fish in the basket and lower it into the hot oil; fry for 2–3 minutes until crisp and golden brown. Drain the fish on layers of crumpled kitchen paper. Sprinkle with salt and pile the fish on to a hot serving dish. Garnish with wedges of lemon and offer the sauce separately.

■ A green salad and crusty bread could be served with the fried fish strips.

Prawns in Curry Sauce

SERVES: 2
PREPARATION: 20 minutes
COOKING: 5 minutes

2 small onions
15 ml/1 tablespoon olive oil
5 ml/1 teaspoon curry powder
15 ml/1 tablespoon plain flour
150 ml/¼ pt fish or chicken stock
5 ml/1 teaspoon tomato paste
5 ml/1 teaspoon mango chutney or
   apricot jam
juice of ½ lemon
25 g/1 oz butter
225 g/8 oz peeled cooked prawns
45 ml/3 tablespoons double cream

Peel and finely chop one of the onions. Heat the oil in a saucepan and add the onion. Cover and fry over low heat for 5 minutes or until the onion is soft, but not brown. Stir in the curry powder and fry gently for a few minutes; blend in the flour and cook for 2–3 minutes. Gradually add the fish or chicken stock and stir until the sauce thickens and comes to the boil. Add the tomato paste, chutney (or apricot jam) and lemon juice. Simmer for 5 minutes, then strain the sauce through a sieve.

Peel and finely chop the remaining onion. Heat the butter in a frying pan and fry the onion until they are soft, then add the prawns. Stir in the curry sauce and bring the mixture to the boil. Remove from the heat at once and stir in the cream.

■ Serve with plain boiled Basmati rice.

POULTRY & GAME

Chicken Pie

SERVES: 4
PREPARATION: 45 minutes
OVEN: 190°C/375°F/gas 5
COOKING: 1–1¼ hours

175 g/6 oz plain flour
pinch of salt
75 g/3 oz hard margarine
about 30 ml/2 tablespoons water
Filling
1 onion
2 boneless chicken breasts
100 g/4 oz streaky bacon
1 small red pepper
50 g/2 oz small button mushrooms
40 g/1½ oz butter
1 bay leaf
2.5 ml/½ teaspoon dried oregano
25 g/1 oz plain flour
60 ml/4 tablespoons dry white wine
60 ml/4 tablespoons milk
300 ml/½ pt water
black pepper
beaten egg or milk to glaze

Mix the flour and salt in a bowl. Rub in the margarine until the mixture resembles fine breadcrumbs. Add enough cold water, mixing it in with a knife, to bind the ingredients, then press together lightly. Wrap in cling film and leave in a cool place, but not in the refrigerator because the pastry will be too firm to roll out.

Peel and dice the onion; skin the chicken and cut it into cubes. Remove the rind from the bacon and cut it into small pieces. Core and deseed the pepper; cut it into dice. Trim the mushrooms. Melt the butter in a saucepan, add the onion and bay leaf, and cook gently for 5 minutes. Stir in the chicken and bacon and cook for a further 5 minutes, then add the red pepper, mushrooms and oregano and cook for a further 3 minutes.

Stir in the flour and cook for 1 minute, then add the white wine. Gradually add the water and milk, stirring constantly until the sauce comes to the boil. Reduce the heat and simmer for 5 minutes. Stir in salt and freshly ground black pepper to taste, then remove the bay leaf. Pour the mixture into a 900 ml/1½ pt pie dish. Allow to cool a little before covering with pastry.

Roll out the pastry on a lightly floured surface, 5 cm/2 in larger than the dish. Trim a 2.5 cm/1 in strip from the edge of the pastry. Dampen the rim of the dish and press on the pastry strip. Dampen the strip, cover with the pastry lid and press into position to seal the edges. Trim the pie, crimping the edges. Re-roll the trimmings and use to decorate the top. Brush with beaten egg or milk to glaze. Cook in a preheated oven at 190°C/375°F/gas 5 for 35–40 minutes until lightly browned.
Note The cooked pie may be frozen. For best results, dice the mushrooms instead of leaving them whole. Thaw the pie in the refrigerator overnight, then reheat thoroughly before serving.

Duck Breasts en Croûte

Duck breast portions are an easy-to-prepare alternative to a whole bird. Cook the breasts by frying them in a little butter, turning once. The liver may be omitted from the stuffing.

SERVES: 4
PREPARATION: about 1 hour
OVEN: 200°C/400°F/gas 6
COOKING: about 2 hours

1 × 2.27 kg/5 lb duck
25 g/1 oz lean bacon
1 duck liver
30 ml/2 tablespoons finely
    chopped onion
grated rind of 1 orange
25 g/1 oz butter
15 ml/1 tablespoon chopped
    green olives
10 ml/2 teaspoons brandy
salt and black pepper
15 ml/1 tablespoon chopped parsley
225 g/8 oz home-made Puff Pastry
    (page 374) or thawed frozen
    puff pastry
beaten egg to glaze

Roast the duck in a preheated oven at 200°C/400°F/gas 6 for 1½ hours. Set aside to cool. Cut the rind off the bacon and chop it finely. Chop the duck liver. Cook the bacon, liver, onion and grated orange rind in the butter for 5 minutes. Add the olives and brandy with salt and pepper to taste, and cook this mixture over moderate heat for about 5 minutes. Stir in the parsley.

Skin the duck and cut the breasts off in two whole portions. Set the duck carcass aside for making Duck Pâté (page 102). Cut each breast into two equal portions. Roll out the puff pastry to a 35 cm/14 in square and cut it into 4 squares. Lay a portion of duck on each pastry square, spread a little of the bacon and onion mixture over the duck and wrap the pastry round each to form a neat parcel.

Seal the joins with egg and place the parcels, seams up, on a wetted baking tray. Brush with egg and bake in a preheated oven at 200°C/400°F/gas 6 for about 25 minutes.

■　Serve with Savoury Orange Sauce (below).

Savoury Orange Sauce

MAKES: about 450 ml/¾ pt
PREPARATION: 10–15 minutes
COOKING: 5 minutes

300 ml/½ pt Espagnole Sauce
    (page 354)
juice of 1 orange
juice of ½ lemon
60 ml/2 fl oz red wine
30 ml/2 tablespoons
    redcurrant jelly
salt, cayenne pepper, sugar

Rub the Espagnole sauce through a fine sieve into a saucepan. Add the orange and lemon juices, the wine and jelly; heat the sauce through and season to taste with salt, cayenne and sugar. Pour into a sauceboat and serve with the duck breasts.

■　This savoury sauce also makes an excellent accompaniment to baked ham.

Pigeons with Forcemeat Balls

Young, tender pigeons can be roasted or grilled, but at this time of the year they are best used for a casserole.

SERVES: 6
PREPARATION: 1 hour
OVEN: 180°C/350°F/gas 4
COOKING: 1½ hours

100 g/4 oz streaky bacon
25 g/1 oz butter
3 pigeons
30 ml/2 tablespoons plain flour
450 ml/¾ pt hot chicken stock
    or water
salt and black pepper
1 bouquet garni*
12 button onions
225 g/8 oz mushrooms

Forcemeat Balls
100 g/4 oz fresh white breadcrumbs
15 ml/1 tablespoon finely
    chopped parsley
50 g/2 oz shredded suet
finely grated rind of ½ lemon
1–2 eggs
chopped parsley to garnish

Remove the rind and dice the bacon. Heat the butter in a deep, heavy-based pan. Fry the bacon over moderate heat until the fat runs and the bacon pieces are crisp. Remove the bacon from the pan with a perforated spoon and leave to drain on crumpled absorbent kitchen paper. Put the pigeons in the pan to brown them, turning them several times. Lift out the pigeons and put them in a casserole.

Stir the flour into the fat remaining in the pan and cook

gently for a few minutes until browned. Gradually stir in the hot stock and bring the sauce slowly to the boil, stirring continuously. Simmer for a few minutes, then strain the sauce over the pigeons in the casserole. Add the bacon pieces, the salt, a few twists of pepper and the bouquet garni. Peel the onions and add them whole to the pigeons. Cover the casserole and place in a preheated oven at 180°C/350°F/gas 4 for 1 hour.

Meanwhile, trim and finely slice the mushrooms. For the forcemeat balls, measure the breadcrumbs, chopped parsley, shredded suet, and lemon rind into a mixing bowl; season with salt and freshly ground pepper. Beat the eggs lightly and stir them into the mixture with a

Pigeons with Forcemeat Balls.

fork until the forcemeat has a moist, but not too wet, texture. Using the tips of the fingers, shape the forcemeat into 8–12 round balls and put these, together with the mushrooms, in the casserole. Replace the lid and continue cooking for 20 minutes until the pigeons are tender and the forcemeat balls cooked.

Lift the pigeons from the casserole, cut them in half and arrange them on a hot serving dish. Surround them with the mushrooms, onions and force-meat balls. Remove the bouquet garni from the sauce before pouring it over the pigeons. Garnish with chopped parsley.

■　Serve with Château Potatoes (page 347).

Casserole of Hare

In March, as the game season is coming to an end, hare is economical to buy. It needs marinating, however, for about 8 hours, to improve the flavour and to draw out the blood.

SERVES: 4–6
MARINATING: 8 hours
PREPARATION: 45 minutes
COOKING: 2–2½ hours

1 hare
3 onions
4 peppercorns
4 bay leaves
150 ml/¼ pt wine vinegar
750 ml/1¼ pt water
plain flour
salt and black pepper
50 g/2 oz butter
600 ml/1 pt light ale
juice of 1 lemon
1 sprig thyme
5 ml/1 teaspoon Dijon mustard
10 ml/2 teaspoons tarragon vinegar
30–45 ml/2–3 tablespoons
*   caster sugar*
8 soaked prunes
10 ml/2 teaspoons cornflour

Ask the poulterer to skin the hare and to joint it into eight evenly sized portions. Wipe the pieces of meat on absorbent kitchen paper and put them in a large bowl.

Peel and slice one of the onions, and add it, with the peppercorns and two bay leaves, to the hare joints. Mix the wine vinegar with the water and pour over the hare, to cover the pieces completely. Leave the hare in the refrigerator to marinate* for about 8 hours, turning the pieces of meat occasionally.

Lift the hare out of the marinade and dry the pieces thoroughly. Season a little flour with salt and freshly ground pepper and use to coat the hare pieces. Melt the butter in a large frying pan, add the hare and cook until evenly brown all over. Put the pieces of hare in a large saucepan or flameproof casserole. Strain the marinade and pour 150 ml/¼ pt of it over the meat.

Peel and finely chop the remaining two onions and add to the hare, together with the light ale, lemon juice, the remaining two bay leaves, thyme, mustard, vinegar and caster sugar; season to taste with salt and freshly ground black pepper. Bring the mixture to the boil; cover the pan and leave to simmer gently for 2 hours.

Add the soaked prunes to the casserole, or use the type that do not need soaking, and cook for a further 20 minutes, or until the hare is tender.

When the hare is cooked, blend the cornflour with a little water to a smooth paste. Add some of the hot liquid from the pan, blend thoroughly before stirring it into the liquid. Bring the mixture back to boiling point, stirring gently until the sauce has thickened.

Remove the pan from the heat, lift the pieces of hare and prunes on to a hot serving dish. Taste and adjust the seasoning, if necessary, and pour the sauce over the hare.

■   Serve with creamed potatoes and spring greens.

MEAT

Steak au Poivre

This classic steak is prepared with crushed whole peppercorns and is served with brandy sauce.

SERVES: 4
PREPARATION: 15 minutes
COOKING: 15–20 minutes

4 fillet or entrecôte steaks
30 ml/2 tablespoons whole black
*   peppercorns*
50 g/2 oz butter
15 ml/1 tablespoon olive oil
30 ml/2 tablespoons brandy
150 ml/¼ pt double cream
salt

Wipe the steaks on absorbent kitchen paper and trim off any fat. Crush the black peppercorns coarsely in a mortar or on a wooden board with a rolling pin. With the fingers, press the crushed peppercorns into the surface of the meat on both sides.

Heat the butter and oil in a heavy-based pan; cook the steaks over high heat for 2 minutes, turning them once. This initial hot frying seals the juices and peppercorns in the meat; lower the heat and cook the steaks for 5 minutes for rare steaks, 8–10 minutes for medium-rare and 12 minutes for well-done steaks.

Lift the steaks from the pan on to a hot serving dish; add the brandy to the butter in the pan

Steak au Poivre.

and set it alight when hot. Draw the pan off the heat and as soon as the flames have died down, gradually stir in the cream. Season the sauce with salt to taste and pour it over the steaks.

■   Freshly cooked broccoli and Potato Croquettes (page 347) or a green salad will go well with these steaks.

Boeuf Bourguignonne

SERVES: 6
PREPARATION: 30 minutes
OVEN: 150°C/300°F/gas 2
COOKING: 3 hours

900 g/2 lb top rump of beef
50 g/2 oz butter
15 ml/1 tablespoon olive oil
1 onion
15 ml/1 tablespoon plain flour
45 ml/3 tablespoons brandy
2 cloves garlic
1 bouquet garni*
salt and black pepper
1 bottle red wine
175 g/6 oz streaky bacon
20 small pickling onions
175 g/6 oz mushrooms
finely chopped parsley to garnish

Cut the meat into 5 cm/2 in cubes. Melt half the butter with the olive oil in a large, flame-proof casserole. Then add the meat and cook over high heat until browned.

Peel and finely slice the onion and add to the meat. Cook until transparent, sprinkle over the flour and continue cooking for a few minutes. Pour over the warmed brandy and set it alight.

Crush the garlic and add it to the pan with the bouquet garni, salt and black pepper. Pour over enough wine to cover the meat. Bring to simmering point, cover and cook in a preheated oven at 150°C/300°F/gas 2 for 2 hours.

Meanwhile, fry the bacon in the remaining butter until crisp, add the small onions and cook until golden, stirring often. Stir the contents of the pan into the casserole and continue cooking for 30 minutes. Slice the mushrooms and add to the casserole. Cook for another 15 minutes.

Remove the bouquet garni, sprinkle generously with finely chopped parsley and serve.

Paddington Puffs

Bought puff pastry is ideal for making these savoury pasties.

SERVES: 4
PREPARATION: 15 minutes
COOKING: 10–15 minutes

225 g/8 oz cooked meat, such as
  beef, lamb, pork or ham
100 g/4 oz lean bacon
50 g/2 oz mushrooms
25 g/1 oz white bread
2 sprigs parsley
1 small onion
40 g/1½ oz butter
15 ml/1 tablespoon tomato ketchup
  (optional)
salt and black pepper
275 g/10 oz home-made Puff
  Pastry (page 374) or thawed
  frozen puff pastry
oil for deep frying

Mince or finely chop the cooked meat, bacon, mushrooms, bread, parsley and peeled onion. Fry the minced mixture in the butter, for 5 minutes, stirring all the time to prevent it sticking to the pan. Stir in the ketchup (if used) and season to taste.

Roll out the pastry to make a 30 cm/12 in square; cut this into 4 strips, then cut in the opposite direction to make 16 squares, each about 7.5 cm/3 in square. Divide the filling between half the squares, placing it in a neat mound in the centre of each square, moisten the edges with water and cover with the rest of the squares. Seal the pastry edges firmly together.

Heat the oil for deep frying to 190°C/375°F or until a cube of day-old bread browns in 1 minute. Deep fry the puffs until they are golden, crisp and the pastry is well puffed. Turn them once or twice to cook the pastry evenly. Drain the pastry puffs thoroughly on absorbent kitchen paper and serve freshly cooked.

Alternatively, the puffs may be baked in a preheated oven at 225°C/425°F/gas 7 for about 25 minutes, until well puffed and golden brown. For a good colour, the pastry should be brushed with a little beaten egg before baking; milk may be used for a paler colour. Baked puffs may be served hot or cold.

Beef Kofta

SERVES: 4
PREPARATION: 20 minutes
COOKING: 55 minutes

2 green chillies
15 ml/1 tablespoon finely chopped
  onion
1 clove garlic
450 g/1 lb lean minced beef
salt and black pepper
2.5 ml/½ teaspoon ground
  cinnamon
10 ml/2 teaspoons ground cumin
1 large egg
60–75 ml/4–5 tablespoons
  ghee* or oil
2 onions
30 ml/2 tablespoons Garam
  Masala (page 239)
600 ml/1 pt fresh Coconut Milk
  (page 239)
lime or lemon juice

Cut the chillies in half, remove the seeds, stalk and pith, and chop the flesh finely. Mix the beef with the chopped chillies, chopped onion and crushed garlic. Season with salt, pepper, cinnamon and cumin, and bind with the beaten egg. Roll the mince into walnut-size meatballs or kofta. Wetting your hands under cold running water occasionally will prevent the meat mixture from sticking to them.

Heat 30–45 ml/2–3 tablespoons ghee and fry a few kofta at a time, turning them carefully, until evenly browned all over. Remove the fried balls and drain.

Thinly slice the 2 onions and fry over low heat in the ghee left in the pan, until it is soft and transparent. Mix in the garam masala and cook for a further 5 minutes, stirring. Gradually stir in the coconut milk, simmer for 2 minutes, correct seasoning, and sharpen with a dash of lime or lemon juice.

Return the kofta to the sauce and simmer gently for 25–30 minutes. Shake the pan gently from time to time.

■ Serve the spicy kofta with plain boiled Basmati rice and a vegetable such as spinach tossed with a little butter.

Moussaka

The aubergine – or egg plant – is the staple vegetable of the Middle East. It is the basic ingredient in this casserole, which usually includes minced beef or lamb.

SERVES: 4
PREPARATION: 45 minutes
OVEN: 180°C/350°F/gas 4
COOKING: 1¼–1½ hours

1 large onion
60–90 ml/4–6 tablespoons olive oil
450 g/1 lb lean minced beef
5 ml/1 teaspoon salt
10 ml/2 teaspoons tomato paste
150 ml/¼ pt beef stock or water
salt and black pepper
4 aubergines
25 g/1 oz butter
25 g/1 oz plain flour
300 ml/½ pt milk
1 egg

Peel and finely chop the onion; heat 15 ml/1 tablespoon of the oil in a heavy-based pan and gently fry the onion for about 5 minutes, covering the pan with a lid. Add the minced beef and fry until brown and thoroughly sealed. Stir in the salt, tomato paste and stock; season to taste with freshly ground pepper. Bring this mixture to the boil, reduce the heat and cover the pan. Simmer for 30 minutes or until the meat is tender and the liquid is almost absorbed.

Meanwhile, peel and thinly slice the aubergines. Layer them in a colander and sprinkle them generously with salt; let the aubergines stand for 30 minutes to draw out the bitter juices. Drain, rinse in cold water and pat thoroughly dry on absorbent kitchen paper. Fry the aubergine slices in the remaining oil until golden, then drain on absorbent kitchen paper. Arrange a layer of aubergines in the bottom of a large buttered ovenproof dish or casserole. Cover with a layer of the meat, then another layer of aubergines and so on, finishing with a layer of aubergines.

Melt the butter in a saucepan over low heat and stir in the flour. Cook gently for 1 minute, then gradually mix in the milk, stirring continuously. Bring this sauce to the boil, season with salt and freshly ground pepper and simmer for 1–2 minutes. Draw the pan off the heat and beat in the egg. Spoon this sauce over the moussaka; place in the centre of a preheated oven and bake at 180°C/350°F/gas 4 for 35–40 minutes or until bubbling hot and browned.

■ This is a rich and substantial meal, best served straight from the casserole. A tomato and onion salad could be served as an accompaniment.

107

Herby Scotch Eggs

Chopped herbs give simple Scotch eggs a lift in flavour. A quick alternative to adding herbs to the meat is to coat the Scotch eggs with packet stuffing mix instead of breadcrumbs.

SERVES: 4
PREPARATION: 20 minutes
COOKING: 5–10 minutes

30 ml/2 tablespoons chopped
    parsley
15 ml/1 tablespoon chopped
    fresh sage
5 ml/1 teaspoon dried thyme
225 g/8 oz sausagemeat
4 hard-boiled eggs
plain flour
beaten egg
40 g/1½ oz dry white breadcrumbs
oil for deep frying

Mix the fresh and dried herbs with the sausagemeat. Divide the sausagemeat into four equal pieces and shape each piece into a flat, round cake, about 10 cm/ 4 in wide.

Dust the eggs lightly with flour and wrap each one in the sausagemeat, moulding the meat evenly over the eggs and pressing the edges firmly together to make a smooth surface. Coat with flour, dip in beaten egg and roll the Scotch eggs in the dry breadcrumbs.

Heat the oil for deep frying to 190°C/375°F or until a cube of day-old bread browns in 1 minute. Fry the eggs until crisp and golden. Drain on absorbent kitchen paper and leave to cool. Cut the eggs in half to serve.

Fricadelles

These egg-shaped spicy mince balls appear regularly on the Danish family menu. They are usually served hot, with a sauce, but are also used, thinly sliced, as toppings for open sandwiches.

SERVES: 4
PREPARATION: 30 minutes
OVEN: 180°C/350°F/gas 4
COOKING: 30 minutes

450 g/1 lb lean veal
1 small onion
5 ml/1 teaspoon chopped parsley
1.25 ml/¼ teaspoon dried thyme
1.25 ml/¼ teaspoon ground mace
    or grated nutmeg
salt and black pepper
2 thin slices white bread
15–30 ml/1–2 tablespoons milk
1 small egg
30 ml/2 tablespoons flour
300 ml/½ pt Tomato Sauce
    (page 354)
50 g/2 oz butter

Trim any fat from the veal and put the meat through the fine blade of the mincer. Peel and finely chop the onion. Put the minced beef in a bowl and add the onion, parsley, thyme, mace or nutmeg and salt and pepper.

Trim off the bread crusts and soak the bread in the milk for a few minutes, then squeeze out the excess liquid. Mash the bread with a fork, and add it to the meat, together with the lightly beaten egg. Pound the ingredients together thoroughly, using the back of a mixing spoon until the mixture is firm. Shape the mixture into 10–12 ovals.

Season a little flour with salt and freshly ground black pepper and use it to coat the fricadelles lightly. Set the meatballs aside while you prepare the tomato sauce. Now melt the butter in a heavy-based pan and fry the meatballs over high heat until they are evenly brown. Turn the fricadelles once only.

Lift the fricadelles from the pan with a perforated spoon and put them in an ovenproof dish. Pour over the hot tomato sauce, cover the dish and cook for 15–20 minutes in a preheated oven at 180°C/350°F/gas 4.

■ Boiled potatoes and broccoli can be served with this dish.

Navarin of Lamb

Navarin is a French cooking term applied exclusively to a casserole of lamb, or mutton, and young root vegetables. Loin can be used, but best end of neck is also suitable and less expensive.

SERVES: 4
PREPARATION: 30 minutes
OVEN: 160°C/325°F/gas 3
COOKING: 1¾ hours

900 g/2 lb best end neck of lamb
flour
salt and black pepper
25 g/1 oz dripping or 30 ml/
    2 tablespoons vegetable oil
450 g/1 lb young carrots
1 onion
450 ml/¾ pt chicken or beef stock
15 ml/1 tablespoon tomato paste
1 bouquet garni*
8 small button onions
8 small new potatoes
chopped parsley to garnish

Ask the butcher to cut the meat into single rib pieces. Trim any fat from the meat. Season a little flour with salt and freshly ground pepper and use it to coat the pieces. Melt the fat in a large frying pan and add the meat. Fry as many ribs as possible at one time, turning them to brown evenly on both sides. Remove from the pan and put them in a large casserole. Scrape and thinly slice the carrots, and peel and roughly chop the onion. Add the carrots and onion to the fat remaining in the pan. Fry for 10 minutes, then transfer the vegetables to the casserole with a perforated spoon. Drain off most of the fat from the frying pan. Stir in 15 ml/1 tablespoon of the seasoned flour; cook over low heat for a few minutes to brown, then gradually stir in the hot stock. Add the tomato paste and bring the sauce to the boil.

Navarin of Lamb.

Draw the pan off the heat and strain the sauce into the casserole; season with salt and freshly ground pepper. Add the bouquet garni. Cover the casserole and place in a preheated oven at 160°C/325°F/ gas 3. Cook the dish for 1¼ hours.

Peel the button onions, leaving them whole. Put them in a saucepan and cover with cold water. Bring this to the boil, then drain the onions at once. Scrape the new potatoes and add, with the onions, to the casserole, placing them on top of the meat. Replace the lid and cook for a further 30 minutes or until the vegetables are tender.

At the end of this time, take out the bouquet garni, sprinkle with chopped parsley and serve the lamb navarin straight from the casserole.

VEGETABLES & SALADS

Swiss Rosti

This potato cake should be made from potatoes boiled in their skins and allowed to cool, preferably overnight. It is usually served with grilled or fried bacon, eggs and sausages.

SERVES: 4
PREPARATION: 30 minutes
COOLING: 12 hours
COOKING: 30–40 minutes

900 g/2 lb potatoes
50–75 g/2–3 oz butter
salt and black pepper

Scrub the potatoes and put them in a saucepan. Pour in cold water to cover and add salt to taste. Bring to the boil. Boil for about 10 minutes, until the potatoes are parcooked. Drain and leave until completely cold, preferably overnight. Skin the potatoes and grate them coarsely.

Melt the butter in a large, heavy-based pan. Add the grated potatoes, sprinkle with salt and freshly ground pepper. Fry the potatoes over moderate heat, stirring to coat the potatoes in butter, then continue to cook for about 15 minutes.

As the potatoes start to go brown underneath, turn them with a spatula. Press down gently on the potato mixture to form a pancake and cook, without turning or stirring, until the pancake becomes crisp and brown on the underside.

Just before serving, loosen the cake with the spatula, place a round serving plate over the pan, and invert the potato cake on to it. Serve at once.

Savoury Potato Pancakes

This is a substantial vegetable dish on its own. The pancakes also go well with grills, fried sausages and bacon.

SERVES: 4–6
PREPARATION: 20 minutes
COOKING: 15 minutes

675 g/1½ lb potatoes
1 small onion
100 g/4 oz corned beef
2 rashers streaky bacon
salt and black pepper
40 ml/1½ tablespoons plain flour
1 egg
oil for frying

Grate the potatoes on the coarse blade of a grater. Place them in a sieve and rinse well under cold running water. Press out as much water as possible with the back of a mixing spoon. Put the potatoes into a bowl. Grate the onion and flake the corned beef. Dice the bacon and add to the bowl with some salt and pepper. Blend the flour into the egg, add to the potato mixture and stir well.

Heat a little oil in a heavy-based pan until it is hot. Drop spoonfuls of mixture well apart in the pan, then flatten them neatly into round cakes, about 7.5 cm/3 in wide. Cook over medium heat until the cakes are browned and crisp underneath. Turn them over carefully and cook the other side until brown and crisp. Drain on crumpled absorbent kitchen paper and keep the first batch warm while frying the remaining potato pancakes.

Aubergines with Yogurt

SERVES: 4–6
PREPARATION: 40 minutes
COOKING: about 10 minutes

2 aubergines
salt
75 g/3 oz ghee* or butter
oil
300 ml/½ pt plain yogurt
1–2 cloves garlic

Cut the washed and dried aubergines crossways into thin slices. Layer the slices in a colander, sprinkling each layer with salt. Leave to stand for 30 minutes to draw out the bitter juices. Rinse in cold water and dry on absorbent kitchen paper.

Heat about a third of the ghee or butter with enough oil to cover the base of a large frying pan. Fry the aubergines, in single layers, until golden on both sides. Add more ghee or butter and oil as necessary. Drain on crumpled absorbent kitchen paper and arrange the fried aubergines on a serving dish. Serve cold with a separate dressing made by crushing the garlic into the yogurt and stirring well.

Creamed Mushrooms

SERVES: 4
PREPARATION: 10 minutes
COOKING: 8–10 minutes

450 g/1 lb button mushrooms
45 ml/3 tablespoons olive oil
15 ml/1 tablespoon plain flour
60 ml/4 tablespoons dry white vermouth
200 ml/7 fl oz fromage frais or single cream
30 ml/2 tablespoons chopped tarragon
salt and black pepper

Trim the mushroom stalks level with the caps. Heat the oil in a large frying pan, add the mushrooms and stir to coat them in the oil. Cook for 3 minutes until the juices start to run, then stir in the flour and cook for 3 minutes. Stir in the vermouth and bring to the boil, stirring.

Reduce the heat to the minimum setting and stir in the fromage frais or cream. Heat through, stirring, until smooth, but do not allow the mixture to boil. Remove the pan from the heat and add the chopped fresh tarragon with seasoning to taste. Serve immediately.
■   The creamed mushrooms may be served on toast, with pasta or as a filling for baked potatoes.

Creamed Mushrooms.

Glazed Carrots

Towards the end of the month, the first young carrots appear. The full flavour of these tender vegetables is retained by cooking them in a buttery glaze. They are suitable for serving with thick meat casseroles, and with roast lamb and pork as well as with grilled chops.

SERVES: 4
PREPARATION: 10 minutes
COOKING: 20–25 minutes

450 g/1 lb young carrots
25 g/1 oz butter
salt and black pepper
5 ml/1 teaspoon caster sugar
5 ml/1 teaspoon chopped parsley

Scrub and scrape the carrots and cut them into slices about 5 mm/ ¼ in thick. Melt the butter in a saucepan, add the carrot slices and season with the freshly ground pepper and the sugar.

Add sufficient cold water to just cover the base of the pan. Bring to the boil, cover the pan tightly and cook for about 10 minutes, shaking the pan every now and then. Keep the lid on the pan to retain the moisture from the steam.

Remove the lid and check the carrots for cooking progress: they should be only just tender but with a bit of crunch. Increase the heat and cook the carrots until the liquid has evaporated and only the butter remains. Stir frequently and do not allow the carrots to brown. Draw the pan off the heat; add the parsley and toss with the glazed carrots.

Broccoli Spears au Gratin

The purple or white sprouting winter broccoli requires under-cooking to preserve its flavour. The spears can be served tossed in butter or, as here, in a sauce.

SERVES: 6
PREPARATION: 10 minutes
COOKING: 15 minutes

salt and black pepper
675 g/1½ lb broccoli spears
60 ml/4 tablespoons grated
* Parmesan cheese*
300 ml/½ pt thick coating White
* Sauce (page 352)*
50 g/2 oz butter
60 ml/4 tablespoons fresh white
* breadcrumbs*

Bring a saucepan of salted water to the boil. Cut away all coarse leaves from the broccoli and trim the stalks. Wash well. Add the broccoli to the water and bring quickly back to the boil. Simmer for 5–12 minutes, according to the size of the spears, until the broccoli is just tender.

Meanwhile, stir the grated Parmesan cheese into the sauce and set the grill to high.

Drain the broccoli well and place in a shallow gratin dish or flameproof dish. Pour over the white sauce to coat the broccoli. Melt the butter in a small pan, mix in the breadcrumbs and cook for 2 minutes, stirring. Sprinkle them over the broccoli. Grind a little pepper over the top and place under the grill for a few minutes until the crumbs are golden brown.

Black-eye Bean Gratin

This tasty gratin can be made with any canned pulses, like chick peas or soya, haricot or flageolet beans; it is easy to prepare and looks appetising. Make small quantities in shell dishes, ramekins or individual gratin dishes if you want to serve the dish as a first course.

SERVES: 4
PREPARATION: 15 minutes
COOKING: 25–30 minutes

225 g/8 oz mushrooms
2 courgettes
1 onion
1 clove garlic
30 ml/2 tablespoons olive oil
400 g/14 oz can chopped tomatoes
2 × 400 g/14 oz cans
* black-eye beans*
salt and black pepper
50 g/2 oz Cheddar cheese
50 g/2 oz fresh breadcrumbs
15 ml/1 tablespoon chopped
* fresh sage or 5 ml/1 teaspoon*
* dried sage*

Thinly slice the mushrooms and courgettes, and finely chop the onion and garlic. Heat the oil in a saucepan, add the onion and garlic and cook, stirring now and then, for 15 minutes. Add the mushrooms and courgettes, and cook for a further 5 minutes, then stir in the tomatoes and drained black-eye beans. Add seasoning to taste and bring the mixture to the boil. Reduce the heat slightly, so that the mixture does not boil too rapidly, then cover the pan and cook for 5 minutes.

Meanwhile, grate the cheese and mix it with the breadcrumbs and sage. Transfer the bean mixture to a gratin dish and top with the breadcrumb mixture. Brown the topping under a hot grill, then serve at once.

Carrot and Gruyère Soufflé

A purée of carrots perfectly complements the slightly dry flavour of Gruyère cheese in this light soufflé, and a crunchy topping of breadcrumbs and walnuts adds an unusual variation in texture.

SERVES: 4
PREPARATION: 30 minutes
OVEN: 190°C/375°F/gas 5
COOKING: 1 hour 10 minutes

225 g/8 oz carrots
salt and black pepper
150 g/5 oz Gruyère cheese
25 g/1 oz butter
25 g/1 oz plain flour
150 ml/¼ pt milk
5 eggs, separated
40 g/1½ oz fresh white
* breadcrumbs*
30 ml/2 tablespoons finely
* chopped walnuts*

Peel and slice the carrots, place them in a saucepan and add a little salt, then pour in enough water to cover the vegetables. Bring to the boil, reduce the heat slightly and cook for 15 minutes, or until the carrots are tender. Drain the carrots well, mash them and press them through a sieve or purée them in a food processor or liquidiser.

Grate the cheese and set aside 25 g/1 oz for the topping. Melt the butter in a large saucepan. Stir in the flour, then gradually add the milk, stirring vigorously at first, then beating the sauce as it thickens. Bring the sauce to the boil and cook for 1 minute, stirring continuously. Beat well to make sure there are no lumps and then remove the pan from the heat. Beat in the cheese and the carrots, then add the egg yolks and two-thirds of the breadcrumbs. Season the mixture well and beat the ingredients until they are thoroughly combined.

Grease an 18 cm/7 in soufflé dish. Whisk the egg whites until they are stiff but not dry. Beat about a quarter, or slightly less, of the egg white into the carrot mixture. Then use a large metal spoon to fold in the remaining white. Transfer the mixture to the soufflé dish, levelling the top lightly. Run the tip of your finger inside the rim of the dish to make a shallow 'gutter' in the mixture. Mix the remaining cheese and breadcrumbs with the walnuts. Sprinkle this mixture evenly over the top of the mixture, avoiding the rim, then bake the soufflé in a preheated oven at 190°C/375°F/gas 5 for 45–50 minutes, until well risen, golden and just firm to the touch. Serve immediately.

Mixed Vegetable Curry

SERVES: 4
PREPARATION: 15 minutes
COOKING: 30 minutes

2–3 cloves garlic
30 ml/2 tablespoons Garam
  Masala (page 239)
juice of ½ lime or lemon
45 ml/3 tablespoons ghee*
1 onion
3 or 4 tomatoes
caster sugar
350 g/12 oz potatoes
225 g/8 oz green beans
225 g/8 oz peas
salt

Crush and pound the garlic, and mix it into a smooth paste with the garam masala and lime or lemon juice.

Heat the ghee and fry the paste over low heat for 5 minutes, stirring constantly. Peel and chop the onion; add it to the paste and cook for a further 2 minutes. Skin the tomatoes (page 302), chop them roughly and stir in to the onions with a pinch of sugar and 30–45 ml/2–3 tablespoons water. Cook for 5 minutes.

Peel and dice the potatoes; slice the beans and add with the potatoes and peas; season with salt and pour over enough water to barely cover the vegetables. Bring to the boil, then lower the heat and simmer, covered, until the potatoes are cooked, after 15–20 minutes.

■ Serve the curry with warmed nan bread and grated cucumber in plain yogurt.

Aubergine and Tomato Ragoût

SERVES: 4
PREPARATION: 20 minutes
STANDING: 30 minutes
COOKING: 40–45 minutes

2 large or 3 small aubergines
salt and black pepper
1 large onion
1 clove garlic
25 g/1 oz butter
5 ml/1 teaspoon fennel seeds
400 g/14 oz can chopped tomatoes
5 ml/1 teaspoon caster sugar

Peel the aubergines and cut them into 2.5 cm/1 in chunks. Layer the aubergine chunks in a colander, sprinkling each layer with salt. Leave to stand for 30 minutes. Rinse the aubergine under cold water, drain and pat dry on absorbent kitchen paper.

Peel and thinly slice the onion. Peel and crush the garlic. Melt the butter in a saucepan, add the onion, garlic and fennel seeds, and cook over low heat for about 10 minutes until the onion is soft, but not brown. Add the aubergine, stir in the tomatoes and season with salt, freshly ground pepper and the sugar. Heat until just boiling, reduce the heat, cover the pan and simmer for 30 minutes, stirring once or twice. Taste for seasoning before serving.

■ Serve the ragoût with grilled or roast lamb, pork or gammon. It may be used to fill baked potatoes or top pasta. Grated Parmesan cheese may be offered with the ragoût and pasta.

Cous Cous with Vegetables

SERVES: 4
PREPARATION: 30 minutes
COOKING: 1 hour

1 large aubergine
salt and black pepper
1 large onion
2 celery sticks
1 green chilli
2 cloves garlic
75 ml/3 fl oz olive oil
1 bay leaf
2 potatoes
1 green pepper
1 red pepper
2 courgettes
5 ml/1 teaspoon dried oregano
15 ml/1 tablespoon ground
  coriander
2 × 400 g/14 oz cans chopped
  tomatoes
2 × 400 g/14 oz cans chick peas
225 g/8 oz cous cous
25 g/1 oz butter
60 ml/4 tablespoons chopped
  parsley or mint
mint sprigs to garnish

Cut the ends off the aubergine, then cut it into 2.5 cm/1 in chunks. Place the pieces in a colander, sprinkling the layers with salt, and leave to stand over a bowl for 30 minutes. Chop the onion and dice the celery. Cut the chilli in half, cut out the stalk, pith and seeds, then rinse the flesh under cold water. Chop the chilli and the garlic.

Heat the oil in a large saucepan or flameproof casserole and add the onion, celery, garlic, chilli and bay leaf. Cook gently while preparing the remaining ingredients. Peel the potatoes and cut them into chunks. Halve the green and red peppers, cut out the stalks, pith and seeds, then dice the flesh. Thickly slice the courgettes. Drain, rinse and dry the aubergine on absorbent kitchen paper.

Add the aubergine, potato and peppers to the onion mixture and cook, stirring, for 5 minutes. Stir in the courgettes, oregano, coriander, tomatoes and drained chick peas. Add seasoning to taste and heat until simmering. Cover and cook gently for 30 minutes, stirring once.

Place the cous cous in a heatproof bowl to fit on top of the cooking pan instead of the lid. Pour in freshly boiling water to cover the cous cous by about 1–2.5 cm/½–1 in; if the cous cous

Cous Cous with Vegetables and Split Pea Biriani (page 113).

forms a shallow layer in a large bowl, then it does not have to be covered by as great a volume of water as when it is placed in a smaller bowl. Stand the bowl over the pan and cover it with a plate or lid. Continue cooking the vegetables for another 20 minutes, by which time the cous cous will have absorbed all the water – the reason for standing the cous cous over the pan is simply to keep it hot.

Fork the butter into the cous cous and transfer it to a warmed large serving bowl, spreading it in a narrow ring. Taste the vegetables for seasoning and stir in the parsley or mint, then pour into the middle of the cous cous. Garnish with mint sprigs.

RICE & PASTA

Almond Rice

SERVES: 4
PREPARATION: 5 minutes
COOKING: 25 minutes

1 onion
25 g/1 oz butter
175 g/6 oz long-grain rice
25 g/1 oz raisins
450 ml/¾ pt chicken stock
2.5 ml/½ teaspoon salt
50 g/2 oz flaked almonds
15 ml/1 tablespoon chopped
    parsley to garnish

Peel and finely chop the onion.
Melt the butter in a saucepan
and add the onion; cover the pan
and cook over low heat for about
5 minutes until the onion is
transparent. Add the rice and stir
it lightly until the grains are
coated with butter. Stir in the
raisins and add the hot stock and
salt. Bring to the boil, stir the rice
once, then reduce the heat to the
lowest setting and cover tightly.
Cook the rice for 15 minutes,
then turn off the heat and leave
it to stand without removing the
lid, for another 10 minutes.

Meanwhile, put the almonds
in a small heavy-based saucepan
or frying pan and cook them over
gentle heat, shaking the pan
frequently, until they are lightly
browned. Fluff up the rice with a
fork, fold in the almonds and
serve sprinkled with parsley.

■ Almond Rice is a useful
accompaniment for fish, poultry
and meat dishes.

Sprouting Broccoli with Fresh Pasta

SERVES: 4
PREPARATION: 20 minutes
COOKING: 15 minutes

450 g/1 lb sprouting broccoli
6 spring onions
100 g/4 oz Lancashire, Cheshire or
    Wensleydale cheese
25 g/1 oz butter
45 ml/3 tablespoons olive oil
45 ml/3 tablespoons pine kernels
salt and black pepper
350 g/12 oz fresh pasta shapes
    or tagliatelle

Trim any tough stalks off the
broccoli, leaving only the tender
stems and the sprouting ends.
Trim and thinly slice the spring
onions. Coarsely grate or finely
crumble the cheese. Heat the
butter and olive oil together in a
large saucepan, then add the
pine kernels and cook them
gently until lightly browned. Stir
in the spring onions and leave
over low heat.

Bring a large pan of salted
water to the boil, add the
broccoli and cook for 5 minutes,
or until just tender. Use a slotted
spoon to remove the broccoli
from the pan and transfer it to
the spring onion mixture. Top up
the water in the large pan if
necessary, then bring it back to
the boil. Add the pasta, bring the
water back to the boil once
again, and reduce the heat to
prevent it from boiling over.
Cook the pasta for about 3
minutes, until tender but not
soft. Drain well.

Stir the broccoli and spring
onion mixture, adding seasoning
to taste. Toss the pasta with the
broccoli, then turn it into a
warmed serving dish. Top with
the cheese and serve at once.

*Sprouting Broccoli with
Fresh Pasta.*

Cannelloni Stuffed with Spinach

Literally 'big pipes', cannelloni
are pasta tubes, about 7.5 cm/3 in
long and 2.5 cm/1 in across. They
are filled with a savoury stuffing
and served with tomato sauce.

SERVES: 4
PREPARATION: 45–60 minutes
OVEN: 180°C/350°F/gas 4
COOKING: 45–60 minutes

450 g/1 lb fresh spinach
225 g/8 oz cooked chicken
25 g/1 oz butter
25 g/1 oz plain flour
200 ml/7 fl oz milk
salt and black pepper
8 cannelloni tubes
450–600 ml/¾–1 pt Tomato
    Sauce (see Stuffed Peppers
    with Pork and Beef, page 229)
75–100 g/3–4 oz grated
    Parmesan cheese

Wash the spinach thoroughly
and put it in a large saucepan –
no water is needed. Cover and
cook the spinach gently for about
10 minutes, shaking the pan
every now and then. Drain the
spinach through a colander,
squeezing down firmly with the
back of a spoon to remove all
the moisture. Chop the spinach
coarsely and set it aside.

Dice the chicken flesh finely
or put it through a mincer.

Melt the butter in a saucepan
and stir in the flour; cook gently
for 1 minute, then gradually stir
in the milk, stirring continuously
until the mixture boils and
thickens to make a smooth sauce.
Season to taste with salt and
freshly ground black pepper, then
simmer gently for 2–3 minutes.
Take the pan off the heat and stir
the spinach and chicken into the
sauce; check seasoning.

Put the cannelloni tubes in a
pan of boiling water and boil for
10 minutes or until the pasta is
just tender. Drain, rinse with
cold water and drain again.
Spoon or pipe the spinach and
chicken mixture into the tubes.

Arrange the cannelloni in a
buttered ovenproof dish, pour
the tomato sauce over them and
sprinkle with half the grated
cheese. Place the casserole in a
preheated oven and cook at
180°C/350°F/gas 4 for 20–30
minutes or until bubbling hot
and brown. Serve at once, with
the remaining cheese in a bowl.

Split Pea Biriani

Paneer, an Indian cheese, is a cross between a hard cheese and cream cheese. It has a firm texture similar to mozzarella but it is not as moist. It can be cut into cubes and fried, forming a deep golden crust on the outside and softening in the middle without actually melting.

SERVES: 4
PREPARATION: 15 minutes
COOKING: about 40 minutes
STANDING: 10 minutes

100 g/4 oz yellow split peas
225 g/8 oz Basmati rice
2 large onions
2 cloves garlic
1 green chilli (optional)
25 g/1 oz fresh root ginger
25 g/1 oz butter
15 ml/1 tablespoon cumin seeds
1 cinnamon stick
6 green cardamoms
1 bay leaf
salt and black pepper
900 ml/1½ pt water
4 hard-boiled eggs
¼ cucumber
5 ml/1 teaspoon Garam Masala
  (page 239)
Fried Paneer
225 g/8 oz paneer
25 g/1 oz butter
flat-leafed parsley to garnish
  (optional)

Place the yellow split peas in a saucepan with plenty of water to cover and bring to the boil. Reduce the heat, part-cover the pan and cook for 15 minutes, then drain the peas well. While the peas are cooking, place the rice in a basin and pour in cold water to cover, swirl the rice gently, let it settle, then pour off the water. Repeat this process of rinsing the rice twice more, then leave it to soak in cold water.

Halve and thinly slice the onions; crush the garlic. Cut the stalk and seeds from the chilli (if used), rinse it under cold water, then chop the flesh. Peel and chop or finely dice the ginger.

Melt the butter in a large saucepan. Add the onions, garlic, chilli, ginger, cumin, cinnamon, cardamoms and bay leaf. Stir well, then cook for 10 minutes, stirring often. Drain the rice and add it with the peas. Stir in salt and pepper to taste, then pour in the water. Bring to the boil, stir once, then cover the pan tightly and reduce the heat to the lowest setting. Leave the biriani to cook for 20 minutes. Remove the pan from the heat and leave it without removing the lid for a further 10 minutes.

Shell and roughly chop the eggs. Peel and dice the cucumber and mix it with the garam masala. If using the paneer, cut it into 1–2.5 cm/½–1 in cubes. Melt the butter in a frying pan and add the paneer. Leave to cook over medium heat for a few minutes, until golden brown underneath, then cook the second side.

Fork the rice mixture, adding the fried paneer (if used), and turn it into a warmed serving dish. Garnish with the cucumber and eggs and serve at once. The cinnamon stick and bay leaf may be removed or picked out to form part of the garnish for the dish, and a parsley sprig may be added.

Glazed Lemon Tart

The fresh flavour of this tart is ideal after a rich main course.

SERVES: 6
PREPARATION: 45 minutes
STANDING: 30 minutes
OVEN: 190°C/375°F/gas 5
COOKING: about 50 minutes
CHILLING: 55–60 minutes

175 g/6 oz Shortcrust Pastry
  (page 365)
15 ml/1 tablespoon plain flour
50 g/2 oz ground almonds
50 g/2 oz unsalted butter
50 g/2 oz caster sugar
1 egg
grated rind of 1 lemon
5 ml/1 teaspoon natural vanilla
  essence
Topping
1 lemon
150 ml/¼ pt boiling water
225 g/8 oz caster sugar

Prepare the topping first. Scrub the lemon thoroughly and cut it into thin slices, discarding ends and pips. Place the slices in a bowl and pour in the water. Allow to stand for 30 minutes. Then drain the lemon and pour the water into a saucepan. Add the sugar and heat, stirring, until it has dissolved. Bring to the boil, then reduce the heat and add the lemon slices to the syrup. Cook the lemon gently for about 15 minutes until tender. If the syrup boils, the centres of the lemon slices will disintegrate. Remove from the heat and let the slices cool in the liquid.

Roll out the pastry and use to line a 18–20 cm/7–8 in flan tin. Prick the base with a fork. Line the pastry case with greaseproof paper and sprinkle with dried beans or baking beans. Bake in a preheated oven at 190°C/375°F/gas 5 for 10 minutes.

Mix the flour and ground almonds. Beat the butter and sugar until soft and light. Beat the egg lightly and stir it into the butter mixture with the grated lemon rind and vanilla essence. Stir in the plain flour and ground almonds. Spread this mixture evenly over the pastry base. Replace the tart in the oven and bake for a further 25–30 minutes or until the filling is golden brown and firm to the touch. Leave to cool.

Carefully lift the soft lemon slices out of the syrup using a perforated spoon and arrange them on the tart. Bring the syrup to the boil and boil it hard for 1 minute, then spoon it over the lemon slices. Leave to cool and chill for 1–2 hours.

Glazed Lemon Tart.

Crème Brûlée

SERVES: 4
PREPARATION: 15 minutes
COOKING: about 20 minutes
CHILLING: 6–15 hours

600 ml/1 pt double cream
8 egg yolks
15 ml/1 tablespoon caster sugar
2.5 ml/½ teaspoon natural
*   vanilla essence*
about 75 g/3 oz caster sugar

Put the cream in the top half of a large double boiler or in a bowl over a pan of gently simmering water. Beat the egg yolks with the caster sugar and vanilla essence, then stir carefully into the warm cream. Continue cooking, stirring continuously, until the custard has become thick enough to coat the back of a wooden spoon. Do not allow the water in the saucepan to boil as this will overheat the custard and make it curdle. Cooking the custard for too long will also make it curdle. Strain the custard through a fine sieve into a soufflé dish or individual dishes which may be placed under the grill. Leave to cool, then chill for several hours or overnight; the custard must be chilled for at least 4 hours.

Cover the top of the cold custard with a thick, even layer of sugar. The exact amount will depend on the size of the dish. Press it down well. Preheat the grill, then place the dish or

Crème Brûlée.

dishes under the heat and cook the sugar until it melts and caramelises. Watch the crème brûlée carefully to prevent it from burning. If the grill is hot enough, and the custard well chilled in advance, the sugar will form a golden layer before the custard has time to do more than run slightly. Cool and chill for 2–3 hours before serving.

Zabaglione

This Italian dish is probably a more popular sweet in countries outside its homeland, where it is chiefly served as a tonic. It is quickly made, but care must be taken to prevent it from curdling while cooking.

SERVES: 4
PREPARATION: 5 minutes
COOKING: 5–7 minutes

4 egg yolks
50 g/2 oz caster sugar
90 ml/3 fl oz Marsala wine
sponge fingers to serve

Put the egg yolks in a mixing bowl, together with the sugar and Marsala wine. Place the bowl over a saucepan half filled with water that has been kept simmering. Whisk the egg mixture continuously over the heat until it is thick and fluffy (about 5–7 minutes). On no account must the egg mixture reach boiling point.

Remove the bowl from the heat and pour the thickened mixture into warmed serving glasses. Serve at once, with sponge fingers.

Velvet Cream

The Elizabethans invented the syllabub – a frothy mixture of sherry, sugar and cream. Velvet Cream is adapted from the original recipe and is a compromise between a syllabub and a whipped jelly.

SERVES: 6
PREPARATION: 40 minutes
CHILLING: about 3 hours

15 g/½ oz powdered gelatine
150 ml/¼ pt water
50 g/2 oz caster sugar
rind of 1 lemon
150 ml/¼ pt medium dry sherry
300 ml/½ pt double cream
crystallised violets to decorate

Sprinkle the gelatine over the water in a small heatproof basin. Do not stir. Leave to stand for 15 minutes until the gelatine has absorbed the water.

Set the basin over a pan of simmering water and add the sugar and the finely grated lemon rind. Stir until both the sugar and the gelatine have dissolved completely.

When the gelatine mixture is cold and beginning to thicken, add the medium dry sherry and mix thoroughly.

Whip the double cream until it is thick, then gradually add the gelatine mixture to the cream. Continue whipping until the cream mixture is thick and beginning to set. Pour the velvet cream into serving glasses and chill for 2–3 hours.

Before serving, decorate each glass with crystallised violets.

Fig Pie

In Lancashire, a fig pie was traditionally served in March on Mothering Sunday. This was the only day on which Lenten fasting could be broken.

SERVES: 6
PREPARATION: 45 minutes
OVEN: 200°C/400°F/gas 6
COOKING: 30 minutes

175 g/6 oz Shortcrust Pastry
*   (page 365)*
225 g/8 oz no-need-to-presoak
*   dried figs*
450 ml/¾ pt water
15 ml/1 tablespoon cornflour
2.5 ml/½ teaspoon ground
*   mixed spice*
25 g/1 oz currants
10 ml/2 teaspoons treacle or
*   golden syrup*

Roll out the pastry on a floured surface, to a thickness of 3mm/⅛ in. Line a deep 20 cm/8 in pie plate with the pastry. Line the pastry with greaseproof paper and cover with dried beans or ceramic baking beans. Bake in a preheated oven at 200°C/400°F/gas 6 for 15 minutes. Meanwhile, place the figs and water in a saucepan. Bring to the boil, turn down the heat and simmer for 10 minutes. Use a perforated spoon to lift the figs from the cooling liquid. Mix the cornflour to a paste with a little cold water (about 15 ml/1 tablespoon), then pour in some of the fig cooking liquor, stirring all the time. Pour the cornflour mixture back into the saucepan and bring to the boil, stirring all the time, then cook for another 2 minutes. Mix in the spice, currants and syrup and remove from the heat.

Remove the baking beans and paper from the pastry case. Arrange the figs over the pastry; pour over the thickened fig liquid, making sure that the currants are evenly distributed. Bake the pie in a preheated oven at 200°C/400°F/gas 6 for about 30 minutes.

■ Serve hot or cold, with cream or Vanilla Ice Cream (page 380).

Marquise Alice

The classic features of Escoffier's set cream dessert are the praline flavouring and the cream and redcurrant jelly decoration.

SERVES: 6
PREPARATION: 1 hour
CHILLING: about 4 hours

100 g/4 oz blanched almonds
175 g/6 oz caster sugar
150 ml/¼ pt water
15 g/½ oz powdered gelatine
4 egg yolks
450 ml/¾ pt milk
8–10 sponge fingers
30 ml/2 tablespoons rum
450 ml/¾ pt double cream
30 ml/2 tablespoons
  redcurrant jelly

Toast the almonds under a moderately hot grill, turning occasionally, until golden. Place 100 g/4 oz of the sugar in a saucepan with half the water and heat, stirring gently, until the sugar has dissolved. Stop stirring and bring the syrup to the boil, then boil hard until it forms a deep golden caramel. Meanwhile, lightly oil a baking tray. As soon as the caramel is ready, add the toasted almonds and turn it out on to the prepared baking tray. Leave until cold, then crush the nuts and caramel with a rolling pin or in a food processor.

Sprinkle the gelatine over the remaining water in a small heat-proof basin. Do not stir. Leave to stand for 15 minutes, until the gelatine has absorbed the water. Set the basin over a pan of simmering water and stir until the powdered gelatine has dissolved completely.

In a mixing bowl, beat the egg yolks with the remaining sugar until light and creamy. Heat the milk until just about to boil, then allow it to cool for a few seconds before gradually stirring it into the eggs. Strain this custard into a saucepan and cook very gently for 2 minutes without boiling. Remove from the heat and stir in the dissolved gelatine. Pour the custard into a bowl, allow to cool, then chill briefly until it is on the point of setting and beginning to thicken.

Meanwhile, place the sponge fingers on a plate and spoon the rum over them. Whip 150 ml/¼ pt of the cream until thick and fold it into the custard. Fold in the crushed nut mixture. Pour half the mixture into a 1.12 litre/2 pt soufflé dish or charlotte mould. Cover with the sponge fingers, cutting some of them to fill any spaces. Pour in the remaining praline custard mixture and chill until set.

Slide a knife around the edge of the mixture to loosen it from the dish or mould, then dip the base in hot water for a few seconds. Invert the mould on to a serving plate and carefully lift it off the marquise. Whip the remaining cream and spoon half of it into a piping bag fitted with a large star nozzle. Cover the top of the marquise with the whipped cream, then pipe swirls around the edge.

Melt the redcurrant jelly in a small saucepan over low heat. Pour it into a small greaseproof paper piping bag or use a spoon to trickle the jelly over the cream swirls or in neat lines across the top of the dessert. Chill until ready to serve.

Banana Charlotte Russe

SERVES: 6
PREPARATION: 45 minutes
CHILLING: 2 hours

1 packet lemon or lime jelly
150 ml/¼ pt boiling water
300 ml/½ pt cold water
5 large bananas
24–26 sponge fingers
juice of ½ lemon
450 ml/¾ pt double cream

Break the jelly into pieces and place in a bowl. Add the freshly boiling water and stir until the jelly has dissolved. Add the cold water. Spoon a little of the jelly into the base of a 20 cm/8 in round, deep cake tin or an 18 cm/7 in charlotte mould (a charlotte mould is deeper than a cake tin – about 10 cm/4 in in depth). Chill until set.

Peel one of the bananas and cut half of it into even, thin rounds; arrange them in a neat circle around the edge of the jelly. Spoon over a little more citrus jelly, being careful not to disturb the banana slices. Chill again until the jelly has set. Stand the sponge fingers closely together, with the sugared sides towards the sides of the tin, around the inside of the tin.

Mash the remaining bananas with the lemon juice. Whip the double cream until thick. Stir in the rest of the jelly which by now should be beginning to set and should resemble a thick syrup in texture. Then fold the mashed bananas into the cream and jelly

Banana Charlotte Russe and Marquise Alice.

mixture. Spoon this into the cake tin or charlotte mould and chill until set firm.

Just before serving, trim the tops of the sponge fingers level with the filling; dip the base of the tin in hot water for a few seconds to loosen it. Place a round serving dish over the tin, invert it and lift the tin away.

Decorate the Charlotte Russe by tying a ribbon around it. This is also a useful way of ensuring that the side of the Marquise Alice (left) does not bulge slightly after it has been standing for some time.

115

A Chinese Meal

Throughout the centuries, the art of Chinese cooking has required infinite patience and attention to detail. This is because the main aim of the cuisine is to achieve a perfect composition of ingredients, while preserving the individual crisp or soft textures of the component parts and enhancing their natural flavours.

In China, a meal served at home consists of several dishes which are arranged on the table like a buffet. The dining table is laid with rice bowls, chopsticks and china spoons, and savoury soup or green tea is drunk throughout the meal.

At parties and banquets, the food is served dish after dish. A traditional Manchu banquet would include 300 dishes; even in modern China, official state banquets seldom have fewer than a dozen dishes. Wine is served at such occasions, usually yellow wine, the best known of which is Shao Shing (a traditional rice wine). For Western tastes, however, dry, light white wines are recommended with Chinese food. (See pages 413–416 for information on choosing wine.)

This menu, for six people, is composed for a Chinese meal at home, with all the dishes served at the same time. Sweet and Sour Pork and Chicken with Water Chestnuts (page 145) can be served with rice and a savoury cucumber soup. Toasted fish and spare ribs are served first, on their own, with wine. The meal concludes, in true Chinese fashion, with a pure, simple dish, in this case, Quick-fried Spinach. Desserts are seldom served in China, except at banquets, but a fruit salad from Peking has been included here.

Using Chopsticks

Place one chopstick where the thumb and forefinger meet. Rest it between the third and little finger. Hold the second chopstick between the thumb and forefinger. Use the middle finger to move the second chopstick up and down.

以 食 為 天

To eat is heaven! – Confucius

Chicken and Cucumber Soup

Good-quality chicken stock cubes can be used, though real home-made stock is best.

SERVES: 4
PREPARATION: 5 minutes
COOKING: 10 minutes

600 ml/1 pt stock from Spare Ribs Hoisin
600 ml/1 pt well-flavoured chicken stock
2 slices of fresh root ginger
45 ml/3 tablespoons dry sherry
½ cucumber
light soy sauce

The pork and chicken stocks can be clarified (page 311), if liked; alternatively strain them through a muslin-lined sieve into a saucepan. Peel the ginger and cut it into fine shreds; add to the stock with the sherry.

Cut the cucumber in half, scoop out the seeds in the centre, then cut into 5 cm/2 in long, thin strips. Add the strips to the soup with soy sauce to taste and simmer gently for 10 minutes to allow the flavours to mingle. Serve at once, spooning a few cucumber strips into each bowl.

Clockwise from centre top: *Fried Rice (page 132); Sweet and Sour Pork; bowls of mustard white wine vinegar, chilli and soy sauces to season the spare ribs if liked; Chicken and Cucumber Soup; Chicken with Water Chestnuts (page 145); and Fish Toasts. In the centre, Quick-fried Spinach, with Spare Ribs Hoisin.*

Fish Toasts

SERVES: 4
PREPARATION: 30 minutes
COOKING: 5–8 minutes

450 g/1 lb plaice fillets
salt and black pepper
5 ml/1 teaspoon lemon juice
5 ml/1 teaspoon sesame oil
15 ml/1 tablespoon egg white
5 thick slices white bread
sesame seeds (optional)
oil for shallow frying

Skin the plaice fillets or ask the fishmonger to do this for you. Pound the fish, using a mortar and pestle, until very fine or process in a food processor. Stir in a little salt and pepper, the lemon juice, sesame oil and egg white. Remove the crusts from the bread and divide the fish mixture between each slice, spreading it evenly over the bread. Sprinkle a few sesame seeds over the fish, if liked.

Heat a little oil in a frying pan. Add as many slices as the pan will hold, placing them bread side down. Cook for about 3 minutes or until golden, then turn the slices over carefully and fry for a few minutes more until the fish topping is cooked. Remove the toasts with a fish slice and keep hot while cooking the remaining slices.

Cut each slice of toast into small squares and serve.

Sweet and Sour Pork

SERVES: 6
PREPARATION: 20 minutes
MARINATING: 30 minutes
COOKING: about 20 minutes

675 g/1½ lb lean boneless pork
60 ml/4 tablespoons soy sauce
5 ml/1 teaspoon sesame oil
60 ml/4 tablespoons dry sherry
30 ml/2 tablespoons white
wine vinegar
1 onion
1 green pepper
1 carrot
30 ml/2 tablespoons cornflour
30 ml/2 tablespoons oil
20 ml/4 teaspoons tomato paste
15 ml/1 tablespoon sugar
227 g/8 oz can pineapple chunks
in syrup

Cut the pork into 1–2 cm/½–¾ in cubes. Mix the soy sauce, sesame oil, sherry and wine vinegar in a basin. Add the pork and mix well, then cover and set aside to marinate* for 30 minutes.

Meanwhile, peel the onion and cut it into 1–2 cm/½–¾ in chunks, then separate the layers into pieces. Remove the stalk from the green pepper, cut it in half and discard the seeds and pith from inside, then cut the flesh into similar-sized pieces. Cut the carrot into 2 cm/¾ in lengths, then slice the pieces lengthways.

Drain the meat, reserving the marinade, and place it in a clean bowl. Sprinkle the cornflour over the meat and mix it well to coat the pieces evenly. Heat the oil in a large frying pan or wok. Stir fry the meat for 5–7 minutes, or until evenly browned. Add the onion, pepper and carrot and continue stir frying for a further 5–7 minutes, until the vegetables are lightly cooked.

Pour in the reserved marinade, then stir in the tomato paste, sugar and pineapple chunks with their syrup. Simmer for 5 minutes, stirring continuously.

Spare Ribs Hoisin

SERVES: 4
PREPARATION: 25 minutes
MARINATING: 45 minutes
OVEN: 200°C/400°F/gas 6
COOKING: 25 minutes

900 g/2 lb pork spare ribs
1.12 litres/2 pt water
Marinade
5 ml/1 teaspoon five-spice powder
90 ml/6 tablespoons Hoisin sauce
30 ml/2 tablespoons oil
10 ml/2 teaspoons lemon juice
60 ml/4 tablespoons clear honey
2 cloves garlic

Place the spare ribs in a saucepan with the water, bring slowly to the boil, then cook gently for 25 minutes. Remove the ribs and arrange in a single layer in a small roasting tin. Strain the stock, reserving 600 ml/1 pt for the soup.

Mix all the marinade ingredients together. Spoon the marinade over the ribs, cover and place in the refrigerator for 45 minutes, turning once.

Cook in a preheated oven at 200°C/400°F/gas 6 for 25 minutes, until browned. Serve piping hot.

Quick-fried Spinach

SERVES: 6
PREPARATION: 3–4 minutes
COOKING: 4–5 minutes

675 g/1½ lb fresh spinach
2 cloves garlic
45 ml/3 tablespoons vegetable oil
45 ml/3 tablespoons soy sauce
5 ml/1 teaspoon caster sugar

Wash the spinach thoroughly in several changes of clean water; drain well. Remove the tough midribs and any bruised leaves. Peel the garlic and crush.

Heat the oil in a large saucepan; add the garlic and all the spinach, stirring it constantly in the hot oil for 3 minutes. Stir in the soy sauce and sugar and continue cooking, turning all the time, for another 2 minutes. Serve immediately.

Ice-mountain Fruit Salad.

Ice-mountain Fruit Salad

SERVES: 8
PREPARATION: 20 minutes

crushed ice
fresh and canned fruit: lychees,
guavas, ginger in syrup,
strawberries, oranges,
mangoes, pineapple,
black grapes
preserving sugar

Drain or clean the various fruits thoroughly, and cut them into small chunks or slices. Arrange the fruit in an attractive colour pattern on a bed of crushed ice. For a special occasion, build the ice up into a miniature ragged mountain and set the fruit on the mountain ledges. To serve, place saucers of sugar on the table. The fruit is dipped into the sugar before it is eaten.

117

APRIL

Avocado and Citrus Salad, Soused Herrings, Rhubarb Crumble.

April

This month brings a culinary change of pace, as fresh produce and quick-cooked dishes replace the long-stewed hotpots of winter. Easter is the focus for seasonal celebrations, with hot cross buns on Good Friday and simnel cake for tea on Easter Sunday. Then there are chocolate Easter eggs which will make any child's day, especially when they have to be hunted out from secret hiding places in the garden. Spring lamb is the speciality for April, when the mouth-watering aroma of a succulent roast and freshly chopped mint fill the kitchen. Welsh and English lamb are prime quality, with the former renowned for its excellent flavour. In spite of the year-round availability of salad potatoes from all over the world, home-grown new potatoes are the essential accompaniment for this traditional first roast lamb of the year, and the combination tastes very special.

Hot-house French beans and salad vegetables, including Chinese leaves, peppery herb-like rocket, and British spinach are now available. Home-grown globe artichokes are still around, usually until June. They are ideal as a light first course or as a main ingredient for a salad to serve with grilled lamb cutlets.

From the fishmonger, Dover and lemon sole are both good value for money in April, while mussels and crab are also on offer. The catch of huss is usually building up at this time of year, but herring and mackerel are often in short supply. Fish is generally a good choice as a main ingredient in April, for lighter meals that are in keeping with both the milder weather and the wish to pay attention to the diet after the indulgences of winter. Together with traditional dishes, this chapter introduces a few alternative ideas for making the best of April produce by tossing together a crunchy stir fry or serving the occasional vegetarian meal.

Menu suggestions Cooking for the Easter weekend is the high point of this chapter, with traditional baking recipes as well as a mouth-watering lunch menu for Easter Sunday. The following suggestions offer ideas for both everyday and special occasions. All the main recipes will be found in the chapter or elsewhere in the book when page references are given.

Simple Supper
~

Imam Bayildi
Turkish Fried Carrots
(page 254)
~
Lamb and Lemon Soup
with Warm Crusty Bread
~
Feta Cheese and Fresh Fruit
~
Coffee and Turkish Delight

This peasant-style menu combines Greek and Turkish recipes in a starter of two vegetable dishes followed by a hearty soup for the main course. Begin the evening by offering small glasses of aniseed-flavoured ouzo with bowls of cucumber sticks, olives and salted almonds as appetisers. Bowls of Turkish delight – as popular in Greece as in their country of origin – are served with coffee after cheese and fruit.

Spring Dinner Party
~

Spinach Ramekins (page 224)
~
Lamb Kebabs
Minted New Potatoes
with Peppers
Green Salad
~
Gâteau St Honoré
or
Biscuit Tortoni (page 155)
~
Cheese Board with Fresh Fruit

The first course and dessert can be made in advance, but two of the main-course dishes will need some attention. Make the green salad and prepare the dressing before guests arrive, ready to be mixed just before serving. Two desserts are included, one a pastry and the other an ice cream; however, the ice cream could be replaced by a bowl of fresh fruit.

Vegetarian Buffet Lunch

Guacamole (page 184)
with
Crudités and Tortilla Chips
~
Cheese and Tomato Roulade
served on a Green Salad
Sauce Vinaigrette
(page 356)
Artichokes with Mushrooms
~
Hot New Potatoes with
Chopped Mint
~
Hungarian Hazelnut Torte
(page 257)
Brandied Apricot Trifle
(page 174)

A cold cheese and tomato roulade makes an easily prepared, colourful and tasty centrepiece for the buffet table. A bowl of buttery, hot new potatoes is the perfect accompaniment: they can be cooked ahead until three-quarters tender, then transferred to a suitable serving dish for heating in the microwave just before serving. This way they will reach tender perfection without having to be boiled at the last minute. If you do not have a microwave, cook the potatoes through, drain them and reheat them in a heatproof serving bowl over a pan of simmering water. The guacamole should not be made too early on as it will discolour on standing. Make it shortly before the guests are due to arrive and cover the bowl with cling film.

Simnel cake (page 136).

SOUPS

Hearty Fish Soup

SERVES: 6–8
PREPARATION: 35 minutes
COOKING: 45 minutes

225 g/8 oz each of grey mullet,
  whiting and plaice fillets
1 large onion
1 clove garlic
90 ml/6 tablespoons olive oil
400 g/14 oz can tomatoes
30 ml/2 tablespoons tomato paste
15 ml/1 tablespoon chopped parsley
900 ml/1½ pt Fish Stock
  (page 310) or water
150 ml/¼ pt dry white wine
1 bay leaf
pared rind of ½ lemon
salt and black pepper
60 ml/2 fl oz double cream
Garnish
tomato slices
peeled cooked prawns

Skin the fish (page 314), using the skin and any trimmings as a base for the fish stock, if liked. Cut the fish fillets diagonally into 5 cm/2 in pieces. Peel and finely chop the onion. Crush the garlic. Heat the oil in a heavy-based pan and cook the onion until soft, but not browned. Add the garlic and fry for 1–2 minutes before adding the tomatoes with their juice, the tomato paste and chopped parsley. Mix well, bring to the boil, then lower the heat and simmer for 15 minutes. Add the fish, the stock or water, wine, bay leaf and lemon rind. Bring back to simmering point, cover and cook for 20 minutes. Discard the bay leaf and lemon rind. Season to taste and leave the soup to cool slightly before liquidising it until smooth.

Stir in the cream and re-heat the soup without bringing it to the boil. Float slices of tomatoes, garnished with a few peeled prawns, on top of each bowl.

Lamb and Lemon Soup

This Greek soup is thick and meaty; almost a meal in itself.

SERVES: 6
PREPARATION: 15 minutes
STANDING: 3–4 hours
COOKING: 3¼ hours

900 g/2 lb scrag end of neck of
  lamb, chopped
2 carrots
1–2 turnips
2 onions
2 leeks
1 stick celery
1 sprig parsley
2 bay leaves
2.5 ml/½ teaspoon dried
  oregano or thyme
2.5 ml/½ teaspoon dried marjoram
50 g/2 oz pearl barley or
  long-grain rice
salt and black pepper
juice of 1 lemon
2 egg yolks
shredded lettuce to garnish

Trim as much fat as possible from the lamb, put the meat into a large saucepan with the water and bring to the boil. While the meat is boiling, wash and scrape the carrots and turnips and chop them roughly; peel and roughly chop the onions. Trim the leeks and clean them by rinsing them under cold running water. Scrub the celery stick and chop this and the leeks roughly.

Remove any scum from the liquid in the pan. Add the vegetables to the lamb, together with the herbs and barley (if using rice, add this 1 hour later). Season to taste with salt and freshly ground pepper. Cover the pan and simmer the soup for 2–2½ hours, or until the meat comes away from the bones.

Remove the bay leaves and parsley and lift out the meat. Leave the soup to simmer while picking the meat off the bones. Chop up the lamb and return it to the pan.

Remove the soup from the heat and allow it to get cold (if possible refrigerate overnight). Lift off the fat which has solidified in a layer on top of the soup. Bring the soup back to the boil and, just before serving, beat the lemon juice and the egg yolks together in a small bowl. Mix in 45–60 ml/3–4 tablespoons of the hot soup and stir this mixture back in to the pan; heat the soup through without boiling.

Serve the soup sprinkled with finely shredded lettuce.

Kashmiri Yogurt Soup

SERVES: 4
PREPARATION: 45 minutes
CHILLING: 30 minutes

1 cucumber
salt
1 clove garlic
15 ml/1 tablespoon white
  wine vinegar
900 ml/1½ pt plain yogurt
15 ml/1 tablespoon olive oil
15 ml/1 tablespoon finely
  chopped mint

Peel the cucumber and dice it finely. Place the diced cucumber in a dish, sprinkle with salt and leave for 30 minutes. Peel and halve the garlic. Rub the inside of a large serving bowl with the cut garlic. Rinse the bowl with the vinegar, and shake it out. Spoon the plain yogurt into the mixing bowl and stir. Drain the cucumber, rinse under cold water and drain again. Stir into the yogurt and chill for 30 minutes. Just before serving, add the olive oil, a few drops at a time, stirring after each addition. Sprinkle the soup with mint and serve.

Kashmiri Yogurt Soup and Walnut and Parsley Bread (page 397).

STARTERS, SAVOURIES & LIGHT DISHES

Danish Liver Pâté

The inexpensive pig liver is not used very much for grilling or frying, but it is ideal for a pâté. This pâté should be left to cool under a heavy weight before serving. It will keep for up to a week in the refrigerator.

SERVES: 6–8
PREPARATION: 35 minutes
OVEN: 160°C/325°F/gas 3
COOKING: 2 hours
CHILLING: 12 hours

300 ml/½ pt milk
1 onion
1 bay leaf
175 g/6 oz fat back bacon rashers
450 g/1 lb pig liver
6 anchovy fillets
salt and black pepper
2.5 ml/½ teaspoon grated nutmeg
1.25 ml/¼ teaspoon each ground
    cloves and allspice
25 g/1 oz butter
25 g/1 oz plain flour
1 egg
228 g/8 oz streaky bacon rashers

Place the milk in a saucepan. Peel the onion and cut in half; add it, with the bay leaf, to the milk and bring to the boil over gentle heat. Remove the pan from the heat and allow the milk to infuse for 15 minutes. Strain through a sieve and set the milk aside while you prepare the meat.

Trim the rind from the back bacon rashers and remove any skin from the liver. Mince the bacon, the liver and anchovy fillets finely. Mix the ingredients thoroughly and season to taste with salt, freshly ground pepper and the spices.

Melt the butter in a saucepan, add the flour and cook over low heat for 1 minute; gradually add the milk, stirring continuously. Bring the mixture to the boil and cook for 2–3 minutes. Draw off the heat and blend in the liver mixture. Lightly beat the egg and stir it into the liver mixture.

Line a 450 g/1 lb loaf tin with the bacon, leaving the rashers to hang over the edges. Spoon the pâté mixture into the tin and fold the bacon over the top.

Cover the tin with a piece of buttered greaseproof paper and place in a large roasting pan containing 2.5 cm/1 in of cold water. Put in a preheated oven and bake for 2 hours at 160°C/325°F/gas 3. The pâté is ready when a stainless steel skewer inserted in it comes away clean.

Remove the pâté from the oven, cover with freshly buttered greaseproof paper and place a heavy weight on top. Leave the pâté until quite cold, then chill it overnight, or at least 12 hours, before turning it out.

■ Serve the pâté, cut into thick slices, with hot toast and butter.

Artichokes with Mushrooms

SERVES: 6
PREPARATION: 25 minutes
COOKING: 25–45 minutes

6 large globe artichokes
12 large mushrooms
1 clove garlic
90 ml/6 tablespoons white
    wine vinegar
salt and black pepper
90 ml/6 tablespoons olive oil

Trim off the artichoke stems (page 342) and rinse the artichokes thoroughly under cold running water. Put them in a large saucepan of boiling water, cover and boil for 25–45 minutes, depending on the size of the artichokes, until a leaf pulls away easily. Remove the artichokes, drain them upside-down and leave to cool.

Trim the mushrooms; cut them into slices, discarding the stalks. Peel and crush the garlic. Whisk the garlic, vinegar, salt and pepper together in a small bowl. Gradually whisk in the oil. Add the mushroom slices to the dressing, turning them gently to coat then evenly.

Pull off and discard all the leaves and the fine filaments from the base of the artichokes. Set the artichoke bottoms on individual serving plates, and arrange the mushroom slices on top; pour over any garlic dressing remaining in the bowl.

Artichokes with Mushrooms.

Avocado and Citrus Salad

SERVES: 6
PREPARATION: 30 minutes

juice of ½ lemon
2.5 ml/½ teaspoon caster sugar
10 ml/2 teaspoons chopped mint
salt and black pepper
45 ml/3 tablespoons grapeseed or
    sunflower oil
3 large avocados
1 large grapefruit
1 large orange
mint sprigs to garnish

First make a dressing by whisking the lemon juice, caster sugar, mint and seasoning together until the sugar has dissolved. Gradually whisk in the oil.

Cut the avocados in half and remove the stones. Cut the avocado halves in half again, so that the peel can be removed easily by starting it off with the point of a knife. Cut the flesh into thin sections and place in a bowl. Pour the dressing over. Cut a slice from top and bottom of the grapefruit and orange so that they stand flat on a board. Cut downwards, in narrow strips, to remove peel and pith. With a sharp knife cut between the segment membranes to remove the flesh, working over the bowl containing the avocados so that no juice is wasted. Add the grapefruit and orange segments to the bowl.

Arrange the avocado, citrus fruits and dressing on individual serving dishes or plates and garnish with sprigs of mint.

Cheese and Tomato Roulade

SERVES: 6
PREPARATION: 1 hour
OVEN: 200°C/400°F/gas 6
COOKING: about 1 hour

4 eggs
75 g/3 oz mature Cheddar cheese
25 g/1 oz butter
15 g/½ oz plain flour
150 ml/¼ pt milk
100 g/4 oz fresh white breadcrumbs
Filling
1 small onion
1 small carrot
1 stick celery
25 g/1 oz butter
1 bay leaf
100 g/4 oz mushrooms
15 ml/1 tablespoon tomato paste
10 ml/2 teaspoons plain flour
400 g/14 oz chopped tomatoes
salt and black pepper
30 ml/2 tablespoons
    chopped parsley
5 ml/1 teaspoon chopped tarragon

Prepare the filling before making the roulade. Finely chop the onion, then dice the carrot and celery. Melt the butter in a small saucepan, add the prepared vegetables and bay leaf, and cook, stirring occasionally, for 10 minutes. Roughly chop the mushrooms, add to the pan and continue to cook for 10 minutes, stirring occasionally. Stir in the tomato paste, then the flour, and cook for 2 minutes. Stir in the tomatoes and seasoning. Bring to the boil, reduce the heat slightly and allow the mixture to bubble steadily for 20 minutes, stirring occasionally. The mixture needs to be reduced and thickened. Remove the pan from the heat, stir in the parsley and tarragon, and set the mixture aside until the roulade is cooked.

Line and grease a 33 x 23 cm/ 13 x 9 in Swiss roll tin, making sure that the lining paper stands above the rim of the tin by 2.5 cm/1 in. Separate the eggs, placing the whites in a large, clean bowl. Grate the cheese. Melt the butter in a fairly large saucepan. Stir in the flour, then gradually stir in the milk and bring the mixture to the boil to make a thick sauce. There is no need to simmer this. Beat in the cheese, then remove the pan from the heat as soon as most of the cheese has melted. Beat in the egg yolks.

Whisk the whites until they stand in stiff but not dry peaks. Mix the breadcrumbs into the cheese sauce, working quickly once they are incorporated as they will quite rapidly absorb moisture and the mixture will be too thick if left to stand. Beat in about a quarter of the egg whites to lighten the mixture, then use a large metal spoon to fold in the remaining whites. Turn the mixture into the prepared tin, spread it out evenly and bake for 20 minutes in a preheated oven at 200°C/400°F/gas 6.

Meanwhile, dampen a clean tea-towel and lay it on the work surface. Place a sheet of grease-proof paper on top of the tea towel. Remove the bay leaf and gently reheat the tomato mixture. When the roulade is golden brown, risen and springy to the touch, turn it out on to the paper-topped tea-towel. Remove the lining paper from the roulade and trim off any crisp edges. Make a shallow cut into the roulade, across the narrow end, and spread the filling over the top. Roll up the roulade from the cut end, tucking the edge in neatly. Use the paper and tea-towel to roll it up neatly. Leave the roulade covered for 1 minute, then remove the tea-towel and paper and use a serrated knife to slice the roulade. Serve at once.

Scrambled Eggs with Smoked Salmon

This is an easily prepared first course for lunch or dinner.

SERVES: 6
PREPARATION: 8 minutes
OVEN: 200°C/400°F/gas 6
COOKING: 25 minutes

175 g/6 oz butter
8 × 1 cm/½ in thick slices of
    white bread
1 pepper (green or red)
7 eggs
3 tablespoons double cream
salt and black pepper
100 g/4 oz smoked salmon,
    shredded
Garnish
red or green pepper, deseeded
    and sliced
6 sprigs parsley
watercress
12 black olives, stoned

Melt 100 g/4 oz of the butter. With a plain or fluted 7.5 cm/

Scrambled Eggs with Smoked Salmon.

3 in pastry cutter, cut six rounds from the bread slices. Cut the other two slices into 1 cm/½ in fingers. Brush the bread rounds and slices with the melted butter and then bake for about 20 minutes in a preheated oven at 200°C/400°F/gas 6, until crisp and golden. Remove the baked rounds and keep them warm on a serving dish.

Meanwhile, remove the seeds from the pepper and chop it coarsely. Melt half the remaining butter in a pan and slowly cook the chopped pepper in it for 15 minutes. Drain on absorbent kitchen paper and keep hot.

Beat the eggs lightly and stir in the cream, black pepper, salt and shredded salmon.

Melt the remaining butter in a large, heavy-based pan over low heat and pour in the egg and salmon mixture. Stir gently and continuously until the eggs are lightly set and creamy. Remove the pan from the heat and quickly arrange the soft scramble over the six rounds of bread.

Scatter the drained pepper over the scrambled eggs and garnish with sprigs of parsley. Decorate the serving dish with thin slices of red and green pepper, small bunches of water-cress and some stoned black olives. Serve with the extra fried bread fingers.

123

Kidney Scramble

SERVES: 4
PREPARATION: 10 minutes
COOKING: 10–15 minutes

4 lamb kidneys
25 g/1 oz butter
1.25 ml/¼ teaspoon
    Worcestershire sauce
5 ml/1 teaspoon tomato ketchup
1.25 ml/¼ teaspoon made
    English mustard
salt and black pepper
6 eggs
60 ml/4 tablespoons milk
4 slices buttered toast

Prepare the kidneys (page 334) and chop them finely. Melt half the butter and fry the kidneys over high heat until lightly browned. Stir in the sauces and mustard; season with salt and pepper and cook over a moderate heat for a further 2 minutes. Keep the kidneys warm.

Lightly beat the eggs with the milk; season. Melt the remaining butter in a clean pan, and cook the eggs over low heat, stirring continuously, until creamy and just beginning to set. Spoon the eggs on to the toast and top with the kidneys. Serve at once.

Club Sandwiches

This triple-decker sandwich is one of America's best-known culinary inventions.

SERVES: 4
PREPARATION: 15 minutes
COOKING: 5 minutes

4 small tomatoes
8 rashers streaky bacon
12 slices white bread
50 g/2 oz butter
8 small lettuce leaves
8 thin slices cooked chicken
    or turkey
45 ml/3 tablespoons mayonnaise

Slice the tomatoes. Remove the rind from the bacon and cook in a frying pan over moderate heat until the fat runs. Raise the heat and cook until the rashers are golden and crisp. Toast the bread and remove the crusts; butter eight slices on one side, the remaining four slices on both sides. Cover four slices with tomato and top with the bacon; put the slices buttered on both sides on top, and cover each with lettuce and cooked meat. Spoon mayonnaise over the meat and complete each sandwich by adding a final slice of toast. Press the sandwiches firmly together and quarter them; spear each quarter with a cocktail stick and serve at once.

FISH, SHELLFISH & SEAFOOD

Soused Herrings

SERVES: 6
PREPARATION: 35 minutes
OVEN: 180°C/350°F/gas 4
COOKING: 15–20 minutes
SOUSING: 2 days

450 ml/¾ pt cider vinegar
450 ml/¾ pt water
3 juniper berries
6 cloves
1 bay leaf
5 black peppercorns
6 large herrings
2 large onions
30 ml/6 teaspoons mild mustard
2 dill-pickled cucumbers
bay leaves to garnish

Put the vinegar, water, juniper berries, cloves, bay leaf and peppercorns in a saucepan and bring to the boil. Simmer this marinade* for 10 minutes, then leave to cool.

Gut and clean the herrings (page 313); remove the heads and backbones but not the tails. (The fishmonger will do this for you, if asked.) Wash the herrings and dry them thoroughly on absorbent kitchen paper. Peel the onions, slice them thinly and separate the slices into rings.

Open the herrings out flat, and spread 5 ml/1 teaspoon of mustard over the inside of each. Cut each cucumber into three slices lengthways and place a piece of cucumber crossways at the head end of each herring. Arrange a few of the smaller onion rings down the length of the body and roll each herring from head to tail, securing them with toothpicks.

Arrange the herring rolls in an ovenproof dish and strain the marinade over the top. Sprinkle with the remaining onion rings. Cover the dish and bake the herrings for 15 minutes in a preheated oven at 180°C/350°F/gas 4. Leave them to cool in the marinade. Transfer the baked herrings to a deep dish and pour the marinade over them, so that the fish rolls are covered. Then cover the dish and set the herrings to souse* in the refrigerator for 2 days.

Remove the toothpicks and serve the herrings on individual plates, garnished with bay leaves.
■ Serve with thin slices of buttered wholemeal bread or rye bread and offer extra dill pickles with the herrings. A simple side salad topped with sliced apple makes an excellent accompaniment.

Soused Herrings.

Whitebait

Whitebait – immature herrings and sprats – are eaten whole and have long been a great tradition in British cookery.

SERVES: 6
COOKING: 6–10 minutes
PREPARATION: 10 minutes

900 g/2 lb whitebait
100 g/4 oz plain flour
salt and black pepper
oil for deep frying
Garnish
lemon wedges
parsley

Pick over the whitebait carefully and remove any damaged fish and pieces of weed. Do not wash or overhandle the fish as they bruise easily.

Season the flour with salt and black pepper and toss the whitebait gently in the flour to coat them thoroughly (the easiest way to do this is by shaking the fish gently with the seasoned flour in a plastic bag).

Heat the oil for deep frying to 190°C/375°F or until a cube of day-old bread browns in 1 minute. Deep fry the whitebait in small batches for about 2 minutes. Drain on crumpled absorbent kitchen paper.

■ Serve the whitebait hot, garnished with lemon wedges and parsley sprigs. Thinly sliced brown bread and butter is the traditional accompaniment.

Brill Soufflé

Brill Soufflé.

SERVES: 4–6
PREPARATION: 30 minutes
OVEN: 200°C/400°F/gas 6
COOKING: 45 minutes

450 g/1 lb brill fillets
salt and black pepper
1 bay leaf
1 blade mace
75 g/3 oz butter
75 g/3 oz plain flour
150 ml/¼ pt milk
grated nutmeg
juice of ½ lemon
3 large eggs

Place the brill fillets in a saucepan and pour in just enough water to cover the fish. Add salt, the bay leaf and mace. Cover the saucepan and bring slowly to simmering point, turn off the heat and leave the fish to stand in the water for 10 minutes. Lift out the fish, set aside 300 ml/½ pt of the liquid.

Remove the skin and any bones from the fish and flake the flesh roughly. Melt the butter in a large saucepan and stir in the flour. Cook over low heat for 2 minutes, stirring continuously, then gradually stir in the fish liquid and milk. Bring to the boil, still stirring, and cook for 2 minutes or until the sauce is thick and smooth. Season to taste with salt, freshly ground pepper and nutmeg. Stir in the lemon juice. Carefully fold the flaked fish into the sauce. Separate the eggs and beat the yolks into the fish mixture. Whisk the egg whites until stiff, but not dry, then gently fold them into the fish sauce.

Spoon the mixture into a greased 1.7 litre/3 pt soufflé dish; cook in a preheated oven at 200°C/400°F/gas 6 for 35–40 minutes or until the soufflé is risen and golden brown on top. Serve immediately.

Turbot au Gratin

Turbot is a large flat fish, similar to halibut, but with creamy-white flesh. The delicate flavour is best retained through simple cooking. Ask the fishmonger to fillet the turbot and to include the skin and bones.

SERVES: 6
PREPARATION: 30 minutes
OVEN: 180°C/350°F/gas 4
COOKING: 1 hour

6 turbot fillets (175 g/6 oz each)
1 small onion
salt and black pepper
bouquet garni*
150 ml/¼ pt dry white wine
250 ml/8 fl oz water
25 g/1 oz butter
25 g/1 oz plain flour
150 ml/¼ pt milk
1 large egg yolk
30 ml/2 tablespoons double cream
50 g/2 oz Cheddar cheese

Wipe the fillets and put them in a single layer in a shallow ovenproof dish. Rinse the fish trimmings supplied by the fishmonger in cold water and put them in a large saucepan. Peel the onion and add it whole to the pan with salt, the bouquet garni, wine and the water. Bring to the boil, lower the heat, cover, and simmer for 15 minutes.

Strain this stock through a fine sieve over the fish. Cover the dish with a piece of buttered foil and bake for 20 minutes in a preheated oven at 180°C/350°F/gas 4.

Remove the fillets from the oven, drain, reserving the cooking liquid, and arrange them in a hot flameproof serving dish. Melt the butter in a saucepan, stir in the flour and cook for 2 minutes.

Gradually stir in the fish liquid and milk, stirring until the sauce comes to the boil. Lower the heat and simmer, stirring all the time, for 2 minutes. Season to taste with salt and freshly ground pepper; remove from the heat. Lightly beat the egg yolk with the cream, blend in a little of the hot sauce and stir the mixture into the sauce; pour it over the fish fillets.

Grate the cheese and sprinkle it over the sauce; put the dish under a hot grill for 5–10 minutes, until the cheese bubbles and is brown on top.

■ Serve the gratin from the dish, with new potatoes and lightly cooked broccoli spears.

POULTRY & GAME

Chicken with Broccoli

SERVES: 4
PREPARATION: 20 minutes
COOKING: about 25 minutes

450 g/1 lb sprouting broccoli
salt and black pepper
3 skinned boneless chicken breasts
45 ml/3 tablespoons plain flour
a little grated nutmeg
1 small onion
30 ml/2 tablespoons olive oil
1 bay leaf
25 g/1 oz flaked almonds
150 ml/¼ pt dry sherry
250 ml/8 fl oz water

Trim off any tough stalks from the broccoli, then slice the tender stalks and break the heads into small florets. Blanch* the broccoli in boiling lightly salted water for 2 minutes and drain well. Cut the chicken breasts crossways into thin slices. Place in a bowl, add plenty of seasoning, the flour and a little nutmeg, and toss until well coated. Finely chop the onion.

Heat the oil in a large frying pan or wok. Add the bay leaf and onion and stir fry for 3 minutes. Add the chicken, reserving any loose flour in the bowl. Continue to stir fry until the pieces of chicken are lightly browned and cooked – this will take about 8 minutes. Add the almonds and broccoli, and stir fry for 3 minutes more.

Stir in any reserved flour, then pour in the sherry and water and reduce the heat slightly, if necessary, to bring the liquid to the boil without cooking the mixture too quickly. Keep stirring until the sauce is slightly thickened and smooth. Then lower the heat and simmer gently for 3 minutes. Add salt and freshly ground black pepper to taste before removing the bay leaf and serving.

■ Serve with rice, pasta or baked potatoes; there is no need for additional vegetables.

Gardener's Chicken

SERVES: 4–6
PREPARATION: 40 minutes
OVEN: 160°C/325°F/gas 3
COOKING: 1¼ hours

1 chicken, about 1.4 kg/3 lb, or
    4–6 chicken portions
50 g/2 oz streaky bacon
2 large onions
2 sticks celery
100 g/4 oz mushrooms
40 g/1½ oz butter
450 g/1 lb small new potatoes
225 g/8 oz turnips
400 g/14 oz can chopped tomatoes
1 bouquet garni*
salt and black pepper
Garnish
2–3 sprigs parsley
pared rind of ½ orange

If using a whole chicken, joint it (page 322) into four or six pieces,

and wipe clean with absorbent kitchen paper. Remove the rind and any bones from the bacon; cut into dice. Peel and thinly slice the onions; scrub and coarsely chop the celery; clean and slice the mushrooms.

Melt the butter in a large, heavy-based pan and fry the bacon, onions, celery and mushrooms for 5 minutes. Tip the frying pan to drain the butter to one side, remove the vegetables with a perforated spoon, and spread them over the base of a large casserole.

Fry the chicken joints in the butter remaining in the pan until they are golden brown. Remove from the pan and place on the bed of vegetables. Scrape the potatoes, peel and slice the turnips and add these, together with the tomatoes and bouquet garni, to the casserole.

Season with salt and freshly ground pepper, and cover the casserole with foil, before securing the lid so that no steam can escape and the moisture is kept in. Cook in a preheated oven at 160°C/325°F/gas 3 for about 1½ hours or until the chicken is tender.

Immediately before serving, chop the parsley and orange rind finely; mix them together and sprinkle over the casserole.

Gardener's Chicken.

Chicken and Cheese Savoury

Cold roast chicken can be turned into a tempting hot supper when combined with a sauce and grilled on toast. The chicken mixture is also an ideal filling for baked potatoes.

SERVES: 4
PREPARATION: 10 minutes
COOKING: 15 minutes

225 g/8 oz cooked chicken
50 g/2 oz mushrooms
50 g/2 oz Cheddar cheese
300 ml/½ pt thick White Sauce
    (page 352)
salt, black pepper and
    cayenne pepper
5 ml/1 teaspoon made
    English mustard
4 slices buttered toast

Dice the cooked chicken, discarding any skin. Slice the mushrooms thinly. Grate the cheese. Season the white sauce with salt, pepper and cayenne to taste, and stir in the mustard. Add the chicken and mushrooms to the sauce and simmer over low heat until heated through, stirring frequently to prevent the mixture sticking the pan.

Spoon the chicken mixture on to the hot toast and sprinkle with the cheese. Grill until the cheese is brown and bubbling.
Note Leftover cooked chicken can be frozen successfully in a thick white sauce for use as a topping in the above recipe. For a thinner mixture to pour over pasta, make a thick pouring white sauce.

MEAT

Steak Diane

This famous dish originated in Australia where tender beef fillet is always used; rump steak is equally suitable, however.

SERVES: 4
PREPARATION: 20 minutes
COOKING: 10 minutes

675 g/1½ lb rump steak
1 small onion
1 large lemon
75 g/3 oz butter
Worcestershire sauce
15 ml/1 tablespoon chopped parsley
60 ml/4 tablespoons brandy

Trim the rump steak and cut it into four even pieces; beat them flat with a rolling pin until they are no more than 5 mm/¼ in thick. Peel and finely chop the onion. Grate the lemon rind finely, squeeze and strain the juice into a jug.

Melt 50 g/2 oz of the butter in a large, heavy-based frying pan; fry the onion for about 5 minutes or until soft and transparent. Lift the onion on to a small plate with a perforated spoon. Add two steaks to the butter remaining in the pan and fry over high heat for 1 minute only on each side. Lift out; keep hot.

Melt the remaining butter until foaming and fry two more steaks. Return the onion to the pan, stir in the lemon rind and juice, add a few drops of Worcestershire sauce and the parsley. Cook lightly, then put in the steaks. Heat the brandy in a small saucepan or metal soup ladle, ignite it and pour it over the steaks. Serve the steaks with the cooking juices.

Veal with Orange

This is reputed to have been Oliver Cromwell's favourite dish. It is prepared with a fruity stuffing and a wine sauce.

SERVES: 6
PREPARATION: 20 minutes
OVEN: 180°C/350°F/gas 4
COOKING: 2½ hours

100 g/4 oz fresh white breadcrumbs
50 g/2 oz raisins
50 g/2 oz currants
50 g/2 oz shredded beef suet
salt and black pepper
grated nutmeg
grated rind of 2 large oranges
1 large egg yolk
75 ml/5 tablespoons water
1.8–2.27 kg/4–5 lb breast of veal
    or belly of pork, boned
25 g/1 oz lard or 30 ml/
    2 tablespoons oil
25 g/1 oz plain flour
600 ml/1 pt vegetable cooking
    water or stock
90 ml/6 tablespoons claret
    or red wine

Mix the breadcrumbs, raisins, currants, suet and a pinch of salt, pepper and nutmeg together in a bowl. Add the orange rind to the mixture. Lightly beat the egg yolk with the water to bind the mixture to a stuffing.

Cut a pocket between the layers of meat on the breast of veal or pork belly, if used. Spoon the stuffing into this pocket, spreading any extra down the middle of the meat. Roll the joint and tie with thin string at 2.5 cm/1 in intervals. Do not tie the roll too tightly or the stuffing will squeeze out, especially when it expands during cooking.

Heat the lard or oil in a roasting tin in a preheated oven at 180°C/350°F/gas 4. Add the veal or pork and roast for 2½ hours. Baste occasionally and cover the meat with foil if it browns too quickly.

Put the meat on a serving dish and keep it hot in the oven. Pour off excess fat from the juices in the roasting tin. Stir the flour into the juices and cook over medium heat for a minute, stirring all the time. Gradually pour in the stock and bring to the boil, stirring continuously until the sauce has thickened. Season to taste with salt, freshly ground pepper and nutmeg. Stir in the claret or red wine and simmer the sauce gently for 3–5 minutes, If necessary, the sauce may be strained through a fine sieve to remove any lumps from the roasting residue. Remove the pith from the oranges and cut the flesh into small sections. Add these to the sauce and heat it.

Cut the veal into thick slices and arrange them on a serving dish; offer the sauce separately.
■ Chicory and Orange Salad (page 292) and Sauté Potatoes (page 347) would both go well with this joint.

Veal with Orange.

Lamb Kebabs

SERVES: 4
PREPARATION: 20 minutes
MARINATING: 30 minutes
COOKING: 10 minutes

675 g/1½ lb boned shoulder of lamb
1 small green chilli (optional)
2.5 cm/1 in piece of fresh
    root ginger
150 ml/¼ pt plain yogurt
2.5 ml/½ teaspoon ground
    coriander
2.5 ml/½ teaspoon ground cumin
1 clove garlic
juice of ½ lemon
5 ml/1 teaspoon salt
lemon wedges to garnish

Trim any excess fat from the lamb and cut it into 2.5 cm/1 in cubes. Halve the chilli, if used, cut out the stalk end and scrape out the seeds. Chop the chilli finely. Peel the ginger and chop it roughly.

Put the yogurt in a bowl and stir in the ground coriander, ground cumin, chilli and ginger. Peel and crush the garlic; add it to the yogurt mixture, then stir in the lemon juice and salt. Add the lamb, mix well and marinate* for at least 30 minutes.

Remove the lamb cubes from the marinade and thread them on to four metal skewers, 20–25 cm/8–10 in long, packing the pieces closely together. Cook the skewers under a hot grill, turning from time to time, for 8–10 minutes, or until browned on the outside and pink in the centre.
■ Arrange the lamb kebabs on a bed of boiled Basmati rice and garnish with lemon wedges.

Guard of Honour

Given a little extra effort, a pair of racks of lamb can become a spectacular main course. The joints are sewn with the cutlet bones interlaced so as to simulate a guard of crossed swords.

SERVES: 6–8
PREPARATION: 30 minutes
OVEN: 180°C/350°F/gas 4
COOKING: about 1½ hours

2 racks of lamb (each with
    8 cutlets)
salt and black pepper
50 g/2 oz lard or 60 ml/
    4 tablespoons oil
900 g/2 lb button onions
900 g/2 lb peas (shelled) or
    450 g/1 lb frozen peas
2.5 ml/½ teaspoon caster sugar
    (optional)

Ask the butcher to chine* the joints and to remove the skin and tissue from the top 4–5 cm/ 1½–2 in of the bones. Sew the two joints together, skin side outwards so that the thick meaty part is at the base and the cutlet bones interlace at the top. Secure with string between every two or three cutlets, and sprinkle with salt and black pepper.

Melt the lard or heat the oil in a roasting tin in a preheated oven at 180°C/350°F/gas 4.

Wrap foil around each cutlet bone to keep it white. Add the joint to the roasting tin, and roast for about 1½ hours, allowing 25 minutes per 450 g/ 1 lb and 25 minutes extra.

Meanwhile, peel the onions, leaving then whole; cook in lightly salted water for 20 minutes, drain and keep hot. Cook the peas in boiling water until just tender, adding the sugar, if liked. Drain the peas and mix with the onions

Take the meat out of the tin, remove the string and foil and set the meat on a warm serving dish. Arrange the peas and onions around the meat and place a cutlet frill on each bone. Pour the pan juices into a sauceboat, after skimming off the fat.

Pork with Lemon

SERVES: 4–6
PREPARATION: 20 minutes
COOKING: 30 minutes

900 g/2 lb pork fillet
25 g/1 oz lard or 30 ml/
    2 tablespoons oil
1 onion
15 ml/1 tablespoon plain flour
20 ml/4 teaspoons ground cumin
10 ml/2 teaspoons ground
    coriander
300 ml/½ pt dry white wine
2 cloves garlic
1 lemon
salt and black pepper

Trim away any fat and the thin outer skin from the fillet, cut the meat into 2.5 cm/1 in cubes.

Heat the lard or oil in a flameproof casserole and brown the meat, turning it continuously to prevent it from sticking to the pan. Peel and chop the onion and add it to the meat, then cook, stirring, for 5 minutes. Add the flour, cumin and coriander, stirring the spices into the fat in the pan. Stir in just over 150 ml/ ¼ pt of the wine. Peel the garlic and crush it over the meat. Trim the ends off the lemon, cut it lengthways into quarters, then slice these across into thin pieces. Add the lemon to the pork and season to taste with salt and freshly ground pepper. Bring the mixture to the boil, reduce the heat and cover the pan, simmer for about 30 minutes or until tender. Add the remaining wine. Continue cooking, stirring until the sauce thickens slightly. Spoon the meat and the sauce on to a dish and serve.

Gammon in Puff Pastry

An impressive gammon hock serves more people when baked in puff pastry. Preparations should begin the day before.

SERVES: 6
PREPARATION: 30 minutes
OVEN: 230°C/450°F/gas 8
        180°C/350°F/gas 4
COOKING: 2¾ hours
CHILLING: 8 hours

1.8 kg/4 lb gammon hock
1 small onion
1 large bay leaf
12 peppercorns
1 blade mace
4–6 parsley stalks
2 sprigs thyme
450 g/1 lb home-made Puff Pastry
    (page 374) or thawed frozen
    puff pastry
beaten egg to glaze

Ask the butcher to bone part of the hock, leaving the end bone

Gammon in Puff Pastry.

in to make carving easier. Gammon does not usually require soaking but it is a good idea to check with the butcher. Peel the onion, leaving it whole.

Place the gammon in a large saucepan. Cover with cold water and add the onion, bay leaf, peppercorns, mace, parsley stalks and thyme. Bring to the boil, lower the heat, then cover the pan with a lid and simmer for 20 minutes per 450 g/1 lb. Remove the pan from the heat and let the gammon cool in the cooking liquid for about 1 hour, then drain and cool the meat completely, chilling in the refrigerator overnight.

Carefully pull off the skin from the gammon. Roll out the puff pastry to an oblong shape, 3 mm/⅛ in thick, and place the gammon on the centre. Brush the pastry edges with some of the lightly beaten egg; wrap the pastry over the gammon, and press the edges together to enclose the meat. Seal the edges, pleating the pastry round the bone. Brush with egg.

Cover the bone with a piece of foil to keep it white while cooking. Use the pastry trimmings to decorate the casing, then carefully lift the gammon on to a baking sheet; brush the pastry with the remaining egg.

Bake the gammon for 20 minutes in a preheated oven at 230°C/450°F/gas 8, then lower the temperature to 180°C/350°F/ gas 4 and continue cooking for a further 30 minutes. Cover the joint loosely with foil as soon as the pastry is golden.

■ Serve the joint hot, with new potatoes and Lettuce and Green Peas (page 168). You can also serve the gammon cold; garnish the dish with spring onions and watercress and offer a variety of salads, including a rice or potato salad, with cold gammon.

Tripe Provençale

Tripe, which is associated with onions and the tripe parlours of the Midlands and the North, has a long history. The Normans introduced it as a food to Britain; the following recipe comes from southern France.

SERVES: 6
PREPARATION: 20 minutes
COOKING: 2¾ hours

900 g/2 lb dressed tripe
600 ml/1 pt chicken stock
   (for boiling tripe)
salt and black pepper
1 onion
1 clove garlic
25 g/1 oz butter
450 g/1 lb tomatoes
dried thyme
60 ml/4 tablespoons dry white wine
15 ml/1 tablespoon chopped parsley

Unless the tripe has been bought ready boiled and cleaned, it needs to be prepared as follows: Wash the tripe thoroughly. Put it in a saucepan and cover with cold water. Bring to the boil. Remove from the heat, drain and rinse under cold running water. Cut into 5 cm/2 in cubes and return them to the saucepan. Pour over the boiling stock and add a pinch of salt. As soon as the stock boils again, reduce the heat. Cover the pan with a lid and simmer the tripe for 2 hours. If using ready boiled tripe simply cut it into 5 cm/2 in cubes.

Peel and roughly chop the onion, and skin and crush the garlic. Melt the butter in a frying pan and gently fry the onion and garlic for about 5 minutes until transparent. Skin the tomatoes (page 302) and chop them roughly; add them, with a pinch of dried thyme, the wine and parsley, to the frying pan. Bring this mixture to the boil, lower the heat, cover the pan with a lid and simmer for 10 minutes. Season to taste with salt and freshly ground pepper.

Drain the cooked tripe. Add it (or the ready-boiled tripe) to the tomato mixture. Mix well. Cook over low heat for a further 30 minutes, stirring occasionally.
■   Serve the tripe on a bed of plain boiled rice.

Savoury Kidneys

Grilled or fried kidneys were once a favourite dish on the British breakfast or tea table. They are now more popular for lunch or a main meal.

SERVES: 4
PREPARATION: 25 minutes
COOKING: 35 minutes

2 large onions
50 g/2 oz butter
12 lamb kidneys
150 g/5 oz button mushrooms
15 ml/1 tablespoon cornflour
15 ml/1 tablespoon tomato paste
60 ml/4 tablespoons port or
   dry sherry
60 ml/4 tablespoons water
salt and black pepper
sprigs of parsley to garnish

Peel and thinly slice the onions. Melt the butter in a large saucepan and add the onions. Cover the pan with a lid and cook gently for 20 minutes, until soft but not browned.

Remove the fat and skin surrounding the kidneys, then cut them in half and snip out the white cores with a pair of scissors. Rinse the kidneys, pat them dry on absorbent kitchen paper, then cut them into 2.5 cm/1 in chunks. Trim and halve the button mushrooms. Add the kidneys and mushrooms to the onions in the pan; cook gently for 3 minutes.

Mix the cornflour, tomato paste, port or sherry and water in a basin. Stir until smooth. Pour this mixture into the saucepan and stir gently until the sauce begins to thicken. Season to taste with salt and freshly ground pepper. Reduce the heat and simmer the kidneys for 7–10 minutes, or until they are tender.

Arrange the kidneys on a hot serving dish, pour over the sauce and garnish with parsley.
■   Serve with triangles of hot toast, brown rice or tagliatelle.

VEGETABLES & SALADS

Artichokes with Hollandaise Sauce

SERVES: 6
PREPARATION: 30 minutes
COOKING: about 45 minutes

6 globe artichokes
300 ml/½ pt Hollandaise Sauce
   (page 355)

Wash the artichokes thoroughly under cold running water. Pull off any ragged outer leaves and snip off the sharp points of the remaining leaves with scissors. Trim the stalks of the artichokes so that they stand level (page 342). Bring a large saucepan of water to the boil, add a little salt and the artichokes and bring back to the boil. Reduce the heat, cover with a lid and simmer for 25–45 minutes, depending on the size of the artichokes, or until a leaf pulls off easily. Drain the artichokes upside-down.

While the artichokes are boiling, make the Hollandaise sauce and keep it hot.

Remove the centre leaves and the 'choke' from each artichoke; stand the artichokes on individual serving plates and serve the sauce separately.
■   Provide finger bowls, and side plates. Guests pull off the artichoke leaves one by one and dip the pale flesh at the bottom of each leaf in the sauce before nibbling it. The rest of the leaf is discarded on the side plate.

Fried Leeks

This dish can be served hot with any lean grilled or roast meat. It can also be served as a side dish or salad with cold ham and cold roast chicken.

SERVES: 4–6
PREPARATION: 10 minutes
COOKING: 25 minutes

900 g/2 lb leeks
4 tomatoes
60–90 ml/4–6 tablespoons olive oil
2 cloves garlic
1 bay leaf
salt and black pepper
juice of ½ lemon

Cut away the roots and any damaged green leaves from the leeks, slit them partway through in half lengthways and wash under cold running water to remove all traces of grit. Cut into 2.5 cm/1 in slices. Skin the tomatoes (page 302). Heat half the oil in a large frying pan and add the leeks. Peel the garlic and crush over the leeks, then add the bay leaf. Season to taste with salt and freshly ground pepper.

Cover the pan with a lid and cook over low heat for 20 minutes, stirring occasionally, until the leeks are tender. Chop the tomatoes, add them to the pan with the rest of the oil and cook for a further 5 minutes. Remove the bay leaf. Spoon the leeks into a serving dish and sprinkle the lemon juice over.

Minted New Potatoes with Peppers

SERVES: 4
PREPARATION: 40 minutes
COOKING: 20–25 minutes

2 red peppers
2 yellow peppers
900 g/2 lb small new potatoes
salt and black pepper
4–5 large mint sprigs
5ml/1 teaspoon caster sugar
15 ml/1 tablespoon cider vinegar
2.5 ml/½ teaspoon Dijon mustard
    or other mild mustard
150 ml/¼ pt fromage frais
30 ml/2 tablespoons finely
    chopped parsley
30 ml/2 tablespoons finely
    snipped chives
25 g/1 oz butter
freshly grated Pecorino or
    Parmesan cheese to serve

Prepare the red and yellow peppers first. Skewer each of them in turn on a metal fork and hold them over a gas burner on the hob until the skin is charred and blistered. Alternatively, char the peppers under a hot grill. Turn the peppers regularly to blister the skin evenly. Scrape and rub off the charred skin under cold water.

Scrape the potatoes and cook then in boiling salted water for 10–15 minutes until they are just tender. Meanwhile, halve the peppers and cut out their cores, seeds and pith, then dice the flesh. Pick the leaves off the mint, place on a board and sprinkle the sugar over, then chop the mint and scrape it, with the sugar, into a small bowl. Stir in the cider vinegar and mustard with salt and pepper to taste. When the sugar and salt have dissolved, stir in the fromage frais, parsley and chives.

Drain the cooked potatoes and return them to the pan. Add the butter and peppers and mix gently over low heat for 1–2 minutes until the butter has melted. Remove the pan from the heat, pour the fromage frais mixture over the potatoes, mix lightly and immediately transfer the vegetables to a heated serving dish. Serve at once, with a bowl of freshly grated Pecorino or Parmesan cheese.

■ Offer crusty French bread or focaccia with the vegetables.

Onion Flan

The recipe for this creamy flan comes from Alsace in France.

SERVES: 6
PREPARATION: 45 minutes
CHILLING: 30 minutes
OVEN: 200°C/400°F/gas 6
       190°C/375°F/gas 5
COOKING: about 1¼ hours

175 g/6 oz Shortcrust Pastry
    (page 365)
450 g/1 lb onions
40 g/1½ oz butter
1 bay leaf
salt and pepper
2 large eggs
grated nutmeg
150 ml/¼ pt single cream

Prepare the shortcrust pastry and roll it out thick, on a lightly floured surface. Line a 20–23 cm/8–9 in loose-bottomed flan tin with the pastry. Trim the edge and prick the base of the pastry case with a fork. Chill the case for 30 minutes. Line the pastry case with greaseproof paper and sprinkle with baking beans to weigh down the paper. Bake the pastry case in a preheated oven at 200°C/400°F/gas 6 for 15 minutes. Remove the greaseproof paper and beans, and cook the pastry case for a further 5 minutes. Reduce the temperature to 190°C/375°F/gas 5.

Meanwhile, peel the onions and slice them thinly. Melt the butter in a large saucepan or a frying pan with a lid and add the onions and bay leaf. Season with salt and pepper and cover the onions closely with a piece of buttered greaseproof paper.

Cover the pan with a tight-fitting lid and cook the onions gently for 30 minutes or until they are soft but not browned. Shake the pan occasionally to prevent the onions from sticking.

Beat the eggs in a large bowl and season with salt, pepper and nutmeg. Stir in the single cream. Remove the bay leaf from the onions and spread them over the pastry case. Strain the egg and cream mixture over the onions.

Bake the filled onion flan for 30–35 minutes. When cooked, the pastry should be golden and the filling set; it will sink slightly as the flan cools.

■ The rich Onion Flan can be served hot or cold with a crisp green salad for a main course. Alternatively, cut the flan into small wedges for a first course.

Braised Soya Beans with Crisp Vegetables

SERVES: 4–6
SOAKING: 24 hours
PREPARATION: 45 minutes
COOKING: about 3¼ hours

225 g/8 oz dried soya beans
2 cloves garlic
2 large onions
4 sticks celery
1 large carrot
45 ml/3 tablespoons olive oil
1 bouquet garni*
2 × 400 g/14 oz cans
    chopped tomatoes
600 ml/1 pt red wine
600 ml/1 pt water
salt and black pepper
1 red pepper
350 g/12 oz cabbage or
    spring greens
100 g/4 oz mange-tout
2 avocados
grated rind and juice of ½ lemon
15 ml/1 tablespoon chopped mint
60 ml/4 tablespoons
    chopped parsley
15–25 g/½–1 oz butter

Soak the soya beans in plenty of cold water for at least 24 hours. The beans may be left to stand for up to 48 hours, but the water should be changed at least once if they are soaked for as long as this. Drain the beans and par-cook them in plenty of boiling water for 1 hour. Do not add salt as this hardens beans and pulses.

Chop the garlic cloves and 1 of the onions, and dice the celery and carrot. Heat 30 ml/2 tablespoons of the oil in a large saucepan. Add the prepared garlic and vegetables with the bouquet garni. Shake the pan well, cover it tightly and cook gently for 10 minutes, shaking the pan occasionally. Stir in the drained boiled beans, then pour in the tomatoes, wine and water. Bring to the boil and then reduce the heat so that the sauce simmers gently, covering the pan while it does this. Cook the beans for a further 1¾ hours, stirring occasionally. By the time the beans are tender, the sauce should be reduced and well flavoured. Stir in salt and pepper to taste and cook, uncovered, for a further 30 minutes. Do not add salt before the beans are tender.

While the beans are cooking, halve and thinly slice the remaining onion. Halve the red pepper, cut out the stalk, core and seeds, then cut the flesh into short thin strips. Shred the cabbage or spring greens finely and top and tail the mange-tout. When the beans are in the final 3 minutes of cooking, halve the avocados, remove their stones and peel, then cut each half across into slices. Place the avocado slices in a bowl and, sprinkle with the lemon rind and juice, the mint and 15 ml/1 tablespoon of the parsley. Cover and set aside.

Heat the remaining olive oil with the butter in a large saucepan. Add the sliced onion and pepper, and cook, stirring, for 10 minutes. Add the cabbage or spring greens with salt and pepper to taste and stir well. Cover the pan tightly and cook for 5 minutes, shaking the pan once or twice. Add the mange-tout and stir over a fairly high heat for a further 5 minutes until the vegetables are cooked but still slightly crisp.

Transfer the cabbage mixture to a serving dish or individual dishes. Mix the remaining chopped parsley with the braised beans and ladle them over the crisp vegetables, discarding the bouquet garni. Top with the avocado and herbs and serve.

Imam Bayildi

This Turkish dish takes its name from an Imam, a Muslim holy man. Imam Bayildi is said to have swooned with pleasure – or from over-eating – after being served this aubergine dish.

SERVES: 6
PREPARATION: 30 minutes
OVEN: 180°C/350°F/gas 4
COOKING: 40 minutes

3 large aubergines
salt and black pepper
olive oil
3 large onions
350 g/12 oz tomatoes
1 clove garlic
2.5 ml/½ teaspoon ground
    cinnamon
5 ml/1 teaspoon caster sugar
15 ml/1 tablespoon chopped parsley
30 ml/2 tablespoons finely chopped
    pine kernels (optional)

Trim the aubergines, wipe them and put them in a large saucepan. Add boiling water to cover and put a lid on the pan; cook the aubergines for 10 minutes. Drain the aubergines,

plunge them into cold water and leave for 5 minutes. Drain the aubergines, cut them in half lengthways and scoop out most of the flesh, leaving a 1 cm/½ in thick shell. Set aside the scooped out flesh. Arrange the shells in a buttered ovenproof dish and sprinkle them with a little salt and freshly ground pepper. Pour 10 ml/2 teaspoons of olive oil in to each shell, trickling it down around the fleshy sides, and cook the aubergines, uncovered, in a preheated oven at 180°C/350°F/gas 4 for 30 minutes.

While the aubergine shells are cooking, peel and finely chop the onions; skin the tomatoes (page 302) and chop them. Peel and crush the garlic. Heat 30 ml/

Imam Bayildi.

2 tablespoons oil in a frying pan, add the onions and garlic and fry gently for 10 minutes, then add the tomatoes, cinnamon, sugar and parsley; season to taste with salt and black pepper. Continue simmering this mixture until the liquid has reduced by half, after about 20 minutes. Chop the aubergine flesh and add to the frying pan, with the chopped pine kernels (if used) and cook for a further 10 minutes.

Remove the aubergine shells from the oven, stuff them with the tomato mixture and serve.

■ Imam Bayildi may be served hot or cold, as a vegetarian dish or with roast or grilled meat.

Bean Sambal

This piquant, spicy side dish of French beans is typical of Malaysian cooking, which combines the spicy elements of Indian dishes with oriental ingredients and methods.

SERVES: 6
PREPARATION: 15 minutes
COOKING: 15 minutes

1 small onion
1–2 cloves garlic
2 fresh red chillies
small piece (2.5 ml/½ teaspoon)
    tamarind
30–45 ml/2–3 tablespoons
    peanut oil
450 g/1 lb French beans
1 small bay leaf
1 dried lemon leaf or a piece
    of lemon grass
5 ml/1 teaspoon brown sugar
salt
300 ml/½ pt Coconut Milk
    (page 239)

Peel and chop the onion and garlic. Deseed and chop the chillies, chop the tamarind. Pound or liquidise the onion, garlic, chillies and tamarind until they are reduced to a smooth paste. Fry the paste in the peanut oil for 5 minutes.

Top, tail and wash the beans, cut them into 5 cm/2 in pieces and stir into the spiced paste. Add the bay and lemon leaves or lemon grass, with sugar and salt to taste. Gradually stir in the coconut milk. Bring the mixture to the boil, then simmer for 10–12 minutes. Remove the bay and lemon leaves before serving.

Apple and Nut Salad

Fromage frais is an excellent ingredient for dressing full-flavoured salads of this type.

SERVES: 4–5
PREPARATION: 30 minutes

4 crisp dessert apples
15 ml/1 tablespoon lemon juice
75 g/3 oz walnuts
150 ml/¼ pt fromage frais or
    soured cream
75 g/3 oz white cabbage
3 sticks celery
12 large radishes
50 g/2 oz raisins
salt and black pepper

Wash and core the apples and roughly chop them into chunks. Put them in a bowl and sprinkle the lemon juice over them to prevent the apples from going brown. Roughly chop the walnuts and set aside one-third for garnish. Pour the fromage frais or soured cream into a bowl and stir in the apples and walnuts.

Remove any damaged and coarse outer leaves from the cabbage, wash it and cut out the thick centre stalk. Shred the cabbage finely, first one way and then the other. Scrub and thinly slice the celery. Remove leaves and roots from the radishes and slice them evenly. Halve the raisins if liked.

Stir all these ingredients into the fromage frais or soured cream mixture and season to taste with salt and freshly ground pepper. Serve the salad garnished with the remaining walnuts.

RICE & PASTA

Orange Rice

This aromatic rice dish goes well with chicken or lamb, and it can also be used cold as a base for a salad.

SERVES: 6
PREPARATION: 10 minutes
COOKING: 30 minutes

1 small onion
3 sticks celery
25 g/1 oz butter
450 g/1 lb long-grain rice
2 large oranges
900 ml/1½ pt water
salt and black pepper
2 sprigs thyme

Peel and finely chop the onion; wash the celery and cut into thin slices. Melt the butter in a large, heavy-based pan and fry the onion and celery for about 10 minutes, until the onion is soft.

Add the rice and cook for 30 seconds, stirring to combine the rice with the other ingredients. Finely grate the rind from the oranges; squeeze and strain the juice. Add the water to the pan, together with the orange rind and juice, a pinch of salt and the thyme. Stir once, then bring to the boil. Stir again, cover the pan tightly and reduce the heat to the lowest setting.

Cook for 25 minutes. Take the pan off the heat and leave it covered for a further 5 minutes. Remove the thyme and season with freshly ground pepper.

Fried Rice

SERVES: 4
PREPARATION: 15 minutes
COOKING: 30 minutes

225 g/8 oz long-grain rice
salt
600 ml/1 pt water
100 g/4 oz frozen peas
4 rashers streaky bacon
1 onion
4 eggs
30 ml/2 tablespoons oil
5 ml/1 teaspoon sesame oil

Place the rice in a saucepan. Add a little salt and pour in the water. Bring to the boil, stir once, then cover the pan. Reduce the heat to the lowest setting and cook the rice for 20 minutes. Cook the peas in the minimum of boiling water for 3 minutes, then drain them and set them aside.

Meanwhile, remove the rind and any bones from the bacon and roughly chop the rashers. Peel and finely chop the onion. Beat the eggs with a little salt. Heat both types of oil in a large frying pan or wok. Stir fry the bacon and onion until the onion has softened and the bacon slightly browned in places. Add the beaten eggs and cook for a few seconds until they are just setting, then break the mixture up into small pieces.

Reduce the heat and stir in the peas, then add the rice and mix it with the other ingredients.

Gnocchi alla Romana

Gnocchi are small dumplings made from a flour, semolina or potato base. The Roman gnocchi are made from a semolina paste which is left to rest before being cut into squares or circles.

SERVES: 6
PREPARATION: 30 minutes
CHILLING: 2–3 hours
OVEN: 180°C/350°F/gas 4
COOKING: 45 minutes

900 ml/1½ pt milk
225 g/8 oz semolina
100 g/4 oz butter
175 g/6 oz Parmesan cheese
salt and black pepper
grated nutmeg
2 eggs

Heat the milk to just below boiling point. Sprinkle in the semolina, stirring continuously, and bring the mixture slowly to the boil, still stirring. Cook for 2 minutes; remove from the heat and stir in 65 g/2½ oz of the butter and 125 g/4½ oz of the grated cheese; season to taste with salt, freshly ground pepper and nutmeg.

Lightly beat the eggs and gradually beat them into the semolina mixture. Pour this paste into an oiled Swiss roll tin and spread it out evenly until it is 1 cm/½ thick.

Set the paste aside until it is cold, then chill it for several hours until it is firm.

Cut the paste into 4 cm/1½ in squares with a cold, wet knife. Alternatively, a round metal cutter can be used to stamp out circles of mixture or spoonfuls of mixture can be rolled into balls,

Gnocchi alla Romana.

using a little dry semolina to prevent them from sticking to the surface. Place the gnocchi in a buttered ovenproof dish overlapping the pieces neatly. Melt the remaining butter in a saucepan and pour it over the gnocchi; sprinkle with the remaining cheese. Cook in a preheated oven at 180°C/350°F/gas 4 for 40 minutes or until pale golden. Serve the gnocchi freshly cooked.

Fettuccine in Cream

The Italians eat huge bowls of egg noodles – fettuccine – for their midday meal. The pasta is usually served simply tossed in butter and cheese or cream.

SERVES: 6
PREPARATION: 5 minutes
COOKING: 12 minutes

450 g/1 lb fresh fettuccine
salt and black pepper
50 g/2 oz butter
300 ml/½ pt single cream

Cook the fettuccine for about 3 minutes in plenty of boiling salted water, preferably in two pans as the pasta needs space to swell. The fettuccine is cooked when a single strand is tender (*al dente**) to the bite. Drain the fettuccine in a colander.

Melt the butter in a large saucepan. Add the fettuccine and stir in the cream until every strand is thoroughly coated. Season to taste with freshly ground pepper; turn on to a hot dish and serve.

Tagliatelle with Smoked Cheese and Grapes

Juicy seedless grapes go well with smoked cheese in this simple dish, which is ideal for supper or as a first course.

SERVES: 4
PREPARATION: 15 minutes
COOKING: 15 minutes

100 g/4 oz seedless green grapes
175 g/6 oz smoked cheese
350 g/12 oz tagliatelle verdi
salt and black pepper
4 spring onions
1 clove garlic
30 ml/2 tablespoons olive oil
250 ml/8 fl oz fromage frais

Cut the grapes in half and slice the smoked cheese into short, thin strips. Cook the tagliatelle verdi in plenty of boiling lightly salted water for 10–12 minutes, or until just tender.

While the pasta is cooking, trim the root ends from the spring onions, then chop the rest finely, including the green parts. Place the spring onions in a small pan. Crush the garlic and add it to the pan, then add the olive oil. Cook gently for about 3 minutes. Stir in the fromage frais with salt and pepper to taste. Immediately remove the pan from the heat.

Toss the fromage frais and onion mixture, grapes and cheese into the pasta and serve at once.
■ Serve a spinach and bacon salad or a crisp mixed salad with the tagliatelle.

PUDDINGS & DESSERTS

Rhubarb Crumble

The tart flavour of rhubarb blends well with a topping of sweet crumble.

SERVES: 4–6
PREPARATION: 20 minutes
OVEN: 190°C/375°F/gas 5
COOKING: 50 minutes

900 g/2 lb rhubarb
175 g/6 oz caster sugar
30 ml/2 tablespoons water
175 g/6 oz plain flour
75 g/3 oz unsalted butter
1 piece preserved ginger
150 ml/¼ pt cream
5 ml/1 teaspoon ginger syrup
  (from jar)

Wash the rhubarb stalks, top and tail them, discard any damaged pieces and remove tough strings. Chop the stalks into 1 cm/½ in sections. Put the rhubarb in a deep baking dish, sprinkle over half the sugar and add the water. Sift the flour into a bowl. Cut the butter into cubes and rub it in until it forms a crumbly mixture; stir in the remaining sugar. Cover the rhubarb with this crumble mixture, patting it down lightly. Bake in a preheated oven at 190°C/375°F/ gas 5 for about 50 minutes or until crisp and golden on top.

Chop the piece of preserved ginger finely. Whip the cream until it stands in soft peaks; flavour with the chopped ginger and the syrup.
■ Serve the crumble warm or cold and offer the cream in a separate dish.

Rhubarb Crumble.

French Apple Flan

Neatly arranged rings of dessert apple top a generous layer of apple purée in this attractive, fruity flan.

SERVES: 4–6
PREPARATION: 1 hour
OVEN: 200°C/400°F/gas 6
      180°C/350°F/gas 4
COOKING: 1 hour

175 g/6 oz plain flour
salt
100 g/4 oz unsalted butter
175 g/6 oz caster sugar
1 large egg yolk
900 g/2 lb cooking apples
3 red-skinned dessert apples
juice of 1 lemon
15 ml/1 tablespoon apricot jam

Sift the flour and a pinch of salt into a mixing bowl. Cut 75 g/3 oz of the butter into small knobs and rub into the flour until the mixture resembles breadcrumbs. Mix in 15 ml/1 tablespoon of the caster sugar. Make a well in the centre of the flour, drop in the egg yolk and mix to a stiff dough with a little cold water.

Wrap the pastry in grease-proof paper and leave to rest for 30 minutes. Meanwhile, peel and core the cooking apples and cut them up roughly. Melt the remaining butter in a saucepan and add the apple pieces and 90 g/3½ oz of the remaining sugar. Cover with a lid and cook gently for 10 minutes. Drain the apples, saving the cooking liquid. Rub the cooked apples through a coarse sieve or process briefly in a liquidiser or food processor.

Allow this purée to cool. Wash the dessert apples; core them before cutting them into 5 mm/ ¼ in rings. Sprinkle with a little lemon juice to prevent them from going brown.

Roll out the pastry on a floured surface and use it to line an 18 cm/7 in loose-bottomed flan tin. Trim the pastry edges and prick the base with a fork. Line the pastry with greaseproof paper and sprinkle some baking beans on top, then bake in a preheated oven at 200°C/400°F/ gas 6 for 15 minutes. Remove the paper and baking beans. Reduce the oven temperature to 180°C/ 350°F/gas 4. Spoon the apple purée over the pastry and smooth the top. Drain the apple rings and arrange in an overlapping pattern on top.

Put the apple cooking liquid, 30 ml/2 tablespoons lemon juice, the jam and the remaining sugar in a saucepan. Cook over low heat until the sugar has dissolved, then bring to the boil and boil briskly for 4 minutes. Brush a little of this glaze over the apple slices.

Bake the flan for a further 45 minutes. If the apple slices brown too quickly, cover the flan loosely with foil. Remove the flan from the oven, brush with the remaining glaze and serve.
■ This flan is delicious hot or cold. Serve with cream or crème fraîche as an accompaniment.

Secret Cake

The title of this Yorkshire sweet refers to the filling which is hidden within a puff pastry case. It is traditionally served hot, with lashings of cream.

SERVES: 4
PREPARATION: 30 minutes
SOAKING: 1 hour
OVEN: 230°C/450°F/gas 8
200°C/400°F/gas 6
COOKING: 35–40 minutes

50 g/2 oz chopped candied peel
225 g/8 oz currants
30 ml/2 tablespoons brandy
375 g/13 oz home-made Puff
Pastry (page 374) or thawed
frozen puff pastry
25 g/1 oz caster sugar

Mix the candied peel and the currants together in a bowl, pour over the brandy and leave them to soak for at least 1 hour. Roll out the puff pastry, 3 mm/⅛ in thick, on a floured surface, and cut out two 20 cm/8 in rounds.

Place one pastry round on a baking sheet and top with the brandy-soaked currants and peel. Moisten the edge of the pastry with water and cover with the other pastry round. Press the edges together to seal them and decorate the top with pastry trimmings. Cut the cake into quarters, keeping them together.

Bake the cake for 15 minutes in a preheated oven at 230°C/450°F/gas 8. Turn the oven down to 200°C/400°F/gas 6 and bake the cake for a further 20–25 minutes until golden brown. Sprinkle with caster sugar.

Gâteau St Honoré

This cake is a Parisian speciality, named after St Honoré, the patron saint of pastry cooks. It is a case of shortcrust and choux pastries, filled with vanilla-flavoured cream.

SERVES: 4–6
PREPARATION: 1 hour
OVEN: 220°C/425°F/gas 7
190°C/375°F/gas 5
COOKING: 25 minutes

190 g/6½ oz plain flour
salt
50 g/2 oz butter
25 g/1 oz lard
300 ml/½ pt water
1 large egg
natural vanilla essence
225 g/8 oz sugar
1 quantity Pastry Cream, see
Greengage Flan (page 236)
Decoration
glacé cherries
angelica

Make the shortcrust pastry (page 365). Sift 100 g/4 oz of the flour and a pinch of salt into a bowl and rub in half the butter and all the lard until the mixture has a crumbly texture. Mix to a stiff dough with cold water. Roll out the pastry on a floured surface, to a 15 cm/6 in circle and trim the edge, using a plate as a guide. Place the pastry on a greased baking sheet and prick it all over.

Sift the remaining flour and a pinch of salt into a clean bowl. Put the remaining butter and 150 ml/¼ pt of the water in a saucepan and bring to the boil. Add the flour all at once and stir until the flour and liquid form a paste. Remove the pan from the heat, stir until the paste forms a ball leaving the side of the pan clean. Do not beat the paste.

Allow the choux pastry to cool for 10–15 minutes, then beat in the egg and a few drops of vanilla essence. Carry on beating hard until the choux paste is smooth and glossy.

Spoon the pastry into a piping bag fitted with a large plain nozzle. Pipe small buns, about 2.5 cm/1 in in diameter, closely around the edge of the

Gâteau St Honoré.

shortcrust pastry circle. Pipe the remaining choux pastry into buns of the same size, on a separate greased baking sheet.

Bake the pastry round and the individual buns in a preheated oven at 220°C/425°F/gas 7 for 10 minutes, then reduce the temperature to 190°C/375°F/gas 5 and continue to cook them for a further 15 minutes or until the pastry is golden brown. Remove both baking sheets from the oven and allow the pastries to cool.

Heat the sugar with the remaining cold water in a small pan until the sugar has dissolved. Bring to the boil, and boil hard until the syrup turns a pale golden colour. Remove the pan from the heat immediately to prevent the caramel from over-cooking. Dip the separate choux buns in this caramel and arrange them on top of the buns on the shortcrust base to form a double layer of pastry buns.

Spoon the pastry cream into the centre of the gâteau. Deco-rate with whole glacé cherries and strips of angelica.

Spiced Vanilla Soufflé

SERVES: 4
PREPARATION: 15 minutes
INFUSING: 30 minutes
OVEN: 180°C/350°F/gas 4
COOKING: 1 hour

300 ml/½ pt milk
1 cinnamon stick
2 bay leaves
10 cardamoms
25 g/1 oz plain flour
30 ml/2 tablespoons caster sugar,
plus extra for dusting dish
3 large eggs
15 ml/1 tablespoon natural
vanilla essence
icing sugar for dredging

Put the milk in a saucepan with the cinnamon stick. Break the bay leaves in half and add them to the pan with the cardamoms. Heat gently to just simmering, remove from the heat and leave to infuse for 30 minutes.

Mix the flour and sugar in a bowl. Separate the eggs. Beat the yolks into the flour mixture to give a smooth paste, then add the vanilla.

Strain the milk. Gradually stir it into the flour mixture, return it to the clean saucepan and bring slowly to the boil, stirring all the time until the mixture begins to thicken. Continue stirring until the custard boils and is really thick. Cook, stirring occasionally, for 3–4 minutes, then transfer the custard to a large bowl and cover the surface with cling film to prevent a skin from forming. Allow to cool slightly.

Lightly butter a 900 ml/1½ pt soufflé dish and sprinkle with caster sugar. Whisk the egg whites until stiff. Stir a little of the whisked egg white into the custard to lighten it, then fold in the remainder. Pour the mixture into the prepared soufflé dish. Run a clean finger around the inside rim of the dish to create a gutter between the mixture and the dish. Sprinkle with icing sugar and bake in a preheated oven at 180°C/350°F/gas 4 for 40–45 minutes or until well risen. Serve at once.

Note When planning the spiced vanilla soufflé as a dinner-party dessert, the custard may be cooked before guests arrive and left, covered, at room temperature. Then the mixture may be finished and baked just before the main course is served. Alternatively, finish the soufflé after the main course and serve a platter of cheeses while it is being baked.

Apple and Ratafia Dessert

SERVES: 4
PREPARATION: 30 minutes
COOKING: 20 minutes
CHILLING: 2–4 hours

675 g/1½ lb cooking apples
150 ml/¼ pt water
100 g/4 oz sugar
juice of 1 lemon
15 ml/1 tablespoon powdered gelatine
1 egg white
150 ml/¼ pt double cream
2.5 ml/½ teaspoon natural vanilla essence
15 ml/1 tablespoon caster sugar
Decoration
about 20 ratafia biscuits
angelica leaves
split blanched almonds

Peel, core and slice the apples, then place them in a saucepan with half the water, the 100 g/4 oz sugar and lemon juice. Heat, stirring occasionally, until the sugar dissolves and the syrup boils, then reduce the heat if necessary and cover the pan. Simmer for 15–20 minutes, until the apples are pulpy. Rub the fruit through a sieve and set it aside to cool.

Sprinkle the gelatine over the remaining water in a small heatproof basin. Do not stir. Leave to stand for 15 minutes until the gelatine has absorbed the water. Stand the basin over a pan of simmering water and stir until the gelatine has dissolved completely. Stir the dissolved gelatine into the apple purée.

Whisk the egg white until stiff, but not dry, and fold it into the apple mixture. Rinse a 900 ml/1½ pt mould with cold water, then pour the apple mixture into it and chill until set.

Dip the mould into hot water for a few seconds and invert it on to a serving platter. Whip the cream with the vanilla essence and caster sugar until it stands in soft peaks. Spoon the cream into a piping bag fitted with a star nozzle and pipe a border of cream around the base of the dessert. Decorate the top of the dessert with swirls of cream. Arrange ratafia biscuits, angelica leaves and split blanched almonds on and around the pudding. Chill until ready to serve.

Chocolate Mousse

SERVES: 6
PREPARATION: 20–30 minutes
CHILLING: 2–3 hours

225 g/8 oz plain chocolate
15 g/½ oz unsalted butter
15 ml/1 tablespoon Cointreau
4 large eggs

Break the chocolate into small pieces and put them in a heatproof bowl. Set the bowl over a pan of hot water and leave the chocolate to melt, stirring occasionally. Cool slightly, then stir in the butter and Cointreau.

Separate the eggs and whisk the whites until stiff. Beat the yolks into the slightly cooled chocolate mixture, then gently fold in the whites. Spoon the mousse into glasses and leave to set in the refrigerator.

Grapefruit in Brandy

SERVES: 6
PREPARATION: 12 minutes
COOKING: 8 minutes

4 large grapefruit
100 g/4 oz caster sugar
150 ml/¼ pt water
5 ml/1 teaspoon cinnamon
60 ml/4 tablespoons brandy

Cut off all the peel and pith from the grapefruit and carefully poke out the pithy core. Slice the grapefruit into 1 cm/½ in thick rounds.

Put the caster sugar in a large saucepan with the water and the ground cinnamon. Cook over a low heat, stirring frequently, until the sugar has dissolved, then boil this syrup briskly for 2 minutes. Lower the heat, add the grapefruit slices and poach them gently in the syrup for 6 minutes, turning once.

Arrange the grapefruit slices on a serving dish, pour over the brandy and serve hot or chilled.

Grapefruit in Brandy.

135

Easter Feasting

*E*aster, which falls between March 22 and April 25, is the most sacred festival in the Christian year, although many of its customs can be traced back to the traditions of pagan religions. The notion of exchanging eggs goes back to pre-Christian times when eggs, as a symbol of renewed life, were exchanged at the pagan spring festivals.

Hot cross buns are thought to have originated from the small wheat cakes eaten at the spring festivals held in honour of Astarte, the Phoenician fertility goddess. Her counterpart in Britain was Eostre, from whom we get the word Easter. The cross on the buns, however, is of Christian origin. The simnel cake, originally made by servant girls for Mothering Sunday, is now baked for Easter in Britain.

Most other countries also have their special Easter fare. The Russian housewife bakes a yeast cake, known as *Kulich*, which she wraps in a spotless napkin to take to church for the priest's blessing. In Portugal, the traditional sweet consists of fine strands of egg yolk called Angel's Hair. The Italians bake *Colomba*, which is similar to the Russian *Kulich*, and the Sicilians make *Cassata alla Siciliana* – a rich layered cake covered with icing.

In Poland, the Easter fare is a huge buffet, each item blessed by the priest. Place of honour goes to the Paschal Lamb, a sculpture of butter or boiled white sugar.

Easter Baking

Hot Cross Buns

Instead of easy-blend yeast, fresh yeast can be used in this recipe following the traditional double-rising method (page 395).

MAKES: 12
PREPARATION: 45 minutes
   plus rising
OVEN: 190°C/375°F/gas 5
COOKING: 15–20 minutes

450 g/1 lb strong white flour
5 ml/1 teaspoon salt
50 g/2 oz butter
50 g/2 oz caster sugar
5 ml/1 teaspoon ground
   mixed spice
10 ml/2 teaspoons fast-action
   easy-blend dried yeast
25 g/1 oz currants
50 g/2 oz chopped mixed peel
150 ml/¼ pt hand-hot water
150 ml/¼ pt hand-hot milk
1 egg
Glaze
50 g/2 oz sugar
30 ml/2 tablespoons water
30 ml/2 tablespoons milk

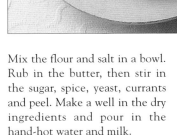

Mix the flour and salt in a bowl. Rub in the butter, then stir in the sugar, spice, yeast, currants and peel. Make a well in the dry ingredients and pour in the hand-hot water and milk.

Beat the egg, add it to the liquids, then gradually work in the flour to make a stiff dough. Knead the dough thoroughly on a lightly floured surface for about 10 minutes, until it is smooth and elastic.

Cut the dough into twelve equal-sized pieces and shape into a ball. Place the balls of dough well apart on greased baking sheets, then flatten them slightly. Cover them loosely with lightly oiled cling film or polythene and leave in a warm place until doubled in size.

Hot Cross Buns and Simnel Cake.

Use a sharp knife to cut a deep cross in the top of each bun. Bake the buns in a preheated oven at 190°C/375°F/gas 5 for 15–20 minutes. Make the glaze while the buns are cooking: heat the sugar with the water and milk until the sugar dissolves, then bring the syrup to the boil and cook, without stirring, until it is reduced and thickened slightly. Brush the hot syrup over the buns as soon as they are taken out of the oven, then put them on a wire rack to cool.

Note Instead of cutting a cross in the top of the buns, a thick paste of flour and water can be piped on the buns to make a more pronounced cross.

Simnel Cake

MAKES: 1×20 cm/8 in cake
PREPARATION: 20 minutes
OVEN: 160°C/325°F/gas 3
COOKING: 2¾–3 hours

225 g/8 oz unsalted butter
   or margarine
grated rind and strained juice of
   2 large lemons
225 g/8 oz caster sugar
4 large eggs
175 g/6 oz chopped mixed peel
175 g/6 oz sultanas
575 g/1¼ lb currants
400 g/14 oz plain flour
salt
baking powder
5 ml/1 teaspoon mixed spice
15–30 ml/1–2 tablespoons milk
900 g/2 lb marzipan
sugar or chocolate eggs to decorate

Cream the butter or margarine with the grated lemon rind and the sugar until light and fluffy. Beat in the eggs, one at a time, and stir in the mixed peel and dried fruit. Sift the flour with a little salt, a good pinch of baking powder and the spice. Fold the flour into the creamed mixture. If necessary, add the milk.

Line and grease a 20 cm/8 in, round, deep cake tin. Roll out half the marzipan to a circle slightly larger than the tin, then, using the tin as a guide, cut out a circle that will fit inside it. Spoon half the cake mixture into the tin and level the top. Place the circle of the marzipan on top, then add the rest of the mixture. Bake in a preheated oven at 160°C/325°F/gas 3 for 2¾–3 hours. Cool on a wire rack.

Roll out two-thirds of the remaining marzipan to a 13 cm/5 in round and place on top of the cooled cake. Smooth the marzipan around the edge of the cake. Shape the remaining marzipan into 11 balls, which represent the Apostles excluding Judas, and set these around the edge of the cake.

The centre of the cake can be decorated with small chocolate eggs and, if liked, golden Easter chicks. A bow of ribbon may be tied around the cake.

Easter Sunday Lunch

Young spring lamb is traditional at Easter. All the recipes for this menu appear here, with the exception of Grapefruit in Brandy (page 135).

Menu

~

Stuffed Eggs

~

Saddle of Lamb with Wine Sauce
Haricots Verts, New Potatoes
Green Salad

~

Grapefruit in Brandy

Stuffed Eggs

SERVES: 8
PREPARATION: 30 minutes

8 hard-boiled eggs
50 g/2 oz can anchovy fillets
10 ml/2 teaspoons drained capers
90 ml/6 tablespoons olive oil
30 ml/2 tablespoons lemon juice
French mustard
black pepper

Cut the eggs in half lengthways and carefully remove the yolks, taking care not to break the egg whites. Mash the yolks in a bowl. Chop the anchovies roughly, add them to the bowl with the remaining ingredients and pound the mixture to a paste. Spoon into a piping bag fitted with a plain nozzle, then pipe it into the egg whites.

Saddle of Lamb with Wine Sauce

SERVES: 8
PREPARATION: 20 minutes
MARINATING: 12 hours
OVEN: 180°C/350°F/gas 4
COOKING: 3¾ hours

2.8 kg/6 lb saddle of lamb
12 sprigs rosemary
50 g/2 oz dripping or lard
25 g/1 oz flour
75 ml/5 tablespoons
  redcurrant jelly
salt and black pepper
Marinade
1 carrot
2 onions
150 ml/¼ pt water
3 parsley sprigs
1 sprig thyme
1 bay leaf
6 peppercorns
2 cloves
1 blade mace
60 ml/4 tablespoons malt vinegar
900 ml/1½ pt red wine
60 ml/4 tablespoons medium sherry
60 ml/4 tablespoons brandy

Make the marinade: Chop the carrot and onions finely and place them in a pan with the water. Add the herbs, spices and vinegar. Boil for 30 minutes, then leave to cool. Stir the red wine, sherry and brandy into the marinade. Pour into a dish large enough to hold the lamb. Add the lamb, spoon the marinade over, cover and marinate in the refrigerator for 12 hours.

Drain the lamb, reserving the marinade. Make small incisions in the lamb and add the rosemary sprigs. Heat the dripping or lard in a roasting tin in a preheated oven at 180°C/350°F/gas 4. Add the lamb and roast. Baste the lamb every now and then with the cooking fat and juices.

Transfer the lamb to a heated serving platter, cover with foil and keep warm. Pour off any excess fat from the roasting tin, leaving a thin covering in the bottom. Stir in the flour, then cook for 2 minutes, scraping the residue off the tin. Gradually pour in the reserved marinade, stirring continuously, and bring to the boil. Reduce the heat and stir in the redcurrant jelly, then simmer the sauce for 5 minutes, stirring often. Taste the sauce for seasoning, adding salt and pepper as necessary. Bring to a full boil, cook for 1 minute, then strain the sauce into a heated sauceboat and serve it with the lamb.

Decorating Eggs

Use only white-shelled eggs for decorating. When hard-boiled in spinach water, they take on a green colour, while those boiled with raw beetroot turn red. Onion or shallot skins wrapped around the eggs and wound on with brown cotton give an orange-brown mottled effect. Flower petals can be placed on damp eggs, covered with onion skin and kept in place with string or tape. The boiled eggs will then bear the imprint of both petals and onion skins.

Add a few drops of vegetable dye or food colouring to the water to dye the egg yellow. Narrow strips of masking tape can be stuck on to the eggs in geometric patterns before dyeing. Peeling off the tapes afterwards will reveal white patterns on a coloured background. Polish all boiled eggs with a little olive oil.

The eggs may be boiled before being decorated with wax crayons, vegetable dyes, water colours or oil paints. Complicated designs for keepsake eggs should be traced on uncooked eggs, first dipped in vegetable dye.

The Ukranians are famous for making decorated eggs that resemble miniature mosaics. The complicated designs are traced on uncooked eggs which are dipped, at various stages, in different vegetable dyes. Only a small part of the egg is coloured at a time, the other areas being masked with wax or cotton tape.

May

Salmon with Fromage Frais, Gooseberry and Elderflower Soufflés.

May

May brings a delicious vegetable treat in the form of home-grown English asparagus. This is wonderfully crisp and juicy when freshly cut from the garden or a pick-your-own farm – and economical as well. Take advantage of its availability while you can, for the season ends before June is out. Look for thick, young shoots that are thin skinned and tender, and cut them cleanly off the plant near their base. This plump and tender, prime-quality asparagus should be eaten fresh as freezing makes the vegetable limp. It is worth freezing some of the thinner, slightly middle-grade spears . These will still be tender, if not quite so plump and succulent, ideal for making soup or adding to sauced dishes such as pasta bakes and pie fillings. Tall, thin and/or woody spears are often sold very cheaply and these are also useful for making soups and sauces.

One of the features of the month's recipes is a selection of ideas and reminders for salads using light dressings and fresh herbs. Salad ingredients are now available throughout the year, but as summer approaches the emphasis moves away from serving them as accompaniments and towards making salad meals. Experiment with more adventurous combinations of classic salad leaves with fish or seafood, poultry or meat, or marinated cheese. Pepper your salads with additional flavours and textures by adding nuts, seeds and spices, and top them with well-mixed dressings.

Oysters, scallops and mussels are now out of season, but they are replaced by lobster and crab, with skate and monkfish tail offering good value for money. Look out for the first young mackerel, especially at small fishing ports where local fishermen sell their catch.

Gooseberries and apricots are the seasonal choice for dessert, but it is worth remembering that both fruit also go well with savoury foods. A simple sauce of sweetened stewed gooseberries is a classic accompaniment for mackerel, the sharp tang of the fruit balancing the rich flavour of the fish. Apricots are a popular fruit to serve with meat. Dried apricots are commonly used in stuffings but the fresh fruit also tastes good with richer poultry and meat, such as duck, lamb, pork and gammon. Poach halved and stoned apricots in a wine sauce made with the cooking juices from a roast joint or grilled cutlets, chops or steaks, and add a little redcurrant jelly or a hint of honey to counteract the sharp apricot flavour.

Menu suggestions *Salads are the focus for this month's feature pages, the emphasis switching to main courses rather than side dishes. The menus that follow take a broader view of early summer entertaining, with ideas for family and formal occasions. The main recipes are included in this chapter unless page references indicate that they are found elsewhere in the book.*

Formal Dinner Party
~
Gravad Lax
~
Lamb Argenteuil
Buttered New Potatoes
Fresh Garden Peas with Mint
~
*Gooseberry and
Elderflower Soufflés*
Gâteau de Pithiviers Feuilleté
~
Cheese Board and Fresh Fruit

This menu is easily prepared, requiring the minimum of attention once guests have arrived. Two desserts are included, but one could be replaced by a fruit salad. Since opinions on when to serve cheese differ, it is quite acceptable to put both cheese, fruit, and dessert on the table together, leaving it to your guests to decide which to eat first.

Vegetarian Meal
~
*Spinach with Flageolets
Freshly Cooked Pasta*
~
*Rhubarb Crumble (page 133)
Custard Sauce (page 338)*

This is an everyday vegetarian menu, with a pasta and vegetable main course followed by a hearty pudding and custard. For a less sugary dessert, a lightly sweetened baked custard is a good choice. If you have any concerns about the protein content of a vegetarian diet, it is worth thinking in terms of the amount eaten across all meals in one day as well as taking a balanced view of the weekly diet. The protein content of this menu can be boosted by serving the spinach and flageolet mixture as a base for poached eggs or grilled tofu, both of which are equally delicious.

Special Supper for Two
~
*Chicken Livers with Grapes
Salad of Mixed Leaves*
~
*Bananas Flambé (page 363)
with
Vanilla Ice Cream (page 380)*

The recipe quantities can be adapted quite easily to make two portions in this quick-to-prepare menu. The main course of livers served with a salad is not too filling, leaving room for the indulgent dessert, which can be served with good-quality bought ice cream – ideal for Friday night supper to round off the week.

Mixed Leaf and Chick Pea Salad (page 157), Courgette and Mozzarella Salad (page152), and Pasta Salad with Stilton Dressing (page157).

SOUPS

French Turnip Soup

SERVES: 6–8
PREPARATION: 20 minutes
COOKING: 50 minutes

350 g/12 oz turnips
225 g/8 oz potatoes
1 leek
1 onion
50 g/2 oz butter
25 g/1 oz plain flour
1.7 litres/3 pt vegetable stock
salt and black pepper
2 egg yolks
45 ml/3 tablespoons single cream
Croûtons (page 313) to garnish

Peel and dice the turnips and potatoes and rinse them in cold water. Remove the roots and coarse outer leaves from the leek, cut in half and rinse thoroughly under cold running water to remove all traces of dirt. Chop up the leek coarsely. Peel and roughly chop the onion.

Melt the butter in a large pan and add the chopped vegetables; cover the pan with a lid and cook them over low heat for about 15 minutes without browning them. Add the flour and cook for a few more minutes, stirring all the time. Gradually stir in the stock and season to taste with salt and freshly ground black pepper. Bring to the boil, then lower the heat and simmer the soup for about 30 minutes, or until the vegetables are tender.

Let the soup cool a little before liquidising it or rubbing it through a fine sieve into the clean pan. Reheat the soup over a low heat.

Beat the egg yolks with the cream in a small bowl, stir in a little of the hot soup and then stir it all back into the soup. Stir over low heat for a few minutes, without allowing the soup to boil. Correct seasoning and serve the soup at once, with a separate bowl of croûtons.

Asparagus Soup

The water and trimmings left after cooking asparagus are excellent for soup. For the best flavour, boil the cooking water from the asparagus until it is reduced to the required quantity.

SERVES: 4–6
PREPARATION: 20 minutes
COOKING: 30–35 minutes

1 large onion
1 small clove garlic
1 large potato
25 g/1 oz butter
15 ml/1 tablespoon plain flour
900 ml/1½ pt cooking water from
*   asparagus or stock*
spear ends from 900 g/2 lb
*   asparagus*
salt and black pepper
150 ml/¼ pt single or double cream
chopped chervil or parsley to garnish

Peel and finely chop the onion and garlic. Peel the potato and cut it into 2.5 cm/1 in cubes. Melt the butter in a large saucepan and cook the onion, garlic and potato in this for 15 minutes, stirring often. Stir in the flour and cook for a few minutes, before blending in the asparagus water or stock bit by bit. Add the asparagus spear ends and bring to the boil. Reduce the heat, cover the pan and simmer the soup for 15 minutes.

Take the pan off the heat, leave the soup to cool slightly, then purée it in a liquidiser or food processor. Rub the purée through a sieve into a clean pan and season to taste with salt and freshly ground pepper. Reheat the soup and stir in the cream, without letting it boil.

Serve the soup in individual bowls and sprinkle the chopped chervil or parsley on top.

Note Asparagus Soup is an excellent freezer candidate. A concentrated soup can be made by by using less asparagus water or stock, reducing the quantity to 600 ml/1 pt. Do not add the egg yolks and cream to the soup before freezing. Add an additional 300 ml/½ pt stock to the thawed soup, then stir in the egg yolks and cream when the soup is hot, as above.

STARTERS, SAVOURIES & LIGHT DISHES

Canapés à la Crème

This starter is quick to prepare. Hot, crisp bread, salty anchovies and cold clotted cream make an unusual savoury too.

SERVES: 4
PREPARATION: 8 minutes
COOKING: 10–12 minutes

8 slices white bread
12 drained canned anchovy fillets
75 g/3 oz clarified butter
*   (page 306)*
60 ml/4 tablespoons clotted cream
parsley sprigs to garnish

Cut a round from each slice of bread with a 7.5 cm/3 in scone cutter. Cut each anchovy fillet in half lengthways. Melt the clarified butter in a heavy-based pan and fry the bread until golden brown. Keep the slices warm on a hot serving dish.

When all the bread has been fried, quickly arrange three anchovy strips on each slice of bread, spoon over the cream and garnish each portion with a small sprig of parsley.

Serve immediately, before the cream melts into the hot bread.

Canapés à la Crème.

Chicken Liver Pâté

Frozen chicken livers are readily available and are excellent for pâtés and terrines.

SERVES: 6
PREPARATION: 15 minutes
COOKING: 10 minutes
CHILLING: 2–3 hours

1 small onion
50 g/2 oz butter
2 bay leaves
10 ml/2 teaspoons chopped thyme
450 g/1 lb chicken livers
salt and black pepper
30 ml/2 tablespoons brandy

Peel and finely chop the onion. Melt the butter and fry the onion, the bay leaves and the thyme for 2–3 minutes. Trim the chicken livers, removing any discoloured parts which may have been in contact with the gall bladder, and cut them into small pieces; add to the pan. Cook gently for 5 minutes or until the livers are cooked through. Discard the bay leaves and liquidise the liver mixture until smooth, or mince it twice.

Season to taste with salt and freshly ground pepper and stir in the brandy. Scrape the pâté into a bowl, cover and leave to cool, then chill in the refrigerator for several hours.

■ If the pâté is not to be served immediately, the surface can be covered with a layer of clarified butter (page 306).

Mushroom Pâté

SERVES: 4
PREPARATION: 30 minutes
COOKING: 30–40 minutes
CHILLING: 2–3 hours

450 g/1 lb closed cap mushrooms
50 g/2 oz butter
2.5 ml/½ teaspoon ground mace
2.5 ml/½ teaspoon paprika
45 ml/3 tablespoons brandy
salt and black pepper
225 g/8 oz cream cheese

Chop up the mushrooms finely. Melt the butter in a saucepan, add the mushrooms and cook, stirring occasionally, until they give up their liquid. Stir in the mace, paprika and brandy. Bring to the boil, then reduce the heat slightly so that the mixture bubbles steadily and cook for about 30–40 minutes. Stir the mixture occasionally to ensure that it does not burn, but keep the mushrooms bubbling so that the cooking liquid evaporates until they form a buttery paste.

Remove the pan from the heat and stir in salt and pepper to taste. Then beat in half the cream cheese. When this first batch of cheese has melted into the mushrooms, gradually work in the remaining cheese. Turn the mixture into a dish (about 450 ml/¾ pt capacity), smooth the top and leave to cool. Cover and chill for at least 2–3 hours or overnight, if possible, before serving. The pâté keeps well in the refrigerator for 2–3 days.

■ Crisp toast, Bath Oliver biscuits, oatcakes or crusty bread are all ideal accompaniments.

The Curé's Omelette

A society beauty, engaged in good works, once visited a priest in one of the poorest parts of Paris, to find him dining on an expensive omelette of luxurious fresh tuna and carp roes. This variation is made with canned tuna and fresh herring roes, but the result is still superb.

SERVES: 4
PREPARATION: 20 minutes
COOKING: 10 minutes

225 g/8 oz soft herring roes
99 g/3½ oz can tuna
1 shallot
50 g/2 oz butter
8 eggs
salt and black pepper

Pour boiling water over the roes and leave them to stand for 30 seconds to blanch*. Drain the roes and chop them roughly, discarding any discoloured parts. Drain the oil from the tuna; flake the fish with a fork. Peel and finely chop the shallot. Heat 25 g/1 oz of the butter and cook the shallot over low heat until soft and transparent.

Add the roes and the tuna to the shallot, crushing the mixture down with a fork. Cook for a few minutes, then remove the pan from the heat and leave the mixture to cool slightly. Beat the eggs in a bowl and stir the fish mixture into them. Season to taste. Melt the remaining butter in an omelette pan and use the egg mixture to make four omelettes (page 337).

FISH, SHELLFISH & SEAFOOD

Gravad Lax

Fresh dill is now readily available in large supermarkets. It is also worth freezing dill as the herb can be used from frozen in the pickle for this salmon. The fish must be perfectly fresh – always check that it is the same day's delivery to the fishmonger.

SERVES: 6
PREPARATION: 30 minutes
CHILLING: 12 hours–5 days

675 g/1½ lb salmon tailpiece
Pickle
75 ml/5 tablespoons sea salt
75 ml/5 tablespoons sugar
10 ml/2 teaspoons crushed black peppercorns
15 ml/1 tablespoon brandy (optional)
75 ml/5 tablespoons dill
Sauce
30 ml/2 tablespoons French or German mustard
15 ml/1 tablespoon sugar
1 large egg yolk
105 ml/3½ fl oz olive oil
30 ml/2 tablespoons wine vinegar
10 ml/2 teaspoons dill
salt and white pepper

Ask the fishmonger to fillet the salmon into two pieces. Mix all the pickling ingredients together and spread a quarter of this mixture over the base of a flat dish. Lay the first piece of salmon, skin down, on top of the mixture and spread half of the remaining pickle over the cut side. Place the other piece of salmon, skin side up, over the first. Spread the top with the remaining mixture, rubbing it well into the skin. Cover the salmon with a piece of foil and a board weighed down with a couple of cans. Leave the salmon to press in the refrigerator for anything up to 5 days, but not less than 12 hours, turning and thoroughly basting the salmon with the pickle once a day.

Drain the salmon and pat it dry on absorbent kitchen paper. Before serving, scrape off the peppercorn mixture. Slice the salmon thinly, either parallel to the skin as with smoked salmon or obliquely to the skin.

For the sauce to go with the fish, beat the mustard with the sugar and egg yolk until smooth. Gradually add the olive oil and the vinegar, mixing thoroughly between each addition. Season to taste with dill, salt and pepper.

Arrange the slices of salmon on individual plates, and serve the sauce separately.

■ Buttered light rye bread makes an excellent accompaniment for gravad lax.

Salmon with Fromage Frais

SERVES: 6
PREPARATION: 15 minutes
OVEN: 190°C/375°F/gas 5
COOKING: 25–30 minutes

150 ml/¼ pt water
150 ml/¼ pt dry white wine
2 parsley sprigs
1 thyme sprig
1 bay leaf
salt and black pepper
6 salmon steaks (each 2.5 cm/
  1 in thick)
150 ml/¼ pt fromage frais
10 ml/2 teaspoons snipped chives
15 ml/1 tablespoon finely
  chopped parsley
lemon wedges to garnish

Place the water, wine, parsley sprigs, thyme and bay leaf in a small saucepan. Add a little seasoning and heat gently until just boiling, then remove from the heat and leave to cool until just warm. Butter an ovenproof dish, large enough to take the salmon steaks in a single layer. Arrange the salmon steaks in the dish, pour over the wine mixture with the herbs and cover the dish with foil.

Bake the salmon steaks in a preheated oven at 190°C/375°F/gas 5 for 20–25 minutes, until the salmon is only just cooked. Transfer the salmon steaks to a warmed serving dish and strain the cooking liquor through a fine sieve into a large saucepan. Boil the liquor hard until it is reduced by half. Remove from the heat and stir a little of the liquor into

the fromage frais, then pour the fromage frais into the pan. Stir. Taste for seasoning, adding salt and pepper if necessary. Reheat the sauce for a few seconds if liked but take extreme care as the fromage frais curdles easily. Stir in the chives and chopped parsley and spoon the sauce over or around the salmon. Garnish the fish with lemon wedges.

Whiting with Orange Sauce

SERVES: 6
PREPARATION: 30 minutes
COOKING: 40 minutes

6 whiting
salt and black pepper
juice of 1 lemon
grated rind and juice of 1 orange
60 ml/4 tablespoons double cream
150 ml/¼ pt dry white wine
4 egg yolks
100 g/4 oz butter
plain flour for coating
Garnish
1 orange
chopped parsley

If the fishmonger has not already done so, clean the whiting, and fillet each into two pieces. Rinse the fillets and dry them on absorbent kitchen paper; season with salt and freshly ground black pepper and sprinkle with half the lemon juice. Mix the orange juice with the rest of the lemon juice in a heatproof bowl.

For the sauce, stir the cream, wine and egg yolks into the fruit juices and set the bowl over a pan of simmering water. Whisk

the sauce mixture continuously until it has the consistency of thin cream. Season to taste with salt and black pepper, and stir in the grated orange rind. Cut half the butter into knobs and beat them one by one into the sauce. Keep the sauce hot, but do not allow it to boil.

Season the flour for coating with salt and pepper; coat the whiting fillets with the flour. Melt the remaining butter in a large, heavy-based pan and fry the fillets until cooked and golden brown on both sides.

Cut the orange into wedges and use as a garnish, with the chopped parsley. The sauce can be served separately or poured over the fish.

■ Offer crusty French bread with which to mop up the sauce.

Baked Trout with Garlic Mushrooms

SERVES: 4
PREPARATION: 15 minutes
OVEN: 190°C/375°F/gas 5
COOKING: 30–35 minutes

175 g/6 oz mushrooms
2 cloves garlic
25 g/1 oz butter
45 ml/3 tablespoons olive oil
30 ml/2 tablespoons chopped
  parsley
4 oven-ready trout
salt and black pepper
lemon wedges to garnish

Slice the mushrooms. Peel and crush the garlic. Melt the butter with the oil in a saucepan. Add the mushrooms and crushed

garlic and cook over high heat for 2 minutes. Using a perforated spoon, transfer the mushroom mixture to an ovenproof dish large enough to hold the trout in a single layer. Reserve the pan juices. Add the chopped parsley and spread the mixture out to cover the base of the dish.

Arrange the trout on top of the mushroom mixture. Pour over the reserved pan juices, season with salt and pepper and cover with foil. Bake in a preheated oven at 190°C/375°F/gas 5 for 30–35 minutes or until the trout are cooked through. Serve hot, garnished with lemon wedges.

Whiting with Orange Sauce.

Soles aux Crêpes

The combination of buttered fillets of sole with featherlight strips of pancake is a speciality from Bayeux, northern France.

SERVES: 6
PREPARATION: 15 minutes
COOKING: 25 minutes

butter or oil for frying pancakes
12 fillets of sole
plain flour for coating
salt and black pepper
75 g/3 oz clarified butter (page 306)
15 ml/1 tablespoon chopped parsley
lemon wedges to garnish
Batter
50 g/2 oz plain flour
1.25 ml/¼ teaspoon salt
1 egg
60 ml/4 tablespoons water
75 ml/5 tablespoons milk

Begin by making the crêpe batter. Sift the flour and salt into a bowl, make a well in the centre and add the lightly beaten egg. Mix thoroughly and add the water and milk gradually, beating well, until the batter is smooth and has the consistency of single cream. Add more water to the batter if necessary.

Grease a clean frying pan with butter or oil and fry three or four crêpes from the batter.

Wipe the sole fillets with absorbent kitchen paper. Season the flour with salt and pepper and coat the sole fillets, shaking off any surplus. Melt 50 g/2 oz of the clarified butter in a large pan and fry the fillets until golden brown on both sides, turning once. Arrange the fillets on a serving dish and keep them hot.

Roll the crêpes up and cut them into 1 cm/½ in strips. Melt the remaining butter and reheat the strips until they are hot and golden. Sprinkle with the parsley and pile the pancake strips over and among the sole fillets. Garnish with wedges of lemon.

■ As a side dish, make Hot and Cold Rice Salad (page 195), omitting the peaches.

Lobster Thermidor

Lobster is the most expensive shellfish and is also regarded by gourmets as the most delicious.

SERVES: 6
PREPARATION: 50 minutes
COOKING: 1½ hours

300 ml/½ pt fish stock
150 ml/¼ pt dry white wine
1 onion
4 peppercorns
1 bay leaf
1 sprig thyme
salt and black pepper
450 ml/¾ pt milk
3 cooked lobsters (575–675 g/ 1¼–1½ lb)
50 g/2 oz butter
50 g/2 oz plain flour
5 ml/1 teaspoon Dijon mustard
2 large egg yolks
150 ml/¼ pt single cream
5 ml/1 teaspoon lemon juice
75 g/3 oz Parmesan cheese
50 g/2 oz dried white breadcrumbs
lettuce leaves to serve

Pour the fish stock and white wine into a saucepan, bring to the boil and then boil the

Lobster Thermidor.

mixture briskly until the liquid has reduced to 150 ml/¼ pt.

Peel the onion, cut it into quarters and put it in another saucepan with the peppercorns, bay leaf, thyme, a pinch of salt and the milk. Bring to the boil, remove the pan from the heat, cover with a lid and leave the milk to infuse for 30 minutes.

Meanwhile, remove the claws from the lobsters (page 318); split each body in half lengthways, through the head and tail and along the centre line of the shell. Set the shells aside, with the feeler claws intact. Discard the grey sac in the head and the black intestinal tube in the body.

Rub any loose coral (or spawn) through a fine sieve. Remove the meat from the shells and the claws and cut it carefully into 2 cm/¾ in cubes.

Melt the butter in a saucepan, stir in the flour and cook gently for 2 minutes; remove the pan from the heat. Strain the infused milk through a fine sieve and gradually stir this and the reduced fish stock into the roux*. Bring this sauce to the boil, stirring continuously, and cook gently for 3 minutes, until the sauce thickens. Leave to cool for 2 minutes, then stir in the mustard, egg yolks, sieved coral and the cream. Season the sauce with salt and freshly ground black pepper, and stir in the lemon juice.

Thoroughly wash and dry the empty lobster shells and coat the inside of each with a little of the sauce. Stir the lobster meat into the sauce and carefully spoon the mixture into the shells.

Grate the Parmesan cheese, mix it with the breadcrumbs and sprinkle the mixture over the lobsters. Place the shells under a hot grill and cook until the cheese topping is golden brown. Arrange the filled lobster shells on a bed of lettuce leaves.

■ Crisp French bread and a tossed green salad are traditionally served with the lobster.

Hot Crab Soufflé

SERVES: 4
PREPARATION: 20 minutes
OVEN: 190°C/375°F/gas 5
COOKING: 40 minutes

25 g/1 oz butter
25 g/1 oz plain flour
250 ml/8 fl oz milk
salt and black pepper
pinch cayenne pepper
50 g/2 oz Cheddar cheese
4 eggs
175 g/6 oz crabmeat, fresh, canned or frozen

Melt the butter in a saucepan; stir in the flour and cook over low heat for a few minutes. Gradually beat in the milk, stirring continuously until the sauce thickens and comes to the boil. Season to taste with salt, freshly ground pepper and cayenne. Grate the cheese and stir into the sauce. Leave to cool for 5 minutes.

Separate the eggs and beat the yolks, one at a time, into the cheese sauce. Flake the prepared crabmeat finely and stir into the sauce. Correct the seasoning if necessary. Whisk the egg whites until stiff, then fold gently into the crab mixture.

Pour the mixture into a buttered 900 ml/1½ pt soufflé dish and level the top. Bake in the centre of a preheated oven at 190°C/375°F/gas 5 for 35–40 minutes, until the soufflé is well risen and golden brown. Serve immediately.

■ A tossed green salad could be served as an accompaniment.

POULTRY & GAME

Chicken Livers with Grapes

Frozen chicken livers are readily available, either fresh or frozen. Here they are served in a wine sauce with grapes and make a good lunch or supper dish.

SERVES: 6
PREPARATION: 25 minutes
COOKING: 10–12 minutes

675 g/1½ lb chicken livers,
thawed if frozen
salt and black pepper
350 g/12 oz seedless green grapes
6 slices white bread
175 g/6 oz butter
30 ml/2 tablespoons oil
90–125 ml/3–4 fl oz Madeira, port
or sweet sherry

Rinse the chicken livers in cold water and pat them dry. Cut away the white, stringy pieces and any discoloured parts which may have been in contact with the gall bladder – they will taste bitter. Season the livers with salt and pepper and set aside.

Peel the grapes (page 360). Remove the crusts from the bread slices. Melt 100 g/4 oz of the butter with the oil in a pan. When hot, fry the bread until golden brown on both sides. Stand the fried bread upright on a baking sheet and keep hot.

Melt the remaining butter in the pan and cook the livers for 5 minutes until they are cooked through. Remove from the pan using a perforated spoon and keep hot. Stir the wine into the pan juices and reduce by rapid boiling until the sauce has thickened to a syrup. Add the grapes to the sauce and let them heat through.

To serve, arrange the hot bread on a serving dish, top with chicken livers and spoon the grapes on top. Serve immediately, before the sauce soaks into the fried bread.

Chicken Livers with Grapes.

Chicken Breasts with Sage

SERVES: 6
PREPARATION: 10 minutes
COOKING: 45 minutes

plain flour for coating
salt and black pepper
6 skinned boneless chicken breasts
15 ml/1 tablespoon olive oil
15 g/½ oz butter
50 g/2 oz thin gammon rashers
150 ml/¼ pt dry white wine
150 ml/¼ pt chicken stock
12 sage leaves

Season the flour for coating with salt and pepper. Add the chicken breasts and coat lightly on both sides. Heat the oil and butter in a frying pan over moderate heat and lightly brown the chicken pieces on both sides.

Cut the gammon into narrow strips and add to the chicken breasts. When the chicken is golden brown, pour in the wine and enough of the stock to come about two-thirds up the chicken breasts. Chop the sage roughly and add it to the pan.

Cover the pan with a lid and simmer the chicken over a moderate heat for 10–15 minutes or until cooked through.

Using tongs, remove the chicken to a serving dish and keep it hot. Increase the heat and rapidly boil the liquid in the pan until it has reduced to a thin coating consistency. Season the sauce to taste with salt and freshly ground pepper.

Pour the sauce over the chicken and serve at once.

Chicken with Water Chestnuts

SERVES: 3–4
PREPARATION: 45 minutes
MARINATING: 30 minutes
COOKING: 12–15 minutes

1.5 cm/½ in piece of fresh
root ginger
1 clove garlic
2 strips lemon rind
5 ml/1 teaspoon cornflour
30 ml/2 tablespoons soy sauce
30 ml/2 tablespoons dry sherry
2 skinless chicken breasts
100 g/4 oz baby sweetcorn
30 ml/2 tablespoons oil
2.5 ml/½ teaspoon sesame oil
2 large spring onions
225 g/8 oz can water chestnuts
75 ml/3 fl oz chicken stock

Peel and shred the ginger. Crush the garlic. Mix the lemon rind, cornflour, soy sauce, dry sherry, ginger and garlic in a large shallow dish. Cut the chicken into thin strips. Add it to the marinade, toss well, cover and leave in a cool place for 30 minutes. Blanch the sweetcorn in boiling salted water for 3 minutes. Drain and refresh under cold water, then drain again. Slice the spring onions and drained water chestnuts.

Heat both types of oil in a wok. Using a perforated spoon, lift the meat out of the marinade and stir fry for 2–3 minutes. Add the spring onions and sweetcorn, stir fry for 2 minutes, then stir in the chicken stock and marinade. Cook, stirring, for 5 minutes. Serve at once with rice.

Turkey Kebabs

SERVES: 4
PREPARATION: 20 minutes
MARINATING: 1–2 hours
COOKING: 20 minutes

4 spring onions
1 lime
15 ml/1 tablespoon chopped
rosemary
30 ml/2 tablespoons chopped mint
30 ml/2 tablespoons olive oil
salt and black pepper
freshly grated nutmeg
675 g/1½ lb boneless turkey breast

Trim and chop the spring onions. Grate the rind off the lime, squeeze the juice and mix both with the spring onions in a bowl. Stir in the rosemary, mint, olive oil, salt, freshly ground black pepper and nutmeg.

Cut the turkey breast into 2.5 cm/1 in cubes and place them in the bowl. Mix well to coat the turkey with the flavouring ingredients. Cover and marinate* the meat for 1–2 hours.

Thread the turkey cubes on to four long, or eight short, metal skewers. Brush the kebabs with any remaining marinade and cook under a hot grill for about 20 minutes, turning once or twice, until the turkey is browned and cooked through.

■ Serve the kebabs with a salad and rice, new potatoes, baked potatoes or warmed crusty bread.

Peking Duck

Several local variations are combined in this version of the classic Chinese recipe. It did not, in fact, originate in Peking, but in Inner Mongolia, and became famous in Peking restaurants only in the last century. The duck was hung in a draughty place for many hours to dry. Serving and eating Peking duck is a matter for some ceremony; the crackling skin is sliced off and served with sliced duck meat, to be wrapped in pancakes, with spring onions and a sauce.

SERVES: 4–6
PREPARATION: 2 hours
DRYING: 45 minutes
OVEN: 200°C/400°F/gas 6
       230°C/450°F/gas 8
COOKING: about 1½ hours

1 large duck (about 2.27 kg/5 lb)
30 ml/2 tablespoons brandy, vodka
    or gin (optional)
18 spring onions
45 ml/3 tablespoons soy sauce
15 ml/1 tablespoon caster sugar
150 ml/¼ pt water
Pancakes
175 g/6 oz plain flour
150 ml/¼ pt boiling water
45 ml/3 tablespoons sesame oil
Sauce
60 ml/4 tablespoons Hoisin
    (or plum) sauce
15 ml/1 tablespoon water
10 ml/2 teaspoons sugar
10 ml/2 teaspoons sesame oil

The essence of Peking duck is the crisp skin which is stripped off the cooked duck and served separately. To obtain this, the skin of the uncooked duck needs to be thoroughly dried. Wipe and dry the duck and pass a length of string under the wings so that it can be suspended from a rod or broom handle, placed across the seats of two chairs. Set a plate under the duck to catch any drips. Rub the skin with brandy, vodka or gin, if liked. This alcohol aids the drying process. Dry the duck by directing a blast of cold air on to it from a fan or a hair-drier, for about 15 minutes. Then leave the duck for a further 30 minutes.

Remove any bits of roots and blemished leaves from the onions – trimming them to a length of 7.5–10 cm/3–4 in. Wash them thoroughly. Use a sharp knife to make two cuts 1–2 cm/½–¾ in long, at the bulb end of each spring onion, then make two similar cuts at right angles to the first cuts. Put the onions in a large bowl of iced water and leave them in the refrigerator until required. The cut end of each spring onion will fan out to resemble a brush.

To make the pancakes, place the flour in a bowl and pour in the boiling water, stirring to make a soft dough. Knead the dough on a lightly floured surface for 5 minutes, until it is smooth. Wrap the dough in cling film and leave it to rest for 10 minutes. Roll the dough into a sausage shape and cut it in half, then cut each half into eight equal slices. Leave the slices on the floured work surface, covering them with cling film to prevent them drying out. Roll out a piece of dough to a circle measuring about 10 cm/4 in in diameter. Roll out a second piece to the same size. Brush one circle of dough lightly with sesame oil and lay the second circle on top. Roll out the pair of circles together to 15 cm/6 in in diameter.

Heat an ungreased heavy-based frying pan or griddle and cook the pair of circles for 2–3 minutes on each side, until they are browned in patches. Allow to cool slightly, then pull the pancakes apart. Continue rolling and cooking the dough, stacking the pancakes when cooked. Wrap the pancakes in cling film or foil and set them aside.

Mix the sauce ingredients together in a small pan and bring

Peking Duck.

to the boil. Reduce the heat and cook, stirring, for 2–3 minutes. Pour the sauce into a dish.

Mix the soy sauce, caster sugar and water in a bowl, then brush this mixture all over the duck. Place the duck, breast upwards, on an open grid or wire rack in a roasting pan. Pour in enough boiling water to reach 5 mm/¼ in up the sides of the pan. Roast the duck in the lower part of a preheated oven at 200°C/400°F/gas 6 for 1¼ hours. Brush with the basting sauce in the pan every 15 or 20 minutes. After 45 minutes increase the oven temperature to 230°C/450°F/gas 8. Place the pancakes in a steamer, removing their foil or cling film wrapping, and reheat them over a pan of boiling water for about 10 minutes.

To assemble the dish, cut off the duck skin with scissors or a sharp knife, cut into 2.5–5 cm/1–2 in squares; place on a serving dish and keep hot. Carve the meat into long thin slivers and arrange on another dish to keep hot. Pile the pancakes on a hot dish and cover with a napkin or folded cloth to keep them warm. Put the spring onion brushes in a dish and arrange all these dishes, with the sauce, on the table.

To eat Peking duck, take a pancake. Dip an onion brush in the sauce and brush it liberally on to the soft moist side of the open pancake. Top with pieces of duck skin and slivers of meat; fold and roll up the pancake.

■ The Chinese use chopsticks to eat the pancakes, but fingers and a fork are just as effective. Fingerbowls are useful.

MEAT

Beef Paupiettes

Paupiettes are thin slices of meat, which are stuffed and rolled into cork shapes. The meat should be cut very thinly: this is most easily achieved by placing the meat in the freezer until it is just firm.

SERVES: 4
PREPARATION: 45 minutes
OVEN: 160°C/325°F/gas 3
COOKING: 1½ hours

675 g/1½ lb topside of beef, cut
    in thin slices
10 ml/2 teaspoons French mustard
salt and black pepper
Stuffing
75 g/3 oz lean bacon
100 g/4 oz cooked chicken or pork
1 shallot
1 large clove garlic
40 g/1½ oz butter
1 egg
50 g/2 oz fresh white breadcrumbs
15 ml/1 tablespoon chopped parsley
2.5 ml/½ teaspoon chopped thyme
45 ml/3 tablespoons brandy
Sauce
450 g/1 lb mixed vegetables
    (onions, carrots, turnips, green
    beans, parsnips)
40 g/1½ oz beef dripping or lard
300 ml/½ pt beef stock
150 ml/¼ pt red wine
15 g/½ oz butter
15 g/½ oz plain flour

Beat the beef slices between two pieces of non-stick paper until they are wafer thin and measure about 10 × 10 cm/4 × 4 in.

Spread a little mustard over each slice and season to taste.

Remove the rind and chop the bacon finely, together with the chicken or pork. Peel and finely chop the shallot and garlic. Melt the butter in a small frying pan over moderate heat and cook the shallot and garlic until soft.

In a mixing bowl, combine the bacon, chicken, shallot and garlic. Beat the egg and add it with the breadcrumbs. Mix well. Stir in the parsley and thyme, and season the stuffing with salt and pepper; stir in the brandy.

Spoon the stuffing equally on the beef slices; roll up each slice and tuck the ends over to keep the stuffing in place. Tie each paupiette securely with fine string. Set the meat aside.

To make the sauce, peel and chop the onion; brown it over moderate heat in the dripping or lard. Wash and prepare the other vegetables, then chop them finely. Add these to the onion and cook for a few minutes to brown slightly. Spoon the vegetables into a large shallow casserole and put the paupiettes on top in a single layer. Pour the stock and wine into the pan in which the vegetables were fried and bring to the boil.

Pour the pan juices over the meat, cover the casserole and cook in a preheated oven at 160°C/325°F/gas 3 for 1¼ hours. Turn the meat once during cooking. Remove the lid and cook for a further 15 minutes.

Lift the paupiettes from the casserole, remove the string and arrange the meat on a warm serving dish. Surround the paupiettes with the vegetables. Keep hot. Pour the cooking liquid into a saucepan and boil rapidly to reduce by a third.

Soften the butter and mix to a paste with the flour. Add small pieces of this beurre manié to the sauce, stirring constantly until thickened. Spoon a little of the sauce over the meat and serve the rest in a sauceboat.

Beef with Olives

Shin or leg of beef is an excellent cut for stewing. The gelatinous part holding the nuggets of meat together adds texture to the sauce and prevents the meat from becoming stringy.

SERVES: 4–6
PREPARATION: 20 minutes
OVEN: 150°C/300°F/gas 2
COOKING: 3¼ hours

1.15–1.4 kg/2½–3 lb shin of beef
plain flour for coating
salt and black pepper
1 large onion
1 large carrot
2 cloves garlic
30 ml/2 tablespoons oil
15 ml/¼ pt red wine
600 ml/1 pt beef stock
bouquet garni*
5 ml/1 teaspoon anchovy essence
100–175 g/4–6 oz black or
    green olives
chopped parsley to garnish

Remove skin and any large lumps of fat from the beef. Cut the meat into 2.5–4 cm/1–1½ in chunks. Season the flour for coating with salt and pepper and coat the meat. Peel and finely slice the onion, carrot and garlic. Heat the oil in a large frying pan; fry the meat and vegetables until brown. Using a perforated spoon, transfer the contents of the pan to a flameproof casserole.

Pour the wine and a little stock into the frying pan. Boil these juices rapidly, scraping in all the residue. Pour into the casserole, adding the remaining stock. Tuck in the bouquet garni, stir in the anchovy essence and plenty of freshly ground pepper. Cover with a lid or foil. Cook in a preheated oven at 150°C/300°F/gas 2 for 3 hours or until the meat is tender.

Using a perforated spoon, remove the cooked meat and vegetables to a shallow warm serving dish. Add a little salt if needed. Boil the liquid in the casserole rapidly until it has reduced and thickened to a rich sauce. Remove the bouquet garni. Add the olives and simmer for 5 minutes. Correct seasoning if necessary. Pour some of the sauce over the meat and serve the remainder in a sauceboat. Garnish the meat with parsley.

■   Serve the meat surrounded with triangles of toast or boiled new potatoes.

Cornish Pasties

SERVES: 4
PREPARATION: 20–30 minutes
OVEN: 200°C/400°F/gas 6
        180°C/350°F/gas 4
COOKING: 1¼ hours

225 g/8 oz braising steak
2 potatoes
1 small turnip
1 onion
salt and black pepper
Shortcrust Pastry (page 365)
beaten egg to glaze

Trim any fat from the steak and cut it into small dice. Peel and dice the potatoes and turnip; chop the onion finely. Mix the meat with the vegetables and season very well with salt and freshly ground black pepper.

Roll out the pastry on a lightly floured surface to a thickness of about 5 mm/¼ in and, using a large saucer as a guide, cut out four circles.

Pile the meat and vegetable filling in the centre of each pastry circle. Dampen the pastry edges with cold water and carefully draw up two edges to meet on top of the filling. Pinch and twist the pastry firmly together to form a neat fluted and curved pattern. Cut a small air vent in the side of each pasty.

Brush the Cornish pasties with the lightly beaten egg and place them on a greased baking sheet. Bake the pasties in a preheated oven at 200°C/400°F/gas 6 for 15 minutes, then lower the oven temperature to 180°C/350°F/gas 4 and cook for a further 50–60 minutes.

Dolmas

The vine leaves used in this Turkish dish are available ready for rinsing and blanching.

SERVES: 4–6
PREPARATION: 40 minutes
COOKING: about 1½ hours

1 onion
75 g/3 oz butter
100 g/4 oz long-grain rice
900 ml/1½ pt White Stock
    (page 310)
450 g/1 lb lean minced lamb
15 ml/1 tablespoon chopped mint
    or parsley
5 ml/1 teaspoon chopped fresh
    or 2.5 ml/½ teaspoon
    dried rosemary
salt and black pepper
12 vine leaves or 185 g/6½ oz can
    vine leaves
juice of ½ lemon
150 ml/¼ pt plain yogurt

Peel the onion and chop it finely. Melt 25 g/1 oz of the butter in a large heavy-based pan and fry the onion and the rice until lightly coloured. Add 300 ml/½ pt of the stock. Bring to the boil, stir the rice once, then cover the pan tightly and reduce the heat to the minimum setting. Cook for 20 minutes. Turn the heat off and leave the rice to stand for 5 minutes with the lid on.

Leave the rice and onion to cool and set. Stir in the minced lamb, the chopped mint or parsley and rosemary and mix thoroughly. Season to taste with salt and freshly ground pepper. Rinse the vine leaves, then blanch* them for a few minutes in boiling water. Drain them well. If using canned vine leaves, separate them carefully without breaking them.

Dolmas.

Spread out the leaves and put a spoonful of the lamb and rice filling on each; fold the vine leaves over to make small, neat parcels. Pack them closely in layers in a flameproof casserole. Add enough white stock to cover, and sprinkle with the lemon juice; dot with the remaining butter. Put a plate on top of the stuffed vine parcels to keep them under the liquid.

Cover the casserole with a lid or foil and simmer over low heat for about 1 hour. Lift out the vine parcels with a perforated spoon and arrange them on a warm serving dish. Serve the yogurt in a separate bowl.

Lamb Argenteuil

In its classic form this recipe uses asparagus, from the district of Argenteuil in France, and cream. Tender English asparagus gives an equally delicate flavour and lighter fromage frais makes a less rich dish.

SERVES: 6
PREPARATION: 30 minutes
COOKING: 1¼ hours

900 g/2 lb asparagus
salt and black pepper
900 g/2 lb boned shoulder of lamb
15 ml/1 tablespoon plain flour
4 small onions
40 g/1½ oz butter
150 ml/¼ pt medium-fat
    fromage frais
lemon juice

Wash and scrape the asparagus, but do not trim; tie in three or four bundles and cook in a large

pan of lightly salted water. When the asparagus is tender, which takes 15–20 minutes, drain well, reserving the cooking liquid. Cut off the asparagus tips about 7.5 cm/3 in down the stems. Put the tips aside. Liquidise the asparagus stems, adding a little of the asparagus cooking liquid if necessary, then press the mixture through a sieve to remove any tough or stringy parts.

Trim as much fat as possible off the lamb and cut the meat into 5 cm/2 in pieces. Season the flour with salt and freshly ground black pepper; toss the meat in this to coat evenly. Peel and roughly chop the onions. Melt the butter in a deep frying or sauté pan, and cook the meat and onions until brown.

Gradually add about 300 ml/½ pt of the reserved asparagus liquid, stirring continuously until the sauce is smooth and creamy. Simmer for about 50 minutes until the meat is tender, stirring occasionally and removing any fat which rises to the surface of the sauce during cooking. If the liquid evaporates too quickly, cover the pan with a lid.

When the meat is cooked, stir in the asparagus purée and heat through. Stir in the fromage frais and heat for only a few seconds. Season to taste with salt, freshly ground pepper and lemon juice. The sauce should be fairly thick.

Arrange the asparagus tips around the edge of a warm serving dish and spoon the meat and sauce into the centre.

■ This tasty dish does not need any accompaniment other than boiled new potatoes.

Lample Pie

The name is an 18th-century corruption of lamb and apple pie.

SERVES: 4–6
PREPARATION: 20 minutes
OVEN: 200°C/400°F/gas 6
      180°C/350°F/gas 4
COOKING: 45 minutes

175–225 g/6–8 oz cooked lamb
100–175 g/4–6 oz cooked ham
    or bacon
225 g/8 oz cooking apples
1 large onion
salt and black pepper
1.25 ml/¼ teaspoon each dried
    rosemary and sage
300–450 ml/½–¾ pt chicken stock
15 ml/1 tablespoon tomato paste
175 g/6 oz Shortcrust Pastry
    (page 365)
beaten egg to glaze

Cut up the lamb and ham or bacon, then mince them together or chop them very finely. Peel and slice the apples; slice the onion thinly. Arrange the apples and onions in layers with the minced or finely chopped meat in a greased 18–20 cm/7–8 in pie dish. Sprinkle each layer with a little salt, pepper and herbs. Mix the stock with the tomato paste and pour it over the pie.

Roll out a pastry lid and cover the pie. Seal the edges, cut a vent in the top and brush the pastry with beaten egg.

Bake the pie in a preheated oven at 200°C/400°F/gas 6 for 15 minutes, then lower the oven temperature to 180°C/350°F/gas 4 and cook for a further 30 minutes.

Pork with Pistachio Nuts

A loin of pork is particularly suitable as part of a cold buffet.

SERVES: 8–10
PREPARATION: 20 minutes
STANDING: 24 hours
OVEN: 180°C/350°F/gas 4
       150°C/300°F/gas 2
COOKING: 2½ hours

30 ml/2 tablespoons salt
30 ml/2 tablespoons brown sugar
1.8–2.2 kg/4–5 lb loin of pork
25 g/1 oz shelled pistachio nuts
black pepper
2 bay leaves
2 mace blades
300 ml/½ pt dry white wine
600 ml/1 pt water

Ask the butcher to cut the skin off the pork and to bone the joint, and to include the skin and bone with the order. Mix together the salt and brown sugar; rub it into the pork, particularly on the boned side. Place the pork, boned side down, in a deep dish, cover and leave in a refrigerator for 24 hours.

Pork with Pistachio Nuts.

Make small incisions with a sharp knife in the fat and press in the pistachio nuts. Sprinkle the meat with plenty of freshly ground black pepper; roll it neatly and tie with string, taking care not to push out the nuts.

For the cooking, use a deep casserole into which the meat fits snugly with the bones and skin tucked around the sides. Add the bay leaves and mace. Pour the wine over it and add the water. Cook, uncovered, in a preheated oven at 180°C/350°F/gas 4 for 30 minutes until the fat has coloured. Then cover the casserole with a double layer of foil; reduce the temperature to 150°C/300°F/gas 2 and continue cooking for a further 2 hours.

When the pork loin is cooked, remove the bones and skin which were added to the casserole for flavour. Leave the meat to cool in the juice, which will set to a jelly. Remove the jelly when set and chop it finely. The fat may be removed from the top of the meat and cooking liquid and reserved to be served with the joint, spread on thickly sliced bread. Carve the cold pork into 5 mm/¼ in thick slices and arrange them on a dish garnished with the chopped jelly.

■ Serve with wholemeal or rye bread and the pork fat, if liked. A mixed leaf salad would go well with the cold pork.

Pork Noisettes with Prunes

SERVES: 6
PREPARATION: 15 minutes
SOAKING: 12 hours
COOKING: 1 hour

450 g/1 lb large prunes
600 ml/1 pt dry white wine
6 slices pork fillet (each 2.5 cm/
    1 in thick) or 6 boned loin
    chops
plain flour for coating
salt and black pepper
25 g/1 oz butter
15 ml/1 tablespoon redcurrant jelly
150 ml/¼ pt single cream
lemon juice

Place the prunes in a bowl with the wine. Soak overnight, then transfer the prunes and the wine to a pan and simmer, covered, for 20–30 minutes or until tender.

Trim excess fat off the pork slices or chops. Season the flour and coat the meat, shaking off any surplus. Melt the butter in a heavy-based pan and brown the meat over gentle heat, turning it once. Cover the pan and cook the pork for 30 minutes.

When the meat is nearly done, pour the prune liquid into the pan. Increase the heat and boil rapidly for a few minutes until the liquid has reduced slightly. Lift the meat on to a warm serving dish and arrange the prunes around it. Keep the meat and prunes hot while making the sauce.

Stir the redcurrant jelly into the juices remaining in the pan, and boil this sauce over high heat until it has the consistency of syrup. Lower the heat and add the cream, stirring continuously until the sauce is smooth and thick. Season with salt, pepper and lemon juice. Pour the sauce over the meat and serve at once.

■ Traditionally, noisettes are served with boiled potatoes only.

Baked Forehock of Bacon

SERVES: 8
PREPARATION: 20 minutes plus
    overnight soaking
OVEN: 180°C/350°F/gas 4
       200°C/400°F/gas 6
COOKING: 2–2¼ hours

1.8 kg/4 lb boned, rolled
    forehock of bacon
8 peppercorns
3 cloves
bouquet garni*
50–75 g/2–3 oz demerara sugar
150 ml/¼ medium dry cider or
    unsweetened apple juice
4 peaches
75 g/3 oz butter
40 g/1 oz honey or dark
    brown sugar
pinch cinnamon

Soak the bacon in cold water overnight. The next day, put the bacon joint in a large pan with sufficient cold water to cover it completely. Add the peppercorns, cloves and bouquet garni. Bring the water to the boil over moderate heat, remove any scum from the surface, and cover the pan with a lid. Reduce the heat, and simmer the bacon joint for 1¼ hours.

Lift the meat from the pan, leave it to cool and firm up, then remove all the string. Cut away the rind from the joint with a sharp knife, score the fat in a diamond pattern, at 1 cm/½ in intervals, and press the demerara sugar firmly all over the fat.

Put the joint in a roasting tin, heat the cider or apple juice and pour it over the meat.

Skin the peaches (page 361), cut them in half and remove the stones, then enlarge the cavities slightly with a pointed teaspoon. Soften the butter and mix it with the honey or dark brown sugar and a pinch of cinnamon until creamy. Spoon this mixture into the peach halves.

Bake the joint in a preheated oven at 180°C/350°F/gas 4 for 30 minutes, basting frequently with the pan juices.

Place the peaches around the joint, raise the oven temperature to 200°C/400°F/gas 6 and bake the joint for 15 minutes more, or until the top of the joint is golden and shiny.

Serve the bacon joint whole or sliced, garnished with the peach halves.

■ Anna Potatoes (page 347) or Carrots Paysanne (page 213) would make good vegetable dishes to go with the bacon.

VEGETABLES & SALADS

Spinach with Flageolets

If preferred, the butter can be replaced by an additional 15–30 ml/1–2 tablespoons olive oil – this is especially good when the spinach mixture is served with freshly cooked pasta.

SERVES: 4
PREPARATION: 15 minutes
COOKING: 10 minutes

450 g/1 lb fresh spinach
6 spring onions
2 × 400 g/14 oz cans
    flageolet beans
15 ml/1 tablespoon olive oil
25 g/1 oz butter
salt and black pepper
grated nutmeg

Trim the stalks from the spinach, discarding any damaged leaves. Wash the rest of the leaves thoroughly. Place the spinach in a large saucepan while it is still wet, cover tightly and cook over high heat for about 5 minutes, shaking the pan every now and then. Reduce the heat and cook for a further 2 minutes, until the spinach is limp. Drain well, pressing the excess liquid from the spinach with the back of a mixing spoon.

Trim the onions, discarding the roots but retaining the green parts, then slice them thinly. Drain the flageolet beans. Shred the drained spinach. Heat the olive oil and butter together in a saucepan. Add the spring onions and flageolets, and cook for 2 minutes, stirring until the beans are hot. Stir in the spinach and heat, stirring, for 1 minute. Season to taste with salt, freshly ground black pepper and a little grated nutmeg. Serve at once.

■ The spinach and bean mixture goes well with rice, pasta or baked potatoes. It may also be served as a base for creamy scrambled eggs or poached eggs, or it can be used as a filling for savoury pancakes.

Asparagus with New Potatoes

English asparagus appears in shops and on roadside stalls just as the first new potatoes make their appearance. If you have an asparagus cooker, there is no need to tent foil over the bundle of spears but the method is useful when boiling the vegetable in a standard-depth saucepan.

SERVES: 6
PREPARATION: 45 minutes
COOKING: 30 minutes

900 g/2 lb asparagus
900 g/2 lb new potatoes
salt
6 thin slices Parma ham
100 g/4 oz butter
lemon juice
chopped parsley to garnish

Wash the asparagus carefully and lightly scrape the spears, away from the tips. Cut off the lower 5–7.5 cm/2–3 in of each spear where the stem begins and set these pieces aside to use for making asparagus soup. Tie the asparagus in bundles.

Wash and scrape the new potatoes, put them in a saucepan and cover with water, then add salt and bring the water to the boil. Cook the potatoes until tender, about 10–15 minutes for small to medium potatoes or up to 20 minutes if they are large.

Meanwhile, bring a large saucepan of salted water to the boil. Stand the asparagus bundles in the pan so that the tips are not in the water. Tent a piece of foil over the top of the asparagus to keep the steam in and cook for about 15 minutes, or until the asparagus is tender (page 343).

Drain the potatoes and keep hot. Drain the asparagus, untie the bundles and divide into six equal portions. Wrap a slice of ham around each portion and arrange around the edge of a serving dish. Put the potatoes in the centre of the serving dish.

Melt the butter over a low heat, pour a little over the potatoes and serve the rest of it, seasoned with a little lemon juice, in a sauceboat. Sprinkle the chopped parsley over the potatoes and serve the dish warm rather than hot.

Asparagus in Filo Pastry

This is an excellent way of presenting asparagus as the main feature of the meal. It is also a good recipe for a vegetarian dinner party.

SERVES: 4
PREPARATION: 15 minutes
OVEN: 180°C/350°F/gas 4
COOKING: about 50 minutes

20 asparagus spears
salt and black pepper
225 g/8 oz ricotta cheese
45 ml/3 tablespoons grated
    Parmesan cheese
60 ml/4 tablespoons snipped chives
30 ml/2 tablespoons chopped
    fresh parsley
4–6 basil leaves
30 ml/2 tablespoons olive oil
25 g/1 oz butter
4 sheets of filo pastry (each about
    50 × 30 cm/20 × 12 in) or
    8 small sheets (each about
    27.5 cm/11 in square)

Trim any woody ends off the asparagus and tie the spears in a bundle. Cook the asparagus spears in boiling salted water for 12–15 minutes, or until they are just tender.

If you do not have a tall asparagus pan, stand the bundle of spears in an ordinary saucepan and tent foil over the top, crumpling it on to the rim to retain the steam that will rise from the boiling water. This way, the bottom of the spears will cook and the tips will remain tender. When cooked, drain the asparagus well and cool slightly.

Season the ricotta cheese to taste, then mix in the Parmesan cheese, chives and parsley. Shred the basil leaves with scissors and stir them into the ricotta and herb mixture.

Heat the olive oil and butter together gently until the butter melts. Brush one side of a sheet of filo with a little of the oil and butter, then fold the pastry in half. If using small sheets, lay one on top of the other.

Place a quarter of the ricotta mixture on the middle of the filo, in a long oblong shape to form a base for the asparagus. Top with 5 asparagus spears. Fold one side of the filo pastry over the asparagus, brush with a little of the oil and butter, then fold the opposite side over. Gently turn the filo over and brush the surface that is now uppermost with a little of the oil mixture, then fold the ends of the pastry over to make a neat package.

Place the package on a baking sheet, with the ends folded underneath. Brush the top with a little more oil and butter. Repeat with the remaining filo, ricotta and asparagus.

Bake the filo packages in a preheated oven at 180°C/350°F/gas 4 for about 40 minutes, or until the pastry is crisp and golden. Serve at once.

■ New potatoes and lightly cooked seasonal vegetables or a salad of tomatoes and courgettes are suitable accompaniments for the asparagus in filo pastry.

Braised Celery

SERVES: 6
PREPARATION: 15 minutes
COOKING: 55 minutes

1 small onion
2 small carrots
25 g/1 oz butter
2 heads of celery
salt and black pepper
300 ml/½ pt chicken stock
Beurre Manié (page 355)
        made with 20 g/¾ oz each
        of butter and plain flour
parsley sprigs to garnish

Finely chop the onion and dice the carrots, and cook both together in the butter in a flameproof casserole for 10 minutes, stirring occasionally. Trim the celery and remove any damaged stalks, then scrub the stalks thoroughly. Cut the stalks into 5–7.5 cm/2–3 in lengths. Add the celery to the casserole with salt and pepper to taste and turn the pieces with the other vegetables to coat them in the cooking juices. Pour in the stock, then heat until just boiling. Reduce the heat until the stock just simmers.

Cover the pan with a lid or foil and simmer the celery over low heat for about 40 minutes, until tender. Use a perforated spoon to transfer the celery to a serving dish, draining it well; cover and keep hot. Bring the cooking liquor to simmering point and gradually whisk in lumps of the beurre manié, allowing each lump to melt into the sauce before adding the next. Bring to the boil, whisking, and

cook for 2 minutes. Taste for seasoning and pour the sauce over the celery. Garnish with parsley sprigs and serve at once.

Peperonata

This colourful casserole of sweet peppers and tomatoes is Italian in origin.

SERVES: 4
PREPARATION: 10 minutes
COOKING: 30–35 minutes

1 onion
4 large red or green peppers
8 large tomatoes
1 clove garlic
salt and black pepper
25 g/1 oz butter
30 ml/2 tablespoons olive oil
10 ml/2 teaspoons caster
        sugar (optional)

Peel and finely chop the onion. Remove the stalks and wash the peppers; cut them in half lengthways and remove the inner ribs and the seeds. Cut the peppers into narrow strips. Skin the tomatoes (page 302) and chop them up coarsely. Peel the garlic clove and pound it to a paste with a little salt.

Heat the butter and oil in a heavy-based pan; add the onion and peppers. Cover the pan and fry the vegetables gently until soft, but not brown. Add the tomatoes, garlic and sugar (if used) and season to taste with freshly ground pepper. Put the lid back on the pan and continue cooking over very low heat, stirring every now and then, for 25 minutes. The mixture should

now be soft; remove the lid and cook for 5 minutes to allow some of the juices from the tomatoes to evaporate. Correct seasoning if necessary.

Spoon the casserole into a dish and serve.

■ Peperonata may be served hot with grilled meat and fish, or cold as a side salad or a starter.

Pissaladière

This strongly flavoured tart from France resembles a pizza, but the pastry base is of lighter texture. It makes a substantial lunch or supper dish on its own.

SERVES: 6–8
PREPARATION: 20 minutes
CHILLING: 30 minutes
OVEN: 200°C/400°F/gas 6
COOKING: 1¼ hours

225 g/8 oz plain flour
5 ml/1 teaspoon ground cinnamon
150 g/5 oz butter
1 egg
900 g/2 lb onions
3 cloves garlic
90 ml/6 tablespoons olive oil
400 g/14 oz can chopped tomatoes
15 ml/1 tablespoon tomato paste
2.5 ml/½ teaspoon sugar
bouquet garni*
salt and black pepper
50 g/2 oz black olives
2 × 50 g/2 oz cans anchovy fillets

Sift the flour and cinnamon into a mixing bowl; cut up the butter and rub it into the flour until the mixture resembles breadcrumbs. Beat the egg lightly and add it with enough cold water to make a firm dough.

Knead the pastry on a floured surface and roll out to a thickness of 5 mm/¼ in. Line a 25–28 cm/ 10–11 in loose-bottomed flan tin with the pastry; prick the base lightly with the prongs of a fork. Chill for 30 minutes. Bake the tart blind (page 367) in a preheated oven at 200°C/400°F/ gas 6 for 15 minutes.

Peel the onions and slice them thinly; peel and finely chop the garlic. Heat the oil in a large, heavy-based pan and cook the onions and garlic over low heat for 30–40 minutes until soft.

Put the tomatoes in a clean pan with the tomato paste, sugar and bouquet garni; boil rapidly to reduce the mixture to a thick

sauce. Remove the bouquet garni and stir the tomatoes into the cooked onions. Season to taste with pepper. It should not be necessary to add salt, in view of the saltiness of the anchovies and black olives.

Spoon the onion and tomato mixture into the tart case and arrange the anchovy fillets in a criss-cross pattern on top; garnish with the olives. Bake the savoury tart in a preheated oven at 200°C/400°F/gas 6 for 20 minutes; brush the top with a little olive oil after 10 minutes. Pissaladière is best served hot as soon as baked.

Pissaladière.

Courgette and Mozzarella Salad

SERVES: 4
PREPARATION: 20 minutes
MARINATING: 30–60 minutes

225 g/8 oz mozzarella cheese
5 small courgettes
salt and black pepper
2.5 ml/½ teaspoon caster sugar
30 ml/2 tablespoons cider vinegar
75 ml/5 tablespoons olive oil
15 ml/1 tablespoon chopped capers
15 ml/1 tablespoon chopped mint
30 ml/2 tablespoons
    chopped parsley
3 spring onions

Slice the mozzarella thinly. Trim the ends off the courgettes, then peel them very thinly, removing only an outer layer of the peel to leave them a bright green colour. Cut the peeled courgettes into thin slices and arrange the slices of mozzarella cheese and courgettes in a shallow serving dish.

Sprinkle some salt and freshly ground black pepper into a bowl. Add the caster sugar and cider vinegar and stir the mixture with a hand whisk until the sugar has dissolved. Gradually whisk in the olive oil to make a slightly thickened dressing. Stir in the capers, mint and parsley.

Trim the roots off the spring onions and chop them finely, including the green parts. Stir the chopped spring onions into the dressing. Spoon the dressing evenly over the courgette and mozzarella salad, cover and allow it to marinate for 30–60 minutes before serving.

Bean Salad

SERVES: 6
PREPARATION: 10 minutes
SOAKING: 8 hours
OVEN: 150°C/300°F/gas 2
COOKING: 2–3 hours
CHILLING: 1 hour

250 g/8 oz dried haricot beans
1 onion
1 carrot
bouquet garni*
salt and black pepper
60 ml/4 tablespoons finely chopped
    parsley, chervil, tarragon,
    chives or spring onions
75 ml/5 tablespoons olive oil
15 ml/1 tablespoon
    tarragon vinegar
5 ml/1 teaspoon French mustard
2.5 ml/½ teaspoon caster sugar

Put the haricot beans in water overnight. Drain the beans and put them in a large flameproof casserole. Peel and quarter the onion and carrot, and add to the beans with the bouquet garni and plenty of black pepper. Pour over water to cover the beans by 1 cm/½ in. Cover and cook in a preheated oven at 150°C/300°F/gas 2 for 3 hours, or simmer on the hob for 2 hours. Top up with water if necessary during cooking.

Season to taste with salt and freshly ground pepper and cook for 5 minutes. Drain the beans, remove the onion, carrot and bouquet garni, and put the beans in a large serving bowl. Add the chopped herbs, oil, vinegar, mustard and sugar to the beans. Stir to blend the ingredients thoroughly. When cool, chill in the refrigerator for about 1 hour.

RICE & PASTA

Rice, Tuna and Fennel Salad

SERVES: 4–6
PREPARATION: 30 minutes
COOKING: 20 minutes
CHILLING: 30 minutes

175 g/6 oz long-grain rice
350 ml/12 fl oz water
2 Florence fennel bulbs
198 g/7 oz can tuna
100 g/4 oz stoned black olives
15 ml/1 tablespoon Pernod
150 ml/¼ pt mayonnaise
Garnish
6 spring onions
3 hard-boiled eggs

Place the rice in a saucepan and pour in the water. Bring to the boil, stir once, then cover the pan tightly and reduce the heat to the minimum setting. Cook for 20 minutes. Turn off the heat and leave the rice to stand for a further 5 minutes, then remove the lid and cool the rice.

Trim, wash and drain the fennel. Cut the bulbs into thin slices. Drain the tuna and break up the flesh with a fork. Mix the rice, fennel, tuna and olives together in a salad bowl. Stir the Pernod into the mayonnaise and fold this dressing into the salad.

Trim the spring onions and cut them in half lengthways. Shell and quarter the eggs. Garnish the salad with the onions and eggs, cover and chill in the refrigerator for 30 minutes.

Spaghetti alle Vongole

Spaghetti with clams is a favourite dish in southern Italy. Canned clams are used here, but the fresh shellfish (page 317) may be used instead.

SERVES: 4–6
PREPARATION: 15 minutes
COOKING: 20–25 minutes

450 g/1 lb spaghetti
salt
4 cloves garlic
15 ml/1 tablespoon olive oil
90 ml/3 fl oz white wine
2 × 290 g/11oz cans baby clams
40 g/1½ oz butter

Cook the spaghetti in a large pan of lightly salted boiling water, uncovered, for 10–15 minutes.

Peel and finely chop the garlic. Heat the oil in a small pan and fry the garlic for 2–3 minutes over moderate heat. Pour the wine over the garlic and increase the heat. Boil the wine to reduce it. Drain the clams, reserving the liquid, and add them to the pan with 30–45 ml/2–3 tablespoons of the liquid. Heat the mixture through over low heat.

As soon as the spaghetti is tender, drain it thoroughly in a colander, and tip it into a heated serving dish. Add the butter and toss the spaghetti. Pour the clams in the sauce over the spaghetti.

■ Serve with crusty bread and a tomato salad.

Tagliatelle alla Carbonara

Many pastas, such as tagliatelle, spaghetti and macaroni, were at one time cooked over a charcoal burner (alla carbonara). The term now applies to a dish cooked with bacon, eggs and cheese.

SERVES: 6
PREPARATION: 10 minutes
COOKING: 15 minutes

50 g/2 oz streaky bacon
50 g/2 oz cooked ham
225 g/8 oz tagliatelle
salt and black pepper
25 g/1 oz butter
15 ml/1 tablespoon olive oil
4 eggs
50 g/2 oz Cheddar cheese
25 g/1 oz Parmesan cheese

Remove the rind and any bones from the bacon and chop the rashers roughly; dice the ham. Cook the tagliatelle in plenty of boiling salted water for 10–15 minutes or until just tender. Drain thoroughly in a colander.

While the pasta is cooking, heat the butter and oil in a pan over moderate heat and fry the bacon and ham until crisp. Beat the eggs in a bowl. Grate in the cheese and mix lightly.

Add the pasta to the meat and stir until evenly coated. Pour in the eggs and continue stirring over gentle heat until the eggs thicken slightly. Be sure to take the pan off the heat before the eggs scramble. Spoon the pasta into a warm dish and serve.

■ Offer Parmesan cheese and a red leaf salad with the pasta.

PUDDINGS & DESSERTS

Croûtes aux Abricots

Croûtes used for a dessert should be made from sweet breads (brioches are the most suitable).

SERVES: 6
PREPARATION: 10 minutes
COOKING: 20 minutes

12 ripe apricots
175 g/6 oz caster sugar
30 ml/2 tablespoons water
3 brioches
175 g/6 oz clarified butter
    (page 306)
150 ml/¼ pt double cream
30 ml/2 tablespoons Kirsch
    (optional)
angelica to decorate

Cut the apricots in half and remove the stones. Bring the sugar and water to the boil in a saucepan, add the apricots and poach them gently for 6–8 minutes; they should be tender and retain their shape.

Using a perforated spoon, carefully lift out the apricots and keep them hot. Turn up the heat and boil the syrup rapidly until it is thick. Do not allow it to caramelise. Let the syrup cool.

Trim the crusts from the brioches or bread and cut into six slices, 1 cm/½ in thick. Heat the clarified butter in a frying pan and fry the bread slices on both sides until they are golden brown. Keep hot. Whip the cream lightly and flavour it to taste by stirring in the apricot syrup and Kirsch (if used).

To serve, arrange the fried bread on a dish and put four apricot halves on each slice. Top each portion with a swirl of the flavoured cream. Chop the angelica finely and use it to decorate the desserts.

Croûtes aux Abricots.

French Toast with Fruit Sauce

Fried bread fritters – a version of classic French toast – can make a delicious family pudding.

SERVES: 6
PREPARATION: 10 minutes
COOKING: 10 minutes

8 thick slices white bread
150 ml/¼ pt milk
2 eggs
50 g/2 oz caster sugar
2.5 ml/½ teaspoon natural
    vanilla essence
227 g/8 oz can apricots
juice of ½ lemon
25–50 g/1–2 oz unsalted butter

Remove the crusts from the bread and cut each slice into 3 fingers. Whisk the milk and eggs, together and stir in the sugar and vanilla essence.

Purée the apricots with their syrup in a liquidiser or food processor, or rub through a coarse sieve into a saucepan. Stir in the lemon juice and heat the purée over moderate heat. Put to one side and keep warm.

Heat the butter in a large frying pan. Dip the bread fingers in the milk and egg mixture, and fry them in the butter until they are golden brown. Drain on crumpled absorbent kitchen paper and arrange on a warm serving dish. When all the fingers are cooked, pour the purée over them and serve.

■ Thick Greek yogurt, crème fraîche or single cream may be offered with the French toast and apricot sauce.

Gâteau de Pithiviers Feuilleté

This puff pastry cake is a speciality of Pithiviers, a small town just south of Paris. The recipe and the petal pattern were invented by the chef Antonin Carême, in the 19th century.

SERVES: 6
PREPARATION: 30 minutes
OVEN: 220°C/425°F/gas 7
        190°C/375°F/gas 5
        230°C/450°F/gas 8
COOKING: 45 minutes

450 g/1 lb home-made Puff
    Pastry (page 374) or thawed
    frozen puff pastry
100 g/4 oz ground almonds
100 g/4 oz caster sugar
40 g/1½ oz unsalted butter
2 egg yolks
30 ml/2 tablespoons double cream
30 ml/2 tablespoons rum (optional)
beaten egg to glaze
20 ml/4 teaspoons icing sugar

Roll out a third of the pastry on a floured surface and cut out a 23 cm/9 in circle, using a plate or dish as a guide. Place the pastry on a baking sheet. Set the remaining pastry aside.

Mix the almonds and caster sugar in a large bowl. Melt the butter and add it to the bowl. Beat in the egg yolks, one at a time, then beat in the cream and lastly the rum (if used). Spread this filling over the pastry, spreading it level, but leaving 2.5 cm/1 in clear around the edge. Roll out the remaining pastry to a 25 cm/10 in round. Brush the pastry rim with water and place the pastry round over the filling. Press the edges firmly together with the fingers to seal.

Using a sharp knife, make 12 evenly spaced nicks around the edge of the pastry. Push up the pastry at each nick, using both thumbs, so that the edge is scalloped into 12 curves or petals. Brush with the beaten egg and leave to stand for 5 minutes.

Make a 1 cm/½ in hole in the centre of the pastry top. Using a sharp knife, lightly mark scallop lines inside the curved edge of the puff pastry lid and cut curving lines from the centre hole to the scallops to look like the petals of a flower.

Bake the cake in a preheated oven at 220°C/425°F/gas 7 for 10–15 minutes or until the pastry is well risen. Then turn down the temperature to 190°C/375°F/gas 5 and bake for a further 20–25 minutes, when the top should be well browned.

Remove the cake from the oven and set it aside; increase the temperature to 230°C/450°F/gas 8. Sift the icing sugar evenly over the cake and return it to the oven for about 2 minutes until the sugar has melted to a golden brown glaze.

■ Serve the gâteau warm or cold with a jug of single cream.

Black Forest Gâteau

PREPARATION: about 1 hour
OVEN: 180°C/350°F/gas 4
COOKING: 25–30 minutes

3 eggs
100 g/4 oz caster sugar
75 g/3 oz plain flour
15 g/½ oz cocoa powder
Filling and Topping
425 g/15 oz can pitted
    black cherries
15 ml/1 tablespoon arrowroot
175 g/6 oz plain chocolate
300 ml/½ pt double cream
90 ml/6 tablespoons kirsch

Line the bases and grease two 20 cm/8 in sandwich cake tins. Place the eggs and sugar in a heatproof bowl over a saucepan of hot water. Whisk until the mixture is thick and pale in colour and the whisk leaves a trail when lifted. Remove the bowl from the heat and continue whisking until cool.

Sift the flour and cocoa together. Using a metal spoon and a gentle action, fold them gradually into the whisked mixture. Divide the mixture evenly between the prepared tins. Bake in a preheated oven at 180°C/350°F/gas 4 for 25–30 minutes. Cool on a wire rack.

Meanwhile, make the filling and topping. Drain the cherries, reserving the juice in a small saucepan. In a heatproof bowl, mix the arrowroot to a paste with a little of the juice, bring the remainder to the boil, then pour it on to the arrowroot and mix well. Pour the mixture back into the pan and bring to the boil, stirring constantly. Remove from the heat as soon as the sauce boils. Stir in all but eight of the cherries. Allow to cool.

Melt half the chocolate in a heatproof bowl over a pan of hot water. Using a palette knife, spread a thin layer of the melted chocolate on to a marble slab or cold surface. When it is just setting, make the chocolate caraque: holding a sharp, thin-bladed knife at both ends, position it at a slight angle to the chocolate, then scrape it along the surface of the chocolate to make curls. Repeat the process with the remaining chocolate. Keep the chocolate caraque cool but do not refrigerate it.

Whip the cream and spoon about half of it into a large piping bag fitted with a large star nozzle. Sprinkle half the kirsch on to the bottom sponge cake, spread the centre with the cooled cherries, then pipe some of the whipped cream around the edge. Cover with the remaining sponge cake and sprinkle with more kirsch. Spread the sides and top with the rest of the cream in the bowl. Place the cake on a plate. Gently press the cool chocolate caraque around the sides of the cake, reserving some of the better curls for the top.

Pipe eight swirls of cream around the top rim of the gâteau, using the cream remaining in the piping bag. Top each swirl with one of the reserved cherries and decorate the centre of the gâteau with the rest of the chocolate caraque.

Gooseberry and Elderflower Soufflés

SERVES: 6
PREPARATION: 50 minutes
CHILLING: 2 hours

450 g/1 lb green gooseberries
4 elderflower heads
120 ml/4 fl oz water
50 g/2 oz granulated sugar
4 large eggs
75 g/3 oz caster sugar
15 ml/1 tablespoon
    powdered gelatine
150 ml/¼ pt double cream
Decoration
25 g/1 oz semi-sweet biscuits
150 ml/¼ pt double cream
18 small Frosted Mint Leaves
    (page 412) or pistachio nuts

Tie a double band of greaseproof paper around each individual 150 ml/¼ pt soufflé dish so that it stands 5 cm/2 in above the rim and sits tightly against the sides of the dish. Where the paper extends above the dish, brush it lightly with oil. Stand the 6 dishes on a tray or baking sheet.

Top and tail the gooseberries. Put them in a medium saucepan. Wash the elderflower heads, shake them dry and tie them in a piece of muslin. Add to the pan with 60 ml/4 tablespoons of the water and the granulated sugar. Cover and simmer until the fruit is just soft, stirring occasionally. Remove the muslin bag. Press the fruit through a sieve into a bowl or liquidise and strain the purée; allow to cool. Separate the eggs, placing the yolks in a large

Gooseberry and Elderflower Soufflés.

bowl and the whites in another. Beat the yolks with the caster sugar until thick and pale. Stir in the gooseberry purée.

Sprinkle the gelatine over the rest of the water in a small heatproof bowl. Do not stir. Leave to stand for 15 minutes, until the gelatine has absorbed the water. Set the bowl over a pan of simmering water and stir until the gelatine has dissolved completely. Stir in about 30 ml/2 tablespoons of the gooseberry mixture, then fold into the remaining gooseberry mixture.

Whip the cream until it holds the shape; fold into the mixture. Using a clean whisk, whisk the egg whites until stiff, then gradually fold into the mixture using a metal spoon. Divide the mixture evenly between the prepared dishes – it should extend about 2.5 cm/1 in above the rim of each dish. Chill for about 2 hours or until the soufflés are set.

Shortly before serving, decorate the soufflés. Place the biscuits in a stout polythene bag and crush with a rolling pin. Carefully take the greaseproof paper off each soufflé, then, using a palette knife, press the crumbs around the sides. Whip the cream and pipe rosettes on the top of each soufflé. Decorate with the frosted mint leaves or the pistachios.

Avocado Fool

The origin of the word 'fool' to describe a purée of pressed fruit mixed with cream or custard goes back to the 16th century. It was then a synonym for a trifling thing – of small consequence. This avocado fool is an unusual, refreshing, sweet, best flavoured with lime juice.

SERVES: 6
PREPARATION: 20 minutes
CHILLING: 2 hours

3 large avocados
2 limes or 1 large lemon
15 ml/1 tablespoon icing sugar
125 ml/4 fl oz double cream

Peel the avocados and remove the stones. Dice the avocado flesh finely. Cut a thin slice from the middle of one lime or the lemon and divide the slice into six small wedges; set aside to decorate the dessert.

Squeeze the juice from all the citrus fruit and put it in the liquidiser with the icing sugar. Process for 30 seconds. Add the diced avocado flesh and liquidise until the mixture has become a smooth purée.

Scrape the purée into a bowl. Whip the cream and fold it into the purée, adding more sugar and fruit juice, if necessary, to taste.

Spoon the avocado fool into six individual glasses and chill in the refrigerator for at least 2 hours. Decorate the avocado dessert with the reserved lime or lemon wedges.

■ Serve with sponge fingers or similar dessert biscuits.

Biscuit Tortoni

In the 19th century, Tortoni's restaurant in Paris was famous for its buffet table, patronised by many great writers.

SERVES: 6–8
PREPARATION: 15 minutes
FREEZING: 8 hours

450 ml/¾ pt double cream
150 ml/¼ pt single cream
50 g/2 oz icing sugar
salt
12 macaroons
75 ml/3 fl oz medium sherry
wafers or ratafia biscuits to serve

About 1 hour before beginning preparations, turn the freezer to its coldest setting.

Whip the creams with the sugar and a pinch of salt, until the mixture is firm but not stiff. Spoon into a 23 cm/9 in loaf tin or plastic box, cover with a lid or a double layer of foil and freeze until half frozen.

Biscuit Tortoni.

Put the macaroons into a plastic or greaseproof paper bag and crush them to fine crumbs with a rolling pin. Alternatively, crumb the macaroons in a food processor. Set aside a third of the crumbs for decoration.

Break up the frozen cream mixture in a bowl and stir in the sherry and remaining macaroon crumbs. The mixture should stay light and bulky; add a little more sugar and sherry if necessary. Spoon the cream mixture into the washed and dried container, cover and return to the freezer for 8 hours or overnight.

Remove the ice cream loaf from the freezer and invert the container on to a serving plate. Rub the container with a cloth wrung out in very hot water until the ice cream drops out. Press the rest of the macaroon crumbs lightly into the top and sides of the ice cream loaf with a broad-bladed knife.

Spanish Cake Dessert

This is an excellent way of using up the remains of a fruit cake; if it is a very rich cake, keep the portions fairly small. Fresh or canned fruit in natural juice adds a refreshing contrast to the richness of the cake.

SERVES: 4–6
PREPARATION: 10 minutes
OVEN: 190°C/375°F/gas 5
COOKING: 10–15 minutes

4 large slices sponge or fruit cake
175 g/6 oz fruit, fresh or canned
150 ml/¼ pt fresh or thawed frozen orange juice
15 ml/1 tablespoon rum
5 ml/1 teaspoon cornflour
300 ml/½ pt single cream
2 egg yolks
50 g/2 oz caster sugar
salt
about 5 ml/1 teaspoon natural vanilla essence

Arrange the slices of sponge or fruit cake in a lightly buttered ovenproof dish and top with the fruit. Pour over the orange juice and rum, and bake in a preheated oven at 190°C/ 375°F/gas 5 for 10–15 minutes.

Mix the cornflour with a little cream. Beat the egg yolks with the remaining cream and stir in the cornflour mixture, sugar and a pinch of salt.

Cook this custard over a low heat, stirring continuously, until smooth and slightly thickened. Add vanilla essence to taste, pour the custard over the warm cake and fruit and serve at once.

Chocolate Cake Mousse

Leftover chocolate cake can be turned into a rich dessert.

SERVES: 6
PREPARATION: 20–30 minutes
CHILLING: 4 hours

2–4 thick slices plain chocolate cake
75 g/3 oz plain chocolate
3 eggs, separated
75 g/3 oz caster sugar
30 ml/2 tablespoons concentrated frozen orange juice, thawed
150 ml/¼ pt double cream
30 ml/2 tablespoons grated chocolate to decorate

Cut the cake into even dice. Melt the plain chocolate in a bowl set over a pan of simmering water. Beat the egg yolks with the sugar until pale and fluffy, and stir in the melted chocolate. Stir in the orange juice and the chocolate cake pieces.

Whip the cream, then fold it into the chocolate and egg mixture. Whisk the egg whites until stiff but not dry, then fold them into the mixture until evenly distributed. Spoon the mousse into a serving bowl or individual dishes. Chill until set.

Sprinkle with coarsely grated chocolate before serving.

Salad Days

*A*lthough the year-round availability of salad produce has encouraged people to try out more vegetable side dishes, it takes a spell of warm weather to spur on most cooks to experiment with more substantial salads as the focal point of a meal. The idea that a salad meal consists of cold meat or cheese flanked by a few lettuce leaves, quartered tomatoes, sliced cucumber and chunks of spring onion without a hint of dressing is now old-fashioned – even the average cold platter is usually more exciting than this.

When good salad ingredients are combined imaginatively, they make a delicious meal. It is worth remembering the current advice that we ought to eat at least five portions of fruit and vegetables every day, with emphasis placed on the inclusion of raw produce in the diet. The ingredients for a salad must be of prime quality. Although this is obvious in the case of leafy vegetables, it is equally true of other ingredients that are served cold, such as cooked fish, poultry and meat. Beans, pulses, rice and pasta must be cooked to perfection so as to contribute their characteristic texture to a salad. It is essential that flavouring ingredients, such as nuts and seeds or fruit, are used while fresh as any bitterness or dull flavour will spoil the salad.

Preparing Ingredients

Cooked foods, such as fish, poultry, meat, potatoes, pasta and rice, should be cooked and cooled no more than a day before making the salad. Leafy vegetables should be prepared as near as possible to serving so that they remain crisp and crunchy. Depending on the recipe, certain ingredients, such as mushrooms, rice and cheese, may benefit from being marinated in a dressing before being tossed with the rest of the salad. Foods that are likely to discolour should be prepared just before the salad is mixed. Apples and avocados fall into this category: toss them with a little lemon juice immediately after peeling, then cover them closely with cling film to help slow down discoloration.

Bitter or tough skins and peel should be removed from fruit and vegetables such as cucumber, peppers or tomatoes for best results. It is generally best to cut foods finely for salads, into small pieces or thin slices, and all the ingredients should be cut to a similar size. Avoid using carbon steel knives as they may react with acidic juices in fruit or vegetables to cause discoloration and/or tainting with a metallic taste. The traditional method of preparing salad leaves is to tear them by hand rather than shredding them with a knife; however, as long as a sharp stainless steel knife is used, the flavour of the vegetables will not be affected, so the choice of method is entirely personal.

Dressings

A dressing is used to moisten the salad and to bring the ingredients together as one dish. The dressing must not spoil the salad's texture nor mask the flavour of the ingredients used. Recipes for classic dressings are given in the section on Sauces and Dressings (page 352–356) but dressing a salad is a highly individual affair. A standard dressing recipe may be adapted to complement a specific salad by varying the choice of oil, vinegar or citrus juice, seasonings, herbs and spices.

There are many types of salad oil, from light safflower oil to strongly flavoured nut oils. Like safflower, grapeseed and sunflower oils are light; their role is to carry the flavour of other ingredients. The flavour of olive oil varies according to the type used, and there are some rich, dark oils which go well with strong vinegars, like balsamic vinegar. Olive oil, even when light, contributes its own flavour to a salad but does not necessarily dominate the dressing. Nut oils, like walnut or hazelnut oil, are very strong, so are usually used in combination with a lighter oil to avoid masking the flavour of the main ingredients. Their role is to flavour rather than moisten the food. Sesame oil and citrus oils are even stronger and should be used in very small quantities if they are added to a dressing – treat these as flavouring essences.

There is an equally wide choice of vinegars, from mild, light cider vinegar to the rich, dark balsamic vinegar aged in oak casks. Wine vinegar is a popular choice for dressings but it is worth remembering that this term covers a wide range of products. Malt vinegar is very harsh and is not usually used for salad dressings; however, some wine vinegars have flavours that are almost as severe. Sherry vinegar has a richer taste than ordinary wine vinegar but it is not as full-flavoured as balsamic vinegar. Cider vinegar is the mildest choice and is less tangy than lemon juice; good balsamic vinegar makes a full, robust dressing which is not too harsh.

In addition to the oil and vinegar in a dressing, seasonings usually include salt and pepper with a little sugar to balance the sour taste of vinegar or citrus juice. Mustard is another classic seasoning which adds a little bite to the dressing. Garlic, herbs and spices may all be added, depending on the composition of the salad. Soured cream, yogurt and fromage frais are also good candidates for salad dressings. Use a low-fat fromage frais or yogurt for a light dressing or make a creamier light dressing by thinning low-fat soft cheese with a little yogurt or milk.

Fruits, Nuts and Seeds

As well as fresh fruit, dried fruit can be used to enrich a salad and to balance sharp dressings – raisins, sultanas and apricots are particularly delicious. All types of nuts can be tossed into salads or sprinkled over them to add flavour and texture. Nuts must be fresh as any that taste bitter will spoil the salad – this is especially true of walnuts. Salted roasted nuts should be used sparingly and the seasoning reduced accordingly. Pine kernels, sesame seeds and sunflower seeds can all be sprinkled over salads or mixed into the dressing. The seeds may be roasted first, if liked, in a heavy-bottomed pan. Place over low to medium heat, shaking the pan often to cook the seeds evenly until lightly browned.

Herbs

Dried herbs can be used sparingly to flavour dressings but fresh herbs are the better choice for salads. Mild fresh herbs, such as parsley, can be used generously to flavour salads but stronger herbs, like tarragon and chives, should be added sparingly. Basil is excellent with tomatoes or cheese and can be used quite liberally, but it is important to prepare it at the last minute and to shred the leaves rather than chop them. Basil leaves quickly wilt and lose flavour when overhandled, chopped or cooked for long periods.

Mixed Leaf and Chick Pea Salad

A variety of salad leaves may be used as a base for the crunchy chick pea mixture: try using curly endive (or frisée) as a base – about half a head will be plenty – adding some lamb's lettuce, a handful of rocket leaves, a head of radicchio and a bunch of watercress. Alternatively, cos, iceberg or oak leaf lettuce may be used instead of curly endive.

SERVES: 4–6
PREPARATION: 30 minutes
COOKING: 10 minutes

30 ml/2 tablespoons
*   sunflower seeds*
30 ml/2 tablespoons sesame seeds
45 ml/3 tablespoons pine kernels
75 g/3 oz walnuts
100 g/4 oz no-need-to-presoak
*   dried apricots*
50 g/2 oz raisins
4 spring onions
2 × 400 g/14 oz cans chick peas
mixed salad leaves (see recipe
*   introduction)*
1 clove garlic
salt and black pepper
pinch of ground mace
30 ml/2 tablespoons cider vinegar
2.5 ml/½ teaspoon caster sugar
5 ml/1 teaspoon Dijon mustard or
*   other mild mustard*
90 ml/6 tablespoons olive oil

Place the sunflower seeds, sesame seeds and pine kernels in a small, heavy-based pan. Cook over low to medium heat, shaking the pan occasionally, until the seeds and pine kernels are lightly browned. Take care not to overbrown the

seeds or they will taste bitter. Allow to cool slightly. Roughly chop up the walnuts, cut up the apricots into small pieces and add both to the seeds and pine kernels with the raisins. Trim the root ends off the spring onions and finely chop the rest, including the green parts. Add the seeds and spring onions to the drained chick peas. Mix well.

Prepare the salad leaves according to type, discarding any stalks and damaged leaves. Shred the leaves and mix them in a serving bowl. Crush the garlic

Mixed Leaf and Chick Pea Salad, Courgette and Mozzarella Salad (page 152) and Pasta Salad with Stilton Dressing.

into a bowl. Add a generous sprinkling of salt and freshly ground black pepper, the mace, cider vinegar and sugar. Stir with a hand whisk until the sugar and salt have dissolved, then stir in the mustard and gradually whisk in the oil. Pour this dressing over the chick pea mixture and stir well. Spoon the mixture over the salad leaves and serve at once.

Pasta Salad with Stilton Dressing

The Stilton mixture may be replaced by a different dressing if preferred; for example, an oil and vinegar dressing flavoured with garlic or a simple yogurt and chive dressing would go well with the pasta mixture.

SERVES: 6
PREPARATION: 20 minutes
STANDING: 30 minutes

225 g/8 oz pasta shapes
salt and black pepper
100 g/4 oz French beans
100 g/4 oz broccoli florets
100 g/4 oz shelled peas
175 g/6 oz Stilton cheese
grated rind and juice of
*   ½ orange*
150 ml/¼ pt plain yogurt
150 ml/¼ pt fromage frais
30 ml/2 tablespoons
*   snipped chives*
15 ml/1 tablespoon
*   chopped tarragon*
½ small head Chinese leaves
2 bunches watercress
4 spring onions
15 ml/1 tablespoon lemon juice
30 ml/2 tablespoons olive oil
orange slices to garnish

Cook the pasta in plenty of boiling lightly salted water for 10–15 minutes. Meanwhile, trim the ends off the beans and cut them into short lengths. Cut the broccoli florets into small pieces. Cook the beans and broccoli together in boiling salted water for 2–3 minutes. Cook the peas in a separate pan of boiling salted water, allowing 10 minutes for

fresh peas or 4–5 minutes for frozen peas. As the vegetables are cooked, drain them, rinse them under cold water, then drain them again. When the pasta is just tender, drain it well and mix with the vegetables.

Crumble the Stilton cheese finely into a bowl. Add the orange rind and juice with some of the yogurt and gradually mash the liquids into the cheese. Continue to add the yogurt, a little at a time, mashing after each addition until the mixture forms a lumpy paste. Beat in the fromage frais. Add freshly ground black pepper, the snipped chives and the tarragon.

Pour this Stilton dressing over the pasta mixture and stir well. Cover and leave to stand until the pasta is cold. If the pasta has already cooled, allow the salad to stand for at least 30 minutes to allow the dressing to flavour the pasta.

Trim and finely shred the Chinese leaves. Pick the leaves off the watercress and mix them with the Chinese leaves in a large bowl. Trim the root ends off the spring onions and finely chop the rest, including the green parts, then add them to the green salad.

Stir salt and pepper to taste into the lemon juice until the salt has dissolved, then whisk in the olive oil. Add this dressing into the green salad and toss lightly. Turn the green salad out on to a large shallow dish or individual bowls. Top with the pasta salad. Garnish with orange slices and serve at once.

JUNE

Fresh Asparagus, Chicken Chaud-froid, Strawberry Ice Cream.

June

The horn of plenty is well and truly filled in June, when home produce is at its best and its most economical. Fish, seafoods, salads, vegetables and fruit are all of excellent quality, allowing for enjoyable cooking sessions and varied eating. It makes sense to use garden-fresh asparagus, peas, carrots, potatoes, cucumbers, radishes and a variety of salad leaves to full advantage by focusing the meal on them; for example, lightly cooked mixed fresh vegetables with a little herb butter and some warm crusty bread make an excellent supper or light lunch. For a main meal, include several different vegetables or new potatoes and a salad with grilled fish or poached salmon steaks. Concentrate on serving vegetables with light cooking juices or simple dressings rather than heavy sauces or thickened gravies.

Although preserving food is traditionally an autumn activity, the availability of freezers in most homes, coupled with access to the increasingly popular pick-your-own farms, means that now is the time to start stocking up on the most successful freezer candidates, such as peas, beans and soft fruit. Plan ahead by checking the contents of the freezer, ensuring there is space for new produce, and pick only as much as you can process on the same day.

The real culinary celebration of June is one of the simplest – strawberries and cream, with just a dusting of icing sugar. When there is a good crop of fruit, a jam-making session provides the perfect excuse for preparing a Sunday cream tea to sample the new preserve, complete with home-baked scones and clotted cream. This chapter also includes recipes for ice cream and a water ice using strawberries, plus an unusual, refreshing cucumber and strawberry salad.

June is a favourite month for weddings and the idea of holding a reception at home or in a local hall is now popular. Two alternative catering suggestions are included here, the first for a sit-down meal for up to 12 people and the second a menu for a buffet for up to 50 guests. There are also background notes on planning ahead and practical guidance on tackling all the chores associated with taking charge of the celebrations., from cooking, presenting and serving the food and drinks to clearing up afterwards.

Menu suggestions There is such a wide variety of fresh produce available in summer that menus tend to be far fresher, and more vegetable based, than in winter. By way of contrast with lighter everyday fare, June is also a traditional time for wedding feasts, as highlighted in this chapter's feature pages. The menus suggested for wedding celebrations are equally suitable for other occasions, such as anniversaries, birthdays or parties. Main recipes in the following menus are either included in the chapter or are found elsewhere in the book, as indicated by the page references.

Celebration Lunch
~

*Fresh Asparagus
Thin Bread and Butter*
~
*Salmon en Croûte
Buttered New Potatoes
Sliced Cucumbers
with Sauce Vinaigrette
(page 356)*
~
Strawberry Ice Cream

This is an ideal menu for a Sunday family gathering, since it is easy to prepare with much of the preparation finished beforehand. When there is a plentiful supply of strawberries, it is a good idea to serve a bowl of the fresh fruit with the ice cream.

Soft Fruit Gâteau (page 174) and Summer Risotto (page 172).

Family Barbecue
~

*Cheese and Chutney Dip
(page 264) with
Crudités*
~
*Barbecued Spare Ribs
Barbecued Sausages
(page 271)
Courgette and Chive Salad
Tomato Salad
Green Salad*
~
*Fresh Fruit or Barbecued
Bananas (page 199)*

This straightforward menu is excellent for a family evening in the garden. The cheese dip with crudités will keep everyone happy while the spare ribs and sausages are cooking on the barbecue. For a more substantial meal, bake potatoes in the oven or skewer boiled new potatoes and crisp them on the barbecue.

Summer Tea Party
~

Cucumber Sandwiches
~
*Scones (page 401)
with
Strawberry Jam (page 407)
Clotted Cream*
~
*Brandy Snaps (page 391)
Swiss Tarts (page 385)
Victoria Sandwich Cake
(page 384)*
~
*Fresh Strawberries
Clotted Cream*

Take advantage of the strawberry season to host a tea party. The brandy snaps should be filled and the sandwiches prepared just before guests arrive, but everything else should be in tip-top order in advance, including a perfectly laid table complete with fresh flowers.

SOUPS

Chilled Watercress Soup

Watercress is most often used as a garnish or as an ingredient in salads. It also makes a good basis for a smooth soup.

SERVES: 6–8
PREPARATION: 20 minutes
COOKING: 45 minutes
CHILLING: 2 hours

2 bunches watercress
375 g/12 oz potatoes
1 onion
1 clove garlic (optional)
25 g/1 oz butter
1 bay leaf
1.12 litres/2 pt chicken stock
salt and black pepper
150 ml/¼ pt single cream or low-fat fromage frais
grated nutmeg to garnish (optional)

Wash the watercress, discard the main stalks and damaged leaves. Peel and cut the potatoes into thick slices, chop the onion and peel the garlic, if used.

Melt the butter in a saucepan. Add the chopped onion and the garlic and cook, stirring every now and then, for about 15 minutes or until the onion is softened but not browned. Stir in the sliced potatoes, watercress and the bay leaf. Cook for 1 minute then pour in the stock. Add salt and pepper to taste and bring to the boil. Reduce the heat, cover the pan and simmer the soup for 30 minutes.

Remove the bay leaf and rub the soup through a coarse sieve. Alternatively, let the soup cool a little, then liquidise it.

Pour the smooth soup in to a large bowl. When it is cool, stir in the cream or low-fat fromage frais. Cover and chill in the refrigerator for at least 2 hours. Serve in chilled bowls, sprinkling each portion with a little freshly grated nutmeg, if liked.

■ Serve with slices of Melba Toast (page 313) or some warm bread rolls.

Summer Pea Soup

SERVES: 6
PREPARATION: 20 minutes
COOKING: 40 minutes

675 g/1½ lb fresh peas
1 onion
1 potato (275–350 g/
     10–12 oz in weight)
25 g/1 oz butter
1 bay leaf
2 thyme or savory sprigs
900 ml/1½ pt chicken
     or ham stock
salt and black pepper
15 ml/1 tablespoon
     chopped mint
15 ml/1 tablespoon
     chopped tarragon
300 ml/½ pt single cream

Shell the peas and rinse them under cold water. Chop the onion and peel and dice the potato. Melt the butter in a saucepan. Add the onion and

potato, and cook for 5 minutes, stirring once or twice. Stir in the peas, bay leaf, thyme or savory and the stock. Add salt and pepper, then bring the soup to the boil. Reduce the heat so that the soup simmers, cover the pan and cook for 30 minutes.

Remove the herbs from the soup before puréeing it in a liquidiser or food processor, or rubbing it through a fine sieve. Stir in the mint and tarragon and reheat the soup, then reduce the heat and stir in the cream. Taste for seasoning and heat the soup gently for a few seconds but do not allow it to boil or the cream will curdle.

■ Serve the soup hot or allow it to cool completely and chill it well before serving. Crisp Melba Toast (page 313) or crusty rolls are suitable accompaniments.
Note Pea soup freezes well for at least 6 months if made with chicken stock. Fresh ham stock does not have a long freezer life and it should be stored for 4–6 weeks. Do not add the cream to the soup before freezing it. Thaw and reheat the soup, then stir in the cream.

STARTERS, SAVOURIES & LIGHT DISHES

Avocado Bristol Fashion

Green avocados and scarlet lobster make an attractive starter. Avocados should be prepared at the last minute, otherwise they turn brown.

SERVES: 4
PREPARATION: 25 minutes

1 cooked lobster
75 ml/3 fl oz double cream or
     fromage frais
10 ml/2 teaspoons lemon juice
cayenne pepper
2 large avocados
salt
paprika

Ask the fishmonger to split the cooked lobster in half. Remove the grey sac in each half of the head and the black intestinal tubes. Prise out all the lobster meat from the body, tail and claws, and set the thin scarlet crawler claws aside for garnish.

Chop the lobster meat finely, put it in a basin and stir in the cream or fromage frais and lemon juice. Season to taste with cayenne pepper.

Cut the avocados in half lengthways and remove the stones. Scoop out the avocado flesh in chunks, using a blunt knife and teaspoon; take care not to puncture the shell. Dice the flesh and fold it into the lobster mixture. Season with salt.

Pile the lobster mixture into the avocado shells and sprinkle with a little paprika. Arrange the claws on top.

Avocado Bristol Fashion.

Fresh Asparagus

Fresh Asparagus.

The English asparagus season lasts for only a brief period over May and June, but in early June, home-grown asparagus is widely available. While you can buy imported asparagus at other times of the year, it lacks the flavour of fresh English asparagus and is much more expensive.

SERVES: 4
PREPARATION: 10 minutes
COOKING: 20–30 minutes

900 g/2 lb asparagus
salt and black pepper
100 g/4 oz butter, melted, or
    French Dressing (page 356)

Wash the asparagus carefully and lightly scrape the lower parts of the stems, away from the delicate tips. Young fresh asparagus needs no further preparation, but if the stems are woody towards the base, trim off the wood, keeping the stems at a uniform length.

Tie the asparagus in bundles of 10–12, using cooking string or tape fairly loosely so as not to damage the stems. Bring a large pan of lightly salted water to the boil. Place the bundle of asparagus upright in it, with the tips above the water. Cover the pan and reduce the heat slightly to prevent the water from boiling over. If the asparagus is too tall for the lid to be positioned, tent foil over the top, folding it on the pan edge. Time of cooking varies according to the age, size and length of the asparagus, but as a general rule asparagus is cooked when the tips are soft. Young asparagus cooks in about 10 minutes, the average is nearer 20 minutes and older spears may take up to 30 minutes.

Untie the asparagus and drain carefully. Serve the asparagus on individual plates, either hot with melted butter or cold with French dressing.

■ Asparagus is traditionally eaten with the fingers. Finger bowls, with lukewarm water and a slice of lemon are required.

Asparagus in Mornay Sauce

SERVES: 4
PREPARATION: 15 minutes
COOKING: 30–40 minutes

900 g/2 lb asparagus
25 g/1 oz butter
25 g/1 oz plain flour
300 ml/½ pt milk
100 g/4 oz Cheddar cheese
30 ml/2 tablespoons double cream
salt and black pepper

Prepare and cook the asparagus as described for Fresh Asparagus (left), keeping back 30 ml/2 tablespoons of the cooking water when draining the spears.

Melt the butter in a saucepan, stir in the flour and cook this roux* for a few minutes. Gradually add the milk, stirring until the sauce boils and then thickens. Stir in the reserved asparagus water and simmer the sauce gently for 2 minutes. Grate the cheese and add 75 g/3 oz to the sauce, stirring until it has melted completely. Stir in the cream, season to taste with salt and freshly ground pepper and remove from the heat.

Put the drained asparagus in a greased flameproof serving dish, and pour over the cheese sauce. Sprinkle with the rest of the cheese and put the dish under a hot grill until bubbly and brown on top. Serve immediately.

Quick Chicken Pâté

Pâté is a popular start to a meal, but it usually takes a long time to prepare. This recipe will quickly transform a small amount of cooked chicken into a well-flavoured pâté.

SERVES: 4
PREPARATION: 10 minutes
COOKING: 5 minutes
CHILLING: 30 minutes

50 g/2 oz streaky bacon
1 clove garlic
100 g/4 oz cooked chicken
125 g/4½ oz liver paste or
    smooth liver pâté
5 ml/1 teaspoon finely
    chopped parsley
5 ml/1 teaspoon finely
    snipped chives
salt and black pepper

Remove the rinds and any bones from the bacon; cut it into small dice. Place in a heavy-bottomed pan over medium heat until the fat runs, then raise the heat and fry for 2–3 minutes more. Crush the garlic, add it to the bacon and cook for 1 minute.

Chop the chicken finely. Put the liver paste or pâté in a bowl. Pour off the fat from the bacon and stir it into the liver paste or pâté; mix in the bacon, garlic, chicken, parsley and chives. Season with salt and pepper.

Pack the pâté in a small earthenware dish, cover and chill for at least 30 minutes in the refrigerator.

■ Serve with hot toast or with warmed pitta bread.

Stuffed Anchovy Eggs

SERVES: 4
PREPARATION: 20 minutes
COOKING: 15 minutes

8 hard-boiled eggs
50 g/2 oz can anchovy fillets
30 ml/2 tablespoons
    tomato ketchup
30 ml/2 tablespoons
    double cream
salt and black pepper
25 g/1 oz butter
25 g/1 oz plain flour
300 ml/½ pt milk
50 g/2 oz Cheddar cheese
2.5 ml/½ teaspoon paprika

Cut the shelled eggs in half lengthways and carefully remove the yolks, keeping the whites intact. Drain the can of anchovy fillets, mash them with a fork, and stir in the egg yolks. Pound to a smooth paste with a pestle or wooden spoon. Stir in the ketchup and cream, and season to taste.

Fill the egg whites with the yolk mixture and arrange them, cut side down, in a greased flameproof dish. Melt the butter in a saucepan, add the flour and cook for 1 minute. Gradually add the milk, stirring until the sauce boils and thickens, then stir in half the cheese.

Pour the cheese sauce over the stuffed eggs. Sprinkle with the remaining cheese and dust lightly with paprika. Brown the dish under a hot grill.

■ Serve as a hot savoury with Creamed Spinach (page 169).

FISH, SHELLFISH & SEAFOOD

Fried Cod Roe

SERVES: 4–6
PREPARATION: 5 minutes
COOKING: 20–30 minutes

450–675 g/1–1½ lb fresh cod roe
salt and black pepper
1 bay leaf
plain flour for coating
1 egg
about 50 g/2 oz fresh white
    breadcrumbs
oil for shallow frying
lemon wedges to garnish

Wash the roe carefully in cold running water. Put it in a saucepan with the bay leaf, and cover with lightly salted water. Bring slowly to the boil, then lower the heat to a bare simmer, cover the pan and cook for 15 minutes. Drain carefully. Place the roe on a board, cover with a weighted plate and leave until cold.

Cut the cold roe into 2.5 cm/1 in thick slices. Season the flour for coating with salt and pepper. Beat the egg lightly. Coat the slices of roe in the seasoned flour, shaking off the excess, dip in egg, then coat evenly with the fresh breadcrumbs.

Heat the oil in a heavy-based pan and fry the slices over moderate heat until golden brown on both sides. Drain on absorbent kitchen paper and serve at once, garnished with wedges of lemon.

Cod Gourmet

SERVES: 4
PREPARATION: 15 minutes
OVEN: 200°C/400°F/gas 6
COOKING: 30 minutes

4 portions cod fillet, each
    about 175g/6 oz
40 g/1½ oz butter
3 shallots
100 g/4 oz mushrooms
salt and black pepper
30 ml/2 tablespoons dry white wine
10 ml/2 teaspoons lemon juice
25 g/1 tablespoon chopped parsley
    to garnish

Skin the cod. Grease a large, shallow, ovenproof dish with a little butter and arrange the fillets in this. Peel and finely chop the shallots. Melt the remaining butter in a pan and fry the shallots for 2–3 minutes, until they are transparent. Wipe and trim the mushrooms, slice them thinly and add to the shallots. Cook for 2 minutes, then season to taste.

Spoon the fried shallot and mushroom mixture over the cod fillets and pour over the white wine. Cover the dish and bake in a preheated oven at 200°C/400°F/gas 6 for 20–25 minutes.

Serve the fish straight from the dish. Sprinkle with lemon juice and garnish with parsley.
■ Tiny new potatoes and young peas go well with this dish.

Haddock Barrie

SERVES: 4
PREPARATION: 15 minutes
OVEN: 200°C/400°F/gas 6
COOKING: 30 minutes

4 portions haddock fillet, each
    about 175 g/6 oz
40 g/1½ oz butter
1 small onion
25 g/1 oz plain flour
400 ml/14 fl oz milk
50 g/2 oz Cheddar cheese
100 g/4 oz peeled cooked prawns
salt and cayenne pepper

Skin the haddock and remove any stray bones. Use a little of the butter to grease a shallow flameproof dish and arrange the fillets in a single layer in this.

Peel and finely chop the onion. Melt the remaining butter in a small pan, add the onion and cook, stirring frequently, for 5 minutes without browning. Stir in the flour, cook for a few minutes, then gradually add the milk, stirring continuously until the mixture boils and thickens to make a white sauce. Grate the Cheddar cheese and stir it into the sauce until it has melted. Chop the prawns roughly and stir them into the cheese sauce. Season the sauce with salt and cayenne pepper.

Pour the cheese and prawn sauce over the fish and bake in a preheated oven at 200°C/400°F/gas 6 for 20–25 minutes until lightly browned on top. Serve the fillets at once.
■ Plain boiled rice or new potatoes and spinach or broccoli go well with this dish.

Monte Carlo Haddock

This dish used to be a favourite with gamblers who had spent the night in the Casino.

SERVES: 4
PREPARATION: 10 minutes
COOKING: 20–30 minutes

450 g/1 lb smoked haddock fillet
600 ml/1 pt milk
1 bay leaf
50 g/2 oz butter
50 g/2 oz plain flour
salt and cayenne pepper
75 g/3 oz Cheddar cheese
4 eggs

Wash and dry the fillet before putting it in a large pan with the milk and bay leaf. Heat until the milk is simmering, then poach the fish, uncovered, for about 10 minutes or until just cooked. Lift out the fish, remove the skin and divide the fish into four. Arrange the pieces in a warm flameproof dish, cover and keep hot.

Strain the milk. Melt the butter in a saucepan, stir in the flour and cook for 1 minute. Add the milk gradually, stirring, until the mixture boils and thickens to form a sauce. Season to taste with salt and cayenne pepper.

Grate the cheese and stir it into the sauce until it has melted. Poach the eggs (page 337) until they are just set. Lift the eggs out with a perforated spoon and place one egg on each haddock portion. Pour over the sauce and place the dish under a hot grill for 2–3 minutes, until lightly browned.

Turbot Duglére

SERVES: 4
PREPARATION: 15 minutes
OVEN: 190°C/375°F/gas 5
COOKING: about 1 hour

4 turbot steaks
fish trimmings
25 g/1 oz butter
juice of 1 lemon
salt and black pepper
120 ml/4 fl oz dry white wine
Sauce
2–3 tomatoes
25 g/1 oz butter
15–30 ml/1–2 tablespoons
    plain flour
20 ml/4 teaspoons chopped parsley
75 ml/2½ fl oz double cream

Wash and trim the fish. Make a Court Bouillon (page 316) with the trimmings. Rub the steaks with lemon juice, place them in a buttered dish and season with salt and freshly ground pepper. Add the wine and sufficient court bouillon to come to the top of the fish. Cover with buttered foil and cook in a preheated oven at 190°C/375°F/gas 5 for about 25 minutes. Put the steaks in a warm dish and set the liquid aside. Skin the tomatoes, remove the pulp and rub it through a sieve. Set the sieved liquid aside and cut the flesh into thin strips.

Melt the butter, remove from heat and stir in flour. Stir in the sieved tomato and 300 ml/½ pt of the fish liquid. Simmer the sauce over low heat for 3–5 minutes. Add the tomato strips, parsley and cream; do not boil the sauce. Adjust the seasoning and pour the sauce over the fish.

Salmon Mousse

SERVES: 6–8
PREPARATION: 25 minutes
COOKING: 10–15 minutes
CHILLING: 2 hours

450 g/1 lb fresh salmon fillet or
*   418 g/14½ oz can red salmon*
300 ml/½ pt water
1 bay leaf
10 ml/2 teaspoons
*   powdered gelatine*
200 g/7 oz fromage frais
100 g/4 oz low-fat soft cheese
15 ml/1 tablespoon lemon juice
30 ml/2 tablespoons chopped dill
2 egg whites
salt and black pepper
cucumber slices to garnish

If using fresh salmon, poach it in the water with the bay leaf for 10–15 minutes, depending on thickness, until cooked. Drain and reserve 45 ml/3 tablespoons of the water; then remove the skin and bones from the salmon and flake the flesh. If using canned fish, drain and reserve 45 ml/3 tablespoons of the liquid; then remove skin and bones.

Sprinkle the gelatine over the reserved cooking water or can liquid in a heatproof basin and leave to stand for 15 minutes. Stand the basin over a saucepan of simmering water until the gelatine has dissolved.

Purée the fish with the fromage frais, soft cheese, lemon juice and dill in a liquidiser or food processor. Scrape into a bowl and stir in the gelatine.

Whisk the egg whites until stiff and fold into the purée. Season to taste with salt and

pepper. Spoon into a 15 cm/6 in soufflé dish, or decorative mould. Chill for 2–3 hours or until set. If the mousse has been made in a soufflé dish, serve spoonfuls on individual plates.

A decorative mould should be dipped briefly in hot water before being unmoulded on a serving platter. Garnish with slices of cucumber.

Salmon en Croûte

SERVES: 4–6
PREPARATION: 45 minutes
OVEN: 220°C/425°F/gas 7
   190°C/375°F/gas 5
COOKING: 40 minutes

1 small grilse or piece of salmon
*   (about 675 g/1½ lb)*
450 g/1 lb asparagus
salt and black pepper
5 ml/1 teaspoon chopped dill
3 thin gammon steaks or rashers
225 g/8 oz home-made Puff
*   Pastry (page 374) or thawed*
*   frozen puff pastry*
1 egg yolk
15 ml/1 tablespoon milk
lemon wedges to garnish

Ask the fishmonger to skin and fillet the fish. Otherwise cut the head off the salmon and wash the fish thoroughly to remove all traces of blood. Carefully peel off the skin with a sharp knife before removing the backbone (page 314). Leave the salmon in two long fillets.

Wash and trim the asparagus (page 343), tie in a bundle and cook upright in a pan of lightly salted water for 20–30 minutes or until the asparagus tips are soft to

the touch (page 343). Drain the asparagus thoroughly, and cut off the soft tips (the stems can be used in an omelette).

Arrange the asparagus over one half of the salmon, sprinkle with dill, salt and pepper and put the fish together. Trim the rind and fat from the gammon. Place it between sheets of greaseproof paper and beat with a rolling pin until the slices are very thin. Wrap the gammon slices around the salmon and set it aside.

Roll out the puff pastry, on a floured surface, to a rectangle that measures about 30 × 25 cm/ 12 × 10 in or one that is large enough to completely enclose the salmon. Place the salmon in the centre of the puff pastry and wrap the pastry over the fish. Beat the egg yolk lightly with the milk and brush the edges of the pastry. Seal the long joint firmly with more egg. Tuck in the short ends of the pastry neatly and seal the edges with egg.

Place the salmon on a baking sheet, with the seam underneath. Cut one or two holes in the pastry for the steam to escape, and decorate the top with leaves made from the pastry trimmings. Brush with the remaining egg and milk. Bake in a preheated oven at 220°C/425°F/gas 7 for 20 minutes, then lower the temperature to 190°C/375°F/gas 5 and bake for a further 20–25 minutes or until the pastry is golden brown. Serve the salmon, hot or cold, cut in slices, and garnish with lemon wedges.

■ New potatoes tossed in butter and dill, and a cucumber salad, are traditional side dishes.

Mackerel with Cucumber

The cool, pale green look of young cucumber heralds summer. Its taste suits oily fish, such as mackerel or trout. The dish can be served hot or cold.

SERVES: 4
PREPARATION: 25 minutes
OVEN: 200°C/400°F/gas 6
COOKING: 35 minutes

4 mackerel (about 225 g/
*   8 oz each)*
25 g/1 oz butter
1 small cucumber
salt and black pepper
30 ml/2 tablespoons cider vinegar
*   or dry white wine*

Gut and clean the mackerel (page 313) and cut off the heads. Wash the fish and pat them dry on absorbent kitchen paper. Grease a shallow, ovenproof dish sparingly with a little of the butter. Wash and dry the cucumber and slice it thinly; put a layer of cucumber slices over

Mackerel with Cucumber.

the base of the dish. Place the mackerel on top and cover with the remaining cucumber slices. Season to taste with salt and freshly ground pepper.

Sprinkle the vinegar or wine over the fish and cucumber, and dot with the remaining butter. Cover the dish and bake in a preheated oven at 200°C/400°F/gas 6 for 30 minutes.

Remove the dish from the oven and transfer the fish and cucumber to a serving dish. Keep it hot unless the mackerel is to be served cold. Strain the juices from the fish through a fine sieve into a saucepan. Boil briskly for a few minutes until it is reduced to a small amount of glaze. Pour this glaze over the mackerel and serve at once or leave to cool.

■ For a hot main course, serve with potatoes tossed in butter and chopped parsley, and with young peas. If served cold, a green salad and Garlic Potatoes (page 290) would complement this mackerel dish.

POULTRY & GAME

Chicken Chaud-froid

This is a French dish which classically consists of a whole cooked chicken coated with aspic sauce (chaud-froid sauce) and then elaborately garnished. Individual chicken joints are, however, easier to coat.

SERVES: 6
PREPARATION: 1 hour
COOKING: 1½–1¾ hours

6 boneless chicken breasts
1 large onion
1 sprig of thyme
1 bay leaf
salt and black pepper
1 small carrot
6 parsley stalks
6 peppercorns
2.5ml/½ teaspoon salt
300 ml/½ pt milk
25 g/1 oz butter
25 g/1 oz plain flour
10 ml/2 teaspoons
    powdered gelatine
300 ml/½ pt Aspic Jelly (page 311)
Garnish
2.5 cm/1 in piece of cucumber peel
pared peel of 1 large tomato
pared rind of 1 small lemon
sprigs of dill

Place the chicken breasts in a large saucepan. Peel the onion and cut it into 2.5 cm/1 in slices. Reserve one slice then add the rest to the pan together with the thyme, bay leaf and enough cold water to just cover the chicken.

Add salt and pepper to taste. Bring slowly to the boil, remove the scum, lower the heat and cover the pan with a lid. Simmer gently for 40–45 minutes or until the chicken breasts are cooked through. Lift out the chicken portions and drain. Save the cooking liquid as the basis of a soup or sauce, if liked.

Scrape the carrot, leaving it whole, and put it in a saucepan with the reserved onion slice, parsley stalks, peppercorns, salt and milk. Bring slowly to the boil, then turn off the heat and leave to infuse for 30 minutes.

Melt the butter in a saucepan, stir in the flour and cook for 2 minutes; strain the infused milk and gradually stir it into the butter and flour roux*. Bring the sauce to the boil over low heat, stirring continuously, and cook gently for 2 minutes. Season to taste. Cover the surface of the sauce with dampened grease-proof paper and set aside until just cooled.

Stir the gelatine into the hot aspic and heat gently, stirring, until it has dissolved completely. Leave to cool, then stir half into the white sauce. Place the sauce in the refrigerator briefly until it is just beginning to thicken as the aspic content sets. Do not chill the remaining aspic and gelatine mixture.

Meanwhile, remove the skin carefully from the chicken portions, pat them dry and place on a wire rack. Stand the rack over a sheet of foil or plate. Coat each portion carefully with the sauce, spooning it evenly over the top of the chicken and allowing any excess to run off. Chill for 15 minutes to set.

Cut the cucumber peel, the tomato peel and lemon rind into narrow strips, dip them in the

Chicken Chaud-froid.

remaining aspic jelly and arrange them in decorative patterns on the chicken. Allow to set before spooning over the remaining aspic jelly; leave the chicken in a cool place to set completely. Add the dill garnish before serving.

If at any stage in the preparations, the aspic or the chaud-froid sauce sets before you have finished coating the chicken, stand the container over hot water and stir until the aspic or sauce is runny again. Leftover sauce which runs down through the rack on to the foil or plate should be scraped up and warmed with the main batch to complete the coating on the chicken.

■ Salads, crusty bread or new potatoes could be served as side dishes with the chicken.

Chicken in Mushroom Sauce

SERVES: 6
PREPARATION: 25 minutes
COOKING: 1½ hours

2 onions
2 sticks celery
15 ml/1 tablespoon oil
1 chicken (about 1.6 kg/3½ lb)
salt and black pepper
1 bay leaf
100 g/4 oz mushrooms
25 g/1 oz butter
45 g/1½ oz plain flour
60 ml/2 fl oz single cream
    (optional)
15 ml/1 tablespoon finely chopped
    parsley to garnish

Peel and finely chop the onions; scrub the celery and chop finely.

Heat the oil in a large heavy-based pan over low heat; cook the onion and celery until soft and just beginning to colour.

Meanwhile, wash and wipe the chicken, inside and out; then truss it (page 321). Clean the giblets and liver (if using); put the chicken, giblets and liver in the pan with the onions and celery; add enough water to cover the chicken. Bring to the boil, remove any scum and add salt, freshly ground pepper and the bay leaf. Cover the pan with a lid, lower the heat and simmer for about 1½ hours, or until the chicken is cooked through. Lift the chicken on to a warm dish and keep it hot. Strain the cooking liquid and set aside.

Trim and thinly slice the mushrooms. Melt the butter in a small pan and cook the mushrooms over low heat for 2–3 minutes. Add the flour and cook, stirring continuously, until all the melted butter has been absorbed. Gradually blend in 450 ml/¾ pt of the strained chicken liquid and bring to the boil, stirring continuously, to make a smooth sauce. Correct seasoning with salt and pepper if necessary. Stir in the cream, if using, and heat the sauce through without boiling.

Carve the chicken as for turkey (page 325), and arrange the slices and joints in a serving dish. Pour the mushroom sauce over the meat and garnish with the finely chopped parsley.

■ Serve with broccoli spears and plain boiled potatoes. Alternatively, serve a mixture of brown rice and wild rice.

Poulet Sauté Marengo

According to legend, this now-classic dish was invented by Napoleon's chef after the Battle of Marengo in 1800. The dish's ingredients, which originally included freshwater crayfish, were apparently available in the war-torn Italian countryside.

SERVES: 6
PREPARATION: 45 minutes
COOKING: 1 hour

1 chicken (about 2.05 kg/4½ lb) or
*   8 chicken portions*
2 onions
1 clove garlic
50 g/2 oz butter
45 ml/3 tablespoons olive oil
25 g/1 oz plain flour
150 ml/¼ pt chicken stock
300 ml/½ pt Marsala
6 tomatoes
12 button mushrooms
1 white truffle (optional)
salt and black pepper
30 ml/2 tablespoons brandy

If using a whole chicken, cut it into eight neat portions (page 322). Peel the onions and garlic, roughly chop the onions, and crush the garlic. Heat the butter and oil in a large flameproof casserole over moderate heat. Brown the chicken pieces all over, then remove them from the pan. Fry the onions and garlic until light golden, then sprinkle in the flour and cook, stirring, until all the fat is absorbed. Gradually add the chicken stock and the Marsala, stirring until the mixture boils. Replace the chicken pieces, carefully pushing them down into the sauce.

Skin the tomatoes (page 302) and roughly chop them; trim the button mushrooms and slice them finely. Chop the truffle finely, if used. Add the tomatoes, mushrooms and truffle to the pan. Season to taste with salt and freshly ground pepper.

Bring the sauce back to the boil, then lower the heat and cover the pan. Simmer the chicken gently for about 1 hour, or until the pieces are cooked through. Stir occasionally to prevent the sauce from sticking. About 10 minutes before the end of cooking time, stir the brandy into the sauce.

■ Serve hot with boiled new potatoes or with plain buttered noodles. For the traditional garnish, place six cooked crayfish around the chicken.

Duck with Redcurrant and Lime

SERVES: 4
PREPARATION: 20 minutes
MARINATING: 2 hours
COOKING: 40–45 minutes

1 lime
60 ml/4 tablespoons white wine
6 juniper berries
2 bay leaves
4 duck breasts
1 large shallot
225 g/8 oz redcurrants
60 ml/4 tablespoons
*   redcurrant jelly*
salt and black pepper
sugar

Pare 2 strips of peel from the lime, then cut it in half. Squeeze the juice from one half, then cut the other half into thin slices. Set aside. Place the wine, the lime juice and strips of lime peel in a small saucepan. Add the juniper berries and bay leaves, heat for a few seconds, then pour into a shallow dish large enough to hold the duck breasts in a single layer. Arrange the duck breasts flesh side down in the marinade. Cover and refrigerate for 2 hours.

Lift the duck out of the marinade, strain and reserve the liquor. Place the duck breasts skin side down in a single layer in a large frying pan. Cook gently for 15 minutes, turn the breasts over and cook for a further 15–20 minutes or until they are cooked through. Transfer to a serving plate and keep hot.

Strain off all but 15 ml/ 1 tablespoon of the duck fat. Finely chop the shallot, add to the pan and cook gently for 5 minutes or until softened.

Meanwhile, strip the redcurrants from their stalks. Add them to the pan, cook for a few minutes until the berries soften slightly, then add the reserved marinade and the redcurrant jelly. Stir gently until the jelly has dissolved and the sauce is hot, then taste and adjust the seasoning with salt and freshly ground black pepper, adding a little sugar if required. Spoon the sauce over the duck, garnish with the lime slices.

Terrine de Campagne.

Terrine de Campagne

This farmhouse-style terrine of calf liver and veal is a good choice for a picnic, lunch or supper. If preferred, pig or lamb liver and minced pork may be used in place of the veal liver.

SERVES: 6–8
PREPARATION: 20 minutes
OVEN: 180°C/350°F/gas 4
COOKING: 2 hours

350 g/12 oz thin rashers
*   streaky bacon*
350 g/12 oz calf liver
1 large onion
675 g/1½ lb minced veal
2 cloves garlic
15 ml/1 tablespoon tomato paste
5 ml/1 teaspoon chopped summer
*   savory or sage*
5 ml/1 teaspoon chopped
*   oregano*
100 g/4 oz butter
150 ml/¼ pt red wine
salt and black pepper
4 bay leaves

166

Remove the bacon rind and any bones from the bacon and stretch the rashers as when making Bacon Rolls (page 331) thinly with the flat blade of a knife. Line a 1.12 litre/2 pt terrine or soufflé dish with the bacon, allowing the rashers to hang over the edges of the dish.

Clean the calf liver, removing any gristle, and put the meat through the coarse plate of a mincer. Peel the onion and chop it finely. Mix together the liver, onion and veal in a large bowl.

Peel the garlic and crush it over the meat mixture. Stir in the tomato paste, summer savory or sage and oregano. Melt the butter and stir into the terrine mixture together with enough red wine to give a moist but not sloppy consistency. Season to taste with salt and freshly ground black pepper.

Spoon the mixture into the terrine or soufflé dish, over the bacon rashers. Arrange the bay leaves on top of the meat mixture and fold over the bacon rashers. Cover the dish with a lid or tight-fitting foil. Cook the terrine in a preheated oven at 180°C/350°F/gas 4 for 2 hours.

When cooked, remove the lid from the dish, cover with fresh foil and a flat board. Place a heavy weight on the board and leave overnight.

Serve the terrine straight from the dish or turn it out on to a serving plate and cut it into thick wedges.

■ Crusty bread and a tossed green salad may be served with this terrine to make a substantial main course.

Lamb in Red Wine

A leg of lamb makes a good choice for a large gathering of guests. Spices and wine give a fresh summer taste to succulent English or Welsh lamb, which is in season at this time of year.

SERVES: 6–8
PREPARATION: 15 minutes
OVEN: 220°C/425°F/gas 7
      180°C/350°F/gas 4
COOKING: 1¾–2 hours

2 cloves garlic
1.8–2.27 kg/4–5 lb leg of lamb
7 g/¼ oz lard
salt and black pepper
ground ginger
2 onions
2 carrots
50 g/2 oz butter
3–4 sprigs of thyme
1 bottle dry red wine

Peel the garlic and cut each clove into three or four slivers. With the point of a sharp knife, make small incisions in the meat and press the garlic into these. Rub the skin with the lard, a little salt and freshly ground pepper; dust with ginger. Peel the onions and carrots and chop them roughly.

Melt the butter in a roasting tin, and quickly brown the meat over moderate heat to seal in the juices. Remove the meat from the pan and cook the onions and carrots for a few minutes in the butter until golden. Add the thyme and place the meat on top of the vegetable mixture. Cover with a lid or foil.

Roast the meat in a preheated oven at 220°C/425°F/gas 7 for 20 minutes, then pour over the red wine and reduce the heat to 180°C/350°F/gas 4. Continue

Lamb in Red Wine.

cooking the lamb for a further 1–1¼ hours. Baste two or three times with the wine.

Remove the joint and keep it warm on a serving dish in the oven. Boil the cooking juices briskly, until they have reduced by about one third. Remove any fat by drawing absorbent kitchen paper over the surface of this gravy. Strain into a clean pan, heat through and correct the seasoning with salt and pepper.

■ Serve boiled new potatoes and young fresh vegetables, such as carrots, mange-tout or sugar snap peas tossed in parsley, with the roasted lamb. Pour the gravy into a sauceboat and serve it separately.

Pork Chops with Apple

Cooking apples are traditionally served with pork to counteract the fattiness of the meat. They appear as stuffings and sauces with roasts, and can also, as here, be used with oven-cooked chops.

SERVES: 4
PREPARATION: 15 minutes
OVEN: 180°C/350°F/gas 4
COOKING: 1¼ hours

4 thick pork chops
25 g/1 oz butter
salt and black pepper
3–4 large cooking apples
juice of 1 lemon

Trim any excess fat from the chops, wipe them dry with absorbent kitchen paper, and put them in a lightly buttered oven-proof dish. Season to taste with salt and freshly ground pepper. Peel, core and thinly slice the apples and arrange over the chops to cover them completely. Melt the remaining butter and brush some of it over the apple slices. Sprinkle with lemon juice and cover the dish closely.

Cook the pork chops in a pre-heated oven, at 180°C/350°F/gas 4 for 45 minutes. Remove the foil, brush the cooking apples with the rest of the butter and cook for a further 10–15 minutes, until the apples are lightly browned, but not dry, and the chops are tender.

■ Serve the chops from the cooking dish. New potatoes and Braised Chicory (page 169) go well with the sharp apple taste.

Barbecued Spare Ribs

This is a substantial first course to be served in the Chinese style and eaten with the fingers. The lean spare ribs are grilled until crisp and served with a spicy barbecue sauce.

SERVES: 4
PREPARATION: 15 minutes
OVEN: 180°C/350°F/gas 4
COOKING: 45 minutes

12 pork spare ribs
60 ml/4 tablespoons clear honey
45 ml/3 tablespoons soy sauce
45 ml/3 tablespoons tomato
  ketchup
Tabasco sauce
1 small clove garlic
mustard powder
paprika
salt and black pepper
juice of 1 small orange
60 ml/4 tablespoons wine vinegar

Ask the butcher for the type of lean spare ribs used in Chinese cookery; thin ends of the ribs, not the chunky chops.

Wipe the meat and, if it has not been done already, separate it into single rib portions. Grill the spare ribs for 10–15 minutes under high heat, or on a barbecue, until they are brown, turning them several times. Arrange them in a single layer in a large roasting tin and pour over the pan juices.

Put the honey, soy sauce, tomato ketchup and few drops of Tabasco sauce into a bowl. Peel and crush the garlic and add it. Stir in the mustard powder,

paprika, salt and freshly ground pepper to taste, then add the orange juice and wine vinegar. Pour over the spare ribs.

Cook the ribs, uncovered, in a preheated oven at 180°C/350°F/gas 4 for 30 minutes.
■ Serve the spare ribs piping hot in the sauce. Provide finger bowls if possible.

Simple Veal & Ham Pie

Veal pies first became popular in Britain during the 18th century. They were often cooked as raised pies or made into jellied moulds – the following recipe is a simpler farmhouse version.

SERVES: 4–6
PREPARATION: 45 minutes
OVEN: 200°C/400°F/gas 6
       180°C/350°/gas 4
COOKING: 2¾ hours

1 shin bone
900 g/2 lb pie veal
900 ml–1.12 litres/1½–2 pt stock
2 bay leaves
bouquet garni*
15 ml/1 tablespoon chopped parsley
6 black peppercorns
salt and black pepper
225 g/8 oz piece cooked gammon
3 hard-boiled eggs
grated rind of 1 lemon
225 g/8 oz home-made Flaky
  Pastry (page 372) or Puff
  Pastry (page 374) or thawed
  frozen puff pastry
1 egg
5ml/1 teaspoon olive oil

Ask the butcher to saw the shin bone into pieces. Place the veal

and the shin bone in a large pan, and cover with the stock. Add the bay leaves, bouquet garni, parsley and peppercorns. Bring to the boil, lower the heat, cover the pan and simmer gently for 2 hours. Allow to cool slightly, then remove the meat from the liquid, cut it into small pieces and remove any pieces of fat. Strain the liquid, season to taste with salt and freshly ground pepper and set it aside.

Cut the gammon into narrow strips and mix with the veal. Shell the hard-boiled eggs, place them in the centre of a 1.12 litre/2 pt pie dish, and pack the veal and gammon around them. Sprinkle the lemon rind over the top. Pour the liquid over the pie filling to just cover it.

Roll out the flaky or puff pastry to a thickness of 1 cm/½ in. Cover the pie with the pastry and make a slit in the centre to allow the steam to escape. Beat the egg with the olive oil, and. brush over the pastry.

Bake the veal and ham pie in a preheated oven at 200°C/400°F/gas 6 for 15 minutes, then lower the oven temperature to 180°C/350°F/gas 4 and bake for a further 30 minutes or until the pastry is golden brown. Give the pie a half turn about halfway through cooking.

Top up the pie filling, if necessary, with more stock, added through the pastry slit.
■ Serve the pie hot with boiled potatoes and mange-tout or sugar snap peas or, ideally, cold with a mixed salad tossed in a French Dressing (page 356), flavoured with tarragon.

VEGETABLES & SALADS

Peas and Spring Onions

Spring onions and young fresh garden peas make an excellent combination to serve with roast lamb or chicken.

SERVES: 4–6
PREPARATION: 15–20 minutes
COOKING: 20–30 minutes

1.15 kg/2½ lb fresh peas
10–12 spring onions
300 ml/½ pt chicken stock
15 g/½ oz butter
15 g/½ oz plain flour
salt and black pepper

Shell the garden peas. Trim the roots and outer leaves from the spring onions; wash them and cut the stems off the onions, leaving about 2.5 cm/1 in of green on each bulb. Put the spring onions in a pan with the chicken stock and bring them slowly to simmering point. Cook the spring onions gently for 2–3 minutes, until they begin to soften, then add the peas and cover the pan. Continue to cook for about 20 minutes over low heat until the peas are tender.

Soften the butter and mix to a paste with the flour. Add small pieces of this beurre manié to the peas, stirring carefully, so that the peas do not break up, and simmer until the stock has thickened to a sauce. Season to taste with salt and freshly ground pepper. Serve hot.

Lettuce and Green Peas

Young peas are traditionally cooked with fresh mint, and this is another classic combination – lettuce with fresh peas. The salad leaves yield the liquid needed to braise the peas.

SERVES: 4–6
PREPARATION: 15 minutes
COOKING: 40 minutes

1 cos lettuce
900 g/2 lb fresh peas
5 ml/1 teaspoon chopped mint
25 g/1 oz butter
pinch of caster sugar
salt and black pepper

Wash the cos lettuce leaves thoroughly, but do not dry them, then coarsely break half of them into a saucepan. Shell the green peas and put them, with the mint, on top of the lettuce. Add the butter, cut into knobs, and the caster sugar. Sprinkle with salt and freshly ground pepper, and break the remaining lettuce leaves into pieces, laying them on top of the peas.

Cover the pan tightly and cook the vegetables over a gentle heat for about 40 minutes or until the peas are tender. Keep shaking the pan every now and then to prevent sticking.

Carefully spoon the lettuce and peas, with the cooking liquid, into a deep warm dish and serve immediately.

Creamed Spinach

Young, crisp spinach leaves should be cooked as soon as possible after buying or picking. You can omit the cream added to the cooked, buttered spinach or substitute a low-fat alternative, such as fromage frais or half-fat cream, if preferred.

SERVES: 4
PREPARATION: 10 minutes
COOKING: 10–15 minutes

900 g/2 lb spinach
25 g/1 oz butter
salt and black pepper
1.25 ml/¼ teaspoon grated nutmeg
90 ml/6 tablespoons single cream

Remove the stalks and the coarse midribs from the spinach and throw away any bruised leaves. Wash the leaves thoroughly in several changes of cold water to get rid of all sand and grit.

Put the spinach in a large saucepan with only the water clinging to the leaves. Cook over medium to high heat, shaking the pan frequently for 5–8 minutes. There is no need for extra water because the spinach cooks in its own liquid and the steam which condenses in the covered pan. Drain the spinach thoroughly through a fine sieve, squeezing out as much liquid as possible with a potato masher.

Chop the spinach roughly on a board. Melt the butter in the saucepan, add the spinach, salt and freshly ground pepper, and nutmeg and heat through before stirring in the cream. Spoon into a hot serving dish.

Braised Chicory

The sharp, clean taste of chicory, also called Belgian endive, goes particularly well with roast pork, goose or duck.

SERVES: 4
PREPARATION: 15 minutes
OVEN: 180°C/350°F/gas 4
COOKING: 40 minutes

4 heads chicory
1 small onion
25 g/1 oz butter
salt and black pepper
150 ml/¼ pt chicken or beef stock
chopped parsley to garnish

Wash the chicory, trim off the root ends and cut each head in half lengthways. Scoop out the small piece of tough core at the base of each heart.

Peel the onion and chop it finely. Melt the butter in a flameproof casserole over low heat and fry the onion in the butter until soft and transparent, but not browned. Add the chicory, fry for 2–3 minutes on each side, then season to taste with salt and pepper.

Remove the pan from the heat. Pour the stock over the chicory, cover closely and cook in a preheated oven at 180°C/350°F/gas 4 for 35 minutes.

Serve the braised chicory straight from the dish, sprinkled with finely chopped parsley.

Ratatouille

A classic ratatouille does not have to be reduced to a pulpy stew after long cooking; with careful, slow simmering the vegetables will be full flavoured but will retain some 'bite'. Herbs, such as chopped fresh marjoram or oregano and bay, may be added to the stew with the tomatoes and plenty of chopped parsley can be sprinkled in just before serving. The aubergines are sliced in this recipe, but they may be cut into 1–2.5 cm/½–1 in cubes for a firmer result.

SERVES: 6–8
PREPARATION: 30 minutes
STANDING: 1 hour
COOKING: 50 minutes

2 large courgettes
2 large aubergines
salt and black pepper
5 large tomatoes
1 large green pepper
1 small red pepper
1 large onion
2 cloves garlic
about 150 ml/¼ pt olive oil

Cut the stalks off the courgettes and the aubergines. Wash well and cut them crossways into 5 mm/¼ in thick slices. Put the aubergines in a colander, and sprinkle them with salt. Skin the tomatoes (page 302) and chop them roughly. Wash the peppers, remove the white inner ribs and all seeds, and dice the flesh. Peel and coarsely chop the onion and garlic. Rinse the aubergines, drain and pat them dry with absorbent kitchen paper.

Heat some of the olive oil in a large frying pan and fry the aubergine slices a few at a time over medium to high heat, turning them once. The slices should be lightly browned on each side but not softened. Use a perforated spoon to remove the slices from the pan as they are cooked and add more olive oil as necessary, heating it between frying batches of aubergine. The oil should be hot enough to brown the slices lightly, but quite quickly; if the oil is too cool the aubergine slices will absorb a large amount of oil and they will soften before they go brown. You must take care not to overheat and burn the oil.

When the aubergine slices have been fried and set aside, add the onion and garlic to the oil in the pan, and cook for 10 minutes until the onion is softened but not browned. Then add the peppers, and cook for a further 5 minutes. Replace the aubergine slices and add the courgettes and tomatoes, then mix the vegetables using a spatula to turn and rearrange them. Season the stew to taste with salt and freshly ground black pepper. Cover the pan and simmer the mixture over low heat for 35 minutes, stirring every now and then, until the vegetables are soft but not pulpy. Correct seasoning.

■ Serve ratatouille hot or cold, on its own as a first course or with grilled or fried meat.

Ratatouille.

Asparagus Quiche

This special quiche is made with crisp Parmesan-enriched pastry and a delicate asparagus and chive filling. It is ideal as a main course for a summer lunch party or the same recipe may be prepared in individual quiche dishes or tins to make a splendid starter. Use only the tender tips from 450 g/1 lb asparagus spears, reserving the remainder for a soup or sauce.

SERVES: 6
PREPARATION: 45 minutes
OVEN: 200°C/400°F/gas 6
        180°C/350°F/gas 4
COOKING: about 1 hour

1 small onion
1 bay leaf
1 blade of mace
450 ml/¾ pt milk
salt and black pepper
350 g/12 oz asparagus tips
3 eggs
3 egg yolks
30 ml/2 tablespoons snipped chives
Parmesan Pastry
100 g/4 oz butter
175 g/6 oz plain flour
50 g/2 oz freshly grated
        Parmesan cheese
45–60 ml/3–4 tablespoons
        cold water

Chop the onion finely and put it in a saucepan with the bay leaf, mace, milk and a good sprinkling of salt and pepper. Heat gently, stirring occasionally, until the milk is just about to boil. Partially cover the pan and cook the mixture very gently for 5 minutes. Then add the asparagus to the pan and raise the heat until the milk is just simmering. Continue cooking the asparagus gently for 10–12 minutes, until the tips are just tender. Check frequently to make sure that the milk does not burn the bottom of the pan. Remove from the heat, cover the pan and set aside.

For the pastry, rub the butter into the flour, then stir in the Parmesan cheese and enough of the water to bind the ingredients into clumps. Press the pastry together, then roll it out on a lightly floured surface and line a 25 cm/10 in flan dish or tin. Prick the pastry base, chill the case for at least 15 minutes, then line it with a piece of greaseproof paper and sprinkle with baking beans. Bake the pastry case in a preheated oven at 200°C/400°F/gas 6 for 15 minutes. Remove the paper and the beans. Turn down the oven to 180°C/350°F/gas 4.

Strain the asparagus tips, keeping the milk. Discard the bay leaf and the blade of mace. Spoon the asparagus tips and the chopped onion into the pastry case. Beat the eggs and yolks with the chives, then gradually beat in the reserved milk. Pour the egg mixture into the pastry case. Bake the quiche for about 45 minutes, until the filling is set and browned on top. Serve the quiche hot or cold.

■ Boiled new potatoes and a salad of cherry tomatoes are ideal accompaniments.

Aromatic Vegetable Packets

This is an excellent dish for making the most of garden-fresh vegetables as a tasty lunch or supper. The canned beans give the vegetables substance but can be omitted if you prefer to serve the vegetables as a light side dish or first course.

SERVES: 4
PREPARATION: 30 minutes
OVEN: 200°C/400°F/gas 6
COOKING: 15 minutes

100 g/4 oz French beans
6 small carrots
4 small turnips
salt and black pepper
4 strips of lime rind
100 g/4 oz shelled peas
400 g/14 oz can haricot beans
15 ml/1 tablespoon
        chopped tarragon
30 ml/2 tablespoons
        chopped parsley
2 spring onions
30 ml/2 tablespoons olive oil
25 g/1 oz butter
2 cloves garlic
4 bay leaves
lime wedges to serve

Trim the French beans. Trim the ends off the carrots, scrape them lightly then cut them lengthways into quarters. If the pieces are long, cut them across in half. Trim the ends off the turnips, peel them and cut them into strips about the same size as the carrots. Bring a saucepan of lightly salted water to the boil. Add the prepared vegetables and the strips of lime rind, bring the water back to the boil and cook for 5 minutes. Then drain the vegetables well, reserving the strips of lime, and mix them with the shelled peas in a bowl. Drain the haricot beans and add them to the bowl. Mix lightly.

Prepare four pieces of foil, each large enough to enclose a quarter of the vegetable mixture. Cup the sides of the foil, then divide the vegetables between the pieces; top each portion with a strip of lime rind. Mix the chopped tarragon and parsley, then sprinkle these herbs over the vegetables.

Trim the root ends off the spring onions and chop up the remainder, including the green parts. Place the oil and butter in a small saucepan. Crush the garlic into the pan and add the spring onions and bay leaves, with salt and pepper to taste. Heat gently, pressing the bay leaves with the back of a spoon, until the butter melts, then cook gently for 2 minutes. Spoon the garlic butter and oil mixture over the vegetables, placing a bay leaf on each portion.

Seal the foil around the vegetables and place the packets on a baking sheet. Bake in a preheated oven at 200°C/400°F/gas 6 for 15 minutes. Transfer each unopened packet to a plate and serve immediately. Have a small dish of lime wedges on the table so that guests may squeeze the juice over the vegetables once they have opened their individual packets.

■ Serve warmed crusty bread or pitta bread with the vegetables to mop up the buttery juices.

Courgette and Chive Salad

Fresh, young courgettes make a refreshing and versatile salad.

SERVES: 4
PREPARATION: 10 minutes
COOKING: 5 minutes
CHILLING: 1 hour

350 g/12 oz courgettes
45 ml/3 tablespoons olive oil
juice of ½ lemon
2.5 ml/½ teaspoon clear honey
salt and black pepper
45 ml/3 tablespoons snipped chives

Wash the courgettes thoroughly and top and tail them.

Cut the courgettes crossways into very thin slices and put them in a small, deep serving dish. Make a salad dressing by whisking the oil, lemon juice and honey together and seasoning with salt and freshly ground black pepper. Pour the dressing over the courgettes. Add the snipped chives and toss them with the courgettes thoroughly. Cover the salad and allow it to marinate for 30 minutes before serving, tossing the courgettes gently in the vinaigrette dressing every now and then.

Mushroom Salad

SERVES: 4–6
PREPARATION: 15 minutes
STANDING: 1 hour

450 g/1 lb mushrooms
salt and black pepper
10 ml/2 teaspoons
 Worcestershire sauce
15 ml/1 tablespoon soy sauce

Trim the mushrooms, and slice them as thinly as possible into a deep serving dish. Season to taste with salt and freshly ground pepper, and sprinkle over the Worcestershire and soy sauces. Mix the salad well and set aside for about 1 hour, turning the mushroom slices occasionally.

The mushrooms will have yielded quite a lot of juice by the time they are ready for serving; this is the dressing and should not be drained off.

Tomato Salad

SERVES: 6
PREPARATION: 20 minutes
CHILLING: 1 hour

12 tomatoes
caster sugar
salt and black pepper
60 ml/4 tablespoons olive oil
20 ml/4 teaspoons white
 wine vinegar
15 ml/1 tablespoon snipped chives
 or chopped tarragon

Skin the tomatoes (page 302), slice them thinly and place them in a serving dish. Sprinkle with a pinch of sugar, and season to taste with salt and freshly ground pepper. Whisk the olive oil and vinegar together, and sprinkle the dressing over the sliced tomatoes. Add snipped chives or chopped tarragon and chill the salad for at least 1 hour before serving. Turn the tomato slices once or twice.

Salad Elona

This unusual salad of cucumber and strawberries is an ideal side dish to serve with cold chicken and turkey, or with delicately flavoured fish such as salmon.

SERVES: 4–6
PREPARATION: 15 minutes
CHILLING: 30 minutes

1 small cucumber
12 large strawberries
salt and black pepper
15–30 ml/1–2 tablespoons dry
 white wine or cider vinegar

Peel the cucumber and slice it thinly. Wash, hull and drain the strawberries, then cut them into thin, even slices. Arrange the slices in a decorative pattern in a shallow serving dish – an outer circle of cucumber overlapped by a circle of strawberry, then more cucumber, finishing with a layer of strawberries in the centre of the dish. Season lightly with salt and freshly ground black pepper. Sprinkle the wine or cider vinegar over the salad and chill for 30 minutes before serving.

Simple salads: clockwise from top left – Courgette and Chive Salad, Mushroom Salad, Tomato Salad and Salad Elona.

RICE & PASTA

Summer Risotto

Fresh young asparagus tips steam perfectly on the surface of the risotto; however, if the asparagus spears are particularly large or if they are slightly tough, they should be blanched in boiling water for 1–2 minutes before being added to the risotto.

SERVES: 4
PREPARATION: 30 minutes
COOKING: 30 minutes
STANDING: 10 minutes

Summer Risotto.

1 onion
30 ml/2 tablespoons olive oil
25 g/1 oz butter
1 bay leaf
strip of lemon rind
225 g/8 oz Italian risotto rice or Arborio rice
salt and black pepper
450 ml/¾ pt hot vegetable or chicken stock
225 g/8 oz shelled peas
5 ml/1 teaspoon saffron threads or 1.25 ml/¼ teaspoon powdered saffron
300 ml/½ pt dry white wine
225 g/8 oz asparagus tips
225 g/8 oz small courgettes
freshly grated Parmesan cheese to serve

Finely chop the onion. Heat the oil and butter in a large, heavy-based saucepan. Add the onion and bay leaf, and cook for 10 minutes. Stir in the lemon rind and rice, stirring until the rice grains are well coated with the fat. Add salt and pepper to taste, then pour in half the stock. Bring to the boil, cover the pan tightly and reduce the heat to the lowest setting. Cook for 5 minutes.

Pour the remaining stock into the pan, stir in the peas and bring to the boil. Reduce the heat so that the stock just simmers, cover the pan tightly and cook the risotto for a further 5 minutes. Meanwhile, pound the saffron threads with a pestle in a mortar until they are reduced to a powder. Stir in a little boiling water from a kettle to dissolve the saffron. Pour the saffron liquid over the risotto, rinse the mortar with some of the wine and add all the wine to the risotto. If you are using powdered saffron, sprinkle it straight into the risotto. Stir well, then bring the liquid back to simmering point. Add the asparagus tips, cover the pan again and cook for 5 minutes.

Wash and trim the ends off the courgettes and slice them thinly. Stir the risotto, then add the courgettes and cover the pan tightly. Cook for a further 5 minutes, then remove the pan from the heat but do not remove the lid. Leave the risotto to stand in the covered pan for 10 minutes before serving. Gently mix the courgettes with the risotto and serve with plenty of freshly grated Parmesan cheese.

Chicken Pilaf

SERVES: 4
PREPARATION: 20 minutes
COOKING: 25–30 minutes

1 onion
2 sticks celery
1 small red pepper
2 cloves garlic
225 g/8 oz boneless chicken breasts
50 g/2 oz no-need-to-presoak apricots
45 ml/3 tablespoons olive oil
1 bay leaf
1 cinnamon stick
1 mace blade
175 g/6 oz long-grain rice
600 ml/1 pt chicken stock
75 g/3 oz sultanas
salt and black pepper
25 g/1 oz pine nuts

Chop the onion and thinly slice the celery. Remove the core and seeds from the pepper; dice the flesh. Peel the garlic clove and chop it. Remove the skin from the chicken breasts if necessary, then cut them into thin strips. Chop the apricots.

Heat the olive oil in a large saucepan. Add the bay leaf, cinnamon stick, mace blade, onion, celery and garlic. Cook, stirring all the time, for 3 minutes, then add the pepper and cook for a further 2 minutes.

Add the chicken strips to the pan. Stir until the chicken has changed colour, then add the rice, stirring to coat the grains in the oil. Add the chicken stock, chopped apricots and sultanas. Bring slowly to the boil, stir once, then cover tightly and reduce the heat to the lowest possible setting. Cook for 20 minutes, then remove the pan from the heat without lifting the lid and leave the pilaf to stand for 5 minutes.

Meanwhile, lightly brown the pine nuts in a small frying pan. Add to the pilaf, forking them in lightly, and add salt and freshly ground pepper to taste.

Seafood Cannelloni

SERVES: 4
PREPARATION: 50 minutes
OVEN: 200°C/400°F/gas 6
COOKING: 25 minutes

15 ml/1 tablespoon oil
8 cannelloni tubes
375 g/12 oz haddock, cod or
*   pollock fillet*
600 ml/1 pt milk
1 bay leaf
1 mace blade
175 g/6 oz peeled cooked prawns
15 ml/1 tablespoon chopped parsley
15 ml/1 tablespoon snipped chives
15 ml/1 tablespoon lemon juice
salt and pepper
40 g/1½ oz butter
40 g/1½ oz plain flour
30 ml/2 tablespoons grated
*   Parmesan cheese*

Bring a large saucepan of lightly salted water to the boil. Add the oil and cannelloni and cook for 5–8 minutes until the pasta is just tender. Drain the cannelloni in a colander, rinse under cold water and drain again.

Place the fish in a large shallow pan. Add the milk, bay leaf and mace. Simmer the fish for 8–10 minutes depending on the thickness of the fish, until tender and cooked through. Carefully remove the fish and transfer it to a plate. Strain the milk into a jug and reserve.

Remove any stray bones from the fish, then flake the flesh off the skin. Use a fork to mash the fish. Chop 100 g/4 oz of the prawns and mix them into the

Lobster Ravioli.

fish with the chopped parsley, snipped chives, lemon juice and salt and pepper to taste.

Melt the butter in a saucepan, add the flour and cook for 1 minute. Little by little add the reserved milk, until the sauce boils and thickens. Cook for 2 minutes, stirring continuously, then add seasoning to taste. Stir 45 ml/3 tablespoons of the sauce into the fish mixture, cover the rest closely and set it aside.

Divide the fish mixture into 8 portions, shape each into a sausage and use to stuff each cooked cannelloni tube. Arrange the pasta in a lightly greased baking dish. Add the remaining prawns to the sauce. Pour it over the cannelloni and sprinkle with the Parmesan cheese.

Bake the cannelloni in a preheated oven at 200°C/400°F/ gas 6 for 25 minutes.

Lobster Ravioli

SERVES: 4
PREPARATION: 1½ hours
STANDING: 2 hours
COOKING: 10 minutes

225 g/8 oz plain flour
1.25 ml/¼ teaspoon salt
2 large eggs
40 g/1½ oz butter
beaten egg
Filling
225–350 g/8–12 oz lobster or
*   crab meat*
15 ml/1 tablespoon double cream
lemon juice
salt and cayenne pepper
Sauce
25 g/1 oz butter
25 g/1 oz plain flour
300 ml/½ pt milk
45 ml/3 tablespoons single cream
*   or fromage frais*
5 ml/1 teaspoon tomato paste
juice of ½ lemon
grated Parmesan cheese to serve

Sift the flour and the salt into a mixing bowl and make a well in

the centre. Lightly beat the 2 eggs and pour into the flour; mix thoroughly. Melt the butter in a small saucepan and add to the flour. Knead the mixture to a stiff dough with a little cold water.

Turn the dough on to a floured surface and knead for 10 minutes until shiny. Wrap the dough in cling film and set it aside to rest for about 1 hour, but do not chill.

Meanwhile, make the filling for the ravioli: chop the lobster or crab meat finely and place in a mixing bowl. Add the cream, with lemon juice, salt and cayenne pepper to taste.

Roll out the dough on a floured surface, to a 61 cm/24 in square. With a teaspoon, drop the filling over one half of the paste, at intervals of 4 cm/1½ in. Brush between the fillings with lightly beaten egg. Turn over the other half of the pasta and press down firmly with the fingers between the filling. Cut through the filled squares with a pastry wheel or knife. Dust the ravioli with flour and set them aside.

Make the pasta sauce before cooking the ravioli. Melt the butter in a saucepan, stir in the flour and cook this roux for 1 minute. Gradually add the milk, stirring until the sauce boils and thickens. Remove from the heat and stir in the cream or fromage frais, tomato paste and lemon juice, with any remaining filling.

When you are ready to cook the ravioli, bring a large pan of lightly salted water to the boil. Drop the ravioli into the water and cook for about 7 minutes. Drain the ravioli on absorbent

kitchen paper and keep them hot in a serving dish.

Reheat the sauce without boiling. Season to taste with salt and cayenne pepper and serve separately. Grate fresh Parmesan cheese into a separate bowl, and pass it around with the hot ravioli and sauce.

Broad Beans with Pasta

SERVES: 4
PREPARATION: 40 minutes
COOKING: about 25 minutes

1.4 kg/3 lb broad beans
225 g/8 oz pasta shapes, such as
*   twists or shells*
salt and black pepper
3 spring onions
50 g/2 oz butter
15 ml/1 tablespoon chopped
*   summer savory*
freshly grated Parmesan
*   cheese to serve*

Shell the beans. Cook the pasta in boiling lightly salted water for about 12 minutes or according to the packet instructions. Cook the broad beans in a separate pan of boiling lightly salted water for 8–10 minutes, until just tender.

Trim the roots off the spring onions and chop the remainder, including the green parts. Drain the cooked pasta in a colander. Melt the butter in the saucepan, add the onions and savory, and cook for 3 minutes. Drain the beans and add them to the butter with the pasta shapes. Toss well, season with pepper and serve with grated Parmesan cheese.

PUDDINGS & DESSERTS

Blackcurrant and Mint Pie

SERVES: 6
PREPARATION: 30 minutes
OVEN: 200°C/400°F/gas 6
COOKING: 35–40 minutes

450 g/1 lb blackcurrants
10 ml/2 teaspoons chopped mint
100 g/4 oz caster sugar plus
    extra for sprinkling
225 g/8 oz Shortcrust Pastry
    (page 365)
a little milk to glaze

Top and tail the blackcurrants and wash them with cold water in a colander. Drain the blackcurrants thoroughly and put them in an 18 cm/7 in pie dish. Mix the finely chopped mint with the sugar and sprinkle it evenly over the blackcurrants.

Roll out the prepared shortcrust pastry on a floured surface to a round about 5 cm/2 in wider than the top of the pie dish. Cut a strip 2.5 cm/1 in wide from around the pastry. Dampen the rim of the dish and press the pastry strip on it, then dampen the strip. Cover the pie with the pastry round. Trim, knock up and seal the edges (page 366) and decorate the top with pastry leaves or flowers cut from the trimmings. Make a slit in the centre of the pastry for the steam to escape. Brush the surface with milk and sprinkle with a little caster sugar.

Bake the pie in a preheated oven at 200°C/400°F/gas 6 for 35–40 minutes or until golden.
■ Serve the pie hot or cold, with a jug of fresh cream.

Blackcurrant and Mint Pie.

Soft Fruit Gâteau

SERVES: 6–8
PREPARATION: 50–60 minutes
OVEN: 190°C/375°F/gas 5
COOKING: 15 minutes

4 eggs
100 g/4 oz caster sugar
100 g/4 oz plain flour
1.25 ml/¼ teaspoon salt
450 g/1 lb mixed soft fruit
    (strawberries, raspberries,
    redcurrants and blueberries)
300 ml/½ pt double cream
225 g/8 oz redcurrant jelly

Lightly grease a rectangular 35 × 20 cm/14 × 8 in sponge tin. Sprinkle lightly with flour, then invert the tin and tap out the excess. Put the eggs and sugar into a deep mixing bowl, and whisk until the eggs are pale and thick enough for the whisk to leave a trail. Sift the flour and salt together, and fold gently into the creamed egg mixture.

Spoon this sponge mixture into the tin, spreading it evenly. Bake in a preheated oven at 190°C/375°F/gas 5 for 15 minutes, or until the sponge is golden and firm to the touch.

Turn the sponge out on to a wire rack and leave to cool. Clean the fruit, wash and drain it thoroughly on absorbent kitchen paper. Whip the double cream until it is thick and fluffy.

Carefully cut the sponge across in half with a sharp knife. Spread with half the whipped cream and top with half the fruit. Cover with the remaining piece of cake. Pipe the remaining cream on top of the gâteau and decorate with the rest of the fruit. Warm the redcurrant jelly in a pan until just melted and brush it generously over the fruit.

The cake will keep for 2–3 hours in a refrigerator, but should not be assembled too far in advance, or the fruit will become mushy and stain the cream.

Brandy Apricot Trifle

SERVES: 4–6
PREPARATION: 20 minutes
CHILLING: 2 hours

600 ml/1 pt Custard Sauce
    (page 338)
450 g/1 lb fresh apricots
150 ml/¼ pt white wine
50 g/2 oz caster sugar
90 ml/6 tablespoons brandy
225 g/8 oz ratafia biscuits
150 ml/¼ pt double cream

Prepare the custard, cover the surface with dampened greaseproof paper and set aside to cool. Wash and dry the apricots, cut them in half and remove the stones. Heat the wine and sugar in a pan until the sugar has dissolved, stirring occasionally, then bring the syrup slowly to the boil. Add the apricots to the syrup and cook them over low heat, until softened; set aside.

Put the apricots in a serving dish and pour over the syrup and brandy. Set aside 6–8 ratafia biscuits for decoration and crush the remainder with a rolling pin. Sprinkle them over the apricots and brandy, stirring carefully to let the biscuits absorb the liquid.

Remove the greaseproof paper and spoon the custard, which should almost have set, over the apricots. Chill the trifle in the refrigerator for about 2 hours.

Just before serving, whip the cream until stiff and pipe it in swirls over the trifle. Decorate the top with the other ratafias.

Banana Fritters

SERVES: 6
PREPARATION: 20 minutes
COOKING: 10 minutes

100 g/4 oz plain flour
salt
1 large egg
150 ml/¼ pt milk or milk and water
oil for deep frying
6 small bananas
caster sugar
300 ml/½ pt whipping cream

Sift the flour with the salt into a mixing bowl. Make a well in the centre and break in the egg. Add half the liquid and gradually beat the flour into the liquids until smooth. Slowly add the rest of the liquid and continue beating until the batter is smooth.

Heat the oil to 190°C/375°F or until a cube of day-old bread browns in 1 minute. Peel the bananas and cut them in half lengthways. Dip them in the batter. With a perforated spoon, lower three banana halves into the oil and fry for 2–3 minutes until golden. Drain the fritters on absorbent kitchen paper.

Serve the fritters on a warmed dish and sprinkle caster sugar over them. Whip the cream and offer it in a separate bowl.

Peach Melba

During the 1892–3 opera season Escoffier, then chef at the Savoy Hotel, London, created this now classic dessert for Dame Nellie Melba, the famous Australian soprano. The sweet originally consisted of peaches and vanilla ice cream, the raspberry purée being a later addition.

SERVES: 4
PREPARATION: 12 minutes

2 large peaches
225 g/8 oz fresh raspberries
50 g/2 oz caster sugar
450 ml/¾ pt Vanilla Ice Cream
  (page 380)

Peach Melba.

Put the two peaches in a bowl and cover with boiling water. Leave for no more than 1 minute, then drain and peel them. Cut the peaches in half, carefully remove the stones and set the fruit aside. Rub the raspberries through a fine sieve into a mixing bowl; sweeten the purée with the sugar.

Place two scoops of vanilla ice cream in each individual serving glass; put one peach half on top, rounded side up, and carefully spoon over a little of the raspberry purée. Serve at once, offering any remaining raspberry purée in a jug.

Strawberry Water Ice

Water ices make a perfect summer sweet after a rich main course. Turn the freezer to its coldest setting before freezing. This recipe is made with bought, fizzy lemonade – check that you are buying a type sweetened with sugar, not a low-calorie drink.

SERVES: 4–6
PREPARATION: 10 minutes
FREEZING: 6–8 hour

450 g/1 lb strawberries
50 g/2 oz icing sugar
5 ml/1 teaspoon lemon juice
450 ml ¾ pt lemonade
2 egg whites

Wash and hull the strawberries, drain them thoroughly in a colander, then cut them into small pieces. Purée the fruit with the icing sugar and lemon juice in a liquidiser or food processor. Alternatively, press the strawberries through a sieve into a bowl; stir in the icing sugar. Add enough lemonade to the purée to make 450 ml/¾ pt liquid. Spoon the mixture into an ice cube tray (without divisions) or a plastic freezing container, cover with foil or a lid and put in the freezer.

When the mixture is starting to freeze around the sides of the container, remove it from the freezer. Tip the mixture into a bowl and use a fork to break up any ice crystals. Whisk the egg whites until stiff, but not dry, and fold them into the strawberry mixture. Return to the freezer, either in the original container or spooned into small moulds. Cover and freeze the ice for 6–8 hours or until set.

Serve the water ice spooned into glasses or in their moulds.

Strawberry Ice Cream

This ice cream is perfect for a warm summer's evening and makes a little fruit go a long way. It is best prepared the day before.

SERVES: 6
PREPARATION: 15–20 minutes
FREEZING: 12 hours

225 g/8 oz strawberries
75 g/3 oz icing sugar
2.5 ml/½ teaspoon lemon juice
300 ml/½ pt double cream
6–8 large strawberries to decorate

Wash and hull the strawberries, drain them in a colander and cut into small pieces. Purée them with the icing sugar and lemon juice in a liquidiser or food processor. Alternatively, rub the strawberries through a fine sieve and add the sugar and lemon juice to the purée. Whip the cream until thick, stir into the purée until totally combined.

Spoon the strawberry mixture into a plastic freezing container, cover with a lid and put in freezing compartment. Leave to freeze for 12 hours. Transfer the strawberry ice cream to the main part of the refrigerator about 45 minutes before serving to allow it to soften slightly.

Scoop the ice cream into individual glasses and decorate with slices of fresh strawberries.

Summer Wedding Reception

Holding a wedding reception at home is a considerable challenge and undertaking all the catering as well as planning the event may seem somewhat formidable. The main advantage is, of course, that it is far less expensive to prepare an impressive, and original, meal at home than it is to entertain guests at an hotel or to commission caterers. However, to achieve success when inviting more than a dozen guests to the wedding reception, careful planning is essential. It is vital that every aspect of the reception is thought through, so that lists may be written, friends canvassed to help in advance and potential problems avoided. A timetable must be worked out and followed to the letter so that the preparation and the party go as smoothly as possible.

The menus given here offer a choice between a sit-down meal for any number up to 12 or a buffet for 50. In both cases, the aim is to complete as much preparation as possible the day before the wedding.

The style of meal depends not only on the number of guests, but also on the house and facilities. If you have a small dining room and furniture to seat no more than eight around a table in comfort, it is pointless organising a formal sit-down meal at which everyone will feel cramped and uncomfortable. Most homes with one large or two average size reception rooms can accommodate 30–40 people for a buffet meal – it may not be spacious but

a good party atmosphere will prevail if the menu you choose allows your guests to eat comfortably while standing.

If the house has one large and a second smaller room, with adequate kitchen and hall space, and, if the wedding is held in the summer, a garden, 50 guests can be entertained without much disruption to your home.

When inviting more than 30 guests to an average-sized home, remember that almost the whole house will have to be utilised; so clear the hallway, make space in one of the bedrooms for ladies to leave hats that have become tiresome, and ensure that the bathrooms and any other toilet facilities are in sparkling order.

Floral decorations should be introduced – pretty swags or small posies on banisters, posies in the toilet and bathroom, and appropriate floral arrangements in the living rooms.

If space and budget permit, a marquee may be the answer to lack of space. It may be possible for the marquee to be connected to a living room with patio doors, making it ideal for both winter and summer weddings.

Village halls, church halls and similar venues can be hired. Check the kitchen and seating facilities, availability of parking space and whether alcohol may be served or music played. Some venues, particularly rooms at private clubs, will have a bar.

A few key points related to catering need to be considered. Before committing yourself to preparing the food, make sure that you have the support of all the other members of the household and select one or two helpers who are reliable and competent enough to assist right up to the final details of preparation and garnishing. One of the key problems of catering for any number at home is refrigerator space, so enlisting the aid of one or two neighbours who will make space to chill food at the last minute is practical.

Plan to have the buffet table in one room and the drinks in another. Keep the main 'bar' in the kitchen with a table in one

Chilled Watercress Soup.

reception room or in the hallway. Delegate the task of bartender to a friend or have one or two people who will hand around trays of drinks.

Linen, crockery, cutlery and glassware can all be hired from catering suppliers, but it is economical to improvise; for example, a white sheet makes an excellent cloth for a buffet table – nobody will notice, even if the only available one is a fitted sheet which has to be pinned up into swags decorated with posies of flowers and bows or ribbon. Crockery can be borrowed from friends. Alternatively buy some heavy-quality, reusable plastic plates, which are sold for picnics and patio use; thin plastic or paper plates should be a last resort as they are inferior and difficult to manage.

Wine merchants usually loan glasses free of charge on a pay-for-breakages basis. Cutlery can be a problem: it usually has to be borrowed or hired; plastic cutlery is nasty and unpleasant to use. China serving platters and dishes can be hired or heavy-quality disposable items, such as large foil platters, can be purchased from catering suppliers. The latter look perfectly acceptable when filled with delicious food and garnished, and they do not have to be washed up afterwards!

You should also consider the practicalities of cooking your chosen menu. For example, will you need a fish kettle for poaching salmon or an enormous saucepan for boiling a joint of ham? Avoid technical hitches by thinking ahead and borrowing or hiring any unusual pieces of kitchen equipment, or arranging to have food, such as a large ham, prepared by the butcher or relevant supplier. Oven and hob space must be considered when there is a good deal of cooking to be done on the day before the wedding. You also need to think about the clearing up after the cooking and when all the guests have left; family and friends may help or a local cleaning company can be called in to give the place a once-over when all the major catering has been completed.

Poached Salmon.

It is also worth considering employing professional help to look after the needs of guests, leaving all the family free to socialise. One or two waiters or waitresses can be employed to assist with drinks, serving food and clearing away used crockery. Remember to show them how to use your dishwasher, if you have one, or hire a third person to wash up and clean the kitchen, arranging for them to be in the kitchen when the party starts. Make sure the clearing up is discreet – there is nothing guaranteed to break up a gathering more rapidly than plates being taken away before guests have quite finished, or the sound of crockery and cutlery crashing about under running water!

Wedding Breakfast for Twelve

Menu
~
Chilled Watercress Soup
~
Cold Poached Salmon
Potato Salad with Chives
Salad Elona
Green Salad with French Dressing
Raspberries with Cream
~
Cheese and Biscuits
Fruit
~
Coffee

Chilled Watercress Soup

Double the quantities for the recipe on page 161. Cook the soup the night before and leave to chill in the refrigerator until just before serving.

Poached Salmon

A 2.72–3.25 kg/6–7 lb salmon will be sufficient. Poach it the day before in Court Bouillon (page 316) and leave it to cool before skinning it. Bone the salmon (page 316), leaving it whole, and refrigerate overnight. Prepare all the garnishes, place them in small dishes or saucers, cover with cling film and chill them. Garnish the salmon next morning. Lay alternate thin slices of cucumber and hard boiled egg down the centre, setting them with a little aspic if liked. Decorate the dish with watercress, prawns in their shells, thinly sliced tomatoes, and Radish Roses (page 412). Cover loosely and chill until needed.

Salads

For the potato salad, you will need 1.8 kg/4 lb small new potatoes, 300 ml/1/2 pt mayonnaise mixed with 150 ml/¼ pt double cream, and a small bunch of chives. Boil the potatoes the night before, and peel them. In the morning, dress the potatoes with the mayonnaise mixture and sprinkle with the snipped chives. Set the salad aside.

For Salad Elona, double the quantities given on page 171.

The green salad requires 2 large cos lettuces, 2 bunches of watercress and 1 large head of celery, but this mixture can be varied to include a range of different salad leaves that are available. Prepare the salad ingredients the day before; pack them in plastic bags and chill. Make the French Dressing (page 356) the day before. Just before serving, tip the salad greens into bowls, add the dressing and toss.

Raspberries with Cream

These must be prepared on the morning of the wedding. Allow 1.8 kg/4 lb raspberries, a serving bowl of caster or sifted icing sugar, and 750 ml/1¼ pt double cream. Wash the raspberries carefully, drain and put in a serving dish. Chill until required. Whip the cream lightly and serve in a separate bowl.

Cheeseboard

There are two alternatives: offer a range of soft and hard cheeses, laying out wedges on a number of boards, each with a bunch of grapes, or buy one or two large cheeses, such as a small whole brie and a half Stilton. Whichever option is taken, order the cheese, if possible, from a good supplier or speak to the manager of the cheese counter at the supermarket to reserve a large cheese in advance. This is vital if you want to secure a ripe brie. There is an amazing choice of

international cheeses in larger supermarkets, but be wary of buying a piece of everything; it is better to select two or three hard cheeses, a blue cheese and two soft cheeses at the most. The same applies to biscuits: it is better to make up a basket of water biscuits and oatcakes rather than a muddle of every type of savoury biscuit.

Drinks

Welcome your guests with medium and dry sherry (allow 2 bottles of each) or offer cool Bavarian Cup (recipe follows). As an alcohol-free alternative, serve Summer Refresher (recipe follows). During the meal, serve a dry white wine and sparkling or still mineral water. Toast the bride and groom in well-chilled champagne. Allow 4 bottles of champagne – each of which will provide 6 glasses – for the toast.

Bavarian Cup.

Bavarian Cup Four jugs of this barely alcoholic drink will be required. Into each jug, slice 10–12 large strawberries and pour over a miniature bottle of Grand Marnier (or other orange-based liqueur). Leave to infuse for 30 minutes, then add a tray of ice cubes. Pour 1 bottle of Riesling wine over the Grand Marnier-soaked strawberries and top up the fruit cup with half as much soda water.

Summer Refresher Make four jugs of this alcohol-free punch. For each jug, slice 1 lemon, 1 orange and 1 lime. Thinly slice 1 cucumber and place a quarter into each jug. Pour 300 ml/½ pt apple juice into each jug and leave to stand for at least 1 hour, or up to 4 hours. Then add a handful of mint sprigs to each jug and pour in a bottle of sparkling mineral water just before serving.

Buffet for Fifty

Menu

~

Filled Vol-au-vents
Roast Stuffed Turkey
Whole Baked Glazed Ham
Mixed Green Salad,
Tomato, Mushroom and
Potato Salads

~

Cheeses
Blue Stilton, Cheddar,
Double Gloucester, Brie,
Camembert, Dolcelatte
French Bread and Butter,
Radishes, Celery

~

Trifles
Fruit Salads and Cream

~

Coffee

Preparations The hard work can be finished the day before: the vol-au-vents baked, the turkey roasted and ham glazed. Trifles and fruit salads can be made and chilled. Arrange tableware, put out glasses and ensure that all non-perishable items are ready.

On the day, fill the vol-au-vents and arrange the food on the buffet. Decorate the trifles and fruit salads, assemble the cheeseboards and chill the wine. Fix paper frills around the turkey legs and ham bone.

If the atmosphere is formal, employ a competent waiter or waitress to carve the meats; otherwise ensure that a few close friends carve for themselves to encourage others to do so.

Filled Vol-au-vents

Order 120 vol-au-vent cases from the baker. Buy good-quality mayonnaise for the fillings and make them the day before the wedding. Fill the vol-au-vents on the day of the wedding.

For a creamy chicken filling, roast a large chicken early on the day before the reception. Use a small sharp kitchen knife and a fork to remove all the meat from the bones, discarding skin. Cover the meat and leave to cool. Chop 225 g/8 oz button mushrooms and cook them in a little olive oil until they are reduced and all the excess liquid has evaporated; set aside to cool. Chop up 2 celery sticks and a bunch of spring onions and mix them into 600 ml/1 pt mayonnaise with the mushrooms. Stir in 300 ml/2 pt Greek yogurt and salt and freshly ground pepper to taste. Mix the chopped cold chicken with the dressing, cover and chill.

For a prawn filling, chop 450 g/1 lb peeled cooked prawns. Mix 30 ml/2 tablespoons tomato paste and the juice of ½ lemon into 600 ml/1 pt mayonnaise. Stir in 300 ml/½ pt Greek yogurt. Add 2 finely chopped spring onions and seasoning to taste, then stir in the prepared prawns. Chill the filling.

Roast Stuffed Turkey

Order a dressed turkey, weighing 10 kg/22 lb and use Forcemeat (page 358) for the body and Chestnut Stuffing (page 358) for the breast. Cook the turkey, wrapped in foil, in a preheated oven at 180°C/350°F/gas 4 for 6 hours, then raise the temperature to 200°C/ 400°F/gas 6, remove the foil and cook for a further 30 minutes, to brown the turkey.

Glazed Ham

Most butchers will supply the ham cooked at no extra charge. Score the top of the ham into a diamond pattern and brush it with a glaze of honey and light brown sugar. Place the ham in a preheated oven at 230°C/450°F/ gas 8 for 30 minutes. Garnish with halved glacé cherries, spiked with white cloves.

A summer setting for a wedding buffet.

Salads

For green salads, allow 8 iceberg and 8 lollo biondo or round lettuces, with 6 bunches of watercress. Make a tomato salad from 3.25 kg/7 lb tomatoes, and for Mushroom Salad (page 171) use 1.4 kg/3 lb mushrooms; for potato salad, use 2.72 kg/6 lb small new potatoes, 600 ml/1 pt mayonnaise mixed with 300 ml/ ½ pt single cream, and a small bunch of chives.

Cheeseboards

Make up at least two cheeseboards from 3.25 kg/7 lb assorted cheeses, 6 bunches of radishes and 6 large heads of celery. Allow 8 long French loaves and 1.15 kg/2½ lb butter.

Trifles and Fruit Salads

Make 5 large Sherry Trifles (page 379) and decorate them on the day with piped whirls of cream. Mix the fruit salads from fresh and drained canned fruit. Choose 6 large cans of superior fruits, such as white peaches, green figs, cherries, pineapple and/or lychees and mix with 675 g/1½ lb dessert apples, 1 large fresh pineapple, 900 g/2 lb strawberries, 450 g/1 lb seedless grapes, 8 large oranges and 8 large pears. Heat, but do not boil, ½ bottle medium dry Sauterne with 45–60 ml/3–4 tablespoons caster sugar. Pour this syrup over the bowls of fruit salad and set aside to cool. Add a few generous shakes of Angostura bitters to give a refreshing flavour.

Vegetarian Suggestions

If you expect a number of vegetarian guests, add Celeriac and Bean Terrine with Pepper Relish (page 71) and Mixed Leaf and Chickpea Salad (page 157) to the buffet menu.

Make five terrines and five times the given quantity of green salad. The terrines can be made one or two days before the wedding reception and chilled; the pepper relish can be made the day before. Serve the terrine and relish as an alternative to the filled vol-au-vents.

The chickpea mixture for the salad can be dressed the day before the wedding, chilled in the refrigerator overnight and transferred to a bed of mixed salad leaves on the day itself.

Drinks

The toast to the happy couple should traditionally be drunk in a sparkling wine, champagne for preference, but a wide choice is available in supermarkets as well as wine merchants. If in doubt about what to choose, speak to the wine manager at the supermarket or ask your wine merchant to recommend a good choice within your price range. Each bottle provides 6 glasses.

A glass of sherry on arrival, and a choice of inexpensive but good-quality red or white wines are suitable. Alternatively, serve jugs of Bavarian Cup (see Wedding Breakfast), and provide fruit juice for the children. Remember to have a selection of alcohol-free drinks for adults.

179

JULY

Raspberry Yogurt Sorbet, Summer Pudding, Coeurs à la Crème.

July

July is the height of the season for home produce, with a wealth of soft fruits to be enjoyed or preserved quickly before they vanish for another year, or these days become too expensive for this to be economic. Large, pink-blushed gooseberries are delicious when lightly poached, and currants and cherries are all readily available for introducing lively flavours to savoury, as well as sweet, dishes. In a good year, there is often a glut of fruit and vegetables, so this is likely to be a busy time for stocking the freezer and making jam or chutney. Those with large vegetable patches think of July as a month to test their culinary ingenuity in dealing with trug loads of green vegetables. Towards the end of the month, and particularly after a good shower of rain, it is easy to imagine that prolific vegetables, such as courgettes and runner beans, seem to grow before your eyes.

From the specialist food counters and shops, shellfish is readily available, with cockles, scallops, crab and lobster giving good value for money. Celery grown in kitchen gardens is ready, needing a thorough wash to rinse out all the dirt, but rewarding the hard work with an excellent flavour both in salads and cooked dishes. This is also a month when heads of British-grown garlic can be plaited and hung in a cool place for early winter use. Take advantage of a plentiful supply of garden herbs by freezing them ready for winter. If time allows chop the herbs first or simply freeze the washed and dried stalks whole – the leaves usually crumble easily when frozen hard.

Warm days and long, light evenings mean that barbecues continue to be popular. This chapter includes family favourites, like burgers, plus suggestions for seasonings, marinades and sauces to pep up a wide variety of plain ingredients. Those who do not eat meat need not feel left out as the recipes include grilled fish, cheese and vegetables.

Menu suggestions *Here is a selection of ideas for midsummer meals. The main recipes are either featured in this chapter or are to be found elsewhere in the book, in which case page references are given.*

Simple Supper Menu
~

Guacamole
with Crudités and
Tortilla Chips
~

Pizza
Green Salad
~

Raspberry Yogurt Sorbet

Home-cooked pizza – thin, crisp and bubbly – is a real family treat and is convenient to prepare since it can be part-baked in advance and frozen, ready to be thawed and heated to crisp perfection in a few minutes. There are lots of topping options, too. When you are entertaining informally, it is a good idea to offer guests a choice of extra toppings (ready prepared) to sprinkle over their chosen pizza which can be baked while they whet their appetites with a spicy dip.

Sunday Lunch
~

Lettuce Soup
~

Spiced Brisket of Beef
Lettuce and Celery Salad
Tomatoes with
Horseradish Mayonnaise
New Potatoes
~

Clafoutis Limousin

A brisket of spiced beef, served cold with salads, replaces the traditional roast in this menu; but the meal ends on a warm note, with a hot cherry dessert – Clafoutis Limousin. The lettuce soup for the first course may be served hot or chilled.

Pizza (page 185).

Mackerel Barbecue
~

Mackerel with
Redcurrant Relish
Courgette and Chive Salad
(page 171)
Tomato Salad
Warmed Crusty Bread
~

Coeurs à la Crème

Mackerel is one of the best fish for barbecuing thanks to its full flavour and natural fat content. In this menu, a tangy redcurrant relish complements the rich fish. Since fish cooks quickly, it is a good candidate for grilling on foil-based portable barbecues which are popular for picnics. If you are planning a visit to a small fishing port where fresh young mackerel are sold on the quayside, remember to take a portable barbecue for having an 'al fresco' feast on the beach.

SOUPS

Cream of Tomato Soup

SERVES: 4–6
PREPARATION: 15 minutes
COOKING: 20 minutes

675 g/1½ lb firm tomatoes
1 onion
1 clove garlic
25 g/1 oz butter
300–450 ml/½–¾ pt chicken stock
salt and black pepper
pinch caster sugar
150 ml/¼ pt double cream
30 ml/2 tablespoons chopped basil
*   or parsley to garnish*

Skin the tomatoes (page 302) and chop them roughly. Peel and finely chop the onion and garlic.

Melt the butter in a heavy-based saucepan and fry the onion and garlic gently for 10 minutes until soft and transparent. Add 300 ml/½ pt of the stock to the pan, with the chopped tomatoes. Bring the soup to the boil, then lower the heat and cover the pan. Simmer for 15 minutes.

Leave the tomato soup to cool slightly before liquidising it. Strain it into the clean pan.

Reheat the soup, adding more stock until it has the desired consistency. Season to taste and add a pinch of sugar.

Stir in the cream. Reheat the soup briefly but do not allow it to approach boiling point or it will curdle. Sprinkle chopped basil or parsley over each portion.

Crème Vichyssoise

SERVES: 6
PREPARATION: 30 minutes
COOKING: 30–40 minutes
CHILLING: 3 hours

900 g/2 lb leeks
450 g/1 lb potatoes
50 g/2 oz butter
1 stick celery
600 ml/1 pt chicken stock
600 ml/1 pt milk
salt and black pepper
freshly grated nutmeg
300 ml/½ pt single cream

Trim the roots and coarse outer leaves from the leeks and wash them thoroughly in cold water. Slice the leeks diagonally into 5 mm/¼ in pieces. Peel and coarsely dice the potatoes. Melt the butter in a large pan and add the leeks and potatoes. Cook them over moderate heat for about 7 minutes, stirring continuously. Add the scrubbed and coarsely chopped celery to the pan. Pour over the stock and milk, and bring the soup to the boil. Season with salt, freshly ground pepper and some grated nutmeg. Lower the heat and simmer for 25 minutes or until the vegetables are tender.

Allow the vichyssoise to cool slightly before rubbing it through a sieve into a bowl or liquidising it. Correct the seasoning and stir in the single cream.

Chill the soup for 2–3 hours before serving.

Lebanese Cucumber Soup

There are many variations of this popular Middle Eastern soup. It can only be served cold, but is refreshing in hot weather and makes a tempting dinner-party starter with a few pink shrimps floating on top.

SERVES: 4–6
PREPARATION: 15 minutes
CHILLING: about 1 hour

1 large cucumber
300 ml/½ pt single cream
150 ml/¼ pt plain yogurt
1 clove garlic
30 ml/2 tablespoons
*   tarragon vinegar*
salt and black pepper
30 ml/2 tablespoons finely
*   chopped mint*
Garnish
15 ml/1 tablespoon finely chopped
*   cocktail gherkins*
sprigs of mint

Wash and dry the cucumber. Do not peel it, but grate it coarsely into a bowl. Stir in the cream and the yogurt.

Peel and crush the garlic, and add to the cucumber, together with the vinegar. Season to taste with salt and freshly ground black pepper. Stir in the chopped mint. Cover the soup and chill for at least 1 hour.

Serve the pale green soup in individual bowls. Garnish each portion with chopped gherkins and/or a sprig of fresh mint.

■ On special occasions, float a few shelled shrimps on top of the soup instead of the green garnish.

Lettuce Soup

A surplus of home-grown lettuce, or those not quite crisp enough for a salad, can be used for this economical soup.

SERVES: 4–6
PREPARATION: 10 minutes
COOKING: 30 minutes

225 g/8 oz lettuce leaves
1 small onion
1 large potato
40 g/1½ oz butter
450 ml/¾ pt chicken stock
salt and black pepper
grated nutmeg
450 ml/¾ pt milk
Croûtons (page 313)

Thoroughly wash the lettuce leaves and shred them. Peel and *Lettuce Soup.*

finely chop the onion. Peel and dice the potato.

Melt the butter in a saucepan, add the onion and fry for 5 minutes, until soft. Add the potato, lettuce and stock. Bring to the boil. Reduce the heat, cover the pan and simmer the soup for 30 minutes.

Allow the lettuce soup to cool slightly before liquidising it or rubbing it through a sieve into a clean pan. Add the milk. Season to taste with salt, freshly ground pepper and nutmeg. Reheat gently and serve with a bowl of crisp croûtons.

■ This soup freezes well. Freeze the puréed soup before adding the milk. Thaw the soup, add the milk and reheat.

183

STARTERS, SAVOURIES & LIGHT DISHES

Guacamole

This avocado dip comes from Mexico. Very ripe avocados, suitable for mashing, are often sold cheaply and they are ideal for this delicious dip.

SERVES: 6–8
PREPARATION: 10 minutes
CHILLING: 30 minutes

½ small onion
2 cloves garlic
3 ripe avocados
15 ml/1 tablespoon lemon juice
15 ml/1 tablespoon olive oil
salt and black pepper
cayenne pepper
Tabasco sauce

Grate the onion and crush the garlic. Cut the avocados in half with a sharp stainless steel knife. Remove the stones. Spoon the avocado flesh into a bowl and mash with the onion and garlic until smooth. Stir in the lemon juice and oil; season to taste with salt, ground pepper, cayenne and Tabasco. Cover the surface of the dip closely with cling film. Chill for 30 minutes.

Serve on lettuce leaves on individual plates or in ramekins.
■ Mixed raw vegetables, such as celery sticks, or slices of carrot, green pepper and radish, could be used as dippers. Lightly spiced tortilla chips are also delicious with guacamole.

Cucumber Cups with Prawns

For a quick cool starter, few ingredients combine so well in terms of flavour and eye-appeal as cucumber and shellfish.

SERVES: 6–8
PREPARATION: 15 minutes
CHILLING: 30 minutes

1 large plump cucumber
2 mint leaves
2 drained canned pimientos
150 ml/¼ pt plain yogurt
225 g/8 oz small peeled
  cooked prawns
salt and black pepper
paprika

Chop the stalk off the cucumber and cut the remainder into eight pieces equal in size. Stand the eight cucumber sections upright on a serving dish and, with a pointed spoon, hollow out the centres to form cup shapes. Leave about 5 mm/¼ in around the sides and base.

Chop the mint leaves and canned pimientos. Add to the yogurt, and fold in the prawns. Season to taste with salt and freshly ground pepper. Spoon the mixture into the cucumber cups and sprinkle with a little paprika. Chill for 30 minutes.
■ Serve with thin slices of buttered brown bread.

Skewered Halloumi

When halloumi, which is a firm ewes' milk cheese, is grilled the outside forms a crisp brown crust while the centre remains soft, making it an excellent candidate for the barbecue.

SERVES: 4
PREPARATION: 15 minutes
MARINATING: 1–2 hours
COOKING: about 10 minutes

grated rind and juice of 1 lime
salt and black pepper
1.25 ml/¼ teaspoon ground mace
60 ml/4 tablespoons olive oil
1 spring onion
1 clove garlic
450 g/1 lb halloumi cheese
2 peaches or nectarines
mixed salad leaves to serve
lime wedges to garnish

Mix the lime rind and juice, the seasoning and mace in a bowl. Whisk until the seasoning dissolves, then gradually whisk in the olive oil. Finely chop the spring onion, peel and finely chop the garlic, then add both to the oil mixture. Cut the cheese into cubes (about 2.5 cm/1 in), add them to the bowl and mix well. Cover and leave to marinate* for 1–2 hours.

Just before you cook the halloumi, place the peaches in a bowl and cover with freshly boiling water. Leave the peaches to stand for 1–2 minutes, then drain and peel them. Nectarines do not have to be peeled. Cut the peaches or nectarines in half and remove their stones. Slice the fruit and arrange it on a bed of mixed salad leaves.

Preheat the grill. Brush two long metal skewers with a little oil. Drain the halloumi, keeping the marinade, and thread the cubes on to the skewers. Spoon the marinade over the salad. Grill the cheese close to the heat source for about 2 minutes on each side, or until golden brown. Quickly slide the cubes off the skewers and serve on the salad.

Skewered Halloumi served on mixed salad leaves.

Garnish with lime wedges so that extra fruit juice can be squeezed over the cheese, if liked. Serve immediately, while the cheese remains soft.

Shrimp and Mushroom Flambé

This is a light and easily made starter for a dinner party.

SERVES: 4
PREPARATION: 10 minutes
COOKING: 10 minutes

225 g/8 oz mushrooms
40 g/1½ oz butter
175 g/6 oz peeled cooked
  shrimps or prawns
pinch nutmeg
black pepper
4 slices brown bread
30 ml/2 tablespoons brandy

Trim and wipe the mushrooms then slice them thinly. Melt the butter in a small frying pan and fry the mushrooms for 2–3 minutes until they have slightly softened. Add the shrimps or prawns to the pan and stir over moderate heat until they are heated through. Season to taste with a little nutmeg and freshly ground black pepper.

Toast the bread and arrange it on individual warmed serving plates; keep hot.

Warm the brandy in a metal soup ladle or small pan, set it alight, then pour it over the shrimp or prawn mixture. As soon as the flames have died down, spoon the mixture on to the hot toast and serve.

Cream Cheese and Bacon Tart

SERVES: 4–6
PREPARATION: 25 minutes
OVEN: 200°C/400°F/gas 6
　　　180°C/350°F/gas 4
COOKING: about 50 minutes

175 g/6 oz Shortcrust Pastry
　(page 365)
4 rashers smoked streaky bacon
3 tomatoes
1 egg
3 egg yolks
225 g/8 oz cream cheese
150 ml/¼ pt double cream
30 ml/2 tablespoons snipped chives
salt and black pepper
snipped chives to garnish

Roll out the pastry on a lightly floured surface and line a 20 cm/ 8 in loose-bottomed flan tin. Prick the pastry case and chill it for 15–30 minutes. Line the pastry with greaseproof paper and sprinkle with baking beans. Bake in a preheated oven at 200°C/ 400°F/gas 6 for 15 minutes. Remove the paper and beans. Keep the oven at the same temperature setting.

Remove the rind from the bacon and cut the rashers crossways into 5 mm/¼ in strips; fry without extra fat in a small pan over a moderate heat for 3 minutes, without browning. Drain on crumpled absorbent kitchen paper, then arrange in the bottom of the pastry case. Skin the tomatoes (page 302) and set them aside.

Gradually beat the egg and egg yolks into the cream cheese and beat until smooth. Stir in the cream and chives a little at a time. Season to taste with salt and pepper and pour the mixture over the bacon. Slice the tomatoes and arrange them on top.

Bake the tart for a further 10 minutes, then reduce the heat to 180°C/350°F/gas 4 and bake for a further 20 minutes or until the filling is set and golden.

■ Serve the tart hot or cold, with a green salad and new or baked potatoes.

Brown Tom

The name of this dish describes a casserole of fresh tomatoes with a crumble topping of bacon and brown breadcrumbs. Serve it on its own, or with grilled sausages.

SERVES: 4
PREPARATION: 20 minutes
OVEN: 200°C/400°F/gas 6
COOKING: 30–35 minutes

1 large onion
4 rashers lean bacon
4 large slices wholemeal bread
15 ml/1 tablespoon chopped parsley
7.5 ml/1½ teaspoons chopped fresh
　marjoram or 2.5 ml/½ teaspoon
　dried marjoram
450 g/1 lb tomatoes
40 g/1½ oz butter
salt and black pepper
caster sugar

Peel and roughly chop the onion; cut the rind off the bacon and chop the rashers roughly. Put the onion and bacon through the fine blade of a mincer. Tip into a bowl. Take the crusts off the bread and crumble it into the bacon. Add the herbs. Skin the tomatoes and slice them thinly.

Put a layer of the bacon and crumb mixture in the bottom of a buttered baking dish. Cover with a layer of tomatoes; season and add a little sugar. Repeat until the ingredients are used up; finish with a crumble layer.

Dot with the rest of the butter and bake in a preheated oven at 200°C/400°F/gas 6 for 30–35 minutes or until crisp and brown on top. Serve at once.

Pizza

SERVES: 4
PREPARATION: 30 minutes
RISING: 30 minutes
OVEN: 220°C/425°F/gas 7
COOKING: 45 minutes

350 g/12 oz strong white flour
5 ml/1 teaspoon salt
25 g/1 oz lard or butter
1 sachet fast-action easy-blend
　dried yeast
250 ml/8 fl oz hand-hot water
Topping
2 large onions
2 cloves garlic
90 ml/6 tablespoons olive oil
1 bay leaf
10 ml/2 teaspoons dried oregano
225 g/8 oz can chopped tomatoes
90 ml/6 tablespoons tomato paste
salt and black pepper
2.5–5 ml/½–1 teaspoon sugar
1 green pepper
350 g/12 oz mozzarella cheese
50 g/2 oz anchovy fillets (optional)
16 black olives

Start by making the sauce for the topping. Peel and chop up the onions and garlic. Heat 60 ml/ 4 tablespoons of the oil in a saucepan, add the onions, garlic and bay leaf and cook for 10 minutes, stirring every now and then, until the onion is soft but not browned. Stir in the dried oregano, chopped tomatoes and tomato paste, with salt and freshly ground pepper to taste. Bring to simmering point, cover and cook for 15 minutes. Add a little sugar to taste and adjust the seasoning if necessary. Set the sauce aside to cool.

Make the base. Sift the flour into a large bowl. Add the salt and rub in the lard or butter until the mixture resembles fine breadcrumbs. Sprinkle in the dried yeast, add the hand-hot water and mix to a firm dough. Turn on to a lightly floured surface and knead for 10 minutes until smooth.

Divide the dough into four and roll each piece out thinly to a 20 cm/8 in round. Place on

Pizza.

lightly greased baking trays and brush the rim of each pizza with the remaining olive oil.

Cut the stalk end off the pepper, discard all the pith and seeds and cut into 12 thin slices. Cut the mozzarella into 12 thin slices. Drain the anchovies, if used, and cut in half lengthways.

Remove the bay leaf from the tomato mixture, then divide it between the rounds, spreading it evenly to within 1 cm/½ in of the edge. Arrange the pepper slices, olives and cheese on top. Finally add the anchovies, if used. Cover the pizzas loosely with cling film or place the trays in polythene bags; leave in a warm place for about 30 minutes or until the dough has doubled in height.

Cook in a preheated oven at 220°C/425°F/gas 7 for 20 minutes or until the pizza crusts are golden and the cheese is golden brown.

FISH, SHELLFISH & SEAFOOD

Smoked Trout Pâté

This creamy pâté can be prepared a day in advance and kept in the refrigerator until needed.

SERVES: 4–6
PREPARATION: 15 minutes
CHILLING: 1 hour

350 g/12 oz smoked trout
100 g/4 oz curd cheese
10 ml/2 teaspoons creamed
  horseradish
15 ml/1 tablespoon lemon juice
salt and black pepper
30 ml/2 tablespoons single
  cream or milk
finely chopped parsley to garnish

Remove the skin and any bones from the trout, and flake the flesh into a liquidiser or food processor. Add the soft cheese and blend the mixture until it is smooth. Alternatively, mash the flaked fish to a smooth paste with a mortar and pestle, then stir in the soft cheese. Add the creamed horseradish, the lemon juice and salt and pepper to taste. Stir in the cream or milk, then spoon the pâté into individual ramekins, cover and chill.

When ready to serve, remove the cover on each ramekin and sprinkle chopped parsley around the edge of the pâté.
■ Serve with fingers or triangles of hot brown toast and butter.

Taramasalata

A Greek hors-d'oeuvre, or *meze* as it is called in Greece, nearly always includes a dish of this delectable creamy pâté.

SERVES: 4–6
PREPARATION: 30 minutes
CHILLING: 45 minutes

225 g/8 oz smoked cod roe
1–2 cloves garlic
4 slices white bread, each
  2 cm/¾ in thick
75 ml/5 tablespoons milk or water
90–120 ml/3–4 fl oz olive oil
juice of 1 large lemon
black pepper

Choose a soft and plump piece of smoked roe. Scoop the roe out of its skin and into a mixing bowl. Peel and crush the garlic.

Remove the crusts from the bread and place it in a large shallow dish. Pour over the milk or water and leave to soak.

Add the garlic to the roe and beat thoroughly with a wooden spoon until the mixture is quite smooth. Squeeze the bread dry and beat it into the mixture.

Add the olive oil gradually, alternately with the lemon juice, as when creating home-made mayonnaise. Beat the mixture vigorously after each addition of liquid until the mixture is a creamy purée.

Alternatively, the pâté can be made in a food processor. Purée the cod roe, garlic, bread and milk. Then gradually trickle in the lemon juice and olive oil with the food processor running.

Season to taste with freshly ground pepper and pack the pâté into a single pot or individual ramekins. Cover and chill lightly for about 45 minutes.
■ Serve taramasalata with hot crisp toast, butter, black olives and lemon wedges.

Smoked Haddock Soufflé

Warm sunny days call for light delicate meals. This smoked fish soufflé is easy to prepare. It can constitute the main course, or it can be made in small individual soufflé dishes and served as a light first course.

SERVES: 4–8
PREPARATION: 30 minutes
OVEN: 200°C/400°F/gas 6
COOKING: about 40 minutes

350 g/12 oz smoked
  haddock fillet
300 ml/½ pt milk
15 ml/1 tablespoon water
65 g/2½ oz butter
50 g/2 oz plain flour
grated rind of ½ lemon
30 ml/2 tablespoons grated
  Parmesan cheese
cayenne pepper
15 ml/1 tablespoon finely chopped
  parsley
4 eggs

Wash the smoked haddock fillet and pat it dry with absorbent

kitchen paper. Put the fish in a large shallow pan and pour over the milk and water. Bring slowly to the boil, then remove the pan from the heat. Lift out the fish, put it on a plate or chopping board and allow it to cool a little; put the cooking liquid to one side. Remove all the skin and bones from the haddock and flake the flesh into a bowl. Mash it finely with a fork.

Melt 50 g/2 oz of the butter in a small pan and stir in the flour. Cook for 1 minute. Gradually add the haddock liquid to this roux, stirring continuously until the sauce boils and thickens to a creamy consistency. Flavour the fish sauce with the lemon rind, Parmesan cheese and cayenne pepper; stir in the haddock. Take the sauce from the heat and allow it to cool for 2–3 minutes.

Use the rest of the butter to grease a 900 ml–1.12 litre/1½–2 pt soufflé dish or 8 individual 150 ml/¼ pt soufflé dishes. Sprinkle the chopped parsley in the dishes.

Separate the eggs and beat the yolks into the sauce, one at a time. Whisk the egg whites until stiff, but not dry, and fold them carefully into the fish mixture.

Spoon the haddock mixture into the dish and bake in a preheated oven at 200°C/400°F/gas 6. The large soufflé will require 30 minutes; individual soufflés about 20 minutes. When ready, the soufflés should be well risen and golden.

Fillets of Sole Dugléré

Invented in the 19th century by the French chef Duglére, this classic dish can also be made with turbot or halibut steaks. If served as a first course, half quantities only are necessary.

SERVES: 4
PREPARATION: 20–30 minutes
COOKING: 25 minutes

4 Dover sole fillets, about 150 g/
  5 oz each (see method)
3 shallots
4 large tomatoes
40 g/1½ oz butter
salt and black pepper
150 ml/¼ pt fish stock
150 ml/¼ pt dry white wine
30 ml/2 tablespoons plain flour
5 ml/1 teaspoon chopped fresh
  tarragon (optional)
lemon juice
chopped parsley to garnish

Ask the fishmonger to fillet the soles and to include the bones and skin with the order. Use these trimmings to make the fish stock, following the method shown on page 310.

Peel and finely chop the shallots. Skin the tomatoes (page 302), remove the seeds and chop the flesh finely. Use 15 g/½ oz of the butter to thoroughly grease a shallow, flameproof casserole, large enough to hold all the fillets of sole in a single layer. Wash the sole fillets and pat them dry with absorbent kitchen paper. Arrange them in the casserole and season with salt and freshly ground pepper.

Sprinkle the shallots over the fish and top with the chopped tomatoes. Strain the stock over the fish and add the white wine. Cover the casserole with a layer of buttered greaseproof paper. Bring the contents of the casserole to simmering point on top of the stove, then lower the heat. Poach* the sole fillets gently for about 7 minutes, or until they are cooked but still firm. Alternatively, bake the fish in a preheated oven at 180°C/350°F/gas 4 for about 15 minutes.

When the sole is cooked, carefully transfer the fillets to a plate. Cover and keep hot. Bring the cooking liquid, with the shallots and tomatoes, to the boil and reduce the volume by at least a quarter. Soften the remaining butter and mix to a paste with the flour. Reduce the heat so that the sauce just simmers, then whisk in the butter and flour (beurre manié), adding the paste in small lumps and whisking in each before adding the next. Simmer for 2–3 minutes until the sauce is thick and the flour cooked. Stir in the tarragon, if used. Sharpen the sauce with a little lemon juice and season to taste with salt and freshly ground pepper. Coat the fillets with the sauce and sprinkle with parsley.

Mackerel with Redcurrant Relish

SERVES: 4
PREPARATION: 20 minutes
COOKING: about 10 minutes

225 g/8 oz redcurrants
1 onion
1 stick celery
1 clove garlic
30 ml/2 tablespoons oil
50 g/2 oz sugar
60 ml/4 tablespoons raspberry
  vinegar or cider vinegar
cayenne pepper
4 mackerel
salt and black pepper
30 ml/2 tablespoons finely
  chopped rosemary

Strip the redcurrants from the stems. Peel and finely chop the onion and scrub and finely chop the celery. Peel and crush the garlic. Heat half the oil in a saucepan, add the onion, celery and garlic, and cook, stirring, for 20 minutes, until the vegetables are soft. Add the redcurrants, sugar and vinegar. Cook, stirring, until the sugar dissolves and the liquid boils. Cook, stirring, for 5 minutes without boiling rapidly. Remove from heat, season to taste with cayenne then cool.

Slit and clean the mackerel; leave the heads and tails but remove the fins. Rinse and dry on kitchen paper. Sprinkle the body cavities with salt, pepper and rosemary. Brush the skin with oil. Grill each side for about 5 minutes until the fish is cooked. Transfer to warm plates and spoon relish beside each fish.

Mackerel with Tomatoes

Mackerel is sometimes known as the poor man's trout – unjustly so, for although both mackerel and trout are oily fish, their flavours are quite distinct. Mackerel is at its best, and most plentiful in summer, and makes an excellent main course.

SERVES: 4–6
PREPARATION: 30 minutes
COOKING: 20 minutes

6 medium mackerel
plain flour for coating
salt and black pepper
1 onion
1 clove garlic
50 g/2 oz mushrooms
350 g/12 oz firm tomatoes
45 ml/3 tablespoons cooking
  or olive oil
10 ml/2 teaspoons chopped parsley
10 ml/2 teaspoons wine vinegar

Clean and fillet the mackerel (page 314). Wash the fillets and pat them dry with absorbent kitchen paper. Season the flour with salt and pepper and coat the fish, shaking off any surplus.

Peel the onion and garlic, and trim the mushrooms. Finely chop the onion and mushrooms, and crush the garlic clove. Skin the tomatoes (page 302) and slice them thinly.

Heat 15 ml/1 tablespoon of the oil in a small saucepan and fry the onion for 10 minutes over moderate heat. Add the mushrooms and garlic, and cook for a further 5 minutes. Season to taste with salt and pepper, then stir in the chopped parsley and vinegar. Leave the pan over very low heat, if necessary, until the mackerel is cooked. While the onions are cooking, heat the rest of the oil in a heavy-based frying pan. Fry the fillets for 7–10 minutes, or until they are golden brown, turning once.

Carefully move the mackerel fillets to a platter and keep hot. Add the tomato slices to the same pan and fry them quickly until they have softened.

Arrange the cooked tomatoes between the mackerel fillets and spoon a little of the onion mixture on to each fillet.
■ Serve at once with buttered new potatoes and a fresh, crisp green salad.

Mackerel with Tomatoes.

POULTRY & GAME

Sesame Chicken with Spiced Rice

Tahini, a smooth paste of sesame seeds and oil, gives the sauce a good flavour to complement the spiced chicken in this recipe.

SERVES: 4
PREPARATION: 40 minutes
COOKING: about 1 hour

225 g/8 oz Thai jasmine rice or
    basmati rice
6 spring onions
45 ml/3 tablespoons oil
1 bay leaf
1 blade of mace
7.5 ml/1½ teaspoons ground
    coriander
7.5 ml/1½ teaspoons ground ginger
salt and black pepper
600 ml/1 pt water
45 ml/3 tablespoons plain flour
1.25 ml/¼ teaspoon ground mace
4 skinless boneless chicken breasts
5 ml/1 teaspoon sesame oil
1 mango
1 lime
45 ml/3 tablespoons tahini
300 ml/½ pt chicken stock
150 ml/¼ pt plain yogurt

Place the rice in a basin and pour in plenty of cold water. Swirl the grains with your fingertips, then drain off most of the water and repeat once or twice until the water runs clear. Drain the rice in a fine sieve. Trim and finely slice the spring onions.

Heat 15 ml/1 tablespoon of the oil in a saucepan and add the spring onions, bay leaf and blade of mace. Cook gently for 5 minutes. Add 5 ml/1 teaspoon each of the coriander and ginger with salt and pepper, stir well, then gently stir in the rice and cook for 2 minutes. Pour in the water and bring to the boil. Stir the rice once, cover the pan tightly and reduce the heat to the minimum setting. Cook for 20 minutes. Turn off the heat and leave the rice to stand for 5 minutes without lifting the lid.

Mix the flour with the remaining coriander and ginger, ground mace and a liberal sprinkling of salt and pepper. Coat the chicken pieces in the spiced flour. Heat the remaining oil with the sesame oil in a large frying pan. Add the chicken and cook for 25–30 minutes, turning the chicken once, until the pieces are lightly browned and cooked through. Reserve any leftover spiced flour from coating the chicken.

Meanwhile, peel the mango and cut the flesh off the stone in large slices, then cut these into small chunks. Cut the lime in half and squeeze the juice from one half. Slice the remaining lime half and set it aside for garnishing the dish.

Use a perforated spoon to remove the chicken from the pan, set it aside and keep hot. Stir the reserved spiced flour into the pan juices and cook them for 1 minute, then stir in the tahini and gradually pour in the chicken stock, stirring continuously. Bring the sauce to the boil and allow it to simmer for 3 minutes. Stir in the lime juice, then reduce the heat to the minimum setting and stir in the yogurt. Heat the yogurt through without allowing the sauce to boil. Taste the sauce and adjust the seasoning if necessary.

Fork the prepared mango into the rice and turn it out on to a serving dish or warmed plates. Arrange the chicken pieces on the rice, then pour the sauce over them. Garnish the sesame chicken with the reserved lime slices and serve at once.

Chicken Salad

SERVES: 4
PREPARATION: 25 minutes
CHILLING: 30 minutes

175 g/6 oz cooked chicken
2 cooked potatoes
½ small cucumber
2 spring onions
2 sticks celery
150 ml/¼ pt French Dressing
    (page 356)
1 clove garlic
5 ml/1 teaspoon paprika
1 small lettuce separated into leaves
4 hard-boiled eggs

Dice the chicken and potatoes. Peel and dice the cucumber, thinly slice the spring onions and chop the celery. Mix the chicken and vegetables in a salad bowl. Whisk the French dressing with the crushed garlic and paprika. Pour over the salad ingredients and toss well.

Arrange the cleaned lettuce leaves on a large flat serving dish and pile the dressed salad in the centre. Halve the hard-boiled eggs lengthways and arrange them around the chicken. Chill the salad for 30 minutes.

Chicken with Calvados

This recipe for a casserole of chicken with a rich cream and calvados sauce comes from Normandy in France.

SERVES: 4–6
PREPARATION: 20 minutes
COOKING: 1¼–1½ hours

1 chicken, 1.4–1.8 kg/3–4 lb
salt and black pepper
2 mild onions
50 g/2 oz cooked ham or lean
    bacon
50 g/2 oz butter
1 bay leaf
2 thyme sprigs
60 ml/4 tablespoons calvados
    or brandy
15 ml/1 tablespoon finely chopped
    celery leaves
300 ml/½ pt dry cider or
    unsweetened apple juice
30 ml/2 tablespoons plain flour
2 large egg yolks
150 ml/¼ pt single cream
Garnish
2 dessert apples
25 g/1 oz butter

Season the chicken with salt and freshly ground black pepper. Peel and finely chop the onions, and dice the ham or bacon after removing the rind.

Melt half the butter in a large pan over moderate heat and cook the onions, bay leaf and thyme until the onions are soft and transparent. Stir in the ham or bacon and cook for 2–3 minutes more. Move the mixture to one side and brown the chicken lightly all over in the butter. Warm the calvados or brandy in a small pan and set alight (calvados will produce a fair amount of flame). Pour the flaming spirit over the chicken. Shake the pan gently until the flames die out.

Sprinkle in the celery leaves and pour over the cider or apple juice; let it come to the boil, then lower the heat and cover the pan tightly. Simmer for about 1¼ hours or until the chicken is cooked through. If preferred, the chicken may be cooked in a casserole in a pre-heated oven at 160°C/325°F/ gas 3 for 1¼–1½ hours. To check if the chicken is cooked, pierce the thick portion of meat on the thigh. If there is any sign of blood in the juices, or if the meat looks pink and undercooked, continue cooking.

While the chicken is cooking, peel and core the apples for the garnish. Cut them, without breaking, into 5 mm/¼ in rings. Melt the butter in a small pan and fry the apple rings until they are golden brown, turning once. Keep the apple rings hot.

When the chicken is cooked, lift it on to a heated serving dish and keep hot. Strain the liquid if liked or retain the onion and bacon if preferred. Skim any excess fat off the surface with a metal spoon. Cream the flour with the rest of the butter to make a paste. Whisk lumps of the butter and flour mixture into the pan juices and continue whisking until the sauce boils. Simmer for 2 minutes. Beat together the egg yolks and the cream; mix in a few spoonfuls of the sauce, then stir the mixture into the sauce and heat gently for 1–2 minutes without simmering.

Pour the sauce over the meat and garnish with the apple slices.
■　Serve with a green salad; add boiled potatoes or rice for a more substantial meal.

Grilled Turkey Cordon Bleu

This is a variation on the popular recipe for escalopes with ham and cheese, usually coated with egg and breadcrumbs and fried. Here the ham and cheese are served as a topping.

SERVES: 4
PREPARATION: 20 minutes
OVEN: 180°C/350°F/gas 4
COOKING: 25 minutes

4 slices lean cooked ham
4 thin slices Gruyère cheese
4 turkey escalopes
100 g/4 oz mushrooms
25 g/1 oz butter
plain flour for coating
salt and black pepper
15 ml/1 tablespoon olive oil
30 ml/2 tablespoons chopped parsley
watercress to garnish (optional)

Cut the ham and cheese slices to fit the turkey escalopes. Slice the

mushrooms thinly. Melt 15 g/ ½ oz of the butter in a small frying pan, add the mushrooms and fry until they are soft. Set aside. Season the flour with salt and freshly ground pepper and coat the turkey escalopes evenly, but not too thickly.

Melt the remaining butter in the oil in a large frying pan over moderate heat. Fry the escalopes for about 5 minutes on each side, until lightly browned and cooked through. Place a slice of ham on each escalope, spoon over a thin layer of mushrooms and season lightly with freshly ground pepper. Sprinkle a little of the parsley over the mushrooms and

cover with a slice of cheese. Place the pan under a moderately hot grill until the cheese is bubbling and lightly browned here and there.

Arrange the turkey escalopes on a hot serving dish or plates. Sprinkle over the remaining chopped parsley or garnish with sprigs of watercress.
■　The richness of the escalopes is best offset by a dish of buttered ribbon noodles or new potatoes and a tossed green salad.

Grilled Turkey Cordon Bleu.

Pigeons with Olives

Small woodpigeons can be roasted or grilled like other game birds. But since this meat is rather dry, they are more suitable for braising or stewing.

SERVES: 4
PREPARATION: 1 hour
OVEN: 150°C/300°F/gas 2
COOKING: 2 hours

4 pigeons
3 onions
1 carrot
100 g/4 oz streaky bacon rashers
2 cloves garlic
plain flour for coating
salt and black pepper
45 ml/3 tablespoons brandy
150 ml/¼ pt dry white wine or vermouth
100 g/4 oz stuffed green olives
bouquet garni*
To Serve
15 ml/1 tablespoon olive oil
4 large slices white bread

Skin the pigeons carefully. Cut along and down either side of the breastbone on each pigeon so that each breast, leg and wing comes away in one piece. Wash the pigeon halves thoroughly in cold water and dry them with absorbent kitchen paper. Clean the pigeon carcasses and giblets thoroughly and put them in a large saucepan.

Peel and finely slice one of the onions, then scrape and roughly chop the carrot. Add to the saucepan and cover with cold water. Bring to the boil, then lower the heat, cover and simmer until all the meat has come

off the bones. Strain the cooking stock into a measuring jug; reserve 450 ml/¾ pt.

Meanwhile, remove the rind from the bacon and cut the meat crossways into 1 cm/½ in wide strips. Put the bacon strips in a large flameproof casserole over moderate heat and cook until the fat runs. Peel and finely chop the remaining onions, and peel and crush the garlic. Add these to the bacon and cook until soft.

Season the flour for coating with salt and pepper. Add the pigeons and coat them thickly. Move the onion mixture aside and brown the pigeon halves well on both sides. Warm the brandy in a metal soup ladle or small pan, set it alight and pour it over the pigeons, shaking the casserole until the flames die down. Add the white wine or vermouth and reserved stock. Put in the olives and bouquet garni and bring to the boil. Remove the casserole from the heat and cover closely with foil and a lid. Transfer the casserole to a preheated oven at 150°C/ 300°F/gas 2 and cook for 2 hours or until tender.

Just before serving, heat the olive oil in a frying pan and fry the bread slices until golden. Drain the bread on absorbent kitchen paper and place on four individual plates. Arrange two pigeon halves on each slice. Top with the bacon strips and olives and a little of the sauce. Serve the remaining sauce separately.
■　Serve with lightly sautéed courgettes and small new carrots. New or mashed potatoes will complement the rich sauce.

MEAT

Spiced Brisket of Beef

As it takes two days to make this dish, you need to plan ahead. The result is a succulent joint with a slightly gamey flavour. The strained cooking liquid makes an excellent stock for soups and casseroles; it may be reduced, then cooled and frozen.

SERVES: 10
PREPARATION: 15 minutes
COOLING AND MARINATING:
   26 hours
COOKING: 3–3¼ hours

1 onion
1 carrot
1 stick celery
2 cloves garlic
30 ml/2 tablespoons oil
10 black peppercorns
10 whole allspice
2 bay leaves
4 juniper berries
2 blades mace
1 small cinnamon stick
1 sprig each thyme and parsley
6 cloves
2 strips orange peel
5 ml/1 teaspoon salt
black pepper
450 ml/¾ pt red wine
60 ml/4 tablespoons brandy
1.8 kg/4 lb piece boned and
   rolled brisket

Peel and chop the onion and carrot; scrub and slice the celery. Peel the garlic cloves and cut them in half. Heat the oil in a saucepan, add the onion, carrot, celery and garlic and cook, stirring every now and then, for 5 minutes or until the vegetables start to soften. Stir in all the spices and herbs with the orange peel, salt and pepper. Add the wine and brandy. Bring to the boil, reduce heat and simmer for 15 minutes. Pour into a bowl and set this marinade* aside to cool.

Put the beef brisket in a deep bowl, large enough to hold it and the marinade. Pour the marinade over, cover and marinate in the refrigerator for 24 hours, turning and basting the meat occasionally.

Drain the beef and place it in a large flameproof casserole or pan (about 4.5 litres/8 pt). Pour in the marinade and add enough water to almost cover the meat. Bring slowly to the boil, remove any scum, then lower the heat and simmer gently for 2¾ hours. To serve hot, lift the meat from the liquid, drain it for a few seconds, then place it on a platter and carve the beef into thick slices. To serve cold, transfer the beef to a large bowl, pour over the cooking liquid and cover. Leave until cool (about 2 hours) before putting the bowl in the refrigerator to get completely cold. Leave the beef overnight if preferred. Drain the meat and cut it into thin slices.

■ Redcurrant, crab apple or rowan jelly may be served with the spiced beef. Hot Cumberland Sauce (page 356) is also a suitable accompaniment.

Spiced Brisket of Beef.

Vitello Tonnato

In Italy, this classic dish of veal in tuna sauce is a standby for hot summer days. In some regions the meat is roasted instead of boiled. The tuna sauce may be served with cold poached or roasted chicken instead of veal; it is also good with hard-boiled eggs. A speedy version of the sauce can be made by making a purée of the tuna and anchovies, then stirring in good-quality bought mayonnaise. This also avoids the use of raw eggs.

SERVES: 6
PREPARATION: 30 minutes
COOKING: 1¾ hours

1.15 kg/2½ lb leg or loin of veal
   (see method)
1 carrot
1 onion
1 stick celery
4 peppercorns
5 ml/1 teaspoon salt
99 g/3½ oz can tuna in oil
4 drained canned anchovy fillets
up to 150 ml/¼ pt olive oil
2 egg yolks
black pepper
20 ml/4 teaspoons lemon juice
Garnish
capers
gherkins
tarragon sprigs

Ask the butcher to bone the meat, tie it in a neat roll and include the bones with the order.

Scrape and wash the carrot and peel the onion; quarter both. Scrub and chop the celery. Put the meat into a large saucepan. Add the veal bones, vegetables, peppercorns, salt and enough water to cover the meat. Bring the water quickly to the boil, lower the heat, cover the pan and simmer for about 1¾ hours, or until the meat is tender. Lift the meat carefully out of the pan and set aside to cool on a plate. Reduce the cooking liquid by fast boiling, strain through muslin or a fine sieve and set aside.

To make the sauce, drain the tuna, reserving the oil. Make up the tuna oil to 150 ml/¼ pt with olive oil. Put the tuna and anchovies in a bowl with 15 ml/1 tablespoon of the oil from the tuna. Mash with a fork until thoroughly mixed. Mix in the egg yolks and season with black pepper. Rub the mixture through a sieve into a bowl. Stir in half the lemon juice, then gradually add the remaining oil, whisking well after each addition. When the sauce is thick and shiny, add more lemon juice to taste. Stir in about 30 ml/2 tablespoons of the veal liquid to give the sauce the consistency of thin cream.

Cut the cold meat into thin slices and arrange in a terrine. Cover the veal slices completely with the tuna sauce, then wrap the dish closely in foil and chill completely overnight.

Before serving, garnish the dish with capers, a few sliced gherkins and a sprig of tarragon.

■ Cold savoury rice or a tossed green salad is a good complement for this meat dish.

Hamburgers Pizzaiola

One of the classic American dishes – the hamburger – is here combined with a classic Italian tomato sauce.

SERVES: 6–8
PREPARATION: 35 minutes
COOKING: 40–45 minutes

900 g/2 lb lean sirloin or
*   rump steak*
salt and black pepper
Pizzaiola Sauce
2 onions
2 cloves garlic
2 green peppers
15 ml/1 tablespoon olive oil
50 g/2 oz mushroom caps
400 g/14 oz can chopped tomatoes
15 ml/1 tablespoon chopped
*   oregano or marjoram*
chilli sauce

Trim any fat from the steak and mince it finely. Lean steak mince may be used instead, but it should be freshly minced and of the best quality. Add salt and freshly ground pepper to taste. Shape the steak into six or eight rounds, each about 4 cm/1½ in thick. Leave the hamburgers to rest while you prepare the pizzaiola sauce.

Peel and finely chop the onions and garlic. Remove the stalks and seeds from the peppers and cut them crossways into thin slices. Heat the oil in a deep, heavy-based frying pan and, over a gentle heat, cook the onions and garlic until pale golden. Add the pepper slices and continue cooking for 15 minutes.

Hamburgers Pizzaiola.

Chop the mushrooms roughly and add to the pan with the tomatoes and the oregano or marjoram. Cover and continue cooking for 10 minutes more. Season to taste with chilli sauce, salt and freshly ground pepper. Leave the pan over low heat while cooking the hamburgers.

Grill the hamburgers for about 3 minutes on each side if you like them rare; for pink-rare, add another minute each side; for medium, add 2 minutes. Alternatively, cook the burgers in a very hot frying pan without extra fat. Bought minced steak *must* be cooked thoroughly before being served. Add salt and pepper.

Put the hamburgers on a hot serving dish and pour the tomato sauce over them.
■ Open freeze raw burgers and pack them when hard. Store for up to 6 months. Cook from frozen, allowing extra time.

Noisettes of Lamb Shrewsbury

Tender noisettes are cut from the loin or best ends of lamb.

SERVES: 4–6
PREPARATION: 15–25 minutes
COOKING: about 2½ hours

8–12 noisettes of lamb, each
*   75 g/3 oz (see method)*
15 ml/1 tablespoon olive oil
Sauce
1 small carrot
1 small onion
2 sticks celery
25 g/1 oz lean back bacon
25 g/1 oz butter
25 g/1 oz plain flour
600 ml/1 pt brown stock
300 ml/½ pt dry white or red wine
15 ml/ tablespoon tomato paste
*bouquet garni**
1 sprig rosemary
30–45 ml/2–3 tablespoons
*   redcurrant jelly*
salt and black pepper

The noisettes can be cut from cutlets from the loin or from best end of neck; the latter are smaller, but have a more delicate flavour. Most butchers will prepare the noisettes on request, but ask for the trimmings to be included with the order. Alternatively, cut the piece of meat into single cutlets, remove the bone from each, and shape each piece of meat into a neat round, about 5 cm/2 in across. Tie each noisette firmly with string.

Prepare the sauce: scrape the carrot, peel the onion and scrub the celery; dice these vegetables. Cut the rind from the bacon and chop the flesh into small dice; blanch* for a few minutes.

Melt the butter in a heavy-based saucepan over moderate heat. Fry the diced vegetables and bacon (with the chopped lamb trimmings, if available) for 10 minutes. Stir in the flour and cook over low heat for a further 10 minutes, stirring constantly, until this sauce base is light brown in colour.

Gradually whisk or stir in the brown stock and the wine. Stir in the tomato paste and add the bouquet garni with the fresh rosemary. Bring to the boil, stirring, then partially cover the pan and simmer the sauce gently for 2 hours, stirring occasionally to prevent sticking. Remove any scum from the surface from time to time. When the sauce is thick, remove it from the heat and strain it through a coarse sieve into a clean pan. Remove any fat which rises to the top.

About 30 minutes before serving, reheat the sauce gently, stir in the redcurrant jelly and simmer the sauce until the jelly has melted. Season to taste and keep the sauce warm.

Heat the oil in a heavy-based frying pan and cook the prepared lamb noisettes over moderate heat for 4–6 minutes on each side, depending on the size. They should be well browned, and slightly pink inside. Alternatively, the noisettes may be grilled, allowing 3–5 minutes on each side. The exact cooking time depends on the thickness of the noisettes and personal preferences, as the lamb may be served slightly pink or well cooked.

Serve the lamb noisettes with the thick, dark brown sauce poured over them.
■ Boiled new potatoes, courgettes or green beans and young carrots are suitable vegetables.

191

Raised Pork Pie

SERVES: 4–6
PREPARATION: 50 minutes
OVEN: 190°C/375°F/gas 5
      180°C/350°F/gas 4
COOKING: 4¼–4½ hours

2 veal knuckles
bouquet garni*
salt and black pepper
6 peppercorns
350 g/12 oz plain flour
1.25 ml/¼ teaspoon salt
100 g/4 oz lard
60 ml/4 tablespoons milk
90 ml/6 tablespoons water
675 g/1½ lb lean pork
beaten egg to glaze

Ask the butcher to chop the veal knuckles into pieces. Rinse them well in cold water, put them in a large saucepan and add the bouquet garni, 2.5 ml/¼ teaspoon salt and peppercorns. Cover with cold water. Bring the water to the boil, and remove the scum. Lower the heat, cover and simmer for 2 hours. Strain the stock through muslin or a fine sieve, leave to cool, then remove the fat from the surface.

Sift the flour and salt into a bowl. Put the lard in a large pan with the milk and 60 ml/ 4 tablespoons of the cold water. Heat gently, without boiling, until the fat melts. Then bring to the boil as quickly as possible and immediately pour the liquid into the flour. Stir quickly until a dough has formed. Knead the dough briefly until it is smooth, taking care to avoid burning your hands. Cut off a third of the hot dough for the pie lid and keep it

warm in a heatproof bowl covered with cling film over a pan of hot water.

Flour the outside of a 900 g/ 2 lb straight-sided jam jar. Alternatively, cover the jar with cling film or a piece of cooking foil. Mould the dough over the bottom of the jar and down the sides, keeping it about 5 mm/¼ in thick. Leave the dough to set, then remove it from the jam jar.

Cut the pork into 1 cm/½ in cubes. Place in a bowl, season with salt and freshly ground pepper and stir in the remaining cold water. Pack the meat into the pie crust to within 1.5 cm/ ¾ in of the top.

Roll out the rest of the pastry to make a lid for the crust, moisten the edge with water, put the lid in position and press the edges tightly together to seal. Make a hole in the top of the pie and tie a band of at least double thick, buttered greaseproof paper around the pie to keep it in shape. Brush the top of the pie with the beaten egg.

Stand the pie on a lightly greased baking sheet and bake in a preheated oven at 190°C/ 375°F/gas 5 for 1 hour. Reduce the heat to 180°C/350°F/gas 4 and cook the pie for another 1¼–1½ hours.

Remove the pie from the oven. When it is almost cold, pour about 120 ml/4 fl oz of the veal stock through a small funnel into the pie through the hole in the top. Set aside for a couple of hours while the stock sets.

Before serving, remove the greaseproof paper. Serve cold, cut into wedges.

VEGETABLES & SALADS

Mushrooms and Prawns

SERVES: 4
PREPARATION: 15 minutes
STANDING: 1 hour

225 g/8 oz large mushrooms
120 ml/4 fl oz olive oil
30 ml/2 tablespoons lemon juice
1–2 cloves garlic
salt and black pepper
100 g/4 oz peeled cooked prawns
45 ml/3 tablespoons
    chopped parsley

Slice the mushrooms thinly into a shallow salad dish. Whisk the oil and lemon juice together in a

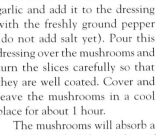

small bowl. Peel and crush the garlic and add it to the dressing with the freshly ground pepper (do not add salt yet). Pour this dressing over the mushrooms and turn the slices carefully so that they are well coated. Cover and leave the mushrooms in a cool place for about 1 hour.

The mushrooms will absorb a lot of olive oil while standing; if necessary add a little more oil just before serving. Add the prawns and sprinkle lightly with salt. Garnish with the parsley.

■   This can be served as a light lunch with thin brown bread and butter, or as a starter.

Mushrooms and Prawns.

Cardamom Vegetable Kebabs

These delicious spiced vegetable kebabs are ideal for a summer lunch party – they can be cooked on a barbecue as well as under the grill.

SERVES: 4
PREPARATION: 40 minutes
MARINATING: at least 1 hour
COOKING: 8–10 minutes

2 aubergines
salt and black pepper
12 green cardamoms
2.5 ml/½ teaspoon turmeric
juice of ½ lemon
90 ml/6 tablespoons olive oil
1 spring onion
2 cloves garlic
14 bay leaves
30 ml/2 tablespoons chopped
    fresh coriander
2 red peppers
2 onions

Trim the ends off the aubergines, then cut them into 2.5 cm/1 in cubes. Place them in a colander, sprinkling the layers with salt. Set the colander aside over a bowl for 15 minutes.

Split the cardamom pods and carefully scrape out the tiny black seeds into a mortar. Use a pestle to grind the seeds to a powder, then mix this with the turmeric and lemon juice in a bowl large enough to hold the aubergine cubes. Whisk salt and freshly ground black pepper into the spice mixture, then gradually whisk in 60 ml/4 tablespoons of the olive oil. Finely chop or snip the spring onion, add it to the mixture. Peel and chop 1 clove garlic and stir it into the mixture. Rinse and dry the aubergine cubes, then toss them with the spice mixture until they are evenly coated.

Tear 2 bay leaves in half and place them in a bowl. Add the rest of the oil. Peel and crush the remaining clove of garlic, then crush the pieces of bay leaf so that they release their flavour. Add the chopped coriander and seasoning. Halve the red peppers, discard the cores, seeds and pith, then cut the flesh into chunks. Peel and quarter the onions, then cut the pieces in half width-ways. Add the red peppers and onions to the oil and bay leaf mixture, tossing them well to coat them evenly.

Leave these vegetables to marinate* for at least 1 hour. They may be placed in the refrigerator for several hours or overnight: the longer the marin-ating time, the better the flavour. Thread the vegetables on to metal skewers, alternating the aubergines with the onions and peppers, and adding the whole bay leaves. Grill the spiced kebabs for about 4–5 minutes on each side, turning them once or twice, or until the vegetables are tender and browned.

■ Serve boiled barley or wheat, or cooked rice with the carda-mom kebabs, adding any leftover oil, crushed bay leaf and spices to the cooking liquid for the grains. A bowl of grated cucumber mixed with plain yogurt (*raita*) and/or a leafy salad (including rocket, parsley and watercress) would be ideal accompaniments.

Spinach with Mushrooms

This combination of spinach purée and mushrooms in a cheese sauce makes a light lunch or supper dish which needs no accompaniment other than fresh crusty bread.

SERVES: 4–6
PREPARATION: 20 minutes
COOKING: 20 minutes

900 g/2 lb fresh spinach
salt and black pepper
75 g/3 oz butter
grated nutmeg
225 g/8 oz button mushrooms
40 g/1½ oz plain flour
450 ml/¾ pt milk
100 g/4 oz Cheddar cheese

Remove any stalks and coarse midribs from the spinach, and wash the leaves thoroughly in several lots of cold water. Put the spinach into a large pan with just the water that clings to the leaves. Salt lightly, cover and cook over moderate heat for 5–7 minutes or until the spinach has softened. Drain thoroughly in a colander, squeezing out all excess moisture. Rub the cooked spin-ach through a coarse sieve or purée it in a liquidiser.

Melt 25 g/1 oz of the butter in a pan and reheat the purée gently. Season to taste with salt, freshly ground pepper and nutmeg. Spread the purée over the base of a buttered flameproof dish. Trim the mushroom stalks. Arrange on top of the spinach, rounded side up, and place the dish under a low grill.

Melt the remaining butter in a saucepan. Stir in the flour and cook for 2 minutes. Gradually add the milk, stirring until the sauce boils and thickens. Grate the cheese. Add salt and pepper to taste. Stir in the grated cheese and cook gently until it melts.

Pour the hot sauce over the spinach and mushrooms and return to the grill. Turn up the heat and grill until the sauce is brown. Serve immediately.

■ For a more substantial meal, serve with rice or pasta.

Cucumber au Gratin

SERVES: 4–6
PREPARATION: 15–20 minutes
OVEN: 200°C/400°F/gas 6
COOKING: 40 minutes

2 cucumbers
salt and black pepper
40–50 g/1½–2 oz butter
175 g/6 oz Gruyère cheese

Peel the cucumbers and cut them into 7.5 cm/3 in pieces. Slice in half lengthways, and remove the seeds. Cook the cucumber in boiling salted water for 10 minutes, then drain and dry.

Arrange a layer of cucumber in the base of a buttered baking dish. Grate the cheese and sprinkle a third of it over the cucumber. Season with salt and freshly ground pepper. Repeat these layers, finishing with cheese. Dot the top with butter.

Bake the cucumber gratin in a preheated oven at 200°C/400°F/gas 6 for 30 minutes.

French Beans Mimosa

Crisp cooked French beans with a light vinaigrette dressing make a refreshing change from a traditional green salad.

SERVES: 4–6
PREPARATION: 10 minutes
COOKING: 3–4 minutes
MARINATING: 30 minutes

450 g/1 lb young French beans
salt
90 ml/6 tablespoons olive oil
30 ml/2 tablespoons lemon juice
1 large hard-boiled egg to garnish

Top, tail and wash the beans, leaving them whole. Cook them in a saucepan of lightly salted

French Beans Mimosa.

boiling water for 3–4 minutes; they should stay crisp. Drain the beans and rinse them under cold water, then drain them well. Arrange the beans in a round shallow serving dish, radiating from the centre.

Whisk the olive oil and the lemon juice together, with salt and pepper to taste; pour over the beans. Cover and set aside to marinate* for 30 minutes.

Separate the white and yolk of the hard-boiled egg. Chop the white finely and rub the yolk through a coarse sieve.

Before serving, decorate the beans. Arrange the egg white in the centre of the dish and scatter the yolk among the beans.

Tomatoes with Horseradish Mayonnaise

For this dish choose large firm tomatoes of even size. Serve this dish chilled as an accompaniment to cold meat or with grilled steaks and chops.

SERVES: 4–6
PREPARATION: 20 minutes
CHILLING: 2 hours

8 firm tomatoes
salt
150 ml/¼ pt double cream
150 ml/¼ pt mayonnaise
lemon juice
30 ml/2 tablespoons fresh
    grated horseradish
chopped chives, chervil, basil or
    parsley to garnish

Skin the tomatoes (page 302), and slice off the tops with a serrated knife. Carefully scoop out the seeds and juice with a teaspoon, without breaking the flesh. Sprinkle the inside of the tomato cups with salt, stand them upside down on absorbent kitchen paper to drain, then chill them for 2 hours.

Lightly whip the double cream and fold it into the mayonnaise; add lemon juice to taste and stir in the fresh grated horseradish (the tomato tops may also be chopped and stirred into the mayonnaise). Chill the mixture for about 1 hour.

Just before serving, spoon the horseradish mayonnaise into the tomato cups and sprinkle with the chopped herbs.

Pepper, Anchovy and Tomato Salad

SERVES: 4
PREPARATION: 35 minutes
CHILLING: 30 minutes

2 large red peppers
3 large tomatoes
2 × 50 g/2 oz cans anchovy fillets
1 small clove garlic
45–60 ml/3–4 tablespoons olive oil
juice of ½ lemon
salt and black pepper

Put the peppers under a hot grill, turning them frequently until the skins are charred and black all over. Place in a bowl, cover with several layers of absorbent kitchen paper and set aside until cold. Rub off the skin under cold running water. Remove the stalk ends and seeds from the peppers and cut out any white pith. Cut the flesh into wide strips. Skin the tomatoes (page 302), cut them into slices and remove the seeds. Drain the anchovy fillets and rinse them in cold water to remove excess oil and salt; ease them apart carefully.

Arrange the pepper strips on a flat serving dish with the sliced tomatoes, and lay the anchovy fillets on top in a lattice pattern.

Peel and crush the garlic and mix with the olive oil. Pour this dressing over the salad and sprinkle with lemon juice and a very small amount of salt and freshly ground black pepper. Chill for at least 30 minutes.

■ This salad can be served as a starter and also goes well with lamb chops and chicken dishes.

RICE & PASTA

Gnocchi Verdi

These dumplings are served in the same way as simple pasta dishes. The quantities here are sufficient for a main course for four or for a first course for six.

SERVES: 4–6
PREPARATION: 20 minutes
CHILLING: 2 hours
COOKING: 15–20 minutes

450 g/1 lb fresh spinach
250 g/9 oz ricotta cheese
1 egg plus 1 yolk
225 g/8 oz plain flour
75 g/3 oz grated Parmesan cheese
salt and black pepper
grated nutmeg
50 g/2 oz butter

Wash the spinach thoroughly in several lots of cold water and remove any thick stalks. Put it in a large pan with just the water that clings to the leaves. Cover with a closely fitting lid. Cook over moderate heat for about 5 minutes or until the spinach is just soft. Drain thoroughly in a sieve, pressing out all moisture. Chop the spinach finely.

Place the spinach in a bowl and mix in the ricotta cheese and eggs. Stir in the flour and 25 g/ 1 oz of the Parmesan cheese. Season to taste with salt, freshly ground black pepper and some grated nutmeg. Turn the gnocchi mixture into a flat dish, smooth the surface and chill for 2 hours or until firm.

Bring a large saucepan of lightly salted water to simmering point. Shape the gnocchi mix-

Gnocchi Verdi.

ture into small balls, no more than 1.5 cm/¾ in wide, between floured hands. Drop the balls into the simmering water, a few at a time. As soon as they puff up and rise to the surface, remove the gnocchi carefully with a perforated spoon.

Arrange the gnocchi in a buttered flameproof dish. Melt the butter and pour over the top. Sprinkle with the remaining cheese and put the dish under a hot grill until the cheese has melted and browned.

Serve at once.

Spaghetti with Beans

This is a simple and delicious way of serving beans for supper. For a special treat, truffle oil is excellent tossed into the pasta.

SERVES: 4
PREPARATION: 15–30 minutes
COOKING: about 25 minutes

450 g/1 lb runner beans,
    French beans or
    haricot beans
1 onion
1 carrot
1 clove garlic
1 stick celery
2 bay leaves
25 g/1 oz butter
30 ml/2 tablespoons olive oil
350 g/12 oz spaghetti
salt and black pepper
30 ml/2 tablespoons truffle oil
    (optional)
about 12 basil leaves
freshly grated Parmesan or
    Pecorino cheese to
    serve (optional)

String and slice the runner beans or cut the French or haricot beans into short lengths and set them aside. Peel and finely chop the onion, carrot and garlic, then scrub and finely chop the celery. Cook these ingredients with the bay leaves in the butter and oil in a covered, large saucepan for 30 minutes. Stir the vegetables occasionally and keep the heat moderate or lower so that they soften but do not brown.

Cook the spaghetti in a large saucepan of boiling salted water for about 12 minutes, or until it is tender but not soft. Cook the beans in boiling salted water for 5–7 minutes, until they are tender but slightly crisp. Drain the beans well and mix them with the other vegetables.

Drain the spaghetti well, turn it into a large warmed serving dish. Add the truffle oil and toss it into the spaghetti, if liked.

Shred the basil leaves into the bean mixture and turn it out on to the spaghetti. Toss the vegetables into the spaghetti and serve at once. Grated Parmesan or Pecorino cheese may be served with the pasta if liked.

Hot and Cold Rice Salad

SERVES: 6
PREPARATION: 20 minutes
COOKING: 20 minutes

1 fennel bulb
4 sticks celery
6 spring onions
2 courgettes
60 ml/4 tablespoons
    chopped parsley
grated rind and juice of 1 lemon
salt and black pepper
2.5 ml/½ teaspoon caster sugar
5 ml/1 teaspoon wholegrain or
    Dijon mustard
120 ml/4 fl oz olive oil
1 green chilli (optional)
225 g/8 oz long-grain rice
1 bay leaf
600 ml/1 pt water
4 peaches

Trim and dice the fennel, celery and spring onions. Trim, thinly peel and halve the courgettes lengthways, then slice them thinly. Mix all these prepared vegetables with the parsley.

Whisk the lemon juice with seasoning, the caster sugar and mustard. Whisk in the olive oil, then pour half this dressing over the vegetables. Mix well.

Cut the stalk end off the chilli, if using, slit it and discard the seeds, then chop the flesh finely. Add the chilli to the remaining dressing.

Place the rice in a saucepan. Add the lemon rind, bay leaf and salt to taste, then pour in the water. Bring to the boil, stir once and cover the pan closely.

Reduce the heat to the minimum setting and cook for 20 minutes.

In the meantime, place the peaches in a bowl, cover with freshly boiled water and leave to stand for 2 minutes. Drain and skin the fruit, then halve, stone and dice it. When the rice is cooked, pour the chilli dressing over it and add the peaches. Lightly fork the fruit into the rice, then arrange it on a serving platter with the vegetable salad. The rice may be served in the centre of the ring of vegetables, or the two salads can be arranged in alternate rows. Serve immediately, while the rice is hot.

Salmon Kedgeree

In the 19th century, kedgeree, which is of Indian origin, was an established country house breakfast dish. Nowadays it more frequently makes its appearance at lunch or supper.

SERVES: 4–6
PREPARATION: 5 minutes
COOKING: 30 minutes

225 g/8 oz cooked salmon
225 g/8 oz long-grain rice
600 ml/1 pt water
salt, black pepper and
    cayenne pepper
1 onion
50 g/2 oz butter
2 hard-boiled eggs
chopped parsley to garnish

Remove any skin and bones from the salmon, and flake it carefully. Place the rice in a saucepan and pour in the water. Add a pinch each of salt, pepper and cayenne.

Bring to the boil, stir the rice once, then cover the pan tightly with a lid or foil, and reduce the heat to the minimum setting. Cook for 20 minutes. Turn the heat off and leave the rice to stand for a further 5 minutes without lifting the lid.

While the rice is cooking, peel and finely chop the onion. Melt a little of the butter in a pan and fry the onion until it is soft and transparent. Set aside. Roughly chop the whites of the hard-boiled eggs, and press the yolks through a sieve.

Cut the remaining butter into small knobs and stir into the cooked rice, with the flaked salmon, onion and egg whites. Season to taste and heat the mixture through gently.

To serve, pile the kedgeree up on a warmed flat dish and decorate with the sieved egg yolks, arranged in a star or cross pattern. Sprinkle the dish with chopped parsley.
■ Serve with fingers of hot buttered toast, if liked.

Salmon Kedgeree.

PUDDINGS & DESSERTS

Baked Stuffed Peaches

SERVES: 4–6
PREPARATION: 20 minutes
OVEN: 180°C/350°F/gas 4
COOKING: 20–30 minutes

20 ml/4 teaspoons caster sugar
15 g/½ oz unsalted butter
1 egg yolk
50 g/2 oz amaretti or
   ratafia biscuits
4 large peaches

Cream together the sugar, butter and egg yolk in a small bowl. Crumb the biscuits in a food processor or crush with a rolling pin. Add to the creamed mixture.

Pour boiling water over the peaches and leave them for 1–2 minutes. Peel off the skins, halve the peaches and take out the stones. Make the cavities slightly larger by scooping out some of the flesh with a pointed teaspoon. Add this pulp to the crumb mixture and mix well.

Pile the crumb stuffing into the peach halves and arrange them in a buttered baking dish. Bake the stuffed peaches in a preheated oven at 180°C/350°F/gas 4 for 20–30 minutes or until the peaches are soft, but still hold their shape.
■ Serve the peaches warm, with whipped cream or ice cream.

Baked Stuffed Peaches.

Clafouti Limousin

A clafouti is a baked batter pudding cooked with fresh fruit. In the Limousin province of France, where it originated, the pudding is traditionally made with black cherries.

SERVES: 6
PREPARATION: 15 minutes
OVEN: 190°C/375°F/gas 5
COOKING: 30 minutes

450 g/1 lb black cherries
3 eggs
100 g/4 oz plain flour
50 g/2 oz caster sugar plus extra
   for sprinkling
450 ml/¾ pt milk
15 ml/1 tablespoon dark rum
   (optional)
unsalted butter for greasing

Remove the stalks from the cherries, stone, wash and drain the fruit thoroughly. Beat the eggs lightly together. Sift the flour into a bowl and stir in the sugar, then make a well in the middle. Pour the eggs into the bowl and add a little milk. Beat the eggs and milk, gradually working in the dry ingredients and adding more milk to make a smooth batter. Add the dark rum if it is being used.

Butter a 1.12 litre/2 pt shallow ovenproof dish thoroughly. Put in the cherries and pour the batter over them. Bake in a preheated oven at 190°C/375°F/gas 5 for 25–30 minutes or until the batter is set and browned on top. Sprinkle the pudding with a little caster sugar and serve warm.

Raspberry Charlotte

SERVES: 6
PREPARATION: 25 minutes
OVEN: 150°C/300°F/gas 2
COOKING: 1–1¼ hours
CHILLING: 6–8 hours

melted butter for greasing
2 eggs plus 2 egg yolks
25 g/1 oz caster sugar
600 ml/1 pt milk
15 ml/1 tablespoon natural
   vanilla essence
45 ml/3 tablespoons sherry
350 g/12 oz Madeira cake or
   sponge cake
350 g/12 oz raspberries
150 ml/¼ pt double cream

Lightly grease a 1.7 litre/3 pt soufflé dish with the melted butter. Beat the eggs and yolks with the sugar. Heat the milk to just below boiling, then gradually beat into the egg mixture. Stir in the vanilla essence and sherry.

Crumble the cake; spoon half the crumbs into the soufflé dish in an even layer. Spread 225 g/8 oz of the raspberries over the top, cover with the rest of the crumbs, then carefully strain the custard mixture over the top. Allow to stand for 10 minutes.

Bake the charlotte in a preheated oven at 150°C/300°F/gas 2 for 1–1¼ hours or until the custard has set in the centre. Remove the charlotte from the oven and allow to cool before chilling it in the refrigerator.

Decorate with the remaining raspberries. Whip the cream and pipe it around the rim.

Coeurs à la Crème

This is a classic French summer sweet, made from cream cheese and cream. Traditionally, it is set in little heart-shaped ceramic moulds and served with cream and soft summer fruit.

SERVES: 6
PREPARATION: 20 minutes
CHILLING: 12 hours

225 g/8 oz cream cheese
300 ml/½ pt double cream
20 ml/4 teaspoons caster sugar
2 egg whites
150 ml/¼ pt single cream
   (optional)
225 g/8 oz soft fruit

Rub or press the cheese through a fine sieve into a bowl. Stir in the double cream, then the sugar. Whisk the egg whites until stiff but not dry, and fold them into the cheese and cream mixture.

Line the heart-shaped moulds with fine muslin, which makes unmoulding easier, or use clean yogurt pots as moulds. Pierce a few holes in the base of each yogurt pot for draining.

Spoon the cheese and cream mixture into the moulds and spread it evenly, smoothing the top. Stand the moulds in a large dish or tin. Leave them in the refrigerator overnight to drain.

Just before serving, unmould the desserts on to individual serving plates and remove the pieces of muslin. Pour over the single cream, if liked, and serve with fresh raspberries or other soft fruit, or with a sweetened fruit sauce.

Raspberry Yogurt Sorbet

A sorbet will be welcome on a hot summer's evening. One of the most delicious is made from raspberries, when these are in plentiful supply. Adding yogurt to this delicious dessert enhances its flavour.

SERVES: 6
PREPARATION: 15 minutes
COOKING: 2–3 hours

225 g/8 oz raspberries
50–75 g/2–3 oz caster sugar
300 ml/½ pt plain yogurt
juice of ½ lemon
15 g/½ oz powdered gelatine
60 ml/4 tablespoons water
2 egg whites
Decoration (optional)
a few raspberries
sprigs of mint

A few hours before preparing the sorbet, set the freezer to the coldest setting. Make a thick purée from the raspberries by rubbing them through a sieve and into a bowl. Sweeten to taste with the sugar. Stir the yogurt and the lemon juice into the sweetened purée.

Sprinkle the gelatine over the water in a small heatproof basin. Do not stir. Leave to stand for 15 minutes, until the gelatine has absorbed the liquid. Set the basin over a pan of simmering water and stir until the gelatine has dissolved completely.

Stir a small amount of the raspberry purée into the liquid gelatine, then add the mixture to the remaining raspberry purée. In a separate bowl, whisk the egg whites until stiff but not dry, then fold them into the purée.

Spoon the mixture into a suitable container for freezing, cover with a lid and place in the freezer. When almost frozen, break up the sorbet by beating it with a rotary whisk or hand-held electric mixer. Return the sorbet to the freezer until firm.

Scoop the sorbet into large or small bowls and decorate each serving with a few raspberries and mint, if liked.

Summer Pudding

The origin of this classic English pudding is unknown, but as early as the 18th century it was served to sick people who had been forbidden rich pastry sweets. This does not in the least make it invalid food – it is a delicious composition of summer fruits.

SERVES: 6
PREPARATION: 30–40 minutes
CHILLING: 8 hours

6–8 slices day-old white bread,
    1 cm/½ in thick, crusts removed
675 g/1½ lb mixed soft fruits
100 g/4 oz caster sugar

Strawberries, raspberries, red- and blackcurrants, as well as black cherries, are all suitable for this dish, and can be mixed according to taste and availability. The more varied the fruits, the tastier the result, but avoid using too many blackcurrants as their flavour and colour will tend to dominate the summer pudding.

Line the bottom of a 900 ml/1½ pt soufflé dish or pudding basin with one or two slices of bread to cover the base completely. Line the sides of the dish with more bread, if necessary cut to shape, so that the bread fits closely together.

Hull* and carefully wash the fruit, removing the stones from cherries, if used. Put the fruit in a wide heavy-based pan and sprinkle the sugar over it. Bring to the boil over very low heat, and cook for 2–3 minutes only, until the sugar melts and the juices begin to run. Remove the pan from the heat and set aside 1–2 tablespoons of the fruit juices. Spoon the fruit and remaining juice into the prepared dish and cover the surface closely with the rest of the bread.

Put a plate that fits the inside of the dish on top of the pudding and weight it down with a heavy

Summer Pudding.

can or jar. Chill the summer pudding for 8 hours.

Before serving, remove the weight and plate. Invert the serving plate over the dish or basin and turn both over together to unmould the pudding. Pour the reserved fruit juice over any parts of the bread which have not been coloured by the fruit juices. Serve with cream.

Summer Barbecues

Eating outdoors is one of the pleasures of warm, sunny summers and cooking outside can be just as much fun. Planning ahead is important for success outdoors, though, particularly when holding a barbecue party. The following guidelines show how to avoid some of the main pitfalls that can face an 'al fresco' chef.

The Fire

Charcoal is available in a wide variety of forms, including small briquettes which are useful for small barbecues, or sealed bags which include lighters and are ignited by setting a match to the outer wrapping. Whatever your choice, make sure you have plenty of fuel. Fuel that is old, and may have absorbed moisture from the atmosphere or which has actually been exposed to rain, will not light easily (if at all). Use a commercial lighting fuel, fire lighters or paper and kindling to light the barbecue. Light up at least 30 minutes before you intend to start cooking; 45 minutes or longer for a large barbecue. The coals are ready when they look ashen.

Alternatively, if you have a gas-fired barbecue, make sure that you have sufficient gas and always read and follow the manufacturer's instructions.

The Food

Prepare the food in advance and keep it chilled until the fire is ready. Consider the cooking space on the barbecue when planning a menu and make sure you will have enough room to cook everything before the coals die completely.

When cooking vegetarian food as well as fish and meat, remember that they should be kept separate. If necessary, buy a small disposable barbecue for the vegetarian food.

Plain foods, such as chops or vegetables, benefit from being marinated in a seasoning mixture before grilling, so prepare the ingredients in plenty of time.

Simple accompaniments are usually best for barbecued foods: fresh salads, new potatoes or baked potatoes and/or fresh bread are ideal. Formal first courses are not necessary, but it is a good idea to have a platter of crudités and/or dips and a few savoury snacks to hand around while the food sizzles on the grill.

Safety First

• NEVER use paraffin or petrol to light a barbecue. NEVER pour fuel (such as methylated spirits) on to a barbecue that has not lit successfully. Even though the fire may appear to have gone out, the residual heat may be sufficient to ignite the fuel and its vapour, causing it to burn back to the container you are holding, with disastrous consequences.

• Always keep an eye on children and NEVER leave the barbecue unattended when there are children present.

• Keep any pets well away from the barbecue.

Food Safety

• Remember that the standard rules of cooking hygiene apply even when enjoying a casual outdoor cooking session.

• Never use the same utensils for raw and cooked foods.

• Keep all raw food in the refrigerator until you are ready to put it on the barbecue.

• Always ensure that poultry is thoroughly cooked; if necessary, part-cook it in the oven before transferring it to the barbecue.

• Hamburgers and other items made with bought minced beef should be cooked through.

• Keep food covered so that flies and other pests are prevented from contaminating it.

• Do not leave food out for long periods in the warm. Take it out of the refrigerator just before cooking or serving and replace any leftovers promptly when the barbecue is over.

Lamb cutlets marinated in the Marinade for Meat, Cardamom Vegetable Kebabs (page 192) and Skewered Halloumi (page 184).

Corn on the Cob

Fold back the husk, but do not remove it, then pull off the silky hairs. Cover the corn with the husks, folding them back carefully to cover the corn kernels, and cook on the hot barbecue for 15–20 minutes, turning every now and then. Remove the husks and serve the corn at once with butter and freshly ground pepper.

Bacon-wrapped Prawns

Wrap some large peeled cooked prawns in rindless bacon; thread three or four prawn packages on to each metal skewer. Grill for about 2–3 minutes on each side, or until the bacon is browned and crisp in places.

Fish

Select firm fish, such as cod, monkfish or salmon, and thicker cuts – steaks rather than thin fillets. Swordfish, tuna and shark steaks are excellent for grilling. Marinate* the fish for about 1 hour in white wine, with the juice of 1 lemon, 1 onion, finely chopped, and chosen seasonings, such as ground cinnamon or mace and a touch of ground cloves. Cook the fish on the grill for 10–15 minutes, turning once. Sprats or sardines can also be marinated, threaded on skewers and grilled for about 10 minutes. **Whole fish** Small trout and mackerel, thoroughly cleaned and dried, may be grilled whole. They may be marinated for 1 hour in a dressing consisting of 120 ml/4 fl oz dry white wine, 60 ml/4 tablespoons olive oil, 2 peeled and crushed garlic cloves, 10 ml/2 teaspoons finely chopped rosemary, thyme or marjoram, 30 ml/2 tablespoons chopped parsley and salt and black pepper to taste.

Grill the fish for 2–5 minutes on each side, turning them carefully using a slice and a fork. A fish-shaped grilling rack that encloses the fish completely makes turning it easier.
Fish in Foil Make three or four slits in the skin of whole fish, sprinkle with fresh dill, fennel or thyme, and wrap in individual foil parcels. Cook at the edge of the grill for about 30 minutes.

Meat

Lean, tender cuts grill well on a barbecue. Beefburgers, sausages, trimmed lamb and pork cutlets, and steaks may all be marinated*. Brush the meat with oil or the marinade and turn it once only during grilling.

Allow 10 minutes for well-done steaks and burgers, and 15 minutes for sausages and cutlets.

Marinade for Meat

Shake the following ingredients together in a screw-top jar: 30 ml/2 tablespoons olive oil, 30 ml/2 tablespoons lemon juice, 30 ml/2 tablespoons tomato juice, 30 ml/2 tablespoons dry white wine, 10 ml/2 teaspoons Worcestershire sauce, 10 ml/2 teaspoons soy sauce. Pour the marinade over the meat, cover and chill for up to 24 hours.

Spicy Barbecue Basting Sauce

Mix together 5 ml/1 teaspoon chilli powder, 5 ml/1 teaspoon celery salt, 30 ml/2 tablespoons soft brown sugar, 30 ml/2 tablespoons wine or tarragon vinegar, 45 ml/3 tablespoons tomato ketchup, 30 ml/2 tablespoons Worcestershire sauce, 150 ml/¼ pt beef stock or water and Tabasco sauce to taste. Bring to the boil and simmer for 5 minutes. Brush over poultry or meat before and during grilling.

Kebabs

Fish (firm cubes), poultry, meat and vegetables can be threaded on skewers and grilled. Leg of lamb, rump steak, lamb kidneys, cocktail sausages or chipolatas, button mushrooms and onions, squares of pepper, fresh bay leaves, rosemary sprigs and slices of courgettes are all suitable.

It is important to use ingredients that cook at the same rate. Tomatoes will over-cook when skewered with meat. Tiny tomatoes can be threaded at the end of the skewers where they will receive the least heat. Cubes of fresh or canned pineapple, dried prunes or apricots and apples also grill well. Marinate* the ingredients in advance, if required, or mix them with seasonings before threading on the skewers.

Brush the ingredients with oil or the seasoning mixture during cooking and turn them several times. Meat kebabs usually cook in 15–20 minutes; fish cooks very quickly – about 5–7 minutes.

Poultry

If the barbecue has a rotating spit attachment, small chickens can be threaded on to the spit, brushed with oil and left to cook for 2 hours. Chicken portions are more popular and boneless breasts are the best choice for even, quick cooking. Always ensure the poultry is cooked through by piercing the thickest part of the flesh with a knife or skewer and checking that the juices are free of any signs of blood.

Devil Seasoning or Basting Sauce

Mix together 5 ml/1 teaspoon dry mustard with 5 ml/1 teaspoon ground ginger and 30 ml/2 tablespoons caster sugar. Rub this over the poultry or meat and leave for 30 minutes.

For the basting sauce, mix 30 ml/2 tablespoons oil with 30 ml/2 tablespoons soy sauce, 30 ml/2 tablespoons fruit sauce, 15 ml/1 tablespoon Worcestershire sauce, 30 ml/2 tablespoons tomato ketchup, the juice of a small orange and a dash of Tabasco sauce.

Desserts

A fresh fruit salad makes a refreshing finish to a barbecued meal. Alternatively, put some unpeeled bananas on the grill and cook them until they have thoroughly blackened. Carefully slit and peel the fruit, then serve them with honey or golden or maple syrup and whipped cream.

Firm peaches, peeled and halved, can be grilled. Sprinkle with soft brown sugar and serve them with ice cream.

AUGUST

Brown-bread Ice Cream, Granita al Caffé, Melon Ice Cream.

August

On the one hand, August is a time for relaxing outdoors and avoiding long hours in the kitchen, but on the other it can be a busy time socially, when family and friends visit, and guests stay for long weekends. With children on holiday from school, outdoor activities and packed lunches are popular, so there are some practical hints and tips for the latter included in this chapter, along with additional ideas for special occasion picnics of a more formal nature.

For some, the important culinary event on the calendar is the 'Glorious Twelfth' – this marks the start of the game season. The four-month season for grouse begins now, but it usually takes a few weeks for the shops to stock oven-ready birds.

Another traditional country pastime at this time of year is blackberrying; an afternoon's picking will provide enough blackberries to make jam or bramble jelly and a tart or two. Plums ripen towards the end of the month, with golden gages ready for jam-making and Victoria plums known for their firm flesh and tangy taste.

August Dinner Party
~

Chilled Carrot Soup

~

Salmi of Grouse
Game Chips (page 347)
Sautéed Courgettes
Creamed Spinach (page 169)

~

Victoria Plums in Wine

Salmi of Grouse is an ideal dish to cook in celebration of the start of the game season. This menu combines a cook-ahead starter, with a main course that requires attention just before it is served. The plums in wine can be prepared ahead of time and reheated before serving or served cold.

Pasta with Pesto (page 214) and Prawns with Mange-tout (page 207).

Sunday Buffet Lunch
~

Plaice with Oranges

~

Boeuf à la Mode en Gelée
French Beans Mimosa
(page 193)
Tomato Salad (page 171)
Buttered New Potatoes

~

Danish Layer Cake
or
Summer Pudding (page 197)

This cold Sunday buffet is an elegant alternative to a hot roast lunch and it is ideal for entertaining outdoors. Lay out the buffet in the kitchen, away from the heat of the day, but set a table outside where everyone can sit and eat in comfort. Serve one plaice fillet per portion as the first course.

Light Lunch
~

Salade Niçoise
New Potatoes
Home-baked Bread Rolls
(page 396)

~

Melon Ice Cream
or
Greengages with Apricot Purée

This is a simple, yet special, light lunch to share with weekend guests. Serve a dish of vegetable crudités – fingers of crunchy carrot, cucumber and pepper, with cauliflower florets and cherry tomatoes – with drinks before lunch and offer some good-quality chocolates when serving coffee. Make a double quantity of the Salade Niçoise as the main course for the lunch. Bake and freeze the bread rolls in advance.

Menu suggestions *Cool dishes and light meals are popular during the heat of August, when a Sunday lunch buffet is the ideal alternative to a wintry roast. The menus featured this month also include a game dinner party. The recipes for the main dishes are included in this chapter and page references are given for those found elsewhere in the book.*

Soups

Gazpacho Andaluz

On a hot summer day, a chilled soup is particularly welcome. This Andalusian soup is also decorative, served with several crisp, colourful garnishes. In Spain, ice cubes are added to each soup bowl before serving.

SERVES: 6
PREPARATION: 35 minutes
CHILLING: 1–2 hours

675 g/1½ lb tomatoes
4 large thick slices day-old white
    bread, about 1 cm/½ in thick
2 large cloves garlic
20 ml/4 teaspoons herb or red
    wine vinegar
45–60 ml/3–4 tablespoons olive oil
450 ml/¾ pt tomato juice
1 large Spanish onion
1 small cucumber
salt and black pepper
450 ml/¾ pt iced water
Garnish
1 small cucumber
2 small peppers
4 large tomatoes
black olives
hard-boiled eggs
raw onion rings
Croûtons (page 313)

Skin the tomatoes (page 302), remove the seeds and chop the flesh finely. Cut the crusts off the bread and crumble it finely into a large bowl. Peel and crush the garlic into the bowl. Stir in the vinegar and gradually add as much olive oil as the crumbs will absorb. Stir in the tomato flesh and juice and mix thoroughly. Peel and grate or finely chop the onion and cucumber and stir both into the tomato mixture. Season to taste with salt and freshly ground pepper. Purée the mixture in a liquidiser until smooth, or rub it through a fine sieve into a bowl.

The soup should be perfectly smooth. Dilute it with iced water until it has the consistency of thin cream. Add more salt and pepper if required. Cover the soup and chill it.

The garnishes are usually served in separate small bowls, so that guests can help themselves. Peel and dice the cucumber. Core, seed and chop the peppers. Skin the tomatoes and cube the flesh. Stone the black olives, if necessary; slice the hard-boiled eggs. Place the onion rings and croûtons in bowls.

Gazpacho Andaluz.

Chilled Carrot Soup

As young, home-grown carrots become more plentiful, it is well worth trying this delicious soup. It can be served hot, but the subtle, creamy flavour is more pronounced if the soup is chilled thoroughly before serving.

SERVES: 6
PREPARATION: 20 minutes
COOKING: 45 minutes
CHILLING: 1 hour

1 onion
3–4 cloves garlic
25 g/1 oz butter
575 g/1¼ lb carrots
1.12 litres/2 pt chicken or
    beef stock
250 ml/8 fl oz double cream
salt and black pepper
finely chopped parsley to garnish

Peel and thinly slice the onion; peel and crush the garlic. Melt the butter in a heavy-based pan, add the onion and garlic and cook over low heat, keeping the pan covered with a lid until the onion is soft and transparent but has not coloured.

Meanwhile, top, tail and scrape the carrots; chop them roughly. Add these to the onion mixture, replace the lid and continue cooking for about 8 minutes more. Pour the stock over the vegetables. Bring to the boil, then simmer gently for about 30 minutes.

Remove the soup from the heat and allow to cool slightly before liquidising it until it is smooth. If you don't have a liquidiser, rub the soup through a fine sieve into a bowl.

In a separate bowl, lightly whip half the cream until it holds its shape. Stir the whipped cream into the soup and season to taste with salt and freshly ground pepper. When it is cold, cover the carrot soup and chill it for at least 1 hour.

Serve the soup in chilled individual bowls, trickling into each about 1 tablespoon of the remaining cream. Garnish each portion with a sprinkling of the finely chopped parsley.

Tomato Ice

The Italians invented the water ice or sorbet, which is usually made from sweetened citrus juice and served as a dessert or to cleanse the palate between courses. This savoury shaved ice version, also known as a granita, makes a refreshing starter.

SERVES: 6
PREPARATION: 10 minutes
COOKING: 25 minutes
FREEZING: overnight

1.4 kg/3 lb ripe tomatoes
1 small onion
30 ml/2 tablespoons chopped
    marjoram
15 ml/1 tablespoon tomato paste
juice of 1 lemon
caster sugar
mint sprigs, lemon twists or
    cucumber slices to garnish

Roughly chop the tomatoes. Peel and roughly chop the onion. Put the tomatoes, onion and the chopped marjoram in a large saucepan. Bring to the boil, cover the pan, lower the heat and simmer for 25 minutes or until the tomatoes are soft. Stir occasionally to prevent the tomatoes from sticking to the pan.

Rub the mixture through a sieve into a large bowl, and stir in the tomato paste, lemon juice and caster sugar to taste.

Leave the mixture to cool, spoon it into a plastic freezer container and cover with a lid. Freeze the tomato ice for several hours or overnight until it is solid. Remove the frozen mixture from the container and either crush it with a rolling pin or process it *briefly* in a food processor fitted with a steel blade. Pile the tomato crystals into individual serving glasses. Garnish with sprigs of mint, lemon twists or cucumber slices.

Cucumber with Prawns and Mushrooms

SERVES: 4
PREPARATION: 15 minutes
COOKING: 15 minutes

1 large or 2 small cucumbers
salt and black pepper
100 g/4 oz mushrooms, sliced
40 g/1½ oz butter
10 ml/2 teaspoons plain flour
75 ml/2½ fl oz chicken stock
75 ml/2½ fl oz single cream
soy sauce (optional)
100 g/4 oz peeled cooked prawns
Garnish
finely chopped chives, basil or dill
cucumber twists

Wash the cucumber, but do not peel it. Cut it into 1 cm/½ in dice and cook for 3–4 minutes in a saucepan of boiling, lightly salted water. Drain the cucumber in a colander, refresh under cold running water and drain again. Trim the mushrooms and cut them into 5 mm/¼ in thick slices.

Melt the butter in a small frying pan and cook the mushrooms for 2–3 minutes or until they are lightly browned. Add the diced cucumber, cover with a lid and simmer for 2–3 minutes. Sprinkle in the flour, stirring until it is absorbed thoroughly. Gradually add the stock and cream, stirring the mixture until it is smooth. Bring the pan gently to the boil, stirring, and season to taste with salt, freshly ground pepper and a few drops of soy sauce, if used. Reduce the heat and simmer for another 2–3 minutes, then stir in the prawns and heat through.

Spoon the mixture into a warmed serving dish or individual deep scallop shells, Sprinkle each serving with the herbs and garnish with thin twists of cucumber. Serve at once.

■ Thinly sliced brown bread and butter, or crisp toast fingers may be served with the cucumber and prawn mixture.

Baked Tomatoes

SERVES: 6
PREPARATION: 20 minutes
OVEN: 190°C/375°F/gas 5
COOKING: 35 minutes

6 firm beefsteak tomatoes or 12
    large tomatoes
1 onion
175 g/6 oz cooked meat
40–50 g/1½–2 oz butter
100 g/4 oz cooked rice
30–45 ml/2–3 tablespoons stock
15 ml/1 tablespoon single cream
10 ml/2 teaspoons
    Worcestershire sauce
30 ml/2 tablespoons
    chopped parsley
black pepper
50 g/2 oz Cheddar cheese
25 g/1 oz breadcrumbs

Cut a thin slice from the top of each tomato. Scoop out the pulp and reserve it for use in another recipe. Place the tomatoes upside down on layers of absorbent kitchen paper to drain.

Chop the onion finely. Mince the meat or chop it finely in a food processor. Melt the butter in a pan and cook the onion until soft. Add the meat, rice, stock, cream, Worcestershire sauce and parsley. Season with pepper and cook for 3 minutes.

Fill the tomato cases with the meat mixture and pack them in a single layer in a lightly greased ovenproof dish. Grate the cheese. Sprinkle the meat mixture with the cheese and breadcrumbs, and bake in a preheated oven at 190°C/375°F/ gas 5 for 15–20 minutes.

Tomato Ice.

Eggs Baked in Tomatoes

This light and colourful starter can also be served as a lunchtime snack. Use beefsteak tomatoes for the best results.

SERVES: 4
PREPARATION: 40 minutes
OVEN: 180°C/350°F/gas 4
COOKING: 15–20 minutes

1 clove garlic
4 large firm tomatoes
salt and black pepper
4 eggs
10 ml/2 teaspoons tomato paste
20 ml/4 teaspoons double cream
15 ml/1 tablespoon grated
    Parmesan cheese
4 slices bread
25 g/1 oz butter
10 ml/2 teaspoons olive oil

Peel the garlic and chop it finely. Wash the tomatoes, wipe them dry and slice off the tops with a sharp knife. Carefully scoop out

Eggs Baked in Tomatoes.

the tomato pulp with a spoon and sprinkle the inside of each shell with salt and a little of the chopped garlic. Turn the tomato shells upside down on layers of absorbent kitchen paper to drain for 30 minutes.

Arrange the tomatoes in a baking dish, hollows uppermost. Break an egg carefully into each, keeping back as much as possible of the white. (Reserve the remaining egg white for use in another recipe.) Season with salt and freshly ground pepper. Stir the tomato paste with the cream in a small bowl; spoon the mixture gently over the eggs. Sprinkle each filled tomato with a little grated Parmesan cheese.

Bake the tomatoes in a preheated oven at 180°C/350°F/gas 4 for 15–20 minutes, or until the eggs have just set.

Meanwhile, cut the bread into rounds with a fluted round cutter. Heat the butter and oil in

a large frying pan and fry the bread until golden brown on both sides. Drain on absorbent kitchen paper, place on a serving platter and keep hot.

As soon as the eggs are set, arrange one tomato on each round of bread and serve at once.

Sundancer Eggs

Baked eggs are one of the classic quick snacks, equally welcome at breakfast or at midnight.

SERVES: 4
PREPARATION: 10 minutes
OVEN: 180°C/350°F/gas 4
COOKING: 8–10 minutes

8 thin rashers lean bacon
100 g/4 oz mushrooms
50 g/2 oz butter
salt and black pepper
8 eggs
60 ml/4 tablespoons double cream
finely chopped chervil

Remove the rinds from the bacon and dice the rashers. Chop the mushrooms finely.

Fry the bacon in the butter, over moderate heat, for 3 minutes. Add the mushrooms and cook for a further 2 minutes. Season with salt and pepper. Divide this mixture between eight small ramekin dishes, and break an egg into each. Top with cream and sprinkle with a little chopped chervil

Bake the eggs in a preheated oven at 180°C/350°F/gas 4 for 8–10 minutes or until the egg whites are just set.

■   Serve two ramekins to each person, with hot toast fingers.

FISH, SHELLFISH & SEAFOOD

Sole Véronique

The term 'Véronique' describes a dish, usually fish, served in a sauce made from white wine and cream. The traditional garnish is muscat grapes, but any type of large white grape may be used.

SERVES: 4–6
PREPARATION: 20 minutes
OVEN: 180°C/350°F/gas 4
COOKING: 25 minutes

8 fillets of sole
2 shallots
3 mushrooms
1 sprig parsley
1 bay leaf
salt and black pepper
15 ml/1 tablespoon lemon juice
150 ml/¼ pt medium dry
    white wine
175 g/6 oz white muscat grapes
20 g/¾ oz butter
30 ml/2 tablespoons plain flour
about 150 ml/¼ pt milk
    (see method)
150 ml/¼ pt double cream

Wash the fish fillets, pat them dry and arrange them in a lightly buttered baking dish.

Peel and finely chop the shallots; trim the mushrooms and slice thinly. Sprinkle both over the fish and add the parsley and bay leaf. Season with salt and pepper and sprinkle with two-thirds of the lemon juice.

Pour the wine over the fish, adding sufficient water to barely cover the fillets. Cover the dish closely with foil, and bake in a preheated oven at 180°C/350°F/gas 4 for 15–20 minutes, or until tender. Meanwhile, peel the grapes (page 360), cut them in half and remove the pips.

Remove the dish from the oven. Carefully move the fillets to a flameproof dish, folding them over, and keep them warm. Strain the cooking liquid into a small saucepan. Boil rapidly over high heat until it has reduced by about half. Melt the butter in a separate saucepan and stir in the flour; mix well and cook over moderate heat for 2 minutes.

Meanwhile make the reduced liquid up to 300 ml/½ pt with the milk. Gradually add it to the flour mixture, stirring all the time until the sauce boils and thickens. Reduce the heat and stir until the sauce has the consistency of thick cream. Stir in the double cream and the rest of the lemon juice and reheat the sauce without boiling. Remove from the heat, add salt and pepper to taste and fold in two-thirds of the grapes.

Pour the sauce over the fish and brown the top under a hot grill. Garnish the sole véronique by arranging the rest of the grapes at either end of the dish and serve immediately.

Spicy Grilled Swordfish

Any firm meaty fish can be used instead of swordfish. Marinating gives the fish extra flavour and helps to prevent the fish from drying out during grilling. This is an excellent recipe for cooking on the barbecue, but take care when basting because the oil-based marinade will cause the fire to flare up.

SERVES: 4
PREPARATION: 10 minutes
MARINATING: 1 hour
COOKING: 8–10 minutes

2 cloves garlic
2.5 cm/1 in piece of fresh
*   root ginger*
2 bay leaves
90 ml/6 tablespoons oil
10 ml/2 teaspoons ground
*   coriander*
juice of 2 lemons
salt and black pepper
4 swordfish steaks

Peel and crush the garlic, peel the ginger and cut it in shreds and crumble the bay leaves between your fingers. Heat the oil, add the garlic, ginger and bay leaves and cook over low heat for 1–2 minutes. Stir in the ground coriander and cook for 1 minute more, then remove the pan from the heat. Add the lemon juice, salt and pepper and pour the marinade into a shallow dish large enough to hold the fish in a single layer. When cool, add the fish, spoon the marinade over, cover and marinate for 1 hour, turning once or twice.

Remove the fish from the marinade and place it on a rack in a grill pan. Strain the marinade into a small saucepan, bring to the boil, then keep hot over low heat. Grill the fish for 6–8 minutes or until cooked through, turning once and basting occasionally with the marinade. Serve with the remaining marinade spooned over the fish.
■ Serve with simple vegetables such as boiled new potatoes and mange-tout.

Plaice with Oranges

Chilled poached plaice fillets coated in mayonnaise make a quick and simple meal on a hot day. The richness of the sauce is balanced by an orange garnish in a sharp French dressing.

SERVES: 4–6
PREPARATION: 20 minutes
OVEN: 180°C/350°F/gas 4
COOKING: 20 minutes
COOLING: 1–2 hours

8 plaice or lemon sole fillets
4 oranges
juice of ½ lemon
salt and black pepper
40 g/1½ oz butter
150 ml/¼ pt mayonnaise
paprika
50 g/2 oz anchovy fillets
30 ml/2 tablespoons French
*   Dressing (page 356)*

Skin the fish fillets or ask the fishmonger to do this. Grate 1 orange finely, taking care not to include any of the pith. Squeeze the juice into a measuring jug. Set the remaining oranges aside.

Sprinkle the fish fillets with the lemon juice and half the orange juice, then season with salt and freshly ground pepper. Sprinkle with orange rind.

Roll up the fillets, beginning at the head, and secure with wooden cocktail sticks. Arrange them in a single layer in a buttered ovenproof dish.

Pour the rest of the measured orange juice over the fish. Dot the fillets with small pieces of butter and cover the dish with buttered greaseproof paper or foil. Bake in a preheated oven at 180°C/350°F/gas 4 for about 20 minutes, or until the fillets are cooked. Remove from the oven and leave to cool.

Meanwhile grate 1 of the remaining oranges and set half the grated rind aside. Cut the orange in half and squeeze the juice from one of the halves. Beat the mayonnaise with the reserved orange rind, then gradually add the juice, drop by drop, beating constantly. Lift the cold fillets carefully on to a shallow serving dish, and remove the cocktail sticks. Coat the fish fillets with the orange-flavoured mayonnaise, sprinkle with paprika and arrange two halved anchovies on each fillet.

Peel the remaining oranges, removing all the pith, and cut them into thin round slices with a sharp serrated knife. Dip the orange slices in the french dressing and serve separately or as a garnish to the fillets.
■ Serve with a salad made from blanched, sliced courgettes with strips of red and green pepper.

Plaice with Oranges.

Sweet-sour Salmon

In German cookery, a sweet-sour sauce is frequently served with fish and with braised meat. This is a light version, using fromage frais instead of cream and cider vinegar which is not as tart as wine vinegar.

SERVES: 4
PREPARATION: 10 minutes
OVEN: 160°C/325°F/gas 3
COOKING: 35–40 minutes
CHILLING: 2–3 hours

4 salmon steaks
salt and black pepper
1 large onion
30 ml/2 tablespoons cider vinegar
15 ml/1 tablespoon soft
*   light-brown sugar*
10 ml/2 teaspoons lemon juice
5 ml/1 teaspoon tomato paste
200 ml/7 fl oz fromage frais
cucumber slices to garnish

Wash and dry the salmon steaks. Season with salt and pepper and arrange in a shallow ovenproof dish. Peel and slice the onion; sprinkle the slices over the fish.

Pour boiling water over the fish to barely cover it. Cover the dish with foil and bake in a preheated oven at 160°C/325°F/gas 3 for 20–25 minutes or until cooked. Carefully transfer the steaks to a serving dish with a perforated spoon.

Mix 45 ml/3 tablespoons of the cooking liquid from the salmon with the cider vinegar, sugar, lemon juice and tomato paste in a small saucepan. Heat, stirring continuously, until the sugar melts. Cool slightly, then stir the tomato mixture into the fromage frais. Pour the sauce over the salmon and cool before chilling for at least 2 hours.

Garnish the salmon with thin slices of unpeeled cucumber.

■ Serve with cherry tomatoes, new potatoes and a green salad.

Salmon Trout in Jelly

This dish makes an impressive, attractive centrepiece for an extra-special dinner party or an elaborate cold buffet, and can be prepared well in advance.

SERVES: 8
PREPARATION: 30 minutes
OVEN: 180°C/350°F/gas 4
  (optional)
COOKING: 1–1½ hours
COOLING AND SETTING:
  3–4 hours

1 salmon trout, about 1.15–
  1.4 kg/2½–3 lb
15 g/½ oz gelatine
15 ml/1 tablespoon white
  wine vinegar
90 ml/3 fl oz dry sherry
2 egg whites
Stock
1 carrot
1 onion
600 ml/1 pt water
bouquet garni*
4 peppercorns
20 ml/4 teaspoons wine vinegar
2.5 ml/½ teaspoon salt
Garnish
100 g/4 oz peeled cooked prawns
watercress

Begin by making the stock. Combine all the ingredients in a large saucepan. Bring to the boil, cover, lower the heat and simmer for 20 minutes. Strain the stock through a muslin-lined sieve into a clean bowl.

Remove the fins and gills from the salmon trout, if the fishmonger has not already done so, and cut a 2.5 cm/1 in deep inverted 'V' out of the tail so that it resembles a mermaid's tail. Wash the fish thoroughly to remove all traces of blood, and put it in a fish kettle, or a large flameproof dish. Pour over the warm stock and cover with a lid or foil. Cook the fish for 25–30 minutes on top of the stove, or for 50 minutes in a preheated oven at 180°C/350°F/gas 4. Baste frequently with the stock. Leave the fish to cool in the liquid.

Skin and bone the cooked fish, keeping it whole or lifting off both fillets and replacing them neatly (page 316).

Strain the fish poaching liquid, through a muslin-lined sieve. Spoon 60 ml/4 tablespoons of the poaching liquid into a cup and pour the rest into a saucepan. Sprinkle the gelatine over the liquid in the cup. Do not stir. Leave to stand for 15 minutes until the gelatine has absorbed the liquid.

Heat the remaining poaching liquid over moderate heat, whisking steadily until it is hot. Stir in the sponged gelatine until it has completely dissolved, then add the wine vinegar, sherry and egg whites; whisk steadily until the mixture comes to the boil Draw the pan off the heat at once and leave the liquid to settle for 5 minutes. Bring to the boil again,

draw it off the heat and leave it to settle once more. The liquid should now look clear; if it does not, repeat the boiling process. Strain the clear liquid through a muslin-lined sieve and set it aside to cool. As it cools, it will start to solidify into a jelly.

Spoon a little of the cool jelly over the base of a serving dish and leave it to set. Set the salmon trout carefully down on top of the jelly. Garnish the fish with the prepared prawns and spoon over a little more of the jelly. When the jelly coating on the prawns has set, spoon more jelly over the whole salmon and leave it to set. Pour any jelly that is left into a shallow dish and put it in the refrigerator until it sets.

Serve the salmon trout garnished with sprigs of watercress and the remaining jelly, chopped into cubes.

Prawns with Mange-tout

SERVES: 4
PREPARATION: 20 minutes
COOKING: 10 minutes

2.5 cm/1 in piece of fresh
  root ginger
1 clove garlic
6 spring onions
1 green pepper
225 g/8 oz mange-tout
5 ml/1 teaspoon cornflour
45 ml/3 tablespoons soy sauce
60 ml/4 tablespoons dry sherry
60 ml/4 tablespoons water
15 ml/1 tablespoon oil
10 ml/2 teaspoons sesame oil
450 g/1 lb peeled cooked prawns
8 whole cooked prawns to garnish
  (optional)

Peel and finely chop the ginger and garlic. Chop or snip the spring onions. Halve the green

Pasta with Pesto (page 214) and Prawns with Mange-tout.

pepper, discard the core, seeds and pith, then cut the flesh across into thin strips. Top and tail the mange-tout. Mix the cornflour to a smooth paste with the soy sauce, sherry and water.

Heat both types of oil in a large frying pan or wok. Add the ginger, garlic, spring onions and pepper, and stir fry for 3 minutes. Add the mange-tout and continue to stir fry for a further 3 minutes. Pour in the cornflour liquid and stir over medium heat until the mixture boils and thickens. Reduce the heat, stir in the prawns and simmer for 2–3 minutes, until the sauce is thickened and the prawns are hot. Serve, garnished with whole cooked prawns, if liked.

■ Chinese egg noodles and plain boiled rice are both suitable accompaniments.

POULTRY & GAME

Galantine of Chicken

A galantine of chicken makes an impressive centrepiece for a summer party. Garnish it in the same way as Chicken Chaud-froid (page 165). This recipe uses a combination of veal and pork for the stuffing, but the veal can be omitted and the quantity of pork doubled if you prefer.

SERVES: 6
PREPARATION: 1½–2 hours
COOKING: 1½ hours
COOLING/PRESSING:
   3–4 hours

1 chicken, about 1.8 kg/4 lb
100 g/4 oz lean cooked ham
8 stoned olives
Stuffing
1 small onion
225 g/8 oz minced veal
225 g/8 oz lean minced pork
salt and black pepper
mixed herbs
grated rind and juice of 1 lemon
100 g/4 oz mushrooms (optional)
1 egg
stock to moisten

Bone the chicken (see page 322). Set the chicken liver aside for use in the galantine stuffing. Use the chicken carcass, the bones and the remaining giblets to make a well-flavoured stock (see page 310).

For the stuffing, peel and finely chop the onion and mince the chicken liver. Put the veal and pork in a bowl, mix in the chopped onion and chicken liver and season with salt and freshly ground pepper. Add mixed herbs to taste, then mix in the rind and lemon juice. If using the mushrooms, chop them finely and add them to the mixture. Beat the egg and stir it into the stuffing, with enough stock to give a firm, moist consistency.

Lay the boned chicken on a board, skin side down, and spread half the stuffing mixture over it, to within 1 cm/½ in of the edges. Top with the cooked ham, cut into 1–2 cm/½–¾ in wide strips, and the olives. Cover with the rest of the stuffing. Draw the long sides of the chicken over the stuffing and sew it together neatly with fine string.

Wrap the stuffed chicken in a double layer of muslin and tie the ends securely. Tie one or two pieces of string around the chicken parcel to keep it in shape. Put it in a large pan and cover with stock. Bring to the boil, cover, lower the heat and simmer for about 1½ hours.

When cooked, lift out the chicken parcel and press it between two plates. Place a heavy weight on top. Leave the galantine until nearly cold, then take off the string and muslin and continue pressing the chicken until it is cold.

Remove the sewing thread from the cold galantine before garnishing it with dill, lemon rind, and cucumber and tomato peel as for Chicken Chaud-froid.

Chicken Turnovers

These savoury pastries make a delicious snack or, served with a green salad, a filling lunch.

MAKES: 4
PREPARATION: 15 minutes
OVEN: 200°C/400°F/gas 6
         180°C/350°F/gas 4
COOKING: 30 minutes

1 carrot
2 spring onions
1 rasher lean bacon
15 ml/1 tablespoon finely
   chopped parsley
2 skinned boneless chicken breasts
   (total weight about 275 g/10 oz)
salt and black pepper
275 g/10 oz home-made Puff
   Pastry (page 374) or thawed
   frozen puff pastry
beaten egg or milk to glaze

Peel and coarsely grate the carrot; trim and chop or snip the spring onions. Remove the rind from the bacon. Combine the carrot, spring onions and the chopped parsley in a bowl. Dice the chicken breasts and the bacon rasher finely and add them to the bowl with salt and freshly ground black pepper to taste.

Roll out the puff pastry on a lightly floured surface and trim to a 30 cm/12 in square. Cut the pastry into four equal squares. Pile a quarter of the chicken filling mixture on to each piece of pastry, spreading it slightly to ensure an even fill. Lightly brush the edges of the pastry with water. Fold each square over diagonally to enclose the filling; crimp the edges.

Brush the chicken turnovers with a little beaten egg or milk and place on a wetted baking sheet. Cook in a preheated oven at 200°C/400°F/gas 6 for 15 minutes, then reduce the oven temperature to 180°C/350°F/gas 4 and cook for 15 minutes more. Serve hot or cold.

Chicken Turnovers.

Chicken and Ham Loaf

SERVES: 6–8
PREPARATION: 1 hour
OVEN: 190°C/375°F/gas 5
COOKING: about 1¼ hours

225 g/8 oz cooked chicken
2 onions
225 g/8 oz mushrooms
175 g/6 oz lean bacon
225 g/8 oz cooked ham
1 crusty sandwich loaf
25 g/1 oz butter
15 ml/1 tablespoon chopped parsley
salt and black pepper
225 g/8 oz sausagemeat
30 ml/2 tablespoons dry sherry
2.5 ml/½ teaspoon each chopped
    sage and thyme

Remove any skin from the chicken and dice the flesh. Chop the onions finely and slice the mushrooms thinly. Remove the rind from the bacon and dice both the bacon and the ham.

Cut a 1 cm/½ in slice off the top of the sandwich loaf (along its length, not from one end) and carefully pull out the soft bread inside. Leave a 1 cm/½ in inner lining of bread to preserve the shape. Crumb the soft bread in a food processor or on a grater; set aside 90 ml/6 tablespoons of the crumbs for the loaf filling. The remaining crumbs may be frozen for use in another recipe.

Melt the butter, cook the onions until they are soft, then add the mushrooms and cook for a further 2 minutes. Stir in the parsley and season with salt and freshly ground pepper.

Mix the sausagemeat, bacon, ham and the reserved bread-crumbs in a bowl. Stir in the sherry, chopped sage and thyme and season to taste. Press half the sausagemeat mixture well down on to the base of the loaf case; cover with half the onion and mushroom mixture. Arrange the chicken on top. Cover with the onion and a final layer of sausagemeat. Replace the 'lid' and wrap the loaf in foil. Bake in a preheated oven at 190°C/375°F/gas 5 for 1 hour.
■ Serve the loaf hot or cold, cut into thick slices.

Duck with Apricots

Bitter-sweet oranges are a classic flavouring and garnish with duck. This recipe provides the sharper tang of fresh apricots; canned apricots may be used instead but the flavour will not be so piquant.

SERVES: 4
PREPARATION: 10 minutes
OVEN: 160°C/325°F/gas 3
COOKING: 2½ hours

1 duck, about 2.27 kg/5 lb
salt and black pepper
75 g/3 oz butter
15 ml/1 tablespoon olive oil
300 ml/½ pt veal or chicken stock
150 ml/¼ pt medium dry
    white wine
450 g/1 lb fresh apricots
juice of ½ orange
15 ml/1 tablespoon apricot brandy
30 ml/2 tablespoons brandy

Wipe the prepared duck inside and out; rub the skin with salt and freshly ground pepper. Heat the butter and oil in a roasting tin and brown the duck on all sides. Lift the duck into a large flameproof casserole.

Add the stock and white wine to the roasting tin and bring to the boil, scraping to incorporate any sediment on the bottom of the tin. Pour the liquid over the duck. Cover the casserole with a lid or foil and cook in a preheated oven at 160°C/325°F/gas 3 for 1½–2 hours.

Wash and dry the apricots, cut them in half and remove the stones. Put half the apricots around the duck after it has been cooking for 45 minutes.

Lift the cooked duck on to a serving dish and keep it hot. Strain the cooking liquid into a bowl, retrieving the cooked apricots from the strainer. Skim off as much fat as possible from the cooking liquid, pour it back into the casserole and boil it briskly until it has reduced by a third.

Meanwhile purée the cooked apricots in a liquidiser or food processor; alternatively, press the apricots through a sieve into a bowl. Add the orange juice and the puréed apricots to the sauce to thicken.

Arrange the remaining fresh apricot halves around the duck. Warm the brandies, pour them over the duck and set alight.
■ Serve the duck at once, with roast potatoes and mange-tout or dwarf French beans. Offer the sauce separately.

Salmi of Grouse

The 'Glorious Twelfth' of August marks the beginning of the grouse season in Britain. The young birds are usually roasted whole and served one per person, on a slice of fried bread. Unless quite young and tender, these birds are better used in a salmi – a cooking method in which the birds are partially roasted before being finished in game stock and served in a wine sauce.

SERVES: 2–4
PREPARATION: 10 minutes
OVEN: 190°C/375°F/gas 5
COOKING: 1½ hours

2 oven-ready grouse (see method)
1 onion
salt and black pepper
100 g/4 oz mushrooms
250 ml/8 fl oz red wine
12 juniper berries
15 g/½ oz butter
15 ml/1 tablespoon plain flour
chopped parsley to garnish

Order the grouse trussed and barded (page 321) and ask the poulterer to include the giblets with the order. Put the grouse, breast down, in a greased roasting tin and cook in a preheated oven at 190°C/375°F/gas 5 for 15 minutes. Remove the grouse from the oven, cut off the barding fat around each bird and carve the breasts off neatly. Slice each breast piece in half and set aside. Peel and chop the onion.

Put the grouse carcasses and chopped onion in a pan, cover with cold water and bring to the boil. Reduce the heat and simmer for about 30 minutes. Strain the stock through a fine sieve into a jug, season with salt and pepper and set aside.

Wipe and trim the mushrooms and slice them thickly.

Put the grouse breasts in a wide shallow pan, add the mushrooms and sufficient stock to cover. Put a lid on the pan and simmer over low heat for about 30 minutes.

Meanwhile stir the wine into the remaining stock. Pour into a small pan; add the grouse giblets and the mashed livers. Crush the juniper berries lightly and add them to the pan. Bring the wine stock to the boil, reduce the heat and simmer for 10–15 minutes.

Lift the cooked grouse breasts from the pan and arrange the pieces on a heated serving dish. Keep them hot. Strain the wine stock into the pan juices, stirring to incorporate any sediment on the bottom of the pan. Soften the butter and mix to a paste with the flour, then add small pieces of this beurre manié to the simmering stock mixture, stirring vigorously or whisking continuously. Whisk in each piece of beurre manié before adding the next, then bring to the boil to thicken the sauce. Reduce the heat and simmer for a few minutes; taste and add salt and freshly ground pepper as required.

Pour the wine sauce over the grouse and sprinkle with finely chopped parsley
■ Traditionally, grouse is served with round Game Chips (page 347), fried breadcrumbs and/or Bread Sauce (page 356) and sprigs of watercress.

MEAT

Boeuf à la Mode en Gelée

Most classic recipes for cold jellied beef use expensive fillet, but topside, poached slowly to a near-jelly consistency, makes an excellent alternative. Calf's foot is the traditional ingredient for providing the required setting qualities, but pig's trotters can be used instead. Alternatively, gelatine can be used to set the stock.

SERVES: 6–8
PREPARATION: 30 minutes
OVEN: 150°C/300°F/gas 2
COOKING: 4½–5 hours

1.4 kg/3 lb topside or top
    rump of beef
100 g/4 oz pork fat (see method)
300 ml/½ pt dry red wine
2 cloves garlic
salt and black pepper
1 calf's foot, chopped in pieces
15–30 ml/1–2 tablespoons
    beef dripping
30 ml/2 tablespoons brandy
2 shallots
2 bay leaves
300 ml/½ pt beef stock or water
15 small onions
10 young carrots

If the butcher has not already done so, lard the beef with the pork fat: cut the pork fat into strips, narrow enough to go through the eye of a larding needle, and long enough to be threaded through the meat. Pull the fat strips through the meat and trim them off at each end. This larding technique is illustrated on page 329.

Put the meat in a deep bowl, pour over the red wine, cover and marinate* for about 4 hours in a cool place, turning the meat frequently.

Peel the garlic cloves, cut them into strips and push these into the meat with the point of a knife. Season to taste with salt and freshly ground pepper.

Bring a large pan of salted water to the boil and blanch* the calf's foot pieces for 10 minutes. Drain and set aside.

Melt half the dripping in a heavy-based deep pan or flame-proof dish over high heat. Drain the meat, reserving the marinade, and add it to the pan. Brown it all over to seal in the juices. Reduce the heat. Pour the brandy over the meat, let it warm through slightly, then set it alight. When the flames have died down, add the calf's foot pieces to the pan.

Peel and finely chop the shallots and add them, with the bay leaves, to the pan. Add the stock or water, with the reserved marinade. Bring the liquid to boiling point, cover the pan tightly with foil and add the lid. Cook in a preheated oven at 150°C/300°F/gas 2 for 3 hours.

Meanwhile, peel the onions, leaving them whole. Wash and scrape the carrots and split them in half lengthways. Heat the rest of the dripping in a small pan and lightly brown the vegetables. Using a slotted spoon, transfer the vegetables to the meat and continue cooking for a further 1–1½ hours.

Lift the meat on to a dish and set aside to cool. Remove the vegetables with a slotted spoon and place them in a bowl. Let the liquid cool, then strain it through a muslin-lined sieve into a bowl. Leave the liquid in the refrigerator overnight to set to a jelly. Cover the vegetables and the meat and refrigerate both of them overnight.

The next day, carefully scrape the surface fat from the jelly with a spoon dipped in hot water. Cut the meat into neat, thin slices and arrange in a deep serving dish with the carrots and onions. Melt the jelly in a saucepan over low heat, then pour it carefully over the meat and vegetables. Leave the dish in a cool place to allow the jelly to set again.

■ Serve the jellied beef with a selection of salads, such as a crisp green salad tossed in French Dressing (page 356), a tomato salad and a cold potato salad.

Braised Shoulder of Lamb

The boned lamb is rolled around a savoury apricot stuffing.

SERVES: 6
PREPARATION: 30 minutes
OVEN: 230°C/450°F/gas 8
        180°C/350°F/gas 4
COOKING: 2½ hours

1.8 kg/4 lb shoulder of lamb, boned
salt and black pepper
600 ml/1 pt lamb stock
2 large onions
6 carrots
6 celery sticks
6 turnips
Stuffing
1 onion
25 g/1 oz butter
100 g/4 oz no-need-to-presoak
    dried apricots
75 g/3 oz fresh white breadcrumbs
30 ml/2 tablespoons
    chopped parsley
10 ml/2 teaspoons finely
    chopped rosemary
45 ml/3 tablespoons milk

To make the stuffing, finely chop the onions. Melt the butter in a frying pan over moderate heat and cook the onions until they are soft and transparent. Chop up the apricots. Remove the pan from the heat and add the bread-crumbs, apricots, parsley, rosemary, and salt and pepper to taste. Stir in enough milk to bind the ingredients.

Sprinkle the cut surface of the shoulder of lamb with salt and freshly ground pepper. Spread the stuffing over the meat, roll it up and tie with string. Place the joint in a large, lightly greased flameproof casserole and roast in a preheated oven at 230°C/450°F/gas 8 for 15 minutes, uncovered. Pour in half the lamb stock and reduce the oven temperature to 180°C/350°F/gas 4. Cover the casserole and cook for a further 45 minutes.

Meanwhile, roughly chop the onions, then cut the carrots, celery and turnips into chunks. Arrange the vegetables around the joint and add the remaining stock. Cover and cook the casserole for a further 1¼ hours. Transfer the meat and vegetables to a serving dish. Keep hot.

Skim the fat from the pan juices and boil them until they are reduced by half. Serve the juices with the meat.

Pork Cooked in Milk

The Italians frequently pot-roast meat or chicken in milk. For this recipe, choose boned leg of pork or, more economically, blade or the fore-end of a hand. It can be served hot or cold.

SERVES: 6
PREPARATION: 10 minutes
COOKING: about 3 hours

900 g/2 lb boned pork, rolled
    (see method)
salt and black pepper
1 clove garlic
12 coriander seeds
2 onions
2 slices cooked ham
15 ml/1 tablespoon olive oil
1 rosemary sprig
600 ml/1 pt milk

Ask the butcher to bone the meat and to take the skin and part of the fat off the pork before rolling it. Wipe the meat with dampened absorbent kitchen paper and rub it all over with salt and freshly ground pepper. Peel the garlic and cut it lengthways into small strips. Make small incisions in the meat with the point of a knife and push in the garlic strips and coriander seeds.

Peel and finely chop the onions; dice the ham. Heat the oil in a heavy-based saucepan into which the meat will fit closely. Fry the onions, ham and rosemary sprig in the oil for a few minutes until they all begin to colour. Put in the meat and fry it until it has lightly browned all over. In a separate pan, bring the milk to boiling point, then pour it over the pork.

Cook the pork, uncovered, over low heat for about 1 hour. The milk should be kept barely at simmering point and will form a cobweb-like skin on the surface which will gradually turn pale golden brown. Break the milk skin and turn the meat over, scraping all the skin from the sides into the bottom of the pan.

Continue cooking the meat slowly for a further 2 hours, turning the joint every 20–30 minutes, or until the milk has reduced to a small amount of creamy thick sauce.

Lift the meat on to a serving dish and spoon the sauce over it. The pork should be perfectly tender and delicately flavoured.

■ Serve this pork dish hot or cold, with boiled potatoes and a selection of simple salads.

Liver with Dubonnet and Orange

Take care not to overcook the liver – when it is tender and still slightly pink it tastes delicious, especially when combined with the fruity, sweet-wine sauce.

SERVES: 6
PREPARATION: 15 minutes
COOKING: 10–15 minutes

450 g/1 lb lamb liver
plain flour for coating
salt and black pepper
1 clove garlic
2 small onions
15 ml/1 tablespoon olive oil
40 g/½ oz butter
Sauce
15 ml/1 tablespoon orange juice
120 ml/4 fl oz red Dubonnet
30 ml/2 tablespoons
    chopped parsley
coarsely grated rind of 1 orange
5 ml/1 teaspoon finely grated
    lemon rind

Rinse the liver, remove the skin and any tubes and dry it thoroughly. Cut the liver into slices 1 cm/½ in thick. Season the flour with salt and freshly ground black pepper, add the liver slices and toss until well coated. The easiest way to do this is in a stout polythene bag.

Peel and finely chop the garlic and onions. Heat the oil and butter in a large, heavy-based pan over a moderate heat and add the onions and garlic. Cover the pan and cook until the onions are soft and beginning to colour.

Liver with Dubonnet and Orange.

Push the onions to the side of the pan and add the liver slices in a single layer. Cook over low heat. As soon as the blood begins to run, turn the liver over and cook the other side for a slightly shorter time.

When the liver is crisp on the outside but still just pink inside, transfer it to a warmed serving dish. Cover with the onion, using a perforated spoon to remove it from the pan. Keep the dish hot.

To make the sauce, stir the orange juice and Dubonnet into the pan juices. Boil rapidly until the liquid has reduced by half. Remove the pan from the heat and stir in most of the chopped parsley, grated orange and lemon rind, reserving a little of these ingredients for the garnish.

Pour the sauce over the liver and sprinkle with the rest of the parsley and orange and lemon rind. Serve at once.

Lamb Kidneys in Sherry

SERVES: 4
PREPARATION: 20 minutes
COOKING: 15 minutes

10–12 lamb kidneys
salt and black pepper
1 onion
1 small clove garlic
45 ml/3 tablespoons olive oil
1 small bay leaf
30 ml/2 tablespoons plain flour
150 ml/¼ pt chicken stock
120 ml/4 fl oz dry sherry
30 ml/2 tablespoons chopped
    parsley, plus extra to garnish

Cut out the fat and outer membranes from the kidneys (page 334), cut them in half lengthways and snip out the cores with scissors. Cut each half into three or four slices and season lightly.

Peel and chop the onion and garlic. Heat the oil in a small frying pan over moderate heat, and fry the kidneys for about 5 minutes to brown them slightly, stirring to prevent them from overcooking. Use a perforated spoon to remove them from the pan. Add the onion, garlic and bay leaf. Cook, stirring often, for about 10 minutes, or until the onion is soft and transparent. Stir in the flour and mix thoroughly. Gradually stir in the stock and sherry, then cook, stirring all the time, until the mixture thickens and boils. Stir in the parsley, reduce the heat and simmer the mixture for 5 minutes, then take out the bay leaf.

Replace the lamb kidneys in the sauce and simmer gently for a further 3–5 minutes, or until the kidneys are cooked. Taste and adjust the seasoning, if necessary, then serve immediately, sprinkled with a little extra parsley.

■ Serve the kidneys on pieces of toast or on a bed of fluffy saffron-flavoured rice.

211

VEGETABLES & SALADS

Black Lentils with Tomatoes

Brown or green lentils can be used instead of the black (Puy) lentils, but red lentils are not suitable as they do not hold their shape when cooked.

SERVES: 4
PREPARATION: 40 minutes
COOKING: about 1 hour

225 g/8 oz black lentils
675 g/1½ lb tomatoes
1 large onion
30 ml/2 tablespoons olive oil
1–2 garlic cloves
50 g/2 oz pitted black olives
15 ml/1 tablespoon capers
grated rind of 1 lemon
2.5 ml/½ teaspoon caster sugar
5 ml/1 teaspoon, Dijon mustard
salt and black pepper
45 ml/3 tablespoons
    chopped parsley
30 ml/2 tablespoons chopped mint

Cook the black lentils in plenty of boiling water, without adding salt, for 40–45 minutes, until they are tender but still whole.

Meanwhile, skin the tomatoes (page 302), cut them in half, remove the seeds, then cut them into chunks. Halve and thinly slice the onion. Heat the olive oil in a large saucepan, add the onion and stir well. Crush the garlic into the pan and cook, stirring occasionally, for about 20 minutes, or until the onion is softened but not browned.

Slice the black olives and chop the capers, then stir them into the onion with the lemon rind, caster sugar and mustard. Add the tomatoes and seasoning to taste, mix well, remove from the heat and set aside until the lentils are cooked.

Drain the lentils. Return the tomato mixture to high heat and stir to heat it through quickly. Stir in the lentils, the chopped parsley and mint. Season to taste with salt and freshly ground pepper and serve at once.

Gratin of Braised Fennel

SERVES: 4
PREPARATION: 15 minutes
COOKING: about 1 hour

1 small onion
1 small carrot
4 fennel bulbs
juice of ½ lemon
50 g/2 oz butter
1 bay leaf
2 thyme sprigs
4 large sage leaves
salt and black pepper
150 ml/¼ pt dry white wine
150 ml/¼ pt chicken or
    vegetable stock
30 ml/2 tablespoons plain flour
50 g/2 oz Lancashire or
    Cheshire cheese
50 g/2 oz fresh white breadcrumbs

Finely chop the onion and carrot. Trim the fennel and cut each bulb in half lengthways. Remove any large pieces of thick core from the base of each piece, then place in a dish and sprinkle with the lemon juice. Cover and set the fennel aside.

Melt half the butter in a saucepan or flameproof casserole. Add the onion, carrot, bay leaf, thyme, sage, salt and pepper. Cook for 5 minutes, then add the fennel and turn the pieces in the pan to coat them lightly with some of the butter. Pour in the wine and stock, bring to the boil, then reduce the heat so that the liquid simmers and cover the pan tightly. Cook for about 45 minutes, or until the fennel is tender, turning the pieces of fennel after 20–30 minutes.

Meanwhile, mix the flour with the remaining butter to form a smooth paste (beurre manié). Grate the cheese and mix it with the breadcrumbs.

Transfer the fennel to a gratin dish using a perforated spoon. Gradually whisk pieces of the butter and flour paste into the cooking liquid, keeping it just simmering. Bring the sauce to the boil, then reduce the heat again and simmer for 2 minutes. Taste for seasoning before pouring the sauce over the fennel. Sprinkle with the breadcrumb and cheese mixture and brown the topping under a hot grill.

■ The gratin is an excellent side dish for grilled poultry or meat. Simple braised fennel is transformed into a tasty dish for lunch or supper with the addition of the crunchy topping.

Courgettes in Hollandaise Sauce.

Courgettes in Hollandaise Sauce

The delicate flavour of young courgettes is best preserved when they are served with melted butter or a simple sauce.

SERVES: 6
PREPARATION: 30 minutes
OVEN: 180°C/350°F/gas 4
COOKING: 30 minutes

450 g/1 lb large courgettes
25 g/1 oz butter
salt and black pepper
juice of ½ lemon
45 ml/3 tablespoons grated
    Parmesan cheese
300 ml/½ pt Hollandaise Sauce
    (page 355)

Trim the courgettes and blanch* them in a pan of boiling water for 1–2 minutes. Drain, wipe dry and cut the courgettes in half lengthway. With a pointed teaspoon, carefully scoop out a shallow groove in each courgette half, removing the seeds.

Use a little of the butter to grease a large, shallow flameproof dish. Arrange the courgettes, cut-side up, in the dish and sprinkle with salt, freshly ground black pepper and the lemon juice. Cut the rest of the butter into small pieces, dot it all over the courgettes and cover the dish tightly. Bake the vegetables in a preheated oven at 180°C/350°F/gas 4 for 25 minutes.

Stir 30 ml/2 tablespoons of the grated Parmesan cheese into the prepared Hollandaise sauce. Spoon the sauce into the grooves in the cooked courgettes, and sprinkle with the rest of the Parmesan. Put the dish under a hot grill until the cheese topping is lightly browned.

■ Serve the courgettes immediately with roast chicken or lean roast meat.

Carrots Paysanne

Sweet young carrots, braised with bacon and onion, make a good accompaniment to grilled meat.

SERVES: 4–6
PREPARATION: 15 minutes
COOKING: 30 minutes

450 g/1 lb small carrots
salt
1 large onion
2 rashers lean bacon
25 g/1 oz butter
150–300 ml/¼–½ pt chicken stock
    or water
5 ml/1 teaspoon caster sugar
60 ml/4 tablespoons double cream
finely chopped parsley to garnish

Trim and scrape the carrots. Blanch* them for 5 minutes in a pan of salted boiling water, then drain in a colander.

Peel and cut the onion into thin slices. Cut off the rinds and dice the bacon. Melt the butter in a wide shallow pan over low heat, and cook the onion and bacon until beginning to colour.

Add the carrot to the bacon and onion, and pour over enough stock or water to barely cover the vegetables. Cover the pan and simmer until the carrots are tender. Using a perforated spoon, transfer the carrots to a heated serving dish and keep them hot.

Boil the liquid over high heat until it has reduced to a few tablespoons. Add the sugar, cream, and salt to taste. Simmer the liquid, uncovered, until the sauce has thickened slightly.

Pour the cream sauce over the carrots and sprinkle with parsley.

Leeks in Yogurt Sauce

The first young leeks appear on market stalls towards the end of the month. This dish can be served cold with chicken or fish.

SERVES: 4–6
PREPARATION: 15 minutes
COOKING: 30 minutes

8 slender leeks
2 shallots
juice of 1 large lemon
2.5 ml/½ teaspoon salt
12 black peppercorns
12 fennel seeds
6 coriander seeds
6 sprigs parsley
450 ml/¾ pt water
chopped parsley to garnish
Sauce
250 ml/8 fl oz plain yogurt
3 egg yolks
10 ml/2 teaspoons lemon juice
salt and black pepper
Dijon mustard

Trim the leeks, slit them halfway down from the top and wash them thoroughly in cold running

Leeks in Yogurt Sauce.

water. Drain them well. Peel the shallots and slice them.

Mix the lemon juice, spices, herbs and shallots in a pan. Add the water, bring to the boil and cook for 10 minutes.

Put the leeks in a frying pan wide enough to take them in one layer; strain the hot lemon juice mixture over them. Cover the pan with a lid and simmer the leeks gently for 10–15 minutes, until soft. Leave them to cool in the cooking liquid.

For the sauce, beat the yogurt, egg yolks and lemon juice together in a heatproof bowl, then place it over a pan of gently simmering water. Cook the sauce, stirring frequently for about 15 minutes or until it has thickened. Season with salt and freshly ground pepper, stir in mustard to taste, and set aside.

Before serving, drain the leeks thoroughly and cut each into two or three diagonal pieces. Arrange them in a serving dish, spoon the yogurt sauce over the leeks and sprinkle with parsley.

Salade Niçoise

There are numerous versions of this classic French salad, but all have in common the basic ingredients of lettuce, eggs, anchovy fillets, black olives and tomatoes. Serve the salad as a starter, a light summer lunch dish or the centrepiece for a picnic.

SERVES: 6
PREPARATION: 25 minutes

2 eggs
225 g/8 oz French beans
350 g/12 oz firm tomatoes
½ onion
1 lettuce heart
½ green pepper
120 ml/4 fl oz garlic-flavoured
    French Dressing (page 356)
99 g/3½ oz can tuna
50 g/2 oz can anchovy fillets
50 g/2 oz small black olives

Hard boil the eggs for 8–10 minutes, then plunge them into cold water. Shell and quarter the eggs, and set them aside to cool. Top and tail the beans. Bring a saucepan of lightly salted water to the boil, add the beans and cook for 5–8 minutes; drain, refresh under cold water and drain again. Set aside to cool.

Skin the tomatoes (page 302) and cut them into quarters. Peel the onion; slice it thinly into rings. Wash and dry the lettuce heart. Core, seed and thinly slice the pepper half.

Put half the French dressing in a shallow bowl and toss the shredded lettuce and beans in it. Drain and flake the tuna; drain the anchovies. Arrange the tuna,

anchovy fillets, olives, green pepper and onion rings on top of the lettuce and beans. Surround with the quartered tomatoes and hard-boiled eggs. Sprinkle over the remaining dressing and serve the salad immediately.

Lettuce and Celery Salad

Rich meat dishes, especially those with fruit stuffings, are often better accompanied by a side salad than by a vegetable dish.

SERVES: 4–6
PREPARATION: 10 minutes

4 lettuce hearts
4 celery sticks
celery leaves to garnish
Dressing
5 ml/1 teaspoon Dijon mustard
2.5 ml/½ teaspoon salt
5 ml/1 teaspoon caster sugar
150 ml/¼ pt single cream
150 ml/¼ pt olive oil
45 ml/3 tablespoons
    tarragon vinegar

Wash and dry the lettuce leaves, tear them into large pieces and put them in a salad bowl. Chop the celery sticks coarsely and add them to the bowl.

To make the dressing, mix the mustard, salt and sugar in a bowl; stir in the cream. Whisk in the olive oil, drop by drop, as for mayonnaise. When all the oil is absorbed, gradually beat in the vinegar until the dressing has the consistency of thick cream. Pour the dressing over the celery and lettuce, toss and serve garnished with a few celery leaves.

RICE & PASTA

Arancini Siciliani

'Sicilian oranges' is the literal translation of this lunch or supper dish. The 'oranges' are crisp rice balls with a savoury filling of cheese and ham.

MAKES: 18
PREPARATION: 45 minutes
COOKING: 30 minutes

225 g/8 oz Arborio or risotto rice
600 ml/1 pt water
salt and black pepper
50 g/2 oz grated Parmesan cheese
2 small eggs
50 g/2 oz mozzarella cheese
50 g/2 oz cooked ham, chicken
   or salami
50 g/2 oz dry white breadcrumbs
oil for deep frying
mint or basil leaves to garnish

Place the rice in a saucepan and pour in the water. Add salt and pepper, then bring to the boil. Stir the rice once, cover the pan tightly and reduce the heat to the minimum setting. Cook for 20 minutes, then leave the rice to stand for 10 minutes, without removing the lid.

Put the rice in a bowl and stir in the Parmesan cheese. Beat the eggs lightly and add them to the rice with a little salt and freshly ground pepper. Stir the ingredients thoroughly, then set the mixture aside until cold.

Cut the mozzarella and the cooked meat into 1 cm/¾ in cubes. Take 15ml/1 tablespoon of the cold rice and mould it in the well-floured palm of your hand; put a cube of cheese and a cube of meat into the hollow, top with a little more rice and shape the filled rice into a ball about 5 cm/ 2 in wide. Shape the remaining rice, cheese and meat to make 18 balls. When all the balls have been shaped, coat them thickly with breadcrumbs.

Heat the oil for deep frying to 190°C/375°F or until a cube of day-old bread browns in 1 minute. Fry the rice balls, two or three at a time, until they are golden brown. Drain on crumpled absorbent kitchen paper and keep hot.

Just before serving, garnish each 'orange' with a herb leaf.

■ A Tomato Sauce (page 354) may be served with the Arancini Siciliani, if liked.

Arancini Siciliani.

Pesto

This intensely flavoured paste should be made while fresh basil is in plentiful supply.

MAKES: about 300 ml/½ pt
   (4–6 servings)
PREPARATION: 10 minutes

40 g/1½ oz fresh basil sprigs (tender
   sprig ends and leaves only)
50 g/2 oz pine kernels
2 cloves garlic
50 g/2 oz Parmesan cheese
150 ml/¼ pt olive oil
salt and black pepper

Place the fresh basil leaves in a food processor. Add the pine kernels and garlic. Cut the Parmesan cheese into small pieces and add them to the mixture, then process the mixture until it is coarsely ground. Gradually add the olive oil, continuing to process the mixture until it forms a coarse paste. Season to taste with salt and pepper.

Pesto can also be made in a liquidiser, but it must be processed in small batches and the Parmesan must be grated first.

The paste can be made in small quantities by hand by gradually pounding the ingredients to a paste in a mortar with a pestle. When making pesto by hand, start by pounding the basil sprigs and garlic, until they are well reduced and combined, and gradually pound in the remaining ingredients.

■ Pesto is traditionally served with pasta, but it is also good with baked potatoes, boiled barley or green lentils.

Pasta with Turkey and Passata

SERVES: 4
PREPARATION: 15 minutes
COOKING: 30 minutes

1 onion
1 leek
½ small green pepper
2 cloves garlic
50 g/2 oz mushrooms
350 g/12 oz skinned boneless
   turkey breast
30 ml/2 tablespoons olive oil
500 g/18 oz carton passata
salt and black pepper
225 g/8 oz penne or rigatoni pasta
6 sprigs basil

Peel and chop the onion. Trim the leek, slice it thinly into a colander and wash thoroughly. Drain well. Remove the core and seeds from the pepper and chop the flesh. Peel and crush the garlic; trim and chop the mushrooms. Cut the turkey breast into thin strips.

Heat the olive oil in a large saucepan. Add the onion, garlic, leek, pepper and mushrooms and cook over low heat for 5 minutes, stirring occasionally. Add the turkey, raise the heat and cook the meat for 3–5 minutes until it is firm and white.

Stir in the passata, with salt and pepper to taste. Bring to the boil, stirring occasionally, then cover and simmer over low heat for 20 minutes.

Cook the pasta in boiling salted water until al dente*. Dried pasta will take 10–12 minutes; fresh pasta will take less time and will be ready when it rises to the surface of the water. Drain well and toss with the sauce in a bowl. Remove any coarse stalks from the basil, shred or tear the leaves and sprinkle them over the pasta. Serve at once.

■ Offer a bowl of freshly grated Parmesan cheese with the pasta and serve a simple green salad as an accompaniment.

Spaghetti with Tuna Sauce

This is a simple and economical everyday dish which can be varied by adding sliced button mushrooms or selecting another type of pasta from the wide selection available.

SERVES: 4
PREPARATION: 10 minutes
COOKING: about 30 minutes

1 clove garlic
1 onion
198 g/7 oz can tuna in oil
25 g/1 oz plain flour
45 ml/3 tablespoons dry white
*   wine or vermouth*
300 ml/½ pt milk
salt and black pepper
350 g/12 oz spaghetti
30 ml/2 tablespoons finely chopped
*   parsley to garnish*

Peel and finely chop the garlic and onion. Heat the oil from the can of tuna in a pan and fry the onion and garlic for 12 minutes. Stir in the flour, then stir in the wine or vermouth and milk. Bring to the boil, stirring, then simmer the sauce for 3 minutes.

Flake the tuna and add it to the sauce. Season with salt and freshly ground black pepper. Set aside over the lowest heat setting, cover the pan and keep the sauce hot without allowing it to cook further.

Bring a large pan of lightly salted water to the boil, add the spaghetti, gradually lowering it into the water as it softens, and bring the water back to the boil. Stir the pasta once to make sure that it does not stick to the bottom of the saucepan, then reduce the heat slightly if necessary. Cook for 7–12 minutes or until the spaghetti is just tender, but resistant to the bite (al dente*). Stir occasionally.

When the spaghetti is ready, drain it thoroughly in a colander, tip it into a serving dish or divide it between individual plates or pasta bowls. Pour over the tuna sauce, sprinkle with the chopped parsley and serve at once.

■ Crusty bread and a simple green salad are ideal accompaniments for the pasta. Offer a bowl of freshly grated Parmesan cheese so that it can be sprinkled over the pasta to taste.

Pasta with Eggs and Anchovies

SERVES: 4
PREPARATION: 20 minutes
COOKING: about 25 minutes

350 g/12 oz tagliatelle verdi or
*   spinach-flavoured pasta shapes*
salt and black pepper
40 g/1½ oz butter
40 g/1½ oz plain flour
600 ml/1 pt milk
45 ml/3 tablespoons snipped chives
30 ml/2 tablespoons
*   chopped parsley*
8 eggs
50 g/2 oz can anchovies
75 g/3 oz mozzarella cheese
60 ml/4 tablespoons grated
*   Parmesan cheese*

Cook the pasta in boiling water for about 12 minutes, or until tender but not soft.

Melt the butter and stir in the flour. Gradually stir in the milk and bring to the boil, still stirring continuously. Add the chives, parsley and seasoning to taste to the sauce and cover its surface with cling film. Boil the eggs for 10 minutes, then drain them and cover them with cold water. Quickly shell the eggs and cut them in half.

Drain the cooked pasta and arrange it on a gratin dish. Top with the eggs. Drain and chop up the anchovies, then sprinkle them over the eggs. Coat with the sauce. Chop the mozzarella, mix it with the Parmesan cheese, then sprinkle the mixture over the pasta and sauce and grill until golden brown.

PUDDINGS & DESSERTS

Victoria Plums in Wine

The slightly acid flavour of these home-grown plums makes them suitable for sweet compôtes and puddings. The flavour is brought out to the full by poaching them in a syrupy wine and serving them while still warm.

SERVES: 6
PREPARATION: 5 minutes
COOKING: 30 minutes

75 g/3 oz caster sugar
300 ml/½ pt water
300 ml/½ pt tawny port, medium
*   dry sherry or Madeira wine*
675–900 g/1½–2 lb firm Victoria
*   plums*
30 ml/2 tablespoons flaked almonds

Combine the sugar and the water in a large shallow pan. Cook over moderate heat, stirring until all the sugar has dissolved. Simmer for 10 minutes. Stir in the wine and bring the syrup to simmering point again.

Remove the stalks from the plums, wash and dry them. Add the plums, one at a time, to the simmering syrup. Cover the pan with a lid and remove from the heat. Leave the plums in the syrup for 10 minutes.

Lift out the plums with a slotted spoon and put them in a serving dish. Cover the dish and keep hot. Boil the syrup over high heat until it has reduced by about one-third and thickened slightly. Pour it over the plums.

Toast the flaked almonds in a grill pan under moderate heat for about 5 minutes until golden. Scatter the toasted almonds over the plums and serve at once, with a jug of single cream.

Victoria Plums in Wine.

Greengages with Apricot Purée

The small, round, golden-yellow greengages make a brief appearance in the latter half of August. They are excellent as dessert fruits, and for puddings.

SERVES: 4
PREPARATION: 25 minutes
OVEN: 180°C/350°F/gas 4
COOKING: 30 minutes

225 g/8 oz fresh or 100 g/4 oz
    dried apricots
25 g/1 oz caster sugar
2.5 ml/½ teaspoon grated
    lemon rind
450 g/1 lb greengages
4 slices white bread
40–50 g/1½–2 oz butter
25–50 g/1–2 oz vanilla sugar* or
    golden granulated sugar

Make the apricot purée first: wash and dry the apricots, cut them in half and remove the stones. If using dried apricots, you may need to soak them overnight in cold water.

Put the apricots in a saucepan, cover with fresh cold water and cook, uncovered, over moderate heat until tender. Drain thoroughly. Purée the apricots in a liquidiser or food processor, or rub through a coarse sieve into a bowl; flavour the purée with the sugar and lemon rind.

Wash and dry the greengages, and cut them in half. Remove the stones. Cut the crusts from the bread and spread the slices with half the butter. Lay the slices, buttered side up, in a greased ovenproof dish. Arrange the greengages on top with a tiny knob of butter in each half; sprinkle with the vanilla sugar or golden granulated sugar.

Bake in a preheated oven at 180°C/350°F/gas 4 for about 30 minutes, or until the greengages are tender. Meanwhile warm the apricot purée in a small pan.
■ Serve the greengage pudding warm, and offer the warmed purée in a separate dish.

Peaches with Soured Cream

Golden peaches make refreshing summer sweets – on their own, poached in white wine or cooked in a pastry case. Here, poached peaches are served cold with a soured cream topping.

SERVES: 6
PREPARATION: 35 minutes
CHILLING: 30 minutes

225 g/8 oz vanilla sugar*
300 ml/½ pt water
6 large peaches
caster sugar
300 ml/½ pt soured cream
25 g/1 oz demerara sugar or
    25 g/1 oz toasted flaked
    almonds to decorate

Combine the vanilla sugar and water in a large shallow pan. Cook over moderate heat, stirring until all the vanilla sugar has dissolved. Simmer this syrup for 5 minutes.

Wash the peaches, dry them thoroughly, then poach* them lightly in the syrup for 5–10 minutes, depending on the ripeness of the fruit.

Using a perforated spoon, lift the peaches from the syrup, leave to cool slightly, then peel off the skins and cut the peaches in half. Remove the stones. Slice the peaches into a serving bowl, one layer at a time, sprinkling each layer with a little caster sugar. Strain the syrup and set aside for use in another recipe.

Cover the top of the peaches with a thick layer of soured cream and chill for 30 minutes. Just before serving, decorate the top by sprinkling over demerara sugar or toasted flaked almonds.

Melon Ice Cream

The Italians introduced water ices or sorbets to Britain during the reign of Charles I, at least two centuries before cream ices became known. Today, virtually any sweetened fruit juice can be made into ice cream with egg custard and cream.

SERVES: 4
PREPARATION: 30–40 minutes
CHILLING: 30 minutes
FREEZING: 12 hours

1 large Ogen melon
4 egg yolks
100 g/4 oz caster sugar
75 ml/5 tablespoons ginger wine
30 ml/2 tablespoons lemon juice
450 ml/¾ pt double cream

Turn the freezer to its coldest setting 1 hour before preparing the ice cream.

Slice about 4 cm/1½ in off the top of the melon; remove the seeds and fibres with a small spoon. Scoop all the melon flesh

into a bowl, taking care not to pierce the shell (which may be wrapped, chilled and used for serving the ice cream, if liked). Mash the melon with a potato masher until it is reduced to a pulp. Alternatively, the melon and sugar can be puréed in a food processor or liquidiser.

Place the egg yolks and sugar in a heatproof bowl, then stand the bowl over a saucepan of hot, not boiling, water and beat the yolks and sugar until pale and creamy. Add them to the melon pulp, stirring well.

Stir in the ginger wine and lemon juice. In a separate bowl, whip the double cream lightly. Fold it into the melon and egg

Melon Ice Cream.

custard mixture, cover the bowl and chill for 30 minutes.

Spoon the melon cream into a freezing container, cover and freeze for 3 hours or until it is half frozen. Beat the ice cream or process it in a food processor until smooth. Return it to the freezer and repeat the process once or twice. Then leave the ice cream to freeze completely for several hours or overnight.

Allow the ice cream to soften in the refrigerator for about 30 minutes before scooping it out of the container. Pile it into glasses or the chilled melon shell and serve at once.

Brown-bread Ice Cream

SERVES: 6–8
PREPARATION: 20 minutes
FREEZING: 12 hours

300 ml/½ pt double cream
150 ml/¼ pt single cream
25 g/1 oz icing sugar
2.5 ml/½ teaspoon natural
*   vanilla essence*
75 g/3 oz crustless brown bread
75 g/3 oz soft dark brown sugar

Mix the double and single cream with the icing sugar and vanilla essence until the cream stands in soft peaks. Spoon the cream into a freezer container, cover and freeze. When the cream is icy around the edges, stir the sides into the middle to break up any ice crystals. Repeat this process twice during freezing.

Reduce the brown bread to fine crumbs and mix with the brown sugar in a large heavy-bottomed pan. Cook, stirring continuously, until the bread is golden and the sugar caramelises. Alternatively, the mixture may be toasted under a moderately hot grill, turning it frequently. Leave to cool, then break up the crumbs with a fork.

When the cream is nearly frozen, turn it into a chilled bowl, beat with an egg whisk and stir in the crumbs. Alternatively, the cream may be processed in a food processor until it is smooth before stirring in the crumbs. Return the mixture to the container and freeze for several hours or overnight until firm.

Granita al Caffé

Strong, bitter black coffee, preferably a continental roast, should be used for this Italian water ice. It can be served with sweetened whipped cream.

SERVES: 4
PREPARATION: 10 minutes
CHILLING: 3–4 hours

75 ml/5 tablespoons caster sugar
150 ml/¼ pt water
450 ml/¾ pt strong black coffee
150 ml/¼ pt whipping cream
10 ml/2 teaspoons icing sugar

Turn the freezer to its coldest setting 1 hour before starting to make the granita. Combine the caster sugar and water in a saucepan. Place over moderate heat, stirring until the sugar has completely dissolved. Bring this syrup to the boil and boil steadily for 5 minutes. Remove from the heat and leave the syrup to cool.

Strain the coffee into the cold syrup, and pour the mixture into ice cube trays. For the best texture, the dividers should be left in the trays so that the ice will set in cubes. Put the trays into the freezer for at least 3 hours. Stir the ice occasionally with a fork or with a skewer to break up the frozen crystals around the edges of the trays.

Turn the frozen cubes into a bowl and crush them lightly with a pestle or break them up with a fork. Spoon the coffee granita into individual glasses and serve at once with a separate bowl of whipped cream, sweetened with the icing sugar.

Danish Layer Cake

There are numerous versions of Danish layer cake, from a plain jam sandwich to an impressive eight-layer concoction of wafer-thin sponge cakes with alternate layers of thick cream and fruit.

SERVES: 6
PREPARATION: 45 minutes
OVEN: 180°C/350°F/gas 4
COOKING: 35 minutes
CHILLING: about 1¼ hours

4 eggs
grated rind and juice of ½ lemon
150 g/5 oz icing sugar
75 g/3 oz plain flour
25 g/1 oz cornflour
2.5 ml/½ teaspoon baking powder
Filling
15 ml/3 teaspoons gelatine
90 ml/6 tablespoons water
600 ml/1 pt double cream
20 ml/4 teaspoons vanilla sugar*
*   or caster sugar*
4 slices fresh or drained
*   canned pineapple*
75 g/3 oz dark bitter chocolate

Line and grease a 20 cm/8 in loose-bottomed round cake tin. Separate the eggs and put the yolks in a large bowl, with the lemon rind and juice. Put the egg whites to one side. Sift the icing sugar into the yolks and beat until they are fluffy and pale.

Whisk the egg whites in a separate bowl until they are stiff but not dry, then fold them carefully into the yolk mixture. Sift the plain flour, the cornflour and the baking powder together and fold them carefully into the egg mixture.

Spoon the cake mixture into the lined tin, smoothing it level around the sides. Bake in a preheated oven at 180°C/350°F/gas 4 for 35 minutes or until the sponge is golden and well risen and has shrunk away from the sides of the tin.

Loosen the edges of the cooked sponge with a sharp knife and turn the cake out on to a wire rack to cool. When it is completely cold, cut the cake into three thin rounds.

Make the filling. Sprinkle the gelatine over the water in a small heatproof basin. Do not stir. Leave to stand for 15 minutes, until the gelatine has absorbed the water. Set the basin over a pan of simmering water and stir until the gelatine has dissolved completely. Leave the gelatine to cool slightly. Whip two-thirds of the cream in a bowl until it stands in soft peaks. Fold a little of the cream into the cooled gelatine, then add to the rest of the whipped cream and sweeten with the vanilla sugar or caster sugar. Peel and trim the pineapple slices (or drain thoroughly if using canned pineapple); set one slice aside and chop up the other three finely. Grate the dark chocolate and fold it into the whipped cream with the chopped pineapple. Chill this filling until lightly set.

Assemble the layer cake about 2 hours before serving. Divide the filling between the sponge layers, spreading it out evenly; sandwich the layers together.

Whip the remaining cream and place it in a piping bag fitted with a star nozzle. Pipe the whipped cream around the rim and down the sides of the cake. Decorate the top of the cake with the reserved pineapple slice, cut into small chunks.

Chill the cake for about 1 hour and serve it cut into wedges.

Danish Layer Cake.

Planning a Picnic

Whether it is an elegant occasion or a simple day out with the children, a picnic should be fun. Eating outdoors is not an occasion for worrying about diet and decorum – it is an excuse to indulge in all your favourite 'al fresco' foods, even if the combinations are slightly off-beat. When planning a formal picnic, such as a dinner party out of doors, choose flamboyant food on which to feast the eyes as well as the palate but make sure the food is easy to eat and serve too. As with all food preparation, there are a few important guidelines for hygiene, safety and success.

Packing and Transporting Food

Containers should prevent the food from being crushed, keep it fresh and enable it to remain presentable until it is served. Liquids must be placed in containers with tight-fitting lids, including items like fruit salads or savoury dishes with liquid dressings. In addition, the packing should be neither too fragile nor too heavy.

Cling film, foil and plastic bags are all invaluable, especially for food which is to be packed in a chiller box, but such wrappings are not suitable for pastries and other foods which can be crushed easily. Delicate pastries are best packed in a rigid container and surrounded by layers of crumpled absorbent kitchen paper to prevent them sliding about.

The right choice of cooking container will often solve any packing problem. For example, a pâté cooked in a terrine or a soufflé dish can simply be wrapped in foil or sealed in a plastic bag; a tart, flan or quiche baked in an ovenproof glass or china dish is ready to go and easier to carry than one baked in a tin with a loose bottom.

Screw-top jars are useful for salad dressings and sauces but must be packed with care – a clean tea-towel wrapped around glassware helps to prevent breakages and provides a useful cloth for wiping hands or utensils at the end of the picnic.

Keeping Cool

It is important to keep perishable foods cool. Chiller bags may not be as attractive as baskets, but they are more practical in terms of food safety. Cooked poultry, fish or meat, mayonnaise, cheese, butter and creamy items are just some examples of foods that must be kept cool. Remember to replace such perishable foods in the chiller bag once individual portions have been removed. Avoid leaving the food out to become warm and attract flies.

Chiller bags designed for bottles are useful for keeping drinks cold, as are vacuum flasks.

Essential Accessories

Simple packed lunches require no more than a roll of absorbent kitchen paper by way of serving equipment. Cornish pasties, filled bread rolls, home-baked individual plain cakes and fresh fruit (bananas, apples, peaches and pears) are just a few examples of familiar foods that taste terrific outdoors and are easy to eat: ideal for an impromptu outdoor meal. Even if not quite so basic, the aim on the majority of family picnics is to keep crockery and utensils, and the clearing up, to a minimum. Most supermarkets stock a choice of paper plates, napkins and disposable plastic cutlery in cheerful designs. If you picnic regularly, it makes sense to invest in a set of rigid plastic plates. These are easier to hold than paper plates and are quite pleasant to eat off, but they are resilient at the same time.

Essentials that tend to be forgotten on picnics include bottle openers and corkscrews; glasses and plastic cups; cutlery, spare plates for desserts; a roll of absorbent kitchen paper for mopping up spills, a few large plastic bags for soiled crockery and a refuse bag for any rubbish.

Children's Picnic Boxes or Bags

A picnic can provide an opportunity to meet up with friends and their families. Making up individual 'tuck bag' containers for youngsters provides a fun treat. The food itself can be quite ordinary – favourite sandwiches, a small pie, some fruit – with a treat, like a chocolate biscuit bar and crisps, but the packaging makes it special. Sandwiches can be cut into letter shapes or fancy shapes using cutters and cakes or biscuits can be decorated with the children's names. Buy individual carrier bags and attach name labels. Small children will feel very privileged with their own particular bags while adults will be able to relax over their food with their friends. Just make sure that all the tuck bags contain the same goodies – or there may be squabbles!

Formal Picnics

There are all sorts of opportunities for formal picnics, from grand occasions, such as a visit to the opera at Glyndebourne, boating trips or romantic evenings not too far from home.

Plan the menu with the same care as you would plan a dinner party. Fresh fruit starters, such as melon with Parma ham, are ideal as they can be packed and transported successfully, then served and eaten easily.

A hamper packed with cold Pizza and Cream Cheese and Bacon Tart (both page 185).

Galantine of Chicken (page 208), Raised Veal and Bacon Pie (page 370) or Chicken Chaudfroid (page 165) are all classic choices for picnics. Remember to pack a strong, sharp serrated knife for cutting a pie or slicing a galantine, and take a board for serving instead of a platter (if you do not have a presentable one, cover a kitchen board with foil).

Taking creamy dressed salads on a picnic can be a mistake as they do not always look as appetising after a long journey as when first tossed. It is better to pack a good mixture of prepared mixed leaves with a separate container of excellent oil and vinegar dressing, then combine them in a large bowl just before they are eaten. Similarly, tiny new potatoes cooked in their skins are an excellent option, with a dressing to pour over as soon as the picnic is unpacked.

Fresh fruit makes a practical dessert (select varieties that are easy to eat rather than messy fruit which is best tackled at a table). A moulded dessert, such as Summer Pudding (page 197), can be turned out just before it is eaten. Tarts and flans are ideal as long as the filling is not too runny or, in the case of flans, below the rim of the dish to allow for easy packing.

Drinks
For family picnics, bottles or cans of fizzy drinks, fruit juice and mineral water are ideal. Vacuum flasks of boiling water can be used to make instant coffee or tea (by using tea bags); sachets of herb and fruit tea can also be used in this way. Tea or coffee can be made beforehand and taken in a vacuum flask, but both tend to taste rather 'stewed'.

Wines are often served at formal picnics and sparkling wine or champagne completes a special picnic menu. Although aperitifs are served on some occasions, a rosé or sparkling wine is usually quite sufficient.

It is essential to include plenty of alcohol-free refreshments for any drivers and others who may not wish to drink wine. Sparkling mineral water, tonic water, fruit juice, or mineral waters flavoured with herbs and fruit are the usual alternatives.

Ricotta and Smoked Salmon Tart

Serve a large tart as the main picnic course or offer small tartlets for a starter.

SERVES: 6
PREPARATION: 15 minutes
OVEN: 200°C/400°F/gas 6
COOKING: about 30 minutes

175 g/6 oz Shortcrust Pastry
    (page 365)
225 g/8 oz ricotta cheese
salt and black pepper
2 eggs
100 g/4 oz smoked salmon
10 ml/2 teaspoons grated
    lemon rind
15 ml/1 tablespoon finely
    chopped parsley
50 g/2 oz Gruyère cheese
Garnish
watercress
black olives

Roll out the pastry on a lightly floured surface. Line a greased 20 cm/8 in loose-bottomed flan tin or dish, or 18 individual tartlet moulds (or patty tins) with the pastry. Prick the pastry, then chill it for 30 minutes. Line the pastry case with greaseproof paper and sprinkle with baking beans. Bake the flan case blind in a preheated oven at 200°C/400°F/gas 6 for 15 minutes.

If making individual tartlets, prick and chill them, then bake them empty for 5 minutes.

Place the ricotta cheese in a bowl, stir until smooth, and season to taste with salt and freshly ground pepper. Beat the eggs lightly and gradually stir them into the ricotta cheese. Chop the smoked salmon and add to the cheese, with the grated lemon rind and parsley. Spoon the mixture into the flan or individual tart cases and smooth level with the edge. Using a cheese slicer or a very sharp knife, cut the Gruyère cheese into thin slivers; lay them on top of the filling.

Bake the flan or tartlets in a preheated oven at 200°C/400°F/gas 6 for 12–15 minutes or until the filling is well risen and golden brown.

Serve hot or cold, garnished with sprigs of watercress and whole black olives.

■ Leave the cooked tart to cool, then wrap it completely in foil. Pack the watercress and olives separately. The tartlets are best packed in a rigid container. The garnish may be omitted for an informal picnic.

Melon and Ham Gondolas

Sweet ripe melon combines perfectly with Italian raw smoked ham, also known as prosciutto, or with the Westphalian variety of smoked ham from Germany.

SERVES: 6
CHILLING: at least 2 hours
PREPARATION: 12 minutes

½ large ripe honeydew melon
6 wafer-thin slices smoked ham
juice of 1 lemon
black pepper
lemon wedges to serve

Chill the melon thoroughly. Cut it into six slim wedges, scoop out the seeds and cut the skin away. Place one piece of melon on each slice of ham and wrap the ham neatly over the melon.

Pack each portion in cling film and place them in a rigid container or wrap in foil in a chiller box. Sprinkle the melon and ham with lemon juice and freshly ground black pepper just before serving.

Serve the melon gondolas with the wedges of lemon.

Melon and Ham Gondolas.

SEPTEMBER

*Roast Pork with Apple and Nut Stuffing, Stuffed Mushrooms, Braised
Patty Pan Squash.*

September

September's cooler mornings and shorter evenings bring the end of lazy summer days and mark the onset of autumn. The culinary response to the changing weather is to move away from salads and light dishes, and to begin cooking proper dinners and spicy meals to meet the revived appetite for hot food.

A good harvest of vegetables, and often a glut of tomatoes, always arouses enthusiasm for pickling and preserving. Chutney-making sessions fill the house with their unique sweet-sour aroma of vinegar and brown sugar heavily laced with onions and spices. It is also time for taking advantage of a plentiful and inexpensive supply of stone fruit; many kitchen work surfaces will have a parade of sparkling pots of jam, lined up ready for labelling and storing.

The 'r' in the month heralds the beginning of the native oyster season and gourmets welcome the return of this delectable shellfish to the menu. In more modest households, the 'r' traditionally meant that joints of pork were bought again, and what a treat that first autumn roast was, with its golden crackling, tasty sage and onion stuffing, and a helping of tangy apple sauce.

Wild duck (mallard and teal) and partridge are in season from September until the end of January, and grouse becomes more readily available and less expensive as the season progresses. Crisp home-grown apples and sweet, juicy pears come into the shops, while the last wild blackberries are picked this month.

Towards the end of the month, it is worth searching out the ripening crop of wild cob nuts when walking in the country. There is a small commercial harvest of cob nuts (usually filberts), which trickle into greengrocers' shops from the end of September or into October, but it is more rewarding to gather a pocketful of hedgerow nuts yourself, lay them out to dry in the sun, then pile them in a small dish to serve with cheese and fruit at the end of a dinner party.

Menu suggestions *The menus for September combine some of early autumn's traditional foods and offer simple ideas for making the most of them. The main dishes are included in this chapter, while page references are given for recipes featured elsewhere in the book.*

Sunday Roast Dinner
~

Roast Pork with Apple and Nut Stuffing
Roast and Boiled Potatoes
Buttered Cabbage
Runner Beans

~

Rice Pudding (page 348)
or
Apple Crumble (page 377)
with
Custard Sauce (page 338)

A first course does not usually feature in the Sunday family meal, but it is traditional to offer a choice of puddings.

Formal Dinner Party
~

Melon and Ham Gondolas
(page 219)

~

Casserole of Grouse
Cauliflower Polonaise
Roast Potatoes

~

Greengage Flan (page 236)

This is a practical dinner party menu which will enable you to entertain in style without having to rush around in the kitchen at the last minute. Since this menu is based on game, check with your guests that they like it: otherwise, keep it in reserve to share with friends with similar tastes to your own.

Vegetarian Family Supper
~

Vegetable Chilli
Boiled Rice
Garlic Bread

~

Baked Custard (page 338)
Fresh Fruit

This spicy menu is colourful and delicious, taking full advantage of the excellent quality produce that is readily available in early autumn. The combination of vegetables, pulses and rice followed by a baked custard and fresh fruit provides a well-balanced meal.

Baked Vegetable Patties and Vegetable Chilli (both page 233).

SOUPS

Borshch

There are numerous variations of this famous Russian and Polish soup, but beetroot is the basic ingredient for every borshch, whether it is served hot or cold.

SERVES: 6
PREPARATION: 25 minutes
COOKING: 1¼ hours

450 g/1 lb uncooked beetroot
1 onion
1 leek
1 carrot
1 turnip
1 large potato
1 stick celery
1.12 litres/2 pt strong beef, chicken
    or duck stock
1 bay leaf
15 ml/1 tablespoon chopped parsley
salt and black pepper
15 ml/1 tablespoon tomato paste
5 ml/1 teaspoon caster sugar
15 ml/1 tablespoon lemon juice
150 ml/¼ pt soured cream
45 ml/3 tablespoons chopped mint
    or snipped chives to garnish

Peel the beetroot, set aside 100 g/ 4 oz and dice the rest of it finely. Peel and thinly slice the onion; trim the roots and coarse outer leaves from the leek, wash it in cold running water and chop it finely. Peel the carrot and turnip, and shred into thin strips. Peel and dice the potato. Scrub the celery and chop it finely.

Put the prepared vegetables in a large pan with the stock, bay leaf, parsley, and season generously with salt and freshly ground black pepper. Bring the soup to the boil, reduce the heat, cover and simmer for about 30 minutes. Mix the tomato paste, sugar and lemon juice in a small bowl and add to the soup. Continue cooking over low heat for 30 minutes more. Purée the soup if you prefer a smoother texture.

About 10 minutes before you serve the soup, grate the reserved beetroot and add it to the soup. Thin with a little more stock if necessary. Tip the soured cream into a bowl. Stir in 60–75 ml/ 4–5 tablespoons of the soup and gradually stir this mixture back into the borshch. Heat the soup through without boiling and serve at once, sprinkled with chopped mint or chives.

To serve the borshch cold, chill the soup thoroughly, after puréeing if preferred, before stirring in the soured cream. Before serving, add a little more lemon juice. Pour the soup into individual bowls, each containing an ice cube, and top with a swirl of soured cream. Finely chopped spring onion, hard-boiled egg and grated cucumber can also be sprinkled on top of the borshch as a garnish.

Borshch.

STARTERS, SAVOURIES & LIGHT DISHES

Egg Mayonnaise Cocktail

This quickly made starter is also excellent as a sandwich filling.

SERVES: 4–6
PREPARATION: 20 minutes

5 hard-boiled eggs
300 ml/½ pt mayonnaise
5 ml/1 teaspoon grated onion
15 ml/1 tablespoon chopped
    green pepper
15 ml/1 tablespoon tomato ketchup
15 ml/1 tablespoon plain yogurt
salt and black pepper
2 spring onions
6 black olives
3 lettuce leaves
lemon slices to garnish

Roughly chop the hard-boiled eggs. Mix the mayonnaise, onion, green pepper, tomato ketchup and yogurt in a bowl; season with salt and freshly ground pepper. Fold in the chopped hard-boiled eggs. Chop the spring onions and black olives, discarding the olive stones, and add them to the mixture. Mix lightly.

Shred the lettuce leaves and divide them between four or six individual serving glasses; pile the egg mixture on top of the lettuce. Garnish each portion with a thin lemon slice.

■ Serve the Egg Mayonnaise Cocktail with brown bread and butter or hot buttered toast. For a sandwich filling, the shredded lettuce can be mixed into the egg cocktail and layered thickly between slices of bread.

North Coast Kipper Pâté

This rich smoky fish pâté keeps well in the refrigerator. It is excellent as a sandwich filling, or as a first course with toast.

SERVES: 4
PREPARATION: 20 minutes

2 boned kippers
15 ml/1 tablespoon double cream
75–100 g/3–4 oz butter
15 ml/1 tablespoon lemon juice
cayenne pepper
1.25 ml/¼ teaspoon ground mace

Place the kippers, head down, in a jug, pour over enough boiling water to cover all but the tails and leave to stand for 5 minutes. Pour off the water, transfer the kippers to a board and remove all skin and any small bones. Set the kippers aside to cool.

Mash the fish until smooth, or process in a liquidiser or food processor. Blend in the cream. Soften the butter and add it to the mixture with the lemon juice. Season with cayenne and mace. Spoon the pâté into an earthenware jar and chill.

Spinach Ramekins

SERVES: 4
PREPARATION: 10–15 minutes
CHILLING: about 1 hour

120 g/4½ oz can sardines in oil
450 g/1 lb spinach
1 onion
2.5 ml/½ teaspoon dried tarragon
30 ml/2 tablespoons finely
    chopped parsley
1 hard-boiled egg
30 ml/2 tablespoons double cream
salt and black pepper
Garnish
1 hard-boiled egg
4 anchovy fillets

Drain and split the sardines, and remove the backbones. Pull the spinach leaves off the stalks and wash in several lots of cold water. Peel and finely chop the onion. Put the wet spinach in a large saucepan with the onion, tar-ragon and parsley; cover with a lid. Cook over low heat, shaking the pan occasionally, for 7–10 minutes, or until softened, then drain thoroughly.

Chop the hard-boiled egg. Chop the fish into small pieces, discarding any remaining bones; mix with the egg and spinach. Purée the mixture in a liquidiser or food processor, or rub it through a coarse sieve into a bowl. Stir in the double cream and season to taste with salt and freshly ground pepper. Spoon the purée into individual ramekins or small serving dishes and chill until it sets.

For the garnish, separate the white and yolk of the hard-boiled egg; chop the white finely and push the yolk through a sieve. Decorate each ramekin with alternate rows of white and yolk.

Spinach Ramekins.

Split the anchovy fillets in half lengthways and lay them on top in a criss-cross pattern.

Squash with Goats' Cheese

A small cylindrical goats' cheese with a brie-like rind is best for this recipe.

SERVES: 4
PREPARATION: 15 minutes
COOKING: 20–25 minutes

2 small butternut squash
salt and black pepper
40 g/1½ oz fresh white
    breadcrumbs
30 ml/2 tablespoons snipped chives
75 g/3 oz cylindrical chèvre
    (goats' cheese)
4 lime wedges to garnish

Wash the butternut squash, then place them in a saucepan with enough water to cover. Add a little salt and bring to the boil. Reduce the heat and simmer the squash for about 15 minutes, until they are just tender. Test them for tenderness by piercing with a fine skewer.

Meanwhile, mix the bread-crumbs, chives and seasoning to taste. Drain the cooked squash and cut them in half lengthways, using a clean tea-towel to protect your hand. Place the squash in a flameproof dish and top with the breadcrumbs, pressing them into the small round holes. Cut the cheese into four slices and put one on each squash half. Place under a hot grill until the cheese is lightly browned. Garnish with lime wedges and serve at once.

Vegetable and Cheese Soufflé

Cooked vegetables are incor-porated into a cheese soufflé to make this light supper dish.

SERVES: 4
PREPARATION: 20 minutes
OVEN: 190°C/375°F/gas 5
COOKING: 25–30 minutes

100 g/4 oz cooked vegetables
40 g/1½ oz butter
15 ml/1 tablespoon plain flour
150 ml/¼ pt milk
3 eggs
50 g/2 oz Cheddar cheese
salt and cayenne pepper

Dice the cooked vegetables and set them aside. Melt 25 g/1 oz butter in a pan over moderate heat. Stir in the flour, and cook the roux* over low heat for 1 minute. Gradually add the milk, stirring continuously until the sauce boils and thickens. Remove the pan from the heat.

Separate the eggs, and beat the yolks, one at a time, into the sauce. Stir in the vegetables. Grate the cheese into the pan and stir until it has melted into the sauce. Season with salt and cayenne. In a clean bowl, whip the egg whites until stiff, but not dry; fold them into the sauce.

Use the remaining butter to grease a 900ml–1.12 litre/1½–2 pt soufflé dish generously and bake in a preheated oven at 190°C/375°F/gas 5 for 25–30 minutes, or until well risen.

Ham and Vegetable Croustades

SERVES: 4
PREPARATION: 20 minutes
OVEN: 200°C/400°F/gas 6
    190°C/375°F/gas 5
COOKING: 15 minutes

16 thin slices white bread
45–60 ml/3–4 tablespoons olive oil
175 g/6 oz cooked ham or chicken
1 small onion
50 g/2 oz lightly cooked vegetables
    (carrots, celery, leek, beans)
15 g/¼ oz butter
150 ml/¼ pt thick coating White
    Sauce (page 352)
salt and black pepper

Cut circles from the bread slices with a 7.5 cm/3 in pastry cutter; brush them on both sides with olive oil and press them into deep patty tins or castle-pudding tins. Bake in a preheated oven at 200°C/400°F/gas 6 for 8–10 minutes or until crisp and golden brown. Remove from the tins and set aside to cool. Reduce the oven temperature to 190°C/375°F/gas 5.

Chop the ham or chicken very finely in a food processor, or mince it. Chop the onion finely and dice the cooked vegetables. Melt the butter in a pan and fry the onion until soft, then add the ham or chicken and vegetables.

Season the white sauce with salt and pepper. Stir in the vegetables and meat, and spoon the mixture into the croustades. Bake for 5 minutes.

■ Serve as a starter, or with vegetables as a main course.

Fish, Shellfish & Seafood

Baked Cod

SERVES: 6
PREPARATION: 10 minutes
OVEN: 180°C/350°F/gas 4
COOKING: 1 hour

6 cod steaks
butter for greasing
salt and black pepper
juice of ½ large lemon
45 ml/3 tablespoons olive oil
1 large onion
1 clove garlic
1 small green pepper
400 g/14 oz can chopped tomatoes
15 ml/1 tablespoon chopped
    marjoram

Wipe the cod steaks thoroughly and arrange in a single layer in a buttered ovenproof dish. Sprinkle with salt and pepper, and strain the lemon juice on top. Add 15 ml/1 tablespoon olive oil and cover with buttered foil. Bake in a preheated oven at 180°C/350°F/gas 4 for 25 minutes.

Peel and finely chop the onion and the garlic. Wash the pepper, remove the stalk, ribs and seeds; chop the flesh into small pieces. Heat the remaining oil in a large frying pan. Add the onion, garlic and pepper and fry over low heat for 15 minutes. Stir in the tomatoes; season to taste with salt, pepper and chopped marjoram. Bring to the boil, reduce the heat and simmer for 10 minutes.

Remove the baked fish from the oven and pour the onion, pepper and tomato mixture over. Bake the dish for a further 10 minutes.
■ Sautéed Potatoes (page 347) and steamed broccoli make ideal accompaniments to this dish.

Pescada a la Marina

The South Americans are great believers in marinating meat and fish. Here, the marinade forms the basis of the sauce.

SERVES: 4–6
PREPARATION: 20 minutes
MARINATING: 1 hour
COOKING: 15 minutes

675 g/1½ lb haddock or cod fillet
1 egg
75–100 g/3–4 oz fresh white
    breadcrumbs
oil for shallow frying
120 ml/4 fl oz dry white wine
2 egg yolks
15 ml/2 tablespoons finely
    chopped parsley
Marinade
60 ml/4 tablespoons olive oil
30 ml/2 tablespoons lemon juice
1 small onion
1 clove garlic
1–2 bay leaves
5 ml/1 teaspoon salt
black pepper
pinch nutmeg

Make the marinade* first by whisking together the olive oil and lemon juice in a bowl. Peel and finely chop the onion and garlic. Add to the oil, with the bay leaves, salt, freshly ground pepper and nutmeg.

Divide the fillet into four or six portions. Place them in a single layer in a shallow dish and pour the prepared marinade over. Cover and leave for about 1 hour, turning the fish occasionally.

Lift out the fish, reserving the marinade in a small pan. Dry the fillets thoroughly on absorbent kitchen paper. Lightly beat the egg in a shallow bowl and spread out the breadcrumbs on a sheet of foil. Dip each fillet in the egg, then coat it evenly in breadcrumbs. Press the crumbs well in.

Bring the marinade to the boil, then strain it through a fine sieve into a heatproof bowl. Add the wine. Beat in the egg yolks and stand the bowl over a saucepan of gently simmering water. Stir continuously with a wooden spoon until the sauce thickens sufficiently to coat the back of the spoon. If the sauce shows signs of curdling, add 15 ml/1 tablespoon of cold water and remove the bowl from the heat immediately.

Heat the oil in a heavy-based pan and fry the fish until golden brown on both sides, turning once. Drain on absorbent kitchen paper. Serve the fish hot, sprinkled with parsley. Serve the sauce separately.
■ Offer creamed potatoes and buttered beans with the fish, or serve cold with Tartare Sauce (page 356) and a green salad.

Moules à la Poulette

In France, the mussels in this classic dish are served in their half shells and eaten with the fingers. Any remaining sauce can be mopped up with bread.

SERVES: 4–6
PREPARATION: 30 minutes
COOKING: 10 minutes

2.72 kg/6 lb mussels
1 bay leaf
1 parsley sprig
1 shallot
6 black peppercorns
450 ml/¾ pt dry white wine
150 ml/¼ pt double cream
2 egg yolks
30 ml/2 tablespoons
    chopped parsley
black pepper
lemon juice

Clean the mussels thoroughly, following the instructions on page 318, discarding any with broken or open shells. Scrape away all grit and remove the beards. Put the mussels in a large, heavy-based saucepan with the bay leaf and parsley sprig. Peel and finely chop the shallot and

Moules à la Poulette.

add it to the pan with the peppercorns. Pour over the wine, cover and cook the mussels over high heat, shaking the pan every now and again, for 5–7 minutes or until the shells open.

As the shells open, remove the mussels from the pan, throw away the empty top halves and place the mussels in their half shells in a warmed dish. Discard any mussels which fail to open. Cover the mussels to prevent them drying out, and to keep them warm. Strain the cooking liquid through muslin and return it to the clean pan.

Mix the cream and egg yolks together in a bowl and stir in 30–40 ml/2–3 tablespoons of the mussel liquid. Add to the rest of the liquid in the pan, with the chopped parsley. Stir in freshly ground black pepper and lemon juice to taste. Reheat the liquid, without boiling, until it has thickened slightly.

Serve the mussels in individual deep soup plates, with the sauce poured over them.
■ Provide finger bowls and a spare bowl or plates for the empty mussel shells.

Crab Puffs

SERVES: 4
PREPARATION: 40 minutes
OVEN: 230°C/450°F/gas 8
COOKING: 15–20 minutes

100 g/4 oz crabmeat
50 g/2 oz mushrooms
25 g/1 oz butter
30 ml/2 tablespoons
    chopped watercress
15 ml/1 tablespoon plain flour
60–90 ml/2–3 fl oz single cream
15 ml/1 tablespoon dry sherry
salt and black pepper
5–10 ml/1–2 teaspoons lemon juice
225 g/8 oz home-made Puff
    Pastry (page 374) or thawed
    frozen puff pastry
beaten egg to glaze
Garnish
lemon wedges
watercress sprigs

Flake the crabmeat. Trim and thinly slice the mushrooms. Melt the butter in a pan over low heat, and fry the mushrooms and the crabmeat for a few minutes. Stir in the chopped watercress. Take the pan off the heat and stir in the flour. Stir in the cream and return the pan to the heat. Cook gently for 4–5 minutes. Remove from the heat and add the sherry, with salt, freshly ground pepper and lemon juice to taste. Set this filling aside until cold.

Roll out the puff pastry on a lightly floured surface to a rectangle measuring 41 × 20 cm/16 × 8 in. Cut the pastry into eight 10 cm/4 in squares with a sharp knife. Put about 15 ml/1 tablespoon of the crabmeat mixture into the centre of each square. Brush the pastry edges with a little beaten egg, and fold each square into a triangle. Press the edges firmly together, completely sealing in the filling. Crimp the edges with a fork and brush the top of each puff with beaten egg. Make two or three slits in the top of each puff to allow the steam to escape.

Place the puffs on a damp baking sheet. Bake in a preheated oven at 230°C/450°F/gas 8 for 10–15 minutes or until the puffs have risen and are golden brown.

Serve the crab puffs hot or cold, garnished with wedges of lemon and sprigs of watercress.

■ These pastry puffs may be served hot or cold as a main course or a buffet dish, allowing two per person. A tossed green salad would be a suitable side dish for a main course.

Crab Puffs.

POULTRY & GAME

Chicken with Papaya and Pistachio Nuts

SERVES: 4
PREPARATION: 20 minutes
COOKING: 15–20 minutes

40 g/1½ oz shelled pistachio nuts
1 papaya
1 orange
4 boneless chicken breasts
45 ml/3 tablespoons plain flour
5 ml/1 teaspoon ground mace
salt and black pepper
25 g/1 oz butter
30 ml/2 tablespoons oil
30 ml/2 tablespoons snipped chives

Place the pistachios in a bowl. Pour over boiling water to cover, allow to soak for a few minutes, then drain and remove the skins. Peel the papaya, cut it in half and remove the seeds. Cut the flesh into slices. Squeeze the orange and set the juice aside. Skin the chicken breasts if necessary. Season the flour with mace, salt and pepper; coat the chicken.

Melt the butter and the oil in a frying pan. Brown the chicken on all sides, then lower the heat and cook for 15–20 minutes or until cooked, turning once. Transfer the chicken to a serving platter and keep hot. Add the papaya to the fat remaining in the pan and stir in the orange juice, pistachios and chives. Heat for 1 minute, then spoon over the chicken and serve.

Casserole of Grouse

Mature grouse are not tender enough for plain roasting. They can, however, be made into a tasty casserole, flavoured with herbs and brandy. The grouse are served, according to the tradition for many such game birds, on fried bread; however, if this is too rich for your taste the fried bread can be omitted.

SERVES: 4
PREPARATION: 30 minutes
COOKING: 1½ hours

4 mature grouse
8–12 button onions
1 stick celery
225 g/8 oz mushrooms
75 g/3 oz butter
30 ml/2 tablespoons plain flour
600 ml/1 pt stock
15 ml/1 tablespoon chopped thyme,
    marjoram and rosemary
salt and black pepper
45–60 ml/3–4 tablespoons
    double cream
30 ml/2 tablespoons brandy
lemon juice
4 small slices white bread
15 ml/1 tablespoon chopped parsley

If the butcher or game supplier has not already done so, truss the grouse neatly (page 321). Peel the button onions, leaving them whole. Scrub the celery stick, trim the mushrooms and chop both roughly. Melt 25 g/1 oz of the butter in a flameproof casserole and, when hot, brown the grouse all over, with the onions.

Lift out the browned grouse and onions, place them on a plate and set them aside. Add the celery and mushrooms to the butter remaining in the casserole and fry until soft. Stir in the flour and cook the roux* until brown, then gradually stir in the stock. Bring to simmering point and season to taste with the herbs, salt and freshly ground pepper.

Return the grouse and onions to the casserole, cover with a lid and cook over low heat on top of the stove for about 1½ hours or until the grouse are tender.

Mix the cream and brandy together in a bowl, stir in 30–45 ml/2–3 tablespoons of the sauce from the grouse, then stir the mixture back into the casserole. Sharpen to taste with lemon juice and adjust the seasoning.

In a large frying pan, melt the remaining butter. Remove the crusts from the bread and fry the slices until they are crisp and golden. Drain the fried bread on crumpled kitchen paper, then arrange them on a hot serving dish. Place one grouse on each fried bread slice, pour over a little sauce and sprinkle with the chopped parsley. Pour the rest of the sauce into a sauceboat.

■ Serve the casserole with fluffy creamed potatoes and Cauliflower Polonaise (page 231).

Mustard Rabbit.

Mustard Rabbit

SERVES: 4–6
CHILLING: 8–12 hours
(optional)
PREPARATION: 15 minutes
COOKING: 1¼–1½ hours

6 rabbit joints
60 ml/4 tablespoons Dijon mustard
50 g/2 oz streaky bacon
1 onion
1 clove garlic
plain flour for coating
salt and black pepper
30 ml/2 tablespoons oil
1 bay leaf
600 ml/1 pt chicken or
vegetable stock
Garnish
chopped chervil or parsley
Croûtons (page 313)

Spread the rabbit joints evenly with mustard, cover and chill overnight if possible.

Remove the rind from the bacon and chop it roughly. Peel and finely chop the onion and garlic. Season the flour for coating with salt and freshly ground pepper. Dust the rabbit joints lightly with the seasoned flour.

Heat the oil in a flameproof casserole and lightly brown the rabbit joints on both sides; lift them out and set them aside. Add the chopped bacon to the fat remaining in the casserole and fry for 2–3 minutes, then add the onion, garlic and bay leaf and continue cooking over low heat until the onion is soft. Pour in the stock and bring the contents of the casserole to the boil. Add a little salt and pepper, then return the rabbit joints to the casserole. Push the joints down into the liquid and reduce the heat so that it simmers. Cover closely with a lid or foil and simmer over low heat for 1¼–1½ hours.

Baste or rearrange the rabbit portions once or twice during cooking. Taste the sauce for seasoning before serving, sprinkled with the fresh chervil or parsley and garnished with croûtons.

■ Noodles or large potato shapes can be served with the rabbit casserole, together with broccoli or green beans.

Roast Saddle of Hare

An entire hare may be too much for the majority of meals, but the saddle can be roasted in one piece, and the legs used for making a pâté.

SERVES: 4
PREPARATION: 25 minutes
OVEN: 190°C/375°F/gas 5
COOKING: 1 hour

saddle of a young hare
(see method)
8 rashers streaky bacon
40 g/1½ oz butter
salt and black pepper
225 g/8 oz egg noodles
30 ml/2 tablespoons brandy or
brown stock
250 ml/8 fl oz soured cream
generous pinch dried rosemary
rosemary sprigs to garnish

When you order the hare, ask the butcher or game supplier to skin it and cut it into the complete saddle and four leg portions.

Insert the point of a sharp knife under the skin or thin membrane which covers the hare saddle and carefully peel the skin off. Place the saddle in a greased roasting tin.

Remove the rind from the bacon and put the rashers over the saddle. Soften the butter and spread it over the bacon. Roast the hare in a preheated oven at 190°C/375°F/gas 5 for about 50 minutes or until tender.

About 15 minutes before the hare is ready, bring a large pan of lightly salted water to the boil and cook the noodles for about 10 minutes. Drain in a colander. Remove the crisp bacon from the hare, chop it finely and mix it into the noodles with 15 ml/1 tablespoon of fat from the roasting tin. Season with freshly ground pepper and keep hot.

Lift the saddle from the tin and keep it hot while making the sauce: carefully pour off the fat, leaving the pan juices in the tin. Add the brandy (or stock) and the soured cream to the pan juices. Crumble in the rosemary. Put the tin over low heat on top of the stove and stir the gravy, scraping the bottom of the tin to incorporate the residue. Season to taste with salt and pepper.

Carve the saddle lengthways along the backbone and arrange the slices on a heated serving dish; surround the slices with the noodles. Pour the sauce over the hare and garnish with sprigs of fresh rosemary.

■ Green beans and carrots make suitable side vegetables, as does braised red cabbage.

227

MEAT

Châteaubriand Steak

This famous dish cannot be served for less than two persons as it is a double fillet steak cut from the thick end of the fillet.

SERVES: 2
PREPARATION: 5 minutes
COOKING: 8–10 minutes

350–400 g/12–14 oz thick
    fillet steak
15 g/½ oz butter
black pepper
Garnish
watercress sprigs
Maître d'Hôtel Butter (page 307)

Trim the fillet steak and, if necessary, flatten it slightly – it should be 4–5 cm/1½–2 in thick. Melt the butter in a small saucepan or in a bowl in the microwave. Brush one side of the fillet with melted butter and season with freshly ground pepper. Do not add salt as this will draw out the meat juices.

Cook the steak, buttered and seasoned side up, under a hot grill to brown the surface and seal in the juices. Turn the steak over, brush with the remaining melted butter and season with pepper. Turn the heat down and grill the steak for a further 4–5 minutes or until cooked to your taste, turning it once only.

Lift the steak on to a board and carve it, at a slight angle, into six even slices. Transfer the steak to a heated serving dish. Garnish with sprigs of watercress and slices of maître d'hôtel butter.

■ A châteaubriand steak is traditionally served with Château Potatoes (page 347) and Béarnaise Sauce (page 355). A tossed crisp green or mixed salad makes an excellent side dish.

Beef Jardinière

Silverside and brisket of beef are not tender enough to oven-roast successfully, but they make excellent pot-roasts.

SERVES: 6
PREPARATION: 25 minutes
COOKING: 3 hours

8 small onions
225 g/8 oz small carrots
2 young turnips
25 g/1 oz beef dripping or
    30 ml/2 tablespoons oil
1.4 kg/3 lb rolled silverside or
    brisket of beef
2 bay leaves
2.5 ml/½ teaspoon mixed herbs
6 peppercorns
salt and black pepper
300 ml/½ pt dry red wine
225 g/8 oz young runner or
    French beans or fresh peas

Peel the onions, leaving them whole. Scrape or peel the carrots, and peel and quarter the turnips. Melt the dripping or heat the oil in a large heavy-based pan or flameproof casserole with a close-fitting lid. Rapidly brown the meat on all sides. Add the onions and fry them until they are golden. Put the carrots and turnips into the pan together with the bay leaves, mixed herbs, peppercorns and 5 ml/1 teaspoon salt. Pour over the wine and bring to the boil.

Reduce the heat so that the wine barely simmers and cover the pan. Cook over low heat for 3 hours or until the meat is tender. If the pan does not have a close-fitting lid, then crumple a band of foil around its rim and seat the lid firmly in it.

Top and tail the beans, string them if necessary and cut them into 2.5 cm/1 in pieces. If you are using peas, they will have to be shelled. Cook the peas or beans in lightly salted boiling water for 10 minutes or until just tender.

Remove the meat from the pan, carve it and arrange the slices on a heated serving dish. Pile the vegetables around the meat and garnish with the beans or peas. Remove the bay leaves from the pan juices; skim off the surface fat or blot it with absorbent kitchen paper. Season the pan juices to taste with salt and freshly ground pepper and pour the gravy into a heated sauceboat.

■ Potatoes (about 450 g/1 lb) may be added to the meat for the last hour of cooking, or cooked and served separately.

Rice-stuffed Shoulder of Lamb

SERVES: 6
PREPARATION: 35 minutes
OVEN: 180°C/350°F/gas 4
COOKING: 1¾ hours plus about
    3 hours for stock

1.4 kg/3 lb shoulder of lamb
    (see method)
1 large onion
2 carrots
1 stick celery
bouquet garni*
salt and black pepper
100 g/4 oz long-grain rice
pinch saffron
100 g/4 oz streaky bacon
1 bunch watercress
50 g/2 oz walnuts
rind of 1 lemon
1 egg
15 ml/1 tablespoon oil
150 ml/¼ pt dry white wine
watercress sprigs to garnish

Ask the butcher to bone out the lamb and to include the bones with the order. Put the bones in a pan. Peel and chop the onion, scrape and chop the carrots and slice the celery. Add the vegetables to the pan and cover with cold water. Add the bouquet garni, salt and pepper. Bring to the boil, then reduce the heat and simmer for about 3 hours, adding more water as necessary. Strain the stock and set it aside.

Place the rice in a pan and pour in 300 ml/½ pt of the prepared stock. Add the saffron. Bring to the boil, stir the rice once, then cover the pan tightly and reduce the heat to the minimum setting. Cook the rice for 20 minutes. Turn the heat off and leave the rice to stand for a further 5 minutes without taking off the lid.

Meanwhile, cut the rind from the bacon. Wash and chop the watercress, finely chop the walnuts and grate the rind from the lemon. Heat the bacon rashers in a frying pan until the fat runs, then raise the heat and fry until crisp. Remove the bacon from the pan, drain on absorbent kitchen paper and chop it.

Put the rice in a mixing bowl, and add the bacon fat from the pan with the bacon, watercress, walnuts and lemon rind. Add salt and pepper to taste. Beat the egg lightly and bind the stuffing.

With a sharp knife, open a cavity in the meat to make a pocket for the stuffing. Spread the stuffing evenly into the pocket, roll up the joint and tie with string.

Heat the oil in a roasting tin and brown the lamb. Pour over the wine and roast in a preheated oven at 180°C/350°F/gas 4 for about 1½ hours. Baste frequently with the wine, adding a little stock if necessary.

Transfer the joint to a heated serving dish and remove the string. Add 150 ml/¼ pt of the remaining stock to the roasting tin, stirring to incorporate any sediment on the bottom of the tin. Boil over high heat until the liquid has reduced by about half. Pour the thickened gravy into a heated sauceboat.

Carve the lamb into neat slices and serve, garnished with sprigs of watercress.

Épigrammes d'Agneau

This classic French recipe illustrates an unusual and highly successful way of cooking breast of lamb. It is also an economical dish, for the stock can be used as the basis for Lamb and Lemon Soup (page 121). The intriguing title is credited to a marquise in the 18th century. Ignorant of the meaning of the word *épigramme*, overheard in a conversation, she ordered her chef to produce a dish of *épigrammes*!

SERVES: 4–6
PREPARATION: 30 minutes
COOKING: 2 hours
STANDING: 3 hours

1 onion
2 leeks
1–2 sticks celery
3–4 carrots
2 breasts of lamb on the bone, total
    weight about 1.4 kg/3 lb
bouquet garni*
10 ml/2 teaspoons salt
6 peppercorns
1 large egg
50–75 g/2–3 oz dry white
    breadcrumbs
25 g/1 oz butter
30 ml/2 tablespoons oil
Garnish
watercress sprigs
lemon wedges

Peel and slice the onion. Cut the roots and coarse outer leaves from the leeks, wash them under cold running water and chop them roughly. Scrub the celery and scrape or peel the carrots; chop both roughly.

Trim as much fat as possible from the breasts of lamb, and put them in a large pan, with the prepared vegetables, the bouquet garni, salt and peppercorns. Add cold water to cover the meat and vegetables and bring to the boil. Remove any scum from the surface, then cover the pan with a lid, reduce the heat and simmer gently for 1½ hours. Remove the meat from the pan, leave to cool slightly, then carefully pull out all the bones. Strain the liquid through a fine sieve and use it as the basis for a soup or sauce.

Lay the meat flat between two boards and place a heavy weight on top. Leave until cold.

Trim off any remaining fat and cut the meat into 5 cm/2 in squares. Beat the egg in a bowl; spread out the breadcrumbs on a sheet of foil. Dip the meat in the egg and coat evenly with the breadcrumbs. Set aside until the coating has firmed up.

Heat the butter and oil in a heavy-based pan and fry the meat for about 20 minutes until crisp and golden on both sides. Drain on crumpled absorbent kitchen paper.

Serve the *épigrammes* on a heated dish and garnish them with sprigs of watercress and wedges of lemon.

■ Broccoli spears, Sautéed Potatoes (page 347), and Béarnaise Sauce (page 356) or Tartare Sauce (page 355) would go well with the *épigrammmes*.

Épigrammes d'Agneau.

Stuffed Peppers with Pork and Beef

SERVES: 4, with about 600ml/
    1 pt Tomato Sauce
PREPARATION: 30 minutes
OVEN: 200°C/400°F/gas 6
COOKING: 40 minutes

4 green peppers
salt and black pepper
1 small onion
1 stick celery
50 g/2 oz mushrooms
30 ml/2 tablespoons oil
1 bay leaf
225 g/8 oz minced pork
225 g/8 oz lean minced beef
2.5 ml/½ teaspoon dried oregano
90 ml/6 tablespoons fresh
    white breadcrumbs
25 g/1 oz Cheddar cheese
Tomato Sauce
1 onion
1 small carrot
1 stick celery
15 ml/1 tablespoon oil
400 g/14 oz can chopped tomatoes
30 ml/2 tablespoons tomato paste
salt and black pepper
2.5–5 ml/½–1 teaspoon sugar

Cut the stalk ends neatly off the peppers. Chop the flesh around the stalk and set it aside; remove the pith and seeds from the peppers, keeping them whole. Bring a large saucepan of lightly salted water to the boil, add the pepper shells and cook for 5 minutes. Drain in a colander, refresh under cold water, drain again and invert the shells on absorbent kitchen paper.

Peel and chop the onion, scrub and slice the celery and trim and chop the mushrooms. Heat the oil in a saucepan. Add the onion, celery, reserved chopped pepper and the bay leaf. Cook over low heat for 5 minutes until starting to soften, then stir in the pork and beef. Cook, stirring, for 5 minutes until the meat is browned. Stir in the mushrooms, oregano and breadcrumbs, with salt and pepper to taste. Remove the bay leaf.

Cut a small slice off the base of any peppers that will not stand upright, then divide the meat filling evenly between them, pressing it down gently. Arrange the peppers in an ovenproof dish just large enough to hold them snugly. Sprinkle the cheese on top of each stuffed pepper and pour water into the dish to a depth of about 2.5 cm/1 in. Tent foil over the peppers and bake in a preheated oven at 200°C/400°F/gas 6 for 40 minutes.

Meanwhile, make the tomato sauce. Peel and chop the onion and carrot; scrub and slice the celery. Heat the oil in a saucepan and cook the onion, carrot and celery for about 7 minutes or until soft but not browned. Stir in the tomatoes and tomato paste with salt and pepper to taste. Bring to the boil, lower the heat, cover and simmer for 30 minutes. Purée the sauce in a liquidiser or food processor, return it to the clean pan and reheat. Add a little sugar to balance the sharp flavour of the tomato and adjust the seasoning if necessary.

Arrange the peppers on individual plates. Pour over a little hot tomato sauce and serve the remainder in a separate bowl.

229

Meat Loaf en Croûte

Golden crisp puff pastry is often used to make a covering for such expensive foods as fillet of beef or salmon. The same delicious crust can be used to turn a simple meat loaf into a special occasion dish. The meat loaf should be made well in advance to allow time for it to cool before enclosing it in the pastry.

SERVES: 6
PREPARATION: 25 minutes
OVEN: 190°C/375°F/gas 5
      230°C/450°F/gas 8
COOKING: 1¾ hours

1 onion
1 clove garlic
900 g/2 lb lean minced pork
30 ml/2 tablespoons
      chopped parsley
salt and black pepper
10 ml/2 teaspoons
      Worcestershire sauce
3 eggs
100 g/4 oz Bel Paese or
      Gouda cheese
175 g/6 oz mushrooms
225 g/8 oz home-made Puff
      Pastry (page 374) or thawed
      frozen puff pastry
watercress sprigs to garnish

Peel and finely chop the onion and crush the garlic clove. Mix together the pork, onion, garlic and parsley in a large bowl; season to taste with salt and freshly ground pepper. Beat the Worcestershire sauce with two of the three eggs and stir into the meat mixture.
    Grease a 900 g/2 lb loaf tin

thoroughly and press in half the meat mixture in an even layer. Dice the cheese finely, trim and chop the mushrooms and put both on top of the meat, then cover with the remaining pork, levelling the surface. Cover the tin with greased foil or greaseproof paper.
    Place the loaf tin in a roasting tin, pour in boiling water to a depth of about 1 cm/½ in, and bake in a preheated oven at 190°C/375°F/gas 5 for 1¼ hours. Remove the roasting tin from the oven. Leave the meat in the loaf tin to cool.
    Beat the remaining egg lightly in a cup and set it aside for glazing the pastry. Roll out the puff pastry on a lightly floured surface to a thin rectangle which measures roughly 30 × 20 cm/ 12 × 8 in. Turn the meat out of the tin and place it in the centre of the pastry rectangle; wrap the pastry over and around the meat, sealing the edges with the lightly beaten egg.
    Put the pastry-wrapped meat loaf, with the join underneath, on a damp baking sheet; brush the top with egg. Decorate the loaf with the pastry trimmings, and cut two or three slits in the pastry, which will allow the steam to escape.
    Bake in a preheated oven at 230°C/450°F/gas 8 for 20–25 minutes or until the pastry is well risen and golden brown.
    Serve the loaf hot, garnished with sprigs of watercress.
■ Surround the garnished loaf with halved grilled tomatoes, grilled mushroom caps and boiled potatoes.

Roast Pork with Apple and Nut Stuffing

SERVES: 6
PREPARATION: 20 minutes
OVEN: 200°C/400°F/gas 6
      180°C/350°F/gas 4
COOKING: 2 hours

1.6 kg/3½ lb blade of pork, boned
1 small onion
50 g/2 oz cashew nuts or almonds
50 g/2 oz white bread
1 cooking apple
1 stick celery
10 ml/2 teaspoons chopped parsley
25 g/1 oz butter
salt and black pepper
2.5 cm/½ teaspoon dried summer
      savory
lemon juice
30–45 ml/2–3 tablespoons
      vegetable oil
150 ml/¼ pt dry cider
fresh herbs to garnish

Score the pork rind (page 331). Peel and finely chop the onion and roughly chop the cashew nuts or almonds. Remove the crusts and dice the bread; peel, core and dice the apple. Finely chop the celery and parsley.
    Melt the butter in a large frying pan and fry the onion and nuts until they are just beginning to colour. Add the bread, apple, celery and parsley to the pan and continue cooking until the apple has softened. Add salt, pepper, the summer savory and lemon juice to taste.
    Open up the pocket in the pork and spread the stuffing evenly over the meat. Roll up the joint and tie securely.
    Place the joint in an oiled roasting tin; brush the rind with oil and sprinkle generously with salt. Roast in a preheated oven

Roast Pork with Apple and Nut Stuffing.

at 200°C/400°F/gas 6 for 20–30 minutes, until the crackling is crisp and golden. Reduce the oven temperature to 180°C/ 350°F/gas 4 and cook for a further 1½ hours or until the juices run clear when a skewer is pushed into the meat.
    Put the joint on a heated serving plate and keep it hot. Leave the residue in the roasting tin to settle, then carefully skim or pour off the fat. Add the cider to the pan juices and bring to the boil over moderate heat, scraping the bottom of the tin to incorporate the residue. When the gravy has coloured, add salt and pepper to taste and pour it into a heated sauceboat. Garnish the pork with fresh herbs such as sage or parsley.

Gammon Steaks in Madeira Sauce

SERVES: 4
PREPARATION: 20 minutes
COOKING: 20–25 minutes

4 gammon steaks, each
      1–2 cm/½–¾ in thick
100–175 g/4–6 oz mushrooms
1 large onion
4 large tomatoes
15 ml/1 tablespoon oil
1.25 ml/¼ teaspoon dried basil
1.25 ml/¼ teaspoon
      dried marjoram
50 ml/2 fl oz Madeira or
      sweet sherry
120 ml/4 fl oz ham or
      vegetable stock
black pepper
caster sugar
lemon juice

Cut the rind off the gammon steaks and snip the fat with a pair of kitchen scissors to prevent it from curling up when fried. Remove the mushroom stalks and chop them roughly, leaving the caps whole. Peel and thinly slice the onion; skin the tomatoes (page 302) and chop them roughly.

Heat the oil in a heavy-based pan over moderate heat. Fry the gammon steaks for about 8 minutes or until they are golden on both sides, turning once only. Remove the gammon from the pan and keep hot.

Fry the onion, mushroom caps and stalks lightly in the pan juices until softened; add the chopped tomatoes, basil and marjoram. Cover the pan with a lid or foil and simmer for about 5 minutes, shaking the pan from time to time.

Return the gammon steaks to the pan and add the Madeira or sweet sherry and stock. Add freshly ground pepper, sugar and lemon juice to taste. The gammon is usually sufficiently salty without the addition of extra salt. Cover the pan again and continue cooking over low heat for 10 minutes or until the sauce is well flavoured.

Arrange the gammon steaks on a hot serving dish and pour the sauce over them.

■ Baby sprouts and fluffy boiled rice or creamed potatoes, to mop up the sauce, would go well with this gammon dish.

VEGETABLES & SALADS

French Fried Cabbage

Use firm white cabbage for this recipe. The deep-fried, crisp, but feather-light shreds are an excellent accompaniment to grilled fish or meat.

SERVES: 4
PREPARATION: 5 minutes
COOKING: 10 minutes

½ medium-sized white cabbage
150 ml/¼ pt milk
50 g/2 oz plain flour
oil for deep frying
salt

Discard any dark or damaged outer leaves, wash the cabbage and cut out the hard central stalk. Shred the cabbage finely.

Dip a few cabbage shreds at a time in the milk, then toss them in the flour in a polythene bag.

Heat the oil for deep frying to 190°C/375°F or until a cube of day-old bread browns in 1 minute. Put a few shreds of coated cabbage into the frying basket and fry for 1–2 minutes until crisp and golden. Drain the shreds on crumpled absorbent kitchen paper and keep hot until all the shreds have been fried.

Sprinkle the fried cabbage with salt and serve at once, before the crispness is lost.

Stuffed Mushrooms

SERVES: 4
PREPARATION: 30 minutes
OVEN: 200°C/400°F/gas 6
COOKING: 30 minutes

4 large open mushrooms or
*   8 medium mushrooms*
1 small onion
1 dessert apple
3 pickled walnuts
100 g/4 oz Stilton cheese
75 g/3 oz fresh white breadcrumbs
salt and black pepper
45 ml/3 tablespoons milk

Cut the stalks off the mushrooms, wipe the caps and place them rounded sides down in one or two ovenproof dishes. Chop the mushroom stalks. Peel and grate the onion and apple, chop the walnuts and crumble the Stilton cheese.

Mix these prepared ingredients and the mushroom stalks with the breadcrumbs and season to taste with salt and freshly ground pepper. Add the milk and mix well. Divide the cheese stuffing between the mushroom caps, pressing it in place and moulding it neatly.

Bake the mushrooms in a preheated oven at 200°C/400°F/gas 6 for about 30 minutes, until the filling is browned and the mushrooms are lightly cooked. Serve at once.

■ The stuffed mushrooms may be served on rounds of toasted bread, if liked.

Cauliflower Polonaise

Plainly prepared cauliflower is an excellent accompaniment to meat or poultry served in a rich sauce. The classic garnish of fried breadcrumbs in this recipe adds an interesting texture and makes the cauliflower a good side dish for grilled main courses.

SERVES: 4–6
PREPARATION: 15 minutes
COOKING: 20 minutes

1 cauliflower
salt and black pepper
2 hard-boiled eggs
50 g/2 oz butter
50 g/2 oz dried breadcrumbs
30 ml/2 tablespoons
*   chopped parsley*
lemon juice

Cauliflower Polonaise.

Cut off the tough outer leaves and thick stalk at the base of the cauliflower. Cook the cauliflower whole in boiling salted water for about 10 minutes or until it is just tender.

Meanwhile, shell the hard-boiled eggs, remove the yolks and rub them through a sieve; chop the whites finely. Melt the butter in a small pan and fry the breadcrumbs until they are crisp. Remove the pan from the heat, stir in the chopped parsley and season with salt, freshly ground pepper and lemon juice.

Drain the cauliflower and place it in a warm serving dish. Sprinkle with the fried breadcrumbs, then garnish with the egg yolks and whites arranged in an attractive pattern.

Stuffed Marrow Rings

SERVES: 4
PREPARATION: 25 minutes
OVEN: 190°C/375°F/gas 5
COOKING: 45 minutes

4 thick slices marrow
40 g/1½ oz butter
100 g/4 oz mushrooms
100 g/4 oz lean cooked ham
15 ml/1 tablespoon chopped parsley
1.25 ml/¼ teaspoon dried
*   summer savory*
salt and black pepper
50 g/2 oz fresh white breadcrumbs

Scoop the middle from the marrow slices to make rings. The rings should be about 4–5 cm/1½–2 in thick. Butter a large baking dish thoroughly and arrange the marrow rings in this in a single layer.

Trim the mushrooms and chop them roughly. Dice the ham. Melt the remaining butter in a pan and lightly fry the mushrooms and ham for 5 minutes. Add the parsley and savory, and season to taste with salt and freshly ground pepper. Stir in the breadcrumbs.

Lightly sprinkle the marrow rings with salt and pepper before filling them with the stuffing. Cover the dish tightly with foil so that the marrow will cook in its own steam. Bake in a preheated oven at 190°C/375°F/gas 5 for 45 minutes or until the rings are tender.

■ Serve the stuffed marrow rings straight from the dish, with a hot cheese or tomato sauce.

Baked Courgettes

The subtle flavour and light consistency of courgettes make them an excellent accompaniment to delicately flavoured fish, chicken or veal dishes.

SERVES: 4
PREPARATION: 5 minutes
OVEN: 190°C/375°F/gas 5
COOKING: 25–30 minutes

6 courgettes
50 g/2 oz butter
40 g/1½ oz Cheddar or
*   Lancashire cheese*
salt and black pepper
60 ml/4 tablespoons double
*   cream (optional)*

Wipe the courgettes with a clean damp cloth; do not peel them, but cut off the stalk ends. Slice each courgette in half lengthways with a sharp knife.

Melt the butter in a shallow, flameproof casserole and fry the courgettes, cut side downwards, until light golden. Grate the cheese. Turn the courgettes over, season them with salt and freshly ground pepper and sprinkle the grated cheese over them.

Cover the casserole with a lid or foil and bake in a preheated oven at 190°C/375°F/gas 5 for 20 minutes.

If using the double cream, heat it gently in a small pan over moderate heat. Do not let it boil. Pour it over the courgettes just before serving.

Onions à la Grecque

SERVES: 6
PREPARATION: 1 hour
COOKING: 40 minutes
CHILLING: 2–3 hours

675 g/1½ lb small onions
45 ml/3 tablespoons chopped
*   parsley to garnish*
Sauce
600 ml/1 pt dry white wine
50 g/2 oz caster sugar
75 ml/5 tablespoons olive oil
8 juniper berries
juice of 1 lemon
1 bay leaf
60 g/2¼ oz can tomato paste
6 sprigs parsley
1.25 ml/¼ teaspoon basil
300 ml/½ pt water
salt and black pepper

Bring a large saucepan of water to the boil. Cut the tops and *Onions à la Grecque.*

bottoms from the onions and drop them into the boiling water. Cook for 1 minute, then drain the onions; cool slightly before slipping off the skins.

Put all the sauce ingredients into a heavy-based pan. Add the onions, bring to the boil, then reduce the heat and simmer for 20 minutes or until the onions are tender, but not disintegrating. Using a perforated spoon, transfer the onions to a shallow dish which is large enough to hold them in a single layer. Boil the sauce briskly for about 15 minutes or until it has reduced to three-quarters of the original amount. Strain the sauce through a sieve over the onions; leave to cool, then cover and chill for 2–3 hours.

■ Serve the onions, in the sauce, in soup plates, garnished with the finely chopped parsley.

Green Beans, Tuscany Style

This traditional Italian method of cooking beans is a useful way of ringing the changes on runner beans towards the end of their season. French beans may also be cooked this way, and both go well with roast or grilled meat and poultry dishes.

SERVES: 4
PREPARATION: 10 minutes
COOKING: 15 minutes

450 g/1 lb runner beans
salt and black pepper
25 g/1 oz butter
15 ml/1 tablespoon olive oil
15 ml/1 tablespoon chopped fresh
*   sage or chopped fresh parsley*
1 large clove garlic
15 ml/1 tablespoon grated
*   Parmesan cheese*

Wash, top, tail and string the runner beans. Cut them into 5 cm/2 in chunks, not fine slices as in the English style. Cook the beans in lightly salted boiling water over low heat until they are just tender. Drain the beans thoroughly and cover them with a cloth to keep them warm.

Heat the butter and oil over moderate heat; stir in half the sage or parsley. Peel and crush the garlic, add it to the pan, fry for 1 minute, then add the beans. Season to taste with salt and freshly ground pepper and toss over low heat until the mixture is hot. Mix in the Parmesan cheese, and serve the beans immediately, sprinkled with the remaining chopped herbs.

Vegetable Chilli

SERVES: 6
PREPARATION: 40 minutes
COOKING: about 45 minutes

1 large onion
1 large carrot
2 cloves garlic
4 celery sticks
1 green pepper
30 ml/2 tablespoons oil
1 bay leaf
30 ml/2 tablespoons
    ground coriander
15–30 ml/1–2 tablespoons
    chilli powder
30 ml/2 tablespoons tomato paste
400 g/14 oz can chopped tomatoes
300 ml/½ pt vegetable stock
2 × 400 g/14 oz cans red
    kidney beans
salt and black pepper
1 small cauliflower
225 g/8 oz courgettes or
    prepared marrow
2 avocados
150 ml/¼ pt plain yogurt
chopped fresh coriander to
    garnish (optional)

Peel and chop the onion, carrot and garlic. Scrub and slice the celery. Halve the pepper, discard the stalk, seeds and pith, then dice the flesh.

Heat the oil in a large saucepan or casserole. Add the prepared ingredients and the bay leaf. Cook, stirring every now and then, for 10 minutes. Stir in the ground coriander, and chilli powder to taste – chilli powder is very hot, so if you are not familiar with it, add only the smaller quantity. Cook for 1 minute, then stir in the tomato paste, tomatoes and stock. Bring to the boil, reduce the heat and cover the pan. Simmer for 10 minutes. Stir in the kidney beans and seasoning, then cook for a further 10 minutes.

Cut the cauliflower into small florets and the courgettes or marrow into chunks. Add both to the chilli and stir well, then continue cooking for a further 15 minutes, stirring once or twice, or until the cauliflower is tender but not too soft.

Halve, stone, peel and slice the avocados just before serving the chilli. Top each portion with a spoonful of yogurt and avocado slices. Sprinkle with coriander if liked and serve at once.

Baked Vegetable Patties and Vegetable Chilli.

Baked Vegetable Patties

MAKES: 8
PREPARATION: 30 minutes
OVEN: 190°C/375°F/gas 5
COOKING: 40 minutes

1 small onion
100 g/4 oz carrot
1 clove garlic
1 stick celery
30 ml/2 tablespoons oil
2 × 400 g/14 oz cans soya beans
45 ml/3 tablespoons
    chopped parsley
5 ml/1 teaspoon dried oregano
2.5 ml/½ teaspoon ground mace
50 g/2 oz fresh wholemeal
    breadcrumbs
salt and black pepper
1 egg

Fresh Tomato Chutney
450 g/1 lb tomatoes
4 spring onions
5 ml/1 teaspoon caster sugar
30 ml/2 tablespoons chopped mint
5 ml/1 teaspoon made
    English mustard
5 ml/1 teaspoon wine vinegar

Peel and finely chop the onion, carrot and garlic. Scrub and finely chop the celery. Then cook these ingredients together in half the oil for 10 minutes, stirring often. Meanwhile, drain and mash the soya beans or grind them in a food processor – they should be slightly coarse rather than smooth. Combine the soya beans, cooked onion mixture, parsley, oregano, mace and breadcrumbs. Stir in plenty of seasoning, then lightly beat the egg and mix it in to bind the ingredients. Divide the mixture into four and shape each portion into two neat round patties. Grease a baking sheet, place the patties on it, and brush them with a little oil. Bake in a preheated oven at 190°C/375°F/gas 5 for about 40 minutes until well browned.

Make the chutney. Skin the tomatoes (page 302), remove the seeds, then roughly chop them. Finely chop the spring onions and mix them with the tomatoes. Stir in the caster sugar, mint, mustard and vinegar. Taste and add seasoning as required. Serve with the patties.

■ Once shaped, the patties may be frozen. Cook them straight from frozen, allowing about 5 minutes extra.

Braised Patty Pan Squash

The small flying-saucer-shaped squashes, known as patty pan, have a good flavour. They are easy to prepare and cook quickly.

SERVES: 4
PREPARATION: 15 minutes
COOKING: 30 minutes

1 onion
1 thin slice of fresh root ginger
1 red pepper
15 ml/1 tablespoon olive oil
15 g/½ oz butter
1 bay leaf
2 sprigs thyme
2 sprigs parsley
450 g/1 lb patty pan squash
15 ml/1 tablespoon plain flour
300 ml/½ pt dry white wine
salt and black pepper

Peel, halve and thinly slice the onion and chop the ginger. Halve the pepper, discard the stalk, seeds and pith, then thinly slice the flesh. Heat the oil and butter in a large saucepan. Add the prepared ingredients, bay leaf, thyme and parsley and stir well. Cover the pan and cook gently for 15 minutes.

Meanwhile trim the stalk ends off the patty pan and slice them in half horizontally. Stir the flour into the parcooked vegetables, gradually pour in the wine and bring the contents of the pan to the boil. Simmer the sauce for 5 minutes, then add the patty pan. Turn the vegetables in the sauce, bring it back to the boil and reduce the heat again. Cover and simmer gently for 8–10 minutes, until the patty pan are tender but not soft. Taste for seasoning before serving.

■ The patty pan may be served as a side dish with grilled poultry or meat. They can also be tossed with pasta or served with rice; grated fresh Parmesan or Cheddar cheese is a tasty addition.

Braised Patty Pan Squash.

RICE & PASTA

Greek Rice Ring

Particularly attractive when moulded in a ring, this spicy rice dish, served hot or cold, makes a light meal on its own.

SERVES: 6
PREPARATION: 20 minutes
COOKING: 20–40 minutes
COOKING: 1 hour

salt and black pepper
225 g/8 oz long-grain rice
lemon juice
2 large ripe tomatoes
30 ml/2 tablespoons finely
    snipped chives
30 ml/2 tablespoons
    chopped parsley
8 green olives
5 ml/1 teaspoon each basil
    and marjoram
1 red pepper
60 ml/4 tablespoons olive oil
30 ml/2 tablespoons
    tarragon vinegar
black olives to garnish

Bring a large pan of salted water to the boil. Add the rice and 5 ml/1 teaspoon lemon juice and cook for about 15 minutes or until the rice is just tender. Drain the rice in a colander and cover with a dry cloth to absorb the steam and keep the rice dry.

Skin the tomatoes (page 302), chop them finely and put them in a large bowl with the chives and parsley. Chop the green olives finely and add them to the bowl with the herbs. Cook the pepper in a saucepan of boiling water for 5 minutes, cut off the stalk end and remove the seeds. Cut the pepper into narrow strips; set eight strips aside and chop the remainder finely. Add them to the tomato mixture.

Stir the still-warm rice into the tomato mixture. Mix the oil and vinegar in a small bowl and season to taste with salt and freshly ground pepper. Add enough of this dressing to the rice to moisten it thoroughly; adjust the seasoning and sharpen to taste with lemon juice. Press the rice firmly into a ring mould, cover and leave in a cool place for at least 1 hour.

To serve the dish hot, cover the rice mould with a fresh piece of buttered foil or greaseproof paper and place it in a roasting tin. Add boiling water to a depth of 1 cm/½ in. Heat on top of the stove for 15–20 minutes, then remove the covering and invert the serving dish over the mould. Holding the plate and mould together, turn both over and give a sharp shake to ease out the rice.

Garnish with black olives and the reserved strips of red pepper. If serving cold, simply unmould the rice ring, as already described, without reheating it.

■ One way of serving the hot Greek rice ring is to invert half a grapefruit in the centre and arrange grilled Lamb Kebabs (page 127) in a fan coming out of the grapefruit.

Paella a la Valenciana

Probably the most famous of all Spanish dishes, paella has many local variations. All, however, contain the basic ingredients of chicken, onion and saffron-flavoured rice. In Spain, paella is cooked in and served straight from a two-handed iron pan (paella) from which the dish takes its name.

SERVES: 6
PREPARATION: 1 hour
COOKING: 1 hour

1 chicken, about 1.15 kg/2½ lb
3 parsley sprigs
1 bay leaf
1 sprig marjoram
salt and black pepper
225 g/8 oz tomatoes
1–2 red or green peppers
225 g/8 oz peas or green beans
400 g/14 oz can artichoke
    hearts (optional)
1 onion
350 g/12 oz mussels
50 ml/2 fl oz olive oil
100 g/4 oz chorizo or garlic
    sausage (optional)
350 g/12 oz long-grain rice
175 g/6 oz large peeled
    cooked prawns
pinch powdered saffron
Garnish
6 large cooked prawns,
    in the shells
6 lemon wedges

Cut the leg and wing portions off the chicken, before severing the whole breast section from the lower carcass. Divide the breast section, lengthways, in two along

the breastbone. Leave the flesh on the bone to prevent shrinkage during cooking.

Put the rest of the chicken carcass and the giblets in a large pan, add the parsley, bay leaf and marjoram and enough cold water to cover. Season thoroughly with salt and freshly ground pepper. Bring the stock to the boil, then reduce the heat, cover and simmer for about 30 minutes. Strain the stock through a fine sieve and set aside.

While the stock is cooking, prepare the vegetables and shellfish: skin the tomatoes (page 302) and chop them roughly. Wash the peppers, cut off the stalk bases, remove the seeds and cut the flesh into narrow slices or strips. Shell the peas. Alternatively, remove any strings from the green beans and cut into 5 cm/2 in lengths. Drain the canned artichokes, if using, and cut them in half. Peel and finely slice the onion.

Clean the mussels and remove their beards (page 318), discarding any open shells. Pour 300 ml/ ½ pt of the reserved stock into a large saucepan and heat it until just simmering. Add the mussels, cover the pan and simmer gently for 5–7 minutes, until all the shellfish are open. Drain the mussels, then strain the stock through a muslin-lined sieve to remove grit. Reserve the mussels, discarding any ones that are still closed. Remove the top shells.

Paella a la Valenciana.

Heat the oil in a paella pan or a large, heavy-based pan over moderate heat. Fry the chicken joints until golden on both sides; remove from the pan and divide each into smaller pieces. Fry the chorizo, if using, until browned, then remove from the pan and cut it into slices. Fry the onion in the oil, stirring constantly, until transparent, then add the rice and fry until it is a pale biscuit colour. Return the chicken pieces and chorizo to the pan, together with the prepared vegetables, except the artichokes.

Pour over the mussel cooking stock and enough extra chicken stock to cover the ingredients.

Bring to the boil, reduce the heat and cover with foil or a lid. Simmer slowly until the stock is absorbed and the rice is just tender – about 30 minutes. Add the prawns and mussels about 5 minutes before the end of cooking to heat them through without toughening them. Stir occasionally during cooking, and add more stock if necessary until the rice is cooked, but not mushy.

Stir the artichokes into the mixture in the pan and then add a pinch of saffron, just enough to give the rice a golden colour. Stir thoroughly and season to taste with salt and freshly ground black pepper.

Serve the paella in the pan, garnished with the prawns in the shells and wedges of lemon.

■ A bowl of green salad can be served as a side dish, but the paella is a substantial meal.

Lumachine con Cozze

This is an Italian dish made from egg pasta shells (*lumachine*) and mussels cooked in wine.

SERVES: 4
PREPARATION: 30 minutes
COOKING: 25 minutes

675 g/1½ lb mussels
450 g/1 lb ripe tomatoes
1 clove garlic
30 ml/2 tablespoons olive oil
15 ml/1 tablespoon chopped parsley
15 ml/1 tablespoon shredded basil
75 ml/2½ fl oz white wine
225 g/8 oz lumachine
salt and black pepper
lemon juice

Scrub and clean the mussels thoroughly (page 318). Remove their beards, and throw away any mussels which have broken or open shells.

Skin the tomatoes (page 302) and chop them roughly. Peel and finely chop the garlic. Heat the oil in a frying pan and lightly fry the garlic. Add the tomatoes, parsley and basil and bring this mixture to simmering point. Simmer for 20 minutes.

Meanwhile, put the cleaned mussels and the white wine in a large shallow pan and cover tightly with a lid. Cook over a moderate heat, shaking the pan every now and then, for 5–7 minutes or until the mussels open. Discard any mussels that remain closed after cooking.

Remove the mussels from the shells and set them aside. Strain the cooking liquid through a muslin-lined sieve to remove any sandy sediment, and stir it into the tomato mixture.

While the tomatoes are cooking, bring a large pan of lightly salted water to the boil, and cook the pasta shells for 12 minutes or until they are tender, but not soft. Drain in a colander and cover with a clean cloth to keep the pasta warm.

Add the mussels to the sauce and heat through. Season to taste with freshly ground pepper, adding salt only if necessary, and sharpen with lemon juice. Put the pasta shells in a warmed deep serving dish and pour the mussels and sauce over them. Serve the pasta immediately.

■ Offer warmed Italian bread, such as ciabatta, with the pasta.

PUDDINGS & DESSERTS

Swiss Blackberry Charlotte

The classic charlotte is a cold dessert of cooked fruit, set in a mould of sponge fingers. The Swiss meringue topping is crisp on top with a soft marshmallow texture underneath.

SERVES: 4–6
PREPARATION: 40 minutes
OVEN: 150°C/300°F/gas 2
COOKING: 25 minutes

450 g/1 lb blackberries
150 g/5 oz caster sugar
300 ml/½ pt water
20 ml/4 teaspoons cornflour
2 eggs
75 ml/2½ fl oz double cream
lemon juice
100 g/4 oz sponge fingers
100 g/4 oz icing sugar

Hull* the blackberries and set aside a dozen of the larger ones for decoration. Put 100 g/4 oz of the caster sugar and the water in a pan over low heat until the sugar has dissolved to a syrup. Add the blackberries to the syrup and cook over very low heat for 10 minutes, or until tender but still whole. Strain the syrup into a measuring jug, and set the blackberries aside.

Put the cornflour in a small pan and gradually stir in 300 ml/½ pt of the blackberry syrup; cook over low heat for 3–4 minutes, stirring all the time, until the mixture is clear and beginning to thicken. Remove the syrup from the heat.

Separate the eggs, setting the whites aside for the meringue. Beat the yolks and cream in a bowl and gradually stir this into the thick syrup mixture. Sharpen with lemon juice and stir in enough of the remaining caster sugar to sweeten the mixture.

Cut one rounded end off each of the sponge fingers. Put a 1 cm/½ in layer of the blackberry cream in the base of a 600 ml/1 pt soufflé dish. Stand the sponge fingers, cut edge downwards, closely around the inside of the dish to make a casing. Put a single layer of blackberries over the cream, followed by another layer of cream and so on finishing with a layer of the blackberry cream.

For the meringue topping, put the egg whites in a dry heatproof bowl with the icing sugar. Add 75 ml/5 tablespoons of the remaining blackberry syrup. Place the bowl over a pan of simmering water and whisk the mixture steadily until it stands in soft peaks. Remove the bowl from the heat and continue whisking until the meringue is cool. Swirl or pipe it over the blackberry cream.

Bake the charlotte in the centre of a preheated oven at 150°C/300°F/gas 2 for 20 minutes or until the meringue topping is delicately coloured. Serve the dessert cold, decorated with the reserved blackberries.

Poires Flambées

This recipe for pears in brandy is an ideal sweet to cook in a chafing dish at the table. Fresh firm peaches and apricots or peeled and thickly sliced fresh pineapple are also excellent cooked in this way.

SERVES: 4
PREPARATION: 15 minutes
COOKING: 10 minutes

4 ripe firm dessert pears
4 pieces preserved ginger
25 g/1 oz unsalted butter
30 ml/2 tablespoons brandy
15–30 ml/1–2 tablespoons ginger syrup (from jar)
30 ml/2 tablespoons double cream

Peel the pears thinly, cut them in half and carefully scoop out the cores with a pointed teaspoon. Quarter each piece of preserved ginger and set aside.

Melt the butter in a chafing dish, a shallow flameproof dish, or a frying pan over moderate heat. Fry the pears, cut side down, until golden brown. Turn the pears over and fry the other side. Pour the brandy into a metal soup ladle or small pan, heat it, then set it alight and pour over the pears.

Using a perforated spoon, transfer the pears to individual plates, placing two ginger pieces in each cavity. Add the ginger syrup and double cream to the pan juices and stir over gentle heat until well blended and heated through. Spoon a little sauce over each portion and serve immediately.

Greengage Flan

Tart greengages are the ideal topping for a rich, pastry-cream-filled flan. This basic recipe can be used with a variety of other fruit as the topping, and a suitable jam to glaze.

SERVES: 6
PREPARATION: 40 minutes
COOKING: 30 minutes

1 flan case (see method)
225 g/8 oz greengages
60 ml/4 tablespoons greengage jam
45 ml/3 tablespoons water
15 ml/1 tablespoon lemon juice
150 ml/¼ pt double cream
icing sugar to sweeten
Pastry Cream
2 eggs
50 g/2 oz caster sugar
25 g/1 oz plain flour
300 ml/½ pt milk
2.5 ml/½ teaspoon natural vanilla essence or 20 ml/4 teaspoons lemon juice

Bake an 18 cm/7 in flan case using either Rich Shortcrust Pastry (365) or Pâte Sucrée (page 376). Leave the baked flan to cool completely before assembling the greengage dessert.

Make the pastry cream next as this too should not be used until quite cold: put 1 whole egg and 1 egg yolk in a mixing bowl (set aside the remaining egg white). Whisk the sugar with the eggs until creamy and pale, then sift in the flour, whisking it into the mixture, and gradually add the milk. Pour the mixture into a small saucepan and bring to the boil, whisking continuously.

Simmer this custard-cream over very low heat for 2–3 minutes to ensure the flour is cooked. Flavour to taste with vanilla essence or lemon juice and pour the cream into a shallow dish to cool. Stir from time to time to prevent the formation of a skin.

Spread the cold pastry cream over the base of the flan case. Cut the greengages in half, remove the stones and arrange the fruit over the cream.

Put the greengage jam in a small, heavy-based pan, with the water and lemon juice. Cook over low heat, stirring until the jam has melted. Increase the heat and bring to the boil. Remove from the heat and rub through a sieve.

Brush the glaze over the greengages, covering them completely; brush the top edge of the flan with the remaining glaze. Set the flan in a cool place until the glaze has set.

Just before serving, whip the remaining egg white in a dry bowl until stiff, but not dry. In a separate bowl, whip the cream into soft peaks. Fold the egg white into the cream, sweeten to taste with a little icing sugar and serve in a separate bowl to accompany the flan.

Berry Lemon Pudding

Late summer fruits such as blackberries and raspberries go well with the lemon flavour of this dessert, which can be eaten hot or cold. The quantities for the lemon topping can be doubled and the mixture baked without a fruit base to make a plain pudding with a creamy lemon sauce.

SERVES: 4
PREPARATION: 25 minutes
OVEN: 190°C/375°F/gas 5
COOKING: 40–45 minutes

175 g/6 oz blackberries or
   raspberries
25 g/1 oz butter
100 g/4 oz caster sugar plus extra
   for decoration
1 large lemon
2 eggs
150 ml/¼ pt milk
25 g/1 oz plain flour
150 ml/¼ pt whipping cream

Cream the butter and 30 ml/ 2 tablespoons of the sugar in a mixing bowl until pale and light. Wash and dry the lemon and finely grate the rind into this mixture; squeeze the lemon and strain the juice in as well. Beat the mixture thoroughly.

Separate the eggs and beat the milk into the yolks. Add this gradually to the creamed mixture, alternately with the sifted flour and remaining sugar, beating until the mixture is thoroughly combined. In a clean bowl, whisk the egg whites until stiff, but not dry; fold them into the mixture.

Hull* the blackberries, setting a few large ones aside for decoration. Put the remaining berries in the bottom of a 1.12 litre/2 pt soufflé dish. Pour the lemon mixture over the berries and set the dish in a roasting tin. Pour in boiling water to a depth of 2.5 cm/1 in. Bake in a preheated oven at 190°C/375°F/gas 5 for 40–45 minutes or until the top is golden brown and set. Test by pressing the top with a finger – the pudding is cooked if the surface springs back and the finger leaves no imprint in the top.

The top of the pudding will have set to a sponge-like mixture over a creamy lemon sauce which covers the berries.

If the pudding is served hot, sprinkle it generously with caster sugar and decorate with the remaining berries. Whip the cream and offer it separately. For a cold dessert, pipe swirls of whipped cream over the top and decorate with the blackberries.

Hazelnut Gantois

A gantois or Flemish pastry, consists of crunchy biscuit rounds, layered with fresh fruit and whipped cream. The pudding is topped with a layer of crisp golden caramel.

SERVES: 4–6
PREPARATION: 1½ hours
OVEN: 180°C/350°F/gas 4
CHILLING: 30 minutes
COOKING: 25–30 minutes

100 g/4 oz toasted hazelnuts
125 g/4½ oz plain flour
50 g/2 oz caster sugar
75 g/3 oz unsalted butter
450 g/1 lb raspberries or
   6–8 peaches
300 ml/½ pt whipping cream
5 ml/1 teaspoon icing sugar
Caramel Topping
75 g/3 oz caster sugar
30 ml/2 tablespoons water

Chop 25 g/1 oz of the toasted hazelnuts coarsely and set them aside. Grind the remainder in a food processor or chop them very finely with a knife.

Sift the flour into a mixing bowl and add the ground nuts and the sugar. Rub in the butter until the mixture resembles fine breadcrumbs, press the mixture together to form a dough, then knead lightly. Wrap the dough and chill it for at least 30 minutes, or until quite firm.

Meanwhile, peel the peaches (page 361), if using, and cut them into thin slices.

On a lightly floured board shape the firm dough into a thick sausage. Divide the dough

into four equal pieces and roll each piece out to an 18 cm/7 in circle, about 3 mm/⅛ in thick. Lift the circles carefully on to greased baking sheets. Bake in a preheated oven at 180°C/ 350°F/gas 4 for 15 minutes or until the biscuit rounds are golden brown and firm. Remove to a wire tray and leave to cool.

For the caramel topping, put the sugar and water in a small pan over low heat. Stir until the sugar has completely dissolved. Turn up the heat and boil the syrup briskly, without stirring, until it is caramel-coloured.

Pour enough of the caramel over one biscuit to cover it, spreading it evenly with an oiled knife. Sprinkle the coarsely

Hazelnut Gantois.

chopped nuts around the edge of the caramel-covered biscuit, and arrange a quarter of the raspberries or peach slices in the centre of the biscuit. Trickle over the remaining caramel or use a fork to pull this into thin threads to decorate the top of the biscuit.

Whip the cream in a bowl and sweeten with the icing sugar. Assemble the cake by spreading an equal amount of the cream over each of the remaining three biscuit layers; divide the fruit between them. Put the biscuit layers on top of each other, finishing with the caramel-topped biscuit. Serve at once.

237

Success with Spices

Just as with the majority of cooking techniques, the way to gain confidence in your use of spices is to practise and experiment: getting to know the individual characteristics of spices as opposed to mixtures, such as curry powder, tandoori spice or garam masala, is important. It is also useful to know something about the basic foods which the spices are intended to flavour and how they are combined in different countries. Indian-style dishes are probably the most popular, although Thai and Malaysian dishes are becoming more well known. There are many familiar Chinese spiced dishes too, particularly those from the Szechuan region, which often include fresh chillies and other spices.

Spices are used in many different cuisines. They are widely used in North African and South American cooking; and many of the opulent dishes of Turkish origins often illustrate the fascinating marriage of Eastern spices with the Mediterranean cuisine.

The cooking styles of both Thailand and Malaysia in Southeast Asia highlight fascinating ways in which different nations have brought together their ingredients to create a wonderful zest for speedy cooking, with exceptional respect for some of the most potent spices. In both cases, Indian and Chinese influences play very powerful roles. Malaysia, in particular is a place where there is a colourful and vigorous mixing of culinary traditions. Indian, Chinese and Malay foods and flavourings are literally thrown together. Many Malaysian dishes combine the stir-fried ingredients of Oriental cooking with the curry spices of India. Pungent dried shrimps are ground to a fine powder, sweet coconut milk is often added and chillies can be used quite liberally with fresh root ginger or the beautiful flower bud of the ginger plant. There are a few basic guidelines to follow which will help to ensure success when cooking with spices.

Handling Spices

Spices are powerful and often expensive flavouring ingredients, which should be treated with respect. They may discolour or sting the skin – chilli juices are a severe irritant to tender skin areas and eyes, and bright turmeric can stain the skin or plastic and wooden cooking utensils.

The rule of little and often, applies when buying spices,. They should be stored in a cool, dark place to keep them fresh and to retain their distinctive flavour and colour.

A heavy pestle and mortar are the ideal tool for grinding small quantities of spices. An ordinary food processor or liquidiser will not usually grind the spices effectively. A small spice mill or coffee grinder reserved for the purpose (otherwise the coffee beans will be flavoured with spices) is useful for grinding large quantities of spices.

Cooking Spices

Very few spices are used raw – paprika, chilli powder and nut-

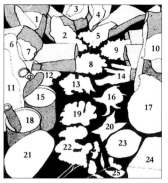

Ingredients used in Malaysian cooking.

1 *Rice flour*
2 *Dried shrimps*
3 *Coriander seeds*
4 *Mustard seeds*
5 *Cardamom pods*
6 *Rose water*
7 *Peanuts*
8 *Almonds*
9 *Pistachio nuts*
10 *Long-grain rice*
11 *Soy sauce*
12 *Pomegranate seeds*
13 *Dried chillies*
14 *Cinnamon bark (cassia)*
15 *Ground cumin*
16 *Fresh chillies*
17 *Coconut*
18 *Ground turmeric*
19 *Fresh root ginger*
20 *Bay leaves*
21 *Mango*
22 *Parsley*
23 *Lemon*
24 *Dried tamarind*
25 *Mint*

meg are a few examples of spices that are added to food in the final stages of cooking or as a garnish. Most spices must be well cooked before they are combined with the main ingredients, or they should be cooked with the ingredients in the first stages of cooking. This is particularly true when making curries and spiced sauces or when using whole spices, such as cumin seeds, to flavour rice dishes.

Always use a heavy-based pan when roasting whole spices or seeds without fat. Heat the pan carefully so that it is hot enough to cook the spices but not sufficiently hot to burn them. Shake the pan to turn and rearrange the spices, then continue to cook until the spices give off their aroma – this is the first sign that they are roasted. Seeds will pop slightly, then the spices should be tipped out of the pan before they turn a dark colour or smell burnt – by this stage they will have developed a bitter flavour. Roasted whole spices are extremely hot, so cool them before grinding them to a powder.

Coconut Milk

Coconut milk can be made from fresh or desiccated coconut.

If using a fresh coconut, drill two or three holes at the top of the coconut and shake out the colourless juice. Crack or saw the coconut in half and scrape out the flesh. Grate it coarsely or shred it finely, pour over boiling water to cover and leave to stand for 20 minutes.

Strain the liquid – called the coconut milk – through a fine sieve, pressing all the moisture from the coconut. The coconut can be soaked once or twice more and the liquid squeezed from it to yield a thinner coconut milk. Desiccated coconut should be treated in the same way.

There are easy alternatives to making coconut milk as above: bought canned milk is the quickest form (make sure it is unsweetened), blocks of creamed coconut are ready to dissolve in boiling water, or instant coconut milk powder is excellent.

Garam Masala

This is a ground mixture of roasted spices. It differs from other spice mixtures and raw spices in that it can be sprinkled over food just before serving, as a garnish.

50 g/2 oz coriander seeds
50 g/2 oz black peppercorns
40 g/1½ oz cumin seeds
20 ml/4 teaspoons whole cloves
2 sticks cinnamon
20 cardamoms

Place all the spices, except the cardamoms, in a heavy-based pan. Split the cardamom pods and scrape the black seeds into the pan. Roast the spices over low heat, stirring or shaking the pan every now and then, until they are aromatic and the small seeds begin to pop. Set aside to cool.

Grind the spices to a powder in a coffee grinder or spice mill. Store in an airtight container.

Mint Chutney

Tangy mint and lime juice combine wonderfully with spices to make this aromatic condiment. Serve the chutney with poultry, meat or vegetable dishes – it also makes a delicious appetiser with hot nan bread and a dish of cooling cucumber raita.

50 g/2 oz fresh mint leaves
8 spring onions
2 small fresh green chillies
salt
5 ml/1 teaspoon sugar
5 ml/1 teaspoon garam masala
15 ml/1 tablespoon pomegranate seeds
15 ml/1 tablespoon lime juice

Wash, drain and finely chop the mint leaves. Chop the spring onions. Discard the stalks, pith and seeds from the chillies, then chop the flesh.

Pound or purée the mint, onion and chillies with the salt, sugar and garam masala. Crush the pomegranate seeds, add to the mixture and continue processing or pounding until smooth. Add the lime juice and spoon the chutney into a bowl.

Chicken with Cardamom Stuffing

Elachi is the Indian name for ground cardamom seeds. It is an expensive spice which may be found in Indian grocers or, sometimes, in wholefood shops. The spice can be ground at home by scraping the tiny black seeds from the pale green cardamom pods and crushing them in a mortar using a pestle.

SERVES: 4–6
PREPARATION: 30 minutes
OVEN: 200°C/400°F/gas 6
COOKING: 45 minutes

2 onions
50 g/2 oz ghee
7.5 ml/1½ teaspoons elachi or ground cardamoms
salt and black pepper
100 g/4 oz chicken livers
40 g/1½ oz fresh white breadcrumbs
2 spring chickens or small chickens

Peel and finely chop the onions, then fry them gently in half the ghee until soft. Add the ground cardamoms and a generous seasoning of freshly ground black pepper. Reduce the heat and continue cooking the onions for 6–7 minutes. Chop the chicken livers and add to the onions, then cook until brown. Season to taste with salt.

Remove from the heat and stir in the breadcrumbs. Stuff the chickens with this spicy filling and set them on a spit or on a trivet in a roasting tin. Melt the remaining ghee and brush a little over the chicken. Roast in a preheated oven at 200°C/400°F/gas 6 for about 45 minutes, basting with the remaining ghee occasionally.

Pierce the thick thigh meat on the chickens to check that they are thoroughly cooked: if there are any signs of blood in the juices or raw meat, continue cooking and check after a further 10 minutes. Use a sharp knife and kitchen scissors to joint the chickens and serve with the stuffing on a platter.

Fried Bananas

Ice cream, sorbet or yogurt are popular cooling desserts to round off a spicy meal. Fresh fruit should always be offered, but anyone requiring a sweet dessert may like to sample this simple banana dish.

Peel six small bananas and cut them in half lengthways. Dip in lemon juice and coat with brown sugar. Fry the bananas in hot groundnut oil in a large shallow pan, until they are crisp and golden. Drain on absorbent kitchen paper and serve at once.

OCTOBER

Rich Pumpkin and Apricot Pie, Glazed Onions, Pheasant Vigneron.

October

October is a month for harvesting orchard fruits and picking potatoes. Earlier this century school holidays were organised to allow country children to help on the farms, when half term was known as 'potato week' or some equally evocative title.

Shorter days and darker evenings are a clear sign that autumn has set in, and traditional cooking activities reflect the need to stock up for winter. Despite the fact that the majority of foods are no longer seasonal, and that the freezer provides the easiest and most popular method for preserving fruit and vegetables, especially in summer, it is still traditional to turn any surplus autumn produce into chutneys and pickled vegetables. Not only do these add zest to meals later in the year, but their glowing colours add a touch of brightness to kitchen and pantry shelves.

British apples and pears are in their crisp and juicy prime, and the last of the plums are still available. The pumpkin makes its brief appearance with piles of the colourful vegetables stacked for sale at roadside farms in time for Halloween. Hollowed-out pumpkins make marvellous lanterns, but it is a shame if the firm, orange-coloured flesh is discarded. It can be prepared in a variety of ways to make delicious savoury and sweet dishes.

October is the beginning of the pheasant season. This game bird is a good choice for a formal dinner party or Sunday lunch gathering. New-season Jerusalem artichokes, those nutty-flavoured knobbly root vegetables that resemble potatoes, go well with game in addition to game chips and other classic accompaniments. Those lucky enough to have access to a crop of crab apples will be able to make a sparkling reserve of tangy jelly – ideal for complementing rich game, pork or ham, and an excellent preserve to pack away for Christmas as it is delicious with cold roast turkey.

Menu suggestions *Celebrate Halloween in style with the supper party menu, which makes full use of the traditional pumpkin, as well as featuring the less well-known Jerusalem artichoke. Alternatively, organise a formal Sunday lunch and make pheasant the focus of the meal. All the main recipes for these autumn menus are to be found within this chapter, with page references given for any additional recipes.*

Halloween Supper Party
~

Savoury Pumpkin Strudel
Buttered Boiled Jerusalem
Artichokes (page 342)
Baked Cabbage
~
Rich Pumpkin and Apricot Pie
or
Damson and Apple Tansy

As a change from the usual pumpkin soup, make a delicious Savoury Pumpkin Strudel, but don't drop the traditional sweet pumpkin pie – for true pumpkin fans it is one of the highlights of Halloween. The pie in this chapter is a departure from tradition, with apricots bringing a tart note to the usual creamy, spicy filling.

Queen of Puddings (page 256) with Damson and Apple Tansy (page 257).

Pasta Supper Party
~

Avocado, Pear and Nut Salad
~
Rigatoni with Hare Sauce
Green Salad
Warmed Crusty Bread
~
Fresh Figs with Yogurt

A main course served with pasta is ideal for informal entertaining. The casserole can be left to cook gently with the minimum of attention, or prepared up to a day ahead, chilled and thoroughly reheated before serving. The pasta can be cooked just before the main course is served and a simple salad really is the best possible accompaniment. Warm crusty bread is ideal for mopping up the delicious casserole juices.

Sunday Lunch
~

Smoked Eel Smetana
(page 264)
~
Pheasant Vigneron
Roast Potatoes
Cauliflower Polonaise
(page 231)
Steamed Pumpkin (page 346)
with Chive Butter (page 307)
~
Chocolate Pears

A seasonal variation on the usual joint, this menu makes the most of young roasting pheasant. Since there is always a certain amount of last-minute work involved in ensuring that a roast reaches the table in peak condition, complete with its sauce, garnish, vegetables and other accompaniments, the first course is very simple and the dessert can be prepared in advance.

SOUPS

Game Soup with Port

This is a rich, sustaining soup for cold autumn days. It can be made from stewing venison or from any game bird, such as pheasant, partridge or grouse, that is too tough for roasting or grilling.

SERVES: 6–8
PREPARATION: 55 minutes
COOKING: 2½ –3 hours

450 g/1 lb stewing venison or a
    900 g/2 lb game bird
1 large onion
1 parsnip or turnip
1 carrot
1 leek
3 sticks celery
225 g/8 oz mushrooms
75 g/3 oz butter
1 bay leaf
pinch each dried thyme, marjoram
    and basil
salt and black pepper
1–2 cloves garlic
1.7 litres/3 pt water
50 g/2 oz plain flour
150 ml/¼ pt port or burgundy
Croûtons (page 313) to garnish

Cut the venison into 5–7.5cm/ 2–3 in chunks, trimming off any fat. If a game bird is being used, chop it through the bone, into small portions; clean thoroughly. Peel and roughly chop the onion, parsnip or turnip and carrot. Wash all the dirt off the leek and the celery sticks under cold running water and chop them roughly as well. Trim and thinly slice the mushrooms.

Melt 25 g/1 oz of the butter in a large pan over moderate heat and fry the meat, turning it frequently, until it begins to colour. Add the onion, leek and celery to the pan and brown evenly. Put the parsnip or turnip into the pan, with the carrot, bay leaf, thyme, marjoram and basil. Season with salt and freshly ground pepper. Crush the garlic and add it to the pan. Pour in the water, which should be sufficient to cover the contents in the pan; bring to the boil over high heat.

Remove any scum which rises to the surface, then add the sliced mushrooms. Cover the pan with a lid and simmer over low heat for about 2 hours or until the meat is perfectly tender.

Strain the stock through a fine sieve or a muslin-lined sieve and leave it to cool slightly. Remove the bay leaf and all bones, then purée the meat and vegetables in a food processor or liquidiser with a little of the soup. It should be quite thick.

Melt the remaining butter in a large, clean pan over moderate heat; blend in the flour and cook, stirring continuously, until the roux* is caramel coloured. Take the pan off the heat and gradually blend in the port and about 300 ml/½ pt of the stock. Return the pan to the heat, bring the soup to simmering point, stirring all the time, then stir in the meat and vegetable purée and about 900 ml/1½ pt of the remaining stock to make a thick soup. Heat the soup through over low heat for about 15 minutes and correct seasoning if necessary.

Serve the game soup garnished with small croûtons.

Mexican Hot Pot Soup

This is the kind of winter soup which is a meal in itself. The ingredients include red kidney beans and chick peas which can be bought canned or dried. Dried beans and peas should be soaked overnight before use.

SERVES: 4
PREPARATION: 10 minutes
OVEN: 180°C/350°F/gas 4
COOKING: ¾–1½ hours

400 g/14 oz can or 100 g/4 oz
    dried red kidney beans
225 g/8 oz can or 50 g/2 oz
    dried chick peas
1 large onion
1 green or red pepper
25 g/1 oz bacon fat or butter or
    30 ml/2 tablespoons oil
225 g/8 oz minced beef
400 g/14 oz can tomatoes
450 ml/¾ pt stock
2.5 ml/½ teaspoon chilli powder
salt
shredded lettuce to garnish

If using dried beans and chick peas, drain off the soaking water and place them in a saucepan. Add plenty of fresh water and bring to the boil. Boil the beans and chick peas for 10 minutes, then reduce the heat and cover the pan; continue to cook for 30 minutes. Drain the beans and chick peas – they will not be tender at this point, but they will finish cooking in the soup.

Peel and finely chop the onion; cut off the stalk base of the pepper, remove the seeds and chop the pepper finely. Heat the fat or oil in a large heavy-based pan, and fry the onion until it begins to colour. Add the minced beef and continue frying over medium heat until the meat is well browned.

Add the tomatoes with their juices, the drained canned or partially cooked dried beans and chick peas and the chopped pepper. Stir in the stock, mixing thoroughly. Season to taste with chilli powder and a little salt. Cover the pan, and simmer the soup for 30 minutes or until the kidney beans or chick peas are very tender. Allow to cool, then purée in a liquidiser or food processor or rub the soup through a coarse sieve.

Reheat the thick soup before serving. Garnish with some finely shredded lettuce and serve with hot garlic bread.

■ Garlic bread goes very well with this soup: cut a French loaf into thick slices and spread each slice with Garlic Butter (page 307). Put the slices back to the original loaf form, wrap it in foil and heat in the oven for about 10 minutes, at 180°C/375°F/gas 4.

Mexican Hot Pot Soup.

STARTERS, SAVOURIES & LIGHT DISHES

Prawn Cocktail

The prawns can be replaced with lobster or white crabmeat, or mixed shellfish can be used to make a seafood cocktail.

SERVES: 4
PREPARATION: 15 minutes
CHILLING: 1 hour

225 g/8 oz peeled cooked prawns
15 ml/1 tablespoon tomato paste
150 ml/¼ pt mayonnaise
10 ml/2 teaspoons creamed
   horseradish
2.5 ml/½ teaspoon Worcestershire
   sauce or a few drops Tabasco
lemon juice
60 ml/4 tablespoons finely shredded
   lettuce heart
4 thin lemon slices to garnish

Select four of the largest prawns to garnish the cocktail and set them aside.

Mix the tomato paste, mayonnaise, creamed horseradish, the Worcestershire sauce or Tabasco and sharpen the dressing to taste with lemon juice.

Divide the shredded lettuce heart between individual serving glasses. Arrange the prawns over the lettuce and cover with the dressing. Chill the cocktails for about 1 hour.

Just before serving, hang one of the reserved prawns and a slit slice of lemon over the rim of each glass.

Honeydew Cups

A well-chilled melon salad is a good choice before a rich main course. Honeydew or cantaloupe melons are the least expensive, but for a special occasion, choose small Ogen or Charentais melons.

SERVES: 6
PREPARATION: 40 minutes
CHILLING: 1 hour

1 cucumber
salt
1 honeydew or cantaloupe melon
6 tomatoes
10 ml/2 teaspoons each chopped
   mint, chives, and chervil or
   parsley to garnish
Dressing
15–30 ml/1–2 tablespoons
   caster sugar
45 ml/3 tablespoons lemon juice or
   tarragon vinegar
90 ml/6 tablespoons salad oil

Peel the cucumber and cut it into 1 cm/½ in dice; sprinkle with salt and leave to stand for about 30 minutes. Cut the melon in half, crossways, and remove the seeds. Carefully scoop out the flesh in small balls, or cut it into small wedges. Skin the tomatoes (page 302), cut them in half and take out the cores and seeds. Chop the tomato flesh roughly.

Whisk the ingredients for the dressing in a bowl, adding the oil last of all. Rinse the cucumber in cold water and pat the dice dry on absorbent kitchen paper.

Put the melon, tomato and cucumber in a large bowl, pour over the dressing and mix well. Chill in the refrigerator for at least 1 hour, stirring occasionally.

Serve the salad in individual glass bowls and sprinkle with the mixed chopped herbs.

Avocado, Pear and Nut Salad

Avocados and dessert pears discolour quickly when peeled. For this salad it is essential to mix the dressing first and sprinkle the diced pears generously with lemon juice before mixing them into the dressing.

SERVES: 6
PREPARATION: 15 minutes
CHILLING: 1 hour

150 ml/¼ pt soured cream
10 ml/2 teaspoons tarragon vinegar
salt and black pepper
French mustard or
   Worcestershire sauce
caster sugar
3 avocados
juice of 1 lemon
1 large or 2 small dessert pears
45 ml/3 tablespoons salted almonds
snipped chives to garnish

Put the soured cream in a mixing bowl and stir in the vinegar. Season to taste with salt, freshly ground black pepper, mustard or Worcestershire sauce and a little sugar. Mix thoroughly.

Cut the avocados in half, take out the stones and carefully cut the flesh lengthways into four strips in each shell. Do not cut through the shell. Then cut the flesh in the opposite direction to make small cubes. Use a knife and teaspoon to loosen the flesh, easing it out of each shell in turn, in cubes. Save the avocado shells. Place the small cubes of avocado in a bowl. Sprinkle with some of the lemon juice. Peel, core and dice the dessert pear, add to the avocado and sprinkle with the remaining lemon juice.

Chop the salted nuts roughly and set a little aside for garnishing. Mix the remainder with the avocado and pears. Pour over the dressing and mix thoroughly. Pile the salad into the avocado shells and wrap each half in foil. Chill for 1 hour.

Just before serving, unwrap the avocado shells, arrange them on small plates and garnish with the chopped almonds and chives.

Savoury Eggs Bénédict

SERVES: 4
PREPARATION: 5 minutes
COOKING: 15–20 minutes

150 ml/¼ pt Hollandaise Sauce
   (page 355)
2.5 ml/½ teaspoon dry mustard
pinch cayenne pepper
pinch mixed herbs
4 slices cooked ham or 4 rashers
   back bacon
4 slices thick white bread
50 g/2 oz butter
4 eggs

First make the Hollandaise sauce (page 355) and season it with the mustard, cayenne and some mixed herbs. Keep it warm.

Trim the ham to fit the bread. If using bacon, fry the rashers in a little butter until they are crisp. Meanwhile, poach the eggs lightly in simmering salted water (page 337) and toast the bread.

Butter the toast, cover each slice with ham or bacon, and top with an egg. Pour over the warm sauce and serve at once.

Swiss Cheese Fondue

SERVES: 4–6
PREPARATION: 5 minutes
COOKING: 15–20 minutes

2 cloves garlic
350 g/12 oz Gruyère cheese
150 ml/¼ pt milk
450 ml/¾ pt dry white wine
15 ml/1 tablespoon Kirsch
salt and white pepper
1 French loaf

Peel the garlic and cut the cloves in half. Dice the cheese. Rub the garlic around the side and base of a flameproof heavy-based fondue pan. Add the cheese and milk and cook over very low heat, stirring all the time, with a wooden spoon, until the cheese melts and the mixture becomes smooth and creamy. Gradually stir in the wine and Kirsch; season with salt and pepper and heat through without boiling.

Heat the loaf in the oven until crisp. Cut it into 2.5 cm/ 1 in cubes and serve with the fondue. Use forks or skewers for dipping the bread in the cheese.

Mushrooms with Bacon

Streaky bacon and mushrooms are inexpensive ingredients for making savoury snacks or meals in a hurry.

SERVES: 4
PREPARATION: 10 minutes
COOKING: 20 minutes

100 g/4 oz sliced button
    mushrooms
15 g/½ oz butter
8 thin rashers streaky bacon
300 ml/½ pt thick coating White
    Sauce (page 352)
1.25 ml/¼ teaspoon mixed herbs
salt and black pepper
pinch cayenne pepper
4 slices buttered white toast

Cook the sliced mushrooms in the butter over low heat for 3 minutes. In a clean pan, fry the bacon until it is crisp – do not use any fat – then drain on absorbent kitchen paper and crumble the bacon into small pieces.

Make the white sauce, adding the mixed herbs. Season with salt, cayenne and freshly ground pepper. Gently fold the cooked mushrooms and bacon into the sauce; heat through. Pile the mixture on to the buttered toast and serve at once.

Tabbouleh with Olives and Bacon

Tabbouleh is a salad made largely of bulgur, a form of crushed and parcooked wheat. Tomatoes, garlic and mint are added and it is usually served with lettuce leaves which are used to scoop up the grain. Here, the basic salad is topped with olives, bacon and lemon, making a robust dish for lunch or supper. Omit the bacon if cooking for vegetarians.

SERVES: 4
PREPARATION: 30 minutes
SOAKING: 30 minutes
MARINATING: 45–60 minutes
COOKING: 15 minutes

225 g/8 oz bulgur
grated rind and juice of 1 lemon
salt and black pepper
2.5 ml/½ teaspoon caster sugar
15 ml/1 tablespoon
    chopped marjoram
75 ml/5 tablespoons olive oil
4 tomatoes
½ small onion
1 large clove garlic
30 ml/2 tablespoons chopped mint
60 ml/4 tablespoons
    chopped parsley
225 g/8 oz streaky bacon
50 g/2 oz black olives
pitta bread to serve

Soak the bulgur in plenty of cold water in a bowl for 30 minutes. Meanwhile, whisk the lemon juice, seasoning, caster sugar and marjoram together in a salad bowl. Gradually whisk in the olive oil. Skin the tomatoes (page 302), halve them and scoop out their seeds, then roughly chop the flesh and add it to the dressing. Peel and finely chop the onion, crush the garlic and add both to the tomatoes with the chopped mint and parsley.

Thoroughly drain the bulgur in a fine sieve, then stir it into the tomato and dressing mixture. Cover and leave to marinate* for 45–60 minutes.

Remove the rind from the bacon and cut the rashers into thin strips. Dry fry the bacon over low heat until the fat runs, then raise the heat and continue to cook until browned and crisp. Drain on absorbent kitchen paper. Stone and slice the olives. Mix the olives, bacon and grated lemon rind together. Pile the tabbouleh on a large shallow serving dish and surround it with the bacon and olive mixture. Serve with warmed pitta bread.

Rillettes of Pork

Most French country towns have their own version of rillettes – a coarse-textured terrine of pork and pork fat. It makes a pleasant change from smooth pâtés and is inexpensive to make.

SERVES: 6
PREPARATION: 30 minutes
OVEN: 140°C/275°F/gas 1
COOKING: 4 hours

900 g/2 lb belly pork
225 g/8 oz pork fat
salt and black pepper
2 cloves garlic
2 bay leaves
2 sprigs parsley
2 sprigs thyme or rosemary
about 150 ml/¼ pt water

Ask the butcher to bone the belly pork. Remove the rind from the pork and cut it into narrow strips. Dice the pork fat finely and season the meat and fat with salt and freshly ground pepper. Peel and crush the garlic and mix it with the meat. Pack the meat and fat into a casserole or terrine. Push the herbs down into the centre of the meat and pour the water over it. Cover the casserole with a lid or foil.

Bake in a preheated oven at 140°C/275°F/gas 1 for 4 hours. Stir the contents of the casserole occasionally to prevent a crusty top forming. When the meat is tender, turn the contents of the casserole into a sieve placed over a mixing bowl; leave until the fat and liquid has dripped through the sieve and into the bowl. Take out the herbs and shred the meat with two forks. Adjust the seasoning if necessary.

Pack the meat into one large earthenware pot, or several small ones. Pour the liquid and fat over to cover the meat by at least 5 mm/¼ in. Cool, cover and chill until the fat on the surface has set solid.

■ Serve the rillettes of pork with crusty French bread for a first course and with a watercress salad for a delicious light lunch or a cold snack.

Rillettes of Pork.

FISH, SHELLFISH & SEAFOOD

Fish Mousse with Bercy Sauce

This soufflé-like mousse can be kept waiting for a short without collapsing because it is steamed instead of baked. Here it is served as a main course, but it can also be served in individual moulds for a first course.

SERVES: 4–6
PREPARATION: 30 minutes
OVEN: 160°C/325°F/gas 3
COOKING: 1½ hours

450 g/1 lb haddock or cod fillets
900 ml/1½ pt Court Bouillon
 (page 316)
75 ml/2½ fl oz milk
25 g/1 oz butter
25 g/1 oz plain flour
2 eggs
75 ml/2½ fl oz double cream
20 ml/4 teaspoons chopped parsley
5 ml/1 teaspoon anchovy essence
lemon juice
salt and black pepper
45 ml/3 tablespoons lightly toasted
 breadcrumbs
Bercy Sauce
1 small onion
50 g/2 oz butter
150 ml/¼ pt dry white wine or cider
300 ml/½ pt fish stock
20 ml/4 teaspoons plain flour
75 ml/2½ fl oz double cream
Garnish
lemon slices
parsley sprigs

Simmer the fish, uncovered, in the court bouillon over low heat for 5–7 minutes or until just firm. Lift the fish out with a perforated spoon and set the liquid aside. Remove skin and any bones from the fish and flake it finely into a bowl. Mash it with a fork or make it into a coarse purée in a liquidiser or food processor.

Make the milk up to 150 ml/ ¼ pt with the fish liquid. Melt the butter in a saucepan, stir in the flour and cook for 2 minutes, then gradually stir in the milk mixture and bring to the boil to make a thick white sauce. Simmer for 2 minutes. Remove from the heat: the sauce should be very thick. Mix in the fish purée and beat well. Separate the eggs, and beat the yolks with the double cream; add them to the fish mixture, together with the chopped parsley, the anchovy essence, lemon juice, salt and freshly ground pepper.

Whisk the egg whites until stiff, but not dry. Beat a spoonful of the whites into the mixture, then use a metal spoon to fold in the rest of the whites. Brush a 600 ml/1 pt charlotte mould* or cake tin with oil and coat it evenly with the toasted crumbs.

Spoon the fish mixture into the mould – it should be three-quarters full. Cover the top with a piece of buttered foil and place the mould in a roasting tin. Pour 1 cm/½ in of water into the roasting tin. Bake in a preheated oven at 160°C/325°C/gas 3, for 1–1¼ hours or until the mousse is risen and set.

About 30 minutes before the mousse is ready, prepare the Bercy sauce. Peel the onion and chop it finely. Fry it over low heat in half the butter until soft, then add the wine or cider and fish stock. Increase the heat and boil the liquid rapidly, uncovered, until it has reduced by half. Cream the remaining butter and the flour to a beurre manié , and drop a few small knobs of the mixture into the gently simmering liquid, whisking all the time. Continue adding the beurre manié, whisking in each addition before adding the next, and bring to the boil. Lower the heat and simmer the sauce for 3 minutes. Stir in the cream and heat for a few seconds. Remove from the heat. Do not allow the sauce to boil. Season to taste with salt and freshly ground pepper.

Unmould the mousse on to a warm serving dish and garnish with lemon slices and sprigs of parsley. The Bercy sauce can be poured over the mousse or into a separate sauceboat.

■ Buttered spinach or Broccoli Spears au Gratin (page 110) are both suitable vegetables to serve with the mousse.

Finnan-filled Pancakes.

Finnan-filled Pancakes

Two pancakes should be allowed per person for a main course; one will be enough for a first course.

SERVES: 4
PREPARATION: 20 minutes
COOKING: about 45 minutes
 plus time for preparing
 pancakes

1 small onion
100 g/4 oz mushrooms
50 g/2 oz butter
30 ml/2 tablespoons chopped celery
400 g/14 oz can chopped tomatoes
2.5 ml/½ teaspoon caster sugar
salt and black pepper
225 g/8 oz cooked smoked
 finnan haddock fillet or
 smoked haddock
lemon juice
8 thin Pancakes (page 339)
45–60 ml/3–4 tablespoons grated
 Cheddar or Gruyère cheese
Garnish
lemon wedges
parsley sprigs

Peel and finely chop the onion. Thinly slice the mushrooms.

Melt half the butter and fry the onion and celery for about 15 minutes, until softened but not browned. Stir in the mushrooms and cook for a further 5 minutes. Add the tomatoes, and season with sugar, salt and pepper. Simmer, uncovered, for 20 minutes.

Meanwhile, skin and flake the haddock. Add the haddock to the tomato mixture, sharpen to taste with lemon juice and adjust the seasoning, if necessary.

Spoon the filling down the centre of the pancakes. Fold the sides over to form an envelope. Arrange the stuffed pancakes in a shallow flameproof dish.

Melt the remaining butter and pour it over the pancakes. Sprinkle with grated cheese. Set the dish under a moderately hot grill until the pancakes are hot and the cheese is golden.

Garnish the pancakes with lemon wedges and parsley sprigs.

Devilled Crab

Devilled dishes first appeared on English menus early in the 19th century. The main ingredient, which may be meat, poultry or fish, is cooked in a sharp hot sauce, topped with breadcrumbs and finished off under the grill or in the oven.

If fresh crab is used for this recipe, allow two medium crabs and reserve the scrubbed shells to use instead of serving dishes.

SERVES: 4
PREPARATION: 20 minutes
COOKING: 5–10 minutes

150 ml/¼ pt single cream
5 ml/1 teaspoon French mustard
5–10 ml/1–2 teaspoons
    anchovy essence
5 ml/1 teaspoon Worcester-
    shire sauce
10–20 ml/2–4 teaspoons
    lemon juice
pinch cayenne pepper
salt and black pepper
350 g/12 oz crabmeat
30 ml/2 tablespoons toasted
    breadcrumbs
30 ml/2 tablespoons grated
    Cheddar cheese
Garnish
watercress
lemon wedges

Mix the single cream, French mustard, anchovy essence and Worcestershire sauce together in a saucepan. Season to taste with lemon juice, cayenne, salt and freshly ground pepper. Stir the crabmeat into the cream and heat the mixture through over moderate heat without boiling.

Spoon the crab mixture into four individual gratin dishes. Mix together the breadcrumbs and grated cheese and sprinkle over the crab. Brown the topping under a hot grill. Garnish with watercress and lemon wedges and serve piping hot.

■ Thin, brown bread and butter is traditional with crab and is sufficient for a first course.

Prawns in Coconut Cream

SERVES: 4
PREPARATION: 10 minutes
COOKING: 45 minutes

2 large onions
45 ml/3 tablespoons ghee*
15 ml/1 tablespoon Garam
    Masala (p239)
1 green pepper
450 g/1 lb peeled cooked prawns
salt
300 ml/½ pt Coconut Milk (p239)

Finely chop the onions and fry over low heat in the ghee, until soft and pale golden – this can take up to 30 minutes. Add the garam marsala and cook for a further 2–3 minutes.

Slice the pepper, discarding the core and seeds and stir it into the onions. Cover and cook gently for 10 minutes. Add the peeled prawns, season with salt, and cook for 1 minute. Keep the heat as low as possible; stir in the coconut milk and cook gently until the prawns and the sauce are heated through.

■ Serve the prawns with plain boiled basmati rice.

Scallop Brochettes

SERVES: 2–4
PREPARATION: 25 minutes
COOKING: 15–20 minutes

2 shallots
1 egg
12 scallops
1 sprig parsley
salt and black pepper
150 ml/¼ pt dry white wine
about 25 g/1 oz dry white
    breadcrumbs
225 g/8 oz thin rashers
    streaky bacon
2 green peppers
16 small mushroom caps
30 ml/2 tablespoons oil
plain or saffron rice to serve
fresh bay leaves to garnish

Peel and halve the shallots. Beat the egg lightly in a shallow bowl. Put the scallops in a saucepan with the shallots and parsley sprig, a little salt and freshly ground pepper; add sufficient wine to cover. Poach the scallops over gentle heat for 1 minute, until just firm.

Lift out the scallops, cut off the orange-coloured roes and coat the roes in the lightly beaten egg and then the breadcrumbs. Set them aside.

Slice each nut of white scallop in half horizontally. Remove the rind from the bacon, stretch the rashers with the blade of a knife and cut each rasher into three pieces. Wrap a piece of bacon around each portion of white scallop.

Remove the stalk ends and seeds from the peppers and cut them into 2.5 cm/1 in squares. Trim the mushrooms, leaving them whole.

Thread the bacon-wrapped scallops, mushroom caps, peppers and breadcrumbed roes alternately on to the skewers. Brush with oil and cook under a hot grill for 8–10 minutes, turning the brochettes several times to grill evenly, until the bacon is browned and the other ingredients are cooked.

Arrange the skewers on a bed of plain or saffron rice and garnish with fresh bay leaves.

■ Serve a fresh, crisp salad with these brochettes.

Scallop Brochettes.

POULTRY & GAME

Chicken Kiev

This classic recipe consisting of deep-fried chicken fillets stuffed with savoury butter comes from the Ukraine. Initial preparations should be done in advance.

SERVES: 4
PREPARATION: 40 minutes
CHILLING: 8–12 hours
COOKING: 15 minutes

100 g/4 oz butter
grated rind and juice of 1
*   small lemon*
30 ml/2 tablespoons chopped
*   tarragon or parsley*
pinch grated nutmeg (optional)
salt and black pepper
4 part-boned chicken breasts,
*   with wing bone only*
1 large egg
100 g/4 oz fresh white breadcrumbs
oil for deep frying
watercress to garnish

Cream the butter with the lemon rind, tarragon (or parsley) and a pinch of nutmeg. Season to taste with salt, freshly ground pepper and a little lemon juice. Shape the butter into a rectangular block, wrap it in foil and chill until it has set solid.

Put one chicken breast between sheets of greaseproof paper, keeping the wing bone to one side, and beat the meat flat. Repeat with the other joints, so that they all have small wing bones attached to large, thin fillets of chicken.

Cut the hard butter into four roughly square pieces and place one in the centre of each flat chicken fillet. Fold the meat over to enclose the butter completely in a neat nugget of meat, still attached to the wing bone.

Beat the egg and coat the chicken with beaten egg and then breadcrumbs; press them on thoroughly. Coat the chicken a second time for a crisper finish; pat the egg on with a brush so as not to disturb the first coating. Chill for several hours or overnight. This will set the coating and help to keep the butter enclosed during cooking.

Heat the oil for deep frying to 190°C/375°C or until a cube of day-old bread browns in 1 minute. Fry the chicken in two batches, until golden brown and cooked through. Do not allow the fat to get too hot or the chicken will brown before it is cooked. Drain the cooked chicken on crumpled absorbent kitchen paper.

Arrange the pieces of chicken Kiev on a warmed serving dish and garnish with small bunches of watercress.

■ Boiled new potatoes and sliced courgettes cooked in butter make good side dishes for this chicken dish.

Faisan au Verger

This method of cooking pheasant with apples and Calvados comes from Normandy. Many supermarkets now sell prepared pheasant joints, which are ideal for use in this casserole.

SERVES: 4
PREPARATION: 40 minutes
OVEN: 160°C/325°F/gas 3
COOKING: 1–1¼ hours

1 pheasant
1 bay leaf
1 sprig parsley
salt and black pepper
1 onion
2 sticks celery
2 cooking apples
30–45 ml/2–3 level tablespoons
*   plain flour*
40 g/1½ oz butter
150 ml/¼ pt cider
30 ml/2 tablespoons Calvados
*   (optional)*
75 ml/2½ fl oz double cream
Garnish
2 dessert apples
butter (see method)
celery leaves

If you are using a whole bird, joint the pheasant by first removing the legs, then cutting away the two breast sections down and along the backbone. Leave the flesh on the bone, so that it will not shrink during cooking, and cut off the wing pinions.

Put the leftover pheasant carcass, the neck and the cleaned giblets into a pan, together with the bay leaf, parsley, and a seasoning of salt and freshly ground pepper. Cover with cold water, put the lid on the pan and bring to the boil, then simmer this stock over low heat for about 20 minutes, then strain the stock into a measuring jug.

Peel and thinly slice the onion. Cut the leafy tops off the celery and set aside for garnish. Scrub the celery sticks and chop them finely. Peel, core and roughly chop the cooking apples.

Coat the pheasant joints lightly with a little flour, and heat the butter in a flameproof casserole or heavy-based pan. Fry the pheasant over high heat until it is golden brown all over, then remove from the casserole. Lower the heat and fry the onion and celery for 5 minutes. Add the cooking apples and fry for a further 5 minutes.

Draw the casserole from the heat and stir in enough of the remaining flour to absorb all the fat. Gradually stir in the cider (and Calvados if used) and 300 ml/½ pt of the strained pheasant stock. Stirring all the time, bring this sauce to simmering point over low heat.

Put the pheasant back into the casserole and, if necessary, stir more stock into the sauce until it almost covers the joints.

Season to taste with salt and freshly ground pepper, and cover the casserole with a lid.

Cook the casserole in the centre of a preheated oven at 160°C/325°F/gas 3, for 45 minutes or until the meat is tender. Remove the pheasant and keep warm. Boil the sauce briskly on top of the stove, stir into the cream and pour this mixture back into the pan; adjust seasoning.

Return the pheasant to the sauce and serve straight from the dish. Alternatively, arrange the joints on a warm deep serving dish and spoon the sauce over them. Surround with the cored, but unpeeled apples, cut into thick slices and fried in a little butter until golden. Push a garnish of celery leaves through the centre of each apple slice.

■ Serve with Scalloped Potatoes (page 252) and courgettes.

Faisan au Verger.

Pheasant or Guinea Fowl Vigneron

In this French recipe, guinea fowl is cooked with white grapes. This domesticated game bird has a flavour similar to that of turkey. Pheasant cooked this way is also delicious. A guinea chick will provide two servings and a fully grown bird three.

SERVES: 3
PREPARATION: 30 minutes
OVEN: 200°C/400°F/gas 6
COOKING: 55 minutes

1 pheasant or guinea fowl
    (with giblets)
1 onion
bouquet garni*
salt and black pepper
225 g/8 oz seedless white grapes
juice of 1 lemon
25 g/1 oz butter
4 rashers fat bacon (optional)
120 ml/4 fl oz dry white wine
2 egg yolks
75 ml/2½ fl oz single cream
Garnish
white grapes
lemon wedges
herb sprigs

Place the giblets in a saucepan with 600 ml/1 pt cold water. Peel and quarter the onion. Add it to the giblets with the bouquet garni and a good seasoning of salt and freshly ground pepper. Bring to the boil, remove any scum, then lower the heat and simmer the stock, covered, for 20 minutes. Strain and set aside.

Meanwhile, peel the grapes (page 360) if they are thick-skinned. Sprinkle them with a

Pheasant Vigneron.

little lemon juice and salt before stuffing them into the guinea fowl. Sew up the vent or spear it with two short metal skewers to keep the grapes inside the bird. Melt the butter and brush it all over the bird. Remove the rind from the bacon and tie the rashers over the breast of the guinea fowl.

Roast the stuffed guinea fowl in the centre of a preheated oven at 200°C/400°F/gas 6 for 30 minutes. Remove the bacon and continue cooking the guinea fowl for a further 15 minutes or until the bird is golden brown and tender. Place on a serving dish and keep the bird warm in the oven.

Pour the white wine into the roasting tin and bring to the boil on top of the stove, scraping up all the residue. Pour it into a measuring jug and make it up to 150 ml/¼ pt with the giblet stock.

Beat the egg yolks with the single cream in a bowl and gradually stir in the wine and stock mixture. Place the bowl over a saucepan containing 1 cm/½ in of gently simmering water. Stir this sauce continuously until it has thickened enough to coat the back of a wooden spoon thinly. Do not let the sauce reach boiling point or it will curdle. Correct seasoning and sharpen to taste with lemon juice.

Garnish the guinea fowl with grapes, lemon wedges and fresh herb sprigs. Pour the sauce into a warmed sauceboat and serve it separately.
■ Château Potatoes (page 347) and Cauliflower Polonaise (page 231) over which the crisp roasted bacon has been crumbled instead of the egg garnish could be served with this dish.

Spatch-cocked Grouse with Rowan Jelly

Spatch-cocking is a distortion of an 18th century Irish term for providing unexpected guests with a quick meal. A farmyard chicken was dispatched (killed), split and fried or grilled. The term has since come to define the cooking method, which is especially suitable for small birds which do not require hanging.

SERVES: 2
PREPARATION: 35 minutes
COOKING: 30 minutes

2 young grouse
30–45 ml/2–3 tablespoons olive oil
15–30 ml/1–2 tablespoons
    lemon juice
salt and black pepper
50 g/2 oz butter
4 rashers streaky bacon
2 large slices white bread
60 ml/2 fl oz dry vermouth
15 ml/1 tablespoon rowan or
    quince jelly
30 ml/2 tablespoons chopped
    parsley to garnish

For spatch-cocking, slit each grouse along the backbone without separating the two halves. Open each bird out in turn and beat it flat. Cut off the feet and push up the flesh on the legs to expose about 2.5 cm/1 in on each drumstick. Make a slit with a sharp knife below each thigh joint, just above the vent. Push up the leg and insert the bare bone in the slit. Fold the pinions underneath the wings so that

they lie flat. Hold each grouse in position by inserting skewers in a crossways pattern from each wing to leg joint.

Mix 30 ml/2 tablespoons olive oil with 15 ml/1 tablespoon lemon juice. Brush this mixture over the grouse and sprinkle with salt and pepper. Set aside for 20 minutes so that the oil soaks in.

Melt the butter in a heavy-based pan and fry the prepared grouse over high heat for 5 minutes on each side. Lower the heat and continue cooking the grouse for another 5–7 minutes on each side. Lift the grouse on to a warm serving plate.

Trim the rind from the bacon. Remove the crusts from the bread and cut each slice into two triangles. Fry the bacon and the bread in the pan until they are quite crisp (adding the rest of the oil if necessary). Lift them out and keep warm. Pour the fat from the pan, leaving about 15 ml/1 tablespoon. Add the vermouth and boil over high heat, scraping up the residue in the bottom of the pan. Stir in the rowan or quince jelly and cook until it has melted. Sharpen the gravy to taste with lemon juice.

Remove the skewers from the grouse, and pour the gravy over the birds. Arrange the crisp bacon and fried bread around the grouse and sprinkle with parsley.
■ Serve the grouse with Game Chips (page 347) and Green Beans Tuscany Style (page 232).

MEAT

Tournedos en Croûte

The small, thick round slices – or tournedos – cut from the fillet of beef are among the most expensive cuts of meat. But for a special occasion, tournedos can be encased in puff pastry, and a 100 g/4 oz portion will then be sufficient for each person.

SERVES: 6
PREPARATION: 30 minutes
OVEN: 220°C/425°F/gas 7
COOKING: 40 minutes

6 tournedos
25 g/1 oz butter
350–375 g/12–13 oz home-made
  Puff Pastry (page 374) or
  thawed frozen puff pastry
100 g/4 oz pâté with mushrooms
  or truffles
1 egg
1 onion
120 ml/4 fl oz red wine
300 ml/½ pt beef stock
salt and black pepper
watercress to garnish

Trim any fat off the tournedos. Heat the butter in a heavy-based pan and brown the meat quickly on both sides to seal in the juices. Set aside to cool, reserving the pan juices.

Roll out the puff pastry on a floured surface, to a rectangle, 3 mm/⅛ in thick. Divide the pastry into six equal squares, each one large enough to wrap around a tournedo. Spread one side of each tournedo with pâté and place it, pâté side down, on a pastry square. Brush the edges of the pastry with cold water and draw them together over the meat to form a neat parcel. Seal the edges carefully.

Place the pastry parcels, with the seams underneath, on a wet baking sheet. Lightly beat the egg and brush over the pastry. Make two or three slits in each parcel for the steam to escape, and decorate with leaves cut from the pastry trimmings. Beat the egg to glaze the pastry.

Bake the tournedos in the centre of a preheated oven at 220°C/425°F/gas 7 for 15–20 minutes. At this point, the pastry should be well risen and golden brown and the meat will be rosy-pink in the middle. For well-done steaks, lower the heat to 180°C/350°F/gas 4 and cook for a further 10 minutes.

Make the sauce while the tournedos are cooking. Peel and finely chop the onion and fry until just coloured in the butter left in the pan. Add the wine and let it bubble over moderate heat for 2–3 minutes, stirring in the residue from the pan. Stir in the stock and simmer for a further 5 minutes. Season with salt and freshly ground pepper.

Arrange the tournedos en croûte on a warm serving dish. Garnish with sprigs of watercress. Pour the sauce into a sauceboat and serve it separately.

Tournedos en Croûte.

Boeuf Stroganoff

SERVES: 4–6
PREPARATION: 10 minutes
COOKING: 25 minutes

675 g/1½ lb fillet or rump steak
1 onion
225 g/8 oz mushrooms
50 g/2 oz butter
15 ml/1 tablespoon French mustard
150 ml/¼ pt soured cream
salt and black pepper
lemon juice

Wipe and trim the steak. If using rump, beat it thin between two sheets of greaseproof paper to make it as tender as possible. Cut it into thin strips.

Peel and finely chop the onion and trim and slice the mushrooms. Heat 25 g/1 oz of the butter and fry the vegetables over low heat until they are soft and just beginning to colour. Use a perforated spoon to remove the vegetables, setting them aside in a bowl with all the cooking juices scraped from the pan.

Heat the remaining butter in the pan and fry the meat over high heat until the strips are brown all over. Replace the vegetables and their juices, and stir in the French mustard. Pour in the soured cream and add salt, freshly ground pepper and lemon juice to taste. Heat through, stirring, then serve immediately.
■ Fluffy boiled rice and green beans, baby Brussels sprouts or peas would go well with this dish.

Hungarian Goulash

Different regions of Hungary have their own favourite goulash recipes, using fresh tomatoes, caraway, garlic or marjoram, but they always contain paprika.

SERVES: 4
PREPARATION: 35 minutes
COOKING: 2–2½ hours

575 g/1¼ lb chuck steak
450 g/1 lb onions
30 ml/2 tablespoons oil or
  25 g/1 oz lard
30 ml/2 tablespoons plain flour
900 ml/1½ pt beef stock or water
salt
45 ml/3 tablespoons tomato paste
15–20 ml/3–4 teaspoons paprika
2.5 ml/½ teaspoon caster sugar
65 ml/2½ fl oz soured cream

Trim the meat and cut it into 3.5 cm/1½ in cubes. Peel and thinly slice the onions.

Heat the oil or melt the lard in a flameproof casserole and fry the meat and onions until the onions are soft and the meat is sealed. Stir in the flour, then pour over the hot stock and bring to simmering point, stirring all the time. Stir in the salt, tomato paste, paprika and sugar.

Cover the stew and leave to cook over gentle heat for about 2 hours or until the meat is tender. Stir every now and then to ensure that the sauce does not burn on the bottom of the pan.

Stir in the soured cream just before serving.
■ Ribbon noodles are the traditional accompaniment.

Beef Satay

Soak bamboo skewers in cold water for 30 minutes before use to prevent them from scorching.

SERVES: 6
PREPARATION: 20 minutes
MARINATING: 2 hours
COOKING: 20 minutes

15 ml/1 tablespoon blanched almonds
15 ml/1 tablespoon sliced fresh root ginger
5 ml/1 teaspoon ground coriander
5 ml/1 teaspoon ground turmeric
300 ml/½ pt Coconut Milk (p239)
675 g/1½ lb fillet or frying steak
salt and black pepper
5 ml/1 teaspoon brown sugar

Purée the almonds, ginger, coriander and turmeric to a paste in a liquidiser. Gradually add the coconut milk.

Cut the meat into bite-size pieces, discarding all the fat; sprinkle the pieces with salt and ground pepper. Marinate* the

Beef Satay.

meat in the spiced coconut milk for 2 hours.

Remove the meat from the marinade and thread on to the drained bamboo skewers; sprinkle lightly with sugar and grill, turning and basting frequently with the marinade. Allow two skewers per person and serve with Satay Sauce.

Satay Sauce

SERVES: 6
PREPARATION: 15 minutes
COOKING: 15 minutes

2 onions
15–30 ml/1–2 tablespoons peanut oil
75 g/3 oz roasted peanuts
2.5 ml/½ teaspoon chilli powder
150 ml/¼ pt warm water
5 ml/1 teaspoon light brown sugar
salt
15 ml/1 tablespoon soy sauce
juice of ½ lime

Peel and thinly slice one onion and fry in the hot peanut oil until brown.

Peel and finely chop the second onion and pound it with the peanuts and chilli powder in a mortar or liquidiser. Add this paste to the browned onion and fry for a further 3 minutes, stirring all the time. Gradually dilute the mixture with the warm water and stir in the sugar. Bring to the boil, reduce the heat and simmer for a few minutes until the sauce has the consistency of single cream. Season to taste with salt, soy sauce and lime juice. Serve the sauce hot, with the beef skewers.

Carré d'Agneau Dordonnaise

Walnuts and liver pâté are both used in this recipe from the Dordogne, which transforms best end of lamb into a party dish.

SERVES: 4–6
PREPARATION: 30 minutes
OVEN: 200°C/400°F/gas 6
        190°C/375°F/gas 5
COOKING: 1¼ hours

2 best end necks of lamb
50–75 g/2–3 oz shelled walnuts
½ small onion
100 g/4 oz fine pâté
60 ml/4 tablespoons fresh white breadcrumbs
30 ml/2 tablespoons finely chopped parsley
salt and black pepper
lemon juice
30 ml/2 tablespoons cooking oil
120 ml/4 fl oz dry white wine
5 ml/1 teaspoon chopped rosemary

Order the best ends skinned and boned and ask the butcher to include the bones with the order. Trim any excess fat off the meat. Chop the walnuts finely or grind them in a food processor. Peel and grate the onion. Stir the walnuts and onion into the pâté. Mix the breadcrumbs and parsley into the stuffing, and season with salt, pepper and lemon juice.

Spread the underside of each best end with the stuffing. Roll the meat neatly and tie with string at 5 cm/2 in intervals. Put the two meat rolls in an oiled roasting tin; brush them with oil.

Cook the lamb in a preheated oven at 200°C/400°F/gas 6 for about 20 minutes, or until golden brown. Reduce the oven temperature to 190°C/375°F/gas 5 and cook for a further 40–50 minutes, or until tender.

Meanwhile, put the bones in a saucepan with salt and pepper. Cover with cold water, bring to the boil and simmer for 30–40 minutes. Strain the stock into a measuring jug.

Remove the meat from the roasting tin, cover with foil and set aside to keep warm. Carefully pour off the excess fat in the roasting tin and add the wine to the meat juices. Bring to the boil, add 600 ml/1 pt of the strained stock and the rosemary. Boil this gravy over high heat until it has reduced by about a quarter. Stir in the sediment off the bottom of the pan occasionally. Correct the seasoning and strain the gravy into a warm sauceboat.

■ Serve the lamb, cut into thick slices, with roast potatoes and Brussels sprouts.

Spare Rib Chops in Cider

With the onset of cool autumn weather, a casserole makes a warming meal.

SERVES: 6
PREPARATION: 30 minutes
OVEN: 200°C/400°F/gas 6
COOKING: 50 minutes

225 g/8 oz mushrooms
1 large onion
75 g/3 oz butter
5 ml/1 teaspoon dried winter savory or thyme
salt and black pepper
6 spare rib chops
200 ml/7 fl oz medium dry cider
50 g/2 oz Cheddar cheese
25 g/1 oz fresh white breadcrumbs
parsley sprigs to garnish

Wipe and slice the mushrooms. Peel the onion and chop it finely. Melt the butter in a small pan and cook the onion for 5 minutes. Stir in the mushrooms, then immediately transfer the mixture to a casserole. Sprinkle with the savory or thyme and season with salt and pepper.

Trim excess fat off the chops and lay them on top of the vegetables. Pour in the cider and bake in a preheated oven at 200°C/400°F/gas 6 for 30 minutes. Baste the chops with the cooking juices.

Grate the cheese and mix it with the breadcrumbs. Spread this mixture evenly over the chops. Cook for a further 15 minutes, until the topping is crisp and lightly browned. Garnish with parsley sprigs.

Hock with Cider and Raisins

SERVES: 6
PREPARATION: 20 minutes
SOAKING: 8 hours
COOKING: 2½ hours

900 g–1.15 kg/2–2½ lb hock or
    shoulder of gammon
225 g/8 oz split peas or chick peas
1 small onion
50 g/2 oz butter
30 ml/2 tablespoons chopped celery
40 g/1½ oz plain flour
300 ml/½ pt dry cider
50 g/2 oz stoneless raisins
10 ml/2 teaspoons Demerara sugar
30 ml/2 tablespoons chopped
    fresh parsley

Wash the hock and soak it with the split or chick peas in cold water for 8 hours or overnight. Drain the meat and peas, put them in a large heavy-based pan and cover with fresh cold water. Bring to the boil, then lower the heat and cover the pan with a lid. Simmer for 1½ hours or until the hock is tender.

Hock with Cider and Raisins.

Lift the meat from the pan and set it aside to cool slightly. Leave the peas to cook for a further 30–40 minutes or until they are quite tender. Skin the hock carefully while still warm, and cut the meat off the bone in small pieces, discarding the fat.

Peel and finely chop the onion. Melt 40 g/1½ oz of the butter in a heavy-based pan and fry the onion and celery for 10 minutes until soft. Stir in the flour, then gradually stir in the cider and bring to the boil, stirring, to make a smooth sauce. Mix in the raisins. Drain the peas, reserving 300 ml/½ pt of the gammon stock. Set the peas aside and stir the reserved stock into the sauce. Add the sugar and meat and continue cooking and stirring over low heat for a further 10 minutes.

Melt the remaining butter in a pan and add the peas. Toss lightly to heat through, then add the parsley. Spoon the meat and sauce into a dish and surround with a border of the peas.

VEGETABLES & SALADS

Baked Cabbage

Firm white winter cabbage is one of the least expensive vegetables.

SERVES: 6
PREPARATION: 30 minutes
OVEN: 220°C/425°F/gas 7
COOKING: 25 minutes

675 g/1½ lb white cabbage
salt and black pepper
50 g/2 oz butter
40 g/1½ oz plain flour
600 ml/1 pt milk
ground mace or grated nutmeg
50 g/2 oz chopped salted
    peanuts (optional)
50–100 g/2–4 oz grated
    Cheddar cheese

Discard any damaged outer leaves and cut the cabbage into quarters. Cut out the centre stalk and shred the cabbage finely. Cook the shredded cabbage in boiling salted water for 5–7 minutes or until cooked, but not soft. Drain thoroughly.

Melt the butter and stir in the flour. Cook over a low heat for 2–3 minutes, stirring constantly. Gradually add the milk and beat continuously until a thick smooth sauce is obtained. Bring to the boil, then lower the heat and simmer for about 3 minutes. Season to taste with salt, pepper and mace or nutmeg.

Butter an ovenproof dish and arrange a layer of cabbage over the base. Cover with some of the sauce and sprinkle with nuts (if used) and Cheddar cheese. Fill the dish with layers of cabbage, white sauce, nuts and cheese, finishing with grated cheese. Bake in a preheated oven at 220°C/425°F/gas 7 for about 15 minutes, or until the cheese is golden brown. Serve the baked cabbage at once.

■ Baked in a cheese sauce, cabbage goes well with sausages or bacon, or it may be served with baked potatoes or pasta.

Glazed Onions

These small buttered onions are both tasty and decorative with elaborate joints of meat, such as fillet of beef en croûte or roast crown of lamb.

SERVES: 4
PREPARATION: 15 minutes
COOKING: 20 minutes

450 g/1 lb button onions or shallots
50 g/2 oz butter
30 ml/2 tablespoons caster sugar

Fill a large saucepan with water, bring to the boil, and put in the washed onions. Cook over low heat for 7 minutes, then drain and peel the onions.

Melt the butter in the saucepan, add the boiled onions and toss them over low heat for 3 minutes. Sprinkle over the sugar and continue tossing the onions for a further 4 minutes until they are evenly glazed and tender. Serve the onions with the glaze.

Scalloped Potatoes

This potato gratin can be served with any type of grilled or roast meat, or it can be made into a main dish by adding chopped cooked ham or flaked cooked fish between the potato layers.

SERVES: 6
PREPARATION: 15–20 minutes
OVEN: 180°C/350°F/gas 4
COOKING: 1½ hours

675 g/1½ lb potatoes
1 onion
100 g/4 oz Cheddar cheese
50 g/2 oz butter
salt and black pepper
1 egg
300 ml/½ pt milk

Peel and thinly slice the potatoes. Peel and finely chop the onion, and grate the Cheddar cheese. Use a little of the butter to grease a shallow, ovenproof dish. Arrange the potato slices in layers in the dish, sprinkling each layer with onion, grated cheese, salt and freshly ground pepper. Finish with a thick layer of cheese and dot with the remaining butter.

Beat the egg and milk together and pour this mixture carefully over the layered potatoes. Cover the dish with buttered grease-proof paper or foil. Bake in a preheated oven at 180°C/350°F/gas 4 for 1 hour. Then remove the paper or foil and continue cooking for a further 30 minutes, or until the potatoes are tender, and the topping is golden. If cooked too quickly, the egg and milk will curdle.

Chestnut and Potato Purée

SERVES: 6–8
PREPARATION: 20 minutes
COOKING: 30 minutes

350 g/12 oz fresh chestnuts or
    225 g/8 oz can chestnut purée
600 ml/1 pt stock
    (for fresh chestnuts)
350 g/12 oz mashed potatoes
50 g/2 oz butter
60–75 ml/4–5 tablespoons
    single cream
salt and pinch grated nutmeg or
    black pepper
60 ml/4 tablespoons chopped
    celery heart

If using fresh chestnuts, make a small cut on the flat side of each chestnut and roast them on the hob in a chestnut pan or on a baking tray near the top of a hot oven. After 5–10 minutes, the skins will crack. Peel the two layers of skin from the chestnuts while still warm.

Put the stock in a saucepan, add the peeled chestnuts and cover the pan with a lid. Bring to the boil, then simmer the chestnuts for 20 minutes or until tender. Drain the chestnuts and rub them through a coarse sieve.

Blend the freshly made or canned chestnut purée with the mashed potato, stir in the butter and heat the mixture through over low heat. Blend in enough cream to give the purée a fluffy texture, and season with salt and grated nutmeg or pepper.

Stir in the chopped celery just before serving.

Broccoli with Poulette Sauce

SERVES: 4–6
PREPARATION: 10 minutes
COOKING: 20–30 minutes

900 g/2 lb broccoli
salt and black pepper
50 g/2 oz butter
15 ml/1 tablespoon plain flour
1 egg yolk
10 ml/2 teaspoons lemon juice
30 ml/2 tablespoons double cream

Trim the tough stalk and any leaves off the broccoli. Boil the broccoli in salted water for about 10 minutes or until just tender. Lift the broccoli carefully into a colander to drain, reserving the liquid. Cover it with a dry cloth to keep warm. Measure 300 ml/½ pt of the liquid and set aside.

Melt the butter in a small saucepan, stir in the flour and cook for 2 minutes. Gradually mix in the broccoli liquid. Bring this sauce to the boil, stirring all the time, then reduce the heat and simmer for 10 minutes. Beat the egg yolk with the lemon juice and 30 ml/2 tablespoons of the hot sauce. Remove the sauce from the heat and stir in the egg.

Stir in the cream. Keep the sauce warm, but do not allow it to boil or the egg and cream will curdle. Season to taste with salt, freshly ground pepper and more lemon juice. Put the broccoli in a warm deep serving dish and pour over the sauce.

Broccoli with Poulette Sauce.

Spiced Marrow with Chick Peas

SERVES: 4–6
PREPARATION: 20 minutes
COOKING: 1–1½ hours

900 g/2 lb peeled and
    deseeded marrow
1 large onion
1 green chilli
25 g/1 oz butter or 30 ml/
    2 tablespoons oil
2 cloves garlic
6 green cardamoms
15 ml/1 tablespoon cumin seeds
1 bay leaf
30 ml/2 tablespoons
    ground coriander
5 ml/1 teaspoon turmeric
2 × 400 g/14 oz cans chick peas
300 ml/½ pt chicken or
    vegetable stock
salt and black pepper
60 ml/4 tablespoons instant
    coconut milk powder
300 ml/½ pt plain yogurt

Cut the marrow into large chunks; peel and chop the onion. Cut the stalk end off the chilli, discard all the seeds and pith, and chop the flesh. Melt the butter or heat the oil in a flameproof casserole. Crush the garlic into the pan. Add the onion, cardamoms, cumin and bay leaf. Cook, stirring, for 15 minutes. Add the marrow, stir well and cook for 5 minutes.

Add the coriander, turmeric, drained chick peas, stock and seasoning. Bring to the boil, cover and simmer for 15 minutes. Remove the lid and continue to simmer for a further 15 minutes.

Gradually stir coconut milk powder into the yogurt, then stir the mixture into the marrow. Bring back to simmering point and cook for a further 10–15 minutes, or until the marrow is well flavoured and tender, but not mushy. Taste for seasoning before serving.

■ Serve the spiced marrow and chick peas with Basmati rice or with warmed nan bread.

Baked Marrow

SERVES: 4–6
PREPARATION: 10 minutes
OVEN: 180°C/350°F/gas 4
COOKING: 30 minutes

1 young marrow (about
    900 g/2 lb)
40 g/1½ oz butter
30 ml/2 tablespoons finely
    chopped, mixed fresh
    herbs – tarragon, mint,
    parsley and chives
salt and black pepper

Cut the marrow into 2.5 cm/1 in thick slices; peel and cut them into rough chunks, discarding the seeds. Butter an ovenproof dish thoroughly. Add the marrow with the remaining butter cut into small knobs and sprinkle with the chopped herbs. Season to taste with salt and freshly ground pepper.

Cover the dish with a lid or foil and bake in a preheated oven at 180°C/350°F/gas 4 until just tender, after about 30 minutes. Be careful not to overcook. Serve the marrow at once, straight from the dish.

Chick Pea Patties

SERVES: 4
PREPARATION: 50 minutes
SOAKING: 8 hours
CHILLING: 30 minutes
COOKING: 2¼–2½ hours

225 g/8 oz dried chick peas or
  2 × 400 g/14 oz cans chick peas
1 onion
25 g/1 oz butter
60 ml/4 tablespoons
  chopped parsley
30 ml/2 tablespoons chopped sage
salt and black pepper
1 large egg
50 g/2 oz bacon fat or dripping or
  60 ml/4 tablespoons oil

Soak dried chick peas for 8 hours or overnight. Drain the chick peas and put them in a saucepan with plenty of cold water. Bring to the boil and boil for 10 minutes. Reduce the heat, cover the pan and simmer for about 2 hours or until tender.

Drain the cooked or canned chick peas and purée them coarsely in a liquidiser or food processor. Peel and finely chop the onion. Fry the onion in the butter over low heat for 5 minutes or until just colouring.

Stir the cooked onion into the chick pea purée, together with the finely chopped parsley and sage. Season to taste with salt and pepper and mix in the beaten egg. Divide the mixture into eight equal portions. Roll each portion into a ball between well-floured hands, then flatten it into a round patty shape on a floured surface. Chill the patties for at least 30 minutes.

Heat the fat or oil in a non-stick frying pan over moderate heat, and fry the patties for 10–12 minutes, until they are golden on both sides, turning once.

Drain the chick pea patties on absorbent kitchen paper.

Turkish Fried Carrots

SERVES: 4
PREPARATION: 15 minutes
COOKING: 20 minutes

450 g/1 lb carrots
salt and black pepper
15 ml/1 tablespoon plain flour
30 ml/2 tablespoons olive oil
300 ml/½ pt plain yogurt
15 ml/1 tablespoon chopped fresh
  mint or 5 ml/1 teaspoon
  caraway seeds to garnish

Cut the carrots crossways, into 5 mm/¼ in thick slices. Bring a pan of salted water to the boil and cook the carrots for about 10 minutes or until nearly tender. Drain in a colander, then dry on absorbent kitchen paper.

Season the flour with salt and pepper, and use it to coat the carrots, shaking off any surplus. Heat the oil in a heavy-based pan and fry the carrots over moderate heat until golden brown. Season to taste with salt and freshly ground pepper. Put the yogurt in a separate pan over low heat, and let it warm through. Do not allow it to reach boiling point or it will curdle.

Put the carrots in a hot dish, pour over the yogurt, and sprinkle with mint or caraway seeds.

Lentil Bake

SERVES: 6
PREPARATION: 45 minutes
OVEN: 200°C/400°F/gas 6
COOKING: 1¼ hours

900 g/2 lb potatoes
salt and black pepper
1 small swede (½ if large)
225 g/8 oz red lentils
450 ml/¾ pt vegetable or chicken
  stock, or water
1 onion
2 celery sticks
2 carrots
225 g/8 oz mushrooms
1 green pepper
30 ml/2 tablespoons oil
50 g/2 oz mature Cheddar cheese

Peel and dice the potatoes. Cook them in a saucepan of boiling salted water for about 10 minutes or until they are tender. Drain and set them aside. Peel and dice the swede and place it in a saucepan with the lentils. Add the stock or water and bring to the boil. Cover the pan, reduce the heat and simmer for 25 minutes, or until all the stock has been absorbed.

Meanwhile, peel and chop the onion, scrub and dice the celery and peel and chop the carrots. Slice the mushrooms. Cut the stalk end off the pepper, discard all the pith and seeds and dice the flesh.

Heat the oil in a saucepan, add the prepared onion, celery, carrots and green pepper and cook, stirring every now and then, for 10 minutes. Stir in the sliced mushrooms and cook for a further 5 minutes.

Stir the lentils into the vegetable mixture and add seasoning to taste. Spoon the mixture into a large ovenproof dish and smooth the top. Cover with the potatoes. Grate the cheese and sprinkle it over the surface. Bake in a preheated oven at 200°C/400°F/gas 6 for about 30 minutes, until golden brown.

■ The lentil bake makes a tasty family supper. It can be frozen after the topping has been added, then thawed for several hours at room temperature or overnight in the refrigerator before being finished in the oven as above.

Savoury Pumpkin Strudel

SERVES: 4
PREPARATION: 40 minutes
OVEN: 180°C/350°F/gas 4
COOKING: 1½ hours

225 g/8 oz leeks
60 ml/4 tablespoons olive oil
450 g/1 lb deseeded and
  peeled pumpkin
100 g/4 oz mushrooms
15 ml/1 tablespoon
  chopped thyme
30 ml/2 tablespoons
  chopped parsley
salt and black pepper
100 g/4 oz Cheddar cheese
3 sheets filo pastry (each measuring
  38 × 30 cm/15 × 12 in)

Trim, slice and wash the leeks. Heat half the oil in a large saucepan, add the leeks and cook for about 5 minutes, until well reduced. Dice the pumpkin and add it to the leeks, then cover it

and cook for about 15 minutes more, or until just tender. Stir occasionally to prevent the base of the mixture from browning.

Remove the pan from the heat. Chop the mushrooms. Add with the thyme and parsley. Stir in seasoning to taste, then leave to cool. Grate the cheese and stir three-quarters of it into the pumpkin mixture.

Brush one of the sheets of filo sparsely with a little of the remaining oil, lay the second sheet on top, brush again with oil and top with the third sheet of pastry. Spread the pumpkin mixture evenly over the pastry, leaving a border of about 2.5 cm/1 in all round. Fold the pastry border over the filling and brush the edge with a little oil. Then roll up both filling and pastry from the long side, like a Swiss roll. Grease a large baking sheet with some of the remaining oil and transfer the strudel to it. Brush the pastry lightly with oil and sprinkle the top with the remaining cheese.

Bake the strudel in a preheated oven at 180°C/350°F/gas 4 for about 1 hour, until the pastry and cheese topping is golden brown and cooked through. Serve piping hot.

■ The pumpkin strudel may be transformed from starter to light meal with the addition of a simple side salad. For a more substantial meal, add potatoes or boiled Jerusalem artichokes.

RICE & PASTA

Rigatoni with Hare Sauce

This rich pasta dish of rigatoni, which is a short, ribbed variety of macaroni, with a rich hare sauce comes from the Tuscan region of central Italy.

SERVES: 4
PREPARATION: 25 minutes
COOKING: 1¼ hours

4 hare legs
100 g/4 oz streaky bacon
1 clove garlic
1 onion
1 stick celery
100 g/4 oz mushrooms
15 ml/1 tablespoon lard or oil
30 ml/2 tablespoons plain flour
120 ml/4 fl oz red wine or 60 ml/
    2 fl oz Marsala or brown sherry
450 ml/¾ pt water
salt and black pepper
5 ml/1 teaspoon dried thyme
5 ml/1 teaspoon dried marjoram
grated rind and juice of ½ lemon
350 g/12 oz rigatoni or
    broad noodles
75–100 g/3–4 oz Parmesan cheese

Slice the meat off the legs of the hare and cut out the tough tendons. Cut the meat into 1 cm/½ in pieces and set aside.

Remove the rind from the rashers and chop the bacon roughly. Peel and finely chop the garlic, and peel and finely slice the onion. Scrub and chop the celery stick, and trim and slice the mushrooms.

Heat the lard or oil in a large, heavy-based pan over moderate heat and fry the bacon, garlic, onion and celery for about 5 minutes, or until just taking colour. Add the hare meat and mushrooms and cook for a few minutes until lightly browned.

Remove the pan from the heat and stir in the flour. Return the pan to the heat and fry the mixture until brown, stirring continuously. Add the wine or sherry and gradually stir in the water, bringing it to the boil to make a thick sauce. Season to taste with salt, freshly ground pepper, thyme and marjoram. Cover the pan with a lid and simmer over low heat for 1 hour. Add the lemon rind and sharpen with lemon juice.

Meanwhile, cook the rigatoni or noodles in a large pan of salted water for 12–15 minutes. Drain the pasta thoroughly in a colander. Arrange the rigatoni around the edge of a serving dish and spoon the sauce into the centre.

Grate the Parmesan cheese and sprinkle a little over the sauce. Serve the remainder in a separate bowl.

■ Serve a tossed green salad or a simple dish of sautéed courgettes or lightly boiled French beans with the pasta.

Schinken-fleckerl

This recipe for noodles with ham is traditional both in Austria and Switzerland.

SERVES: 4
PREPARATION: 15 minutes
COOKING: 40–45 minutes

10 ml/2 teaspoons olive oil
30 ml/2 tablespoons toasted
    breadcrumbs
salt and black pepper
225 g/8 oz pasta squares or
    short cut noodles
225 g/8 oz lean ham
2 shallots or 1 small onion
50 g/2 oz butter
225 ml/7½ fl oz soured cream
2 eggs
50 g/2 oz grated Gruyère or
    Cheddar cheese
1 small green pepper to garnish

Grease a 15 cm/6 in cake tin with the oil and coat it evenly with the breadcrumbs.

Bring a large pan of salted water to the boil and add the pasta squares or noodles. Bring the water back to the boil and cook over a high heat for 10–15 minutes or until the pasta is al dente*. Drain thoroughly in a colander and put the pasta in a large bowl.

While the pasta is cooking, dice the ham and peel and finely chop the shallots or the onion. Melt the butter in a small frying pan and cook the shallots or onion over moderate heat for about 5 minutes or until they are soft and transparent. Stir the contents of the pan into the drained pasta.

Whisk the soured cream and eggs in a small bowl, stir in the ham and cheese, and add this mixture to the onions and pasta. Mix thoroughly, but lightly, and season to taste with salt and freshly ground pepper.

Spoon the pasta mixture into the prepared mould or tin and place it in a roasting tin with enough cold water to reach 2.5 cm/1 in up the sides of the mould. Bake in a preheated oven at 200°C/400°F/gas 6 for 30 minutes, or until the mixture has set and is light brown on top.

Remove the mould from the oven and allow the mixture to cool and shrink slightly before unmoulding it on to a warmed serving dish. Garnish the pasta with wedges or small squares of lightly grilled green pepper.

■ Lightly grilled halved tomatoes and trimmed mushroom caps would be suitable accompaniments to this dish

Schinken-fleckerl.

PUDDINGS & DESSERTS

Crêpes Georgette

These pancakes with a rum-flavoured pineapple filling are said to have been created for Georgette Leblanc, close friend of the Belgian poet Maeterlinck.

SERVES: 6
PREPARATION: 30 minutes
COOKING: 30 minutes

50 g/2 oz butter
6 drained canned pineapple rings
60 ml/4 tablespoons rum
300 ml/½ pt vanilla-flavoured
    pastry cream (see Greengage
    Flan, page 236)
12 very thin Pancakes (page 339)
icing sugar to dredge

Melt the butter and use a little to grease a flameproof dish. Drain and finely chop the pineapple rings. Add 15 ml/1 tablespoon of the rum to the pastry cream with the chopped pineapple and mix together well.

Fill the pancakes with this mixture and place them in the prepared dish. Brush the pancakes with the rest of the melted butter, and dredge them generously with sifted icing sugar. Heat a metal skewer and press it on to the sugar coating to make a criss-cross pattern.

Set the dish under a hot grill for about 5 minutes to glaze the sugar topping. Just before serving the dessert, warm the remaining rum, set it alight and pour it over the pancakes.

Rich Pumpkin and Apricot Pie

SERVES: 8
PREPARATION: 1 hour
OVEN: 200°C/400°F/gas 6
      180°C/350°F/gas 4
COOKING: about 1¼ hours

350 g/12 oz deseeded and
    peeled pumpkin
225 g/8 oz Shortcrust Pastry
    (page 365)
175 g/6 oz caster sugar
100 g/4 oz chopped
    toasted hazelnuts
3 eggs
5 ml/1 teaspoon natural
    vanilla essence
15 ml/1 tablespoon ground
    cinnamon
300 ml/½ pt double cream
225 g/8 oz no-need-to-presoak
    dried apricots

Cut the pumpkin into large chunks and cook them in boiling water for 15–20 minutes or until just tender. Drain thoroughly.

Meanwhile, make the pastry following the recipe instructions, but adding 50 g/2 oz of the caster sugar and the hazelnuts to the rubbed-in mixture before mixing in the water. Roll out the pastry and use it to line a 28–30 cm/11–12 in loose-bottomed flan tin or dish. Prick the pastry all over, line it with greaseproof paper and baking beans and chill the flan for 10 minutes. Bake the pastry in a preheated oven at 200°C/400°F/gas 6 for 20 minutes. Turn down the oven temperature to 180°C/350°F/gas 4.

Purée the drained pumpkin in a food processor or liquidiser or press it through a sieve. Beat the eggs with the remaining sugar, vanilla and cinnamon. Stir in the cream. Chop the apricots or snip them into pieces using a pair of kitchen scissors. Sprinkle the apricots over the base of the pastry case and pour in the pumpkin mixture.

Bake the filled pie for about 45 minutes, or until the filling is set and golden brown.

■ The pumpkin and apricot pie may be served warm or cold, with pouring or whipped cream or vanilla ice cream.

Queen of Puddings

SERVES: 4–6
PREPARATION: 15 minutes
OVEN: 180°C/350°F/gas 4
COOKING: 30–35 minutes

100 g/4 oz white bread, crusts
    removed
600 ml/1 pt milk
50 g/2 oz unsalted butter
3 eggs, separated
grated rind of 1 lemon
150 g/5 oz caster sugar
60 ml/4 tablespoons apricot or
    strawberry jam

Cut the bread into 1 cm/½ in cubes and put them in a lightly buttered baking dish. Heat the milk and butter until just warm. Beat the egg yolks, the lemon rind and 75 g/3 oz of the sugar in a bowl, then stir in the warmed milk mixture. Pour this custard over the bread.

Bake the pudding in a preheated oven at 180°C/350°F/gas 4 for about 20 minutes or until it is set. Remove from the oven and spread the apricot or strawberry jam over the pudding.

Whisk the egg whites until stiff, and fold in the remaining sugar. Pile this meringue over the jam, and return the pudding to the oven for another 10 minutes or until the top is crisp.

Queen of Puddings with Damson and Apple Tansy (opposite).

Damson and Apple Tansy

This English pudding recipe dates back to the 15th century.

SERVES: 4
PREPARATION: 15 minutes
COOKING: 40 minutes
CHILLING: 1 hour

225 g/8 oz damsons
225 g/8 oz cooking apples
50 g/2 oz unsalted butter
75 ml/2½ fl oz water
100 g/4 oz caster sugar
30–45 ml/2–3 tablespoons fresh
    white breadcrumbs
10 ml/2 teaspoons lemon juice
150 ml/¼ pt double cream

Wash the damsons and cut them in half. Peel, core and thinly slice the apples. Melt the butter in a saucepan with the cold water. Add the fruit. Cover with a lid and cook the fruit over low heat until it is soft, stirring from time to time.

Remove the pan from the heat and rub the fruit through a coarse sieve. Return the purée to the pan and stir in sugar to taste. If the purée is thin, cook it over low heat until it has reduced and thickened to a dropping consistency. Take the pan off the heat and stir in the breadcrumbs. Stir the mixture over low heat until thick, then leave to cool. Sharpen with lemon juice.

Whisk the cream lightly and fold it through the cooled purée so that it is partly mixed with the fruit mixture. Spoon the mixture into serving glasses and chill in the refrigerator for 1 hour.

Chocolate Pears

SERVES: 4
PREPARATION: 30 minutes
COOKING: 20 minutes
CHILLING: 2–3 hours

4 ripe dessert pears
15 g/½ oz shelled walnuts
15 g/½ oz glacé cherries
100 g/4 oz dark plain chocolate
30 ml/2 tablespoons cold
    black coffee
25 g/1 oz unsalted butter
20 ml/4 teaspoons rum
2 eggs
Decoration
angelica
whipped cream
chopped pistachio nuts

Peel the pears and cut out the cores from the base leaving the stem and top intact. Cut a small sliver from the base of each pear so that it will stand upright. Roughly chop and mix the walnuts and cherries and press a little of this mixture into the

Chocolate Pears.

core cavities of the pears. Stand the pears upright in one large or four small shallow serving dishes.

Break up the chocolate and put it in a bowl with the coffee. Stand the bowl over a saucepan of boiling water and stir every now and then until the chocolate has melted. Remove the bowl from the heat and stir in first the butter and then the rum. Separate the eggs and beat the yolks, one at a time, into the chocolate mixture. Whisk the egg whites until stiff, but not dry, and fold them carefully into the chocolate. The mixture should have a consistency similar to that of a mousse.

Spoon the chocolate mixture over the pears until they are evenly coated. Soften the angelica strips in hot water, cut into 1 cm/½ in lengths and slice them crossways into eight diamond shapes. Make a small slit on either side of each pear stalk and

insert an angelica diamond. Chill the chocolate pears for 2–3 hours or overnight.

Decorate with whipped cream and chopped pistachio nuts.

Hungarian Hazelnut Torte

Hungarian dessert cakes (torte) are internationally famous, and several of them were perfected by Dobos, a Hungarian confectioner in the 19th century . This classic hazelnut torte has a chocolate cream filling and a caramel topping. It improves in flavour if kept for a day or two in a completely airtight tin.

SERVES: 6
PREPARATION: 30 minutes
OVEN: 180°C/350°F/gas 4
COOKING: 30–40 minutes

100 g/4 oz unblanched hazelnuts
4 eggs
150 g/5 oz caster sugar
Filling
50 g/2 oz unsalted butter
50 g/2 oz icing sugar
10 ml/2 teaspoons drinking
    chocolate powder
5 ml/1 teaspoon instant
    coffee powder

Topping
30 ml/2 tablespoons water
75 g/3 oz caster sugar
12 hazelnuts

Lightly grease two round 18 cm/ 7 in sandwich tins. Grind the unblanched hazelnuts finely in a liquidiser or grinder. Separate the eggs and whisk the whites until stiff, but still moist. Whisk the egg yolks with the caster

sugar until pale lemon in colour and the mixture trails off the whisk in ribbons.

Fold the ground nuts and whisked egg whites alternately into the egg yolks. Divide the mixture equally between the two sandwich tins and bake in the centre of a preheated oven at 180°C/350°F/gas 4 for about 30 minutes, or until set. Test by pressing the top of the cakes with a finger – it should leave no impression. Remove the cakes from the oven, and allow them to shrink slightly before turning them out to cool on a wire rack.

Meanwhile, prepare the filling. Cream the butter until fluffy; sift the icing sugar, chocolate and coffee powders together; beat the mixture gradually into the butter. When the cakes are cool, sandwich them together with the butter filling. Set the torte aside while preparing the caramel topping.

Put the water and caster sugar in a small, heavy-based saucepan. Stir over low heat until the mixture has dissolved into a clear syrup. Increase the heat and boil the syrup rapidly, without stirring, until it is a golden colour.

Remove the pan from the heat immediately and pour most of the caramel over the top of the cake. Spread it evenly with an oiled knife and mark the topping into portions with an oiled knife. Garnish the top with the whole nuts before the caramel hardens. As the rest of the caramel cools it can be trickled over the nuts or pulled into fine strands using a fork to make a fine spun sugar veil on the cake.

The Great British Breakfast

Traditional breakfast dishes: Devilled Kidneys, Kedgeree, Cod Roe and Bacon and Kippers with Scrambled Eggs.

The British are renowned for the quality and quantity of their breakfasts. Despite the social changes and dietary reforms that have tamed the habit of regularly feasting at breakfast time, by continental standards the British breakfast is still a meal of many choices. Wisely, most people now reserve the traditional fried breakfast for the occasional weekend treat, but it remains very popular. In content, it varies widely, from a couple of rashers of bacon with a fried egg to a platter of devilled kidneys, sausages, black pudding, bacon, eggs, tomatoes, mushrooms, fried potatoes and fried bread. Regional specialities may also be included, such as fried oatcakes from the Peak District, laver bread from South Wales or potato cakes from Ireland. But it is the Scots who enjoy the reputation of feasting on the most formidable breakfasts, featuring foods such as the legendary kipper, piping-hot porridge served with thick cream and toast spread with delicious Dundee marmalade.

Everyday Breakfasts

Elaborate breakfasts are both a treat and a practical option for holidays and weekends, when generous portions may be justified on the grounds that only one meal – the leisurely brunch – is served some time between dawn and the evening meal. However, on a daily basis, starting the day with a satisfying but fairly light meal is more healthy. Foods such as cereals, porridge and toast, which provide plenty of starch-based carbohydrate, are the best choice, providing a good source of energy that will keep you going through the day ahead. This is particularly important for children and those who have an active way of life. Breakfast is also important as a regular source of dietary fibre, from cereals, wholemeal bread and fresh fruit.

Thanks to the availability of a wide variety of enriched breads, yogurts and other dairy produce, cereals and fruits, it is possible to devise dozens of different menus, none of them difficult to prepare. For a well-balanced breakfast, eat a good variety of foods.

- Eat starchy foods at the start of the day.
- Limit your intake of fats at breakfast time.
- Avoid eating too much sugar. Children are especially vulnerable as many breakfast cereals and yogurts are extremely sweet, far too sweet to be eaten on a regular basis, let alone every morning at breakfast.

Muesli

It is easy to make delicious, light breakfast muesli. Use porridge oats as the base, adding a few raisins, chopped nuts (almonds, brazils, hazelnuts and pecans) and chopped no-need-to-presoak dried apricots. Other dried fruits can be added if liked – but the fruit and nut content should be quite small. Keep a jar of this dry fruit and nut mix ready for daily use at breakfast.

Moisten the dry muesli mix with water, unsweetened apple juice or plain yogurt and leave it to stand for 15 minutes. Then mix fresh fruit with the muesli – sliced banana, orange segments, diced apple, strawberries or raspberries are all delicious. Top with a dollop of plain yogurt, if liked.

Fruit for Breakfast

Fruit makes a refreshing breakfast. Grapefruit and melon are traditional choices but unsweetened fruit salad with plain yogurt or fromage frais also gets the day off to a good start. A platter of exotic fruits looks attractive and makes a welcome weekend treat, especially when you are entertaining guests. Select from star fruit, mango, passion fruit, fresh dates, papaya, kiwi fruit, pineapple and melon. Alternatively, offer a compôte of dried fruits, made simply by soaking mixed dried fruits overnight in water and then stewing them in their soaking liquid until they are tender. Canned prunes (in syrup or unsweetened fruit juice) are another easy option, especially when served well chilled with fresh orange segments.

Porridge

This is the traditional Scottish breakfast, described by Robert Burns as 'Chief o' Scotia's food'. It was eaten with horn spoons from birch bowls. Porridge takes little time to prepare and cook. For four generous helpings allow 150 g/5 oz medium oatmeal to 1.12 litres/2 pt of water.

Bring the water to the boil over medium heat and, as soon as it is bubbling, pour in the oatmeal in a steady but slow stream, with one hand, stirring constantly with the other hand. As soon as the mixture comes back to the boil, pull the pan to the side of the heat, cover with a lid and simmer gently for 10 minutes. Stir in 1.25 ml/¼ teaspoon salt, re-cover the saucepan and continue simmering the porridge for about 10 minutes.

■ In Scotland, porridge is traditionally served with cream and salt, although brown sugar is the preferred option south of the Scottish border.

Kedgeree

This is an English breakfast or high tea dish, of Indian origin. *Khicharbi* (or kedgeree) originally consisted of rice, onion, lentils, spices, limes, butter and fish.

For four persons, take 2 hard-boiled eggs, 450 g/1 lb cooked smoked haddock, 225 g/8 oz boiled rice, a pinch of grated nutmeg, lemon juice, salt, a pinch of cayenne pepper, 150 ml/¼ pt single cream and 50 g/2 oz butter, with some chopped fresh parsley to garnish.

Cut the eggs into small wedges and mix them with the flaked fish and the rice. Season to taste with nutmeg, lemon juice, salt and cayenne. Stir in the cream. Butter a deep, oven-proof dish and spoon in the kedgeree mixture. Dot with the remaining butter, cover the dish with a lid and bake in a pre-heated oven at 180°C/350°F/gas 4 for about 30 minutes. Garnish the hot kedgeree with chopped parsley.

Kippers with Scrambled Eggs

This combination is a highly popular breakfast dish throughout Britain. The finest, pale oak-smoked kippers come from the Isle of Man, but are, unfortunately, seldom exported. For grilled kippers with scrambled eggs, allow 1 pair of kippers and 1 egg per person.

Scissor the heads and tails off the kippers, place them on a layer of foil, skin upwards, on the grill pan and grill them under high heat until the skin begins to curl. Turn the kippers over and grill the other side, allowing 2–3 minutes on each side.

Meanwhile, beat the eggs lightly and season with freshly ground pepper only. Melt a little butter in a small saucepan and scramble the eggs for about 2 minutes, until they are creamy and moist. Serve at the side of the grilled kippers.

Cod Roe and Bacon

This is a favourite breakfast dish in Cornwall, the north of England and Ireland.

Peel the skin off 450 g/1 lb pressed cod roe and cut the roe into 1 cm/½ in thick slices. Coat these in lightly seasoned flour and fry them in a little lard or dripping until they are golden brown. Fry bacon rashers in the pan with the cod roe.

Alternatively, mash the roe with an equal amount of cooked mashed potatoes; season with salt and freshly ground pepper and bind with 2 lightly beaten eggs. Shape the mixture into round cakes, about 5 cm/2 in wide and 1.5 cm/¾ in thick. Fry for about 10 minutes or until golden brown on both sides.

Devilled Kidneys

These have been popular in Britain since the 18th century, when the thrifty housewife invented a spicy sauce to add sparkle to jaded palates.

SERVES: 4
PREPARATION: 30 minutes
COOKING: 7 minutes

8 lambs' kidneys
10 ml/2 teaspoons
    Worcestershire sauce
10 ml/2 teaspoons
    mushroom ketchup
15 ml/1 tablespoon dry mustard
50 g/2 oz butter, melted
salt and white pepper
pinch cayenne
30 ml/2 tablespoons oil or
    25 g/1 oz butter

Clean and halve 8 lamb kidneys (page 334). Prepare the devil sauce by mixing the Worcestershire sauce, mushroom ketchup and mustard with the melted butter. Season with salt, white pepper and cayenne.

Heat the oil or butter in a pan and fry the kidneys for 3 minutes on each side. Arrange them in a flameproof serving dish, spread the devil sauce evenly on top of the kidneys and put under a hot grill for 1 minute.

Fresh Figs with Yogurt

This refreshing combination of sweet fresh figs and creamy yogurt is ideal for breakfast or as a dessert. For breakfast, double the quantity of yogurt and omit the cream.

SERVES: 4
PREPARATION: 15 minutes
CHILLING: 2 hours

8 fresh figs
150 ml/¼ pt double cream
150 ml/¼ pt plain yogurt
45–60 ml/3–4 tablespoons soft
    brown sugar

Put the figs in a large bowl of hot water for 1 minute. Drain them thoroughly, peel off the skins and quarter each fig. Whisk the cream lightly and blend it into the yogurt.

Spoon a little of the cream mixture into four small serving glasses. Top with a layer of figs, followed by more cream and figs, and finish with a layer of cream mixture. Sprinkle each layer with brown sugar.

If time allows, or when serving the dish as a dessert, chill it for at least 2 hours to allow the sugar to melt into the cream.

Fresh Figs with Yogurt.

NOVEMBER

Roasted Onions, Stuffed Cabbage Leaves, Middle Eastern Chicken Stew.

November

Cold, foggy November cries out for hot soups and substantial stews. Guy Fawkes' night brings bonfires, fireworks and all the fun of bobbing for apples. Steaming mugs of hot soup, grilled sausages, baked potatoes and toffee apples are traditional treats for this quintessentially English celebration.

For everyday meals, mussels, sprats and huss are usually good buys from the fishmonger. The game season is at its height in November, with pheasant, partridge, snipe and mallard in prime condition, and these are perfect fare for entertaining. Root vegetables, winter cabbage, cauliflower and Brussels sprouts are in plentiful supply, as are quality British apples.

November is a month for settling down indoors and enjoying afternoon tea in front of the fire. For pure nostalgia there is nothing quite like the flavour of muffins or crumpets toasted on a long-handled fork and served with butter, or the aroma of roasting chestnuts. With the weather turning colder, reviving the old-fashioned idea of high tea makes a cheery start to a dark and dismal evening, especially after a long Saturday afternoon of shopping.

Conscientious cooks will be planning ahead and spending a few hours in the kitchen busily preparing for Christmas. Shops may have been sporting cards and decorations for several weeks, but authentic preparations for the festive season cannot possibly begin until bonfire night is over – then there is a sudden flurry of activity as mincemeat, Christmas pudding and the cake are made.

Menu suggestions: This selection of menus offers ideas for everyday meals as well as special occasions. The main recipes are included in this chapter; others carry a page reference.

Soup Supper
~

Pumpkin Soup
Savoury Olive and Sun-dried
Tomato Bread
~
Grilled Bananas
(page 199, cooked under
the grill instead of on the
barbecue) with
Maple Syrup

Impromptu suppers are easy to organise if you have a well-stocked freezer. The main elements of this menu – pumpkin soup and a speciality bread – can be made in bulk and frozen, ready for thawing and heating at a moment's notice, either in the microwave or using a conventional oven and hob.

November Supper Party
~

Buckling with
Horseradish Cream
~
Savoury Game Pie
Baked Potatoes
Brussels Sprouts
Glazed Carrots (page 110)
~
Orange Caramel Custards

A pâté of smoked fish and a hearty pie make up this simple menu for informal entertaining. The pie filling can be made with venison, hare or any game bird, depending on what is available.

Traditional high tea dishes (page 278), clockwise from top left: Ham and Haddie, Dublin Coddle, Anglesey Eggs, Mackerel with Gooseberry Sauce and potted shrimps.

Italian Menu
~

Parma Ham with Celeriac
Salad (page 91)
~
Escalopes with Artichokes
and Lemon Sauce
Risotto Bianco
French Beans
Green Salad
~
Baked Stuffed Peaches
(page 196)
or
Zabaglione (page 114)

This is a wholesome, country-style menu. It is not over-fussy but the choice of ingredients is sufficiently sophisticated to make it suitable for an informal dinner party. The escalopes, which can be veal or pork, may be cooked in advance, but the simple risotto that accompanies it should be made at the last minute.

SOUPS

Pumpkin Soup

This spicy soup is ideal for cold winter days.

SERVES: 6–8
PREPARATION: 30 minutes
COOKING: about 1 hour

1 large onion
1 clove garlic
900 g/2 lb deseeded and
    peeled pumpkin
25 g/1 oz butter or 45 ml/
    3 tablespoons oil
2 bay leaves
2 blades mace
1 cinnamon stick
salt and black pepper
600 ml/1 pt unsweetened
    apple juice
600 ml/1 pt chicken or
    vegetable stock
150 ml/¼ pt plain yogurt

Peel and chop the onion, peel the garlic and cut the pumpkin into 2.5 cm/1 in cubes. Heat the fat in a large saucepan. Add the onion, bay leaves, mace and cinnamon. Crush in the garlic. Cook, stirring occasionally, for 5 minutes. Add the pumpkin cover and cook for 10 minutes.

Add seasoning, then pour in the apple juice and stock. Bring to the boil, reduce the heat and cover. Simmer the soup for 45 minutes. Discard the bay leaves and whole spices, then purée the soup in a liquidiser or rub it through a sieve. Reheat the soup and taste for seasoning again. Serve hot, with a little plain yogurt swirled into each portion.

Pumpkin Soup with Savoury Olive and Sun-dried Tomato Bread (page 265).

Mulligatawny Soup

There seem to be several ways of making this soup; this version is based on chicken, but lean minced beef could be used. It can be served hot or cold.

SERVES: 6
PREPARATION: 15–20 minutes
COOKING: 1¼–1½ hours

1 onion
5 cloves garlic
2.5 cm/1 in piece of fresh
    root ginger
1 small potato
60 ml/4 tablespoons oil
10 ml/2 teaspoons ground cumin
15 ml/1 tablespoon ground
    coriander
2.5 ml/½ teaspoon ground turmeric
175 g/6 oz red lentils
1.12 litres/2 pt chicken stock
1 skinned boneless chicken breast
    (about 150 g/5 oz)
25 g/1 oz Basmati rice
300 ml/½ pt water
pinch cayenne pepper
2.5 ml/½ teaspoon salt
5 ml/1 teaspoon lemon juice

Peel and finely chop the onion, garlic cloves and ginger. Peel and dice the potato. Heat 45 ml/ 3 tablespoons of the oil in a large saucepan. Stir in the cumin, coriander and turmeric; cook for 30 seconds, then stir in the onion, garlic and ginger. Cook for 3 minutes, add the lentils, potato and chicken stock and bring to the boil. Stir, lower the heat, cover the pan and simmer for 45 minutes.

Meanwhile, finely shred the chicken breast. Rinse the rice well. Heat the remaining oil in a frying pan, add the chicken and sauté for 3 minutes. Drain the rice and add to the pan, stirring to coat the grains in the oil. Pour in the water and set the pan aside, off the heat.

Purée the lentil mixture in a liquidiser, return it to a clean pan and tip in the contents of the frying pan. Sprinkle in the cayenne and salt, bring to a gentle simmer and cook for a further 30 minutes. Stir in the lemon juice. Before serving, taste the soup and add more salt and pepper if liked.

New England Fish Chowder

The traditional chowder or fish soup cum stew is a perfect cold-weather dish which takes less than an hour to prepare and cook. Any type of white fish fillet may be used, and prawns can be substituted for the crab.

SERVES: 4–6
PREPARATION: 20 minutes
COOKING: 30 minutes

450 g/1 lb cod fillet
1 large onion
225 g/8 oz potatoes
50 g/2 oz mushrooms
600 ml/1 pt water
salt and black pepper
75 g/3 oz streaky bacon
25 g/1 oz butter
20 ml/4 teaspoons plain flour
300 ml/½ pt milk
50 g/2 oz chopped white crab meat
lemon juice
30 ml/2 tablespoons chopped
    parsley to garnish

Skin the fish and cut it into three or four pieces. Peel and roughly chop the onion. Peel the potatoes and cut them into 1 cm/ ½ in cubes; trim and slice the mushrooms. Bring the water to the boil, add a little salt and the fish and simmer over low heat for 10 minutes. Drain the fish and set the liquid aside.

Remove the rind from the bacon and dice the meat. Fry the bacon in a pan over low heat until the fat runs. Raise the heat and cook the bacon until crisp, then add the butter to the pan. When it has melted, stir in the potatoes, onion and mushrooms and fry for a further 5 minutes.

Stir in the flour, then gradually add the milk. Bring the mixture to the boil, then stir in 450 ml/¾ pt of the reserved fish stock. Add the fish, which will break up naturally, and the crab meat. Simmer for 10 minutes, season to taste with salt, freshly ground pepper and lemon juice; stir in the parsley.

Serve the chowder soon after it is cooked because prolonged simmering or standing will overcook the fish.

■ Crisp Croûtons (page 313) may be served as a garnish for the chowder. Warm, crusty bread, cut into thick slices, is the ideal accompaniment.

STARTERS, SAVOURIES & LIGHT DISHES

Smoked Eel Smetana

This starter is reputed to have been a favourite of the Czech composer Smetana. Smoked eel makes a change from smoked trout or salmon.

SERVES: 4
PREPARATION: 15 minutes

225 g/8 oz smoked eel fillets
2 hard-boiled eggs
5 ml/1 teaspoon French mustard
45 ml/3 tablespoons olive oil
15 ml/1 tablespoon
*   tarragon vinegar*
45 ml/3 tablespoons soured cream
salt and black pepper
caster sugar
30 ml/2 tablespoons chopped
*   cooked beetroot*

Peel off any skin and arrange the fillets on four individual serving plates. Cut the eggs in half and rub the yolks through a coarse sieve; chop the whites finely. Mix together the yolks, mustard, oil, vinegar and cream. Season to taste with salt, freshly ground pepper and sugar. Add the beetroot to the dressing.

Arrange the beetroot dressing along one side of the eel fillets and sprinkle with the chopped egg white.

■ Serve the eels with thin slices of brown bread and butter.

Cheese and Chutney Dip

This savoury dip can be made very quickly for a first course or to serve with drinks. Tangy yogurt lightens the cream cheese base or single cream may be used with a low-fat soft cheese.

SERVES: 6
PREPARATION: 10 minutes
CHILLING: 30 minutes

30 ml/2 tablespoons plain yogurt
225 g/8 oz cream cheese
5–10 ml/1–2 teaspoons curry paste
15 ml/1 tablespoon tomato ketchup
10 ml/2 teaspoons lemon juice
60 ml/4 tablespoons finely chopped
*   chutney or sweet pickle*
celery leaves to garnish

Mix the yogurt into the cream cheese until the mixture is smooth. Stir the curry paste into the tomato ketchup, with the lemon juice, and add to the cheese mixture, together with the chutney or pickle.

Stir the dip well before piling it into a serving dish. Chill for about 30 minutes. Garnish the cheese dip with celery leaves.

■ Serve the cheese and chutney dip with crisp crackers, cheese biscuits or potato crisps. Alternatively, offer strips of fresh carrots, celery, green pepper and cauliflower florets.

Buckling with Horseradish Cream

Whole smoked herrings, known as buckling, are inexpensive appetisers. Dressed in a cream sauce, the flaked fish can be served in deep scallop shells, and can be prepared well in advance.

SERVES: 4
PREPARATION: 15 minutes

2 large buckling
60 ml/4 tablespoons double cream
10–15 ml/2–3 teaspoons
*   lemon juice*
10 ml/2 teaspoons grated
*   horseradish*
5 ml/1 teaspoon tarragon vinegar
salt and black pepper
caster sugar
½ cucumber
lemon slices to garnish

Fillet each buckling into two halves, carefully removing the roe, skin and all bones, or ask the fishmonger to do this for you. Break the fillets up into bite-sized pieces.

Blend the double cream with the lemon juice, grated horseradish and vinegar, and season to taste with salt, freshly ground pepper and sugar.

Cut the unpeeled cucumber into thin slices and use it to line four deep scallop shells or four individual shallow serving dishes. Mix the buckling carefully into the creamy dressing and pile the mixture into the centre of the shells or dishes. Top each portion with a lemon slice.

■ Serve with slices of brown bread and butter.

Buckling with Horseradish Cream.

Grilled Tofu with Mushrooms

SERVES: 4
PREPARATION: 15 minutes
MARINATING: 45–60 minutes
COOKING: 15–20 minutes

5 ml/1 teaspoon ground mace
10 ml/2 teaspoons dried thyme
grated rind and juice of 1 orange
45 ml/3 tablespoons olive oil
salt and black pepper
1 clove garlic
6 fresh sage leaves
450 g/1 lb firm tofu
225 g/8 oz closed cap mushrooms
2 bunches watercress

Mix the mace, thyme, orange rind and juice in a bowl with 30 ml/2 tablespoons of the olive oil. Add seasoning to taste. Peel the garlic and crush it into the mixture, then finely shred the sage leaves and stir them in. Place the tofu, which will probably be in two blocks, on a shallow flameproof dish. Spoon half the herb mixture over the top then carefully turn the blocks of tofu over and cover with the remaining herb mixture. Cover and leave to marinate* for at least 45 minutes.

Thinly slice the mushrooms and place them in a bowl. Pick the leaves off the watercress and mix them with the mushrooms.

Preheat the grill. Baste the tofu with the juices in the dish, then grill it until well browned on top. Use a fish slice and a palette knife to turn the tofu over, baste and cook the second side until well browned.

While the tofu is grilling, heat the remaining oil in a large frying pan. Sauté the mushroom and watercress mixture for 1–2 minutes, until heated. Season lightly and transfer to four plates.

Slice the grilled tofu and arrange the slices on top of the mushrooms. Spoon any remaining juices over and serve.

■ Rice or pasta goes well with the tofu and mushrooms.

Savoury Olive and Sun-dried Tomato Bread

Use either sun-dried tomatoes that come in a packet or a jar of sun-dried tomatoes in olive oil. If using the latter, substitute the oil from the jar for the olive oil.

MAKES: 2 loaves
PREPARATION: 45 minutes
    plus proving
OVEN: 220°C/425°F/gas 7
COOKING: about 1 hour

1 large onion
90 ml/6 tablespoons olive oil
1 clove garlic
5 ml/1 teaspoon finely
    chopped rosemary
5 ml/1 teaspoon dried oregano
12 sun-dried tomatoes
100 g/4 oz black olives
100 g/4 oz Parma ham
675 g/1½ lb strong white flour
10 ml/2 teaspoons salt
2 sachets fast-action easy-blend
    dried yeast
350 ml/12 fl oz hand-hot water

Peel and finely chop the onion. Heat the olive oil in a small saucepan and add the onion. Peel the garlic and crush it into the pan. Cook, stirring every now and then, for 10 minutes. Remove the pan from the heat and stir in the rosemary and oregano. Chop the sun-dried tomatoes or snip them into the onion mixture using kitchen scissors. Stone and roughly chop the olives, then add them to the pan. Chop the Parma ham and stir it into the mixture.

Mix the flour, salt and dried yeast in a bowl. Make a well in the middle of the dry ingredients and pour in the water, than add the contents of the saucepan. Stir until the ingredients are combined well, then turn the mixture out on to a floured surface and knead well until the dough is springy and elastic.

Grease two baking sheets. Divide the dough in half and shape each portion into a long oval loaf. Place the loaves on the baking sheets and cover loosely with oiled polythene. Leave in a warm room for several hours, until doubled in bulk.

Bake the loaves in a pre-heated oven at 220°C/425°F/gas 7 for about 40 minutes, until they are crisp and well browned. Rap the base of the loaves with your knuckles – if they sound hollow, the bread is cooked. Transfer the loaves to a wire rack and leave to cool until warm. Serve thickly sliced.

■ The bread may be frozen when cold. It will keep for up to 1 month. The Parma ham may be omitted, in which case the bread will keep for up to 3 months in the freezer.

FISH, SHELLFISH & SEAFOOD

Filets de Sole Walewska

This dish is named after the Polish Countess Maria Walewska, who was so devoted to Napoleon that she begged in vain to be allowed to accompany him into exile on Elba.

SERVES: 4
PREPARATION: 40 minutes
OVEN: 190°C/375°F/gas 5
COOKING: 1¼ hours

2 Dover sole (575 g/1¼ lb each)
1 bay leaf
1 large parsley sprig
1 small onion
6 peppercorns
salt and black pepper
juice of 1 large lemon
120 ml/4 fl oz dry white wine
4 peeled cooked crawfish tails or
    8 large peeled cooked prawns
100 g/4 oz butter
40 g/1½ oz plain flour
150 ml/¼ pt milk
75–100 g/3–4 oz grated Cheddar
    or Gruyère cheese
75 ml/2½ fl oz double cream
Garnish
8 thin slices of truffle or 8 small
    flat mushrooms
lemon slices
parsley sprigs

Ask the fishmonger to skin and fillet each sole into four. Put the bones and skin into a pan with the bay leaf, parsley, onion, peppercorns and some salt. Cover with water. Simmer for 20–30 minutes, strain and set aside.

Rub the fillets with lemon juice, then arrange them in a buttered shallow ovenproof dish. Pour over the wine and stock almost to cover the fillets. Cover the dish with lightly buttered greaseproof paper, and cook in a preheated oven at 190°C/375°F/gas 5 for 20–25 minutes.

Cut each crawfish tail in half lengthways. Lift out the sole carefully with a perforated slice and keep them warm. Pour the liquid into a pan, boil over high heat for 5 minutes to reduce it, and strain off 250 ml/8 fl oz.

Melt half the butter in a saucepan and stir in all the flour.

Gradually stir in the milk and bring this sauce to simmering point. Stir in the reserved fish liquid and cook for a further 5 minutes. Stir in the grated cheese until it has melted. Gradually add the cream. Season to taste, cover and keep warm without further cooking.

Heat the remaining butter and fry the crawfish tails or prawns for about 3 minutes.

Arrange the sole fillets in a circle on a warm dish, with the tail ends towards the centre, and set the crawfish or prawns around the edge of the dish. Coat the fillets carefully with the sauce and put the dish under a hot grill for 1 minute to glaze the sauce.

Garnish each fillet with a slice of truffle – if mushrooms are used, fry them lightly in a little butter and place them, dark side uppermost, on the fillets. Add lemon twists (page 412) and tiny sprigs of parsley.

Filets de Sole Walewska.

Bream Plaki

Large fish such as grey mullet, bream, brill and John Dory are well suited to being cooked by this traditional Greek method. In a plaki, the fish is baked whole in the oven, and tomatoes and lemon are added.

SERVES: 4–6
PREPARATION: 15 minutes
OVEN: 190°C/375°F/gas 5
COOKING: 55 minutes

1 large onion
1 large clove garlic
5 ml/1 teaspoon fennel or
 coriander seeds
900 g–1.4 kg/2–3 lb bream
45 ml/3 tablespoons olive oil
salt and black pepper
1 large lemon
15–30 ml/1–2 tablespoons
 chopped parsley
400 g/14 oz can tomatoes
120 ml/4 fl oz dry white wine

Peel and thinly slice the onion and peel the garlic. Crush the

Bream Plaki.

fennel or coriander seeds in a mortar or with a broad-bladed knife. Scale and clean the fish (page 313) and place it whole in an oiled baking dish; sprinkle generously with seasoning and the juice from half the lemon.

Heat the remaining oil in a pan and fry the onion and crushed garlic over medium heat, until soft and transparent. Stir in the tomatoes, with their juice; add the parsley, crushed seeds and wine. Cook this sauce for a few minutes, stirring until well mixed, then season to taste.

Pour the sauce over the bream, topping up with a little water, if the baking dish is large. Cut the remaining lemon into thin slices and lay them on top of the fish. Cover with foil or a lid, and bake in a preheated oven at 190°C/375°F/gas 5 for about 45 minutes. Serve the bream in the sauce, straight from the dish.

■ Jacket or floury boiled potatoes go well with this dish.

Fisherman's Cobbler

A savoury scone topping makes a substantial meal of fish in sauce and the combination of smoked and white fish gives the dish a good flavour.

SERVES: 4–6
PREPARATION: 25 minutes
OVEN: 220°C/425°F/gas 7
COOKING: 25–30 minutes

350 g/12 oz white fish fillet
350 g/12 oz smoked haddock fillet
600 ml/1 pt milk plus extra
 for glazing
65 g/2½ oz butter
25 g/1 oz plain flour
salt and black pepper
30 ml/2 tablespoons
 chopped parsley
2 hard-boiled eggs
75 g/3 oz Cheddar cheese
175 g/6 oz self-raising flour
10 ml/2 teaspoons dry mustard

Skin both types of fish fillet and remove any stray bones, then

place the fish in a frying pan or in a large saucepan and pour in 450 ml/¾ pt of the milk. Heat until simmering, then poach the fish for 5 minutes or until it is just firm, but not cooked through. Use a fish slice or perforated spoon to remove the fish from the pan, reserving the milk, and flake it coarsely or cut it into bite-sized pieces.

Melt 25 g/1 oz of the butter in a saucepan. Stir in the plain flour, then slowly pour in milk from cooking the fish, stirring continuously. Bring the sauce to the boil, stirring, then taste and season with a little salt, if necessary, and pepper. Remove the pan from the heat.

Stir the parsley and the fish into the sauce. Chop the eggs and add them to the fish and sauce, then pour the mixture into a 1.7 litre/3 pt ovenproof dish or gratin dish measuring about 25 cm/10 in in diameter.

Grate the cheese. Place the self-raising flour in a bowl and rub in the remaining butter, then stir in the mustard and cheese with a good sprinkling of salt and pepper. Mix in the remaining milk to make a soft dough. Roll out the dough on a floured surface into a circle large enough to fit on top of the fish mixture, inside the rim of the dish. Cut the dough circle into eight wedges and arrange these on the fish mixture, with their points towards the middle of the dish. Brush with milk and bake the cobbler in a preheated oven at 220°C/425°F/gas 7 for about 25 minutes, until the topping is risen and golden brown.

Winter Garden Plaice

The distinctive flavour of Jerusalem artichokes blended with leeks is an excellent combination with plaice or other white fish.

SERVES: 4
PREPARATION: 25 minutes
COOKING: 50 minutes

2 plaice (each 575 g/1¼ lb)
450 g/1 lb Jerusalem artichokes
225 g/8 oz leeks
50 g/2 oz butter
120 ml/4 fl oz dry cider or dry
 white wine
1 lemon
salt and black pepper
75 ml/2½ fl oz double cream

Skin the plaice (page 314) and fillet each into four or ask the fishmonger to do this for you. Use the trimmings to make a Court Bouillon (page 316).

Peel the Jerusalem artichokes and thinly slice them into water to which a little lemon juice has been added. Wash and trim the leeks and slice them thinly. Melt the butter in a shallow flameproof casserole, add the drained artichokes and leeks, cover and cook gently for 5 minutes. Add the cider or wine, the juice of half the lemon and strain in sufficient court bouillon to just cover the vegetables. Cover again and simmer gently for 30 minutes or until the artichokes are just tender.

Trim and wipe the fillets, season with salt, freshly ground pepper and lemon juice; fold them in half and place on top of the vegetables. Cover and simmer gently for 15 minutes. Transfer the fish to a warm plate; reduce the liquid in the pan slightly, then stir in the cream. Adjust the seasoning and replace the fish; heat through.

■ Serve the plaice from the casserole, with peas and grilled tomatoes as an accompaniment.

Fritto Misto Mare

This is a dish of mixed fried seafood. There are other versions which can quite easily include a mixture of savoury ingredients and pieces of plain Italian cake, all battered and fried together in the same batch.

SERVES: 6
PREPARATION: 30 minutes
COOKING: 35 minutes

225 g/8 oz smelts
225 g/8 oz sprats
225 g/8 oz prawns
oil for deep frying
Batter
20 ml/4 teaspoons vegetable oil
300 ml/½ pt tepid water
100 g/4 oz plain flour
salt
1 egg white
Garnish
parsley sprigs
lemon wedges

Make the batter first so that it has time to rest while the fish is being prepared. Blend the oil with the tepid water and gradually stir it into the flour sifted with a pinch of salt. Beat the batter until quite smooth. Just before using the batter, fold

in the stiffly beaten, but still moist egg white.

Cut the heads off the smelts and sprats and shell the prawns. Heat the oil to 190°C/375°F or until a cube of day-old bread will crisp in 1 minute. Dip the fish and the prawns, one at a time, in the batter, using either tongs or a small perforated spoon. Hold them over the bowl for a moment to allow the surplus batter to drip off, then put them into the basket in the hot oil and fry for 5–6 minutes, until crisp and golden. Fry the fish in small batches and drain on crumpled absorbent paper.

Serve the fish on a warm dish, garnished with parsley sprigs, lightly fried in the oil until they are crisp and bright green, and lemon wedges.

Note Cooked shelled mussels, shelled scallops (halved or sliced if large), cleaned squid (sliced into rings or cut into pieces) and chunks of skinned white fish fillet are all suitable ingredients for including in Fritto Misto Mare. Frozen mixed seafood is available prepared ready for cooking and is quite suitable for an 'everyday' version of this dish.

Scallops in the Shell

SERVES: 2–4
PREPARATION: 20 minutes
COOKING: 35 minutes

4 large scallops
100 g/4 oz button mushrooms
300 ml/½ pt water
150 ml/¼ pt dry white wine or
    dry cider
1 slice lemon
1 bay leaf
450 g/1 lb potatoes
50 g/2 oz butter
25 g/1 oz plain flour
salt and black pepper
1 egg yolk
30 ml/2 tablespoons double cream
chopped parsley to garnish

Slide a knife under the scallops to remove them from the shells, wash them well under running cold water and remove the black beards and intestines. Clean

the scallop shells and set them aside. Cut each scallop into four or six slices.

Wipe and slice the button mushrooms thinly. Put the scallops and mushrooms in a pan. Add the water, white wine (or cider), lemon slice and bay leaf. Bring to the boil, cover with a lid and simmer gently for 15-20 minutes. Strain through a colander and set aside 300 ml/½ pt of the fish liquid for the sauce. Remove the lemon slice and bay leaf, and keep the scallops and mushrooms hot.

Cook the potatoes in boiling salted water. Meanwhile, melt 25 g/1 oz of the butter in a saucepan over low heat, stir in the flour and cook gently for a few minutes. Gradually mix in the reserved fish liquid, stirring continuously until the sauce is smooth. Bring to the boil, then simmer gently for 2–3 minutes.

Add the mushrooms and scallops; season to taste with salt and freshly ground black pepper and reheat gently. Lightly mix the egg yolk and cream, remove the pan from the heat and stir the egg into the fish mixture.

Drain the potatoes, mash with the remaining butter and season well with salt and freshly ground pepper. Using a large piping bag fitted with a large star nozzle, pipe a border of mashed potato around the edges of the deep scallop shells. Brush the potato border with melted butter and place the shells under a hot grill for a few minutes until the potatoes are golden brown.

Spoon the scallops into the centre of each shell and sprinkle them with chopped parsley.

■ Serve with a tossed green salad for a main course, or on their own as a first course for a dinner party.

Scallops in the Shell.

POULTRY & GAME

Middle Eastern Chicken Stew

When pumpkin is out of season, butternut squash is an excellent alternative for this stew. If preferred, boneless chicken breasts may be substituted for the thighs, in which case allow 4 portions, one per serving.

SERVES: 4–6
PREPARATION: 1 hour
COOKING: 1 hour

1 small aubergine
salt and black pepper
1 large onion
1 red pepper
1 green chilli
450 g/1 lb peeled and deseeded
    pumpkin
60 ml/4 tablespoons olive oil
8 chicken thighs
2 cloves garlic
1 cinnamon stick
2 bay leaves
25 g/1 oz raisins
15 ml/1 tablespoon ground
    coriander
grated rind and juice of 1 lemon
400 g/14 oz can chick peas
600 ml/1 pt chicken stock

Trim the ends off the aubergine and cut it into small cubes. Place these in a colander, sprinkle with salt and leave to stand over a bowl for 15 minutes. Rinse and drain well.

Peel and chop the onion. Cut the stalk end off the pepper and chilli, then remove all pith and seeds from both and chop the flesh. Cut the pumpkin into small cubes.

Heat about a quarter of the olive oil in a large flameproof casserole. Brown the chicken thighs all over, then use a perforated spoon to transfer them to a plate. Add the rest of the oil to the pan. Peel the garlic and crush it. Add all the prepared vegetables and the chilli and fry, stirring often, for 10 minutes.

Add the cinnamon stick, bay leaves, raisins, coriander, grated lemon rind and juice. Drain the chick peas and stir them in. Pour in the stock and bring to the boil. Season the mixture well. Stir well, replace the chicken pieces, pushing them down between the vegetables, and reduce the heat so that the stew simmers very gently. Cover the pan and cook for about 45 minutes, or until the chicken pieces are cooked through and the vegetables are tender. Taste for seasoning before serving.

■ Serve this Middle Eastern stew with cous cous, rice or pasta.

Savoury Game Pie

The pie filling may be venison, hare or game bird, all of which should be prepared, boned if necessary and marinated.

SERVES: 6
PREPARATION: 45 minutes
MARINATING: 8 hours
OVEN: 220°C/425°F/gas 7
        190°C/375°F/gas 5
COOKING: about 3 hours

Marinade
1 onion
1 stick celery
7 coriander seeds
7 allspice or juniper berries
2 bay leaves
2 sprigs parsley
pinch marjoram
300 ml/½ pt red wine
75 ml/2½ fl oz olive oil
Pie Filling
675 g/1½ lb haunch or shoulder of
    venison
50 g/2 oz streaky bacon
225 g/8 oz mushrooms
15 g/½ oz butter
30 ml/2 tablespoons plain flour
salt and black pepper
Puff Pastry
225 g/8 oz home-made Puff Pastry
    (page 374) or thawed frozen
    puff pastry
beaten egg to glaze

Prepare the vegetables and spices for the marinade*: peel and finely chop the onion, scrub the celery and chop it finely, and crush the coriander seeds and allspice or juniper berries.

Cut the venison into 2.5cm/ 1 in cubes, removing all the fat. Place in a large bowl, in layers with the prepared vegetables and crushed spices. Add the bay leaves, parsley sprigs and a pinch of marjoram and pour over the wine mixed with the oil. Cover the bowl and leave the venison to marinate for at least 8 hours. Lift the venison out of the marinade and strain the liquid through a sieve. Set it aside.

Precook the pie filling to avoid over-baking the pastry: remove the rind from the bacon and dice it, then fry it over low heat to extract all the fat. Slice the mushrooms, and cook them for 2 minutes in the bacon fat. Add the butter to the pan, together with the mushrooms. Stir in the flour. Gradually stir in the reserved marinade and bring to the boil. Add salt and freshly ground pepper to taste, then stir in the venison. Cover the pan with a lid and simmer over low heat for 1½ hours. Leave the venison to cool.

Spoon the cold venison and sauce into a deep pie dish, setting a pastry funnel in the centre. Roll out the pastry on a floured surface, to a thickness of 5 mm/ ¼ in. Cut off 1 cm/½ cm wide pastry strips and place them on the moistened rim of the pie dish. Brush with water before covering the filling with the remaining pastry. Seal and scallop the edges (page 367) and brush the pastry with lightly beaten egg; decorate with leaves cut from the pastry trimmings and brush with more egg. Make a few slits in the pastry for the steam to escape.

Bake the pie in a preheated oven at 220°C/425°F/gas 7 for 20 minutes, then reduce the heat to 190°C/375°F/gas 5 and bake for a further 30 minutes or until the pie is golden brown.

■ Serve the game pie hot, with boiled potatoes, Brussels sprouts and roasted or creamy mashed parsnips.

Venison in Whisky Sauce

Whisky sauce lends a distinctive flavour to the game in this main course dish.

SERVES: 6
PREPARATION: 20 minutes
OVEN: 160°C/325°F/gas 3
COOKING: 1¾–2 hours

6 venison cutlets or steaks
50 g/2 oz streaky bacon
1 onion
2 carrots
2 sticks celery
juice of 1 lemon
12 juniper berries
5 ml/1 teaspoon dried marjoram
    or thyme
salt and black pepper
40 g/1½ oz butter
25 g/1 oz plain flour
150–300 ml/¼–½ pt stock or water
30 ml/2 tablespoons whisky
20 ml/4 teaspoons cranberry sauce
juice of 1 small orange
Garnish
Croûtons (page 313)
whole cranberries or orange wedges

Beat the venison cutlets or steaks lightly, if necessary, to flatten them. Remove the rind from the bacon and chop the rashers roughly. Peel and finely chop the onion, carrots and celery.

Rub the venison with about half the lemon juice. Crush the juniper berries in a mortar. Mix with the marjoram or thyme, and add a few twists of pepper; rub this mixture into both sides of each cutlet or steak.

Heat the butter in a flame-proof casserole and fry the bacon over low heat until the fat runs. Turn up the heat and brown the venison on both sides, then remove from the casserole. Fry the onion, carrots and celery until they are lightly coloured; season with salt. Sprinkle the flour over the vegetables and cook over low heat until the mixture is light brown. Stir in the stock and the whisky, bring the sauce to simmering point. Put the venison back in the sauce, making sure that it just covers the top of the meat – if necessary add a little more stock.

Cover the dish with a lid and cook in a preheated oven at 160°C/325°F/gas 3 for about 1½ hours or until the meat is tender. Remove the venison from the dish and keep hot. Add the cranberry sauce and orange juice to the sauce, adjust seasoning and sharpen to taste with the remaining, lemon juice. Serve at once with the venison.

■ The cutlets may be arranged around a mound of Celeriac and Potato Purée (page 273) and garnished with croûtons and cranberries or orange wedges.

Chilli con Carne

Banish November shivers with a bowl of warming chilli. If preferred the wine may be omitted and additional stock added to make 600 ml/1 pt.

SERVES: 6–8
SOAKING (optional): 12 hours
PREPARATION: 20 minutes
COOKING: about 2¼ hours

175 g/6 oz dried kidney beans
    or 2 × 400 g/14 oz cans
    kidney beans
1 large onion
2 cloves garlic
1 large chilli
1 small red pepper
30 ml/2 tablespoons oil
675 g/1½ lb lean minced beef
10 ml/2 teaspoons chilli powder
150 ml/¼ pt red wine
400 g/14 oz can chopped tomatoes
450 ml/¾ pt beef stock
60 ml/4 tablespoons tomato paste
salt and black pepper

If you are using dried kidney beans, soak them in cold water to cover for 12 hours. Drain, tip the beans into a saucepan and cover with fresh cold water. Bring to the boil, boil hard for 10 minutes, then reduce the heat and cook the beans for a further 30 minutes.

Meanwhile, peel and chop the onion and garlic. Cut the chilli and red pepper in half; carefully remove the seeds and any pith. Chop the chilli finely and dice the pepper.

Heat the oil in a large flameproof casserole. Add the onion, garlic, chilli and pepper and cook over low heat for 5 minutes. Add the minced beef and cook, stirring, until it browns. Stir in the chilli powder and the red wine. Cook for 3 minutes, stirring constantly, then add the tomatoes, stock and tomato paste. Mix well.

Chilli con Carne.

Drain the partially cooked beans and stir them into the meat mixture. Bring to the boil, reduce the heat to a simmer, cover the pan and cook the chilli for 1½ hours, stirring every now and again. After cooking for 1 hour, test the beans; if they are still slightly firm, do not add the salt until the final 5 minutes' cooking. If using canned beans, drain and add for the last 30 minutes of the cooking time.

■ Serve the chilli with plain boiled rice or baked potatoes. Add a crisp celery, cucumber and lettuce salad for a pleasing contrast in texture.

Tournedos Rossini

The Italian composer Rossini enjoyed a great reputation not only as a musician, but also as a creator of gourmet dishes. The following is one of his best-known culinary masterpieces, which is traditionally garnished with truffles or flat mushrooms.

SERVES: 6
PREPARATION: 15 minutes
COOKING: 20 minutes

6 tournedos of beef
6 slices white bread
100–150 g/4–5 oz butter
15 ml/1 tablespoon oil
60 ml/2 fl oz Madeira, Marsala or
    cream sherry
150 ml/¼ pt Espagnole Sauce
    (page 354)
150 ml/¼ pt brown stock
salt and black pepper
Garnish
6 slices pâté de foie gras
6 slices truffle or 6 flat mushrooms

Ask the butcher to trim the tournedos and tie them neatly. Cut six circles from the bread to fit the tournedos exactly.

Heat 50 g/2 oz of the butter and the oil in a large frying pan over medium heat and fry the bread until it is crisp and golden. Drain the fried bread on crumpled absorbent kitchen paper and keep it hot.

Heat 40 g/1½ oz of the remaining butter in a pan and fry the tournedos over high heat, turning once, for 1½–2 minutes on each side. They should be rich brown on the outside and rosy-pink inside. Lift out and keep warm. Add the wine to the pan, stirring to scrape up all the residue on the bottom. Cook the tournedos for about 2 minutes, until the juices have reduced. Stir in the prepared espagnole sauce and the stock and leave the sauce to cook, uncovered, until it has thickened.

Meanwhile make the garnish. Heat the remaining butter in a clean pan and fry the slices of pâté over high heat, until golden. Lift out and keep warm. Lightly fry the truffles or mushrooms in the remaining butter.

To serve, arrange the bread circles on a warmed dish, set a tournedo on each and top with a slice of foie gras and truffle or mushroom, dark side uppermost.

Correct the seasoning of the sauce. Pour sufficient around the bread to cover the bottom of the dish and spoon the remainder into a warm sauceboat.

■ Serve with Matchstick Chips (page 347) and buttered spinach or baby Brussels sprouts.

Osso Buco

This appetising, inexpensive stew comes from Italy. It is usually made with veal on the bone, although stewing veal, in boneless cubes, can be substituted if preferred. The traditional garnish – known as *gremolata* – adds a colourful appearance and fresh flavour to the finished stew.

SERVES: 6
PREPARATION: 30 minutes
COOKING: 1¾–2 hours

1.15 kg/2½ lb shin of veal
plain flour
salt and black pepper
3 carrots
2 sticks celery
1 onion
2 cloves garlic
50 g/2 oz butter
250 ml/8 fl oz dry white wine
250 ml/8 fl oz chicken or veal stock
400 g/14 oz can chopped tomatoes
pinch caster sugar
1 sprig fresh rosemary or 2.5 ml/
  ½ teaspoon dried rosemary
Garnish
60 ml/4 tablespoons finely
  chopped parsley
finely grated rind of 2 large lemons
2–3 cloves garlic

Ask the butcher to saw the veal into pieces, about 3.5 cm/1½ in thick. Remove any chips of bone. Season a little flour with salt and pepper and use to coat the veal pieces. Peel or scrub the vegetables and chop them finely.

Melt the butter in a heavy-based pan, large enough to take all the meat in one layer. Brown the meat and the vegetables.

Osso Buco.

Stand each piece of meat upright to prevent the marrow from falling out during cooking. Pour over the wine, stock and tomatoes. Season to taste with salt, freshly ground pepper and sugar. Then add the rosemary. Simmer, covered, for 1½ hours, or until the meat is tender.

While the veal is cooking, mix the parsley and lemon rind. Peel and finely chop the garlic and add to the mixture.

Transfer the meat to a platter, pour the sauce over and sprinkle with the garnish. The marrow is usually left inside the bones, but it can also be extracted and spread on toast.

■ Osso Buco can be served with Risotto alla Milanese (page 275), or with buttered noodles.

Escalopes with Artichokes and Lemon Sauce

If small veal or pork escalopes are used, double the number and allow two per portion.

SERVES: 4
PREPARATION: 15 minutes
COOKING: 25 minutes

4 veal or pork escalopes
plain flour
salt and black pepper
50 g/2 oz butter
15 ml/1 tablespoon chopped
  shallots or onion
350 g/12 oz can artichoke bottoms
120 ml/4 fl oz dry white wine
300 ml/½ pt chicken stock
juice and rind of 2 small lemons
150 ml/¼ pt double cream

Trim any fat from the escalopes. Season a little flour with salt and black pepper and use it to coat the escalopes. Heat the butter in a heavy-based pan over medium heat and fry the escalopes for a few minutes, until golden brown, turning once. Add the finely chopped shallots or onion. Drain the artichoke bottoms and add them with the white wine.

Bring the mixture to simmering point. Add sufficient stock to cover the escalopes completely. Grate the rind from the lemons and set aside; squeeze the juice and add it to the sauce. Cover the pan and cook over low heat for 20 minutes or until the meat is tender.

Stir in the cream and heat gently for a few minutes without boiling. Taste and add salt and freshly ground pepper if required.

Arrange the escalopes in the centre of a warmed serving dish and surround with a border of noodles or rice. Pour the sauce over the meat and top with a scattering of grated lemon rind.

Crown of Pork

This is an impressive and colourful main course for a large dinner party. The crown is cut from the loin of pork and cannot be constructed from less than 12 cutlets. The crown should have the fat carefully trimmed off by the butcher, as it cannot crisp when filled with a stuffing.

SERVES: 10–12
PREPARATION: 35 minutes
OVEN: 190°C/375°F/gas 5
COOKING: 2½–3 hours

1 crown of pork (12 cutlets)
lard
Rice Stuffing
1 large onion
1 celery stick
175 g/6 oz carrots
2 × 350 g/12 oz cans pineapple
  rings in syrup
30 ml/2 tablespoons corn oil
75 g/3 oz cooked rice
30–45 ml/2–3 tablespoons
  chopped parsley
5 ml/1 teaspoon dried savory
5–10 ml/1–2 teaspoons paprika
75 g/3 oz sultanas
salt and black pepper
lemon juice
300 ml/½ pt water
watercress sprigs to garnish

Prepare the stuffing first. Peel and finely chop the onion, celery and carrots. Drain the pineapple, reserving the juice from both cans. Reserve half the pineapple rings for garnish and finely chop the remainder.

Heat the oil and fry the onion and celery until just turning colour. Add the rice, carrots, parsley, savory, paprika, pineapple and sultanas. Mix well and heat through. Season to taste with salt, pepper and lemon juice. Set the stuffing aside to cool.

Stand the crown of pork in a greased roasting tin and brush the outside of the meat thoroughly with melted lard. Spoon the stuffing into the centre of the crown and cover it with a piece of foil. Wrap foil around each cutlet bone to prevent it from charring. Roast the crown in the centre of a preheated oven at 190°C/375°F/gas 5 for 2¼ hours or until amber-coloured juice runs out when a skewer is inserted in the meat. Lift out the crown and keep warm.

Fry the reserved pineapple rings in the hot fat in the roasting tin for about 4 minutes or until golden on both sides, then arrange around the pork.

Pour excess fat carefully from the roasting tin and add the pineapple juice and water (vegetable boiling water may be used) to the residue in the pan. Bring to the boil, stirring continuously and scraping the cooking residue off the pan to flavour the gravy. Boil for about 3 minutes, until the gravy is well flavoured and has reduced slightly. Taste for seasoning, pour into a warm sauceboat and serve with the pork. Remove the foil from the tips of the cutlets and replace

with paper frills. Garnish with small sprigs of watercress placed between the pineapple rings.
■ Serve the crown with roast potatoes and green beans.

Orange-glazed Roast Lamb

A fruit-flavoured glaze and stuffing transform a leg of lamb into a dish fit for a special occasion. Ask the butcher to bone the lamb, but not to roll it.

SERVES: 6–8
PREPARATION: 20 minutes
OVEN: 190°C/375°F/gas 5
COOKING: 2¼ hours

1.8–2.05 kg/4–4½ lb leg
    of lamb (boned)
Fruit Stuffing
1 large onion
25 g/1 oz butter
75 g/3 oz fresh white breadcrumbs
50 g/2 oz sultanas
50 g/2 oz raisins
50 g/2 oz currants
grated rind of 2 oranges and juice
    of 1 orange
2.5 ml/½ teaspoon dried rosemary
2.5 ml/½ teaspoon dried thyme
salt and black pepper
Glaze
50 g/2 oz soft brown sugar
juice of ½ lemon
juice of 1 orange
30 ml/2 tablespoons
    Worcestershire sauce
Sauce
120 ml/4 fl oz red wine
300 ml/½ pt chicken, vegetable
    or beef stock
Garnish
orange slices
watercress

Prepare the stuffing for the lamb first. Peel and finely chop the onion. Melt the butter in a pan over medium heat and fry the onion for 3 minutes. Mix the breadcrumbs, sultanas, raisins, currants and the fried onion. Stir in the orange rind, rosemary and thyme. Season to taste. Bind the stuffing with the orange juice.

Pack the stuffing into the lamb. Tie the joint into a neat shape, securing it with string. Put it in a greased roasting tin.

Place the glaze ingredients in a small pan and cook over low heat for 1 minute, then spoon the glaze over the meat. Roast in the centre of a preheated oven at 190°C/375°F/gas 5 for 2 hours, basting frequently.

Orange-glazed Roast Lamb.

Remove the joint to a serving dish and keep it warm. Pour off any excess fat from the roasting tin. Stir the wine and stock for the sauce into the pan juices and boil over high heat, scraping up all the residue from the glaze. Continue boiling briskly until the sauce has reduced down and thickened slightly. Season with salt and pepper if necessary.

Garnish the joint with thin orange twists (page 412) and sprigs of watercress. Pour the sauce in a warm sauceboat.
■ Galette Lyonnaise (page 273) and buttered baby Brussels sprouts or salsify would go well with the lamb joint.

Barbecued Sausages

A spicy basting sauce, more often used with outdoor grills, adds tang to grilled sausages. English mustard gives the sausages a slight kick, but a mild French or American mustard can be substituted, if preferred.

SERVES: 4
PREPARATION: 10 minutes
MARINATING: 1 hour
OVEN: 200°C/400°F/gas 6
COOKING: 20 minutes

450 g/1 lb pork sausages
30 ml/2 tablespoons oil
30 ml/2 tablespoons tomato
    ketchup
10 ml/2 teaspoons made
    English mustard
2.5 ml/½ teaspoon
    Worcestershire sauce
salt and black pepper

Pierce the skin of the sausages with the prongs of a fork. Arrange them in one layer in a roasting tin or ovenproof dish.

Mix together the oil, ketchup, mustard and Worcestershire sauce. Season with salt and pepper and pour this marinade* over the sausages. Cover and place in the refrigerator, then leave the sausages for at least 1 hour, turning them occasionally.

Bake the sausages in a preheated oven at 200°C/400°F/gas 6 for 20 minutes, basting frequently, until the sausages are well browned.
■ Serve hot with creamed potatoes and grilled tomatoes, or cold in buttered rolls.

Braised Hearts with Apples

SERVES: 4
PREPARATION: 20 minutes
MARINATING: 30 minutes
OVEN: 150°C/300°F/gas 2
COOKING: 1–1½ hours

4 lamb hearts
juice of 1 lemon
225 g/8 oz onions
2 medium cooking apples
30–45 ml/2–3 tablespoons
    plain flour
40 g/1½ oz butter
salt and black pepper
2 bay leaves
150 ml/¼ pt cider
5 ml/1 teaspoon crushed
    coriander seeds
5 ml/1 teaspoon caster sugar
2 thin slices unpeeled lemon

Cut the hearts in slices, about 1 cm/½ in thick, and remove all the fat and blood vessels. Put the slices in a basin with the lemon juice and leave to marinate* for 30 minutes.

Meanwhile, peel and slice the onions; peel, core and slice the cooking apples.

Dry the heart slices and coat them with flour, then fry them in the butter in a flameproof casserole over high heat. Add the onions and continue frying until they are pale golden. Season well with salt and freshly ground black pepper. Add the bay leaves and the cider. Cover the heart slices with the apple and sprinkle them with coriander seeds and sugar. Lay the lemon slices on top of the apples.

Put the lid on the casserole and simmer over low heat on top of the stove or in a preheated oven at 150°C/300°F/gas 2 for about 1 hour or until the meat is tender. When the casserole is cooked, remove the lemon slices and bay leaves and stir the apple slices into the sauce.

■ Serve the casseroled hearts with creamed potatoes.

Toad-in-the-hole

A traditional British dish, which consists of sausage baked in batter, toad-in-the-hole is economical and easy to prepare.

SERVES: 4
PREPARATION: 20 minutes
OVEN: 220°C/425°F/gas 7
        180°C/350°F/gas 4
COOKING: about 1 hour

450 g/1 lb pork sausages
300 ml/½ pt Basic Pancake Batter
    (page 339)

Grease a roasting tin (about 25 × 30 cm/10 × 12 in) and place the sausages in it. Put the tin in a preheated oven at 220°C/425°F/gas 7 for 10 minutes until the fat runs from the sausages and is sizzling. Reduce the oven temperature to 180°C/350°F/gas 4.

Pour the batter over the sausages, and return to the oven. Cook for about 45 minutes, until the batter is well-risen and golden brown. The larger the tin, and the thinner the layer of batter, the shorter the cooking time. If a small tin is used, the batter may require an additional 5–10 minutes. Serve at once.

Vegetables & Salads

Stuffed Cabbage Leaves

Buy a large, open cabbage for this savoury supper dish. You need at least eight good-sized leaves.

SERVES: 4
PREPARATION: 30 minutes
COOKING: 40–45 minutes

1 large cabbage
salt and black pepper
½ onion
450 g/1 lb minced lamb
50 g/2 oz cous cous
25 g/1 oz seedless raisins
15 g/½ oz pine kernels
30 ml/2 tablespoons chopped mint
grated nutmeg
Tomato Sauce
1 onion
1 small carrot
1 stick celery
15 ml/1 tablespoon oil
400 g/14 oz can chopped tomatoes
salt and black pepper
2.5–5 ml/½–1 teaspoon sugar

Separate the cabbage leaves. Set aside eight of the largest undamaged leaves, if necessary using smaller ones in pairs to make up the number. Cut out the thick stalks. Bring a large saucepan of salted water to the boil. Add the leaves. When the water boils again, blanch the leaves for 2 minutes, making sure that they remain beneath the water. Drain well, refresh under cold water and drain again. Pat dry on absorbent kitchen paper.

Peel the onion and chop it finely. Mix with the lamb, cous cous, raisins and pine kernels. Add the mint with salt and pepper to taste, plus a generous amount of grated nutmeg.

Spread out the leaves. Place an equal amount of stuffing in the centre of each leaf. Fold over and tuck in the edges, then roll up the filled leaves, completely enclosing the stuffing. Place the cabbage rolls in a single layer in a large frying pan or flameproof casserole. Pour in enough water to come halfway up the rolls. Bring to the boil, cover the pan, reduce the heat and simmer for about 45 minutes. Check the water level in the pan frequently and top up as necessary.

Meanwhile, make the sauce. Peel and chop the onion and carrot; scrub and slice the celery. Heat the oil in a saucepan and cook the onion, carrot and celery

Stuffed Cabbage Leaves.

for about 7 minutes or until soft but not browned. Stir in the tomatoes with salt and pepper to taste. Bring to the boil, lower the heat, cover and simmer for 30 minutes. Add a little sugar to balance the sharp flavour of the tomato and adjust the seasoning if necessary.

When the leaves are tender and the stuffing cooked through, transfer them to a serving dish with a perforated spoon. Pour the hot sauce over the stuffed cabbage leaves and serve at once.

Countryside Potatoes

SERVES: 4
PREPARATION: 10 minutes
OVEN: 200°C/400°F/gas 6
COOKING: 25–30 minutes

4 large baked potatoes
2 rashers back bacon
100 g/4 oz cream cheese
15–30 ml/1–2 tablespoons milk
10 ml/2 teaspoons chopped parsley
salt and black pepper
50 g/2 oz grated Cheddar cheese

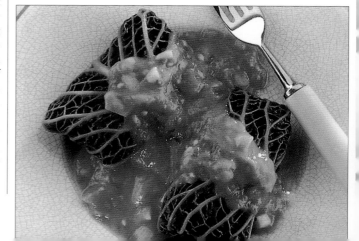

Cut the potatoes in half, scoop out the flesh and mash it finely. Quickly fry the bacon, without any fat, until it is crisp; drain on absorbent kitchen paper and crumble the bacon into the mashed potato. Mix in the softened cream cheese, the milk and parsley. Stir thoroughly and season with salt and freshly ground black pepper.

Pile the mixture back into the potato skins and sprinkle with grated cheese. Bake in a preheated oven at 200°C/400°F/gas 6 for about 20 minutes.

Galette Lyonnaise

This savoury potato dish with its classic Lyonnaise flavouring of onion and cheese is an excellent accompaniment to both fish and meat main courses. Extra grated Cheddar or Parmesan cheese may be mixed with the potato in addition to the topping.

SERVES: 4
PREPARATION: 35 minutes
OVEN: 200°C/400°F/gas 6
COOKING: 25–30 minutes

450 g/1 lb potatoes
225 g/8 oz onions
65 g/2½ oz butter
1 egg
salt and black pepper
pinch nutmeg
30 ml/2 tablespoons grated
    Cheddar or Parmesan cheese
parsley sprigs to garnish

Peel the potatoes, cut them into even sized pieces and boil them in lightly salted water. Rub the potatoes through a coarse sieve. Peel the onions then finely chop them.

Heat 50 g/2 oz of the butter and cook the onions over low heat until they are soft and golden. Stir the contents of the pan into the potatoes. Beat the egg and add it to the potatoes with salt, freshly ground pepper and nutmeg to taste.

Spoon the onion and potato mixture into a greased, shallow ovenproof dish; smooth the top, sprinkle over the grated cheese and dot with the remaining butter. Bake the potatoes in a preheated oven at 200°C/400°F/gas 6 for about 20 minutes or until golden brown on top.

Serve the potatoes straight from the dish, garnished with sprigs of parsley.

Leeks à la Niçoise

French vegetable dishes or salads prepared à la Niçoise usually include tomatoes and garlic.

SERVES: 4
PREPARATION: 15 minutes
COOKING: 20 minutes

900 g/2 lb young leeks
225 g/8 oz tomatoes
45–60 ml/3–4 tablespoons olive oil
salt and black pepper
1 large clove garlic
15 ml/1 tablespoon chopped parsley
lemon juice

Cut the roots and most of the green tops off the leeks, so they are of even length. Rinse the leeks thoroughly under cold running water to get rid of any grit and then dry them on absor-

Celeriac and Potato Purée.

bent kitchen paper. Skin the tomatoes (page 302) and chop them up roughly.

Heat the oil in a flameproof casserole over medium heat and put in the leeks side by side. Fry them until they are lightly coloured underneath, then turn them over and season with salt and freshly ground pepper. Cover the casserole with a lid, and cook the leeks over gentle heat for 10 minutes or until the thick white part is tender. Lift out the leeks and keep them warm.

Add the tomatoes, crushed garlic and parsley to the casserole and cook briskly for 2 or 3 minutes, stirring continuously. Adjust seasoning and sharpen to taste with lemon juice. Put the leeks back into the sauce and serve hot or cold.

■ This vegetable dish can be served hot with grilled fish, meat or chicken, or cold as a first course, with plenty of crusty bread to mop up the juices.

Celeriac and Potato Purée

SERVES: 4–6
PREPARATION: 10 minutes
COOKING: 45 minutes

450 g/1 lb celeriac
salt and black pepper
350 g/12 oz mashed potatoes
40 g/1½ oz butter
45 ml/3 tablespoons double cream

Scrub the celeriac thoroughly in cold water to remove all traces of dirt, but do not peel it. Put it in a pan of boiling salted water and cook for 35–40 minutes or until it is quite tender. Leave to cool slightly, then peel the celeriac and chop it roughly. Purée in a liquidiser or food processor or press through a sieve.

Mix the celeriac purée with the mashed potatoes, add the butter and cream, and season to taste with salt and freshly ground pepper. Heat the purée through over low heat before serving.

Roasted Onions

The sweet flavour of Spanish, or other mild-flavoured, onions is particularly enhanced by roasting them whole. In this recipe, the tender onions are dressed with a delicate herb butter.

SERVES: 6
PREPARATION: 5 minutes
OVEN: 180°C/350°F/gas 4
COOKING: 2½–3 hours

6 large Spanish onions
75 g/3 oz butter
30 ml/2 tablespoons
    chopped parsley
15 ml/1 tablespoon chopped
    thyme or sage
salt and black pepper
herb sprigs to garnish (optional)

Line a deep roasting tin with foil to prevent the onions from sticking to the tin. Wash but do not peel the onions, cut away the roots and stand them upright in the tin. Bake the whole onions in a preheated oven at 180°C/350°F/gas 4 for about 2½ hours or until they are tender when tested with a skewer.

Cream the butter with the parsley and thyme or sage in a bowl. Add salt and pepper to taste and set aside.

To serve, slit the top of each onion with a sharp knife and push the halves aside slightly. Place a knob of herb butter in the middle of each onion and serve them immediately. The soft centre is scooped out and eaten with a teaspoon. The onions may be garnished with herb sprigs, if liked.

273

RICE & PASTA

Bangkok Chicken and Rice

SERVES: 6–8
PREPARATION: 35 minutes
COOKING: 2¼ hours

1.6 kg/3½ lb chicken
450 g/1 lb onions
1 bay leaf
1 sprig parsley
salt and black pepper
450 g/1 lb long-grain rice
45 ml/3 tablespoons olive or
  vegetable oil
30 ml/2 tablespoons peanut butter
2.5 ml/½ teaspoon chilli powder
100 g/4 oz peeled cooked prawns
100 g/4 oz diced cooked ham
5 ml/1 teaspoon cumin seeds
7.5 ml/1½ teaspoons
  coriander seeds
1 clove garlic
pinch ground mace
Garnish
½ cucumber
2 hard-boiled eggs
8–12 unpeeled cooked prawns

Put the chicken in a large pan, with one whole peeled onion, the bay leaf and parsley sprig. Add a seasoning of salt and freshly ground black pepper and enough cold water to cover the chicken. Bring the water to the boil, scoop off any scum from the surface with a slotted spoon, then cover the pan with a lid and simmer over gentle heat for about 1½ hours or until the chicken is tender.

Lift out the chicken and leave to cool slightly. Strain the stock through a fine sieve and use it to cook the rice. Place the rice in a saucepan and pour in 1.12 litres/2 pt stock. Bring to the boil, stir once, then cover the pan tightly and reduce the heat to the minimum setting. Cook for 20 minutes. Turn the heat off and leave the rice to stand for a further 5 minutes without taking off the lid.

Remove the skin from the chicken and cut the meat into small pieces. Peel and thinly slice the remaining onions. Heat the oil in a large pan, and fry the onions over low heat until they begin to colour. Stir in the peanut butter and chilli powder. Add the peeled prawns, diced ham, chicken and rice, which should now be dry and fluffy. Continue frying over low heat, stirring frequently until the rice is slightly brown. Crush the cumin and coriander seeds; peel and crush the garlic, and stir them, with the mace, into the rice. Season to taste with salt.

Pile the rice and chicken mixture on to a hot serving dish and garnish with thin slices of unpeeled cucumber, wedges of hard-boiled egg and prawns.

■ Arrange a number of small side dishes or bowls around the Bangkok chicken. A suitable selection might include apricot and mango chutney; sliced tomatoes, dressed with sugar and lemon juice; peeled, sliced oranges; and sliced green and red pepper with raw onion rings, both served in Sauce Vinaigrette (page 356). Other bowls could contain small wedges of fresh pineapple; fried sliced bananas with lemon juice; and fresh shredded and toasted coconut. Shelled almonds or cashew nuts fried in a little butter are also frequently served with this dish.

Bangkok Chicken and Rice.

Risotto Bianco

This quick and simple risotto is cooked by the one-stage method.

SERVES: 4–6
PREPARATION: 10 minutes
COOKING: about 30 minutes

1 small onion
1 small clove garlic
75 g/3 oz butter
10 ml/2 teaspoons olive oil
225 g/8 oz risotto rice
900 ml/1½ pt White Stock
  (page 310)
salt and black pepper
100 g/4 oz grated Parmesan cheese

Peel and finely chop the onion and garlic. Heat 50 g/2 oz of the butter with the oil in a deep pan and cook the onion and garlic until soft and just beginning to colour. Add the rice to the pan. Cook over low heat, stirring continuously, until the rice is yellow and shiny.

Add the hot stock to the rice; bring to the boil, stir, then cover the pan with a lid. Reduce the heat to the minimum setting and cook for 20 minutes. Turn off the heat and leave the rice to stand, covered, for a further 5 minutes. The rice should be tender and creamy. Watch the risotto carefully while cooking to see that it does not dry out.

Season the risotto to taste with salt and freshly ground pepper. Stir in the remaining butter and half the grated cheese. Spoon the risotto bianco into a warm shallow dish, stir lightly with a fork, and sprinkle with the rest of the cheese.

Risotto alla Milanese

Serve this rich risotto on its own for lunch or supper. It is also the traditional accompaniment to Osso Buco (page 270).

SERVES: 6
PREPARATION: 20 minutes
COOKING: 20 minutes

1 small onion
75 g/3 oz butter
450 g/1 lb risotto rice
150 ml/¼ pt dry white wine
1.12 litres/2 pt beef or
   chicken stock
2.5 ml/½ teaspoon powdered
   saffron
75 g/3 oz Parmesan cheese

Peel and finely chop the onion. Melt half the butter in a large pan, add the onion and fry over moderate heat until transparent. Add the rice and sauté, stirring continuously, until it begins to change colour. Pour in the wine and bring to the boil.

Stir in a quarter of the stock, bring to the boil and stir. Cover the pan and reduce the heat to the lowest setting. Bring the remaining stock to the boil in a separate saucepan. Gradually add it to the risotto at intervals when the previous addition has been absorbed. The last batch will not be absorbed completely as the risotto should be quite moist. Finally stir in the saffron. The rice should be tender after about 20 minutes.

Stir in the remaining butter. Grate the Parmesan cheese, stir it into the rice and serve at once.

Lasagne Verde al Forno

SERVES: 6
PREPARATION: 30 minutes
OVEN: 200°C/400°F/gas 6
COOKING: 1½ hours

50 g/2 oz lean gammon or bacon
1 small onion
1 carrot
50 g/2 oz button mushrooms
25 g/1 oz butter
175 g/6 oz minced beef
50–75 g/2–3 oz chicken livers
   (optional)
15 ml/1 tablespoon tomato paste
150 ml/¼ pt dry white wine
300 ml/½ pt beef stock
salt and black pepper
225 g/8 oz green lasagne
450 ml/¾ pt Béchamel Sauce
   (page 353)
50 g/2 oz grated Parmesan cheese

Remove the rind and chop the gammon or bacon. Peel and finely chop the onion and carrot and trim the mushrooms before slicing them thinly.

Melt half the butter in a large, heavy-based pan over low heat. Fry the gammon or bacon for 2 minutes, then add the prepared vegetables and fry them lightly. Crumble in the minced beef. Trim and chop the chicken livers (if used) and add them to the minced beef. Stir in the tomato paste. Continue frying, and stir continuously until the meat has browned.

Add the wine and let the mixture bubble for a few minutes before adding the stock. Season to taste. Cover the pan with a lid

and simmer over low heat for 30–40 minutes.

Meanwhile cook the lasagne in a large pan of boiling salted water for 10–15 minutes or until just tender, stirring occasionally. Drain the pasta through a colander and drop it into a large basin of cold water to prevent the sheets from sticking together. If you are using dried lasagne which requires no pre-cooking, follow the instructions on the packet.

Thoroughly butter a shallow ovenproof dish, about 25 × 30cm/ 10 × 8 in. Cover the base with a thin layer of meat mixture, then Béchamel sauce and lastly the drained lasagne. Repeat these layers until all the ingredients are used up, finishing with Béchamel sauce. Sprinkle the top with the Parmesan cheese.

Bake in a preheated oven at 200°C/400°F/gas 6 for about 15–20 minutes or until the top is crisp and bubbly. Serve straight from the dish.

■ A tossed green salad is the ideal accompaniment for this baked lasagne, as the crisp leaves contribute a contrasting texture and, when tossed with a slightly sharp dressing, the salad balances the richness of the meat and Béchamel sauces.

Meat Tortellini with Tomato Sauce

SERVES: 6–8
PREPARATION: 1 hour
COOKING: 12–15 minutes

1 quantity Pasta Dough
   (page 351)
100 g/4 oz lean boneless pork
100 g/4 oz rump steak
1 small onion
2 cloves garlic
25 g/1 oz fresh white breadcrumbs
5 ml/1 teaspoon tomato paste
2.5 ml/½ teaspoon ground mace
30 ml/2 tablespoons
   chopped parsley
1.25 ml/¼ teaspoon dried oregano
salt and black pepper
30 ml/2 tablespoons brandy
   or sherry
1 small egg
a little plain flour
Tomato Sauce (see Stuffed Peppers
   with Pork and Beef, page 229)

Make the pasta dough and cut it into quarters so that it is easier to roll out. Wrap each portion in cling film and set aside but do not chill the dough.

Finely mince or process the pork and steak. Peel and grate the onion; peel and crush the garlic, then mix both with the meats. Add the breadcrumbs, tomato paste, mace, parsley and oregano. Season the meat mixture generously, add the brandy or sherry and pound the ingredients until evenly combined.

Roll out a portion of dough into a square which is slightly larger than 15 cm/6 in. Trim the edges of the dough neatly,

then cut it into 5 cm/2 in strips and cut these across to make 5 cm/2 in squares. Beat the egg and brush a little over each of the squares. Place a small mound of the meat mixture in the middle of each square. Take one square and fold the dough over the filling to make a tiny triangular pasty. Pinch the edges together to seal in the meat. Then wrap the long side of the pasty around the end of your little finger and pinch the overlapping corners together to make the characteristic tortellini shape. Seal all the other squares in the same way. Place the filled pasta on a floured plate, cover loosely with cling film and chill. Roll out and fill the remaining portions of dough in the same way.

Cook the tortellini in batches in plenty of boiling salted water for 12–15 minutes. Test one piece of pasta to check that the meat filling is cooked through. Drain well and transfer to a warmed serving dish. Cover and keep hot. Serve with the hot tomato sauce.

Note Filled, uncooked tortellini freeze very well. Cover a baking tray with cling film and spread the filled pasta out in a single layer. Cover the tortellini loosely with cling film and freeze them for several hours, or overnight, until they are hard. Then pack them in an airtight bag. The tortellini will not freeze in a solid block, so the required number can be removed and cooked from frozen. Allow a few minutes' extra boiling to ensure that the meat filling is cooked through.

PUDDINGS & DESSERTS

Tutti-frutti Pudding with Orange Foam Sauce

A steamed pudding is an ideal warming winter sweet, especially when it is composed of a light-textured sponge and colourful dried fruits. This pudding is also served with a light, orange-flavoured sauce.

SERVES: 6
PREPARATION: 40 minutes
COOKING: 2 hours

50 g/2 oz no-need-to-
    presoak prunes
50 g/2 oz apricots
50 g/2 oz glacé cherries
25 g/1 oz angelica
100 g/4 oz unsalted butter
100 g/4 oz caster sugar
grated rind and juice of 1 orange
2 eggs
75 g/3 oz self-raising flour
50 g/2 oz fresh white breadcrumbs
30 ml/2 tablespoons golden syrup
6 drained canned apricot halves
Orange Foam Sauce
25 g/1 oz unsalted butter
grated rind and juice of 1 orange
10 ml/2 teaspoons plain flour
50 g/2 oz caster sugar
1 egg
lemon juice

Stone and finely chop the dried prunes. Chop the dried apricots, glacé cherries and the angelica. Thoroughly grease a 900 ml/ 1½ pt pudding basin.

Cream the butter and sugar until light and fluffy, then add the grated orange rind. Beat the eggs lightly and gradually stir them into the mixture. Combine the sifted flour and the bread-crumbs and lightly fold them into the mixture. Add the orange juice and fold in the fruit.

Coat the bottom of the pudding basin with golden syrup and arrange the apricot halves in a circle over the syrup. Spoon over the pudding mixture and cover the bowl with buttered foil or a double layer of greaseproof paper. Tie securely with string. Place the pudding basin in a steamer or in a pan with boiling water reaching two-thirds up the basin. Steam for 1¾–2 hours or until the pudding is risen and set.

Tutti-frutti Pudding with Orange Foam Sauce.

While the pudding is steaming, prepare the orange-flavoured sauce: cream the butter with the grated orange rind and gradually beat in the flour and the sugar. Separate the egg and beat the yolk into the butter and flour mixture. Measure the orange juice, make it up to 150 ml/¼ pt with water and add it to the sauce, mixing well. Do not worry if the mixture curdles at this stage; it will become smooth again as it cooks.

Cook the sauce in a small heavy-based saucepan over low heat, stirring constantly until it thickens. Add a little extra water if necessary to keep the sauce to a pouring consistency. Remove the pan from the heat and cover with a lid to keep warm.

Just before serving, fold the stiffly whisked egg white into the sauce and sharpen with a little lemon juice.

Unmould the pudding on to a hot serving dish, and serve the orange foam sauce separately.

Lemon Meringue Pie

SERVES: 4–6
PREPARATION: 40 minutes
OVEN: 200°C/400°F/gas 6
        150°C/300°F/gas 2
COOKING: 1–1¼ hours

175g/6 oz Shortcrust Pastry
    (page 365)
40 g/1½ oz cornflour
20 ml/4 teaspoons plain flour
225 g/8 oz caster sugar
300 ml/½ pt water
grated rind and juice of 2 lemons
2 eggs

Roll out the pastry on a lightly floured surface and line a deep 20 cm/8 in or a shallower 23 cm/ 9 in loose-bottomed flan tin. Bake blind (page 367) in a preheated oven at 200°C/400°F/gas 6 for 15 minutes, then remove the lining paper and beans, return the flan case to the oven and bake for a further 5 minutes. Remove from the oven and lower the temperature to 150°C/300°F/gas 2.

Prepare the filling. Mix the cornflour, flour and 100 g/4 oz of the sugar in a saucepan. Stir in a third of the water, beat until smooth, then add the remaining water. Bring to the boil, then reduce the heat and cook for 2 minutes, stirring. The mixture will be thick. Remove from the heat and add the lemon rind and strained juice, mixing well.

Separate the eggs. Beat the yolks into the lemon mixture, then pour the filling into the flan case, spreading it evenly. Whisk the egg whites until stiff peaks

form, then add the remaining caster sugar, 5 ml/1 teaspoon at a time, whisking after each addition. Pile the stiff meringue mixture over the lemon filling and spread it evenly to the edges, making sure that it seals in all the filling. Bake for 30–40 minutes or until the meringue is crisp and lightly coloured. Serve hot or cold, with cream.

Linzertorte

This classic Austrian torte, which is named after the town of Linz, is popular both as a dessert and as an accompaniment to morning or afternoon coffee. It is tradi-tionally served with another dish – *Schlagsahne*. This consists of 150 ml/¼ pt of sweetened whip-ped cream into which stiffly whisked egg white is folded just before serving.

SERVES: 6
PREPARATION: 30 minutes
CHILLING: 1½ hours
OVEN: 180°C/350°F/gas 4
COOKING: 50–60 minutes

175 g/6 oz plain flour
2.5 ml/½ teaspoon ground
    cinnamon
75 g/3 oz caster sugar
75 g/3 oz ground almonds
    or hazelnuts
grated rind of ½ lemon
100 g/4 oz unsalted butter
2 egg yolks
1.25 ml/¼ teaspoon natural
    vanilla essence
350 g/12 oz raspberry jam
Glaze
1 egg yolk
15 ml/1 tablespoon milk

Sift the flour and cinnamon into a mixing bowl. Stir in the sugar, ground almonds or hazelnuts and grated lemon rind. Rub in the butter until the mixture resembles breadcrumbs.

Beat the egg yolks with the vanilla essence and stir into the flour and almond mixture to bind it into a soft dough. Wrap in cling film and chill for 1 hour.

Grease a 20 cm/8 in loose-bottomed flan tin. Knead the dough lightly to soften it slightly. Use two-thirds of the dough to line the tin, rolling it out on a lightly floured surface, then pressing it into the tin and up the sides. The dough is too short to be rolled out large enough to cover the base and line the sides of the tin. Trim off the excess dough neatly with a knife. Spread the jam evenly over the base of the flan.

Knead the trimmings with the reserved dough and roll it out on a well-floured surface to a rectangle measuring 20 × 7.5 cm/ 8 × 3 in. Cut this into six strips, each cm/½ in wide. Lay the strips across the filling in a lattice pattern. Press the ends of the strips on to the pastry lining and fold the edges down, if necessary, to neaten any excess height of pastry and make an even border.

For the glaze, beat the egg yolk and milk together and brush it over the lattice. Chill the flan for 30 minutes, then bake it in a preheated oven at 180°C/350°F/ gas 4 for 50–60 minutes until crisp and golden.

Leave the Linzertorte to cool and shrink slightly, then loosen the edge with a knife. Place the tin on a jar and gently push down the rim of the tin. Slide the torte on to a serving plate.
■ Serve the Linzertorte warm or cold with whipped cream, soured cream, fromage frais or thick Greek yogurt.

Orange Caramel Custards

Caramel custard is a favourite international dessert, especially after a rich or spicy main course. In this Spanish recipe, the caramel custard is given additional flavour by the use of fresh or frozen orange juice.

SERVES: 4
PREPARATION: 30–35 minutes
OVEN: 180°C/350°F/gas 4
COOKING: about 40 minutes
CHILLING: 12 hours

grated rind of 1 orange
300 ml/½ pt fresh orange juice
3 eggs plus 3 egg yolks
30 ml/2 tablespoons caster sugar
Caramel
100 g/4 oz caster sugar
45 ml/3 tablespoons water

Mix the orange rind and juice. Warm but do not grease four heatproof ramekins, which have about 150ml/¼ pt capacity, and make the caramel. Put the sugar and water in a small, heavy-based pan over low heat; stir gently until the syrup is clear. Turn up the heat and boil briskly, without stirring, until the syrup turns a deep golden caramel colour. Pour a little caramel into each dish. Twist the moulds quickly until they are coated with the caramel (use thick oven gloves to handle the moulds as they will be very hot).

Heat the orange juice and rind in a pan over low heat. Beat the whole eggs, egg yolks and sugar until the mixture is creamy. When the orange juice is on the point of boiling, strain it into the eggs, stirring briskly. Pour the mixture into the prepared ramekins and set them in a roasting tin. Pour in hot water to come about 2.5 cm/1 in up the outside of the ramekins.

Cover the ramekins with buttered greaseproof paper or foil and bake in a preheated oven at 180°C/350°F/gas 4 for about 30 minutes or until completely set.

Remove the ramekins from the oven, leave them to cool and then chill overnight. Just before serving, unmould the caramel custards on to individual plates.
■ Serve the caramel custards with single cream.

Chestnut Meringue

SERVES: 6
PREPARATION: 35 minutes
OVEN: 140°C/275°F/gas 1
COOKING: 1 hour

2 egg whites
100 g/4 oz caster sugar
Filling
50 g/2 oz unsalted butter
25 g/1 oz caster sugar
225 g/8 oz sweetened
 chestnut purée
15–30 ml/1–2 tablespoons
 dry sherry
lemon juice
300 ml/½ pt whipping cream
25 g/1 oz pistachio nuts to garnish

Line a large baking tray with non-stick baking parchment and draw two 18 cm/7 in pencil circles on it.

Whisk the egg whites until they are stiff and dry, add 20 ml/ 4 teaspoons of the sugar and whisk again until stiff. Lightly fold in the remaining sugar. Put this meringue mixture into a piping bag fitted with a large rose nozzle. Pipe a ring of meringue inside one of the marked circles, and spread the other circle completely with meringue, about 5 mm/¼ in thick. Pipe the remaining meringue into eight small rosettes.

Bake the meringue in a preheated oven at 140°C/275°F/ gas 1 for about 1 hour or until the meringues are crisp and dry. Leave on a wire rack to cool.

For the filling, cream together the butter and sugar; stir the chestnut purée until smooth and beat it into the creamed butter and sugar, adding it gradually or it will curdle. Flavour to taste with sherry and lemon juice.

To assemble the sweet, place the meringue base on a flat serving dish. Whip the cream. Fit a piping bag with a plain nozzle and pipe a little of the whipped cream around the edge of the meringue base; set the ring on top. Fill the centre of the case with the chestnut mixture, piling it up into a mound. Pipe a little of the whipped cream on the base of each meringue rosette and arrange them on top of the meringue ring. Pipe the rest of the cream over the chestnut mound to resemble snow and scatter the blanched, chopped pistachio nuts over the purée.

Chestnut Meringue.

277

High Teas

*H*igh tea is a substantial meal that combines delicious sweet foods, such as tea breads, with tempting savouries, such as cheese on toast. It is a direct survival of the 17th-century eating habit of having dinner at 5 p.m.; later in the evening a small supper, known as 'rear supper' was served. This established eating pattern suited equally the hardworking labourer who, hungry after a long day's work, wanted his meal as soon as he came home, and the 'gentleman about town' who, after his early dinner, would play cards or frequent taverns or theatres.

Weekend Teas

High tea has survived mainly as a weekend meal, particularly for a Saturday evening when the family comes together after a busy day playing, shopping, gardening or enjoying other pastimes and tasks. High tea provides the opportunity for serving tempting savouries, such as cheese on toast, toasted crumpets, cold meats and pickles or poached eggs on toast, followed by afternoon tea favourites, such as scones, cakes, buns or teabreads. This is a meal to satisfy all tastes – the only tradition is that it should consist of at least one savoury dish followed by baked items rather than a dessert. Tea is the essential beverage.

Suitable Savouries

Traditionally, high tea had close ties with breakfast in terms of the choice of dishes. Bacon and eggs, kippers and grilled kidneys were as likely to be served for this tea-cum-supper meal as they were to be included in a country-house breakfast. There are many popular savouries to suit the menu. Here are a few suggestions.

- Canned salmon served with snipped chives, chopped hard-boiled egg and mayonnaise. Lemon wedges should be used for garnish so that their juice can be squeezed over the salmon. Serve with brown bread and butter.
- Grilled or poached kippers or smoked haddock, topped with poached eggs.
- Cauliflower cheese served with crusty bread.
- Poached eggs on toast. The eggs may also be served on grilled cheese on toast.
- Potato cakes or grated potato pancakes with grilled bacon.
- Toasted crumpets topped with tomatoes and cheese, grilled until golden. Serve with bacon rolls, if liked.
- Grilled tomatoes or mushrooms on toast.
- Toasted sandwiches make a quick and tasty savoury for high tea; cheese, ham, banana and ham or mozzarella cheese and salami are all good fillings.
- Quiche with salad.
- Cold meats with pickles. As well as, or instead of, the traditional boiled or baked ham and cold roast beef or pork, a selection of salamis and continental meats may be served.
- Pickled onions, pickled cabbage, pickled eggs, chutneys, relishes and mustards are all excellent with a selection of cold meats, cheese and bread.
- For a lighter savoury, offer potted prawns or shrimps, or pâté with toast or crusty rolls.

Ham and Haddie

This comes from the Moray Firth area of Scotland. It is an unusual combination of smoked ham and haddock.

SERVES: 4
PREPARATION: 40 minutes
COOKING: 15 minutes

225–350 g/8–12 oz
  smoked haddock
40 g/1½ oz butter
4 slices smoked ham
black pepper
45 ml/3 tablespoons single cream

Poach* the smoked haddock in water for 5 minutes. Remove all skin and bones, and cut the fish into four equal portions. In a frying pan which can be used under a hot grill, melt the butter until it is foaming, and lightly fry the ham. Put the haddock on top of the ham, and season with black pepper. Cover with a lid and cook gently for 5 minutes. Pour the cream over the haddock and brown the dish under a hot grill for about 2 minutes.

Anglesey Eggs

This is a happy combination of two favourite Welsh foods: leeks and cheese.

SERVES: 4
PREPARATION: 45 minutes
OVEN: 200°C/400°F/gas 6
COOKING: about 30 minutes

6 leeks
450 g/1 lb mashed potato
25 g/1 oz butter
salt and black pepper
8 hard-boiled eggs
75 g/3 oz Cheddar cheese
300 ml/½ pt hot thin coating White
  Sauce (page 352)

Trim and clean the leeks, chop them into 1 cm/½ in slices and cook in boiling salted water for 10 minutes. Drain thoroughly and add the leeks to the hot mashed potatoes, together with the butter and salt and freshly ground black pepper to taste. Beat the leek and potato mixture thoroughly until it is pale green and fluffy.

Slice the eggs and arrange them in the centre of a large shallow flameproof dish; spoon the potato mixture around them. Keep the dish hot. Grate the Cheddar cheese. Stir two thirds of it into the hot white sauce; set the rest aside for the topping.

Pour the cheese sauce over the eggs and sprinkle with the rest of the grated Cheddar cheese. Bake the dish in a preheated oven at 200°C/400°F/gas 6 for about 20 minutes or until the cheese is golden brown on top.

Dublin Coddle

This substantial cold-weather dish is ideal for serving at high tea or supper.

SERVES: 6
PREPARATION: 30 minutes
OVEN: 180°C/350°F/gas 4
COOKING: 2–2½ hours

450 g/1 lb gammon or bacon
450 g/1 lb pork chipolata sausages
3–4 large onions
900 g/2 lb potatoes
60 ml/4 tablespoons
  chopped parsley
salt and black pepper
250 ml/8 fl oz milk or water

Trim the rind from the gammon or bacon. Cut the gammon into 2.5 cm/1 in pieces or cut the bacon into wide strips. Cook the chipolata sausages under a hot grill until they are lightly browned all over. Chop up the onions and slice the potatoes.

Layer the gammon or bacon, sausages, onions and potatoes in a deep ovenproof dish, sprinkling each layer with a little parsley, a little salt and some pepper and reserving sufficient potato slices for the top layer. Pour the milk or water over and cover the dish with a lid or foil.

Bake the pork and potato caddle in a preheated oven at 180°C/350°F/gas 4 for 1½–2 hours. Remove the lid and dot the potatoes with the butter, then continue cooking, with the dish uncovered, until the vegetables are tender and golden brown on top, and most of the liquid has evaporated. The mixture should be juicy and moist.

■ Traditionally, fresh soda bread would be served with this Irish supper dish.

Mackerel with Gooseberry Sauce

SERVES: 4
PREPARATION: 40 minutes
OVEN: 190°C/375°F/gas 5
COOKING: 35–40 minutes

4 mackerel
75 g/3 oz fresh white breadcrumbs
15 ml/1 tablespoon chopped parsley
grated rind of 1 lemon
pinch of grated nutmeg
salt and black pepper
1 egg
15–25 g/½–1 oz butter
Gooseberry Sauce
225 g/8 oz gooseberries
90 ml/3 fl oz water
30 ml/2 tablespoons sugar
25 g/1 oz butter
15 ml/1 tablespoon chopped fennel

Clean and bone the mackerel, discarding their heads and tails. Rinse under cold water and pat dry on absorbent kitchen paper.

Mix the breadcrumbs, parsley, lemon rind, nutmeg, seasoning and egg, then divide this stuffing into four and place a portion in

Clockwise from top left: crumpet with cheese; ham, cheese and pickle; Drop Scones (page 403) and jam; and Barm Brack with butter.

each fish. Close the fish around the stuffing and secure them with wooden cocktail sticks. Place the stuffed mackerel in a lightly greased ovenproof dish and dot with a little butter. Bake at 190°C/375°F/gas 5 for 25–30 minutes, until the mackerel are cooked and lightly browned.

Meanwhile, cook the gooseberries with the water and sugar for about 10 minutes or until they are tender. Then stir in the butter and chopped fennel. Serve the sauce hot with the baked stuffed mackerel.

Potato Cakes

These cakes originated in Ireland, but they are a traditional treat for high tea in Scotland and parts of the North of England.

MAKES: about 8
PREPARATION: 30 minutes
OVEN: 230°C/450°F/gas 8
COOKING: 20–25 minutes

225 g/8 oz self-raising flour
5 ml/1 teaspoon baking powder
2.5 ml/½ teaspoon salt
75 g/3 oz butter or margarine
175 g/6 oz mashed potato
75 ml/2½ fl oz milk
caraway seeds (optional)

Dust a baking tray with flour. Mix the flour, baking powder and salt in a bowl. Rub in the butter or margarine, then make a well in the middle and add the mashed potatoes. Pour in the milk and stir it into the potatoes, gradually mixing in the flour, to make a soft dough.

Roll out the potato dough on a floured surface to about 1 cm/½ in thick and cut out 7.5 cm/3 in rounds, kneading the trimmings together and rolling or pressing them out again. Place the potato cakes on the floured baking tray and sprinkle with a few caraway seeds, if liked. Bake the potato cakes in a preheated oven at 230°C/450°F/gas 8 for 20–25 minutes. Cool on a wire rack, then serve warm, split and spread with butter.

Barm Brack

MAKES: 900 g/2 lb loaf
SOAKING: 12 hours
PREPARATION: 40 minutes
OVEN: 180°C/350°F/gas 4
COOKING: 1¼ hours

175 g/6 oz sultanas
175 g/6 oz raisins
175 g/6 oz light soft brown sugar
200 ml/7 fl oz cold tea
90 ml/3 fl oz whisky (or
*   Irish whiskey)*
275 g/10 oz self-raising flour
5 ml/1 teaspoon ground
*   mixed spice*
1 egg

Mix the sultanas, raisins and sugar in a bowl. Pour in the tea and whisky, stir well, then cover the bowl and leave the fruit to soak overnight.

Next day, grease a 900 g/2 lb loaf tin (about 23 × 13 × 6 cm/ 9 × 5 × 2¾ in). Mix the flour and spice in a bowl and make a well in the middle. Turn the fruit mixture into the flour, scraping all the juice from the bowl. Beat the egg and pour it into the fruit, then gradually stir the flour into the moist ingredients and mix until thoroughly combined. Turn the mixture into the tin and smooth the top.

Bake the loaf in a preheated oven at 180°C/350°F/gas 4 for about 1¼ hours, or until it is risen, well browned and firm to the touch. Leave the loaf in the tin for a few minutes, then turn it out on to a wire rack to cool.

■ Serve the barm brack sliced and buttered.

DECEMBER

Mulled Wine, Christmas Pudding, Orange Mince Pies.

December

A time for celebrating and sharing, December is probably the most sociable month of the entire year. Feasting and entertaining are all part of the festivities in the weeks leading up to Christmas, and although much of the cooking is time consuming, all of it is extremely enjoyable for you and your guests.

Fast refrigerated transport means that the majority of fresh produce is available all year round, even in the depths of winter. During December the larger supermarkets and specialist shops are stocked with a wonderful array of foods, including fruit and vegetables from all over the world. Nuts (including chestnuts) and fresh or preserved dates all play their part in preserving Christmas traditions, and delicatessens display whole or half Stilton cheeses alongside other familiar – and unfamiliar – cheese varieties.

Speciality preserves, confectionery and other luxury comestibles that tend to be confined to gourmet food shops during the rest of the year, now appear on supermarket shelves at competitive prices, so it can be worth stocking up on items that have a long shelf life.

Salmon and smoked salmon are often offered at exceptionally good prices at this time of year. Fishmongers will readily order freshwater fish, such as carp. As well as the seasonal poultry such as goose (easily obtained during December), butchers will usually be well stocked with whole hams, pickled tongues, venison and well-hung beef joints, such as standing rib roasts.

Vegetarians are not forgotten during the Christmas celebrations and this chapter includes suggestions for delicious vegetarian dishes so that they can take part in the festive feeding.

Menu suggestions *This selection of menus provides ideas for the whole of the festive season, and for a variety of occasions, from a fireside supper to a buffet party. Recipes that are not included in this chapter can be located by referring to the page references.*

Formal Dinner Party

Cream of Jerusalem
Artichoke Soup

~

Salmon Mousse (page 164)
Melba Toast (page 313)

~

Rollatine de Manzo al Forno
Anna Potatoes (page 347)
Cauliflower with Almonds
(page 71)
French Beans

~

Champagne Charlie
Fresh Fruit Salad
or
Paris-Brest

~

Cheese and Biscuits

Keep the portions modest in this menu or the guests will be too full to enjoy the whole meal. The choice of desserts depends on the number of guests.

Light Supper Party

Mushroom Pâté (page 142)
Crisp Hot Toast Triangles

~

Turbot with Sweetcorn
Creamed Potatoes
Steamed or Glazed Carrots
(page 110)

~

Apple-Rum Meringue

If the formal dinner party feast seems a bit too elaborate for the time of year, invite friends to share a simple supper. This light menu will make a change from the many 'Christmas dinners' enjoyed (or endured) with colleagues and acquaintances.

Roast turkey with all the trimmings (page 296).

Hot Buffet

Vegetable Crudités
Anchovy Mayonnaise
(page 356)
Soured Cream with Chives

~

Boeuf Bourguignonne
(page 106)
Buttered Pasta
Parsnips Molly Parkin
Green Salad

~

Paris-Brest
Caramelised Oranges Grand
Marnier (page 94)

~

Cheese and Biscuits

This is a practical menu for a weekend buffet lunch, when a substantial, warming meal goes down well as old friends catch up. Boeuf Bourguignonne makes an ideal centrepiece as the ingredients can be increased according to the number of guests, and the dish can be prepared and frozen in advance, ready for thawing overnight. The parsnip casserole is an interesting side dish, which doubles as a vegetarian main course. Select pasta shapes that are easy to eat with a fork: twists or rigatoni rather than spaghetti or noodles. Offer a selection of dips and nibbles instead of a formal first course and include several cheeses with grapes, so that guests can carry on nibbling after the main course has been cleared away. Greet guests with a warming bowl of mulled wine, with the option of alcohol-free drinks. Offer a choice of red or white wine with the buffet.

SOUPS

Cream of Jerusalem Artichoke Soup

Delicately flavoured Jerusalem artichokes, which are available in late autumn and early winter, make delicious soup.

SERVES: 8
PREPARATION: 30 minutes
COOKING: 35 minutes

675 g/1½ lb Jerusalem artichokes
juice of 1 lemon
1 onion
50 g/2 oz butter
900 ml/1½ pt chicken stock
300 ml/½ pt dry white wine
6 parsley stalks
salt and black pepper
300 ml/½ pt double cream
45 ml/3 tablespoons
    chopped parsley

Peel the Jerusalem artichokes, cut them into 1 cm/½ in chunks. Strain the lemon juice. Leave the artichokes in a bowl of cold water to which the lemon juice has been added. Peel and thinly slice the onion.

Drain the artichokes and dry them on absorbent kitchen paper. Melt the butter in a large pan and add the artichokes and onion. Cook for 5 minutes over low heat – do not allow them to colour. Pour over the stock and wine. Bring the soup to the boil and add the parsley stalks. Season with salt and freshly ground pepper. Cover the pan and reduce the heat.

Simmer the soup for about 20 minutes, or until the vegetables are soft. Remove the pan from the heat and cool slightly before liquidising or rubbing it through a sieve. Taste for seasoning, then reheat. Add the cream, and heat the soup for a few minutes without boiling. Serve at once, sprinkled with parsley. This soup is also good chilled.

Note Cream of Jerusalem artichoke soup freezes well but the cream should not be added until the soup has been thawed.

Eliza Acton's Apple Soup

In 1845, Eliza Acton published her *Modern Cookery*, the first important English cookery book. It included this recipe for a tart apple soup which can be made with mutton stock. Miss Acton gives Burgundy as the place of origin, but a similar soup was known in medieval Britain.

SERVES: 6
PREPARATION: 10 minutes
COOKING: 30 minutes

1.12 litres/2 pt Brown Stock
    (page 310)
350g /12 oz cooking apples
2.5 ml/½ teaspoon ground ginger
salt and black pepper
60 ml/4 tablespoons long-grain rice

Remove all the fat from the surface of the stock. Wash the apples and chop them roughly, without removing the peel or core. Bring the stock to the boil in a large pan, add the apples and cover. Lower the heat and simmer the soup until the apples are tender.

Pour the soup through a sieve, rubbing through as much of the fruit pulp as possible. Stir in the ginger and season with salt and ground pepper. Reheat the soup and remove any scum.

While the soup is cooking, cook the rice in plenty of boiling water. Drain thoroughly through a sieve and keep the rice warm.

Divide the rice between six serving bowls, pour in the soup and serve at once.

Scallop Chowder

SERVES: 4
PREPARATION: 40 minutes
COOKING: 25 minutes

100 g/4 oz lean streaky bacon or
    175 g/6 oz boned belly of pork
1 large onion
1 green pepper
1 large carrot
225 g/8 oz potatoes
1 stick celery
1 bay leaf
1 blade mace
600 ml/1 pt milk
300 ml/½ pt fish stock or water
12 large scallops
15 g/½ oz butter
15 ml/1 tablespoon plain flour
juice of 1 lemon
salt and black pepper
paprika

Remove the rind from the bacon or the skin from the belly of pork. Chop the flesh. Peel and finely dice the onion. Cut the stalk end off the pepper, discard all the seeds and pith; slice the flesh. Peel and slice the carrot; peel and dice the potatoes. Scrub the celery and slice it finely.

Cook the bacon or pork in a large heavy-based saucepan until the fat runs. Add the pepper, cook for 2 minutes, then add the carrot, potatoes and celery, with the bay leaf and mace. Cook gently, stirring occasionally, for 2 minutes more.

Add the milk and stock or water. Bring to the boil, stir, lower the heat and simmer for about 15 minutes or until the vegetables are cooked.

Meanwhile, prepare the scallops (page 319). Cut each roe into about four pieces; any smaller and they risk being lost in the chowder sauce.

Soften the butter and mix it to a paste with the flour. Add small pieces of this beurre manié to the cooked vegetable mixture, stirring constantly until it boils. Lower the heat and gently stir in the scallops. Cook for about 5 minutes until the scallops are tender and the sauce has thickened slightly. Stir in the lemon juice, with salt and pepper to taste. Dust with paprika and serve at once.

Scallop Chowder.

STARTERS, SAVOURIES & LIGHT DISHES

Roquefort and Walnut Mousse with Fresh Dates

SERVES: 4
PREPARATION: 45 minutes
CHILLING: 3 hours

225 g/8 oz fresh dates
30 ml/2 tablespoons olive oil
coarsely grated rind and juice
*   of ½ lemon*
1 spring onion, chopped
5 ml/1 teaspoon powdered gelatine
30 ml/2 tablespoons water
50 g/2 oz walnuts
175 g/6 oz Roquefort cheese
45 ml/3 tablespoons sherry
100 g/4 oz cream cheese or
*   medium-fat soft cheese*
150 ml/¼ pt whipping cream
salt and black pepper
1 egg white
4–8 small lettuce leaves

Slide the papery skins off the dates, slit them and discard their stones, then cut them crossways into slices and place in a bowl. Shake the olive oil and lemon juice together in a screw-topped jar. Sprinkle the lemon rind and spring onion over the dates, pour over the dressing and mix well. Cover and set aside.

Sprinkle the gelatine over the water in a heatproof bowl. Set aside for 15 minutes until it has sponged. Then stand the bowl over a pan of hot water and stir until the gelatine has dissolved.

Coarsely grind or finely chop the walnuts. Mash the Roquefort cheese with the sherry, then work in the cream cheese or soft cheese. Stir the walnuts and dissolved gelatine into the cheese mixture. Whip the cream until it stands in soft peaks, then fold it into the cheese mixture. Add seasoning to taste. Whisk the egg white until it is stiff, but not dry, and use a metal spoon to fold it into the mixture. Transfer the mousse to a serving dish, cover and chill for at least 3 hours, or overnight if preferred.

To serve, scoop out spoonfuls of the mousse and arrange them on four individual serving plates. Arrange one or two small lettuce leaves on each plate beside the mousse. Stir the date mixture and spoon it into the lettuce.

Pears with Tarragon Cream

SERVES: 4
PREPARATION: 10 minutes
CHILLING: 1 hour

4 dessert pears
150 ml/¼ pt double cream
15 ml/1 tablespoon
*   tarragon vinegar*
caster sugar
salt and black pepper

Chill the dessert pears in the refrigerator. Whip the double cream and the tarragon vinegar together until the mixture is thick, but not too stiff. Season the tarragon cream to taste with sugar, salt and freshly ground black pepper. Peel and halve the pears and scoop out the centre cores with a teaspoon.

Serve the pears, rounded side up, on individual small plates, with the tarragon cream spooned over them.

Croque-Monsieur

This hot, fried cheese and ham sandwich, which is a speciality of France, may be served either as a quick snack, an hors-d'oeuvre or as a savoury.

SERVES: 4
PREPARATION: 10 minutes
COOKING: 10 minutes

75 g/3 oz butter
8 square slices white bread
*   (8 mm/⅓ in thick)*
4 slices lean ham
100 gl4 oz grated Cheddar
*   cheese*
fat or oil for frying

Butter the bread and cover four of the slices with the ham and cheese. Top with the remaining bread, and press the sandwiches firmly together.

Trim off the crusts, and cut each sandwich into three even-sized fingers. Fry the bread fingers in hot fat until they are golden brown on both sides. Drain the bread on absorbent kitchen paper before serving.

Quail Eggs in Pâté

SERVES: 6
PREPARATION: 45 minutes
CHILLING: 2 hours

295 g/10½ oz can beef consommé
10 ml/2 teaspoons powdered
*   gelatine*
6 quail eggs
175 g/6 oz pâté de foie gras or
*   smooth pâté*
24 stoned black olives
parsley sprigs to garnish

Pour the beef consommé into a heatproof bowl and sprinkle the powdered gelatine over. Leave to stand for 15 minutes. Set the bowl over a pan of simmering water and stir until the gelatine has dissolved in the consommé completely. Remove from the heat and leave to cool.

Quail Eggs in Pâté

Add the quail eggs to a pan of boiling water and boil them gently for 4 minutes. Lift out the eggs and plunge them into cold water. Remove the shells and put the eggs in a bowl of cold water.

Brush six shallow ramekin dishes with oil. Divide the pâté into six equal portions and spread it over the base and up the sides of the ramekins. Nest an egg in each portion of pâté and surround it with four olives. Spoon the jellied consommé over the boiled eggs and olives and leave to set in the refrigerator for about 2 hours. Remove the ramekins about 30 minutes before serving and decorate with sprigs of parsley.

■ Serve the quail eggs with hot French bread and butter.

Red Flannel Hash

An American favourite, this colourful hash is often served with poached or fried eggs.

SERVES: 4
PREPARATION: 15 minutes
COOKING: 15–20 minutes

50 g/2 oz lean streaky bacon
1 onion
225 g/8 oz corned beef
25 g/1 oz dripping or lard
350 g/12 oz mashed potatoes
100–175 g/4–6 oz cooked beetroot
30 ml/2 tablespoons finely
*   chopped parsley*
30 ml/2 tablespoons double cream
salt and black pepper

Finely chop the bacon and onion. Flake the corned beef. Heat the lard and fry the bacon and onion for 2 minutes or until the onion is transparent. Lift the bacon and onion out of the pan, place them in a mixing bowl and stir in the potatoes, diced beetroot, corned beef, parsley and cream. Season with salt and ground pepper.

Reheat the fat in the pan, add the hash mixture and press it down firmly and evenly with the back of a spoon. Cook over high heat for 15 minutes or until it is well browned on the bottom. Turn the hash out, upside-down, on to a warmed serving dish.

FISH, SHELLFISH & SEAFOOD

Turbot with Sweetcorn

SERVES: 6
PREPARATION: 15 minutes
OVEN: 180°C/350°F/gas 4
COOKING: about 30 minutes

50 g/2 oz butter
6 turbot steaks or fillets
*   (100–175 g/4–6 oz each)*
10 ml/2 teaspoons lemon juice
black pepper
400 g/14 oz can sweetcorn
300 ml/½ pt Béarnaise Sauce
*   (page 355)*

Lightly butter two large sheets of foil. Place the turbot on one sheet. Sprinkle with lemon juice, grind over a little pepper and dot the fish with knobs of butter. Cover with the second piece of foil and seal tightly to form a loose parcel. Bake the turbot for 25 minutes in a preheated oven at 180°C/350°F/gas 4.

Heat the corn over moderate heat, then drain and season with pepper. Spread over the base of a shallow serving dish. Arrange the turbot on the sweetcorn, pour over the juices from the foil parcel, and coat each steak with Béarnaise sauce.

■ Serve with lightly cooked broccoli spears or French beans.

Turbot with Sweetcorn.

Lobster Newburg

SERVES: 4
PREPARATION: 15 minutes
OVEN: 150°C/300°F/gas 2
COOKING: 30 minutes

2 large cooked lobsters
6 large slices white bread
175 g/6 oz butter
salt and black pepper
150 ml/¼ pt sherry or Madeira
15 ml/1 tablespoon brandy
*   (optional)*
3 egg yolks
300 ml/½ pt double cream
pinch paprika

Carefully extract the meat from the tails and claws of the lobsters and cut it into 3.5–5 m/1½–2 in pieces. Cut six circles from the bread. Melt 100 g/4 oz of the butter, add the bread circles and leave to soak until the butter has been absorbed. Bake the butter-soaked bread on a baking tray in a preheated oven at 150°C/300°F/gas 2 for 25 minutes.

Melt the remaining butter in a heavy-based pan, add the lobster meat and season with salt and pepper. Heat through over very low heat for 5 minutes, then pour over the sherry or Madeira and brandy, if used. Continue cooking over very low heat for about 10 minutes until the wine has reduced by half. While the lobster is cooking, beat the egg yolks and stir in the cream.

Remove the pan from the heat and pour the egg and cream mixture over the lobster. Shake the pan until the cream has mixed thoroughly with the wine, then move it gently to and fro over gentle heat until the sauce has the consistency of thick cream. Do not stir, or the meat will disintegrate and the sauce curdle. After about 3 minutes the lobster should be ready. Adjust seasoning and spoon the lobster and sauce on to the bread rounds. Sprinkle the lobster with a little paprika and serve at once.

Crab with Mushrooms

SERVES: 4–6
PREPARATION: 10 minutes
COOKING: 1 hour

225 g/8 oz mushrooms
2 cloves garlic
juice of 1½ lemons
Tabasco sauce
90 ml/6 tablespoons olive oil
1.25 ml/¼ teaspoon caster sugar
salt and black pepper
225 g/8 oz crabmeat
150 ml/¼ pt fromage frais
Garnish
75 g/3 oz stoned black olives
chopped fresh parsley

Trim the mushrooms and finely slice them into a deep bowl. Crush the garlic and add to the mushrooms. Strain in the lemon juice and add a few drops of Tabasco and the olive oil. Season to taste with sugar, salt and freshly ground pepper. Mix all the ingredients thoroughly, spoon them into a shallow serving dish; chill for 1 hour.

Just before serving, stir the flaked crabmeat and the fromage frais into the mushrooms. Garnish with olives and parsley.

285

POULTRY & GAME

Chicken and Cider Pudding

There are two ways of cooking this warming winter pudding; the traditional method is steaming, but there is also a baked version.

SERVES: 4
PREPARATION: 40 minutes
OVEN: 200°C/400°F/gas 6
COOKING: 1¼–1¾ hours

2 skinned boneless chicken
breasts (total weight
about 275 g/10 oz)
1 carrot
1 shallot
1 bay leaf
1 sprig parsley
salt and black pepper
300 ml/½ pt dry cider
1 small leek
25 g/1 oz butter or margarine
45 ml/3 tablespoons plain flour
100 g/4 oz smoked sausage
½ eating apple
1.25 ml/¼ teaspoon dried sage
Suet Pastry
225 g/8 oz self-raising flour
100 g/4 oz shredded suet
150 ml/¼ pt water

Cut the chicken breasts into 2.5 cm/1 in cubes and place in a saucepan. Peel and slice the carrot and shallot, add to the pan with the bay leaf, parsley, salt, pepper and cider. Bring to the boil, then simmer over low heat for 10 minutes or until the chicken is cooked. Strain, reserving the stock in a measuring jug. You

should have 300 ml/½ pt; make up with water if necessary. Set the chicken aside with the carrot and shallot, but discard the bay leaf and parsley.

Trim the leek, slice thinly into a colander and wash thoroughly. Drain well. Melt the butter or margarine in a saucepan and cook the leek for 5 minutes until soft. Stir in the flour and cook for 1 minute, then gradually stir in the reserved stock. Bring to the boil and cook for 3 minutes, stirring all the time, then remove the pan from the heat. Slice the sausage into the pan. Core the apple, chop the flesh and add to the sauce with the reserved cooked chicken, carrot and shallot. Stir in the sage, taste and add extra seasoning if necessary.

Lightly grease a 1.12 litre/2 pt ovenproof basin. Sift the flour into a bowl. Add the suet with a little salt and freshly ground black pepper. Mix in the water with a palette knife and bring the mixture together with one hand. Knead on a lightly floured surface. Cut off one third for the lid of the pudding and roll the remainder out to a circle 7.5 cm/3 in larger than the top of the basin.

Line the basin carefully with the suet pastry, making sure that it comes to the top. Spoon in the filling, pressing it down. Roll out the remaining pastry to a round large enough to fit

the top of the basin. Dampen the edges and cover with the lid.

Either bake the pudding, uncovered, on a baking sheet in a preheated oven at 200°C/400°F/gas 6 for 50 minutes, or cover the basin with greased greaseproof paper and foil (pleated in the centre to allow the pudding to rise, and twisted around the rim) and place on a trivet in a saucepan. Pour in boiling water to come half-way up the basin and steam the pudding for 1¼ hours, topping up the water as required. Serve hot, with carrots and broccoli.

Duck with Cherries.

Duck with Cherries

SERVES: 4
PREPARATION: 20 minutes
COOKING: 1¼–1½ hours

4 duck quarters
salt and black pepper
25 g/1 oz butter
120 ml/4 fl oz Madeira or
sweet sherry
284 g/10½ oz can morello or
black cherries
150 ml/¼ pt port
15 ml/1 tablespoon cornflour
lemon juice (optional)
45 ml/3 tablespoons chopped
parsley (optional)
sage or other herb sprigs to garnish

Prick the skin on the duck quarters and season with salt and freshly ground pepper. Melt the butter in a large pan and fry the duck over medium heat for about 20 minutes or until brown all over. Drain the fat from the pan

and pour the Madeira and the juice from the tin of cherries over the duck. Bring the contents of the pan to simmering point, cover tightly with a lid and continue simmering the duck for 45–55 minutes.

Lift the duck portions from the pan, drain on crumpled absorbent kitchen paper, transfer to a serving dish and keep hot.

Skim as much fat as possible from the pan juices and stir in the port. Mix the cornflour with 30 ml/2 tablespoons of cold water, and stir into the pan juices. Taste for seasoning and add a little lemon juice if liked. Bring to the boil, stirring. Add the cherries and heat through.

Pour the cherry sauce over the duck portions, sprinkle with the parsley, if used, and serve garnished with fresh herb sprigs.
■ French beans or Jerusalem Artichokes in Butter (page 342) are both suitable side dishes.

Teal à la Normande

SERVES: 4
PREPARATION: 20 minutes
OVEN: 160°C/325°F/gas 3
COOKING: 50 minutes

4 teal
75 g/3 oz butter
4 russet apples
juice of 1 lemon
300 ml/½ pt single cream
30 ml/2 tablespoons brandy
1.25 ml/¼ teaspoon crushed
*   coriander seeds*
salt and black pepper
Garnish
apple peel
watercress

Wipe the teal inside and out with absorbent kitchen paper. Melt the butter in a large, heavy-based pan. Fry the teal, covered, over low heat for about 10 minutes, turning occasionally, until they are browned all over. Transfer the birds to a dish and keep them hot.

Core, but do not peel the apples, chop them coarsely and fry in the pan juices, with the lemon juice, for about 5 minutes, until they colour slightly. Put the apples in the bottom of a casserole dish just large enough to take the teal. Place the teal on top of the apples and pour over the cream and brandy. Sprinkle the crushed coriander seeds over the birds, together with a little salt and freshly ground pepper. Cover the casserole with a lid and cook in a preheated oven at 160°C/325°F/

gas 3 for 35 minutes. Baste the birds three times during cooking.

Remove the casserole from the oven, lift out the teal and spread the apple mixture over the base of a warm serving dish. Set the teal on the apples and garnish each bird with a freshly cut spiral of apple peel; garnish with sprigs of watercress.
■ Fried Rice and Leeks (page 73), or braised red cabbage would go well with this casserole.

Jugged Hare

The term 'jugged' refers to the method of stewing or boiling meat in a closed earthenware jug or pot. This stew is thickened with the blood of the hare.

SERVES: 6
PREPARATION: 25 minutes
COOKING: 2½–3 hours

1 hare
1 large onion
2 carrots
2 sticks celery
50 g/2 oz streaky bacon
50 g/2 oz butter
salt and black pepper
bouquet garni*
grated rind of ½ lemon
900 ml–1.12 litres/
*   1½–2 pints stock*
25 g/1 oz plain flour
60 ml/4 tablespoons port

Order the hare already jointed and ask the butcher to include the blood with the order. Peel and roughly chop the onions and carrots, scrub and chop the celery, and remove the rind from the bacon. Chop the bacon and

fry it in a deep, heavy-based pan until the fat runs. Add half the butter and fry the hare joints until they are well browned, then add the prepared vegetables, salt and freshly ground pepper, the bouquet garni and finely grated lemon rind. Pour over enough stock to cover the meat and bring to the boil. Cover the pan tightly with a lid and cook over very low heat for 2½–3 hours, or until the meat is tender.

Mix the flour to a smooth paste with the remaining butter and gradually stir this beurre manié into the stew in small pieces. Only add a new piece when the piece before has melted into the sauce. Bring to the boil, stirring and cook for a further 2–3 minutes. Mix together the port and blood, remove the pan from the heat and carefully stir in the blood mixture. Do not reheat the stew but serve at once.
■ Pasta or boiled or mashed potatoes will go well with rich jugged hare.

MEAT

Beef Curry

A paste of onions, garlic and spices is used in this classic-style curry. Frying the spices is important for a rich, well-balanced result and to prevent their raw flavour from dominating the finished dish.

SERVES: 4–6
PREPARATION: 45 minutes
COOKING: 3–3½ hours

675 g/1½ lb stewing beef or
*   lamb fillet*
2 large onions
6 cloves garlic
5 cm/2 in piece of fresh root ginger
1–2 chillies
15 ml/1 tablespoon ground cumin
10 ml/2 teaspoons ground
*   coriander*
5 ml/1 teaspoon ground turmeric
1.25 ml/¼ teaspoon chilli powder
250 ml/8 fl oz water
60 ml/4 tablespoons oil
2 dried red chillies
15 ml/1 tablespoon cumin seeds
5 ml/1 teaspoon coriander seeds
5 ml/1 teaspoon ground fenugreek
225 g/8 oz can chopped tomatoes
5 ml/1 teaspoon salt

Trim the meat and cut it into 2.5 cm/1 in cubes. Peel the onions. Slice one onion thinly and set it aside. Quarter the second onion. Peel and roughly chop the garlic and ginger. Slit the chilli or chillies, remove the seeds and chop roughly. Combine the onion quarters, garlic,

cloves, ginger and chilli in a food processor or liquidiser. Add the ground cumin, ground coriander, turmeric and chilli powder; process to a smooth paste, adding a little of the measured water if necessary.

Heat 45 ml/3 tablespoons of the oil with the whole dried chillies in a flameproof casserole. Stir in the reserved onion slices. Cook for about 10 minutes until the onions are soft and have begun to turn brown. Using a perforated spoon, transfer them to a plate lined with absorbent kitchen paper. Set aside.

Remove and discard the chillies from the casserole. Add the remaining oil. When hot, fry the meat in batches, one third at a time. As the cubes brown, transfer them to a plate with a perforated spoon. Stir the cumin and coriander seeds into the pan with the fenugreek. Cook for 30 seconds, then stir in the onion and spice paste. Cook for 5 minutes, stirring. Add the tomatoes, the rest of the water and the salt, then return the meat cubes to the casserole. Bring to the boil, cover and simmer over low heat for 2–2½ hours or until the meat is tender and flavoursome.

Serve the curry sprinkled with the browned onions
■ Suitable accompaniments for the curry would be pilau rice, diced cucumber in plain yogurt, chopped tomatoes and chutney or lime pickle. Offer nan bread or parathas too.

287

Rollatine de Manzo al Forno

The name of this dish means 'beef rolls cooked in the oven'.

SERVES: 6
PREPARATION: 45 minutes
OVEN: 190°C/375°F/gas 5
COOKING: 1 hour

12 thin slices sirloin of beef (each
about 10 × 7.5 × 0.5 cm/
4 × 3 × ¼ in)
12 wafer-thin slices Parma ham
or cooked ham
3 cloves garlic
12 thin slices salami
4 hard-boiled eggs
150 g/5 oz raisins
50 g/2 oz grated Parmesan cheese
120 ml/8 tablespoons finely
chopped parsley
2.5 ml/½ teaspoon grated nutmeg
2.5 ml/½ teaspoon dried oregano
salt and black pepper
25 g/1 oz butter
300 ml/½ pt beef stock
300 ml/½ pt dry white wine
4 bay leaves
6 cloves
30 ml/2 tablespoons Marsala wine

Place each slice of beef between sheets of waxed or greaseproof paper and flatten with a rolling pin. Cover the beef slices with ham, trimmed to fit, and spread with peeled and crushed garlic.

Finely chop the skinned salami, the hard-boiled eggs and raisins, and put them in a bowl. Stir in the Parmesan cheese, parsley, nutmeg and oregano, and season with salt and freshly ground pepper.

Divide this mixture equally and spread it over the beef and ham slices. Fold over the long sides to keep the stuffing in place and roll the slices up. Tie the parcels with fine string.

Place the rolls in a buttered ovenproof dish. Pour over the stock and wine and cook for 30 minutes in a preheated oven at 190°C/375°F/gas 5. Add the bay leaves, cloves and Marsala, and cook for further 30 minutes.

■ Serve these Italian beef and ham rolls with Fettuccine in Butter (page 351) or Cauliflower with Almonds (page 71).

Rollatine de Manzo al Forno.

Filet de Boeuf en Croûte

SERVES: 8
PREPARATION: 1 hour
OVEN: 220°C/425°F/gas 7
CHILLING: 1 hour
COOKING: 1½ hours

1.8 kg/4 lb fillet of beef
½ clove garlic (optional)
25 g/1 oz butter
675 g/1½ lb Puff Pastry
(page 374) or thawed frozen
puff pastry
50 g/2 oz pâté de foie gras
2.5 ml/½ teaspoon dried thyme
1 egg
10 ml/2 teaspoons olive oil
Mushroom Sauce
225 g/8 oz mushrooms
300 ml/½ pt chicken stock
1 onion
25 g/1 oz butter
10 ml/2 teaspoons plain flour
150 ml/¼ pt milk
salt and black pepper
30 ml/2 tablespoons Madeira
(optional)
1 egg yolk
watercress to garnish

Trim any fat from the fillet, roll it into a neat shape, and tie it at intervals with fine string.

If using the garlic, cut it into slivers and insert them into the beef with the point of a sharp knife. Soften the butter and spread it over the top of the fillet. Cook the meat for 10 minutes in a roasting tin in a preheated oven, at 220°C/425°F/gas 7. Remove the beef from the oven and leave to cool. When the beef is quite cold, remove the string.

Roll out the puff pastry, 3mm/⅛ in thick, to an oblong 3½ times the width of the fillet, and its length plus 18 cm/7 in. Spread the pâté over the top of the fillet, then place the meat, pâté-side down, in the centre of the pastry. Sprinkle with the thyme. Fold the pastry over and under the meat, brushing the seams with water and sealing them thoroughly. Turn the pastry over so that the join is underneath; prick the top with a fork and decorate with leaves cut from the pastry trimmings. Cover the pastry with a clean cloth and leave it in the refrigerator for at least 1 hour.

To make the mushroom sauce, finely chop the mushrooms. Put in a saucepan with the chicken stock and bring to the boil. Reduce the heat and simmer for 30 minutes. Cool slightly, then purée the mushrooms with the stock in a liquidiser or food processor.

Chop the onion finely. Melt the butter in a pan and cook the onion for 5 minutes. Stir in the flour and cook for 3 minutes, stirring continuously. Gradually stir in the milk, and bring the

sauce to boiling point over low heat. Mix in the mushroom purée, season with salt and freshly ground pepper, and stir in the Madeira. Simmer for a further 10 minutes, then remove from the heat and allow to cool slightly. Stir in the beaten egg yolk just before serving.

Beat the egg with the oil and brush it over the pastry to glaze it during cooking. Set the pastry roll on a wet baking tray, and bake in the centre of a preheated oven at 220°C/425°F/gas 7 for 35 minutes. The pastry should then be golden brown, and the beef rosy-pink inside. Place the boeuf en croûte on a bed of watercress. Serve the sauce separately.

■ Serve with Broccoli Spears au Gratin (page 110).

Note If you prefer meat which is well cooked throughout, rather than pink in the middle, increase the initial cooking time slightly. The final cooking in pastry should not be too long as the crust will overcook.

Lamb à la Grecque

SERVES: 6
PREPARATION: 1½–2 hours
OVEN: 180°C/350°F/gas 4
COOKING: 1¾ hours

225 g/8 oz aubergines
salt and black pepper
60 ml/4 tablespoons olive oil
1.4 kg/3 lb boned shoulder of lamb
2 large onions
400 g/14 oz can chopped tomatoes
60 ml/4 tablespoons tomato paste
4 bay leaves
1.25 ml/¼ teaspoon crushed
    coriander seeds
1.25 ml/¼ teaspoon grated nutmeg
15 ml/1 tablespoon chopped parsley
juice of 1 lemon
432 g/15½ oz can apricot halves
    in syrup
75 g/3 oz butter
225 g/8 oz long-grain rice
600 ml/1 pt chicken stock
2.5 ml/½ teaspoon curry powder
Garnish
100 g/4 oz stoned black olives
orange peel

Remove the stalk ends and wipe the aubergines; cut them lengthways into 5 mm/¼ in thick slices. Layer the aubergine slices in a bowl with 2 teaspoons salt, to draw out the excess water. Cover with a clean cloth and leave for 45 minutes. Rinse the aubergines thoroughly, drain and pat dry on absorbent kitchen paper.

Heat the olive oil in a heavy-based pan and fry the aubergine slices for just 1 minute, then drain the slices on absorbent kitchen paper.

Trim any excess fat from the lamb, cut the meat into 2.5 cm/ 1 in cubes and fry over low heat in a dry pan, turning frequently, until the fat runs and the meat turns a light brown.

Peel and finely chop the onions, add them to the lamb and continue cooking until the onions are transparent. Add the chopped tomatoes with their juice, the tomato paste, bay leaves, coriander seeds, nutmeg, parsley, salt, freshly ground black pepper and lemon juice. Drain the apricots and set them aside. Top up the syrup from the can with water to make 300 ml/½ pt, pour the mixture over the lamb and bring to boiling point.

Line the base of a large buttered casserole with the aubergine slices and spoon over the lamb mixture. Cover the casserole tightly with foil and the lid. Cook for 1 hour in a preheated oven at 180°C/350°F/ gas 4. Remove the covering from the casserole, lay the apricots over the lamb and return the casserole to the oven while preparing the rice.

Place the rice in a pan, pour in the chicken stock and add a little salt. Bring to the boil, stir and cover with a close-fitting lid. Reduce the heat to the minimum setting and cook the rice for 15–20 minutes. Turn the heat off and remove the pan from the heat but do not remove the lid. Leave the rice to stand for a further 5 minutes.

Melt the remaining butter in a saucepan and stir in the curry powder. Cook for 2 minutes, then add the cooked rice and stir to mix. Spoon the rice in a ring on to a warm serving dish and fill the centre of the ring with the lamb and aubergines. Garnish the rice with the black olives, the apricots, and narrow strips of orange peel.

■ Serve with a lettuce and tomato salad tossed in an oil and orange juice dressing.

Crown Roast of Lamb

The crown is formed by joining two best ends of lamb, and the hollow between them is stuffed with a savoury filling. The cutlet bones are frequently decorated with cutlet frills, but glazed onions make an unusual, and edible, garnish for this meat dish.

SERVES: 6
PREPARATION: 45 minutes
OVEN: 190°C/375°F/gas 5
    180°C/350°F/gas 4
COOKING: 2 hours

2 best ends of lamb (6 cutlets each)
15 ml/1 tablespoon redcurrant jelly
    or cranberry sauce
Glazed Onions (page 252)
    to garnish
Stuffing
225 g/8 oz cranberries
150 ml/¼ pt chicken stock
25 g/1 oz caster sugar
1 onion
100 g/4 oz mushrooms
25 g/1 oz butter
1 clove garlic
225 g/8 oz minced pork
60 ml/4 tablespoons finely
    chopped parsley
7.5 ml/1½ teaspoons dried thyme
100 g/4 oz fresh white breadcrumbs
1 egg
salt and black pepper

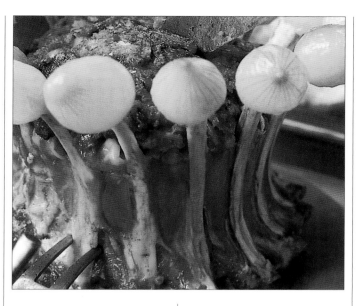

Ask the butcher to trim off any excess fat and to shape the best ends of lamb into a crown.

For the stuffing, put the cranberries, stock and sugar in a saucepan; if necessary, top up the stock with sufficient water to cover the fruit. Bring the cranberries to the boil and cook until they burst open, and the liquid has reduced to a thick sauce.

Peel and finely chop the onion, trim and coarsely chop the mushrooms. Melt the butter in a pan and fry the onion until it is soft but not coloured. Peel and crush the garlic, add it to the onion and cook for 1 minute. Add the mushrooms, turning them in the butter until they are lightly coloured.

In a mixing bowl, combine the cranberries and the onion and mushroom mixture with the minced pork. Mix in the chopped parsley, dried thyme and breadcrumbs. Beat the egg

Crown Roast of Lamb.

lightly and use to bind the stuffing. Season with salt and freshly ground pepper.

Spoon the cranberry stuffing into the hollow crown. Wrap some foil around the cutlet bones to protect them during roasting. Roast in a preheated oven at 190°C/375°F/gas 5, for 10 minutes. Reduce the heat to 180°C/ 350°F/gas 4 and carry on roasting. Allow 30 minutes to the pound, and baste frequently.

Remove the crown roast and keep it warm. Skim off as much fat as possible and boil the pan juices to make a gravy. Sweeten the gravy with the redcurrant jelly or cranberry sauce, and pour it into a warm sauceboat. Spike a glazed onion on the end of each cutlet bone.

■ Serve the roast with Garlic Potatoes (page 290) and Chicory and Orange Salad (page 292).

Pork Chops with Almonds and Sherry

When a special main course is required at short notice, this dish is the ideal solution.

SERVES: 4
PREPARATION: 10 minutes
COOKING: 20 minutes

4 pork chops
1 clove garlic
5 ml/1 tablespoon crushed dill seeds
15 ml/1 tablespoon olive oil
25 g/1 oz butter
100 g/4 oz flaked almonds
120 ml/4 fl oz dry sherry

Trim any excess fat off the chops, leaving 5 mm/¼ in around the edge. Peel and crush the garlic and rub this and the dill seeds into both sides of each chop.

Brush the chops all over with olive oil and put them under a hot grill, for 8 minutes each side or until cooked through. Brush the chops again with oil when they are turned.

Meanwhile, melt the butter in a small pan and cook the flaked almonds over a low heat until they are straw-coloured. Pour in the sherry, boil, then reduce the heat to simmering point and continue cooking the sauce for 5 minutes.

Arrange the pork chops on a serving dish, with the sherry sauce and flaked almonds poured over them.

■ Creamed potatoes and Brussels sprouts would be suitable vegetable side dishes.

Stuffed Hearts

With a little care and long slow cooking, the humble heart can make a succulent supper dish. In this recipe, the lean meat is complemented by a flavourful stuffing and the rich pan juices.

SERVES: 4
PREPARATION: 45 minutes
OVEN: 160°C/325°F/gas 3
COOKING: about 3 hours

4 lamb hearts
45 ml/3 tablespoons plain flour
salt and black pepper
40 g/1½ oz unsalted butter
450 ml/¾ pt lamb or beef stock
1 large onion
225 g/8 oz carrots
1 celery heart
Stuffing
1 onion
1 stick celery
50 g/2 oz minced pork
50 g/2 oz fresh white breadcrumbs
15 ml/1 tablespoon finely chopped
   fresh parsley
5 ml/1 teaspoon ground cumin
grated rind of 1 lemon
salt and black pepper
15 ml/1 tablespoon honey
25 g/1 oz butter

Prepare the stuffing first: peel and finely chop the onion, scrub and dice the celery. Mix these ingredients with the minced pork, breadcrumbs, parsley, cumin and lemon rind. Season to taste with salt and plenty of freshly ground black pepper. Stir in the honey. Melt the butter and use it to bind the stuffing.

Rinse the hearts thoroughly under cold running water to remove all traces of blood. Snip out the tubes with scissors and trim off any fat, then fill the hearts with the stuffing. Be careful not to stuff the hearts too tightly, as the filling will swell during cooking. Sew up the openings. Season the flour with salt and freshly ground pepper and use it to coat the hearts. Reserve any remaining flour.

Melt the butter in a heavy-based pan and fry the hearts over high heat, turning them until they are evenly browned. Lift the hearts into an ovenproof dish. Stir the reserved seasoned flour into the pan and cook for a few minutes, then gradually stir in the stock and bring to the boil. Add seasoning to taste and pour the sauce over the hearts.

Cover the casserole and cook in a preheated oven, at 160°C/325°F/gas 3 for 2 hours.

Meanwhile, peel and thinly slice the onion; peel or scrape the carrots and chop them and the washed celery heart. Add the vegetables to the casserole after 2 hours and continue cooking, at the same temperature, for another 45 minutes. Serve the stuffed hearts, vegetables and sauce straight from the casserole.

■ Fluffy boiled rice or buttered noodles would go well with this substantial dish.

VEGETABLES & SALADS

Garlic Potatoes

Mashed or creamed potatoes are given additional flavour by adding a garlic sauce.

SERVES: 6
PREPARATION: 20 minutes
OVEN: 200°C/400°F/gas 6
COOKING: 2 hours

1.4 kg/3 lb baking potatoes
5 cloves garlic
50 g/2 oz butter
25 g/1 oz plain flour
300 ml/½ pt milk
45 ml/3 tablespoons double cream
45 ml/3 tablespoons finely
   chopped parsley
salt and black pepper

Wash and dry the potatoes, prick them with a fork, and bake for 1½ hours or until they are tender in a preheated oven, at 200°C/400°F/gas 6.

Put the garlic in a small pan, cover with water; boil for 5 minutes, then drain and peel. Melt the butter in a saucepan and crush the garlic into it. Stir in the flour and cook over low heat for 2 minutes. Gradually stir in the milk and bring to the boil, stirring constantly. Simmer for 3 minutes, until the sauce is smooth and thick.

Scoop the flesh from the baked potatoes, press it through a sieve and stir in the double cream, sauce and parsley. Add seasoning to taste.

Heat the mashed garlic potato through gently on the hob if necessary, pile it back into the potato skins and serve at once.

Sweet Potatoes with Apples

Sweet potatoes are a staple vegetable in the southern United States. This recipe is a Creole dish which can be served on its own or with roast lamb.

SERVES: 6
PREPARATION: 20 minutes
OVEN: 200°C/400°F/gas 6
COOKING: 40 minutes

450 g/1 lb sweet potatoes
450 g/1 lb cooking apples
50 g/2 oz butter
5 ml/1 teaspoon salt
75 g/3 oz soft brown sugar
5 ml/1 teaspoon grated nutmeg
15 ml/1 tablespoon lemon juice

Peel and thinly slice the sweet potatoes; peel, core and thinly slice the apples. Butter a casserole, and in it arrange alternate layers of sweet potatoes and apples, starting and finishing with sweet potatoes. Sprinkle each layer with salt, sugar, nutmeg and lemon juice, and dot with the remaining butter.

Place the casserole in a preheated oven, at 200°C/400°F/gas 6. Cover and cook for about 40 minutes or until the potatoes are tender. Serve straight from the casserole

Parsnips Molly Parkin

SERVES: 6
PREPARATION: 40 minutes
OVEN: 160°C/325°F/gas 3
COOKING: 45 minutes

900 g/2 lb parsnips
450 g/1 lb tomatoes
75 ml/5 tablespoons oil
50 g/2 oz butter
45 ml/3 tablespoons soft brown
    sugar
salt and black pepper
300 ml/½ pt single cream
175 g/6 oz Gruyère cheese
60 ml/4 tablespoons fresh white
    breadcrumbs

Peel the parsnips, then cut away and discard any hard central cores. Slice the parsnips thinly. Skin the tomatoes (page 302), remove the seeds and cut the flesh into slices. Heat the oil in a pan and lightly fry the parsnips for 4 minutes.

Grease a 1.12 litre/2 pt casserole dish generously with butter, and place a layer of parsnips over the base. Sprinkle with a little sugar, salt, and freshly ground pepper. Add a little cream, before covering with a layer of tomatoes. Grate the cheese. Spread a little more cream over the tomatoes, sprinkle with some of the cheese and repeat these layers until all the ingredients are used up, finishing off with cream and cheese. Top with the breadcrumbs and dot with the remaining butter.

Cook the parsnip casserole for 40 minutes in a preheated oven at 160°C/325°F/gas 3. Serve straight from the casserole.

■ Serve this vegetable casserole as a lunch or supper dish, or to complement plain grilled meat.

Parsnips Molly Parkin.

Brussels Sprouts with Chestnut and Apples

SERVES: 6
PREPARATION: 45 minutes
OVEN: 180°C/350°F/gas 4
COOKING: 30–40 minutes

900 g/2 lb Brussels sprouts
salt and black pepper
1 small onion
juice of 1 lemon
2 sweet, dessert apples, such as
    Cox's Orange Pippins
25 g/1 oz butter
30 ml/2 tablespoons oil
45 ml/3 tablespoons
    redcurrant jelly
400 g/14 oz can whole chestnuts in
    brine or 225 g/8 oz peeled
    cooked chestnuts

Trim the sprouts, cut a cross in the base of each, then cook them in boiling salted water for 8–10 minutes or until just tender. Drain well.

Peel and finely chop the onion. Place the lemon juice in a bowl. Quarter, peel and core the apples, cut them into thick slices and add them to the bowl. Toss in the lemon juice.

Heat the butter and oil in a large, heavy-based pan. Add the onion and cook for 10 minutes. Drain the apple slices, reserving the lemon juice, and add them to the onion. Continue to cook until the apple slices are lightly browned in places. Stir in the reserved lemon juice, redcurrant jelly, sprouts and chestnuts and cook gently, stirring every now and then, for 5 minutes.

Cauliflower Charlotte

SERVES: 4
PREPARATION: 20 minutes
OVEN: 160°C/325°F/gas 3
COOKING: about 1¼ hours

1 large cauliflower
1 onion
50 g/2 oz butter
75 g/3 oz fresh white breadcrumbs
300 ml/½ pt milk
50 g/2 oz Gruyère cheese
salt and black pepper
pinch of grated nutmeg
5 eggs

Cut away the coarse outer leaves from the cauliflower and break into florets. Bring a large pan of lightly salted water to the boil. Add the florets, cover the pan with a lid, and simmer for 5 minutes until just tender, but still crisp. Drain.

Meanwhile, finely chop the onion. Melt 25 g/1 oz butter and fry the onion for 10 minutes. Butter the inside of a 2.3 litre/ 4 pt ovenproof dish and line it with 25 g/1 oz of breadcrumbs.

Bring the milk to the boil. Meanwhile, grate the Gruyère cheese and add it to the milk with the remaining butter, breadcrumbs and fried onion. Season to taste with salt, pepper and a little nutmeg. Remove from the heat. Beat the eggs, then stir them into the mixture. Stir in the cauliflower and spoon the mixture into the baking dish.

Bake in a preheated oven, at 160°C/325°F/gas 3 for about 1 hour until firm and browned.

Vegetable Charlotte with Brandied Mushroom Sauce

SERVES: 6–8
PREPARATION: 1 hour
SOAKING: 20 minutes
OVEN: 180°C/350°F/gas 4
COOKING: 2½–2¾ hours

1 aubergine
salt and black pepper
900 g/2 lb swede
about 60 ml/4 tablespoons olive oil
450 g/1 lb leeks
25 g/1 oz butter
2 cloves garlic
5 ml/1 teaspoon finely
    chopped rosemary
50 g/2 oz fresh white breadcrumbs
50 g/2 oz mature Cheddar cheese
3 eggs

Brandied Mushroom Sauce
12 dried morels
1 bay leaf
2 sprigs thyme
2 sprigs parsley
1 small onion
100 g/4 oz button mushrooms
40 g/1½ oz butter
40 g/1½ oz plain flour
300 ml/½ pt milk
45 ml/3 tablespoons brandy
30 ml/2 tablespoons finely
    chopped parsley

Trim the ends off the aubergine, then slice it thinly. Place the slices in a colander, sprinkling each layer with salt. Set the aubergines aside over a bowl for 15 minutes. Meanwhile peel and dice the swede, then cook it in boiling salted water until tender. This will take about 15 minutes if the dice are small and evenly

sized. Drain the swede, reserving 200ml/7 fl oz of the cooking water, and mash well. If a fine texture is preferred, rub the cooked swede through a sieve into a large bowl.

Rinse the aubergine slices and pat them dry on absorbent kitchen paper. Heat some of the olive oil in a large frying pan and cook one batch of aubergine slices quickly, turning once, until tender but not soft. Use a fish slice to transfer them to a plate. Fry the remaining aubergine slices, adding more olive oil as necessary. Set aside.

Slice and wash the leeks. Melt the butter in a large frying pan or saucepan. Add the leeks and cook, stirring often, until they are tender and all the liquid they yield has evaporated – this will take about 20 minutes. Mix the leeks with the swede. Peel the garlic, crush it into the swede mixture, then add the rosemary, breadcrumbs, cheese, seasoning to taste and the eggs. Mix well.

Grease a 20 cm/8 in round deep cake tin and line the base with non-stick baking parchment. Arrange aubergine slices in the base of the tin, starting with one neat round slice in the centre and overlapping the others around the edge. Press the slices down with the back of a metal spoon. Spoon a layer of swede mixture on top, spreading it carefully and evenly to keep the aubergine slices neatly in place. Repeat the layers until all the aubergine slices and swede mixture are used, ending with the swede mixture. Smooth the top neatly.

Bake the vegetable charlotte in a preheated oven at 180°C/350°F/gas 4 for about 1–1¼ hours, or until it is set and feels firm in the middle.

Make the sauce while the charlotte is baking. Rinse the morels in two changes of cold water, then place them in a small pan with the bay leaf, thyme and parsley sprigs. Pour in the cooking water from the swede. Heat gently until warm, remove from the heat and leave to soak for 20 minutes. Drain and set the morels aside. Strain the liquid through a muslin-lined sieve or coffee filter to remove any grit.

Peel and finely chop the onion; quickly rinse the button mushrooms. Melt the butter in a saucepan and cook the onion with the soaked herbs from the morels for about 15 minutes, until softened. Stir in the button mushrooms and cook for a further 15 minutes, or until the liquor from the mushrooms has evaporated. Stir in the flour, then pour in the strained morel liquid and the milk. Bring to the boil, stirring all the time, then lower the heat and simmer for 3 minutes, stirring occasionally. Discard the bay leaf and herb sprigs, stir in the brandy and morels and simmer gently for 3 minutes. Add seasoning to taste and stir in the chopped parsley.

To serve, slide a knife around between the charlotte and the tin, then invert it on to a flat serving dish. Spoon some of the sauce around the charlotte, if liked, or serve it all in a separate jug. Cut the charlotte into wedges to serve.

Winter Vegetable Stir Fry

Soya beans or chick peas are a useful source of protein and should be included if this dish is to be served as a main course; however, they are not essential for a lighter stir fry which is intended to be an accompaniment.

SERVES: 4
PREPARATION: 30 minutes
COOKING: about 40 minutes

450 g/1 lb swede
salt and black pepper
1 large onion
1 large leek
1 fennel bulb
350 g/12 oz white cabbage
30 ml/2 tablespoons olive oil
1 bay leaf
15 ml/1 tablespoon sesame seeds
2 × 400 g/14 oz cans soya beans or
    chick peas (optional)
10 ml/2 teaspoons cornflour
60 ml/4 tablespoons dry sherry
150 ml/¼ pt vegetable stock

Peel and dice the swede, then cook it in a saucepan of boiled salted water for 10 minutes. Drain and set aside. Peel the onion, cut it in half and slice it thinly. Trim, thinly slice and wash the leek, trim and thinly slice the fennel and shred the cabbage. Heat the oil in a wok, large frying pan or saucepan. Add the bay leaf, onion, leek and fennel. Stir fry these vegetables for 15 minutes, until quite well cooked. Then add the cabbage and swede and stir fry for a further 5 minutes. Stir in the sesame seeds and drained soya

beans or chick peas (if used) and leave to cook for 5 minutes.

Stir the cornflour to a smooth paste with the sherry and stock, then pour the liquid over the vegetables. Add seasoning and stir until the liquid boils. Lower the heat and simmer for 3 minutes. Check the seasoning before serving.

■ Serve the stir fried vegetables in baked potatoes, with rice or pasta, or in taco shells. Grated cheese may be sprinkled over the top of the vegetables.

Chicory and Orange Salad

A slightly sharp, refreshing salad which goes well with most kinds of game, cold meats or stuffed joints. Make the French dressing with orange juice instead of vinegar to complete this salad.

SERVES: 6
PREPARATION: 20 minutes

4 heads of chicory
3 oranges
French Dressing (page 356)

Remove any brown outer leaves and the root ends from the chicory. Wash and drain thoroughly, then cut the chicory into thin slices, crossways. Peel the oranges with a sharp knife, removing all the white pith with the peel. Slice the oranges thinly in cross-section and remove the pips. If the oranges are large, cut each slice in two.

Mix the chicory and orange slices in a serving bowl, and pour over the French dressing.

Waldorf Salad

This American salad was created at the Waldorf-Astoria Hotel in New York. The tart combination of apple and celery makes it an excellent counter-balance to rich meats such as duck, lamb and pork.

SERVES: 6
PREPARATION: 20 minutes
STANDING: 30 minutes

30 ml/2 tablespoons lemon juice
5 ml/1 teaspoon caster sugar
150 ml/¼ pt mayonnaise
450 g/1 lb tart red dessert apples
½ head celery
50 g/2 oz walnuts
1 lettuce

Make a dressing by combining the lemon juice, caster sugar and 15 ml/1 tablespoon of the mayonnaise in a bowl. Set one apple aside for the garnish. Core and dice the remainder, toss them in the dressing and let the mixture stand for 30 minutes.

Wash, core and thinly slice the remaining apple. Dip the slices in the dressing to prevent them from discolouring, then set them aside briefly while you assemble the salad.

Scrub and chop the celery and chop the walnuts. Add the celery and walnuts to the diced apple, with the rest of the mayonnaise, and mix well.

Trim, wash and shred the lettuce. Line a serving bowl with the prepared lettuce leaves, pile the apple, celery and walnut salad into the centre and garnish with the apple slices.

RICE & PASTA

Savoury Rice Cakes

A good way of using up leftover rice, these cakes taste delicious with Tomato Sauce (page 354) and a green salad.

SERVES: 4
PREPARATION: 25 minutes
OVEN: 200°C/400°F/gas 6
COOKING: 30–40 minutes

250 g/9 oz cooked rice or 100 g/
   4 oz easy-cook long-grain rice
3 large spring onions
100 g/4 oz button mushrooms
50 g/2 oz Cheddar cheese
60 ml/4 tablespoons oil
100 g/4 oz ricotta cheese
50 g/2 oz fresh white breadcrumbs
salt and black pepper
plain flour for coating

If you have no cooked rice to hand, bring a saucepan of salted water to the boil, stir in the rice and cook for 12–15 minutes. Drain but do not rinse as a sticky rice is ideal for this recipe.

Trim and slice the spring onions; chop the mushrooms. Grate the Cheddar cheese. Heat 30 ml/2 tablespoons of the oil in a saucepan. Add the chopped spring onions and mushrooms and cook gently, stirring, for 2–3 minutes or until the vegetables are beginning to soften. Remove the pan from the heat and mix in the Cheddar and ricotta, breadcrumbs, cooked rice, salt and freshly ground pepper.

Using your hands, mould the mixture into eight patties, flatten with a palette knife and coat lightly in flour. Place on a baking tray, brush with a little of the remaining oil; turn the patties over and brush with oil again.

Bake in a preheated oven at 200°C/400°F/gas 6 for 15–20 minutes until sizzling hot.

Spaghettini with Mussels

The fine strands of spaghetti, known as spaghettini, make a lighter-then-usual pasta dish. It is here served in an unusual sauce for a main course.

SERVES: 4–6
PREPARATION: 1 hour
COOKING: 15–20 minutes

2.3 litres/4 pt mussels
120 ml/4 fl oz olive oil
3 cloves garlic
450 g/1 lb spaghettini
salt and black pepper
150 ml/¼ pt fish stock
15 ml/1 tablespoon finely
   chopped parsley

Scrub the mussels under cold running water, scraping the shells to remove barnacles and dirt. Carefully pull out the brown or black beards that just protrude from the shells. Discard any open shells which do not shut when tapped and any with broken shells. Place the mussels in a bucket of cold water.

Heat 45 ml/3 tablespoons of the oil in a large pan. Peel and chop 2 cloves of garlic and fry in the oil for 30 seconds. Drain the mussels and put them in the pan. Put the pan over high heat, and cover with a lid. Shake the pan for 5 minutes, or until the shells have opened. Remove the pan from the heat and discard any mussels that remain closed. Strain the contents through a muslin-lined colander into a bowl and ease the mussels from the shells, retaining the liquid.

Cook the spaghettini in fast boiling salted water for 7–10 minutes, stirring every now and then, until it is just tender. Drain thoroughly in a colander.

Heat the remaining oil in the pan over low heat. Peel and crush the remaining garlic and fry until golden. Pour half the oil and garlic over the spaghettini in a warm serving bowl and toss until it gleams. Keep hot. Add the mussels and the strained liquid to the pan and heat through gently. Add the fish stock and continue cooking for 1–2 minutes until thoroughly heated. Add salt and pepper to taste, and stir in the parsley.

Spoon the mussels and liquid over the spaghettini, toss and serve at once, with slices of warm crusty bread.

Spaghettini with Mussels.

PUDDINGS & DESSERTS

Bread and Butter Pudding

Slightly dry buttered bread is the basis for this favourite traditional English pudding.

SERVES: 4
PREPARATION: 15 minutes
STANDING: 15 minutes
OVEN: 180°C/350°F/gas 4
COOKING: 45 minutes

8 slices buttered white bread
50 g/2 oz sultanas
grated rind of 1 lemon
2 eggs
45 ml/3 tablespoons caster sugar
2.5 ml/½ teaspoon natural vanilla essence
600 ml/1 pt milk

Remove the crusts and cut the bread into 2.5 cm/1 in squares. Place them in a lightly buttered baking dish, with alternate layers of sultanas mixed with grated lemon rind.

Beat the eggs lightly with 2 tablespoons of the sugar, the vanilla and the milk. Pour this custard mixture over the bread and leave to stand for at least 15 minutes. Sprinkle the rest of the sugar over the top, and bake the pudding in a preheated oven at 180°C/350°F/gas 4 for about 45 minutes or until it is set and golden brown.

Soured Cream Flan

This flan, with a texture reminiscent of cheesecake, makes a good weekday dessert and may be served hot or cold.

SERVES: 6
PREPARATION: 30 minutes
CHILLING: 30 minutes
OVEN: 200°C/400°F/gas 6
    220°C/425°F/gas 7
    180°C/350°F/gas 4
COOKING: 55 minutes

175 g/6 oz Shortcrust Pastry (page 365)
2 eggs
100 g/4 oz caster sugar
150 g/5 oz sultanas
2.5 ml/½ teaspoon cinnamon
1.25 ml/¼ teaspoon ground cloves
1,25 ml/¼ teaspoon salt
150 ml/¼ pt soured cream
grated rind of 1 lemon

Roll out the prepared shortcrust and use it to line a 23 cm/9 in flan tin. Prick the base with a fork and leave it to rest in the refrigerator for 30 minutes. Line the flan case with greaseproof paper and baking beans and bake it in a preheated oven, at 200°C/400°F/gas 6 for 15 minutes. Take the flan case out of the oven and increase the oven temperature to 220°C/425°F/gas 7.

Separate the eggs and beat the yolks with the caster sugar until the mixture is pale and thick. Finely chop the sultanas

and beat them into the eggs with the cinnamon, cloves, salt, soured cream and lemon rind.

Beat the egg whites in a separate bowl until stiff, but not dry. Fold the egg whites carefully and evenly into the yolk mixture, and spoon it into the flan case. Bake for 15 minutes in the preheated oven at 220°C/425°F/gas 7, then reduce the heat to 180°C/350°F/gas 4 for a further 25 minutes.

Leave the flan to stand for about 10 minutes before serving.

Orange Chiffon Cream

The taste of fresh oranges is predominant in this flan case filled with a fluffy mixture of eggs and cream. For a dinner party, cover the chilled flan with extra whipped cream.

SERVES: 6
PREPARATION: 45 minutes
OVEN: 200°C/400°F/gas 6
    190°C/375°F/gas 5
COOKING: 30 minutes
CHILLING: 1 hour

175 g/6 oz Shortcrust Pastry (page 365)
10 ml/2 teaspoons powdered gelatine
75 ml/5 tablespoons water
4 eggs
75 ml/5 tablespoons caster sugar
150 ml/¼ pt fresh orange juice
15 ml/1 tablespoon lemon juice
grated rind of 1 orange
150 ml/¼ pt double cream
Decoration
plain chocolate
orange matchsticks

Roll out the prepared shortcrust pastry 4mm/⅙ in thick, and use it to line a 20–23 cm/8–9 in wide flan ring. Prick the base with a fork and bake blind (page 367) for 10 minutes in a preheated oven at 200°C/400°F/gas 6. Reduce the heat to 190°C/375°F/gas 5 for a further 20 minutes. Cool on a wire rack.

Sprinkle the gelatine over the cold water in a small bowl. Do not stir. Leave to stand for 15 minutes until the gelatine has absorbed the water. Separate the eggs and beat the yolks with the sugar in a heatproof bowl, until they are pale and thick. Beat in the orange and lemon juice. Set the bowl over a pan of barely simmering water. Cook over low heat, stirring continuously, until the mixture thickens. Remove from the heat and mix in the orange rind and the dissolved gelatine. Blend thoroughly and leave to cool slightly.

Whip the cream and egg whites, in separate bowls, until stiff, and carefully fold first the cream, then the egg whites into the orange mixture.

Spoon the mixture into the flan case and smooth the top. Chill for at least 1 hour.

Just before serving, grate plain chocolate over the cream and decorate the flan with orange matchsticks.

Apple-Rum Meringue

Meringue is a favourite topping for many sweets. In this recipe, it covers tart cooking apples on a bed of rum-soaked ratafia biscuits. Macaroons or sponge fingers may be used instead of ratafias.

SERVES: 6
PREPARATION: 30 minutes
OVEN: 180°C/350°F/gas 4
COOKING: 30 minutes

100 g/4 oz ratafia biscuits
60 ml/4 tablespoons white rum
675 g/1½ lb cooking apples
25 g/1 oz unsalted butter
2.5 ml/½ teaspoon cinnamon
100 g/4 oz soft brown sugar
30–45 ml/2–3 tablespoons water
3 egg whites
1.25 ml/¼ teaspoon salt
75 g/3 oz granulated sugar
75 g/3 oz caster sugar

Cover the base of a china flan dish with the ratafias, and pour the rum over them. Peel, core and thinly slice the apples into a saucepan; add the butter, cinnamon, brown sugar and water. Simmer for 10–15 minutes or until the apples are just cooked. Leave to cool, then spoon them over the ratafias.

Beat the egg whites with the salt until stiff, but not dry. Stir in the granulated sugar and beat for about 2 minutes or until the meringue mixture is smooth and glossy. Fold in the caster sugar, and immediately spoon the meringue over the apples in the flan dish. Swirl the meringue into soft peaks with a spatula.

Bake the flan for about 15 minutes in a preheated oven at 180°C/350°F/gas 4 until the meringue is pale beige.

■ Serve the apple meringue hot or cold with a bowl of cream.

Meringue à la Reine

These small meringue boats (barquettes), with a cream filling, were first served at the French court in the 18th century.

SERVES: 6
PREPARATION: 15 minutes
OVEN: 140°C/275°F/gas 1
COOKING: 1½–2 hours

3 egg whites
salt
75 g/3 oz granulated sugar
75 g/3 oz caster sugar
25 g/1 oz lightly toasted
  flaked almonds
300 ml/½ pt double cream
45 ml/3 tablespoons sweet sherry
juice of 1 orange
crystallised fruit to decorate

In a warm dry bowl, whisk the egg whites, with a pinch of salt, until stiff but not dry. Add the granulated sugar and continue whisking for 2 minutes until the meringue mixture is smooth and glossy. Gently fold in the caster sugar and almonds.

Spoon the meringue into a piping bag, fitted with a 1 cm/ ½ in wide rosette nozzle. Pipe out 7.5 cm/3 in long oval shapes (the barquettes) on to a lightly floured baking tray. Bake the meringues in a preheated oven at 140°C/275°F/gas 1 for 1½–2

hours. The meringues should then have a faint tint of beige. Leave the barquettes on a wire rack to cool.

Whip the cream and beat in the sherry and strained orange juice. Fill the hollows in the barquettes with the whipped cream mixture and decorate with crystallised fruit.

Champagne Charlie

SERVES: 6
PREPARATION: 30 minutes
COOKING: 10 minutes
FREEZING: 5 hours

175 g/6 oz caster sugar
150 ml/¼ pt water
2 oranges
2 lemons
600 ml/1 pt chilled champagne
600 ml/1 pt double cream
175 ml/6 fl oz brandy
36 ratafia biscuits
lemon peel to garnish

Put the caster sugar in a pan with the water. Bring to the boil and boil rapidly for 6 minutes to make a syrup.

Meanwhile, grate the rind from one orange and squeeze the juice from the oranges and lemons. Add the rind and the strained juice to the syrup and leave to cool. Stir in the chilled champagne.

Pour the mixture into a plastic container, and cover with the lid or a double layer of foil. Freeze for 2 hours or until frozen around the edges. Scoop the mixture into a chilled bowl and

whip until smooth. In a separate bowl, whip the double cream until it is stiff. Stir the cream slowly into the champagne mixture until it is smooth and uniform in colour. Stir in 30 ml/ 2 tablespoons of brandy. Spoon the mixture into the container, cover and freeze overnight.

About 30 minutes before serving the dessert, place six ratafia biscuits in the bottom of six serving dishes or champagne glasses if you have them. Pour 10ml/2 teaspoons of brandy over the biscuits in each glass and leave them to soak. Scoop the ice cream into the glasses or dishes. Hang a thin spiral of lemon peel from the rim of each glass and pour 5 ml/1 teaspoon of brandy over each portion. Serve immediately. Serve with langues de chat biscuits or sponge fingers.

Paris-Brest

In the late 19th century, this sweet was created in honour of a famous bicycle race which was run between Paris and Brest. It is a concoction of choux pastry filled with Chantilly cream.

SERVES: 4
PREPARATION: 30 minutes
OVEN: 220°C/425°F/gas 7
       190°C/375°F/gas 5
COOKING: 30 minutes

1 quantity Choux Pastry
  (page 371)
40 g/1½ oz flaked almonds
Chantilly Cream
300 ml/½ pt double cream
45 ml/3 tablespoons icing sugar
1 egg white

Spoon the choux pastry into a piping bag fitted with a large

Paris-Brest.

plain nozzle. Pipe a ring, about 3.5 cm/1½ in wide and 20 cm/ 8 in diameter, on to a greased baking tray. Sprinkle the flaked almonds over the dough and bake the pastry ring at 220°C/ 425°F/gas 7 for 10 minutes. Reduce the oven temperature to 190°C/375°F/gas 5 and cook for a further 20 minutes or until crisp and golden.

Split the choux ring in half horizontally but do not separate the halves. Cool on a wire rack.

For the Chantilly cream filling, whip together the double cream, 30 ml/2 tablespoons sifted icing sugar and the egg white until light and fluffy. Spoon the cream into the hollow bottom half of the ring. Cover with the lid, and dust the ring with the remaining icing sugar.

Cooking for Christmas

December has always been a time for celebration. In Northern Europe, Odin and his fellow gods were worshipped at this time of year with an orgy of eating and drinking. The Romans celebrated Saturnalia, and the peoples of Egypt and Persia adored their gods of plenty. The early Christian Church wisely refrained from banishing the pagan festivities and named December 25th as the date when Christ was born. Mid-winter, with its solstice celebrations, was already an established time for feasting. The feasting continues today with our traditional Christmas meal – roast turkey with all the trimmings followed by Christmas pudding.

The British took to the Christian celebrations as enthusiastically as they had once enjoyed the old Celtic festival. The whirlwind of merry-making continued until abruptly halted by the Puritans in the 17th century – even plum pudding was declared food fit for heathens only, and carols were condemned as evil chants. Charles II, however, restored the custom of merry-making at Christmas.

Two famous 19th century figures, Charles Dickens and Prince Albert, helped create the traditions of a Victorian Christmas – Dickens with *A Christmas Carol*, and Prince Albert by popularising the Christmas tree.

A white Christmas is more often seen on Christmas cards than in reality. This is largely due to a reform of the calendar in 1752, when 11 days were 'lost' so that Christmas Day fell earlier in the year. Snow is more common in January than in December.

In Elizabethan days, Christmas dinner always began with fresh oysters served on a bed of cracked ice. For a main course, the Victorians had turkey or roast goose, a fatty bird with succulent flesh. Nowadays, turkey is the highlight of Christmas dinner in Britain, its popularity owing much to the classic English stuffings and the accompanying sauces, such as bread sauce, spiced cranberry sauce and gravy or port wine sauce. Lastly comes the Christmas pudding, shrouded in a blue haze of brandy flames, and served with brandy butter and/or cream. Mince pies, crystallised fruits, dates, figs and nuts, and port are all traditional ingredients for rounding off the Christmas meal.

Spiced Cranberries

SERVES: 8
PREPARATION: 10 minutes
COOKING: 45 minutes

450 g/1 lb cranberries
2.5 cm/1 in piece of fresh
    root ginger
1 stick cinnamon
15 ml/1 tablespoon whole allspice
6 cloves
300 ml/½ pt cider vinegar
225 g/8 oz Demerara sugar

Put the cranberries in a pan with all the spices tied in muslin. Pour over the vinegar and bring to the boil. Lower the heat and simmer the cranberries until the skins begin to pop, about 25 minutes. Stir in the sugar and simmer for 20 minutes. Remove the spices and store the preserve in small jars. Serve cold with roast turkey.

Chestnut Stuffing for Turkey

1 onion
turkey heart and liver
175 g/6 oz mushrooms
50 g/2 oz butter
225 g/8 oz chestnut purée
50 g/2 oz can pâté de foie gras
1 stick of celery
100 g/4 oz bacon
15 ml/1 tablespoon chopped parsley
salt and black pepper
50 g/2 oz fresh white breadcrumbs

Peel and chop the onion. Chop the turkey heart and liver; slice the mushrooms. Fry these ingredients in the butter, until this has been absorbed. Mix in the chestnut purée with the pâté.

Chop the celery and bacon and add with the parsley. Season and add enough breadcrumbs to bind the stuffing. Fill the breast end of the turkey with the chestnut stuffing and fill the body cavity with sausage stuffing.

Sausage Stuffing

100 g/4 oz belly pork
2 shallots
100 g/4 oz fresh white breadcrumbs
675 g/1½ lb pork sausagemeat
1 egg
salt and black pepper

Mince the belly pork. Chop the shallots and mix with the breadcrumbs, minced pork and sausagemeat. Beat the egg and stir into the stuffing to bind. Season to taste.

A roast turkey with all the trimmings.

Apricot Stuffing for Goose and Duck

350 g/12 oz apricots
juice of 1 lemon
15 ml/1 tablespoon soft
    brown sugar
1 large cooking apple
1 large green pepper
4 sticks celery
100 g/4 oz fresh white breadcrumbs
grated rind of 1 orange
75 g/3 oz butter
2 eggs
salt and black pepper

Put the apricots in a pan with the lemon juice and the sugar; bring to the boil, then simmer for 20 minutes. Set aside to cool.

Strain the apricots, reserving the cooking juices, and chop them roughly. Peel, core and dice the apple; finely chop the pepper and celery. Mix with the apricots. Stir in the breadcrumbs and orange rind. Melt the butter; beat the eggs. Stir both into the stuffing. Season to taste and bind the stuffing with about 90 ml/ 6 tablespoons of the reserved apricot juice.

Prune and Apple Stuffing for Goose and Duck

20 no-need-to-presoak stoned,
    dried prunes
250 ml/8 fl oz water
grated rind and juice of ½ lemon
15 ml/1 tablespoon soft
    brown sugar
2 large cooking apples
goose liver
1 stick celery
50 g/2 oz cooked rice
2.5 ml/½ teaspoon ground mace
15 ml/1 tablespoon chopped parsley
salt and black pepper
1 egg

Put the prunes with the water, lemon juice and sugar into a pan, bring to the boil, then simmer for 20 minutes. Set aside to cool. Drain the prunes, reserving the juice, and cut them into quarters.

Peel, core and roughly chop the cooking apples. Chop the goose liver and celery stick. Mix the quartered prunes with all the rest of the ingredients, adding the beaten egg last. Stir in as much of the prune juice as the stuffing will absorb.

Forcemeat Stuffing for Goose

1 small onion
2 large slices white bread,
    crusts removed
120 ml/4 fl oz milk
100 g/4 oz veal
100 g/4 oz lean pork
1 goose liver
15 g/½ oz butter
15 ml/1 tablespoon chopped parsley
15 ml/1 tablespoon chopped thyme
120 ml/4 fl oz red wine
1 large egg
salt and black pepper

Peel the onion. Soak the bread in the milk for 10 minutes. Put the veal, pork, goose liver and onion through the fine blade of a mincer. Fry this mixture in the butter until it is golden brown. Remove from the heat.

Drain the bread, squeezing it to remove the excess milk, then add it to the minced meat and onion mixture. Stir in the herbs and wine. Beat the egg and use it to bind the stuffing. Season to taste with salt and freshly ground black pepper.

Note All the Christmas stuffings featured here can be made in advance and frozen, saving time on last-minute preparations.

Stuffings made with bacon should not be frozen for longer than 1 month as the bacon will turn rancid with prolonged freezing. The other stuffings can be frozen for 2–3 months. Thaw stuffing overnight in the refrigerator, or for several hours at room temperature.

Christmas Pudding

The ingredients listed below will make enough for two large Christmas puddings.

MAKES: 2 large puddings
PREPARATION: 1¼ hours
COOKING: 10 hours

450 g/1 lb raisins
50 g/2 oz mixed peel
50 g/2 oz blanched almonds
225 g/8 oz currants
225 g/8 oz sultanas
100 g/4 oz plain or
    self-raising flour
2.5 ml/½ teaspoon grated nutmeg
2.5 ml/½ teaspoon mixed spice
2.5 ml/½ teaspoon cinnamon
5 ml/1 teaspoon salt
50 g/2 oz ground almonds
450 g/1 lb shredded suet
225 g/8 oz fresh white breadcrumbs
100 g/4 oz soft brown sugar
6 large eggs
60 ml/4 tablespoons brandy
250 ml/8 fl oz milk
25 g/1 oz unsalted butter

Chop the raisins, mixed peel and blanched almonds. Mix together, in a large bowl, all the fruits, the sifted flour, spices, salt and ground almonds. Mix thoroughly until all the fruit is well coated (this is easiest done with the hands). Work in the suet, breadcrumbs and sugar. Beat the eggs lightly and stir them into the mixture. Add the brandy and milk, stirring until the pudding has a soft dropping consistency. (If you prefer a darker-coloured pudding, decrease the quantity of suet to 275 g/10 oz and increase the flour to 275 g/10 oz).

Butter well two 1.15 kg/2½ lb pudding basins, spoon in the pudding and cover each basin with a pleated, double layer of buttered greaseproof paper. Tie down with a pudding cloth.

Set the pudding basins in one or two large pans of boiling water, reaching two-thirds up the sides of the basins. Boil steadily for 6 hours, topping up with boiling water as necessary. Remove the puddings, leave them to cool, then cover them with fresh greaseproof paper and cloths. Allow to mature by storing the puddings in a cool place, for at least two months.

On Christmas Day, boil the puddings for a further 4 hours. Turn them out of the basins and garnish each pudding with a sprig of holly. Pour over warmed brandy and set alight. Serve with brandy butter.

Brandy Butter

SERVES: 4
PREPARATION: 15 minutes
CHILLING: 2–3 hours

75 g/3 oz unsalted butter
75 g/3 oz caster sugar
grated rind of ½ orange
30–45 ml/2–3 tablespoons brandy

Cream the butter until soft and pale in colour. Beat in the sugar and orange rind. Gradually beat in the brandy until the mixture is frothy. Chill in the refrigerator for 2–3 hours or until solid.

Christmas Pudding with Destiny Sauce

A Christmas pudding can look a sorry sight on Boxing Day, but if slices are fried and served with a chilled sauce, it becomes a mouth-watering new dessert.

SERVES: 4–6
PREPARATION: 5–10 minutes
COOKING: 5 minutes

150 ml/¼ pt double cream
15 ml/1 tablespoon sifted
    icing sugar
30 ml/2 tablespoons port
8 thin slices Christmas pudding
40 g/1½ oz unsalted butter
30 ml/2 tablespoons caster sugar

Beat the cream until thick, then stir in the icing sugar and port until well combined. Chill in the refrigerator until required.

Fry the slices of Christmas pudding in the butter, over medium heat, for 4 minutes, turning it once. Arrange the slices on a warm serving dish, dust with the caster sugar and serve the chilled cream in a separate bowl.

Orange Mince Pies

MAKES: 20
PREPARATION: 30 minutes
OVEN: 200°C/400°F/gas 6
COOKING: 15 minutes

275 g/10 oz plain flour
75 g/3 oz butter
50 g/2 oz lard
grated rind of 1 orange
45 ml/3 tablespoons orange juice
Filling
450 g/1 lb mincemeat
1 small Cox's apple
15 ml/1 tablespoon Cointreau

Sift the flour into a large bowl. Rub in the butter and lard until the mixture resembles fine bread-crumbs. Add the grated orange rind and juice. With your fingers, draw the pastry mixture together; knead the dough lightly until smooth. Wrap in cling film and chill while preparing the filling.

Spoon the mincemeat into a bowl. Peel the apple if preferred, cut into quarters, remove the core and grate the flesh into the mincemeat. Stir in the Cointreau.

Roll out the pastry on a lightly floured surface. Cut out 20 rounds, each large enough to line a tartlet tin, then cut out 20 slightly smaller round shapes as lids, re-rolling the pastry trimmings as necessary.

Fit the pastry bases into the tins, divide the filling between them and cover with the lids, sealing well. Bake in a preheated oven at 200°C/400°F/gas 6 for 15 minutes, until golden brown. Leave in the tins for 5 minutes before transferring the mince pies to wire racks to cool.

Oat Biscuits

MAKES: 24 biscuits
PREPARATION: 15 minutes
OVEN: 160°C/325°F/gas 3
COOKING: 20–25 minutes

75 g/3 oz plain flour
2.5 ml/½ teaspoon bicarbonate of soda
75 g/3 oz Demerara sugar
75 g/3 oz rolled porridge oats
75 g/3 oz unsalted butter
15 ml/1 tablespoon golden syrup
15 ml/1 tablespoon rum

Sift the flour and bicarbonate of soda into a bowl; thoroughly mix in the sugar and oats. Melt the butter with the syrup and the rum. Stir into the flour mixture.

Shape the dough into balls, 2.5 ml/1 in wide, between floured hands. Set the balls well apart on greased baking trays. Bake in a preheated oven at 160°C/325°F/gas 3 for 20–25 minutes or until golden brown. Serve when cool with Wassail Cup.

Wassail Cup

SERVES: 16–20
PREPARATION: 5 minutes
COOKING: 20 minutes

3.4 litres/6 pt brown ale
450 g/1 lb soft brown sugar
1 large stick cinnamon
2 lemons
5 ml/1 teaspoon grated nutmeg
2.5 ml/½ teaspoon ground ginger
900 ml/1½ pt medium-dry sherry

Pour 1.12 litres/2 pt of the ale into a large pan. Add the sugar and cinnamon stick, and heat the mixture slowly over low heat until the sugar has dissolved. Thinly slice the lemons and add to the pan with the spices, sherry and remaining ale. Heat through gently and serve hot.

Christmas Cake

PREPARATION: 2½ hours plus standing time
OVEN: 150°C/300°F/gas 2
COOKING: 4 hours

150 g/5½ oz chopped, ready-to-eat dried pineapple
125 g/4½ oz cut mixed peel
250 g/9 oz glacé cherries, halved
500 g/1 lb 2 oz sultanas
500 g/1 lb 2 oz seedless raisins
300 g/10½ oz currants
finely grated rind of 1 large orange
finely grated rind of 1 large lemon
150 ml/5 fl oz brandy
250 g/9 oz butter
250 g/9 oz molasses or dark muscovado sugar
7 large eggs, beaten
250 g/9 oz plain flour
10 ml/2 teaspoons mixed spice
200 g/7 oz ground almonds
For the marzipan and icing
90 ml/6 tablespoons apricot glaze (see page 391)
1 kg/2 lb 4 oz bought marzipan
royal icing (see page 390)
To decorate
leaves and candles, made from rolled out, coloured marzipan
1 m/39 in of red ribbon, 2.5 cm/1 in wide (optional)

Put the fruit, orange and lemon rind and 6 tablespoons of the brandy into a large bowl – saving the remaining brandy for later. Mix well, cover and leave to stand for 3 hours.

Grease and line a 25 cm/10 in round or square cake tin with nonstick baking paper. Tie a double band of brown paper round the outside. Turn on the oven.

In a very large mixing bowl, cream the butter and sugar together until fluffy, then gradually beat in the eggs. (If the mixture curdles slightly, don't worry.) Sift the flour and spice into the bowl, add the ground almonds and mix well. Then mix in the soaked fruit. Spoon the mixture into the prepared tin and level the top.

Bake the cake in the centre of the oven for 4 hours, or until a skewer inserted into the centre comes out clean. Remove from the oven and cool in the tin for 1 hour. Then carefully turn out the cake onto a wire rack to cool completely.

Without removing the baking paper, wrap the cold cake in cling film; overwrap in foil and store in an airtight container in a cool, dry, airy cupboard until one week before Christmas.

Decorating the cake Remove the wrappings from the cake and place it upside down on a 33 cm/13 in cake board or large cake plate. Prick holes in the base of the cake with a skewer, carefully spoon on the reserved 4 tablespoons of brandy and allow it to soak in.

Bring the apricot glaze to the boil and brush it evenly all over the cake. Cover with marzipan and leave to dry at room temperature for 24 hours before icing.

Spread the royal icing all over the marzipan, swirling it up into peaks with a palette knife. If you intend using a ribbon, smoothe the sides. Decorate while the icing is soft, and add the ribbon when the icing is quite dry.

Marzipan can be coloured with concentrated food colouring, rolled out and used to make attractive decorations.

The slightly spicy roulade tastes particularly festive and looks most appealing. Since it is simple to prepare, it is also an extremely useful recipe for anyone who is combining a vegetarian menu with a traditional turkey dinner.

The roquefort and walnut mousse is an ideal first course before turkey, and the vegetable accompaniments for the main course will suit both the roulade and the traditional roast poultry. Remember to roast some potatoes separately from the meat, basting them with a mixture of vegetable oil and melted butter, not the juices from the roast, so that the potatoes can be eaten with the vegetarian main course.

When preparing the Christmas pudding, buy vegetarian suet. Similarly, remember to use vegetarian suet for the mincemeat used in mince pies.

Chestnut Roulade

Small cans of chestnut purée are sometimes available, but they are often sweetened; if you cannot find a small can of unsweetened purée, use half a large, 425 g/ 15 oz, can instead. The rest of the purée can be placed in a small rigid container and frozen for future use; or, try the recipe for Peaches with Brandied Chestnut Cream (page 74).

SERVES: 4–6
PREPARATION: 45 minutes
OVEN: 200°C/400°F/gas 6
COOKING : about 50 minutes

1 small onion
40 g/1½ oz butter
25 g/1 oz plain flour
150 ml/¼ pt milk
3 eggs
225 g/8 oz unsweetened chestnut purée
90 ml/6 tablespoons grated Parmesan cheese
salt and black pepper
pinch of ground cloves
5 ml/1 teaspoon ground mace
2.5 ml/½ teaspoon ground cinnamon
50 g/2 oz fresh white breadcrumbs
Tomato Sauce to serve (see Stuffed Peppers with Pork and Beef, page 229)

Filling
1 small onion
25 g/1 oz butter
225 g/8 oz broccoli
175 g/6 oz ricotta cheese

Line and grease a 33 × 23 cm/ 13 × 9 in Swiss roll tin, so that the paper stands about 2.5 cm/ 1 in above the rim of the tin.

Prepare the filling before making the roulade. Finely chop the onion and cook it in the butter for 10 minutes. Cook the broccoli in boiling salted water for 10 minutes, drain and chop it finely. Stir the broccoli into the onion, remove from the heat and mix in the ricotta cheese. Season to taste and set the filling aside.

Make the chestnut roulade. Finely chop the onion. Melt 25g/ 1 oz of the butter in a saucepan, add the onion and cook for 5 minutes, stir in the flour, then gradually stir in the milk until evenly combined. Remove the pan from the heat without bringing the sauce to the boil and thickening it.

Separate the eggs. Place the chestnut purée in a bowl and break it into pieces, then gradually beat it until smooth.

Beat in the egg yolks and Parmesan cheese with seasoning to taste, the ground cloves, mace and cinnamon. Gradually mix in the sauce.

Whisk the egg whites until stiff but not dry. Stir the breadcrumbs into the sauce. As soon as the breadcrumbs are incorporated, stir in about a quarter of the whisked whites. Use a metal spoon to fold in the remaining whites. Turn the mixture into the prepared tin, spread it evenly and bake in a preheated oven at 200°C/400°F/ gas 6 for about 20 minutes, or until the roulade has risen, set and browned.

Lay a clean tea-towel on the work surface and cover it with a piece of foil, shiny side underneath. Melt the remaining butter and brush it over the foil. Turn

A vegetarian Christmas dinner: Roquefort and Walnut Mousse with Fresh Dates, followed by Chestnut Roulade with tomato sauce and Braised Red Cabbage.

the roulade out on to the foil, remove the lining paper and trim off any crisp edges. Make a shallow slit across one long end about 1 cm/½ in from the edge. Spread the filling over the roulade, then roll it up using the foil and tea-towel as a guide. Tuck the cut edge in neatly so that the roulade rolls up tightly at the beginning, but take care not to squeeze out the filling.

Pinch the foil loosely at the ends of the roll, place the roulade on a baking tray and put it in the oven for 10 minutes to set and to heat the filling. Serve sliced, with the hot tomato sauce.

METHODS AND

TECHNIQUES

FOOD PREPARATION & COOKING METHODS

This section explains and illustrates the essential techniques that form the starting point for most cooking. There is information on the equipment you need, how to prepare the basic ingredients and how and when to use the different cooking methods.

WEIGHING AND MEASURING

The need for accuracy when weighing and measuring depends on the type of recipe and food being cooked. It can be vital to use ingredients in the correct proportion for baking, and good results with everyday dishes also depend on carefully measuring certain ingredients. For example, using a few too many vegetables in a stew is unlikely to cause a problem, but adding too much flour to thicken the sauce can give a very stodgy result. Getting into the habit of always using proper measuring spoons, jugs and scales when a recipe specifies an exact amount ensures that the finished dish tastes as good as it did when it was first cooked. Guessing and being creative with seasonings and flavourings is all part of the fun of cooking but following a recipe closely is sensible when trying new dishes or complex mixtures and recipes.

Measuring Spoons

Proper measuring spoons are essential equipment. Using table cutlery or serving spoons, which are usually larger than measuring spoons, as substitutes will cause problems. Use a set with either British Standard teaspoon and tablespoon volumes or millilitre measures. All spoon measures should be level unless the recipe states otherwise. Dip the measuring spoon into dry ingredients, then level it off with a knife without packing the ingredient into the bowl of the spoon.

Measuring Jug

A glass jug with clear markings is best. Remember to check the level of the liquid from the side, rather than from above, which will give an inaccurate reading: pour in the liquid, stand the jug on a level surface and bend down to check the volume.

Weighing Scales

Good balance scales are the most accurate. Digital scales, depending on their quality, are particularly useful for weighing small amounts and some give consistently accurate results, but make sure they include a form of warning to let you know when the batteries are wearing out. Spring scales tend to be less precise and they do vary enormously in quality. Whatever your choice, look for scales which give a clear indication of the weight and allow for weighing out quantities of less than 25 g/1 oz with a reasonable degree of accuracy.

FOOD PREPARATION

The basic techniques given here are for common foods and simple meals, and they will be a useful source of reference for less-confident cooks or for checking methods which are not used everyday, like skinning tomatoes or cutting julienne strips. More complex methods are always explained in the recipes.

Trimming and Cleaning

The best way of cleaning and trimming fresh produce depends on the type of food, its quality and age, and on the personal preferences of the cook. Before cooking, food should be washed, if necessary, and any inedible parts which are not required in the cooked dish, like bones, should be removed. Trim away any damaged areas or tough parts of vegetables; sometimes the inferior pieces can be used for making stock or flavouring soup – woody asparagus stalks or tough sprouting broccoli stems both make tasty soup so long as they are sieved out when cooked.

Washing Wash any fruit which is used with its peel or skin. Wash dirty vegetables before peeling or trimming them, then rinse them in clean water when they are prepared. Do not allow foods to soak as this results in the loss of water-soluble nutrients.

Wiping Mushrooms should be wiped with dampened absorbent kitchen paper to remove dirt before trimming. Button mushrooms or slightly larger closed cap mushrooms can be cleaned by rinsing them briefly in a colander under cold running water, but do not wash open mushrooms or allow the undersides of the caps to absorb water.

Scrubbing or peeling Young vegetables with fine skins are usually scrubbed before cooking, older produce is usually peeled. As the peel and area immediately beneath it contain the valuable nutrients, it is a good idea to cook even older vegetables with their peel on for everyday dishes where presentation is not such a high priority; this is particularly true of potatoes which can be baked in their jackets.

Trimming Remove stalks and tough parts, blemishes, damaged areas, excess fat and inedible parts, except bones which are to be cooked with meat or fish.

Skinning Tomatoes and peppers may be skinned before use for some dishes, particularly salads, and strips of curled tomato skin are also unpleasant in a stew or meaty sauce. There are two methods of removing fine skins.

Place tomatoes in a bowl and cover with freshly boiled water from a kettle. Leave for 30–60 seconds, then remove the fruit and slit the skins which will slide off easily. The riper the fruit, the more quickly the skins will loosen. Do not leave the fruit in boiling water for too long as the flesh will soften and cook.

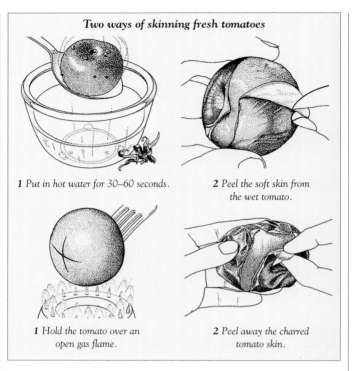

Two ways of skinning fresh tomatoes

1 Put in hot water for 30–60 seconds.

2 Peel the soft skin from the wet tomato.

1 Hold the tomato over an open gas flame.

2 Peel away the charred tomato skin.

Alternatively, char each tomato by skewering it on a fork and holding over a gas burner on the hob. When the peel is blistered and charred in places, rub the skin off under cold water.

Peppers are charred over a glass hob or under a hot grill until blistered all over. Then the skin may be rubbed off under cold water, using a small knife to remove any stubborn areas. The peppers may also be put into a polythene bag and closed with a twist tie, then left for a few minutes after grilling so that the condensation loosens the skin.

Cleaning The majority of dried fruits and other groceries are sold clean and ready for use, but it is sometimes necessary to pick over foods like dried pulses to remove any discoloured pieces or foreign material which may be present.

Slicing

There are two ways of slicing food and, although this may seem to be a pedantic point, the method used can make quite a difference to the result.

The tip of the knife may be held still on the cutting board while the knife blade is pivoted up and down to slice the food. This method is used for the majority of firm foods to cut thin and/or even slices.

The other method is to use a sawing action, especially when using a serrated knife and cutting foods that are likely to fall apart, such as breads, cooked pastries and cakes. The sawing method is also useful for cutting the finest slices off a side of smoked salmon or off a joint of part-frozen

uncooked meat. The vigour with which you slice the food depends on its texture; it can be better to slice quickly through a fine-crumbed bread or cake, whereas slow, careful strokes of the knife are more suitable if you want to avoid damaging delicate smoked salmon or a dessert such as lemon meringue pie.

Cutting Fingers, Strips or Julienne

Slice the food thickly for fingers, moderately thickly or thinly for strips, and finely for julienne. After slicing, trim the slices to the length required for the pieces. Fingers should be even in width and thickness but strips, which are usually smaller than fingers, may be slightly wider than they are thick. Julienne are always finely cut, they are all of similar size with neatly trimmed ends and they are even in width and in thickness.

Cutting Chunks or Cubes

First slice the food thickly, then cut it into large fingers and, finally, cut the fingers across into chunks or cubes. Chunks can be random in shape, but for neat cubes, the food should be trimmed before it is sliced to make sure that all the pieces have square corners.

Cutting Dice

These are cut in the same way as cubes, but the slices are thinner, the fingers finer and the dice are far smaller. Dicing is a more precise technique to give pieces that are always even in shape and size for a neat appearance.

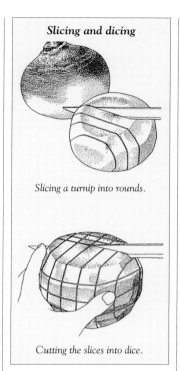

Slicing and dicing

Slicing a turnip into rounds.

Cutting the slices into dice.

Chopping

Chopped food is finely cut into small, uneven pieces. Often the best method is to cut slices, then to stack them and cut fingers, and, finally, to cut across the fingers to make small pieces. The pieces may be larger than dice if the food is 'roughly chopped'. Onions are chopped by halving, slicing and cutting across the slices to free small pieces off each ring of the onion flesh.

For very finely chopped food, a large, smooth-bladed and well-sharpened cook's knife may be used in a pivot action. The point of the blade should be held firmly on the cutting board and the handle used to pivot the blade quickly up and down. This chopping method is most often used

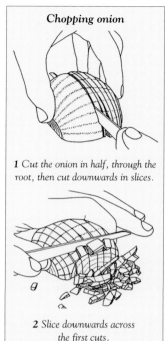

Chopping onion

1 *Cut the onion in half, through the root, then cut downwards in slices.*

2 *Slice downwards across the first cuts.*

for herbs and it is also useful for meat or other foods which are already cut into small pieces that are not too thick or large to fit under the fast-moving knife blade. Scrape the food together occasionally and clean the blade of the knife to keep the pieces together in a neat pile. This ensures even chopping.

Shredding

This is a method of cutting into very coarse or fine, short, even strips. Slice the food thinly, then cut it into strips of the width required for the shreds and cut across these strips to make fine shreds. For example, to shred citrus rind, cut strips off the fruit and cut fine shreds off across the strips. To shred cabbage, cut

wedges, then slice them finely; large, thick wedges will give long shreds while slim wedges yield short pieces.

COOKING METHODS

Boiling

This is a moist, rapid and fairly harsh cooking method used most often for foods with a high starch content and a resilient texture, such as potatoes, rice and pasta. The food is cooked in boiling water or other liquid, either by covering with cold liquid and bringing to the boil or by adding the food to boiling liquid. Foods suitable for boiling include root vegetables, which are covered with cold water and brought to the boil, and pasta, which is added to boiling water.

Boiling is not suitable for delicate foods, such as fish. These foods should be simmered, otherwise they may begin to break up. Simmering is used for cooking large joints, such as gammon, because boiling toughens meat.

Salt and flavouring ingredients, such as herbs, spices or lemon rind, may be added to the liquid. During long cooking, for example when boiling meat or a pudding, remember to check that the water has not evaporated below the required level and top it up with fresh boiling water. When boiling foods such as pasta for a short period, the pan is usually left uncovered, otherwise the water boils over. A saucepan of root vegetables should be partly covered, allowing steam to escape, but preventing too much water from evaporating.

303

Simmering

Simmering is another moist method of cooking, but it is a more gentle method than boiling. The liquid is usually brought to the boil before the heat is regulated so that the liquid simmers steadily. Sometimes, for delicate foods or those that will toughen easily in boiling water, the cooking temperature must be regulated very quickly when the liquid first appears to boil so that it barely bubbles. When food is 'simmered gently', the bubbles should not break the surface of the liquid regularly, but the surface should simply ripple and move slightly with the very occasional bubble surfacing at most; this is important when cooking delicate shellfish or dumplings that may disintegrate.

Steaming

This is a method of cooking food in the steam from boiling liquid. The term is also used when food is placed on a plate, covered and cooked over a pan of boiling water. Steaming is gentle in that the food is not stirred or vigorously moved about during cooking, but it can be hotter than boiling, for example when a steamer is placed over a pan full of rapidly boiling water, it can provide a hotter environment for the food than the water itself.

Steaming can be a bland cooking method if the food is not seasoned or flavoured. However, it is a good way of preserving the full, natural flavour of vegetables and it is also a useful, classic method for fish and seafood which are seasoned with Chinese sauces or with spices. Chicken can be steamed in a similar way, with soy sauce, root ginger and other fairly powerful condiments, such as black bean sauce.

Savoury and sweet puddings, always a favourite in traditional British kitchens, are steamed for many hours, allowing flavours to develop and starchy foods to become light in texture.

The term 'steaming' is also used when foods are cooked in a small amount of liquid in a covered pan. This method is used for vegetables and shellfish, such as mussels. Although some of the food is immersed in the liquid, the majority is piled above it and cooked in the steam from the simmering or boiling liquid.

Sweating

A moist cooking method, usually used for vegetables. The food is tossed with the minimum of fat or oil – sometimes sufficient only to grease the base of the pan – then the pan is covered and the food cooked in the steam it produces. The pan is shaken occasionally to reposition the food, keeping the lid on so that the steam does not escape. Depending on the food, the heat initially has to be quite high in order to encourage the water content of the food to evaporate and condense, providing the moisture necessary for cooking.

Stewing

A slow, moist cooking method for tough foods. The food is immersed in liquid and cooked over low heat or at a low temperature in the oven for long periods. This encourages the breakdown of tough connective tissue in meat and causes the gelatinous areas to soften. Vegetables are also stewed, but for shorter periods than meat.

Before stewing, the ingredients are often fried or sautéed to enrich the mixture and improve the flavour of the finished dishes; this is particularly important when onions, leeks or peppers are used, otherwise you will still be able to detect their 'raw', boiled flavour in a cooked sauce. Thickening can be added at the beginning of cooking or at the end, just before serving; sometimes the main ingredients, like vegetables or pulses, break down to thicken the cooking liquor.

Braising

This is a moist cooking method, though the food is not immersed in liquid. The ingredients and main food are usually fried or browned in a little fat, then some liquid is added and the cooking pan is tightly covered so that the steam from the gently simmering liquid is kept in the pan. The partly immersed food is then cooked by a combination of gentle simmering and steaming. Braising can be long and slow in the oven – ideal for larger cuts of meat – or gentle and fairly brief for smaller portions of meat or delicate ingredients.

Poaching

A moist cooking method similar to simmering without allowing the small amount of liquid to boil. Poaching is used for delicate foods that cook quickly, like fish fillets or tender shellfish that are cooked very gently in milk. A completely different example of poaching is when cooking eggs by this method, where the water is boiled, then the heat reduced to prevent it bubbling before the eggs are added. Once the eggs are in the water it must not be allowed to bubble but it has to be hot enough to poach the eggs quickly to keep them in shape.

Frying

This fierce method of cooking at high temperatures in fat is used only for tender foods and ingredients that cook quickly. There are various methods of frying: shallow frying, sautéing, stir frying and deep frying.

Shallow frying Enough fat is used to cover the base of the pan and, in some cases, to baste the food. Many foods have to be protected by a coating before frying. Seasoned flour or egg and breadcrumbs are the most usual coatings, with batter being used occasionally and mainly for deep frying. Eggs, meats, poultry, bacon and vegetables can be shallow fried without a coating.

Heat enough fat to coat the base of the frying pan: the fat is hot enough when it runs freely and begins to shimmer slightly on the surface. Then add the food and cook it until the underside is browned and crisped before turning it over and cooking the second side in the same way. Eggs are usually basted to cook the top of the whites or they may be turned and cooked for a few seconds to seal the top of the yolks and whites.

When shallow frying, regulate the temperature according to the food. The fat must be very hot at first to seal the outside of the food, then the heat can be reduced when this initial stage is complete to allow time for the food to be cooked through without over-browning the outside. It is important to reduce the heat for thicker foods, such as fillets of chicken, chops or thick slices of vegetables, such as aubergines.

Sautéing This is a method of frying food quickly over high heat until it is browned. The food is turned and rearranged often to ensure that it cooks and browns evenly. Sautéing is useful for foods like courgettes, boiled potatoes or mushrooms.

Stir frying This is a fast method of frying finely cut pieces of food in a small amount of fat over high heat. The food is stirred constantly as it cooks; for this reason a large pan is essential. A wok is best, as the deep sides contain the food and allow it to be tossed in and out of the centre of the pan; however a large frying pan or wide saucepan may also be used. Stir-fried dishes often include a variety of ingredients, so those that require the longest cooking are put into the pan first, and others added in order according to how quickly they cook. For good results, it is important that the food is cut into fine, even-sized pieces.

Deep frying For deep frying, use a deep, heavy-based saucepan or a special deep fryer fitted with a wire basket. Fill the pan no more than one-third with oil or melted lard, and warm over a moderate heat. The general temperature of 190°C/375°F is suitable for most deep frying. The temperature can be accurately assessed from a cooking thermometer, but if this is not available, drop a cube of day-old bread into the hot oil. It should sink to the bottom, then rise to the surface and brown in 60 seconds.

Fritters and croquettes are best fried at 190°C/375°F, while potato chips and crisps should be fried at 195°C/385°F. At this heat a bread cube should brown in 40 seconds. The higher heat is necessary because the high water content of potatoes lowers the temperature of the oil. However, for best results, deep fry potatoes twice, at 190°C/375°F. Fry them for 2–3 minutes to extract the water, drain thoroughly and re-heat the oil before frying the second time to crisp the outside.

Frying times vary according to the size and type of food. For foods made up of previously cooked ingredients, such as croquettes, allow only 2–3 minutes. Fritters need 3–5 minutes; potato chips, 4–6 minutes; and coated chicken joints should be fried for about 15 minutes.

Oil and lard can be used several times for deep frying, depending on the amount of food cooked, the type of ingredients and the cooking temperature. Fat which has darkened or over-heated or which is tainted with strong flavours should be thrown away. After cooking, leave the oil or lard to cool, then strain it into a bowl or jar. Store lard, covered, in the refrigerator, and store oil in a cool cupboard.

Coating Batter

PREPARATION: 10 minutes

100 g/4 oz plain flour
pinch of salt
1 egg
150 ml/¼ pt milk

Sift the flour and a pinch of salt into a bowl. Make a hollow in the centre of the flour, and add the egg. Gradually beat in the milk. Beat steadily until the batter is smooth and free of lumps.

For a lighter coating batter, which gives a crisper finish to the fried fish, add 15 ml/1 tablespoon olive oil to the flour and salt. Beat in the egg yolk, with 45–60 ml/3–4 tablespoons milk, until the batter is smooth. Whisk the egg white until stiff and fold it into the batter; use at once. The food should be dipped in seasoned flour, then in batter.

Egg and Breadcrumb Coating

Roll the prepared fish in seasoned flour, then dip it in beaten egg. Coat with dry breadcrumbs, pressing them in well and shaking off any surplus.

Before frying, check the temperature of the oil in the deep fryer. Use the frying basket only for fish coated with eggs or breadcrumbs – batter-coated fish will stick to the basket. Fry only a few pieces at a time as overcrowding the pan lowers the temperature of the oil and ruins the coating. Fry the fish for 5–10 minutes, until crisp and golden.

As soon as the fish is fried, lift it out with a perforated spoon and leave to drain on crumpled absorbent kitchen paper.

Grilling

This is a fierce, dry cooking method, useful for tender foods that cook quickly. The food may be flavoured or moistened by marinating* before cooking. Oil or other fat is usually brushed over the food to prevent it from drying out during grilling.

Slide the grill rack into position and preheat the grill; foods which cook very quickly may be placed on a high rack close to the heat source, items which take slightly longer should be cooked further away from the heat, in a lower position so that they cook through before browning. Some foods should be sealed on the outside quickly under fierce heat to stop them losing their moisture and juices, then lowered away from the heat to finish cooking through. Grill one side of the food, then turn it over and grill the second side.

Sometimes, the grill may be heated on a moderate setting and the food cooked less quickly – this method is useful for vegetables and to crisp toppings before they are well browned.

Barbecuing This is a method of grilling over a heat source, and traditionally over burning charcoal. Electric and gas-fired barbecues are also available. This is not a precise cooking method nor one which can be easily controlled, but its distinctive flavour is valued for a wide range of ingredients. The information on grilling applies to barbecuing; a feature is also included on page 198, giving details of fuel, lighting a barbecue, safety and suitable recipes.

Roasting

This is a dry oven cooking method using high temperatures to cook tender, large portions of food, like joints of meat. The food should be prepared according to type, placed on a rack in a roasting tin and seasoned outside. Brushing the food with oil or fat keeps it moist and promotes browning. Any delicate areas which may overcook should be covered with a piece of foil or barded* with fat.

During roasting, the fat in the roasting tin should be spooned over the meat occasionally; this is known as basting*. The higher the temperature and the less fat the food contains, the more it should be basted; so a fatty goose does not have to be basted as frequently as a joint of beef. Food may be roasted at a very high temperature initially to seal the outside, then the heat reduced and the cooking continued more slowly to cook the food through.

The food is sometimes placed directly in the roasting tin, without using a rack. This is not strictly correct in the traditional use of the method but it does mean that other ingredients can be placed around the food, and/or flavourings and a little liquid added towards the end of cooking to make a sauce. A covering of foil may also be laid loosely over the food for part of the cooking time, to prevent it from over-browning and to reduce the frequency of basting. Roasting bags keep food moist and well basted during cooking, but they do hold in steam so the results are not as crisp.

Spit roasting The food is skewered on a rotating spit and cooked in a hot oven. The spit turns slowly so that the fat and cooking juices baste the food automatically. This is one of the best methods for cooking kebabs and whole chickens and it is also useful for joints of meat.

Pot Roasting

This is a method of roasting less-tender joints of meat on a bed of finely cut prepared vegetables and herbs in a covered casserole. A very little liquid or fat may be added and the pot is kept tightly covered. The moisture from the food evaporates on the lid, keeping the meat moist and allowing more opportunity for tenderising than cooking by roasting. The cooking temperature is usually slightly lower than for roasting and the cooking time is longer.

Pressure Cooking

This is a moist method based on the use of high temperatures achieved by controlling the escape of steam from a sealed cooking pan with a weight. As the pressure of steam builds up in the pan, the temperature rises and the food cooks more quickly than by ordinary steaming or boiling. The standard pressure, traditionally referred to as high pressure, is 15 lb, at which water will boil at 121°C/250°F (at ordinary atmospheric pressure water boils at 100°C/212°F). Some pressure cookers provide the facility for cooking at lower pressures, which are best for dishes like sponge puddings.

Pressure cookers now incorporate automatic timers and pressure release mechanisms. Always read and follow the manufacturer's instructions. The pressure cooker must always contain a minimum of 300 ml/ ½ pt of water or similar liquid (not fat) for the first 15 minutes' cooking time and this should be increased for longer cooking. The cooker should never be filled to more than half its capacity with liquids or two-thirds with solid food. This is particularly important when cooking in milk, for example when making a milk pudding. For foods which froth up easily during cooking, such as dried beans and pulses, the cooker should be no more than one-third full. Overfilling the cooker can cause the vents and safety mechanisms to clog.

Tough meats tenderise quickly by pressure cooking, making this an excellent method of preparing stews and casseroles. Dried beans can be cooked quickly in a pressure cooker without pre-soaking. Steamed puddings and other foods which would require lengthy cooking are excellent candidates for pressure cooking; however, some delicate mixtures, such as sponge puddings, first require a short period of steaming without pressure to allow raising agents to work successfully.

Slow Cooking

This is a method of cooking at a very low temperature for a long time. Pots incorporating heating elements and thermostats are used. Always follow the manu-facturer's instructions. Take particular care on points of food safety, as the low temperature, moist environment and long cooking time can provide ideal conditions for incubating the bacteria that cause food poisoning. For this reason, foods should be brought to a high temperature before being put into the slow cooker and left for the recommended time. The method is not recommended for items such as a whole chicken. Slow cooking is useful for dried beans and pulses.

Microwave Cooking

This cooking method is totally different from all conventional methods as it does not employ a heat source but uses microwaves to generate heat within the food. The waves cause the molecules in the food to vibrate and this generates heat and cooks the food. Microwave cooking is a fierce method with many uses and certain distinct limitations. Apart from the different results obtained by microwaving, metal utensils and dishes with metal trims or decoration generally cannot be used in the microwave. There are certain conditions under which metal can be used, and these are outlined by individual manufacturers for their own appliances.

Steam is produced by the water content of food, so microwave cooking is a moist method and, as such, results resemble those of boiling or steaming rather than grilling, roasting or baking. Food does not become brown or crisp, and a crust or skin will not form as when baking in a conventional oven. Special cooking devices can be used to encourage browning, like dishes coated with a substance that becomes very hot or a cooking paper that browns food by a similar method, but the results cannot be compared to conventional methods. As a general guide, foods which cook quickly and are not too delicate are excellent candidates for microwave cooking. Many vegetables, some fish dishes, rice, lentils and many sauces cook extremely well in a microwave. Never attempt to fry in fat in a microwave as this is dangerous and impractical. Eggs cannot be boiled in a microwave as they burst. Tough meats and other foods which rely on long slow cooking for good results cannot be cooked as well in a microwave without the aid of specific appliances, such as a microwave pressure cooker.

Defrosting and reheating foods
A microwave is a useful tool for rapidly defrosting and reheating food. Always follow the manufacturer's guidelines.

Combination microwave cooking
This is an excellent method for many foods, including roasting poultry and meat, pastry and some baking. A combination microwave cooker combines conventional heat with microwave energy simultaneously. There are also appliances on the market which include browning elements or heat sources that cannot be used at the same time as the microwave energy and these do not give the same standard of results as a combination oven.

FATS & OILS

Fats and oils play many important roles in cooking. Fat is an essential ingredient in many baking mixtures, contributing flavour and having a vital role in achieving the required texture. As a cooking medium, for frying, grilling or roasting, fat alters the flavour and texture of the food.

FATS

Butter
This is made from the fatty substances skimmed from full-cream milk. It is churned and then pressed to squeeze out the water, and salt is added. Unsalted butter is also produced, though the majority is salted for British consumption. It is used as the cooking medium for egg dishes, for sautéed vegetables, for shallow frying and in the baking of cakes and biscuits. Unsalted butter is used for some cooking, particularly when making sweet dishes and in baking.

Clarified butter This type of fat is sometimes used in recipes for frying and grilling. It is an expensive cooking medium, as 225 g/8 oz of butter produces only about 150 g/5 oz of clarified butter. Melt 225 g/8 oz of salted butter in a small pan over gentle heat and cook, without stirring, until the butter begins to foam. Continue to cook the butter without browning until the spitting and foaming stops. During cooking, the water content of the butter evaporates and the solids separate out in a deposit. Remove the pan from the heat and let it stand until the milky deposits have sunk to the bottom of the pan, leaving a clear yellow liquid on top. Pour this liquid carefully, through a piece of muslin, into a bowl. Clarified butter can be used in liquid or solid form.

Beurre meunière This sauce is made from the butter in which fish has been shallow-fried. Add a little extra butter to the pan juices and cook until lightly brown. Stir in a squeeze of lemon juice and add a little finely chopped parsley.

Beurre noir This is melted butter heated until it becomes nut brown, but not black. Add 30 ml/2 tablespoons of finely chopped parsley, 15 ml/1 tablespoon of wine vinegar and 15 ml/1 tablespoon of chopped capers to every 100 g/4 oz of butter. It is served with eggs, brains, poached skate, fish roe and boiled vegetables.

Beurre noisette Melted butter allowed to brown lightly before being seasoned. Serve with the same types of food as beurre noir.

Savoury butters These butters have a wide variety of uses; for example, to garnish meat, fish and vegetable dishes, or they may be added to sauces (see chart, right).

SAVOURY BUTTERS

Butter (100 g/4 oz)	Flavouring	Preparation	Serving suggestions
FISH BUTTERS:			
Anchovy butter	6 anchovy fillets	Rinse the anchovies in cold water to remove salt and oil. Dry. Rub through a sieve and combine with the butter	Grilled meat or fish. As a garnish for cold hors-d'oeuvre, or added to a white sauce
Crab or shrimp butter	100 g/4 oz crabmeat or 100 g/4 oz peeled cooked shrimps	Rub the crabmeat or shrimps through a sieve and combine with the butter	As a garnish for cold hors-d'oeuvre, or cold fish, or add to fish sauces
FRUIT BUTTERS:			
Lemon butter	grated rind of ½ lemon salt and black pepper	Combine the grated lemon rind with the butter. Season to taste with salt and pepper	As a garnish for cold hors-d'oeuvre
HERB BUTTERS:			
Chive butter	50 g/2 oz chives	Chop chives finely and pound to a paste. Combine with the butter	Grilled meat or fish
Chivry (ravigote) butter	5 ml/1 teaspoon each chervil, chives, parsley and tarragon 15 ml/1 tablespoon chopped shallot	Wrap the herbs in muslin and blanch* in scalding hot water for 3 minutes. Drain, dip the bag in cold water, drain again, and wring dry. Blanch the shallots and pound, with the herbs, to a paste. Combine with the butter	As a garnish for cold hors-d'oeuvre, or added to white sauces
Maître d'hôtel butter	15 ml/1 tablespoon chopped parsley salt and black pepper lemon juice	Combine the parsley with the butter and season to taste with salt, pepper and a few drops of lemon juice	Grilled meat or fish, boiled vegetables and coated fried fish
Tarragon butter	50 g/2 oz tarragon leaves	Blanch* the tarragon in scalding-hot water, drain and dry. Pound to a paste and combine with the butter	As a garnish for cold hors-d'oeuvre
VEGETABLE BUTTERS:			
Garlic butter	4 cloves garlic	Combine the crushed garlic with the butter	As a garnish for cold hors-d'oeuvre, or added to white sauces
Horseradish butter	60 ml/4 tablespoons grated horseradish	Pound the horseradish until smooth in a mortar, with the butter	As a garnish for cold hors-d'oeuvre, or added to white sauces
Shallot butter	100 g/4 oz shallots	Blanch* the shallots in scalding-hot water and drain thoroughly. Peel and chop them finely. Pound to a paste, then combine with the butter	Grilled meat or fish
MISCELLANEOUS BUTTERS:			
Mustard butter	15 ml/1 tablespoon dry mustard	Beat the dry mustard thoroughly into the softened butter	Grilled meat or fish
Snail butter	15 ml/1 tablespoon chopped shallot 5 ml/1 teaspoon chopped parsley 1 clove garlic salt and black pepper	Chop the shallot and parsley finely. Combine the crushed garlic and herbs with the butter and season with salt and pepper	Stuffed into snail shells

Dripping

This is the rendered fat from beef or mutton. It is sold already rendered down. Dripping from home-cooked meat may also be strained and reserved for roasting and shallow frying.

Lard

This is processed from pure pork fat and is traditionally used for both shallow and deep frying. It can be used in pastries and in some cakes.

Margarine

This fat is made from a blend of oils and fats with emulsifiers, added vitamins and other ingredients. Some margarines are made solely from vegetable fats while others may include fish oils or other fats of animal origin. It is not suitable for frying.

Suet

The fat deposits from the loins and around the kidneys of beef or lamb. It is sold fresh for grating or already shredded and packed. Suet is used in some pastries, in mincemeat, Christmas puddings and stuffings. A vegetarian alternative to suet is readily available; this has the same appearance and texture as animal suet, and gives equally good results.

OILS

Edible oils are liquid forms of fat, derived from fish, vegetables, cereals, fruit, nuts and seeds. Oils vary in colour and flavour, as well as in cooking qualities. Most oils are suitable for frying, and sometimes for baking, but lighter oils or olive oil are usually selected for making mayonnaise and salad dressings.

Cooking in Oil

Fats and oils can be heated to a higher temperature than water before they undergo changes. Water evaporates when heated. When fat is heated to a very high temperature, it becomes more fluid and, eventually, it begins to smoke. When this point is reached, the flavour of the fat changes, becoming bitter or, in some cases, tasting burnt.

Different fats smoke at different temperatures. For deep frying, fats and oils which can be heated to high temperatures without smoking are best. Corn, sunflower and groundnut oils are popular for deep frying. Blended vegetable oils are also commonly used. Olive oil smokes at a lower temperature, so its use in cooking is usually restricted to shallow frying. Some classic methods rely on deep frying in olive oil but these are rare and the distinctive flavour is not usually required.

Vegetable oils (and lard) or oil in combination with butter can be used for shallow frying.

HERBS & SPICES

Herbs and spices are widely used in a variety of ways to flavour sweet and savoury dishes according to the origins of the recipes. There are literally hundreds of varieties and mixtures within each group. So this section is only an introduction to the most commonly used ones. Keep a small supply of spices and selected dried herbs in your kitchen, storing them in a cupboard or darkened glass jars to keep them fresh. Use the herbs and spices up quickly and buy a fresh supply instead of keeping large quantities which will go stale after a few months.

Fresh herbs and dried spices are excellent candidates for the freezer too. Pack washed, dried and chopped herbs in small airtight containers, and place them in a polythene bag. Whole bay leaves and sprigs of woody herbs, such as thyme or savory, also freeze well. Pack ground spices, or spice mixtures, in airtight containers and place them in a tightly closed polythene bag to prevent their aroma tainting other foods in the freezer. Packed in this way, herbs and spices will keep well for up to a year.

HERBS

Fresh – or dried – herbs are much used in cooking to impart flavour to dishes. Certain herbs go particularly well with certain foods and some have a quite distinctive flavour which can be used with a wide variety of ingredients. Fresh herbs should always be used in preference to dried ones if they are available.

Basil Use this herb with oily fish, roast lamb, chicken, duck and goose. Also with tomato dishes and cheese. Fresh basil is far superior to the dried herb which is pungent. Do not chop basil as it quickly loses its flavour. Shred it and add it towards the end of the cooking time.

Bay Use in bouquet garni*; with oily fish, pork, veal, goose and in pâtés and terrines. Also essential in many sauces, stews, soups and spiced dishes. Bay has a very pronounced flavour.

Chervil This aromatic herb is used in soups, with delicate fish and shellfish. Also used in salads and herb butters.

Chives Grass-like herb with rounded blades and a noticeable onion-like flavour. Excellent raw in salads, savoury butters and spreads. Also good in sauces and stuffings. Chive flowers may be added to salads.

Coriander leaves Bright green plant with leaves that look like flat-leafed parsley. Coriander is usually sold in large bunches with the roots on in Indian and Chinese stores. It has a distinct aroma and flavour that complements a wide variety of spiced dishes and curries. The chopped herb is usually sprinkled over cooked dishes or added to mixtures for stuffing Indian breads or making fritters and similar snacks.

Dill Excellent with fish and seafood; also good with lamb and mutton. Used to flavour sauces, salad dressings and mayonnaise. Avoid dried dill which is vastly inferior to the fresh herb.

Fennel This aniseed-flavoured herb can be used with roast lamb and mutton, oily fish and to flavour sauces.

Garlic A widely used flavouring ingredient which is not, strictly speaking, a herb. Used particularly with tomato and shellfish dishes. Much used in stews, dressings and herb butters.

Marjoram Strongly flavoured herb. Ideal with oily fish, also with roast lamb, pork and veal, chicken, duck and partridge. This is a favourite herb addition to tomato dishes and is good with beans and pulses.

Mint Fresh mint sauce is a traditional complement to roast lamb and mutton. Use to flavour peas, new potatoes and carrots. Fresh leaves are used as a garnish with fruit salads and iced tea.

Oregano A strongly flavoured herb, similar to, but with a more pronounced flavour than, marjoram. Excellent with vegetables and pulses as well as with meat and poultry. Dried is a good substitute for the fresh herb.

Parsley The traditional garnish with fish and many soups. Used to flavour sauces and vegetable dishes. A necessary ingredient of bouquet garni* and maître d'hôtel butter (page 307).

There are two distinct types of parsley used in cooking. Curly parsley is dark green, with curly, slightly spiky, leaves and a full flavour. This herb is excellent in stews and soups or wherever a pronounced parsley flavour is required. It is usually chopped fairly finely.

Flat-leafed parsley is similar in appearance to, and often confused with, coriander. It has a more delicate flavour than the curly-leafed variety and is often used in sauces or light dishes. It does not have to be chopped as finely as the curly-leafed variety.

Rosemary A favourite powerful herb with oily fish, and much used to flavour roast lamb, pork, duck and goose. May also be added to casseroled potatoes.

Sage Used in stuffings for pork, chicken and duck. Also used to flavour oily fish, especially eel, and excellent with full-flavoured vegetable dishes or cheese.

Savory Summer savory has a more delicate flavour than winter savory. The winter herb has a stronger flavour and is reminiscent of thyme. Both are used to flavour salads, soups and stews, grilled fish and egg dishes. Summer savory is especially good with broad beans.

Tarragon French tarragon is a full-flavoured, aniseed-like herb; some varieties have little or no flavour, which is worth bearing in mind when buying a plant. This herb is excellent with fish, chicken and eggs and in sauces, salad dressings and mayonnaise.

Thyme One of the traditional components of a bouquet garni. Thyme is a strongly flavoured herb which is widely used in cooking: for soups, sauces, stuffings, in casseroles, with roasts and with vegetables.

SPICES

The majority of spices are used in a dried form, either whole or ground. They are usually cooked with food, or before adding to food. Spices should be used to enhance the flavour of food, or to marry with the food in a well-balanced dish; they should not entirely mask the main ingredients of a dish.

Allspice Also known as Jamaican pepper, the flavour of allspice resembles a combination of nutmeg, cinnamon and cloves. It is used in sweet cooking and pickling as well as in some savoury dishes. The whole spice is similar in size to peppercorns, but darker in colour.

Aniseed Dark seeds with a strong flavour. Used in Chinese cooking, this is also one of the spices making up five-spice powder.

Caraway These small, curved and striped seeds have a strong flavour. Caraway complements pork, lamb and cabbage. It is also used in baking to flavour cakes, biscuits and crackers.

Cardamom There are three types of cardamom: green, white and black. Green and white cardamoms are small pear-shaped pods with slight ridges. The white pods are a bleached form of the green spice. Used in savoury and sweet cooking, primarily in Indian dishes, they contribute a fresh, lemon-eucalyptus flavour. The whole pods may be used or the tiny black seeds scraped out from them. The seeds may be ground to a fine powder. Black cardamoms are large and hairy with a coarse flavour. They are used only in savoury dishes, such as meat curries.

Cayenne pepper This is one of the hottest of chillies in a dried and ground form and it should be used sparingly. Cayenne is a useful seasoning for pepping up cheese dishes and other savouries.

Chillies One of the spices used fresh as well as dried and ground to a powder. There are many types of chilli, from large, mild, peppery vegetables to small fiery spices. The standard green and red chillies sold fresh are hot, but are not usually the most fiery. They may be used raw as well as cooked. Small dried red chillies are usually added whole during cooking. They are very hot.

When handling fresh chillies, discard the stem and cut out all the seeds, which are especially hot. Rinse the chillies and chop or slice them. Always wash your hands thoroughly after handling chillies, as their juices are a severe irritant to skin and will cause burning to any tender areas. Never touch your eyes after handling chillies.

Chilli powder This is dried and ground chillies. The strength of chilli powder varies; the majority are hot, there are some very hot powders and mild chilli powder is also available.

Cinnamon Bark (cassia), sticks and ground are available. Used in savoury and sweet cooking. The loose pieces of bark are not as good quality as the rolled sticks and do not give as much flavour.

Cloves Small dark buds with a strong, fresh flavour. Used in savoury and sweet cooking, to mull drinks and flavour pickles. Ground cloves make a strong spice which should be used sparingly. Especially good with apples in pies.

Coriander Small round pale seeds about the size of peppercorns. A sweet, strong flavour useful in savoury cooking and pickling. The seeds are used whole, crushed or ground.

Cumin Small slim seeds of a pale colour. Black cumin seeds are smaller. Used whole or ground in savoury cooking, especially in Indian rice or vegetable dishes.

Curry powder A mixture of spices devised to flavour curried dishes. Authentically, each cook would roast and grind a selection of spices for any one particular dish. The quality of curry powders varies enormously, and some of the better products are useful for savoury cooking if not for preparing authentic curries.

Fennel Small pale curved seeds with a mild aniseed flavour. This spice goes well with vegetables, lamb and pork.

Fenugreek This makes up a major component in the flavouring of some curries. The seeds look like tiny stones and they are extremely hard. They should be used ground rather than whole; as they are difficult to grind, buy the spice ready ground. A strong spice which can make a dish bitter if used too generously.

Five-spice A Chinese powder with a strong flavour. Star anise, cloves, cinnamon, peppercorns and fennel are the spices ground into the powder. Especially good with duck, but also used with steamed fish. Use with care until the flavour is familiar.

Garam masala An Indian spice mixture consisting of a combination of whole spices, roasted together and then ground to a powder. Usually including cinnamon, cumin, coriander, cloves, cardamom and a bay leaf. Authentically, the spice mixture would vary according to the requirements of the dish and the cook. It is a mild spice and, because it has been roasted, it is one which may be sprinkled over food just before serving.

Ginger Fresh root, dried root, ground, Chinese pickled, crystallised stem ginger, candied chopped ginger and stem ginger preserved in syrup are all readily available. Ginger is widely used in savoury and sweet cooking all over the world. When buying fresh ginger look for plump, thin-skinned roots and avoid any wrinkled or soft ones. Ginger has a peppery, fresh flavour and it can be quite hot when used in quantity, particularly in the ground form.

Juniper berries Small, dark, glossy berries which are slightly larger than peppercorns. They are pliable rather than hard and easily crushed in a mortar with a pestle. Used sparingly to flavour pâtés, game and meat. Juniper is the spice which flavours gin.

Mace The outer covering of the nutmeg, this orange, net-like spice is used whole or ground. The whole piece is referred to as a blade of mace. Useful in savoury cooking, the blade may be added to boiling water for meats, while the ground spice is useful for pâtés, stews and for flavouring sausagemeat.

Mustard There are many types of mustard seeds as well as various forms of the ground powder. Used in savoury cooking, the whole dark seeds are not as hot as the English, ground yellow powder would suggest. Mustard powder is mixed to a paste with water, vinegar or a mixture of both and allowed to stand for about 15 minutes before being used. Various other flavourings may be added, including wine, beer, brandy, other spices, horseradish or herbs, such as chives. Mustard seeds are used with vegetables in Indian cooking and in pickling; the powder is especially useful as a seasoning for cheese dishes.

Nutmeg A large oval spice best used freshly grated, but also available ground, in which form it. is useful when measured in large amounts for cake-making and other baking. Nutmeg is one of the sweet spices, and one of the few which may be sprinkled over food as a final seasoning just before serving.

Paprika Dried and ground sweet peppers. Paprika is best known as a flavouring for the Hungarian stew, goulash; it is also useful with cheese dishes, and it may be sprinkled over food as a final seasoning just before serving.

Saffron This is one of the most expensive and highly prized spices, but the quality varies enormously. Ground or in strands, saffron gives a delicate but distinct flavour and yellow colour to savoury and sweet dishes. It may be used to marinate* some foods or be added towards the end of cooking, for example, to savoury rice dishes. The powdered form can be sprinkled directly into the food; saffron strands must be pounded in a mortar and dissolved in a little boiling water before adding to a dish.

Turmeric A bright yellow spice with a peppery flavour, usually used in the powdered form for savoury cooking. The dried root is sometimes available and the fresh root, which resembles ginger in appearance but with a finer texture and bright yellow colour, is occasionally available from ethnic stores. A main spice for flavouring piccalilli.

Vanilla This is another highly prized spice. It is in the same price bracket as saffron, but is used in sweet cooking. Vanilla is extracted from a long, dried seed pod. The pod looks black in colour with a crystal deposit on it which actually contributes the vanilla flavour. The whole pod may be added to a jar of sugar and allowed to infuse for several weeks to make vanilla sugar. Infusing the pod in milk is another method of extracting the vanilla flavour.

Liquid vanilla flavouring is the more common form of the spice, but the quality varies immensely. Use only natural vanilla flavouring and avoid the intense, artificial essence which is synthetic and not an extract from the true spice. Always check the label, as the synthetic flavouring is vastly inferior and infinitely stronger in flavour.

STOCKS & SOUPS

There are six basic stocks: brown (or household stock), white, fish, chicken, vegetable and game stock. Brown stock or chicken stock can be used for most soups, although fish, vegetable and game soups all gain in flavour when prepared with their own type of stock.

Fresh bones and meat are essential ingredients for brown, white and chicken stocks. Use marrow bone and shin of beef for brown stock, and knuckle of veal for a white stock and ask the butcher to chop the bones into manageable pieces. The chopped bones release gelatine while cooking, which gives body to the stock.

A meaty carcass from a roast chicken can be used to make stock but the best flavour is obtained by using the carcass from a boned raw bird or by boiling a whole fowl, or a portion of a chicken.

Vegetables give additional flavour, but avoid potatoes which make the stock cloudy. Strong-flavoured vegetables, such as turnips, swedes and parsnips, should be used sparingly.

There are an enormous number of classic and international soups which all fall into two distinct categories, according to their consistency: thin soups and thick soups. Thin soups are again divided into consommés and broths; and thick soups into puréed and cream soups. Thick soups also include classic velouté soups which are based on a velouté sauce, but these are seldom made today.

Chicken Stock

MAKES: 1.7 litres/3 pt
PREPARATION: 20 minutes
COOKING: 2 hours

carcass from boning 1 uncooked
    chicken or 1 meaty carcass
    from roast chicken or 1
    chicken quarter
1 onion
2 carrots
2 sticks celery
bouquet garni*
salt
10 black peppercorns
2 litres/3½ pt water

Chop or break the chicken car-cass into pieces so that it fits in a large saucepan. Alternatively, chop the chicken quarter into two small portions. Peel and slice the onion, peel or scrub and slice the carrots, and scrub and slice the celery. Add the prepared vegetables to the pan with the bouquet garni. Sprinkle in a little salt and add the peppercorns.

Pour in the water which should cover the bones. Bring to the boil, skimming any scum off the surface. Allow the stock to boil for 2 minutes and continue removing scum that rises to the surface. Reduce the heat, cover and simmer for about 2 hours. Cool the stock before straining it through a fine sieve or muslin.

Brown Stock

MAKES: 3.4 litres/6 pt
PREPARATION: 20 minutes
OVEN: 220°C/425°F/gas 7
COOKING: 5 hours

450 g/1 lb marrow bones
900 g–1.4 kg/2–3 lb shin of beef
40 g/1½ oz butter or dripping
1–2 leeks
1 large onion
1–2 sticks celery
225 g/8 oz carrots
2 bouquets garnis*
salt and black peppercorns

Blanch* the bones for 10 min-utes in boiling water, then put them, with the chopped meat and butter or dripping, in a roasting tin. Brown the bones in a preheated oven at 220°C/425°F/gas 7 for 30–40 minutes.

Turn them over occasionally to brown them evenly. Put the roasted bones in a large pan, add the cleaned and sliced vegetables, bouquets garnis and peppercorns. Cover with cold water, to which 2.5 ml/½ tea-spoon salt has been added.

Bring the contents slowly to boiling point, remove any scum from the surface and cover the pan with a tight-fitting lid. Simmer the stock over the lowest possible heat for about 4 hours to extract all the flavour from the bones. Top up with hot water if the level of the liquid should fall below the other ingredients.

Strain the stock through a fine sieve or muslin, into a large bowl. Leave the stock to settle for a few minutes, then remove the fat from the surface by drawing absorbent kitchen paper over it. If the stock is not needed immediately, leave the fat to settle in a surface layer which can then be easily lifted off.

Once the fat has been re-moved from the stock, correct seasoning if necessary.

White Stock

This is made like brown stock, but the blanched veal bones are not browned. Place all the in-gredients in a large pan of water and proceed as for brown stock.

Game Stock

The ingredients for this stock can be the carcass of a game bird, together with the scalded feet of the bird, and the cleaned giblets. Cook as for brown stock, sim-mering for 2–3 hours. Strain and remove the fat.

Fish Stock

The basis for this stock is bones and trimmings, such as the head and the skin. White fish such as cod, haddock, halibut, whiting and plaice can all be used.

MAKES: 600 ml/1 pt
PREPARATION: 10 minutes
COOKING: 30 minutes

450 g/1 lb fish trimmings
600 ml/1 pt water
salt
1 onion
bouquet garni* or 1 large leek
    and 1 stick celery

Wash the trimmings thoroughly in cold water and put them into a large pan, with the lightly salted water. Bring to the boil over low heat and remove any scum from the surface. Meanwhile, peel and finely chop the onion and add to the stock with the bouquet garni or the cleaned and chopped leek and celery. Cover the pan with a lid and simmer over low heat for 30 minutes. Strain the stock through a sieve or muslin. Store, covered, in the refrigerator.

Fish stock does not keep well and should preferably be used on the day it is made.

Vegetable Stock

Uncooked vegetables are used for this stock. For a lightly flavoured stock, care should be taken in the selection of ingredients, avoiding using large quantities of cabbage or other strongly flavoured ingredients. Swede, parsnips and cauliflower will all impart their distinct flavour to the stock, so they should be used with care. Leafy green veget-ables, such as spinach, will also colour the stock. Onion, carrot and celery should make up the basic ingredients. A vegetable stock may also include the outer leaves of cabbage, lettuce and other greens, cauliflower stalks and parsnips.

Chop the vegetables and/or trimmings roughly. Heat the minimum of butter or oil in a large pan. Add the vegetables and cover the pan. Sweat the vegetables for about 10 minutes, shaking the pan occasionally. Pour in water to cover the vegetables and add a little salt. Cover and bring just to the boil. Simmer the stock over low heat for about 45 minutes. A bouquet garni* and 6–8 peppercorns may be added for extra flavour. Strain the stock through muslin.

Cooking Stock in a Pressure Cooker

Place the stock ingredients, with lightly salted water, in the pressure cooker – it must not be more than two-thirds full. Bring to the boil and remove the scum from the surface before fixing the lid. Lower the heat and bring to 15 lb pressure. Reduce the heat quickly and cook steadily for 1 hour. Strain the stock and remove the fat.

Storing Stocks

If not required for immediate use, store prepared stocks in the refrigerator. After the fat has been removed, pour the cooled stock into a container and cover with a lid. It should be used within 2 days.

Freezing Stocks

Stocks can be satisfactorily stored in a freezer, where they will keep for 3–6 months. Boil the prepared stock over high heat to reduce it by half. Pour the concentrated cooled stock into ice-cube trays, freeze quickly and transfer the stock cubes to polythene bags. Alternatively, pour the stock into 300 ml/½ pt or 600 ml/1 pt freezing containers, leaving a 2.5 cm/1 in space at the top.

To use frozen stock, leave it to thaw at room temperature, or simply turn it into a saucepan and heat over low heat, stirring occasionally. Add water to thin down concentrated stock.

Ready-made Stocks

Many ready-made stock preparations are available. The best alternatives to home-made stocks are chilled commercial stocks. The most common form of commercial stock is a cube. Bouillon cubes, meat extracts, and meat-and-vegetable extracts vary enormously in quality. On the whole, they are highly seasoned and over-flavoured with herbs and spices which can dominate any soup or sauce in which they are used. They also lack body and jelling qualities. Stock cubes should always be regarded as an emergency ingredient and should be used with care in everyday cooking.

THIN SOUPS
Consommés

A consommé is a clear soup made from meat, poultry, fish or vegetables and clarified stock. The basic stock must be accentuated by the main ingredient, so that a beef consommé is made from brown stock and lean beef, a chicken consommé from chicken stock and chicken flesh. Consommés may be served hot or chilled as a jellied soup.

Beef Consommé

SERVES: 6
PREPARATION: 15 minutes
COOKING: 1½–2 hours

225 g/8 oz lean beef
1 small carrot
1 small onion or leek
1.7 litres/3 pt brown stock
bouquet garni*
salt and black pepper
1 egg white

Shred the meat finely, and peel and chop the vegetables. Put all

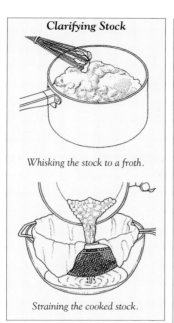

Clarifying Stock

Whisking the stock to a froth.

Straining the cooked stock.

the ingredients into a large pan, adding the egg white last. Heat gently, whisking continuously with a wire whisk, until a thick froth forms on the surface. Stop whisking, reduce the heat immediately and simmer the beef consommé very slowly for 1½–2 hours. Do not let the liquid reach boiling point, as the foam layer will break up and cloud the consommé.

Strain the consommé into a bowl through a double layer of muslin, or a scalded jelly bag. Strain the consommé again through the egg foam in the muslin – it should now be perfectly clear and sparkling.

Reheat, taste for seasoning and serve hot or cold.

Clarifying Stock

Strain the cooked stock into a clean pan and check the seasoning. For a crystal clear aspic, all utensils should be washed, then scalded. Line a metal sieve with muslin and place it over a clean bowl. For about 600 ml/1 pt stock, whisk 2 egg whites and their crushed shells into the stock over low heat until frothy. Stop whisking and heat gently until a crust forms on the stock. Bring to the boil, then reduce heat or remove the pan from heat immediately the crust rises. Allow to subside, then repeat once or twice. Strain through the muslin-lined sieve.

Aspic Jelly

Aspic is a clear stock that is set with gelatine.

Sprinkle 15 ml/3 teaspoons gelatine over 600 ml/1 pt hot stock and stir until dissolved, standing the bowl over a pan of hot water if necessary.

For coating purposes, allow the jelly to set to the consistency of unbeaten egg white, then place the item to be coated on a wire rack over a plate or baking tray. Spoon over the jelly until an even layer adheres. Leave until set, and repeat if necessary. Dip pieces of garnish – such as tarragon, carrot, olives or truffle slices – in a little cool, but liquid, aspic before setting them in position. When set, glaze with more aspic. For chopped aspic turn the jelly on to a piece of wet greaseproof paper and chop it up with a wet knife.

Broths

These semi-clear soups are easy to make and consist of uncleared brown or white stock with added meat, vegetables, rice or barley. Broths are often a by-product of the main course, pot-au-feu being a classic example.

Scotch Broth

This broth is a nourishing, easily prepared soup which is a complete meal in itself.

SERVES: 8
PREPARATION: 25 minutes
COOKING: 2½–3 hours

450 g/1 lb flank of mutton or scrag end or middle neck of lamb
3.4 litres/6 pt water
50 g/2 oz pearl barley
2 onions
225 g/8 oz carrots
225 g/8 oz turnips
3 leeks
salt and black pepper
finely chopped parsley

Ask the butcher to chop the mutton or lamb into small pieces. Put the meat into a large pot with the water. Bring to the boil and remove any scum from the surface. Reduce the heat, add the pearl barley and simmer for 20–30 minutes.

Meanwhile peel and finely chop the onions, carrots and turnips. Trim and thoroughly wash the leeks, then cut them into thin rounds. Add all the vegetables to the pot, with 5 ml/ 1 teaspoon salt and several grinds of pepper. Cover the pot and simmer for 2 hours. Lift out the bones, strip off as much meat as possible and stir this back into the broth. Adjust the seasoning to taste and serve the Scotch broth sprinkled with finely chopped parsley.

Pot-au-feu

SERVES: 6–8
PREPARATION: 20 minutes
COOKING: 2½ hours

900 g/2 lb topside of beef
2.9 litres/5 pt brown stock
2 large carrots
1 turnip
2 large onions
2–3 leeks
1 stick celery
1 small cabbage
1 set of chicken giblets (optional)

Tie the meat firmly with string to keep its shape during cooking. Put it in a large deep pan or casserole and add the cold stock. Cover the pan with a lid and bring the stock slowly to boiling point. Remove any scum.

Meanwhile, peel the carrots, turnip and onions and cut them into even chunks. Remove the roots and outer coarse leaves from the leeks and cut the white part into rounds. Clean and roughly chop the celery, wash and quarter the cabbage. Add all the vegetables, except the cabbage, to the pan and simmer gently for 1½ hours. Add the cleaned chicken giblets, if used, continue simmering for another 30 minutes before adding the cabbage. Cook until the cabbage is tender, about 15–20 minutes.

Lift out the cooked meat and vegetables, and keep them hot on a serving dish. Remove the string from the beef and carve the meat into slices.

■ Serve the broth first with the vegetables, followed by the meat served with boiled potatoes and Horseradish Sauce (page 357).

THICK SOUPS

This group includes puréed soups which are thickened with starchy ingredients, such as flour, cereals, pulses and potatoes. Cream soups are thickened or enriched with butter, cream and/or egg yolks.

The thickening agents, which are known as liaisons, also enrich the texture of a soup and change its colour. Liaisons must be added in correct proportions to the liquid, otherwise the soup may curdle or become too starchy.

LIAISON TO LIQUIDS	
7–15 g/¼–½ oz flour	600 ml/1 pt liquid (for purées rich in starch)
15–25 g/½–1 oz flour	600 ml/1 pt liquid (for purées with little starch)
1–2 egg yolks	600 ml/1 pt liquid
150 ml/¼ pt single cream	600 ml/1 pt liquid

Puréed Soups

These soups are usually made from vegetables but can also be prepared from meat, poultry, game, fish and even fruit.

A purée made from starchy vegetables, such as dried peas, split peas, haricot and butter beans, or potatoes, will produce a thick soup that needs little or no additional starch. It can be adjusted to soup consistency by adding stock or water. A thin purée made from spinach or watercress will need thickening with flour, or potatoes may be cooked with the soup to thicken it. This also prevents the purée from sinking to the bottom. Mix the correct liaison of flour with a little hot soup, then stir it back into the soup, and bring to boiling point over gentle heat.

Making puréed soups

Sieving the cooked vegetables.

Scraping the purée off the sieve.

Soup can be puréed by rubbing it through a fine sieve or it may be puréed in a liquidiser. A food processor does not give as smooth a result as a liquidiser. Sometimes the puréed soup may be rubbed through a sieve to remove traces of skins or seeds.

Potato Soup

SERVES: 4–6
PREPARATION: 20 minutes
COOKING: 20 minutes

2 leeks
450 g/1 lb potatoes
40 g/1½ oz butter
1.12 litres/2 pt white stock
salt and black pepper

Wash and finely chop the leeks and peel and roughly chop the potatoes. Cook the leeks in 25 g/1 oz of the butter in a large pan until soft, but not coloured. Add the potatoes, and pour over the stock; season lightly with salt and black pepper. Bring the ingredients to the boil, cover with a lid and simmer until the potatoes are quite tender.

Remove the soup from the heat and leave it to cool slightly. Rub the soup through a sieve or purée in a liquidiser, a little at a time. Reheat the puréed soup over low heat, adjust seasoning and stir in the remaining butter.

Cream Soups

These thick soups are a puréed soup thickened with flour or starchy ingredients and enriched with cream, egg yolks or both.

Most cream soups are based on a vegetable purée, but chicken or fish can also be used as the main ingredient. A Béchamel Sauce (page 353) can be used as a base for thickening a broth or thin purée. For creamed chicken soup, the meat is cooked separately in white stock. It is then minced finely, added to a Béchamel sauce and thinned down, if necessary, with stock to the required consistency.

Cream soups take little time to prepare and are excellent for storing in a freezer.

Care is required when thickening with cream or egg yolks to make sure the soup does not curdle. Put the cream or yolks into a small bowl and beat in a little hot soup until the liaison has the same temperature as the soup. Blend the liaison slowly into the soup, stirring all the

Enriching soup with cream or egg yolks

Ladle a little of the hot soup into a bowl of cream or egg yolks.

time, but do not let the soup reach boiling point. The soup can also be reheated in the top of a double saucepan.

Cream of Vegetable Soup

SERVES: 4
PREPARATION: 20 minutes
COOKING: 25 minutes

450 g/1 lb mixed vegetables (such as carrots, celery, leeks and cabbage)
1 onion
25 g/1 oz butter or 15 ml/ 1 tablespoon oil
600 ml/1 pt Béchamel Sauce (page 353)
300–450 ml/½–¾ pt milk
salt and black pepper
150 ml/¼ pt single cream

Peel or scrape and wash the vegetables before chopping them finely. Peel and chop the onion.

Melt the butter or heat the oil in a heavy-based pan, add the onion and cook for 10 minutes, stirring occasionally. Add all the remaining vegetables and stir well. Cover the pan and cook the vegetables for 15 minutes, until they are tender. Stir in the Béchamel sauce and cook gently for 15 minutes.

Rub the thick vegetable mixture through a sieve or purée in a liquidiser. Reheat the soup without boiling, over low heat, thinning with milk to the desired consistency. Correct seasoning, stir in the cream and serve.

SOUP GARNISHES AND ACCOMPANIMENTS

Garnishes are added to soups either as an embellishment to improve the flavour or to provide a contrasting texture.

Consommé julienne Garnished with julienne (narrow) strips of carrot, celery, leek and turnip. These strips are boiled until tender in lightly salted water, then rinsed in cold water and added to hot consommé just before serving.

Consommé royale A garnish of firm savoury egg custard cut into tiny fancy shapes. Beat 1 egg with 15 ml/1 tablespoon of cleared stock and pour into a small bowl or dariole* moulds. Bake the moulds in a pan of water in a preheated oven at 180°C/350°F/gas 4 for 20 minutes or until firm.

Pasta Used to garnish thin soups. Macaroni, tagliatelle and spaghetti can be broken into short pieces and added to soups for the last 20 minutes of cooking. Tiny soup pasta shapes can be used instead and added for the last 10–20 minutes, according to the instructions on the packet. For hot consommés, cook the pasta separately so that the starch will not cloud the soup.

Thin slices of lemon or orange An excellent garnish for clear soups and tomato soup.

Vegetable and fruit garnishes These add colour to plain cream soups. Celery leaves, watercress and parsley should be trimmed and washed before floating them on top of the soup.

Thinly sliced mushrooms These lend extra texture and flavour to cream soups. Fry the mushroom slices in butter until they are soft, but not coloured. Drain before spooning over the soup.

Cucumber Cut into julienne strips as a garnish for chilled soups. For hot soups fry cucumber strips, or thin rounds of leeks, in a little butter.

Thin onion rings These add more flavour to soups. They can be fried like cucumber strips and leek rounds; alternatively, coat them in milk and flour, and deep fry them until crisp and golden.

Croûtons A classic garnish for thick soups. Remove the crusts from 1 cm/½ in thick slices of white bread; cut the slices into 1 cm/½ in cubes and toast or fry them in a little butter until crisp and golden.

Cheese This makes a pleasant accompaniment to most vegetable soups. Choose a well-flavoured hard cheese, and serve it finely grated in a separate dish.

Dumplings These are ideal for turning a meat or vegetable soup into a substantial family meal. Mix 100 g/4 oz self-raising flour with 50 g/2 oz shredded suet and a sprinkling of salt and pepper. Bind the mixture with sufficient cold water to make a soft dough. Shape the dough into 16 balls

and drop them into the simmering soup for the last 15–20 minutes of cooking.

Melba toast This soup accompaniment is simple and quick to make. Toast thin slices of white bread, cut off their crusts and quickly slice them through the middle. Toast the uncooked surfaces under a hot grill until they are crisp and curling. Alternatively, bake the slices.

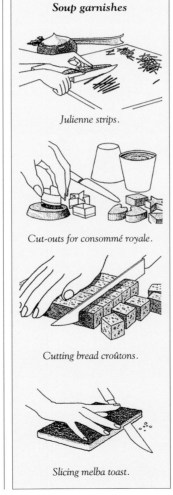

Soup garnishes

Julienne strips.

Cut-outs for consommé royale.

Cutting bread croûtons.

Slicing melba toast.

FISH, SHELLFISH & SEAFOOD

Fish are sold fresh, frozen, smoked, canned, pickled or salted. Flat fish, such as plaice, are sold whole, filleted, or, in the case of larger fish, as steaks; round fish, such as cod, haddock and hake, are also sold as steaks and cutlets. Many shellfish are sold boiled and prepared. The exceptions are oysters which must be bought live.

Cook fish within 24 hours of purchasing it. Allow 200–225 g/ 7–8 oz per person for a main course, or one good-sized fillet, steak or cutlet. A medium-sized mackerel or trout will serve one person.

STORAGE AND PREPARATION

Preparation of fish for cooking includes scaling, cleaning, skinning and sometimes filleting. Fishmongers will usually clean and fillet whole fish ready for cooking. But if this has not been done, a few simple preparations are necessary.

Storing Fish

Unwrap and prepare the fish, if necessary, as soon as possible after purchase. Place the fish in an airtight container, such as a polythene bag or plate covered with cling film, in the refrigerator and cook within 24 hours.

Scaling

Cover a board with several sheets of greaseproof paper. Lay the fish on the paper and, holding it by the tail, scrape away the scales from the tail towards the head, using the blunt edge of a knife. Rinse the scales off under cold water. Alternatively, scrape off the scales directly into the sink, under gently running water. The

fish can also be cooked without removing the scales, and skinned before serving.

Cleaning

Once scaled, the fish must be cleaned, or gutted. This process is determined by the shape of the fish – in round fish the entrails lie in the belly, in flat fish in a cavity behind the head. Work on a board covered with several sheets of greaseproof paper.

Round fish (cod, herring, mackerel, trout, for example) Slit the fish, with a sharp knife, along the belly from behind the gills to just above the tail. Scrape out the cavity and discard the entrails. Rinse the fish under cold running water and, with a little salt, gently rub away any black skin inside the cavity.

The head and tail may be left on but the eyes should be taken out. Use a sharp knife or scissors to cut off the lower fins on either side of the body and the gills below the head. Alternatively, cut the head off just below the gills and slice off the tail.

313

Cleaning round fish

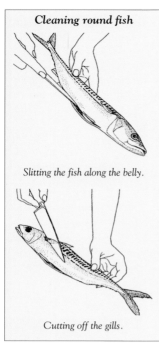

Slitting the fish along the belly.

Cutting off the gills.

Cleaning flat fish

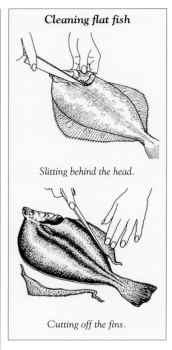

Slitting behind the head.

Cutting off the fins.

Skinning round fish

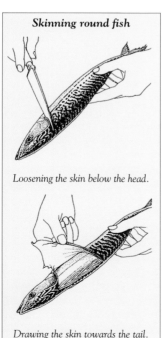

Loosening the skin below the head.

Drawing the skin towards the tail.

Skinning flat fish

Slitting the skin above the tail.

Drawing the skin towards the head.

Small round fish, such as smelts, sardines and sprats, need less preparation. Cut off the heads below the gills, leaving the tails intact. Squeeze out the entrails.

Fresh eels are sold live; the fishmonger will cut off the heads and skin the fish. Otherwise, loosen the skin at the head with the tip of a knife. Grip the skin in a rough cloth and peel it down and over the tail. Cut the skinned eel into pieces and rinse in cold water to remove blood.

Flat fish (plaice or sole, for example) Make a semi-circular slit just behind the head, on the dark skin side. This opens up the cavity which contains the entrails. Scrape these out and wash the fish. Cut off the fins, and cook the fish whole.

Skinning
Again, the method varies according to the type of fish.

Round fish These are usually cooked with the skin on, but it is also possible to remove the skin before cooking. Using a sharp knife, loosen the skin round the head and then gently draw it down towards the tail. Cut it off. Repeat on the other side.

Flat fish Lay the fish, dark skin uppermost, on the board. Make a slit across the skin just above the tail. Slip the point of the knife under the edge of the skin to loosen it, or do this with your thumb. Holding the fish firmly by the tail, pull the skin quickly towards the head (dip the fingers in a little salt to get a better grip), and cut it off. The white skin on the other side may be removed in the same way.

Filleting and Boning
The fish can now be filleted, boned and cut into serving portions. Fillets of both round and flat fish provide a solid piece of fish without bones.

Filleting round fish To fillet a large fish, such as salmon or haddock, cut the head off the cleaned fish, and cut along the backbone, towards the tail. Insert the knife at a slight angle to the bone and, keeping the sharp edge towards the tail, gently ease the flesh away from the bone with slicing movements.

Continue cutting in line with the backbone, until the whole fillet is freed. Open out the fish and cut off the fillet at the tail. With the tip of the knife, ease off the backbone to reveal the other fillet, and cut off the tail. If the fish is large, the fillets can be cut into serving-size portions.

Boning small round fish To bone a cleaned mackerel or herring, cut off the head and fins; the tail may also be removed. Open out the split fish and spread it flat, skin side up. Press firmly along the centre back of the fish to loosen the backbone, then turn the fish over. Starting at the head, ease away the backbone with the tip of the knife, removing at the same time as many of the small bones as possible. The fish can now be folded back into its original shape or cut into two long fillets.

Steaks and cutlets Large round fish are often sold in thick cutlets, from the middle of the fish, or as steaks, from the tail end. The small central bone is

Cutting a round fish into two fillets

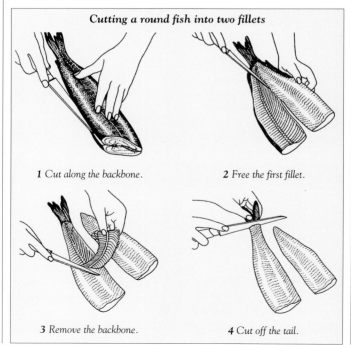

1 Cut along the backbone.

2 Free the first fillet.

3 Remove the backbone.

4 Cut off the tail.

Boning a herring

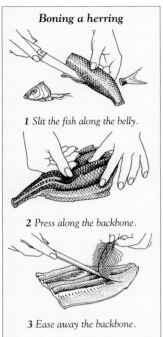

1 *Slit the fish along the belly.*

2 *Press along the backbone.*

3 *Ease away the backbone.*

Removing the four fillets from a flat fish

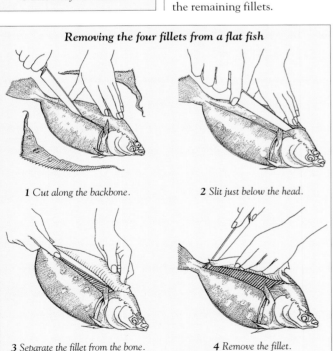

1 *Cut along the backbone.*

2 *Slit just below the head.*

3 *Separate the fillet from the bone.*

4 *Remove the fillet.*

best removed after cooking. If the bone is removed before cooking, the centre should be stuffed. **Filleting flat fish** A large sole or plaice will yield four small fillets, two from each side. Lay the fish, dark side up, on the board and with a sharp knife cut off the fins. Make the first cut along the backbone, working from the head towards the tail. Then make a semi-circular cut, just below the head, through half the thickness of the fish. Slant the knife against the backbone, and with short strokes of the knife separate the left-hand fillet from the bone. Make a thick cut just above the tail and remove the fillet. Turn the fish round and remove the right-hand fillet in the same way. Turn the fish over and remove the remaining fillets.

COOKING METHODS

A number of basic cooking methods are suitable for all fish whether they are whole, filleted or cut into steaks. But whatever cooking method is chosen, fish must not be overcooked. Prolonged cooking time and too fierce a temperature destroy the texture and flavour.

Frying

Frying is suitable for steaks and fillets of cod, haddock, hake and eel and for small whole fish such as herrings, mackerel, sprats, whitebait and trout. The fish may be shallow or deep fried.

It is especially important that the delicate flesh of fish is protected by a coating before it is fried. Flour seasoned with salt and pepper, egg and breadcrumb coating and batter (page 305) are the usual coatings.

Shallow frying (eels, herrings, mackerel, mullet, plaice, sole, trout, sprats) Coat the prepared fish in seasoned flour or dip them first in lightly beaten egg, then in dry breadcrumbs, shaking off any surplus. Heat an equal amount of butter and cooking oil in a frying pan over moderate heat. Put in the fish and fry until brown on one side; turn it over with a fish slice. Allow about 10 minutes frying depending on the thickness of the fish. Remove from the frying pan and drain on absorbent kitchen paper.

Deep frying (fillets, smelts, sprats, sardines, whitebait) A deep pan, ideally one fitted with a wire basket, is essential. The frying medium is oil. Olive oil imparts its distinct flavour, but a good-quality vegetable oil is usually used. The deep fryer should be no more than half-filled with oil and heated over moderate heat to 190°C/375°F. A cooking thermometer will give the accurate temperature; if this is not available, test by frying a 2.5 cm/1 in cube of day-old bread in the hot oil. If the cube of bread browns in 60 seconds the oil has reached the correct temperature.

Grilling

This quick cooking method is suitable for small whole fish, round or flat, and fillets, cutlets and steaks. Whole fish should be scored with three or four diagonal cuts on each side of the body. This allows the heat to penetrate more evenly and prevent the fish splitting.

Brush white fish, such as plaice or sole, with melted butter or oil, and sprinkle them with lemon juice or a little finely chopped onion. Baste two or three times during grilling.

Grill all fish under a preheated grill at moderate heat. Allow 4–5 minutes for fillets, and 10–15 minutes for thick steaks, cutlets and whole fish. The fish is cooked when the flesh flakes easily when tested with a knife.

During grilling, whole fish and thick steaks should be turned over once to ensure that both sides are evenly cooked. Thin steaks and fillets need to be cooked on one side only.

Baking

This method is suitable for small whole fish and for individual cuts, such as fillets and steaks.

Fish is usually baked in a covered dish to retain moisture. Alternatively, the fish should be basted frequently during baking or covered with streaky bacon rashers to provide fat and prevent the surface of the fish from drying out.

Brush the prepared fish with melted butter and season with lemon juice, salt and freshly ground pepper. Make three or four diagonal score marks on each side of whole round fish so that they will keep their shape. Lay the fish in a well-buttered, shallow ovenproof dish. Bake in a preheated oven at 180°C/350°F/gas 4, allowing 25–30 minutes for whole fish and 10–20 minutes for fillets and steaks.

Baking in foil Baking can also be done in foil, which is excellent for sealing-in both flavour and aroma. Place the prepared fish on buttered foil and sprinkle with lemon juice, salt and pepper. Wrap the foil loosely over the fish, place in a baking tin, and cook in a preheated oven at 180°C/350°F/gas 4. Allow 20 minutes for steaks, and about 8 minutes per 450 g/1 lb for large fish plus 10 minutes extra in all.

Baking en papillote This term is used for fish (or any other food) cooked in paper; it is also sometimes used when a foil casing is applied. Brush greaseproof paper or non-stick parchment with melted butter or oil. Place the fish on the paper and sprinkle with salt and pepper. Wrap the paper loosely around the fish and fold the edges together to close the packet. Bake the fish as when wrapped in foil (above).

Stuffed fish Before baking, fish may be stuffed with a filling of fine breadcrumbs seasoned with salt, pepper, herbs or parsley and bound with a little melted butter. Spoon the filling loosely into the cavity, as it tends to swell during cooking. Close the opening on round fish with cocktail sticks.

Whole flat fish have only small cavities which must be opened up to allow room for stuffing. To do this, make an incision down the centre of the back. Ease the flesh from the backbone on either side, as far as the fins, with the knife blade to form a cavity and loosely stuff this. Leave the pocket open.

For individual stuffed fish fillets, spread the mixture over the fish, roll it up and secure with wooden skewers.

Poaching

This is ideal for all types of fish, whether whole, filleted or cut into steaks. Poaching, or slow simmering in liquid, can be done in a large saucepan or fish kettle on top of the stove, or in a shallow covered dish in a preheated oven at 180°C/ 350°F/ gas 4. For easy removal, tie fish loosely in muslin.

Cover the fish completely with lightly salted water (7.5 ml/ 1½ teaspoons salt to 1.12 litres/ 2 pt water). Add to the pan a few parsley or mushroom stalks, a good squeeze of lemon juice, a slice of onion and a slice of carrot, together with a bay leaf and 6 black peppercorns.

Heat the liquid gently until it is just about to boil, then cover the pan and lower the heat so that the liquid simmers gently. Simmer the fish until it flakes when tested with a fork, allowing 8–10 minutes per 450 g/1 lb. Lift out the cooked fish with a perforated spoon, and use the poaching liquid as the base for making a sauce.

Wine, a mixture of wine and water, milk, or milk and water, may be used instead of water. Small portions of fish do not have to be completely submerged in liquid during poaching. Lightly seasoned cooking liquid can be used to make a sauce to be served with the fish.

Whole fish, such as salmon, trout and salmon trout, are often poached in a classic preparation known as a court bouillon.

Court bouillon is discarded after cooking and should not be confused with stock.

Court Bouillon

MAKES: 1.12 litres/2 pt
PREPARATION: 15 minutes
COOKING: 20 minutes

2 carrots
1 onion
2 sticks celery
2 shallots
1 bay leaf
3 parsley stalks
2 sprigs thyme
30 ml/2 tablespoons lemon juice
300 ml/½ pt dry white wine
900 ml/1½ pt water
salt and black pepper

Peel and finely chop the vegetables. Put them in a large saucepan with the rest of the ingredients. Bring to the boil, cover with a lid and simmer over low heat for 15 minutes. Leave the court bouillon to cool slightly, then strain it and pour over the fish to be poached.

Braising

Large flat fish, such as brill and turbot, can be cooked by this method which adds flavour to their somewhat dry flesh. Peel and finely chop 2 carrots, 1 onion and 1 leek or parsnip. Fry these vegetables in a little butter or oil for about 10 minutes to soften them slightly and spread them over the base of an ovenproof dish. Lay the prepared fish on top and sprinkle with salt and black pepper. Add a few sprigs of fresh herbs, such as parsley or thyme, or a bay leaf. Pour over enough fish stock or white wine to come just level with the fish.

Cover the dish and cook in a preheated oven at 180°C/350°F/ gas 4 until the fish flakes when tested with a fork. Lift out the fish carefully and strain the cooking liquid. This may be used as a sauce and can be thickened with egg yolks or cream, or it can be reduced by fast boiling until the flavour is more concentrated.

Steaming

Fillets and small portions of fish are ideal for steaming. Plain steamed fish has a rather drab image, but flavouring ingredients, such as celery, carrots and fresh herbs, are often added to impart a delicate flavour to the cooked fish. Stronger condiments and spices, such as soy sauce and fresh root ginger, are used to flavour steamed fish in oriental cooking.

Fish may be enclosed in greased foil, double-thick greaseproof paper or wrapped in nonstick parchment before steaming. Alternatively, a shallow dish or deep plate may be used to hold the fish above the boiling liquid.

Plain steamed fish is easily digested by invalids or young children. It can be used in more complicated recipes once it is lightly steamed, for example, to make fish cakes or croquettes, or in a pie or mousse.

Roll the fillets or lay them flat in the perforated steamer compartment and sprinkle lightly with salt and black pepper. Set the steamer over a pan of boiling water and cook the fish for about 10–15 minutes.

If a steamer is not available, the simplest method of steaming thin portions of fish is by placing them between two plates over a saucepan of boiling water.

Boning Cooked Large Round Fish

(salmon and salmon trout) Prepare the fish and poach it in a home-made court bouillon (left). If the fish is to be served cold, allow it to cook in its cooking liquid. There are two methods of removing the bones: the first is less time-consuming than the second but it is a difficult technique and some bones may remain in the fish; the second method is a little more complicated but it is usually far more successful, especially for a less-experienced cook.

Lift the poached fish on to a board, and with a sharp knife or scissors snip the skin just below

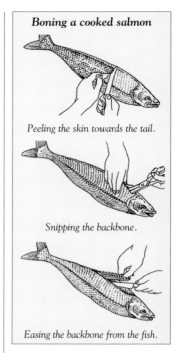

Boning a cooked salmon

Peeling the skin towards the tail.

Snipping the backbone.

Easing the backbone from the fish.

the head and above the tail. Carefully peel off the skin, leaving head and tail intact. Snip the backbone below the head and above the tail, then with the blade of a sharp knife split the fish along the backbone. Ease the bone out from the back without breaking the fish.

Alternatively, the fillets may be removed from the top of cooked fish, then the bones lifted out. Lift the poached fish on to a board and peel off the skin as above. Place the skinned fish on a serving platter. Using a fine-bladed knife, cut through the flesh as far as the bone along the fish, from the side of the head to the tail. Then cut sideways into the fish from the tail to the head along the backbone: cutting close to the bone, slide the knife between the bone and flesh to free the fillet. Cut the fish fillet around the head and across the tail end. Use a large palette knife to lift the fillet off the fish, taking care to keep it in one piece, and lay it on a board. Cut off the remaining top fillet, this time sliding the knife between the bone and fish working from the middle out towards the slit along the belly of the fish. Remove this second fillet and lay it flat on a board.

When both fillets have been taken out, snip the exposed backbone with scissors at head and tail ends. Carefully lift the backbone away and it will bring most of the other bones with it. Remove any stray bones. When all the bones are removed, use a large palette knife to replace the fillets on top of the fish. If you are concerned about breaking the fish fillets, cut them across to make four sections, which are easily removed and replaced without flaking the flesh. A garnish of cucumber slices will conceal the cuts in the fish.

SHELLFISH

Shellfish are most readily available cooked, for example prawns, crabs and lobsters are sold ready boiled by the majority of fishmongers and supermarkets. Live mussels are also readily available; while live crabs and lobsters are offered by the better, and busier, fishmongers; notice of a day or so is usually necessary when ordering them from supermarkets. Oysters, which are often eaten raw, are the one exception: they are always sold live. All shellfish must be chilled quickly after purchase and used within 24 hours. Live shellfish should be scrubbed, cooked and prepared promptly after purchase.

Small shellfish are served as hors-d'oeuvre, and in soups and sauces. Large shellfish, such as crabs, lobsters and crawfish, can be served either as a first or a main course. If they are bought ready-prepared, they must be used on the day of purchase.

It is important to remember that shellfish will require only a short cooking time, and over-boiling causes the flesh to become tough and fibrous.

Most shellfish have indigestible or unwholesome parts, such as the beard of the mussel, and the 'dead men's fingers', or gills, in crabs or lobsters. These parts, together with the stomach sac and the intestinal tubes, must be removed during preparation.

Clams

There are many varieties of clam, in vastly differing sizes, including soft-shell clams. Small clams with hard shells may be served raw, like oysters, or they may be prepared and cooked in the same way as mussels. Allow 12 small clams per person. Large clams are cooked, shelled and diced or chopped before being added to dishes such as soups, casseroles and sauces.

Cockles

These small shellfish are usually sold already cooked. If fresh cockles are available, the tightly closed shells should be left in a large bucket of lightly salted water for about 3 hours. Ensure that the cockles are covered by plenty of water and leave them in a cool place. Change the water every 2–3 hours if leaving the cockles for any longer or use a large container overnight. This process of purging removes sand.

Scrub the shells with a stiff brush, and put them in a large pan with 1 cm/½ in water in the bottom. Cover the pan with a lid and cook over low heat, shaking the pan frequently. As soon as the shells open, remove the cockles from the pan.

Serve the cooked cockles cold, with malt vinegar and brown bread and butter.

Crab

This is usually bought cooked, and has often been dressed by the fishmonger. When buying a fresh crab, make certain that it has two claws and that it is heavy for its size. The edible parts of a crab are the white meat in the claws and the creamy-brown meat in the body shell. Allow 225–275 g/ 8–10 oz dressed crab per person.

Wash the crab and put it in a large saucepan with plenty of cold water seasoned with 15 ml/ 1 tablespoon lemon juice, a few parsley stalks, 1 bay leaf, a little salt and a few black peppercorns. Cover the pan with a lid and bring the water slowly to boiling point. Cooking time is short – a 1.15–1.4 kg/2½–3 lb crab, about 20 cm/8 in across the body shell, should be boiled for only 15–20 minutes. Leave the crab to cool in the cooking fluid.

Dressed crab Place the cooked crab on a board and twist off the legs and two large claws. Twist off the crab's pincers and crack each claw open with a claw cracker, a hammer or the handle of a heavy knife.

Empty the white meat into a bowl and use a skewer or the handle of a teaspoon to scrape all the white meat from the crevices in the claws. Set the small legs

Dressing a cooked crab

1 Twist off the legs and claws.

2 Crack and empty the claws.

3 Scrape the meat from the legs.

4 Pull the body from the shell.

5 Remove the stomach and gills.

6 Scrape out the brown meat.

7 Trim the shell.

8 Replace the meat in the shell.

aside for garnish or, if they are large, crack them open with a hammer and extract the white meat with a skewer.

Place the crab on its back and firmly pull the body (to which the legs were attached) away from the shell. Remove and discard the greyish-white stomach sac which lies behind the head in the shell, and the grey feathered gills, which are known as 'dead men's fingers'.

Using a spoon, gently scrape the soft brown meat from the shell and put it in another bowl until required.

Cut the body part in two and pick out the white meat left in the leg sockets. Using the handle of a knife, tap and trim away the shell edge along the natural dark line round the rim. Scrub the inside of the shell thoroughly under cold water, dry, brush it with oil and set aside.

Finely chop the white meat and season it to taste with salt, black pepper, cayenne and a few drops of white wine vinegar. Mix the brown meat with 15–30 ml/1–2 tablespoons fresh white breadcrumbs and season with salt, freshly ground black pepper, lemon juice and finely chopped parsley. Place the brown crab meat in the centre of the shell and arrange the white meat on either side.

Lobsters

These are usually sold ready-cooked, but live lobsters can be ordered in advance. The shells are then grey-blue, but turn bright red during cooking. Fish-mongers supply live lobsters with the fierce pincers secured with rubber bands. An average-size lobster will serve two people.

Rinse the lobster under cold running water. Grip it firmly round the body part and drop it into a large pan of boiling salted water. Cover with a lid and bring back to the boil. Simmer over low heat, allowing 20 minutes for a 450 g/1 lb lobster and 30 minutes for a 675 g/1½ lb lobster. Leave to cool.

Dressed lobster Twist the claws and pincers off the boiled lobster. Using a hammer, a sturdy nut cracker or a specially designed lobster cracker, break the large claws and carefully extract the meat inside. Remove the thin membrane from the centre of each claw. The head may be cut off or left on.

Place the lobster on a board, back upwards, and split in half along its entire length with a sharp knife. Open out the two halves and remove the gills, the dark intestinal vein which runs down the tail, and the small stomach sac which lies in the head. The green creamy liver in the head is a delicacy and should not be discarded. The spawn – or roe – in a female lobster should also be kept; it is bright coral red and contained in the tail. It is usually added to the accompanying sauce.

Extract the meat from the tail, and with a small skewer pick out the meat from the feeler claws or set them aside for a garnish. Wash and polish the empty half shells and put all the meat back in them. Garnish with the claws.

■ Serve cold with mayonnaise or a Sauce Vinaigrette (page 356) or grilled with a Savoury Butter (page 307).

Mussels

As soon as possible put live mussels into a large bucket of cold salted water and throw away any mussels with open or broken shells. If time allows, sprinkle a little oatmeal or flour into the water and leave the mussels in a cool place for 2–3 hours. The live mussels will feed on the oatmeal and excrete their dirt. Throw away any mussels that float to the surface. Check with the fishmonger when buying mussels, as the majority are now sold ready purged.

Scrub the shells with a stiff brush to remove all the grit. With a sharp knife, scrape away the beard or seaweed-like strands protruding from each shell, and also scrape off the barnacles growing on the shells. Rinse the mussels in several changes of cold water to remove any remaining grit. Discard any open or broken shells.

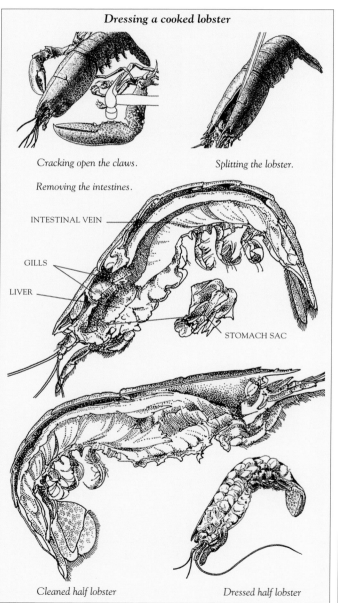

Dressing a cooked lobster

Cracking open the claws.

Splitting the lobster.

Removing the intestines.

INTESTINAL VEIN

GILLS

LIVER

STOMACH SAC

Cleaned half lobster

Dressed half lobster

Cleaning mussels

1 Scrub the shell.

2 Scrape the shell clean.

3 Remove the beard.

Put the cleaned mussels in a large, heavy-based saucepan containing 1 cm/½ in of water or white wine, chopped parsley and shallots or onions. Cover the pan with a lid and heat until the liquid boils. Reduce the heat so that the liquid does not boil too rapidly, then steam the mussels for about 5 minutes, shaking the pan occasionally. As soon as the shells open, take the pan off the heat and remove a half shell from each mussel. Discard any mussels that are still closed. Keep the mussels warm under a dry cloth, and strain the cooking liquid through muslin. Serve with the liquid poured over them.

Oysters

Oysters must be purchased live and opened just before they are served if they are to be eaten raw. Live oysters have firmly closed shells and they should be kept in the refrigerator until they are used, which should always be on the same day as purchase.

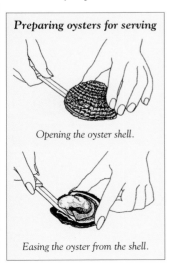

Preparing oysters for serving

Opening the oyster shell.

Easing the oyster from the shell.

Scrub the tightly closed shells with a stiff brush and scrape them, if necessary, to remove all sand and dirt.

Oysters contain a delicately flavoured juice that is served with the raw shellfish or reserved for use in a sauce if the oysters are to be cooked. To open an oyster, use a strong, short-bladed knife, preferably a proper oyster knife.

Protect your hand with a thick cloth; a folded ovenglove is ideal. Hold the oyster in one hand, rounded shell down, over a bowl to catch any juices. If the oysters are to be served raw, the juices should be kept in the shells. Insert the tip of the oyster knife into the hinge. Twist the knife to prise the shell apart at the hinge and cut the two muscles which lie above and below the oyster. Run the knife blade between the shells to open them and lift off the top shell. After opening the shell, loosen the oyster with a knife.

Serve the oysters in their shells, lightly seasoned with salt and ground pepper and on a bed of cracked ice. They are traditionally served with lemon wedges and with thin slices of brown bread and butter.

Alternatively, drain the juices from the oyster shells and trickle a little melted butter over the oysters, then grill them briefly until they are just opaque and firm – this should take about 3–4 minutes. Grilled oysters may be served very plain; with a little pepper and lemon juice, or they may be dressed with cream and cheese or a sauce before grilling.

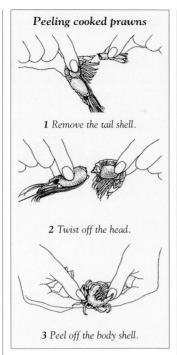

Peeling cooked prawns

1 *Remove the tail shell.*

2 *Twist off the head.*

3 *Peel off the body shell.*

Prawns and Shrimps

These small shellfish are available all year round and are usually sold ready-cooked and often shelled. Frozen uncooked prawns are more readily available than the fresh, live shellfish. Live prawns and shrimps are grey-brown in colour, but turn bright pink during cooking. Drop the live prawns or shrimps into a pan of boiling water, cover with a lid and boil for 5 minutes. Leave prawns and shrimps to cool in the cooking liquid.

The large Dublin Bay prawns are often sold as scampi, though correctly this name should be applied only to the large prawns from the Bay of Naples. Scampi are only available ready-cooked and frozen, but Dublin Bay prawns should be boiled for

10–15 minutes if purchased alive ready for cooking.

To peel cooked prawns and shrimps, hold the shellfish between two fingers, then gently pull off the tail shell and twist off the head. Finally, peel away the soft body shell, with the small crawler claws attached.

These shellfish are served hot or cold, as hors-d'oeuvre, in seafood cocktails, salads, curries, soups and sauces. The large prawns may be coated in batter or in beaten egg and breadcrumbs and then deep fried.

Scallops

Fresh scallops are often sold already opened and cleaned, with the beards and all the intestines removed.

Wash and scrub the tightly closed shells of live scallops in cold water. Place the scallops, rounded shells uppermost, on a baking tray in a preheated oven at 150°C/300°F/gas 2 until the shells open; this will take about 5 minutes.

Once the shells have opened, cut through and remove the hinge muscles, and detach the rounded shells. Clean the shells thoroughly and set them aside – they make excellent small hors-d'oeuvre containers. The scallop, attached to the flat shell, is surrounded by a beard-like fringe which must be scraped off. The black intestinal thread must also be removed. Slide a sharp knife blade under the scallop and carefully ease off the white flesh with the coral attached.

Put the white and orange scallop flesh in a pan of cold

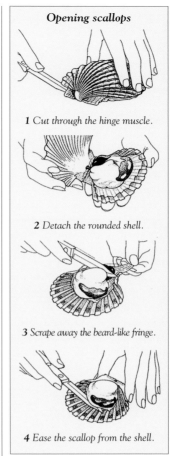

Opening scallops

1 *Cut through the hinge muscle.*

2 *Detach the rounded shell.*

3 *Scrape away the beard-like fringe.*

4 *Ease the scallop from the shell.*

water. Bring to the boil, remove any scum from the surface and simmer the scallops for 5–10 minutes, being careful not to overcook them.

Scallops may also be baked, deep fried or grilled, or served in a cheese or mushroom sauce (page 352).

Whelks and Winkles

These molluscs with snail-like shells resemble each other closely, but winkles are smaller. Both are sold ready-cooked, from stalls at the seaside and in London streets, where they are served cold, with salt, black pepper and vinegar. Whelks are shelled before they are served, but winkles are left in their shells and they must be extracted with a long pin.

SMOKED AND PRESERVED FISH

A small group of fish are preserved or cured by salting, brining and/or smoking. There are two methods of smoking, cold and hot. Cold-smoked fish require cooking, but hot-smoked fish are ready for the table, because they have been partially cooked during smoking.

Cooked, cold-smoked fish, such as haddock, may be served simply: poached and with a little butter, pepper and lemon juice. Smoked haddock is also flavoursome in fish cakes and pies.

Cod, smoked
Cold-smoked; should be cooked as smoked haddock.

Cod Roe, smoked
Ready to eat; serve as an hors-d'oeuvre or appetiser on lettuce leaves with lemon wedges and crisp fingers of toast.

Coley, smoked
Cold-smoked; should be cooked as smoked haddock.

Eel, smoked
Hot-smoked; this fish is available whole or in fillets to serve as an hors-d'oeuvre.

Haddock, smoked
Cold-smoked. Poach fillets on top of the stove in a pan of milk,

or milk and water, allowing 8 minutes per 450 g/1 lb. Alternatively, put the haddock in a buttered ovenproof dish, dot with butter and add 45–60 ml/3–4 tablespoons milk. Cover the dish and bake in a preheated oven at 180°C/350°F/gas 4 for 15 minutes. Smoked haddock is also suitable for grilling.

Arbroath smokies are small, whole, cold-smoked haddock or whiting. Brush the smokies with melted butter or oil and put them under a hot grill for about 3 minutes on each side.

Herrings, salted
These include rollmops and Bismarck herrings. Both are boned herring fillets preserved in spiced vinegars. Rollmops are rolled round a stuffing of onions, gherkins and peppercorns, Bismarck herrings are flat fillets. Both are bought ready for serving as an appetiser.

Herrings, smoked
These include bloaters, bucklings and kippers. Bloaters are lightly salted before being cold-smoked without gutting. Clean the bloaters before grilling them in the same way as Arbroath smokies (see Haddock, smoked). Bloaters should be used on the day they are purchased.

Bucklings are hot-smoked and ready for eating. Serve as an hors-d'oeuvre with a sharp sauce.

Kippers can be bought with the bone in, or filleted and packed in vacuum-sealed bags ready for cooking. Grill kippers under a hot grill for 3 minutes on each side. Cook vacuum-packed

fillets according to the instructions on the packet.

Mackerel, smoked
Hot-smoked, ready for serving. Use for an hors-d'oeuvre or as a main course with a soured cream dressing and new potatoes.

Salmon, smoked
Cold-smoked and ready for eating. Serve in very thin slices, with lemon wedges and brown bread and butter. Hot-smoked salmon is also available. Unlike traditional smoked salmon, the hot-smoked variety is cooked and cut in thick slices across the fillet rather than at an angle along its length.

Sprats, smoked
Cold-smoked. Brush the sprats with melted butter and put under a hot grill for 4 minutes, turning once. Cut off the heads and ease out the bones from the back. Serve as an appetiser.

Fillets of salted sprats are sometimes called Norwegian anchovies. Soak in milk for 1–2 hours to remove excess salt.

Trout, smoked
Hot-smoked and ready for serving cold as a first or main course. Either sharp or mild Horseradish Sauce (page 357) may be served with filleted smoked trout.

POULTRY & GAME

Poultry is available all year, with goose being the only exception, as it is difficult to obtain outside the Christmas season. Probably the most dramatic change in the availability of poultry is in the increased choice of cuts – joints, boneless portions and prepared fillets of breast meat are now sold in most large supermarkets as well as by independent butchers. There is also a choice of types of birds, such as free-range and corn-fed chickens. Conversely, game is still a truly seasonal food despite the, limited, year-round availability of some frozen birds. The section on choice of game at the front of the book outlines the different seasons (page 19).

PREPARATION OF POULTRY

Most poultry is sold ready for cooking – that is hung, plucked, drawn and trussed. Oven-ready frozen poultry should be unwrapped and placed in a deep, covered container in the refrigerator until thawed. Particular attention must be paid to thawing large birds, such as turkey, ensuring that the liquid which drips from them is regularly drained and that they are properly thawed before cooking. Poultry must never be thawed using hot water.

Stuffing
Stuffing improves the flavour and appearance of poultry, and makes the meat go further.

Stuffing can be placed in the body cavity and/or under the skin which covers the breast. Stuffing must not be inserted in the bird more than about 2 hours before cooking. When the body of a large bird is stuffed, it is essential that ample cooking time is allowed so that both

stuffing and bird are thoroughly cooked through to a high temperature when served.

Two stuffings may be used in a large bird, such as a turkey. Use a small spoon to stuff the thoroughly rinsed and dried body cavity. Do not overpack the bird's cavity because the stuffing will expand on cooking.

To stuff the area over the breast meat, snip between the skin and flesh, then gently ease your fingers under the skin to loosen it. Loosen the skin all over the breast meat. Use a small spoon to insert stuffing between the skin and meat, pushing it from the outside.

Trussing
After stuffing, the bird should be trussed so as to keep it in shape during cooking, and to make it look attractive when it reaches the table. To tie up a bird, use a trussing needle, which has an eye large enough to take a piece of fine string. If a trussing needle is not available, use poultry skewers and string to secure the bird.

Using a trussing needle Place the chicken, breast down, on a board. Fold the loose neck skin over the back, closing the neck opening. Fold the wing tips over the body so as to hold the neck skin in position. Turn the chicken, breast side up.

Make a slit in the skin above the opening at the vent of the body, and put the tail (parson's nose) through this.

Thread the trussing needle with string. Insert the needle through the second joint of the right wing, push it through the body, and out through the corresponding joint on the left side. Insert the needle through the first joint, where the wing is attached to the body, on the left side. Pass the needle through the body again and then out through the corresponding joint on the right side. Tie the ends of the string securely.

To truss the legs, press them close to the body; thread the needle again and pass it through the right side of the parson's nose. Loop the string first around the right leg and then around the left leg. Pass the needle through the left side of the parson's nose, pull the string tightly to draw the legs together and tie the ends.

Trussing with a skewer Fold the neck skin and wing tips over the back of the bird as already explained, and pull the parson's nose through the slit above the vent of the body.

Lay the bird on its back and, pushing the legs up towards the neck, insert a poultry skewer just below the thigh bone. Push the skewer through the body so that

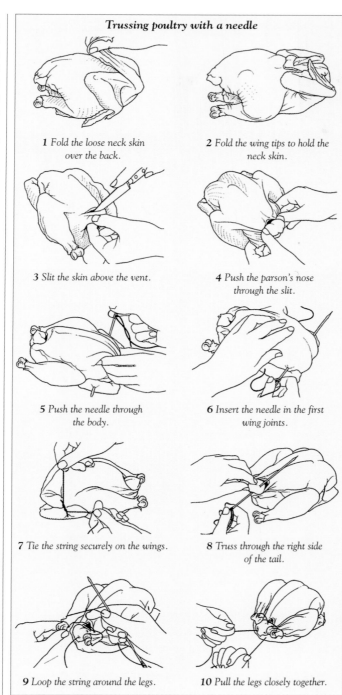

Trussing poultry with a needle

1 Fold the loose neck skin over the back.

2 Fold the wing tips to hold the neck skin.

3 Slit the skin above the vent.

4 Push the parson's nose through the slit.

5 Push the needle through the body.

6 Insert the needle in the first wing joints.

7 Tie the string securely on the wings.

8 Truss through the right side of the tail.

9 Loop the string around the legs.

10 Pull the legs closely together.

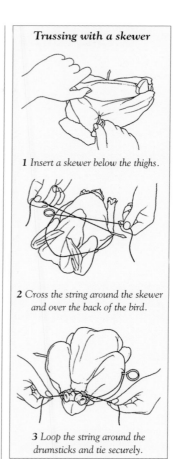

Trussing with a skewer

1 Insert a skewer below the thighs.

2 Cross the string around the skewer and over the back of the bird.

3 Loop the string around the drumsticks and tie securely.

it comes out below the thigh bone on the other side.

Turn the bird on its breast. Pass a piece of string over the wing tips and beneath and up over the ends of the skewer. Cross the string over the back of the bird.

Turn the bird on to its back again, loop the string around the drumsticks and parson's nose, then tie the string securely.

Barding

After trussing, the bird is ready for cooking. If it is to be roasted, the lean breast flesh may be

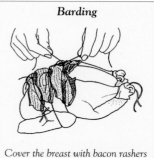

Barding

Cover the breast with bacon rashers and secure with string.

protected to prevent it from drying out and reduce the need for basting. This is particularly important for large birds which require lengthy cooking, such as turkey, or for very lean birds, such as pheasant, which have a tendency to dry out quickly during roasting. This process is known as barding and consists of covering the breast with fatty bacon rashers.

During cooking, the fat from the bacon melts and bastes the flesh, thus keeping the meat moist. About 20 minutes before the end of cooking time, remove the crisp bacon rashers and return the bird to the oven.

Jointing

A chicken – or duck – can be cooked whole or cut into joints. A small bird can be halved by placing it, back down, on a board and cutting lengthways down and through the breastbone and then through the backbone.

Each half bird can be further divided into two. Tuck the blade of the knife underneath the leg joint and slice this away from the wing portion, holding the knife at an angle of 45 degrees.

321

To joint a chicken, pull the chicken leg away from the body, and slice down to where the thigh joins the carcass. Break the bone and cut the whole leg away with a knife. A large leg joint can be cut into the drumstick and thigh. Next, cut down from the breast towards the wing joint, severing the wing from the body, and fold the breast meat over the wing joints. Cut along the natural break in the rib cage to separate the top of the breast from the lower carcass. Divide the top. Divide this breast meat into two or three pieces. The remaining carcass can be used for making stock.

Boning

For a classic galantine of chicken, the bird must be boned whole. Lay the drawn bird on its breast, and remove the wing pinions (the lower parts of the wings) at the second joint. The feet and first joint of the legs should have been removed when it was drawn.

Using a small knife, make a cut down the centre of the back, starting at the neck end. Carefully cut the flesh away from the rib cage down to the wing joints. Nick the sinews where the wing joins the carcass.

Holding the exposed wing bone in one hand, scrape the flesh away along the wing bone. Cut off the sinews at the end of the bone and pull the bone from the flesh. The flesh of the wing has now been pulled inside out. Repeat with the other wing.

Cut along and down the carcass until the leg joint is

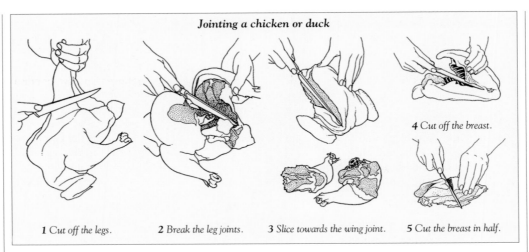

Jointing a chicken or duck

1 *Cut off the legs.* 2 *Break the leg joints.* 3 *Slice towards the wing joint.* 4 *Cut off the breast.* 5 *Cut the breast in half.*

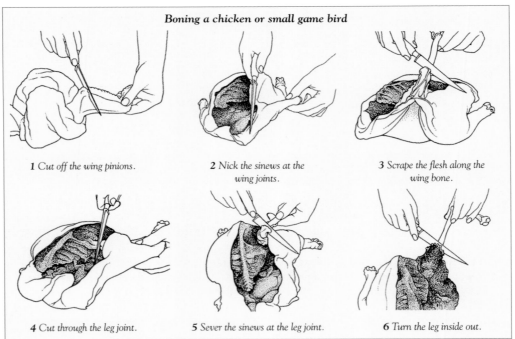

Boning a chicken or small game bird

1 *Cut off the wing pinions.* 2 *Nick the sinews at the wing joints.* 3 *Scrape the flesh along the wing bone.*

4 *Cut through the leg joint.* 5 *Sever the sinews at the leg joint.* 6 *Turn the leg inside out.*

reached. Nick the sinews between the ball-and-socket joint. Pulling at the end of the leg bone with one hand, scrape along the bone until the next joint in the leg is reached. Sever the sinews around this joint and pull the bone from the flesh, scraping down with the knife. The legs are also turned inside out as the bone is pulled away. Repeat with the other leg, then continue working down either side of the breastbone, being careful not to puncture the bird's skin. Finally, work the flesh carefully away from the tip of the breastbone and remove the carcass.

COOKING METHODS FOR POULTRY

Roasting is the most popular and widely used method of cooking a whole duck, chicken, goose, guinea fowl and turkey.

Boiling and steaming are suitable methods for cooking older birds and joints. The cooked flesh is mainly used in other dishes, such as fricassées and curries. Casseroling and braising are ideal, but slow, methods of cooking older birds or joints.

Grilling and frying are mainly used for cooking whole small and young birds, and for joints or fillets of meat from a bird.

CHICKEN

Boiling

Boiling fowl are available from good butchers but they are rarely found in supermarkets and high-street chains or smaller family butchers. These older birds have a good flavour but they are extremely tough. Long boiling tenderises the meat and yields a full-flavoured broth. The meat may be cut from the bone and served in a sauce or used for a flavoursome pie filling.

Rub the surface of a whole chicken with lemon juice to preserve the colour, and place it in a pan. Add a bouquet garni*, a peeled carrot and onion, and sufficient water to just cover the bird. For every 450 g/1 lb of poultry add 2.5 ml/½ teaspoon salt. Bring the water to the boil, and remove any scum from the surface. Reduce the heat to a gentle simmer, then cover with a lid and cook until the bird is tender, after about 2–3 hours; chicken joints need only 15–20 minutes. Lift the chicken from the pan and serve hot or cold with a white sauce. Use the cooking liquid in a sauce or soup.

Braising and Casseroling
Lightly fry a whole bird or joints in a little butter until golden. Remove the bird from the pan and fry about 450 g/1 lb of cleaned, roughly chopped vegetables, such as carrots, onions, celery and turnips, in the butter. Replace the poultry on the bed of vegetables, and cover the pan tightly with a lid. Cook over low heat on top of the stove or in a preheated oven at 160°C/325°F/ gas 3, until tender. Braising is a slow process, up to 3 hours, but cooking time depends on the size and age of the bird.

For a chicken casserole, fry the joints in butter until golden, then put them in a flameproof casserole. Pour stock, wine or a mixture of both over the base of the dish to a depth of 2.5 cm/ 1 in. Add seasoning, chopped herbs or a bouquet garni*, and cover the dish with a lid. Cook as for braising, on top of the stove or in the oven, for 1–1½ hours or until tender. A selection of lightly fried vegetables, such as button onions and mushrooms, baby carrots and small new potatoes, may be added halfway through cooking.

Grilling and Frying
Spring chickens, poussins and small guinea fowl are excellent for grilling. One average bird (weight about 675 g/1½ lb) will serve two people. To prepare a whole bird for grilling, place it on its breast, cut through the backbone and open the bird out. Flatten the bird with a meat mallet, breaking the joints.

Brush the bird all over with melted butter, and season lightly with salt and freshly ground black pepper. Cook the bird on the grill pan under moderate heat for 20–30 minutes, turning it over frequently.

Before frying chicken joints, coat them with seasoned flour, or with beaten egg and breadcrumbs. For shallow frying, brown the joints quickly in hot fat, then lower the heat and fry gently until the meat is tender, after 15–20 minutes. For deep frying, heat the oil to 190°C/ 375°F and cook the coated joints for 10–15 minutes or until tender and crisp on the outside.

Roasting
A roasting chicken weighing up to 1.6 kg/3½ lb will serve 3–4 persons. Place the barded* chicken in a roasting tin in a preheated oven at 190°C/375°F/ gas 5. Allow 20 minutes per 450 g/1 lb, plus 20 minutes over. A chicken weighing 1.8–2.72 kg/ 4–6 lb will give 4–6 servings. It should be roasted in a preheated oven at 160°C/325°F/gas 3, allowing 25 minutes per 450 g/ 1 lb plus 25 minutes over.

Alternatively, loosely wrap the chicken in foil and roast in a preheated oven at 200–220°C/ 400–425°F/gas 6–7, allowing 20 minutes per 450 g/1 lb, plus an extra 20 minutes. Open the foil 20 minutes before cooking is completed to allow the bird to brown. Use a skewer to test that the bird is thoroughly cooked. Insert the skewer into the thickest part of the thigh; if clear juices run out, the bird is cooked. If there is any sign of pink flesh near the bone or blood in the juices, continue to cook the bird.

Steaming
Place the trussed but unstuffed chicken on a wire rack or trivet over a deep pan of boiling water. Cover the chicken with foil and steam for 3–4 hours, topping up with more water when necessary. Remove the skin from the cooked chicken and use the flesh as required. A whole chicken or chicken portions may also be seasoned with fresh root ginger, lemon grass, spring onions and soy sauce before steaming to give aromatic, oriental results. Fermented black beans and dry sherry are other ingredients used to flavour steamed chicken in Chinese recipes.

Roast Boned Chicken
Proceed as for the Galantine of Chicken (page 208), but do not tie the stuffed chicken in muslin. Instead, place it seam downwards in a greased roasting tin; brush the top generously with melted butter or oil and sprinkle with salt and black pepper.

Cover the chicken with buttered greaseproof paper and roast in a preheated oven at 200°C/ 400°F/gas 6, for 1¼–1½ hours. Remove the paper after 1 hour to brown the skin.

Serve the boned chicken hot or cold, cut into slices.

DUCK
Duck is prepared for roasting in the same way as chicken. Because duck is a fatty bird, it does not need barding* or brushing with butter before cooking, but the skin should be pricked all over with a needle to allow the fat to run out of the bird during cooking. Season the duck with salt and pepper, and cook in a preheated oven at 200°C/400°F/ gas 6, allowing 20 minutes per 450 g/1 lb.

A whole duck can also be jointed and braised for about 1 hour in a preheated oven at 180°C/350°F/gas 4.

Because the meat is very rich, duck is best served with sharply flavoured sauces and fruit, such as oranges, peaches and cherries. When buying, allow 450 g/1 lb of duck per person.

GOOSE
Goose is more fatty than chicken or turkey and therefore does not need to be brushed with melted butter before cooking. For its weight, goose yields a small number of portions because so much is lost as fat melting down during cooking. A 4.5 kg/10 lb goose will serve 6–8.

Before roasting a young bird, stuff it from the neck end and sprinkle with salt. Loosely cover the bird with a piece of foil and roast in a preheated oven at 200°C/400°F/ gas 6, allowing 15 minutes per 450 g/1 lb, plus an extra 15 minutes. Alternatively, slow-roast the goose in a preheated oven at 180°C/350°F/ gas 4, allowing 25 minutes per 450 g/1 lb. Drain excess fat from the tin every now and then during cooking and remove the foil 30 minutes before the end of the cooking time. Serve with apple sauce.

GUINEA FOWL
All the methods of cooking chicken can be applied to guinea fowl, particularly braising. When roasting the bird, bard* the lean breast meat well, otherwise the flesh will dry out. An average guinea fowl serves three to four people while a guinea chick will only serve two people.

TURKEY
A turkey is usually filled with two different stuffings. The neck end can be stuffed with chestnut or veal forcemeat, and the body cavity filled with a Sausage Stuffing (page 358). An average 4.5–5.45 kg/10–12 lb turkey will require stuffing made from at least 900 g/2 lb of sausagemeat.

ROASTING TIMES FOR TURKEY

Weight of bird	Method 1 (160°C/325°F/gas 3)	Method 2 (230°C/450°F/gas 8)
2.72–3.62 kg/6–8 lb	3–3½ hours	2¼–2½ hours
3.62–4.5 kg/8–10 lb	3½–3¾ hours	2½–2¾ hours
4.5–6.35 kg/10–14 lb	3¾–4¼ hours	2¾–3 hours
6.35–8.15 kg/14–18 lb	4¼–4¾ hours	3–3½ hours
8.15–9 kg/18–20 lb	4¾–5¼ hours	3½–3¾ hours
9–10.9 kg/20–24 lb	5¼–6 hours	3¾–4¼ hours

Roasting

Before roasting the stuffed and trussed turkey, it should be generously coated with softened butter and barded* with fat bacon strips. Roasting methods depend on the size of the bird and the time available. At the low oven temperature, the turkey must be frequently basted. At the higher temperature, wrap the bird loosely in foil to prevent the flesh from drying out. About 30 minutes before cooking is complete, open the foil to allow the bird to brown.

When buying turkey, allow 350 g/12 oz oven-ready weight per person, and 450 g/1 lb if the bird is not drawn and trussed.

PREPARATION OF GAME BIRDS

All game birds can be bought already hung, plucked and trussed (and sometimes barded).

Young birds are excellent candidates for roasting; older and tougher birds are better braised or casseroled.

COOKING METHODS FOR GAME BIRDS

Braising

Before cooking, cut the bird into joints, coat with seasoned flour and brown in hot fat in a pan. Remove the browned game from the pan and place the joints in a casserole. Rinse the pan with 150 ml/¼ pt dry red wine or game stock. Add the liquid to the casserole, cover tightly with a lid and cook in a preheated oven at 160°C/325°F/ gas 3 for 1 hour, or until the meat is tender.

ROASTING TIMES FOR GAME BIRDS		
Bird	Temperature	Time
Capercaillie	200°C/400°F/gas 6	30–45 minutes
Grouse	200°C/400°F/gas 6	30–45 minutes
Ortolan	220°C/425°F/gas 7	20 minutes
Partridge	200°C/400°F/gas 6	30–45 minutes
Pheasant	220°C/425°F/gas 7	Allow 20 minutes per 450 g/1 lb
Pigeon	220°C/425°F/gas 7	Allow 20 minutes per 450 g/1 lb
Plover	220°C/425°F/gas 7	30–45 minutes
Ptarmigan	200°C/400°F/gas 6	30–45 minutes
Quail	220°C/425°F/gas 7	20 minutes
Snipe	220°C/425°F/gas 7	20 minutes
Woodcock	220°C/425°F/gas 7	20 minutes

Grilling

Small, tender game birds, such as grouse, partridge and quail, can be grilled. Split them through lengthways along the breastbone and flatten them out; brush generously with melted butter. Place under a hot grill and cook for 25–30 minutes, basting continuously and turning frequently.

Roasting

Before roasting, game birds must be barded* with strips of fat pork or bacon. Sprinkle the inside of the bird with salt and black pepper and put a large knob of butter inside the bird to keep it moist. Place the prepared game bird on a piece of toast in the roasting tin. Baste frequently during cooking and remove the fat strips for the last 10–15 minutes. Sprinkle the breast lightly with flour and continue cooking until brown.

SERVING ROAST GAME BIRDS

Small birds, such as grouse, partridge, quail, snipe and woodcock, are served whole on their toast or fried bread, and gar- nished with watercress. One bird should be allowed per person. Larger birds are split through lengthways to give two portions. Chips or Matchstick Chips (page 347) are traditional with roast game and so too are fried breadcrumbs or Bread Sauce (page 356). A well-flavoured brown gravy, a tossed crisp green salad, buttered sprouts or Braised Celery (page 151) are served separately.

WILD DUCK

These game birds, which include mallard, teal and widgeon, should be hung for only 2–3 days. After hanging, the wild birds are plucked, drawn and trussed just like other game.

Wild duck should not be overcooked. Coat the bird with softened butter, and roast in a preheated oven at 220°C/425°F/ gas 7, allowing about 20 minutes for teal, and 30 minutes for mallard and widgeon. For extra flavour, baste with a little orange juice or port.

Serve wild duck with Game Chips (page 347), fried bread- crumbs and an orange salad.

CARVING POULTRY AND GAME

The technique for carving poultry follows certain basic steps which consist of first removing the legs and wings and then carving the breast meat downwards in thick or thin slices. When carving turkey, serve each person with both white meat – from the breast – and brown meat – from the body or legs.

Chicken and the larger game birds, such as pheasant, blackcock and capercaillie, are carved in the same way as turkey. Small game birds, for example grouse, widgeon and partridge, are either served whole, one served to each person, or they may be cut in half in the same way as duckling.

Whole saddle of hare and venison are carved in the same way as a saddle of lamb (page 333).

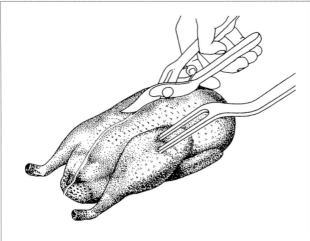

Duckling

Small duckling – and some larger game birds – are often jointed after cooking and half a bird is served to each person. Remove the trussing string or skewers from the roast duckling, then split the bird in half with a carving knife or with a pair of poultry shears or strong kitchen scissors. Insert the scissors in the neck end and cut along the centre of the breastbone to the vent; split the bird in half by cutting through the backbone.

Duck

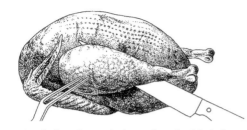

1 *First cut off the leg joints from either side of the body.*

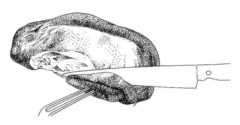

2 *Remove the wings on either side of the breast, and detach the wishbone and meat from the neck end.*

3 *Slice down through the centre of the breast meat.*

4 *Holding the knife blade at an angle of 45° to the breast, carve the meat in fairly thick, slightly wedge-shaped slices. Make them parallel to the first cut along the breast bone.*

Goose

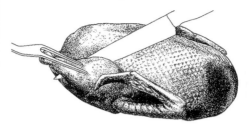

1 *Begin by carving the legs from the bird at the point where the thigh bones meet the body.*

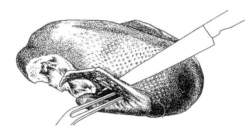

2 *Remove the wing joints from either side of the breast.*

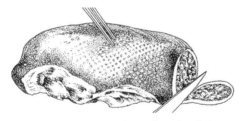

3 *If the goose has been stuffed from the neck end, first cut thick slices across the stuffing.*

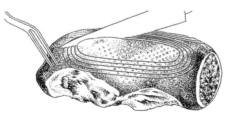

4 *Fairly thick slices are then taken from both sides of the breast bone along the whole length of the bird. To remove these slices, carve downwards with the knife blade held almost flat against the body of the bird.*

Turkey

1 *Cut the large drumsticks from either side of the body.*

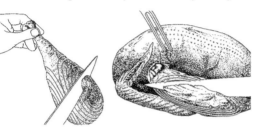

2 *Hold the knuckle end of the drumstick in one hand and slice the meat downwards following the direction of the bone. Rotate the drumstick and carve off all the meat. Next, carve thin slices from the thigh bones.*

3 *Cut off both wing joints and set them aside.*

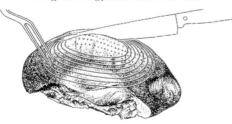

4 *Carve the white breast meat in long, thin downwards slices, from either side of the breast bone.*

FURRED GAME

This term covers hare, which is a true game animal, and rabbit which is now specially bred for the table. The butcher or game dealer will sell the hare prepared for cooking and jointed, if required. If you want the blood to thicken the sauce for jugged hare, remember to ask the butcher to save it for you when you place the order.

Rabbit is eaten when it is 3–3½ months old. Fresh or frozen prepared rabbits are sold ready for cooking. As well as rabbit portions, boneless cuts of rabbit are also available.

COOKING METHODS

Braising

This is a suitable cooking method for a jointed hare or rabbit. Coat the joints in seasoned flour and brown them in hot fat in a pan. Remove the joints from the pan and place in a casserole. Rinse the pan with 300 ml/½ pt red wine or game stock, scraping up the pan residues. Pour this liquid over the joints, cover tightly with a lid and cook in a preheated oven at 160°C/325°F/gas 3 for about 2 hours, or until the meat is tender. Add a little more stock or wine, if necessary, and thicken the juices with a little of the reserved blood, soured cream or beurre manié (page 355) before serving.

Roasting

Fill the body cavity of the animal with Forcemeat Stuffing (page 358) and sew the flesh together. Lay slices of fatty bacon over the back and add 50 g/2 oz dripping to the pan. Roast the hare in a preheated oven at 180°C/350°F/gas 4 for 1½–2 hours. Frequent basting is necessary. The bacon should be removed 15 minutes before cooking is completed to allow the hare to brown.

VENISON

Venison is now farmed and is available in a wide choice of cuts. Wild game venison is also stocked by butchers and supermarkets, as well as game dealers.

Meat from a young deer is delicate and can be cooked without marinating*, but the flesh of an older animal is tougher and is usually steeped in a marinade* for 12–48 hours before cooking.

All fat should be removed from venison before cooking as it has an unpleasant taste.

COOKING METHODS

Frying

Chops or cutlets taken from the loin of venison are suitable for frying. Trim any surplus fat and gristle from the cutlets or chops and flatten them slightly with a meat cleaver. Season lightly with salt and freshly ground black pepper and fry the cutlets over high heat, in oil or butter, for about 12 minutes or until tender, turning them once only.

The fillet, cut into 5 cm/2 in thick slices, can also be fried. Flatten the slices a little, then fry over high heat, without fat, for 1 minute on each side to seal the meat. Add butter and reduce the heat; continue cooking the meat for about 8 minutes, turning once.

Roasting

Shoulder, haunch and saddle of venison are large joints which are suitable for roasting after marinating* for a long period of time. Cover the joint with a thick paste of flour and water, to keep the meat moist, before roasting in a preheated oven at 190°C/375°F/gas 5, allowing 35 minutes per 450 g/1 lb. Remove the paste 20 minutes before cooking is completed to allow the venison joint to brown.

Alternatively, brush the joint generously with oil, then wrap it in foil before roasting.

Serve roast venison with a sharp redcurrant jelly.

Marinade for Venison

PREPARATION: 10 minutes

1 large onion
1 carrot
1 stick celery
1–2 cloves garlic
bouquet garni*
6 black peppercorns
900 ml/1½ pt red wine
150 ml/¼ pt olive oil

Peel and chop the onion, carrot and celery and crush the garlic cloves. Put these ingredients into a bowl, together with the bouquet garni, peppercorns, wine and oil. Mix together thoroughly and pour the marinade over the venison in a shallow dish. Leave the dish, covered, in a cool place and turn the meat frequently. Venison should be marinated for several hours or overnight and, depending on the freshness of the meat, it can be left for up to 48 hours, or longer.

MEAT

Fresh meat will keep for up to 2 days in the refrigerator or according to packet instructions. Where there is a 'use by' date, always observe it. Remove the wrapping paper and place the meat in a deep, covered dish in the refrigerator as soon as possible after purchase.

Minced meat and offal do not keep well and preferably should be used on the day of purchase. Once meat has been cooked, it should be cooled as quickly as possible before storing. For a detailed guide to joints and cuts of meat, see pages 21–31.

COOKING METHODS

There are no set rules for cooking meat, as each cut lends itself to preparation, cooking and presentation in several different ways. In general, however, the tender cuts are roasted, grilled or fried, while the tougher cuts are more suitable for pot-roasting, boiling, braising and stewing.

Roasting

This is the traditional method for cooking large joints of meat. It can be done in several ways, oven roasting being the most common, and again there are two methods. With quick-roasting, the meat is cooked at a high temperature which quickly seals in the juices, thus preserving the full flavour. At the same time, however, the joint shrinks.

Slow-roasting is done at a low temperature over a long period. This method reduces the shrinkage of the meat and usually produces a joint that is more tender than a quick-roasted one.

Whichever roasting method is used, the joint must first be weighed and the cooking time calculated. Put the meat, fat side up, on a wire rack in a shallow roasting tin. Rub a lean joint with dripping or lard first.

Place the tin in the centre of the oven. During roasting the melting fat on some cuts of meat naturally bastes the joint; otherwise spoon the pan juices over it from time to time. A cooked joint should be allowed to rest for 10–20 minutes before carving.

Times and temperatures for roasting The size and shape of a joint and the way in which it has been prepared influence cooking times. Large joints require less roasting time per 450 g/1 lb than small ones.

Some joints on the bone cook more quickly than boned joints because the depth of meat as far as the bone may be shallower than the distance to the middle of a neatly tied and compacted joint. However, it is not easy to generalise because the shape, size and cut of meat will also influence the cooking time.

A joint on the bone is considered to have a better flavour than a piece of boned and rolled meat. Joints on the bone, especially from the loin and breast, usually have the chine bone removed by the butcher.

Joints which weigh less than 1.4 kg/3 lb should always be slow-roasted for at least 1½ hours. Very small joints tend to shrink and dry out.

Meat thermometer A meat thermometer, which registers the internal temperature of meat, is useful for assessing the cooking progress of a joint. The scale on the thermometer indicates the extent to which different types of meat will be cooked when a given internal temperature has been reached.

Before cooking, insert the thermometer into the middle of the thickest part of the meat, but make certain that it does not touch the bone or fat. When the meat thermometer registers the required temperature, the joint will be cooked to taste.

Foil-roasting Roasting in foil has become popular, mainly because it prevents the oven from being splattered with the roasting juices. Wrap the joint loosely in foil, sealing the edges firmly; basting is unnecessary, but remove the foil for the last 20–30 minutes of cooking to brown the joint. Foil wrapping is particularly useful for slightly tough joints because the moist heat that the foil traps helps to tenderise the meat. At the same time, foil deflects heat, and the oven temperature should consequently be raised.

Clear plastic roasting bags are also available. These bags completely eliminate splashing of the oven, and the joint bastes and browns during roasting.

COOKING TIMES FOR MEAT

Cooking methods	Quick-roasting at 220°C/425°F/gas 7	Slow-roasting at 180°C/350°F/gas 4	Stuffed joints	Meat thermometer recommended internal temperatures	Boiling	Grilling and frying
Beef	On the bone 15 minutes per 450 g/1 lb + 15 minutes extra Off the bone 20 minutes per 450 g/1 lb + 20 minutes extra	On the bone 20 minutes per 450 g/1 lb + 20 minutes extra Off the bone 30 minutes per 450 g/1 lb + 30 minutes extra	+ 5–10 minutes per 450 g/1 lb	Rare (flesh and juice are bloody): 60°C/140°F Medium (juices are bloody): 71°C/160°F Well done (flesh brown and dry): 76°C/170°F	20 minutes per 450 g/1 lb + 20 minutes extra Salt beef: 25 minutes per 450 g/1 lb + 25 minutes extra	Steaks (2.5 cm/1 in thick) Rare: 7 minutes Medium: 10 minutes Well done: 15 minutes
Veal	On the bone 25 minutes per 450 g/1 lb + 25 minutes extra Off the bone 30 minutes per 450 g/1 lb + 30 minutes extra	On the bone 35 minutes per 450 g/1 lb + 35 minutes extra Off the bone 40 minutes per 450 g/1 lb + 40 minutes extra	+ 5–10 minutes per 450 g/1 lb	82°C/180°F	20 minutes per 450 g/1 lb + 20 minutes extra	Chops: 12–15 minutes Escalopes (beaten and crumbed): 2 minutes each side
Lamb	On the bone 20 minutes per 450 g/1 lb + 20 minutes extra Off the bone 25 minutes per 450 g/1 lb + 25 minutes extra	On the bone 25 minutes per 450 g/1 lb + 25 minutes extra Off the bone 35 minutes per 450 g/1 lb + 35 minutes extra	+ 5–10 minutes per 450 g/1 lb	82°C/180°F	Mutton: 20 minutes per 450 g/1 lb + 20 minutes extra	Cutlets: 7–10 minutes Chops: 12–15 minutes Kidneys: 5–10 minutes Liver (1 cm/½ in thick slices): 4–6 minutes
Pork	On the bone 25 minutes per 450 g/1 lb + 25 minutes extra	Off the bone at 190°C/375°F/gas 5 35 minutes per 450 g/1 lb + 35 minutes extra	+ 5–10 minutes per 450 g/1 lb	87°C/190°F	20 minutes per 450 g/1 lb + 20 minutes extra	Chops: 15–20 minutes Sausages: 10–15 minutes
Bacon and Gammon				71°C/160°F	Cured bacon and ham 25 minutes per 450 g/1 lb + 25 minutes extra. Weigh after soaking	Bacon rashers (5 mm/¼ in thick): 5–10 minutes Gammon steaks: 10–15 minutes Bacon chops: 10–15 minutes

There is no need to remove the bag until the joint is finished, but it is a good idea to cut a small slit in the bag to allow steam to escape during cooking. Alternatively, slit the bag down the middle for the final 15–30 minutes of cooking time.

Pot-roasting

This is a particularly suitable method for cooking smaller and slightly tougher joints, such as brisket and topside of beef. Melt enough fat to cover the base of a deep, heavy-based pan, put in the meat and brown it over high heat. Lift out the meat, put a wire rack or a bed of root vegetables in the bottom of the pan, and replace the joint.

Cover the pan with a tight-fitting lid and cook over low heat until the meat is tender; allow 45 minutes per 450 g/1 lb. Turn the meat frequently.

Alternatively, put the browned meat in a deep baking dish, cover it tightly and cook in a preheated oven at 160°C/325°F/gas 3; allow 45 minutes per 450 g/1 lb. Lift out the cooked meat, drain the fat from the juices and use them for gravy or sauce.

Braising

This cooking method is used for smaller cuts of meat, such as less tender chops and steaks, and for large offal, such as hearts. Coat the meat with seasoned flour and brown it evenly in hot fat. Place the meat on a bed of diced, lightly fried root vegetables in a casserole or heavy-based saucepan. Pour over enough water or stock to cover the vegetables; add herbs and seasoning.

Cover the casserole with a tight-fitting lid and cook in a preheated oven at 160°C/325°F/gas 3, or on the stove until tender – about 2–3 hours. Add more liquid if necessary.

Stewing

This long, slow-cooking method is suitable for the tougher cuts of meat. Cut the meat into 2.5 cm/1 in cubes, coat them in seasoned flour and brown them quickly, in a pan of very hot fat.

Lift the meat on to a plate and fry a few sliced carrots, onions and turnips in the fat until golden. Sprinkle in 15–30 ml/1–2 tablespoons flour, or enough to absorb all the fat; fry until the mixture is pale brown.

Stir in sufficient warm stock or water to give a pouring consistency, season with salt, black pepper and herbs and bring the sauce to the boil.

Put the meat in a flameproof casserole, pour over the sauce and vegetables and cover with a tight-fitting lid. Simmer the stew on top of the stove or in a preheated oven at 160°C/325°F/gas 3, until the meat is tender, for 1½–3 hours.

Boiling

This method is suitable for whole joints, tongues and salted joints, Bring a pan of water, in which the joint will fit snugly, to the boil. Add salt (10 ml/2 teaspoons to each 450 g/1 lb meat), a bouquet garni*, a large onion studded with cloves, and the meat. Bring to the boil, remove any scum from the surface, then cover the pan with a tight-fitting lid and lower the heat.

Simmer the meat over very low heat until tender. Add a selection of chopped root vegetables to the pan for the last 45 minutes of cooking, if the joint is to be served hot. For a cold, boiled joint, leave the meat to cool in the cooking liquid. Drain the joint of meat thoroughly before serving.

Salted joints should be placed in cold water and brought quickly to the boil. Drain the meat and proceed as already described. A very salty joint should be soaked in water for several hours before being boiled. Modern curing methods often give less salty results, so joints of meat, such as gammon, which would always be soaked by tradition, do not necessarily need soaking these days. Check with the butcher if you are uncertain whether to soak a joint. The majority of pre-packed supermarket joints do not require soaking and may well lose flavour if they are soaked.

Grilling

This quick-cooking method is suitable for small tender cuts, such as prime steaks and chops, and for sausages, liver, kidney, bacon and gammon rashers.

Brush the meat with oil or melted butter, and sprinkle with a little salt and pepper (omit salt on beef steaks as this draws out the juices, and on bacon and gammon rashers). On pork chops, snip the outer layer of fat or rind at 2.5 cm/1 in intervals to prevent curling and shrinkage during grilling.

Grease the grill rack with oil or butter to prevent the meat from sticking to it. Put the meat on the pan and set it under a preheated grill. Turn the meat once only during grilling and baste with the pan juices if the meat begins to dry out.

Frying

Another quick-cooking method for the same types of meat as suggested for grilling, and frying times are the same.

Melt just enough butter or oil to cover the base of a frying pan (dripping may be used for beef and lard for pork), and heat it quickly. A combination of a little butter and oil provides a good cooking medium. Put the meat in the pan and cook it on a high heat, turning once only. For thick cuts, lower the heat after the meat has browned and continue frying until tender.

Lift out and drain the fried meat and keep it warm while making the gravy. Pour the fat from the pan, and stir a little stock or wine into the pan juices. Bring the liquids to the boil, correct seasoning and pour the gravy into a warm sauce boat.

Bacon rashers need little or no extra fat for frying. Place the rashers so that the lean parts overlap the fat in a cool pan, then fry over a moderate heat, turning over, until the rashers are cooked. Grilling is the better method for bacon.

Sausages may be fried but grilling gives better results. They may also be cooked most successfully on a rack in a roasting tin in the oven. If the sausages are fried, the skins may be pricked to prevent them bursting. This is unnecessary if the sausages have natural skins or if they are fried over moderate or low heat for about 20 minutes.

BEEF

Allow 225–350 g/8–12 oz per person from a joint on the bone, and 175–225 g/6–8 oz per person from boned joints. For average portions, allow 150–175 g/5–6 oz steak per person.

Boning and Rolling Sirloin

Lay the joint, bones down, on a steady board. Using a sharp, broad knife, cut the joint across the grain at the thick bone at the top of the joint (chine bone). Insert the knife at the top of the bone where the meat has been loosened and move it downwards, following the bones carefully in sawing movements until the meat comes away from the bones in one piece. Use the bones for stock or a soup.

Lay the boned joint on the board, skin side up, and roll it tightly from the thickest end. Tie it securely with a piece of string to hold its shape. Cut 5 cm/2 in strips of pork fat and tie them, slightly overlapping, around the joint. A wider strip of fat may be tied over the top of the rolled joint to provide extra fat during roasting. Remove this piece of fat before carving.

Larding

Larding is a technique used to introduce fat to an especially lean joint of meat, such as a fillet of beef, or game, such as venison roasting joints.

A whole piece of beef fillet is an excellent, if expensive, joint for roasting. As it has no fat, this must be added in some form to prevent the meat from drying out during roasting. First trim any skin or sinews from the fillet,

Boning and rolling sirloin

1 *Cut the meat from the bone.*

2 *Roll up the boned meat.*

3 *Wrap pork fat around the joint.*

4 *Rolled joint with fat tied on top.*

Larding

Lard beef fillet by threading short lengths of fat through the meat.

then cut pork fat or fatty bacon rashers into strips narrow enough to be threaded through the eye of a larding needle. Thread short lengths of the fat at intervals through the fillet, about 1 cm/½ in deep and on all four sides. A fillet encased in pastry does not need larding.

Alternatively, wrap thin fatty bacon rashers, slightly over-lapping, around the fillet and secure with thin string. Fillet should be quick-roasted, for 12–15 minutes per 450 g/1 lb, or roasted on a spit when 15–20 minutes per 450 g/1 lb should be allowed for cooking.

Roasting

The best beef joints for roasting include sirloin, the rib joints, thick flank and whole fillet. Topside and rump, too, may be slow-roasted, but are more suit-able for pot-roasting.

Sirloin and rib joints are sold on the bone or as rolled joints. Boning and rolling may also be done at home without a great deal of trouble.

Pot-roasting and Braising

Flank, brisket, topside, rump and silverside are the best joints for braising or pot-roasting; for cooking these joints, follow the directions given on page 327.

Boiling

Silverside and brisket are ideal for slow boiling with vegetables. These joints can also be bought salted or pickled.

Grilling and Frying

These cooking methods are suit-able for all steaks – fillet, sirloin, rump, porterhouse and T-bone. Follow the general directions (page 328), but never sprinkle beef with salt as this draws out the juices. Both fillet and rump steaks are also used for the classic Russian dish Boeuf Stroganoff (page 250).

Stewing

This slow-cooking method is ideal for all the tougher cuts of beef, such as flank, chuck, clod and shin. Stews are ideal for winter meals, they store well in a domestic freezer, and many people consider them best if cooked a day in advance. A pre-cooked stew must, however, be heated through thoroughly before being served.

The Hungarian stews, known as goulash (page 250), are inter-nationally famous and differ from a British stew in their piquant, slightly sweet and spicy flavour, due to the use of paprika. These stews are ideally made from chuck steak, but lean boned shoulders of lamb or pork may also be used.

VEAL

Opinions vary widely about the rearing and slaughtering of calves for their meat. Many people will not eat veal and others are conscientious about buying only British meat. It is wise to check that veal is acceptable to guests if it is to be served at a dinner party. As a general rule, pork can be substituted for veal in the majority of recipes.

The flavour of veal is delicate, and the flesh tends to be dry unless carefully cooked. It does not keep well and should be used on the day of purchase. Allow 225 g/8 oz per person from veal on the bone, and about 175 g/6 oz per person of boneless veal.

Roasting

This method is suitable for large joints such as shoulder and loin, both of which may be roasted on the bone or boned and stuffed with Forcemeat (page 358). As the meat is fairly dry, it must be basted frequently. Boned breast is the most economical veal joint. It is ideal for stuffing – allow 450 g/1 lb stuffing to a 2.72 kg/6 lb breast. Use the slow-roasting method rather than the quick-roasting one.

Pot-roasting and Braising

Boned and stuffed shoulder and middle neck can be pot-roasted or braised. Stuffed breast is also recommended for braising, allow-ing approximately 3 hours for a 2.72 kg/6 lb stuffed joint.

Boiling and Stewing

Veal sold for stews and pies usually comes from the neck and knuckle. Both of these contain a large amount of bone, and if bought on the bone, allow 450 g/1 lb per serving.

Grilling and Frying

Thick cutlets cut from best end of neck are suitable for grilling, frying and braising.

For frying, the most popular veal cuts are escalopes. These are cut from the tender fillet, or frequently from the top of the leg. The latter are less tender than fillet slices, and as both are frequently sold ready prepared it is often difficult to see the difference between them.

For veal escalopes, purchase 5 mm/¼ in thick slices from the butcher. Put them between

Preparing veal escalopes

1 Place the escalope between paper.

2 Beat the escalope out thinly.

sheets of waxed paper and beat them flat with a meat hammer or rolling pin. Dip in beaten egg and coat with fresh white breadcrumbs. Fry in hot butter, oil or a mixture of oil and butter for 5 minutes, turning once.

LAMB AND MUTTON

Lamb is a rich, full-flavoured meat. Allow 350 g/12 oz lamb on the bone per person, and 175–225 g/6–8 oz of boned lamb per serving.

Roasting

The double or single loin, with the kidneys attached, can be roasted whole.

Whole leg and shoulder of lamb are among the most popular cuts. They are usually sold on the bone, but may also be purchased boned for stuffing and rolling. Give the butcher 1–2 days' notice to bone the meat.

Best end of neck is probably the most versatile joint of all meats. It is relatively inexpensive and can be used in a number of ways. It is the basis of many classic stews – Lancashire Hot Pot (page 87), Navarin of Lamb (page 108), Scotch Broth (page 311), to name but a few – but the joint is also excellent for roasting when prepared in classic ways, such as a crown roast or a guard of honour.

Crown Roast

Many butchers will prepare a crown roast if given a few days' notice, but if this is not possible, buy two matching pieces of best end, each containing seven to eight rib portions or cutlets.

Preparing a crown roast

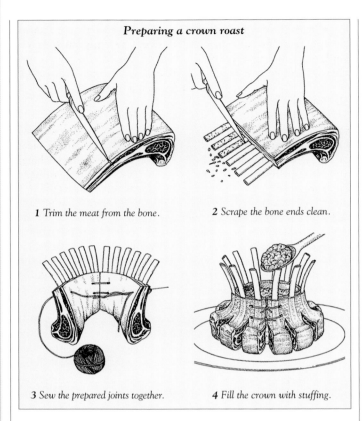

1 Trim the meat from the bone.

2 Scrape the bone ends clean.

3 Sew the prepared joints together.

4 Fill the crown with stuffing.

Guard of honour

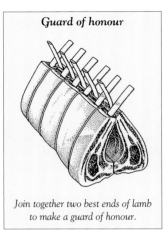

Join together two best ends of lamb to make a guard of honour.

Preparing noisettes of lamb

1 Cut out the rib bones.

2 Roll up the boned joint.

3 Trim the excess fat.

4 Tie and slice the joint.

Trim as much fat as possible from the thick part of each best end, and with a sharp knife cut the top 3.5–5 cm1/½–2 in layer of meat from the thin end of the bones. Scrape off all gristle and meat to leave the bone ends clean. When the two pieces of meat have been prepared, sew them together, with a trussing needle and fine string, having the thick ends of the meat as the base of the crown.

Slit the lower half of the formed crown between each bone, about two-thirds up from the base and, if necessary, tie a piece of string around the middle. Fill the cavity of the crown with a vegetable, rice or Cranberry Stuffing (page 289) and slow-roast the joint.

Butchers who sell prepared crowns often put the trimmings of the joint into the hollow crown. These should be removed before stuffing and roasting. The circle of fat covering the trimmings may be placed on top of the stuffing as it bastes the joint during roasting, but it should be removed for the last 30 minutes.

Guard of Honour

This impressive joint is also prepared from two best ends, but the bones are trimmed clean to about 6–7.5 cm/2½–3 in. The two pieces of meat are then joined and sewn together, skin side up, along the bottom meaty part of the joints. Fold the meat together, skin outside, so that the cleaned bones meet and criss-cross on top. Protect these with foil. Fill the cavity with a savoury stuffing, and tie the joint at intervals to keep its shape during roasting, at low temperature.

Pot-roasting and Braising

Boned breast of lamb is the best joint for pot-roasting and braising. It is usually bought already boned, stuffed and rolled, but make sure most of the fat has been trimmed off.

Stewing and Boiling

Breast of lamb, middle and scrag are the best and most economical cuts for stews and casseroles. As they are all fatty, they should be trimmed of as much fat as possible before cooking.

Grilling and Frying

Cutlets, from best end of lamb and with a high proportion of bone, may be grilled or fried. Chops from the loin are thicker and less bony than cutlets, and chump chops have even less bone. Both types of chops are excellent for grilling and frying.

Noisettes

These are trimmed, round slices from a best end of lamb. Cut off the thick chine bone at the thick end of the best end and trim away all excess fat from the meat. Using a sharp pointed knife, cut along either side of each rib bone and ease it out. Roll up the boned joint, lengthways, trim it and tie with string at 1 cm/½ in intervals. Cut the rolled joints into 5 cm/2 in thick slices and fry or grill them for about 6 minutes on each side.

PORK

A pork joint should have a moderate amount of fat – lean pork is generally lacking in flavour, and fatty pork is wasteful. Allow 225–350 g/8–12 oz of pork on the bone per person, 175 g/6 oz of boned meat.

Roasting

All pork joints are suitable for roasting, on or off the bone. The leg and the loin, both large and expensive joints, together with the more reasonably priced blade

Loin of pork

Scoring a loin of pork, making even cuts through the rind.

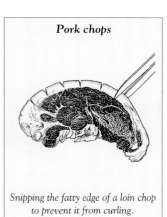

Pork chops

Snipping the fatty edge of a loin chop to prevent it from curling.

joint, have the largest area of skin which gives good crackling.

To obtain the characteristic crackling, the skin on these joints must be evenly and deeply scored. The butcher will usually do this, but before roasting, make sure that all the score marks penetrate the depth of the skin and that they follow the grain of the meat. Rub the skin with olive or vegetable oil and with coarse salt to ensure crisp crackling. This can be removed to make carving easier.

Leg and the fore-end of loin are often boned, stuffed and rolled before roasting; hand of pork, which is an awkward joint to carve, should also be boned and rolled before roasting.

Grilling and Frying

All types of chops are suitable for these methods. Large loin chops have a thick strip of fat around the outer edge. This fat tends to curl during cooking, and to prevent this, snip the fat with scissors at 2.5 cm/1 in intervals.

Lean spare rib cutlets of pork are usually grilled or braised, as

are Chinese spare ribs which are cut from the lower rib section of the pig's belly.

Belly pork may be cut into 1 cm/½ in thick slices and grilled or coated with beaten egg and breadcrumbs and then fried in oil. Slices of lean fillet may be cooked in the same way, but pork fillet is usually stuffed and roasted or braised.

BACON, GAMMON AND HAM

These cured meats are sold as whole joints or as rashers and steaks. Bacon, gammon and ham are all suitable for boiling and for grilling and frying.

Boiling and/or Roasting

Whole joints of gammon should be soaked in cold water for 2–3 hours before being roasted or baked. The majority of bacon and gammon does not need lengthy soaking before boiling as it is not as salty as it used to be. If in doubt, check with the butcher or read the information on pre-packed joints. Joints suitable for boiling and roasting include the

fore hock, collar, back and ribs, and the gammon cuts.

Put the joint in a large pan, cover with cold water and bring slowly to boiling point. Cover the pan with a lid and reduce the heat so that the meat is cooked at a slow simmer. Fast boiling hardens the tissue and causes shrinkage of the meat. For a boiled joint, follow the times given in the chart on page 327.

Lift out the boiled joint, allow it to cool and set slightly, then peel off the skin and serve the bacon hot. Alternatively, leave the bacon to cool in the cooking liquid, peel off the skin and cover the joint with toasted breadcrumbs. Serve cold.

To roast or bake a bacon joint, first simmer it for half the cooking time. Then wrap the joint in foil and cook in a preheated oven at 180°C/350°F/ gas 4 for the remaining cooking time. Half an hour before cooking is completed, remove the foil and peel off the skin.

To finish the joint, score a diamond pattern in the exposed fat, insert whole cloves in the intersections and pat brown sugar over the top of the joint to glaze it. Return the joint to the oven and roast at 220°C/425°F/gas 7 for the last 30 minutes.

Honey, golden syrup or marmalade may be used for glazing the bacon joint instead of brown sugar. Large gammon joints may also be studded with canned half pine-apple rings or apricot halves and basted with the syrups from these fruits.

Cured hams are sold with cooking instructions which vary

according to the curing methods. Be sure to follow the manufacturer's instructions carefully when cooking these hams.

Grilling and Frying

All bacon rashers (streaky, long and short back, best back) and corner gammon rashers, usually cut 5 mm/¼ in thick, are suitable for both grilling and frying. Thicker rashers, such as bacon chops, 1–1.5 cm/½–¾ in thick and cut from best back, and gammon steaks, are also ideal for grilling. To prevent the fatty edges of the bacon rashers curling up during cooking, snip them as for pork chops.

Grilling and Frying

Before cooking bacon rashers, the rind and any small bones must be cut off. The easiest way to remove the rind is to use sharp kitchen scissors.

Bacon Rolls

Streaky bacon rashers are used for barding* (preventing meat from drying out during cooking) and are also rolled up, grilled or baked, and used as a garnish with poultry. Before rolling or tying streaky bacon rashers, they must be stretched. Lay the rasher on a board and run the blade of a knife over each rasher. For bacon rolls, rind must be removed, but this is not necessary for barding.

Preparing gammon for serving or baking

Skinning a gammon joint.

Studding the joint with cloves.

Preparing bacon rolls

Removing bacon rind.

Cutting away small pieces of bone.

Stretching the rasher.

CARVING MEAT

Boned and rolled joints present no carving problems because the bones have already been removed. But for many people, carving meat with the bone in can be daunting. However, knowing about the position of the bones in the joints makes carving them less difficult. When carving, it is essential to use a sharp knife and a two-pronged fork with a thumb guard. With this equipment, the carver can produce neat slices which leave the joint looking respectable enough to serve cold at another meal. Meat may be carved across the grain, because this makes it more tender. Beef should be thinly sliced; pork and veal should be slightly thicker than beef; and lamb should be cut fairly thickly.

Whole gammon

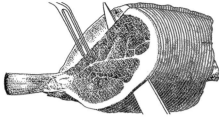

1 Remove a triangular section next to the knuckle end. Carve in a 'V' formation along the bone, taking a slice first from one side, then from the other.

2 Continue carving, with the knife held at an oblique angle, and cutting long thin slices from either side of the bone until the gammon is used up.

Pork loin

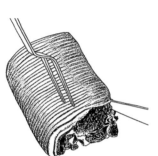
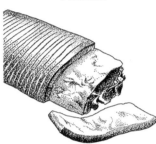
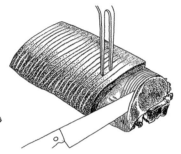

1 Using a small, sharp knife, remove the chine bone and free the meat. Leave the crackling on.

2 Alternatively, remove the crackling in sections from the top of the joint to make carving easier.

3 Slice the loin at a slight angle so that the pieces are not too small. Carve pork thicker than beef.

Hand of pork

1 Detach the ribs from the underside and the crackling from the top. Carve downwards from each side of the bone. Slice the crackling.

2 The joint is fatty on one side, lean on the other. Carve from both sides until the bone is reached; turn the joint over and carve across the grain.

Middle gammon

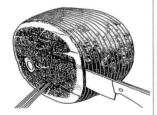

This is the prime cut of the whole gammon. It narrows towards the bone end, so the cuts made into the joint opposite the bone should be thicker at the outside, then taper towards the bone.

Wing rib of beef

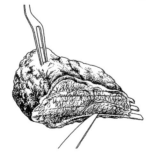

1 Remove the chine bone at the thick end of the joint and loosen the meat from the narrow ribs.

2 Carve the meat in thin downward slices; they should come away easily from the rib bones.

Sirloin of beef

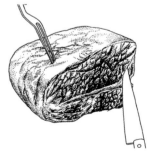
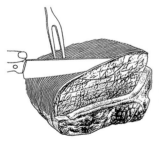

1 Loosen the meat from the bone by inserting a sharp knife between the meat and the bone.

2 Carve down to the bone; turn over the joint, remove the bone and carve the remaining meat.

Leg of lamb

1 Use a cloth to hold the shank end of the joint and turn the meatiest side of the joint uppermost. Take out two slices, about 5 mm/¼ in thick, from the centre of the leg, cutting to the bone.

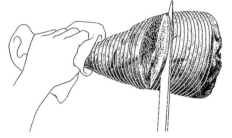

2 Continue slicing from both sides of the first cut, and gradually angling the knife to obtain longer slices. Turn the joint over, remove any unwanted fat and carve horizontal slices along the leg.

Lamb loin

Remove the chine bone to loosen the meat from the bone. Carve the joint downward, in thick slices or chops, following the natural divisions of the bones. Boned, rolled and stuffed loin of lamb can be carved in thinner slices.

Saddle of lamb

1 Cut across the base of the chump and at a right angle down the centre of the saddle, thus forming a 'T' shape.

2 To carve the French way, cut fairly thick even slices down the length of the saddle.

3 The English way is to remove the meat completely before it is carved. The chump end is carved from each side in turn, slanting the knife towards the middle. Turn the joint over and slice the fillet lengthways.

Shoulder of lamb

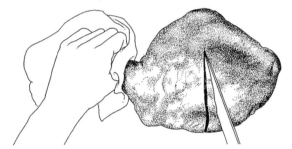

1 Use a cloth to hold the shank end of the joint. Turn the joint so that the thickest part – with the crisp skin – is uppermost. Cut a long slice, about 5 mm/¼ in thick, from the centre of the joint right down to the bone.

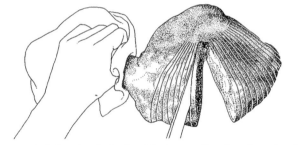

2 Carve thick slices from both sides of the first cut. Slices from the wedge of the blade bone will be smaller.

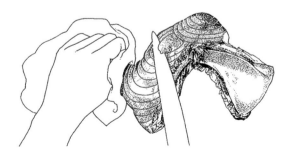

3 Cut horizontal slices from the shank bone until all the meat has been carved from the top of the joint.

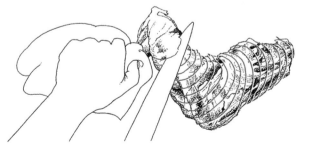

4 Turn the joint over, remove unwanted pieces of fat from the underside of the shoulder, and carve thin horizontal slices from the remaining meat.

333

OFFAL

For a variety of reasons, the range of offal which is available and popular is now smaller than it was some years ago. Few supermarkets and local butchers offer a complete range, partly due to handling and purchasing restrictions. However, large specialist butchers who have both the resources and custom can still supply offal such as brains and sweetbreads.

Brains

There is only limited availability of brains. Cattle brains (calf) are not currently available from British wholesale suppliers, only from imported supplies. Calf, lamb and pork brains may all be prepared and cooked in the same manner. Soak the brains in lightly salted cold water to remove all traces of blood. Snip off any pieces of bone and all fibres. Put the brains in a pan of well-flavoured stock, bring to the boil and simmer over low heat for about 20 minutes. Drain thoroughly, then leave the brains to cool and press under a weight.

Cut the cold brains into 1 cm/½ in slices, coat them in beaten egg and breadcrumbs and fry in butter until golden brown. Alternatively, coat the slices in batter (page 305) and deep fry them. Allow 2 sets of brains per person.

Hearts

Ox, calf and lamb hearts are all used. They are usually stuffed and pot-roasted, braised or stewed. Ox heart, however, being very tough and muscular, is better chopped and used in casseroles. Calf and lamb hearts are more tender; allow one heart per person.

Rinse off all the blood under cold running water and snip out the stumps from the arteries and the tendons with scissors. Stuff the hearts with an onion or sage stuffing and sew up the opening. Pot-roast or braise the hearts for 1½–2 hours or until tender.

Kidneys

Ox kidneys are strongly flavoured and are used, when chopped, for braising, or in pies and puddings. Calf, lamb and pig kidneys are all suitable for grilling and frying, although pork kidneys are less tender than calf and lamb. Allow 2–3 lamb kidneys per person.

Kidneys are sometimes sold in a thick layer of solid fat; this must be removed, and the thin transparent skin surrounding the kidneys must be peeled off. Cut the kidney in half lengthways and snip out the central core.

Brush the kidneys with melted butter, sprinkle with salt and pepper, and grill or fry them for not more than 6 minutes, turning them once only.

Fat from lamb kidneys can be rendered down for frying and roasting; fat from ox kidneys is used for suet crust and, after rendering down, is also suitable for deep-frying.

Liver

Ox liver, which is slightly coarse and tough, should be soaked for at least 1 hour in cold water to remove excess blood. It is best braised, although it can be sautéed like lamb liver.

Cut ox liver into 5 mm/¼ in slices, coat with seasoned flour and brown in butter together with thinly sliced onion and a few bacon rashers. Put the liver in a casserole, with the onion and bacon, cover with stock or tomato sauce. Cover and cook in a preheated oven at 180°C/350°F/gas 4 for 45 minutes.

For grilling and frying, calf and lamb liver are preferable. Cut off any gristly portions and remove, with a knife or scissors, any central cores. Wash and dry the liver thoroughly, then cut into 5 mm/¼ in thick slices. Brush with melted butter and sprinkle with salt and pepper before grilling the liver.

Alternatively, coat the slices in seasoned flour and fry them in butter over gentle heat. Avoid overcooking liver as this toughens it – as soon as blood begins to run, turn over the slices and cook the other side for a shorter time.

Pork liver may be prepared and cooked as calf and lamb liver, and is also used in pâtés, stews and casseroles.

Paunch

The stomach of a sheep is used for the traditional Scottish dish haggis. It is turned inside out and thoroughly cleaned and scrubbed before being stuffed. The stuffing consists of the cooked, minced heart, lungs and liver, seasoned with salt, pepper, cayenne, nutmeg and grated onion. This is mixed with 225 g/8 oz oatmeal and 225 g/8 oz shredded beef suet. The stuffing should only fill half the paunch as it swells during cooking. Add 30 ml/2 tablespoons white stock and sew up the opening. Wrap the haggis in a clean cloth and boil over gentle heat for 3 hours.

Sweetbreads

Sweetbreads, also known as the thymus gland, are no longer widely available. They are not processed from British cattle (calves), only from imported supplies. Calf and lamb sweetbreads are prepared in the same way. One pair of sweetbreads will serve two people. Soak the sweetbreads in cold water for 1–2 hours to remove all blood. Drain and put in a pan with cold water.

Bring to the boil and drain off the liquid immediately; cover the

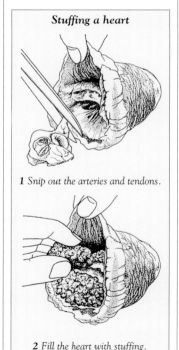

Stuffing a heart

1 *Snip out the arteries and tendons.*

2 *Fill the heart with stuffing.*

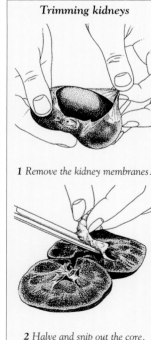

Trimming kidneys

1 *Remove the kidney membranes.*

2 *Halve and snip out the core.*

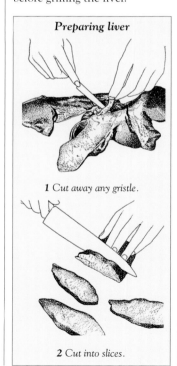

Preparing liver

1 *Cut away any gristle.*

2 *Cut into slices.*

sweetbreads with cold salted water and bring them to the boil again over low heat. As soon as boiling point is reached, lift out the sweetbreads and rinse under cold running water. Remove the black veins which run through the sweetbreads and as much as possible of the thin membranes which cover them.

Put the sweetbreads in a pan, barely cover with white stock and add a knob of butter and a squeeze of lemon juice. Bring to the boil, cover the pan with a lid and simmer gently for 15–20 minutes. Leave the sweetbreads to cool in the liquid, then drain. Coat with seasoned flour, beaten egg and breadcrumbs and fry in butter or bacon fat until golden brown. Serve with a creamy sauce and sautéed mushrooms.

Tongues

Ox tongue is the largest and weighs 1.8–2.72 kg/4–6 lb. It can be purchased salted or fresh, and is cooked whole and usually served cold. Soak a salted tongue overnight in cold water, drain and put in a large pan. Cover with cold water, bring to the boil, then drain thoroughly. Return the tongue to the pan, cover with fresh cold water and add 6 peppercorns, 1 bouquet garni* and a sliced onion. Bring to the boil, cover with a lid and simmer for 2–3 hours or until tender (cook a fresh tongue for 5–6 hours).

Plunge the cooked tongue into cold water, then peel off the skin, starting from the tip end. Remove bones and gristle from the root end and trim it off

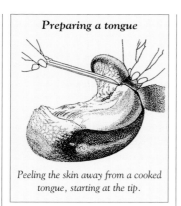

Preparing a tongue

Peeling the skin away from a cooked tongue, starting at the tip.

neatly. Arch the tongue into a round shape and press it into a deep, round cake tin, about 18 cm/7 in wide. Spoon over a little of the strained stock, cover the tongue with a weighted board and leave to set.

Lamb tongues are a great deal smaller, weighing only about 225 g/8 oz each. Soak them for 1–2 hours in lightly salted water. Boil the tongues, with 1 sliced onion, a bouquet garni*, a few peppercorns and enough water to cover, for about 2 hours.

Peel the lamb tongues and serve them hot with a parsley sauce made from the cooking stock. Alternatively, press the tongues in jellied stock as for ox tongue and serve cold.

Tripe, Ox

This is sold blanched, cleaned and partly cooked. Additional cooking time varies according to the pre-cooking – tripe sold in the supermarket is usually boiled until tender, so further cooking is necessary only for enhancing flavour. Always check with the butcher how much longer the tripe should be cooked.

Tripe and Onions

SERVES: 4
PREPARATION: 10 minutes
COOKING: about 2¼ hours

450 g/1 lb tripe
3 large onions
600 ml/1 pt milk
25 g/1 oz butter
25 g/1 oz plain flour
salt and black pepper
15 ml/1 tablespoon finely
chopped parsley

Cut the tripe into 1.5 cm/¾ in pieces, and peel and roughly chop the onions. Place these ingredients in a heavy-based pan, pour over the milk to cover (if necessary, top up with water). Cover the pan tightly with a lid and cook over gentle heat for about 2 hours or until the tripe is tender. Drain in a coarse sieve over a large bowl and set aside about 600 ml/1 pt of the liquid.

Make a roux* from the butter and flour and gradually blend in the liquid. Bring to the boil and season to taste with salt and ground pepper. Reheat the tripe and onions in the sauce, add the parsley and serve.

Veal Bones

The bones of young calves contain a large quantity of gelatine which sets to jelly after boiling. Calf's head and feet are ideal for jellied stocks and brawns; they are, however, scarce and pigs' trotters, which also contain gelatine, may be used instead.

Oxtail

Although not strictly offal, this is often classed as such. It is sold

skinned and jointed into about 5 cm/2 in pieces and is ideal for rich stews. As oxtail has a high proportion of fat and bone allow one oxtail for 3–4 servings.

Stewed Oxtail

SERVES: 4
PREPARATION: 25 minutes
OVEN: 150°C/300°F/gas 2
COOKING: 3–3¼ hours

1 oxtail
25 g/1 oz flour
salt and black pepper
50 g/2 oz dripping or 45 ml/
3 tablespoons oil
2 onions
225 g/8 oz carrots
2 sticks celery
300 ml/½ pt brown stock
bouquet garni*

Trim as much fat as possible from the jointed oxtail and toss in the flour seasoned with salt and pepper. Heat the dripping or oil in a heavy-based pan and brown the oxtail over high heat. Lift out the oxtail and put in a casserole. Fry the sliced onions, carrots and celery in the fat or oil until lightly browned, sprinkle in the remaining seasoned flour and cook until it has absorbed all the fat. Stir in the stock gradually, then pour this sauce over the oxtail. Add the bouquet garni, cover the casserole tightly with a lid and cook in a preheated oven at 150°C/300°F/gas 2 for about 3 hours or until tender. Add more stock during cooking if the oxtail is drying out.

Pig's Head

This is used for making brawn. It

must be soaked for 24 hours in cold salted water before being boiled. A good butcher will supply a half or whole head, cleaned, trimmed and chopped into pieces ready for cooking. The boiled meat, cooked with vegetables, herbs and seasonings, is set in the strained and reduced cooking liquid.

Sausages

Originally, sausages consisted of equal amounts of lean minced meat and fat, seasoned with salt, pepper and herbs. Commercial sausages contain up to one-third of their weight in breadcrumbs.

Pork – and beef – sausages are rarely home-produced today. The sausage mixture is stuffed into the skins (blanched intestines) with the aid of a sausage funnel attached to a food processor. Twist the filled intestines every 7.5–10 cm/3–4 in.

Black and White Puddings

Black puddings are made from seasoned pig's blood and suet, and white puddings from white minced pork meat and fat. These mixtures are stuffed into skins (blanched pig intestines) and slowly poached before being marketed. Cut black and white puddings in half lengthways or into thick slices and fry the pieces in hot butter.

Trotters

Pig's feet or trotters contain a large amount of gelatine and are used, with pig's head, to produce brawn or jellied stock. They are also excellent for flavouring soups and hotpots.

EGGS

Eggs are probably the most useful of all foods. There is no waste on them apart from the shell and they can be cooked very simply – they can be boiled, fried, baked, poached or scrambled.

In combination with other foods, eggs play many vital roles in cooking. They are used to set or to bind mixtures; they act as raising agents when beaten or when separated and whisked. They are an emulsifying agent in mayonnaise and a thickening agent for some soups and sauces.

BUYING AND USING EGGS

Eggs have been associated with food poisoning caused by salmonella bacteria. Uncooked poultry contain the bacteria and they may also be present in eggs.

To avoid any danger of food poisoning, always buy eggs from a reputable source. Store them in a refrigerator, as noted below, and use them within the recommended time, which will be given on the box.

Take particular care when preparing dishes in which the eggs are never completely cooked, for example in cold soufflés and mousses, lightly poached eggs or in fresh mayonnaise. Dishes containing raw eggs must be handled with care: they should be chilled and must never be allowed to stand for long periods at room temperature where any small number of bacteria may multiply to dangerous levels. They should be eaten promptly. It is also worth remembering that the elderly, infirm and other susceptible persons should not eat dishes containing unpasteurised raw egg. Official recommendations are even more stringent than this and suggest that these vulnerable individuals should also avoid dishes that contain lightly cooked eggs.

Egg Sizes

Sizes 1 and 2 are thought of as large eggs, sizes 3 and 4 are medium and size 5 are small. For baking purposes, size 3 is considered to be a standard egg. Commercially, eggs are graded by their metric weight.

Size 1: 70 g and over
Size 2: 65–70 g
Size 3: 60–65 g
Size 4: 55–60 g
Size 5: 50–55 g

Freshness

Test an egg for freshness by lowering it into a bowl of water. If it lies on its side it is quite fresh; if it stands on end it is less fresh; and if it floats to the top it is stale and possibly bad. When it is broken, a fresh egg smells pleasant, the yolk is round and firm and the white is evenly distributed. A stale egg usually has a slight smell, and spreads out thinly when broken.

Storing Eggs

Always store eggs in the refrigerator, keeping them in the container in which they were purchased. Use by the date recommended on the box. Remove the required number of eggs from the refrigerator 30–40 minutes before cooking them.

Separating Eggs

Knock the egg sharply against the rim of a bowl or cup to break the shell in half. Slip the yolk from one half-shell to the other until all the white has drained into the bowl, then slide the yolk into another bowl.

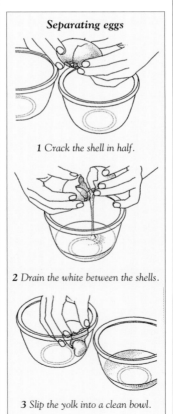

Separating eggs

1 Crack the shell in half.

2 Drain the white between the shells.

3 Slip the yolk into a clean bowl.

Beating and Whisking Eggs

Whole eggs should be beaten vigorously; keep turning them over with upward movements, using a fork, spoon, whisk or electric mixer. Beating draws in air and so increases the volume of the eggs.

When mixing egg yolks and sugar, beat the yolks first, then add the sugar and continue beating until the mixture drops in broad ribbons.

Egg whites, when whisked to a stiff but not dry foam, are used to make soufflés or meringues. Use a spotlessly clean and dry bowl, of a shape which keeps the whisk in constant contact with the egg whites.

Folding in Egg Whites

Egg whites that are to be folded into a mixture should be whisked until they are stiff but not dry. Usually, a little of the egg white is beaten into a stiff mixture before the bulk of the whites are folded in – this softens the mixture and allows the whites to be folded in more easily.

Pile the beaten egg whites on top of the mixture, and with a metal spoon draw part of the mixture from the bottom of the bowl over the whites. Continue folding in the eggs in a figure-of-eight movement, working carefully so that the whites do not lose their air content.

COOKING METHODS

Baked Eggs

(Oeufs en Cocotte)
Melt 15 g/½ oz of butter in a small, fireproof dish, break an egg into a cup and slide it into the dish. Season lightly with salt and black pepper. Bake in a preheated oven at 180°C/350°F/gas 4 for 8–10 minutes or until the white is just set. Serve immediately.

Alternatively, spoon 30 ml/2 tablespoons of cream over the seasoned egg and set the dishes in a pan of hot water. Bake in the same way as before.

Boiled Eggs

Eggs may be soft boiled (softly set white, with a runny yolk), medium boiled (firm white, with a just-soft yolk), or hard boiled (firm white, dry, solid yolk).

COOKING TIMES FOR EGGS	
Soft boiled	
Large eggs	4½ minutes
Standard eggs	4 minutes
Medium eggs	3–3½ minutes
Medium boiled	
Large eggs	6½ minutes
Standard eggs	6 minutes
Medium eggs	4–5 minutes
Hard boiled	
Large eggs	12 minutes
Standard eggs	11 minutes
Medium eggs	10 minutes

Soft-boiled eggs Bring a pan of cold water to boiling point over gentle heat and, with a spoon, carefully lower each egg into the water. To boil a large number of eggs, put them in a wire basket or egg holder so that all the eggs can be immersed in the water at the same time.

Medium-boiled eggs Put the eggs in a saucepan and cover them with cold water; bring to the boil over low heat. As soon as it boils, remove the pan from the heat, cover it with a lid and leave the eggs to stand in the hot water for the necessary time.

Hard-boiled eggs Cook the eggs in boiling water for 10–12 minutes. Plunge them into cold water immediately to prevent further cooking and to make shelling easier. Tap the eggs round the middle with the back of a knife, and pull away the two half-shells. Shelled eggs should not be exposed to air for long as they become tough; put eggs to be served cold in iced water.

Fried Eggs

Melt a knob of butter (25–50g/ 1–2 oz is sufficient for 4 eggs), or equal amounts of oil and butter, in a frying pan over low heat. Break the eggs, one by one, on to a saucer and slide them into the fat. Reduce the heat immediately and baste the eggs with the butter to ensure they cook evenly. Fry the eggs for 3–5 minutes, or until the whites are firm.

Poached Eggs

Fill a heavy-based frying pan with cold water to a depth of 2.5 cm/1 in, add a pinch of salt

Preparing poached eggs

For poached eggs, gather the egg whites around the yolks.

and bring to the boil. Reduce the heat and keep the water just simmering. Break the eggs, one by one, on to a saucer, swirl the water with a knife and slide the egg carefully into the middle of the swirl. Using two spoons quickly gather the whites over and round the yolks. Cover the pan with a lid and cook the eggs for 4–5 minutes, or until the yolk is set and the white firm.

For more regularly shaped poached eggs, round pastry cutters may be set in the pan and the eggs slid inside them. Alternatively, an egg poacher can be used: half fill the pan of the poacher with water, bring to the boil, then reduce the heat and keep the water simmering. Melt a knob of butter or margarine in each egg container and break an egg into them. Season lightly with salt and black pepper. Cover the pan with the lid and cook the eggs for 2 minutes or until they just set.

Scrambled Eggs

Use 2 eggs per person, and for each egg allow 15 g/½ oz butter and 15 ml/1 tablespoon cream or top of the milk. Beat the eggs with a little salt and black pepper in a bowl. Melt the butter in a heavy-based pan but do not heat it fiercely. Pour in the egg mixture and cook over low heat, stirring continuously until the mixture begins to thicken. Continue cooking and stirring until the eggs are lightly set to a creamy consistency. Do not overcook or the eggs will clump into dry curds and a whey-like liquid will separate from them. The

eggs may be cooked in a double saucepan or in a heat-proof bowl over simmering water.

Remove the pan from the heat and stir in the cream or top of the milk.

Omelettes

There are two types of omelette – plain and fluffy (soufflé). Plain omelettes are usually served as part of a savoury course, while fluffy omelettes may be savoury or sweet. Cook omelettes in a special omelette pan or in a small frying pan.

Plain Omelette

SERVES: 1
PREPARATION: 3 minutes
COOKING: 1½–2 minutes

2 eggs
15 ml/1 tablespoon milk or water
1.25 ml/¼ teaspoon salt
black pepper
knob of butter

Break the eggs into a bowl, add the milk or water, salt and pepper; beat until blended, but not foamy. Melt the butter in the pan without letting it brown, and pour in the egg mixture. Cook the omelette over moderate heat and lift it up round the edges with a spatula so that the liquid egg runs underneath. When the omelette is almost set, but still slightly runny on top, allow the underside to become golden. Fold the omelette in half with the spatula and quickly slide it out on to a warm plate. Serve the omelette immediately.

Savoury Omelettes

Many ingredients can be added

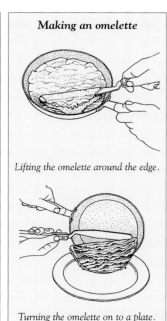

Making an omelette

Lifting the omelette around the edge.

Turning the omelette on to a plate.

to the omelette mixture before cooking, or they can be cooked separately and spooned over the omelette before folding it over.

Cheese Add 25 g/1 oz finely grated cheese to the beaten egg mixture before cooking.

Ham Sprinkle 15 ml/1 tablespoon of finely chopped ham over the omelette before folding.

Fluffy Omelette

This can be filled, like a plain omelette, with savoury ingredients, or it can be served as a sweet course.

SERVES: 2
PREPARATION: 5 minutes
COOKING: 3–5 minutes

2 eggs
1.25 ml/¼ teaspoon salt
black pepper
15 g/½ oz butter

Separate the eggs and whisk the whites until they are stiff, then beat in the salt and a few grinds of pepper. Beat the egg yolks with 30 ml/2 tablespoons water until they are thick, and fold them into the whites.

Melt the butter in a frying pan or omelette pan and spoon in the egg mixture. Cook over moderate heat until the underside is golden. Place the omelette, in the pan, under a hot grill to brown the top lightly. Add any savoury filling, and fold the omelette in half.

For a sweet omelette, omit salt and pepper and whisk the egg whites with 1.25 ml/¼ teaspoon natural vanilla essence to the creamed egg yolks, if liked, then cook the omelette as already described. Spread the omelette with a thin layer of warm jam or fruit purée, before folding it in half. Sprinkle with caster sugar before serving.

Soufflés

These light airy egg dishes may be sweet or savoury and are served either hot or cold. Hot soufflés are based on a thick white sauce to which egg yolks are added before the whisked whites are folded in. To allow even rising during baking, always use a straight-sided buttered soufflé dish and let the soufflé mixture come no more than three-quarters up the sides of the dish. It is not necessary to prepare a hot soufflé with a paper collar (see Cold Soufflés, overleaf), but it is very important to serve the soufflé the moment it is taken from the oven.

Cheese Soufflé

SERVES: 4–6
PREPARATION: 20 minutes
OVEN: 180°C/350°F/gas 4
COOKING: 40–45 minutes

3 eggs
300 ml/½ pt thick coating
    White Sauce (page 352)
salt and black pepper
100 g/4 oz mature Cheddar
    cheese, grated

Butter an 18 cm/7 in soufflé dish. Separate the eggs, and prepare the white sauce. Cool it slightly, then stir in the grated cheese. Beat the egg yolks, one at a time, into the basic sauce, and whisk the whites in a bowl until stiff. Fold the whites carefully into the soufflé mixture, using a metal spoon, and pour it into the dish.

Set the prepared soufflé dish in a roasting tin of hot water and bake in a preheated oven at 180°C/350°F/gas 4 for 40–45 minutes or until well risen and golden brown.

Hot soufflé variations

Corn Mix 50 g/2 oz sweetcorn kernels and 50 g/2 oz grilled, chopped bacon into the sauce.
Fish Add 75 g/3 oz cooked, finely flaked haddock to the sauce.
Ham Mix 75 g/3 oz cooked chopped ham into the sauce.
Caramel Omit salt and black pepper from the white sauce. Heat 45 ml/3 tablespoons caster sugar until it is melted and brown, and stir into the sauce, before adding the eggs.
Chocolate Omit salt and pepper from the sauce and stir in 50 g/2 oz melted plain chocolate.

Cold Soufflés

These soufflés are not baked but are left to set in the refrigerator. To achieve the characteristic risen look of a soufflé, the dish is prepared with a paper collar extending above the rim.

Cut a band 7.5 cm/3 in deeper than the dish from a double layer of greaseproof paper, and fold up 2.5 cm/1 in along one of the long edges. Wrap the band round the dish, with the folded edge of the paper level with the base and the upper edge extending above the rim by 5 cm/ 2 in. Tie the band securely in place with string. Spoon the prepared soufflé mixture into the dish until it reaches almost to the top of the collar.

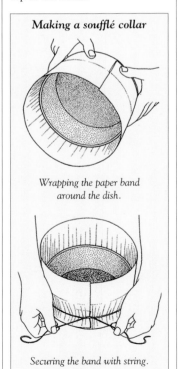

Making a soufflé collar

Wrapping the paper band around the dish.

Securing the band with string.

When the soufflé has set, remove the paper collar. The easiest way to do this is to run a warmed knife blade between the set soufflé and the paper.

Lemon Soufflé

SERVES: 4
PREPARATION: 25 minutes
CHILLING: 2 hours

2 lemons
3 eggs, separated
75 g/3 oz caster sugar
10 ml/2 teaspoons gelatine
30 ml/2 tablespoons water
150 ml/¼ pt double cream

Grate the rind from the lemons and squeeze out the juice. Beat the egg yolks, sugar, lemon rind and juice in a bowl until thick.

Sprinkle the gelatine over the cold water and leave to stand for 15 minutes. Set the bowl over a pan of hot water until the gelatine has dissolved and is clear. Allow to cool slightly, then pour into the lemon mixture. Whip the cream, until it just holds its shape, then fold it into the mixture. Whisk the egg whites until stiff and fold them carefully into the mixture when it is nearly set. Spoon into a prepared 15 cm/6 in soufflé dish and chill until set.

Cold Sweet Soufflés

Chocolate Melt 50–75 g/2–3 oz dark chocolate and stir into the yolk mixture, with 15 ml/1 tablespoon brandy or rum.
Coffee Add 60–75 ml/4–5 tablespoons strong black coffee and 15 ml/1 tablespoon Tia Maria or Curaçao liqueur to the egg yolks.

Orange Add the grated rind of a large orange and 60 ml/4 tablespoons orange juice.

EGG CUSTARDS

There are two types of custard: a set mixture which is baked or steamed, and the softer pouring custard which is used as a sauce.

Egg whites set a baked custard, and the yolks give it the creamy consistency. However, as the yolks thicken at a higher temperature (65°C/149°F) than the egg whites (62°C/144°F), it is important to cook custards at the correct heat. Too much heat, especially direct heat, will cause an egg custard to curdle. Use a double saucepan for making a pouring custard and bake a set custard in a container with a little hot water. If a double saucepan is not available, use a heatproof bowl over a saucepan.

For baked custards, 2 whole eggs plus 2 egg yolks will set 600 ml/1 pt of milk. For a thin pouring custard use 4 egg yolks to every 600 ml/1 pt of milk.

Custard Sauce

MAKES: 600 ml/1 pt
PREPARATION: 10 minutes
INFUSING: 10 minutes
COOKING: 10 minutes

600 ml/1 pt milk
½ vanilla pod
30 ml/2 tablespoons caster sugar
4 egg yolks

Put the milk in a saucepan with the vanilla pod and heat over very gentle heat without boiling. Remove the pan from the heat, cover and leave to infuse for 10 minutes. Remove the vanilla pod and stir in the sugar.

Beat the yolks in a bowl, and gradually stir in the hot milk. Strain the custard back into the pan or into a double saucepan with hot, not boiling, water in the base. Sir the custard continuously over very low heat until it is creamy and slightly thickened, enough to coat the back of a wooden spoon. If the custard is to be used cold, pour it into a bowl and sprinkle with sugar to stop a skin forming.

Simple custard sauce To make a quick, reliable custard sauce, mix 30 ml/2 tablespoons cornflour with a little of the milk, the sugar, egg yolks and 5 ml/1 teaspoon natural vanilla essence to make a smooth thin paste. Heat the remaining milk in a saucepan until it is just beginning to skin over, then pour it into the cornflour mixture, stirring all the time. Pour the custard back into the saucepan and bring it slowly to the boil, stirring continuously. Simmer gently for 2 minutes. This gives a thicker pouring sauce; the cornflour stabilises the mixture by stopping it curdling.

Baked Custard Pudding

SERVES: 4
PREPARATION: 15 minutes
OVEN: 180°C/350°F/gas 4
COOKING: 35 minutes

15–25 g/½ oz butter
600 ml/1 pt milk
strip of lemon rind
2 whole eggs
2 egg yolks
20 ml/4 teaspoons caster sugar
grated nutmeg

Butter the inside of a 900 ml/ 1½ pt pie dish. In a saucepan, bring the milk and lemon rind (free of all pith) to just below boiling point, then remove from the heat. Beat the eggs and yolks in a bowl, using a fork, until well mixed but not frothy. Beat in the sugar. Pour the milk over the eggs, then stir and strain the custard into the pie dish. Dot the custard with tiny flakes of butter, and sprinkle the surface with grated nutmeg.

Set the pie dish in a shallow baking or roasting tin, with about 2.5 cm/1 in of water. Bake the custard in a preheated oven at 180°C/350°F/gas 4, for about 35 minutes or until the custard is set and the top golden brown. Serve warm or cold.

BATTERS

Batters provide the basis for a large number of dishes ranging from simple, traditional pancakes served with lemon and sugar to Russian Blinis (page 61), French Crêpes Suzette (page 93) and American Waffles (page 377).

Batter is a mixture of flour, salt, egg, milk or other liquid. The proportions vary, depending on the consistency required for the batter. Pancakes, for instance, need a thin batter, while fritters need a thick coating batter. For crisp coating batters, 15 ml/1 tablespoon oil may be used with 150 ml/¼ pt of water, or the liquid may be half milk and half water.

Coating batters and batters which are aerated by folding in whisked egg white should be used as soon as they are prepared.

Batter for baked puddings may be used freshly prepared or it may be allowed to stand for up to about 1 hour. Batter for pancakes is best left to stand for 30–60 minutes before use: this is not essential but it does allow some of the air beaten into the mixture to disperse and the starch has time to absorb as much liquid as possible. When the batter has been allowed to stand, a little additional liquid is usually added to thin the batter again just before cooking begins or part-way through making the pancakes. This makes pancakes that are fine and flat.

Basic Pancake Batter

When a recipe refers to this batter, the volume required is judged by the quantity of milk, not the total amount of prepared batter. For example, when a dish calls for 300 ml/½ pt of the batter, make the quantity given below.

MAKES: 8–10 pancakes
PREPARATION: 10 minutes

100 g/4 oz plain flour
pinch of salt
2 eggs
300 ml/½ pt milk

Sift the flour and salt into a large bowl. Using a wooden spoon, make a hollow in the centre of the flour and drop in the lightly beaten eggs. Slowly pour half the milk into the flour, gradually working the flour into the milk. When all of it is incorporated, beat the mixture with a wooden spoon, whisk, or rotary beater, until it becomes smooth and free of lumps. Allow

the batter to stand for a few minutes. Then add the rest of the of the milk, beating continuously until the batter is bubbly and has the same consistency as single cream.

Basic Coating Batter

PREPARATION: 10 minutes

100 g/4 oz plain flour
pinch of salt
1 egg
150 ml/¼ pt milk

Follow the method given for Basic Pancake Batter.

Fritter Batter

PREPARATION: 10 minutes
RESTING: 1 hour

100 g/4 oz plain flour
pinch of salt
15 ml/1 tablespoon oil
150 ml/¼ pt water
1 egg white

Sift the flour and salt together into a bowl. Make a well in the centre, add the oil and water, beating until smooth. Allow the batter to rest for 1 hour.

Whisk the egg white until stiff, but not dry, then fold it evenly into the batter with a metal spoon.

Pancakes

MAKES: 8 pancakes
PREPARATION: 10 minutes
COOKING: 25 minutes

2 lemons
300 ml/½ pt Basic Pancake Batter
50 g/2 oz caster sugar
butter or oil (for frying)

Finely grate the rind from 1 lemon and mix with the sugar. Squeeze the juice from both lemons. To make 8 pancakes, use an 18 cm/7 in heavy-based shallow frying pan with sloping sides. Add just enough butter or oil (or use a mixture of both) to gloss the pan to prevent the batter sticking. Fierce heat is necessary, and the pan should be really hot before the pancake batter is poured in.

Pour in just enough batter to flow in a thin film over the base – tilting the pan to spread it. Use a jug or ladle for pouring in the batter. The heat is right if the underside of the pancake turns

golden in 1 minute; adjust the heat to achieve this. Flip the pancake over with a palette knife or spatula, or toss by flicking the wrist and lifting the pan away from the body. The other side of the pancake should also be done in about 1 minute.

Turn the pancake out on to sugared paper, sprinkle with lemon and sugar, fold it in half, then in half again; keep warm until all the pancakes are fried.
■ Serve immediately, sprinkled with sugar and lemon juice.

Cooking pancakes

1 Coat the hot pan with batter.

2 Cook until the pancake is browned underneath.

3 Turn the pancake with a palette knife.

4 Invert the pancake out of the pan.

To store pancakes If they are to be kept for a short time, stack them in a pile and cover with a clean tea towel. If they are to be stored for 1–2 days, put oiled greaseproof paper between each pancake, stack them and wrap the whole pile in foil and store in the refrigerator.

To freeze pancakes Stack the pancakes with layers of absorbent kitchen paper between them. When cold, re-stack the pancakes with layers of freezer film or clean absorbent kitchen paper, wrap them in foil, then seal them in a polythene bag. Freeze for up to 6 months.

To reheat pancakes If pancakes are to be served with lemon and sugar, wrap three or four pancakes in foil and heat through in a preheated oven at 150°C/300°F/gas 2. Remove the foil, sprinkle each pancake with sugar and squeezed lemon, then fold up, place on a hot dish and dust with sugar. Alternatively, brush a flat tin with melted butter, arrange overlapping pancakes on it, brush with butter and put into a preheated oven at 190°C/375°F/gas 5 for 4–5 minutes. Alternatively, heat the pancakes in a frying pan in, for example, an orange sauce as for Crêpes Suzette (page 93).

For savoury, stuffed pancakes, fill them with a freshly made filling, top with a sauce or grated cheese, and heat the pancakes through under a moderate grill. Alternatively, stuff the pancakes, place them in a flat baking dish or tin, cover with foil and heat in a preheated oven at 190°C/375°F/gas 5 for about 30 minutes.

Yorkshire Pudding and Popovers

SERVES: 4
PREPARATION: 20 minutes
OVEN: 220°C/425°F/gas 7
PREPARATION:
Popovers: 20 minutes
Pudding: 35–40 minutes

25 g/1 oz dripping or lard
300 ml/½ pt Basic Pancake Batter made with milk (page 339)

To make a Yorkshire pudding, heat the dripping in a small baking tin in a preheated oven at 220°C/425°F/gas 7 until smoking hot. Pour in the prepared batter, through a strainer, and bake for 35–40 minutes.

To make popovers, grease 12 individual patty* tins with a knob of fat in each. When the fat is hot, pour in the batter so that the tins are about two-thirds full. Return the tins to a preheated oven at 220°C/425°F/gas 7 for about 20 minutes or until well risen and crisp. Serve the popovers or pudding at once.

A Yorkshire pudding can also be cooked underneath a joint of beef: place the meat on a rack so that the fat and meat juices drip down into the pudding.

MERINGUES

Meringue forms the basis for many desserts: shells and baskets can be filled with cream or fresh fruit. Meringue is also a favourite topping for sweet pies and flans.

Meringue is quite easy to make provided a few points are observed – the whisk and bowl must be absolutely clean and dry, and the eggs quite free from yolk.

Ideally, use 2–3-day-old eggs. The shapes of whisk and bowl also influence a good meringue; a balloon whisk gives the greater volume but takes longer to whisk the whites than a rotary hand whisk. An electric mixer is the quickest, but gives the smallest volume. Choose a wide bowl when using a balloon whisk, and a narrow deep bowl for a rotary hand whisk.

The sugar for a meringue must be fine. Caster sugar is generally used, but equal quantities of caster and icing sugar produce a meringue of pure white colour and crisp melting texture. Do not use granulated sugar, as the coarse crystals break down the egg albumen, thus reducing the volume of the meringue.

Basic Meringue

PREPARATION: 10 minutes

2 egg whites
100 g/4 oz caster sugar

Put the egg whites in a bowl and whisk them until they are stiff and dry. Tip in half the sugar and continue whisking the stiff whites until the texture is smooth and close, and the mixture stands in stiff peaks when the whisk is lifted. Lightly but evenly fold in the rest of the caster sugar with a metal spoon.

Meringue Shells

Line a baking tray with non-stick paper. Using two dessertspoons, set the meringue in six to eight small mounds on the prepared tray, and shape them into neat ovals with the spoons.

Alternatively, spoon the mixture into a piping bag fitted with 1 cm/½ in wide plain or star nozzle: turn the top of the bag down over the hand to form a cuff, then fill the bag using a metal spoon. Ease the meringue down towards the nozzle by twisting the top of the bag. Pipe six to eight meringue whirls on to the baking tray.

Sprinkle the meringues lightly with caster sugar and set the tray in the coolest part of the oven. Dry the meringues, in a preheated oven, at the lowest possible heat for 2–3 hours.

Halfway through drying, the meringues may be taken out and the base of the shells pressed in lightly to make more space for a cream filling. Return the shells, placed on their sides, to the oven until completely dry.

Cool the meringues on a wire rack. Unfilled, they will keep for about a week in an airtight container. To serve the sweet, fill the hollows of the meringues with sweetened cream.

Meringue Cuite

This is made with icing sugar and has a firmer texture than basic meringue; it is ideal for making hollow basket shapes, to be filled with cream or fruit.

MAKES: 6 baskets
PREPARATION: 20 minutes

225–250 g/8–9 oz icing sugar
4 egg whites
2.5–5 ml/½–1 teaspoon natural vanilla essence

Sift the icing sugar on to a sheet of greaseproof paper. Whisk the

egg whites until frothy with a hand rotary or electric beater. Whisk in the sugar, a little at a time, and last of all flavour with vanilla essence.

Set the bowl over a pan half-filled with simmering water, and whisk the meringue until it holds its shape and leaves a thick trail when the whisk is lifted out.

Meringue Baskets

Line one or two baking trays with non-stick paper. Pencil six circles, 7.5 cm/3 in wide and a little apart on the paper. Turn the paper over, so that the pencil marks are underneath but are still visible. Spread about half the prepared Meringue Cuite evenly over the pencilled circles to form the bases for the baskets, and spoon the rest of the meringue into a piping bag fitted with a 6–8 point star nozzle. Pipe two layers, one on top of each other, round the edge of each basket base. Dry the meringue baskets in a cool oven at 140–150°C/275–300°F/gas 1–2 for about 45 minutes or until the baskets come away easily. Cool on a wire rack.

A large meringue basket can be made in the same way as these small baskets, by drawing a large circle on the non-stick paper. Spread the meringue mixture quite thickly over the base. A larger meringue is best dried out at the lowest possible oven temperature for about 3 hours to stop it cracking.

■ Serve filled with Chantilly Cream (page 411) or Vanilla Ice Cream (page 380), and with fresh or canned and drained fruit.

VEGETABLES

Vegetables are at their best for food value and flavour when freshly harvested, so they should always be used as soon as possible after purchase. Buy only good-quality produce, avoiding any limp, tired-looking vegetables or damaged items. The majority of vegetables are best stored in the refrigerator. Certain fruits and vegetables should not be stored together: carrots stored next to apples will take on a bitter taste, and potatoes quickly spoil if they are stored with onions. Cut the leaves from root vegetables before storing, to prevent the sap rising from the roots. Potatoes should be stored in a thick, brown paper bag in a cool, dry place away from light. Potatoes which are turning green or sprouting must be discarded.

Choose vegetables that are crisp and firm rather than hard. The size is sometimes an indication of age and quality. For example, very small vegetables may be flavourless because they are immature, whereas over-large vegetables may be old, and therefore coarse.

PREPARATION

Prepare vegetables immediately before cooking by thorough washing and, if necessary, scrubbing with a brush. But do not soak vegetables at any stage during preparation because their mineral salts and vitamins are soluble in water. Because the most nutritious part of root vegetables and onions lies just under the skin, only a thin outer layer should be peeled away with a knife. If the vegetables are young, just scrape the surface lightly. For everyday cooking, many prefer to cook potatoes in their skins.

Vegetables can be used whole or can be cut up for quicker cooking. The more the vegetables are cut and the smaller the pieces, the greater the surface area from which nutrients can be lost. To cut vegetables, use a sharp kitchen knife; never use a carbon steel knife.

Some vegetables – cabbages, for example – may be merely halved and quartered before cooking; but most can be prepared by slicing, dicing, shredding, chopping or cutting into rounds. These techniques are described on page 303.

FREEZING VEGETABLES

Freeze fresh vegetables when in prime condition. Green beans, peas, mange-tout, broccoli, cooked spinach and corn-on-the-cob are all examples of vegetables that freeze well. Asparagus, cauliflower, courgettes and carrots have an inferior texture when thawed. Tomatoes can be puréed and sieved, but not frozen whole. Generally, vegetables such as potatoes and parsnips are only acceptable when mashed or puréed. Celery, aubergines and mushrooms do not freeze well; however, finely diced celery, cut and cooked aubergines and diced or chopped mushrooms are acceptable in some frozen and thawed cooked dishes.

Broad beans, peas and cauliflower should be blanched for about 2 minutes in boiling water and refreshed in iced water, then drained before freezing. However, other vegetables can be frozen without blanching – French or runner beans keep just as well for up to a year without being blanched.

COOKING METHODS

After preparing vegetables, do not soak them. Only peeled potatoes need to be kept in water; otherwise they will turn brown. Dried peas and beans are quicker to cook if soaked.

Boiling

Use only a minimum of salted water, enough to part-steam green vegetables or to just cover root vegetables. For each 300 ml/ ½ pt of water, add 2.5 ml/½ teaspoon of salt or reduce this according to taste. Root vegetables are put into a pan of cold salted water, and all other vegetables into boiling water.

Bring the water to the boil. Add the prepared vegetables, cover the pan and quickly return to the boil. Reduce the heat and boil at moderate heat until the vegetables are tender but firm. The vegetable liquid can be used to make a stock, sauce or gravy.

Steaming

Place the prepared vegetables in a steamer above rapidly boiling water. Sprinkle with a little salt, if liked. Cover the steamer with a tight-fitting lid, and steam until just tender, usually 3–5 minutes longer than the vegetables would take to boil.

Pressure Cooking

Pressure cook older vegetables and dried peas and beans. Follow the manufacturer's instructions, and time the cooking with care. Vegetables will quickly overcook by this method.

Sweating

Use a wide, shallow pan. Melt 25 g/1 oz butter in the pan, and add the prepared vegetables. Stir well, cover the pan with a tight-fitting lid, and cook over moderate heat until steam forms. Reduce the heat and cook until the vegetables are tender, shaking the pan occasionally.

Vegetables can be cooked by this method using the minimum of fat – simply enough to grease the base of the pan – or without any fat. If the vegetables are cooked without any fat, add 15 ml/1 tablespoon water and heat the vegetables very gently at first, until they provide their own steam and cooking juices.

Shallow Frying

This method is suitable for very tender vegetables such as aubergines, courgettes and tomatoes, or for onion slices. Cook these vegetables in olive oil or butter, or in a mixture of both in an uncovered pan.

Most other vegetables must be precooked or parboiled before frying. Heat butter, oil or other fat in a heavy-based pan, add the prepared and thoroughly drained precooked vegetables, and fry until tender and golden brown.

Stir Frying

Suitable for vegetables that have a good texture and flavour when lightly cooked, such as leeks, onions, carrots, baby sweetcorn, cauliflower, mange-tout, courgettes, cabbage, celery and so on.

Cut the vegetables into fine pieces and cook them in a little oil over high heat, stirring and tossing them continuously.

Deep Frying

Potatoes are often deep fried without a coating to make chips. This method can also be used for other vegetables, such as onions, courgettes or aubergines, which are usually coated with flour or batter, or egg and breadcrumbs, before frying.

Heat the fat or oil in a deep, heavy-based pan to 190°C/ 375°F or until a day-old cube of bread browns in 1 minute.

Before placing the vegetables in the fat, dry them on absorbent kitchen paper or a clean tea towel. Place a few pieces of vegetable at a time in the fat; cook until crisp.

Braising

This method of cooking is suitable for root vegetables and onions. After preparing the vegetables, blanch them by plunging them into a pan of boiling water for 2–3 minutes.

Lightly fry the drained vegetables in butter in a pan. Then add 150–300 ml/¼–½ pt of stock to each 450 g/1 lb of prepared vegetables. Season lightly with salt and pepper, add a knob of butter and cover with a tight-fitting lid. Cook until tender.

Lift the vegetables out of the pan and reduce the juices by rapid boiling, or thicken the juices with cornflour.

Baking

Vegetables may be baked in several different ways. The simplest method, for whole unpeeled vegetables, is to brush them with a little oil and place them on a baking tray. Bake in a preheated oven at 200°C/400°F/gas 6 until tender. Potatoes, small whole squash (such as butternut), courgettes, part-peeled onions and marrow may all be cooked by this method. It is best to cut a large marrow in half and scoop out the seeds, then cover the top with foil.

The popular method of baking prepared and cut vegetables is by placing them in a covered dish. Sliced courgettes, slices or cubes of marrow, cubes of pumpkin, fingers of cucumber and sliced aubergines may be baked in a covered dish. Sprinkle a little salt and pepper over the vegetables and dot them with a little butter. Turn or rearrange the vegetables occasionally while they are cooking.

Another very satisfactory method is to wrap the vegetables in greased foil. Cut vegetables should be placed on a large square of foil and sprinkled with salt and pepper. Dot with butter, if liked, close the foil around the vegetables to seal them in a neat packet. Place this on a baking tray. Individual portions are usually served in their foil packets. An excellent method for courgettes.

Roasting

This method is applied to roots and tubers, usually cooked around a meat joint. Place the prepared vegetables in the hot fat and roast in a preheated oven at 220°C/425°F/gas 7 for 45–60 minutes. Alternatively, parboil the vegetables for 10 minutes, drain, and then add to the hot fat. Roast for 20–30 minutes.

EASY DRESSINGS FOR VEGETABLES

Butter is one of the simplest and most popular dressings for vegetables. Whether steamed or boiled, the flavour of plain-cooked vegetables is always enhanced by tossing them with butter. However, in order to maintain a balanced diet, on a daily basis it is best to use a variety of cooking techniques and serving methods.

Sweating and stir frying are popular methods, which use the minimum of fat and still give an excellent flavour. Quick-cook methods of this type also help to conserve nutrients which are otherwise lost in the cooking water when boiling or steaming vegetables. The following are suggestions for toppings or dressings which may be served with plain boiled or steamed vegetables. Consider the main dish of the meal, which often provides a sauce or dressing that may also complement the vegetable side dishes.

Fromage Frais

Low-fat fromage frais makes a creamy dressing for vegetables. It is particularly good with snipped chives, chopped dill or finely chopped parsley. Turn the cooked vegetables into a heated serving dish and top with the herb-flavoured fromage frais, then toss the vegetables with the dressing as they are served.

Plain Yogurt

Plain yogurt, freshly ground black pepper and a little freshly grated Parmesan cheese combine well to make a savoury topping. Top the vegetables with the yogurt and sprinkle with a little Parmesan; a little paprika or grated nutmeg may be added instead of pepper.

Chopped Egg

Finely chop the white of a hard-boiled egg and sieve the yolk, keeping both separate. Mix snipped chives or chopped parsley with the white. Toss the vegetables with a little butter, fromage frais or low-fat soft cheese. Top with lines of chopped egg white and sieved yolk.

PREPARATION AND COOKING OF VEGETABLES

Artichokes, Globe

PREPARATION:
Cut off stalk and, using scissors, trim off point from each outer leaf; rinse and drain. Rub cut surfaces with lemon. Chokes can be removed before or after cooking. Spread apart top leaves and pull out inside leaves to reveal hairy choke. Using a teaspoon, scrape away hairs to expose the heart or fond. Remaining leaves around the base can also be stripped away leaving just the fond.

COOKING METHODS:
Boiling Whole artichokes: For 40–45 minutes, in salted water. Without chokes: for 15–20 minutes. Drain upside-down.
Braising Blanch* for 5 minutes. Refresh in cold water. Place on a bed of sautéed vegetables, moistened with wine or stock and add a bouquet garni*. Cover and cook for 1 hour.
Steaming Whole artichokes: for 50–55 minutes. Without chokes: for 20–25 minutes. Stuffed artichokes: for 30–35 minutes.

SERVING SUGGESTIONS:
Hot: with melted butter or Hollandaise Sauce (page 355). To eat, pull out one leaf at a time and dip edible base of leaf in the sauce. Scrape off fleshy base of leaf between the teeth. When leaves are removed, eat the heart with a knife and fork.
Cold: with Mayonnaise (page 355), French Dressing (page 356) or Tartare Sauce (page 356).

Artichokes, Jerusalem

PREPARATION:
Scrub and thinly peel the artichoke

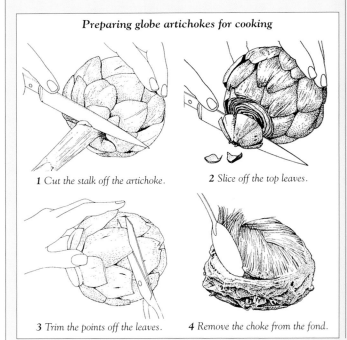

Preparing globe artichokes for cooking

1 Cut the stalk off the artichoke.

2 Slice off the top leaves.

3 Trim the points off the leaves.

4 Remove the choke from the fond.

under running water; place in acidulated water*.

COOKING METHODS:
Boiling For 25–30 minutes in salted acidulated water. Drain. Artichokes can also be boiled in their skins and then peeled.
Steaming Whole artichokes: steam for 35–40 minutes. Quartered: steam for 30 minutes.
Deep frying Parboil for 20 minutes, dry, cut in thick slices, dip in a light batter; deep fry for 3–4 minutes.
SERVING SUGGESTIONS:
Boiled or steamed with melted butter, Béchamel Sauce (page 353) or Cheese Sauce (page 352).

Asparagus

PREPARATION:
Cut off woody parts from base of stems. Using knife, scrape white part of stems downwards. Tie asparagus in bundles, all heads together.

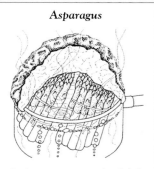

Cooking in a pan tented with foil.

Placing in an asparagus steamer.

COOKING METHOD:
Boiling For 15–20 minutes in salted water to just below the heads.
SERVING SUGGESTIONS:
Serve 8–10 stems per portion: an average bundle gives 3–4 portions. Hot: with melted butter, Mornay Sauce (page 353) or Hollandaise Sauce (page 355).
Cold: with French Dressing (page 356) or Mayonnaise (page 355).

Aubergines

PREPARATION:
Wipe, trim both ends and peel if necessary. Slice, dice or halve. Sprinkle cut surfaces with salt and leave for 30 minutes. Rinse and dry.
COOKING METHODS:
Frying Coat the prepared slices in seasoned flour or leave plain. Fry in olive oil.
Grilling or baking Brush aubergine slices with melted butter or oil.
SERVING SUGGESTIONS:
Fried or grilled with meat; stuffed with Parmesan cheese topping, tomato or cheese sauce.

Avocado

PREPARATION:
Just before serving, slice in half lengthways, round the stone, using a stainless steel or silver knife to prevent discoloration of the flesh. Leave the skins on if avocados are to be served as a first course with a filling or dressing. The flesh can also be carefully scooped out and mixed with salad vegetables or seafood.

If avocado is to be left for any length of time, toss the flesh in lemon juice to prevent discoloration.
COOKING METHOD:
Baking Place the halved avocados on a baking dish, supporting them with crumpled foil to keep them upright. Fill with a savoury mixture of fresh breadcrumbs, chopped parsley, crushed garlic and a little melted butter or olive oil. Grated Parmesan cheese may be added. Bake in a preheated oven at 190°C/375°F/gas 5 for about 20 minutes, until the filling is brown and crisp. This is a good method for cooking slightly under-ripe avocados.
SERVING SUGGESTIONS:
Usually served fresh with Sauce Vinaigrette (page 356), as a savoury dip or a mousse.

Beans, Broad

PREPARATION:
Young and tender beans: wash, top and tail, and cook in their pods. Mature beans: remove from pods. Large beans: remove from their skin after cooking and make into a pureé.
COOKING METHODS:
Boiling For 15–20 minutes, both in and out of their pods. Mature beans, up to 30 minutes.
Steaming For 10–15 minutes.
SERVING SUGGESTIONS:
Serve small beans shelled or in their pods, tossed in butter, and sprinkled with finely chopped parsley or savory. Serve more mature beans with a white or parsley sauce.

Beans, French

PREPARATION:
Young beans: wash, top and tail; leave whole or cut into 3.5–5 cm/ 1½–2 in lengths. Mature beans: top, tail and string before slicing.
COOKING METHODS:
Boiling For 5–10 minutes in salted water. Refresh with cold water. Drain well, then serve at once with butter and herbs.
Steaming For 10–15 minutes.
Stir frying Blanch for 2 minutes in boiling water, then stir fry with other vegetables or with spring onion.
SERVING SUGGESTIONS:
Dress with Garlic, Anchovy or Herb Butters (page 307).

Beans, Runner

PREPARATION:
Wash, top, tail and string. Cut into oblique slices 3.5–5 cm/1½–2 in long.

COOKING METHODS:
Boiling For 5–10 minutes in salted water.
Steaming For 20 minutes.
SERVING SUGGESTIONS:
As for French beans.

Beetroot

PREPARATION:
Cut off leaf stalks 2.5–5 cm/1–2 in above the root, but do not trim off tapering root. Wash carefully to prevent the beetroot 'bleeding'.
COOKING METHODS:
Boiling Depending on the size, for 1–2 hours, in salted water. Drain, cover with cold water and slide off the skin immediately.
Steaming For about 2 hours.
Baking Wrap beetroots in buttered paper. Bake the beetroots in a preheated oven at 160°C/325°F/gas 3 for 30–60 minutes.
SERVING SUGGESTIONS:
Cooked beetroot can be sliced or diced, and served cold in salads.

Broccoli

PREPARATION:
Wash thoroughly in cold water; drain well. Remove any coarse outer leaves and tough parts of the stalk.
COOKING METHODS:
Boiling For 15–20 minutes in salted water.
Steaming For 20–25 minutes.
Stir frying Cut into small florets, discarding or thinly slicing large stalks. Stir fry with thinly sliced onion and braise with a little vegetable or chicken stock before serving.
SERVING SUGGESTIONS:
Serve with butter or Béarnaise Sauce (page 355).

Brussels Sprouts

PREPARATION:
Wash, trim off damaged outer leaves. Make an 'X' cut in base of stems.
COOKING METHODS:
Boiling For 10 minutes in a minimum of salted water.

Braising Parboil in salted water for 5 minutes. Drain. Fry thinly sliced onion rings. Add a little stock and seasoning. Simmer for 5 minutes. Add sprouts; simmer for further 5 minutes, and baste occasionally.
Steaming For about 15 minutes.
Stir frying Shred large sprouts or halve small ones. Stir fry with fine sticks of carrots and chopped onion.
SERVING SUGGESTIONS:
Tossed with butter and freshly ground black pepper. Mix with freshly cooked or reheated chestnuts or sprinkle with flaked almonds browned in a little butter or oil.

Cabbages

PREPARATION:
Remove the coarse outer leaves; cut cabbage into quarters and remove hard centre core. Wash thoroughly, drain and cook either in wedges or finely shredded.

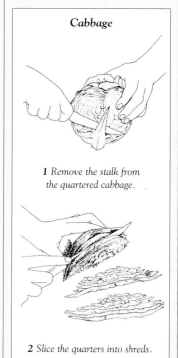

Cabbage

1 *Remove the stalk from the quartered cabbage.*

2 *Slice the quarters into shreds.*

COOKING METHODS:
Boiling Shredded cabbage: cook in salted water for 5–8 minutes. Cabbage wedges: for 10–15 minutes.
Braising Parboil cabbage wedges in salted water for 10 minutes. Refresh in cold water. Place on a bed of fried vegetables. Add bouquet garni* and enough stock to cover. Bake in a preheated oven at 180–190°C/350–375°F/gas 4–5 for 1 hour. Red cabbage: braise shredded cabbage in butter, add chopped apples, vinegar and sugar to taste. Simmer, covered, for 1 hour.
Steaming Shredded cabbage: for 10 minutes. Cabbage wedges: for 20 minutes.
Stir frying An excellent method. Stir fry finely shredded cabbage in butter or oil and butter, adding salt and pepper to taste. Serve crunchy.
SERVING SUGGESTION:
Toss boiled white and green cabbage with butter and seasoning.

Carrots
PREPARATION:
Top and tail; scrub in cold water. Scrape young carrots; peel old ones with a potato peeler. Small carrots can be left whole; large ones can be cut into quarters, rings, sticks or cubes.
COOKING METHODS:
Boiling For 10–30 minutes in salted water or stock.
Steaming For 15–40 minutes, depending on age and size.
Stir frying With a mixture of vegetables, such as spring onions and celery, in a little oil.
SERVING SUGGESTION:
Toss boiled carrots with butter, chopped parsley or mint, or serve with Béchamel Sauce (page 353).

Cauliflowers
PREPARATION:
Cut off damaged outer leaves. If cauliflower is to be cooked whole, cut an 'X' in base of stalk. Alternatively,

Trimming Cauliflower

1 *Remove the tough stalk and leaves.*

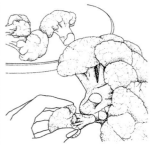

2 *Break away the small florets.*

separate cauliflower into individual florets. Wash well in cold water.
COOKING METHODS:
Boiling For 12–15 minutes, in salted acidulated* water, partially covered with saucepan lid.
Steaming For 15–25 minutes.
Frying Parboil florets for 10 minutes. Drain and cool; dip in egg and breadcrumbs, and deep fry for 3 minutes.
SERVING SUGGESTIONS:
With a white, cheese or parsley sauce. Serve deep fried florets with Tartare Sauce (page 356).

Celeriac
PREPARATION:
Wash, slice, then peel, dice or cut into matchstick strips.
COOKING METHODS:
Boiling For 25–30 minutes in salted acidulated water* with lid on. Drain.
Steaming For 35 minutes.

Frying Fry matchstick strips in butter for 30 minutes.
Stir frying With finely chopped onion. Stir fry coarsely grated or matchstick strips in oil or butter for a few minutes.
SERVING SUGGESTIONS:
Boiled celeriac with Béchamel Sauce (page 353) or Hollandaise Sauce (page 355). Celeriac can also be puréed, or grated fresh as a salad vegetable.

Celery
PREPARATION:
Trim away root end and remove damaged outer stalks and green tops. Separate stalks and scrub clean in cold water. Remove any coarse fibres and cut stalks into even lengths; 5–6 cm/2–2½ in for boiling, 7.5–10 cm/3–4 in for braising.
COOKING METHODS:
Boiling For 15–20 minutes in salted water, covered with lid.
Braising Blanch halved or whole heads of celery for 10 minutes. Fry diced bacon, sliced onions and carrots in buttered casserole. Add celery and enough stock to cover. Bring to the boil, cover and simmer 1½–1¾ hours.
Stir frying An essential ingredient in mixed vegetable stir fries. Thinly sliced or in short, fine strips, with sesame oil for an oriental flavour.
SERVING SUGGESTIONS:
Boiled with a cheese or parsley sauce, made from half the cooking liquid and the same quantity of milk. Fresh as a salad vegetable.

Chicory
PREPARATION:
Trim away outside damaged or wilted leaves. Separate into spears or slice across. If chicory is green, it should be blanched before cooking to reduce its bitterness.
COOKING METHODS:
Boiling For 15–20 minutes in salted, acidulated* water.

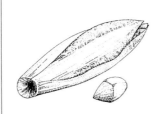

Chicory

Cut out the white bitter root at the base of blanched chicory.

Braising Scoop out the hard core at the base and leave chicory whole. Blanch* and drain. Butter casserole, arrange chicory in base and dot with more butter. Add 30–45 ml/2–3 tablespoons water and a little lemon juice and salt. Cover and bake in a preheated oven at 180°C/350°F/gas 4 for 1–1¼ hours.
SERVING SUGGESTIONS:
Serve boiled chicory with Cheese Sauce (page 352), Béchamel (page 353) or Tomato Sauce (page 354).

Corn
PREPARATION:
Strip the husks off the cobs and remove the silky threads.
COOKING METHODS:
Boiling Cook whole corn cobs in water for 5–10 minutes. Add salt halfway through the cooking time.

Corn on the cob

Strip the green husks and silky threads from corn on the cob.

Steaming For 10–15 minutes.
SERVING SUGGESTION:
Serve with butter and freshly ground black pepper.

Corn, baby
PREPARATION:
Rinse well and pat dry; may be sliced or cooked whole.
COOKING METHODS:
Boiling Cook in lightly salted water for 3–5 minutes.
Stir frying In oil, with other vegetables, for 5 minutes.
SERVING SUGGESTIONS:
With snipped chives and butter or plain stir fried with spring onions.

Courgettes
PREPARATION:
Wash, trim both ends; cook without peeling, either whole, sliced into rounds, or halved with the centres scooped out before filling with a savoury mixture.
COOKING METHODS:
Boiling For 2–5 minutes in salted water.
Steaming Whole courgettes: for 15–20 minutes. Sliced: for 5–10 minutes.
Stir frying In olive oil or butter and oil for 2–3 minutes.
Baking Parboil hollowed-out courgettes for 5 minutes. Drain, brush with butter and season. Bake in a preheated oven at 190°C/375°F/gas 5 for 25 minutes.
SERVING SUGGESTION:
Sprinkled with tarragon or chopped parsley.

Cucumbers
PREPARATION:
Peel cucumber, cut into strips, slice or dice. If cucumber is to be stuffed, cut in half lengthways and scoop out the seeds.
COOKING METHODS:
Boiling For about 10 minutes in salted water.
Braising For about 30 minutes in stock.

Steaming For 20 minutes.
Baking Peel, slice thickly, dot with butter and freshly chopped herbs. Bake in a preheated oven at 190°C/375°F/gas 5 for 30 minutes.
SERVING SUGGESTIONS:
Boiled cucumber with a white or cream sauce flavoured with dill, tarragon or celery seeds. Cucumber is also used as a raw vegetable or garnish.

Endive, Early or Frisée
PREPARATION:
Discard damaged outer leaves. For salads, separate remaining leaves and wash thoroughly in cold water. Leave vegetable whole for braising.
COOKING METHOD:
Braising As for lettuce.
SERVING SUGGESTIONS:
Fresh, as a salad vegetable; braised, with Béchamel Sauce (page 353).

Fennel
PREPARATION:
Trim off top stems and slice off base. Scrub well in cold water.
COOKING METHODS:
Braising As for celery.
Stir frying Cut in half lengthways, then cut into thin slices. Stir fry in a little olive oil. Good with courgettes and leeks.
SERVING SUGGESTIONS:
Thinly sliced as a salad vegetable or as a garnish.

Kale
PREPARATION:
Separate leaves from stems, remove mid-rib from the leaves. Wash thoroughly in cold water. Cut leaves into pieces.
COOKING METHODS:
Braising In minimum salted water and a little butter for 8–10 minutes. Drain.
Steaming For about 15 minutes.
SERVING SUGGESTIONS:
With butter or Béchamel Sauce (page 353).

Kohl-rabi
PREPARATION:
Cut off leaves around bulb and trim off tapering roots. Scrub in cold water, then peel thickly. Small kohl-rabi globes can be left whole. Slice or dice large ones.
COOKING METHODS:
Boiling Depending on size, for 30–60 minutes in salted water. Drain.
Braising Parboil in salted water for 5 minutes. Braise with a little chopped onion and bacon; moisten with white wine or stock. Cook for 1 hour or until tender, depending on size.
SERVING SUGGESTIONS:
Kohl-rabi can be mashed, puréed, baked au gratin and used for fritters. Toss boiled kohl-rabi in melted butter, or serve with a white sauce.

Leeks
PREPARATION:
Cut off roots and green tops; remove coarse outer leaves if necessary. Cut down through the white part and wash carefully to remove dirt from leaves. Leeks can be left whole or halved, sliced into thick rings or 5 cm/2 in lengths.
COOKING METHODS:
Boiling Boil 5 cm/2 in pieces of leeks in salted water for 15 minutes. Sliced into rings: for 10 minutes. Whole: for 20 minutes.
Braising Blanch leeks in boiling salted water for 5 minutes. Drain, fry in butter for 5 minutes. Add stock or water to cover and a bouquet garni*. Cover and cook for 1 hour.
Steaming For about 25 minutes depending on the size of leeks.
Stir frying Cut in thin slices, in oil or oil and butter. Good in mixed vegetable stir fries where it can be used instead of onion.
Frying Prepared leeks may be blanched for 5 minutes, drained and marinated in lemon juice. Dip in a light batter before deep frying.
SERVING SUGGESTIONS:
Boiled with Béchamel Sauce (page 353) or Mornay Sauce (page 353). Use young leeks as a salad vegetable.

Lettuce
PREPARATION:
Trim off base and remove any damaged outer leaves. Separate the leaves and wash in cold water; drain well if used for salad. Leave whole if lettuce is to be braised.
COOKING METHODS:
Boiling For 10 minutes in salted water. Drain thoroughly and chop finely. Melt butter in a pan and add a little chopped onion, garlic and cream. Stir in chopped lettuce and season with salt and pepper.
Braising Blanch* for 5–6 minutes. Refresh under cold running water, and drain thoroughly. In a casserole, melt butter and fry a little chopped bacon, carrot and onion. Fold in tops of lettuce to make a neat shape and lay on fried vegetables. Add stock to depth of 1 cm/½ in, cover, and bake at 160–180°C/325–350°F/gas 3–4 for 40–45 minutes. Pour over reduced pan juices.
SERVING SUGGESTIONS:
Boiled with Mornay Sauce (page 353) or Hollandaise Sauce (page 355). Fresh, shredded in green salads, tossed in dressing. Lettuce is also used for garnishes.

Mange-tout
PREPARATION:
Trim off both ends. Wash and drain.
COOKING METHODS:
Boiling For about 3 minutes in lightly salted water.
Steaming For about 10 minutes.
Stir frying For 3–5 minutes in a little oil.
SERVING SUGGESTIONS:
Toss with snipped chives and/or a little melted butter if boiled.

Marrows
PREPARATION:
Marrow may be peeled, seeded and cubed for boiling, or cut into thick

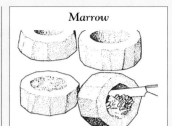

Marrow

Scraping out the seeds from peeled marrow slices.

rings for stuffing. It may also be halved lengthways and deseeded before filling.
COOKING METHODS:
Boiling For about 10 minutes in salted water.
Steaming For 20–40 minutes, depending on the age and size of the marrows.
Frying Marrow can be fried in butter and herbs for 7–10 minutes. Shake the pan occasionally.
Baking Whole or halved stuffed marrow can be baked for 45–60 minutes. Serve with a tomato sauce. Marrow rings can be stuffed with a savoury filling and baked in a well-buttered dish covered with foil in a preheated oven at 180°C/350°F/gas 4 for 35–45 minutes.
SERVING SUGGESTIONS:
Toss in butter, or serve with a white or cheese sauce.

Mushrooms
PREPARATION:
Cultivated mushrooms: trim the base of the stalks, rinse mushrooms in cold water; dry well. Field mushrooms: peel, and trim stems. Leave whole, quarter or slice thinly.
COOKING METHODS:
Frying and grilling Field mushrooms and flat cultivated mushrooms are suitable for frying and grilling. Button mushrooms can be dipped in fritter batter and fried. Fry sliced mushrooms in butter for 3–5 minutes,

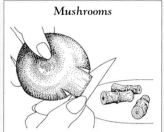

Mushrooms

Trim by removing stalks, and peeling ragged skin.

serve with juices. Brush whole mushrooms with butter or oil, grill under moderate heat for 6–8 minutes, turning once.
SERVING SUGGESTIONS:
Fried, with pan juices, cream and thyme. Button mushrooms are used as a garnish or fresh in salads.

Okra
PREPARATION:
Wash thoroughly but do not remove the stems.
COOKING METHODS:
Braising Parboil okra in boiling salted water for 5 minutes; braise for a further 30–45 minutes.
Stir frying Cut in thin slices, then stir fry very briskly in oil until crisp, allowing only 2–3 minutes.
SERVING SUGGESTIONS:
Toss in melted butter or serve with Hollandaise Sauce (page 355).

Onions
PREPARATION:
Trim roots and peel away papery skins. Onions can be left whole or chopped, sliced or diced. Spring onions need the root removed and the green tops trimmed.
COOKING METHODS:
Boiling Cook in salted water for 20–30 minutes, depending on size.
Braising Cook button onions in white stock or wine, butter and seasoning for 40 minutes.
Shallow frying Cut onions in thin

slices and fry gently in hot fat.

Deep frying Slice onions thinly, dip in milk and seasoned flour before deep frying for about 3 minutes.

SERVING SUGGESTIONS:
Boiled with a white or cheese sauce; glazed button onions on their own, with chopped parsley or in Béchamel Sauce (page 353).

Parsnips

PREPARATION:
Cut off roots and tops, peel. If young, cut in thick slices; if mature, cut in quarters and remove the hard core.

COOKING METHODS:
Boiling For 30–40 minutes in salted water.

Roasting Parboil for 5 minutes. Drain and roast with a joint of meat, or braise in butter with a little stock.

Steaming For about 35 minutes; this method should be used only with young parsnips.

Purée Parsnips can be boiled with carrots and pumpkin, then puréed with a little butter and nutmeg.

Deep frying Cut parsnips into thin slivers and deep fry like crisps.

SERVING SUGGESTION:
Tossed with butter and parsley.

Peas

PREPARATION:
Shell fresh peas.

COOKING METHODS:
Boiling Gently for 15–20 minutes in salted water with a sprig of mint and 5 ml/1 teaspoon of sugar. A little lemon juice helps to preserve the colour of the vegetable.

Steaming For about 25 minutes.

SERVING SUGGESTION:
Tossed with butter and chopped mint or walnuts.

Peppers

PREPARATION:
Wash, cut in half lengthways and remove the stalk, seeds and whitish membrane around the sides. Slice or dice as required. If peppers are to be

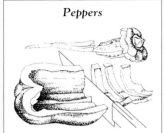

Peppers

Slicing peppers from which the stalk and seeds have been removed.

filled with a savoury mixture, cut around the stalk and lift away the core. Scoop out membrane and seeds.

COOKING METHODS:
Baking Parboil in salted water for 10 minutes. Drain, fill with savoury meat or vegetable filling. Add a little stock and bake in a preheated oven at 180°C/350°F/gas 4 for 25–30 minutes.

Stir frying Cut in thin slices or strips, in oil or butter, or a mixture of both.

SERVING SUGGESTIONS:
Hot: with a Cheese Sauce (page 352) or Tomato Sauce (page 354). Cold: with French Dressing (page 356). Diced or sliced fresh pepper is used in salads or as a garnish.

Pumpkin

PREPARATION:
Wash and cut pumpkin into bite-size pieces. Peel off skin, and remove pith and seeds.

COOKING METHODS:
Boiling For 20–30 minutes in salted water.

Steaming For 35–40 minutes.

Roasting For 45–50 minutes around a joint of meat.

SERVING SUGGESTION:
With a Cheese Sauce (page 352).

Radicchio

PREPARATION:
Discard all the damaged leaves, separate and wash the leaves thoroughly, cutting off the ends of the

stalk at the base of the leaves. Drain the leaves well.

SERVING SUGGESTION:
Combine radicchio with other salad leaves that complement its bitter flavour.

Radishes

PREPARATION:
If served whole, cut off the tops, leaving 1 cm/½ in of stalk, and remove tapering root; wash thoroughly in cold water.

COOKING METHOD:
Boiling Cook large radishes whole in salted water for about 10 minutes.

SERVING SUGGESTIONS:
As a raw salad vegetable or as a garnish for savoury dishes. Serve boiled radishes with a well-seasoned Parsley Sauce (page 352).

Salsify

PREPARATION:
Scrub well in cold water, cut off top and tapering root end. Scrape off the skin, cut into 2.5–5 cm/1–2 in lengths. Plunge immediately into cold, acidulated* water.

COOKING METHOD:
Boiling For 45 minutes in salted water.

SERVING SUGGESTIONS:
With a butter, white or Béarnaise Sauce (page 355). Use leaves in salads or cooked as a green vegetable.

Seakale

PREPARATION:
Trim roots; wash thoroughly under cold running water. Tie the stalks in bundles.

COOKING METHODS:
Boiling For 25 minutes in salted acidulated* water. Drain.

Steaming For 30 minutes.

SERVING SUGGESTIONS:
Boiled or steamed with a cheese sauce, Béchamel Sauce (page 353) or Béarnaise Sauce (page 355). Cold with French Dressing (page 356). The leaf ends can be used in salads.

Seakale Beet or Chard

PREPARATION:
Prepare and cook leaf stalks as for seakale; the green leaves as spinach.

Shallots

PREPARATION:
Prepare and cook as for onions.

SERVING SUGGESTIONS:
Used to flavour stocks and soups.

Spinach

PREPARATION:
Wash spinach several times in cold water. Do not dry, but place in a saucepan with no extra water.

COOKING METHOD:
Sweating In the water left clinging to the leaves after washing. Place in tightly covered pan and cook for about 5 minutes, shaking pan frequently.

SERVING SUGGESTIONS:
Drain well and toss in a little olive oil with chopped cooked onion. Top with fromage frais or yogurt. Reheat with cream and seasoning, chop finely or make into a purée.

Swedes

PREPARATION:
Trim stalk and root ends, peel thickly and cut into 1–2.5 cm/½–1 in cubes.

COOKING METHOD:
Boiling For 30–40 minutes in salted water. Drain and dry out over a gentle heat.

SERVING SUGGESTIONS:
Toss with melted butter and salt and freshly ground pepper; or mash with butter, nutmeg and ginger. Use in stews and casseroles.

Sweet Potatoes

PREPARATION:
Scrub well and peel, if necessary.

COOKING METHOD:
Boiling Cook in their jackets in salted water, covered, for about 25 minutes. If peeled, cut the sweet potatoes into chunks or slices and cook uncovered for 15 minutes.

SERVING SUGGESTIONS:
Serve as potatoes. Toss with stir fried onion, bacon and garlic, sprinkle with nutmeg.

Tomatoes

PREPARATION:
Remove stalk if necessary. To skin, cover with boiling water and leave for 30–60 seconds. Drain, slit skins and slide them off.

COOKING METHODS:
Grilling Cut tomatoes in half, top with a small knob of butter and season. Grill under moderate heat for 5–10 minutes.

Baking Prepare tomatoes as above or leave whole. Arrange in a shallow greased baking dish. Bake in a preheated oven at 180°C/350°F/gas 4 for 15 minutes. Whole tomatoes should be placed stalk end down, cut crossways on top and brushed with oil, before baking.

SERVING SUGGESTIONS:
Hot: as first course. Cold: sliced or quartered in salads and as garnish.

Turnips

PREPARATION:
Wash, trim stalk ends and tapering roots. Large turnips should be quartered; small ones can be left whole.

COOKING METHODS:
Boiling For 25–30 minutes in salted water.

Steaming For 30–40 minutes.

SERVING SUGGESTIONS:
Toss in parsley and butter, or serve with a white sauce.

Watercress

PREPARATION:
Wash thoroughly in cold water and drain well.

SERVING SUGGESTIONS:
Watercress is used in salads or as a garnish for savoury dishes. Chopped watercress can be mixed with salad vegetables or mixed into sauces and mayonnaise. It also makes a refreshing cold soup.

POTATOES

Early potatoes are best boiled or used in salads. When buying early potatoes, check that any soil on them is damp and that the skin rubs off; these are signs of freshness.

Reject potatoes that are green or show signs of yellow-green patches. Avoid buying sealed polythene bags of slightly damp-looking vegetables. When sealed in polythene bags and displayed in a warm environment, potatoes sweat and rot.

Maincrop potatoes can be jacket-baked, roasted, made into chips and used in potato salads.

A selection of different types of maincrop and new potatoes are available throughout the year, including large scrubbed potatoes selected for baking and small, full-flavoured vegetables recommended for use in salads. Supermarkets and greengrocers label the vegetables clearly, indicating the variety and, often, suggested cooking methods.

PREPARATION OF POTATOES

New potatoes need only be washed, scraped lightly, and then washed again. They may also be boiled in their skins. Old potatoes should be washed well, peeled thinly, and then cut into even-sized pieces, and cooked as soon as possible.

Assessing portions is difficult as it depends on the cooking method. It is usual to serve 1 baked potato per portion but for family meals it makes sense to serve ½ large potato each, depending on the main dish.

As a guide for serving boiled potatoes, 900 g/2 lb old potatoes will provide 4 portions while the same weight of new potatoes will serve 4–6.

COOKING METHODS

Boiled

Cut the potatoes into even-sized pieces and put into cold salted water; bring to the boil and simmer, covered, for 10–15 minutes for new potatoes, depending on size, and about 20 minutes for old potatoes.

Mashed

Boil old potatoes. Drain well, and dry the potatoes in the pan over low heat. Using a potato masher or a fork, mash the potatoes in the pan until free of lumps. Alternatively, rub the potatoes through a sieve.

Creamed

Put mashed potatoes in a clean pan. To each 450 g/1 lb of potatoes add 25 g/1 oz of butter, a little milk and seasoning, and put the pan over gentle heat; beat the mixture until light and fluffy.

Sautéed

Boil potatoes until they are almost cooked, and cut them into slices about 5 mm/¼ in thick. Fry in hot fat, turning them until they are crisp and golden brown on both sides.

Jacket-baked

Select good-sized old potatoes, allowing one per person. Scrub, wash, dry and prick all over with a fork. Cut a small cross through the skin on the upper side of the potato. Bake in a preheated oven at 200°C/400°F/gas 6. When it is cooked, cut through the cross and open up the potato. Top with soured cream, low-fat soft cheese or butter.

Roasted

Select old potatoes. Peel and cut them into even-sized pieces. Parboil for 5 minutes, then drain well. Place in a roasting tin with melted lard or dripping, and roast in a preheated oven at 220°C/425°F/gas 7 for 40 minutes, turning them once.

Alternatively, put the cut potatoes around a meat joint to roast for the last 50–60 minutes.

Duchesse Potatoes

Prepare a portion of creamed potatoes with an egg and put the mixture in a piping bag. Pipe into mounds, about 5 cm/2 in high, on a lightly greased baking tray, or into a border round a shallow ovenproof dish. Bake at 200°C/400°F/gas 6 for about 25 minutes, or until golden.

Potato Croquettes

Prepare creamed potatoes. Roll the mixture into cork shapes, and coat each one thickly with egg and breadcrumbs. Heat the fat to 190°C/375°F or until a day-old cube of bread browns in 1 minute. Fry the croquettes for 2–3 minutes, drain thoroughly and fry again, at the same temperature, for 2–3 minutes.

Chips

Peel old potatoes and cut them into 5 mm–1 cm/¼–½ in slices. Cut these slices into strips 5 mm–1 cm/¼–½ in wide. Soak in cold water. Drain well and dry thoroughly before using. Put some fat into a fryer (or a deep saucepan) and heat to 196°C/385°F. When a chip dropped in the fat rises to the surface, surrounded by bubbles, the fat is hot enough for frying.

Place a layer of chips in a wire basket and lower into the fryer or deep saucepan. Cook for 4–6 minutes, or until golden. Drain the chips thoroughly on absorbent kitchen paper. Just before serving, fry all the chips again, at the same temperature, for 1–2 minutes. Drain, sprinkle with a little salt, and serve.

Matchstick Chips

Peel old potatoes and cut them into very small chips, about the size of matchsticks. Cook in the same way as chips, allowing a shorter cooking time – about 3 minutes for the first frying.

Game Chips or Crisps

Peel and wash the potatoes thoroughly. Cut them into thin rounds. Soak in cold water, dry, and deep fry once only in hot fat for about 3 minutes.

Anna Potatoes

Peel old or new potatoes and slice them thinly. Arrange the potato slices in layers in a well-greased ovenproof dish. Sprinkle each layer with salt and pepper and dot with butter. Cover lightly with buttered greaseproof paper or foil and bake in a preheated oven at 190°C/375°F/gas 5 for 1 hour.

Château Potatoes

Shape peeled potatoes into 3.5–5 cm/1½–2 in ovals. Coat thoroughly with melted butter and cook in a covered casserole for 30–35 minutes. Shake the casserole occasionally.

Potato Salad with Mayonnaise

Scrub old potatoes and boil them in their skins for 25–30 minutes, until tender, depending on size. Drain, rinse under cold water, then peel and leave to cool, covered. Slice the potatoes thickly, and then cut them into large dice.

Dress with mayonnaise thinned with single cream or plain yogurt, allowing 150 ml/5 fl oz mayonnaise and 60 ml/4 tablespoons cream or plain yogurt for every 900 g/2 lb potatoes. Finally add 45–60 ml/3–4 tablespoons snipped chives and salt and pepper to taste.

New Potato Salad

Scrub and boil small, evenly sized new potatoes for 10-15 minutes, or until tender. Drain and rinse under cold water, then peel if liked. Thin, even peel may be left on the potato. Dress the hot potatoes with French Dressing (page 356) and sprinkle with plenty of chopped parsley and snipped chives or finely chopped spring onions. Mix well, cover and leave to cool.

This new potato salad may be flavoured with crushed garlic, chopped black olives, shredded basil and/or a little chopped tarragon. Mix in these ingredients well before serving.

RICE, CEREALS & PULSES

The interest in carbohydrate foods, particularly those that are high in fibre, has increased with the growing awareness of healthy eating. There is a wide range of grains and pulses available from supermarkets as well as specialist stores, such as wholefood shops and ethnic grocers.

RICE

Many varieties of rice are grown in the USA, the Far East, Italy and other Mediterranean countries and they can be loosely grouped according to the length of the grain. Long-grain rice is the most widely used for savoury cooking as the grains tend to remain separate when cooked.

Medium-grain rice includes risotto rice, which is more glutinous than long-grain rice; although the individual grains retain their shape when cooked, they form a creamy mass and stick together lightly.

Short-grain rice is sometimes known as round-grain or pudding rice; it is used to make a creamy milk pudding. Glutinous rice is another example of a short, round-grain variety. It is used in Chinese cooking to make steamed rice balls, while in Japanese cooking a similar sticky, rice is used to make sushi. The following are examples of different types of rice.

Long-grain White Rice

White rice has had the outer husk and bran removed before being polished. Patna rice, which is named after its Indian region of origin, was once popular but the majority of white rice is now imported from the USA. Long-grain white rice can be cooked by boiling or by the absorption method. Care must be taken not to overcook the rice as the grains swell and stick together.

Ordinary long-grain rice can be used to make a milk pudding, as with prolonged cooking it will reduce to a thick porridge-like consistency.

Easy-cook White Rice

Easy-cook rice is processed by steaming under pressure to par-cook the grain and remove excess starch. It should be cooked by the absorption method, using just enough water to soften the grains without leaving any excess to be drained away at the end of cooking. Easy-cook rice does not stick together when cooked. It has more flavour than ordinary white rice.

Brown Rice

Brown rice is not as highly refined as white varieties and it still has part of its outer covering or bran layer. It takes longer to cook than white rice and it should have slightly more bite when cooked. It has a slightly nutty flavour. Easy-cook brown rice cooks more quickly than ordinary brown rice and has slightly less bite. Brown basmati rice is also available.

Basmati Rice

An Indian rice with a distinct scent and delicious flavour. It is used to make pullau and biriani dishes, or can be cooked and served plain as an accompaniment to spiced dishes. Basmati rice should be washed gently before cooking; ideally it should also be soaked in cold water for 15 minutes but this is not essential. Washing removes the excess starch which can make the rice sticky when cooked. Care must be taken not to damage the delicate grains.

Camargue Red Rice

This is a French, red-husked variety of long-grain rice with a strong, nutty flavour. Use in combination with other rice and cook as for wild rice.

Thai Fragrant Rice or Jasmine Rice

A delicately flavoured and scented rice which should be washed gently before cooking.

Risotto Rice

This is a medium-grain rice which absorbs more liquid during cooking and gives a slightly creamy result even though the grains retain their shape. Arborio is one of the best types; there are also brown varieties.

Glutinous Rice

Short-grain rice which becomes sticky on cooking. Chinese and Japanese types are readily available from oriental stores.

Pudding Rice

Short-grain or round-grain rice, at one time called Carolina rice after its American origins, this is used to make puddings. With prolonged cooking in a comparatively large volume of liquid, the rice forms a creamy porridge.

Wild Rice

This is not a true rice, but the seeds from an aquatic grass from North America. The grains are long, slim and coated in a dark brown-black husk. Wild rice should be cooked for 40–45 minutes, when the grains will still have some bite. It can be slightly strong in both flavour and texture if eaten on its own, so it is best mixed with other types of rice.

Convenience Forms of Rice

Boil-in-the-bag rice is packed in portions in perforated boilable bags, ready to be dropped into boiling water. The idea is to prevent the rice sticking to the pan and to allow it to be drained easily by lifting the bag out of the water by the loop provided.

Canned cooked rice is ready to reheat following the label instructions. Frozen rice is also ready-cooked for reheating following the instructions provided on the packet. Pre-cooked convenience rice, however, does not have as good a flavour or texture as freshly cooked rice.

COOKING RICE

Rice may be boiled in a large quantity of water, then drained or it may be cooked by the absorption method. The latter is the most practical and popular method for the majority of rice: a measured volume of water is added to the rice, the, pan is covered tightly when the water boils and the heat reduced to a minimum setting. At the end of cooking, the water is absorbed, leaving the rice tender. Allow 50 g/2 oz uncooked rice per person. After cooking, rice almost trebles in bulk.

Boiling Rice

Boiling rice in a large quantity of water, draining and rinsing it, leaves the grains quite separate; however, the rice does not have as much flavour as when cooked by the absorption method. Boiling is usually used for rice which is an ingredient in stuffings or for salads. It is also used for ordinary long-grain rice which is served as an accompaniment but is not flavoured with additional ingredients.

Use 600 ml/ 1 pt of water and 5 ml/1 teaspoon salt to each 50 g/2 oz of rice. Measure the water into a large pan with the salt and bring to the boil; add the rice. Boil the rice rapidly for 12–15 minutes, or until soft, but not mushy. To test the rice, squeeze a grain between thumb and forefinger – when cooked, the centre will be just soft.

Drain the rice in a sieve and rinse it under hot water. Return it to the pan, with a knob of butter, and toss the rice.

Cover the pan with a lid and leave for 10 minutes to dry the rice. Shake the pan to prevent the grains sticking together. Alternatively, put the drained rice in a shallow, buttered baking dish, cover it tightly and dry in a preheated oven at 160°C/ 325°F/ gas 3 for 10 minutes.

Absorption Method

This is the most popular cooking method which ensures tender separate grains. Allow 600 ml/ 1 pt water for each 225 g/8 oz rice. Put the rice in a pan, pour in the water and add a little salt – up to 5 ml/1 teaspoon for a well-seasoned result. Bring the water to the boil, stir the rice and cover the pan with a tight-fitting lid.

Reduce the heat to the minimum setting and cook for the recommended time for the type of rice: 15 minutes for easy-cook white rice; 15–20 minutes for other types of white rice; 30–35 minutes for brown rice. At the end of cooking, turn the heat off or remove the pan from the heat but do not remove the lid. Leave the rice to stand for a further 5 minutes. Fork up the grains and serve.

Cooking Wild Rice

This should be cooked in salted boiling water for about 40–45 minutes, then drained and dried in the same way as boiled rice. When cooking wild rice in combination with other types of rice by the absorption method, the wild rice should be boiled for 15–20 minutes and drained before it is combined with the other grain. Then the volume of

water added for the quantity of wild rice at the absorption stage should be reduced by half to allow for the fact that the rice is partly cooked.

Fried Rice

Fried rice can be made with uncooked or cooked rice. The uncooked rice can be fried in oil or butter, or a combination of both, until the grains look transparent. Then the liquid should be added and the rice cooked by the absorption method. Alternatively, drained cooked rice can be added to heated butter or oil and stir fried, in which case additional flavouring ingredients are usually cooked before the rice is added.

Rice Moulds

Cooked rice can be made into attractive hot or cold moulds. A sauce or dressing may be tossed with the rice or cooked vegetables may be mixed with it.

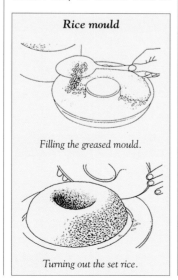

Rice mould

Filling the greased mould.

Turning out the set rice.

Pack the dressed rice into a greased ring mould and smooth the top. If the rice is to be served hot, set the ring mould in a roasting tin of boiling water. Cover the mould with foil and simmer on top of the stove for 10–15 minutes. Place a serving dish on top of the mould and turn it upside-down.

If the rice is to be served cold, leave the rice to cool, then put the mould in the refrigerator for about 1 hour or until firm. Turn the mould upside-down on to a serving dish. The centre of a rice mould may be filled with a hot mixture, such as prawns or chicken in a sauce, or a cold salad.

Rice Salads

Cold, cooked rice makes a good basis for a variety of salads. Toss the cold rice in a well-flavoured Sauce Vinaigrette (page 356) or a thinned-down Mayonnaise (page 355), and serve with cold meat, fish or poultry. For a more substantial dish, mix the dressed rice with chopped ham or chicken, flaked fish and chopped pimentos, cooked peas and sweetcorn kernels.

OTHER GRAINS

Barley

Pot barley is the whole grain and pearl barley is the husked and polished grain. Both can be cooked in the same way as rice, boiling pot parley in plenty of salted water or cooking pearl barley by the absorption method. For 225 g/8 oz pearl barley use 900 ml/1½ pt water and cook for about 30 minutes, until tender

but with bite. Pot barley should be boiled for 1 hour, or until tender. Pearl barley is a traditional ingredient for thickening soups and stews. It is added in small amounts and simmered until the grains break down, release their starch into the cooking liquid and become quite soft.

Buckwheat

A small, brown grain, also known as kasha, buckwheat is sold roasted but raw. It must be cooked with care as it rapidly forms a porridge-like mass if boiled or cooked for too long.

The buckwheat should be washed in cold water before cooking, then placed in a pan with 600 ml/1 pt cold water and a little salt. Bring to the boil, stir once, and cover the pan tightly. Remove the pan from the heat or turn the heat off and leave the buckwheat to stand for 30 minutes without removing the lid. Fork up the grains, add a knob of butter and serve.

Cous Cous

Cous cous is a semolina product, made by steaming the semolina and rolling it until it forms tiny balls. Traditionally, the semolina was steamed in a couscousière, a stew pot with a steamer on top, allowing a meat and vegetable stew to be prepared in the pan while the semolina was cooked in the cloth-lined upper steamer. Cous cous is sold prepared, ready for the minimum of steaming or it can be soaked in boiling water until the grains are swollen.

Place the cous cous in a bowl and cover with freshly boiling

water, add a knob of butter and cover the bowl. Leave it to stand for about 15 minutes, or until the water is absorbed and the grain swollen. The bowl can be placed over a pan of simmering water to keep the cous cous hot or the cous cous can be reheated briefly, if necessary, in a microwave before serving. If freshly boiling water is used and the cous cous served promptly, it is not usually necessary to reheat it.

Oats

Rolled oats are the steamed and flattened grain. They can be used to make porridge: allow 900 ml/ 1½ pt water to each 175 g/6 oz oats. Place the oats and water in a pan with 2.5 ml/½ teaspoon salt. Bring to the boil, stirring, then reduce the heat and simmer for 5–10 minutes, stirring occasionally, until thick and smooth.

Jumbo oats are large rolled oats that require slightly longer cooking than ordinary porridge oats. They should be simmered for 8–10 minutes.

Oatmeal The grain may be ground to a fine, medium or coarse meal. Porridge is made by cooking oatmeal gently for several hours. The grain is also used in baking, to make oatcakes, or as a coating for herrings.

Wheat

The whole grain can be cooked in plenty of boiling salted water for 50 minutes, until tender, then drained and served in the same way as rice. Wheat can also be added to casseroles or combined with other ingredients and cooked by the absorption method.

Cracked wheat The grains of wheat are crushed or cracked open but they are not cooked. Cracked wheat can be cooked in the same way as rice, by the absorption method. The broken wheat may be sprinkled over home-made bread before baking. Kibbled wheat is a form of broken wheat grain.

Bulgur Also called pourgouri, bulgur is wheat which has been crushed and par-cooked. It is soaked in water, drained and used in salads. Tabbouleh is a salad made from bulgur which is flavoured with garlic, parsley, olive oil and lemon, and served on a bed of cos lettuce.

BEANS AND PULSES

These are particularly valuable as a source of protein, particularly in a vegetarian diet. There are many types of beans and pulses, and they are widely available in supermarkets and wholefood stores.

As well as the dried form of beans, a good range of beans is available canned and most of them are excellent quality, with the exception of butter beans and haricot beans which tend to be too soft.

Soaking Dried Beans

The majority of dried beans should be soaked before cooking. Place the beans in a bowl, cover with plenty of cold water and leave to stand overnight until the water has soaked through. Drain the beans and cook them in fresh water. Soya beans should be soaked for a full 24 hours before cooking.

Cooking Dried Beans

Place the drained, soaked beans in a large pan and pour in plenty of cold water. Do not add salt as it will harden the beans and they will never become tender. Bring to a full boil and boil for 10 minutes. It is important to boil beans as some contain natural toxins which are destroyed by boiling but not by soaking, nor by cooking gently.

Reduce the heat, cover the pan, leaving a small gap for steam to escape if necessary, and boil until the beans are tender. The cooking times given are in addition to soaking overnight and boiling for 10 minutes unless otherwise stated.

Popular Beans and Pulses

Aduki beans Small, round red beans with a nutty flavour. Boil for 30 minutes.

Black kidney beans Similar to red kidney beans but with black skins. Boil for 45–50 minutes.

Black-eye beans Small, round creamy-white beans with a black mark; they have a nutty flavour. Boil for 30 minutes.

Brown beans Known as ful medames, these small round pale-brown beans have a nutty flavour. Boil for 30 minutes.

Butter beans Large, white beans which become very soft if overcooked. Boil for 40 minutes.

Cannellini beans Small oval haricot beans. Boil for about 40 minutes.

Chick peas Round, creamy-coloured peas which have a good nutty flavour. Boil for 1 hour. Canned chick peas are excellent.

Flageolet beans Small, oval, pale green beans with a delicate flavour. Boil for 30 minutes. Canned flageolet beans usually have a good texture. Delicious with lamb.

Haricot beans A large family of beans but the term refers to small, oval white beans. Boil for 30 minutes.

Lentils There are many types of lentils: red, green, brown and black (Puy) lentils can all be cooked without soaking. Red lentils become very soft on cooking, reducing to a thick purée and should be cooked by the absorption method as for rice, allowing 600 ml/1 pt water for each 225 g/8 oz lentils and simmering gently for about 20 minutes. Salt can be added to red lentils before cooking.

Green, brown and black lentils can be cooked by boiling in plenty of water or by the absorption method. They require 30–40 minutes cooking.

Peas, dried There are many types, including some which cook quickly. Be sure to follow the instructions on the packet. Allow 40–45 minutes boiling for ordinary dried peas.

Red kidney beans Dark red, kidney-shaped beans with a firm texture. Boil for 50 minutes. Canned red kidney beans have a good texture.

Soya beans Small, oval, beige-gold beans which require lengthy boiling – for about 2 hours. Top up with more boiling water as necessary. Canned soya beans usually have a good texture.

Split peas Do not have to be soaked before cooking. Boil for about 45 minutes.

PASTA

There are many types of pasta of oriental and Italian origins. Italian pasta is made from a flour of hard durum wheat mixed to a stiff dough with oil, water and sometimes egg. Oriental pasta may be made with wheat flour and eggs. Other forms of flour, such as rice flour or mung bean flour, are also used as the base to make a wide variety of noodles and rice sticks. This section concentrates on Italian-style pasta, which can be served simply dressed with olive oil or butter and garlic, with a Tomato Sauce (see Stuffed Peppers with Pork and Beef, page 229) or with a meat sauce such as classic Bolognese Sauce (see Tagliatelle alla Bolognese, page 93).

Cooking Pasta

Allow 75–100 g/3–4 oz pasta per person. Pasta must be boiled in a large volume of water with salt and a little oil added. The oil helps to prevent the water from frothing over when it boils and the pasta sticking together; if enough water is used, the pasta will not stick unless it is overcooked. Bring the water to the boil with the salt and oil, add the pasta and stir. Bring the water back to the boil, reduce the heat so that it does not boil over and stir once more.

Cook dried pasta for the time recommended on the packet. This ranges from 10–20 minutes, with the average being 12–15 for most shapes or noodles. The pasta is cooked when it is tender, not soft. Taste a piece to check whether it is cooked: it must not taste hard or floury but there should be some resistance to the bite; this is known as *al dente*. Drain at once and serve freshly cooked or use it to make the dish.

When cooking long pasta, such as spaghetti, hold the pasta and lower it into the pan of boiling water as it softens.

Fresh Pasta

Fresh pasta is readily available or can be made at home easily. Noodles and unfilled shapes cook quickly – in about 3 minutes – when brought back to the boil. Filled pasta, such as ravioli, require longer to allow time for the filling to cook.

Serving

When served plain, as an accompaniment, toss with a little melted butter or warmed olive oil and season with pepper. Turn into a warmed dish and serve.

Home-made Pasta

Pasta can be made quite easily at home: prepare the dough and knead it until it is smooth, then roll it out thinly and cut it into wide or narrow noodles. The dough may also be cut into strips or squares to make cannelloni or lasagne, or it can be filled and covered to make ravioli or other pasta shapes.

Coloured and Flavoured Pasta

Spinach is used to colour pasta green, making pasta verde, and some of the better-quality pasta actually taste of spinach. Tomatoes are used to make red pasta. Other flavourings and/or colouring ingredients added to pasta include beetroot, chilli powder, garlic, black olives, squid ink and dried ceps (porcini). A wide variety of flavours are available, but they are expensive, and the flavour of some does not warrant their cost.

Pasta Dough

MAKES: 5 75 g/1¼ lb
PREPARATION: 30 minutes
RESTING: 15 minutes
COOKING: 5 minutes

3 eggs
30 ml/2 tablespoons water
45 ml/3 tablespoons olive oil
350 g/12 oz strong plain flour
5 ml/1 teaspoon salt

Beat the eggs with the water and oil. Mix the flour and salt in a bowl and make a well in the centre. Pour in the egg mixture. Gradually work the flour into the liquid to make a stiff mixture. Gather the mixture together with your hand and turn it out on to a lightly floured surface.

Knead the dough thoroughly until it is smooth. Keep the dough moving all the time to prevent it sticking to the surface, pressing the dough with the heel of your hand, then folding the front end of the dough back and pressing it down again. When the dough is smooth, wrap it in cling film and set it aside to rest for 15 minutes. Do not chill.

Cut the dough in half or into four portions. Roll it out firmly on a lightly floured surface, lifting and turning the sheet of dough occasionally. Try to keep the dough in a fairly neat oblong or square shape. The dough for making noodles should be as thin as a sheet of thick paper. If the dough is too thick, the cooked pasta will taste stodgy.

Using a Pasta Machine

Mechanical pasta machines are moderately priced and useful for kneading as well as rolling out the pasta. Adjustable rollers are opened to a wide setting for kneading the pasta, then their width is gradually reduced once the pasta is rolled until smooth and the dough is rolled into a thin sheet. Cutting rollers can be used to cut noodles of different widths, while a hod and ravioli roller attachment fills and seals ravioli shapes.

Cutting Noodles by Hand

Dust the surface of the pasta dough with flour, then roll it up loosely. Cut the roll into slices, 5–10 mm/¼–½ in wide. Shake out the slices so that they fall into long noodles and place them on a floured plate. Cook the noodles as soon as possible. If they are to be kept for any length of time, dust them with flour and pile them loosely on a covered plate in the refrigerator.

Popular Types of Pasta

There are hundreds of types of dried and fresh pasta. You will find a vast range of shapes and flavours in supermarkets and delicatessens.

Anellini Tiny rings.
Cannelloni Large tubes of pasta for stuffing.
Capelletti Small, round, indented 'hat' shapes.
Capellini Thread-like spaghetti.
Conchiglie Available in many sizes, from tiny ones (conchigliette) to very large shells which can be stuffed and baked.
Elbow macaroni Short, bent lengths of macaroni.
Farfalle Butterfly shapes.
Fedelini Thicker than capellini.
Fettuccine Thin noodles similar to tagliatelle.
Fusilli Spirals which vary in length, from long spaghetti-like strands to short shapes.
Lasagne Square or oblong sheets of pasta which are layered with sauces and baked. The majority do not require boiling before layering with the sauce. If you can find a supplier of pasta which does need boiling, then it is worth the effort as the pasta has a better texture.
Macaroni Thicker than spaghetti and hollow.
Mafalde Fluted ribbon pasta.
Ravioli Small, filled squares or rounds.
Rigatoni Short ridged tubes.
Ruote Wheel shapes.
Semini Grain-like pasta pieces.
Short-cut macaroni Short pieces of macaroni.
Soup pasta Tiny shapes for adding to soup.
Spaghetti Familiar long thin strands, available in two lengths.
Spaghettini Thicker than fedelini, thinner than spaghetti.
Tagliatelle Ribbon noodles.
Tortellini Filled pasta, semi-circles or triangles with the ends of the long side folded over where they meet and pressed together.
Tortiglioni Corkscrew shapes.

Filled Pasta Shapes

Some types of pasta are filled with a stuffing before being cooked, ravioli and tortellini being the two classic examples.

For ravioli, roll out two similar-sized sheets of pasta. Dot the chosen filling over the first sheet in small, evenly spaced mounds. Brush the pasta with beaten egg between the filling, then lay the second sheet over the top. Working from one end, press the two sheets of pasta together between the mounds of filling, pressing out the air as you work. When all the mounds of filling are sealed between pasta, cut between them with a large sharp knife or a pastry wheel.

For tortellini, stamp out circles of rolled-out pasta using a small pastry cutter. Place a little filling in the middle of the circle, brush the edge of the pasta with beaten egg and fold it in half to seal the filling in a semi-circle of pasta. Wrap the straight side of the stuffed pasta shape around your finger, pinching the points together to seal them in place. Alternatively, squares of pasta may be cut, filled and folded to make triangular stuffed shapes, then the corners folded over the finger and pinched together.

A ravioli tin and rolling pin may be used for filling ravioli. A sheet of pasta is laid over the tin which is made up of a number of small round cups. The filling and pasta are pressed into the cups, then a second sheet laid over the top and rolled to seal in the filling. Small serrations between the cups cut through the pasta to separate the individual ravioli.

A roller and hopper attachment to fill and seal ravioli is available for pasta machines. A sheet of pasta is folded into the hopper and the stuffing placed on top. The pasta and stuffing are then rolled through the machine to make small ravioli.

When cooking filled pasta shapes, allow sufficient time for the filling to cook through. Unfilled fresh pasta cooks in about 3 minutes, whereas filled shapes can take up to 15 minutes, depending on filling.

Classic fillings include a mixture of ground or minced beef or veal with pork, seasoned with minced or grated onion, garlic and marjoram. Ricotta cheese and spinach, seasoned with grated nutmeg and a little freshly grated Parmesan, is a familiar filling, or finely chopped or minced ham combined with grated Parmesan and ricotta. Parma ham or prosciutto can be used in the filling or cooked ham is a more economical choice.

The pasta dough recipe can be rolled out to make two sheets, each measuring about 38 cm/15 in square, or slightly larger, and this will make 45–49 ravioli. As a guide to quantities of filling, 175–225 g/6–8 oz ground or minced meat will fill this number of ravioli.

SAUCES, DRESSINGS & STUFFINGS

Sauces first came into widespread use in the Middle Ages, to disguise the flavour of long-stored meat that had been inadequately cured. Today, they are used to add flavour to bland food, colour to simple meals and moisture to otherwise dry foods.

There are two main groups of sauces: savoury and dessert. The first group includes white, brown and egg-based sauces; and the cold sauces and salad dressings. Horseradish, mint and the puréed fruit sauces are other savoury sauces which do not belong in any particular sub-group.

French chefs have created most of the hundreds of variations on the basic savoury sauces. Most dessert sauces, on the other hand, originated in England or America.

The main ingredient of all sauces is the basic liquid, which may be milk, wine, stock, vegetable or fruit juices. These are thickened with fat, flour, arrowroot, eggs, cream or blood, or they may be boiled down (reduced) to the desired consistency.

SAUCE CONSISTENCIES

Consistency	Uses	Ingredients Butter, flour	Milk/liquid
Thin sauce	Basis for soups or thin pouring sauces, such as gravy	15 g/½ oz each	300 ml/½ pt
Pouring sauce and fine or thin coating sauce	For accompanying savoury foods, like sausages, boiled ham, poached fish. For coating fish, chicken, pancakes, pasta or other fairly dry foods. For dessert sauces	20 g/¾ oz each	300 ml/½ pt
Thick coating sauce	Coating sauce for cauliflower, leeks, courgettes and similar ingredients which thin the sauce with their own juices. As a base to which ingredients may be added as a filling for pastries, such as vol-au-vent	25 g/1 oz each	300 ml/½ pt
Panada sauce (*very thick*)	For binding croquettes and as a basis for soufflés	50 g/2 oz each	300 ml/½ pt

SIMPLE WHITE SAUCES

		Other ingredients	Method of preparation	Serving suggestions
Butter sauce	300 ml/½ pt pouring white sauce (use milk or stock)	1 egg yolk 15 ml/1 tablespoon water 50 g/2 oz butter	Beat the egg yolk with water and blend into the sauce. Cook gently for 1–2 minutes, stirring without boiling. Beat in the butter cut into knobs	*Fish or vegetables*
Caper sauce	300 ml/½ pt pouring white sauce (use half milk and half white or fish stock)	15 ml/1 tablespoon caper vinegar or lemon juice 15 ml/1 tablespoon finely chopped capers	Add caper vinegar or lemon juice to the stock before making the sauce. Add the capers to the sauce just before serving	*Boiled fish or mutton*
Cheese sauce	300 ml/½ pt thick coating or pouring white sauce (use milk)	50 g/2 oz mature Cheddar cheese 2.5 ml/½ teaspoon dry mustard (optional) pinch cayenne	Beat the grated cheese into the sauce and heat gently until smooth. Season with mustard and cayenne	*Eggs, fish, pasta and vegetables*
Egg sauce	300 ml/½ pt pouring white sauce (use milk)	1 hard-boiled egg 30 ml/2 tablespoons chopped chives	Finely chop the egg and the chives and add to the sauce	*Poached or steamed fish*
Fish sauce	300 ml/½ pt pouring white sauce (made from half milk and half fish stock, simmered with a bay leaf and the rind of ½ lemon, then strained)	50 g/2 oz shrimps or 5 ml/1 teaspoon anchovy essence	Peel and chop the shrimps. Before seasoning the sauce, add the shrimps or anchovy essence	*Poached or steamed fish*
Mushroom sauce	300 ml/½ pt thick coating white sauce (use milk)	50 g/2 oz mushrooms squeeze lemon juice	Trim and slice the mushrooms. Add to the thickened sauce before simmering gently for 3–5 minutes	*Fish, meat, poultry*
Onion sauce	300 ml/½ pt pouring white sauce (use milk)	1 onion	Fry the finely chopped onion in the butter for the roux for about 15 minutes over gentle heat, or until softened but not browned. Stir in the flour and continue making the sauce	*Sausages, bacon, mutton and tripe*
Parsley sauce	300 ml/½ pt pouring white sauce (use milk)	30–45 ml/2–3 table-spoons parsley	Finely chop the parsley and add to the sauce just before serving	*Bacon, boiled or steamed fish, and vegetables*

WHITE SAUCES

This is a sauce made with milk and prepared either by the roux or the blending method. A roux is the usual and most successful method for a savoury sauce made with flour. The blending method is used when thickening with cornflour. The sauce consistencies chart gives proportions of ingredients for sauces of different thicknesses: the same method may be used for all thicknesses. **Note** When a recipe calls for a volume of white sauce, one of its variations, or Béchamel sauce, the quantity on the chart refers to the volume of milk used to make the sauce, not the exact amount of finished sauce.

Roux Method

A roux is usually composed of equal amounts of butter, or other fat, and flour to which liquid is added to the required consistency. Melt the fat in a heavy-based pan, stir in the flour, and cook over low heat for 2–3 minutes, stirring constantly.

Gradually add the liquid to the roux, which will at first thicken to a near solid mass. Beat the roux vigorously between small additions of liquid, allow-

Roux method white sauce

1 *Blend the butter with the flour.*

2 *Beating in a little milk.*

3 *Add the remaining milk.*

ing the mixture to thicken between each addition. When the thick mixture is smooth, the liquid can be added more quickly. Continuous beating, or vigorous stirring as the sauce thins, is essential to obtain a smooth sauce. When all the liquid has been added, bring the sauce to the boil; let it simmer for about 3–5 minutes and add the seasoning.

One-stage Method

A basic white sauce can also be made by the one-stage method. This consists of whisking the basic ingredients (fat, flour and liquid) together in a pan. Cook over low to medium heat, whisking continuously until the sauce has thickened. Boil for 3–5 minutes and season. It is essential that a whisk is used for a one-stage sauce; beating or vigorous stirring will not give a smooth result.

Blending Method

For this method of making a sauce, the thickening agent is mixed to a paste with a little cold liquid. This method is usually used with cornflour. Although flour can also be added in this way, the roux method is preferable as there is less chance of the sauce forming lumps as it begins to cook. Mix the cornflour or flour with a few tablespoons taken from the measured liquid. Blend to a smooth paste in a bowl, and bring the remaining liquid to the boil.

Pour the hot liquid over the paste and return the mixture to the pan. Bring to the boil over

low heat, stirring continuously. Simmer the sauce for 2–3 minutes, until thick. Add a knob of butter and seasoning and cook for 3 minutes.

Variations on a Basic White Sauce

A basic white sauce can be made into other savoury sauces. Delicately flavoured rich sauces, such as Béchamel and Velouté (page 354) have evolved from the basic white sauce. These sauces are, in turn, the main components for the compound white sauces.

COMPOUND WHITE SAUCES

	Ingredients	Method of preparation	Serving suggestions
Allemande sauce	300 ml/½ pt Velouté sauce 2 egg yolks 150 ml/¼ pt white stock 40 g/1½ oz butter	Beat the egg yolks with the stock and blend into the sauce. Simmer gently, stirring until thick, smooth and reduced by one-third. Stir in the butter (cut into pieces) and adjust seasoning	*Chicken, eggs, fish, vegetables*
Aurora sauce	300 ml/½ pt Velouté sauce 60 ml/4 tablespoons tomato purée or 15 ml/ 1 tablespoon tomato paste 40 g/1½ oz butter	Blend the tomato purée or tomato paste into the sauce. Stir in the butter (cut into pieces), and correct the seasoning	*Eggs, poultry, sweetbreads, fish, vegetables*
Chantilly sauce	300 ml/½ pt Suprême sauce 150 ml/¼ pt double or whipping cream	Whip the cream until light and fluffy. Fold into the Suprême sauce	*Serve immediately with poultry or offal*
Chaud-froid sauce	300 ml/½ pt Velouté sauce 300 ml/½ pt jellied white stock 60 ml/4 tablespoons single cream	Add the stock and cream to the sauce. Cook over gentle heat until reduced to coating consistency. Adjust the seasoning	*Cold as a coating for chicken, eggs and fish*
Mornay sauce	300 ml/½ pt Béchamel sauce 50 g/2 oz grated Parmesan or Gruyère cheese	Mix the cheese into the sauce. Do not reheat	*Chicken, eggs, veal, fish, vegetables and pasta*
Suprême sauce	300 ml/½ pt Velouté sauce 2 egg yolks 30 ml/2 tablespoons double cream 25 g/1 oz butter	Beat the egg yolks and cream together. Blend into the sauce and heat without boiling. Stir in the butter (cut into pieces)	*Serve immediately with eggs, poultry and vegetables*

Béchamel Sauce

MAKES: 300 ml/½ pt
PREPARATION: 10 minutes
INFUSING: 15 minutes
COOKING: 5–10 minutes

300 ml/½ pt milk
½ small bay leaf
1 sprig thyme
½ small onion
1.25 ml/¼ teaspoon grated nutmeg
25 g/1 oz butter
25 g/1 oz plain flour
salt and black pepper
30–45 ml/2–3 tablespoons single cream (optional)

Put the milk with the bay leaf, thyme, onion and nutmeg in a pan, and bring slowly to the boil. Remove from the heat, cover and leave the milk to infuse for 30 minutes.

Strain the milk through a fine sieve. In a clean heavy-based pan, melt the butter, stir in the flour and cook the roux for 3 minutes. Gradually stir the strained milk into the roux. Bring to the boil, stirring continuously, then simmer gently for 3–5 minutes. Adjust seasoning and stir in the cream, if using.

Velouté Sauce

MAKES: 300 ml/½pt
PREPARATION: 5–10 minutes
COOKING: 1 hour

25 g/1 oz butter
25 g/1 oz plain flour
600 ml/1 pt white stock
salt and black pepper
15–30 ml/1–2 tablespoons single or
   double cream (optional)

Make the roux with the butter and flour. Gradually stir in the hot stock until the sauce is quite smooth. Bring to boiling point, lower the heat, and let the sauce simmer for about 1 hour until reduced by half. Stir the sauce occasionally. Strain through a

Making Espagnole sauce

1 Blend in the flour.

2 Stir in the stock.

3 Strain the sauce.

sieve, season to taste, and stir in the cream, if using.

BROWN SAUCES

A basic brown sauce is made by the roux method, using the same proportions of flour, fat and liquid (brown stock) as for a basic white sauce. Melt the fat in a pan and stir in the flour. Cook the roux over low heat, stirring continuously with a wooden spoon, until the roux is light brown in colour. Gradually stir in the brown stock and proceed as for a white sauce.

Espagnole Sauce

This classic sauce, made from a brown roux, is the basis of many compound brown sauces.

MAKES: 300 ml/½ pt
PREPARATION: 10 minutes
COOKING: 1¼ hours

1 carrot
1 onion
50 g/2 oz streaky bacon
25 g/1 oz butter
25 g/1 oz plain flour
450 ml/¾ pt brown stock
bouquet garni*
30 ml/2 tablespoons tomato paste
salt and black pepper

Peel and dice the carrot and onion. Remove rind from the bacon and chop the rashers. Melt the butter in a heavy-based pan, and cook the vegetables and bacon over low heat for 10 minutes or until light brown.
   Blend in the flour, stirring the roux until brown. Gradually blend in 300 ml/½ pt of the stock, stirring constantly until the mixture has cooked through and

COMPOUND BROWN SAUCES

	Ingredients	Method of preparation	Serving suggestions
Demi-glace sauce	300 ml/½ pt Espagnole sauce 150 ml/¼ pt jellied brown stock	Add the jellied stock to the Espagnole sauce. Bring to the boil and cook until the sauce is shiny and thick enough to coat the back of a spoon	*Game:* add 45 ml/3 tablespoons Madeira to finished sauce *Poultry:* add 100 g/4 oz mushrooms and 15 ml/1 tablespoon Madeira
Devilled sauce	300 ml/½ pt Espagnole sauce 1 small onion 300 ml/½ pt white wine 15 ml/1 tablespoon wine vinegar sprig of thyme small bay leaf 15 ml/1 tablespoon parsley cayenne	Finely chop the onion and mix with the wine, vinegar, thyme and bay leaf. Bring to the boil and reduce by half. Strain and add to the Espagnole sauce. Boil for a few minutes, add the chopped parsley and cayenne to taste	*Grilled chicken*
Red wine sauce	300 ml/½ pt Espagnole sauce ½ onion 50 g/2 oz butter 300 ml/½ pt red wine bouquet garni*	Fry the finely chopped onion in 25 g/1 oz of the butter until clear. Add the rest of the ingredients and boil to reduce by half. Strain and add to Espagnole sauce. Cook until reduced by one-third. Stir in 25 g/1 oz of the butter and serve immediately	*Game*
Robert sauce	300 ml/½ pt Espagnole sauce 1 onion 15 g/½ oz butter 120 ml/4 fl oz red wine 5 ml/1 teaspoon mustard	Fry the chopped onion in the butter. Add the red wine and boil until reduced by half. Strain and add to the Espagnole sauce. Heat gently and stir in the mustard	*Roast pork*
Tomato sauce	300 ml/½ pt Espagnole sauce (made from tomato juice instead of brown stock) 100 g/4 oz ham	Dice the ham and add to the finished sauce	*Grilled chicken, meat leftovers, chops, pasta, meat patties*

has thickened. Add the bouquet garni, cover and simmer gently for 30 minutes. Add the remaining stock and the tomato paste. Cover the pan again, and continue cooking for 30 minutes, stirring frequently. Strain the sauce through a sieve, skim off fat, and adjust seasoning.

Gravies

The most frequently used brown sauce is gravy, made from the

pan residues of a roast joint, boiled up with brown stock. Gravies may be thick or thin.

Thick gravy

Pour off most of the fat from the roasting tin, leaving the sediment and just enough fat, if necessary, to cover the base of the tin thinly. Stir in about 30 ml/2 tablespoons plain flour and blend thoroughly with the fat. Stir constantly over medium

heat to brown the flour slightly if possible and scrape all sediment off the roasting tin. Gradually add 600 ml/1 pt hot stock or vegetable cooking water. Bring the gravy to boiling point and simmer, stirring often, for about 5 minutes. Season to taste, strain and serve hot with a roast.

Thin gravy

Pour all the fat from the pan, leaving only the pan residues.

Add 600 ml/1 pt hot vegetable liquid or stock. Stir well to remove all sediment from the roasting tin and boil for about 5 minutes to reduce slightly. A hot thin gravy is traditionally served with roast beef.

Thickening Agents for Sauces

Basic white and brown sauces can be thickened or enriched with various liaisons: cornflour or arrowroot with water; beurre manié (kneaded butter and flour); egg yolks and cream.

Cornflour and arrowroot

To thicken 300 ml/½ pt of liquid to a sauce of coating consistency, stir 15 ml/1 tablespoon cornflour with 30 ml/2 tablespoons cold water, and mix into a smooth paste. Blend a little of the hot liquid into the liaison, then return this to the sauce. Bring the sauce to the boil, stirring constantly for 2–3 minutes to allow the starch to cook through.

Arrowroot is best used to thicken clear sauces that are to be served at once. To thicken 300 ml/½ pt sauce, use 11.25 ml/2¼ teaspoons arrowroot mixed to a paste with water. As soon as a sauce thickened with arrowroot boils, it should be removed from the heat, as it will thin down with further cooking. The sauce cannot be reheated and quickly loses its thickening qualities.

Beurre manié

This is a mixture of butter and flour, used to thicken sauces, casseroles and stews at the end of cooking. Mix an equal amount of butter and flour to a paste with a spoon or fork. The weight of butter and flour depends on the volume of sauce and type of dish: 25 g/1 oz in 600 ml/1 pt gives a thin sauce; 40 g/1½ oz in 600 ml/1 pt gives a coating sauce.

To use beurre manié, the liquid to be thickened should be just simmering. It must not boil but it should be sufficiently hot to melt the butter quickly and take up the flour. Add small pieces of the beurre manié to the liquid, whisking continuously to dissolve the butter and disperse the flour. Bring the sauce to the boil, then reduce the heat and simmer for 3–5 minutes to lose the starchy taste of raw flour.

Egg yolks and cream

These are used when enriching a sauce. Mix 1 egg yolk with 30–45 ml/2–3 tablespoons cream in a bowl. Blend in a little of the hot sauce. Remove the sauce from the heat or reduce the heat to a very low setting to ensure that the sauce does not simmer and stir in the liaison. Return the pan to the heat and cook the sauce over low heat for about 2 minutes without simmering or boiling. Over-heating causes the eggs to over-cook and the sauce to curdle.

EGG-BASED SAUCES

These rich sauces require care and practice to prevent them curdling. They are made from egg yolks and a high proportion of butter. Through continuous whisking, these two main ingredients are emulsified to a thick and creamy consistency.

Hollandaise Sauce

MAKES: 300 ml/½ pt
PREPARATION: 10 minutes
COOKING: 10 minutes

*45 ml/3 tablespoons white
    wine vinegar*
15 ml/1 tablespoon water
6 black peppercorns
1 bay leaf
3 egg yolks
175 g/6 oz soft butter
salt and black pepper

Boil the vinegar and water with the peppercorns and the bay leaf in a small pan, until reduced to 15 ml/1 tablespoon. Leave to cool. Cream the egg yolks with 15 g/½ oz of the butter and a pinch of salt. Strain the vinegar into the eggs, and set the bowl over a pan of boiling water. Turn off the heat. Whisk in the remaining butter, 7 g/¼ oz at a time, until the sauce is shiny and has the consistency of thick cream. Season to taste.

Until the technique has been mastered, a Hollandaise sauce may sometimes curdle during preparation. This is usually because the heat is too sudden or too

Making Hollandaise sauce

Whisking in pieces of butter to thicken Hollandaise sauce.

high, or because the butter has been added too quickly. If the finished sauce separates, it can often be saved by removing from the heat and beating in 15 ml/1 tablespoon of cold water.

Béarnaise Sauce

This sauce is similar to Hollandaise, with a sharper flavour. It is served with grilled meat and fish.

MAKES: 300 ml/½pt
PREPARATION: 10 minutes
COOKING: 10 minutes

*30 ml/2 tablespoons
    tarragon vinegar*
*30 ml/2 tablespoons white
    wine vinegar*
½ small onion
2 egg yolks
75–100 g/3–4 oz butter
salt and black pepper

Put the vinegars and finely chopped onion in a small saucepan; boil steadily until reduced to 15 ml/1 tablespoon. Strain and set aside to cool. Follow the method used for making Hollandaise sauce.

COLD SAUCES

Mayonnaise and its variations are the most widely used savoury cold sauces. They are served with hors-d'oeuvre, salads, cold meat, poultry and vegetable dishes. Mayonnaise, like Hollandaise and Béarnaise sauces, is based on eggs and fat, but oil is used instead of butter. (See page 336 for advice on dishes containing raw eggs.)

All ingredients and equipment should be at room temperature. Assemble them 1 hour before making the mayonnaise.

Mayonnaise

MAKES: 150 ml/¼pt
PREPARATION: 20 minutes

1 egg yolk
1.25 ml/¼ teaspoon salt
2.5 ml/½ teaspoon dry mustard
pinch caster sugar
black pepper
150 ml/¼ pt olive or salad oil
*15 ml/1 tablespoon white wine
    vinegar or lemon juice*

Beat the egg yolk in a bowl until thick. Beat in the salt, mustard, sugar and a few grinds of freshly ground pepper. Add the oil, drop by drop, whisking vigorously between each addition of oil so that it is absorbed completely before the next drop. As the mayonnaise gradually thickens, and becomes shiny, the oil may be added in a thin stream. Finally, blend in the vinegar or lemon juice.

The flavour of the mayonnaise can be varied by using a tarragon, garlic or chilli vinegar, or by substituting lemon juice for vinegar. Chopped herbs such as parsley or chives, or crushed garlic, may also be added when the mayonnaise is finished.

Alternatively, fold in 150 ml/¼pt of whipped cream into the finished mayonnaise.

Mayonnaise may curdle if the oil was cold or added too quickly, or if the egg yolk was stale. To save a curdled mayonnaise, beat a fresh yolk in a clean bowl, and gradually beat in the curdled mayonnaise. Alternatively, beat in 5 ml/1 teaspoon tepid water until the mayonnaise becomes thick and shiny.

MAYONNAISE SAUCES

	Ingredients	Method of preparation	Serving suggestions
Anchovy mayonnaise	150 ml/¼ pt mayonnaise 30 ml/2 teaspoons anchovy essence	Mix the anchovy essence thoroughly into the finished mayonnaise	*Fish and vegetable salads*
Orange mayonnaise	150 ml/¼ pt mayonnaise *grated rind of 1 orange* *15–30 ml/1–2 tablespoons lightly whipped cream*	Fold the grated orange rind and lightly whipped cream into the mayonnaise	*Salads*
Remoulade sauce	150 ml/¼ pt mayonnaise *5 ml/1 teaspoon each chopped capers, chervil, gherkins, parsley, tarragon, onion*	Mix the finely chopped herbs and vegetables and blend into the mayonnaise	*Cold shellfish and egg dishes*
Tartare sauce	150 ml/¼ pt mayonnaise *10 ml/2 teaspoons capers* *3 cocktail gherkins* *5 ml/1 teaspoon chives* *15 ml/1 tablespoon double cream*	Finely chop the gherkins and chives. Add all the ingredients to the mayonnaise	*Fried or grilled fish*

Using a Liquidiser or Food Processor for Mayonnaise

A liquidiser or food processor simplifies the process of emulsifying egg yolks and oil when making mayonnaise. Put the yolk, seasonings and a little oil in the machine and process until pale. With the machine running on slow speed (if possible) gradually trickle in the oil, very slowly at first, then more quickly as the mixture thickens.

SALAD DRESSINGS

A good dressing is essential to a salad, but it must be varied to complement the salad ingredients. A sharp vinaigrette sauce is probably best for a green salad, but egg, fish, meat and vegetable salads will nearly always need extra flavouring. Chopped fresh herbs, such as parsley, chives, dill or tarragon, are all excellent in salad dressings.

French Dressing

MAKES: 200 ml/7 fl oz
PREPARATION: 3 minutes

120 ml/4 fl oz oil
60 ml/4 tablespoons vinegar
10 ml/2 teaspoons French mustard
2.5 ml/½ teaspoon each salt, black pepper
caster sugar (optional)

Whisk or shake all the dressing ingredients together, seasoning with sugar (optional).

Any of the following ingredients can be added to a basic French dressing, according to the salad or the dish it accompanies: 1–2 crushed garlic cloves; 30ml/ 2 tablespoons chopped tarragon or chives; 15 ml/1 tablespoon tomato paste and a pinch of paprika; 30 ml/2 tablespoons each finely chopped parsley and onion; 5 ml/1 teaspoon anchovy essence (for cold fish).

Sauce Vinaigrette

MAKES: 150 ml/¼ pt
PREPARATION: 3 minutes

90 ml/6 tablespoons oil
30 ml/2 tablespoons vinegar
10 ml/2 teaspoons finely chopped herbs
salt and black pepper

Put the oil and vinegar in a bowl or in a screw-top jar. Whisk with a fork or shake vigorously before seasoning to taste with herbs, salt and pepper.

MISCELLANEOUS SAUCES

Cumberland Sauce

MAKES: 600 ml/1 pt
PREPARATION: 15 minutes
COOKING: 10 minutes
STANDING: 24 hours

2 oranges
2 lemons
450 g/1 lb redcurrant jelly
250 ml/8 fl oz port or red wine
15ml/1 tablespoon arrowroot

Thinly peel one orange and one lemon. Remove pith and shred the peel finely. Bring a pan of water to the boil, add the shreds and boil for 3 minutes. Drain and cover with cold water for 1 minute; drain again and set aside.

Squeeze and strain all the fruit juices into a pan, add the jelly and bring slowly to the boil. Simmer for 5 minutes, then add the port and bring the sauce back to the boil. Remove the sauce from the heat.

Mix the arrowroot to a smooth paste with a little cold water. Stir in a little of the hot sauce, then pour the mixture into the hot sauce, stirring continuously. Return to the heat and bring just to the boil. Remove the pan from the heat immediately. Add the blanched peel and serve at once.

If the sauce is to be used later, cover the surface with a piece of dampened greaseproof paper or cling film to stop a skin forming. Leave to cool before serving.

■ Serve hot with boiled bacon, ham or grilled gammon, or cold with pork, ham or game pies.

Apple Sauce

MAKES: 300 ml/½ pt
PREPARATION: 10 minutes
COOKING: 10 minutes

450 g/1 lb cooking apples
25 g/1 oz unsalted butter
caster sugar (optional)

Peel, core and slice the apples. Put them in a saucepan with 30–45 ml/ 2–3 tablespoons water and cook over low heat for about 10 minutes. Rub the cooked apples through a coarse sieve or purée them in a liquidiser. Stir in butter and sweeten with sugar.

■ Serve with roast pork and goose, grilled sausages and bacon.

Bread Sauce

MAKES: 600 ml/1 pt
PREPARATION: 10 minutes
INFUSING: 15 minutes
COOKING: 15 minutes

1 onion
1–2 cloves
1 bay leaf
600 ml/1 pt milk
75 g/3 oz fresh white breadcrumbs
25 g/1 oz butter
salt and black pepper

Peel the onion. Stick the cloves into the onion and put into a pan with the bay leaf and milk. Bring to the boil. Remove the pan from the heat, cover with a lid and leave to infuse for 15 minutes. Add the breadcrumbs and the butter. Cook the sauce, uncovered, over lowest possible heat for 15 minutes, then remove the onion and bay leaf. Season to taste with salt and pepper.

■ Serve with chicken or turkey.

Horseradish Sauce

Fresh horseradish root can be bought in the shops in autumn. It should be scrubbed, then peeled. Horseradish is a harsh irritant and causes the eyes to water, so it is best peeled under gently running cold water. It can even sting the fingers or delicate areas under the fingernails, so always wash the hands well after handling the root.

MAKES: 200 ml/7 fl oz
PREPARATION: 10 minutes

75 ml/5 tablespoons fresh coarsely grated horseradish
150 ml/¼ pt soured cream
salt and black pepper
pinch dry mustard

Fold the freshly grated horseradish root into the soured cream and season to taste with salt, pepper and mustard.
■ Serve with roast beef.

Mint Sauce

SERVES: 4–6
PREPARATION: 10 minutes
STANDING: 30 minutes

small handful mint leaves
5–10 ml/1–2 teaspoons caster sugar
30 ml/2 tablespoons boiling water
30 ml/2 tablespoons vinegar

Carefully wash and dry the mint leaves. Put them on a board, sprinkle with the sugar, and chop them finely. Place the chopped mint in a jug and stir in the boiling water. Add the vinegar and leave the sauce to stand for 30 minutes.
■ Serve with roast lamb.

DESSERT SAUCES

Custard Sauce is given on page 338, under Egg Custards.

Apricot Sauce

MAKES: 300 ml/½pt
PREPARATION: 6 minutes
COOKING: 4 minutes

½ lemon
7.5 ml/1½ teaspoons arrowroot
150 ml/¼ pt water
60 ml/4 tablespoons apricot jam
25 g/1 oz caster sugar (optional)

Pare the rind from the lemon. Squeeze out the juice. Blend the arrowroot with the water in a small pan, and stir in the jam. Cook gently until the jam has melted, then stir in the lemon rind and juice. Bring to the boil, stirring continuously. Strain and reheat the sauce; sweeten to taste.
■ Serve hot with steamed or baked puddings or cold with ice cream, in which case reduce the arrowroot to 5 ml/1 teaspoon.

Honey Sauce

MAKES: about 150 ml/¼pt
PREPARATION: 3 minutes
COOKING: 5 minutes

50 g/2 oz unsalted butter
7.5 ml/1½ teaspoons cornflour
175 g/6 oz thin clear honey

Melt the butter in a small pan over low heat, without browning it; stir in the cornflour.
   Gradually blend in the honey and bring the sauce to the boil, stirring all the time. Heat for 1 minute to cook the cornflour.
■ Serve warm with ice cream or banana splits.

Brandy Sauce

MAKES: 300 ml/½pt
PREPARATION: 5 minutes
COOKING: 5 minutes

15 ml/1 tablespoon cornflour
300 ml/½ pt milk, less 30 ml/ 2 tablespoons
15 ml/1 tablespoon caster sugar
30 ml/2 tablespoons brandy

In a bowl, blend the cornflour to a smooth paste with 15 ml/ 1 tablespoon of the milk. Bring the remaining milk to the boil; pour it over the cornflour, stirring well. Return the sauce to the pan, add the caster sugar and brandy and cook over low heat for 2–3 minutes.
■ Serve hot with steamed fruit puddings. Brandy sauce is traditionally served with Christmas pudding and mince pies.

Butterscotch Sauce

MAKES: 300 ml/½pt
PREPARATION: 10 minutes
COOKING: 15 minutes

75 g/3 oz granulated sugar
90 ml/6 tablespoons boiling water
7.5 ml/1½ teaspoons arrowroot
60 ml/4 tablespoons cold water
25 g/1 oz unsalted butter

Heat the sugar over gentle heat in a heavy-based pan, until dissolved. Increase the heat and let the sugar bubble until it caramelises to a golden brown. Remove the pan from the heat, add (without stirring) the boiling water and return the pan to the heat. Simmer the caramel for a few minutes, stirring all the time, until dissolved.

Blend the arrowroot with the cold water and stir into the caramel. Bring the mixture to the boil, over low heat. Add the butter, cut into small pieces, and cook the sauce until thick and clear, stirring all the time to prevent the sauce burning.
■ Serve warm with ice cream and sundaes, baked apples and plain steamed sponge puddings.

Chocolate Sauce

MAKES: 200 ml/7 floz
PREPARATION: 5 minutes
COOKING: 5 minutes

100 g/4 oz plain dark chocolate
15 g/½ oz unsalted butter
30 ml/2 tablespoons golden syrup or clear honey
5 ml/1 teaspoon natural vanilla essence (optional)
2 tablespoons water

Break the chocolate into pieces and put them into a pan with the butter, water and syrup or honey. Cook over low heat until the chocolate has melted, then stir in the vanilla essence if using.
■ Serve hot with vanilla ice cream or warm with profiteroles.

Sauce Sabayon

MAKES: 300 ml/½pt
PREPARATION: 7 minutes
COOKING: 5 minutes

2 egg yolks
50 g/2 oz caster sugar
1.25 ml/¼ teaspoon arrowroot
75 ml/2½ fl oz sherry, white wine, fruit juice or strong black coffee

In a deep bowl, beat the yolks and sugar until thick, creamy and

pale in colour. Blend the arrowroot to a paste with a little of your chosen liquid, then beat it with the rest of the liquid into the eggs. Place the bowl over a pan of gently simmering water and whisk the sauce until it is thick and frothy.
■ Serve at once with fruit puddings and apple pie.

Soured Cream Sauce

MAKES: 300 ml/½pt
PREPARATION: 10 minutes
CHILLING: 30 minutes

150 ml/¼ pt double cream
150 ml/¼ pt soured cream
5 ml/1 teaspoon caster sugar

Whip the cream until it just holds its shape, then fold in the soured cream and the sugar. Refrigerate for about 30 minutes.
■ Serve with cooked fruit, fruit pies, mince pies and fruit salads.

Syrup Sauce

MAKES: 200 ml/7 fl oz
PREPARATION: 3 minutes
COOKING: 5 minutes

10 ml/2 teaspoons arrowroot
150 ml/¼ pt water
60 ml/4 tablespoons golden syrup
30 ml/2 tablespoons lemon juice

Blend the arrowroot to a smooth paste with the water in a small pan. Add the syrup and lemon juice. Bring the sauce to the boil, over low heat, stirring all the time, and remove from the heat at once.
■ Serve hot with light steamed puddings, and warm with ice cream, pancakes and waffles.

STUFFINGS

Stuffings are based on breadcrumbs, meat and rice to which butter or chopped suet is added together with herbs and seasoning. Stuffings are used in a variety of ways to fill small or large portions of food with the intention of flavouring the food. The stuffing should not dominate the dish; it should simply complement the flavour of the main ingredient and absorb cooking juices; it may also give the dish extra body or bulk, for example when used to fill fish fillets or thin slices of meat.

Whole fish or fillets of fish may be stuffed. It is usually best to make a delicate stuffing for fish. Poultry and game birds may be filled with a variety of stuffings, from delicate herb and citrus mixtures to highly spiced ingredients. The body cavity of a bird can be filled with stuffing and/or the stuffing may be inserted under the skin covering the breast meat. As a breadcrumb-based stuffing expands during cooking, it is necessary to stuff the bird loosely; a basic 100 g/ 4 oz stuffing mixture is sufficient for a 1.6 kg/3½ lb chicken.

The prepared food should not be stuffed too far in advance. This is particularly important when preparing poultry as the warmth of a stuffing provides the ideal environment for bacteria to multiply. When cooking a large bird, like a turkey, it takes some time for the stuffing to heat through, again presenting a potential food safety problem. So, never stuff the food more than 2–3 hours in advance, always ensure that the stuffing is cold if the food is to stand before cooking, and chill the stuffed food until it is put in the oven or cooked.

Basic Breadcrumb Stuffing

PREPARATION: 15 minutes

100 g/4 oz white breadcrumbs
25 g/1 oz butter
1 small onion
salt and black pepper
1 egg
stock or milk

Put the breadcrumbs in a bowl. Melt the butter and stir it into the breadcrumbs. Peel and finely chop the onion and stir into the breadcrumbs. Season with salt and pepper; beat the egg lightly and mix into the breadcrumbs. Add enough stock or milk to give a moist but firm consistency.

Using a small spoon, fill the cavity of the bird with the stuffing. Chicken is stuffed from the neck end, duck and goose from either neck or vent end. Turkey is usually stuffed from both neck and vent ends.

Variations on Basic Breadcrumb Stuffing

Sage and onion stuffing Add 30 ml/2 tablespoons finely chopped fresh sage or 15 ml/ 1 tablespoon dried sage.
Celery stuffing Chop 3 sticks of celery finely and cook them in a little butter for 5 minutes. Add to the basic stuffing.
Celery and apricot stuffing Make the celery stuffing as above and add 100 g/4 oz finely chopped dried apricots.

Apple stuffing Peel, core and finely chop 2 medium cooking apples. Replace the butter in the basic stuffing recipe with 25 g/ 1 oz bacon fat or 100 g/4 oz finely chopped, lightly cooked streaky bacon and mix in the apples.
Mushroom stuffing Trim and chop 100 g/4 oz mushrooms and cook them in the melted butter for the basic stuffing for 2 minutes. Mix the mushrooms with the breadcrumbs, onion, egg and seasonings.
Sausage stuffing For a large bird, a meaty stuffing helps to keep the flesh moist. Make up the basic stuffing and mix it with 225 g/ 8 oz sausagemeat.

Alternatively, melt 25 g/1 oz butter and lightly fry 1 finely chopped onion and 450 g/1 lb sausagemeat for 2–3 minutes. Turn the mixture into a bowl and add 25 g/1 oz fresh white breadcrumbs, salt and freshly ground black pepper to taste, 1 beaten egg and milk to bind. Leave the mixture to cool before stuffing the bird.

Rice stuffing Melt 25 g/1 oz butter and lightly fry 1 small finely chopped onion until it is transparent. Add 100 g/4 oz long-grain rice and fry with the onion, stirring occasionally, for a further 2–3 minutes.

Season the rice stuffing with salt and freshly ground black pepper, and pour in 300 ml/½ pt stock or water. Bring to the boil, then cover the pan and reduce the heat to the lowest setting. Cook the stuffing for 20 minutes, then leave it to stand off the heat, without removing the lid, for a further 10 minutes.

Apple and Orange Stuffing

Full-flavoured, sweet dessert apples and tangy orange complement each other well in this breadcrumb-based stuffing.

Tarragon may be added to give a hint of aniseed. Use the stuffing with poultry, or rich meat, such as pork and lamb, or with oily fish, such as mackerel.

PREPARATION: 15 minutes
COOKING: 10 minutes

2 sweet dessert apples
1 onion
25 g/1 oz butter
100 g/4 oz fresh white breadcrumbs
60 ml/4 tablespoons
    chopped parsley
15ml/1 tablespoon chopped
    tarragon (optional)
grated rind and juice of 1 orange
salt and black pepper

Peel, core and coarsely grate the apples and finely chop the onion. Melt the butter in a small pan over low heat. Add the apple and onion and cook, stirring often, for 10 minutes.

Mix in the breadcrumbs, parsley, tarragon (if used), orange rind and seasoning to taste. Remove from the heat. Stir in enough orange juice to bind the ingredients.

Forcemeat Stuffing

PREPARATION: 20 minutes

25 g/1 oz butter
75 g/3 oz fresh white breadcrumbs
1 small onion
100 g/4 oz lean veal or pork
50 g/2 oz lean bacon
salt and black pepper
1 egg
stock

Melt the butter and stir it into the breadcrumbs. Finely chop the onion, then add it to the breadcrumbs. Put the veal and bacon through the fine blade of a mincer or process them in a food processor until they are finely minced and add to the breadcrumbs. Season with salt and freshly ground pepper, then mix in the egg and enough stock to bind the stuffing.

Chestnut Stuffing

Boiled, puréed fresh chestnuts or canned unsweetened purée may be used in this stuffing.

PREPARATION: 20 minutes

1 quantity Forcemeat Stuffing
30 ml/1 tablespoon
    chopped parsley
50 g/2 oz streaky bacon
225 g/8 oz chestnut purée
grated rind of 1 lemon

Make up the forcemeat stuffing and stir in the parsley.

Cut the rind off the bacon and chop it finely. Dry fry the bacon for 2–3 minutes until crisp.

Mix the drained bacon into the stuffing. Add the chestnut purée and finely grated lemon rind and mix well.

FRUIT

Fresh fruit makes delicious eating on its own, in fruit salads and with cheese. This section includes basic recipes and suggestions on how to prepare and serve, stew, poach and bake fruit. Various types of fruit are also used for jams and jellies, pickles and chutneys as well as in many savoury and sweet recipes throughout this book.

Apples

Having varieties of sour apples set aside specifically for cooking is one of the great characteristics of British desserts. Dessert apples are used for pies, flans and other puddings in most countries but the sharp, full flavour of a Bramley apple pie is something very special and very British. Unlike dessert apples, cooking apples soften quickly to form a purée when cooked, making them ideal for apple sauce.

Continental apple flans and the French classic tarte Tatin have to be made with fruit that retains its shape when baked. Dessert apples are also useful for poaching until tender but still whole, not floury.

Apples can be baked, stewed, made into purées or used as fillings for pastry, baked and steamed puddings, cream-based foods and mousses. Without additional sugar and water, 450 g/1 lb cooking apples make 300 ml/½ pt purée. Dip sliced apples for decoration in lemon juice to prevent discoloration.

For a purée, wash, peel and core 450 g/1 lb of apples. Cook them over gentle heat, with a piece of pared lemon peel and 30–45 ml/2–3 tablespoons of water, until soft. Liquidise the pulp or rub it through a sieve.

Apricots

Perfect ripe fruit are excellent served as a dessert fruit. They can also be poached in sugar syrup or

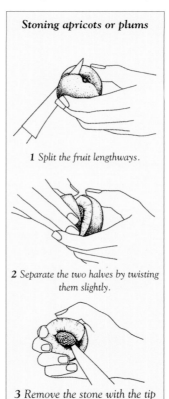

Stoning apricots or plums

1 Split the fruit lengthways.

2 Separate the two halves by twisting them slightly.

3 Remove the stone with the tip of a knife.

used in pie fillings, sweetened with vanilla sugar. Stone apricots by cutting them in half with a sharp knife, following the slight indentation line. Twist the two halves in opposite directions to separate them; remove the stone.

Bananas

Once peeled, bananas discolour rapidly. Sprinkling them with lemon, lime or orange juice prevents bananas from rapidly turning brown but this can change their flavour.

Bananas may be used in trifles, to flavour ice cream, or in jellies. They make delectable fritters and they are also good baked or grilled, especially over a barbecue, when they should be cooked in their skins until thoroughly blackened, by which time the soft flesh will be hot.

Blackberries

These berries go extremely well with apples, and are used as pie fillings, in apple snow, fruit puddings, jams and jellies.

Cherries

Both white and black heart cherries are served as a dessert fruit. For cooking in puddings, pies, compôtes and jams, choose morello cherries. Strip them of the stalks and ideally push out the stones with the special tool known as a cherry stoner.

Currants

Blackcurrants are usually served cooked, in pies, suet and sponge puddings and in ice creams and sorbets. They are also used for jams, jellies and fruit syrups.

Redcurrants may be eaten fresh, or in a sugar frosting (see Garnishes and Decorations, pages 411–412). Redcurrants are also suitable for compôtes, fruit salads, pastries and jams. White currants can be eaten fresh.

Before cooking, strip all currants off the stalks by running a fork down the stalk.

Damsons

These are used, stoned, in pies and puddings. They are also used to make jams and jellies or an old-fashioned preserve, Damson Cheese (page 408).

Dates, fresh

Serve these as a dessert fruit or use in fresh fruit salads. They are also an excellent fruit to serve with cheese, especially soft goats' cheese. Squeeze the stem end to remove the date from its slightly tough skin.

Figs, fresh

These dessert fruits are served fresh; they may be cut open with a knife and fork and only the soft red flesh inside eaten. Alternatively, the stalk and thin skin may be removed and the figs may be cut into wedges, then used in flans or other desserts. Figs are delicious with soft cheese, such as Camembert or Brie, or tangy goats' cheese.

Gooseberries

Dessert varieties are served on their own, but acid gooseberries are cooked. They are used for favourite desserts such as gooseberry fool and in pies, puddings, jams, jellies and chutneys.

Preparing gooseberries

Top and tail gooseberries by snipping off the stalk and flower ends

Gooseberries may be stewed to make a tart sauce as an accompaniment for mackerel, duck or rich meats like pork and lamb. Top and tail the gooseberries by pinching off the ends.

Grapefruit

This popular citrus fruit is usually served fresh as a breakfast dish or a first course. To prepare a grapefruit, cut the fruit in half 'crossways' and use, ideally, a curved, saw-edged grapefruit knife to cut round inside the skin to loosen the flesh. Make deep cuts between the grapefruit segments close to the membranes dividing them. Flip out any pips with the point of the knife. The central core may be cut away, but this is not essential. Serve with or without sugar or honey.

Grilled grapefruit Sprinkle the halves with a little sherry and demerara or soft brown sugar, and put under a hot grill for a few minutes to glaze.

Vandyke cutting Empty half grapefruit shells look attractive as serving 'dishes'. Use kitchen scissors to cut out a series of small V's round the edge of the shells

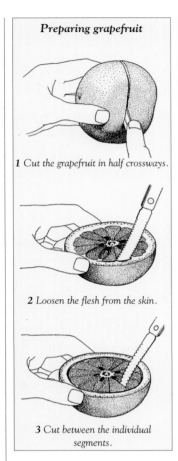

Preparing grapefruit

1 *Cut the grapefruit in half crossways.*

2 *Loosen the flesh from the skin.*

3 *Cut between the individual segments.*

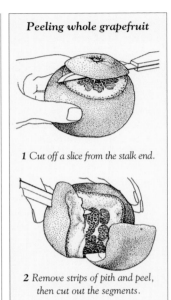

Peeling whole grapefruit

1 *Cut off a slice from the stalk end.*

2 *Remove strips of pith and peel, then cut out the segments.*

Removing pips from grapes

Remove pips from grapes by inserting a new hair grip from the stalk end.

or halve the fruit by making short cuts at alternate angles in as far as the centre. Work all around the fruit to give two zig-zag halves, then gently pull the fruit halves apart. This is known as vandyking.

Peeling grapefruit To peel a whole grapefruit, hold the fruit firmly with the tips of the fingers and cut a thin slice from the stem end of the fruit until the flesh just shows. Place the grapefruit, cut side down, on a board and with a sawing action cut the peel and pith off in strips to reveal the flesh of the grapefruit. Trim off any remaining pith.

Segmenting grapefruit To remove the individual segments without any membranes, hold the fruit in one hand over a basin to catch spilt juices. Carefully cut close to the membrane beside one fruit segment and cut through to the centre. Then work the knife from the middle of the segment and around to cut outwards on the other side, keeping the knife as close as possible up against the next membrane. The action involves cutting in towards the centre of the fruit, then using a combination of cutting and scraping to work back out to the edge.

This method gives neat fruit segments and leaves the core with the membranes in one piece – squeeze any remaining juice from core and membranes before discarding them.

Grapes
These delicious fruits are served for dessert, plain or in a sugar frosting (see Garnishes and Decorations pages 411–412). They also make a good addition to fresh fruit salads. They are also the classic garnish in savoury dishes known as à la Véronique.

Most grapes are easily peeled away from the stem end using a fine, sharp paring knife. If the skins are difficult to remove dip a few grapes at a time in boiling water for 30 seconds, then plunge them immediately into cold water. Seedless varieties are now readily available.

Greengages
Ripe fruits are served fresh and are also delicious halved and stoned as pie fillings. These varieties of plums are also popular ingredients for jams.

Kiwi Fruit or Chinese Gooseberries
These are widely used in fruit salads, flans, cheesecakes and gâteaux. They may also be served very simply as a dessert fruit – cut them in half crossways and scoop out the juicy flesh with a teaspoon. They can also be used for jams and jellies.

Kumquats
Miniature orange-like fruits. These are cooked whole, including the skin, and are also used as a garnish for duck or in other savoury cooking. They may be preserved whole in syrup and served with cream.

Lemons
Lemons are one of the most useful fruits in the kitchen and both the rind and juice are used in a large number of dishes. They make an attractive garnish for food and long drinks. Rub sugar lumps over the skin of a lemon until they are well coloured and use the lumps whole or crushed in iced drinks.

Lemon juice can be substituted for vinegar in many recipes, except pickling, and can be used to sour fresh cream: add 15 ml/1 tablespoon lemon juice to 150 ml/¼ pt. Store lemons in the refrigerator and, if cut, wrap in cling film.

Limes
These are used in a similar way to lemons, and lime juice is particularly good squeezed over melon wedges. It also gives a fresh flavour to salad dressings.

Limquats
Similar to kumquats, these are miniature limes.

Lychees
Lychees are served as a dessert fruit on their own or added to a fruit salad. Pinch the parchment-like outer skin to crack it and peel it off. Slit the opaque, soft white flesh down one side and gently part the slit so that the large shiny seed in the middle slips out.

Mangoes
These tropical fruits should not be cut too long before serving as mangoes tend to discolour, depending on use.

Peel the fruit, then cut slices of the flesh off the stone, working from the bottom. The stone is large and flat, and some flesh clings to the edges of it. Very ripe fruit is quite pulpy and difficult to slice. The fruit may be cut in half, off the stone, then the flesh may be scored into squares and turned inside-out so that the skin curves inwards.

Mango chutney Indian mango chutney is made from small, hard fruits which have not grown large stones. They are green, sour and similar in size to small tomatoes. Ripe, but firm, sweet mangoes can also be used in British-style chutneys.

Melons
Cool ripe melon is served as a first course as well as for dessert. The fruit may be served plain, or sweetened if liked, with finely chopped stem ginger or a squeeze of fresh lemon or lime juice. Fine slices of prosciutto (such as Parma ham) may be served with plain melon to make a delicious, refreshing starter.

Refrigerate melon only long enough to chill it, or the delicate flavour will be lost.

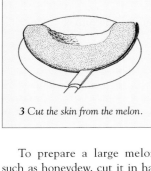

Preparing melon

1 Cut the melon in half lengthways.

2 Remove the pips from the melon segments.

3 Cut the skin from the melon.

To prepare a large melon, such as honeydew, cut it in half lengthways with a sharp knife. Cut each half lengthways into segments and scoop out the pips with a spoon or fork. A fully ripe melon segment may be served with the skin attached or the skin may be loosened by running the knife blade between flesh and skin. Leave the skin underneath the melon segment.

A small melon, such as Charentais or Ogen, usually only serves two persons. Cut across in half and scoop out the pips.

Melon basket To shape a large melon into a basket, first cut a thin slice from the base so that the melon will stand upright. From the top, make one vertical cut 1 cm/½ in from the centre to halfway down the melon; make a similar cut 1 cm/½ in to the other side. Cut the melon horizontally, stopping at the downward cuts and lift out the two sections, leaving a 2.5 cm/1 in wide handle. Remove the pips from the melon, and take out the flesh with a small ball scoop.

Nectarines

These tender dessert fruits need no peeling. Serve with dessert knives and forks, cut the fruits in half and slip out the stones.

Oranges

The most widely available citrus fruits, oranges are served fresh on their own and in fruit salad. They are much used in cooking, especially in sauces and stuffings.

Peel and cut oranges as described under grapefruit. Alternatively, peel oranges in round strips, remove all pith and cut the orange into slices across the grain. If oranges do not peel easily, chill them for 1 hour or cover them with boiling water and leave for a few minutes.

Passion Fruit

The sharp, tangy, pulpy flesh of this tropical fruit is used to flavour cocktails, punches or fresh fruit cups, as well as being used to fill fruit pies. Depending on the fruit, the juice may be yellow or pink, with small, dark, edible seeds that have a crunchy texture. The seeds can be overwhelming in some dishes, so the pulpy flesh is often sieved and the seeds discarded or only a few added. The sieved pulp makes an excellent dessert sauce. The fruit can also be served plain, cut in half and arranged on a platter to display its tempting flesh, then eaten with small teaspoons.

Pawpaws

Prepare ripe pawpaws (papayas) as melon, cutting them in half and removing the black seeds. Serve plain as a dessert or breakfast fruit, or cut up and mixed into a fruit salad.

Peaches

These fruits are usually served whole as a dessert, but are also excellent in fruit salads, flans and pies. Peach purée can be used as base for ice creams, soufflés and other sweet recipes. To peel fresh peaches, dip them in a bowl of boiling water, count up to ten, then drain and put the peaches at once in a bowl of cold water. Peel off the skin in downward strips with a knife.

Pears

Really ripe dessert pears can be eaten on their own or served in fruit salads. They may also be poached. To prepare pears for poaching, cut them in half lengthways with a sharp knife. Fresh pears discolour quickly, so they should not be allowed to stand for any length of time once cut. Lemon or orange juice helps to slow down the process of discoloration. Scoop out the core and pips with a pointed spoon. Poach the pears for 20–30 minutes, until tender, in a syrup made by dissolving 175 g/6 oz sugar in 600 ml/1 pt water. Add a strip of pared lemon rind, if like.

Persimmons

For serving fresh, wash and lightly chill the fruits and serve with a pointed spoon, to dig the juicy flesh out of the skin. A squeeze of lemon or lime juice may be added, and the skin can be marked in quarters and peeled back for an attractive presentation. The pulp may be used as a basis for ice creams, milk drinks, jellies and sauces.

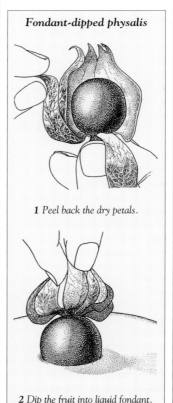

Fondant-dipped physalis

1 Peel back the dry petals.

2 Dip the fruit into liquid fondant.

Physalis, Cape Gooseberries or Goldenberries

These are sometimes served as a sweetmeat dipped in Fondant Icing (page 390). Peel the calyx back to form petals round the berry and dip in liquid fondant; leave to set and serve in tiny paper cases. The fruit may be part-dipped in melted chocolate instead of fondant.

Pineapple

A ripe pineapple is best served as a dessert fruit. Slice off the leaf and the stem ends, and cut the

Preparing pineapple

Slicing off the leaf top.

Removing the skin from the pineapple slices.

Stamping out the central woody cores.

pineapple across into 1 cm/½ in thick slices. Using a sharp knife, cut off the skin and the woody 'eyes' in the flesh of each slice. Remove the tough centre core with a small, plain pastry cutter or an apple corer. Arrange the pineapple slices on a flat dish, sprinkle with caster sugar and 30 ml/2 tablespoons of liqueur. Leave to marinate* for about 2 hours before serving.

For a spectacular party sweet, slice off the leaf end only and, without splitting the skin, cut round the edge of the pineapple between the flesh and skin, loosening it at the base as well. Extract the pineapple flesh, remove the core and cut the flesh into wedge-shaped pieces. Set the pineapple shell on a serving dish, replace the wedges and cover with the pineapple top. Pineapple shells also make attractive containers for fruit salads, pineapple sorbet, water ices and ice creams.

Plums

A few plum varieties are excellent as dessert fruits. All types of plums are suitable for pies, fruit salads, flans, baked and steamed puddings, jams and chutneys, as well as pickles.

Pomegranates

These fruits are served fresh as a dessert. Cut them into quarters and scoop the seeds from the bitter membranes with a pointed spoon. The small, dark, edible seeds are surrounded by a clear layer of juicy flesh, usually pink or bright red. The seeds and flesh are sweet, yet tangy, and very

juicy. Pomegranates are not easy to eat and they are certainly not a popular dessert fruit for dinner parties. They taste best when the seeds are bitten from the wedges, but this is thoroughly inelegant! One old-fashioned method of eating the fruit was to pick out each seed carefully with a pin. The most successful method of using the fruit for dessert is to remove all seeds over a basin to catch the juice, then add them to a fruit salad or serve them with other fruit.

Raspberries

Like other soft fruit, ripe raspberries should be used as soon as possible after picking. If it is necessary to wash them, put them in a colander and let water flow gently through them. Drain and use at once.

To make raspberry purée, rub the fruit through a nylon sieve, pressing it with a wooden spoon, or liquidise and then sieve the purée to remove the seeds – 450 g/1 lb fresh raspberries will give 300 ml/½ pt purée.

Rhubarb

Particularly suitable for pie fillings, baked puddings, fools and jams, rhubarb blends well with many flavours, such as orange rind, ginger and cinnamon. Forced tender rhubarb needs little preparation apart from cutting off the root ends and the leaves. Older rhubarb is somewhat coarser, and tough strings of skin must be peeled off before cooking. Wash and drain before use.

Poached rhubarb makes a quick and tasty dessert served

with cream, yogurt or home-made custard. Cut the trimmed rhubarb into 2.5 cm/1 in pieces. Put 75–100g/3–4 oz sugar in a saucepan with 60 ml/4 tablespoons water. Heat gently, stirring, until the sugar dissolves. Add the rhubarb and bring the syrup to the boil, stirring once or twice. Then reduce the heat and cover the pan. Poach the fruit gently, stirring occasionally, for about 15 minutes, or until tender but not pulpy.

Orange rind and juice may be added to the syrup instead of water, if preferred. The rhubarb may also be baked: layer the fruit in an ovenproof dish with the sugar. Sprinkle with the juice and grated rind of an orange. Cover and cook in a preheated oven at 180°C/350°F/gas 4 for about 35 minutes.

Strawberries

These soft fruits are best eaten soon after picking but they are not quite as perishable as raspberries. The calyxes at the stalk ends are sometimes left on the berries for decoration, but strawberries are usually hulled*. Serve whole or sliced. Strawberry purée is made in the same way as raspberry purée and yields the same amount. There is no need to sieve the purée if it is made in a liquidiser as strawberries do not contain large seeds.

Ugli Fruits

These may be prepared and served in the same way as grapefruit halves; because they are sweeter than grapefruit, they do not need any sugar.

Fresh Fruit Salad

This is the classic, British, fresh fruit salad; with the greater availability of exotic fruit and less use of sugar, a wider variety of fruit is usually mixed for a salad and a little icing sugar or honey may be used to sweeten the salad instead of syrup.

SERVES: 6
PREPARATION: 30 minutes
STANDING: 1–2 hours

100 g/4 oz granulated sugar
150 ml/¼ pt water
30 ml/2 tablespoons lemon juice
15 ml/1 tablespoon orange liqueur or Kirsch
225 g/8 oz seedless white or black grapes
2 dessert apples
2 ripe dessert pears
2 oranges
2 bananas

Put the sugar and water in a small pan, heat gently to dissolve the sugar, then bring to the boil for 2–3 minutes. Cool, then add the lemon juice and liqueur and pour into a large serving bowl.

Peel the grapes (page 360), if liked. Add the grapes to the sugar syrup in the bowl. Wipe the apples, quarter them, discard the cores and thinly slice the apple quarters into the bowl. Halve and peel the pears, remove the cores and cut the pears into chunks. Add to the bowl. Peel and segment the oranges (as for grapefruit, page 360), add to the bowl and squeeze the orange membranes into the bowl. Turn the fruit in the syrup. Cover and leave in a cool place, preferably not the refrigerator, for 1–2

hours to develop the flavours. Just before serving the salad, peel and slice the bananas and mix them with the fruit.

When fresh strawberries are available, use 1 apple and 1 pear and include 225 g/8 oz hulled* and halved small strawberries. Cherries, plums and greengages with stones removed, halved apricots, sliced peaches, redcurrants, pineapple, grapefruit and melon are all suitable.

Baked Apples

SERVES: 4
PREPARATION: 10 minutes
OVEN: 180°C/350°F/gas 4
COOKING: 30–45 minutes

4 large cooking apples
juice of 1 lemon
60–90 ml/4–6 tablespoons soft brown sugar
40 g/1½ oz butter

Wipe the apples and remove the cores, using a sharp knife or apple corer. Make a cut in the skin around the middle of each apple. Place the apples in an ovenproof dish and sprinkle with the lemon juice. Fill the cavity of each apple with sugar and top with a knob of butter. Cover and bake in a preheated oven at 180°C/350°F/gas 4 for about 50–60 minutes, basting occasionally with the apple juices, until tender.

Fillings Baked apples may be filled with diced fruit, such as sultanas, currants or raisins, and honey may be used instead of sugar. Ground mixed spice or ground cinnamon may be used to flavour the filling.

Banana Flambé

SERVES: 6
PREPARATION: 5 minutes
COOKING: 5 minutes

6 firm bananas
50–75 g/2–3 oz unsalted butter
45 ml/3 tablespoons
   demerara sugar
45 ml/3 tablespoons orange
   liqueur, brandy or rum

Peel the bananas and cut them in half lengthways. Fry quickly in hot butter, turning once, until they are just beginning to colour. Sprinkle with sugar, add the liqueur and set it alight. Burn for a few seconds, then serve at once, with the pan juices.

Blackcurrant Brûlée

SERVES: 4
PREPARATION: 12 minutes
COOKING: 8–10 minutes

225 g/8 oz stripped blackcurrants
75 ml/5 tablespoons water
75 g/3 oz demerara sugar
7.5 ml/1½ teaspoons arrowroot
150 ml/¼ pt double cream
light soft brown sugar
ground cinnamon

Simmer the stripped blackcurrants in 60 ml/4 tablespoons of the water until tender; add the demerara sugar, bring to the boil and simmer for a few more minutes. Blend the arrowroot with the remaining water, stir it into the currants and heat gently, stirring continuously, until the sauce thickens and just boils. Remove the pan from the heat immediately as the sauce will thin down if it is allowed to simmer. Cover the surface of the fruit with a piece of dampened greaseproof paper or cling film and allow it to cool.

Divide the fruit between four individual flameproof dishes. Whip the cream until it stands in peaks. Divide the cream between the dishes, spreading it to cover the fruit completely. Sprinkle a little cinnamon over the cream, then cover it completely with a generous layer of brown sugar. Press the sugar down evenly with the back of a spoon and chill the desserts for at least 2–3 hours. They are best chilled overnight.

To serve, preheat the grill on the hottest setting. Set the dishes under the grill for a few seconds until the sugar bubbles and caramelises. Serve immediately.

Compôte of Redcurrants

SERVES: 4–6
PREPARATION: 15 minutes
CHILLING: 2–3 hours

450 g/1 lb redcurrants
200 g/7 oz caster sugar
30 ml/2 tablespoons water

Strip the currants from the stems, rinse and drain. Put the currants in a pan, together with the sugar and water. Shake the pan over low heat until the fruit juice begins to run and the sugar has dissolved. Stir carefully occasionally, taking care not to pound the currants. Cook gently for about 5 minutes to soften the currants slightly without reducing them to a purée. Then set aside until lukewarm. Chill.
■ Serve with Chantilly Cream (page 411).

Peaches in Wine

SERVES: 4
PREPARATION: 20 minutes
CHILLING: 20 minutes

4 ripe yellow peaches
20 ml/4 teaspoons caster sugar
90–120 ml/3–4 fl oz sweet
   white wine

Peel the peaches, cut them in half and remove the stones. Slice the peaches into individual serving glasses, sprinkle with the sugar and spoon the wine over. Chill for about 20 minutes.

Pears in Red Wine

SERVES: 4
PREPARATION: 10 minutes
OVEN: 180°C/350°F/gas 4
COOKING: about 1 hour

4 firm dessert pears
50 g/2 oz demerara sugar
300 ml/½ pt red wine
300 ml/½ pt water

Halve the pears lengthways, scoop out the cores and peel the pears. Lay them in a single layer in an ovenproof dish and sprinkle with the sugar. Mix the wine and water and pour it over the pears. Cover the dish with foil and cook in a preheated oven at 180°C/350°F/gas 4 for about 50 minutes, or until the pears are tender.

Lift the pears out with a perforated spoon and set them in a serving dish. Boil the cooking liquid until reduced by half, then spoon it over the pears.
■ Serve the cooked pears hot or cold, with cream or Chantilly Cream (page 411).

Pineapple in Kirsch

SERVES: 8
PREPARATION: 20 minutes
CHILLING: 1 hour

1 small pineapple
2 large oranges
8 maraschino cherries
30 ml/2 tablespoons caster sugar
30 ml/2 tablespoons water
30 ml/2 tablespoons Kirsch

Cut the pineapple into eight rounds; slice off the skin and remove woody eyes and centre cores. Slice the peel and white pith from the oranges and cut each one into eight slices, crossways. Arrange one slice of pineapple and two of orange on dessert plates and top with a cherry. Dissolve the sugar in the water in a pan over gentle heat, add the Kirsch and spoon the syrup over the pineapple. Chill.
■ Serve with chilled cream.

Poached Apricots

SERVES: 4
PREPARATION: 10 minutes
COOKING: 5 minutes

450 g/1 lb fresh apricots
75–100 g/3–4 oz granulated sugar
300 ml/½ pt water
lemon rind or cinnamon stick

Wash and dry the apricots. Put the sugar, water and thinly pared lemon rind or cinnamon stick in a saucepan and place over low heat until the sugar has dissolved. Bring to the boil and cook for 2 minutes. Strain this syrup through a sieve.

Cut the apricots in half with a small sharp knife. Twist the two halves to separate. Discard the stones. Return the syrup to the pan, place the apricot halves, rounded side down, in the syrup and bring slowly to the boil. Reduce the heat, cover and simmer gently until the apricots are tender but not soft, which will take about 5 minutes. Leave to cool. Plums may be cooked in a similar way.

Baked Fruit Flambé

SERVES: 6
PREPARATION: 30 minutes
OVEN: 200°C/400°F/gas 6
COOKING: 20 minutes

1 medium pineapple
450 g/1 lb plums
60 ml/4 tablespoons marmalade
grated rind and juice of 1 lemon
2.5 ml/½ teaspoon ground
   cinnamon
100 g/4 oz soft brown sugar
50 g/2 oz unsalted butter
60 ml/4 tablespoons white rum

Slice, peel and core the pineapple. Cut the slices in half. Cut the plums in half, and remove the stones. Place the pineapple slices and plums in a wide, shallow casserole.

Heat the marmalade, lemon rind and juice, cinnamon, sugar and butter, stirring until melted. Pour the mixture over the fruit. Cover and cook in a preheated oven at 200°C/400°F/gas 6 for about 20 minutes.

Just before serving, place the rum in a metal ladle and warm it over a gas hob. Alternatively, warm the rum in a small saucepan. Ignite the rum and pour, it flaming, over the fruit.

FREEZING FRUIT

The majority of home-grown fruit freezes well, providing an excellent supply of prepared ingredients for making savoury dishes, cooked puddings and sauces as well as cold desserts.

Apples, rhubarb, currants and gooseberries all freeze well. Raspberries, strawberries and other soft fruits also keep well in the freezer but they become very soft on thawing, particularly strawberries. If they are used while frozen, or if they are puréed, this is not a problem.

Apricots, plums and similar stone fruits also become very soft on thawing, so they are useful only for purées or well-cooked pie fillings.

As a general rule, bananas do not freeze well (they become black) but they can be used to make ice cream for short-term storage. On the whole, exotic fruit are not good candidates for the freezer as their texture is spoilt and they may discolour. Mangoes and kiwi fruit may be puréed, and frozen, adding a little lemon juice.

Preparing fruit Always prepare fruit before freezing it, discarding skin, stones or any other inedible parts of the fruit.

Packing There are many ideas for packing fruit in syrup or sugar, but the most practical and popular method is to leave the fruit plain.

Open freezing Open freeze soft fruits on baking trays, then pack them in polythene bags when hard, to avoid crushing them.

Storage time Fruit keeps very well for up to a year.

PASTRY

The many different kinds of pastry made in Britain today have evolved over the centuries from a crude flour and water dough mixture invented by the Romans. The paste was wrapped around meat and game before roasting and was not intended to be eaten. It served only to retain the meat juices and aroma.

As time passed, the paste was enriched with fat and milk and began vaguely to resemble today's shortcrust pastry. By medieval times, pastry-making was well-established and rich-crust pastry coverings, known as coffers, became as important as the contents of the huge fruit, fish, meat and game pies they covered.

As different areas and localities developed their own puddings and pies, many pastry variations emerged from the basic fat, flour and water recipe. Perhaps the most famous of all is the 14th-century raised hot water crust. This was indigenous to Britain and was used with meat and game pies. It was moulded from the inside with a clenched fist, in the same way as a clay pot, and then filled and baked until crisp and brown. The method is perpetuated in the Melton Mowbray pork pies.

By the 17th century both flaky and puff pastries were being used to make elaborate pies, and the decorations and intricate patterns on the finished pies were works of art. Later still, continental pastry-making was added to the ever-growing number of recipes, and yet today the basic art of pastry-making is much as it has been for centuries.

Pastry is no longer used principally to retain the juices of the filling it covers. Its chief purpose is to complement the flavour of the filling and at the same time to provide a convenient casing in which anything from a steak and kidney pudding to a lemon meringue pie may be cooked. It also helps to eke out a limited amount of meat, fish, game or fruit.

Although much mystique surrounds pastry-making, there are no great secrets to guarantee instant success, for pastry-making techniques are mastered by care, patience and practice. There are, however, a few essentials which must be observed before good results can be achieved. The kitchen, working surface and utensils should be cool, and the recipe must always be strictly adhered to, especially in regard to measurements. Pastry should be made as quickly as possible, and handling kept to a minimum. Many pastries are best rested in a cool place before they are cooked.

Shortcrust pastry, with its variations, is probably the best known and most commonly used pastry. Traditionally, suet crust

was also widely used; however, with the widespread availability of good-quality ready-mixed puff pastry, the latter has become very popular. Many home cooks who loathe pastry-making will opt to buy puff pastry for almost all pies and tarts. Puff pastry is time-consuming and difficult to prepare, but rough puff and flaky pastries are easily within the scope of the good home baker.

Although hot water crust is not difficult to make, it can be difficult to shape and use. Choux pastry has a totally undeserved reputation for being difficult when it is, in fact, the easiest of pastries to make. Unlike other recipes, choux is literally a paste and the only techniques involved in its preparation are accurate measuring, stirring and beating. Choux is not 'handled', it is spooned or piped into shape. Given that the cook reads and follows a good recipe closely, choux pastry is usually successful.

SHORTCRUST PASTRY

This popular and versatile pastry is used for savoury and sweet pies, tarts, flans and tartlets. Shortcrust pastry is made by the 'rubbing-in' method, but there are alternative methods which have been devised.

Flour

Plain flour should always be used to make a short, slightly crisp pastry. Self-raising flour makes the pastry rise during cooking, giving a thick crust with a soft, more cake-like texture. Pastry made with self-raising flour has a more open, lighter, texture and

it lacks crispness: it is not 'short' in texture.

Fat

Fat is used in the proportion of 'half fat to flour', so 100 g/4 oz fat is used for every 225 g/8 oz plain flour. The traditional, and best, combination of fat is lard and butter used in equal amounts. The lard has excellent shortening properties while butter gives the pastry a good flavour. However, with such a wide choice of fats, shortcrust pastry is now often made with all margarine or a combination of white vegetable fat and margarine. Block margarine may be used in combination with a white fat; tub margarine may be used on its own, but the very soft whipped margarines are not ideal. Some vegetable-fat spreads may be used for pastry, but they usually require a specially tested recipe. Low-fat spreads are totally unsuitable for use in traditional pastry recipes.

Standard Recipe

The standard recipe uses 225 g/8 oz flour to 100 g/4 oz fat. The proportions should remain the same: half the fat to the amount of flour. This standard recipe is referred to as '225 g/8 oz shortcrust pastry' reflecting the weight of flour **not** the weight of the finished dough. This will yield sufficient pastry to line a 23–25 cm/9–10 in flan tin, or to line and cover an 18 cm/7 in tart plate, or to prepare and cover a 1.12 litre/2 pt pie dish. It is also enough to make 24 small tartlets or 12 small pies, like mince pies.

Freezing Shortcrust Pastry

The rubbed-in flour and fat may be frozen before water is added. Although the prepared, uncooked pastry may be frozen, the most practical method is to freeze raw or part-baked made-up items, such as pies, pasties, flan cases and so on. Cooked shortcrust pastry items also freeze well. Pastry will keep for 3–6 months, depending on the other ingredients included in the dish.

Shortcrust Pastry

PREPARATION: 15 minutes
CHILLING: 30 minutes

225 g/8 oz plain flour
pinch salt
50 g/2 oz lard or white
*   vegetable fat*
50 g/2 oz butter or block margarine
30–45 ml/2–3 tablespoons
*   cold water*

Sift the flour and salt into a wide bowl. Cut up the firm fats and rub them into the flour, using the tips of the fingers, until the mixture resembles fine breadcrumbs. Lift the dry mixture well out of the bowl and let it trickle back through the fingers to keep the pastry cool and light.

Sprinkle the water evenly over the surface and mix the dough lightly with a round-bladed knife until it clumps together. The mixture is dampened, not wetted.

Gather the dough together with the fingers into a ball which leaves the sides of the bowl clean. Press the pastry together into a smooth ball, flattening it into a smooth pat. Do not knead

Preparing traditional shortcrust pastry

1 *Rub the fat into the flour.*

2 *Mix in enough water to bind the dry ingredients. Knead lightly.*

3 *Roll out pastry.*

the pastry as this toughens it – press it together only sufficiently to ensure that it is well bound and smooth. Wrap the pastry in cling film and chill it for 15 minutes before use. If the pastry is chilled for a long period, it should be brought to room temperature again before rolling,

otherwise it will be too hard and brittle to handle.

Roll the pastry out as required on a lightly floured surface, using short, light strokes and rotating the pastry regularly to keep it an even shape. Gently press or pinch the edges together if they begin to break and try to keep the pastry as near as possible to the required finished shape to avoid wastage.

One-stage (Fork) Pastry

A shortcrust pastry using tub margarine to give a pastry with a smooth texture and soft crumb.

PREPARATION: 10 minutes
CHILLING: 30 minutes

150 g/5 oz margarine
225 g/8 oz plain flour
30 ml/2 tablespoons water

Put the margarine with 30 ml/2 tablespoons of the flour and the water in a deep mixing bowl. Cream these ingredients with a fork until well mixed. Still using the fork, work in the remaining flour to form a manageable

Preparing one-stage pastry

Cream the margarine, flour and water with a fork.

dough. Turn this on to a floured surface and knead lightly until smooth. Chill for 30 minutes.

Rich Shortcrust Pastry

PREPARATION: 10 minutes
CHILLING: 30 minutes

150 g/5 oz plain flour
pinch salt
75 g/3 oz unsalted butter
1 egg yolk
7.5 ml/1½ teaspoons caster sugar
15–20 ml/3–4 teaspoons water

Sift the flour and salt into a wide bowl. Cut up the fat and rub it into the flour with the fingertips until the mixture resembles breadcrumbs. Beat the egg yolk, sugar and 10 ml/2 teaspoons of the water in a separate bowl and pour it into the flour mixture. Stir with a round-bladed knife, adding the remaining water as necessary until the mixture begins to form a dough. Gather this into a ball and turn it on to a floured surface. Knead lightly. Use as required, then chill for 30 minutes before baking.

Pastry with Oil

This recipe produces a pastry with a tender, flaky crumb. It must be mixed and used quickly – if left or chilled, it dries out and cannot be rolled.

PREPARATION: 15 minutes

225 g/8 oz plain flour
1.25 ml/¼ teaspoon salt
75 ml/5 tablespoons oil
90 ml/6 tablespoons cold water

Sift the flour and salt together. Whisk the oil and water together

in a large, clean bowl until they are evenly mixed.

Use a palette knife to mix the flour gradually into the oil and water mixture. Then turn the dough out on to a floured surface. Knead the pastry lightly and quickly until smooth and shiny. Roll out and bake as for traditional shortcrust pastry.

Cheese Pastry

This shortcrust pastry is ideal for cheese straws, as a crust for vegetable pies, and for savoury flan cases. This standard recipe is referred to as '100 g/4 oz', reflecting the weight of the flour, not the total weight of the finished dough.

PREPARATION: 10 minutes
CHILLING: 30 minutes

100 g/4 oz plain flour
salt and cayenne pepper
50 g/2 oz butter or block margarine
50 g/2 oz Cheddar, Lancashire or
*   Cheshire cheese, grated*
1 egg yolk
10–15 ml/2–3 teaspoons
*   cold water*

Sift the flour, a pinch of salt and a shake of cayenne into a wide bowl. Cut up the fat and rub it into the flour with the fingertips until the mixture resembles fine breadcrumbs. Blend in the grated cheese. Lightly whisk the egg yolk with 10 ml/2 teaspoons of the water and mix this into the ingredients to bind them into a short dough. Add more water if necessary.

Knead the dough lightly on a floured surface and chill it lightly before using.

PASTRY TECHNIQUES

Covering a Pie Dish

Roll out the pastry to the required thickness (no more than 5 mm/¼in thick) and 5 cm/2 in wider than the pie dish, using the inverted dish as a guide. Cut a 2.5 cm/1 in wide strip from the outer edge of the pastry and place it on the moistened rim of the pie dish. Brush the whole strip with water.

Fill the pie dish and set a pie funnel in the centre; lift the remaining pastry on the rolling pin and lay it over the pie dish. Press the pastry strip and lid firmly together with the fingers. Trim any excess pastry with a knife blade held at a slight angle to the dish.

Knocking up and finishing a pastry edge

To seal the pastry edges firmly so that they do not come apart during baking, hold the blunt edge of the knife blade horizontally towards the pie dish. Press the pastry edge gently outwards with the front of your index finger and tap the pastry with the knife to mark, rather than cut, the edge. Work around the pie so that the very edge of the pastry is slightly raised and the two layers are no longer obvious. This process is called 'knocking up' pastry.

Finally, give the pie a decorative edge by pressing down on the pastry with a fingertip and drawing the knife against the edge to make a scallop. Make large scallops on savoury pies; small one on sweet pies. Use the pastry trimmings to cut decorative shapes for the top of the

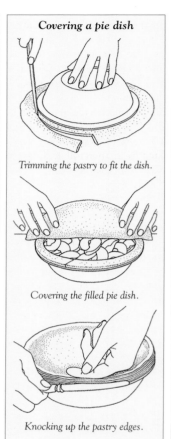

Covering a pie dish

Trimming the pastry to fit the dish.

Covering the filled pie dish.

Knocking up the pastry edges.

pie. Cut a slit into the centre of the pastry for the steam to escape, and decorate the edges.

Preparing a Double-Crust Pie

Divide the pastry into two portions, one slightly larger than the other. Shape the larger portion into a ball and roll it out on a lightly floured surface. Rotate the pastry occasionally to keep the edge round; if the edge begins to break, pinch the pieces together. Roll out the pastry about 2.5 cm/1 in wider than the inverted pie plate.

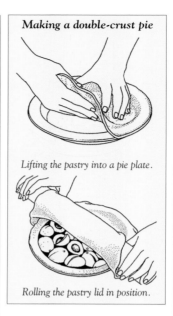

Making a double-crust pie

Lifting the pastry into a pie plate.

Rolling the pastry lid in position.

Fold the pastry in half and lift it on to the pie plate; unfold and loosely ease the pastry into position, being careful not to stretch the pastry. Put the cold filling over the pastry base, keeping it slightly domed in the centre. Roll out the remaining pastry for the lid, allowing about 1 cm/½ in beyond the rim. Brush the edge of the pastry lining with water, then lift the lid on the rolling pin and place in position over the filling.

Trim the edges of the pastry almost level with the plate and knock them up with a knife. Cut a slit in the centre of the pastry lid for the steam to escape.

Lining a Pie Plate

For an open tart, roll out the pastry 2.5 cm/1 in wider than the pie plate. Lift the pastry into the plate and ease it loosely over the base and sides. Trim off excess

Lining a flan ring

1 Lay the pastry over the flan.

2 Roll off any surplus pastry.

3 Press the pastry into the fluted ridges.

pastry. Flute the edge of the pastry (see Finishing and Decorations, opposite) so that the points protrude from the plate rim.

Lining a Flan Tin or Ring

Flans are baked in flan dishes, loose-bottomed flan tins or plain fluted rings set on baking trays. Roll the pastry out to about 5 cm/2 in wider than the dish, tin or ring. With the rolling pin, lift the pastry and lower it loosely into the flan tin without pressing the pastry down on the rim. Lift the edges carefully and press the

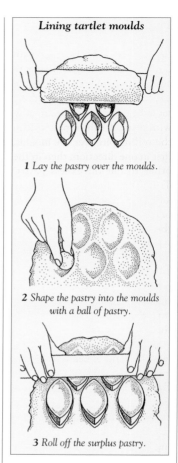

Lining tartlet moulds

1 Lay the pastry over the moulds.

2 Shape the pastry into the moulds with a ball of pastry.

3 Roll off the surplus pastry.

pastry gently into the base of the dish, tin or ring with the fingers, taking care that no air pockets are left between the container and the pastry. Trim the pastry in a plain dish, tin or ring with a knife or scissors, just above the rim. On a fluted flan dish, tin or ring, press the pastry back over the rim slightly, then roll the rolling pin across the top of the container then cut off the excess pastry. Finally, press the top of the pastry into the flutes to give a neat edge. Chill for at least 15 minutes before baking.

Lining Tartlet Moulds

Set the small moulds closely together on a baking tray. Roll out the pastry large enough to cover the whole area of moulds. Lay the pastry loosely over the moulds, press it into the moulds with a small ball of pastry. Run the rolling pin over the moulds, first in one direction, then in the other to cut off excess pastry. Trim the edge of the pastry around each mould, if necessary, or press it neatly into place. Prick the bases of the pastry tartlets.

To line a sheet of patty tins, use a plain or fluted cutter – 1–1.5 cm/ ½–¾ in wider than the patty – to cut out rounds from the pastry. Ease the pastry rounds into the patty tins and prick them with a fork.

Chill the pastry tartlets for at least 15 minutes before baking.

Baking Blind

Sometimes pastry, especially flan cases and individual tartlets, has to be part-baked before the filling is put in to prevent the base of the case remaining soft and undercooked when served.

To bake blind, cover pastry with paper and weigh down with beans.

If a pastry shell is baked empty, it tends to bubble up in the middle and sag slightly around the sides unless it is lined with paper and weighted down – this is known as baking blind. Line the pastry case with grease-proof paper cut roughly to shape and weigh it down with dried beans (if kept specially for this purpose, the beans can be used again and again) or ceramic baking beans. A piece of lightly crumpled foil may be placed in the pastry shell, in which case there is no need to use baking beans. Bake the pastry case in a preheated oven at 200°C/400°F/ gas 6 for about 15 minutes.

Alternatively, and especially for tartlets, prick the base and sides of the pastry with a fork before lining it with foil.

Baking an empty pastry case until cooked For fresh fruit flans or tartlets, where an uncooked filling is used, the pastry should be baked blind as above, then the paper and beans should be removed and the pastry baked for a further 5 – 10 minutes, until it is lightly browned on the base, and pale golden around the edge.

Flan cases and tartlet moulds should be left on a wire rack to cool and shrink slightly before being eased out of their moulds. It is sometimes best to leave the pastry in the mould until the filling is added – or even until just before serving the pastry – to prevent damage.

Finishing and Decorations

The edge of a covered pie can be finished in many decorative ways. Scalloped or fluted pattern

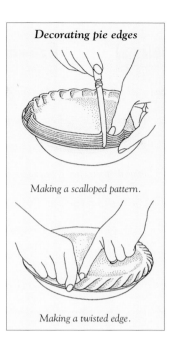

Decorating pie edges

Making a scalloped pattern.

Making a twisted edge.

is classic, with large scallops or flutes used on savoury pastries and small ones for sweet pastries.

To flute a pastry edge, use a thumb and finger to press the edges together and to lift small peaks at regular intervals into a neat fluted pattern. To make a flat scalloped edge, press the pastry outwards slightly over the rim of the dish at intervals of 1–1.5 cm/½–¾ in. Draw pastry inwards using the blunt edge of a knife without cutting the edge.

To make a twisted edge, twist and slightly turn the pastry between a thumb and index finger, at 1 cm/½ in intervals.

Alternatively, seal the edges with the tines of a fork; however, this method is only suitable for pies that have a short cooking time as the forked edge tends to overbrown and become very crisp on long-cooked pastries.

Pastry leaves To make leaves, cut the pastry into 2.5–3.5 cm/ 1–1½ in wide strips and cut these into diamond shapes. With the back of a knife, trace the ribs.

Pastry tassel For a tassel, cut a 2.5 cm/1 in wide pastry strip about 15 cm/6 in long. Make cuts 1.5 cm/¾ in long, at intervals of 5 mm/¼ in, then roll up the strip, place it on the pie and open out.

Finishing open tarts Finish the edges of open tarts by fluting or crimping. A simple method, using a pair of scissors, is to make cuts just over 5 mm/¼ in deep and a little over 5 mm/¼ in apart around the pastry edge. Fold alternate pieces of pastry inwards and bend the remaining pieces outwards. Or the edges can be decorated with thin pastry strips that have been twisted or plaited. Moisten the pastry edge with water first.

Pastry lattice A lattice pattern is a traditional decoration for any open flans. The trimmings left after lining a flan tin or tart plate are not usually sufficient for making a neat lattice, so allow a little extra pastry and press the trimmings together with it. Cut the rolled out pastry into 1 cm/ ½ in wide strips (a pastry wheel gives an attractive edge) and long enough to cover the middle

Lattice pattern

Lay pastry strips over the flan top; interleave the crossing strips.

of the flan. Moisten the edges, then lay half the strips over the filling, 2.5 cm/1 in apart, and lay the remaining strips criss-crossing the first. Trim the strips to shape at the outer edge, or fold the pastry lining down over them for a neater finish. For a really professional touch, the pastry strips should be interwoven by laying them over the filling 2.5 cm/1 in apart, and a strip of pastry at a right angle across the centre. Lift alternate lengths of the first strips of pastry on one half of the flan and place a strip at right angles. Replace the top strips and repeat with the other side of the flan to complete the interwoven effect.

Pastry flowers Pies can be decorated with pastry flowers. Simple flowers are made by rolling a small piece of pastry to the size and shape of an acorn.

Cut out two diamond shapes and pinch the edges to round them to a petal shape. Dampen the base of the petals and wrap around the wide base of the acorn shape. Pinch the pastry to seal the pieces together, then bend the tip of each petal slightly outwards.

More ornate flowers can be made by making a cross with a knife on a small, flattened round of pastry. Set the round on a square of dampened pastry; set this in turn on another square of dampened pastry, similar in size, to form a star pattern. Shape the corners of the squares to resemble petals. Pinch and shape each point of the central round of pastry into a petal to complete the flower.

Glazing

Brush the decorated pie or flan before baking to give a shiny golden look. Brush savoury pies with beaten whole egg or with egg yolk diluted with a little water or milk, and a pinch of salt. Glaze sweet pies with milk or egg white and dust with caster sugar.

Cheese Straws

MAKES: about 60
PREPARATION: 10 minutes
OVEN: 200°C/400°F/gas 6
COOKING: 12 minutes

*100 g/4 oz Cheese Pastry
  (page 365)*

Roll out the pastry into a 23 cm/ 9 in square. Trim the edges then cut the pastry into strips, 5 mm/ ¼ in wide and 7.5 cm/3 in long, using a floured knife. Place on baking trays and bake in a preheated oven at 200°C/400°F/ gas 6 for 10–12 minutes, or until golden. Leave to cool.

Cheese and Bacon Quiche

SERVES: 4–6
PREPARATION: 30 minutes
OVEN: 200°C/400°F/gas 6
    180°C/350°F/gas 4
COOKING: 40 minutes

*175 g/6 oz Shortcrust Pastry
  (page 365)
1 small onion
15 g/½ oz butter
100 g/4 oz lean streaky bacon
100 g/4 oz Cheddar cheese
2 large eggs
250 g/8 fl oz milk or single cream
salt and black pepper
15 ml/1 tablespoon freshly chopped
  parsley (optional)*

Roll out the shortcrust pastry and use it to line a 20 cm/8 in loose-bottomed flan tin. Prick the pastry base and chill the flan case in the refrigerator for at least 15 minutes. Then line the pastry with greaseproof paper and baking beans and bake it blind in a preheated oven at 200°C/ 400°F/gas 6 for 15 minutes. Remove the paper and beans. Reduce the oven temperature to 180°C/350°F/gas 4.

Peel and finely chop the onion, fry it in the butter over low heat for 5–10 minutes until transparent. Set aside. Remove the rind from the rashers and cut the bacon into small pieces. Fry until the fat runs and the bacon begins to crisp.

Mix the onion and bacon and arrange it in the flan case. Grate the cheese and sprinkle it into the flan.

Lightly beat the eggs with the milk or cream; add the chopped parsley and season to taste. Spoon this mixture over the flan filling and bake for about 40 minutes, until the filling is set and lightly browned.

Apple Pie

SERVES: 4–6
PREPARATION: 20 minutes
OVEN: 200°C/400°F/gas 6
    180°C/350°F/gas 4
COOKING: 40 minutes

*675 g/1½ lb cooking apples
175–225 g/6–8 oz Shortcrust
  Pastry (page 365)
50–75 g/2–3 oz caster or
  demerara sugar
4–6 cloves (optional)
milk*

Peel and core the apples and cut them into chunky slices. Place a pie funnel in the centre of a 900 ml/1½ pt pie dish, arrange half the apple slices in the dish, sprinkle over the sugar and cloves, if used, then add the remaining fruit with the water.

Roll out the pastry to about 5 cm/2 in larger than the dish and cut a 2.5 cm/1 in strip from around the edge. Dampen the rim of the dish and press the pastry strip on it. Cover the pie with the remaining rolled-out pastry. Trim and knock-up the edge, then finish it in a decorative pattern. Brush the top with milk and dust with caster sugar, if liked. Make a slit in the centre of the pastry lid for the steam to escape.

Set the pie on a baking tray and bake in a preheated oven at 200°C/400°F/gas 6 for 30 minutes. Reduce the oven temperature to 180°C/350°F/gas 4 and cook for a further 20 minutes, until the pastry becomes golden brown and the apples are tender.

For variation, the water may be replaced with orange juice and the grated rind of ½ orange mixed with the sugar.

SUET CRUST PASTRY

This traditional British pastry is used for steamed or boiled savoury and sweet puddings, and for roly-poly puddings and dumplings. Suet is available already shredded and pre-packed, both in traditional form and as a vegetable fat, ideal for vegetarian dishes. Fresh beef suet is also available from some butch-

ers: the skin should be removed and the fat chopped finely or coarsely grated. Keep the suet dusted with flour to prevent it sticking. Light, speedy mixing and handling achieve a pastry of a light spongy texture. For an even lighter texture replace 50 g/2 oz of the measured flour with 50 g/2 oz fresh white breadcrumbs.

Standard Recipe

The quantities given in the following recipes make enough suet crust pastry to line and cover a 1.12 litre/2 pt pudding basin or to make 16 dumplings. This standard recipe is referred to as '225 g/8 oz suet crust pastry', reflecting the weight of flour **not** the weight of the finished dough.

Suet Crust Pastry

PREPARATION: 15 minutes
RESTING: 15 minutes

*225 g/8 oz self-raising flour
  or 225 g/8 oz plain flour
  and 15 ml/1 tablespoon
  baking powder
2.5 ml/½ teaspoon salt
100 g/4 oz shredded suet
175 ml/6 fl oz cold water*

Sift the flour and salt into a bowl (together with the baking powder if plain flour is used). Mix in the shredded suet. Using a round-bladed knife, stir in the water to form a soft dough. Turn the dough on to a lightly floured surface, and sprinkle it with a little flour. Knead the dough lightly into a smooth ball using just your fingertips. Use the pastry as required.

Lining a Pudding Basin

Grease a 1.12 litre/2 pt pudding basin. Cut one quarter from the prepared suet pastry and set it aside for the lid. Roll out the remaining pastry, on a floured surface, to a circle, 5 cm/2 in wider than the top of the basin and about 5 mm/¼ in thick. Sprinkle the pastry with flour, fold it in half and then in half again to form a triangle.

Put the pastry triangle inside the basin, point downwards, and unfold it, moulding it to shape of the basin. Spoon in the prepared filling. Turn the pastry which is overhanging the rim of the basin in over the pudding filling and brush with water.

Roll out the remaining pastry to a circle that fits the top of the basin. Lift the pastry lid on the rolling pin and lay it over the filling. Press the edges firmly together to seal them.

Fold a pleat in a square of buttered greaseproof paper – the pleat allows the cover to expand as the pastry rises during cooking. Place the paper over the pudding and twist it under the rim of the basin. Cover the top of the pudding with a clean napkin or cloth, tie it securely with string below the rim of the basin and tie the ends into a knot on top of the pudding. Alternatively, cover the top of the pudding with foil instead of the cloth, pleating it as when using the greaseproof paper.

Freezing Suet Crust Pastry

Uncooked suet crust does not freeze. Cooked suet crust pastry dishes may be frozen; puddings keep for as long as the shortest freezer life of ingredients they contain. Suet dumplings are good freezer candidates as they can be reheated from frozen in soup or a moist stew.

Beef and Carrot Pudding

SERVES: 4
PREPARATION: 25 minutes
COOKING: 2 hours

225 g/8 oz onions
25 g/1 oz dripping or 30 ml/
*   2 tablespoons oil*
450 g/1 lb lean minced beef
225 g/8 oz carrots
5 ml/1 teaspoon mixed herbs
30 ml/2 tablespoons plain flour
300 ml/½ pt beef stock
salt and black pepper
Worcestershire sauce
225 g/8 oz Suet Crust Pastry
*   (page 368)*

Peel and finely chop the onions. Melt the dripping or heat the oil in a pan over moderate heat and fry the onions until they begin to colour. Stir in the minced beef and continue to cook, stirring occasionally, until the meat is lightly cooked. Meanwhile, peel and coarsely grate the carrots, then add them to the pan. Cook for a further 5 minutes, stirring occasionally. Stir in the herbs, flour and stock. Bring to the boil, stirring, and cook for 2 minutes, until the gravy is thickened. Season to taste with salt and pepper, and add a dash of Worcestershire sauce. Remove the pan from the heat. Leave the beef mixture to cool.

Line a 1.12 litre/2 pint pudding basin with three-quarters of the prepared suet crust and spoon the mince mixture into the basin. Cover with the pastry lid, and seal the edges. Cover the pudding with greaseproof paper and foil or a napkin, and set the basin in a large saucepan. Pour boiling water into the pan until the water reaches half-way up the sides of the basin.

Cover the saucepan with a lid and simmer for 2 hours. Top up the pan with boiling water when necessary.

■ Serve the beef and carrot pudding straight from the basin, with boiled potatoes and additional vegetables, such as boiled cabbage or broccoli.

Dumplings

Dumplings can be left plain or flavoured with parsley, as here. Other chopped fresh herbs, such as dill, thyme or tarragon, may be added in small quantities to flavour the pastry. A generous pinch of dried mixed herbs may be used if liked. For a more 'savoury' result mix 25 g/1 oz finely grated cheese with the flour and suet.

MAKES: 8
PREPARATION: 5 minutes
COOKING: 15 minutes

100 g/4 oz Suet Crust Pastry
*   (page 368)*
45 ml/3 tablespoons
*   chopped parsley*

Half fill a large saucepan with water and put it to boil. Make the pastry as described in the basic recipe, adding the parsley to the flour and suet before mixing in the water. Divide the pastry into eight equal pieces, and shape these into balls.

Put the dumplings into the boiling water, bring it back to the boil, then reduce heat and cover the pan. Simmer gently for 15 minutes – the dumplings will break up if the water is allowed to boil rapidly.

The dumplings can be served with soups or stews. If the dish is sufficiently moist and the cooking pan large enough, then the dumplings may be cooked in the soup or on top of the stew instead of being cooked separately.

Apple and Ginger Roll

SERVES: 8
PREPARATION: 30 minutes
COOKING: 1½ hours

450 g/1 lb cooking apples
2.5–5 ml/½–1 teaspoon
*   ground ginger*
50 g/2 oz demerara sugar
225 g/8 oz Suet Crust Pastry
*   (page 368)*
50 g/2 oz sultanas
caster sugar

Put a large saucepan, half full of water, on to boil. Peel and core the apples, then cut them into even, not too thin, slices and put them in a bowl. Mix the ginger, demerara sugar and the apples.

Roll the prepared suet crust pastry into a rectangle about 25 × 20 cm/10 × 8 in and about 5 mm/¼ in thick. You must have a saucepan large enough to hold the roll – about 5 cm/2 in wider than the pastry. A deep roasting tin can be used instead of a saucepan, with a sheet of foil firmly folded over the rim of the tin in place of a lid. Spread the apple filling over the pastry to within 1 cm/½ in of the edges, and sprinkle with the sultanas. Turn the edges in over the filling and brush them with water. Roll up the pastry from the longest side and wrap it in greased foil, making a pleat in it to allow for expansion during cooking. Leave a short space at each end and twist the foil tightly to seal.

Place a heatproof inverted plate in the pan. Lower the roll into the water and bring it back to the boil. Reduce the heat, cover the pan and boil gently for 1½ hours. Add more boiling water, if necessary, to keep the roll covered. If using a roasting tin, roll two or three tightly crumpled foil 'sausages' on which to stand the roll and turn the roll over halfway through cooking.

Lift the roll from the pan with a fish slice. Leave to stand for a few minutes, then remove the foil. Put the roll on a hot dish and dredge with caster sugar.

■ Serve with a Butterscotch Sauce (page 357) or custard.

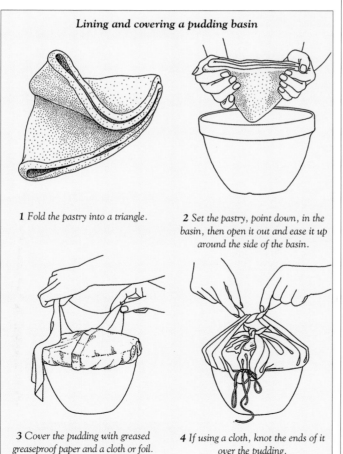

Lining and covering a pudding basin

1 Fold the pastry into a triangle.

2 Set the pastry, point down, in the basin, then open it out and ease it up around the side of the basin.

3 Cover the pudding with greased greaseproof paper and a cloth or foil.

4 If using a cloth, knot the ends of it over the pudding.

HOT WATER CRUST PASTRY

This pastry has evolved from the original coffer paste. It is used for raised savoury meat and game pies and is usually served cold. The pastry is moulded while still hot, traditionally by hand, or fitted into a loose-bottomed cake tin or pie mould.

Raw hot water crust pastry can be frozen only when it has been shaped and filled. The cooked pies may be frozen, depending on the filling.

Hot Water Crust Pastry

PREPARATION: 15 minutes
RESTING: 20 minutes

350 g/12 oz plain flour
2.5 ml/½ teaspoon salt
100 g/4 oz lard
60 ml/4 tablespoons water
60 ml/4 tablespoons milk

Sift the flour and salt into a bowl. Make a well in the flour.

Put the fat, water and milk into a small saucepan over low heat until the fat has melted, then bring to the boil as quickly as possible. Remove from the heat immediately the mixture reaches a full boil and pour it into the flour. Quickly stir the flour into the liquid and mix until a fairly lumpy dough is formed. The dough is very hot but it should be lightly kneaded into a ball at this stage, working in the bowl. Take care not to burn your hand. The dough cools quickly to a manageable temperature once the flour absorbs the liquid and expands.

Turn the dough on to a lightly floured surface and knead it briefly until smooth and pliable. The pastry must be used while hot to give smooth results. As the dough cools, it becomes difficult to mould or roll, it cracks easily and does not seal together well. It is at its most manageable when it has cooled and firmed up slightly – usually after a few seconds' shaping or kneading and rolling. Place the pastry in a bowl, cover it closely with cling film and stand the bowl over a pan of hot water to keep it soft until required.

To mould the pastry, cut off and set aside one-third of the dough over hot water for the lid. Roll out the pastry thickly and use to line a hinged pie mould or a loose-bottomed cake tin set on a baking tray, both thoroughly greased. It is not possible to roll out the hot pastry large enough to completely line the tin. The technique is to lower the thick dough into the tin, gradually moulding and thinning it into shape. Try to keep the edge of the pastry near the top, so that it can be smoothed down to the base and up to the rim.

Alternatively, flour an empty 900 g/2 lb jam jar, place the ball of warm dough on its base and carefully mould the dough two-thirds down the outside of the jar. Set the jar aside while the dough cools and sets, then carefully ease out the jar.

Spoon the filling into the pastry, roll out the remaining pastry for the lid, moisten the edges with water or egg glaze and cover the pie. Seal the edges firmly: the warm, fresh pastry softens the rim of the pastry case. Cut a slit in the lid and garnish.

Pastry moulded around a jar should have a protective band of double-thick foil or greaseproof paper tied around it to prevent the pie collapsing during baking.

Raised Veal and Bacon Pie

Cook the pie the day before to give the jellied stock time to set.

SERVES: 8
PREPARATION: 1 hour
OVEN: 180°C/350°F/gas 4
COOKING: about 6 hours

Pastry
1½ quantities Hot Water
    Crust Pastry
Jellied Veal Stock
900 g/2 lb veal bones, chopped
1 carrot
1 onion
2 bay leaves
6 peppercorns
Filling
225 g/8 oz lean streaky bacon
1 onion
450 g/1 lb lean pork
350 g/12 oz pie veal
2.5 ml/½ teaspoon salt
1.25 ml/¼ teaspoon black pepper
2.5 ml/½ teaspoon dried sage
grated rind of ½ lemon
30 ml/2 tablespoons
    chopped parsley
225 g/8 oz pork sausagemeat
egg for glazing

Make the stock: put the chopped veal bones, cleaned carrot and peeled onion in a large saucepan. Add the bay leaves, peppercorns and enough water to cover. Bring to the boil, remove the scum from the surface, then cover the

Moulding and filling a raised hot water crust pie

1 Flour a large jam jar or cover it with a piece of cling film or foil.

2 Mould the dough over the base and down the outside of the jar.

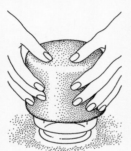

3 Leave to cool on the jar until the pastry is set.

4 Ease out the jar, removing the cling film or foil.

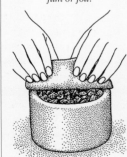

5 Fill the pie and cover with a lid of warm pastry, sealing the edges well.

6 Garnish the top of the pie and cut a hole in the lid.

7 Tie a band of double-thick foil or greaseproof paper around the pie to strengthen the side during cooking.

8 Pour in liquid stock when the pie is cooked.

pan. Reduce the heat and simmer the stock for 2½ hours. Strain the stock through muslin, pour it into a clean pan and reduce to about 300 ml/½ pt by fast boiling. Leave to cool.

For the filling, cut the rind off the bacon and peel the onion. Put the pork, veal, half the bacon and the peeled onion through the coarse blade of a mincer. Mix it thoroughly in a large bowl, then add the salt, freshly ground pepper, sage, lemon rind and parsley. Moisten the mixture with 45 ml/3 tablespoons of the veal stock.

For the pie use a greased pie frame, 14.5 × 19 × 9 cm/5¾ × 7½ × 3¼ in, or an 18 cm/7 in loose-bottomed cake tin lined with foil. Roll out two-thirds of the pastry into a thick oval or circle about half or two-thirds the size required to line the chosen mould. Lower the pastry halfway down into the mould, then ease it smoothly and evenly into the base and up the sides. Press the dough well into any indentations in the pie frame.

Line the pastry base with the sausagement and top with the remaining chopped bacon. Spoon the minced meat mixture over the top, pressing it down lightly and keeping it slightly domed. Beat the egg with salt and brush over the pastry edge. Roll out the remaining pastry to form a lid, lift it on the rolling pin over the filling. Press the lid on to the pie edge and pinch the edges firmly together to seal. Trim the pastry.

Glaze the top of the pie by brushing with egg; roll out the pastry trimmings and cut them into leaf shapes. Arrange these in a pattern on the lid and brush with more egg. Make a wide hole in the centre of the pie lid.

Set the pie on a baking tray and bake in a preheated oven at 180°C/350°F/gas 4 for 3 hours. Check the pie occasionally and cover the top loosely with foil once it is a deep golden brown to prevent further browning. Carefully remove the sides of the tin if using a raised pie mould and brush the pastry immediately with beaten egg.

It is important to work very quickly at this stage because the soft pastry tends to bulge outwards. The layer of beaten egg sets on the pie to strengthen the pastry and the pastry quickly becomes firm when it is put back in the oven.

Continue cooking for a further 30 minutes, until the sides of the pie are golden. Leave the pie to cool in the mould or tin until quite firm. Remove the mould or tin, and when the pie is nearly cold, pour the cool liquid stock slowly through a small funnel into the pie.

Leave the pie to set completely, which will generally take several hours, when the stock will have set to jelly around the meat. Serve the pie cold, cut into slices or wedges.

Note A filling of pork and bacon can be used instead of veal: use 800 g/1¾ lb lean pork. Instead of veal bones for the stock, use the bones from a leg of pork or boil 450 g/1 lb of lean belly or spare rib pork. Dissolve 15 g/½ oz gelatine in the strained stock.

CHOUX PASTRY

This pastry is a French speciality and is used for a variety of recipes, including cream buns, chocolate eclairs and profiteroles. During cooking, the paste rises, then it sets to a crisp, hollow crust. The centre should be slightly moist when baked. Split the crust immediately to allow steam to escape or the pastry softens.

Freezing Choux Pastry

Baked, unfilled choux pastries freeze well for up to 3 months. Crisp for 1–2 minutes in a hot oven when thawed, then cool again before filling.

Choux Pastry

PREPARATION: 20 minutes

65 g/2½ oz plain flour
pinch salt
50 g/2 oz butter
150 ml/¼ pt water
2 eggs, beaten

Sift the flour and salt on to a sheet of greaseproof paper. Put the butter and the liquid in a heavy-based pan and cook over low heat until the butter melts, then raise the heat and rapidly bring the mixture to the boil. Draw the pan off the heat and pour in all the flour. Stir quickly with a wooden spoon until the flour has been absorbed by the liquid and comes away from the sides of the pan. Do not beat at this stage or the paste will become greasy.

Cool paste slightly, then beat in the beaten eggs, a little at a time, beating well after each addition. Continue beating until the paste is shiny. The paste should be thick enough to hold its shape, but not too stiff to pipe.

Cheese Aigrettes

Beignets are the sweet equivalent of these cheese aigrettes. They usually consist of fruit coated in choux pastry and fried.

MAKES: 24
PREPARATION: 20 minutes
COOKING: 15–20 minutes

1 quantity Choux Pastry
75 g/3 oz Cheddar cheese
pinch cayenne pepper
oil for deep frying
extra grated Cheddar cheese
* for dusting*

Make the pastry, following the basic recipe. Finely grate the cheese and beat it into the paste with the cayenne pepper after the eggs.

Heat the oil for deep frying to 190°C/375°F or until a cube of bread turns golden in 60 seconds. Drop teaspoonfuls of the paste into the hot fat, about six at a time depending on the size of pan, and fry for 4–6 minutes until puffed and golden brown. Lift the cheese puffs out with a perforated spoon and leave to drain on absorbent kitchen paper. Pile the cheese aigrettes on to a hot serving dish and dust with more grated Cheddar cheese. Serve freshly cooked.

Making choux pastry

1 Heat the butter and liquid gently.

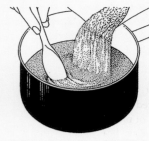

2 Bring the liquid to a full boil, then stir in the flour and remove the pan from the heat.

3 Stir the flour into the liquid to make a smooth paste which leaves the sides of the pan clean. Do not beat.

4 Gradually beat in the eggs, and continue to beat until the paste is glossy.

Chocolate Eclairs

MAKES: 12–14
PREPARATION: 20 minutes
OVEN: 220°C/425°F/gas 7
     190°C/375°F/gas 5
COOKING: 30 minutes

1 quantity Choux Pastry
   (page 371)
300 ml/½ pt double cream
15 ml/1 tablespoon caster sugar
100 g/4 oz plain chocolate

Spoon the choux paste into a piping bag fitted with a 1 cm/½ in plain nozzle. Pipe out 7.5cm/3 in lengths on to a greased baking tray, starting with the end of the nozzle touching the tray and lifting it while pressing the mixture out. Cut off the required lengths with a wet knife.

Bake the eclairs in a preheated oven at 220°C/425°F/gas 7 for 15 minutes. Reduce the oven temperature to 190°C/375°F/gas 5 and continue baking for 20–25 minutes or until crisp. Slit the eclairs down one side and leave on a wire rack to cool.

Whip the cream with the sugar, then spoon it into a piping bag fitted with a plain nozzle. Fill the cold eclairs with cream.

Break the chocolate into squares and place them in a heat-proof basin. Stand the basin over a pan of hot water, stirring occasionally, until the chocolate melts. Coat the tops of the eclairs with melted chocolate.

Piping out chocolate eclairs

1 Spoon choux into a piping bag.

2 Pipe out 7.5 cm/3 in lengths.

Profiteroles

MAKES: 20
PREPARATION: 1 hour
OVEN: 220°C/425°F/gas 7
    180°C/350°F/gas 4
COOKING: 15 minutes

1 quantity Choux Pastry
   (page 371)
300 ml/½ pt double or
   whipping cream
icing sugar
Chocolate Sauce (page 357)

Make up the choux pastry and spoon it into a piping bag fitted with a plain 1 cm/½ in plain nozzle. Pipe 20 small buns, well apart, on to greased baking trays, and bake in a preheated oven at 220°C/425°F/gas 7 for 15–20 minutes until well risen, puffed and crisp. Split the buns halfway through to allow the steam to escape; cool on a wire rack.

Whip the cream until it stands in soft peaks, then spoon it into a piping bag fitted with a plain nozzle. Fill the hollow buns with whipped cream and dust the tops with sifted icing sugar. To serve, pile the profiteroles into a pyramid on a serving dish and pour a little chocolate sauce over them; serve the rest separately.

FLAKED OR LAYERED PASTRIES

These include flaky pastry, rough puff pastry and puff pastry, all of which are characterised by fat and air being trapped between thin layers of dough. During baking the trapped air expands and lifts the pastry layers.

Certain procedures are common to all three pastries to ensure crisp flakes.
1 Handle the pastry as lightly as possible and do not overwork it.
2 The fat and the dough should have the same consistency – the fat is therefore softened and kept cool but not chilled hard.
3 To prevent the fat from melting during rolling, the pastry must be chilled during preparation. The pastry must also be chilled before rolling and before the completed item is baked.
4 Roll out the pastry evenly without squashing the edges flat and losing the layers as this will force out the air. Never stretch the pastry.

Freezing Layered Pastries

These freeze very well when raw, but they are easily damaged when cooked. Also, when frozen after baking, the pastry layers tend to collapse and lose their crisp texture when thawed.

Bought frozen puff pastry is an excellent freezer standby and it can be used instead of any of the flaked or layered pastries.

FLAKY PASTRY

This pastry is used for pie crusts, Eccles cakes, sausage rolls, jam puffs and cream horns. Flaky pastry can be used instead of puff pastry in most recipes of this type but it does not rise as high nor does it have as many layers as puff pastry.

Flaky Pastry

MAKES: about 675 g/1½ lb
PREPARATION: 30 minutes
RESTING: about 2 hours

225 g/8 oz plain flour
2.5 ml/½ teaspoon salt
75 g/3 oz lard
75 g/3 oz butter or block margarine
105–120 ml/7–8 tablespoons
   iced water
5 ml/1 teaspoon lemon juice

Sift the flour and salt into a wide bowl. Work the lard and butter or margarine on a plate until evenly blended, and divide it into quarters. Lightly chill three quarters. Rub the remaining quarter of the fat into the flour with the fingertips until the mixture resembles breadcrumbs. Add the water and lemon juice and mix the ingredients with a round-bladed knife to a soft, manageable dough. Turn it out on to a lightly floured surface and knead briefly until it is smooth. Cover the dough with cling film and leave it to rest in a cool place for 20 minutes.

On a lightly floured surface roll out the dough into an oblong measuring about 35 × 15 cm/14 × 6 in. Cut another quarter of the fat into small lumps and dot them evenly over the top two-

Preparing flaky pastry

1 Roll out the cooled dough.

2 Dot fat over two-thirds of the pastry.

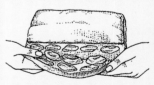

3 Fold the unbuttered end of the dough over the middle of the pastry.

4 Fold the buttered end over.

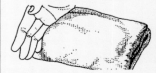

5 Seal the pastry edges by pressing them with the side of the little finger.

thirds of the pastry and to within 1 cm/½ in of the edges. Fold the unbuttered third of the pastry over the middle of the pastry and fold the buttered top third down. Turn the dough so that the folded edge points to the left and seal all the edges by pressing them together firmly with the side of your little finger.

Cover the pastry with a polythene bag and leave it to rest again in a cool place for about 20 minutes.

Turn the pastry so that the fold points to the right-hand side. Roll the pastry out as before, cover two-thirds with another quarter of fat, and repeat the folding, sealing and resting as before. Continue with the rest of the fat, giving the pastry a half-turn between each rolling.

Finally, roll out the pastry to the original rectangle, brush off any surplus flour, fold it up and wrap it loosely in polythene. Leave it to rest in a cool place for at least 30 minutes before shaping. Flaky pastry is usually baked in a preheated oven at 220°C/425°F/gas 7.

Cream Horns

MAKES: 8 .
PREPARATION: 30 minutes
OVEN: 220°C/425°F/gas 7
COOKING: 10 minutes

½ quantity Flaky Pastry
1 egg
raspberry or blackcurrant jam
250 ml/8 fl oz whipping cream
icing sugar

Roll the prepared pastry out to a strip 61 cm/24 in long and 10 cm/4 in wide. Beat the egg and brush it over the pastry. Cut the pastry into eight strips, 61 cm/24 in long and 1 cm/½ in wide, using a sharp knife. Wind each pastry strip around a cream horn tin, starting at the tip and with the glazed side of the pastry outside; overlap each turn by about 3 mm/⅛ in. As it rises during baking, the pastry should come just short of the metal rim of the horn. Set the moist horns on a baking tray, join downwards.

Bake in a preheated oven at 220°C/425°F/gas 7 for 8–10 minutes, until the horns are light golden. Leave to cool for a few minutes, then with one hand grip the rim of each tin with a clean cloth and carefully twist the tin. Hold the pastry lightly in the other hand and ease it off the tin. Leave the horns to cool completely.

To fill the horns, put a teaspoonful of jam into the base of each. Whip the cream and spoon it into the horns. Dust with icing sugar. Serve soon after filling as the pastry will soften if allowed to stand for long periods.

Eccles Cakes

MAKES: 10–12
PREPARATION: 30 minutes
OVEN: 220°C/425°F/gas 7
COOKING: 15 minutes

25 g/1 oz unsalted butter
25 g/1 oz soft brown sugar
25 g/1 oz mixed peel
50 g/2 oz currants
½ quantity Flaky Pastry
1 egg white
caster sugar

Make the filling for these little cakes first: beat the butter and sugar until pale and fluffy. Chop the peel finely and add to the creamed butter, together with the currants. Roll out the prepared pastry, 5 mm/¼ in thick. Cut it into rounds with a 7.5 cm/3 in plain cutter.

Put a teaspoonful of the fruit filling in the centre of each pastry round and bring the edges together over the top to cover the filling completely, pinching them to seal in the filling. Re-shape each cake into a round. Turn the cakes over and roll them lightly into flat rounds until the shapes of the currants just show through the pastry. Lightly score the tops of the cakes into a lattice pattern.

Leave the cakes to rest on greased baking trays for about 10 minutes in the refrigerator. Then brush them with lightly beaten egg white and sprinkle generously with caster sugar. Bake in a preheated oven at 220°C/425°F/gas 7 for about 15 minutes or until the cakes are golden and puffed.

ROUGH PUFF PASTRY

A cross between flaky and puff pastry, rough puff pastry is easier to make than puff pastry but slightly more difficult to handle than flaky pastry. However, it rises more than flaky pastry, but becomes heavy when cold. Rough puff is not as rich in butter as puff pastry and the butter is added all at once, in lumps, to the dough mixture. It is an excellent pastry for savoury pie crusts, sausage rolls and tarts.

Rough Puff Pastry

MAKES: about 675 g/1½ lb
PREPARATION: 30 minutes
RESTING: 50 minutes

175 g/6 oz butter
225 g/8 oz plain flour
5 ml/1 teaspoon salt
5 ml/1 teaspoon lemon juice
150 ml/¼ pt iced water

The butter should be cold and firm but not hard and long-chilled. Cut the butter into walnut-sized pieces. Sift the flour and salt into a bowl and add the butter, lemon juice and water. Mix lightly with a knife to form a soft dough.

Turn the dough on to a floured surface and knead it lightly – as the dough is soft it needs careful handling. Shape it into a rectangle then roll it into a strip about 1.5 cm/¾ in thick, 30 cm/12 in long and 10 cm/4 in wide, keeping the edges straight. The butter will be seen clearly as lumps in the pastry. Fold the bottom third of the pastry up, and the upper third down. Turn the pastry so that the fold points towards the left-hand side, and seal the edges lightly with the edge of the little finger. Roll out the pastry again, keeping it 1 cm/½ in thick and to a 46 × 15 cm/18 × 6 in rectangle. Repeat the folding, rolling and turning four times.

Place in a polythene bag and chill for 20 minutes after every two rollings. Rest the finished pastry for 10 minutes.

Rough puff pastry is usually baked in a preheated oven at 220°C/425°F/gas 7.

Making rough puff pastry

1 *Add the lumps of butter to the sifted flour.*

2 *Mix in iced water to make a soft dough.*

3 *Roll the dough into a long oblong.*

4 *Fold the dough in three.*

Sausage Rolls

MAKES: 18
PREPARATION: 20 minutes
OVEN: 220°C/425°F/gas 7
COOKING: 30 minutes

1 quantity Rough Puff Pastry
    (page 373)
450 g/1 lb sausagemeat
plain flour
1 egg

Roll out the prepared pastry into an oblong measuring 46 × 15 cm/ 18 × 6 in and cut it lengthways into two strips 7.5 cm/3 in wide.

Divide the sausagemeat in half, roll it on a floured surface into two long rolls to fit the pastry strips. Lay the sausagemeat in the centre of the pastry strips, brush the edges with beaten egg and fold the pastry over. Seal the two long edges firmly.

Sausage rolls

Covering the sausagemeat with the pastry.

Scoring the tops of the sausage rolls.

Brush the two pastry lengths with beaten egg and cut them into 5 cm/2 in long pieces. Score the top of the pastry lightly with the point of a knife. Set the sausage rolls on baking trays and bake in a preheated oven at 220°C/425°F/gas 7 for 25–30 minutes or until golden brown and puffed.

PUFF PASTRY

This is regarded as the finest and most professional pastry. It is time-consuming to prepare but well-made puff pastry has a excellent flavour and texture. Uncooked puff pastry may also be stored in a freezer for up to 3–4 months.

There is a good choice of commercially frozen and chilled puff pastry, so it is rarely prepared at home these days. Bought puff pastry is available in blocks or ready rolled in fine sheets. However, for a special dish or a superb vol-au-vent, it is worth making your own pastry.

Puff pastry, which is used for savoury pie crusts, as wrappings for meat and poultry, for vol-au-vent cases, cream horns, mille feuilles and palmiers, must be rolled out six times.

Vol-au-vent cases, patties and pastry crusts, which need the greatest rise and flakiness, should always be shaped from the first rolling of the finished dough. Second rolling, including trimmings from the first rolling, can be used for small items such as palmiers and crescents.

Prepared but uncooked puff pastry can be stored for 2–3 days in the refrigerator.

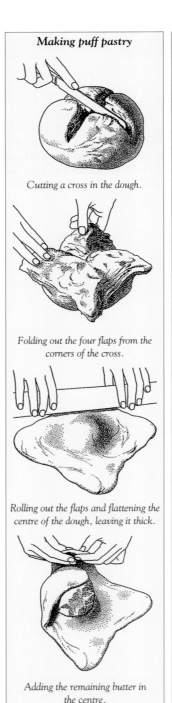

Making puff pastry

Cutting a cross in the dough.

Folding out the four flaps from the corners of the cross.

Rolling out the flaps and flattening the centre of the dough, leaving it thick.

Adding the remaining butter in the centre.

Standard Recipe

Throughout the book, when puff pastry is used, a weight of the finished dough is listed in the ingredients. This allows for the option of buying or making the pastry.

Puff Pastry

MAKES: about 1.4 kg/3 lb
PREPARATION: 1 hour
RESTING: 2½ hours

450 g/1 lb plain flour
10 ml/2 teaspoons salt
450 g/1 lb butter
300 ml/½ pt iced water
5 ml/1 teaspoon lemon juice

Sift the flour and salt into a large bowl. Cut 100 g/4 oz of the butter into small pieces and rub it into the flour with the fingertips. Add the water and lemon juice and using a round-bladed knife, mix the ingredients to a firm but pliable dough. Turn the dough on to a lightly floured surface and lightly knead it until the dough is smooth.

Shape the pastry into a thick round and cut through half its depth in the form of a cross. Open out the four flaps and roll them out until the centre is four times as thick as the flaps. Flatten the centre slightly.

Shape the remaining firm butter to fit the centre of the dough, leaving a clear 1 cm/½ in all round. Fold the flaps over the butter, envelope-style, and press the edges gently together with a rolling pin. Roll the dough into a 41 × 20 cm/16 × 8 in rectangle, using quick short strokes. Roll lightly but firmly, back and forth,

so as not to squeeze out the butter. Brush off any surplus flour between rollings. Fold the dough into three and press the edges with the edge of the little finger. Wrap the pastry in greaseproof paper, cover with cling film and chill for 20 minutes.

Roll out the pastry, raw edge pointed to the left, to a rectangle as before. Fold and chill for 20 minutes. Repeat rolling, folding and resting four times, giving the dough a half-turn every time. Chill the dough for 30 minutes before shaping it.

Puff pastry, properly made, should rise about six times in height and should generally be baked in a preheated oven at 230°C/450°F/gas 8.

Vol-au-vent

The following quantity makes one large 18 cm/7 in wide vol-au-vent case, eight 7.5 cm/3 in cases for individual servings, 12–14 small bouchée cases for cocktail snacks.

PREPARATION: 20 minutes
OVEN: 230°C/450°F/gas 8
          180°C/350°F/gas 4
COOKING: 40 minutes

450 g/1 lb prepared puff pastry
1 egg
175–225 g/6–8 oz diced, cooked
    chicken or flaked salmon, or
    100 g/4 oz peeled cooked
    prawns
300 ml/½ pt Béchamel Sauce
    (page 353)

For a large case, roll out the pastry to a 19 cm/7½ in square. Using an 18 cm/7 in plate or lid as a guide, cut round it with a sharp knife, held at an oblique angle to give a bevelled edge. Set the pastry upside-down on a moistened baking tray.

Brush the top of the pastry with beaten egg and mark a 15 cm/6 in wide circle on the pastry with a knife. Cut through half the depth of the pastry, following the mark of the inner circle. Draw a lattice pattern with the knife on the centre of the pastry triangles on the rim; rest for 15 minutes.

Bake the vol-au-vent case in a preheated oven at 230°/450°F/gas 8 for about 20 minutes or until it is risen and brown, then reduce the oven temperature to 180°C/350°F/gas 4 and cook for a further 20 minutes.

When cooked, carefully ease out the pastry lid and discard any soft pastry from the centre. Fill the case with chicken, salmon or prawns in Béchamel sauce.

Small vol-au-vent cases are made in a similar way. The pastry should be rolled out 1 cm/½ in thick and cut into 7.5 cm/3 in rounds for the cases and 3.5 cm/1½ in rounds for the lids. Bake in a preheated oven at 230°C/450°F/gas 8 for 20 minutes.

For bouchée cases, roll the pastry out, 5 mm/¼ in thick. Use 5 cm/2 in cutters or cases and 2.5 cm/1 in cutters for lids. Bake for about 15 minutes.

Fleurons

These are small crescents of puff pastry. They can be made from pastry trimmings and frozen raw, ready for cooking when required.

Roll the pastry trimmings out, 5 mm/¼ in thick, and cut out small crescents using a cutter. If you do not have a crescent cutter, use a round cutter to stamp out the shapes. Set on a moist baking tray and brush with beaten egg. Bake in a preheated oven at 230°C/450°F/gas 8 for barely 10 minutes, until puffed and golden. Cool on a wire rack.

Use as a garnish for soups, fish dishes and casseroles.

Mille Feuilles

MAKES: 6
PREPARATION: 40 minutes
OVEN: 230°C/450°F/gas 8
COOKING: 20 minutes

225 g/8 oz prepared puff pastry
100 g/4 oz raspberry jam
300 ml/½ pt Pastry Cream
  (page 236)
175 g/6 oz icing sugar
pink food colouring
15–30 ml/1–2 tablespoons water

Roll out the pastry to a 25 × 23 cm/10 × 9 in rectangle. Prick it all over with a fork. Lift the pastry on to a moistened baking tray and bake in a preheated oven at 230°C/450°F/gas 8 for 20 minutes or until well risen and golden brown. Cool the pastry on a wire rack. Use a sharp serrated knife to cut the pastry in half lengthways. Spread the top of one piece with two-thirds of the raspberry jam; cover with pastry cream.

Put the icing sugar in a bowl and beat in just enough cold water to give a thick coating consistency. Colour about 15 ml/1 tablespoon icing pale pink.

Spread the remaining raspberry jam over the second piece of pastry and turn it upside-down on to the pastry cream. Press the pastries together, then cover the top of the pastry with white icing. Pipe thin lines of pink icing at 1 cm/½ in intervals, lengthways, over the white icing. Draw the tip of a knife quickly across the width of the pastry, at 1 cm/½ in intervals to give the icing a feathered effect. Leave the mille feuille to set, then cut it into six equal slices.

Palmiers

MAKES: 12
PREPARATION: 15 minutes
OVEN: 220°C/425°F/gas 7
COOKING: 14 minutes

225 g/8 oz prepared puff pastry
25 g/1 oz caster sugar

On a lightly floured surface, roll out the pastry to a 30 × 25 cm/12 × 10 in rectangle. Sprinkle the pastry with caster sugar. Fold the long sides so that they meet in the centre. Sprinkle with the remaining sugar, and fold the pastry in half, lengthways, hiding the first folds. Press lightly and evenly with the fingertips along the pastry. Cut the pastry across into twelve slices.

Place the palmiers on a moist baking tray, cut side down and well apart to give them room to spread. Open out the top of each palmier slightly and flatten the whole slice lightly with a round-bladed knife. Bake the palmiers in a preheated oven at 220°C/425°F/gas 7 for 10 minutes, then turn them over and bake for about a further 4 minutes. Cool on a wire rack.

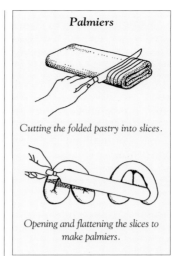

Palmiers

Cutting the folded pastry into slices.

Opening and flattening the slices to make palmiers.

FILO PASTRY

This paper-thin pastry is readily available frozen. The sheets vary in size, from 28 cm/11 in squares to 38 × 30 cm/15 × 12 in oblongs. Follow the maker's instructions for thawing the pastry; usually it is enough to leave it in the refrigerator for a few hours. Do not attempt to unroll part-thawed pastry as any hard sheets will crack and break.

Using Filo

Filo can be used for savoury and sweet dishes, and it can be baked or deep fried. The thin pastry dries out quickly, so once a sheet is opened out it must be used quickly; any pastry which is not actually in use must be covered with cling film, otherwise it dries and crumbles.

Work on a clean dry surface – if the filo becomes damp it sticks. Filo pastry is used in layers, not as a single sheet. The pastry can be layered in a dish or on top of a filling; individual pastries can be made by folding one end of a strip of filo pastry over a filling, then folding the pastry over and over until the strip is wrapped around the filling.

Brushing with Fat

To give its characteristic crisp texture and browned crust when baking, filo is brushed with melted butter. Oil or a mixture of oil and butter can be used instead of all butter – olive oil and butter are a good combination for many savouries.

There is no need to use generous quantities of fat as a very light brushing is sufficient. The fat keeps the layers of pastry separate during cooking, prevents them from becoming dry rather than crisp, and also seals the edges of the pastry together.

Do not brush filo pastry with egg or milk to seal the ends or keep the layers in place – the fat will do this.

Filo Toppings

As a wrapping for food, filo forms fine, even layers and it can be used to make large as well as small 'pasties' in this way. To make a filo pastry topping more attractive, and to give more variety in texture, the top sheet of pastry can be loosely pinched into pleats and irregular folds.

Alternatively, roll and shred a sheet of filo pastry, then sprinkle it over the top of the dish. This may be used as the top layer on a filo pie, or the shredded pastry can be sprinkled over food and baked as a crisp topping. This can also be used on savoury dishes, such as sauced fish or stews, or on sweets, such as stewed or poached fruit. Trickle a little melted butter over some of the pastry shreds before baking.

Freezing Filo

Filled, uncooked pastry freezes well. Although cooked items can be frozen, the pastry is fragile and it breaks easily. Very thickly layered pastries also tend to lose their texture on thawing.

PÂTE SUCRÉE

This type of pastry is the French equivalent of British rich shortcrust pastry. It is thin and crisp, yet melting in texture, and does not shrink or spread during baking. Pâté sucrée is usually baked blind, but flan cases and moulds need not be weighted down.

The authentic method of mixing is by lightly kneading all the ingredients together on a marble slab; however, the technique of rubbing fat into flour and then mixing in the egg yolks can be used if preferred.

Pâte Sucrée

PREPARATION: 15 minutes
RESTING: 1 hour

100 g/4 oz plain flour
pinch salt
50 g/2 oz caster sugar
50 g/2 oz butter
2 egg yolks

Sift together the flour and salt on to a cool working surface or, preferably, a marble slab. Make a well in the centre of the flour and put in the sugar, soft butter and the egg yolks.

Using the fingertips of one hand, pinch and work the sugar, butter and egg yolks together until they are well blended. Gradually work in all the flour from the sides and knead the pastry lightly until it is smooth. Leave the pastry in a cool place for at least 1 hour to rest before rolling it out.

Bateaux aux Fruits

MAKES: 6
PREPARATION: 20 minutes
OVEN: 190°C/375°F/gas 5
COOKING: 5–7 minutes

⅓ quantity Pâte Sucrée
400 g/14 oz canned fruit (apricot halves, pineapple pieces, cherries)
45 ml/3 tablespoons Apricot Glaze (page 388)
15 g/½ oz pistachio nuts

Roll out the pâte sucrée and line six boat-shaped moulds. Prick the pastry bases several times with a fork. Set the lined moulds on a baking tray and bake the pastry bases blind in a preheated oven at 190°C/375°F/gas 5 for 5–7 minutes or until tinged brown around the edges and cooked. Cool slightly, then ease the pastry boats out of the moulds and cool on a wire rack.

Brush the inside of the pastry boats with hot apricot glaze. Drain the canned fruit mixture thoroughly, cut the apricot halves in two and, if cherries are used, remove the stones. Arrange the fruit in the pastry boats, brush with more apricot glaze and decorate with blanched pistachio nuts.

COMMON PROBLEMS IN PASTRY MAKING

Heavy handling and overworking dough are two common mistakes that result in pastry with an inferior, coarse – or heavy – texture. Another general point for success with rolled-out pastry doughs is to pay attention to the working temperature of the ingredients, the environment and your hands.

Poor-quality pastry can be the result of preparation in conditions that are too warm (or using ingredients that are not cool enough); however, sometimes fats that have been chilled for too long can make pastry difficult to manage and this results in the dough being overworked. The following specific faults relate to different types of pastry.

Shortcrust

Hard and/or tough pastry: due to too much liquid and too much flour when rolling out; too little fat; over-handling; or insufficient rubbing in.

Soft and crumbly pastry: too little water; or self-raising flour used instead of plain.

Shrunk pastry: excess stretching during rolling out and not allowing the pastry to rest or chill before baking.

Speckled pastry: undissolved sugar grains in enriched pastry crust, usually caused by using coarser granulated sugar instead of caster sugar.

Soggy, uncooked pastry base: pastry not baked blind before filling added to flan or tartlets; fruit juices cause the base of a double-crust pie to soften but if

the tart plate conducts heat well the pastry should not taste raw. Brushing the pastry base with a little egg white helps but the best solution is to use a metal tart plate (enamel) or an ovenproof glass dish.

Hot Water Crust

Cracked pastry: liquid not boiling when added to flour; pastry not kneaded together until it is smooth; dough allowed to cool before being rolled or used.

Dry, difficult-to-mould pastry: liquid not boiling when added to flour; dough allowed to cool before being used.

Very soft, difficult-to-mould pastry: too little flour or too much water or fat; pastry not kneaded together until smooth; pastry still too hot and soft to roll out (allow to stand or knead gently for 1–2 minutes).

Hard pastry when cooked: insufficient fat or liquid; heavy handling or repeated moulding and rolling.

Suet Pastry

Heavy pastry: insufficient baking powder; too little suet or too much flour; water not kept on the boil during cooking.

Tough pastry: dough has been handled too much and rolled out excessively.

Soggy pastry: paper and cloth covering over filled pie too loose, and water not kept boiling during cooking. Foil is the best choice of covering.

Choux Pastry

Flour does not form paste leaving pan clean: liquid not

fully boiling when flour added; flour added in stages instead of all at once; too much water or fat used.

Greasy flour, fat and water paste: mixture beaten before eggs added, causing the fat to separate out.

Mixture too soft: too much water used; liquid not boiling when water added; eggs too large.

Pastry did not rise: self-raising flour used; paste not beaten enough once eggs added; oven too cold.

Sinking after removal from oven: insufficient baking; oven temperature too hot, browning paste before cooking it through or oven temperature not reduced part-way through baking.

Flaky, Rough Puff and Puff Pastries

Too few layers: insufficient rolling, resting and chilling; heavy rolling causing fat to break through and intermingle with the pastry; fat too soft.

Fat running out during baking: oven too cool.

Hard and tough pastry: too little fat; too little rolling; heavy handling; too cool an oven.

Shrinking pastry: over-stretching during rolling pastry and insufficient resting.

PUDDINGS & DESSERTS

Family favourites include sweet pies, tarts and flans (see pastry, pages 364–376), as well as steamed puddings and custards. For party occasions, jellies, mousses and home-made ice creams are ideal desserts. In Britain, desserts are served before cheese, although gourmets maintain that desserts should follow the cheese.

STEAMED, BOILED AND BAKED PUDDINGS

Puddings can be steamed in a steamer over a saucepan of boiling water or in a large saucepan. If using the latter, stand the pudding on a trivet or inverted heatproof saucer so as to raise it off the base of the pan. Pour water into the pan until it reaches halfway up the basin. Keep at least 2.5 cm/1 in space around the basin.

Whichever method is used, the water must be kept boiling throughout cooking. Top up with boiling water at intervals.

Preparing a Pudding Basin

Butter the basin lightly and cut and butter a disc of greaseproof paper to fit the base; this prevents the pudding from sticking. Fill the basin no more than two-thirds with mixture. Butter a piece of greaseproof paper thoroughly and make a 2.5 cm/1 in pleat in the centre to allow for the pudding to rise. Lay the paper over the basin and cover it with pleated foil. Tie the paper and foil covering securely with string below the lip of the basin. Make a string handle to lift the pudding out.

Filling a pudding cloth

1 Place a floured pudding cloth over a colander.

2 Spoon in the mixture and tie up the cloth.

3 The pudding, ready for boiling.

Many regional and traditional suet puddings are boiled rather than steamed. The pudding basin is covered tightly with a pudding cloth and immersed completely in a pan of boiling water. More usually, however, the pudding mixture is placed inside a scalded and flour-dusted pudding cloth. This is easiest done by laying the cloth over a colander, spooning in the mixture and tying the corners tightly. The two knots help to lift the pudding.

Turning Out a Pudding

Uncover the pudding basin. Leave to cool and shrink slightly, then loosen the pudding at one side of the basin. Place a dish over the basin, and turn it upside-down.

Baked Puddings

Apart from steaming and boiling, puddings can also be baked in the oven. The pudding mixture should be a little softer than for steamed puddings to give a crisp surface. To prevent jam-based puddings from caramelising, set the dish in a shallow tin of water.

Steamed Jam Pudding

SERVES: 4–6
PREPARATION: 20 minutes
COOKING: 1¾ hours

100 g/4 oz butter or margarine
100 g/4 oz caster sugar
2 eggs
175 g/6 oz self-raising flour
30 ml/2 tablespoons jam
Jam Sauce
225 g/8 oz jam
60 ml/4 tablespoons water

Cream the butter or margarine with the caster sugar until pale and light. Beat in the eggs, then fold in the flour. Grease a 1.12 litre/2 pt pudding basin and place the jam in it. Spoon the sponge mixture on top of the jam and spread it out evenly. Cover the basin with greaseproof paper and a piece of foil, crumpling the foil tightly around the rim.

Stand the basin in a steamer and set it over a pan of boiling water. Steam the pudding for 1¾ hours, checking the water level occasionally and adding more boiling water as necessary.

For the jam sauce, heat the jam and water together, stirring, until combined and just boiling. Turn the pudding out on to a serving dish and pour a little of the jam sauce over the top. Serve the remaining sauce separately.

Apple Crumble

SERVES: 4–6
PREPARATION: 25 minutes
OVEN: 200°C/400°F/gas 6
COOKING: 45 minutes

675 g/1½ lb cooking apples
75 g/3 oz caster sugar
grated rind of ½ lemon
Topping
175 g/6 oz plain flour
75 g/3 oz margarine
50 g/2 oz caster sugar
15 g/½ oz demerara sugar

Peel, core and slice the apples thinly. Put them, sprinkled with caster sugar, into a 1.7 litre/3 pt pie dish; top with lemon rind.

For the topping, sift the flour into a mixing bowl, cut up the margarine and rub it lightly into the flour with the tips of the fingers. Mix in the caster sugar. Spoon the crumble mixture over the apples and press it down lightly. Sprinkle the demerara sugar on top. Place the dish on a baking tray and bake in a preheated oven at 190°C/375°F/gas 5 for 45 minutes.

WAFFLES AND FRITTERS

Waffles and fritters are both batter-based puddings. They are served hot, with honey, maple or golden syrup; butter and/or jam may be served with waffles.

Waffles

MAKES: about 12
PREPARATION: 12 minutes
COOKING: 20 minutes

175 g/6 oz self-raising flour
pinch salt
45 ml/3 tablespoons caster sugar
3 eggs, separated
200 ml/7 fl oz milk
40 g/1½ oz butter
5 ml/1 teaspoon natural vanilla essence

Sift the flour and salt into a bowl and stir in the sugar. Make a well in the centre and drop in the egg yolks; mix thoroughly, then gradually beat in the milk and butter alternately. Stir in the vanilla essence. Whisk the egg whites until stiff, but not dry, and fold them evenly into the batter with a metal spoon or spatula.

Heat a well-greased waffle iron until it is hot. Pour in a little batter and cook for about 30 seconds until golden brown on each side.

Fruit Fritters

SERVES: 6
PREPARATION: 15 minutes
OVEN: 150°C/300°F/gas 2
COOKING: 12 minutes

150 ml/¼ pt Fritter Batter
(page 339)
822 g/28 oz can peach halves or
pineapple rings or 675 g/1½ lb
bananas or 3 cooking apples
caster sugar

Drain and dry canned fruit. Cut bananas into chunks. Peel, core and thickly slice apples. Prepare the fritter batter and heat the oil to 190°C/375°F or until a day-old cube of bread browns in 60 seconds.

Dip the fruit into the batter and fry in the hot oil for 2–3 minutes, turning them halfway through cooking. Fry only a few pieces at a time. Drain on absorbent kitchen paper. Keep warm in a preheated oven at 150°C/300°F/gas 2 until all are cooked. Dredge with caster sugar.

Frying fruit fritters

Draining batter from a fritter.

Draining fried fritters.

JELLIES, MOULDS AND MOUSSES

These cold desserts are all made with gelatine, an extract from animal bones, tendons and skin. Gelatine is available in powdered and leaf form.

Some fresh fruit – pineapple and papaya (also called paw paw) for example – contains enzymes which act on gelatine to reduce its setting power. Depending on the type and amount of fresh fruit used, the gelatine may not set at all. Also, a mixture which has set, and has been allowed to stand for any length of time, can soften again. Cooking destroys the enzyme, so canned fruit does not create a problem. Lemon juice is usually used in quantities sufficiently small to avoid significant setting problems.

Using Powdered Gelatine

Jellies and mousses made in individual glasses may be softer and made with less gelatine than a dessert made in a mould for turning out later. In general, one sachet (15 ml/1 tablespoon) will set 600 ml/1 pt of liquid.

In order to dissolve powdered gelatine, sprinkle it over a small amount of water (about 30–60ml/ 2–4 tablespoons for 1 sachet) in a small heatproof basin. Do not stir. Leave to stand for 15 minutes until the gelatine has absorbed the water and becomes spongy in appearance. Stand the basin over a pan of simmering water and stir until the gelatine has dissolved.

Once the gelatine has dissolved it may be added to liquid but not to a very cold or chilled

liquid which will rapidly set in into unpleasant strings. It is often best to stir some of the liquid or mixture to be set into the gelatine, then mix it into the bulk of the mixture.

For coating and glazing with jelly (for whisked jellies and for setting fruit decorations) use the jelly when it has set to the same consistency as unbeaten egg white.

Leaf Gelatine

Thin leaf gelatine must be soaked in cold water until soft, after 15–20 minutes. Squeeze the softened gelatine lightly to extract surplus water, and place it in a bowl with the measured amount of liquid used in the recipe or a small amount of water. Stand the bowl over hot water and heat, without boiling, until the gelatine has dissolved. Six sheets of leaf gelatine equal 25 g/ 1 oz of powdered gelatine.

Agar Agar

Agar agar is a vegetarian alternative to gelatine, derived from seaweed rather than animal sources. It has quite different setting qualities from those of gelatine, so always check the manufacturer's instructions for a guide to quantity.

The main properties to remember are that agar agar gives a firmer set than gelatine and that it sets at a higher temperature. So take particular care not to add dissolved agar agar to a very cool mixture as it sets rapidly. Also, remember this when folding whipped cream into agar agar mixtures.

Grape Jelly

SERVES: 4
PREPARATION: 40 minutes
CHILLING: about 3 hours

30 ml/2 tablespoons caster sugar
60 ml/4 tablespoons water
7.5 ml/1½ teaspoons powdered
gelatine
juice of 2 oranges
juice of 1 lemon
575 g/1¼ lb seedless white grapes
150 ml/¼ pt single cream

Dissolve the sugar with 30 ml/ 2 tablespoons water in a small pan over low heat. Dissolve the gelatine in the remaining water. Stir the hot sugar liquid into the gelatine, blend thoroughly and stir into the strained fruit juices. Make up to 300 ml/½ pt with cold water if necessary. Cool until beginning to set.

Peel the grapes; this is easiest done by dipping the whole bunch in boiling water for 30 seconds, then skinning them.

Divide the grapes equally between four sundae glasses, and spoon the jelly over them. Chill until set, and just before serving pour a thin layer of cream on top of each dessert.

Honeycomb Mould

SERVES: 6
PREPARATION: 45 minutes
CHILLING: 3 hours

rind of 1 lemon
600 ml/1 pt milk
2 eggs
50 g/2 oz caster sugar
15 ml/3 teaspoons powdered
gelatine
30 ml/2 tablespoons water

Peel the rind from the lemon as thinly as possible. Put the milk in a saucepan with the lemon rind and heat over very low heat for about 10 minutes.

Meanwhile, separate the eggs and beat the yolks with the sugar until thick and creamy. Strain the hot, not boiling, milk into the egg yolk mixture, and stir thoroughly. Return this custard to the pan and cook over low heat until it begins to thicken. Remove the pan from the heat.

Dissolve the gelatine in the water, leave it to cool slightly, then stir it into the custard. Put aside until it begins to set. Whisk the egg whites until stiff; then fold them into the custard.

Rinse a 900 ml–1.12 litre/ 1½–2 pt jelly mould with cold water, and spoon the mixture into the mould. Chill until set. To turn out, dip the mould in hot water for 5 seconds, place a serving dish over the mould and turn upside-down.

Raspberry Mousse

SERVES: 6
PREPARATION: 45 minutes
CHILLING: 2 hours

450 g/1 lb raspberries
3 whole eggs
100 g/4 oz caster sugar
15 ml/1 teaspoon gelatine
45 ml/3 tablespoons water
150 ml/¼ pt double cream
grated chocolate

Set aside about 8 raspberries for decorating the mousse.

Pureé the remaining raspberries, then rub the purée through a sieve.

Put the eggs in a bowl with the sugar. Place the bowl over a pan of hot water and whisk the eggs until thick and fluffy. Set the bowl in a basin of chilled water or ice cubes. Whisk the mixture until cool.

Sprinkle the gelatine over the water in a heatproof basin and set aside for 15 minutes. Stand the basin over a saucepan of simmering water and stir until the gelatine has dissolved completely. Stir the dissolved gelatine into the raspberry pureé, and then whisk this into the egg mixture. Whip the cream lightly and fold it into the raspberries when beginning to set. Spoon the mousse into a serving dish and chill until set.

Just before serving, sprinkle coarsely grated chocolate over the mousse and decorate with the whole raspberries.

SYLLABUBS AND TRIFLES

Syllabubs, which date back to Elizabethan times, were originally a drink, consisting of a bubbling wine, Sill or Sille, mixed with frothing cream. They later developed into a rich sweet with the addition of brandy and sherry, cream and sugar. The trifle, developed from the syllabub in the 18th century, became a little more substantial by the addition of sponge cake and jam.

Both syllabubs and trifles are ideal for dinner parties, as they can be made well in advance and chilled overnight. The basis is still wine or liqueur or both, with eggs and cream.

Syllabub

SERVES: 6
PREPARATION: 30 minutes
CHILLING: 1–3 hours

1 lemon
90 ml/6 tablespoons white wine or sherry
30 ml/2 tablespoons brandy
75 g/3 oz caster sugar
300 ml/½ pt double cream

Grate the lemon rind and squeeze out the juice. Put the rind and 60 ml/4 tablespoons of lemon juice in a bowl, add the wine (or sherry) and brandy. Stir in the sugar until it has dissolved Pour the cream slowly into the liquid, stirring all the time. Whisk the syllabub until it stands in soft peaks, then spoon it into tall glasses. Chill for at least 1 hour but serve within 2–3 hours.

■ Serve with soft sponge fingers or ratafia biscuits.

Sherry Trifle

SERVES: 6–8
PREPARATION: 30 minutes
CHILLING: 2 hours

6–8 trifle sponge cakes
100 g/4 oz strawberry or other red jam
2 x 400 g/14 oz cans sliced peaches
60 ml/4 tablespoons sherry
60 ml/4 tablespoons peach juice
30 ml/2 tablespoons nibbed almonds
600 ml/1 pt Custard Sauce (page 338)
300 ml/½ pt double cream
50 g/2 oz small macaroons

Split the sponge cakes in half, spread them with jam and sandwich them together. Cut the sponge cakes into 1 cm/½ in slices and arrange them over the base of a deep trifle bowl.

Drain the peach slices, set a few aside for decoration and arrange the remainder on the sponge. Sprinkle the sherry and peach juice over the sponge. Scatter the almonds over the sponge and peaches, and spoon the warm custard over them.

Cover the surface of the custard with cling film and leave until cold. Whip the cream until it just holds its shape and spoon it over the custard. Swirl the cream with a knife and decorate with the reserved peach slices and macaroons. Chill well.

ICE CREAM AND SORBETS

Home-made cream ices and water ices (or sorbets) are quite different in both texture and flavour to the commercial varieties. A basic ice cream is often based on a custard enriched with double cream. The basis of a water ice is a sugar syrup flavoured with fruit juice or purée.

Pointers to Success

1   The amount of sugar in the mixture is important – if vastly too much, the ice cream will not freeze, and if too little it will be hard and tasteless. In sorbets or water ices it is even more important to have the correct amount of sugar, as the soft yet firm consistency depends on the sugar content.
2   Whichever method is used for freezing the cream, it has a

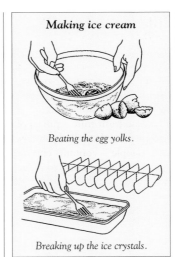

Making ice cream

Beating the egg yolks.

Breaking up the ice crystals.

better texture if frozen quickly. Turn the freezer to the fast-freeze setting, if possible, before making the ice cream. Use the fast-freeze compartment, if available.
3   Chill the equipment as well as the ingredients before starting.
4   Once the ice cream is frozen, it should be transferred to a shelf in the refrigerator for a little while before serving. Rock-hard ice creams are never pleasant and lose much of their flavour. This is sometimes known as ripening. The length of time for standing depends on the individual recipe.

Making Ice Cream in a Freezer

Set the dial to the fast-freeze about 1 hour before the ice cream is ready to be frozen or according to the manufacturer's instructions for using the fast-freeze facility.

Prepare the ice cream mixture according to the recipe, place it in a suitable container and freeze it until mushy.

Remove the container from the freezer and whisk the mixture thoroughly with an electric beater or in a food processor to break up the ice crystals. Freeze the mixture again and repeat the whisking, then freeze the ice cream until it is firm. Set the freezer back to normal after a few hours or as recommended by the manufacturer's instructions.

Using an Ice Cream Maker

The advantage of using an ice cream maker is that it churns the mixture it is freezing continuously which gives extremely smooth results. The other significant difference compared to putting the ice cream mixture in the freezer is that the whole process is far quicker.

There are various types of ice cream makers, including models which have a built-in refrigeration unit. The majority of domestic ice cream makers have containers that are placed in the freezer well in advance of making the ice cream. Then the ingredients are churned in the container and the ice cream is ready well within an hour.

It is important to read carefully and follow the manufacturer's instructions and to make ice creams in quantities suited to the appliance.

Vanilla Ice Cream

SERVES: 6
PREPARATION: 25 minutes
FREEZING: about 3 hours

300 ml/½ pt milk
vanilla pod
1 whole egg
2 egg yolks
75 g/3 oz caster sugar
300 ml/½ pt double cream

Bring the milk almost to the boil with the vanilla pod, then leave to infuse off the heat for about 15 minutes. Remove the vanilla pod. Cream the whole egg, yolks and sugar until pale. Stir in the vanilla-flavoured milk and strain this mixture through a sieve into a clean pan. Heat the custard mixture slowly over gentle heat, stirring all the time, until the mixture thickens enough to just coat the back of a wooden spoon. Pour into a bowl.

Whip the cream lightly and fold into the custard. Spoon into a container, cover and freeze until half frozen. Whisk thoroughly; freeze until firm.

Variations

Praline Ice Cream Make a caramel topping (see Orange Caramel Custard, page 275) and pour it over 50 g/2 oz lightly toasted blanched almonds on a greased baking tin. When cold, crush the mixture. Add 50 g/2 oz of praline to the half-frozen ice cream.
Coffee Ice Cream Add 15 ml/ 1 tablespoon coffee essence to the cooled custard mixture.
Pineapple Ice Cream Canned crushed pineapple may be added at half-frozen stage.

Rich Chocolate Ice Cream

SERVES: 6
PREPARATION: 20 minutes
FREEZING: 4 hours

75 g/3 oz caster sugar
90 ml/6 tablespoons water
4 egg yolks
600 ml/1 pt single cream
vanilla pod
200 g/7 oz plain chocolate

Put the sugar and water in a small pan and heat gently until the sugar is dissolved. Bring to the boil and continue boiling until the sugar has reached the thread stage, at about 105°C/ 220°F. Beat the egg yolks in a mixing bowl, then pour in the syrup in a thin stream, whisking all the time.

Put the cream, vanilla pod and chocolate, broken into small pieces, in a pan and cook over low heat until just below boiling point. Remove the vanilla pod and pour the chocolate cream into the egg mixture, whisking until it is thoroughly mixed. Cool and freeze, whisking once or twice during freezing.

Blackcurrant Sorbet

SERVES: 6
PREPARATION: 30 minutes
FREEZING: 3–4 hours

450 ml/¾ pt plus 30–45 ml/
2–3 tablespoons water
100 g/4 oz caster sugar
225 g/8 oz fresh or frozen
blackcurrants
2 egg whites

Put the water in a saucepan together with the sugar. Heat over low heat until the sugar has dissolved, then bring to the boil and boil for 10 minutes. Set aside to cool.

Meanwhile, strip and wash the fresh blackcurrants. Put the fresh or frozen currants, with 30–45 ml/2–3 tablespoons of water, in a pan and cook over low heat for 10 minutes. Purée and sieve the currants. Leave until quite cool. Pour the mixture into a freezing container. Freeze until half frozen and mushy.

Whisk the egg whites until stiff, but not dry. Beat the frozen mixture until smooth or process it in a food processor, and carefully fold in the egg whites. Return the sorbet mixture to its container and freeze until firm.

Granita

A true Italian granita is a fruit- (or coffee-) flavoured, coarse-textured water ice.

SERVES: 4
PREPARATION: 15 minutes
FREEZING: 3–4 hours

100 g/4 oz caster sugar
300 ml/½ pt water
250 ml/ 8 fl oz fresh lemon juice
finely grated rind of 2 lemons

Put the sugar and water in a pan. Bring to the boil over gentle heat until the sugar has dissolved, then continue boiling, without stirring, for 5 minutes. Remove the syrup from the heat and leave it to cool.

Stir the fruit juice and rind into the cooled syrup and pour the mixture into ice-cube trays, with the dividers left in. Set the trays in the freezer compartment and freeze until mushy. Remove the trays and scrape the ice crystals with a fork from the sides towards the centre. Repeat twice at 30 minute intervals, then return the trays to the freezing compartment and leave to freeze solid.

Remove the frozen cubes from the trays – an easy way to do this is to rub a cloth wrung out in hot water over the base and sides of the ice trays. Crush the cubes coarsely with a pestle, and spoon them into glasses. Serve at once.

BISCUIT CRUSTS

Biscuit crusts are made from crushed sweet or semi-sweet biscuits bound with melted butter. They are set as a base or as a flan case, either in a loose-bottomed tin or in a serving dish. A biscuit crust may be filled with a mousse or soufflé-type mixture, a cheesecake mixture or with ice cream and fruit.

Flavoured or chocolate-coated biscuits may be used – almond or coconut macaroons are suitable. Crush the biscuits finely and evenly for best results; a food processor is ideal for this. Chill the biscuit crust well before adding the filling.

Biscuit Crust

This uncooked crust is ideal for flan cases with fluffy chiffon-type fillings or it may be used as a base for cheesecake mixtures.

MAKES: 18–20 cm/7–8 in crust
PREPARATION: 15 minutes
CHILLING: 2 hours

225 g/8 oz plain biscuits, such
as digestive, rich tea or
gingernut biscuits
150 g/5 oz butter

Crush the plain biscuits by placing them in a polythene bag and rolling them with a rolling pin. Alternatively, crush them in a food processor. Melt the butter in a large saucepan over low heat. Add the biscuit crumbs and mix well.

Turn the biscuit mixture into a 18–20 cm/7–8 in flan dish; alternatively, use a loose-bottomed flan tin. With the back of a spoon, press the crumbs over the base and up the sides to form a shell.

Chill the flan case for at least 2 hours in the refrigerator or for about 20 minutes in the freezer until the mixture is firm.

Preparing a biscuit crust

Crushing biscuits in a large, loosely closed polythene bag.

Pressing the mixture up around the sides of a flan dish or tin with the back of a spoon.

CAKE-MAKING

The key to successful cake-making lies in following every recipe extremely carefully, and in understanding how the various ingredients work together. The basic ingredients are fat, flour, raising agents, eggs, sugar and often fruit. Using the right size tins, correct oven position and temperature are also important factors.

Basically cakes fall into two categories: those made with fat, and the sponge types made without fat. The exception to sponge mixtures is the Genoese sponge which combines the two methods.

In fat-type cakes, the fat is either rubbed in, creamed or melted. Rubbed-in mixtures are generally used for plain cakes while creamed cakes are rich and soft with a fairly close even grain and soft crumb.

In melted cakes, such as gingerbread, the fat, often with liquid, sugar, syrup or treacle added, is poured into the dry ingredients to give a batter-like consistency.

Preparations
Always use the right size tin. Bigger, smaller or shallower tins than those called for can cause a cake to fail. Prepare the tin either by greasing, lining and greasing, or by greasing and sprinkling with flour according to the type of cake and recipe instructions. Set the oven to the correct temperature and assemble the ingredients – eggs, butter and margarine should be at room temperature.

Fats
Butter, margarine, whipped-up white fat, lard and corn oil are all used in cakes of one type or another. However, they are not always interchangeable.

Butter, preferably unsalted butter, gives the best flavour but margarine can be used in place of butter in most recipes, with only a slight difference in flavour.

Specific recipes have been devised using other fats, such as oil or white fats, and for low-fat spreads. These ingredients cannot simply be used as substitutes for butter or margarine in a classic cake mixture; they must only be used according to recipes tested for them.

Flour and Raising Agents
Plain or self-raising flour or a mixture of both are used for cakes. Self-raising flour is popular, as it eliminates errors in calculating the exact amount of raising agents, which are already evenly blended throughout the flour.

A mixture of plain and self-raising flour is ideal for semi-rich cakes, such as Dundee Cake, which would rise too much if only self-raising flour were used. Other cakes, and in particular whisked cakes such as sponges, should be made only with plain flour, as they have their own natural raising agent – air. Substituting self-raising flour throws the balance of ingredients and some whisked mixtures will flop if a chemical raising agent is used.

In some melted cakes, bicarbonate of soda is used as a raising agent. Always follow the method closely as the stage at which the bicarbonate of soda is added is important for success.

Baking powder is a ready-made blend of soda and cream of tartar, and these together act as a powerful raising agent. Baking powder is used with plain flour or it may be added with self-raising flour when preparing a one-stage mixture, to give additional lift and compensate for the fact that air is not incorporated by creaming the fat and sugar.

Increasing the amount of chemical raising agent does not improve the success of the cake: over a certain proportion, the additional baking powder will make the mixture rise excessively and too rapidly, so destroying the texture of the cake, causing it to flop and sink in the middle.

A combination of cream of tartar and bicarbonate of soda is sometimes used as an alternative to baking powder, in the proportion of 2:1, usually only for scones.

Eggs
When whisked, eggs act as a raising agent by trapping air which expands on heating.

Cakes with a high proportion of egg, such as sponge cakes, need little, if any, raising agent.

In creamed mixtures, the eggs are beaten in, not whisked, and a little additional raising agent is required.

The other main function of eggs in many light cakes is to set the mixture and trap the gas, be it air or carbon dioxide produced by chemical raising agents, giving the cake its characteristic texture. The eggs also enrich the cake and contribute to the flavour even when they merely bind ingredients together rather than make the cake rise.

Sugar
Granulated sugar is the least expensive white sugar; it can be used in rubbed-in cakes, but as it is coarse it takes longer to dissolve and may give a spotted appearance to the cake crust. Caster sugar, being finer, creams more easily with fats and gives a finer, softer cake.

Demerara sugar should only be used in recipes for melted cakes, where sugar is dissolved, unless otherwise recommended.

Soft brown sugar, medium or light brown in colour, is good for rubbed-in, melted and fruit cakes. The colour and flavour add richness and the soft, moist quality helps to keep certain cakes in good condition longer.

Barbados or muscovado sugar is very dark brown, full-flavoured and moist, and it is used in rich fruit mixtures.

Syrup, honey and treacle, often combined with sugar, are used to sweeten, colour and flavour a variety of cakes. They promote a close, moist texture.

Fruit and Peel
Always choose good-quality dried fruit. Seedless raisins are similar in size to sultanas, but ready-prepared seeded or stoned raisins are large and juicy. Wash any syrup from glacé cherries, drain them well and dry them thoroughly.

Peel can be bought ready-chopped, but make sure that it looks soft and moist. Coarsely chopped, thin cut peel sometimes needs more chopping to make it finer. 'Caps' of candied orange, lemon, grapefruit and citron peel should be stripped of sugar before being shredded, grated, minced or chopped.

Preparing Cake Tins
There are many different finishes applied to baking tins. Read and follow the manufacturer's instructions for success and to ensure that the tins perform well for as long as possible. The following traditional methods apply to standard baking tins.

Greasing The most common method of preparation. Use oil and a brush to grease corners and curves well.

Greasing and flouring For fatless sponges, dust the greased tin with flour, tapping and tilting the tin well to coat it thinly and evenly. Then shake any excess flour out of the tin. This coating provides a surface for very light whisked sponges to cling to as they rise, without baking on to the tin. If the tin is greased and not floured, the side of a whisked sponge tends to wrinkle as it slips down the tin slightly during rising and baking.

Base lining Cut a piece of greaseproof paper to fit the base of the tin. Brush with oil. This is a useful method of preparing most tins to avoid the danger of a cake sticking to the base.

Non-stick paper or baking parchment Non-stick baking paper or baking parchment can be used instead of greaseproof paper. There are various types of non-stick papers, including reusable non-stick papers which may be wiped or washed and dried after baking.

Lining a round cake tin Cut a strip of greaseproof paper as long as the circumference of the tin and 5 cm/2 in wider than the depth of the tin. Make a fold about 2.5 ml/1 in deep along one of the long edges, and cut this at 1 cm/½ in intervals up to the fold, at a slight angle. Curve the strip around and slip it against the side of the tin, nicked fold downwards so that this lies flat, overlapping neatly against the base of the tin.

Cut a circle of paper slightly smaller than the bottom of the tin and drop it in over the nicked paper. Brush with oil as you line the tin – this helps to keep the paper in place as you work. Grease well when lined. For rich cakes with long cooking times, double-line the tin.

Lining a rectangular or square tin Measure the length and width of the tin and add twice the tin's depth to each of these measurements. Cut a sheet of greaseproof paper to this size and place the tin squarely in the centre. At each corner, make a cut from the angle of the paper as far as the corner of the tin.

Put in the paper so that it fits the inside of the tin, closely overlapping at the corners. Brush again with oil.

Skewer Test
To check if a large rubbed-in, creamed or rich cake is cooked, insert a clean metal skewer into the middle of the cake. If it comes out free of mixture, the cake is cooked. If there is sticky mixture on the skewer, continue to bake the cake.

Cooling Cakes
After baking, most cakes are best left to settle in their tins for 5 minutes before being turned out. Rich fruit cakes are allowed to cool completely in their tins.

Run a small palette knife or rounded-bladed knife between the cake and tin. Place a wire rack over the cake and invert both the cake and rack, then lift off the tin carefully. Peel off the lining paper. Turn the cake with the aid of a second rack or the hand so that the top is uppermost. Leave the cake to cool completely on the wire rack.

To prevent the wire mesh marking the surface of a soft-textured cake place a tea towel over the rack before turning the cake out.

Storing Cakes
Storage time depends on the type of cake. Fatless sponges should preferably be eaten on the day of baking as they go stale quickly. However, this type of cake freezes well for up to a year.

Creamed cakes keep well for up to a week in an airtight container in a cool place. Light fruit cakes, depending on their exact proportions, keep well for 2–3 weeks. Rich fruit cakes keep for long periods (years) and are not at their best until they have matured for 1–2 months.

Store both plain and iced cakes in airtight cake tins or similar containers.

Cream-filled cakes must be kept chilled.

Wrap rich fruit cakes with the lining paper left on in fresh greaseproof paper and then in foil before storing.

Foil
Never wrap fruit cakes in foil without first enclosing them completely in greaseproof paper. The acid from the fruit breaks down the foil which disintegrates on the surface of the cake in a fine dust.

Freezing
As already noted, fatless sponges freeze extremely well for long periods. Since rich fruit cakes keep for years without freezing, they are not prime freezer candidates. Creamed, rubbed-in and melted cakes keep for 1–6 months, depending on the ingredients. Plain cakes, as a rule, freeze better than flavoured types. Remember that some nuts, particularly coconut which has a high saturated fat content, do not freeze well for more than about 1–2 months as they can become rancid.

Decorated cakes, with a filling or icing, do not always freeze well as the filling and/or icing may separate or weep slightly.

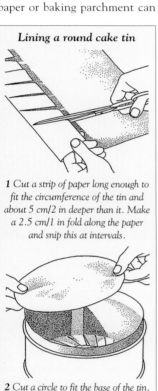

Lining a round cake tin

1 *Cut a strip of paper long enough to fit the circumference of the tin and about 5 cm/2 in deeper than it. Make a 2.5 cm/1 in fold along the paper and snip this at intervals.*

2 *Cut a circle to fit the base of the tin.*

3 *Brush the tin and lining paper with oil.*

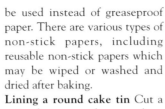

Lining a tin with corners

1 *Cut a sheet of paper large enough to fit in the base and up the sides of the tin. Place the tin on the paper and cut it in from the corners of the paper to the corners of the tin.*

2 *Place the paper in the greased tin, greasing and overlapping the corners so that they fit squarely in place.*

Turning out cakes

1 *Run a knife along the inner edge of the tin.*

2 *Invert the cake on to a covered rack.*

RUBBED-IN CAKES

As the proportion of fat to flour is half or less, rubbed-in mixtures are best eaten when fresh or within 2–3 days of baking. Rubbing in consists of blending flour and fat to a crumb-like mixture, using the fingertips.

To keep the mixture cool, raise the hands high when letting the crumbs drop back into the bowl. Shake the bowl occasionally to bring bigger crumbs to the surface. Make sure the texture is even, but do not handle more than necessary, or the crumbs will toughen and the fat become soft and oily.

The amount of liquid added can be critical: too much results in a doughy texture, whereas too little gives a crumbly cake which quickly dries out. For a large cake, the mixture should only just drop off the spoon when gently tapped.

Strawberry Shortcake

MAKES: 18 cm/7 in round cake
PREPARATION: 25 minutes
OVEN: 220°C/425°F/gas 7
COOKING: 20 minutes

225 g/8 oz plain flour
5 ml/1 teaspoon cream of tartar
2.5 ml/½ teaspoon bicarbonate
of soda
pinch salt
100 g/4 oz butter
50 g/2 oz caster sugar
1 egg
30 ml/2 tablespoons milk
Filling
450 g/1 lb strawberries
300 ml/½ pt double cream
15 ml/1 tablespoon milk
caster sugar

Sift together the flour, cream of tartar, bicarbonate of soda and salt into a bowl. Rub the butter into the flour until the mixture resembles fine breadcrumbs. Stir in the sugar. Make a well in the centre, stir in the beaten egg and enough milk to give a soft but manageable dough. Knead lightly on a floured surface, then roll out to an 18 cm/7 in circle.

Place on a greased baking tray, dust lightly with flour and bake in a preheated oven at 220°C/425°F/gas 7 for about 20 minutes. Cool on a wire rack.

For the shortcake filling, keep back 6 strawberries for decoration and hull, then slice the remainder thickly. Whip the cream and milk with caster sugar to taste, until it holds its shape in soft peaks. Cut the warm shortcake horizontally into two layers, using a serrated knife.

Spread the base with most of the whipped cream. Top with the sliced strawberries and the second layer of shortcake. Add piped cream and the reserved strawberries.

Cherry and Coconut Cake

MAKES: 20 cm/8 in round cake
PREPARATION: 30 minutes
OVEN: 180°C/350°F/gas 4
COOKING: 1¼ hours

350 g/12 oz self-raising flour
pinch salt
175 g/6 oz margarine
225 g/8 oz glacé cherries
50 g/2 oz desiccated coconut
175 g/6 oz caster sugar
2 large eggs
about 150 ml/¼ pt milk
granulated sugar

Grease a 20 cm/8 in round cake tin. Sift the flour and salt into a bowl, and rub in the cut-up margarine. Quarter the cherries, toss them in the coconut and add, with the sugar, to the flour, stirring lightly to combine. Beat the eggs and stir them into the mixture, together with sufficient milk to give a stiff but dropping consistency.

Turn the mixture into the prepared tin, level the surface, dust with granulated sugar and bake in a preheated oven at 180°C/350°F/gas 4 for about 1¼ hours or until well risen and golden brown. Cover the top of the cake loosely with a piece of foil if it browns too quickly – check after 1 hour.

Tyrol Cake

MAKES: 15 cm/6 in round cake
PREPARATION: 25 minutes
OVEN: 160°C/325°F/gas 3
COOKING: 1¾–2 hours

225 g/8 oz plain flour
pinch salt
5 ml/1 teaspoon ground cinnamon
90 g/3½ oz block margarine
50 g/2 oz caster sugar
50 g/2 oz currants
50 g/2 oz sultanas
5 ml/1 teaspoon bicarbonate
of soda
150 ml/¼ pt milk
45 ml/3 tablespoons clear honey

Grease a 15 cm/6 in round cake tin. Sift the flour, salt and cinnamon into a bowl, cut up the margarine and rub into the flour until the mixture resembles fine breadcrumbs. Stir in the sugar, currants and sultanas and make a well in the centre. Dissolve the bicarbonate of soda in the milk, stir in the honey and pour this mixture into the well in the flour. Using a wooden spoon, gradually work in the dry ingredients, adding more milk if necessary to give a firm dropping consistency.

Spoon the cake mixture into the prepared tin and level the top. Bake in a preheated oven at 160°C/325°F/gas 3 for 1¾–2 hours or until well risen and cooked through.

Raspberry Buns

MAKES: 10
PREPARATION: 25 minutes
OVEN: 220°C/425°F/gas 7
COOKING: 10–15 minutes

200 g/7 oz self-raising flour
pinch salt
25 g/1 oz ground rice
75 g/3 oz caster sugar
75 g/3 oz butter or block margarine
1 egg
15 ml/1 tablespoon milk
raspberry jam
beaten egg

Grease two baking trays. In a bowl, sift together the flour, salt, ground rice and sugar. Add the butter or margarine, cut into small pieces, and rub into the flour with the fingertips until the mixture resembles fine breadcrumbs. Beat the egg lightly with the milk and mix this in with a round-bladed knife, until the mixture forms a light and manageable dough.

Shape the dough between the palms of the hands into 10 even-sized balls. Make a hole with a floured finger in the centre of each ball and drop in a little raspberry jam. Close up the opening, pinching the edges.

Place the buns well apart on the baking trays, as they double in size. Brush with egg and bake in a preheated oven at 220°C/425°F/gas 7 for 10–15 minutes. Cool on a wire rack.

Rock Buns

MAKES: 12
PREPARATION: 15 minutes
OVEN: 200°C/400°F/gas 6
COOKING: 15 minutes

225 g/8 oz plain flour
pinch salt
10 ml/2 teaspoons baking powder
100 g/4 oz butter or margarine
100 g/4 oz mixed dried fruit
100g/4 oz demerara sugar
grated rind of ½ lemon
1 large egg
15–30 ml/1–2 tablespoons milk

Grease two baking trays. Sift together flour, salt and baking powder into a bowl. Rub butter or margarine into the flour until the mixture resembles fine breadcrumbs. Stir in fruit, sugar and lemon rind. Beat egg with 15 ml/1 tablespoon milk. Using a fork, stir the egg mixture into the dry ingredients, adding more milk if necessary to give a stiff dough – the mixture should just bind.

Place the mixture in 12 small heaps on greased baking trays. Keep mixture rough to give a rocky appearance which will remain after baking. Bake in a preheated oven at 200°C/400°F/gas 6 for 20 minutes, or until golden. Cool on a wire rack.

CREAMED CAKES

These are all made from the basic method of blending fat with sugar. Put the softened butter or block margarine into a bowl. Add the sugar and beat or cream the mixture until fluffy and pale. After 7–10 minutes the volume should have increased greatly and the mixture should drop easily from the spoon.

An electric mixer speeds up the preparation. A hand-held mixer is suitable for most recipes, but a larger stand-mounted mixer is essential for large cakes.

One-stage Cakes

A comparatively new method, the one-stage idea was invented by the manufacturers of soft margarine. It is an excellent way of quickly making creamed cakes using soft margarine or softened butter and an electric mixer. The standard Victoria sandwich ingredients are used with 2.5 ml/ ½ teaspoon baking powder added.

Victoria Sandwich

MAKES: 18 cm/7 in sandwich cake
PREPARATION: 20 minutes
OVEN: 160°C/325°F/gas 3
COOKING: 25–30 minutes

100 g/4 oz butter or margarine
100 g/4 oz caster sugar
2 large eggs
100 g/4 oz self-raising flour

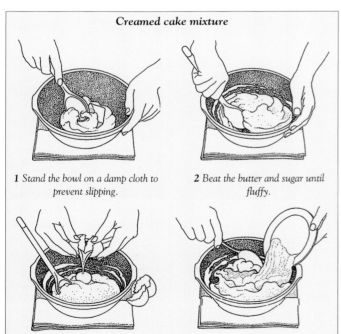

Creamed cake mixture

1 Stand the bowl on a damp cloth to prevent slipping.

2 Beat the butter and sugar until fluffy.

3 Gradually stir in the egg, adding a little of the measured flour to prevent the mixture curdling

4 Fold in the sifted flour using a metal spoon.

Base line and grease two 18 cm/ 7 in straight-sided sandwich tins. In a bowl, beat the butter or margarine until soft, then add the sugar and cream until light and fluffy. Lightly mix in the eggs, one at a time, adding a little of the measured flour to prevent the mixture curdling. Use a metal spoon to fold in the flour.

Divide this mixture equally between the two tins, and level off the surface. Bake the cakes in a preheated oven at 160°C/ 325°F/gas 3 for 25–30 minutes. Cool on a wire rack.

Sandwich the cakes with jam and dust with caster sugar.

Chocolate Layer Cake

MAKES: 20 cm/8 in layer cake
PREPARATION: 25 minutes
OVEN: 160°C/325°F/gas 3
COOKING: 30 minutes

100 g/4 oz butter or margarine
100 g/4 oz caster sugar
2 large eggs
100g/4 oz self-raising flour
30 ml/2 tablespoons cocoa
Filling
40 g/1½ oz butter or margarine
75 g/3 oz icing sugar
10 ml/2 teaspoons coffee essence
15 ml/1 tablespoon milk

Base line and grease two 18 cm/ 7 in sandwich tins.

Beat the butter until soft, then add the sugar and cream the mixture until light and fluffy. Beat the eggs before beating them into the mixture, a little at a time, adding a little of the measured flour to prevent the mixture curdling. Sift the remaining flour and cocoa

Chocolate layer cake

1 Sift icing sugar thickly over the cake.

2 Draw a lattice pattern across the sugar using the point of a knife.

together, then fold the mixture into the cake using a metal spoon. Turn the cake mixture into the prepared tins, level the surface and bake in a preheated oven at 160°C/325°F/gas 3 for about 30 minutes or until well risen and springy to the touch.

Meanwhile, make the filling. Beat the butter until soft and creamy, sift the icing sugar and beat it in a little at a time. Stir in the coffee essence and milk.

Turn the cake on to a wire rack, and remove the lining paper. Leave to cool. Cut the cold cake in half horizontally, and spread the bottom half with the filling; place the top in position and lightly press the two halves together. Dust the top with sifted icing sugar. Using the back of a knife blade, draw a lattice pattern across the sugar.

Dundee Cake

MAKES: 20 cm/8 in round cake
PREPARATION: 20 minutes
OVEN: 150°C/300°F/gas 2
COOKING: 3½–4 hours

175 g/6 oz plain flour
150 g/5 oz self-raising flour
pinch salt
225 g/8 oz butter or margarine
225 g/8 oz caster sugar
4 large eggs
350 g/12 oz sultanas
350 g/12 oz currants
175 g/6 oz chopped mixed peel
100 g/4 oz small glacé cherries
grated rind of ½ lemon
50–75 g/2–3 oz blanched almonds

Line and grease a 20 cm/8 in round cake tin. Tie a band of brown paper around the outside of the tin and let it extend about 5 cm/2 in above the rim. Set the tin on a double piece of brown paper on a baking tray.

Sift both types of flour and the salt. Cream the butter or margarine with the sugar until light and fluffy. Beat in the eggs a little at a time. Fold in the flours. Fold in the sultanas, currants, peel, cherries and lemon rind. Chop 25 g/1 oz of the almonds and add them to the cake mixture. Spoon into the tin.

Split the rest of the almonds lengthways, and arrange them, rounded side up, over the cake. Bake in a preheated oven at 150°C/300°F/gas 2 for 3½–4 hours. To check if the cake is cooked, insert a metal skewer into the centre. If there is any sticky mixture on the skewer, return the cake to the oven and check after a further 5 minutes.

Cool in the tin for 30 minutes, then on a wire rack. Wrap the cake in greaseproof paper and cling film. Keep for at least 1 week and up to 1 month.

Madeleines

These are the traditional British cakes covered with jam and coconut. They are not related to the French sponge Madeleines baked in small fluted tins.

MAKES: 6–8
PREPARATION: 20 minutes
OVEN: 180°C/350°F/gas 4
COOKING: 20 minutes

100 g/4 oz butter or margarine
100 g/4 oz caster sugar
2 eggs
100 g/4 oz self-raising flour
pinch salt
60 ml/4 tablespoons red jam
15 ml/1 tablespoon water
50 g/2 oz desiccated coconut
6 glacé cherries
angelica leaves

Grease six dariole moulds*. Cream the butter or margarine with the sugar until light and fluffy. Beat in the beaten eggs. Fold in the flour and salt. Divide between the moulds, filling them no more than two-thirds full. Set on a baking tray and bake in a preheated oven at 180°C/350°F/gas 4 for 20 minutes or until golden. Cool on a wire rack.

When the cakes are cold, heat the jam and water, stirring until boiling. Level the wide bases of the cakes if necessary, brush them all over with the jam and roll in coconut. Decorate with a cherry and angelica leaves.

Orange Butterflies

MAKES: 12
PREPARATION: 15 minutes
OVEN: 200°C/400°F/gas 6
COOKING: 10–15 minutes

75 g/3 oz butter or margarine
75 g/3 oz caster sugar
1 large egg
150 g/5 oz self-raising flour
5 ml/1 teaspoon grated orange rind
15 ml/1 tablespoon orange juice
orange-flavoured Butter Cream
(page 389–90)

Grease 12 patty tins. Beat the butter or margarine until soft, then add the sugar, and cream until light and fluffy. Add the beaten egg. Sift the flour, add the orange rind and fold this in alternately with the orange juice. Fill the patty tins to half their depths. Bake in a preheated oven at 200°C/400°F/gas 6 for 10–15 minutes or until well-risen and golden. Cool on a wire rack.

Cut a slice from the top of each cake and pipe or spoon in a little butter cream. Cut each top slice in half and insert these in the butter cream to resemble the wings of butterflies.

Swiss Tarts

MAKES: 6
PREPARATION: 25 minutes
OVEN: 180°C/350°F/gas 4
COOKING: 20 minutes

100 g/4 oz butter
25 g/1 oz caster sugar
5 ml/1 teaspoon natural
vanilla essence
100 g/4 oz plain flour
icing sugar
redcurrant jelly

Place six paper baking cases in a sheet of patty tins and set on a baking tray. Beat the butter until soft, add the sugar, and cream until light and fluffy. Beat in the vanilla essence and gradually add the flour, beating well between each addition.

Put the mixture in a piping bag fitted with a large star vegetable nozzle. Pipe the mixture into the paper cases, starting at the centre, and piping with a spiral motion around the sides, leaving a shallow depression in the centre. Chill well. Bake in a preheated oven at 180°C/350°F/gas 4 for about 20 minutes or until set and very lightly browned in places.

Leave the cakes in their paper cases to cool on a wire rack. Dredge with icing sugar and top each tart with a little red-currant jelly.

Farmhouse Fruit Cake

MAKES: 20 cm/8 in round cake
PREPARATION: 10 minutes
OVEN: 180°C/350°F/gas 4
COOKING: about 1½ hours

175 g/6 oz margarine
175 g/6 oz caster sugar
75 g/3 oz sultanas
75 g/3 oz seedless raisins
75 g/3 oz glacé cherries, chopped
350 g/12 oz self-raising flour
pinch salt
5 ml/1 teaspoon mixed spice
45 ml/3 tablespoons milk
3 eggs

Base line and grease a 20 cm/8 in round cake tin. Mix the margarine and all the dry ingredients in a bowl, then add the milk and eggs and beat the mixture with an electric mixer or wooden spoon until well mixed. Turn the mixture into the prepared tin and level the top.

Bake in a preheated oven at 180°C/350°F/gas 4 for about 1½ hours. Test with a skewer (page 382). Leave the cake in the tin for 15 minutes before turning out on to a wire rack to cool.

Coffee Walnut Cake

MAKES: 18 cm/7 in
sandwich cake
PREPARATION: 20 minutes
OVEN: 160°C/325°F/gas 3
COOKING: 35–40 minutes

100 g/4 oz margarine
100 g/4 oz caster sugar
2 large eggs
50 g/2 oz walnuts, chopped
15 ml/1 tablespoon coffee essence
100 g/4 oz self-raising flour
5 ml/1 teaspoon baking powder
Filling
75 g/3 oz butter or margarine
225 g/8 oz icing sugar
10 ml/2 teaspoons milk
10 ml/2 teaspoons coffee essence
walnut halves

Base line and grease two 18 cm/7 in straight-sided sandwich tins. Put the margarine and sugar, eggs, chopped walnuts and coffee essence in a bowl. Add the self-raising flour and baking powder. Beat until the ingredients are well combined.

Divide the mixture between the prepared tins, level the surface and bake in a preheated oven at 160°C/325°F/gas 3 for 35–40 minutes, or until well-risen and springy to the touch.

When baked, turn the cakes out on a wire rack to cool before removing the lining paper.

Meanwhile make the filling: beat the butter or margarine, sifted icing sugar, milk and coffee essence in a bowl until smooth. Sandwich the cakes together with two-thirds of the filling, top with the remaining filling and mark the surface with the prongs of a fork in a decorative pattern. Place walnut halves on the cake.

Madeira Cake

MAKES: 18 cm/7 in round cake
PREPARATION: 20 minutes
OVEN: 160°C/325°F/gas 3
COOKING: 1–1¼ hours

175 g/6 oz butter or margarine
175 g/6 oz caster sugar
3 large eggs
150 g/5 oz self-raising flour
100 g/4 oz plain flour
grated rind and juice of ½ lemon
citron peel

Line and grease an 18 cm/7 in round cake tin. Beat the butter until soft, then add the sugar and cream until light and fluffy. Add the eggs, one at a time, beating well between each addition and adding a little of the measured flours to prevent curdling. Fold in the flours alternately with the rind and strained lemon juice. Turn the mixture into the prepared tin and level the surface. Arrange a large slice of thinly cut citron peel on top of the mixture.

Bake in a preheated oven at 160°C/325°F/gas 3 for 1–1¼ hours. Leave to cool in the tin for 10 minutes, then turn out on to a wire rack.

WHISKED CAKES

These are the lightest of all cake mixtures.

Use an electric mixer or rotary whisk and stand the bowl of eggs and sugar over a pan of hot water. The heat cooks the eggs very lightly, allowing them to increase in volume slightly by trapping more air as they thicken. The water must not boil nor simmer as this will overcook the eggs or thicken them too quickly, hindering the process rather than allowing more air to enter the mixture. The mixture should be thick enough to leave a trail when the whisk is lifted.

Continue whisking after removing the bowl from the pan. Although this method is the quickest for achieving a good volume, it is not essential to whisk over hot water. The mixture will be slightly less thick and it will not achieve as good a volume if cold, but the cake will certainly be a success. Fold in the flour carefully to avoid knocking out the air which has been beaten in. Use a metal spoon in a figure-of-eight movement.

■ Whisked, fatless sponges freeze well for up to a year if they are carefully wrapped.

Enriched Sponge Cakes

Melted butter may be folded into the whisked sponge cake alternately with, or after, the flour. This enriches the cake and improves its keeping qualities. A Genoese sponge is the classic example of a whisked cake with melted butter added. Unsalted butter should be used whenever possible for a whisked sponge.

Swiss Roll

MAKES: 20 cm/8 in Swiss roll
PREPARATION: 15 minutes
OVEN: 220°C/425°F/gas 7
COOKING: 10 minutes

3 large eggs
75 g/3 oz caster sugar
75 g/3 oz plain flour
about 75 ml/5 tablespoons jam
caster sugar for dusting

Line and grease a Swiss roll tin measuring 30 × 20 cm/12 × 8 in.

Put the eggs and sugar in a large bowl over a pan of hot water, and whisk until the mixture is pale and holds a thick trail. Remove from the heat and continue whisking until cooled.

Fold in the flour using a large metal spoon. Turn the mixture into the prepared tin, and spread it out evenly. Bake at once in a preheated oven at 220°C/425°F/gas 7 for about 10 minutes or until light golden and springy.

Prepare a sheet of sugar-dredged greaseproof or non-stick paper on a clean, dampened tea-towel. Warm the jam in a small saucepan. Turn the cake out on to the paper. Remove the lining paper and quickly trim off the crisp edges from the sponge with a sharp knife. Make a shallow cut across the narrow end of the sponge, about 1 cm/½ in from the end. Spread with the jam. Roll up the sponge at once, tucking in the 1 cm/½ in at the end to form a tight middle to the roll. Use the

Making a Swiss roll

1 Spread the mixture evenly.

2 Remove the lining paper from the cooked cake.

3 Spread the warm jam over the cake.

4 Roll up the sponge on sugared paper; a damp tea-towel helps to prevent the sponge from cracking.

paper and damp tea-towel as a guide. Leave for 30 seconds, then remove the paper and tea-towel. Cool on a wire rack, with the join of the sponge underneath. Dust with caster sugar.

Cream-filled Swiss Roll

The Swiss roll may be spread with a cream filling. In this case, lay a sheet of clean greaseproof paper on the sponge instead of spreading it with jam. Roll the clean paper inside the sponge and leave to cool as above.

When cold, carefully unroll the sponge, then spread with the chosen filling and roll up again.

Strawberry Cream Sponge

MAKES: 18 cm/7 in
    sandwich cake
PREPARATION: 20 minutes
OVEN: 190°C/375°F/gas 5
COOKING: 15 minutes

3 eggs
75 g/3 oz caster sugar
75 g/3 oz plain flour
strawberry jam
150 ml/¼ pt double or whipping
    cream
caster or icing sugar for dusting

Grease and flour two 18 cm/7 in straight-sided sandwich tins. Place a deep mixing bowl over a pan of hot water, break the eggs into the bowl and add the sugar. Whisk until the mixture is pale, and thick enough to hold a trail.

Carefully fold in the flour. Divide the mixture equally between the two tins. Bake in a preheated oven at 190°C/375°F/gas 5 for about 15 minutes or until pale brown and springy to

the touch. Carefully ease away the edges of the baked cakes with a palette knife, and cool on a tea-towel on a wire rack.

When cold, spread the bases of both sponges with a thin layer of jam, cover one sponge with whipped cream and place the other cake, jam downwards, on top. Press lightly together and dust with caster or sifted icing sugar. Chill until serving.

Genoese Sponge

MAKES: 18 cm/7 in
    sandwich cake
PREPARATION: 15 minutes
OVEN: 190°C/375°F/gas 5
COOKING: 25–30 minutes

40 g/1½ oz unsalted butter
65 g/2½ oz plain flour
15 ml/1 tablespoon cornflour
3 large eggs
75 g/3 oz caster sugar

Line and grease two 18 cm/7 in sandwich tins. Heat the butter in a pan over low heat until melted but not hot; remove from the heat and leave to stand for a few minutes. Sift together the flour and cornflour. Put the eggs in a large bowl over a pan of hot water, whisk for a few seconds, then add the sugar and continue whisking until the mixture is pale and holds a thick trail when the whisk is lifted out.

Remove the bowl from the heat and whisk for a few minutes longer, until the mixture is cool. Using a metal spoon, carefully fold in half the sifted flour, then pour in the melted butter in a thin stream. Fold in the remaining sifted flour. Turn this mixture into the prepared tin and bake in a preheated oven at 190°C/375°F/gas 5 for 25–30 minutes or until well-risen and springy to the touch. Cool on a wire rack covered with a clean tea-towel. Sandwich the cakes together when cold: a variety of fillings may be used, including jam and/or whipped cream.

Deep Genoese Sponge

The sponge, if placed in a deep round 18 cm/7 in tin, should be baked at the lower temperature of 160°C/325°F/gas 3 for about 45–50 minutes. The cold cake can be split horizontally into three equal layers and sand-wiched together with a cream and fruit or Butter Cream (page 389) filling, and the top decorated with cream.

Shallow Sponge

A sponge baked in a Swiss roll tin can be cut into fancy individual shapes.

Iced Fancies

MAKES: 24–30
PREPARATION: 1¼ hours
OVEN: 190°C/375°F/gas 5
COOKING: 30 minutes

1 shallow Genoese sponge, baked
in a Swiss roll tin and cooled
Apricot Glaze (page 391)
450 g/1 lb marzipan
Glacé Icing (page 390), made
from 450 g/1 lb icing sugar
food colourings
cake decorations, such as silver
dragees, angelica, sugar
mimosa balls, glacé cherries,
crystallised violets and rose
petals, and/or nuts

Coating of iced fancies

1 Stamp out small fancy shapes from the Genoese sponge.

2 Brush the fancies with apricot glaze.

3 Top with thinly rolled marzipan.

4 Coat with glacé icing and decorate with bought cake decorating ingredients.

Cut the sponge into 24–30 small shapes, such as squares, diamonds, rounds and crescents. Roll out the marzipan thinly on a surface lightly dusted with icing sugar. Brush the fancies with warm apricot glaze. Cut the marzipan into the same shapes as the fancies and lay them on the brushed cakes. Stand the cakes on a wire rack over a sheet of foil.

Make up the glacé icing beating in enough water to give a thick coating consistency. Divide it into four portions and colour three of these green, pink or lemon. Carefully spoon the icing over the cakes, using a teaspoon to tease the icing down the sides.

When the icing is set completely, decorate the cakes with pieces of glacé cherry, angelica, mimosa balls, silver dragees, nuts, or crystallised violets and rose petals.

After decorating the cakes, put the fancies in small paper cases and serve.

MELTED CAKES

Unlike other raw cake mixtures, a melted mixture has a pouring consistency, similar to a thick batter. When baked, the cakes have a close texture, are moist, and quite rich.

Treacle or syrup is often a key ingredient and bicarbonate of soda may be used as a raising agent. When using bicarbonate of soda, take care to measure it accurately, as too much will give the cake a bitter taste and very dark colour. These cakes keep well for 2–3 weeks and improve after maturing for 1 week.

Gingerbread

MAKES: 23 cm/9 in square cake
PREPARATION: 20 minutes
OVEN: 180°C/350°F/gas 4
COOKING: 1½ hours

450 g/1 lb plain flour
15 ml/1 tablespoon ground ginger
15 ml/1 tablespoon baking powder
5 ml/1 teaspoon bicarbonate
of soda
5 ml/1 teaspoon salt
225 g/8 oz demerara sugar
175 g/6 oz butter
175 g/6 oz black treacle
175 g/6 oz golden syrup
300 ml/½ pt milk
1 large egg

Line and grease a 23 cm/9 in square cake tin, about 5 cm/2 in deep. Sift all the dry ingredients, except the sugar, into a large bowl. Warm the sugar, butter, treacle and syrup in a pan over low heat until the butter has just melted. Stir the melted ingredients into the centre of the dry mix, together with the milk and beaten egg. Beat thoroughly with a wooden spoon. Pour the mixture into the prepared tin and bake in a preheated oven at 180°C/350°F/gas 4 for about 1½ hours, or until well-risen and just firm to the touch. Leave to cook in the tin for 15 minutes, then turn out to cool on a wire rack.

When the cake is cold, do not remove the lining paper, and wrap the gingerbread in clean greaseproof paper, then in foil or a polythene bag.

Store gingerbread for 4–7 days to give both the flavour and the texture time to mellow and improve before serving.

Parkin

MAKES: 25 × 20 cm/
10 × 8 in cake
PREPARATION: 20 minutes
OVEN: 180°C/350°F/gas 4
COOKING: 45 minutes

225 g/8 oz plain flour
pinch salt
10 ml/2 teaspoons baking powder
10 ml/2 teaspoons ground ginger
50 g/2 oz butter or margarine
50 g/2 oz lard
225 g/8 oz medium oatmeal
100 g/4 oz caster sugar
175 g/6 oz golden syrup
175 g/6 oz black treacle
60 ml/4 tablespoons milk

Line and grease a 25 × 20 × 3.5 cm/10 × 8 × 1½ in tin. Sift together the flour, salt, baking powder and ginger into a bowl. Cut the butter or margarine and lard into small pieces and rub into the flour until the mixture resembles fine breadcrumbs. Stir in the oatmeal and sugar. Warm the syrup and treacle, pour it into the centre of the dry ingredients, together with the milk, and beat lightly with a wooden spoon until thoroughly blended.

Turn the mixture into the prepared tin, and bake in a preheated oven at 180°C/350°F/gas 4 for about 45 minutes or until the mixture has begun to shrink away from the sides of the tin. It often sinks slightly. Cool on a wire rack. Leave the lining paper in place, wrap the cake in clean paper and foil or a polythene bag and store for at least a week.

■ Serve the parkin cut into thick slices.

CAKE FILLINGS & TOPPINGS

Fillings and toppings contribute to the taste and texture of a cake as well as to its appearance. There are many types of fillings and coatings, from simple whipped cream to classic royal icing. It is important to match any filling, coating, topping and decoration to the cake. A heavy icing on a light cake gives a poor result; a clash of flavour, sweetness or texture in the choice of filling or topping can ruin a perfectly good plain cake.

Dairy Cream
Whipped double cream or whipping cream may be used plain or lightly sweetened with icing sugar to fill whisked sponges or creamed cakes. Keep chilled and eat within 2 days.

Confectioner's Custard or Crème Pâtissière
A soft cream based on a sweet milk sauce or custard, enriched with eggs and whipped cream. Use on light whisked sponge cakes. Keep chilled and eat within 2 days.

Butter Cream
Icing sugar, or sometimes a mixture of caster and icing sugar, is beaten with butter until soft, smooth and pale. Various flavours may be added and the butter cream may be coloured. Butter cream may be used as a filling or topping; it can be piped or swirled. This is a rich, very sweet filling. Used for Victoria sandwich cakes, Madeira mixes and small cakes. Butter cream keeps well for up to a week in a cool place or it may be frozen.

Crème au Beurre
A rich butter cream made by gradually creaming butter into a mixture of egg yolks and sugar (see Buying and Using Eggs on page 336 for notes on dishes containing raw eggs). Crème au beurre is soft and lighter in texture than butter cream even though it has a richer taste. Used as for butter cream, also on light whisked sponges. Crème au beurre must be chilled and eaten within 2 days. It does not freeze.

Soft Cheese Fillings
Cream, curd, quark, low-fat soft and mascarpone cheeses may all be beaten with icing sugar and flavouring, such as grated lemon rind, to make luscious fillings and toppings for sponge cakes and Madeira-type cakes. Chill and eat within 2–3 days.

Cooked Fudge Frosting
This needs careful attention, as the soft fudge sets quickly and makes spreading difficult. It is used as a topping rather than a filling. A sugar mixture is cooked to a given temperature, cooled, then beaten until creamy. If the frosting sets too quickly, the bowl can be placed over hot water and a teaspoon or two of warm water or milk beaten in. Used on creamed cakes rather than light sponge cakes. Fudge frosting should be kept in a cool place and eaten within 2–3 days.

Fluffy Cooked Frosting
For this type of frosting, sugar, egg whites, water and flavourings are beaten over boiling water until the mixture stands in stiff peaks. A similar frosting can be made by cooking a syrup from sugar and water, then beating it slowly into whisked egg whites. Both types of frosting must be used immediately they are made and allowed to cool before serving, then eaten within 2 days. Used on creamed cakes or light whisked sponges. Keep in the refrigerator.

Glacé Icing
The simplest of icings, this is icing sugar mixed with liquid (water or fruit juice) to a coating consistency. The icing is poured over the cake and left to find its own level. Used on creamed and whisked cakes, both large and small, glacé icing keeps well but cracks once cut.

Fondant Icing
A boiled icing made by kneading a sugar syrup, then melting it again before pouring it over a cake. A difficult icing to make. Traditionally used to coat fancies and petits fours or light sponge cakes. Fondant icing gives a glossy finish and it keeps well.

Royal Icing
Made from egg whites or dried albumen powder and icing sugar, this is a crisp icing which is used for rich fruit cakes. It is applied over a coating of marzipan and keeps for several months in a cool, dry place.

Sugarpaste or Roll-out Icing
There are various types of soft icings which are best bought rather than made at home. The quality of these bought icings varies: specialist cake decorating suppliers offer a wide range of high quality coatings in a variety of colours.

Marzipan or Almond Paste
Excellent quality commercial paste is readily available. This is used as a base for applying fondant, sugarpaste or royal icing; it can also be used as a coating in its own right.

Apricot Glaze
A glaze of sieved apricot jam. Use to coat fruit toppings on gâteaux, as a base coat before applying glacé icing or to attach marzipan to rich fruit cakes.

BASIC TECHNIQUES
Apart from complicated methods that are necessary for serious cake decorating, there are a few classic techniques which are used when decorating everyday cakes and gâteaux for desserts.

Preparing the Cake
Allow the cake to cool completely before decorating it. A warm cake will make most coatings run. Before the crust is cold and set, thin icings may sink into the cake. Brush off any loose crumbs which tend to get into the coating and spoil the appearance of the cake.

If a cake has to be sliced into layers, place it on a flat surface and use a large serrated knife. Do not work from one side across to the other as it is difficult to cut evenly thick layers; cut all around the cake first, making sure the layers are even and cutting only partway towards the centre of the cake. When there is a complete cut around the outside of the cake, slice evenly through the centre of the cake.

For a good finish on a special cake, apply a thin coat of boiling-hot apricot glaze before covering with glacé icing. Leave the glaze to cool and it provides a smooth base for the icing.

Coating a Gâteau Side
Fill and stack the layers. Use a palette knife or round-bladed knife to spread the cream evenly around the cake in a thin layer. If the cake and filling is sufficiently firm, sprinkle the chosen topping (chopped nuts, biscuit crumbs, grated chocolate or chocolate vermicelli) over a sheet of greaseproof paper and roll the cake side over the topping. Hold the cake firmly between the palms of your hands when doing this.

For a gâteau with a soft filling, such as fruit, place the cake on a board or sheet of greaseproof paper and use a plastic spatula or large palette knife to press the topping on to the cream-coated side.

Coating a Gâteau Top with Cream

Drop spoonfuls of the cream on the middle of the cake, then use a palette knife to cover the top of the cake by a combination of pressing the cream down and spreading it across. When using whipped cream, take care not to overwork it as it will separate and look curdled. It is better to leave the top looking very 'rough' than to continue trying to swirl the cream once it begins to thicken.

Decorate a cream topping simply: draw it into large swirls with a palette knife or smooth the knife across the top in even lines. Do this once – or twice at the most when using butter cream – then leave well alone.

Finish the edge by piping stars or swirls to neaten the cream topping. Use a large star nozzle (the same as for piping mashed potato) when piping whipped cream; use a small star nozzle for butter cream.

Coating with Glacé Icing or Fondant

The cake must be smooth and free of loose crumbs. Glaze with apricot glaze and allow to cool if liked. To coat a cake completely, place it on a rack over a sheet of foil or paper. Icing can be scraped off foil – this is important if you want to re-use fondant.

Remember that the icing will run down the cake, so a cake which has a severely domed top may end up with a sparse coating on the top. A gently curved cake is best, allowing the icing to coat the sides evenly but retaining a good covering on top.

Feather icing

1 *Coat the cake with glacé icing. Immediately pipe lines of contrasting coloured icing across the cake.*

2 *Drag the coloured icing at regular intervals by drawing a pointed knife across the cake in straight lines.*

3 *Turn the cake and drag the knife across between the previous rows of feathering but in the opposite direction.*

Pour the icing on to the cake, then work quickly before it sets. Tease the icing down the side using the point of a knife or a skewer to give an even coating.

To coat just the top of the cake, simply pour a puddle of icing on the middle and quickly spread it with a palette knife, easing it towards the edge but not right up to the rim of the cake as it might flow over and down the side. The top of the cake must not be domed if the

icing is to stay on top in an even layer. One way of preventing the icing from flowing over the edge is to pipe a neat border of butter cream around the cake before pouring on the icing.

Coffee Essence

This is very strong coffee. Dissolve 15 ml/1 tablespoon instant coffee in 30 ml/2 tablespoons boiling water and allow the mixture to cool.

Natural Vanilla Essence

Natural vanilla essence should always be used, as its flavour is greatly superior to synthetic flavouring which is highly concentrated and traditionally used by the drop.

Confectioner's Custard

Also known as crème pâtissière or pastry cream, this mixture is primarily used as a filling for pastry flans and tarts, instead of whipped cream. It can be used to fill and decorate gâteaux. The custard must be well chilled if it is to be piped. This amount is sufficient to fill and decorate a 20–23 cm/8–9 in gâteau.

PREPARATION: 10 minutes

600 ml/1 pt milk
100 g/4 oz caster sugar
50 g/2 oz plain flour
15 ml/1 tablespoon cornflour
2 large eggs
50 g/2 oz unsalted butter

Heat the milk in a pan over low heat. In a bowl blend together the sugar, flour, cornflour and beaten eggs; gradually stir in the warm milk. Return the mixture

to the pan over low heat and stir continuously until it thickens and just comes to the boil. Remove from the heat and stir in the butter. Cool the custard in the pan, covered closely with dampened greaseproof paper to prevent skin forming. Chill and beat well before using.

Crème au Beurre

This is a rich, French butter cream. This amount is sufficient to fill and cover the top of an 18 cm/7 in cake.

PREPARATION: 20 minutes

75 g/3 oz caster sugar
60 ml/4 tablespoons water
2 egg yolks
100 g/4 oz unsalted butter

Put the sugar and water in a heavy-based pan and dissolve over low heat without boiling. When dissolved, bring the syrup to the boil and boil steadily for 2–3 minutes until 107°C/225°F is reached.

Beat the egg yolks in a deep bowl and pour in the syrup in a thin steady stream, whisking all the time until pale and light. Continue to whisk until the mixture is cool (the bowl may be stood in iced water).

Cream the butter until very soft. Gradually beat the egg mixture into the butter, a little at a time.

Flavouring Crème au Beurre

To vary the flavour, add 50 g/2 oz plain chocolate, melted and cool but still liquid; 15–30 ml/1–2 tablespoons coffee essence; or grated orange or lemon rind.

Butter Cream

This recipe uses the classic proportions of twice the weight of icing sugar to butter. For a slightly less sweet result, use 175 g/6 oz icing sugar instead of 225 g/8 oz. This amount will be enough to coat the sides and top of an 18 cm/7 in cake.

PREPARATION: 10 minutes

100 g/4 oz unsalted butter
225 g/8 oz icing sugar
2.5 ml/½ teaspoon natural vanilla essence (optional)
15–30 ml/1–2 tablespoons milk

Beat the softened butter with half the sifted icing sugar until thoroughly combined. Gradually beat in the remaining sugar and the vanilla essence. The butter cream should be pale and soft, with a spreading consistency slightly firmer than whipped cream. Beat in the milk to soften the butter cream.

Flavouring Butter Cream
Almond Add 30 ml/2 tablespoons finely chopped, toasted almonds. Substitute a few drops of almond essence for vanilla essence.
Chocolate Add 25–40 g/1–1½ oz melted chocolate and omit 15 ml/1 tablespoon milk; alternatively, blend 15 ml/1 tablespoon cocoa with 15 ml/1 tablespoon hot water, cool and add, omitting the milk.
Coffee Omit vanilla essence and milk; flavour with 10 ml/2 teaspoons instant coffee blended with 5 ml/1 teaspoon water.
Ginger Omit vanilla essence; add 50 g/2 oz finely chopped stem ginger.

Liqueur Omit milk and vanilla essence; add 10–15 ml/2–3 teaspoons liqueur.

Mocca Omit vanilla essence, mix 10 ml/2 teaspoons cocoa with 10 ml/2 teaspoons instant coffee powder to a smooth paste with freshly boiled water, cool before adding and omit milk.

Orange Omit vanilla essence and milk; beat in 30 ml/2 tablespoons fresh orange juice, the finely grated rind of 1 small orange and, if liked, 5 ml/1 teaspoon orange bitters.

Quick American Frosting

This amount of icing is sufficient to coat the top and side of a 20 cm/8 in cake.

PREPARATION: 10 minutes

1 egg white
175 g/6 oz caster sugar
pinch salt
30 ml/2 tablespoons water
pinch cream of tartar

Put all the ingredients in a deep bowl and using a rotary or electric mixer, whisk for a few minutes. Place the bowl over a pan of hot water and continue to whisk until the mixture is thick enough to stand in 'peaks', after about 7 minutes. Use at once.

Chocolate Fudge Frosting

This is sufficient to coat the top and side of a 20 cm/8 in cake.

PREPARATION: 30 minutes

450 g/1 lb caster sugar
300 ml/½ pt water
30 ml/2 tablespoons golden syrup
50 g/2 oz unsalted butter
50 g/2 oz cocoa

Place all the ingredients in a saucepan and heat, without boiling, until the sugar has dissolved. Bring to the boil and continue boiling until the sugar thermometer registers 114°C/238°F.

To prevent sticking, draw a wooden spoon across the base of the pan, but do not beat. Remove the pan from the heat and leave the mixture until cool, then beat until thick. Use at once.

Honey Butter Frosting

This amount of frosting is sufficient to lightly fill and top an 18 cm/7 in cake.

PREPARATION: 15 minutes

75 g/3 oz unsalted butter
175 g/6 oz icing sugar
15 ml/1 tablespoon clear honey
15 ml/1 tablespoon lemon juice

Beat the butter, which should be at room temperature, until soft but not oily. Gradually sift in the icing sugar, beating well. Halfway through, beat in the honey and lemon juice.

Glacé Icing

This amount is sufficient to coat about 20 small cakes or the top of a 20 cm/8 in cake.

PREPARATION: 10 minutes

225 g/8 oz icing sugar
30–45 ml/2–3 tablespoons
  warm water

Sift the icing sugar into a deep bowl. Stir in the water, a little at a time, beating well once the icing sugar has dissolved and before adding the final 15 ml/

1 tablespoon. Check the consistency and gradually beat in the remaining water until the icing is as thin as required for the cake.

Flavoured Glacé Icing

The basic glacé icing may be flavoured with, for example, 15 ml/1 tablespoon of lemon juice to replace 15 ml/1 tablespoon water, 5–7.5 ml/1–1½ teaspoons coffee essence as part of the amount of water. Strained orange juice may replace all the water and a few drops of orange colouring may also be added. Alternatively, blend 10 ml/2 teaspoons of cocoa with 15 ml/1 tablespoon boiling water, or replace 15 ml/1 tablespoon water with 15 ml/1 tablespoon liqueur.

Caramel Icing

PREPARATION: 20 minutes

350 g/12 oz icing sugar
100 ml/3½ fl oz milk
75 g/3 oz unsalted butter
30 ml/2 tablespoons caster sugar

Sift the icing sugar and set it aside. Warm the milk and butter in a small saucepan. In a medium saucepan, heat the caster sugar over a medium heat until it turns to a golden caramel. Take care as the sugar will burn quickly if not watched. Immediately remove both pans from the heat, pour the milk mixture over the caramel. Hold the pans at arm's length as the caramel spits violently when the milk is added. Return the mixture to low heat. Continue heating until the caramel has dissolved, stirring occasionally. Remove the pan

from the heat. Gradually stir in the sifted icing sugar, beating until the icing is smooth and of a spreading consistency. Use fairly quickly.

Fondant Icing

This traditional pouring icing is difficult to make if you are unfamiliar with sugar work. However, once a batch is made, the firm crystallised icing can be stored in an airtight container for weeks. It is, in fact, possible to buy fondant icing mix from specialist cake decorating suppliers and shops.

This amount is sufficient to coat about 24 petits fours or an 18–20 cm/7–8 in cake.

PREPARATION: 30 minutes

150 ml/¼ pt water
450 g/1 lb caster sugar or
  lump sugar
pinch cream of tartar or
  25 g/1 oz glucose

Put the water in a large heavy-based pan, add the lump sugar and dissolve to a syrup, without boiling, over low heat. Using a brush dipped in cold water, wipe round the pan at the level of the syrup to prevent crystals from forming. Add the cream of tartar or glucose dissolved in a little water. Bring the syrup to the boil and continue boiling steadily until the syrup registers 115°C/240°F (read the thermometer at eye level). Pour the syrup very slowly into a heat-resistant bowl; leave until a skin forms on top.

Using a wooden spatula work the icing in a figure-of-eight movement until it becomes

opaque and firm. Knead the icing until smooth and store in an airtight container until required.

Before using, heat the fondant icing in a bowl over hot water, adding a little sugar syrup until the icing has the consistency of double cream.

Royal Icing

You need a heavy-duty food mixer to make royal icing in this quantity. Mixing by hand does not give the required light texture and volume.

For special cakes, bridal icing sugar may be purchased from cake decorating suppliers.

This amount is sufficient to coat a 23–25 cm/9–10 in cake with about three layers of icing.

PREPARATION: 15 minutes

800–900 g/1¾–2 lb icing sugar
4 egg whites
15 ml/1 tablespoon lemon juice
10 ml/2 teaspoons glycerine

Sift the icing sugar twice. Whisk the egg whites in a large food mixer, using the beater attachment, not the whisk. The whites should be only very lightly frothy on the surface. Add the icing sugar in small batches, beating in each addition thoroughly. Add the lemon juice and glycerine and beat well. The icing should stand in soft peaks which fall over slightly at the top.

Place the icing in an airtight container and leave for 24 hours. Beat by hand before using. Kept in an airtight container in a cool place (not the refrigerator), royal icing will remain workable for up to a week.

Uncooked Marzipan

This quantity makes enough paste to cover the top and side of an 18 cm/7 in cake.

PREPARATION: 10 minutes

100 g/4 oz icing sugar
100 g/4 oz caster sugar
225 g/8 oz ground almonds
5 ml/1 teaspoon lemon juice
almond essence
1 egg

Sift the icing sugar into a bowl and mix in the caster sugar and ground almonds. Add the lemon juice and a few drops of almond essence. Gradually stir in the beaten egg until the mixture forms a firm but manageable dough. Knead the dough lightly, and roll out as required.

Apricot Glaze

PREPARATION: 15 minutes

450 g/1 lb apricot jam
15 ml/1 tablespoon lemon juice
60 ml/4 tablespoons water

Bring all the ingredients slowly to the boil, stirring until the jam melts. Rub the mixture through a sieve, return it to the pan and boil for 2 minutes. Cool the apricot glaze before storing it in a screw-top jar. Use as required to glaze fruit tarts or to hold marzipan on cakes.

BISCUITS

The word 'biscuit' comes from the French bis cuit, *'twice cooked', which is a literal description of what happened in the early days of biscuit-making. At the start of a long sea voyage, small, hard cakes were taken aboard, to form part of the crew's daily diet. These cakes had to be cooked before loading, otherwise they would have gone mouldy, and before eating their 'hard tack', the sailors would have the cakes cooked again.*

Biscuits today are only 'once cooked', and although usually at their best when freshly baked, some can be stored in airtight containers for about 1 week. Cool freshly baked biscuits on a wire rack, lifting them from the baking trays as soon as cooked. Some biscuits, however, especially those made with syrup or honey, are soft when baking is complete – leave these biscuits on the trays to settle for a few minutes.

Generally, biscuits fall into one of half a dozen main groups: bar types, drop biscuits, shaped biscuits, piped doughs, refrigerator biscuits and rolled biscuits.

DROP BISCUITS

Baked drop biscuits can be soft with a cake-like texture, or crisp and even brittle. The soft dough is dropped in mounds on to a baking tray.

Brandy Snaps

MAKES: 16
PREPARATION: 20 minutes
OVEN: 180°C/350°F/gas 4
COOKING: 20–30 minutes

50 g/2 oz butter
50 g/2 oz caster sugar
30 ml/2 tablespoons golden syrup
50 g/2 oz plain flour
2.5 ml/½ teaspoon ground ginger
5 ml/1 teaspoon brandy
finely grated rind of ½ lemon

Filling
175 ml/6 fl oz double cream
15 ml/1 tablespoon milk

Grease two baking trays and grease the handles of a few wooden spoons thoroughly. Melt the butter, with the sugar and syrup, over low heat. Stir until smooth, then remove.

Sift the flour and ginger, and stir it into the melted ingredients, together with the brandy and lemon rind. Mix thoroughly with a wooden spoon, and cool for 1–2 minutes.

Drop the mixture in teaspoonfuls at 10 cm/4 in intervals, on to the baking trays. Bake in a preheated oven at 180°C/350°F/gas 4 for 7–10 minutes or until the biscuits are bubbly, lacy and golden. Rotate the baking so that not too many will be ready for rolling at the same time.

Remove the biscuits from the oven and allow them to stand for a few seconds, until the mixture is firm enough to cling together when lifted. Quickly roll each snap loosely around a greased spoon handle. Leave the snaps on the handles until set, then twist them off gently and cool on a wire rack. If the biscuits set before they have all been shaped into snaps, return them to the oven for few seconds until soft and pliable again.

Finishing brandy snaps

1 *Roll the snaps around spoon handles as soon as the mixture has set enough not to fall apart when lifted.*

2 *Remove the brandy snaps from the spoons when set.*

3 *Pipe cream into the brandy snaps when they have cooled completely. Do not fill with cream more than 1 hour before serving.*

Just before serving, whip together the cream and milk until light and fluffy. Pipe or spoon the cream into both ends of each snap. Unfilled brandy snaps will keep in an airtight container for up to 1 week.

SHAPED BISCUITS

The dough for shaped biscuits is fairly soft and needs quick and light handling. Alternatively, it can be chilled and moulded in the palms of the hands.

Jumbles

MAKES: 14
PREPARATION: 30 minutes
OVEN: 200°C/400°F/gas 6
COOKING: 12–15 minutes

65 g/2½ oz butter
65 g/2½ oz caster sugar
1 small egg
150 g/5 oz self-raising flour
5 ml/1 teaspoon finely grated lemon rind
25 g/1 oz ground almonds

Grease two baking trays. Beat the butter until soft, then add the sugar and cream until light and fluffy. Beat the egg, then add 30 ml/2 tablespoons of it to the creamed mixture with the sifted flour, lemon rind and ground almonds. Form the mixture into three rolls, 1 cm/½ in wide; cut these into 10 cm/4 in long pieces and form them into 'S' shapes.

Place on the baking trays, and brush with the remaining beaten egg. Bake in a preheated oven at 200°C/400°F/gas 6 for about 12 minutes, or until risen and pale brown. Cool for a few minutes, then transfer to a wire rack.

Coconut Wafers

MAKES: 18
PREPARATION: 20 minutes
OVEN: 180°C/350°F/gas 4
COOKING: 12 minutes

50 g/2 oz butter
50 g/2 oz caster sugar
15 ml/1 tablespoon golden syrup
10 ml/2 teaspoons lemon juice
50 g/2 oz plain flour
25 g/1 oz fine desiccated coconut

Grease two or three baking trays. Cream the butter and sugar until light and fluffy, then beat in the syrup. Add the lemon juice, sifted flour and the coconut. Drop the dough in teaspoonfuls on to the baking trays, setting them well apart as the wafers spread during cooking.

Bake in a preheated oven at 180°C/350°F/gas 4 for about 12 minutes, when the edges of the wafers should be golden brown and the centres lightly coloured. Cool the wafers slightly on the baking trays before lifting carefully on a palette knife from the trays to a wire rack.

Ginger Nuts

MAKES: 24
PREPARATION: 15 minutes
OVEN: 190°C/375°F/gas 5
COOKING: 15 minutes

100 g/4 oz self-raising flour
2.5 ml/½ teaspoon bicarbonate
of soda
5 ml/1 teaspoon ground ginger
2.5 ml/½ teaspoon ground
cinnamon
10 ml/2 teaspoons caster sugar
50 g/2 oz butter
75 g/3 oz golden syrup

Grease two or three baking trays. Sift the flour, bicarbonate of soda, ginger and cinnamon into a bowl; add the sugar. In a small pan, melt the butter, without boiling, and stir in the syrup. Mix this into the dry ingredients, using a wooden spoon. Shape the dough between the hands into a thick sausage shape before cutting it into 24 even pieces. Roll each piece into a small ball, set them well apart on the baking trays and flatten slightly.

Bake in a preheated oven at 190°C/375°F/gas 5 for about 15–20 minutes, or until the tops have cracked and are golden brown. Cool for a few minutes on the baking tray before lifting on to a wire rack. As soon as quite cold, store in an airtight tin, as they go soft quickly.

Orange Creams

MAKES: 18
PREPARATION: 30 minutes
OVEN: 190°C/375°F/gas 5
COOKING: 20 minutes

100 g/4 oz butter
100 g/4 oz caster sugar
10 ml/2 teaspoons golden syrup
1 egg yolk
finely grated rind of 1 orange
200 g/7 oz plain flour
2.5 ml/½ teaspoon cream of tartar
5 ml/1 teaspoon baking powder
Filling
50 g/2 oz butter
75 g/3 oz icing sugar
orange juice
orange food colouring

Grease two or three baking trays. Cream the butter and sugar, using a wooden spoon, until light and fluffy. Beat in the syrup, egg yolk and orange rind. Sift the flour, cream of tartar and baking powder over the creamed ingredients and fold in with a metal spoon to give a soft dough.

Shape the dough into 36 balls about the size of large marbles and set them well apart on the baking trays. Bake in a preheated oven at 190°C/375°F/gas 5 for about 20 minutes, or until the biscuits are lightly coloured and risen. Cool on a wire rack.

For the filling, beat the butter until soft, then gradually beat in the sifted icing sugar with as much orange juice as the filling will take without becoming too soft. Colour it pale orange.

Spread the filling over half the biscuits, and then sandwich them together.

PIPED DOUGHS

The dough for piping is fairly soft and should be piped through a star-shaped vegetable nozzle.

Lemon Meltaways

MAKES: about 20
PREPARATION: 30 minutes
OVEN: 160°C/325°F/gas 3
COOKING: 30 minutes

100 g/4 oz butter or margarine
25 g/1 oz icing sugar
finely grated rind of ½ lemon
100 g/4 oz plain flour
sieved apricot jam
Glaze
30 ml/2 tablespoons icing sugar
about 10 ml/2 teaspoons
lemon juice

Grease two baking trays. In a deep bowl, beat the butter or margarine with a wooden spoon until creamy, add the sifted icing sugar and cream until the mixture is pale and fluffy. Stir in the lemon rind and flour to give a soft dough. Spoon the mixture into a piping bag, fitted with a medium star vegetable nozzle, and pipe out about 20 shell shapes, a little apart from each other. Chill for 30 minutes.

Bake in a preheated oven at 160°C/325°F/gas 3 for about 25 minutes or until lightly browned. For the glaze, blend the sifted icing sugar with enough lemon juice so that the mixture gives a coating consistency.

Leave the baked biscuits on the baking trays, brush them with soft sieved jam and then with the lemon glaze. Return the biscuits to the oven for a further 5 minutes, then set them on a wire rack to cool and crisp.

Short Fingers

MAKES: 12
PREPARATION: 45 minutes
OVEN: 190°C/375°F/gas 5
COOKING: 10–15 minutes

115 g/4½ oz butter
25 g/1 oz icing sugar
150 g/5 oz plain flour
75 g/3 oz plain cooking chocolate
Butter cream
25 g/1 oz butter
50 g/2 oz icing sugar
1.25 ml/¼ teaspoon natural
vanilla essence

Grease two baking trays. Beat the butter with a wooden spoon until soft, but not oily, then cream in the sifted icing sugar. Stir in the sifted flour. Put the mixture in a piping bag, fitted with a medium star vegetable nozzle. Pipe the biscuit mixture in 5 cm/2 in fingers on to the baking trays. Bake in a preheated oven at 190°C/375°F/gas 5 for 10–15 minutes or until pale golden brown.

Break the chocolate into small pieces and place them in a bowl over hot water until melted. To make the butter cream, cream the butter until soft, then beat in the sifted icing sugar and the natural vanilla essence.

Short fingers

Piping out 5 cm/2 in fingers.

Sandwiching the cooled biscuits together with butter cream.

Coating the tips of the biscuits in chocolate.

Leave the baked biscuits to cool completely on a wire rack. When cold, sandwich them in pairs with the butter cream. Dip one end of each biscuit in the melted chocolate and place them on a rack with the chocolate end protruding over the edge. When the chocolate has set, repeat the procedure with the other ends. Leave the biscuits for about 1½ hours before serving.

Macaroons

MAKES: 24
PREPARATION: 10 minutes
OVEN: 190°C/375°F/gas 5
COOKING: 15 minutes

rice paper
100 g/4 oz ground almonds
175 g/6 oz caster sugar
2 egg whites
15 ml/1 tablespoon cornflour
few drops of almond essence
10 ml/2 teaspoons water
12 blanched almonds

Line two or three baking trays with rice paper. Mix the ground almonds with the sugar. Lightly break up the egg whites with a fork and set aside 15 ml/1 tablespoon. Using a wooden spoon, work the whites into the mixture until the ingredients are evenly blended. Stir in the cornflour, almond essence and water.

Spoon the mixture into a piping bag fitted with a 1 cm/½ in plain nozzle. Pipe the biscuits on to the rice paper in large round buttons; top each with half an almond. Brush lightly with the remaining egg white.

Bake the macaroons in a preheated oven at 190°C/375°F/

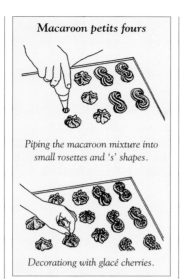

Macaroon petits fours

Piping the macaroon mixture into small rosettes and 's' shapes.

Decorationg with glacé cherries.

gas 5 for about 15 minutes or until lightly browned, risen and slightly cracked. Cut the rice paper to fit round each macaroon and leave to cool on a wire rack.

Macaroon Petits Fours

The macaroon mixture can be used to make petits fours. The above quantities will make about 30 petits fours, depending on their size and shape.

Spoon the mixture into a piping bag fitted with a large star nozzle and pipe it on to the baking trays in small rosettes and 'S' shapes. Decorate the petits fours with glacé cherries or strips of angelica.

ROLLED BISCUITS

The dough must be stiff enough to be rolled to a thickness of 3–5 mm/⅛–¼ in before cutting out a variety of shapes. Dough that is difficult to handle is best rolled between sheets of non-stick baking parchment.

Butter Shorts

MAKES: 16
PREPARATION: 20 minutes
OVEN: 150°C/300°F/gas 2
COOKING: 25 minutes

100 g/4 oz butter
50 g/2 oz caster sugar
175 g/6 oz plain flour
caster sugar for dredging

Grease two baking trays. Beat the butter with a wooden spoon until it is soft, but not oily, add the caster sugar and cream until the mixture is pale and fluffy. Work in the sifted plain flour and knead lightly together with the fingertips to form a ball. Roll the dough out to 3mm/⅛ in thick, on a lightly floured surface or between sheets of non-stick baking parchment.

Using a 6–6.5 cm/2½–2¾ in fluted pastry cutter, stamp out rounds and lift them on to the baking trays with a small palette knife. Prick each biscuit with a fork twice, and bake in a preheated oven at 150°C/300°F/gas 2 for about 25 minutes or until faintly tinged with brown. Cool on a wire rack and serve the biscuits dredged with caster sugar. Butter shorts will keep in an airtight container in a cool place (but not the refrigerator) for about 10 days.

Easter Biscuits

MAKES: 24
PREPARATION: 25 minutes
OVEN: 180°C/350°F/gas 4
COOKING: 15–20 minutes

100 g/4 oz butter or block margarine
150 g/5 oz caster sugar
1 egg
1 egg yolk
50 g/2 oz currants
175 g/6 oz plain flour
50 g/2 oz rice flour
5 ml/1 teaspoon mixed spice
15–30 ml/1–2 tablespoons milk

Line two or three baking trays with non-stick baking parchment or greased greaseproof paper. Beat the butter or margarine with a wooden spoon until soft, add 100 g/4 oz of the sugar and cream thoroughly until pale and fluffy. Separate the egg and beat in the two egg yolks, and then stir in the currants. Sift the flours, together with the spice, into the creamed ingredients, a little at a time. Stir to combine, adding a little milk if necessary to bind the mixture to make a soft but manageable dough.

Knead the dough lightly on a floured board, then roll it out 3–5 mm/⅛–¼ in thick. Cut into rounds with a 6 cm/2½ in fluted cutter, and set the biscuits on the baking trays. Mark lines, about 5 mm/¼ in apart, with the back of a knife. Bake in a preheated oven at 180°C/350°F/gas 4 for 15–20 minutes. After 10 minutes, brush the biscuits with the egg white and dredge with the remaining sugar. Cool slightly, then lift on to a wire rack.

BAR-TYPE BISCUITS

These have a cake-like texture, with the exception of shortbread, and are baked in one complete piece before being cut up.

Boston Brownies

MAKES: 16–20
PREPARATION: 15 minutes
OVEN: 180°C/350°F/gas 4
COOKING: 35 minutes

65 g/2½ oz butter or block margarine
50 g/2 oz cooking chocolate
175 g/6 oz caster sugar
65 g/2½ oz self-raising flour
pinch salt
2 eggs
2.5 ml/½ teaspoon natural vanilla essence
50 g/2 oz shelled walnuts

Grease and flour a shallow 20 cm/8 in square tin. Melt the butter or margarine and chocolate in a bowl over hot water, and add the sugar. Sift the flour and salt into a bowl, and stir in the chocolate mixture, beaten eggs, vanilla essence and chopped walnuts. Beat the mixture until smooth, then spoon into the prepared tin.

Bake in a preheated oven at 180°C/350°F/gas 4 for about 35 minutes or until the brownie mixture is risen and beginning to leave the sides of the tin. Leave in the tin to cool before cutting the brownies into 3.5–5cm/1½–2 in squares.

Shortbread

MAKES: 8
PREPARATION: 20 minutes
OVEN: 150°C/300°F/gas 2
COOKING: 1 hour

150 g/5 oz plain flour
pinch salt
25 g/1 oz rice flour or ground rice
50 g/2 oz caster sugar
100 g/4 oz butter

Sift the flour, salt and rice flour or ground rice into a bowl. Add the sugar and grate the butter, taken straight from the refrigerator, into the dry ingredients. Work the mixture with the fingertips until it resembles

Shortbread

Grating the butter into the flour and rice flour mixture.

Marking the mixture into portions before baking.

breadcrumbs. Press the mixture into an 18 cm/7 in straight-sided sandwich tin and level the top. Prick the top all over with a fork and mark the mixture into eight equal portions, cutting through to the base of the tin.

Chill the shortbread for 1 hour, then bake in a preheated oven at 150°C/300°F/gas 2 for about 1 hour or until pale-straw coloured. Leave in the tin to cool for 10 minutes before cooling on a wire rack. Break into wedges.

REFRIGERATOR BISCUITS

These are usually round and thin, with a crisp texture. The soft dough is shaped into a long roll, wrapped in waxed, non-stick paper or foil and chilled for at least 2 hours. The roll is then cut into thin slices and baked. As the dough will keep for about 1 week in the refrigerator, the biscuits can be sliced and baked as required.

Refrigerator Biscuits

MAKES: 48
CHILLING: 2 hours
PREPARATION: 20 minutes
OVEN: 190°C/375°F/gas 5
COOKING: 10 minutes

225 g/8 oz plain flour
5 ml/1 teaspoon baking powder
150 g/5 oz butter
175 g/6 oz caster sugar or light, soft brown sugar
5 ml/1 teaspoon natural vanilla essence
1 egg
50 g/2 oz plain chocolate
50 g/2 oz ground hazelnuts
caster sugar for dusting

Sift together the flour and baking powder. Beat the butter with a wooden spoon until soft, add the sugar and cream until light and fluffy. Beat in the vanilla essence and the beaten egg. Add the flour, and grate the chocolate finely into the mixture; lastly add the nuts. Stir just enough to combine the ingredients. Share the dough, on a lightly floured surface, into a sausage about 5 cm/2 in wide. Wrap in foil or paper, secure the ends and chill.

To bake the biscuits, slice off as many thin rounds as required from the roll. Set them, well spaced out, on a greased baking tray. Sprinkle with sugar and bake in a preheated oven at 190°C/375°F/gas 5 for about 10 minutes. Cool on a wire rack.

Flavourings for Refrigerator Biscuits

Plain Omit the chocolate and ground hazelnuts; increase the natural vanilla essence to 10 ml/ 2 teaspoons.
Orange Omit the chocolate; the hazelnuts may be added if liked. Add the grated rind of 1 large orange with the nuts. When cold, the biscuits may be coated with Glacé Icing (page 390) flavoured with the grated rind of ½ orange.
Almond Substitute a few drops of almond essence for the vanilla essence. Omit the chocolate and use ground almonds instead of the hazelnuts.

BAKING WITH YEAST

Bread is composed of such basic ingredients as flour, yeast, salt and liquid; enriched dough mixtures for buns and tea breads also include butter, spices, dried fruits and/or nuts. Strong flour is essential for well-made loaves.

INGREDIENTS FOR YEAST DOUGHS

Flour
Strong flour has a high gluten content. It is this protein substance which makes bread dough become elastic when kneaded. The tough, stretchy nature of the dough ensures that the bubbles of gas produced by the fermenting yeast are trapped. The trapped gas makes the dough rise before baking and again when heated as the gas expands. This gives bread or other yeast mixtures their characteristic texture.

Wholemeal flour contains 100 per cent wheat, and wheatmeal flour has 80–90 per cent wheat including all the germ and some bran. Both these types of flour give the characteristic mealy taste to bread.

Fresh Yeast
Fresh yeast should have a creamy-beige colour, and a firm consistency which crumbles easily when broken up. It can be stored in a loosely tied polythene bag in the coldest part of a refrigerator for up to a month, or in a freezer for up to a year.

Fresh yeast is not usually mixed directly with the flour as it is first blended with liquid or added as a batter. Lukewarm liquid should be used with fresh yeast; if the liquid is too cold the yeast will not work; too hot and it will be killed.

Blending with liquid Blend the yeast with part of the measured lukewarm liquid. Stir in about 2.5 ml/½ tsp sugar and leave the mixture in a warm place until it is frothy, then add to the flour and salt, together with the rest of the liquid. Blending with liquid is the basic way and is suitable for all recipes.

Batter method Blend the yeast with some of the warm liquid, then gradually stir in the rest of the liquid. Mix one-third of the measured flour with this liquid and add 5 ml/1 teaspoon sugar. Leave the mixture in a warm place until it is bubbly, which takes about 20 minutes, then add the rest of the flour, salt and any other ingredients. The batter method is best used when making rich yeast doughs.

Easy-blend Dried Yeast
This is probably the most popular and most readily available form of bakers' yeast. It comes in the form of very fine granules that are mixed with the flour or other dry ingredients before any liquid is added.

The liquid used with easy-blend dried yeast should be hand-hot (not lukewarm) for the majority of recipes, that is doughs and stiff batters.

If using fast-action easy-blend dried yeast, once it is incorporated, only one rising stage is necessary. There is no need to knock back the dough, it can be shaped after the first kneading. Check the packet instructions as some easy-blend yeasts are not fast-action, and they need two rising stages.

Dried Yeast
Dried and easy-blend dried yeasts are more concentrated than fresh yeast: 15 g/½ oz or 20 ml/4 teaspoons of dried or easy-blend dried yeast is the equivalent of 25 g/1 oz of fresh yeast.

Ordinary dried yeast, in the form of granules, should be sprinkled over lukewarm water with a little sugar added and allowed to stand in a warm place for about 15 minutes. It is usually best to avoid stirring the yeast until after standing: this allows the granules to rehydrate separately. Sometimes, stirring the yeast into the water makes it clump together and it takes longer to dissolve.

Salt
Salt improves the flavour of bread and it also helps to prevent gluten from breaking down, thereby assisting in the making of a strong, light dough. If there is significantly too much salt, the yeast is inhibited, it will not work, and the bread will be heavy or uneven in texture. Always measure the salt.

Liquid
Water is the most common liquid used in standard bread recipes. Milk, eggs and wine are all added to different doughs. Milk and eggs enrich a dough.

Fat
A little fat is added to keep bread moist. Additional fat may be added to enriched yeast doughs for buns, croissants and tea breads which have a soft outer crust. Fat makes a dough soft and also slows down yeast action so that the dough rises less than plain bread dough.

Sugar
A little sugar provides 'food' for yeast and speeds up its action. However, in significant quantities, sugar slows down fermentation of the yeast, so sweet doughs require longer proving and they do not rise as high as savoury doughs.

STAGES IN MAKING BASIC YEAST DOUGH
There are distinct stages in making any yeast dough or batter. The following outline lists the key techniques in the order in which they are used.

Yeast Preparation
Prepare the yeast liquid or yeast batter if using fresh or ordinary dried yeast.

Flour and Dry Ingredients
Mix the flour and the salt in a bowl. **Add easy-blend dried yeast at this stage.** Make a well in the centre and add all the liquid at once, including the

1 *Pour the liquid into the flour, mixing with a spoon at first.*

2 *Knead until the dough is elastic – there are many styles of kneading, but the important thing is to stretch, fold and press the dough back into a ball.*

3 *When rising, dough needs a warm place and it must be covered to prevent the surface from crusting.*

Making bread dough

yeast liquid. Mix with a spoon at first, then use your hand to bring the dough together. Roll the dough around the inside of the bowl to pick up all the flour. The dough should feel very dry at this stage.

Kneading
Kneading is vital to develop the gluten and strengthen the dough. Smooth the dough into a ball, press down on the dough and

away from the body with the knuckles. Lift the front of the dough back over the middle and press down with the palm of the hand. Give the dough a quarter-turn and repeat the kneading. As you work, the process of pressing, stretching and folding the dough should be quite speedy, and the dough should be turning in an anti-clockwise direction most of the time.

Knead the dough for about 10 minutes until the dough feels firm, smooth and elastic and no longer sticks to the fingers or work surface – it is better to knead the dough too much rather than too little.

Rising or Proving with Fast-action Easy-blend Yeast
When using fast-action easy blend yeast, the dough only needs one set of kneading. Once it is smooth and elastic, set it into the required shape and place in its prepared tin. Cover loosely with oiled polythene (a slit bag is ideal) or a slightly dampened, warm tea-towel and leave in a warm place until doubled in volume. The dough is then ready for baking.

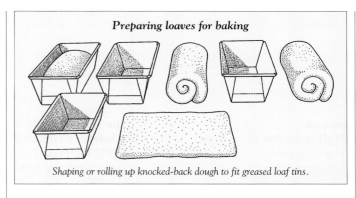

Preparing loaves for baking

Shaping or rolling up knocked-back dough to fit greased loaf tins.

First Rising or Proving
After kneading, dough made with fresh yeast or ordinary dried yeast must be set aside for rising twice. The dough must be covered – place in a bowl and cover with cling film or place it in a loosely closed and lightly oiled polythene bag. Leave the dough until it has doubled in size and springs back when lightly pressed with a finger.

The time depends on the temperature of the surroundings. Allow 12 hours in a cold room; about 2 hours in a normal (warm) room temperature or less if the dough is placed near a radiator or in a very warm place. Dough may be left to rise in a refrigerator for 24 hours.

Do not try to speed up the proving by placing the dough in too hot a place as this may kill the yeast. For example, too hot a grill or right on a radiator.

Knocking Back
After the initial rising the dough has to be lightly kneaded again, to knock out the air bubbles and to ensure a good rise and even texture. This is very brief: do not knead too much at this stage.

Second Rising or Proving

Shape the knocked-back dough as required and put it into tins or on to baking trays. Cover with oiled polythene bags and leave to rise until doubled in size.

Baking

Remove the tins or baking trays from the polythene bags and bake in a preheated oven at 200–230°C/400–450°F/gas 6–8, according to the individual recipes. A bowl of hot water placed in the bottom of the oven creates steam, which improves the bread's texture.

Checking That Bread is Cooked

Protect your hand with a folded tea-towel and turn the loaf out of the tin into your hand. Tap the base of the loaf: if the bread is cooked through, it will sound hollow; if the bread sounds heavy, dull and damp, return it to the oven and check again after a further 5 minutes' cooking.

Freezing Bread

Plain breads freeze well for up to a year. To prevent the bread drying out wrap it in cling film, then seal it in a freezer bag. There is no need to wrap the loaf in cling film if it is to be frozen for only a few weeks.

Sliced breads and rolls are useful freezer candidates as small quantities can be thawed as required. Unpack bread and thaw at room temperature for several hours or overnight. To thaw one roll or slice of bread in the microwave, allow 30–60 seconds on full power.

White Bread

MAKES: 4 loaves
PREPARATION: 25 minutes
 (plus rising)
OVEN: 230°C/450°F/gas 8
COOKING: 30–40 minutes

1.4 kg/3 lb strong plain flour
15 ml/1 teaspoon salt
25 g/1 oz lard
25 g/1 oz fresh yeast or 20 ml/
 4 teaspoons dried yeast or
 20 ml/4 teaspoons easy-blend
 dried yeast
900 ml/1½ pt water less 45 ml/
 3 tablespoons

Sift the strong plain flour and salt together into a large bowl and rub in the lard.

Prepare the yeast according to type: adding easy-blend directly to the flour, making a yeast liquid using 300 ml/½ pt of the measured liquid and the fresh yeast or ordinary dried yeast. Leave the yeast liquid until it becomes frothy.

Make a well in the centre of the flour and pour in the yeast liquid and the remaining water or all the water. Mix to a dough and knead until smooth and elastic. Cover and leave the dough to rise until it has doubled in size. If you are using fast-action easy blend yeast, shape the dough at this stage without rising first.

Knock back the risen dough. Divide the dough into quarters and shape each piece to fit a greased 450 g/1 lb loaf tin, rolling the dough neatly and placing the seam underneath. Score the top of the dough with a sharp knife.

Brush the top of the dough with lightly salted warm water. Place the tins in lightly oiled polythene bags and leave in a warm place to rise, until the dough reaches the top of the tins. Remove the polythene, brush the top of the dough with salted water again and set the tins on baking trays.

Bake the loaves in a preheated oven at 230°C/450°F/gas 8 for about 30 minutes, or until the loaves shrink slightly from the sides of the tins and the upper crust is a deep golden brown. For really crusty bread, turn the loaves out of the tins on to a baking tray and return them to the oven for a further 5–10 minutes. Leave the bread to cool on a wire rack.

SHAPING BREAD DOUGH

For a golden crust, fancy breads may be glazed with egg yolk. Use a fork to lightly whisk the yolk with a little salt and 15 ml/1 tablespoon water. Brush over the risen dough.

Cob Loaf

Divide the dough into quarters. Roll each piece of dough into a ball, flatten it and place on a floured baking tray.

Crown Loaf

Divide a quarter of the dough into five or six balls. Set these in a greased 13 cm/5 in round cake tin or a deep sandwich tin.

Fancy Loaf

Divide a quarter of the dough into four equal pieces; shape

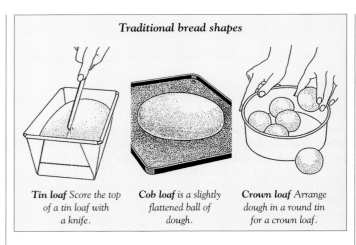

Traditional bread shapes

Tin loaf *Score the top of a tin loaf with a knife.*

Cob loaf *is a slightly flattened ball of dough.*

Crown loaf *Arrange dough in a round tin for a crown loaf.*

them into rolls the width of a greased 450 g/1 lb loaf tin and fit them, side by side, into the tin.

Rolls

Divide a quarter of the knocked-back dough into eight equal pieces. Roll each into a round on an unfloured surface, using the palm of one hand. Shake a little flour on to the palm of the hand, and press the dough down, hard at first, easing up until the rounds have the shape of a roll. Set the rolls well apart on floured baking trays, put them into oiled polythene bags and leave in a warm place until doubled.

Remove the polythene and bake the rolls in a preheated oven for 15–20 minutes. Cool on a wire rack.

For soft rolls, set the shaped rolls 1.5 cm/¾ in apart on the baking trays and sprinkle generously with flour. The rolls will bake into contact with each other along the sides and the flour will give a soft top.

FLAVOURINGS FOR SAVOURY BREADS

The wide variety of international breads on offer in specialist bakers, Italian delicatessens and, even, on supermarket shelves provides a source of inspiration for simple variations on white bread. The following ingredients may all be added to a quarter portion of the plain white bread dough. Shape the loaf into an oval cob, rather than into the shape of a conventional loaf.

Olive and Rosemary Bread

Knead 50 g/2 oz roughly chopped, stoned black olives and 5 ml/1 teaspoon finely chopped fresh rosemary into the dough before shaping the loaf. Before baking, brush a little olive oil over the risen bread and sprinkle with fennel seeds.

Sun-dried Tomato and Garlic Bread

Use sun-dried tomatoes packed in a jar of olive oil. Chop 12 tomatoes. Peel and finely chop 1 clove garlic. Knead the tomatoes and garlic into the dough before shaping the loaf. Brush with a little oil from the tomatoes before baking.

Spicy Lemon Bread
Knead 30 ml/2 tablespoons cumin seeds into the dough. When ready to shape the loaf, pat the dough out rather like a thick pizza base and sprinkle with 30 ml/2 tablespoons chopped fresh coriander leaves and the grated rind of 1 lemon. Roll up the dough and pat the ends together to shape it into an oval. Serve warm with spiced dishes.

Walnut and Parsley Bread
Mix 50 g/2 oz finely chopped walnuts and 45 ml/3 tablespoons chopped parsley with 30 ml/ 2 tablespoons olive oil. A finely chopped garlic clove may be added if liked. When the dough is ready for shaping, press it flat rather like a thick pizza base. Spread the walnut mixture over and roll up the dough. Pat the ends to shape an oval cob.

Floury Baps
MAKES: 4
PREPARATION: 15 minutes
  (plus rising)
OVEN: 200°C/400°F/gas 6
COOKING: 25 minutes

150 ml/¼ pt water
150 ml/¼ pt milk
450 g/1 lb strong plain flour
5 ml/1 teaspoon salt
50 g/2 oz lard
15 g/½ oz fresh yeast or 10 ml/
  2 teaspoons dried yeast, or
  10 ml/2 teaspoons easy-blend
  dried yeast

Mix the water and milk, heat both together until lukewarm if using fresh yeast or ordinary dried yeast, or until hand hot if using easy-blend dried yeast. Follow the method for White Bread to make the dough.

Divide the risen dough into four, shape into balls and roll out to flat rounds, 1–1.5 cm/ ½–¾ in thick. Set the rounds on a well-floured baking tray, dredge the tops with more flour and cover with polythene. Leave the dough to rise at room temperature until doubled in size, for about 45 minutes.

Press each bap lightly in the centre with the knuckles. Bake in a preheated oven at 200°C/ 400°F/gas 6 for 25 minutes. Cool on a wire rack.

Wholemeal Bread
MAKES: 4 loaves
PREPARATION: 20 minutes
  (plus rising)
OVEN: 230°C/450°F/gas 8
COOKING: 30–40 minutes

1.4 kg/3 lb strong plain
  wholemeal flour
15 ml/1 tablespoon caster sugar
15–20 ml/3–4 teaspoons salt
25 g/1 oz lard
50 g/2 oz fresh yeast or 40 ml/
  4 teaspoons dried yeast or
  40 ml/4 teaspoons easy-blend
  dried yeast
900 ml/1½ pt warm water

Sift the flour, sugar and salt into a large bowl. Rub in the lard.

Prepare the yeast according to type: adding easy-blend directly to the flour, making a yeast liquid using 300 ml/½ pt of the

measured liquid and the fresh yeast or ordinary dried yeast. Leave the yeast liquid until it becomes frothy.

Make a well in the centre of the flour and pour in the yeast liquid and the remaining water or all the water. Mix to a dough and knead until smooth and elastic. Cover and leave to rise until doubled in size. If using fast-action easy blend yeast, shape the dough at this stage without rising first. Follow the instructions for White Bread.

Half and Half Bread
Use half wholemeal and half white strong plain flours. Alternatively, use half brown instead of wholemeal flour. Follow the instructions given for White Bread.

Enriched White Bread
PREPARATION: 35 minutes
  (plus rising)
OVEN: 190°C/375°F/gas 5
COOKING: 30–45 minutes

450 g/1 lb strong plain flour
5 ml/1 teaspoon salt
50 g/2 oz margarine
5 ml/1 teaspoon caster sugar
1 sachet fast-action easy-blend
  dried yeast
1 egg
250 ml/8 fl oz hand-hot milk
Glaze
1 egg
5 ml/1 teaspoon caster sugar
15 ml/1 tablespoon water
poppy seeds (optional)

Sift the flour and salt into a bowl and rub in the margarine. Stir in the caster sugar and fast-action

easy blend yeast. Make a well in the centre. Beat the egg and add it with the milk. Mix to make a fairly soft dough, then use your hand to roll the dough and leave the side of the bowl clean.

Turn the dough out on to a lightly floured surface, knead it for about 10 minutes until smooth, then shape it as required and place on a greased baking tray. Cover with oiled polythene and leave the dough to rise until doubled in size.

Brush the eggs with the sugar and water for the glaze. Glaze the risen bread and sprinkle with poppy seeds, if used. Bake according to the instructions for the particular shape of loaf.

SHAPING ENRICHED WHITE BREAD

Poppy-seed Plaits
Divide the dough into three, and roll each into a 30 cm/12 in long strand. Set the three strands side by side on a flat surface, and pass the left strand over the centre strand, then the right strand over

Plaited loaf

For a three-strand plait, begin crossing the dough near the top.

the centre strand. Continue like this until the whole length is plaited. Finally join the short ends neatly together and tuck them under. Place on greased baking trays and leave to rise. Glaze before baking.

Bake the loaves in a preheated oven at 190°C/375°F/ gas 5 for 35–40 minutes.

Crown Loaf
Divide all the risen dough into 12 equal pieces – about 50 g/ 2 oz each. Shape these with the palm of the hand, one by one, and put them in a greased, 23 cm/9 in sandwich tin and place the balls in a circle around the inner edge of the tin, with three or four balls in the centre. Prove and glaze, then bake as for Poppy-seed Plaits (above) for 45–60 minutes.

Fancy Rolls
Shape the rolls as described below. Brush with egg glaze and set them aside to rise until doubled in size. Bake the rolls in a preheated oven at 190°C/ 375°F/gas 5 for 10–15 minutes or until golden.

Twists Use about 50 g/2 oz of risen dough for each roll. Roll a piece of dough out, about 10 cm/4 in long, cut it in half lengthways and, holding each strip at both ends, twist it about three times.

Knots Roll strips of dough as for Twists, then roll each strip into a strand and tie it into a knot in the centre.

Plaits Roll three thin strips and plait them together, pinching their ends.

Miniature loaves Shape 50 g/ 2 oz pieces of dough into oblong miniature loaves and score the surface with five or six marks, at even intervals. With a scissor-point, make triangular cuts between the score marks, through the dough, so that the points are slightly raised.

Trefoil Divide a 50 g/2 oz piece of dough into three, shape into balls and set them on a baking tray in such a way that all three balls touch each other.

S-rolls Roll a 5 cm/2 in piece of dough into a thick strand and shape into a snail or 'S' form.

Fancy rolls

Twists Twisting strips of dough.

Miniature loaves Snipping small cuts in rolls.

Trefoil Arranging small balls of dough close together in threes so that they join up when risen.

Yorkshire Tea Cakes

Easy-blend dried yeast may be used instead of fresh yeast in these tea cakes. Add fast-action easy blend yeast to the flour and shape the tea cakes as soon as the dough has been kneaded.

MAKES: 5
PREPARATION: 20 minutes (plus rising)
OVEN: 200°C/400°F/gas 6
COOKING: 20 minutes

450 g/1 lb strong plain flour
5 ml/1 teaspoon salt
25 g/1 oz caster sugar
25 g/1 oz lard
50 g/2 oz currants
15 g/½ oz fresh yeast
300 ml/½ pt warm milk (43°C/110°F)

Sift the flour and salt together into a large bowl, add the sugar and rub in the lard until evenly blended. Stir in the currants, then make a well in the centre.

In a small bowl, blend the yeast with the milk until smooth and creamy. Pour this liquid into the well, mix the ingredients together, beating the dough against the bowl until it leaves the sides clean (add a little extra flour if necessary).

Turn the dough out on to a lightly floured surface and knead for about 10 minutes. Put the dough in a lightly oiled polythene bag and set aside to rise at room temperature for about 1½ hours or until it has doubled in size. Remove the polythene, place the risen dough on a lightly floured surface and knead well. Divide the dough into five equal portions and shape each portion into a round; roll each of these into a 18 cm/7 in wide, flat cake.

Set the cakes well apart on lightly greased baking trays and brush the tops with milk. Cover the trays with sheets of oiled polythene. Leave the cakes to rise in a warm place for 45 minutes or until doubled in size.

Bake the cakes in a preheated oven for about 20 minutes. Cool on a wire rack.

■ Serve the cakes split and buttered. The tea cakes may be toasted if liked.

Bath Buns

Fast-action easy-blend dried yeast may be used in these buns. Add it to the flour, salt and sugar omitting the yeast batter stage. Use hand-hot milk. The dough can be shaped immediately after kneading as the fast-action easy-blend yeast does not need two rising stages.

MAKES: 6
PREPARATION: 20 minutes (plus rising)
OVEN: 190°C/375°F/gas 5
COOKING: 15 minutes

450 g/1 lb strong plain flour
25 g/1 oz fresh yeast or 1 tablespoon dried yeast
75 g/3 oz plus 5 ml/1 teaspoon caster sugar
150 ml/¼ pt warm milk
90 ml/6 tablespoons warm water
5 ml/1 teaspoon salt
50 g/2 oz butter or margarine
2 eggs
175 g/6 oz sultanas
25–50 g/1–2 oz chopped mixed peel
crushed lump sugar

Sift 100 g/4 oz of the measured flour into a large mixing bowl. Add the yeast, crumbling it if fresh, and 5 ml/1 teaspoon of sugar. Make a well in the centre of the flour, add the warm milk and water and stir thoroughly with a wooden spoon to incorporate all the ingredients. Set the bowl aside in a warm place until contents are frothy, about 20–30 minutes.

Meanwhile sift the remaining flour and the salt into a bowl, and add the remaining sugar. Melt the butter or margarine in a small pan, but do not let it boil. Beat the eggs. Stir the fat and the eggs into the yeast mixture with a wooden spoon, then gradually mix in the sifted flour, the sultanas and peel. Beat the dough, with one hand, against the sides of the bowl, then turn it on to a lightly floured surface. Knead the soft dough until smooth and no longer sticky, about 5 minutes.

Put the dough in a large bowl inside a lightly oiled polythene bag and leave it in a warm place until it has doubled in size. Remove the polythene bag and beat the dough in the bowl with a wooden spoon or the hand. Place 12 tablespoonfuls of the dough on greased baking trays, cover them with polythene and leave to rise again until doubled in size.

Remove the polythene, brush the buns with beaten egg and sprinkle the tops with coarsely crushed lump sugar. Bake the buns in a preheated oven at 190°C/375°F/gas 5 for about 15–20 minutes.

Chelsea Buns

Easy-blend dried yeast can be used instead of fresh yeast. Add it to the flour after rubbing in the margarine. Once the dough is well kneaded, the filling can be rolled into it and the buns shaped and proved.

MAKES: 6
PREPARATION: 20 minutes (plus rising)
OVEN: 190°C/375°F/gas 5
COOKING: 30–35 minutes

225 g/8 oz strong plain flour
2.5 ml/½ teaspoon caster sugar
15 g/½ oz fresh yeast
120 ml/4 fl oz warm milk (43°C/110°F)
2.5 ml/½ teaspoon salt
15 g/½ oz margarine or lard
1 egg
75 g/3 oz dried fruit (sultanas, currants or seedless raisins)
25 g/1 oz chopped mixed peel
50 g/2 oz light soft brown sugar
15–25 g/½–1 oz melted butter
clear honey

Sift 50 g/2 oz of the flour into a bowl and add the caster sugar. Crumble in the yeast and beat in the milk with a wooden spoon. Leave this yeast mixture in a warm place for about 20 minutes or until frothy. Sift together the remaining flour and the salt and rub in the margarine or lard. Make a well in the centre, add the beaten egg and pour in the yeast mixture. Using one hand, gradually work in the flour.

Beat the dough in the bowl until it leaves the sides clean; it should be fairly soft and pliable. Turn the dough on to a lightly floured surface and knead it for

10 minutes, until smooth. Put it in a lightly oiled polythene bag and leave to rise at room temperature for 1–1½ hours or until it has doubled in size.

Knead the risen dough on a lightly floured surface until smooth, then roll it out with a well-floured rolling pin, to a 30 × 23 cm/12 × 9 in rectangle. Mix the dried fruit, peel and soft brown sugar together, brush the dough with melted butter and spread the fruit mixture on top to within 1 cm/½ in along the longer edges. Roll up the dough from the long sides and press the join to seal it.

Cut the roll into nine equal slices and lay them flat, in rows of three, in a greased, 18 cm/7 in square cake tin. Leave to rise in a polythene bag, in a warm place, for about 30 minutes.

Remove the polythene bag and bake the buns in a preheated oven for 30–35 minutes. Turn the buns on to a wire rack and, while still hot, brush them with clear honey.

Lardy Cake

MAKES: 25 × 20 cm/
    10 × 8 in cake
PREPARATION: 30 minutes
    (plus rising)
OVEN: 220°C/425°F/gas 7
COOKING: 30 minutes

⅓ quantity white bread dough
100 g/4 oz lard
100 g/4 oz caster sugar
5 ml/1 teaspoon mixed spice
75 g/3 oz sultanas
cooking oil

Roll out the risen dough with a

rolling pin, on a lightly floured surface, to a strip 5 mm/¼ in thick. If using fast-action easy-blend yeast do not leave the dough to rise first.

Cut the lard or margarine into flakes and put one-third of these over the dough to within 1 cm/½ in of the edges. Mix the sugar with the spice and sultanas and sprinkle one-third over the fat. Fold the dough up loosely from one of the short sides.

Roll out the dough again into a strip and cover with another third of the lard or margarine and half the remaining sugar, spice and sultanas. Roll up the dough again, then roll it out into a strip for the third time. Cover the dough with the remaining lard, sugar and sultanas.

Roll up the dough, then roll out and shape it to fit a greased roasting tin, 25 × 20 cm/10 × 8 in. Lift the dough into the tin and press it down well, especially in the corners. Place the tin in an oiled polythene bag and leave the dough to rise until it has doubled in size.

Remove the polythene, brush the top of the dough lightly with oil and sprinkle with a little extra sugar. Score a criss-cross pattern across the surface of the dough with the point of a sharp knife. If necessary for clean cuts, wipe the blade of the knife on a hot, damp cloth between cuts.

Bake in a preheated oven at 220°C/425°F/gas 7 for 30 minutes. Turn the cake out of the tin and leave to cool on a wire rack.

■ Serve lardy cake sliced, plain or buttered.

Preparing a lardy cake

1 *Sprinkle spiced sultanas over the dough.*

2 *Fold the dough loosely.*

3 *Press the dough into the corners of the tin.*

4 *Score the surface of the dough with a knife.*

Brioches

Fast-action easy-blend dried yeast may be used instead of fresh yeast. Mix it with the flour instead of creaming it with liquid. Once the brioche dough is kneaded, it can be shaped and proved once before baking.

MAKES: 12
PREPARATION: 25 minutes
    (plus rising)
OVEN: 230°C/450°F/gas 8
COOKING: 10 minutes

225 g/8 oz strong plain flour
2.5 ml/½ teaspoon salt
15 ml/1 tablespoon caster sugar
15 g/½ oz fresh yeast
22.5 ml/4½ teaspoons warm water
2 eggs
50 g/2 oz butter, melted

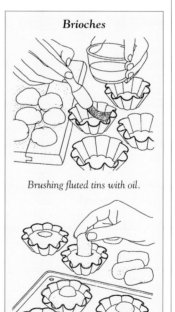

Brioches

Brushing fluted tins with oil.

Inserting a knob of dough in the centre of the brioches.

Sift the flour and salt into a bowl and add the sugar. Cream the yeast with the water in a small bowl, and stir it, together with the beaten eggs and the melted butter, into the flour with a wooden spoon. Beat the dough until it leaves the sides of the bowl clean, then turn it out on to a lightly floured surface and knead for 5 minutes.

Put the dough in an oiled polythene bag and leave it to rise at room temperature for 1–1½ hours or until it has doubled in size. Turn the risen dough on to a lightly floured surface and knead it until smooth. Shape the dough into a sausage and divide it into 12 equal pieces.

Brush 7.5 cm/3 in fluted deep patty tins or individual brioche moulds with oil and shape three-quarters of each piece of dough into a ball; place it in a patty tin. Using a floured finger, press a hole in the centre of the dough as far as the base of the tin. Shape the remaining piece of dough into a knob and insert it in the hole. Press lightly with the fingertip to unite the two pieces of dough.

When all 12 brioches have been shaped, set the patty tins on a baking tray and cover them loosely with lightly oiled polythene. Leave to rise until the dough is puffy and the brioches are nearly doubled in size.

Remove the polythene and bake the brioches in a preheated oven at 230°C/450°F/gas 8 for about 10 minutes or until they are golden brown. Transfer the brioches on to a wire rack and serve warm.

Croissants

MAKES: 12
PREPARATION: 1–1½ hours
(plus rising)
RESTING: 1 hour
OVEN: 220°C/425°F/gas 7
COOKING: 15–20 minutes

450 g/1 lb strong plain flour
5 ml/1 teaspoon salt
275 g/10 oz butter
10 ml/2 teaspoons fast-action
easy-blend dried yeast
2.5 ml/½ teaspoon caster sugar
250 ml/8 fl oz hand-hot water
1 egg

Sift the flour and salt into a bowl. Rub in 50 g/2 oz of the butter. Stir in the yeast and sugar, then mix in the water to make a stiff dough.

Transfer the dough to a lightly floured surface and knead it for about 10 minutes, until smooth. Roll out the dough to a strip measuring about 51 × 20 cm/20 × 8 in. Soften the remaining butter with a knife until pliable but not creamy, and divide it into three portions. Dot one portion of the butter over the upper two-thirds of the dough, leaving a 1 cm/½ in border round the edges.

Fold the dough into three, bringing up first the unbuttered part of the dough, then folding the opposite part over. Give the dough a half turn, and seal the edges by pressing with the rolling pin. Shape into a long strip again by gently pressing the dough at intervals with the rolling pin, and rolling out. Dot as before with the second portion of flaked buttery then fold, turn the pastry and roll again before adding the last of the butter. Continue folding and rolling the dough a further three times without adding butter. Between each rolling, it is important to chill the dough for 10–15 minutes to prevent the fat melting and the dough becoming too sticky to handle. Leave the dough to rest for a final 10–15 minutes when all the butter is incorporated.

Cut the dough in half. Roll out one portion on a lightly floured surface, to a rectangle about 56 × 17 cm/22 × 6½ in. Trim the edges with a sharp knife, to a 56 × 15 cm/22 × 6 in rectangle. Cut the dough into six triangles, 15 cm/6 in wide at the base.

Beat the egg with a few drops of water and brush over the triangles. Roll up each triangle loosely, finishing with the tip underneath, then carefully curve the pastry into a crescent shape. Place the croissants, well spaced, on ungreased baking trays.

Brush the tops with a little more egg glaze, cover them with oiled polythene and leave at room temperature to rise until doubled in size. Brush again with egg before baking in a preheated oven at 220°C/425°F/gas 7 for 15–20 minutes. Use a palette knife to ease the croissants off the baking tray, and transfer them to a wire rack to cool. Serve them while still warm.

■ Uncooked, risen croissants freeze well. Open freeze them, then pack them in a bag or rigid containers when hard. Bake from frozen, allowing a few minutes extra cooking time.

Making croissants

1 Dot butter on two-thirds of dough.

2 Fold the dough into three, taking the lower portion over the middle of the dough, then folding the top down.

3 Turn the dough sideways and seal the edges with a rolling pin.

4 Cut out and roll up triangles.

5 Curve the dough into a crescent.

Babas

MAKES: 6
PREPARATION: 40 minutes
(plus rising)
OVEN: 200°C/400°F/gas 6
COOKING: 15–20 minutes

100 g/4 oz strong white flour
10 ml/2 teaspoons fast-action
easy-blend dried yeast
1.25 ml/¼ teaspoon salt
15 g/½ oz caster sugar
2 eggs
45 ml/3 tablespoons hand-hot milk
50 g/2 oz butter
50 g/2 oz currants
150 ml/¼ pt whipping cream
to decorate

Syrup

60 ml/4 tablespoons clear honey
60 ml/4 tablespoons water
about 45 ml/3 tablespoons rum

Mix the flour, easy-blend yeast, salt and sugar in a large bowl. Beat the eggs and milk, then gradually beat this mixture into the dry ingredients. Melt the butter and beat it in until smooth. Continue beating the mixture for 15 minutes, until it is quite elastic. Beat the currants into the mixture.

Grease 8 small ring moulds and, using a teaspoon, spoon in the batter. Set the ring moulds on baking trays and cover them with sheets of lightly oiled cling film or polythene.

Leave the babas to rise in a warm place until the dough has risen about two-thirds up the sides of the ring moulds.

Bake the babas in a preheated oven at 200°C/400°F/gas 6 for about 10–15 minutes or until they are golden brown.

Meanwhile, prepare the syrup: heat the honey and water in a small pan over low heat; stir in rum to taste.

Leave the baked babas to cool for a few minutes in the moulds before turning them out on to a plate. While the babas are still hot, spoon the warm syrup over them until the syrup has soaked in. Leave to cool, then transfer the rum-soaked babas to a serving dish or individual plates.

Fill the centres of the babas with cream just before serving.

■ Babas may be frozen before they are soaked in syrup. Thaw and heat them until warm, then soak in hot syrup and cool.

Making babas

Spooning the batter into the moulds.

Pouring warmed syrup over the cooked babas.

Decorating the babas by filling with spooned or piped cream.

Danish Pastries

MAKES: 8 squares, 16 crescents or about 20 pinwheels
PREPARATION: 45 minutes (plus rising)
CHILLING: 50 minutes
OVEN: 220°C/425°F/gas 7
COOKING: 10 minutes

225 g/8 oz strong white flour
175 g/6 oz butter
5 ml/1 teaspoon caster sugar
10 ml/2 teaspoons fast-action easy-blend dried yeast
120 ml/4 fl oz hand-hot water
Glacé Icing (page 390) to decorate
Fillings
50 g/2 oz marzipan
25 g/1 oz butter
25 g/1 oz caster sugar
5 ml/1 teaspoon cinnamon
40 g/1½ oz currants
15 g/½ oz chopped mixed peel

Place the flour in a large bowl. Rub in 25 g/1 oz of the butter. Stir in the sugar and yeast, and make a well in the centre of the flour. Pour in the water, then gradually work in the flour by hand to make a soft dough.

Turn the dough out on to a lightly floured surface and knead it for about 10 minutes until the dough is smooth.

Soften the remaining butter until soft but not oily. Fold the butter into the rolled-out dough following the method for making Croissants (opposite): roll out the dough into an oblong measuring about 23 × 15 cm/9 × 6 in and dot two-thirds with a portion of the butter. Fold and roll the dough until all the butter is added, then repeat the rolling twice more without the butter.

Rest the dough for 10 minutes between each rolling and before shaping the pastries.

The dough can be shaped into any of the following traditional pastries.
Almond squares Roll out half the dough to a 25 cm/10 in square, then cut it into four equal squares. Fold two corners of each square to meet in the centre, envelope-style, and repeat with the other two corners. Press down firmly to seal. Place a small round of marzipan in the centre.
Crescents Roll out the dough as for almond squares, and cut each square diagonally in half. Place a small piece of marzipan at the base of each triangle, then roll it up from the base and curve into a crescent shape.
Pinwheels Roll out half a portion of pastry dough to a 30 × 20 cm/12 × 8 in rectangle. Cream the butter with the sugar and cinnamon and spread over the dough to within 5 mm/¼ in of the edges. Scatter the currants and mixed peel over the butter. Roll up the dough from the shorter end and cut into 1–2 cm/½–¾ in slices.

Alternatively, make cuts, 2.5 cm/1 in apart, through three-quarters of the depth of the rolls. Ease the near-cut pinwheels apart so that they overlap each other slightly.

Set the pastry shapes well apart on greased baking trays and cover with sheets of oiled cling film or polythene. Leave the pastries to rise in a warm place until doubled in size. Remove the polythene and brush the pastries with lightly beaten egg.

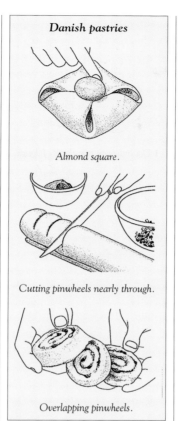

Danish pastries

Almond square.

Cutting pinwheels nearly through.

Overlapping pinwheels.

Bake in a preheated oven at 220°/425°F/gas 7 for about 10–12 minutes or until golden brown. Cool on a wire rack and, while still warm, brush the almond squares, crescents and pinwheels with glacé icing. Leave to set before serving.

Scones & Teabreads

This section includes breads made without yeast, mainly scones, and a good basic teabread. Scones are quick and easy to make, and ideal for tea, served with butter or thick clotted cream and home-made fruit preserves.

Many traditional scones are baked on a griddle or girdle. This is a thick, round iron plate, heated on top of the cooker. The correct heat is important – if too hot, the outside crust of the scones becomes too brown, leaving the centre uncooked. The first batch of griddle scones should be cooked with great caution, checking often on their progress by lifting them slightly. Regulate the heat so that the scones cook neither too fast nor too slowly, then the following batches can be cooked with confidence.

Teabreads, halfway between a bread and a cake, are also popular for tea, as they keep well and can be made in advance. Soda bread is a good substitute for yeast bread in an emergency, and can be made shortly before it is required.

Plain Scones

MAKES: 10–12
PREPARATION: 15 minutes
OVEN: 230°C/425°F/gas 8
COOKING: 10 minutes

225 g/8 oz plain flour
pinch salt
2.5 ml/½ teaspoon bicarbonate of soda
5 ml/1 teaspoon cream of tartar
40 g/1½ oz block margarine
about 60 ml/4 tablespoons each milk and water mixed
milk for glazing

Sift together the flour, salt, bicarbonate of soda and cream of tartar into a wide bowl. Cut up the margarine and rub it into the flour. Gradually add the milk and water and mix with a round-bladed knife to give a soft but manageable dough.

Knead the dough quickly on a lightly floured surface, to remove all cracks. Roll the dough out 1 cm/½ in thick, and cut out 5 cm/2 in rounds with a plain or fluted pastry cutter. Knead the trimmings together, roll them out and cut out as many scones as possible. Set the scones on a heated, ungreased baking tray, brush them with milk and bake them in a preheated oven at 230°C/450°F/gas 8 for about 10 minutes, until well risen and light golden brown.

Sweet Sultana Scones

MAKES: 12
PREPARATION: 15 minutes
OVEN: 230°C/450°F/gas 8
COOKING: 10 minutes

225 g/8 oz plain flour
2.5 ml/½ teaspoon bicarbonate
    of soda
2.5 ml/½ teaspoon cream of tartar
pinch salt
40 g/1½ oz block margarine
25 g/1 oz caster sugar
50 g/2 oz sultanas
10 ml/2 teaspoons lemon juice
about 150 ml/¼ pt milk
milk for glazing

Sift together the flour, bicarbonate of soda, cream of tartar and salt. Cut up the margarine and rub it into the flour with the fingertips until the mixture looks like fine breadcrumbs. Add the sugar and sultanas.

Stir the lemon juice into the milk, then gradually mix it into the dry ingredients, adding enough to make a light, manageable dough. Use a round-bladed knife to mix the dough.

Turn the dough on to a floured surface and knead lightly until smooth. Roll out 1 cm/½ in thick and cut out the scones with a 5 cm/2 in plain or fluted pastry cutter. Re-knead the trimmings lightly to cut more scones. Set on an ungreased heated baking tray, brush the tops with milk and bake in a preheated oven at 230°C/450°F/gas 8 for about 10 minutes. Cool on a rack.

Cheese Scones

MAKES: 12
PREPARATION: 10 minutes
OVEN: 220°C/400°F/gas 7
COOKING: 15 minutes

225 g/8 oz plain flour
2.5 ml/½ teaspoon salt
12.5 ml/2½ teaspoons baking
    powder
50 g/2 oz butter or block
    margarine
100 g/4 oz Cheddar cheese, grated
about 150 ml/¼ pt milk

Sift together the flour, salt, and baking powder. Rub the butter or margarine into the flour until it resembles fine breadcrumbs. Blend in the cheese. Gradually add the milk, mixing it with a round-bladed knife until the dough is soft and manageable.

Turn the dough on to a lightly floured surface, divide into two equal portions and knead them lightly with the fingertips. Shape each portion into a round, 1.5 cm/¾ in thick. Cut each round into six triangular portions and set them on a greased baking tray; prick the tops with a fork.

Bake scones in a preheated oven at 220°C/425°F/gas 7 for 12–15 minutes. Cool slightly before serving.

Savoury Scones

Snipped chives, chopped mixed herbs, chopped thyme or tarragon may all be added to cheese scones. Dried mixed herbs or dried oregano may be added in small quantities. Chopped cooked ham or fried and well drained chopped bacon may also be added with, or instead of, the cheese.

Wholemeal Scone Round

SERVES: 6
PREPARATION: 10 minutes
OVEN: 230°C/450°F/gas 8
COOKING: 15 minutes

50 g/2 oz plain flour
15 ml/1 tablespoon baking powder
pinch salt
175 g/6 oz plain wholemeal flour
50 g/2 oz block margarine
50 g/2 oz caster sugar
about 150 ml/¼ pt milk

Sift the plain flour, baking powder and salt into a mixing bowl. Blend in the wholemeal flour and cut the margarine into knobs; rub the butter into the flour with the fingertips, until the mixture resembles fine breadcrumbs. Mix in the sugar. Add sufficient milk to give a light, soft dough, using a round-bladed knife for mixing.

Turn the dough on to a lightly floured surface. Knead it lightly until smooth, then shape it into a flat round, 15 cm/6 in wide. Mark it into six equal triangles with the back of a floured knife blade.

Set the scone round on a heated, lightly floured baking tray and bake in a preheated oven at 230°C/450°F/gas 8 for about 15 minutes.
■ Serve the scones warm, split and buttered.

Welsh Cakes

MAKES: 16
PREPARATION: 15 minutes
COOKING: 25 minutes

225 g/8 oz plain flour
5 ml/1 teaspoon baking powder
pinch salt
40–50 g/1½–2 oz butter or
    block margarine
40–50 g/1½–2 oz lard
75 g/3 oz caster sugar
50–75 g/2–3 oz currants
1 egg
about 30 ml/2 tablespoons milk
caster sugar for dusting

Heat the griddle, heavy-based frying pan or hot plate. Sift the flour, baking powder and salt into a bowl; cut up the butter or margarine and lard and rub into the flour with the fingertips until the mixture resembles fine breadcrumbs. Stir in the sugar and currants. Beat the egg lightly and add it to the flour mixture, with just enough milk to give a firm paste similar to shortcrust pastry.

Roll the dough 5 mm/¼ in thick, on a floured surface, and cut out rounds using a 7.5 cm/3 in plain or fluted pastry cutter. Bake the cakes on the greased griddle, over low heat for about 3 minutes on each side, until golden brown. Cool on a wire rack, and serve with a dusting of caster sugar.

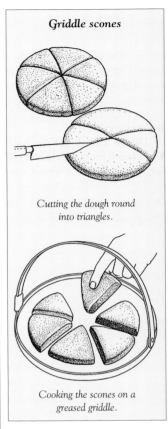

Griddle scones

Cutting the dough round into triangles.

Cooking the scones on a greased griddle.

Griddle Scones

MAKES: 12
PREPARATION: 5 minutes
COOKING: 10 minutes

225 g/8 oz plain flour
5 ml/1 teaspoon bicarbonate
    of soda
10 ml/2 teaspoons cream of tartar
2.5 ml/½ teaspoon salt
25 g/1 oz lard or block margarine
25 g/1 oz caster sugar
about 150 ml/¼ pt milk

Heat a griddle or a heavy-based frying pan. Sift the flour, bicarbonate of soda, cream of tartar and salt into a bowl; cut up the lard or margarine and rub it into the flour with the fingertips until the mixture resembles fine bread-crumbs. Stir in the caster sugar, and gradually add the milk, mixing the dough with a round-bladed knife until it is soft but manageable.

Divide the dough in half. Knead each piece lightly and roll into two rounds, 5 mm–1 cm/ ¼–½ in thick. Cut each round into six even triangles and cook on the greased griddle until evenly brown on one side, then turn and cook on the second side; allow about 5 minutes for each side. Cool on a wire rack.

Drop Scones

MAKES: 15–18
PREPARATION: 5 minutes
COOKING: 3–5 minutes
    per batch

100 g/ 4 oz self-raising flour
pinch salt
15 ml/1 tablespoon caster sugar
1 egg
about 150 ml/¼ pt milk
butter or lard for cooking

Set a griddle or heavy-based frying pan over heat. While it is warming, sift the flour and salt into a bowl and stir in the sugar. Make a well in the centre and drop in the egg; gradually add the milk, working in the flour to make a smooth batter.

Grease the heated surface lightly with a little butter or lard. When a slight haze appears, pour on small rounds of batter, well apart, from a spoon, lifting the spoon high and pouring the batter off its tip.

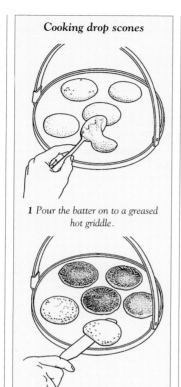

Cooking drop scones

1 *Pour the batter on to a greased hot griddle.*

2 *Turn the drop scones when bubbling on top and browned underneath.*

As soon as the scones are bubbling, part-set and golden underneath, turn them with a palette knife and cook until set and brown on the other side.

Serve at once, or place the scones between folds in a clean tea-towel until ready to serve.

■ Brush with melted butter and sprinkle with caster sugar.

Soda Bread

MAKES: 18 cm/7 in loaf
PREPARATION: 15 minutes
OVEN: 200°C/400°F/gas 6
COOKING: 30 minutes

450g/1 lb plain flour
10 ml/2 teaspoons bicarbonate
    of soda
10 ml/2 teaspoons cream of tartar
5 ml/1 teaspoon salt
25 g/1 oz lard
5–10 ml/1–2 teaspoons caster
    sugar (optional)
300 ml/½ pt soured milk, or
    275 ml/9 fl oz buttermilk made
    up to 300 ml/½ pt with milk

Sift the flour, bicarbonate of soda, cream of tartar and salt into a bowl. Cut up the lard and rub it into the flour with the fingertips until the mixture resembles fine breadcrumbs. Mix in the sugar if used. Make a well in the centre of the flour, add the milk (soured with 15 ml/1 tablespoon of lemon juice) or the buttermilk, and mix to a soft but manageable dough, working the ingredients with a round-bladed knife. Add more milk if necessary.

Turn the dough on to a floured surface, knead it lightly and shape it into an 18 cm/7 in round; flatten it slightly. Mark the round into four with the back of a knife, set it on a floured baking tray and bake in a preheated oven at 200°C/400°F/ gas 6 for about 30 minutes.

Cool on a wire rack and serve fresh, as a teabread.

Fruit and Nut Teabread

MAKES: 1 loaf
PREPARATION: 20 minutes
OVEN: 180°C/350°F/gas 4
COOKING: 1¼ hours

5 ml/1 teaspoon bicarbonate
    of soda
2.5 ml/½ teaspoon cream of tartar
275 g/10 oz plain flour
100 g/4 oz butter
2.5 ml/½ teaspoon ground ginger
5 ml/1 teaspoon ground mace
2.5 ml/½ teaspoon ground allspice
75 g/3 oz light soft brown sugar
50 g/2 oz chopped glacé ginger
50 g/2 oz seedless raisins
50 g/2 oz hazelnuts
50 g/2 oz glacé pineapple
1 egg
150 ml/¼ pt milk

Grease and line a 20 × 13 × 7.5 cm/ 8 × 5 × 3 in loaf tin. Sift the bicarbonate of soda, cream of tartar and flour into a large bowl. Rub in the butter until the mixture resembles fine bread-crumbs. Stir in the ginger, mace, allspice, sugar, glacé ginger and raisins. Chop the hazelnuts and glacé pineapple and mix them into the dry ingredients.

Beat the egg and stir it into the dry ingredients with the milk to give a fairly soft mixture. Spread the mixture evenly in the tin and bake in a preheated oven at 180°C/350°F/gas 4 for about 1¼ hours or until the teabread is well risen, browned and firm to the touch.

To check if the loaf is cooked, insert a fine metal skewer into the centre; if there is any sticky mixture on it then continue cooking for a further 5 minutes.

Leave the teabread in the tin for 5 minutes, then turn it out on to a wire rack to cool. Serve sliced and buttered.

■ Teabreads freeze well. Pack a loaf whole or slice it and separate the slices with freezer film so that they can be thawed individually, then pack the re-shaped loaf.

Bran Teabread

MAKES: 23 × 13 cm/9 × 5 in loaf
PREPARATION: 10 minutes
RESTING: 8 hours
OVEN: 190°C/375°F/gas 5
COOKING: 1¼–1½ hours

75 g/3 oz All Bran
225 g/8 oz sultanas
225 g/8 oz light soft brown sugar
300 ml/½ pt milk
175 g/6 oz self-raising flour
5 ml/1 teaspoon baking powder

Mix the All Bran, sultanas, brown sugar and milk in a bowl and leave to stand overnight, covered with a cloth.

Grease and line a loaf tin (23 × 13 cm/9 × 5 in top measurements). Sift the flour and the baking powder into the soaked ingredients, blend thoroughly and spoon into the tin. Level the top of the mixture and bake in a preheated oven at 190°C/375°F/ gas 5 for about 1¼ hours until the bread is risen and just firm to the touch. If the loaf browns too quickly, cover it with a double sheet of grease-proof paper.

Turn out the loaf, remove the paper and cool on a wire rack. Serve the loaf sliced and buttered. It is best left for a day or two to mature before serving, and will keep for a week in a tin.

CONFECTIONERY

Home-made sweets, packed in decorative boxes, make ideal presents for Christmas and birthdays. Set the individual sweets in paper cases and put waxed paper between the layers.

Many traditional sweets, such as fudge and toffee, are based on concentrated sugar syrup, boiled to high temperatures. A sugar thermometer and a large, heavy-based pan are essential. Use a wooden spoon when needed, to move the mixture backwards and forwards while the syrup is reducing without stirring as such.

Chocolate-covered Sweets

For chocolate-covered sweets, use good-quality plain chocolate. Put it, broken into small pieces, in a bowl and place this over a pan of hot water. Stir the chocolate until melted and never allow the water underneath to boil or it will overheat the chocolate, causing it to separate. Dip the sweets into the chocolate, holding each between two forks, and brush off any excess on the side of the bowl. Leave to set on non-stick or waxed paper.

Marzipan Sweets

Good-quality bought marzipan is popular for many sweets. The marzipan may be coloured pink, green or yellow with a little food colouring, and used as a base or filling for sweets.

Stuffed dates Make a slit in the top of the dates and remove the stones. Fill the cavities with a small piece of plain or coloured marzipan; roll the stuffed dates in granulated sugar or decorate them with blanched almonds.

Ginger marzipan Shape pieces of marzipan into marble-sized balls, dip the bases in melted chocolate and top with stem ginger.

Peanut Brittle

PREPARATION: 1 hour

350 g/12 oz loaf or cube sugar
150 ml/¼ pt water
225 g/8 oz golden syrup
10 ml/2 teaspoons powdered glucose
25 g/1 oz butter
75 g/3 oz browned peanuts
2.5 ml/½ teaspoon lemon essence
10 ml/2 teaspoons bicarbonate of soda

Dissolve the sugar in the water, together with the syrup and glucose, in a large, heavy-based pan set over low heat. Bring to the boil and boil gently until the thermometer registers 149°C/300°F (read at eye level).

Add the butter, warmed nuts (rub the skins off first) and lemon essence; heat until the butter is just melted. Stir in the bicarbonate of soda (the mixture will froth rapidly for a few minutes), and pour it quickly on to an oiled marble slab or large clean baking tray.

When cold, break the peanut brittle into pieces; store in single layers between waxed or non-stick paper.

Coconut Ice

MAKES: 24–30
PREPARATION: 30 minutes

450 g/1 lb caster sugar
150 ml/¼ pt milk
150 g/5 oz desiccated coconut
pink food colouring

Oil or butter a shallow tin, 20 × 15 cm/8 × 6 in. Dissolve the sugar in the milk over low heat, then bring to the boil and boil gently for about 10 minutes or until the temperature reaches 115°C/240°F (read the thermometer at eye level). Remove the pan from the heat and stir in the coconut.

Pour half the mixture quickly into the tin, spreading it evenly. Colour the remainder pale pink and pour quickly over the first layer. Leave until half-set, then mark the coconut into 2.5 cm/1 in squares with a knife. Cut up when quite cold.

Chocolate-covered Pineapple

PREPARATION: 20 minutes

220 g/7½ oz can pineapple rings
175–200 g/6–7 oz plain chocolate decorations

Drain the pineapple rings thoroughly and cut them into halves or quarters. Break up the chocolate and melt in a bowl over a pan of hot water. Using two forks, carefully dip the pineapple chunks in the chocolate, coating them evenly.

Dry on waxed or non-stick paper, and before the chocolate sets, decorate with crystallised violets, mimosa balls or dragees.

Honey Fruit Nut Caramels

PREPARATION: 30 minutes
SETTING: 24 hours

75 g/3 oz butter
150 g/5 oz golden syrup
175 g/6 oz clear honey
100 g/4 oz walnut halves
100 g/4 oz stoned dates

Grease and line with non-stick paper a shallow tin measuring 20 × 13 cm/8 × 5 in. Melt the butter in a large, heavy-based pan set over low heat; add the syrup and honey. Bring the mixture to the boil and continue boiling over gentle heat until the thermometer registers 132°C/270°F. Meanwhile, chop the walnuts and dates finely.

Remove the pan from the heat and add the nuts and dates. Beat the mixture vigorously with a wooden spoon until opaque in colour. Pour it into the tin and leave to cool. When almost set, cut through the caramel with a buttered knife, into 1.5–2.5 cm/¾–1 in squares. Leave to set for about 24 hours, then break the squares apart; wrap them in waxed paper and store.

Toffee Apples

Cored, quartered apples coated in caramel make delicious sweets. You will need one quantity of caramel per apple (see Orange Caramel Custards, page 277). Holding an apple quarter with two forks, dip it in the caramel and leave to set on waxed paper. When cool, the apple can be coated again. Whole apples can be skewered on wooden sticks and turned in the caramel.

Peppermint Creams

MAKES: 25
PREPARATION: 30 minutes
DRYING: 24 hours

225 g/8 oz icing sugar
1 egg white
peppermint essence

Sift the icing sugar into a bowl and blend with enough beaten egg white to form a stiff paste. Add a few drops of peppermint essence to taste.

Knead the paste lightly in the bowl, using the fingertips. Roll the paste out 5 mm/¼ in thick, between sheets of non-stick or waxed paper. Stamp out 2.5 cm/1 in rounds with a plain cutter, and leave the mints to dry for about 24 hours.

Rum Truffles

MAKES: 12
PREPARATION: 35 minutes
CHILLING: 1 hour

75 g/3 oz plain chocolate
1 egg yolk
15 g/½ oz butter
5 ml/1 teaspoon rum
5 ml/1 teaspoon single cream
50 g/2 oz chocolate vermicelli, cocoa or drinking chocolate

Melt the chocolate in a small bowl over a pan of hot water. Add the egg yolk, butter, rum and cream. Beat the mixture until thick, then chill until firm enough to handle.

Shape the mixture into 12 balls and toss at once in vermicelli or drinking chocolate.

Chocolate Fudge

MAKES: 1½ lb
PREPARATION: about 1 hour

450 g/1 lb caster sugar
300 ml/½ pt water
1 large can condensed milk
115g /4½ oz chocolate dots or plain
  cooking chocolate (grated)
50 g/2 oz seedless raisins (optional)

Put the sugar and water in a heavy-based 3.4 litre/6 pt pan and dissolve the sugar over low heat. Bring to the boil, add the condensed milk and boil gently until the thermometer registers 115°C/240°F. Stir occasionally to prevent sticking. Remove the pan from the heat and add the chocolate, and raisins if used.

Beat the mixture with a wooden spoon until thick and creamy; pour this into a buttered tin, about 20 × 15 × 2.5 cm/ 8 × 6 × 1 in.

Leave to cool for several hours, then cut the fudge into 2.5 cm/1 in squares with a sharp knife. Wrap in waxed paper.

PRESERVING

Fruit can be made into jams, jellies and cheeses. It may also be made into pickles and chutneys, or it may be bottled. The most suitable methods of preserving depend on the type of fruit and its quality and ripeness. Only the finest-quality fruit should be used for bottling and freezing, while bruised and under-ripe fruit can be used to make chutneys, jams and jellies. Over-ripe fruit is ideal for syrups and chutneys but unsuitable for jams and jellies.

JAMS AND JELLIES

Both these types of preserves are a combination of fresh fruit, sugar and water, which are all boiled together until setting point is reached.

A good set depends on the presence of pectin, acid and sugar in correct proportions. Pectin, which is found in the fruit cells, reacts with sugar to give a gel. Acid speeds the release of pectin.

Fruits have natural pectin and acid in varying quantities. Tart cooking apples, blackberries, damsons, gooseberries and redcurrants are rich in pectin and acid, and are therefore excellent for jams and jellies. Fruits such as apricots, greengages, loganberries, plums and raspberries are less rich in pectin and acid. They make good jams, but set less firmly than pectin-rich fruit.

Fruits lacking in both pectin and acid include cherries, melons and strawberries. These do not give a good set on their own, therefore pectin and/or acid must be added to give a firm set.

Lemon juice is the ingredient which is usually added to increase the acid content. Lemons are also rich in pectin; however, this is found mainly in the seeds and pith.

Under-ripe fruit contains more pectin than ripe fruit, and over-ripe fruit has a poor pectin content. Seeds, pith and peel are often rich in pectin, therefore trimmings are usually tied in muslin and cooked with the fruit.

Testing for Pectin

Put 5 ml/1 teaspoon of the cooked, but unsweetened, fruit pulp in a glass and leave to cool. Add 15 ml/1 tablespoon methylated spirit and shake gently. If a large clot forms, the fruit has sufficient pectin for the jam to set; if there are numerous small clots the pectin content is too low. This sample is not edible.

Missing pectin can be supplemented by adding lemon juice, which is rich both in pectin and acid content. Allow 30 ml/2 tablespoons lemon juice to each 1.8 kg/4 lb of fruit. Alternatively, add 2.5 ml/½ teaspoon of citric or tartaric acid to the fruit before cooking.

Commercial pectin may also be used in the proportions of 60–120 ml/2–4 fl oz liquid pectin or 7 g/¼ oz powdered pectin to 450 g/1 lb of fruit. The more pectin present, the more sugar it will set, but too much pectin spoils the fruit flavour.

Sugar

Use preserving or granulated sugar, as these dissolve quickly. This is important as the quicker the sugar dissolves, the clearer the jam and the less scum that it produces. The sugar should be warmed in the oven before use.

Sugar has a hardening effect on fruit so it must **never** be added until the fruit is thoroughly softened. Strawberries, which quickly lose their shape during cooking, are best sprinkled with sugar and left overnight.

Sugar with pectin Preserving sugar with added pectin is now a useful ingredient when making preserves using fruit that is naturally lacking in pectin. Follow the packet instructions carefully as the pectin-enriched sugar must be cooked for a specific time, not over-boiled.

Preserving Pans

Choose a large, heavy-based pan made from stainless steel. The pan should be wide in relation to its depth to allow for rapid evaporation before the sugar is added, and for quick boiling.

Preparing the Fruit

Select fresh, slightly under-ripe fruit and cut out any bruised or damaged parts. Berries should be hulled*, currants stripped from their stems and gooseberries topped and tailed.

Wash and drain the fruit carefully. Soft fruit is easiest cleaned by placing it in a sieve or colander, and immersing this in cold water several times. Large fruit such as apples should be chopped, and stone fruits should be halved and quartered and the stones removed.

Cooking the Fruit

Put the prepared fruit in the preserving pan, and add the water if specified. Bring the fruit and water to simmering point over very gentle heat. Simmering softens the skin and breaks down the flesh while releasing the pectin. When the fruit has been reduced to a pulp and the volume has decreased by one-third, remove the pan from the heat and add the warmed sugar. Stir thoroughly until the sugar has dissolved. The addition of 15 ml/1 tablespoon of glycerine after the sugar has dissolved prevents scum forming.

Return the pan to the heat and boil rapidly until setting point is reached. This varies from 3–20 minutes, according to the type and quantity of the fruit. If fruit is over-boiled, the jam becomes sticky and flavourless, and its colour darkens; if boiled too little, it fails to set.

Setting Point

The most accurate method of testing for setting is with a sugar thermometer. Jams and jellies have generally reached setting point when the thermometer registers 104°C/220°F.

Alternatively, use the saucer test: put a teaspoonful of jam on

Making jams and jellies

1 Cook the fruit in a heavy-based, wide-topped pan.

2 Add warmed preserving sugar.

3 Flake test for setting point.

4 Saucer test for setting point.

5 Remove the scum from the finished jam.

6 Pour the jam into warmed jars.

a cold saucer. As the jam cools, a skin forms. If the skin crinkles when pushed with a finger, setting point has been reached.

Another method is the flake test; however, this is the least reliable. Stir the jam with a wooden spoon and hold it flat so that the jam in the bowl of the spoon can cool. Turn the spoon on its side and allow the jam to drop: if the jam sets partly on the spoon and falls away in large flakes, rather than drops, setting point is reached.

If you make jam regularly, it is worth buying a sugar thermometer. A combination of the saucer test and temperature test usually gives reliable results.

Potting and Covering

As soon as setting point is reached remove the pan from the heat. Do this even while testing for setting as the jam can be spoilt by over-boiling. Pour the jam into thoroughly cleaned and dried, warmed jars.

Put a waxed disc (wax-side down) on top of the jam, and press gently to release any air bubbles. Wipe the rim of the jar with absorbent kitchen paper and cover **immediately** with airtight lids. If using cellophane covers, wet them before putting them over the jars; as the cellophane dries, it contracts to an airtight fit.

If the jars of preserve are not covered while boiling hot, then they must be allowed to cool completely before lids are put on. If lids are put on while the jam is hot but not fresh off the boil, condensation can form inside the pots. Without sufficient temperature to kill yeasts and moulds, the jam may become mouldy.

Leave the jam-filled jars to cool completely before labelling them.

Store in a cool, dark place.

JAMS

Apple

MAKES: 4.5 kg/10 lb

2.72 kg/6 lb cooking apples
1.12 litres/2 pt water
grated rind and juice of 4 lemons
*40 g/1½ oz ground ginger
  (optional)*
2.72 kg/6 lb sugar

Peel, core and chop the apples. Tie peel and core in muslin and put with the apple and water into the preserving pan. Add the finely grated lemon rind and the juice, together with the ginger if used. Cook until pulpy, then squeeze out and discard the muslin bag. Stir in the sugar and boil to setting point.

Apricot

MAKES: 2.27 kg/5 lb

1.4 kg/3 lb apricots
juice of 1 lemon
450 ml/¾ pt water
1.4 kg/3 lb sugar

Cut the washed and drained apricots in half, and remove the stones. Quarter the apricots and put them, with the lemon juice and water, in the pan. Simmer until the fruit is pulpy, stir in the sugar and boil rapidly until setting point is reached.

Blackberry

MAKES: 4.5 kg/10 lb

2.72 kg/6 lb blackberries
150 ml/¼ pt water
grated rind and juice of 2 lemons
2.72 kg/6 lb sugar

Put the cleaned fruit, water and lemon rind and juice in the pan. Simmer until the fruit is soft. Stir in the sugar and boil rapidly until setting point is reached.

Blackcurrant

MAKES: 4.5 kg/10 lb

1.8 kg/4 lb blackcurrants
1.7 litres/3 pt water
2.72 kg/6 lb sugar

Put the cleaned fruit in the pan with the water. Bring to the boil and simmer until soft. Stir in the sugar and boil rapidly until setting point is reached.

Cherry

MAKES: 3.25 kg/7 lb

*2.95 kg/6½ lb dark (morello)
  cherries*
juice of 3 lemons
1.6 kg/3½ lb sugar

Stone the cherries, and tie the stones in muslin. Put them in the pan, with the cherries and lemon juice. Simmer over low heat until the juices begin to run and the fruit is tender. Remove the muslin bag, stir in the sugar, and proceed in the usual way.

Gooseberry

MAKES: 2.72 kg/6 lb

1.4 kg/3 lb gooseberries
600 ml/1 pt water
1.8 kg/4 lb sugar

Bring the cleaned gooseberries and water to the boil and simmer until tender. Stir in the sugar and proceed in the usual way.

Marrow

MAKES: 4.5 kg/10 lb

3.62 kg/8 lb marrow
grated rind and juice of 4 lemons
2.72 kg/6 lb sugar

Peel the marrow and remove pith and seeds. Dice the marrow – it should weigh 2.72 kg/6 lb. Put in a steamer and cook until just tender. Leave the cooked marrow in a bowl, and add the lemon rind and juice, together with the sugar. Cover and leave for 24 hours. Boil the marrow over gentle heat until the sugar has dissolved. Continue cooking until the marrow is transparent and the syrup thick.

Plum

MAKES: 4.5 kg/10 lb

2.72 kg/6 lb plums
600 ml/1 pt water
2.72 kg/6 lb sugar

Follow the instructions given for apricot jam.

Raspberry

MAKES: 4.5 kg/10 lb

2.72 kg/6 lb raspberries
2.72 kg/6 lb sugar

Put the cleaned fruit in the pan without any water, and heat gently until the fruit begins to break up and the juices run. Simmer until reduced by a third, stir in the sugar; proceed as usual.

Rhubarb

MAKES: 2.27 kg/5 lb

2.05 kg/4½ lb rhubarb
juice of 3 lemons
1.4 kg/3 lb sugar

Wipe and trim the rhubarb, and cut the stems into 2.5 cm/1 in pieces. (The prepared weight of the rhubarb should be 1.4 kg/ 3 lb.) Layer the chopped rhubarb with sugar in a large bowl, and add the lemon juice. Leave overnight. Put the contents of the bowl into the pan, bring them to the boil, and boil rapidly until setting point is reached.

For extra flavour, wrap a piece of root ginger in muslin and add to the rhubarb before boiling.

Strawberry

MAKES: 2.95 kg/6½ lb

1.8 kg/4 lb strawberries
1.8 kg/4 lb sugar

Hull*, wash and drain the strawberries. Layer with the sugar in a large bowl. Cover with a cloth and leave in a cool place for 24 hours. Bring the contents of the bowl to the boil in a pan, and boil for 5 minutes. Leave the strawberries in the bowl for 48 hours, then boil for 20 minutes or until setting point is reached.

JELLIES

Fruit jellies should be bright and clear, with a good flavour and not too firmly set. Jellies, like jams, are best made from fruit rich in pectin and acid.

Prepare the fruit in the same way as for jams, then simmer it in water – the amount depends on the hardness of the fruit. Cook the fruit slowly for 45–60 minutes or until quite tender, then strain it through a scalded jelly bag and leave to drip for several hours, preferably overnight. Do not squeeze the bag as this makes the jelly cloudy.

Measure the quantity of strained juice and add sugar. Bring the juice and sugar to boiling point and boil rapidly until setting point is reached. Take the pan off the heat and remove any scum.

The amount of sugar used depends on the pectin content of the fruit. Test as for jam and allow 450–575 g/ 1–1¼ lb of sugar to each 600 ml/1 pt of juice rich in pectin. For juice of lesser pectin quality, allow 350 g/12 oz of sugar to each 600 ml/1 pt. Correct yield cannot be given, as this depends on the quantity of juice obtained. Pot and cover jellies as for jams.

Blackberry

1.8 kg/4 lb blackberries
600 ml/1 pt water
juice of 2 lemons
sugar

Simmer the fruit with the water and lemon juice until quite tender. Strain it through a jelly bag and measure the juice. Allow 450 g/1 lb of sugar to each 600 ml/1 pt of juice, then follow general instructions.

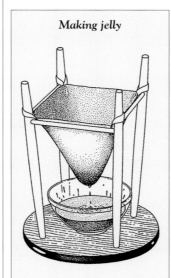

Making jelly

Up-end a stool to strain fruit juice through a scalded jelly bag.

Blackcurrant

1.8 kg/4 lb blackcurrants
1.7 litres/3 pt water
sugar

Simmer the fruit with the water. Strain it through a jelly bag and measure the juice. Allow 575 g/ 1¼ lb of sugar to each 600 ml/ 1 pt of juice, then follow general instructions.

Crab Apple

1.8 kg/4 lb crab apples
1.7 litres/3 pt water
sugar

Simmer the washed and chopped fruit with the water until the apples have cooked to a pulp, and the liquid has reduced by one-third. Strain it through a jelly bag and measure the juice. Allow 450 g/1 lb of sugar to each 600 ml/1 pt of juice, then follow the general instructions.

Damson

2.72 kg/6 lb damsons
1.7 litres/3 pt water
sugar

Simmer the fruit with the water. Strain it through a jelly bag and measure the juice. Allow 450 g/ 1 lb of sugar to each 600 ml/1 pt of juice, then follow general instructions.

Gooseberry

1.8 kg/4 lb gooseberries
1.7 litres/3 pt water
sugar

For jelly, there is no need to top and tail the gooseberries. Simmer the gooseberries with the water.

Strain it through a jelly bag and measure the juice. Allow 575 g/ 1¼ lb of sugar to each 600 ml/ 1 pt of juice, then follow the general instructions.

Quince

900 g/2 lb quinces
1.7 litres/3 pt water
7 g/¼ oz citric acid
sugar

Chop or mince the fruit. Simmer the fruit with the water. Strain it through a jelly bag and measure the juice. Allow 450 g/ 1 lb of sugar to each 600 ml/ 1 pt of juice, then follow the general instructions.

Redcurrant

2.72 kg/6 lb redcurrants
1.7 litres/3 pt water
sugar

Simmer the fruit with the water. Strain it through a jelly bag and measure the juice. Allow 575 g/ 1¼ lb of sugar to each 600 ml/ 1 pt of water, then follow the general instructions.

FRUIT CHEESES

Fruit cheeses are concentrated, sweet purées of fruit. They are only practicable when there is a glut of fruit, as a large quantity is needed to give a small amount of preserve. Stone fruits, such as damsons, plums or quinces, or fruits with strong flavours are the best choice. The finished preserve has a firm solid consistency and should be left to mature for at least 2 months. A fruit cheese is turned out of its mould and sliced for serving.

Making fruit cheese

Fruit cheese is ready for potting when a spoon leaves a clear line.

Damson Cheese

MAKES: 2.27–2.72 kg/5–6 lb

2.72 kg/6 lb damsons
300 ml/½ pt water
sugar

Remove any stalks and leaves from the damsons; wash thoroughly. Put the fruit and water in a heavy-based pan and cover with a lid. Simmer over gentle heat until reduced to a pulp, then rub through a sieve. Meanwhile, brush straight-sided pots with a little glycerine to prevent the cheese sticking.

Weigh the fruit pulp and return it to a clean, dry pan. Boil rapidly until the pulp is thick and has reduced by about one-third. Add the sugar, allowing 450 g/ 1 lb sugar to 450 g/1 lb of pulp. Continue cooking, stirring all the time, until a spoon drawn across the base of the pan leaves a firm line.

Pour into the pots and cover as for jam.

FRUIT CURDS

Curds are made with eggs, which diminish their keeping qualities. They are of soft spreading consistency and should be made only in small quantities. Use within 1 month.

Lemon Curd

MAKES: 450 g/1 lb

3 eggs
grated rind and juice of 2 large
lemons
100 g/4 oz butter
225 g/8 oz sugar

Beat the eggs lightly and mix in the lemon rind and juice, butter and sugar. Place in the top of a double boiler or in a bowl over hot water. Heat gently, stirring occasionally until the sugar has dissolved and the curd thickens. Pour into small, clean, dry jars and cover immediately.

MINCEMEAT

This is a Christmas preserve. It is steeped in brandy or rum, and left to mature for about 1 month.

Mincemeat

MAKES: 2.05–2.27 kg/4½–5 lb

225 g/8 oz cooking apples
225 g/8 oz currants
225 g/8 oz stoned raisins
225 g/8 oz sultanas
100 g/4 oz glacé cherries
100 g/4 oz chopped mixed peel
100 g/4 oz shelled walnuts
225 g/8 oz shredded suet
450 g/1 lb demerara sugar
10 ml/2 teaspoons mixed spice
90–120 ml/3–4 fl oz brandy
or rum

Peel, core and chop the apples, clean and mince the dried fruits; mix in a large bowl with the nuts and apples. Blend in the suet, sugar and spice. Add enough brandy or rum to give a moist mixture. Cover the bowl with a cloth and leave for 48 hours to allow the fruit to swell.

Stir well and put the mincemeat into clean jars. Seal and cover as for jam.

FRUIT SYRUPS

Syrups are made from the sweetened juices of berry fruits, such as blackberries, currants and strawberries. Syrup is a useful way of preserving ripe fruit.

Wash and drain the fruit thoroughly. Put in a pan and cook over gentle heat until the juices run freely. Most fruits require no additional water, but blackcurrants need 300 ml/½ pt of water to each 450 g/1 lb of fruit, and blackberries 300 ml/ ½ pt of water to each 2.72 kg/6 lb of fruit. Use a wooden spoon to crush whole fruit. Bring the fruit rapidly to the boil, then boil for 1 minute and remove the pan from the heat.

Strain through a scalded jelly bag and leave to drain overnight. Press the pulp in the bag to squeeze out any remaining juices.

Measure the quantity of extracted juice, and allow 350 g/ 12 oz sugar to each 600 ml/1 pt of juice. Cook over very gentle heat until the sugar has dissolved, stir and strain the mixture through muslin. Pour into sterilised bottles to within 3.5 cm/1½ in of the top, and seal with scalded screw caps or corks.

Making fruit syrups

Straining the fermented syrup.

Sealing caps on the bottled syrup.

Corks and stoppers should be boiled for 15 minutes before using. Secure the corks with insulating tape to prevent them blowing off during processing.

Place the filled bottles on a trivet in a deep pan. Fill the pan with water to within 2.5 cm/1 in of the top of the bottles. Heat the water to 77°C/170°F and hold at this temperature for 30 minutes. Alternatively, bring the water to simmering point and hold; simmer for 20 minutes.

Lift out the bottles, tighten the screw caps or press in the corks, and leave to cool. When the corks are dry, brush the top of each bottle with melted paraffin wax, covering the corks and 1 cm/½ in of the neck.

To serve, dilute one part syrup with five parts water.

Fermented Syrups

These are made from the same types of berries as fruit syrups, but no heat is applied, and a fuller fruit flavour is thus obtained.

Place the fruit, without any water, in a large earthenware bowl or jar and crush it well. Cover the bowl with a cloth and leave the fruit to ferment. When bubbles appear on the surface of the crushed fruit, fermentation is complete. Most fruits ferment within 24 hours if kept in a warm place, but blackcurrants take about 4 days.

Strain the fermented fruit through a jelly bag and leave to drip overnight; then squeeze the bag to obtain any remaining juice. Add 450 g/1 lb of sugar to each 600 ml/1 pt of juice, stir until dissolved, then strain the syrup through muslin. Pour into clean bottles, and seal with sterilised caps or corks.

Fermented syrups can be processed by heating the sealed bottles as for fruit syrups. Alternatively, a chemical preservative, such as sulphur dioxide, can be added to the syrups. Allow one fruit-preserving tablet (dissolved in 15 ml/1 tablespoon of water) to each 600 ml/1 pt of juice. Stir into the strained syrup before bottling and sealing.

Fermented strawberry syrup is low in acid, and requires citric acid in the proportions of 20 g/ ¾ oz to each 2.3 litres/4 pints of juice. Add this with the sugar.

BOTTLING

This preserving method involves sterilising the fruit. It must be of the finest quality, fresh and ripe.

All types of fruit are suitable for bottling. Berrie should be carefully cleaned, stalks, stems and leaves being removed; gooseberries should be topped and tailed, and rhubarb cut into even lengths. Apples, pears and quinces should be peeled, cored, quartered or sliced, while peeled apricots and peaches can be bottled whole or in halves and the stones removed. Plums are usually bottled whole.

Food Safety

The importance of hygiene and accuracy cannot be over-stressed in the context of bottling. The containers **must** be good quality and in good condition. The temperatures must be achieved and all procedures followed with care if the bottled fruit is to be safely preserved.

The rule of thumb when handling bottled fruit must be to discard any doubtful bottles. Always check the seal carefully before storing the bottles: if there is any question as to its effectiveness, then do not store the fruit. Instead, put it into the freezer (transferring it from the bottle, of course) or chill it and use it within 2–3 days.

Syrup and Jars for Bottling

Fruit may be preserved in water, but the flavour and colour is improved when fruit is bottled in syrup made from 225 g/8 oz of sugar to 600 ml/1 pt of water.

Pack the prepared fruit into

Bottling fruit

1 Pack fruit firmly into jars.

2 Pour sugar syrup over fruit.

3 Release air bubbles from the filled jars.

4 Process fruit at 74–88°C/ 165–190°F.

5 Maintain 5 lb pressure.

sterilised bottling jars. Do not dry the insides of the jars; the fruit slips more easily into place when jars are wet. Allow 275–350 g/10–12 oz fruit to each 450 g/1 lb jar. Pack the fruit as closely as possible without squashing it, and pour the syrup over it. Release any air bubbles by inserting a sterilised knife blade down the side of the jar or by jerking the filled jar. Add a little more syrup if necessary.

Seal the jars with glass or metal discs and with clips or screw bands. If using screw bands, screw down and then give a quarter turn to loosen. This allows steam to escape from the jars during processing, and prevents them from bursting. Bottling jars and clips and screw bands can be used again, but new sealing discs **must** be bought every time.

Methods of Bottling

Processing of the fruit can be done in a water bath or pressure cooker.

For the water-bath method an accurate thermometer is necessary. Place the filled jars on a trivet in a large pan, making sure that the jars do not touch each other. Pour in enough water to reach the level of the syrup in the jars. Heat the water gently, gradually raising the temperature until it reaches 54°C/130°F in 1 hour and the required temperature in 1½ hours. Soft berry fruits and apple slices must be held at 74°C/165°F for 10 minutes; all other fruit should be held at 82°C/180°F for 15 minutes, with the exception of figs and pears which should be held at 88°C/190°F for 30 minutes.

When the fruit has been processed, remove the jars from the pan on to a dry warm surface. Tighten the screw bands **immediately** and leave the jars undisturbed overnight.

When using a pressure cooker, make sure that it is deep enough to take the preserving jars and that there is a reliable control to maintain a steady 5 lb pressure. Cover the bottom of the pan with water to a depth of 2.5 cm/1 in, put in the trivet and set the prepared jars on top. Cover the cooker but leave the vent open, and heat until the steam flows – this should take between 5 and 10 minutes.

Close the vent and raise the pressure to 5 lb. Hold this pressure for 1 minute or, if the fruit is tightly packed, hold for 3 minutes. Pears and figs need 5 minutes. Remove the pan from the heat. Leave to cool for 10 minutes before releasing the pressure. Remove the jars and tighten the screw bands.

Testing the Seal

Always test the seal when the jars have cooled overnight and before storing the preserves.

If the jars are properly sealed, you should be able to lift them by their glass lids, without the screw bands in place. This can only be checked when the jars are cold. Remove the screw bands and check each jar by lifting it by the glass lid. If the lid comes off, the seal is not good enough and the fruit must be used up or frozen.

PICKLING

Pickles are fresh vegetables or fruit preserved in vinegar. White vinegar shows off the colour and texture of pickles, but malt vinegar gives a better flavour. Whichever vinegar is chosen it is usually flavoured with spices.

Preparing Spiced Vinegar

To make spiced vinegar, add 15 g/½ oz each of whole allspice, whole cinnamon, cloves, whole bruised ginger and white peppercorns to 1.12 litres/2 pt of vinegar. Steep the spices in the vinegar for 1–2 months and shake the bottle occasionally. Strain before use.

For immediate use, spiced vinegar can be prepared by a quicker method. Put the spices and vinegar into a bowl, cover and stand it in a pan of cold water. Bring the water to the boil, remove the pan from the heat, and leave the spices in the warm vinegar for about 2 hours. Keep the bowl covered so that no flavour is lost. Strain the vinegar before use.

Methods of Pickling

Wash and prepare the vegetables or fruit according to the recipe. Vegetables must be liberally sprinkled with coarse salt to draw out excess water which would otherwise dilute the vinegar.

Put the vegetables in layers with the salt or immerse them completely in a brine solution of 450 g/1 lb coarse salt to 4.5 litres/8 pt of water.

Leave the vegetables to steep in the salt for 24–48 hours, then rinse in cold water and drain

409

thoroughly. Do not use metal sieves or colanders.

Pack the vegetables into clean, dry jars to within 2.5 cm/1 in of the top. Pour over enough spiced vinegar to come 1 cm/½ in above the vegetables. Seal the jars tightly with vinegar-proof metal caps, greaseproof paper and muslin dipped in melted paraffin wax, or with preserving skins. It is essential that the jars are sealed airtight, otherwise the vinegar will evaporate and the pickle dry out.

The number of jars needed depends on the size of the pickled vegetable and how tightly they are packed. In general, 450 g/1 lb solid ingredients will fill a 450 g/1 lb jar.

Label and date the jars. Store in a cool, dry place for at least 1 month before using.

Sweet Pickles

For sweet pickles, omit the peppercorns when preparing the spiced vinegar, and use this as a base for a syrup, allowing 900 g/2 lb of sugar to each 600 ml/1 pt of spiced vinegar. Simmer the fruit in the syrup until just tender. Pack the fruit or vegetables in jars, pour over the syrup and seal.

When sweet-pickling whole fruit, prick them lightly to prevent shrinkage.

Pickled Beetroot

1.4 kg/3 lb uncooked beetroot
about 600 ml/1 pt spiced vinegar

Wash the beetroot carefully without damaging the skins. Cook in lightly salted water until

tender, after about 2 hours. Drain the beetroot, then pour cold water into the pan and rub off the peel under the water. Drain. Cut the beetroot into small dice or slices. Pack into jars and cover with cold spiced vinegar.

Pickled Cucumber

3 large cucumbers
4 large onions
60 ml/4 tablespoons coarse salt
600 ml/1 pt distilled vinegar
175 g/6 oz granulated or
  preserving sugar
5 ml/1 teaspoon celery seeds
5 ml/1 teaspoon mustard seeds

Wash, dry and thinly slice the cucumbers. Peel and slice the onions. Mix the two ingredients together in a bowl and sprinkle with the salt. Leave for 2 hours, then rinse and drain.

Bring the vinegar, sugar and spices to the boil and simmer for 3 minutes. Pack the drained cucumber and onion loosely in warm jars. Cover with the spiced vinegar and seal immediately.

Pickled Peaches

1.8 kg/4 lb peaches
600 ml/1 pt spiced vinegar syrup

Peel the peaches (page 361). Cut away any discoloured parts of the fruit, then halve and quarter the peaches, removing the stones. Poach fruit in the hot spiced vinegar syrup for 10 minutes or until tender.

Pack the fruit tightly into warm jars. Boil the syrup rapidly for 2–3 minutes to reduce it, remove any scum, and pour the syrup over the fruit. Seal at once.

Pickled Onions

2.72 kg/6 lb small onions
1.12 litres/2 pt spiced vinegar

Select small, even-sized onions and put them, unpeeled, in brine. Leave for 12 hours, then peel the onions and immerse them in fresh brine for a further 24–36 hours. Remove from the brine, rinse and drain thoroughly. Pack into clean jars and cover with cold spiced vinegar. Seal. Leave for 2–3 months before using.

Pickled Red Cabbage

1 large red cabbage
about 1.7 litres/3 pt spiced vinegar

Select a firm, brightly coloured cabbage. Remove outer leaves and centre stalk. Shred the cabbage finely, and layer it with salt in a large bowl. Leave for 24 hours, then drain and rinse thoroughly. Pack the cabbage loosely into jars; cover with cold spiced vinegar and seal. Use within 3 months.

Piccalilli

MAKES: about 3.2 kg/7 lb

2.72 kg/6 lb prepared vegetables
  (cucumber, marrow, small
  onions, cauliflower, beans)
1.7 litres/3 pt white vinegar
30 ml/2 tablespoons dry mustard
10 ml/2 teaspoons ground ginger
250 g/9 oz granulated sugar
40 g/1½ oz plain flour
20 ml/4 teaspoons turmeric

Clean and prepare the vegetables. Cut the cucumber and marrow into 2.5 cm/1 in cubes;

peel the onions, break the cauliflower into florets; and cut the beans into 2.5 cm/1 in lengths. Immerse the vegetables in brine and leave overnight.

Spice the vinegar with dry mustard and ginger, and also add the sugar.

Rinse and drain the vegetables thoroughly. Put them in a pan, pour over the hot vinegar syrup, and simmer for about 20 minutes. Lift the vegetables out with a slotted spoon and pack into warmed jars.

Mix the flour and turmeric to a smooth paste with a little vinegar. Stir this into the hot syrup. Boil for 2 minutes, then pour over the vegetables and seal.

Tomato Sauce

MAKES: 1.7 litres/3 pt

2.72 kg/6 lb ripe tomatoes
225 g/8 oz granulated sugar
300 ml/½ pt spiced vinegar
5 ml/1 teaspoon paprika
10 ml/2 teaspoons salt
cayenne pepper

Wash and quarter the tomatoes. Cook them over gentle heat until the juices run, then turn up the heat and boil them rapidly until they are reduced to a pulp.

Rub the tomato pulp through a nylon sieve and return the purée to a clean pan. Stir in the sugar, vinegar, paprika, salt and a pinch of cayenne. Bring to the boil and cook until the mixture has a sauce consistency.

Pour the tomato sauce into warmed bottles and seal. Process the bottles for 30 minutes (see Fruit Syrups).

CHUTNEYS

These are usually made from fruit such as apples, gooseberries plums and tomatoes. Flavourings are added in the form of spices, onions, garlic and salt, and the preserve is sweetened with sugar, or sugar and dried fruits. Chutneys require long, slow cooking in a stainless steel pan. The preserve should be smooth and pulpy with a mellow flavour. Pour the chutney into warmed, clean jars, and cover with vinegar-proof tops. Leave for 2–3 months before using.

Apple Mint Chutney

MAKES: 3.6 kg/8 lb

1.8 kg/4 lb cooking apples
100 g/4 oz onions
450 g/1 lb ripe tomatoes
600 ml/1 pt vinegar
450 g/1 lb sugar
100 g/4 oz chopped, candied ginger
  or 10 ml/2 teaspoons ground
  ginger
2.5 ml/½ teaspoon mixed spice
pinch cayenne pepper
2.5 ml/½ teaspoon salt
450 g/1 lb seedless raisins
50 g/2 oz finely chopped mint

Peel, core and chop the apples, peel and chop the onions, and skin (page 302) and chop the tomatoes. Cook the apples with 300 ml/½ pt of the vinegar until thick and pulpy, then stir in the remaining vinegar, the tomatoes, sugar, ginger, spice, cayenne, salt and raisins.

Cook for a further 15 minutes, then stir in the mint and cook for 5 more minutes or until thick. Pot and cover.

Tomato Chutney

MAKES: 3.62 kg/8 lb

2.72 kg/6 lb ripe tomatoes
225 g/8 oz onions
20 ml/4 teaspoons whole allspice
5 ml/1 teaspoon cayenne pepper
15 ml/1 tablespoon salt
300 ml/½ pt vinegar
350 g/12 oz soft brown sugar

Skin (page 302) and quarter the tomatoes and put them in a large pan, together with the peeled and thinly sliced onions. Add the allspice, tied in muslin, and the cayenne and salt. Cook over gentle heat until the mixture is pulpy, then stir in the remaining ingredients. Simmer until thick. Pot and cover.

Apple Chutney

MAKES: 2.72 kg/6 lb

1.8 kg/4 lb cooking apples
225 g/8 oz onions
600 ml/1 pt vinegar
2–3 cloves garlic
675 g/1½ lb soft brown sugar
100 g/4 oz chopped, candied ginger
  or 10 ml/2 teaspoons ground
  ginger
2.5 ml/½ teaspoon mixed spice
cayenne pepper
2.5 ml/½ teaspoon salt

Peel, core and chop the apples. Peel and chop the onions. Cook with 300 ml/½ pt of the vinegar and the crushed garlic until thick and pulpy. Add the remaining vinegar, the sugar, ginger, mixed spice, a good pinch of cayenne, and salt; continue cooking for a further 20 minutes or until thick. Pot and cover.

GARNISHES & DECORATIONS

A well-chosen garnish or decoration adds texture, colour and flavour to a dish. It should be fresh and simple rather than cluttered, and if the dish is hidden by a sauce, the garnish or decoration should give a clue to what is in the sauce. For instance, a dish served à la véronique – that is, with a sauce containing white grapes – is always garnished with small bunches of grapes. Many garnishes are classic – lemon and parsley, for example, are traditional with fried fish. Fried breadcrumbs are another classic garnish for adding a crisp texture to soft foods.

The garnish or decoration should be planned alongside the rest of the menu to avoid duplication in texture and colour. The ingredients must be prepared in advance and set out ready for adding to the food just when it is to be served. Garnishes or decorations which have to be cooked just before they are served – for example, fried parsley – should be organised to ensure that the food does not have to stand and cool while the garnish is prepared.

See also Soup Garnishes and Accompaniments (page 313).

Angelica
Use to decorate sweets and puddings. Buy angelica that has a good green colour, without too much sugar. Excess sugar can be removed by placing angelica for a short time in hot water; drain and dry. Use chopped, cut into strips, diamond or leaf shapes.

Aspic Jelly
This is used for coating and for holding a garnish in position. It is also used chopped to garnish a cold dish. See page 311.

Bacon Rolls
See page 331.

Bread Croûtons
See Soup Garnishes, page 313.

Breadcrumbs
Fried crumbs are a traditional garnish for game and *au gratin* dishes. Melt 25 g/1 oz butter in a frying pan, stir in 100 g/4 oz fresh white breadcrumbs and fry over moderate heat until the crumbs are evenly browned and golden. Turn frequently.

Bread Triangles
Remove the crusts from 1 cm/½ in thick slices of white bread. Cut each slice into four triangles and dip in egg beaten with 15–30 ml/1–2 tablespoons of milk. Coat the triangles with fresh white breadcrumbs and deep fry in hot oil until crisp and golden. Drain and use to garnish fish dishes.

Carrot Curls

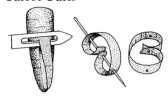

Cold buffet items may be decorated with these. Clean the carrots, and with a potato peeler pare down the length of each carrot to remove a wafer-thin strip. Twist the strip, fasten with wooden cocktail sticks and put in iced water to curl.

Celery Tassels

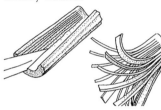

Edible garnish used with dips. Scrub the celery sticks, cut them into 5 cm/2 in lengths, then cut down the lengths at narrow intervals almost to the base. Leave the sticks in a bowl of iced water to curl.

Chantilly Cream
Used as a piped or spooned decoration for sweets. Whip 300 ml/½ pt of chilled double or whipping cream in a deep, cold basin. When the cream shows the first signs of thickening, add 15–20 ml/3–4 teaspoons caster sugar and 5 ml/1 teaspoon natural vanilla essence and continue to whip slowly until the cream just holds its shape. Whipped cream thickens by the pressure needed to force it through a nozzle, so it should stand in soft peaks to begin with. Pipe the cream through a piping bag and use a large star nozzle.

Chocolate
This takes on many forms as a decorative finish to cold desserts, classic gâteaux and simple cakes. Stored in an airtight tin in a cool place, chocolate shapes will keep for about 1 week.

Squares Break cooking chocolate into a bowl, place over a pan of hot water and allow the chocolate to melt slowly. Line a baking tray with non-stick or waxed paper. Pour the melted chocolate in a thin stream over the paper, and with a small palette knife spread the chocolate to a thin smooth layer. Leave to cool until firm, then cut the chocolate into squares with a warm, sharp knife. Peel the paper away carefully from the squares.

Leaves Melt the chocolate as for squares and meanwhile clean and dry small rose leaves. Hold each leaf with fine tweezers and dip the underside in the melted chocolate. Leave to dry, chocolate side up. When the chocolate has set, ease the leaves away carefully.

Cucumber

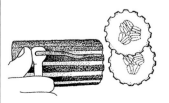

Sliced cucumber is traditional garnish to a cold mousse or

terrine. Deckled or ridged cucumber makes a more unusual decoration: wipe but do not peel a piece of cucumber; score it along the length with a fork or canelling knife, so that it has a serrated edge when sliced.

Gherkin Fans

Drain cocktail gherkins thoroughly, then slice each three or four times lengthways almost to the stalk end. Ease the slices apart to open out like a fan.

Glacé Cherries

These should be washed, in warm water, to remove the sticky syrup, and dried before being used whole, halved or chopped. Maraschino cherries also make an attractive decoration; they must be well dried to prevent the colour bleeding.

Grapes and Redcurrants

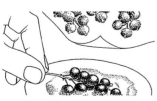

These are used frosted, either singly or in small clusters, to decorate sweet mousses, fruit soufflés and ice creams, or as a dessert fruit on their own. Brush single or small clusters of black or white grapes or strips of red-currants with lightly beaten egg white; dredge heavily with granulated or caster sugar. Leave on a wire rack to dry.

Lemon and Orange Spirals

Used to decorate long drinks and the plain surface of desserts, such as cheese cake. Using a potato peeler, pare off lemon or orange rind, free of white pith, in a continuous spiral. Hang the twisting peel from the rim of the glass or lay on the cake.

Mint Leaves

Frosted with sugar, these are seasonal delicacies with summer fruits. Select firm small sprigs of leaves, or individual leaves, brush them lightly with egg white and dredge thoroughly with caster sugar. Dry on a wire rack and use on the same day.

Mushrooms

'Turned', these are a traditional garnish with grilled meat. Choose large button mushrooms, wipe with a damp cloth and trim the stem level with the cap. With a sharp knife make a series of curving cuts 5 mm/¼ in apart, following the natural shape of the cap and from the top to the base. Remove a narrow strip along each indentation. Fry the mushrooms in a little butter.

Nuts

Almonds are sold whole, halved or finely chopped (nibbed almonds), or flaked. Plain or roasted, almonds make quick finishes for trifles, gâteaux and sweet soufflés. Whole almonds, bought with or without their skins, can be used whole, split in two along their natural seam, cut into slivers or chopped.

For slivered almonds, blanch whole unskinned almonds in boiling water for 2–3 minutes; rub off the skins and, while they are still soft, cut the almonds into strips.

For toasted almonds, spread the nuts, cut to the required shape, in a shallow pan and brown under a grill until golden.

Pistachio nuts should always be blanched to remove the skin. Put the nuts into boiling water and soak for about 5 minutes. Pour off the hot water and add some cold water. Ease off the skins by pinching each nut between thumb and forefinger, and dry the nuts before using them for garnish.

Hazelnuts need to be toasted before the skins can be removed. Place the shelled nuts in a single layer in a shallow pan and toast under a medium grill until the skins are dry and the nuts begin to colour. Cool slightly, place the nuts in a polythene bag, then rub them against each other to loosen the skins.

Fried Parsley

Fried parsley makes an attractive and well-flavoured garnish for fried fish. Allow 4 sprigs of parsley per person, and remove the long stems from the perfectly dry parsley. Heat oil to about 190°C/375°F, put the parsley in a frying basket and immerse it in the hot oil. As soon as the hissing ceases lift out the parsley. Drain on kitchen paper.

Radish Roses

Used to garnish cold entrées, open sandwiches, hors d'oeuvre and salads. Make 6–8 cuts lengthways through a radish from the base towards the stalk; put the radishes in a bowl of iced water until they open like flowers. Long radishes look attractive when cut at intervals along the length to open out concertina-fashion.

Tomatoes

Serrated or ivandyked tomatoes can be stuffed or used as a garnish for salads, flans, fried or grilled fish and meat. Choose firm tomatoes of even size. Using a small, sharp knife, make a series of small V-shaped indentations round the circumference of the tomato. Carefully pull the two halves apart. Oranges, grapefruit and melons may also be separated in this way.

Twists and Butterflies

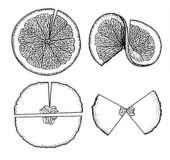

Tomatoes, cucumbers, lemons and oranges make attractive garnishes to any number of dishes, both savoury and sweet. Slice the vegetable or fruit thinly, though not wafer-thin.

For twists, cut each slice through to the centre, then twist the two halves in opposite directions and place in position.

For butterflies, cut two deep V-shaped incisions to meet near the centre of each round lemon slice. Remove the two wedges to leave a butterfly shape. Cucumber butterflies are easily made by cutting a slice in half, then cutting the semi-circle almost to the middle and twisting the wedges apart to lie opposite.

Watercress

Another favourite garnish for meat, poultry and fish dishes. Trim off the stems, and wash the watercress leaves in plenty of salted water. Lift out, rinse and shake well. Discard any ragged and yellow leaves, and arrange the watercress in small bunches to be added as garnish just before the dish is served. Washed watercress, with part of the stem left on, will keep for 1 day in a polythene bag in the refrigerator.

WINE WITH FOOD

Wine and food are natural partners, so choosing the right wine or wines can really turn a carefully cooked meal into a gourmet feast. While there are long-established rules laid down to stipulate which wine should be served with what food, the choice is really a matter of personal taste. There is no reason, for instance, why, if you prefer it, you should not drink red wine with certain types of fish such as salmon, though the textbooks say white is always preferable.

Buying Wine

The range of wines available in the high street is also very much wider than it used to be. Europe is no longer the dominant wine-producing area; the choice is world-wide and many of the newer wines are real value for money.

Where to buy You can buy wine in supermarkets, high street off-licences, traditional wine merchants and wine warehouses. Wines can also be bought by direct mail. Deciding which outlet to use depends on how much you are prepared to pay, how much information you want, how many bottles you need and whether you want the wine delivered.

Supermarkets and, to a lesser extent, off-licence chains are less expensive than traditional wine merchants. This is because they tend to stock many more economical wines from non-classic areas and also have the advantage of buying in greater quantities. So shop here for everyday wines.

Traditional wine merchants deal in fine wines, though increasingly they are offering good wines at the cheaper end of the market. The advantage of traditional merchants is that they provide a personal service. You can talk to knowledgeable staff who will be able to match wine from their stock to your requirements. They will also deliver. Buy wine here for special occasions or to lay down for future drinking.

Wine warehouses can offer bargain prices because the minimum amount you can buy at a time is a dozen bottles. You can often buy a mixed case, which means you can try sample bottles at home before buying in larger quantities. Such warehouses frequently arrange tastings and the staff are generally helpful.

Buying wine by direct mail from a catalogue is convenient but to benefit from free delivery you may have to order two or three cases of wine at a time. This is fine if you know and trust the company (or club) producing the list, but otherwise you are taking a gamble.

Buying wine in advance This makes wine sense. Some red wines, and a few white wines, improve with six months or a year in bottle. Others take five or ten years to reach maturity. Due to the cost of cellaring wine, many fine wines are simply not available for more than one to two years after the vintage and even if they are on sale they will cost a good deal more than the young wine.

A small cellar or collection of wine stored at home not only saves money, it is also extremely convenient. You will always have something to offer to both expected and unexpected guests and to drink yourself.

Choose wines from areas that you know and like. If you prefer drinking Italian or Spanish wines, disregard the general popularity of claret. Look for wines which are not quite ready to drink. Wine list notes such as 'still very young', 'full of promise' or 'will benefit from keeping' point the way. Avoid everyday wines which are not made to last.

Reading Labels

Wherever and whatever you are buying, the label on the bottle provides clues as to the contents. This will tell you which country the wine comes from and probably which wine-growing region. It may even tell you which vineyard, depending on the quality of the wine.

In Europe the cheapest level of wine is labelled table wine, *vin de table*, *vino de tavola*, *vino corriente* or *Konsumwein*. This simple everyday wine comes from anywhere in the country named. Next in line is the easy-drinking regional *vin de pays* or country wine. Above these are the quality wines from smaller designated wine-producing areas.

This kind of geographical classification is not used in the New World. Here grape varieties are more important and usually take precedence over the estate names. In Europe the name of the grape variety only appears on the labels of country wines and wines from Alsace.

The vintage or year the grapes were harvested is shown on the label. Vintages are not very important at the lower end of the wine scale. Ordinary table and country wines should be drunk within a year of the harvest. Quality wines may improve with the time spent in the bottle. The better the wine, the longer it may take to mature.

Labels also carry a certain amount of hype. Growers are fond of phrases like *extra réserve*, *cuvée speciale*, *grand vin* and *sélection speciale* but these do not mean very much. Where the wine is bottled is a much more useful piece of information. Look out for the phrase *mis en bouteille au château/domaine* at the base of the label. This means that the grower has bottled his own wine.

There is also a good deal to be learnt from the label on the back of the bottle and from any description given on the shelf or in the catalogue. Here is a short guide to some common terms.

Acidity This gives zest and freshness to a wine and helps to balance sweeter wines which would be too cloying without it. Too much and the wine is sharp and unpleasant; too little and the wine is flat and dull.

Appellation Contrôlée This is the general description given to wines which come from geographically designated areas. It comes from the French *Appellation d'Origine Contrôlé* or AOC (sometimes shortened in descriptions to AC).

Equivalent categories in other European countries are:
Denominazione di Origine Controllata (DOC) and the higher grade *Denominazione di Origine Controllata e Garantita* (DOCG) in Italy
Denominación de Origen (DO) and the higher grade *Denominación de Origen Calificada* (DOC) in Spain
Denominacão de Origem Controlada (DOC) in Portugal
Qualitätswein bestimmter Anbaugebiete (QbA) and the higher grade *Qualitätswein mit Prädikat* (QmP) in Germany

Balance The all-important ratio between all the different characteristics of a wine such as fruit flavours, acidity, tannin and alcohol. These should harmonise to give a pleasing rounded effect.

Barrique A barrel, usually made of oak, used for ageing wine.

Beerenauslese German wine made from individually selected grapes that are overripe and very sweet. They may be affected by noble rot.

Blanc de Noir White wine made from black grapes.

Body The feel of the wine in the mouth due both to the fullness of flavour and the alcoholic content. It may be described as light, medium or full.

Brut Usually the driest style of Champagne and sparkling wines.

Cava The collective name given to Spanish sparkling wine.

Complex A wine with many facets.

Crisp Often a euphemism for very sharp-tasting or acidic wine.

Cru An area which reflects a particular soil and climate.

Cuvée A selection of wine which may or may not have been blended.

Demi-sec Medium dry wine.

Flowery A fragrant, perfumed or flower-like aroma and flavour.

Fruity The predominant flavour of the wine which may not necessarily be that of fresh grapes. The flavour may be reminiscent of other fruit, for example, hints of apples, citrus fruits, pineapple, melon and tropical fruit occur in white wines; blackcurrant, raspberry, strawberry, cherry and blackberry flavours may be detected in red wines.

Grand Cru A top quality wine from France. The term is used differently in the classic regions.

Kabinett The basic level of German quality wines.

Négociant Merchant who buys grapes or wine from other growers to mature and market it.

Noble rot A mould called *Botrytis cinerea* which attacks the ripe grape and causes it to shrivel up, concentrating the juice.

Oaky A vanilla-like flavour imparted to wines by ageing in oak barrels.

Pétillant Slightly sparkling.

Sekt The collective name given to German sparkling wine.

Sin crianza Spanish term for wines not aged in oak.

Soft Means that the acidity, and in red wine the tannin, levels are quite low.

Sur lie Refers to wines such as Muscadet which have been left on their lees until bottling.

Tannic Indicates a high level of tannin which tends to leave a furry impression on the teeth and gums. Some tannin can be pleasant; too much is not. Tannins can soften with age.

Vendange Means grape harvest.

Dry or Sweet Wine?

The level of sweetness is one of the most important flavour characteristics of a wine, so in the UK a sweetness/dryness guide is widely used by retailers to help you find the level you prefer. The guide is based on a simple scale of 1–9 with 1 representing very dry and 9 very sweet. This scale is used in a large number of supermarkets and wine shops.

It is often claimed that a dry wine is the most sophisticated choice. In fact it depends on the wine. Some dry white wines may be too sharp and acidic, while some sweet wines are so enjoyable that you will be looking for more occasions on which to serve them.

Buying on Price

Price is one of the most important factors in choosing wine, but beware of buying on price alone. With cheap wines very little of the money you spend finds its way to the winemaker. Most of it goes to the taxman and the middlemen. But because these are fixed costs, even a relatively small increase in the amount you pay more than doubles the portion going to the producer. This will certainly be reflected in the quality of the wine.

Choice of Wine

The range of wine on offer in Britain has never been greater. The classic wine-growing areas of Europe continue to flourish and France, Italy and Spain are also developing non-classic country wines. In Eastern Europe, Hungary, Romania, Bulgaria, Moldova, Slovakia and the Czech Republic are all producing good everyday wines.

Wines from California, Australia and New Zealand go from strength to strength. Joining them on the international scene are those from Chile, Argentina and South Africa. At one time it was easy to generalise about the style of wine you might expect. Old World wines were restrained and elegant, whereas New World wines were fulsome and bursting with lush fruit. But winemakers are learning from each other. Old World wines are finding more fruit and the New World has learnt restraint.

Nor is it possible to generalise about the reliability of any particular wine-producing regions. Claret is not always up to the top-estates standard and cheap red wine from Bulgaria can challenge wines with a far greater reputation.

Styles of Wine

It may be that you generally buy a particular wine such as French Chablis or Australian Shiraz. This is fine for the best wines are the ones you like. But you may want to try other wines for a change or to suit a specific occasion. To do this you need to think about the style of a wine.

Light and easy-drinking wines These are wines which are easy to drink on their own at parties and with light meals and simple food. They feel light in the mouth and are usually low in alcohol and tannin. Most are dry but some, like the majority of German white wines, are medium-dry.

White wines include:
- Muscadet, Sauvignon de Touraine, Sancerre, Pouilly-Fumé, Chablis, Bordeaux Blanc, Mâcon, Entre-deux-Mers, Graves, French *vin de pays* wines
- German and English white wines
- Soave, Frascati, Orvieto, Verdicchio and Italian country wines
- Panades and most Rioja wines, La Mancha, and Navarre from Spain
- *Vinho verde* from Portugal
- White wines from Bulgaria, Hungary, Moldova, Slovakia and the Czech Republic
- Sauvignon Blanc wines from California, Chile and South Africa

Red wines include:
- Touraine Rouge, Saumur, Chinon, Beaujolais, young Bourgogne Rouge, Roussillon and French *vin de pays* wines
- Bardolino and Valpolicella from Italy
- Valdepeñas, Valencia and Navarre wines from Spain
- Pinot Noir wines from most wine-producing areas

Medium-bodied all-purpose wines. These wines taste a little fuller than the light and easy-drinking wines. They will partner most types of food and can be served at dinner and buffet parties. Or they can be drunk enjoyably, by the glass, on a quiet evening at home.

White wines include:
- Bourgogne Blanc, Alsace Pinot Blanc and Riesling, Vouvray and Chenin Blanc from France
- Spätlese and Auslese wines from Germany
- Light Chardonnay/Semillon and other blends from South Africa, Chile, Australia and New Zealand

Red wines include:
- Bordeaux Rouge (claret), Bergerac, Fitou, Corbières, Minervois, Côtes-du-Rhône from France
- Chianti and country wines from Italy
- Light young Rioja and some country wines from Spain
- Red wines from Bulgaria, Hungary, Moldova, Slovakia, the Czech Republic, California, Chile and South Africa
- Some Cabernet Sauvignon/Shiraz blends from Australia

Heavier or very distinctive wines This category takes in wine with strongly distinctive flavours. They may be high in alcohol. Some are dry, others are very sweet.

White wines include:
- Alsace Pinot Gris and Gewürztraminer from France
- Some Sauvignon Blanc (Fumé), Chardonnay, Semillon

and Rhine Riesling wines from California, Australia and New Zealand

- Trockenauslese and Trockenbeerenauslese sweet wines from Germany
- Sauternes, Barsac, Premières Côtes de Bordeaux, Loupiac, Monbazillac sweet wines from France.
- Late harvest or botrytised wines from the New World

Red wines include:

- Châteauneuf-du-Pape, Hermitage and Crozes-Hermitage from France
- Mature Rioja and Jumilla from Spain
- Barolo from Italy
- Dão, Bairrada and most Portuguese red wines
- Mature Cabernet Sauvignon and Shiraz wines from California and Australia

Serving Wine

Choose a good corkscrew with a curved ending to the screw. Remove the capsule (foil cover) and wipe the top of the bottle before pulling the cork. If your corkscrew has a straight ending, you may find that small pieces of cork fall into the wine. This does affect the wine. Pick out the cork pieces or strain the wine into a decanter.

Sometimes the cork is infected with a fungal growth which makes both the cork and the wine smell mouldy. This is known as 'corked wine' and it should not be drunk. Once you have encountered a corked wine, you will immediately recognise the smell again. Take the bottle back and ask for a replacement.

Opening bottles of Champagne or sparkling wine does require extra care. The contents of the bottle are under pressure and the cork could come flying out, with dangerous results. Press your thumb over the top of the cork as you twist the bottle with your other hand and keep the bottle pointing at the ceiling.

Decanting Wine

Apart from some very expensive clarets and vintage port which throw a sediment in the base of the bottle, it is not necessary to decant wine. If you do buy one of these wines, decant it by pouring the wine very carefully from the bottle into the decanter in one continuous movement. Position a bright light behind the bottle so that you can see when the sediment reaches the neck of the bottle and then stop pouring.

You may also decide to decant a young wine (with no sediment) to let it breathe. This allows the wine to take up oxygen from the air and so age quickly. However, it is very much a matter of personal preference. Some people simply open the bottle and leave it to stand for 30–60 minutes, others believe that simply pouring it out into a glass is enough!

Temperature Control

The old adage that red wine should be served at room temperature and white wine at cellar temperature is not really applicable in these days of central heating and efficient refrigeration. One hour in the refrigerator will be sufficient to

bring most white wines down to the correct temperature.

Ideally, wine should be served at approximately the following temperatures:

Mature red wines
   15–17°C/59–62°F
Young red wines and country wines
   13–16°C/55–60°F
Beaujolais and Valpolicella
   10–11°C/50–52°F
Sherry
   10°C/50°F
Champagne and dry white wines
   9–11°C/48–52°F
Sweet white wines
   6–7°C/43–45°F

Glasses

Choose a glass which has a stem long enough to give a comfortable grip and a foot wide enough to give a steady base. The glass should funnel gently inwards and be large enough to hold a normal portion without being full. This allows you to enjoy the aroma of the wine.

Serve Champagne and sparkling wines in slightly taller fluted glasses. Old-fashioned saucer-shaped Champagne glasses are easy to spill and their shape does not trap the aroma long enough for it to be enjoyed.

Matching Food and Wine

In an ideal world the wine and food should so complement one another that both gain from the match. Of course, most people do not have the time or the wine stocks for an ideal culinary match at every meal. Nevertheless, it is always worth considering how the wine you have picked will react with what

you are cooking. Does one have a more dominant flavour than the other? Will they harmonise or will they fight?

In the days of elaborate four-, five- and six-course meals rules were developed about which wines went with certain foods. White wine partnered the fish course and red wine the meat. These were useful guidelines but they were not always successful.

Today meals are simpler and the choice of wine is very much wider. In addition, most people are unlikely to serve more than one wine at a meal unless it is a very special occasion.

The modern approach, therefore, is to try to match styles of wine with types of food. For example, full-bodied wines with plenty of character and flavour (such as Syrah-based wines from the French Rhône, Australian Shiraz or Rioja) go well with spicy casseroles. Simple dishes such as grills and roasts will not fight for attention when you serve your very best wines.

Here are some useful questions to ask yourself when planning a match:

Is the dish particularly strongly flavoured or spicy or is it relatively mild? Choose a full-bodied or fine classic wine accordingly.

What are the component flavours of the dish? Can you match them with any of the flavours you might find in different wines? For example, you might match fruity flavours in the dish with similar flavours in the wine.

Does the dish (including

savoury dishes) **have any sweet ingredients?** If it does, you will need to choose a slightly sweeter wine. A very dry wine can taste astringent if served with something sweeter. This is particularly important with dessert wines.

Is the dish oily or fatty? A wine with good acidity is the answer here. For example, Italian wines are often very acidic but they are designed to partner Italian food which can often be rich.

Does the dish have a well-flavoured sauce? Remember that sauces can affect the flavour of mild foods such as chicken and fish. Wines with a lower level of tannin (such as white wine or red wines from Burgundy and north-eastern Italy) go better with most sauces than the tannic wines of Bordeaux, California or Tuscany.

Some foods are notoriously difficult to match. Vinegar in pickles or a salad dressing kills the taste of good wine as do hot chillies.

Wine as an Aperitif

Wines like sherry, white port and vermouth were the original aperitifs. These are basically wines which have been enriched with grape brandy to increase their alcoholic content. Table wines also make very good aperitifs and the same wine can often be served with the first course or even through the meal. Champagne or sparkling wines are good examples of wines to serve as an aperitif and with the first course, and they give a lift to any occasion.

This is also a good time to serve slightly sweeter wines (not as sweet as those to match with dessert), such as a German Spätlese, a French Vouvray or an Australian Rhine Riesling. You can continue to serve these wines with the first course if you choose a rich liver pâté or a fruity hors d'oeuvre.

Wine and Cheese

When you decide to serve the cheese may well affect the choice of wine. In France the cheese traditionally comes before the dessert and red wine is usually served. In the UK the tradition is to serve the dessert before the cheese. This, of course, means that red wine is not suitable as your palate will have been affected by eating the pudding. Port is the answer. It is a very good accompaniment to both mature Cheddar and Stilton.

Other sweet wines are well worth trying with cheese, particularly blue cheese. Good combinations include Sauternes with Roquefort and 'Late Harvest' wines from Australia with Blue Brie.

Serving Dessert Wines

Dessert wines are now often known as 'pudding' wines. They tend to be very sweet. They are often made from the Muscat grape (also known as Moscatel) which produces wine with a distinctively grapey flavour. Other grape varieties widely used include Riesling and Semillon.

Some dessert wines are made from grapes which have been affected by a mould known as 'noble rot'. This gives a very distinctive and intense raisiny flavour to the wine. Others, like port, Marsala and Madeira, are fortified with grape brandy.

The same principles apply to matching dessert wines to pudding dishes as to making any other food and wine partnership. The wine must be sweeter than the dessert or it will be swamped.

Storing Wine

Short-term storage If you have not finished the wine in the bottle you can simply re-cork it and store in the refrigerator until the next day. However, it is certainly worth investing in a proprietary bottle stopper. These remove air from the bottle and so stop the wine from oxidising. Vacuum pump closures and gas both work well.

Longer-term storage While few people today have a cellar where wine can be stored, a recess under the stairs or a discarded cupboard in the garage can provide useful storage. A wine rack can even be kept in the kitchen providing it is placed away from refrigerators, freezers and cookers.

Ideally, wine should be stored in the dark at a temperature of around 12°C/54°F. If this is not possible, try to ensure that any changes in temperature are gradual. Wine suffers more from sudden temperature change than it does from being stored in an area that is a little too warm or too cold.

Always store wine bottles on their sides. This stops the corks from drying out.

ALTERNATIVES TO WINE

Always offer an alcohol-free alternative to wine, or other alcoholic drinks, at dinner or drinks parties.

Water

Water is now drunk in addition to wine with a meal so include a water glass as well as wine glasses at each place setting. Serve iced tap water or still mineral water in a jug with slices of lemon or lime to flavour the water slightly.

Sparkling mineral water is a popular choice for aperitifs or drinks parties, when it should be served with ice and lemon.

Flavoured Mineral Water

There is a wide choice of mineral waters flavoured with fruit, herbs and/or spices. Many of these drinks are sweetened and some have a strong, quite distinctive or 'scented' flavour which does not complement savoury dishes, particularly very light fish or chicken dishes or very rich, meaty main dishes.

These are ideal for serving at drinks parties, or as an aperitif. Select a lightly sweetened and delicately flavoured water to go with a meal.

Fruit Juice

Fruit juice has a pronounced flavour and it is usually too sweet to complement food, so it is not a good choice of drink to serve with a meal. Orange juice should, however, always be offered as one of a selection of aperitifs. Grape, apple and grapefruit juice are all light and,

depending on the brand chosen, not too sweet, so they make good aperitifs or party drinks.

There are many strongly flavoured juices and exotic mixes which can make good alternatives to cocktails, but they tend to be quite sweet and they are not really suitable for drinks parties or buffets.

Fizzy Drinks

Tonic water is the classic alternative to an alcoholic aperitif; served with ice and lemon, it is not too sweet. Russian, a pomegranate-flavoured, lightly sweetened mixer, makes an excellent alcohol-free aperitif. Coke is also popular with many adults and it is a classic mixer for rum. Some of the less-sweet carbonated fruit drinks, ginger beer and lemonade are all suitable for adults.

Alcohol-free Beer

Take care to check whether you are buying alcohol-free beer or a low-alcohol beer as they can be easily confused. It is a good idea to keep a stock of alcohol-free beer for aperitifs, parties and informal gatherings, such as barbecues.

Mixing Alcohol-free Drinks

Sparkling mineral water mixers Shake a good dash of bitters (for example, Angostura) into a tall glass and top up with sparkling mineral water. Add ice and a slice of lemon for a sophisticated alcohol-free aperitif.

A little fresh lime juice and a sprig of mint also brightens up a glass of plain mineral water.

Fruit cocktails Different fruit juices can be combined or diluted with sparkling mineral water or tonic water. Exotic fruit juices which tend to be very sweet, such as mango, pineapple or passion fruit, are ideal for diluting and they can be sharpened with a squeeze of lime or lemon, and decorated with slices of citrus fruit.

Punches and fruit cups Fresh fruit macerated in a light fruit juice is a good base for an alcohol-free punch. Select a mixture of fruit according to the season: strawberries, redcurrants and raspberries are ideal for summer; oranges, lemons and limes for winter. Thinly sliced cucumber and/or mint, borage and lemon balm may be added to the fruit. Cover the fruit with apple or grape juice and leave it to stand for a few hours before the punch is required. Then add plenty of ice and top it up with sparkling mineral water or a mixture of mineral water and tonic water or lemonade, depending on how sweet you want the punch to be.

Tea punches Herb and fruit teas are useful for making summer punches. Cool and chill the tea, then add sliced fresh fruit, mint and sparkling mineral water, tonic water or lemonade to make a light punch.

Mulled fruit drink Make a bowl of mulled fruit punch by mulling apples and oranges with cinnamon, cloves and nutmeg in unsweetened apple juice. Freshly brewed cinnamon and apple tea or another fruit tea can be added to make the drink less sweet.

A TO Z OF COOKERY TERMS

Letters in brackets indicate the country of origin. A stands for Austria; F for France; G for Germany; Gr for Greece; H for Hungary; I for Italy; In for India; R for Russia; S for Spain; T for Turkey; and US for the United States.

A

acidulated water Water with a little lemon juice or vinegar added. Used to help prevent discoloration of some fruits and vegetables. About 5 ml/1 teaspoon lemon juice or vinegar is sufficient for 300 ml/½ pt water. The ingredients may be drained and the water discarded before cooking.

à la (F) In the style of; for example, à la russe, which means 'in the Russian style'.

à la carte (F) 1. Bill of fare from which the diner selects individual dishes. 2. Dishes cooked to order.

à l'anglaise (F) In the English style.

à la crème (F) Served with cream or a cream sauce.

al dente (I) Of pasta; cooked – but firm to the bite.

alla (I) In the style of; for example, alla parmigiana, meaning 'in Parmesan style'.

allumettes (F) Matchstick-sized strips of vegetables.

amandine (F) Cooking or coating with almonds.

antipasti (I) Italian hors d'oeuvre of mixed meats, marinated ingredients, salads or hot dishes.

à point (F) Of meat, medium cooked.

arrowroot Starch similar to cornflour, used for thickening sauces.

Arrowroot is tasteless and gives a clear sauce. Maximum thickness is achieved when the sauce boils; further simmering causes arrowroot to thin down slightly.

aspic Clear jelly made from fish, chicken or meat stock.

au bleu (F) Blue; fish cooked immediately after being caught has a natural coating on the skin which will turn slightly blue.

au gratin (F) Dish with a crisp topping of browned crumbs and/or grated cheese.

B

bain marie (F) A container of hot water, or 'bath', in which a smaller cooking dish or pan is placed. The outer container of water prevents the base and/or sides of the dish or pan of food from becoming too hot. Used for cooking, melting or mixing delicate ingredients or fragile mixtures, or for keeping food hot without further cooking.

barding Covering lean meat, game and poultry with thin slices of pork fat or bacon to prevent drying out during cooking.

basting Moistening food during cooking by spooning over cooking juices or fat.

beating Mixing food vigorously with a wooden or plastic spoon or electric mixer to soften it and, usually, to introduce air to make it lighter in texture.

binding Mixing a minimum amount of liquid into dry ingredients to hold them together.

blanching To plunge into boiling liquid (usually water) and bring back to the boil rapidly, then drain immediately or boil briefly. To loosen the skin from nuts, fruit and vegetables; kill enzymes prior to freezing; or remove strong or bitter flavours.

blanquette (F) White stew of veal, poultry or rabbit in a creamy sauce.

blini, bliny (R) Pancake made of buckwheat and yeast, and traditionally served with caviar and soured cream.

boiling Cooking rapidly in liquid which bubbles steadily. Water boils at a temperature of 100°C/212°F.

boning Removing bones of fish, poultry, game or meat.

bouchée (F) Small puff-pastry case filled with a savoury or sweet mixture.

bouquet garni (F) A bunch of herbs used for flavouring dishes like soups and stews. Bay, parsley, thyme and a celery leaf or short piece of celery stick are tied together to make a basic bouquet garni. Sage, marjoram, savory or rosemary may be added according to the type of dish and main ingredients. Bought sachets or muslin bags of dried herbs are usually far stronger in flavour than a fresh bouquet garni and they can dominate a sauce or soup rather than giving it a delicate herb flavour.

bourguignonne (F) In the style of Burgundy, cooked in red wine.

braising Cooking gently with a small amount of liquid, with flavouring ingredients (such as diced vegetables) in a covered pan or dish on the hob or in the oven.

brine Salt and water solution used for pickling and preserving.

brioche (F) Soft bread made of rich yeast dough, slightly sweetened.

brochette (F) Metal skewer used for kebabs.

broiling (US) Grilling.

brûlé (F) Applied to dishes such as cream custards finished with sugar caramelised quickly under the grill.

C

canapé Bite-sized savoury usually on a base of fresh or fried bread, toast or a cracker.

cannelloni (I) Large pasta tubes for stuffing.

capers Flower buds of the caper bush with a slightly peppery flavour. Usually pickled in vinegar, also available salted.

caponata (I) Sicilian dish of aubergines, tomatoes, onions, capers and black olives, often including fish.

carbonnade (F) Beef stew made with beer.

casserole Ovenproof or flameproof cooking pot with lid. Also term used for a stew cooked in a casserole.

cassoulet (F) Stew of mixed meats and goose or duck with haricot beans and French sausage. Topped with browned crust of breadcrumbs.

champignon (F) Mushroom.

Chantilly (F) Whipped cream, slightly sweetened and sometimes flavoured with vanilla.

charlotte 1. Hot moulded pudding made of buttered bread and filled with fruit. 2. Cold, moulded, set dessert consisting of sponge fingers with cream and/or custard.

charlotte mould A straight-sided, deep mould, sloping out slightly towards the top

chasseur (F) Cooked with mushrooms, shallots and white wine.

chaudfroid (F) Cold dish offish or poultry, masked with a creamy sauce set with aspic. Highly garnished, glazed with aspic, and may be surrounded with chopped aspic.

chiffonade (F) Shredded lettuce, sorrel, spinach or salad leaves used as a garnish or base on which to serve food.

chilling Cooling food in the refrigerator.

chine Of pork; a pair of loins left undivided.

chining Sawing through the backbone along the base of the ribs in a joint of meat to make carving easier.

chinois (F) 1. In the Chinese style. 2. Applied to a conical-shaped sieve with a fine mesh.

chorizo (S) Spicy sausage flavoured with paprika.

chowder (US) Hearty fish soup, almost as substantial as a stew.

civet (F) Brown game stew.

clarified butter Butter which has been heated gently until its water content evaporates and spitting ceases, then strained to remove the white residue of salt and milk protein. Clarified butter keeps well in a covered container in the refrigerator for up to a month. It does not burn as readily as ordinary butter, therefore it is useful for frying. See also *ghee*.

clarifying 1. Clearing fats by heating and filtering. 2. Clearing liquids such as stock or fruit jelly by heating with whisked egg white and crushed egg shell, then straining through a sieve which is lined with muslin.

cocotte (F) Small ovenproof dish, used for baking individual portions, such as eggs or soufflés.

coddling Cooking whole eggs in barely simmering water or by allowing them to stand in a pan of boiling water that has been removed from the heat. The whites are softly set, not firm like those of boiled eggs. An egg coddler is a container in which to boil a shelled egg while keeping it in the shape of a whole egg.

colander Perforated metal or plastic container for draining away liquids.

compôte (F) Fruit cooked in syrup.

concassé (F) Roughly but evenly chopped. Applied to vegetables, such as tomatoes.

condé (F) 1. Cold dessert made with cooked rice. 2. Pastry biscuits topped with icing and glazed in the oven.

conserve (F) Fruit preserve with large pieces of fruit or whole fruit. Conserve is similar to jam, but may be softly set.

coquille (F) 1. Scallop. 2. Shell-shaped ovenproof dish used to serve fish, shellfish or poultry.

corn starch (US) American term for cornflour.

corn syrup (US) American equivalent of golden syrup. Clear corn syrup is the American term for liquid glucose.

coupe (F) Goblet used for serving savoury or dessert cocktails or ice cream.

crème brûlée (F) Cream custard with caramelised topping.

crème caramel (F) Egg custard cooked in a caramel-lined mould; cooked, chilled and turned out so that the caramel forms a topping.

crème fraîche (F) Cream that is cultured to give it a light tang, less so than soured cream.

creole Of Caribbean cookery; prepared with ingredients such as chillies, peppers, tomatoes, okra and rice.

crêpe (F) Thin pancake.

crêpes Suzette (F) Thin pancakes cooked in orange sauce and flamed in liqueur.

crimping 1. Making a decorative border to pie crusts. 2. Gashing fresh skate, then soaking it in cold water and vinegar before cooking, so that the flesh firms.

croquettes (F) Small cylindrical or wedge-shaped patties coated in egg and crumbs, and deep-fried. The mixture is traditionally a thick sauce with fish, chicken or meat added, chilled until set and shaped. Creamed vegetables may also be shaped into croquettes.

croûstade (F) Small case of fried or baked bread filled with a savoury mixture.

croûte (F) 1. Pastry covering around ingredients. 2. Slice of bread fried or baked until crisp and brown.

curdle To separate into small lumps of solids and a thin liquid. Milk curdles when acid is added to it. Eggs curdle when beaten and overheated. Mixtures to which eggs are added or which contain raw egg curdle if overheated or if incompatible ingredients are added too quickly or in large proportions. In raw ingredients curdling is usually irreversible. Some curdled mixtures, such as mayonnaise, can be brought back together.

curds Solids separating out when milk or eggs curdle, leaving the whey or a thin liquid.

cure To preserve by drying, salting or smoking.

D

dariole Small deep, straight-sided metal mould, slightly wider across the top than the base. For baking or setting cold mixtures.

darne (F) Thick slice cut from large fish.

daube (F) Stew of meat and vegetables.

deep-frying Frying food by immersing it in hot fat or oil.

déglacer (F) Diluting concentrated pan juices and cooking residue or sediment by adding a small amount of wine, water or stock and boiling rapidly until reduced and well flavoured. The juices may be served as a thin gravy, added to the dish or used as the basis of a sauce.

devilling Flavouring with piquant or hot seasonings, such as chilli powder, mustard, Worcestershire sauce or Tabasco. Tomato paste is often added.

dice Cut into small even cubes.

dredging Sprinkling generously with flour or sugar.

dress 1. To pluck, draw and truss poultry or game. 2. To prepare and cook crab and lobster in their shells.

dressing 1. Sauce for a salad. 2. Stuffing for meat or poultry.

dripping Fat which drips from meat, poultry or game during roasting.

dumpling 1. Small balls of suet pastry which are poached or steamed. Various other ingredients are used to make dumplings, including potatoes, breadcrumbs, semolina and ricotta cheese. 2. Whole fruit encased in short-crust pastry and baked.

dusting Sprinkling lightly with flour, sugar or other ingredients.

E

en croûte Food encased in pastry.

en papillote (F) Food wrapped, cooked and often served in greased paper or foil.

entrée 1. Third course in a formal meal, following the fish course. 2. Main dish, sauced and garnished.

entremet (F) Sweet or pudding.

escalope Thin slice of poultry or meat which is beaten flat.

F

faggot 1. Small meatball of pork offal, traditionally wrapped in caul and baked. 2. A small bunch; for example, of herbs which are tied with string.

farina (I) Fine flour made from wheat, nuts and potatoes.

farle Round, flat oatmeal cake baked on a griddle.

fines herbes (F) Mixture of finely chopped fresh parsley, chervil, tarragon and chives.

flake Separating cooked fish into individual flakes.

flambé (F) Flamed with burning brandy or other alcohol.

florentine 1. Of fish and eggs; served on a bed of buttered spinach and coated with cheese sauce. 2. Thin biscuit made of brandy-snap type mixture with nuts and glacé fruit; coated with chocolate when cooled.

foie gras (F) The liver of specially fattened goose or duck.

folding in Combining one ingredient or mixture with another by using a large metal spoon to cut and fold the main batch of mixture in a figure-of-eight movement around the ingredient which is being added.

fool Cold dessert consisting of fruit purée and custard or whipped cream.

fricassée (F) A white stew of poultry, veal, meat or vegetables. The term is also used for ready cooked veal or poultry reheated in a white sauce.

frost 1. To coat a cake with an icing of confectioner's sugar. 2. To dip the rim of a glass in egg white and caster sugar and then chill until set.

fumet (F) Concentrated broth or stock obtained from fish, meat or vegetables.

G

galantine (F) Dish of boned and stuffed poultry, game or meat glazed with aspic and served cold.

galette (F) 1. A flat pastry cake traditionally baked for Twelfth Night. 2. A flat cake of cooked sliced or mashed potato.

garnishing Adding 'decoration' to a savoury dish.

gelatine Animal-based setting agent for savoury or sweet use. Powdered gelatine should be sprinkled over a little cold liquid and allowed to stand without stirring until it becomes spongy in texture. Then it can be dissolved by standing the basin over hot water and stirring often. Leaf gelatine must be softened in cold water, drained and dissolved as for powdered gelatine.

génoise (F) A rich whisked sponge with melted butter folded in after the flour has been added.

ghee (In) Clarified butter. Vegetable ghee made from oil is now widely available.

giblets Edible internal organs and trimmings of poultry and game, which include the liver, heart, gizzard, neck, pinions and sometimes the feet and cockscomb.

glacé (F) Glazed, frozen or iced.

glace de viande (F) Meat glaze or residue in the bottom of a pan after roasting or frying meat. Or concentrated meat stock.

glaze A glossy finish given to food by brushing with beaten egg or milk before cooking or by coating with sugar syrup, sieved jam or jelly after cooking.

gnocchi (I) Small dumplings made from semolina, potatoes or ricotta cheese.

goujon (F) Small strips of fish

fillet, coated in egg and breadcrumbs and fried. Taken from gudgeons, small fish fried whole.

goulash (H) Stew flavoured with paprika and tomato.

granita (I) Water ice.

granité (F) Sorbet.

gratiné (F) See *au gratin*.

gravy 1. Juices exuded by roasted meat and poultry. 2. A sauce made from these juices by thickening with flour and boiling with stock.

grecque, à la (F) In the Greek style.

griddle Heavy flat metal plate used to cook pancakes, scones and cakes on the hob.

grissini (I) Breadsticks.

Gugelhupf (G) Sweetened yeast cake with dried fruit, baked in a deep fluted ring mould.

H

haggis Scottish sausage-type mixture of chopped calf's or sheep's offal, suet, onions, spices and oatmeal, which is traditionally boiled in the stomach lining of a sheep, but often cooked in synthetic casing today.

hamburger (US) Minced beef patty.

hard sauce Sweetened butter flavoured with brandy, rum or whisky. Also known as brandy butter. Served with Christmas pudding or minced pies.

hash Dish of chopped leftover meat, potatoes or other vegetables, fried together.

hors d'oeuvre (F) Hot or cold appetisers served at the start of a meal.

hulling Removing green calyx from strawberries and raspberries.

I

icing Sweet coating for cakes, made with icing sugar.

infusing Steeping a flavouring ingredient, such as herbs, tea leaves or coffee, in water or other liquid to extract the flavour.

J

jardinière, à la (F) Garnish of diced and cooked vegetables.

joint To divide meat, game or poultry into individual pieces.

jugged Stew of game, thickened with the blood of the animal as when jugged hare is thickened with the blood of the hare.

jus (F) Juices from roasting meat used as gravy.

K

kebab (T) Skewered food, usually grilled.

kosher Food prepared according to Orthodox Jewish law.

L

langue de chat (F) Flat, finger-shaped crisp biscuit served with cold desserts.

lard Natural or refined pork fat.

larding Threading strips of fat through lean meat, using a special needle. This prevents the meat becoming dry during roasting.

leavening agent Substance, such as yeast, which causes mixture to rise.

légumes (F) 1. Vegetables. 2. Plants with seed pods, such as peas and beans.

lyonnaise (F) In the Lyons style; usually with onions.

M

macaroni (I) Tubular-shaped pasta of varying lengths and shapes.

macedoine (F) Mixture of fruit or vegetables.

macerate To soak sweet ingredients in liquid, such as fruit soaked in alcohol.

marinade Blend of oil, wine or vinegar, herbs and spices. Used to flavour and/or tenderise ingredients which are soaked in it.

marinate To soak ingredients in marinade. A savoury term.

marinière (F) 1. Of mussels; cooked in white wine and herbs, and served in half shells. 2. Of fish; cooked in white wine and garnished with mussels.

marmite (F) Earthenware stock pot.

matelote (F) In the sailor's style; fish stew made with wine or cider.

medallions (F) Small circular cuts of meat, fish or pâté.

meunière (F) In the style of a miller's wife; fish cooked in butter, seasoned, and sprinkled with parsley and lemon juice.

milanese (I) In the Milan style; of escalopes coated in egg, bread-crumbs, seasoned with grated Parmesan cheese, and fried in butter.

mirabelle (F) 1. Small yellow plum, used as tart filling. 2. A liqueur made from this fruit.

mirepoix (F) Mixture of finely diced vegetables used as a base for braising ingredients or flavouring cooking liquids and sauces.

mocha A blend of coffee and chocolate.

moules (F) Mussels.

mousse Light savoury or sweet cold dish lightened with whisked egg whites and set with gelatine.

N

navarin (F) Stew of lamb and vegetables.

Neapolitan (I) Ice creams and sweet cakes in layers of different colours and flavours.

niçoise (F) In the Nice style, cooked with tomatoes, onion, garlic and black olives.

normande, à la (F) In the Normandy style, cooked with cider and cream.

nouilles (F) Noodles.

O

offal Edible internal organs of meat, poultry and game.

P

paella (S) Dish of saffron rice, chicken and shellfish, which is named after the large shallow pan in which it is traditionally cooked.

panada Very thick sauce made of fat, flour and liquid, used as a base for dishes like baked soufflés or to bind mixtures.

panettone (I) Rich, sweet, vanilla-flavoured bread with candied and dried fruit and nuts. Baked for Christmas.

paprika (H) Ground, sweet red pepper.

parboiling Boiling for a short time to half-cook food.

parfait (F) Frozen dessert made of whipped cream.

Parmentier (F) Applied to dishes containing potatoes; the term is derived from Antoine Parmentier who introduced the potato to France.

pasteurising Method of sterilising by heating to destroy bacteria.

pastry wheel Small, serrated wooden or metal wheel for cutting and fluting pastry.

pasty Oval pastry with pointed ends, containing a savoury filling.

pâté (F) 1. Savoury mixture which is baked in a casserole or terrine, and served cold. 2. Savoury mixture baked in a pastry case and served hot or cold.

pâte (F) Pastry.

pâte à choux (F) Choux pastry.

patty 1. Small, flat, round or oval-shaped cake of food, such as potato cake or fish cake, which is served hot. 2. Small, flat, individual pie, such as a chicken patty, which is served hot or cold.

paupiette (F) Thin slice of meat rolled around a savoury filling.

pavé (F) 1. Cold mixture set in a square or oblong mould. Includes savoury and sweet mixtures, and frozen mixtures or sponge cake, filled and iced.

pease pudding Purée of cooked, dried peas, made into puddings, boiled and served sliced.

pectin Setting agent for jams, jellies and marmalades, found naturally in some fruit, particularly citrus fruit and cooking apples.

perdrix (F) Partridge.

petits fours (F) Miniature cakes, biscuits and sweet items served at the end of a meal with coffee, including tiny iced sponge cakes, grapes and cherries coated in sugar and marzipan coloured and shaped to resemble miniature fruits.

petits pois (F) Tiny green peas.

pickle To preserve vegetables in vinegar.

pilaf, pilau (T) Near-eastern dish of cooked rice mixed with spiced, cooked meat, chicken or fish.

pimento Green or red pepper; term usually used to describe canned or bottled vegetables.

pintade (F) Guinea fowl.

piquant Pleasantly sharp and appetising.

pith In citrus fruit, the white cellular lining to the rind.

pizzaiola (I) Meat or chicken, cooked in red wine, tomato sauce and flavoured with garlic.

plat du jour (F) Dish of the day.

pluck 1. Offal. 2. To remove the feathers from a bird.

poaching Cooking food in gently simmering liquid.

polenta (I) Corn meal, made from maize, which is dried and ground.

potage (F) Thick soup.

praline (F) Toasted almonds in caramel, crushed with a rolling pin when cold.

printanier (F) Garnish of spring vegetables.

prosciutto (I) Raw smoked ham, served finely sliced, eg, Parma ham.

provençale (F) In the Provence style, cooked with garlic and tomatoes.

pudding 1. Hot dessert. 2. Hot savoury dish made by lining a pudding basin with suet crust pastry and filling it with meat.

purée (F) 1. Sieved or processed raw or cooked food reduced to a smooth paste.

Q

quenelles (F) Poached light savoury dumplings made of meat or fish and used as a garnish.

quiche (F) Open-faced pastry case filled with a savoury mixture.

R

ragoût (F) Stew of meat and vegetables.

ramekins 1. Individual ovenware dishes. 2. Small pastry cases with cream-cheese filling.

ratafia 1. Flavouring made from bitter almonds. 2. Liqueur made from fruit kernels. 3. Tiny almond macaroon.

ratatouille (F) French stew made by cooking aubergines, onions, peppers, courgettes and tomatoes in olive oil.

reducing Concentrating a liquid by boiling hard in an open pan so that some of the water content evaporates.

relish Sharp or spicy sauce made with fruit or vegetables which adds a piquant flavour to other foods.

rendering Slowly cooking meat tissues or fat and trimmings to obtain liquid fat.

rennet Substance extracted from the stomach lining of calves. Used to coagulate milk for junket and for making cheese curd.

rice paper Edible, thin glossy white paper made from rice starch. Used to line tins on which macaroons are based, it bakes into the mixture.

risotto (I) Savoury rice, fried and then cooked with stock or wine and additional ingredients according to the recipe.

rissole Small patty of cooked minced meat.

roasting Cooking on a rack in a tin in the overt or on a spit.

roe 1. Milt of the male fish, called soft roe. 2. Eggs of the female fish, called hard roe. 3. Shellfish roe, called coral because of its colour.

romano (I) In the style of Rome.

rôtisserie Rotating spit used for roasting or grilling meat or poultry.

roulade (F) Roll of meat, vegetables, chocolate cake and so on.

roux Paste of fat and flour to which liquid is added when making a sauce or soup.

S

saignant (F) Of meat; underdone.

salami (I) Spiced, cured sausage. There are many varieties.

salmi (F) Stew made by first roasting game and then cooking it in wine sauce.

sauté (F) To fry food rapidly in shallow, hot fat, tossing and turning it until evenly browned.

savarin (F) Rich yeast cake, which is baked in a ring mould and soaked in liqueur-flavoured syrup. Served cold filled with fruit, if liked, with cream.

scald 1. To heat milk or cream to just below boiling point. 2. To plunge fruit or vegetables in boiling water to remove the skins.

scaloppine (I) Small escalopes of veal.

Schnitzel (G) Thin veal slice; see escalope, also *Wiener Schnitzel*.

scoring 1. Cutting shallow gashes or narrow grooves in the surface of food; for example, in pork rind. 2. Cutting a shallow pattern of squares or diamonds on pastry crust.

searing Browning meat rapidly with fierce heat to seal in the juices.

seasoned flour Flour flavoured with salt and pepper.

seasoning Salt, pepper, spices or herbs, which are added to food to improve flavour.

sifting Passing flour through a sieve to remove lumps.

simmering Cooking in liquid which is just about boiling and bubbling only occasionally.

skewer Metal or wooden pin used to hold meat, poultry or fish in shape during cooking.

skimming Removing cream from the surface of milk, or fat or scum from broth or jam.

sorbet (F) Water ice made with fruit syrup and/or purée.

soufflé dish Straight-sided circular dish used for cooking and/or serving soufflés.

sousing Pickling food or poaching it gently in vinegar; for example, soused herrings.

spit Revolving skewer or metal rod on which meat, poultry or game is roasted over a fire or under a grill.

spring-form mould Baking tin with hinged sides, held together by a metal clamp or pin, which is opened to release the cake or pie.

steaming Cooking food in the steam rising from boiling water or other steam-producing liquid.

steeping 1. Soaking in liquid until saturated with a soluble ingredient. 2. Soaking to remove an ingredient, such as salt from salt cod.

stewing To simmer food slowly for a long period in a covered pan or casserole on the hob or in the oven.

stirring Mixing with a circular movement, using a spoon.

straining Separating solids from liquids by passing the mixture through a sieve, colander or muslin.

Strudel (A) Thin leaves of pastry dough, filled with fruit, nuts or savoury mixtures, which are rolled and baked.

suet Fat around beef or lamb kidneys. Sold trimmed and shredded ready for use. Vegetarian suet is made from vegetable fat.

syllabub Cold dessert of sweetened cream, white wine, sherry or fruit juice, whipped until thick.

syrup A thick sweet liquid made by boiling sugar with water and/or fruit juice.

T

table d'hôte (F) Meal of three or more courses at a fixed price.

terrine (F) 1. Earthenware pot used for cooking and serving pâté. 2. Food cooked in a terrine.

timbale (F) 1. Cup-shaped metal or earthenware mould. 2. Dish prepared in such a mould.

truffle Mushroom-like fungus, black or white in colour, with a firm texture and delicate taste.

trussing Tying a bird or joint of meat in a neat shape with skewers and/or string before cooking.

tube-pan Ring-shaped tin for baking cakes.

turnover Sweet or savoury pastry made by folding a circle or square of pastry in half to form a semi-circle or triangle.

U

unleavened bread Bread made without a raising agent. When baked, unleavened bread is thin, flat and round.

V

vanilla sugar Sugar flavoured with vanilla by standing a vanilla pod in a closed jar of caster sugar.

velouté (F) 1. Basic white sauce made with chicken, veal or fish stock. 2. Soup of creamy consistency.

vinaigrette (F) Mixture of oil, vinegar, salt and pepper, which is sometimes flavoured with herbs.

vol-au-vent (F) Light case of puff pastry.

W

wafer Thin biscuit made with rice flour; served with ice cream.

waffle Batter cooked on a hot greased waffle iron until risen and crisp.

whey Liquid which separates from the curd when milk curdles.

whipping Whisking cream until thick.

whisk Looped wire utensil used to beat air into eggs, cream or batters.

Wiener Schnitzel (A) Veal slice cooked in the Viennese style, coated in egg and breadcrumbs, fried in butter and garnished with anchovies and capers.

Y

yeast Fungus cells used to produce alcoholic fermentation, or to cause dough to rise.

Z

zabaglione (I) Dessert consisting of egg yolks, white wine or marsala and sugar, which are whisked together in the top of a double boiler over boiling water until thick and foamy.

zest The natural oils and juices found in the rind of citrus fruit, escaping when the peel is removed or punctured. The term is also used occasionally to refer to the rind of the fruit itself.

Editorial Adviser: ELIZABETH POMEROY
Photographer: PHILIP DOWELL
Home Economist: JOY MACHELL

Writers: **Artists:**
  Ena Bruinsma   *Colour:*
  Margaret Coombes   Roy Coombs
  Derek Cooper   Pauline Ellison
  Margaret Costa   Hargrave Hands
  Denis Curtis   Denys Ovenden
  Theodora FitzGibbon   Charles Pickard
  Nina Froud   Josephine Ranken
  Jane Grigson   Charles Raymond
  Nesta Hollis   Rodney Shackell
  Kenneth H.C. Lo   Faith Shannon, MBE
  Elizabeth Pomeroy   John Wilson
  Zena Skinner   *Black and white:*
  Katie Stewart   David Baird
  Marika Hanbury Tenison   Brian Delf
  Silvino S. Trompetto, MBE   Gary Hincks
  Suzanne Wakelin   Richard Jacobs
  Kathie Webber   Rodney Shackell
  Harold Wilshaw   Michael Woods
                                       Sidney Woods
                                     Black and white photography:
                                       Michael Newton

The Publishers also wish to acknowledge the help of the following people and organisations:

Aga Cookers & Boilers; Albrizzi Ltd; Argentine Meat Board; Arts and Crafts of China; Austrian Commercial Delegation; Australian Meat Board; John Baily & Son (Poulterers) Ltd; G. Bettley; R.A. Bevan (Butcher); John Blagden; Bombay Emporium; Alan Bowen; British Agricultural Export Council; British Field Sports Society; British Safety Council; L. Burkett Ltd (Fishmongers); Casa Pupo Ltd; Cecil & Co (Fishmongers); Citrus Marketing Board of Israel; Clare's Handmade Chocolates; College of Distributive Trades; Commercial Rabbit Association; Danish Agricultural Producers; Elizabeth David Ltd; Heino Dorner; Jane Dorner; Barbara Dowell; Caroline Dowling; Edwin Ducat; Dutch Counter Ltd; Dutch Dairy Bureau; Electricity Council; Norma English; Fawkham Church; Fishmonger's Company; *Fish Trades Gazette*; Floris Bakeries Ltd; Fresh Fruit and Vegetable Information Bureau; Nick Frewing; Doreen Fulleylove; Judith Fulleylove; Gas Corporation; General Trading Co. (Mayfair) Ltd; George Gallefant; Gered, Wedgwood & Spode; German Food Centre Ltd; Good Housekeeping Institute; Stephen Gottlieb; Grants of St James's Ltd; Anthony Guyatt; Valerie Hall; Doreen Hare; Susan Harris; Harrods Ltd; Harvey Nichols & Co. Ltd; Roy Hay, MBE; Eric Humphrey; Indiacraft Ltd; Italian Institute for Foreign Trade; Jacksons of Piccadilly; Delilah Jennis; Ellen Keeley; Kraft Foods Ltd; Meg Lake; *Larousse Gastronomique*; Lawleys Ltd; T. & S. Lemkow; Caroline Liddell; Bruno di Lucia; Mac Fisheries; Paul Manousso; Meat and Livestock Commission; David Mellor, Ironmonger; Ministry of Agriculture, Fisheries & Food; Constance Morley; Mostra Design Ltd; National Dairy Council; National Federation of Fruit and Potatoes Trades Ltd; New Zealand Meat Producers Board; William Page and Company Ltd; Paxton & Whitfield Ltd; *Poultry World*; T.J. Poupart Ltd; Reject China Shop; Cathy Roache; Rosenthal Studio House Ltd; G. Rushbrooke Ltd; The Scottish Merchant: Strand Palace Hotel; Summit Art Studios Ltd; Josiah Wedgwood & Sons; White Fish Authority; Wildfowlers' Association of Great Britain and Ireland; Olena Yenkala.